ENCYCLOPEDIA
of JESUS' LIFE
and TIME

AMG
Publishers

ENCYCLOPEDIA
of JESUS' LIFE
and TIME

Compiled by

Mark Water

AMG Publishers
6815 Shallowford Road
Chattanooga, Tennessee 37421

Copyright © 2005 John Hunt Publishing Ltd
Text © 2005 Mark Water
Typography: BookDesign™, London, UK

ISBN: 0–89957–476–9

First Printing, November 2005

Printed in the United States
10 09 08 07 06 05 –MV– 6 5 4 3 2 1

*"Let our chief effort, therefore,
be to study the life of Jesus Christ."
Thomas à Kempis, 1380–1471*

INTRODUCTION

This new "Life of Christ" has collected together much of the best of the classic and contemporary writings and sermons about Jesus Christ that have been written or spoken by more than two hundred people, over the past two thousand years.

1. THE ENCYCLOPEDIA'S OUTLINE

Part One   The person of Jesus
Part Two   The life of Jesus
Part Three   The death of Jesus
Part Four   The resurrection, ascension and return of Jesus
Part Five   Devotional responses to Jesus

The Encyclopedia of Jesus' Life and Time follows a straightforward structure. Most of the encyclopedia focuses on the life of Jesus. So the birth, hidden years and ministry of Jesus come in Part Two, while Part Three covers the death of Jesus, and Part Four the resurrection, ascension and return of Jesus.

Part One, "The person of Jesus," acts as an extended introduction to the life of Jesus. It gives an understanding about who Jesus was, before moving on to Parts Two, Three and Four, which detail what Jesus did and said.

Part Five, "Devotional responses to Jesus," acts as a conclusion to the encyclopedia, with its various testimonies to Jesus from a wide variety of people throughout the centuries.

2. THE ENCYCLOPEDIA'S HEADINGS

Most of the material in *The Encyclopedia of Jesus' Life and Time* has been grouped under one of the five following headings:

a. Comparing modern viewpoints
b. Theologians and Christian writers
c. Poems, hymns, meditations, and prayers
d. Quotation collection
e. Check-lists

a. Comparing modern viewpoints
Under this heading, leading Christians from the twentieth and twenty-first centuries, such as Billy Graham, C.S. Lewis, M. Lloyd-Jones, J.I. Packer, and John Stott, give summaries of some of their views on the person of Jesus, the death of Jesus and the resurrection of Jesus.

b. Theologians and Christian writers
The major part of *The Encyclopedia of Jesus' Life and Time* consists of some of the most helpful writings and sermons of faithful Christian theologians, pastors, Bible teachers and evangelists from throughout the Christian era. In the main, these entries are in chronological order of the birth of the writers.

c. Poems, hymns, meditations, and prayers

Christian communicators agree with Emily Dickinson's advice: "Tell all the Truth but tell it slant," which is found in her poem:

> Tell all the Truth but tell it slant–
> Success in Circuit lies
> Too bright for our infirm Delight
> The Truth's superb surprise
>
> As Lightning to the Children eased
> With explanation kind
> The Truth must dazzle gradually
> Or every man be blind–

Emily Dickinson, *Complete Poems,* No. 1129

Poems, hymns, meditations, and prayers about Jesus have been collected together under the following headings:

> Poems, hymns, meditations, and prayers on Jesus' birth
> Poems, hymns, meditations, and prayers on the life of Jesus
> Poems, hymns, meditations, and prayers on the death of Jesus
> Poems, hymns, meditations, and prayers on the resurrection of Jesus
> Poems, hymns, meditations, and prayers on the ascension of Jesus
> Poems, hymns, meditations, and prayers on the return of Jesus

In Part Five, "Devotional responses to Jesus," there is also a section of poems, hymns, meditations, and prayers.

d. Quotation collection

Nearly six hundred one-liners and quotations only a sentence or two in length about Jesus are found in the following seven places:

> Quotation collection on the person of Jesus
> Quotation collection on the teaching of Jesus
> Quotation collection on the cross of Jesus
> Quotation collection on the resurrection of Jesus
> Quotation collection on the ascension of Jesus
> Quotation collection on the return of Jesus
> Quotation collection of devotional responses to Jesus

e. Check-lists

Check-lists about the person and work of Jesus are in the form of Bible studies. The following nine studies are found scattered throughout *The Encyclopedia of Jesus' Life and Time*:

> Old Testament prophecies fulfilled in Jesus Christ
> 50 specific prophecies fulfilled in Jesus
> 92 prophecies in the psalms fulfilled in Jesus
> 121 Messianic prophecies of Isaiah fulfilled in Jesus Christ
> Bible study on the attributes/character of Jesus
> Bible study on Jesus' names and titles
> Check-list: the second coming of Jesus
> Check-list: on being "in Christ"
> Check-list: instances in the New Testament of faith in Christ

3. THE ENCYCLOPEDIA'S FEATURES

TYPES OF MATERIAL
A wide variety of material is found in *The Encyclopedia of Jesus' Life and Time,* including:
> Stories
> Sermons
> Articles
> Theological books
> Commentaries
> Hymns
> Poems
> Essays
> Allegories
> Songs
> Statements of belief, councils, catechisms and confessions of faith
> Lists, charts, tables
> Quotation collections

Contributors
Contributions from the early church fathers to twenty-first century New Testament scholars are found in *The Encyclopedia of Jesus' Life and Time.* Contributors include:

> Bible commentators
> Early church fathers
> Evangelists
> Martyrs
> Medieval saints
> Missionaries
> Novelists
> Pastors
> Philosophers
> Poets
> Politicians
> Preachers
> Reformers
> Soldiers
> Spiritual/devotional writers
> Theologians
> Writers from the Middle Ages

C.S. Lewis once likened looking at the portrait of Jesus in the New Testament to viewing a work of art. He wrote:

> We must look, and go on looking, till we have certainly seen exactly what is there. We sit down before the picture in order to have something done to us, not that we may do things with it. The first demand any work of art makes upon us is surrender. Look. Listen. Receive. Get yourself out of the way.
>
> C.S. Lewis, *An Experiment in Criticism*

The Encyclopedia of Jesus' Life and Time aims to assist us to "Look. Listen. Receive." as we study the New Testament portrait of the incomparable Jesus.

CONTENTS

PART ONE
THE PERSON OF JESUS

1. Portraits of Jesus
2. Biblical prophecies about Jesus
3. The historical Jesus
4. Comparing modern viewpoints on the person of Jesus
5. The person of Christ
6. The deity of Jesus
7. The character/attributes of Jesus
8. Jesus and the New Testament
9. Quotation collection on the person of Jesus

PART TWO
THE LIFE OF JESUS

1. Jesus and the Gospels
2. Jesus' birth
3. Poems, hymns, meditations, and prayers on Jesus' birth
4. Jesus' hidden years
5. Jesus' ministry
6. Jesus' miracles
7. Jesus' teaching
8. Quotation collection on the teaching of Jesus
9. Incidents in Jesus' life
10. Jesus' transfiguration
11. The Last Supper
12. Jesus in Gethsemane
13. Poems, hymns, meditations, and prayers on the life of Jesus

PART THREE
THE DEATH OF JESUS

1. Comparing modern viewpoints on the death of Jesus
2. Jesus' physical death
3. The meaning of Jesus' death
4. Poems, hymns, meditations, and prayers on the death of Jesus
5. Quotation collection on the cross of Jesus

PART FOUR
THE RESURRECTION, ASCENSION
AND RETURN OF JESUS

1. Comparing modern viewpoints on the resurrection of Jesus
2. Theologians and Christian writers on the resurrection of Jesus
3. Poems, hymns, meditations, and prayers on the resurrection of Jesus
4. Quotation collection on the resurrection of Jesus
5. Jesus' ascension
6. Poems, hymns, meditations, and prayers on the ascension of Jesus
7. Quotation collection on the ascension of Jesus
8. Jesus' return
9. Poems, hymns, meditations, and prayers on the return of Jesus
10. Quotation collection on the return of Jesus

PART FIVE
DEVOTIONAL RESPONSES TO JESUS

1. Jesus and Christians
2. Jesus' continuing presence
3. Testimonies to Jesus
4. Theologians and Christian writers and devotional responses to Jesus
5. Poems, hymns, meditations, and prayers
6. Quotation collection of devotional responses to Jesus

INDEXES

CONTENTS IN DETAIL

PART TWO, THE LIFE OF JESUS

PART THREE, THE DEATH OF JESUS

PART FOUR, THE RESURRECTION, ASCENSION AND RETURN OF JESUS

1. Comparing modern viewpoints on the resurrection of Jesus

PART FIVE, DEVOTIONAL RESPONSES TO JESUS

3. Testimonies to Jesus

Check-list

Testimonies in the Bible

Testimonies from the past 2,000 years

4. Theologians and Christian writers and devotional responses to Jesus

5. Poems, hymns, meditations, and prayers

6. Quotation collection of devotional responses to Jesus   808

Indexes

Part One

THE PERSON OF JESUS

INTRODUCTION

Desiderius Erasmus, 1466-1536, the famous Dutch humanist, scholar, Roman Catholic priest and editor of the first Greek New Testament, which was published in 1516, wrote: "Do we desire to learn, is there any authority better than Christ? We read and reread the works of a friend, but there are thousands of Christians who have never read the gospels and the epistles in all their lives. The Mohammedans study the Koran, the Jews peruse Moses. Why do we not the same for Christ? He is our only teacher. On him the Spirit descended and a voice said, 'Hear ye him!' What will you find in Thomas [Aquinas], what in [Duns] Scotus to compare with his teaching? Let us then thirst for it, embrace it, steep ourselves in it, die in it, be transformed thereby.

"If any one shows us the footprints of Christ we Christians fall down and adore. If his robe is placed on exhibition do we not traverse the earth to kiss it? A wooden or a stone image of Christ is bedecked with jewels and should we not place gold gems and whatever may be more precious on the Gospels which bring Christ closer to us than any paltry image? In them we have Christ speaking, healing, dying and rising and more genuinely present than were we to view him with the eyes of the flesh."

Erasmus' question: "Is there any authority better than Christ?" is addressed in this first part of *The Encyclopedia of Jesus' Life and Time*.

By way of introduction, there are three contrasting entries under the first heading: "Portraits of Jesus." Charles Dickens' *The Life of our Lord*, although originally intended for Dickens' own family, gives a simple and appealing overview of the life of Jesus. John Bunyan's *Christ* is much more didactic, as is Philip Schaff's *The portrait of Jesus*.

To emphasize the fact that Jesus did not just appear as a baby in Bethlehem out of the blue, unannounced, the second section, "Biblical prophecies about Jesus" now follows.

Then, in addition to a section on the person of Jesus, important sections on the historical Jesus and the deity of Jesus follow. They explain why Christian theologians have always insisted that Jesus was both 100% God and 100% man.

The section about the characteristics and attributes of Jesus includes one of C. H. Spurgeon's most renowned sermons. For his first sermon in the new Metropolitan Tabernacle, London, on March 25, 1861, he deliberately chose to preach on Christ Jesus. In this sermon, he states: "I would propose that the subject of the ministry of this house, as long as this platform shall stand, and as long as this house shall be frequented by worshippers, shall be the person of Jesus Christ. I am never ashamed to avow myself a Calvinist, although I claim to be rather a Calvinist according to Calvin, than after the modern debased fashion. I do not hesitate to take the name Baptist. You have there [pointing to the baptistery] substantial evidence that I am not ashamed of that ordinance of our Lord Jesus Christ; but if I am asked to say what is my creed, I think I must reply—'It is Jesus Christ.' My venerable predecessor, Dr. Gill, has left a body of divinity, admirable and excellent in its way; but the body of divinity to which I would pin and bind myself for ever, God helping me, is not his system of divinity or any other human treatise, but Christ Jesus, who is the sum and substance of the Gospel; who is in himself all theology, the incarnation of every precious truth, the all-glorious personal embodiment of the way, the truth, and the life."

The four substantial entries under the section heading "Jesus and the New Testament" further emphasize how the whole of the New Testament teaches both the divinity and humanity of Jesus.

PORTRAITS OF JESUS

1.1 THE LIFE OF OUR LORD, CHARLES DICKENS

This charming little manuscript was written in 1849 by Charles Dickens twenty-one years before his death. It was intended solely for the eyes of his young family. Dickens often told his children the gospel story, and this led him to write down the life of our Lord in his own words. It was never corrected and prepared for publication, and when it was found, after Dickens' death, it was simply bound with a few ribbons, which held the pages together.

CHAPTER THE FIRST

My dear children, I am very anxious that you should know something about the History of Jesus Christ. For everybody ought to know about Him. No one ever lived, who was so good, so kind, so gentle, and so sorry for all people who did wrong, or were in anyway ill or miserable, as he was. And as he is now in Heaven, where we hope to go, and all to meet each other after we are dead, and there be happy always together, you never can think what a good place Heaven is without knowing who he was and what he did.

He was born, a long long time ago—nearly Two Thousand years ago—at a place called Bethlehem. His father and mother lived in a city called Nazareth, but they were forced, by business to travel to Bethlehem. His father's name was Joseph, and his mother's name was Mary.

And the town being very full of people, also brought there by business, there was no room for Joseph and Mary in the Inn or any house; so they went into a Stable to lodge, and in this stable Jesus Christ was born. There was no cradle or anything of that kind there, so Mary laid her pretty little boy in what is called the Manger, which is the place the horses eat out of. And there he fell asleep.

While he was asleep, some Shepherds who were watching Sheep in the Fields, saw an Angel from God, all light and beautiful, come moving over the grass towards Them.

At first they were afraid and fell down and hid their faces. But it said, "There is a child born to-day in the city of Bethlehem near here, who will grow up to be so good that God will love him as his own son; and he will teach men to love one another, and not to quarrel and hurt one another; and his name will be Jesus Christ; and people will put that name in their prayers, because they will know God loves it, and will know that they should love it too." And then the Angel told the Shepherds to go to that Stable, and look at that little child in the Manger. Which they did; and they kneeled down by it in its sleep, and said "God bless this child!"

Now the great place of all that country was Jerusalem—just as London is the great place in England—and at Jerusalem the King lived, whose name was King Herod. Some wise men came one day, from a country a long way off in the East, and said to the King, "We have seen a Star in the Sky, which teaches us to know that a child is born in Bethlehem who will live to be a man whom all people will love." When King Herod heard this, he was jealous, for he was a wicked man. But he pretended not to be, and said to the wise men, "Whereabouts is this child?" And the wise men said, "We don't know. But we think the Star will shew us; for the Star has been moving on before us, all the way here, and is now standing still in the sky." Then Herod asked them to see if the Star would shew them where the child lived, and ordered them, if they found the child, to come back to him. So they went out, and the Star went on, over their heads a little way before them, until it stopped over the house where the child was. This was very wonderful, but God ordered it to be so.

When the Star stopped, the wise men went in, and saw the child with Mary his Mother. They loved him very much, and gave him some presents. Then they went away. But they did not go back to King Herod; for they thought he was jealous, though he had not said so. So they went away, by night, back into their own country. And an Angel came, and told Joseph and Mary to take the child into a Country called Egypt, or Herod would kill him. So they escaped too, in the night—the father, the mother, and the child—and arrived there, safely.

But when this cruel Herod found that the wise men did not come back to him, and that he could not, therefore, find out where this child, Jesus Christ, lived, he called his soldiers and captains to him, and told them to go and Kill all the children in his dominions that were not more than two years old. The wicked men did so. The mothers of the children ran up and down the streets with them in their arms trying to save them, and hide them in caves and cellars, but it was of no use. The soldiers with their swords killed all the children they could find. This dreadful murder was called the Murder of the Innocents. Because the little children were so innocent.

King Herod hoped that Jesus Christ was one of them. But He was not, as you know, for He had escaped safely into Egypt. And he lived there, with his father and mother, until Bad King Herod died.

CHAPTER THE SECOND

When King Herod was dead, an angel came to Joseph again, and said he might now go to Jerusalem, and not be afraid for the child's sake. So Joseph and Mary, and her Son Jesus Christ (who are commonly called The Holy Family) travelled towards Jerusalem; but hearing on the way that King Herod's son was the new King, and fearing that he, too, might want to hurt the child, they turned out of the way, and went to live in Nazareth. They lived there, until Jesus Christ was twelve years old.

Then Joseph and Mary went to Jerusalem to attend a Religious Feast which used to be held in those days, in the Temple of Jerusalem, which was a great church or Cathedral; and they took Jesus Christ with them. And when the Feast was over, they travelled away from Jerusalem, back towards their own home in Nazareth, with a great many of their friends and neighbours. For people used, then, to travel a great many together, for fear of robbers; the roads not being so safe and well guarded as they are now, and travelling being much more difficult altogether, than it now is.

They travelled on, for a whole day, and never knew that Jesus Christ was not with them; for the company being so large, they thought he was somewhere among the people, though they did not see Him. But finding that he was not there, and fearing that he was lost, they turned back to Jerusalem in great anxiety to look for him. They found him, sitting in the temple, talking about the goodness of God, and how we should all pray to him, with some learned men who were called Doctors. They were not what you understand by the word "doctors" now; they did not attend sick people; they were scholars and clever men. And Jesus Christ showed such knowledge in what he said to them, and in the questions he asked them that they were all astonished.

He went, with Joseph and Mary, home to Nazareth, when they had found him, and lived there until he was thirty or thirty-five years old.

At the time there was a very good man indeed, named John, who was the son of a woman named Elizabeth—the cousin of Mary. And people being wicked, and violent, and killing each other, and not minding their duty towards God, John (to teach them better) went about the country, preaching to them, and entreating them to be better men and women. And because he loved them more than himself, and didn't mind himself when he was doing them good, he was poorly dressed in the skin of a camel, and ate little but some insects called locusts, which he found as he travelled: and wild honey, which the bees left in the Hollow Trees. You never saw a locust, because they belong to that country near Jerusalem, which is a great way off. So do camels, but I think you have seen a camel? At all events they are brought over here, sometimes; and if you would like to see one, I will shew you one.

There was a River, not very far from Jerusalem, called the River Jordan; and in this water, John baptized those people who would come to him, and promise to be better. A great many people went to him in crowds. Jesus Christ went too. But when John saw him, John said, "Why should I baptize you, who are so much better than I!" Jesus Christ made answer, "Suffer it to be so now." So John baptized him. And when he was baptized, the sky opened, and a beautiful bird like a dove came flying down, and the voice of God, speaking up in Heaven, was heard to say, "This is my beloved Son, in whom I am well pleased!"

Jesus Christ then went into a wild and lovely country called the Wilderness, and stayed there forty days and forty nights, praying that he might be of use to men and women, and teach them to be better, so that after their deaths, they might be happy in Heaven.

When he came out of the Wilderness, he began to cure sick people by only laying his hand upon them; for God had given him power to heal the sick, and to give sight to the blind, and to do many wonderful and solemn things of which I shall tell you more bye and bye, and which are called "The Miracles" of Christ. I wish you would remember that word, because I shall use it again, and I should like you to know that it means something which is very wonderful and which could not be done without God's leave and assistance.

The first miracle which Jesus Christ did, was at a place called Cana, where he went to a Marriage-Feast with Mary his Mother. There was no wine; and Mary told him so. There were only six stone water-pots filled with water. But Jesus turned this water into wine, by only lifting up his hand; and all who were there, drank of it.

For God had given Jesus Christ the power to do such wonders; and he did them, that people might know he was not a common man, and might believe what he taught them,

and also believe that God had sent him. And many people, hearing this, and hearing that he cured the sick, did begin to believe in him; and great crowds followed him in the streets and on the roads, wherever he went.

CHAPTER THE THIRD

That there might be some good men to go about with Him, teaching the people, Jesus Christ chose Twelve poor men to be his companions. These twelve are called The apostles or Disciples, and he chose them from among Poor Men, in order that the Poor might know—always after that; in all years to come—that Heaven was made for them as well as for the rich, and that God makes no difference between those who wear good clothes and those who go barefoot and in rags. The most miserable, the most ugly, deformed, wretched creatures that live, will be bright Angels in Heaven if they are good here on earth. Never forget this, when you are grown up. Never be proud or unkind, my dears, to any poor man, woman, or child. If they are bad, think that they would have been better, if they had had kind friends, and good homes, and had been better taught. So, always try to make them better by kind persuading words; and always try to teach them and relieve them if you can. And when people speak ill of the Poor and Miserable, think how Jesus Christ went among them and taught them, and thought them worthy of his care. And always pity them yourselves, and think as well of them as you can.

The names of the Twelve apostles were, Simon Peter, Andrew, James the son of Zebedee, John, Philip, Bartholomew, Thomas, Matthew, James the son Alphaeus, Labbaeus, Simon, and Judas Iscariot. This man afterwards betrayed Jesus Christ, as you will hear bye and bye.

The first four of these, were poor fishermen, who were sitting in their boats by the seaside, mending their nets, when Christ passed by. He stopped, and went into Simon Peter's boat, and asked him if he had caught many fish. Peter said No; though they had worked all night with their nets, they had caught nothing. Christ said, "Let down the net again." They did so; and it was immediately so full of fish, that it required the strength of many men (who came and helped them) to lift it out of the water, and even then it was very hard to do. This was another of the miracles of Jesus Christ.

Jesus then said, "Come with me." And they followed him directly. And from that time the Twelve disciples or apostles were always with him.

As great crowds of people followed him, and wished to be taught, he went up into a Mountain and there preached to them, and gave them, from his own lips, the words of that Prayer, beginning, "Our father which art in Heaven," that you say every night. It is called The Lord's Prayer, because it was first said by Jesus Christ, and because he commanded his disciples to pray in those words.

When he was come down from the Mountain, there came to him a man with a dreadful disease called the leprosy. It was common in those times, and those who were ill with it, were called lepers. This Leper fell at the feet of Jesus Christ, and said, "Lord! If thou wilt, thou cans't make me well!" Jesus, always full of compassion, stretched out his hand, and said, "I will! Be thou well!" And his disease went away, immediately, and he was cured.

Being followed, wherever he went, by great crowds of people, Jesus went, with his disciples, into a house, to rest. While he was sitting inside, some men brought upon a bed, a man who was very ill of what is called the Palsy, so that he trembled all over from head to foot, and could neither stand, nor move. But the crowd being all about the door and windows, and they not being able to get near Jesus Christ, these men climbed up to the roof of the house, which was a low one; and through the tiling at the top, let down the bed, with the sick man upon it, into the room where Jesus sat. When he saw him, Jesus, full of pity, said, "Arise! Take up thy bed, and go to thine own home!" And the man rose up and went away quite well; blessing him, and thanking God.

There was a Centurion too, or officer over the Soldiers, who came to him, and said, "Lord! My servant lies at home in my house, very ill." Jesus Christ made answer, "I will come and cure him." But the Centurion said,

"Lord! I am not worthy that Thou shoulds't come to my house. Say the word only, and I know he will be cured." Then Jesus Christ, glad that the Centurion believed in him so truly said, "Be it so!" And the servant became well, from that moment.

But of all the people who came to him, none were so full of grief and distress, as one man who was a Ruler or Magistrate over many people, and he wrung his hands, and cried, and said, "Oh Lord, my daughter—my beautiful, good, innocent little girl, is dead!" Oh come to her, come to her, and lay Thy blessed hand upon her, and I know she will revive, and come to life again, and make me and her mother happy. Oh Lord we love her so, we love her so! And she is dead!"

Jesus Christ went out with him, and so did his disciples and went to his house, where the friends and neighbours were crying in the room where the poor dead little girl lay, and where there was soft music playing; as there used to be, in those days, when people died. Jesus Christ, looking on her, sorrowfully, said—to comfort her poor parents—"She is not dead. She is asleep." Then he commanded the room to be cleared of the people that were in it, and going to the dead child, took her by the hand, and she rose up, quite well, as if she had only been asleep. Oh what a sight it must have been to see her parents clasp her in their arms, and kiss her, and thank God, and Jesus Christ his son, for such great Mercy!

But he was always merciful and tender. And because he did such Good, and taught people how to love God and how to hope to go to Heaven after death, he was called Our Saviour.

CHAPTER THE FOURTH

There were in that country where Our Saviour performed his Miracles, certain people who were called Pharisees. They were very proud, and believed that no people were good but themselves; and they were all afraid of Jesus Christ, because he taught the people better. So were the Jews, in general. Most of the Inhabitants of that country, were Jews.

Our Saviour, walking once in the fields with his disciples on a Sunday (which the Jews called, and still call, the Sabbath) they gathered some ears of the corn that was growing there, to eat. This, the Pharisees said, was wrong; and in the same way, when our Saviour went into one of their churches—they were called Synagogues—and looked compassionately on a poor man who had his hand all withered and wasted away, these Pharisees said, "Is it right to cure people on a Sunday?" Our Saviour answered them by saying, "If any of you had a sheep and it fell into a pit, would you not take it out, even though it happened on a Sunday? And how much better is a man than a sheep!" Then he said to the poor man, "Stretch out thine hand!" And it was cured immediately, and was smooth and useful like the other. So Jesus Christ told them, "You may always do good, no matter what the day is."

There was a city called Nain into which Our Saviour went soon after this, followed by great numbers of people, and especially by those who had sick relations, or friends, or children. For they brought sick people out into the streets and roads through which he passed, and cried out to him to touch them, and when he did, they became well. Going on, in the midst of this crowd, and near the Gate of the city, He met a funeral. It was the funeral of a young man, who was carried on what is called a Bier, which was open, as the custom was in that country, and is now in many parts of Italy. His poor mother followed the bier, and wept very much, for she had no other child. When Our Saviour saw her, he was touched to the heart to see her so sorry and said, "Weep not!" Then, the bearers of the bier standing still, he walked up to it and touched it with his hand, and said, "Young Man! Arise." The dead man, coming to life again at the sound of The Saviour's Voice, rose up and began to speak. And Jesus Christ leaving him with his mother—Ah how happy they both were!—went away.

By this time the crowd was so very great that Jesus Christ went down to the waterside, to go in a boat, to a more retired place. And in the boat, He fell asleep, while his Disciples were sitting on the deck. While he was still sleeping a violent storm arose, so that the waves washed over the boat, and the howling wind so rocked and shook it, that they thought it would sink. In their fright the disciples awoke Our Savior, and said "Lord! Save us, or we are lost!" He stood up, and raising his arm, said to the rolling Sea and to the whistling wind, "Peace! Be still!" And immediately it was calm and pleasant weather, and the boat went safely on, through the smooth waters.

When they came to the other side of the waters they had to pass a wild and lonely burying-ground that was outside the City to which they were going. All burying-grounds were outside cities in those times. In this place there was a dreadful madman who lived among the tombs, and howled all day and night, so that it made travellers afraid, to hear him. They had tried to chain him, but he broke his chains, he was so strong; and he would throw himself on the sharp stones, and cut himself in the most dreadful manner; crying and howling all the while; When this wretched man saw Jesus Christ a long way off, he cried out, "It is the son of God! Oh son of God, do not torment me!" Jesus, coming near him, perceived that he was torn by an Evil Spirit, and cast the madness out of him, and into a herd of swine (or pigs) who were feeding close by, and who directly ran headlong down a steep place leading to the sea and were dashed to pieces.

Now Herod, the son of that cruel King who murdered the Innocents, reigning over the people there, and hearing that Jesus Christ was doing these wonders, and was giving sight to the blind and causing the deaf to hear, and the dumb to speak, and the lame to walk, and that he was followed by multitudes and multitudes of people—Herod, hearing this, said, "This man is a companion and friend of John the Baptist." John was the good man, you recollect, who wore a garment made of camel's hair, and ate wild honey. Herod had taken him Prisoner, because he taught and preached to the people; and had him then, locked up, in the prisons of his Palace.

While Herod was in this angry humour with John, his birthday came; and his daughter, Herodias, who was a fine dancer, danced before him, to please him. She pleased him so much that he swore on oath he would give her whatever she would ask him for.

"Then", said she, "father, give me the head of John the Baptist in a charger." For she hated John, and was a wicked, cruel woman.

The King was sorry, for though he had John prisoner, he did not wish to kill him, but having sworn that he would give her what she asked for, he sent some soldiers down into the Prison, with directions to cut off the head of John the Baptist, and give it to Herodias. This they did, and took it to her, as she had said, in a charger, which was a kind of dish. When Jesus Christ heard from the apostles of this cruel deed, he left that city, and went with them (after they had privately buried John's body in the night) to another place.

CHAPTER THE FIFTH
One of the Pharisees begged Our Saviour to go into his house, and eat with him. And while our Saviour sat eating at the table, there crept into the room a woman of that city who had led a bad and sinful life, and was ashamed that the Son of God should see her; and yet she trusted so much to his goodness, and his compassion for all who, having done wrong were truly sorry for it in their hearts, that, by little and little, she went behind the seat on which he sat, and dropped down at his feet, and wetted them with her sorrowful tears, then she kissed them and dried them on her long hair, and rubbed them with some sweet-smelling ointment she had brought with her in a box. Her name was Mary Magdalene.

When the Pharisee saw that Jesus permitted this woman to touch Him, he said within himself that Jesus did not know how wicked she had been. But Jesus Christ, who knew his thoughts, said to him, "Simon"—for that was his name—"if a man had debtors, one of whom owed him five hundred pence, and one of whom owed him only fifty pence, and he forgave them, both, their debts, which of those two debtors do you think would love him most?" Simon answered, "I suppose that one whom he forgave most." Jesus told him he was right, and said, "As God forgives this woman so much sin, she will love Him, I hope, the more." And he said to her, "God forgives you!" The company who were present wondered that Jesus Christ had power to forgive sins, but God had given it to Him.

And the woman thanking Him for all his mercy, went away.

We learn from this, that we must always forgive those who have done us any harm, when they come to us and say they are truly sorry for it. Even if they do not come and say so, we must still forgive them, and never hate them or be unkind to them, if we would hope that God will forgive us.

After this, there was a great feast of the Jews, and Jesus Christ went to Jerusalem. There was, near the sheep market in that place, a pool, or pond, called Bethesda, having five gates to it; and at the time of the year when that feast took place great numbers of sick people and cripples went to this pool to bathe in it: believing that an Angel came and stirred the water, and that whoever went in first after the Angel had done so, was cured of any illness he or she had, whatever it might be. Among these poor persons, was one man who had been ill, thirty eight years; and he told Jesus Christ (who took pity on him when he saw him lying on his bed alone, with no one to help him) that he never could be dipped in the pool, because he was so weak and ill that he could not move to get there. Our Saviour said to him, "Take up thy bed and go away." And he went away, quite well.

Many Jews saw this; and when they saw it, they hated Jesus Christ the more; knowing that the people, being taught and cured by him, would not believe their Priests, who told the people what was not true, and deceived them. So they said to one another that Jesus Christ should be killed, because he cured people on the Sabbath Day (which was against their strict law) and because he called himself the Son of God. And they tried to raise enemies against him, and to get the crowd in the streets to murder Him.

But the crowd followed Him wherever he went, blessing him, and praying to be taught and cured; for they knew He did nothing but Good. Jesus going with his disciples over a sea, called the Sea of Tiberias and sitting with them on a hill-side, saw great numbers of these poor people waiting below, and said to the apostle Philip, "Where shall we buy bread, that they may eat and be refreshed, after their long journey?" Philip answered, "Lord, two hundred penny-worthy of bread would not be enough for so many people, and we have none." "We have only", said another apostle—Andrew, Simon Peter's brother— "five small barley loaves, and two little fish, belonging to a lad who is among us. What are they, among so many!" Jesus Christ said, "Let them all sit down!" They did; there being a great deal of grass in that place. When they were all seated, Jesus took the bread, and looked up to Heaven, and blessed it, and broke it, and handed it in pieces to the apostles, who handed it to the people. And of those five little loaves, and two fish, five thousand men, besides women, and children, ate, and had enough; and when they were all satisfied, there were gathered up twelve baskets full of what was left. This was another of the Miracles of Jesus Christ.

Our Saviour then sent his disciples away in a boat, across the water, and said he would follow them presently, when he had dismissed the people. The people being gone, he remained by himself to pray; so that the night came on, and the disciples were still rowing on the water in their boat, wondering when Christ would come. Late in the night, when the wind was against them and the waves were running high, they saw Him coming walking towards them on the water, as if it were dry land. When they saw this, they were terrified, and cried out, but Jesus said, "It is I, Be not afraid!" Peter taking courage, said, "Lord, if it be thou, tell me to come to thee upon the water." Jesus Christ said, "Come!" Peter then walked towards Him, but seeing the angry waves, and hearing the wind roar, he was frightened and began to sink, and would have done so, but that Jesus took him by the hand, and let him into the boat. Then, in a moment, the wind went down; and the Disciples said to one another, "It is true! He is the Son of God!"

Jesus did many more miracles after this happened and cured the sick in great numbers; making the lame walk, and the dumb speak, and the blind see. And being again surrounded by a great crowd who were faint and hungry, and had been with him for three days eating little, he took from his disciples seven loaves and a few fish, and again divided them among the people who were

four thousand in number. They all ate, and had enough; and of what was left, there were gathered up seven baskets full.

He now divided the disciples, and sent them into many towns and villages, teaching the people, and giving them power to cure, in the name of God, all those who were ill. And at this time He began to tell them (for he knew what would happen) that he must one day go back to Jerusalem where he would suffer a great deal, and where he would certainly be put to Death. But he said to them that on the third day after he was dead, he would rise from the grave, and ascend to Heaven, where he would sit at the right hand of God, beseeching God's pardon to sinners.

CHAPTER THE SIXTH

Six days after the last Miracle of the loaves and fish, Jesus Christ went up into a high Mountain, with only three of the Disciples— Peter, James, and John. And while he was speaking to them there, suddenly His face began to shine as if it were the Sun, and the robes he wore, which were white, glistened and shone like sparkling silver, and he stood before them like an angel. A bright cloud overshadowed them at the same time; and a voice, speaking from the cloud, was heard to say, "This is my beloved Son in whom I am well pleased. Hear ye him!" At which the three disciples fell on their knees and covered their faces; being afraid.

This is called the Transfiguration of our Saviour. When they were come down from this mountain, and were among the people again, a man knelt at the feet of Jesus Christ, and said, "Lord have mercy on my son, for he is mad and cannot help himself, and sometimes falls into the fire, and sometimes into the water, and covers himself with scars and sores. Some of Thy Disciples have tried to cure him, but could not." Our Saviour cured the child immediately; and turning to his disciples told them they had not been able to cure him themselves, because they did not believe in Him so truly as he had hoped.

The Disciples asked him, "Master, who is greatest in the Kingdom of Heaven?" Jesus called a little child to him, and took him in his arms, and stood him among them, and answered, "A child like this. I say unto you that none but those who are as humble as little children shall enter into Heaven. Whosoever shall receive one such little child in my name receiveth me. But whosoever hurts one of them, it were better for him that he had a millstone tied about his neck, and were drowned in the depths of the sea. The angels are all children." Our Saviour loved the child, and loved all children. Yes, and all the world. No one ever loved all people so well and so truly as He did.

Peter asked Him, "Lord, How often shall I forgive any one who offends me? Seven times?" Our Saviour answered, "Seventy time seven times, and more than that. For how can you hope that God will forgive you, when you do wrong, unless you forgive all other people!"

And he told his disciples this Story—He said, there was once a Servant who owed his master a great deal of money, and could not pay it, at which the Master, being very angry, was going to have this servant sold for a Slave. But the servant kneeling down and begging his Master's pardon with great sorrow, the Master forgave him. Now this same servant had a fellow-servant who owed him a hundred pence, and instead of being kind and forgiving to this poor man, as his Master had been to him, he put him in prison for the debt. His master hearing of it, went to him, and said, "Oh wicked Servant, I forgave you. Why did you not forgive your fellow servant!" And because he had not done so, his Master turned him away with great misery. "So," said Our Saviour; "how can you expect God to forgive you, if you do not forgive others!" This is the meaning of that part of the Lord's prayer, where we say, "Forgive us our trespasses"—that word means faults—"as we forgive them that trespass against us."

And he told them another story, and said, "There was a certain Farmer once, who had a vineyard and he went out early in the morning and agreed with some labourers to work there all day, for a Penny. And bye and bye, when it was later, he went out again and engaged some more labourers on the same terms; and bye and bye went out again; and so on, several times, until the afternoon. When the day was over, and they all came to be paid,

those who had worked since morning complained that those who had not begun to work until late in the day had the same money as themselves, and they said it was not fair. But the Master, said, "Friend, I agreed with you for a Penny; and is it less money to you, because I give the same money to another man?"

Our Saviour meant to teach them by this, that people who have done good all their lives long, will go to Heaven after they are dead. But that people who have been wicked, because of their being miserable, or not having parents and friends to take care of them when young, and who are truly sorry for it, however late in their lives, and pray God to forgive them, will be forgiven and will go to Heaven too. He taught His disciples in these stories, because he knew the people liked to hear them, and would remember what He said better, if he said it in that way. They are called Parables. I wish you to remember that word, as I shall soon have some more of these Parables to tell you about.

The people listened to all that our Saviour said, but were not agreed among themselves about Him. The Pharisees and Jews had spoken to some of them against Him, and some of them were inclined to do Him harm and even to murder Him. But they were afraid, as yet, to do Him any harm, because of His goodness, and His looking so divine and grand—although he was very simply dressed; almost like the poor people—that they could hardly bear to meet his eyes.

One morning, He was sitting in a place called the Mount of Olives, teaching the people who were all clustered round Him, listening and learning attentively, when a great noise was heard, and a crowd of Pharisees, and some other people like them, called Scribes, came running in, with great cries and shouts, dragging among them a woman who had done wrong, and they all cried out together, "Master! Look at this woman. The law says she shall be pelted with stones until she is dead. But what say you? what say you?"

Jesus looked upon the noisy crowd attentively, and knew that they had come to make him say the law was wrong and cruel; and that if He said so, they would make it a charge against Him and would kill him. They were ashamed and afraid as He looked into their faces, but they still cried out, "Come! What say you Master? what say you?"

Jesus stooped down, and wrote with his finger in the sand on the ground, "He that is without sin among you, let him throw the first stone at her." As they read this looking over one another's shoulders, and as He repeated the words to them, they went away, one by one, ashamed, until not a man of all the noisy crowd was left there; and Jesus Christ, and the woman, hiding her face in her hands, alone remained.

Then said Jesus Christ, "Woman, where are thine accusers? Hath no man condemned Thee?" She answered, trembling, "No Lord!" Then said our Saviour, "Neither do I condemn Thee. Go! and sin no more! "

CHAPTER THE SEVENTH
As Our Saviour sat teaching the people and answering their questions, a certain Lawyer stood up, and said, "Master what shall I do, that I may live again in happiness after I am dead?" Jesus said to him, "The first of all the commandments is, the Lord our God is one Lord: and Thou shalt love the Lord Thy God with all Thy heart, and with all Thy Soul, and with all Thy mind, and with all thy Strength. And the second is like unto it. Thou shalt love thy neighbour as thyself. There is none other commandment greater than these."

Then the Lawyer said, "But who is my neighbour? Tell me that I may know." Jesus answered in this Parable:

"There was once a traveller," he said, "journeying from Jerusalem to Jericho, who fell among Thieves; and they robbed him of his clothes, and wounded him, and went away, leaving him half dead upon the road. A Priest, happening to pass that way, while the poor man lay there, saw him, but took no notice, and passed by, on the other side. Another man, a Levite, came that way, and also saw him; but he only looked at him for a moment, and then passed by, also. But a certain Samaritan who came travelling along that road, no sooner saw him than he had compassion on him, and dressed his wounds with oil and wine, and set him on the beast he

rode himself, and took him to an Inn, and next morning took out of his pocket Two pence and gave them to the Landlord, saying, "Take care of him and whatever you may spend beyond this, in doing so, I will repay you when I come here again."—Now which of these three men," said our Saviour to the Lawyer, "do you think should be called the neighbour of him who fell among the Thieves?" The Lawyer said, "The man who showed compassion on him." "True," replied our Saviour. "Go Thou and do likewise! Be compassionate to all men. For all men are your neighbours and brothers."

And he told them this Parable, of which the meaning is, that we are never to be proud, or think ourselves very good, before God, but are always to be humble. He said, "When you are invited to a Feast or Wedding, do not sit down in the best place, lest some more honoured man should come, and claim that seat. But sit down in the lowest place, and a better will be offered you if you deserve it. For whosoever exalteth himself shall be abased, and whosoever humbleth himself shall be exalted."

He also told them this Parable: "There was a certain man who prepared a great supper, and invited many people, and sent his Servant round to them when supper was ready to tell them they were waited for. Upon this, they made excuses. One said he had bought a piece of ground and must go to look at it. Another that he had bought five yoke of Oxen, and must go to try them. Another, that he was newly married, and could not come. When the Master of the house heard this, he was angry, and told the servant to go into the streets, and into the high roads, and among the hedges, and invite the poor, the lame, the maimed, and the blind to supper instead."

The meaning of Our Saviour in telling them this Parable, was, that those who are too busy with their own profits and pleasures, to think of God and of doing good, will not find such favour with him as the sick and miserable.

It happened that our Saviour, being in the city of Jericho, saw, looking down upon him over the heads of the crowd, from a tree into which he had climbed for that purpose, a man named Zacchaeus, who was regarded as a common kind of man, and a Sinner, but to whom Jesus Christ called out, as He passed along, that He would come and eat with him in his house that day. Those proud men, the Pharisees and Scribes, hearing this, muttered among themselves, and said, "He eats with Sinners." In answer to them, Jesus related this Parable, which is usually called:

THE PARABLE OF THE PRODIGAL SON

"There was once a Man," he told them, "who had two sons: and the younger of them said one day, "Father, give me my share of your riches now, and let me do with it what I please? The father granting his request, he travelled away with his money into a distant country, and soon spent it in riotous living.

When he had spent all, there came a time, through all that country, of great public distress and famine, when there was no bread, and when the corn, and the grass, and all the things that grow in the ground were all dried up and blighted. The Prodigal Son fell into such distress and hunger, that he hired himself out as a servant to feed swine in the fields. And he would have been glad to eat, even the poor coarse husks that the swine were fed with, but his Master gave him none. In this distress, he said to himself, "How many of my father's servants have bread enough, and to spare, while I perish with hunger! I will arise and go to my father, and will say unto him, Father! I have sinned against Heaven, and before thee, and am no more worthy to be called Thy Son!"

And so he travelled back again, in great pain and sorrow and difficulty, to his father's house. When he was yet a great way off, his father saw him, and knew him in the midst of all his rags and misery, and ran towards him, and wept, and fell upon his neck, and kissed him. And he told his servants to clothe his poor repentant Son in the best robes, and to make a great feast to celebrate his return. Which was done; and they began to be merry.

But the eldest Son, who had been in the field and knew nothing of his brother's return, coming to the house and hearing the music and Dancing, called to one of the Servants, and asked him what it meant. To this the Servant made answer that his brother had come home, and that his father was joyful because of his return. At this, the elder brother was angry and would not go into the house; so the father, hearing of it, came out to persuade him.

"Father", said the elder brother, "you do not treat me justly, to shew so much joy for my younger brother's return. For these many years I have remained with you constantly, and have been true to you, yet you have never made a feast for me. But when my younger brother returns, who has been prodigal, and riotous, and spent his money in many bad ways, you are full of delight, and the whole house makes merry!"—"Son" returned the father, "you have always been with me, and all I have is yours. But we thought your brother dead, and he is alive. He was lost, and he is found; and it is natural and right that we should be merry for his unexpected return to his old home."

By this, our Saviour meant to teach, that those who have done wrong and forgotten God, are always welcome to him and will always receive his mercy, if they will only return to Him in sorrow for the sin of which they have been guilty.

Now the Pharisees received these lessons from our Saviour, scornfully; for they were rich, and covetous, and thought themselves superior to all mankind. As a warning to them, Christ related this Parable:

OF DIVES AND LAZARUS

"There was a certain man who was clothed in purple and fine linen, and fared sumptuously every day. And there was a certain beggar, named Lazarus, who was laid at his gate, full of sores and desiring to be fed with crumbs which fell from the rich man's table. Moreover, the dogs came and licked his sores.

"And it came to pass that the Beggar died, and was carried by the angels into Abraham's bosom—Abraham had been a very good man who lived many years before that time, and was then in Heaven. The rich man also died, and was buried. And in Hell, he lifted up his eyes, being in torments, and saw Abraham afar off, and Lazarus. And he cried and said, "Father Abraham have mercy on me, and send

Lazarus that he may dip the tip of his finger in water and cool my tongue, for I am tormented in this flame." But Abraham said, "Son, remember that in thy life time thou receivedst good things, and likewise Lazarus evil things. But now, he is comforted, and thou art tormented!"

And among other Parables, Christ said to these same Pharisees, because of their pride, That two men once went up into the Temple, to pray; of whom, one was a Pharisee, and one a Publican. The Pharisee said, "God I thank Thee, that I am not unjust as other men are, or bad as this Publican is!" The Publican, standing afar off, would not lift up his eyes to Heaven, but struck his breast, and only said, "God be merciful to me, a Sinner!" And God,—our Saviour told them—would be merciful to that man rather than the other, and would be better pleased with his prayer, because he made it with a humble and lowly heart.

The Pharisees were so angry at being taught these things, that they employed some spies to ask Our Saviour questions, and try to entrap Him into saying something which was against the Law. The Emperor of that country, who was called Caesar, having commanded tribute-money to be regularly paid to him by the people, and being cruel against any one who disputed his right to it, these spies thought they might, perhaps, induce our Saviour to say it was an unjust payment, and so to bring himself under the Emperor's displeasure. Therefore, pretending to be very humble, they came to Him and said, "Master you teach the word of God rightly, and do not respect persons on account of their wealth or high station. Tell us, is it lawful that we should pay tribute to Caesar?"

Christ, who knew their thoughts, replied, "Why do you ask? Shew me a penny." They did so. "Whose image, and whose name, is this upon it?" he asked them. They said, "Caesar's." "Then," said He, "Render unto Caesar, the things that are Caesar's."

So they left him; very much enraged and disappointed that they could not entrap Him. But our Saviour knew their hearts and thoughts, as well as He knew that other men were conspiring against him, and that he would soon be put to Death.

As he was teaching them thus, he sat near the Public Treasury, where people as they passed along the street, were accustomed to drop money into a box for the poor; and many rich persons, passing while Jesus sat there, had put in a great deal of money. At last there came a poor Widow who dropped in two mites, each half a farthing in value, and then went quietly away. Jesus, seeing her do this as he rose to leave the place, called his disciples about him, and said to them that that poor widow had been more truly charitable than all the rest who had given money that day; for the others were rich and would never miss what they had given, but she was very poor, and had given those two mites which might have bought her bread to eat.

Let us never forget what the poor widow did, when we think we are charitable.

CHAPTER THE EIGHTH

There was a certain man named Lazarus of Bethany, who was taken very ill; and as he was the Brother of that Mary who had anointed Christ with ointment, and wiped his feet with her hair, She and her sister Martha sent to him in great trouble, saying, "Lord, Lazarus whom you love is sick, and like to die."

Jesus did not go to them for two days after receiving this message; but when that time was past, he said to his Disciples, "Lazarus is dead. Let us go to Bethany." When they arrived there (it was a place very near to Jerusalem) they found, as Jesus had foretold, that Lazarus was dead, and had been dead and buried, four days.

When Martha heard that Jesus was coming, she rose up from among the people who had come to condole with her on her poor brother's death, and ran to meet him: leaving her sister Mary weeping, in the house. When Martha saw Him she burst into tears, and said, "Oh Lord if Thou hads't been here, my brother would not have died."—"Thy brother shall rise again," returned Our Saviour. "I know he will, and I believe he will, Lord, at the Resurrection on the Last Day," said Martha.

Jesus said to her, "I am the Resurrection and the Life. Dost thou believe this?" She answered, "Yes Lord"; and running back to her sister Mary, told her that Christ was come. Mary hearing this, ran out, followed by all those who had been grieving with her in the house, and coming to the place where he was, fell down at his feet upon the ground and wept; and so did all the rest. Jesus was so full of compassion for their sorrow, that He wept too, as he said, "Where have you laid him?"— They said, "Lord, come and see!"

He was buried in a cave; and there was a great stone laid upon it. When they all came to the Grave, Jesus ordered the stone to be rolled away, which was done. Then, after casting up his eyes, and thanking God, he said, in a loud and solemn voice, "Lazarus, come forth!" and the dead man, Lazarus, restored to life, came out among the people, and went home with his sisters. At this sight, so awful and affecting, many of the people there, believed that Christ was indeed the Son of God; come to instruct and save mankind. But others ran to tell the Pharisees; and from that day the Pharisees resolved among themselves—to prevent more people from believing in him, that Jesus should be killed. And they agreed among themselves—meeting in the Temple for that purpose—that if he came into Jerusalem before the Feast of the Passover, which was then approaching, he should be seized.

It was six days before the Passover, when Jesus raised Lazarus from the dead; and, at night, when they all sat at supper together, with Lazarus among them, Mary rose up, and took a pound of ointment (which was very precious and costly, and was called ointment of Spikenard) and anointed the feet of Jesus Christ with it, and, once again, wiped them on her hair; and the whole house was filled with the pleasant smell of the ointment. Judas Iscariot, one of the Disciples, pretended to be angry at this, and said that the ointment might have been sold for Three Hundred Pence, and the money given to the poor. But he only said so, in reality, because he carried the Purse, and was (unknown to the rest, at that time) a Thief, and wished to get all the money he could. He now began to plot for betraying Christ into the hands of the chief Priests.

The Feast of the Passover now drawing very near, Jesus Christ, with his disciples, moved forward towards Jerusalem. When they were come near to that city, He pointed to a village and told two of his disciples to go there, and they would find an ass, with a colt, tied to a tree, which they were to bring to Him. Finding these animals exactly as Jesus had described, they brought them away, and Jesus, riding on the ass, entered Jerusalem. An immense crowd of people collected round him as he went along, and throwing their robes on the ground, and cutting down green branches from the trees, and spreading them in His path, they shouted, and cried, "Hosanna to the Son of David!" (David had been a great King there.) "He comes in the name of the Lord! This is Jesus, the Prophet of Nazareth!" And when Jesus went into the Temple, and cast out the tables of the money-changers who wrongfully sat there, together with people who sold Doves; saying, "My father's house is a house of prayer, but ye have made it a den of Thieves!"—and when the people and children cried in the Temple, "This is Jesus the Prophet of Nazareth," and would not be silenced—and when the blind and lame came flocking there in crowds, and were healed by his hand—the chief Priests and Scribes, and Pharisees were filled with fear and hatred of Him. But Jesus continued to heal the sick, and to do good, and went and lodged at Bethany; a place that was very near the City of Jerusalem, but not within the walls.

One night, at that place, he rose from Supper at which he was seated with his Disciples, and taking a cloth and a basin of water, washed their feet. Simon Peter, one of the Disciples, would have prevented Him from washing his feet: but our Saviour told Him that He did this, in order that they, remembering it, might be always kind and gentle to one another, and might know no pride or ill-will among themselves.

Then, he became sad, and grieved, and looking round on the Disciples said, "There is one here, who will betray me." They cried out, one after another, "Is it I, Lord!—"Is it I!" But he only answered, "It is one of the Twelve that dippeth with me in the dish." One of the disciples, whom Jesus loved, happening to be leaning on His Breast at that moment listening to his words, Simon Peter beckoned to him that he should ask the name of this false man. Jesus answered, "It is he to whom I shall give a sop when I have dipped it in the dish," and when he had dipped it, He gave it to Judas Iscariot, saying, "What thou doest, do quickly." Which the other disciples did not understand, but which Judas knew to mean that Christ had read his bad thoughts.

So Judas, taking the sop, went out immediately. It was night, and he went straight to the chief Priests and said, "What will you give me, if I deliver him to you?" They agreed to give him thirty pieces of Silver; and for this, he undertook soon to betray into their hands, his Lord and Master Jesus Christ.

CHAPTER THE NINTH

The feast of the Passover being now almost come, Jesus said to two of his disciples, Peter and John, "Go into the city of Jerusalem, and you will meet a man carrying a pitcher of water. Follow him home, and say to him,The Master says where is the guest-chamber, where he can eat the Passover with his Disciples?' And he will shew you a large upper room, furnished. There, make ready the supper."

The two disciples found that it happened as Jesus had said; and having met the man with the pitcher of water, and having followed him home, and having been shown the room, they prepared the supper, and Jesus and the other ten apostles came at the usual time, and they all sat down to partake of it together.

It is always called The Last Supper, because this was the last time that Our Saviour ate and drank with his Disciples.

And he took bread from the table, and blessed it, and broke it, and gave it to them; and he took the cup of Wine, and blessed it, and drank, and gave it to them, saying, "Do this in remembrance of Me!" And when they had finished supper, and had sung a hymn, they went out into the Mount of Olives.

There, Jesus told them that he would be seized that night, and that they would all leave him alone and would think only of their own safety. Peter said, earnestly, he never would, for one. "Before the cock crows," returned Our Saviour, "you will deny me thrice." But Peter answered, "No Lord. Though I should die with Thee, I will never deny Thee." And all the other Disciples said the same.

Jesus then led the way over a brook, called Cedron, into a garden that was called Gethsemane; and walked with three of the disciples into a retired part of the garden. Then he left them as he had left the others, together; saying, "Wait here, and watch!"— and went away and prayed by Himself, while they, being weary, fell asleep.

And Christ suffered great sorrow and distress of mind, in his prayers in that garden, because of the wickedness of the men of Jerusalem who were going to kill Him; and He shed tears before God, and was in deep and strong affliction.

When His prayers were finished, and He was comforted, He returned to the Disciples, and said, "Rise! Let us be going! He is close at hand, who will betray me!"

Now, Judas knew that garden well, for Our Saviour had often walked there, with his Disciples; and, almost at the moment when Our Saviour said these words, he came there, accompanied by a strong guard of men and officers, which had been sent by the chief Priests and Pharisees. It being dark, they carried lanterns and torches. They were armed with swords and staves too; for they did not know but that the people would rise and defend Jesus Christ; and this had made them afraid to seize Him boldly in the day, when he sat teaching the people.

As the leader of this guard had never seen Jesus Christ and did not know him from the apostles, Judas had said to them, "The man whom I kiss, will be he." As he advanced to give this wicked kiss, Jesus said to the soldiers, "Whom do ye seek?" "Jesus of Nazareth," they answered. "Then," said Our Saviour, "I am He. Let my disciples here, go freely. I am He." Which Judas confirmed, by saying, "Hail Master!" and kissing Him. Whereupon Jesus said, "Judas, Thou betrayest me with a kiss!"

The guard then ran forward to seize Him. No one offered to protect Him, except Peter, who, having a sword, drew it, and cut off the right ear of the High Priest's Servant, who was one of them, and whose name was Malchus.

But Jesus made him sheath his sword, and gave himself up. Then, all the disciples forsook Him, and fled; and there remained not one—not one—to bear Him company.

CHAPTER THE TENTH

After a short time, Peter and another Disciple took heart, and secretly followed the guard to the house of Caiaphas the High Priest, whither Jesus was taken, and where the Scribes and others were assembled to question Him. Peter stood at the door, but the other disciple, who was known to the High Priest, went in, and presently returning, asked the woman, who kept the door, to admit Peter too. She, looking at him said, "Are you not one of the Disciples?" He said, "I am not." So she let him in; and he stood before a fire that was there, warming himself, among the servants and officers who were crowded round it. For it was very cold.

Some of these men asked him the same question as the woman had done, and said, "Are you not one of the disciples?" He again denied it, and said, "I am not." One of them, who was related to that man whose ear Peter had cut off with his sword, said, "Did I not see you in the garden with him?" Peter again denied it with an oath, and said, "I do not know the man." Immediately the cock crew, and Jesus turning round, looked steadfastly at Peter. Then Peter remembered what He had said—that before the cock crew, he would deny Him thrice—and went out, and wept bitterly.

Among other questions that were put to Jesus, the High Priest asked Him what He had taught the people. To which He answered that He had taught them in the open day, and in the open streets, and that the priests should ask the people what they had learned of Him. One of the officers struck Jesus with his hand for this reply; and two false witnesses coming in, said they had heard Him say that He could destroy the Temple of God and build it again in three days. Jesus answered little; but the Scribes and Priests agreed that He was guilty of blasphemy, and should be put to death; and they spat upon, and beat him.

When Judas Iscariot saw that His Master was indeed condemned, he was so full of horror for what he had done, that he took the Thirty Pieces of Silver back to the chief Priests, and said, "I have betrayed innocent blood! I cannot keep it!" with those words, he threw the money down upon the floor, and rushing away, wild with despair, hanged himself. The rope, being weak, broke with the weight of his body, and it fell down on the ground, after Death, all bruised and burst—a dreadful sight to see! The chief Priests, not knowing what else to do with the Thirty Pieces of Silver, bought a burying-place for strangers with it, the proper name of which was The Potters' Field. But the people called it The Field of Blood ever afterwards.

Jesus was taken from the High Priests' to the Judgment Hall where Pontius Pilate, the Governor, sat, to administer Justice. Pilate (who was not a Jew) said to Him, "Your own Nation, the Jews, and your own Priests have delivered you to me. What have you done?" Finding that He had done no harm, Pilate went out and told the Jews so; but they said, "He has been teaching the People what is not true and what is wrong; and he began to do so, long ago, in Galilee." As Herod had the right to punish people who offended against the law in Galilee, Pilate said, "I find no wrong in him. Let him be taken before Herod!"

They carried Him accordingly before Herod, where he sat surrounded by his stern soldiers and men in armour. And these laughed at, Jesus, and dressed him, in mockery, in a fine robe, and sent him back to Pilate. And Pilate called the Priests and People together again, and said, "I find no wrong in this man; neither does Herod. He has done nothing to deserve death." But they cried out, "He has, he has! Yes, yes! Let him be killed!"

Pilate was troubled in his mind to hear them so clamorous against Jesus Christ. His wife, too, had dreamed all night about it, and sent to him upon the Judgment Seat saying, "Have nothing to do with that just man!" As it was the custom of the feast of the Passover to give some prisoner his liberty, Pilate endeavoured to persuade the people to ask for the release of Jesus. But they said (being very ignorant and passionate, and being told to do so, by the Priests), "No, no, we will not have him released. Release Barabbas, and let this man be crucified!"

Barabbas was a wicked criminal, in jail for his crimes, and in danger of being put to death.

Pilate, finding the people so determined against Jesus, delivered him to the soldiers to be scourged—that is beaten. They plaited a crown of thorns, and put it on his head, and dressed Him in a purple robe, and spat upon him, and struck him with their hands, and said, "Hail, King of the Jews!"—remembering that the crowd had called him the Son of David when he entered into Jerusalem. And they ill-used him in many cruel ways; but Jesus bore it patiently, and only said, "Father! Forgive them! They know not what they do!"

Once more, Pilate brought Him out before the people, dressed in the purple robe and crown of thorns, and said, "Behold the man!" They cried out, savagely, "Crucify him! Crucify him!" So did the chief Priests and officers. "Take him and crucify him yourselves," said Pilate. "I find no fault in him." But they cried out, "He called himself the Son of the God; and that, by the Jewish Law is Death! And he called himself King of the Jews; and that is against the Roman Law, for we have no King but Caesar, who is the Roman Emperor. If you let him go, you are not Caesar's friend. Crucify him! Crucify him!"

When Pilate saw that he could not prevail with them, however hard he tried, he called for water, and washing his hands before the crowd, said, "I am innocent of the blood of this just person." Then he delivered Him to them to be crucified; and they, shouting and gathering round Him, and treating him (who still prayed for them to God) with cruelty and insult, took Him away.

CHAPTER THE ELEVENTH

That you may know what the People meant when they said, "Crucify him!" I must tell you that in those times, which were very cruel times indeed (let us thank God and Jesus Christ that they are past!) it was the custom to kill people who were sentenced to Death, by nailing them alive on a great wooden Cross, planted upright in the ground, and leaving

them there, exposed to the Sun and Wind, and day and night, until they died of pain and thirst. It was the custom too, to make them walk to the place of execution, carrying the cross-piece of wood to which their hands were to be afterwards nailed; that their shame and suffering might be the greater.

Bearing his Cross, upon his shoulder, like the commonest and most wicked criminal, our blessed Saviour, Jesus Christ, surrounded by the persecuting crowd, went out of Jerusalem to a place called in the Hebrew language, Golgotha; that is, the place of a skull. And being come to a hill called Mount Calvary, they hammered cruel nails through his hands and feet and nailed him on the Cross, between two other crosses on each of which, a common thief was nailed in agony. Over His head, they fastened this writing "Jesus of Nazareth, the King of the Jews"—in three languages; in Hebrew, in Greek, and in Latin.

Meantime, a guard of four soldiers, sitting on the ground, divided His clothes (which they had taken off) into four parcels for themselves, and cast lots for His coat, and sat there, gambling and talking, while He suffered. They offered him vinegar to drink, mixed with gall; and wine, mixed with myrrh, but he took none. And the wicked people who passed that way, mocked him, and said, "If Thou be the Son of God, come down from the cross." The Chief Priests also mocked Him, and said, "He came to save Sinners. Let him save himself!" One of the Thieves too, railed at him, in his torture, and said,If Thou be Christ, save thyself, and us." But the other Thief, who was penitent, said, "Lord! Remember me when Thou comest into Thy Kingdom!" And Jesus answered, "Today, thou shalt be with me in Paradise."

None were there, to take pity on Him, but one disciple and four women. God blessed those women for their true and tender hearts! They were, the mother of Jesus, his mother's sister, Mary, the wife of Cleophas, and Mary Magdalene who had twice dried his feet upon her hair. The disciple was he whom Jesus loved—John, who had leaned upon his breast and asked Him which was the Betrayer. When Jesus saw them standing at the foot of the Cross, He said to His mother that John would be her son, to comfort her when He was dead; and from that hour John was as a son to her, and loved her.

At about the sixth hour, a deep and terrible darkness came over all the land, and lasted until the ninth hour, when Jesus cried out, with a loud voice, "My God, My God, why has Thou forsaken me!" The soldiers, hearing him, dipped a sponge in some vinegar, that was standing there, and fastening it to long reed, put it up to His Mouth. When He had received it, He said, "It is finished!"— And crying, "Father! Into thy hands I commend my Spirit!"—died.

Then, there was a dreadful earthquake; and the Great wall of the Temple, cracked; and the rocks were rent asunder. The guard, terrified at these sights, said to each other, "Surely this was the Son of God!"—and the People who had been watching the cross from a distance (among whom were many women) smote upon their breasts, and went fearfully and sadly, home.

The next day, being the Sabbath, the Jews were anxious that the Bodies should be taken down at once, and made that request to Pilate. Therefore some soldiers came, and broke the legs of the two criminals to kill them; but coming to Jesus, and finding Him already dead, they only pierced his side with a spear. From the wound, there came out, blood and water.

There was a good man named Joseph of Arimathaea—a Jewish City—who believed in Christ, and going to Pilate privately (for fear of the Jews) begged that he might have the body. Pilate consenting, he and one Nicodemus, rolled it in linen and spices—it was the custom of the Jews to prepare bodies for burial in that way—and buried it in a new tomb or sepulchre, which had been cut out of a rock in a garden near to the place of Crucifixion, and where no one had ever yet been buried. They then rolled a great stone to the mouth of the sepulchre, and left Mary Magdalene, and the other Mary, sitting there, watching it.

The Chief Priests and Pharisees remembering that Jesus Christ had said to his disciples that He would rise from the grave on the third day after His death, went to Pilate and prayed that the sepulchre might be well taken care off until that day, lest the disciples should steal the Body, and afterwards say to the people that Christ was risen from the dead. Pilate agreeing to this, a guard of soldiers was set over it constantly, and the stone was sealed up besides. And so it remained, watched and sealed, until the third day; which was the first day of the week.

When that morning began to dawn, Mary Magdalene and the other Mary, and some other women, came to the sepulchre, with some more spices which they had prepared. As they were saying to each other, "How shall we roll away the stone?" the earth trembled and shook, and an angel, descending from Heaven, rolled it back, and then sat resting on it. His countenance was like lightning, and his garments were white as snow; and at sight of him, the men of the guard fainted away with fear, as if they were dead.

Mary Magdalene saw the stone rolled away, and waiting to see no more, ran to Peter and John who were coming towards the place, and said, "They have taken away the Lord and we know not where they have laid him!" They immediately ran to the Tomb, but John, being the faster of the two, outran the other, and got there first. He stooped down, and looked in, and saw the linen cloths in which the body had been wrapped, lying there; but he did not go in. When Peter came up, he went in, and saw the linen clothes lying in one place, and a napkin that had been bound about the head, in another. John also went in then, and saw the same things. Then they went home, to tell the rest.

But Mary Magdalene remained outside the sepulchre, weeping. After a little time, she stooped down, and looked in, and saw Two angels, clothed in white, sitting where the body of Christ had lain. These said to her, "Woman, why weepest Thou?" She answered, "Because they have taken away my Lord, and I know not where they have laid him." As she gave his answer, she turned round, and saw Jesus standing behind her, but did not Then know Him. "Woman," said He, "Why weepest Thou? what seekest thou?" She, supposing Him to be the gardener, replied,

"Sir! If thou hast borne my Lord hence, tell me where Thou hast laid him, and I will take him away." Jesus pronounced her name, "Mary." Then she knew him, and, starting, exclaimed, "Master!"—"Touch me not," said Christ; "for I am not yet ascended to my father; but go to my disciples, and say unto them, I ascend unto my Father, and your Father; and to my God, and to your God!"

Accordingly, Mary Magdalene went and told the Disciples that she had seen Christ, and what He had said to her; and with them she found the other women whom she had left at the sepulchre when she had gone to call those two disciples Peter and John. These women told her and the rest, that they had seen at the Tomb, two men in shining garments, at sight of whom they had been afraid, and had bent down, but who had told them that the Lord was risen; and also that as they came to tell this, they had seen Christ, on the way, and had held him by the feet, and worshipped Him. But these accounts seemed to the apostles at that time, as idle tales, and they did not believe them.

The soldiers of the guard too, when they recovered from their fainted-fit, and went to the Chief Priests to tell them what they had seen, were silenced with large sums of money, and were told by them to say that the Disciples had stolen the Body away while they were asleep.

But it happened that on that same day, Simon and Cleopas—Simon one of the twelve Apostles, and Cleopas one of the followers of Christ were walking to a village called Emmaus, at some little distance from Jerusalem, and were talking, by the way, upon the death and resurrection of Christ, when they were joined by a stranger, who explained the Scriptures to them, and told them a great deal about God, so that they wondered at his knowledge. As the night was fast coming on when they reached the village, they asked this stranger to stay with them, which he consented to do. When they all three sat down to supper, he took some bread, and blessed it, and broke it as Christ had done at the Last Supper. Looking on him in wonder they found that his face was changed before them, and that it was Christ himself; and as they looked on him, he disappeared.

They instantly rose up, and returned to Jerusalem, and finding the disciples sitting together, told them what they had seen. While they were speaking, Jesus suddenly stood in the midst of all the company, and said, "Peace be unto ye!" Seeing that they were greatly frightened, he showed them his hands and feet, and invited them to touch Him; and, to encourage them and give them time to recover themselves, he ate a piece of broiled fish and a piece of honeycomb before them all.

But Thomas, one of the Twelve Apostles, was not there, at that time; and when the rest said to him afterwards, "We have seen the Lord!" he answered, "Except I shall see in his hands the print of the nails, and thrust my hand into his side, I will not believe!" At that moment, though the doors were all shut, Jesus again appeared, standing among them, and said, "Peace be unto you!" Then He said to Thomas, "Reach hither thy finger, and behold my hands; and reach hither thy hand, and thrust it into my side; and be no faithless, but believing." And Thomas answered, and said to him, "My Lord and my God!" Then said Jesus, "Thomas, because thou hast seen me, thou has believed. Blessed are they that have not seen me, and yet have believed."

After that time, Jesus Christ was seen by five hundred of his followers at once, and He remained with others of them forty days, teaching them, and instructing them to go forth into the world, and preach His gospel and religion; not minding what wicked men might do to them. And conducting his disciples at last, out of Jerusalem as far as Bethany, he blessed them, and ascended in a cloud to Heaven, and took His place at the right hand of God. And while they gazed into the bright blue sky where He had vanished, two white-robed angels appeared among them, and told them that as they had seen Christ ascend to Heaven, so He would, one day, come descending from it, to judge the World.

When Christ was seen no more, the Apostles began to teach the People as He had commanded them. And having chosen a new apostle, named Matthias, to replace the Wicked Judas, they wandered into all countries, telling the People of Christ's Life and Death—and of His Crucifixion and Resurrection—and of the Lessons he had taught—and baptizing them in Christ's name. And through the power He had given them they healed the sick, and gave sight to the Blind, and speech to the Dumb, and Hearing to the Deaf, as he had done. And Peter being thrown into Prison, was delivered from it, in the dead of night, by an Angel: and once, his words before God caused a man named Ananias, and his wife Sapphira, who had told a lie, to be struck down dead, upon the Earth.

Wherever they went, they were persecuted and cruelly treated; and one man named Saul who had held the clothes of some barbarous persons who pelted one of the Christians named Stephen, to death with stones, was always active in doing them harm. But God turned Saul's heart afterwards; for as he was travelling to Damascus to find out some Christians who were there, and drag them to prison, there shone about him a great light from Heaven; a voice cried, "Saul, Saul, why persecutest thou me!" and he was struck down from his horse, by an invisible hand, in sight of all the guards and soldiers who were riding with him. When they raised him, they found that he was blind; and so he remained for three days, neither eating nor drinking, until one of the Christians (sent to him by an angel for that purpose) restored his sight in the name of Jesus Christ. After which, he became a Christians, and preached, and taught, and believed, with the apostles, and did great service.

They took the name of Christians from Our Saviour Christ, and carried Crosses as their sign, because upon a Cross He had suffered Death. The religions that were then in the World were false and brutal, and encouraged men to violence. Beasts, and even men, were killed in the churches, in the belief that the smell of their blood was pleasant to the Gods—there were supposed to be a great many Gods—and many most cruel and disgusting ceremonies prevailed. Yet, for all this, and though the Christian Religion was such a true, and kind, and good one, the Priests of the old Religions long persuaded the people to do all possible hurt to the Christians; and Christians were hanged, beheaded, burnt, buried alive, and devoured in Theatres by Wild Beasts for the public amusement, during many years. Nothing would silence them, or terrify them though; for they knew that if they did their duty, they would go to Heaven. So thousands upon thousands of Christians sprung up and taught the people and were cruelly killed, and were succeeded by other Christians, until the Religion gradually became the great religion of the world.

Remember!—It is Christianity TO DO GOOD always—even to those who do evil to us. It is Christianity to love our neighbour as our self, and to do to all men as we would have them Do to us. It is Christianity to be gentle, merciful, and forgiving, and to keep those qualities quiet in our own hearts, and never make a boast of them, or of our prayers or of our love of God, but always to shew that we love Him by humbly trying to do right in everything. If we do this, and remember the life and lessons of Our Lord Jesus Christ, and try to act up to them, we may confidently hope that God will forgive us our sins and mistakes, and enable us to live and die in Peace.

Charles Dickens,
The Life of our Lord, 1849

1.2 Christ, John Bunyan

John Owen (1616-1683), one of the great Puritans of the seventeenth century, ranks as one of the most remarkable theologians in the history of Christianity. Owen, though a powerful preacher in his own right, nevertheless frequently went to listen to Bunyan's sermons, standing with the thousands of others who came to hear Bunyan preach.

King Charles, learning that Owen went to listen to Bunyan whenever he could, asked the great theologian how a learned man like himself could "go to hear a tinker prate," to which Owen replied, "May it please your majesty, could I possess the tinker's abilities for preaching, I would willingly relinquish all my learning."

In 1850 The American Tract Society published a long book called The Riches of Bunyan *in which it collected together much of Bunyan's doctrinal teaching from his many books. In the preface to this book, the Rev. Jeremiah Chaplin, wrote: "Many of the Christians of our time, though conversant with the* PILGRIM'S PROGRESS, *and* HOLY WAR, *are apparently little aware of the glowing genius, and fervent piety, and strong sense, and picturesque imagery, and racy, vigorous English, that mark the many other writings of the honored tinker of Elstow. These last, if less known than the story of the pilgrimage to the Celestial City, and of the siege and recovery of the good town of Mansoul, yet bear all of them the traces of the same vivid fancy, the same earnest heart, and the same robust and sanctified intellect. To save from comparative disuse and consequent unprofitableness—from being buried in an undeserved seclusion, if not oblivion, many sparkling truths, and pithy sayings, and pungent rebukes, likely to do great good if they could but have, in our busy day, a more general currency over the wide mart of the world; and to bespeak a new circle of influence, and a broader sphere of notoriety and usefulness for these overlooked legacies of a good and great man of a former age, has been the editor's object in the prolonged sifting to which he has subjected all Bunyan's writings. Of that patient and conscientious study the present selection has been the result."*

THE INCARNATION OF CHRIST

The first main design of the life and conversation of the Lord Jesus, was that thereby God, the Eternal Majesty, according to his promise, might be seen by, and dwell with, mortal men. For the Godhead being altogether in its own nature invisible, and yet desirous to be seen by and dwell with the children of men, therefore was the Son, who is the self-same substance with the Father, clothed with or tabernacled in our flesh, that in that flesh the nature and glory of the Godhead might be seen by and dwell with us. "The word was made flesh and dwelt among us, and we beheld his glory;" what glory? "the glory as of the only begotten of the Father, full of grace and truth." Again, "The life"—that is, the life of God in the works and conversation of Christ—"was manifest, and we have seen it and bear witness, and show unto you that

eternal life which was with the Father and was manifested unto us." And hence he is called the image of the invisible God; or he by whom the invisible God is most perfectly presented to the sons of men.

Did I say before that the God of glory is desirous to be seen of us? Even so also have the pure in heart a desire that it should be so. "Lord," say they, "show us the Father, and it sufficeth us." And therefore the promise is for their comfort, that "they shall see God." But how then must they see him? Why, in the person, and by the life and works of Jesus, When Philip, under a mistake, thought of seeing God some other way than in and by this Lord Jesus Christ, what is the answer? "Have I been so long time with you," saith Christ, "and hast thou not known me, Philip? He that hath seen me, hath seen the Father; and how sayest thou then, Show us the Father?

Believest thou not that I am in the Father, and the Father in me? The words that I speak unto you, I speak not of myself; but the Father, that dwelleth in me, he doeth the works. Believe me that I am in the Father, and the Father in me, or else believe me for the very work's sake."

See, here, that both the words and works of the Lord Jesus were not to show you, and so to call you back to the holiness we had lost, but to give us visions of the perfections that are in the Father. "He hath given us the knowledge of the glory of God in the face of Jesus Christ." And hence it is that the apostle, in that brief collection of the wonderful mystery of godliness, places this in the front thereof: "God was manifest in the flesh"—was manifested in and by the person of Christ, when in the flesh he lived among us; manifest, I say, for this as one reason, that the pure in heart, who long after nothing more, might see him. "I beseech thee," said Moses, "show me thy glory." "And will God indeed dwell with men on the earth?" saith Solomon.

Though Adam be called the image or similitude of God, yet but so as that he was the shadow of a more excellent image. Adam was a type of Christ, who only is the express image of his Father's person, and the likeness of his excellent glory; for those things that were in Adam were but of a human, but of a created substance; but those things that were in Christ, of the same divine and eternal excellency with the Father.

Is Christ then the image of the Father, simply as considered of the same divine and eternal excellency with him? Certainly not; for an image is doubtless inferior to that of which it is a figure. Understand, then, that Christ is the image of the Father's glory, as born of the Virgin Mary, yet so as being very God also: not that his Godhead in itself was a shadow or image, but by the acts and doing of that man, every act being infinitely perfect by virtue of his Godhead, the Father's perfections were made manifest to flesh. An image is to be looked upon, and by being looked upon, another thing is seen; so by the person and doings of the Lord Jesus, they that indeed could see him as he was, discovered the perfection and glory of the Father. "Philip, he that hath seen me, hath seen the Father; and how sayest

thou then, Show us the Father?" Neither the Father nor the Son can by us at all be seen, as they are simply and entirely in their own essence. Therefore the person of the Father must be seen by us through the Son, as consisting of God and man; the Godhead, by working effectually in the manhood, showing clearly there through the infinite perfection and glory of the Father. "The word was made flesh, and" then "we beheld his glory, the glory of the only begotten of his Father"—he being in his personal excellencies, infinitely and perfectly, what is recorded of his Father, "full of grace and truth."

When Jesus Christ came down from glory, it was that he might bring us to glory; and that he might be sure not to fail, he clothed himself with our nature—as if we should take a piece out of the whole lump instead of the whole, Heb. 11:14—and invested it with that glory which he was in before he came down from heaven, Eph. 2:6.

THE HUMANITY OF CHRIST

We perceive love, in that the human nature, the nature of man, not of angels, is taken into union with God. Whoso could consider this as it is possible for it to be considered, would stand amazed till he died with wonder. By this very act of the heavenly Wisdom we have an inconceivable pledge of the love of Christ to man; for in that he hath taken into union with himself our nature, what doth it signify but that he intends to take into union with himself our persons? For this very purpose did he assume our nature. Wherefore we read that in the flesh he took upon him, in that flesh he died for us, "the just for the unjust, that he might bring us to God."

The psalmist saith of Christ, that "he was fairer than the children of men;" and that, as I believe in his outward man as well as in his inward part, he was the exactest, purest, completest, and beautifulest creature that ever God made, till his visage was so marred by his persecutions; for in all things he had, and shall have the preeminence.

THE HUMILIATION OF CHRIST

Christ did not only come into our flesh, but also into our condition, into the valley and shadow of death, where we were, and where we are, as we are sinners.

That which would have been death to some—the laying aside of glory, and the King of princes becoming a servant of the meanest form—this he of his own goodwill was heartily content to do. Wherefore he that was once the object of the fear of angels, is now become a little creature, a worm, an inferior one, born of a woman, brought forth in a stable, laid in a manger, scorned of men, tempted of devils, was beholden to his creatures for food, for raiment, for harbor, and a place wherein to lay his head when dead. In a word, he made himself of no reputation, took upon him the form of a servant, and was made in the likeness of men, that he might become capable to do this kindness for us, to give himself a ransom for us.

And it is worth your noting, that all the while that he was in the world, putting himself upon those other preparations which were to be antecedent to his being made a sacrifice for us, no man, though he told what he came about to many, had, as we read of, a heart once to thank him for what he came about. No; they railed on him they degraded him, they called him devil, they said he was mad and a deceiver, a blasphemer of God and a rebel against the state; they accused him to the governor; yea, one of his own disciples sold him, another denied him, and they all forsook him, and left him to shift for himself in the hands of his horrible enemies, who beat him with their fists, spat on him, mocked him, crowned him with thorns, scourged him, made a gazing-stock of him, and finally, hanged him up by the hands and feet alive, and gave him vinegar to increase his affliction, when he complained that his anguish had made him thirsty. And yet all this could not take his heart off the work of our redemption. To die he came, die he would, and die he did, before he made his return to the Father, for our sins, that we might live through him.

When Christ betook himself to his ministry, he lived upon the charity of the people; when other men went to their own houses, Jesus went to the mount of Olives.

THE GLORY OF CHRIST

Christ is rich indeed, both in his blood, resurrection, intercession, and all his offices, together with his relations, and all his benefits; all which he bestoweth upon every one that receiveth him, and maketh them unspeakably wealthy.

The pearl, as it is rich, and so worth much, so again it is beautiful and amiable, even to take the eyes of all beholders; it hath, I say, a very sweet and sparkling light and glory in it, enough to take the eye and affect the heart of all those that look upon it. And thus is Christ to all that come to him, and by him to the Father. "My Beloved is white and ruddy, the chiefest of ten thousand; his mouth is most sweet, he is altogether lovely."

THE LOVE OF CHRIST

Here is love, that God sent his Son, his darling, his Son that never offended, his Son that was always his delight. Herein is love, that he sent him to save sinners; to save them by bearing their sins, by bearing their curse, by dying their death, and by carrying their sorrows. Here is love, in that while we were yet enemies, Christ died for us; yea, here is love, in that while we were yet without strength, Christ died for the ungodly.

Oh, blessed Jesus, how didst thou discover thy love to man in thy thus suffering! And, O God the Father, how didst thou also declare the purity and exactness of thy justice, in that, though it was thine only, holy, innocent, harmless, and undefiled Son Jesus, that did take on him our nature and represent our persons, answering for our sins instead of ourselves; thou didst so wonderfully pour out thy wrath upon him, to the making of him cry out, "My God, my God, why hast thou forsaken me?" And, O Lord Jesus, what a glorious conquest hast thou made over the enemies of our souls—even wrath, sin, death, hell, and devils—in that thou didst wring thyself from under the power of them all. And not only so, but hast led them captive which would have led us captive; and also hast received for us that glorious and unspeakable inheritance that eye hath not seen, nor ear heard, neither hath it entered into the heart of man to conceive.

The great Bringer of the gospel is the good Lord Jesus Christ himself; he came and preached peace to them that the law proclaimed war against. And to touch a little upon the dress in which, by the gospel, Christ presents himself unto us, while he offers unto sinful souls his peace by the tenders thereof:

He is set forth as born for us, to save our souls, Is. 9:6; Luke 2:9-12; 1 Cor. 15:3; Gal. 3:13; Rom. 10:4; Dan. 9:24.

He is set forth before us as bearing our sins for us, and suffering God's wrath for us.

He is set forth before us as fulfilling the law for us, and as bringing everlasting righteousness to us for our covering.

Again, as to the manner of his working out the salvation of sinners for them, that they might have peace and joy, and heaven and glory for ever:

He is set forth as sweating blood while he was in his agony, wrestling with the thoughts of death, while he was to suffer for our sins, that he might save the soul, Luke 22:24.

He is set forth as crying, weeping, and mourning under the lashes of justice that he put himself under, and was willing to bear for our sins.

He is set forth as betrayed, apprehended, condemned, spit on, scourged, buffeted, mocked, crowned with thorns, crucified, pierced with nails and a spear, to save the soul from being betrayed by the devil and sin; to save it from being apprehended by justice and condemned by the law; to save it from being spit on in a way of contempt by holiness; to save it from being scourged with guilt of sins as with scorpions; to save it from being continually buffeted by its own conscience; to save it from being mocked at by God; to save it from being crowned with ignominy and shame for ever; to save it from dying the second death; to save it from wounds and grief for ever.

Dost thou understand me, sinful soul? He wrestled with justice, that thou mightest have rest; he wept and mourned, that thou mightst laugh and rejoice; he was betrayed, that thou mightest go free; was apprehended, that thou mightst escape; he was condemned, that thou mightest be justified, and was killed, that thou mightest live; he wore a crown of thorns, that thou mightest wear a crown of glory; and was nailed to the cross with his arms wide open, to show with what freeness

all his merits shall be bestowed on the coming soul, and how heartily he will receive it into his bosom.

All this he did of mere good-will, and offers the benefit thereof unto thee freely. Yea, he comes unto thee in the word of the gospel, with the blood running down from his head upon his face, with his tears abiding upon his cheeks, as with the holes fresh in his hands and his feet, and as with the blood still bubbling out of his side, to pray thee to accept of the benefit, and to be reconciled to God thereby.

By this we may see his love, in that as a forerunner he is gone into heaven to take possession thereof for us; there to make ready and prepare for us our summer-houses, our mansions and dwelling-places; as if we were the lords, and he the servant. Oh, this love!

Thou Son of the Blessed, what grace was manifest in thy condescension! Grace brought thee down from heaven; grace stripped thee of thy glory; grace made thee poor and despicable; grace made thee bear such burdens of sin, such burdens of sorrow, such burdens of God's curse as are unspeakable.

O Son of God, grace was in all thy tears; grace came bubbling out of thy side with thy blood; grace came forth with every word of thy sweet mouth; grace came out where the whip smote thee, where the thorns pricked thee, where the nails and spear pierced thee. O blessed Son of God, here is grace indeed! unsearchable riches of grace! unthought of riches of grace! grace to make angels wonder, grace to make sinners happy, grace to astonish devils!

And what will become of them that trample under foot this Son of God?

Christ is the desire of nations, the joy of angels, the delight of the Father. What solace then must that soul be filled with, that hath the possession of him to all eternity.

Who can tell how many heart-pleasing thoughts Christ had of us before the world began? Who can tell how much he then was delighted in that being we had in his affections, as also in the consideration of our beings, believings, and being with him afterwards?

Christ was never so joyful in all his life, that we read of, as when his sufferings grew near; then he takes the sacrament of his body and blood into his own hands, and with thanksgiving bestows it among his disciples; then he sings a hymn, then he rejoices, then he comes with a "Lo, I come." O the heart, the great heart that Jesus had for us to do us good! He did it with all the desire of his soul.

When a man shall not only design me a purse of gold, but shall venture his life to bring it to me, this is grace indeed. But, alas, what are a thousand such short comparisons to the unsearchable love of Christ?

Christ Jesus has bags of mercy that were never yet broken up or unsealed. Hence it is said, he has goodness laid up; things reserved in heaven for his. And if he breaks up one of these bags, who can tell what he can do?

It is not exaltation, nor a crown, nor a kingdom, nor a throne that shall make Christ neglect his poor ones on earth; yea, because he is exalted and on the throne, therefore it is that such a river of life, with its golden streams, proceeds with us. And it shall proceed, to be far higher than ever were the swellings of Jordan, Rev. 22:1.

How the brave sun doth peep up from beneath, Shows us his golden face, doth on us breathe; Yea, he doth compass us around with glories Whilst he ascends up to his highest stories, Where he his banner over us displays And gives us light to see our works and ways.

Nor are we now, as at the peep of light, To question is it day or is it night; The night is gone, the shadow's fled away, And now we are most certain that it is day.

And thus it is when Jesus shows his face, And doth assure us of his love and grace.

This makes Christ precious, if I consider how he did deliver me: it was:

1. With his life, his blood; it cost him tears, groans, agony, separation from God; to do it, he endured his Father's wrath, bare his Father's curse, and died thousands of deaths at once.

2. He did this while I was his enemy, without my desires, without my knowledge, without my deserts; he did it unawares to me.

3. He did it freely, cheerfully, yea, he longed to die for me; yea, heaven would not hold him for the love he had to my salvation, which also he has effectually accomplished for me at Jerusalem.

Honorable Jesus! precious Jesus! loving Jesus! Jonathan's kindness captivated David, and made him precious in his eyes for ever. "I am distressed for thee, my brother Jonathan," said he; "very pleasant hast thou been to me; thy love to me was wonderful, passing the love of women." Why, what had Jonathan done? Oh, he had delivered David from the wrath of Saul. But how much more should He be precious to me, who hath saved me from death and hell— who hath delivered me from the wrath of God? "The love of Christ constraineth us." Nothing will so edge the spirit of a Christian as, "Thou wast slain, and hast redeemed us to God by thy blood." This makes the heavens themselves ring with joy and shouting.

THE RIGHTEOUSNESS OF CHRIST

Many there are who, in the day of grace and mercy, despise those things which are indeed the birthright to heaven, who yet when the declining days appear will cry as loud as Esau, "Lord, Lord, open to us;" but then, as Isaac would not repent, no more will God the Father, but will say, "I have blessed these, yea, and they shall be blessed; but as for you, Depart, you are workers of iniquity."

When I had thus considered these scriptures and found that thus to understand them was not against, but according to the Scriptures, this still added further to my encouragement and comfort, and also gave a great blow to that objection—to wit, that the Scriptures could not agree in the salvation of my soul.

And now remained only the hinder part of the tempest, for the thunder was gone beyond me, only some drops did still remain that now and then would fall upon me; but because my former frights and anguish were very sore and deep, therefore it oft befell me still, as it befalleth those that have been seared with the fire, I thought every voice was, "Fire, fire!" Every little touch would hurt my tender conscience.

But one day, as I was passing into the field, and that too with some dashes on my conscience, fearing lest yet all was not right, suddenly this sentence fell upon my soul: "Thy righteousness is in heaven;" and methought withal I saw with the eyes of my soul Jesus Christ at God's right hand—there, I say, as my righteousness; so that wherever I was, or whatever I was doing, God could not say to me, he wanted my righteousness, for that was just before him. I also saw, moreover, that it was not my good frame of heart that made my righteousness better, nor yet my bad frame that made my righteousness worse; for my righteousness was Jesus Christ himself, "the same yesterday, to-day, and for ever."

Now did my chains fall off my legs indeed; I was loosed from my afflictions and irons; my temptations also fled away; so that from that time those dreadful scriptures of God [Num. 15:30; Jer. 7:16; Heb. 10:31; 12:27] left off to trouble me: now went I also home rejoicing, for the grace and love of God. So when I came home, I looked to see if I could find that sentence, "Thy righteousness is in heaven," but could not find such a saying; wherefore my heart began to sink again, only that was brought to my remembrance, "He is made unto us of God wisdom, righteousness, sanctification, and redemption." By this word I saw the other sentence true.

For by this scripture I saw that the man Christ Jesus, as he is distinct from us as touching his bodily presence, so he is our righteousness and sanctification before God. Here, therefore, I lived for some time very sweetly at peace with God through Christ. Oh, methought, Christ! Christ! There was nothing but Christ that was before my eyes. I was now not only for looking upon this and the other benefits of Christ apart, as of his blood, burial, or resurrection, but considering him as a whole Christ—as he in whom all these, and all his other virtues, relations, offices, and operations met together, and that he sat on the right hand of God in heaven.

Further, the Lord did also lead me into the mystery of the union with the Son of God—that I was joined to him, and that I was flesh of his flesh and bone of his bone; and now was that a sweet word to me in Eph. 5:30. By this also was my faith in him as my righteousness, the more confirmed in me; for if he and I were one, then his righteousness was mine, his merits mine, his victory also mine. Now, I could see myself in heaven and earth at once: in heaven, by my Christ, by my Head, by my Righteousness and Life, though on earth by body or person.

Let divine and infinite justice turn itself which way it will, it finds One that can tell how to match it. For if it say, "I will require the satisfaction of man," there is a man to satisfy its cry; and if it say, "But I am an infinite God, and must and will have an infinite satisfaction," here is One also that is infinite, even "fellow" with God; fellow in his essence and being; fellow in his power and strength; fellow in his wisdom; fellow in his mercy and grace, together with the rest of the attributes of God. So that, let justice turn itself which way it will, here is a complete person and a complete satisfaction.

"The law," sayst thou, "must be obeyed." I answer, "Christ Jesus has done that in his own person, and justified me thereby; and for my part, I will not labor now to fulfill the law for justification, lest I should undervalue the merits of the man Christ Jesus, and what he has done without me; and yet will I labor to fulfill, if it were possible, ten thousand laws, if there were so many. And Oh, let it be out of love to my sweet Lord Jesus; for the love of Christ constraineth me."

Though no man can be justified by the works of the law, yet unless the righteousness and holiness by which they attempt to enter into this kingdom be justified by the law, it is in vain once to think of entering in at this strait gate. Now, the law justifieth not, but upon the account of Christ's righteousness; if therefore thou be not indeed found in that righteousness, thou wilt find the law lie just in the passage into heaven to keep thee out.

CHRIST A COMPLETE SAVIOR

"This is the Father's will which hath sent me, that of all which he hath given me, I should lose nothing, but should raise it up again at the last day." John 6:39

The Father therefore, in giving them to him to save them, must needs declare unto us the following things:

1. That he is *able* to answer this design of God to save them to the uttermost sin, the uttermost temptation. Hence he is said to "lay help on one that is mighty," mighty to save. Sin is strong, Satan is also strong, death and the grave are strong, and so is the curse of the law; therefore it follows, that this Jesus must needs be by God the Father accounted almighty, in that he hath given his elect to him to save them from these, and that in despite of all their force and power. And he gave us testimony of this his might, when he was employed in that part of our deliverance that called for a declaration of it. He abolished death; he destroyed him that had the power of death; he was the destruction of the grave; he hath finished sin, and made an end of it; he hath vanquished the curse of the law, nailed it to his cross, triumphed over them upon his cross, and made a show of these things openly. Yea, and even now, as a sign of his triumph and conquest, he is alive from the dead, and hath the keys of death and hell in his own keeping.

2. The Father's giving them to him to save them, declares unto us that he is and will be *faithful* in his office of Mediator, and that therefore they shall be secured from the fruit and wages of their sins, which is eternal damnation. And of this the Son hath already given a proof; for when the time was come that his blood was by divine justice required for their redemption, washing, and cleansing, he as freely poured it out of his heart as if it had been water out of a vessel; not sticking to part with his own life, that the life which was laid up for his people in heaven might not fail to be bestowed upon them.

3. The Father's giving of them to him to save them, declares that he is and will be *gentle and patient* towards them under all their provocations and miscarriages. It is not to be imagined, the trials and provocations that the Son of God hath all along had with these people that have been given to him to save. Indeed, he is said to be *a tried stone*; for he has been tried not only by the devil, guilt of sin, death, and the curse of the law, but also by his people's ignorance, unruliness, falls into sin, and declining to errors in life and doctrine. Were we but capable of seeing how this Lord

Jesus has been tried, even by his people, ever since there was one of them in the world, we should be amazed at his patience and gentle carriages to them. It is said indeed, "The Lord is very pitiful, slow to anger, and of great mercy." And indeed, if he had not been so, he could never have endured their manners as he has done, from Adam hitherto. Therefore are his pity and bowels towards his church preferred above the pity and bowels of a mother towards her child. "Can a woman forget her sucking child, that she should not have compassion on the son of her womb? Yea, they may forget, yet will I not forget thee, saith the Lord."

God did once give Moses, as Christ's servant, a handful of his people to carry them in his bosom, but no further than from Egypt to Canaan; and this Moses, as is said of him by the Holy Ghost, was the meekest man that was then to be found upon the earth. God gave them to Moses that he might carry them in his bosom, that he might show gentleness and patience towards them, under all the provocations wherewith they would provoke him from that time till he had brought them to their land. But he failed in the work; he could not exercise it, because he had not that sufficiency of patience towards them. But now it is said of the person speaking in the text, that "he shall gather his lambs with his arm, shall carry them in his bosom, and shall gently lead them that are with young."

4. The Father's giving them to him to save them, declares that he hath a *sufficiency of wisdom* to wage with all those difficulties that would attend him in his bringing his sons and daughters unto glory. He hath made him to us to be wisdom; yea, he is called Wisdom itself. And God saith, moreover, that he "shall deal prudently." And indeed, he that shall take upon him to be the Savior of the people, had need be wise, because their adversaries are subtle above any. Here they are to encounter the serpent, who for his subtlety outwitted our father and mother when their wisdom was at highest. But if we talk of wisdom, our Jesus is wise, wiser than Solomon, wiser than all men, wiser than all angels; he is even "the wisdom of God." And hence it is that he turneth sins, temptations,

persecutions, falls, and all things, for good unto his people.

I do not doubt but there is virtue enough in the blood of Christ, would God Almighty so apply it, to save the souls of the whole world. But it is the blood of Christ, his own blood, and he may do what he will with his own. It is also the blood of God, and he also may restrain its merits, or apply it as he sees good. But the coming soul, he shall find and feel the virtue thereof, even the soul that comes to God by Christ, for he is the man concerned in its worth.

There is sufficiency of merit in Christ to save a thousand times as many more as are like to be saved by him.

No man needs at all to go about to come at life and peace and rest: let him come directly from sin to grace, from Satan to Jesus Christ.

The cross, it stands and hath stood from the beginning as a way-mark to the kingdom of heaven. Art thou inquiring the way to heaven? Why, I tell thee Christ is the way; into him thou must get, into his righteousness to be justified; and if thou art in him, thou wilt presently see the cross: thou must go close by it, thou must touch it, nay, thou must take it up, or else thou wilt quickly go out of the way that leads to heaven, and turn up some of those crooked lanes that lead down to the chambers of death.

Many there be that begin with grace and end with works, and think that is the only way. Indeed, works will save from temporal punishments, when their imperfections are purged from them by the intercession of Christ; but to be saved and brought to glory, to be carried through this dangerous world from my first moving after Christ until I set foot within the gates of paradise, this is the work of my Mediator, of my High-priest and Intercessor. It is he that fetches us again when we are run away; it is he that lifts us up when the devil and sin have thrown us down; it is he that quickens us when we grow cold; it is he that comforts us when we despair; it is he that obtains fresh pardon when we have contracted sin, and that purges our consciences when they are laden with guilt. I know that rewards do wait for them in heaven, that believe in

Christ, and shall do well on earth; but this is not a reward of merit, but of grace. We are saved by Christ, brought to glory by Christ, and all our works are no other ways made acceptable to God but by the person and personal excellencies and works of Christ; therefore, whatever the jewels are, and the bracelets and the pearls, that thou shalt be adorned with as a reward of service done for God in the world, for them thou must thank Christ, and before all confess that he was the meritorious cause thereof.

Christ must be helpful to thee every way, or he will be helpful to thee no way; thou must enter in by every whit of Christ, or thou shalt enter in by never a whit of him. Wherefore look not to have him thy Savior, if thou take him not for King and Prophet; nay, thou shalt not have him in any one, if thou dost not take him in every one of these.

Christ shall bear the glory of our salvation from sin, preservation in the midst of all temptations, and of our going to glory; also he shall bear the glory of our labor in the gospel, of our gifts and abilities, of making our work and labor effectual to the saving of sinners, that in all things he might have the preeminence.

If you have indeed laid Christ, God-man, for your foundation, then you do lay the hope of your felicity and joy on this, that the Son of Mary is now absent from his children in his person and humanity, making intercession for them and for thee in the presence of his Father, 2 Cor. 5:6.

And the reason that thou canst rejoice hereat is, because thou hast not only heard of it with thine ear, but dost enjoy the sweet hope and faith of it in thy heart; which hope and faith are begotten by the Spirit of Christ, which Spirit dwelleth in thee if thou be a believer, and showeth those things to thee to be the only things.

And God having shown thee these things thus within thee, by the Spirit that dwells in thee, thou hast mighty encouragement to hope for the glory that shall be revealed at the coming again of the man Christ Jesus; of which glory thou hast also greater ground to hope for a share, because that Spirit which alone is able to discover to thee the truth of these things, is given to thee of God as the first fruits of that glory which is hereafter to be revealed—being obtained for thee by the man Christ Jesus' death on Calvary, and by his blood that was shed there, together with his resurrection from the dead out of the grave where they had laid him.

Also, thou believest that he is gone away from thee in the same body which was hanged on the cross, to take possession of that glory which thou, through his obedience, shalt at his the very same man's return from heaven the second time, have bestowed upon thee, he having all this while prepared and preserved it for thee; as he saith himself, "I go to prepare a place for you. And if I go and prepare a place for you, I will come again and receive you to myself; that where I am, there ye may be also."

Again, if thou hast laid Christ, God-man, for thy foundation, though thou hast the Spirit of this man Christ within thee, yet thou dost not look that justification should be wrought out for thee by that Spirit of Christ that dwells within thee; for thou knowest that salvation is already obtained for thee by the man Christ Jesus without thee, and is witnessed to thee by his Spirit which dwells within thee. And thus much doth this man Christ Jesus testify unto us, where he says, "He shall glorify me," saith the Son of Mary. But how? Why, "he shall take of mine"—what I have done and am doing in the presence of the Father—"and shall show it unto you." John 16:14

THE DEATH OF CHRIST

We never read that Jesus Christ was more cheerful in all his life on earth, than when he was going to lay down his life for his enemies; now he thanked God, now he sang.

Christ died and endured the wages of sin, and that without an intercessor, without one between God and him. He grappled immediately with the eternal justice of God, who inflicted on him death, the wages of sin; there was no man to hold off the hand of God; justice had his full blow at him, and made him a curse for sin.

A second thing that demonstrates that Christ died the cursed death for sin, is the frame of spirit that he was in at the time he was to be taken. Never was poor mortal so

beset with the apprehensions of approaching death as was this Lord Jesus Christ; amazement beyond measure, sorrow that exceeded seized upon his soul: "My soul is exceeding sorrowful, even unto death. And he began to be sore amazed, and to be very heavy." Add to this that Jesus Christ was better able to grapple with death, even alone, than the whole world joined all together.

1. He was anointed with the Spirit without measure.

2. He had all grace perfect in him.

3. Never had any so much of his Father's love as he.

4 Never one so harmless and without sin as he, and consequently never man had so good a conscience as he.

5. Never one prepared such a stock of good works to bear him company at the hour of death as he.

6. Never one had greater assurance of being with the Father eternally in the heavens than he. And yet, behold, when he comes to die, how weak is he, how amazed at death, how heavy, how exceeding sorrowful! and, I say, no cause assigned but the approach of death.

Alas, how often is it seen that we poor sinners can laugh at destruction when it cometh; yea, and rejoice exceedingly when we find the grave, looking upon death as a part of our portion, yea, as that which will be a means of our present relief and help, 1 Cor. 3:22.

This Jesus could not do, considered as dying for our sin; but the nearer death, the more heavy and oppressed with the thoughts of the revenging hand of God; wherefore he falls into an agony and sweats—not after the common rate, as we do when death is severing body and soul: "His sweat was as it were great drops of blood falling down to the ground."

What should be the reason but that death assaulted him with his sting? If Jesus Christ had been to die for his virtues only, doubtless he would have borne it lightly.

How have the martyrs despised death, having peace with God by Jesus Christ, scorning the most cruel torments that men and hell could devise and invent! but Jesus Christ could not do so, as he was a sacrifice for sin; he died for us, he was made a curse for us. O, my brethren, Christ died many deaths at once; he made his grave with the wicked, and with the rich in his death.

It was because of sin, the sin that was put into the death he died, and the curse of God that was due to sin, that that death was so bitter to Jesus Christ; it is Christ that died. The apostle speaks as if never any died but Christ; nor indeed did there, so wonderful a death as he. Death, considered simply as a deprivation of natural life, could not have these effects in a person personally more righteous than an angel; yea, even carnal wicked men, not awakened in their conscience, how securely they can die! It must therefore he concluded that the sorrows and agony of Jesus Christ came from a higher cause, even from the curse of God that was now approaching for sin.

At last they condemn him to death, even to the death of the cross, where they hang him up by wounds made through his hands and feet, between the earth and the heavens; where he hanged for the space of six hours. No God yet appears for his help. While he hangs there some rail at him, others wag their heads, others tauntingly say, "He saved others, himself he cannot save." Some divide his raiment, casting lots for his raiment before his face; others mockingly hid him come down from the cross; and when he desires succor, they give him vinegar to drink. No God yet appears for his help.

Now the earth quakes, the rocks are rent, the sun becomes black, and Jesus still cries out, that he was forsaken of God; and presently boweth his head and dies.

And for all this there is no cause assigned from God, but sin. "He was wounded for our transgressions, he was bruised for our iniquities; the chastisement of our peace was upon him, and by his stripes we are healed."

THE RESURRECTION OF CHRIST

You shall have the testimony of the holy angels by the Scriptures, to the resurrection of the Son of God. And first, in Mark 16:3-7, the words are these: "And they said among themselves, Who shall roll away the stone?" They had a good mind to see their Lord; but

they could not, as they thought, get away the stone which covered the mouth of the sepulcher. "And when they had looked," that is, towards the sepulcher, "they saw the stone rolled away, for it was great; and entering into the sepulcher, they saw a young man," that is, an angel, "sitting on the right side, clothed with a long white garment; and they were affrighted. And he saith unto them, Be not afraid," you have no cause for it; "you seek Jesus of Nazareth, who was crucified; he is not here, he is risen: behold the place where they laid him." What scripture can be plainer spoken than this? Here is an angel of the Lord ready to satisfy the disciples of Jesus that he was risen from the dead. And lest they should think it was not the right Jesus he spoke of, Yes, saith he, it is the same Jesus that you mean; you seek Jesus of Nazareth, do you not? Why, "he is risen, he is not here." But do you speak seriously and in good earnest? Yea, surely; if you will not believe me, "behold the place where they laid him." This scripture is very clear to our purpose.

But again, in Matt. 28:3-7, there is an angel as before bearing witness of the resurrection of Jesus. "His countenance was like lightning, and his raiment white as snow. And for fear of him the keepers did shake, and became as dead men. And the angel answered and said unto them," the women who came to seek Jesus, "Fear you not; but let them that seek to keep the Lord in his grave fear if they will, for you have no ground of fear who seek the Jesus that was crucified: he is not here, he is risen; he cannot be here, in body, and risen too: if you will not believe me, come, see where the Lord lay. And go quickly and tell his disciples that he is risen from the dead; and behold, he goeth before you into Galilee, there shall you see him." But shall we be sure of it? "Yea," saith the angel; "lo, it is I that have told you." See how plainly this scripture also doth testify of Christ's resurrection. "Here," saith the angel, "you seek a Savior, and none will content you but he, even the same that was crucified: well, you shall have him, but he is not here." Why, where is he then? "He is risen from the dead." But are you sure it is the same that we look for? "Yea, it is the same that was crucified." But where shall we find him? Why, "he goeth before you into Galilee, where he used to be in his lifetime, before he was crucified. And that you might be sure of it there to find him, know that he is an angel of God that has told you."

THE GLORIFICATION OF CHRIST

For God to adorn his Son with all this glory in his ascension, thus to make him ride conqueror up into the clouds, thus to go up with sound of trumpet, with shout of angels and with songs of praises, and let me add, to be accompanied also with those that rose from the dead after his resurrection, who were the very price of his blood—this does greatly demonstrate that Jesus Christ, by what he has done has paid a full price to God for the souls of sinners, and obtained eternal redemption for them: he had not else rode thus in triumph to heaven.

Consider those glorious circumstances that accompany his approach to the gates of the everlasting habitation. The everlasting gates are set, yea, bid stand open: "Be ye open, ye everlasting doors, and the King of glory shall come in." The King of glory is Jesus Christ, and the words are a prophecy of his glorious ascending into the heavens, when he went up as the High-priest of the church, to carry the price of his blood into the holiest of all.

THE OFFICES OF CHRIST

Christ as a Savior is not divided. He that hath him not in all, shall have him in none at all of his offices in a saving manner.

CHRIST AS INTERCESSOR

Study the priesthood, the high-priesthood of Jesus Christ, both the first and second part of it.

The first part was that when he offered up himself without the gate, when he bore our sins in his own body on the tree.

The second part is that which he executes there whither he is now gone, even into heaven itself, where the throne of grace is. I say, study what Christ has done and is doing. Oh, what is he doing now? He is sprinkling his blood, with his priestly robes on, before the throne of grace. That is too little thought on by the saints of God: "We have such a High-priest, who is set down on the right

hand of the Majesty in the heavens, a minister of the sanctuary and of the true tabernacle, which the Lord pitched and not man." Busy thyself, fellow-Christian, about this blessed office of Christ. It is full of good, it is full of sweet, it is full of heaven, it is full of relief and succor for the tempted and dejected.

The priestly office of Christ is the first and great thing that is presented to us in the gospel; namely, how he died for our sins, and gave himself to the cross, that the blessing of Abraham might come upon us through him. But now because this priestly office of his is divided into two parts, and because one of them, to wit, this of his intercession, is to be accomplished for us within the veil, therefore—as we say among men, out of sight, out of mind—he is too much as to this forgotten by us. We satisfy ourselves with the slaying of the sacrifice; we look not after our Aaron as he goes into the holiest, there to sprinkle the mercy-seat with blood upon our account.

But since his dying is his laying down his price, and his intercession the urging and managing the worthiness of it in the presence of God against Satan, there is glory to be found therein, and we should look after him into the holy place. The second part of the work of the high-priests under the law, had great glory and sanctity put upon it. Forasmuch as the holy garments were provided for him to officiate in within the veil, also it was there that the altar stood on which he offered incense. Also there were the mercy-seat and the cherubim of glory, which were figures of the angels, that love to be continually looking and prying into the management of this second part of the priesthood of Christ in the presence of God. For although themselves are not the persons so immediately concerned therein as we, yet the management of it, I say, is with so much grace and glory, and wisdom and effectualness, that it is a heaven to the angels to see it. O, to enjoy the odorous scent and sweet memorial, the heart-refreshing perfumes that ascend continually from the mercy-seat to the throne where God is, and also to behold how effectual it is to the end for which it is designed, is glorious; and he that is not somewhat let into this by the grace of God, there is a great thing lacking to his faith, and he misseth of many a sweet bit that he might otherwise enjoy. Wherefore, I say, be exhorted to the study of this part of Christ's work in the managing of our salvation for us.

They who are justified by the blood of Christ, should still look to him for the remaining part of their salvation; and let them look for it with confidence, for it is in a faithful hand. And for thy encouragement to look and hope for the completing of thy salvation in glory, let me present thee with a few things.

1. The hardest or worst part of the work of thy Savior is over: his bloody work, his bearing thy sin and curse, his loss of the light of his Father's face for a time. His dying upon the cursed tree, that was the worst, the sorest, the hardest, and most difficult part of the work of redemption; and yet this he did willingly, cheerfully, and without thy desires; yea, this he did, as considering those for whom he did it in a state of rebellion and enmity to him.

2. Consider also that he has made a beginning with thy soul to reconcile thee to God, and to that end has bestowed his justice upon thee, put his Spirit within thee, and begun to make the unwieldable mountain and rock, thy heart, to turn towards him and desire after him, to believe in him and rejoice in him.

3. Consider also that some comfortable pledges of his love thou hast already received; namely, as to feel the sweetness of his love, as to see the light of his countenance, as to be made to know his power in raising thee when thou wast down, and how he has made thee to stand while hell has been pushing at thee utterly to overthrow thee.

4. Thou mayst consider also, that what remains behind of the work of thy salvation in his hands, as it is the most easy part, is so the most comfortable, and that part which will more immediately issue in his glory; and therefore he will mind it.

5. That which is behind is also more safe in his hand than if it was in thine own. He is wise, he is powerful, he is faithful, and

therefore will manage that part that is lacking to our salvation well, until he has completed it. It is his love to thee has made him that he putteth no trust in thee: he knows that he can himself bring thee to his kingdom most surely, and therefore has not left that work to thee, no, not any part thereof.

Live in hope, then, in a lively hope, that since Christ is risen from the dead he lives to make intercession for thee; and that thou shalt reap the blessed benefit of this twofold salvation that is wrought and that is working out for thee by Jesus Christ our Lord.

Every believer may say, Christ did not only die and rise again, but he ascended into heaven to take possession thereof for me, to prepare a place for me. He standeth there in the second part of his suretyship to bring me safe thither, and to present me in a glorious manner, "not having spot or wrinkle, or any such thing." He is therefore exercising his priestly office for me, pleading the perfection of his own righteousness and the virtue of his blood.

He is there ready to answer the accusations of the law, the devil, and sin, for me. Here a believer may through faith look the devil in the face and rejoice, saying, "O Satan, I have a precious Jesus, a soul-comforting Jesus, a sin-pardoning Jesus." Here he may listen to the thunders of the law, and yet not be daunted. He may say, "O law, thou mayest roar against sin, but thou canst not reach me; thou mayest curse and condemn, but not my soul; for I have a righteous Jesus, a holy Jesus, a soul-saving Jesus; and he hath delivered me from thy threats, thy curses, and thy condemnation. I am brought into another covenant, under better promises of life and salvation, freely to comfort me without my merit, through the blood of Jesus; therefore though thou layest my sins to my charge and provest me guilty, yet so long as Christ hath brought in everlasting righteousness and given it to me, I shall not fear thy threats. My Christ is all, hath done all, and will deliver me from thine accusations." Thus also thou mayest say, when death assaulteth thee, "O death, where is thy sting? Thou canst not devour; I have comfort through Jesus Christ, who hath taken thee captive and taken away thy strength; he hath pierced thy heart and let out all thy soul-destroying poison. Though I see thee, I am not afraid of thee; though I feel thee, I am not daunted; for thou hast lost thy sting in the side of the Lord Jesus, through whom I overcome thee. Also, O Satan, though I hear thee make a hellish noise, and though thou threaten me highly, yet my soul shall triumph over thee so long as Christ is alive and can be heard in heaven—so long as he hath broken thy head and won the field—so long as thou art in prison and canst not have thy desire. When I hear thy voice, my thoughts are turned to Christ my Savior; I hearken to what he will say, for he will speak comfort: he hath gotten the victory and doth give me the crown, and causeth me to triumph through his most glorious conquest.

"And I beheld, and lo, in the midst of the throne stood a Lamb as it had been slain." Rev. 5:6. That in the midst of the throne is our sacrifice, with the very marks of his death upon him, showing to God that sitteth upon the throne the holes of the thorns, of the nails, of the spear; and how he was disfigured with blows and blood when at his command he gave himself a ransom for his people; for it cannot be imagined that either the exaltation or glorification of the body of Jesus Christ should make him forget the day in which he died the death for our sins; especially since that which puts worth into his whole intercession is the death he died, and the blood he shed upon, the cross for our trespasses.

Since Christ is an intercessor, I infer that believers should not rest at the cross for comfort: justification they should look for there; but being justified by his blood, they should ascend up after him to his throne. At the cross you will see him in his sorrows and humiliations, in his tears and blood; but follow him to where he is now, and then you shall see him in his robes, in his priestly robes, and with his golden girdle about him. There you shall see him wearing the breastplate of judgment, and with all your names written upon his heart. Then you shall perceive that the whole family in heaven and earth is named of him, and how he prevails with God

the Father of mercies for you. Stand still awhile and listen, yea, enter with boldness unto the holiest, and see your Jesus as he now appears in the presence of God for you; what work he makes against the devil and sin, and death and hell, for you. Ah, it is brave following of Jesus Christ to the holiest: the veil is rent; you may see with open face as in a glass the glory of the Lord.

This then is our High-priest; this is intercession—these the benefits of it. It lies in our part to improve it; and wisdom to do so—that also comes from the mercy-seat or throne of grace where he, even our High-priest, ever liveth to make intercession for us. To whom he glory for ever and ever.

CHRIST AN ADVOCATE

"We have an advocate with the Father, Jesus Christ the righteous." This consideration will yield relief, when by Satan's abuse of some other of the offices of Christ, thy faith is discouraged and made afraid. Christ, as a prophet, pronounces many a dreadful sentence against sin; and Christ, as a king, is of power to execute them: and Satan, as an enemy, has subtlety enough to abuse both these to the almost utter overthrow of the faith of the children of God.

This consideration will help thee to put by that vizor wherewith Christ by Satan is misrepresented to thee, to the weakening and affrighting thee. There is nothing more common among saints, than thus to be wronged by Satan; for he will labor to fetch fire out of the offices of Christ to burn us: so to present him to us with so dreadful and so ireful a countenance, that a man in temptation and under guilt shall hardly be able to lift up his face to God.

But now, to think really that he is my advocate, this heals all. Put a vizor upon the face of a father, and it may perhaps for a while fright the child; but let the father speak, let him speak in his own fatherly dialect to the child, and the vizor is gone, if not from the father's face, yet from the child's mind; yea, the child, notwithstanding that vizor, will adventure to creep into its father's bosom.

Why, thus it is with the saints when Satan deludes and abuses them by disfiguring the countenance of Christ to their view: let them but hear their Lord speak in his own natural dialect—and he doth so indeed when we hear him speak as an advocate—and their minds are calmed, their thoughts settled, their guilt vanished, and their faith revived.

Is Christ Jesus the Lord my advocate with the Father? Then awake, my faith, and shake thyself like a giant; stir up thyself and be not faint: Christ is the advocate of his people; and as for sin, which is one great stumble to thy actings, O my faith, Christ has not only died for that as a sacrifice, nor only carried his sacrifice unto the Father into the holiest of all, but is there to manage that offering as an advocate, pleading the efficacy and worth thereof before God against the devil for us.

The modest saint is apt to be abashed, to think what a troublesome one he is, and what a make-work he has been in God's house all his days; and let him be filled with holy blushing, but let him not forsake his advocate.

If thy foot slippeth, if it slippeth greatly, then know thou it will not be long before a bill be in heaven preferred against thee by the accuser of the brethren; wherefore then thou must have recourse to Christ as advocate, to plead before God thy Judge against the devil thine adversary for thee. And as to the badness of thy cause, let nothing move thee save to humility and self-abasement, for Christ is glorified by being concerned for thee; yea, the angels will shout aloud to see him bring thee off. For what greater glory can we conceive Christ to obtain as advocate, than to bring off his people when they have sinned, notwithstanding Satan's so charging of them as he doth?

He gloried when he was going to the cross to die; he went up with a shout and the sound of a trumpet to make intercession for us; and shall we think that by his being an advocate he receives no additional glory?

Christ, when he pleads as an advocate for his people in the presence of God against Satan, can plead those very weaknesses of his people for which Satan would have them damned, for their relief and advantage. "Is not this a brand plucked out of the fire?" This is part of the plea of our advocate against Satan, for his servant Joshua, when he said, "The

Lord rebuke thee, O Satan." Zech. 13:2. Now, to be a brand plucked out of the fire, is to be a saint—impatient, weakened, defiled, and made imperfect by sin. This then is the next plea of our goodly advocate for us: "O Satan, this is a brand plucked out of the fire." As if he should say, "Thou objectest against my servant Joshua, that he is black like a coal, or that the fire of sin at times is still burning in him. And what then? The reason why he is not totally extinct as tow, is not thy pity but my Father's mercy to him. I have plucked him out of the fire, yet not so out but that the smell thereof is yet upon him; and my Father and I, we consider his weakness and pity him; for since he is as a brand pulled out, can it be expected by my Father or me, that he should appear before us as clear and do our biddings as well as if he had never been there? This is a brand plucked out of the fire, and must be considered as such, and must be borne with as such."

His righteousness Christ presents to God for us; and God, for this righteousness' sake, is well pleased that we should be saved, and for it can save us and secure his honor and preserve the law in its sanction.

For Christ, in pleading against Satan as an advocate with, the Father for us, appeals to the law itself if he has not done it justice; saying, "Most mighty law, what command of thine have I not fulfilled? What demand of thine have I not fully answered? Where is that jot or tittle of the law that is able to object against my doings for want of satisfaction?"

Here the law is mute; it speaks not one word by way of the least complaint, but rather testifies of this righteousness that it is good and holy, Rom. 3:22, 23; 5:15-19.

Now then, since Christ did this as a public person, it follows that others must be justified thereby; for that was the end and reason of Christ's taking on him to do the righteousness of the law. Nor can the law object against the equity of this dispensation of heaven; for why might not that God who gave the law its being and its sanction, dispose as he pleases of the righteousness which it commends? Besides, if men be made righteous, they are so; and if by a righteousness which the law commends, how can fault be found with them by the law? Nay, it is "witnessed by the law and the prophets," who consent that it should be "unto all and upon all them that believe," for their justification, Rom. 3:20, 21.

And that the mighty God suffereth the prince of the devils to do with the law what he can against this most wholesome and godly doctrine, it is to show the truth, goodness, and permanency thereof; for this is as if it were said, Devil, do thy worst.

When the law is in the hand of an easy pleader, though the cause that he pleads be good, a crafty opposer may overthrow the right; but here is the salvation of the children in debate, whether it can stand with law and justice: the opposer of this is the devil, his argument against it is the law; he that defends the doctrine is Christ the advocate, who in his plea must justify the justice of God, defend the holiness of the law, and save the sinner from all the arguments, pleas, stops, and demurs that Satan is able to put in against it. And this he must do fairly, righteously, simply, pleading the voice of the self-same law for the justification of the soul that he standeth for, which Satan leads against it; for though it is by the new law that our salvation comes, yet by the old law is the new law approved of, and the way of salvation thereby consented to.

John Bunyan, The Riches of Bunyan
selected from his works, for the American
Tract Society, by Jeremiah Chaplin

1.3 The portrait of Jesus, Philip Schaff

Philip Schaff, 1819-1893, the Swiss-American theologian and church historian helped set standards in the United States for scholarship in church history.

"In the development of the discipline of church history in the United States, few scholars played a more important role than the Swiss-born, German-educated immigrant Philip Schaff. Known best for his multi-volume History of the Christian Church, *which is still in print, Schaff spent his career arguing for and demonstrating the importance of studying the Christian past. Along the way, he founded the discipline of American church history. Born in Chur, Switzerland, on New Year's Day in 1819, Schaff had a difficult childhood. He experienced poverty and life in an orphanage, where he was sent after his father died and his mother remarried. Fortunately, a series of benefactors cared for him and provided warm Christian nurture that would shape the rest of his life." Stephen R. Graham*

His Christ-centered approach to all his writing is typified in the following two quotations of his. "Jesus of Nazareth, without money and arms, conquered more millions than Alexander, Caesar, Mahomet, and Napoleon; without science and learning, He shed more light on things human and divine than all philosophers and schools combined; without the eloquence of schools, He spoke words of life such as never were spoken before or since, and produced effects which lie beyond the reach of any orator or poet; without writing a single line, He has set more pens in motion, and furnished themes for more sermons, orations, discussions, learned volumes, works of art and sweet songs of praise, than the whole army of great men of ancient and modern times. Born in a manger, and crucified as a malefactor, He now controls the destinies of the civilized world, and rules a spiritual empire, which embraces one-third of the inhabitants of the globe. There never was in this world a life so unpretending, modest, and lowly in its outward form and condition, and yet producing such extraordinary effects upon all ages, nations, and classes of men. The annals of history produce no other example of such complete and astonishing success in spite of the absence of those material, social, literary, and artistic powers and influences which are indispensable to success for a mere man."

"If Christians are ever to be united, they must be united in Christ, their living head and the source of their spiritual life."

1. GOSPEL PORTRAIT OF CHRIST NOT INVENTED

This portrait may itself be confidently adduced as its own warranty. It is not too much to say with Nathaniel Lardner that "the history of the New Testament has in it all the marks of credibility that any history can have." But apart from these more usually marshaled evidences of the trustworthiness of the narratives, there is the portrait itself which they draw, and this can not by any possibility have been an invention. It is not merely that the portrait is harmonious throughout—in the allusions and presuppositions of the epistles of Paul and the other letter-writers of the New Testament, in the detailed narratives of the Synoptics and John, and in each of the sources which underlie them. This is a matter of importance; but it is not the matter of chief moment; there is no need to dwell upon the impossibility of such a harmony having been maintained save on the basis of simple truthfulness of record, or to dispute whether in the case of the Synoptics there are three independent witnesses to the one portrait, or only the two independent witnesses of their two most prominent "sources." Nor is the most interesting point whether the aboriginality of this portrait is guaranteed by the harmony of the representation in all the sources of information, some of which reach back to the most primitive epoch of the Christian movement. It is quite certain that this conception of Christ's person and career was the conception of his immediate followers, and indeed of himself; but, important as this conclusion is, it is still not the matter of primary import. The matter of primary significance is that this portrait thus imbedded in all the authoritative sources of information, and thus proved to be the conception of its founder cherished by the whole of primitive Christendom, and indeed commended to it by that founder himself, is a portrait intrinsically incapable of invention by men. It could never have come into being save as the revelation of an actual person embodying it, who really lived among men. "A romancer," as even Albert Réville allows, "can not attribute to a being which be creates an ideal superior to what be himself is capable

of conceiving." The conception of the God-man which is embodied in the portrait which the sources draw of Christ, and which is dramatized by them through such a history as they depict, can be accounted for only on the assumption that such a God-man actually lived, was seen of men, and was painted from the life. The miracle of the invention of such a portraiture, whether by the conscious effort of art, or by the unconscious working of the mythopeic fancy, would be as great as the actual existence of such a person. Of this there is sufficient a posteriori proof in the invariable deterioration this portrait suffers in its secondary reproductions—in the so-called "Lives of Christ," of every type. The attempt vitally to realize and reproduce it results inevitably in its reduction. A portraiture which cannot even be interpreted by men without suffering serious loss can not be the invention of the first simple followers of Jesus. Its very existence in their unsophisticated narratives is the sufficient proof of its faithfulness to a great reality.

2. THE PORTRAIT OF JESUS
a. His humiliation

Only an outline of this portrait can be set down here. Jesus appears in it not only a supernatural, but in all the sources alike specifically a divine, person, who came into the world on a mission of mercy to sinful man. Such a mission was in its essence a humiliation and involved humiliation at every step of its accomplishment. His life is represented accordingly as a life of difficulty and conflict, of trial and suffering, issuing in a shameful death. But this humiliation is represented as in every step and stage of it voluntary. It was entered into and abided in solely in the interests of his mission, and did not argue at any point of it helplessness in the face of the difficulties which hemmed him in more and more until they led him to death on the cross. It rather manifested his strong determination to fulfill his mission to the end, to drink to its dregs the cup he had undertaken to drink. Accordingly, every suggestion of escape from it by the use of his intrinsic divine powers, whether of omnipotence or of omniscience, was treated by him first and last as a temptation of the evil one. The death in which his life ends is conceived, therefore, as the goal in which his life culminates. He came into the world to die, and every stage of the road that led up to this issue was determined not for him but by him: he was never the victim but always the master of circumstance, and pursued his pathway from beginning to end, not merely in full knowledge from the start of all its turns and twists up to its bitter conclusion, but in complete control both of them and of it.

b. His Messiahship and deity

His life of humiliation, sinking into his terrible death, was therefore not his misfortune, but his achievement as the promised Messiah, by and in whom the kingdom of God is to be established in the world; it was the work which as Messiah he came to do. Therefore, in his prosecution of it, he from the beginning announced himself as the Messiah, accepted all ascriptions to him of Messiahship under whatever designation, and thus gathered up into his person all the preadumbrations of Old-Testament prophecy; and by his favorite self-designation of "Son of Man," derived from Daniel's great vision (7:13), continually proclaimed himself the Messiah he actually was, emphasizing in contrast with his present humiliation, his heavenly origin and his future glory. Moreover, in the midst of his humiliation, he exercised, so far as that was consistent with the performance of his mission, all the prerogatives of that "transcendent" or divine Messiah which he was. He taught with authority, substituting for every other sanction, his great "But I say unto you," and declaring himself greater than the greatest of God's representatives whom he had sent in all the past to visit his people. He surrounded himself as he went about preaching the Gospel of the kingdom with a miraculous nimbus, each and every miracle in which was adapted not merely to manifest the presence of a supernatural person in the midst of the people, but, as a piece of symbolical teaching, to reveal the nature of this supernatural person, and to afford a foretaste of the blessedness of his rule in the kingdom he came to found. He assumed plenary authority over the religious ordinances of the people, divinely established though they were; and exercised absolute control over the laws of nature themselves. The divine prerogative of forgiving sins he claimed for himself, the divine power of reading the heart he frankly exercised, the divine function of judge of quick and dead he attached to his own person. Asserting for himself a superhuman dignity of person, or rather a share in the ineffable Name itself, he represented himself as abiding continually even when on earth in absolute communion with God the Father, and participating by necessity of nature in the treasures of the divine knowledge and grace; announced himself the source of all divine knowledge and grace to men; and drew to himself all the religious affections, suspending the destinies of men absolutely upon their relation to his own person. Nevertheless he walked straight onward in the path of his lowly mission, and, bending even the wrath of men to his service, gave himself in his own good time and way to the death he had come to accomplish. Then, his mission performed, he rose again from the dead in the power of his deathless life; showed himself alive to chosen witnesses, that he might strengthen the hearts of his people; and ascended to the right hand of God, whence he directs the continued preparation of the kingdom until it shall please him to return for its establishment in its glorious eternal form.

3. CENTRAL CONCEPTIONS

It is important to fix firmly in mind the central conception of this representation. It turns upon the sacrificial death of Jesus to which the whole life leads up, and out of which all its issues are drawn, and for a perpetual memorial of which he is represented as having instituted a solemn memorial feast. The divine majesty of this Son of God; his redemptive mission to the world, in a life of humiliation and a ransoming death; the completion of his task in accordance with his purpose; his triumphant rising from the death thus vicariously endured; his assumption of sovereignty over the future development of the kingdom founded in his blood, and over the world as the theater of its development;

his expected return as the consummator of the ages and the judge of all—this is the circle of ideas in which all accounts move.

It is the portrait not of a merely human life, though it includes the delineation of a complete and a completely human life. It is the portrayal of a human episode in the divine life. It is, therefore, not merely connected with supernatural occurrences, nor merely colored by supernatural features, nor merely set in a supernatural atmosphere: the supernatural is its very substance, the elimination of which would be the evaporation of the whole. The Jesus of the New Testament is not fundamentally man, however divinely gifted: he is God tabernacling for a while among men, with heaven lying about him not merely in his infancy, but throughout all the days of his flesh.

Philip Schaff
New Schaff-Herzog Encyclopedia of
Religious Knowledge

2

BIBLICAL PROPHECIES ABOUT JESUS

1.4 JESUS WAS PREFIGURED IN THE OLD TESTAMENT, IRENAEUS

By these [Old Testament prophecies] Christ was typified, and acknowledged, and brought into the world; for He was prefigured in Joseph: then from Levi and Judah He was descended according to the flesh, as King and Priest; and He was acknowledged by Simeon in the temple: through Zebulon. He was believed in among the Gentiles, as says the prophet, "the land of Zabulon;" and through Benjamin [that is, Paul] He was glorified, by being preached throughout all the world.

Irenaeus , Fragments from the Lost Writings of Irenaeus

1.5 THE OFFICES OF CHRIST: PROPHET, KING, AND PRIEST
JOHN CALVIN

In about 1533 Calvin had a "sudden conversion." He said: "God subdued and brought my heart to docility." Apparently he had encountered the writings of Luther. He broke from Catholicism, left France, and settled in Switzerland as if he was in exile. In 1536, Calvin published the first edition of one of the greatest works ever written, The Institutes of the Christian Religion. *At the age of twenty-seven he had already produced a major systematic theology, a clear articulation of Reformation teachings.*

No other Reformer ever stated Protestantism's beliefs so clearly. Luther wrote much, but never in one book did he bring all key beliefs together. Calvin's book, which he kept enlarging throughout his life, covered all the bases.

He was sent to perform the office,

1. Of a Prophet, by preaching the truth, by fulfilling the prophecies, by teaching and doing the will of his Father;

2. Of a King, by governing the whole Church and every member of it, and by defending his people from every kind of adversaries;

3. Of a Priest, by offering his body as a sacrifice for sins, by reconciling God to us though his obedience, and by perpetual intercession for his people to the Father.

He performed the office of a Redeemer by dying for our sins, by rising again for our justification, by opening heaven to us through his ascension, by sitting at the right hand of the Father whence he will come to judge the quick and the dead; and, therefore, he procured for us the grace of God and salvation.

Three things briefly to be regarded in Christ—viz. his offices of prophet, king, and priest.

The principal parts of this chapter are—

1. Of the Prophetical Office of Christ, its dignity and use, sections 1, 2.

2. The nature of the Kingly power of Christ, and the advantage we derive from it, sections 3-5.

3. Of the Priesthood of Christ, and the efficacy of it, section 6.

SUMMARY OF SECTIONS

1. Among heretics and false Christians, Christ is found in name only; but by those who are truly and effectually called of God, he is acknowledged as a Prophet, King, and Priest. In regard to the Prophetical Office, the Redeemer of the Church is the same from whom believers under the Law hoped for the full light of understanding.

2. The unction of Christ, though it has respect chiefly to the Kingly Office, refers also to the Prophetical and Priestly Offices. The dignity, necessity, and use of this unction.

3. From the spirituality of Christ's kingdom its eternity is inferred. This twofold, referring both to the whole body of the Church, and to its individual members.

4. Benefits from the spiritual kingdom of Christ.
   a. It raises us to eternal life.
   b. It enriches us with all things necessary to salvation.
   c. It makes us invincible by spiritual foes.
   d. It animates us to patient endurance.
   e. It inspires confidence and triumph.
   f. It supplies fortitude and love.

5. The unction of our Redeemer heavenly. Symbol of this unction. A passage in the apostle reconciled with others previously quoted, to prove the eternal kingdom of Christ.

6. What necessary to obtain the benefit of Christ's Priesthood. We must set out with the death of Christ. From it follows,
   a. His intercession for us.
   b. Confidence in prayer.
   c. Peace of conscience.
   d. Through Christ, Christians themselves become priests. Grievous sin of the Papists in pretending to sacrifice Christ.

SECTION 1

Though heretics pretend the name of Christ, truly does Augustine affirm (*Enchir. ad Laurent.* cap. 5), that the foundation is not common to them with the godly, but belongs exclusively to the Church: for if those things which pertain to Christ be diligently considered, it will be found that Christ is with them in name only, not in reality.

Thus in the present day, though the Papists have the words, Son of God, Redeemer of the world, sounding in their mouths, yet, because contented with an empty name, they deprive him of his virtue and dignity; what Paul says of "not holding the head," is truly applicable to them (Col. 2:19). Therefore, that faith may find in Christ a solid ground of salvation, and so rest in him, we must set out with this principle, that the office which he received from the Father consists of three parts. For he was appointed both Prophet, King, and Priest; though little were gained by holding the names unaccompanied by a knowledge of the end and use. These too are spoken of in the Papacy, but frigidly, and with no great benefit, the full meaning comprehended under each title not being understood. We formerly observed, that though God, by supplying an uninterrupted succession of prophets, never left his people destitute of useful doctrine, such as might suffice for salvation; yet the minds of believers were always impressed with the conviction that the full light of understanding was to be expected only on the advent of the Messiah. This expectation, accordingly, had reached even the Samaritans, to whom the true religion had never been made known. This is plain from the expression of the woman, "I know that Messiah cometh, which is called Christ: when he is come, he will tell us all things," (John 4:25). Nor was this a mere random presumption which had entered the minds of the Jews. They believed what sure oracles had taught them. One of the most remarkable passages is that of Isaiah, "Behold, I have given him for a witness to the people, a leader and commander to the people," (Is. 54:4); that is, in the same way in which he had previously in another place styled him "Wonderful, Counselor," (Is. 9:6). For this reason, the apostle commending the perfection of gospel doctrine, first says that "God, at sundry times and in divers manners spake in times past unto the prophets," and then adds, that he "has in these last days spoken unto us by his Son," (Heb. 1:1, 2). But as the common office of the prophets was to hold the Church in suspense, and at the same time support it until the advent of the Mediator; we read, that the faithful, during the dispersion, complained that they were deprived of that ordinary privilege. "We see not our signs: there is no more any prophet, neither is there among us any that knoweth how long," (Ps. 74:9). But when Christ was now not far distant, a period was assigned to Daniel "to seal up the vision and prophecy," (Daniel 9:24), not only that the authority of the prediction there spoken of might be established, but that believers might, for a time, patiently submit to the want of the prophets, the fulfillment and completion of all the prophecies being at hand.

SECTION 2

Moreover, it is to be observed, that the name Christ refers to those three offices: for we know that under the law, prophets as well as priests and kings were anointed with holy oil. Whence, also, the celebrated name of Messiah was given to the promised Mediator. But although I admit (as, indeed, I have elsewhere shown) that he was so called from a view to the nature of the kingly office, still the prophetical and sacerdotal unctions have their proper place, and must not be overlooked. The former is expressly mentioned by Isaiah in these words: "The Spirit of the Lord God is upon me: because the Lord has anointed me

to preach good tidings unto the meek; he has sent me to bind up the broken-hearted, to proclaim liberty to the captive, and the opening of the prison to them that are bound; to proclaim the acceptable year of the Lord," (Is. 60:1, 2). We see that he was anointed by the Spirit to be a herald and witness of his Father's grace, and not in the usual way; for he is distinguished from other teachers who had a similar office. And here, again, it is to be observed, that the unction which he received, in order to perform the office of teacher, was not for himself, but for his whole body, that a corresponding efficacy of the Spirit might always accompany the preaching of the Gospel. This, however, remains certain, that by the perfection of doctrine which he brought, an end was put to all the prophecies, so that those who, not contented with the Gospel, annex somewhat extraneous to it, derogate from its authority. The voice which thundered from heaven, "This is my beloved Son, hear him" gave him a special privilege above all other teachers. Then from him, as head, this unction is diffused through the members, as Joel has foretold, "Your sons and your daughters shall prophesy, your old men shall dream dreams, and your young men shall see visions," (Joel 2:28). Paul's expressions, that he was "made unto us wisdom," (1 Cor. 1:30), and elsewhere, that in him "are hid all the treasures of wisdom and knowledge," (Col. 2:3), have a somewhat different meaning, namely, that out of him there is nothing worth knowing, and that those who, by faith, apprehend his true character, possess the boundless immensity of heavenly blessings. For which reason, he elsewhere says, "I determined not to know any thing among you, save Jesus Christ and him crucified," (1 Cor. 2:2). And most justly: for it is unlawful to go beyond the simplicity of the Gospel. The purpose of this prophetical dignity in Christ is to teach us, that in the doctrine which he delivered is substantially included a wisdom which is perfect in all its parts.

SECTION 3

I come to the Kingly office, of which it were in vain to speak, without previously reminding the reader that its nature is spiritual; because it is from thence we learn its efficacy, the benefits it confers, its whole power and eternity. Eternity, moreover, which in Daniel an angel attributes to the office of Christ (Dan. 2:44), in Luke an angel justly applies to the salvation of his people (Luke 1:33). But this is also twofold, and must be viewed in two ways; the one pertains to the whole body of the Church the other is proper to each member. To the former is to be referred what is said in the Psalms, "Once have I sworn by my holiness, that I will not lie unto David. His seed shall endure for ever, and his throne as the sun before me. It shall be established for ever, as the moon, and as a faithful witness in heaven," (Ps. 89:35, 37). There can be no doubt that God here promises that he will be, by the hand of his Son, the eternal governor and defender of the Church. In none but Christ will the fulfillment of this prophecy be found; since immediately after Solomon's death the kingdom in n great measure lost its dignity, and, with ignominy to the family of David, was transferred to a private individual. Afterwards decaying by degrees, it at length came to a sad and dishonorable end. In the same sense are we to understand the exclamation of Isaiah, "Who shall declare his generation?" (Isaiah 53:8). For he asserts that Christ will so survive death as to be connected with his members. Therefore, as often as we hear that Christ is armed with eternal power, let us learn that the perpetuity of the Church is thus effectually secured; that amid the turbulent agitations by which it is constantly harassed, and the grievous and fearful commotions which threaten innumerable disasters, it still remains safe. Thus, when David derides the audacity of the enemy who attempt to throw off the yoke of God and his anointed, and says, that kings and nations rage "in vain," (Ps. 2:2-4), because he who sitteth in the heaven is strong enough to repel their assaults, assuring believers of the perpetual preservation of the Church, he animates them to have good hope whenever it is occasionally oppressed. So, in another place, when speaking in the person of God, he says, "The Lord said unto my Lord, Sit thou at my right hand, until I make thine enemies thy footstool," (Ps. 110:1), he reminds us, that however numerous and powerful the enemies who conspire to assault the Church, they are not possessed of strength sufficient to prevail against the immortal decree by which he appointed his Son eternal King. Whence it follows that the devil, with the whole power of the world, can never possibly destroy the Church, which is founded on the eternal throne of Christ. Then in regard to the special use to be made by each believer, this same eternity ought to elevate us to the hope of a blessed immortality. For we see that every thing which is earthly, and of the world, is temporary, and soon fades away. Christ, therefore, to raise our hope to the heavens, declares that his kingdom is not of this world (John 18:36). In fine, let each of us, when he hears that the kingdom of Christ is spiritual, be roused by the thought to entertain the hope of a better life, and to expect that as it is now protected by the hand of Christ, so it will be fully realized in a future life.

SECTION 4

That the strength and utility of the kingdom of Christ cannot, as we have said, be fully perceived without recognizing it as spiritual, is sufficiently apparent, even from this, that having during the whole course of our lives to war under the cross, our condition here is bitter and wretched. What then would it avail us to be ranged under the government of a heavenly King, if its benefits were not realized beyond the present earthly life? We must, therefore, know that the happiness which is promised to us in Christ does not consist in external advantages—such as leading a joyful and tranquil life, abounding in wealth, being secure against all injury, and having an affluence of delights, such as the flesh is wont to long for—but properly belongs to the heavenly life. As in the world the prosperous and desirable condition of a people consists partly in the abundance of temporal good and domestic peace, and partly in the strong protection which gives security against external violence; so Christ also enriches his people with all things necessary to the eternal salvation of their souls and fortifies them with courage to stand unassailable by all the attacks of spiritual foes. Whence we infer, that he reigns more for us than for himself, and that both within us and without us; that being replenished, in so far as God knows to be expedient, with the gifts of the Spirit, of which we are naturally destitute, we may feel from their first fruits, that we are truly united to God for perfect blessedness; and then trusting to the power of the same Spirit, may not doubt that we shall always be victorious against the devil, the world, and every thing that can do us harm. To this effect was our Savior's reply to the Pharisees, "The kingdom of God is within you." "The kingdom of God cometh not with observation," (Luke 17:21, 22). It is probable that on his declaring himself to be that King under whom the highest blessing of God was to be expected, they had in derision asked him to produce his insignia. But to prevent those who were already more than enough inclined to the earth from dwelling on its pomp, he bids them enter into their consciences, for "the kingdom of God" is "righteousness, and peace, and joy in the Holy Ghost," (Rom. 14:17). These words briefly teach what the kingdom of Christ bestows upon us. Not being earthly or carnal, and so subject to corruption, but spiritual, it raises us even to eternal life, so that we can patiently live at present under toil, hunger, cold, contempt, disgrace, and other annoyances; contented with this, that our King will never abandon us, but will supply our necessities until our warfare is ended, and we are called to triumph: such being the nature of his kingdom, that he communicates to us whatever he received of his Father. Since then he arms and equips us by his power, adorns us with splendor and magnificence, enriches us with wealth, we here find most abundant cause of glorying, and also are inspired with boldness, so that we can contend intrepidly with the devil, sin, and death. In fine, clothed with his righteousness, we can bravely surmount all the insults of the world: and as he replenishes us liberally with his gifts, so we can in our turn bring forth fruit unto his glory.

SECTION 5

Accordingly, his royal unction is not set before us as composed of oil or aromatic perfumes; but he is called the Christ of God, because "the Spirit of the Lord" rested upon him; "the Spirit of wisdom and understanding, the Spirit of counsel and might, the Spirit of knowledge and of the fear of the Lord," (Isaiah 11:2). This is the oil of joy with which the Psalmist declares that he was anointed above his fellows (Ps. 45:7). For, as has been said, he was not enriched privately for himself, but that he might refresh the parched and hungry with his abundance. For as the Father is said to have given the Spirit to the Son without measure (John 3:34), so the reason is expressed, that we might all receive of his fullness, and grace for grace (John 1:16). From this fountain flows the copious supply (of which Paul makes mention, Eph. 4:7) by which grace is variously distributed to believers according to the measure of the gift of Christ. Here we have ample confirmation of what I said, that the kingdom of Christ consists in the Spirit, and not in earthly delights or pomp, and that hence, in order to be partakers with him, we must renounce the world. A visible symbol of this grace was exhibited at the baptism of Christ, when the Spirit rested upon him in the form of a dove. To designate the Spirit and his gifts by the term "unction" is not new, and ought not to seem absurd (see 1 John 2:20, 27), because this is the only quarter from which we derive life; but especially in what regards the heavenly life, there is not a drop of vigor in us save what the Holy Spirit instills, who has chosen his seat in Christ, that thence the heavenly riches, of which we are destitute, might flow to us in copious abundance. But because believers stand invincible in the strength of their King, and his spiritual riches abound towards them, they are not improperly called Christians. Moreover, from this eternity of which we have spoken, there is nothing derogatory in the expression of Paul, "Then cometh the end, when he shall have delivered up the kingdom to God, even the Father," (1 Cor. 15:24); and also, "Then shall the Son also himself be subject unto him that put all things under him, that God may be all in all" (1 Cor. 15:28); for the meaning merely is, that, in that perfect glory, the administration of the kingdom will not be such as it now is.

For the Father has given all power to the Son, that by his hand he may govern, cherish, sustain us, keep us under his guardianship, and give assistance to us. Thus, while we wander far as pilgrims from God, Christ interposes, that he may gradually bring us to full communion with God. And, indeed, his sitting at the right hand of the Father has the same meaning as if he was called the vicegerent of the Father, entrusted with the whole power of government. For God is pleased, mediately (so to speak) in his person to rule and defend the Church. Thus also his being seated at the right hand of the Father is explained by Paul, in the Epistle to the Ephesians, to mean, that "he is the head over all things to the Church, which is his body," (Eph. 1:20, 22). Nor is this different in purport from what he elsewhere teaches, that God has "given him a name which is above every name; that at the name of Jesus every knee shall bow, of things in heaven, and things in earth, and things under the earth, and that every tongue should confess that Jesus Christ is Lord, to the glory of God the Father," (Phil. 2:9-11). For in these words, also, he commends an arrangement in the kingdom of Christ, which is necessary for our present infirmity. Thus Paul rightly infers that God will then be the only Head of the Church, because the office of Christ, in defending the Church, shall then have been completed. For the same reason, Scripture throughout calls him Lord, the Father having appointed him over us for the express purpose of exercising his government through him. For though many lordships are celebrated in the world, yet Paul says, "To us there is but one God, the Father, of whom are all things, and we in him; and one Lord Jesus Christ, by whom are all things, and we by him," (1 Cor. 8:6). Whence it is justly inferred that he is the same God, who, by the mouth of Isaiah, declared, "The Lord is our Judge, the Lord is our Lawgiver, the Lord is our King: he will save us," (Is. 33:22). For though he every where describes all the power which he possesses as the benefit and gift of the Father, the meaning simply is, that he reigns by divine authority, because his reason for assuming the office of Mediator was, that

descending from the bosom and incomprehensible glory of the Father, he might draw near to us. Wherefore there is the greater reason that we all should with one consent prepare to obey, and with the greatest alacrity yield implicit obedience to his will. For as he unites the offices of King and Pastor towards believers, who voluntarily submit to him, so, on the other hand, we are told that he wields an iron scepter to break and bruise all the rebellious like a potter's vessel (Ps. 2:9). We are also told that he will be the Judge of the Gentiles, that he will cover the earth with dead bodies, and level down every opposing height (Ps. 110:6). Of this examples are seen at present, but full proof will be given at the final judgment, which may be properly regarded as the last act of his reign.

SECTION 6

With regard to his Priesthood, we must briefly hold its end and use to be, that as a Mediator, free from all taint, he may by his own holiness procure the favor of God for us. But because a deserved curse obstructs the entrance, and God in his character of Judge is hostile to us, expiation must necessarily intervene, that as a priest employed to appease the wrath of God, he may reinstate us in his favor. Wherefore, in order that Christ might fulfill this office, it behoved him to appear with a sacrifice. For even under the law of the priesthood it was forbidden to enter the sanctuary without blood, to teach the worshipper that however the priest might interpose to deprecate, God could not be propitiated without the expiation of sin. On this subject the Apostle discourses at length in the Epistle to the Hebrews, from the seventh almost to the end of the tenth chapter. The sum comes to this, that the honor of the priesthood was competent to none but Christ, because, by the sacrifice of his death, he wiped away our guilt, and made satisfaction for sin. Of the great importance of this matter, we are reminded by that solemn oath which God uttered, and of which he declared he would not repent, "Thou art a priest for ever, after the order of Melchizedek," (Ps. 110:4). For, doubtless, his purpose was to ratify that point on which he knew that our salvation chiefly hinged. For, as has been said, there is no access to God for us or for our prayers until the priest, purging away our defilements, sanctify us, and obtain for us that favor of which the impurity of our lives and hearts deprives us. Thus we see, that if the benefit and efficacy of Christ's priesthood is to reach us, the commencement must be with his death. Whence it follows, that he by whose aid we obtain favor, must be a perpetual intercessor. From this again arises not only confidence in prayer, but also the tranquility of pious minds, while they recline in safety on the paternal indulgence of God, and feel assured, that whatever has been consecrated by the Mediator is pleasing to him. But since God under the Law ordered sacrifices of beasts to be offered to him, there was a different and new arrangement in regard to Christ—viz. that he should be at once victim and priest, because no other fit satisfaction for sin could be found, nor was any one worthy of the honor of offering an only begotten son to God. Christ now bears the office of priest, not only that by the eternal law of reconciliation he may render the Father favorable and propitious to us, but also admit us into this most honorable alliance. For we though in ourselves polluted, in him being priests (Rev. 1:6), offer ourselves and our all to God, and freely enter the heavenly sanctuary, so that the sacrifices of prayer and praise which we present are grateful and of sweet odor before him. To this effect are the words of Christ, "For their sakes I sanctify myself," (John 17:19); for being clothed with his holiness, inasmuch as he has devoted us to the Father with himself (otherwise we were an abomination before him), we please him as if we were pure and clean, nay, even sacred. Hence that unction of the sanctuary of which mention is made in Daniel (Dan. 9:24). For we must attend to the contrast between this unction and the shadowy one which was then in use; as if the angel had said, that when the shadows were dispersed, there would be a clear priesthood in the person of Christ. The more detestable, therefore, is the fiction of those who, not content with the priesthood of Christ, have dared to take it upon themselves to sacrifice him, a thing daily attempted in the Papacy, where the mass is represented as an immolation of Christ.

John Calvin
Institutes of Christian Religion, Book 2,
Chapter 15
Henry Beveridge translation

1.6 The Sufferings of the Messiah, John Gill

Spurgeon maintained that John Gill, 1697—1771, the English Baptist theologian, was "one of the most able Hebraists of his day. He was always at work; it is difficult to say when he slept, for he wrote 10,000 folio pages of theology."

To say that Dr. Gill influenced evangelical Christians in general and Baptists in particular is like saying the sun influences the daytime. He was the first Baptist to write a complete systematic theology and the first to write a verse-by-verse commentary of the entire Bible. Gill wrote so much that he was known as Dr. Voluminous. Tom Nettles has written of him, "His loss was felt keenly by the whole denomination of Baptists, a group still small and despised . . . His outstanding scholarship, zeal for truth and pious polemics had greatly encouraged Baptists."

Concerning the sufferings of the Messiah; wherein Psalm 22 and Isaiah 53 are particularly considered: as also the several circumstances which were to attend these sufferings.

The writers of the New Testament, as they give an account of the sufferings of Jesus, so they appeal to the books of the Old Testament, as containing prophecies which speak of the Messiah's sufferings; from whence they reasoned with the Jews (Acts 17:2, 3), opening and alleging, that Christ must needs have suffered and risen again from the dead; and that that Jesus whom they preached was Christ. They aver, that the divine Spirit in the prophets (1 Pet. 1:11) testified beforehand the sufferings of Christ unto them, as well as the glory that should follow; and that when they spoke of the sufferings of Jesus, they said (Acts 26:22, 23), none other things than those which the prophets and Moses did say, should come to pass; and that, in what the Jews did to Jesus, was fulfilled, what (Acts 3:18) God before had showed by the mouth of all his prophets. Nay, Jesus himself, in reproving some of his disciples for their dullness and unbelief, said unto them (Luke 24:25-27), O fools and slow of heart to believe all that the prophets have spoken; ought not Christ to have suffered these things, and to enter into his glory? therefore beginning at Moses, and all the prophets, he expounded unto them in all the scriptures, the things concerning himself; that is, those things which chiefly concerned his sufferings. Now, seeing there are such manifest appeals to the books of the Old Testament, as containing prophecies of a suffering Messiah, which had their fulfillment in Jesus, my business in this chapter will be,

First, To consider those prophecies which speak of him as such, and attempt to approve that they belong to him, and him only.

Secondly, To point out the several parts of his sufferings according to these prophecies. And,

Thirdly, Take a view of the several circumstances which were to attend those sufferings.

First, I shall consider those prophecies which speak of the Messiah as suffering, and attempt to prove that they belong to him, and him only. Now the principal prophecies which speak of this affair, and are generally understood to belong thereunto, are contained in Psalm 22 and Isaiah 53 which I shall particularly consider.

1st, The Twenty Second Psalm is commonly understood by Christian interpreters to be a prophecy of the Messiah as suffering; and indeed it cannot with any tolerable color or pretense be applied to any other. That one single individual person is spoken of, throughout the Psalm, the whole series and connection thereof manifestly shew, and therefore the whole body of the Jewish nation, or the congregation of Israel, cannot be intended. Besides, this person is not only distinguished from the viler sort of the people, by whom he was reproached and reviled, verse 6-8 but also from those who are called the brethren, the congregation of Israel, and those who fear the Lord, verse 22, 23 before whom he was to praise the Lord. And as a single person, so a suffering person is certainly intended, as is manifest from his being represented as one forsaken of God, despised by men, encompassed by his enemies, by whom he is cruelly racked and tortured, his bones dislocated, his hands and feet pierced, and he even brought to the dust of death. Now this single and suffering person can be no other than the Messiah. And that the Messiah is intended in this Psalm, may be collected from the title; upon, or concerning Aijeleta Shahar, which respects the subject thereof, and may be rendered, the hind of the morning, which well agrees with the Messiah, and is expressive of his swiftness and readiness in appearing for the salvation of his people, and with our Jesus, who in the very morning of his infancy, was hunted after by Herod, and his agents, to take away his life; Others render it the morning star, which is one of the titles of Jesus (Rev. 22:16). The Targum expresses it by the daily morning sacrifice, which was typical of the Lamb of God which taketh away the sin of the world, and is very justly taken notice of here, where the sufferings of the Messiah are so particularly set forth, which were to be a propitiatory sacrifice for the sins of men. Besides, the person treated of in this Psalm, is one in whom the happiness of God's people was much concerned; by whom the meek were to be satisfied, and enjoy eternal life, as the consequence of his sufferings, and therefore are called upon to praise the Lord on that account, verse 23-26. Moreover, the conversion of the Gentiles through the preaching of the gospel, which was peculiar to the days of the Messiah, was to follow upon the sufferings of this person. Nay, even some Jewish writers have been obliged to apply some parts of this Psalm to the Messiah, which they evidently saw could not in any tolerable sense be referred to any other.

2dly, The fifty-third chapter of Isaiah is another prophecy, which is generally understood by Christian interpreters of the Messiah and his sufferings. The modern Jews, indeed, not being able to make it suit with their now generally received notions of the Messiah, have endeavored to substitute some other person as the subject thereof. . . . But all and every part of this prophecy exactly agrees with the Messiah Jesus, whose first appearance was mean and abject, on the account of which he was despised by men, by whom he suffered many things, which he bore with inexpressible patience, and at last death itself, which was an expiatory sacrifice for the sins of all his people, which being laid on him, he bore in his own body on the tree, and being raised from the dead, is now exalted, extolled, and made very high, at his Father's right hand, where he ever lives to intercede for transgressors; and has ever since had a large number of disciples, who have embraced his doctrines, and espoused his cause; a seed which have served him, and will continue to do so, till time shall be no more.

Secondly, Having considered those two remarkable prophecies which speak of the Messiah as suffering; I proceed to consider the several parts of his sufferings, as they are pointed out in those prophecies, and observe their fulfillment in Jesus.

1st, He was to undergo much reproach from men, to be despised, (Is. 53:3; Ps. 22:6) and rejected by them; nay, to be accounted a worm and no man. How much Jesus was slighted and disesteemed by the men of his generation, on the account of his mean parentage, education, outward poverty, the despicableness of his followers, etc. is notorious enough; as well as how he was flouted, jeered, and scoffed at, when upon the cross, by his enemies, who used the very words in Psalm 22:8 wagging their heads at him.

2dly, He was to be smote and buffeted; this judge of Israel was to be smote with a rod upon the cheek (Micah 5:1), as Jesus was, both by the Jewish and Roman soldiers, which he very patiently endured; and, as was prophesied of him (Is. 1:6), gave his back to the smiters, and his cheeks to them that plucked off the hair, and hid not his face from shame and spitting.

3dly, He was to suffer death for the sins of his people; he was not only to be wounded (Is. 53:5, 8, 12; Ps. 22:15) and bruised for their transgressions, but to be cut off out of the land of the living, his soul was to be poured out unto death, and he brought into the dust thereof; accordingly Jesus died for our sins; (1 Cor. 15:3) according to these scriptures.

4thly, As he was to die, so he was to die the death of the cross, which might be collected from the piercing of his hands and feet, the disjointing of his bones, and the prodigious fever which was to seize him, and dry up his strength like a potsherd, and cause his tongue to cleave to his jaws, all which circumstances, usually attending the crucifixion of persons, were prophesied of in the twenty-second Psalm. Now it is manifest enough that Jesus was obedient unto death, even the death of the cross; though it was very unlikely that he ever should have died in that manner, that not only being a Roman punishment, but also what was not usually inflicted on persons guilty of the crime with which he was charged, and for which he was condemned; but so it was, that these prophecies might be fulfilled, as well as his own predictions be verified.

5thly, He was to be buried and laid in the grave, which was the finishing part of his humiliation. Isaiah says of the Messiah, (Is. 53:9) that he made his grave with the wicked, and with the rich in his death, which words may be rendered thus, he put, or placed his grave with the wicked, but, his tombstone, or sepulchral monument, was with the rich; which was literally fulfilled in Jesus, whose grave, though it was put under the care and custody of the wicked soldiers, who were placed there to watch, lest the disciples should remove the body, and say he was risen from the dead, which circumstance attending his interment, might seem somewhat dishonorable, yet, there being a famous tomb erected over it, at the charge of Joseph of Arimathea, a rich man, rendered his burial honorable, which honor was done him, because he had done no violence, neither was any deceit in his mouth. Hereby another prophecy appears to be fulfilled, which speaks of the Messiah's burial, in Isaiah 11:10 and his rest shall be glorious, this may very well be understood of the grave, which is a place of rest, where, as Job says, Job 3:17, The wicked cease from troubling, and the weary be at rest. The Vulgate renders the words thus, *erit sepulchrum ejus gloriosum*, "his grave shall be glorious." I have already proved, that this prophecy belongs to the Messiah. Abarbinel owns it, and not only so, but also acknowledges, that this clause may be expounded of the Messiah's honorable burial. The author of The Scheme of Literal Prophecy ought to take this as a full answer to his exception, out of Grotius and White, against the prophecy in Isaiah.

To conclude this head; the occasion, nature, efficacy, and intent of the Messiah's sufferings, as delivered in those prophecies, appear to be the very same as those of the sufferings of Jesus, delivered in the New Testament. The occasion of the Messiah's sufferings was not to be for any sin of his own, but for the sins of others, for which his death was to be a propitiatory sacrifice, whereby sin was to be abolished and done away, peace and pardon procured, and an everlasting righteousness brought in, and this upon the account of all the people of God; for he was to bear the sins of many, and be stricken for the transgressions of his people; all which perfectly agrees with those doctrines respecting the occasion, nature, efficacy, intent, and extent of the sufferings of Jesus, which the New Testament abounds with. But I proceed,

Thirdly, To consider the several circumstances which were to attend the death and sufferings of the Messiah. And I shall begin,

1st, With the hypocrisy and treachery of one of his familiar friends; that Jesus was betrayed by Judas, one of his disciples, not only the evangelists affirm, but the Jews themselves acknowledge in the account which they themselves gave of the life and actions of Jesus. Now this, Jesus says, was to come to pass, (John 13:18) that the scripture might be fulfilled, He that eateth bread with me hath lift up his heel against me. The scripture referred to is Psalm 41:9 which Psalm, in its literal, and obvious sense, wholly belongs to the Messiah. In verse 1-3, the happiness of those persons is set forth, who should consider the poor, that is, the Messiah in his low estate, one of whose characters is lowly or poor, Zechariah 9:9 in verse 5, his enemies are represented wishing for his death, saying, When shall he die and his name perish? which was the thing the Jews so earnestly desired, and so much longed for, with respect to Jesus, and never left plotting till they had effected it; which hypocrisy, perfidy, treachery, and vile designs of theirs, are very aptly described in verses 6, 7 where the true complexion and actions of the Jews, in the times of Jesus, are expressed to the life; see Matthew 22:15-18 and chapter 26:3, 4 and this thing which they so much desired, they brought about by suborning false witnesses, and bringing a wrong charge, and false accusation against him, which is signified in verse 8 an evil disease, a word of Belial, a wicked word, or false accusation, say they, cleaveth fast unto him, which was that of making himself a king, forbidding to give tribute to Caesar (Luke 23:2), which succeeded according to their wishes, to the taking away of his life; and therefore, in an exulting and triumphing manner, they say, And now that he lieth, that is, in the grave, he shall rise up no more, that is, from the dead, though that was a mistake of theirs, for he was raised from the dead, for which he prays, verse 10 that he might requite these his enemies, as he did, by destroying their city, temple, and nation. Now all these things must needs be very afflicting to the Messiah, and he mentions them here by way of complaint; but yet what was an aggravation of them, and made them still more heavy, was the deceitfulness and treachery of one of his disciples, who betrayed him into the hands of his enemies; and he complains of it as such in verse 9. Yea mine own familiar friend, in whom I trusted, which did eat of my bread, hath lift up his heel against me. Though he concludes the Psalm with joy and thankfulness for God's raising him from the dead, exalting him with his own right hand, and setting him before his face for ever, verse 11-13. There is indeed one thing which may seem to render this Psalm inapplicable to the Messiah, and so to Jesus, and that is, this person confesses himself to be a sinner in verse 4, I said, Lord be merciful unto me, and heal my soul, for I have sinned against thee. The words may be rendered thus, heal my soul, that is, delivered me out of my sorrows and afflictions, because I have made an offering for sin unto thee. This well agrees with the Messiah, who was to make his soul an offering for sin (Is. 53:10), and with Jesus, who was made sin (2 Cor. 5:21), that is, an offering for sin, for us, who knew no sin, that we might be made the righteousness of God in him. From the whole it appears, that this Psalm is a literal prophecy of the Messiah, and that Judas's betraying of Jesus, was a literal accomplishment of the passage referred to in it. I proceed,

2dly, To consider another circumstance which was to attend the Messiah as suffering, and that is his being sold, by the same person that betrayed him, for thirty pieces of silver. That Jesus was sold at such a price, cannot well be denied, neither is it: Judas agreed with the chief priests to deliver him into their hands, on this consideration, who, having done his work, receives his wages; but his conscience afterwards accusing him for this vile and barbarous action, he returned them the money, acknowledging his guilt; but they not judging it lawful put this money into the treasury, because it was the price of blood, bought the potter's field with it, to bury strangers in; all which was exactly according to the prophecies of the Old Testament. . . .

3dly, Another circumstance which was to attend the Messiah's sufferings, is, his being forsaken by the rest of his disciples. That the disciples of Jesus forsook him and fled, when he was apprehended by his enemies, not only the evangelist, but the Jews themselves affirm. Now this was foretold by Jesus, who declares that so it should be, because it is written (Matthew 26:31, 56), I will smite the shepherd, and the sheep of the flock shall be scattered abroad. The place referred to, where these words are written, is Zechariah 13:7, Awake, O sword, against my shepherd, and against the man that is my fellow, saith the Lord of hosts: smite the shepherd, and the sheep shall be scattered; which prophecy is a manifest prophecy of the Messiah, as appears not only from the character of a shepherd, which is frequently given to the Messiah in the Old Testament, and is what Jesus bears in the New; but also from his being God's fellow, which cannot be said of any other, and is justly applicable to him, who, (Philippians 2:6), being in the form of God thought it not robbery to be equal with him. Many Jewish writers refer those words of Zechariah to the days of the Messiah, even to Messiah the son of Joseph.

4thly, The Messiah was not only to be forsaken by his disciples, but also by his God; this dereliction is prophesied of in Psalm 22 which Psalm has been proved to belong to the Messiah. Accordingly Jesus, while he was suffering on the cross, was deserted by his Father, and in his agony used the very words with which the Psalm begins, My God, my God, why hast thou forsaken me?

5thly, The Messiah was to be numbered with transgressors; accordingly, with Jesus, the Jews crucified two thieves (Mark 15:15, 27, 28), the one on his right hand, and the other on his left; and the scripture was fulfilled, which saith, And he was numbered with the transgressors. Nothing could more effectually do it, than their placing him between them, and his dying with them, which was a manifest indication, that he was reckoned as a malefactor, and so was numbered with them.

6thly, His garments were to be parted, and lots cast upon his vesture, according to Psalm 22:18 which was literally fulfilled in Jesus, Matthew 27:35.

7thly, It was prophesied of him, that gall would be given him for his meat, and vinegar for him to drink, and accordingly these were given to Jesus, when upon the cross; and therefore, in order to bring it about, and that this scripture might be fulfilled, he said, I thirst; which was not fulfilled by a mere accommodation of such a phrase found in the

Psalms, for this does not suppose that there was a prophecy of him, that he should say, I thirst, but his saying so, was an evidence of that thirst being upon him, prophesied of in Psalm 22:15, which was the occasion of fulfilling the prophecy, concerning the gall and vinegar, which were to be given him in this distress. Psalm 69:21.

8thly, A bone of him was not to be broken. Now it is very remarkable, that whereas it was a custom to break the legs of the crucified, and accordingly the legs of the thieves, which were crucified with Jesus, were broken; but when they came to him, finding him dead, notwithstanding all their rage and malice against him, they brake not his legs; and the evangelist observes (John 19:36), that these things were done that the scripture should be fulfilled, A bone of him shall not be broken. The scripture referred to is Psalm 34:20, he keepeth all his bones, not one of them is broken. Which, if understood of the righteous in general, had a very particular and remarkable completion in Jesus, though it seems rather to regard some particular person, and who can be so well supposed to be understood as the Messiah? To understand it of the righteous in general, will not hold good, for such a calamity sometimes befalls them as well as the wicked; and when under such a distress of body, they would be liable to a greater distress of mind; for from hence they would be apt to conclude, that they were not righteous persons, nor under the special care and protection of God, otherwise this promise would be made good to them, he keepeth all his bones: not one of them is broken.

9thly, The Messiah was to be pierced, at the time of his suffering, and accordingly Jesus was; for one of the soldiers, with a spear, pierced his side; whereby, as the evangelist observes (John 19:37), that scripture was fulfilled, they shall look upon him whom they have pierced: the scripture is Zechariah 12:10. Which prophecy, by many Jewish writers, is understood of the Messiah, and of the piercing him. The author of The Scheme of Literal Prophecy, says, that the words "manifestly appear not to concern Jesus; his reasons are, because there was to be a war in Judea, and a siege of Jerusalem, and then a deliverance of the Jews, by the destruction of all the nations that should come up at that time against Jerusalem." And Mr. Sykes asks, "Did any one circumstance of all this happen to the Jews about the time of the death of Jesus? or rather, was not every thing the reverse of what Zechariah says; and instead of all nations being destroyed that came about Jerusalem, Jerusalem itself was destroyed; instead of a spirit of grace and supplications, the Jews have had their hearts hardened against the Christ; instead of mourning for him whom they pierced, they curse him and his followers even to this day." To both which I reply, that these things instanced in, were not according to this prophecy, to come to pass at the time of the piercing of the Messiah, but at the time of the Jews looking to him, and mourning for him, on the account thereof, when brought under a conviction of their evil in so doing; now whereas the piercing of the Messiah has been literally fulfilled in Jesus, and though the Jews, even to this very day, are hardened against him; yet there is no reason to conclude, but that that part of the prophecy, which concerns their looking to him, and a mourning for him, on the account of his being pierced by them, will also, in God's own time be fulfilled; when we may reasonably expect all these circumstances, attending it, will have their full accomplishment.

John Gill

1.7 OLD TESTAMENT PROPHECIES FULFILLED IN JESUS CHRIST, JEROME DOMINGUEZ

Jerome Dominguez, M.D., (1935-), a Roman Catholic, is author of over 90 books, including The Jerome Bible Commentary *400 web sites, weekly radio and TV programs for 35 years. He was born in Spain, and has been a medical doctor in New York since 1961, and is leader of the Cursillo Movement and the Charismatic Renewal. One of his children, Jerome, died at the Twin Towers on Sept. 11, 2001.*

There are over three hundred prophecies in the Old Testament about the first coming of the Messiah, all of them made hundreds of years before the birth of Jesus and fulfilled to the letter in Jesus Christ, the Messiah.

George Heron, a French mathematician, calculated that the odds of one man fulfilling only 40 of those prophecies are 1 in 10 to the power of 157. That is a 1 over a 1 followed by 157 zeros.

Another mathematician, Dr. Peter S. Ruckman, claims the odds of just 60 of these prophecies being fulfilled by the only person who claimed to be the Son of God, and who died on a "tree" on Calvary, and who rose the third day are 1 in 10 to the 895th power. That is a 1 over a 1 followed by 895 zeros.

MOSES AND THE PROPHETS

Philip found Nathanael and told him, "We have found the one Moses wrote about in the Law, and about whom the prophets also wrote—Jesus of Nazareth, the son of Joseph." (John 1:45)

MOSES

If you believed Moses, you would believe me, for he wrote about me. (John 5:46)

MOSES AND ALL THE PROPHETS

And beginning with Moses and all the Prophets, he explained to them what was said in all the Scriptures concerning himself. (Luke 24:27)

THE LAW OF MOSES, THE PROPHETS AND THE PSALMS

(These are the three Jewish divisions of the Old Testament Scriptures)

He said to them, This is what I told you while I was still with you: Everything must be fulfilled that is written about me in the Law of Moses, the Prophets and the Psalms. (Luke 24:44)

WHAT IS WRITTEN

He told them, This is what is written: The Christ will suffer and rise from the dead on the third day. (Luke 24:46)

Jerome Dominguez

1.8 50 SPECIFIC PROPHECIES FULFILLED IN JESUS, JEROME DOMINGUEZ

JESUS' ANCESTORS

1. The "seed of a woman:" Genesis 3:15, compare with Galatians 4:4.

2. Descendent of Abraham: Genesis 12:3; 18:18, compare with Acts 3:25; Matthew 1:1.

3. Descendent of Isaac: Genesis17:19; Luke 3:34.

4. Descendent of Jacob: Numbers 24:17, compare with Luke 3:34; Matthew1:2.

5. From the Tribe of Judah: Genesis 49:10; Luke 3:33.

6. Heir of the throne of David: Isaiah 9:7, compare with Luke 1:32-33.

JESUS' BIRTH AND CHILDHOOD

7. Born in Bethlehem: Micah 5:2, compare with Matthew 2:1 and Luke 2:4-7.

8. To be born of a virgin: Isaiah 7:14; Matthew 1:18; Luke 1:26-35.

9. Time of his birth: Daniel 9:25, compare with Luke 2:1.

10. Slaughter of the innocent children: Jeremiah 31:15, compare with Matthew 2:16-18.

11. Flight to Egypt: Hosea 11:1, compare with Matthew 2:14-15.

12. He shall be called a Nazarene: Judges 13:5, compare with Matthew 2:23.

JESUS' PASSION

13. Triumphal entry in Jerusalem on a donkey: Zechariah 9:9, compare with John 12:13-14.

14. Entry through the "Golden Gate," which will be shut for ever after his entrance: Ezekiel 44:1-2, compare with Mark 11:7-8.

15. Betrayed by a friend, for 30 pieces of silver: Zechariah 11:12; Psalm 41:9, compare with Mark 14:10; Matthew 26:14-15.

16. Money to be returned for a potter's field: Zechariah 11:13, compare with Matthew 27:6-7.

17. Judas' position to be taken by another: Psalm 109:7-8, compare with Acts 1:18-20.

18. Accused by false witnesses: Psalms 27:12; 35:11, compare with Matthew 26:60-61; Mark 14:57.

19. Silent to accusations: Isaiah 53:7, compare with Matthew 26:62-63; Mark15:4-5.

20. Spat on and struck: Isaiah 50:6; Matthew 26:67.

21. Hated without reason: Psalms 35:19; 69:4; 109:3-5, compare with John15:24-25.

22. Soldiers divided his garments and gambled for his clothing: Psalm 22:18; Matthew 27:35 (2 prophecies).

23. Crucified, "pierced through hands and feet:" Zechariah 12:10; Psalm 22:16, compare with Matthew 27:35, John 20:27.

24. Crucified with criminals: Isaiah 53:12, compare with Mark 15:27-28.

25. Experienced extreme thirst: Psalm 22:15, compare with John 19:28.

26. Given gall and vinegar: Psalm 69:21, compare with Matthew 27:34, 48; John 19:19.

27. No bones broken: Psalm 34:20, compare with John 19:32-36.

28. His side pierced: Zechariah 12:10, compare with John 19:34.

29. Deserted by God: Psalm 22:1, compare with Matthew 27:46; Psalm 22:1.

30. Vicarious sacrifice: Isaiah 53:4-5, 6, 12, compare with Matthew 8:16-17, Romans 4:25; 5:6-8; 1 Corinthians 15:3.

31. Buried with the rich: Isaiah 53:9; Matthew 27:57-60.

32. Deserted by his followers: Zechariah 13:7, compare with Mark 14:27.

33. Time of his death: Daniel 9:25, compare with Luke 2:1; Matthew 2:1.

JESUS' RESURRECTION

34. Resurrection of Jesus: Hosea 6:2; Psalms 16:10; 49:15, compare with Luke 24:6-7; Mark 16:6-7.

35. Other dead raised with Messiah: Isaiah 26:19; Ezekiel 37:7-10, compare with Matthew 27:52-53.

JESUS' ASCENSION

36. Ascension to heaven: Psalms 68:18; 24:3, compare with Luke 24:50-51; Acts 1:11; Mark 16:19.

37. Christ at the right hand of the Father: Psalm 110:1, compare with Hebrews 1:2, 3.

JESUS' MINISTRY

38. The way prepared by John the Baptist: Isaiah 40:3, 5, compare with John 1:23; Luke 3:3-6.

39. Preceded by a forerunner: Malachi 3:1; Luke 7:24-27.

40. Preceded by Elijah: Malachi 4:5-6; Matthew 11:13-14.

41. Declared the Son of God: Psalm 2:7; Matthew 3:17.

42. Galilean ministry: Isaiah 9:1-2; Matthew 4:13-16.

43. Speaks in parables: Psalm 78:2-4; Matthew13:34-35.

44. A prophet: Deuteronomy18:15; John 6:14; Acts 3:20-22.

45. Priest after the order of Melchizedek: Psalm 110:4; Hebrews 5:5-6.

46. To bind up the brokenhearted: Isaiah 61:1-2; Luke 4:18-19.

47. Rejected by his own people, the Jews: Isaiah 53:3; John 1:11.

48. Not believed: Isaiah 53:1; John 12:37.

49. Adored by infants: Psalm 8:2; Matthew 21:15-16.

50. Anointed and eternal: Psalm 45:6-7; Hebrews 1:8-12.

Jerome Dominguez

1.9 92 PROPHECIES IN THE PSALMS FULFILLED IN JESUS CHRIST, JEROME DOMINGUEZ

Psalm Prophecies	OT Scripture	NT Fulfillment
The Messiah would also be rejected by Gentiles.	Psalm 2:1	Acts 4:25-28
Political/religious leaders would conspire against the Messiah.	Psalm 2:2	Matthew 26:3-4 Mark 3:6
The Messiah would be King of the Jews.	Psalm 2:6	John 12:12-13 John 18:32
The Messiah would be the Son of God.	Psalm 2:7a	Luke 1:31-35 Matthew 3:16-17 Hebrews 1:5-6
The Messiah would reveal that He was the Son of God.	Psalm 2:7b	John 9:35-37
The Messiah would be raised from the dead and be crowned King.	Psalm 2:7c	Acts 13:30-33 Romans 1:3-4
The Messiah would ask God for His inheritance.	Psalm 2:8a	John 17:4-24
The Messiah would have complete authority over all things.	Psalm 2:8b	Matthew 28:18 Hebrews 1:1-2
The Messiah would not acknowledge those who did not believe in Him.	Psalm 2:12	John 3:36
Infants would give praise to the Messiah.	Psalm 8:2	Matthew 21:15-16
The Messiah would have complete authority over all things.	Psalm 8:6	Matthew 28:18
The Messiah would be resurrected.	Psalm 16:8-10a	Matthew 28:6 Acts 2:25-32
The Messiah's body would not see corruption (natural decay).	Psalm 16:8-10b	Acts 13:35-37
The Messiah would be glorified into the presence of God.	Psalm 16:11	Acts 2:25-33
The Messiah would come for all people.	Psalm 18:49	Ephesians 3:4-6
The Messiah would cry out to God.	Psalm 22:1a	Matthew 27:46
The Messiah would be forsaken by God at His crucifixion.	Psalm 22:1b	Mark 15:34
The Messiah would pray without ceasing before His death.	Psalm 22:2	Matthew 26:38-39

Psalm Prophecies	OT Scripture	NT Fulfillment
The Messiah would be despised and rejected by His own.	Psalm 22:6	Luke 23:21-23
The Messiah would be made a mockery.	Psalm 22:7	Matthew 27:39
Unbelievers would say to the Messiah, "He trusted in God, let Him now deliver Him."	Psalm 22:8	Matthew 27:41-43
The Messiah would know His Father from childhood.	Psalm 22:9	Luke 2:40
The Messiah would be called by God while in the womb.	Psalm 22:10	Luke 1:30-33
The Messiah would be abandoned by His disciples.	Psalm 22:11	Mark 14:50
The Messiah would be encompassed by evil spirits.	Psalm 22:12-13	Colossians 2:15
The Messiah's body would emit blood and water.	Psalm 22:14a	John 19:34
The Messiah would be crucified.	Psalm 22:14b	Matthew 27:35
The Messiah would thirst while dying.	Psalm 22:15a	John 19:28
The Messiah would thirst just prior to His death.	Psalm 22:15b	John 19:30
The Messiah would be observed by Gentiles at His crucifixion.	Psalm 22:16a	Luke 23:36
The Messiah would be observed by Jews at His crucifixion.	Psalm 22:16b	Matthew 27:41-43
Both the Messiah's hands and feet would be pierced.	Psalm 22:16c	Matthew 27:38
The Messiah's bones would not be broken.	Psalm 22:17a	John 19:32-33
The Messiah would be viewed by many during His crucifixion.	Psalm 22:17b	Luke 23:35
The Messiah's garments would be parted among the soldiers.	Psalm 22:18a	John 19:23-24
The soldiers would cast lots for the Messiah's clothes.	Psalm 22:18b	John 19:23-24
The Messiah's atonement would enable believers to receive salvation.	Psalm 22:22	Hebrews 2:10-12 Matthew 12:50 John 20:14
The Messiah's enemies would stumble and fall.	Psalm 27:2	John 18:3-6
The Messiah would be accused by false witnesses.	Psalm 27:12	Matthew 26:59-61
The Messiah would cry out to God, "Into thy hands I commend my spirit."	Psalm 31:5	Luke 23:46

Psalm Prophecies	OT Scripture	NT Fulfillment
There would be many attempts to kill the Messiah.	Psalm 31:13	Matthew 27:1
The Messiah would have no bones broken.	Psalm 34:20	John 19:32-33
The Messiah would be accused by many false witnesses.	Psalm 35:11	Mark 14:55-59
The Messiah would be hated without cause.	Psalm 35:19	John 18:19-23 John 15:24-25
The Messiah would be silent as a lamb before His accusers.	Psalm 38:13-14	Matthew 26:62-63
The Messiah would be God's sacrificial lamb for redemption of all mankind.	Psalm 40:6-8a	Hebrews 10:10-13
The Messiah would reveal that the Hebrew scriptures were written of Him.	Psalm 40:6-8b	Luke 24:44 John 5:39-40
The Messiah would do God's (His Father's) will.	Psalm 40:7-8	John 5:30
The Messiah would not conceal His mission from believing people.	Psalm 40:9-10	Luke 4:16-21
The Messiah would be betrayed by one of His own disciples.	Psalm 41:9	Mark 14:17-18
The Messiah would communicate a message of mercy.	Psalm 45:2	Luke 4:22
The Messiah's throne would be eternal.	Psalm 45:6-7a	Luke 1:31-33 Hebrews 1:8-9
The Messiah would be God.	Psalm 45:6-7b	Hebrews 1:8-9
The Messiah would act with righteousness.	Psalm 45:6-7c	John 5:30
The Messiah would be betrayed by one of His own disciples.	Psalm 55:12-14	Luke 22:47-48
The Messiah would ascend back into heaven.	Psalm 68:18a	Luke 24:51 Ephesians 4:8
The Messiah would give good gifts unto believing men.	Psalm 68:18b	Matthew 10:1 Ephesians 4:7-11
The Messiah would be hated and rejected without cause.	Psalm 69:4	Luke 23:13-22 John 15:24-25
The Messiah would be condemned for God's sake.	Psalm 69:7	Matthew 26:65-67
The Messiah would be rejected by the Jews.	Psalm 69:8a	John 1:11
The Messiah's very own brothers would reject Him.	Psalm 69:8b	John 7:3-5

Psalm Prophecies	OT Scripture	NT Fulfillment
The Messiah would become angry due to unethical practices by the Jews in the temple.	Psalm 69:9a	John 2:13-17
The Messiah would be condemned for God's sake.	Psalm 69:9b	Romans 15:3
The Messiah's heart would be broken.	Psalm 69:20a	John 19:34
The Messiah's disciples would abandon Him just prior to His death.	Psalm 69:20b	Mark 14:33-41
The Messiah would be offered gall mingled with vinegar while dying.	Psalm 69:21a	Matthew 27:34
The Messiah would thirst while dying.	Psalm 69:21b	John 19:28
The potter's field would be uninhabited (Field of Blood).	Psalm 69:25	Acts 1:16-20
The Messiah would teach in parables.	Psalm 78:2	Matthew 13:34-35
The Messiah would be exalted to the right hand of God.	Psalm 80:17	Acts 5:31
The Messiah would come from the lineage of David.	Psalm 89:3-4	Matthew 1:1
The Messiah would call God His Father.	Psalm 89:26	Matthew 11:27
The Messiah would be God's only "begotten" Son.	Psalm 89:27	Mark 16:6 Colossians 1:18 Revelation 1:5
The Messiah would come from the lineage of David.	Psalm 89:29	Matthew 1:1
The Messiah would come from the lineage of David.	Psalm 89:35-3	Matthew 1:1
The Messiah would be eternal.	Psalm 102:25-27a	Revelation 1:8 Hebrews 1:10-12
The Messiah would be the creator of all things.	Psalm 102:25-27b	John 1:3 Ephesians 3:9 Hebrews 1:10-12
The Messiah would calm the stormy sea.	Psalm 107:28-29	Matthew 8:24-26
The Messiah would be accused by many false witnesses.	Psalm 109:2	John 18:29-30
The Messiah would offer up prayer for His enemies.	Psalm 109:4	Luke 23:34
The Messiah's betrayer (Judas) would have a short life.	Psalm 109:8a	Acts 1:16-18 John 17:12
The Messiah's betrayer would be replaced by another.	Psalm 109:8b	Acts 1:20-26

Psalm Prophecies	OT Scripture	NT Fulfillment
The Messiah would be mocked by many.	Psalm 109:25	Mark 15:29-30
The Messiah would be Lord and King.	Psalm 110:1a	Matthew 22:41-45
The Messiah would be exalted to the right hand of God.	Psalm 110:1b	Mark 16:19 Matthew 22:41-46
The Messiah would be a Priest after the order of Melchizedec.	Psalm 110:4	Hebrews 6:17-20
The Messiah would be exalted to the right hand of God.	Psalm 110:5	1 Peter 3:21-22
The Messiah would be the "Stone" rejected by the builders (Jews).	Psalm 118:22	Matthew 21:42-43
The Messiah would come in the name of the Lord.	Psalm 118:26	Matthew 21:9
The Messiah would come from the lineage of David.	Psalm 132:11	Matthew 1:1
The Messiah would come from the lineage of David.	Psalm 132:17	Matthew 1:1 Luke 1:68-70

Jerome Dominguez

1.10 121 MESSIANIC PROPHECIES OF ISAIAH FULFILLED IN JESUS CHRIST, JEROME DOMINGUEZ

Isaiah Prophecies	OT Scripture	NT Fulfillment
The Jews would reject the Messiah.	Isaiah 6:9-10a	John 12:37-40
The Messiah would teach in parables.	Isaiah 6:9-10b	Matthew 13:13-15
The Messiah would be born of a virgin.	Isaiah 7:14a	Luke 1:34-35
The Messiah would be called Immanuel, "God With Us."	Isaiah 7:14b	Matthew 1:21-23, John 12:45
The Messiah would be God.	Isaiah 7:14c	1 Timothy 3:16
The Messiah would have wisdom from His childhood.	Isaiah 7:15	Luke 2:40
The Messiah would be a "Stumbling Stone" for the Jews.	Isaiah 8:14	Matthew 21:43-44
The Messiah would minister in Galilee.	Isaiah 9:1-2a	Matthew 4:12-17
The Messiah would be a light to the Gentiles.	Isaiah 9:1-2b	Luke 2:28-32
The birth of the Messiah.	Isaiah 9:6a	Luke 2:11
The Messiah would be the Son of God.	Isaiah 9:6b	Luke 1:35
The Messiah would be both man and God.	Isaiah 9:6c	John 10:30 John 12:45 John 14:7
The Messiah would be from everlasting.	Isaiah 9:6d	Colossians 1:17
The Messiah would come from the lineage of Jesse.	Isaiah 11:1a	Luke 3:23-32
The Messiah would grow up in Nazareth.	Isaiah 11:1b	Matthew 2:21-23
The Messiah would have the Spirit of God upon Him.	Isaiah 11:2a	Matthew 3:16-17
The Messiah would have the Spirit of knowledge and wisdom.	Isaiah 11:2b	Matthew 13:54
The Messiah would have the Spirit of knowledge and fear of God.	Isaiah 11:2c	Matthew 11:27 John 15:10
The Messiah would have a quick understanding in the fear of the Lord.	Isaiah 11:3a	Luke 2:46-47 Luke 4:31-32 John 14:31

Isaiah Prophecies	OT Scripture	NT Fulfillment
The Messiah would not judge on the basis of outward appearance.	Isaiah 11:3b	John 2:24-25 John 7:24
The Messiah would judge the poor with righteousness.	Isaiah 11:4	Mark 12:41-44 Luke 13:30
The Messiah would come from the lineage of Jesse.	Isaiah 11:10a	Luke 3:23-32
The Messiah would come for all people.	Isaiah 11:10b	Acts 13:47-48
The Messiah would have the key of David.	Isaiah 22:22	Revelation 3:7
The Messiah would defeat death (sin).	Isaiah 25:8	Revelation 1:18 2 Timothy 1:10
Several saints would rise to life at the resurrection of the Messiah.	Isaiah 26:19	Matthew 27:52-53
The Messiah would be the cornerstone.	Isaiah 28:16	1 Peter 2:4-6
The Messiah would heal the blind.	Isaiah 35:5a	Mark 10:51-52 John 9:1-7
The Messiah would heal the deaf.	Isaiah 35:5b	Mark 7:32-35
The Messiah would heal the lame.	Isaiah 35:6a	Matthew 12:10-13 John 5:5-9
The Messiah would heal the dumb.	Isaiah 35:6b	Matthew 9:32-33 Matthew 15:30
The forerunner (John The Baptist) of the Messiah would live in the wilderness.	Isaiah 40:3a	Matthew 3:1-4
The forerunner (John The Baptist) would prepare people for the coming of the Messiah.	Isaiah 40:3b	Matthew 3:11 Luke 1:17 John 1:29 John 3:28
The Messiah would be God.	Isaiah 40:3c	John 10:30 Philippians 2:5-7
The Messiah would be as a shepherd.	Isaiah 40:11	John 10:11 Mark 9:36-37
The Messiah would be God's messenger.	Isaiah 42:1a	John 4:34 John 5:30
The Messiah would have the Spirit of God upon Him.	Isaiah 42:1b	Matthew 3:16-17

Isaiah Prophecies	OT Scripture	NT Fulfillment
The Messiah would please God.	Isaiah 42:1c	Matthew 3:16-17
The Messiah would not desire personal attention for Himself.	Isaiah 42:2	Matthew 12:15-21
The Messiah would have compassion for the poor and needy.	Isaiah 42:3	Matthew 11:4-5 Matthew 12:15-20
The Messiah would receive direction from God.	Isaiah 42:6a	John 5:19-20 John 14:10-11
The Messiah would be ministered to by God.	Isaiah 42:6b	John 8:2 Luke 22:42-43
The Messiah would be the "New Covenant."	Isaiah 42:6c	Matthew 26:28
The Messiah would be a light to the Gentiles.	Isaiah 42:6d	John 8:12
The Messiah would heal the blind.	Isaiah 42:7	Matthew 9:27-30 Matthew 21:14
The Messiah would be the "First and the Last."	Isaiah 44:6	Revelation 1:17-18
The Messiah would be from everlasting.	Isaiah 48:16	John 17:24
The Messiah would come for all people.	Isaiah 49:1a	1 Timothy 2:4-6
The Messiah would be called by God while in the womb.	Isaiah 49:1b	Matthew 1:20-21
The Messiah would be called by His name before he was born.	Isaiah 49:1c	Luke 1:30-31
The Messiah's words would be as a sharp as a two-edged sword.	Isaiah 49:2a	Revelation 2:12-16 John 12:48
The Messiah would be protected by God.	Isaiah 49:2b	Matthew 2:13-15
The Messiah would be empowered for the judgment of mankind.	Isaiah 49:2c	John 5:22-29
The Messiah would be God's servant.	Isaiah 49:3a	John 17:4
The Messiah's life and death would glorify God.	Isaiah 49:3b	Matthew 15:30-31
The Messiah would be sorrowful because of the Jew's unbelief.	Isaiah 49:4	Luke 19:41-42
The Messiah would be God's servant.	Isaiah 49:5a	John 6:38 John 8:29
The Messiah would come to bring Israel back to God.	Isaiah 49:5b	Matthew 15:24 Matthew 10:5-7

Isaiah Prophecies	OT Scripture	NT Fulfillment
The Messiah would be God's servant.	Isaiah 49:6a	John 1:49-50
The Messiah would be a light to the Gentiles.	Isaiah 49:6b	Acts 13:47-48
The Messiah would be despised.	Isaiah 49:7	John 10:20 Matthew 27:22
The palms of the Messiah would be a witness.	Isaiah 49:16	John 20:25-28
The Messiah would speak with God given knowledge.	Isaiah 50:4	John 12:49 Matthew 7:28-29
The Messiah would not be rebellious to God's will.	Isaiah 50:5	John 12:27
The Messiah's back would be lashed (stripped).	Isaiah 50:6a	Matthew 27:26
The Messiah's face would be beaten and spit upon.	Isaiah 50:6b	Matthew 26:67
The Messiah would not waver from His mission.	Isaiah 50:7	Luke 9:51-53
The Messiah would be justified by His righteousness.	Isaiah 50:8	1 Timothy 3:16 Hebrews 8:32-34
The Messiah would completely trust in God.	Isaiah 50:8-10	John 11:7-10
The Messiah would proclaim the gospel from the mountain tops.	Isaiah 52:7	Matthew 5:1-7:29 John 14:31
The Messiah would be God's servant.	Isaiah 52:13a	John 9:4 John 14:31
The Messiah would be highly exalted by God.	Isaiah 52:13b	Philippians 2:9-11
The Messiah's face would be disfigured from extreme beatings during His trial.	Isaiah 52:14	Matthew 26:67-68 Matthew 27:26-30
The Messiah's blood would be shed to make atonement for all mankind.	Isaiah 52:15	Revelation 1:5
The Messiah's own people would reject Him.	Isaiah 53:1	John 12:37-38
The Messiah would grow up in Nazareth.	Isaiah 53:2a	Matthew 2:21-23
The Messiah would appear as an ordinary man.	Isaiah 53:2b	Philippians 2:7-8
The Messiah would be despised.	Isaiah 53:3a	Luke 4:28-29
The Messiah would be rejected.	Isaiah 53:3b	Matthew 27:21-23

Isaiah Prophecies	OT Scripture	NT Fulfillment
The Messiah would suffer great sorrow and grief.	Isaiah 53:3c	Luke 19:41-42 Matthew 26:37-38 Matthew 27:46
Men would deny association with the Messiah.	Isaiah 53:3d	Mark 14:50-52 Matthew 26:73-74
The Messiah bore our sorrows and sufferings.	Isaiah 53:4a	Luke 6:17-19 Matthew 8:16-17
The Messiah would bear the sins of the world upon Himself.	Isaiah 53:4b	1 Peter 2:24 1 Peter 3:18
Many would think the Messiah to be cursed by God. The Messiah would bear the penalty of death for man's sins.	Isaiah 53:4c Isaiah 53:5a	Matthew 27:41-43 Luke 23:33 Hebrews 9:28
The Messiah would be bruised for our iniquities.	Isaiah 53:5b	Colossians 1:20 Ephesians 2:13-18
The Messiah's back would be lashed at His trial.	Isaiah 53:5c	Matthew 27:26 1 Peter 2:24
The Messiah would be the sin-bearer for all mankind.	Isaiah 53:6	Galatians 1:4
The Messiah would be oppressed and afflicted.	Isaiah 53:7a	Matthew 27:27-31
The Messiah would be silent as a lamb before His accusers.	Isaiah 53:7b	Matthew 27:12-14
The Messiah would be God's sacrificial lamb.	Isaiah 53:7c	John 1:29 John 19:14-18
The Messiah would be condemned and persecuted.	Isaiah 53:8a	Matt. 26:47-27:31
The Messiah would be judged.	Isaiah 53:8b	John 18:13-22 Matthew 26:57-66 Matthew 27:1 Matthew 27:22 Luke 23:11
The Messiah would be killed.	Isaiah 53:8c	Matthew 27:35
The Messiah would die for the sins of the world.	Isaiah 53:8d	1 John 2:2
The Messiah would be buried in a borrowed rich man's tomb.	Isaiah 53:9a	Matthew 27:57
The Messiah would be completely innocent.	Isaiah 53:9b	Mark 15:3
The Messiah would have no deceit or guile in His mouth.	Isaiah 53:9c	John 18:38 Luke 23:33-34 1 Peter 2:21-22

Isaiah Prophecies	OT Scripture	NT Fulfillment
God's will would be that the Messiah should die for all mankind.	Isaiah 53:10a	John 18:11 Romans 3:23-26
The Messiah would be a sin offering.	Isaiah 53:10b	Matthew 20:28 Ephesians 5:2
The Messiah would be resurrected and live for ever.	Isaiah 53:10c	Mark 16:16 Revelation 1:17-18
The Messiah would prosper.	Isaiah 53:10d	John 17:1-5 Revelation 5:12
God would be completely satisfied with the suffering of the Messiah.	Isaiah 53:11a	John 12:27 Matthew 27:46
The Messiah would be God's servant.	Isaiah 53:11b	Romans 5:18-19
The Messiah would justify man before God.	Isaiah 53:11c	Romans 5:8-9
The Messiah would be the sin offering for all mankind.	Isaiah 53:11d	Hebrews 9:28
The Messiah would be exalted by God for his sacrifice.	Isaiah 53:12a	Matthew 28:18
The Messiah would freely lay down His life to save mankind.	Isaiah 53:12b	Luke 23:46
The Messiah would be counted with the criminals.	Isaiah 53:12c	Luke 23:32
The Messiah would be the sin offering for all mankind.	Isaiah 53:12d	2 Corinthians 5:21
The Messiah would intercede for man to God.	Isaiah 53:12e	Luke 23:34
The Messiah would be resurrected by God.	Isaiah 55:3	Acts 10:40-41 Acts 13:34
The Messiah would be a witness.	Isaiah 55:4	John 3:10-12 John 18:37
The Messiah would come to provide salvation for all mankind.	Isaiah 59:15-16a	John 6:40 1 Thess. 5:8-10
The Messiah would intercede between God and man.	Isaiah 59:15-16b	Matthew 10:32-33 Romans 8:34
The Messiah would come to Zion as their Redeemer.	Isaiah 59:20	Luke 2:38 John 10:11
The Messiah would have the Spirit of God upon Him.	Isaiah 61:1	Matthew 3:16-17
The Messiah would preach the gospel of "Good News."	Isaiah 61:1-2	Luke 4:18-21
The Messiah would come to provide salvation.	Isaiah 63:5	John 3:17 Colossians 2:13-15

Isaiah Prophecies	OT Scripture	NT Fulfillment
The Messiah would be revealed to a people who were not seeking Him.	Isaiah 65:1	Matthew 15:22-28 Romans 10:18-20
The Messiah would be rejected by His own (Jews).	Isaiah 65:2	John 5:37-40

Jerome Dominguez

3

THE HISTORICAL JESUS

1.11 EARLY EXTRA-BIBLICAL REFERENCES TO JESUS

1. Flavius Josephus
2. Tacitus
3. Pliny the Younger
4. Lucian
5. Suetonius

1. FLAVIUS JOSEPHUS (C. 37-C. 100) JEWISH HISTORIAN

Jesus, wise man and teacher
Now there was about this time Jesus, a wise man, if it be lawful to call him a man; for he was a doer of wonderful works, a teacher of such men as receive the truth with pleasure. He drew over to him both many of the Jews and many of the Gentiles. He was [the] Christ. And when Pilate, at the suggestion of the principal men amongst us, had condemned him to the cross, those that loved him at the first did not forsake him; for he appeared to them alive again the third day; as the divine prophets had foretold these and ten thousand other wonderful things concerning him. And the tribe of Christians, so named from him, are not extinct at this day.
Flavius Josephus, Antiquities, *Book 18, 3, 3*

2. CORNELIUS TACITUS (C. 56-C. 120) ROMAN HISTORIAN

Christus suffered at the hands of Pilatus
Consequently, to get rid of the report, Nero fastened the guilt and inflicted the most exquisite tortures on a class hated for their abominations, called Christians by the populace. Christus, [a reference to Christ] from whom the name had its origin, suffered the extreme penalty during the reign of Tiberius at the hands of one of our procurators,

Pontius Pilatus, and a most mischievous superstition, thus checked for the moment, again broke out not only in Judea, the first source of the evil, but even in Rome, where all things hideous and shameful from every part of the world find their center and become popular.
Tacitus, Annals, *15.44.2-8*

3. PLINY THE YOUNGER (C. 62-C. 114) GOVERNOR OF BITHYNIA IN ASIA MINOR

Sang a hymn to Christ
They [the Christians] were in the habit of meeting on a certain fixed day before it was light, when they sang in alternate verses a hymn to Christ, as to a god, and bound themselves by a solemn oath, not to any wicked deeds, but never to commit any fraud, theft or adultery, never to falsify their word, nor deny a trust when they should be called upon to deliver it up; after which it was their custom to separate, and then reassemble to partake of food—but food of an ordinary and innocent kind.
Pliny, Letters, *10. 96*

4. LUCIAN SAMOSATA (C. 120-C. 180) GREEK WRITER, SATIRIST, AND RHETORICIAN

The man who was crucified
The Christians, you know, worship a man to this day—the man who was crucified in

Palestine because he introduced this new cult into the world. . . . You see, these misguided creatures start with the general conviction that they are immortal for all time, which explains the contempt of death and voluntary self-devotion which are so common among them; and then it was impressed on them by their original lawgiver that they are all brothers, from the moment that they are converted, and deny the gods of Greece, and worship the crucified sage, and live after his laws. All this they take quite on faith, with the result that they despise all worldly goods alike, regarding them merely as common property.

Lucian, The Death of Peregrine

5. SUETONIUS (75-160) ROMAN HISTORIAN AND BIOGRAPHER

"Jews" expelled from Rome in c. 48 AD

As the Jews were making constant disturbances at the instigation of Chrestus [that is, Christus], he expelled them from Rome.

Suetonius, Life of Claudius, 25.4

Punishment by Nero was inflicted on the Christians, a class of men given to a new and mischievous superstition.

Suetonius, Lives of the Caesars, 26.2

1.12 CONSIDERATION OF THE SOURCES, PHILIP SCHAFF

1. HEATHEN WRITERS

The rise of Christianity was a phenomenon of too little apparent significance to attract the attention of the great world. It was only when it had refused to be quenched in the blood of its founder, and, breaking out of the narrow bounds of the obscure province in which it had its origin, was making itself felt in the centers of population, that it drew to itself a somewhat irritated notice. The interest of such heathen writers as mention it was in the movement, not in its author. But in speaking of the movement they tell something of its author, and what they tell is far from being of little moment.

He was, it seems, a certain "Christ," who had lived in Judea in the reign of Tiberius (A.D. 14-37), and had been brought to capital punishment by the procurator, Pontius Pilate (cf. Tacitus, *Annals, 15:44*). The significance of his personality to the movement inaugurated by him is already suggested by the fact that he, and no other, had impressed his name upon it. But the name itself by which he was known particularly attracts notice. This is uniformly, in these heathen writers, "Christ," not "Jesus." In Josephus, *Ant. 18.3.3, 20.9.1*, "Jesus," "Jesus, surnamed

Christ," occur. But the authenticity of the passages is questionable, especially that of the former. Suetonius (*Claudius, 25*) not unnaturally confuses this "Christus" with the Greek name "Chrestus"; but Tacitus and Pliny show themselves better informed and preserve it accurately. "Christ," however, is not a personal name, but the Greek rendering of the Hebrew title "Messiah." Clearly, then, it was as the promised Messiah of the Jews that their founder was reverenced by "the Christians"; and they had made so much of his Messiahship in speaking of him that the title "Christ" had actually usurped the place of his personal name, and he was everywhere known simply as "Christ." Their reverence for his person had, indeed, exceeded that commonly supposed to be due even to the Messianic dignity. Pliny records that this "Christ" was worshiped by "the Christians" of Pontus and Bithynia as their God (Pliny, *Epist., 96 to Trajan*). Beyond these great facts the heathen historians give little information about the founder of Christianity.

Philip Schaff
New Schaff-Herzog Encyclopedia of Religious Knowledge

1.13 THE HISTORICAL CHRIST, B. B. WARFIELD

Benjamin Breckinridge Warfield was born at "Grasmere" near Lexington, Kentucky, November 5, 1851, and died at Princeton, New Jersey, February 17, 1921.

Caspar Wistar Hodge, his immediate successor at Princeton Seminary and long his associate, in his Inaugural Address after referring to the illustrious men who had given the institution fame throughout the world for sound learning and true piety, such as Archibald Alexander, Charles Hodge and Archibald Alexander Hodge, spoke of Warfield as "excelling them all in erudition."

John DeWitt, long the professor of Church History in Princeton Seminary and himself a man of no mean scholarship, knew intimately the three great Reformed theologians of America of the preceding generation—Charles Hodge, W. G. T. Shedd and Henry B. Smith. DeWitt was not only certain that Warfield knew a great deal more than any one of them but that he was disposed to think that he knew more than all three of them put together.

Otto A. Piper, professor of New Testament Literature and Exegesis at Princeton Seminary, once wrote: "Aided by an indefatigable study of the New Testament Criticism and interpretation, patristics, church history and Reformed theology and familiar with all that had been written in foreign languages, Warfield expounded in innumerable articles the truths of the Bible and, based on the Bible, those of the Westminster Confession."

"Warfield's intellectual capacity, diversity of interests, and penetrating analysis could be placed at the apex of the scholarly pyramid of his contemporaries. Consider the course of academic events in his life. When he accepted the position in New Testament at Western Seminary, the previous year he had already turned down an appointment at the same institution to teach Old Testament. When he went from Western to Princeton Seminary, he went from New Testament to a position combining the disciplines of Systematic Theology and Apologetics. When we consider that he was also known for his historical studies on the background and editions of the Westminster Confession, as well as the relationship between Augustine and John Calvin, it is not going too far to say that he could have qualified, in his era, as a one man seminary faculty with abilities in Old Testament, New Testament, Apologetics, Systematics, and Church History." Barry Waugh, Ph.D.

When Benjamin Warfield died, there were notices, memorial services, and eulogies in many parts of the nation. Warfield's own denomination, the Presbyterian Church in the United States of America, adopted a statement at its General Assembly that described his loss as "irreparable" and described him as "probably the most distinguished and learned theologian of the Reformed Faith in our day."

The rise of Christianity was a phenomenon of too little apparent significance to attract the attention of the great world. It was only when it had refused to be quenched in the blood of its founder, and, breaking out of the narrow bounds of the obscure province in which it had its origin, was making itself felt in the centers of population, that it drew to itself a somewhat irritated notice. The interest of such heathen writers as mention it was in the movement, not in its author. But in speaking of the movement they tell something of its author, and what they tell is far from being of little moment. He was, it seems, a certain "Christ," who had lived in Judea in the reign of Tiberius (A.D. 14-37), and had been brought to capital punishment by the procurator, Pontius Pilate (q.v.; cf. Tacitus,

Annals, 15:44). The significance of His personality to the movement inaugurated by Him is already suggested by the fact that He, and no other, had impressed His name upon it. But the name itself by which He was known particularly attracts notice. This is uniformly, in these heathen writers, "Christ," not "Jesus." Suetonius (*Claudius*, 25:) not unnaturally confuses this "Christus" with the Greek name "Chrestus"; but Tacitus and Pliny show themselves better informed and preserve it accurately. "Christ," however, is not a personal name, but the Creek rendering of the Hebrew title "Messiah." Clearly, then, it was as the promised Messiah of the Jews that their founder was reverenced by "the Christians"; and they had made so much of his Messiahship in speaking of Him that the title "Christ" had actually usurped the place of his personal name, and He was everywhere known simply as "Christ." Their reverence for His person had, indeed, exceeded that commonly supposed to be due even to the Messianic dignity. Pliny records that this "Christ" was worshipped by "the Christians" of Pontus and Bithynia as their God. Beyond these great facts the heathen historians give little information about the founder of Christianity.

What is lacking in them is happily supplied, however, by the writings of the Christians themselves. Christianity was from its beginnings a literary religion, and documentary records of it have come down from the very start. There are, for example, the letters of the Apostle Paul (q.v.), a highly cultured Romanized Jew of Tarsus, who early (A.D. 34 or 35) threw in his fortunes with the new religion, and by his splendid leadership established it in the chief centers of influence from Antioch to Rome. Written occasionally to one or another of the Christian communities of this region, at intervals during the sixth and seventh decades of the century, that is to say, from twenty to forty years after the origin of Christianity, these letters reflect the conceptions which ruled in the Christian communities of the time. Paul had known the Christian movement from its beginning; first from the outside, as one of the chief agents in its persecution, and then from the inside, as the most active leader of its propaganda. He was familiarly acquainted with the Apostles and other immediate followers of Jesus, and enjoyed repeated intercourse with them. He explicitly declares the harmony of their teaching with his, and joins with his their testimony to the great facts which he proclaimed. The complete consonance of his allusions to Jesus with what is gathered from the hints of the heathen historians is very striking. The person of Jesus fills the whole horizon of his thought, and gathers to itself all his religious emotions. That Jesus was the Messiah is the presupposition of all his speech of Him, and the Messianic title has already become his proper name behind which His real personal name, Jesus, has retired. This Messiah is definitely represented as a divine being who has entered the world on a mission of mercy to sinful man, in the prosecution of which He has given Himself up as a sacrifice for sin, but has risen again from the dead and ascended to the right hand of God, henceforth to rule as Lord of all. Around the two great facts, of the expiatory death of the Son of God and his rising again, Paul's whole teaching circles. Jesus Christ as crucified, Christ risen from the dead as the first fruits of those that sleep here is Paul's whole gospel in summary.

Into the details of Christ's earthly life Paul had no occasion to enter. But he shows himself fully familiar with them, and incidentally conveys a vivid portrait of Christ's personality. Of the seed of David on the human, as the Son of God on the divine side, He was born of a woman, under the law, and lived subject to its ordinances for His mission's sake, humbling Himself even unto death, and that the death of the cross. His lowly estate is dwelt upon, and the high traits of His personal character manifested in His lowliness are lightly sketched in, justifying not merely the negative declaration that "He knew no sin," but his positive presentation as the model of all perfection. An item of His teaching is occasionally adverted to, or even quoted, always with the utmost reverence. Members of His immediate circle of followers are mentioned by name or by class whether His brethren according to the flesh or the twelve apostles whom He appointed. The institution by Him of a sacramental feast is described, and that of a companion sacrament of initiation by baptism is implied. But especially His sacrificial death on the cross is emphasized, His burial, His rising again on the third day, and His appearances to chosen witnesses, who are cited one after the other with the greatest solemnity. Such details are never communicated to Paul's readers as pieces of fresh information. They are alluded to as matters of common knowledge, and with the plainest intimation of the unquestioned recognition of them by all. Thus it is made clear not only that there underlies Paul's letters a complete portrait of Jesus and a full outline of his career, but that this portrait and this outline are the universal possession of Christians. They were doubtless as fully before his mind as such in the early years of his Christian life, in the thirties, as when he was writing his letters in the fifties and sixties. There is no indication in the way in which Paul touches on these things of a recent change of opinion regarding them or of a recent acquisition of knowledge of them. The testimony of Paul's letters, in a word, has retrospective value, and is contemporary testimony to the facts.

Paul's testimony alone provides thus an exceptionally good basis for the historical verity of Jesus' personality and career. But Paul's testimony is far from standing alone. It is fully supported by the testimony of a series of other writings, similar to his own, purporting to come from the hands of early teachers of the Church, most of them from actual companions of our Lord and eyewitnesses of His majesty, and handed down to us with credible evidence of their authenticity. And it is extended by the testimony of a series of writings of a very different character; not occasional letters designed to meet particular crises or questions arising in the churches, but formal accounts of Jesus' words and acts.

Among these attention is attracted first by a great historical work, the two parts of which bear the titles of "the Gospel according to Luke" and "the Acts of the Apostles." The first contains an account of Jesus' life from His birth to His death and resurrection; or, including the opening paragraphs of the second, to His ascension. What directs attention to it first among books of its class is the uncommonly full information possessed concerning its writer and his method of historical composition. It is the work of an educated Greek physician, known to have enjoyed, as a companion of Paul, special opportunities of informing himself of the facts of Jesus' career. Whatever Paul himself knew of the acts and teachings of his Lord was, of course, the common property of the band of missionaries which traveled in his company, and could not fail to be the subject of much public and private discussion among them. Among Paul's other companions there could not fail to be some whose knowledge of Jesus' life, direct or derived, was considerable; an example is found, for instance, in John Mark, who had come out of the immediate circle of Jesus' first followers, although precise knowledge of the meeting of Luke and Mark as fellow companions of Paul belongs to a little later period than the composition of Luke's Gospel. In company with Paul Luke had even visited Jerusalem and had resided two years at Caesarea in touch with primitive disciples; and if the early tradition which represents him as a native of Antioch be accepted, he must be credited with facilities from the beginning of his Christian life for association with original disciples of Jesus. All that is needed to ground great confidence in his narrative as a trustworthy account of the facts it records is assurance that he had the will and capacity to make good use of his abounding opportunities for exact information. The former is afforded by the preface to his Gospel in which he reveals his method as a historian and his zeal for exactness of information and statement; the latter by the character of the Gospel, which evinces itself at every point a sincere and careful narrative resting upon good and well-sifted information. In these circumstances the determination of the precise time when this narrative was actually committed to paper becomes a matter of secondary importance; in any event its material was collected during the period of Paul's missionary activity. It may be confidently maintained, however, that it was also put together during this period, that is to say, during the earlier years of the seventh decade of the century. Confidence in its narrative is strengthened by the complete accord of the portrait of Jesus, which its detailed account exhibits with that which underlies the letters of Paul. Not only are the general traits of the personality identical, but the emphasis falls at the same places. In effect, the Jesus of Luke's narrative is the Christ of Paul's epistles in perfect dramatic presentation, and only two hypotheses offer themselves in possible explanation. Either Luke rests on Paul, and has with consummate art invented a historical basis for Paul's ideal Christ; or else Paul's allusions rest on a historical basis and Luke has preserved that historical basis in his careful, detailed narrative. Every line of Luke's narrative refutes the former and demonstrates the latter supposition.

Additional evidence of the trustworthiness of Luke's Gospel as an account of Jesus' acts and teaching is afforded by the presence by its side of other narratives of similar character and accordant contents. These narratives are two in number and have been handed down under the names of members of the earliest circle of Christians of John Mark, who was from the beginning in the closest touch with the apostolic body, and of Matthew, one of the apostles. On comparison of these narratives with Luke's, not only are they found to present, each with its own peculiar point of view and purpose, precisely the same conception and portrait of Jesus, but to have utilized in large measure also the same sources of information. Indeed, the entire body of Mark's Gospel is found to be incorporated also in Matthew's and Luke's.

This circumstance, in view of the declarations of Luke's preface, is of the utmost significance for an estimate of the trustworthiness of the narrative thus embodied in all three of the "Synoptic" Gospels. In this preface Luke professes to have had for his object the establishment of absolute "certainty," with respect to the things made the object of instruction in Christian circles; and to this end to have grounded his narrative in exact investigation of the course of events from the beginning. In the prosecution of this task, he knew himself to be working in a goodly company to a common end, namely, the narration of the Christian origins on the basis of the testimony of those ministers of the word who had been also "eyewitnesses from the beginning." He does not say whether these fellow narrators had or had not been, some or all of them, eyewitnesses of some or of all the events they narrated; he merely says that the foundation on which all the narratives he has in view rested was the testimony of eyewitnesses. He does not assert for his own treatise superiority to those of his fellow workers; he only claims an honorable place for his own treatise among the others on the ground of the diligence and care he has exercised in ascertaining and recording the facts, through which, he affirms, he has attained a certainty with regard to them on which his readers may depend. Now, on comparing the narrative of Luke with those of Matthew and Mark, it is discovered that one of the main sources on which Luke draws is also one of the main sources on which Matthew draws and practically the sole source on which Mark rests. Thus Luke's judgment of the value and trustworthiness of this source receives the notable support of the judgment of his fellow evangelists, and it can scarcely be doubted that what it contains is the veritable tradition of those who were as well eyewitnesses as ministers of the Word from the beginning, in whose accuracy confidence can be placed. If the three Synoptic Gospels do not give three independent testimonies to the facts which they record, they give what is, perhaps, better, three independent witnesses to the trustworthiness of the narrative, which they all incorporate into their own. A narrative lying at the basis of all three of these Gospels, themselves written certainly not later than the seventh decade of the century, must in any event be early in date, and in that sense must emanate from the first followers of Christ; and in the circumstances of the large and confident use made of it by all three of these Gospels cannot fail to be an authentic statement of what was the conviction of the earliest circles of Christians.

By the side of this ancient body of narrative must be placed another equally, or perhaps, even more ancient source, consisting largely, but not exclusively, of reports of "sayings of Jesus." This underlies much of the fabric of Luke and Matthew where Mark fails, and by their employment of it is authenticated as containing, as Luke asserts, the trustworthy testimony of eyewitnesses. Its great antiquity is universally allowed, and there is no doubt that it comes from the very bosom of the Apostolic circle, bearing independent but thoroughly consentient testimony, with the narrative source which underlies all three of the Synoptists, of what was understood by the primitive Christian community to be the facts regarding Jesus. This is the fundamental fact about these two sources that the Jesus which they present is the same Jesus; and that this Jesus is precisely the same Jesus found in the Synoptic Gospels themselves, presented, moreover, in precisely the same fashion and with the emphases in precisely the same places. This latter could, of course, not fail to be the case since these sources themselves constitute the main substance of the Synoptic Gospels into which they have been transfused. Its significance is that the portrait of Jesus as the supernatural Son of God who came into the world as the Messiah on a mission of mercy to sinful men, which is reflected even in the scanty notices of him that find an incidental place in the pages of heathen historians, which suffused the whole preaching of Paul and of the other missionaries of the first age, and which was wrought out into the details of a rich dramatization in the narratives of the Synoptic Gospels, is as old as Christianity itself and comes straight from the representations of Christ's first followers.

Valuable, however, as the separation out from the Synoptic narrative of these underlying sources is in this aspect of the matter, appeal cannot be made from the Synoptics to these sources as from less to more trustworthy documents. On the one hand, these sources do not exist outside the Synoptics; in them they have "found their grave." On the other hand, the Synoptics in large part are these sources; and their

trustworthiness as wholes is guaranteed by the trustworthiness of the sources from which they have drawn the greater part of their materials, and from the general portraiture of Christ in which they do not in the least depart. Luke's claim in his preface that he has made accurate investigations, seeking to learn exactly what happened that he might attain certainty in his narrative, is expressly justified for the larger part of his narrative when the sources which underlie it are isolated and are found to approve themselves under every test as excellent. There is no reason to doubt that for the remainder of his narrative (and Matthew too for the remainder of his narrative) not derived from these two sources which the accident of their common use by Matthew, Mark, and Luke, or by Matthew and Luke, reveals, he (or Matthew) derives his material from equally good and trustworthy sources which happen to be used only by him. The general trustworthiness of Luke's narrative is not lessened but enhanced by the circumstance that, in the larger portion of it, he has the support of other evangelists in his confident use of his sources, with the effect that these sources can be examined and an approving verdict reached upon them. His judgment of sources is thus confirmed, and his claim to possess exact information and to have framed a trustworthy narrative is vindicated. What he gives from sources which were not used by the other evangelists, that is to say, in that portion of his narrative which is peculiar to himself (and the same must be said for Matthew, *mutatis mutandis*), has earned a right to credit on his own authentication. It is not surprising, therefore, that the portions of the narratives of Matthew and Luke which are peculiar to the one or the other bear every mark of sincere and well-informed narration and contain many hints of resting on good and trustworthy sources. In a word, the Synoptic Gospels supply a threefold sketch of the acts and teachings of Christ of exceptional trustworthiness. If here is not historical verity, historical verity would seem incapable of being attained, recorded, and transmitted by human hands.

Along with the Synoptic Gospels there has been handed down by an unexceptionable line of testimony under the name of the Apostle John, another narrative of the teaching and work of Christ of equal fullness with that of the Synoptic Gospels, and yet so independent of theirs as to stand out in a sense in strong contrast with theirs, and even to invite attempts to establish a contradiction between it and them. There is, however, no contradiction, but rather a deep-lying harmony. There are so-called Synoptical traits discoverable in John, and not only are Johannine elements imbedded in the Synoptical narrative, but an occasional passage occurs in it which is almost more Johannine than John himself. Take, for example, that pregnant declaration recorded in Matt. 11:27-28, which, as it occurs also in Luke 10:21, 22, must have had a place in that ancient source drawn on in common by these two Gospels which comes from the first days of Christianity. All the high teaching of John's Gospel, as has been justly remarked, is but "a series of variations" upon the theme here given its "classical expression." The type of teaching which is brought forward and emphasized by John is thus recognized on all hands from the beginning to have had a place in Christ's teaching; and John differs from the Synoptics only in the special aspect of Christ's teaching which he elects particularly to present. The naturalness of this type of teaching on the lips of the Jesus of the Synoptists is also undeniable; it must be allowed and is now generally allowed that by the writers of the Synoptic Gospels, and, it should be added, by their sources as well, Jesus is presented, and is presented as representing Himself, as being all that John represents Him to be when he calls Him the Word, who was in the beginning with God and was God. The relation of John and the Synoptists in their portraiture of Jesus somewhat resembles, accordingly, that of Plato and Xenophon in their portraiture of Socrates; only, with this great difference that both Plato and Xenophon were primarily men of letters and the portrait they draw of Socrates is in the hands of both alike eminently a sophisticated and literary one, while the Evangelists set down simply the facts as they appealed to them severally. The definite claim which

John's Gospel makes to be the work of one of the inner circle of the companions of Jesus is supported, moreover, by copious evidence that it comes from the hands of such a one as a companion of Jesus would be a Jew, who possessed an intimate knowledge of Palestine, and was acquainted with the events of our Lord's life as only an eyewitness could be acquainted with them, and an eyewitness who had been admitted to very close association with Him. That its narrative rests on good information is repeatedly manifested; and more than once historical links are supplied by it which are needed to give clearness to the Synoptical narrative, as, for example, in the chronological framework of the ministry of Jesus and the culminating miracle of the raising of Lazarus, which is required to account for the incidents of the Passion-Week. It presents no different Jesus from the Jesus of the Synoptists, and it throws the emphasis at the same place on His expiatory death and rising again; but it notably supplements the narrative of the Synoptists and reveals a whole new side of Jesus' ministry, and if not a wholly new aspect of His teaching, yet a remarkable mass of that higher aspect of His teaching of which only occasional specimens are included in the Synoptic narrative. John's narrative thus rounds out the Synoptical narrative and gives the portrait drawn in it a richer content and a greater completeness.

This portrait may itself be confidently adduced as its own warranty. It is not too much to say with Nathaniel Lardner that "the history of the New Testament has in it all the marks of credibility that any history can have." But apart from these more usually marshaled evidences of the trustworthiness of the narratives, there is the portrait itself which they draw, and this cannot by any possibility have been an invention. It is not merely that the portrait is harmonious throughout in the allusions and presuppositions of the Epistles of Paul and the other letter-writers of the New Testament, in the detailed narratives of the Synoptists and John, and in each of the sources which underlie them. This is a matter of importance; but it is not the matter of chief moment; there is no need to dwell upon the impossibility of such a harmony having been maintained save on the basis of simple truthfulness of record, or to dispute whether in the case of the Synoptics there are three independent witnesses to the one portrait, or only the two independent witnesses of their two most prominent "sources." Nor is the most interesting point whether the aboriginality of this portrait is guaranteed by the harmony of the representation in all the sources of information, some of which reach back to the most primitive epoch of the Christian movement. It is quite certain that this conception of Christ's person and career was the conception of his immediate followers, and indeed of himself; but, important as this conclusion is, it is still not the matter of primary import. The matter of primary significance is that this portrait thus imbedded in all the authoritative sources of information, and thus proved to be the conception of its founder cherished by the whole of primitive Christendom, and indeed commended to it by that founder himself, is a portrait intrinsically incapable of invention by men. It could never have come into being save as the revelation of an actual person embodying it, who really lived among men. "A romancer," as even Albert Reville allows, "can not attribute to a being which he creates an ideal superior to what he himself is capable of conceiving." The conception of the God-man which is embodied in the portrait which the sources draw of Christ, and which is dramatized by them through such a history as they depict, can be accounted for only on the assumption that such a God-man actually lived, was seen of men, and was painted from the life. The miracle of the invention of such a portraiture, whether by the conscious effort of art, or by the unconscious working of the mythopeic fancy, would be as great as the actual existence of such a person. Of this there is sufficient a posteriori proof in the invariable deterioration this portrait suffers in its secondary reproductions in the so-called "Lives of Christ," of every type. The attempt vitally to realize and reproduce it results inevitably in its reduction. A portraiture which cannot even be interpreted by men without suffering serious loss cannot be the invention of the first simple followers of Jesus.

Its very existence in their unsophisticated narratives is the sufficient proof of its faithfulness to a great reality.

Only an outline of this portrait can be set down here. Jesus appears in it not only a supernatural, but in all the sources alike specifically a divine, person, who came into the world on a mission of mercy to sinful man. Such a mission was in its essence a humiliation and involved humiliation at every step of its accomplishment. His life is represented accordingly as a life of difficulty and conflict, of trial and suffering, issuing in a shameful death. But this humiliation is represented as in every step and stage of it voluntary. It was entered into and abided in solely in the interests of His mission, and did not argue at any point of it helplessness in the face of the difficulties which hemmed Him in more and more until they led Him to death on the cross. It rather manifested His strong determination to fulfill His mission to the end, to drink to its dregs the cup He had undertaken to drink. Accordingly, every suggestion of escape from it by the use of His intrinsic divine powers, whether of omnipotence or of omniscience, was treated by Him first and last as a temptation of the evil one. The death in which His life ends is conceived, therefore, as the goal in which His life culminates. He came into the world to die, and every stage of the road that led up to this issue was determined not for Him but by Him: He was never the victim but always the Master of circumstance, and pursued His pathway from beginning to end, not merely in full knowledge from the start of all its turns and twists up to its bitter conclusion, but in complete control both of them and of it.

His life of humiliation, sinking into His terrible death, was therefore not his misfortune, but His achievement as the promised Messiah, by and in whom the kingdom of God is to be established in the world; it was the work which as Messiah he came to do. Therefore, in his prosecution of it, He from the beginning announced himself as the Messiah, accepted all ascription's to him of Messiahship under whatever designation, and thus gathered up into His person all the preadumbrations of Old-Testament prophecy;

and by His favorite self-designation of "Son of Man," derived from Daniel's great vision (7:13), continually proclaimed Himself the Messiah he actually was, emphasizing in contrast with His present humiliation His heavenly origin and His future glory. Moreover, in the midst of His humiliation, He exercised, so far as that was consistent with the performance of his mission, all the prerogatives of that "transcendent" or divine Messiah which He was. He taught with authority, substituting for every other sanction His great "But I say unto you," and declaring Himself greater than the greatest of God's representatives whom He had sent in all the past to visit His people. He surrounded Himself as He went about preaching the Gospel of the kingdom with a miraculous nimbus, each and every miracle in which was adapted not merely to manifest the presence of a supernatural person in the midst of the people, but, as a piece of symbolical teaching, to reveal the nature of this supernatural person, and to afford a foretaste of the blessedness of His rule in the kingdom He came to found. He assumed plenary authority over the religious ordinances of the people, divinely established though they were; and exercised absolute control over the laws of nature themselves. The divine prerogative of forgiving sins he claimed for Himself, the divine power of reading the heart He frankly exercised, the divine function of judge of quick and dead he attached to His own person. Asserting for Himself a superhuman dignity of person, or rather a share in the ineffable Name itself, He represented Himself as abiding continually even when on earth in absolute communion with God the Father, and participating by necessity of nature in the treasures of the divine knowledge and grace; announced Himself the source of all divine knowledge and grace to men; and drew to Himself all the religious affections, suspending the destinies of men absolutely upon their relation to His own person. Nevertheless he walked straight onward in the path of His lowly mission, and, bending even the wrath of men to his service, gave Himself in his own good time and way to the death He had come to accomplish. Then, His mission

performed, He rose again from the dead in the power of His deathless life; showed Himself alive to chosen witnesses, that He might strengthen the hearts of His people; and ascended to the right hand of God, whence He directs the continued preparation of the kingdom until it shall please Him to return for its establishment in its glorious eternal form.

It is important to fix firmly in mind the central conception of this representation. It turns upon the sacrificial death of Jesus to which the whole life leads up, and out of which all its issues are drawn, and for a perpetual memorial of which he is represented as having instituted a solemn memorial feast. The divine majesty of this Son of God; His redemptive mission to the world, in a life of humiliation and a ransoming death; the completion of his task in accordance with His purpose; His triumphant rising from the death thus vicariously endured; His assumption of sovereignty over the future development of the kingdom founded in His blood, and over the world as the theater of its development; His expected return as the consummator of the ages and the judge of all this is the circle of ideas in which all accounts move. It is the portrait not of a merely human life, though it includes the delineation of a complete and a completely human life. It is the portrayal of a human episode in the divine life. It is, therefore, not merely connected with supernatural occurrences, nor merely colored by supernatural features, nor merely set in a supernatural atmosphere: the supernatural is its very substance, the elimination of which would be the evaporation of the whole. The Jesus of the New Testament is not fundamentally man, however divinely gifted: he is God tabernacling for a while among men, with heaven lying about Him not merely in his infancy, but throughout all the days of His flesh.

The intense supernaturalism of this portraiture is, of course, an offense to our anti-supernaturalistic age. It is only what was to be expected, therefore, that throughout the last century and a half a long series of scholars, imbued with the anti-supernaturalistic instinct of the time, have assumed the task of desupernaturalizing it. Great difficulty has been experienced, however, in the attempt to construct a historical sieve which will strain out miracles and yet let Jesus through; for Jesus is Himself the greatest miracle of them all. Accordingly in the end of the day there is a growing disposition, as if in despair of accomplishing this feat, boldly to construct the sieve so as to strain out Jesus too; to take refuge in the counsel of desperation which affirms that there never was such a person as Jesus, that Christianity had no founder, and that not merely the portrait of Jesus, but Jesus Himself, is a pure projection of later ideals into the past. The main stream of assault still addresses itself, however, to the attempt to eliminate not Jesus Himself, but the Jesus of the Evangelists, and to substitute for Him a de-de-super-naturalized Jesus.

The instruments which have been relied on to effect this result may be called, no doubt with some but not misleading inexactitude, literary and historical criticism. The attempt has been made to track out the process by which the present witnessing documents have come into existence, to show them gathering accretions in this process, and to sift out the sources from which they are drawn; and then to make appeal to these sources as the only real witnesses. And the attempt has been made to go behind the whole written record, operating either immediately upon the documents as they now exist, or ultimately upon the sources which literary criticism has sifted out from them, with a view to reaching a more primitive and presumably truer conception of Jesus than that which has obtained record in the writings of His followers. The occasion for resort to this latter method of research is the failure of the former to secure the results aimed at. For, when, at the dictation of anti-supernaturalistic presuppositions, John is set aside in favor of the Synoptics, and then the Synoptics are set aside in favor of Mark, conceived as the representative of "the narrative source" (by the side of which must be placed-though this is not always remembered the second source of "Sayings of Jesus," which underlies so much of Matthew and Luke; and also though this is even more commonly forgotten whatever

other sources either Matthew or Luke has drawn upon for material), it still appears that no progress whatever has been made in eliminating the divine Jesus and His supernatural accompaniment of mighty works although, chronologically speaking, the very beginning of Christianity has been reached. It is necessary, accordingly, if there is not to be acknowledged a divine Christ with a supernatural history, to get behind the whole literary tradition. Working on Mark, therefore, taken as the original Gospel, an attempt must be made to distinguish between the traditional element which he incorporates into his narrative and the dogmatic element which he (as the mouthpiece of the Christian community) contributes to it. Or, working on the "Sayings," discrimination must first be made between the narrative element (assumed to be colored by the thought of the Christian community) and the reportorial element (which may repeat real sayings of Jesus); and then, within the reportorial element, all that is too lofty for the naturalistic Jesus must be trimmed down until it fits in with his simply human character. Or, working on the Gospels as they stand, inquisition must be made for statements of fact concerning Jesus or for sayings of his, which, taken out of the context in which the Evangelists have placed them and cleansed from the coloring given by them, may be made to seem inconsistent with "the worship of Jesus" which characterizes these documents; and on the narrower basis thus secured there is built up a new portrait of Jesus, contradictory to that which the Evangelists have drawn.

The precariousness of these proceedings, or rather, frankly, their violence, is glaringly evident. In the processes of such criticism it is pure subjectivity which rules, and the investigator gets out as results only what he puts in as premises. And even when the desired result has thus been wrested from the unwilling documents, he discovers that he has only brought himself into the most extreme historical embarrassment. By thus desupernaturalizing Jesus he leaves primitive Christianity and its supernatural Jesus wholly without historical basis or justification. The naturalizing historian has therefore at once to address himself to supplying some account of the immediate universal ascription to Jesus by his followers of qualities which he did not possess and to which he laid no claim; and that with such force and persistence of conviction as totally to supersede from the very beginning with their perverted version of the facts the actual reality of things. It admits of no doubt, and it is not doubted, that supernaturalistic Christianity is the only historical Christianity. It is agreed on all hands that the very first followers of Jesus ascribed to him a supernatural character. It is even allowed that it is precisely by virtue of its supernaturalistic elements that Christianity has made its way in the world. It is freely admitted that it was by the force of its enthusiastic proclamation of the divine Christ, who could not be holden of death but burst the bonds of the grave, that Christianity conquered the world to itself. What account shall be given of all this? There is presented a problem here, which is insoluble on the naturalistic hypothesis. The old mythical theory fails because it requires time, and no time is at its disposal; the primitive Christian community believed in the divine Christ. The new "history-of-religions" theory fails because it can not discover the elements of that "Christianity before Christ" which it must posit, either remotely in the Babylonian inheritance of the East, or close by in the prevalent Messianic conceptions of contemporary Judaism. Nothing is available but the postulation of pure fanaticism in Jesus' first followers, which finds it convenient not to proceed beyond the general suggestion that there is no telling what fanaticism may not invent. The plain fact is that the supernatural Jesus is needed to account for the supernaturalistic Christianity which is grounded in him. Or if this supernaturalistic Christianity does not need a supernatural Jesus to account for it, it is hard to see why any Jesus at all need be postulated. Naturalistic criticism thus overreaches itself and is caught up suddenly by the discovery that in abolishing the supernatural Jesus it has abolished Jesus altogether, since this supernatural Jesus is the only Jesus which enters as a factor into the historical development.

It is the desupernaturalized Jesus which is the mythical Jesus, who never had any existence, the postulation of the existence of whom explains nothing and leaves the whole historical development hanging in the air.

It is instructive to observe the lines of development of the naturalistic reconstruction of the Jesus of the Evangelists through the century and a half of its evolution. The normal task which the student of the life of Jesus sets himself is to penetrate into the spirit of the transmission so far as that transmission approves itself to him as trustworthy, to realize with exactness and vividness the portrait of Jesus conveyed by it, and to reproduce that portrait in an accurate and vital portrayal. The naturalistic reconstructors, on the other hand, engage themselves in an effort to substitute for the Jesus of the transmission another Jesus of their own, a Jesus who will seem "natural" to them, and will work in "naturally" with their naturalistic world-view. In the first instance it was the miracles of Jesus which they set themselves to eliminate, and this motive ruled their criticism from Reimarus (1694-1768), or rather, from the publication of the Wolfenbuettel Fragments (q.v.), to Strauss (1835-36). The dominant method employed which found its culminating example in H. E. G. Paulus (1828) was to treat the narrative as in all essentials historical, but to seek in each miraculous story a natural fact underlying it. This whole point of view was transcended by the advent of the mythical view in Strauss, who laughed it out of court. Since then miracles have been treated ever more and more confidently as negligible quantities, and the whole strength of criticism has been increasingly expended on the reduction of the supernatural figure of Jesus to "natural" proportions. The instrument relied upon to produce this effect has been psychological analysis; the method being to rework the narrative in the interests of what is called a "comprehensible" Jesus. The whole mental life of Jesus and the entire course of his conduct have been subjected to psychological canons derived from the critics' conception of a purely human life, and nothing has been allowed to him which does not approve itself as "natural" according to this standard. The result is, of course, that the Jesus of the Evangelists has been transformed into a nineteenth-century "liberal" theologian, and no conceptions or motives or actions have been allowed to him which would not be "natural" in such a one.

The inevitable reaction which seems to be now asserting itself takes two forms, both of which, while serving themselves heirs to the negative criticism of this "liberal" school, decisively reject its positive construction of the figure of Jesus. A weaker current contents itself with drawing attention to the obvious fact that such a Jesus as the "liberal" criticism yields will not account for the Christianity which actually came into being; and on this ground proclaims the "liberal" criticism bankrupt and raises the question, what need there is for assuming any Jesus at all. If the only Jesus salvable from the debris of legend is obviously not the author of the Christianity which actually came into being, why not simply recognize that Christianity came into being without any author and was just the crystallization of conceptions in solution at the time? A stronger current, scoffing at the projection of a nineteenth-century "liberal" back into the first century and calling him "Jesus," insists that "the historical Jesus" was just a Jew of his day, a peasant of Galilee with all the narrowness of a peasant's outlook and all the deficiency in culture which belonged to a Galilean countryman of the period. Above all, it insists that the real Jesus, possessed by those Messianic dreams which filled the minds of the Jewish peasantry of the time, was afflicted with the great delusion that He was Himself the promised Messiah. Under the obsession of this portentous fancy He imagined that God would intervene with His almighty arm and set him on the throne of a conquering Israel; and when the event falsified this wild hope, he assuaged his bitter disappointment with the wilder promise that he would rise from death itself and come back to establish his kingdom. Thus the naturalistic criticism of a hundred and fifty years has run out into no Jesus at all, or worse than no Jesus, a fanatic or even a paranoiac. The "liberal" criticism which has had it so long its own way is called sharply to its defense against the fruit

of its own loins. In the process of this defense it wavers before the assault and incorporates more or less of the new conception of Jesus of the "consistently eschatological" Jesus into its fabric. Or it stands in its tracks and weakly protests that Jesus' figure must be conceived as greatly as possible, so only it be kept strictly within the limits of a mere human being. Or it develops an apologetic argument which, given its full validity and effect, would undo all its painfully worked-out negative results and lead back to the Jesus of the evangelists as the true "historical Jesus."

It has been remarked above that the portrait of Jesus drawn in the sources is its own credential; no man, and no body of men, can have invented this figure, consciously or unconsciously, and dramatized it consistently through such a varied and difficult life-history. It may be added that the Jesus of the naturalistic criticism is its own refutation. One wonders whether the "liberal" critics realize the weakness, ineffectiveness, inanition of the Jesus they offer; the pitiful inertness they attribute to him, his utter passivity under the impact of circumstance. So far from being conceivable as the molder of the ages, this Jesus is wholly molded by his own surroundings, the sport of every suggestion from without. In their preoccupation with critical details, it is possible that its authors are scarcely aware of the grossness of the reduction of the figure of Jesus they have perpetrated. But let them only turn to portray their new Jesus in a life-history, and the pitiableness of the figure they have made him smites the eye. Whatever else may be said of it, this must be said that out of the Jesus into which the naturalistic criticism has issued in its best or in its worst estate the Christianity which has conquered the world could never have come.

The firmness, clearness, and even fullness with which the figure of Jesus is delineated in the sources, and the variety of activities though which it is dramatized, do not insure that the data given should suffice for drawing up a properly so-called life of Jesus." The data in the sources are practically confined to the brief period of Jesus' public work. Only a single incident is recorded from His earlier life, and that is taken from His boyhood. So large a portion of the actual narrative, moreover, is occupied with His death that it might even be said the more that the whole narrative also leads up to the death as the life's culmination that little has been preserved concerning Jesus but the circumstances which accompanied His birth and the circumstances which led up to and accompanied His death. The incidents which the narrators record, again, are not recorded with a biographical intent, and are not selected for their biographical significance, or ordered so as to present a biographical result: in the case of each Evangelist they serve a particular purpose which may employ biographical details, but is not itself a biographical end. In other words the Gospels are not formal biographies but biographical arguments, a circumstance which does not affect the historicity of the incidents they select for record, but does affect the selection and ordering of these incidents. Mark has in view to show that this great religious movement in which he himself had a part had its beginnings in a divine interposition; Matthew, that this divine interposition was in fulfillment of the promises made to Israel; Luke, that it had as its end the redemption of the world; John, that the agent in it was none other than the Son of God himself. In the enforcement and illustration of their several themes each records a wealth of biographical details. But it does not follow that these details, when brought together and arranged in their chronological sequence, or even in their genetic order, will supply an adequate biography. The attempt to work them up into a biography is met, moreover, by a great initial difficulty. Every biographer takes his position, as it were, above his subject, who must live his life over again in his biographer's mind; it is of the very essence of the biographer's work thoroughly to understand his subject and to depict him as he understands him. What, then, if the subject of the biography be above the comprehension of his biographer? Obviously, in that case, a certain reduction can scarcely be avoided. This in an instance like the present, where the subject is a superhuman being, is the same as to say that a

greater or lesser measure of rationalization, "naturalization," inevitably takes place. A true biography of a God-man, a biography which depicts His life from within, untangling the complex of motives which moved Him, and explaining His conduct by reference to the internal springs of action, is in the nature of the case an impossibility for men. Human beings can explain only on the basis of their own experiences and mental processes; and so explaining they instinctively explain away what transcends their experiences and confounds their mental processes. Seeking to portray the life of Jesus as natural, they naturalize it, that is, reduce it to correspondence with their own nature. Every attempt to work out a life of Christ must therefore face not only the insufficiency of the data, but the perennial danger of falsifying the data by an instinctive naturalization of them. If, however, the expectation of attaining a "psychological" biography of Jesus must be renounced, and even a complete external life can not be pieced together from the fragmentary communications of the sources, a clear and consistent view of the course of the public ministry of Jesus can still be derived from them. The consecution of the events can be set forth, their causal relations established, and their historical development explicated. To do this is certainly in a modified sense to outline "the life of Jesus," and to do this proves by its results to be eminently worth while.

A series of synchronism's with secular history indicated by Luke, whose historical interest seems more alert than that of the other evangelists, gives the needed information for placing such a "life" in its right historical relations. The chronological framework for the "life" itself is supplied by the succession of annual feasts which are recorded by John as occurring during Jesus' public ministry. Into this framework the data furnished by the other Gospels which are not without corroborative suggestions of order, season of occurrence, and relations fit readily; and when so arranged yield so self-consistent and rationally developing a history as to add a strong corroboration of its trustworthiness. Differences of opinion respecting the details of arrangement of course remain possible; and these differences are not always small and not always without historical significance. But they do not affect the general outline or the main drift of the history, and on most points, even those of minor importance, a tolerable agreement exists. Thus, for example, it is all but universally allowed that Jesus was born c. 5 or 6 BC (year of Rome 748 or 749), and it is an erratic judgment indeed which would fix on any other year than A.D. 29 or 30 for his crucifixion. On the date of His baptism which determines the duration of his public ministry more difference is possible; but it is quite generally agreed that it took place late in A.D. 26 or early in 27. It is only by excluding the testimony of John that a duration of less than between two and three years can be assigned to the public ministry; and then only by subjecting the Synoptical narrative to considerable pressure. The probabilities seem strongly in favor of extending it to three years and some months. The decision between a duration of two years and some months and a duration of three years and some months depends on the determination of the two questions of where in the narrative of John the imprisonment of John the Baptist (Matthew 4:12) is to be placed, and what the unnamed feast is which is mentioned in John 5:1. On the former of these questions opinion varies only between John 4:1-3 and John 5:1. On the latter a great variety of opinions exists: some think of Passover, others of Purim or Pentecost, or of Trumpets or Tabernacles, or even of the day of Atonement. On the whole, the evidence seems decisively preponderant for placing the imprisonment of the Baptist at John 4:1-3, and for identifying the feast of John 5:1 with Passover. In that case, the public ministry of Jesus covered about three years and a third, and it is probably not far wrong to assign to it the period lying between the latter part of A.D. 26 and the Passover of A.D. 30.

The material supplied by the Gospel narrative distributes itself naturally under the heads of (1) the preparation (2) the ministry, and (3) the consummation. For the first twelve or thirteen years of Jesus' life nothing is recorded except the striking circumstances connected with His birth, and a general statement of His remarkable growth. Similarly for His youth, about seventeen years and a half, there is recorded only the single incident, at its beginning, of His conversation with the doctors in the temple. Anything like continuous narrative begins only with the public ministry, in, say, December, A.D. 26. This narrative falls naturally into four parts which may perhaps be distinguished as (a) the beginning of the Gospel, forty days, from December, 26 to February, 27; (b) the Judean ministry, covering about ten months, from February, 27 to December, 27; (c) the Galilean ministry, covering about twenty-two months, from December, 27 to September, 29; (d) the last journeys to Jerusalem, covering some six months, from September, 29 to the Passover of (April) 30. The events of this final Passover season, the narrative of which becomes so detailed and precise that the occurrences from day to day are noted, constitute, along with their sequences, what is here called "the consummation." They include the events which led up to the crucifixion of Jesus, the crucifixion itself, and the manifestations which He gave of Himself after His death up to His ascension. So preponderating was the interest which the reporters took in this portion of the "life of Christ," that is to say, in His death and resurrection, that about a third of their whole narrative is devoted to it. The ministry which leads up to it is also, however, full of incident. What is here called "the beginning of the Gospel" gives, no doubt, only the accounts of Jesus' baptism and temptation. Only meager information is given also, and that by John alone, of the occurrences of the first ten months after His public appearance, the scene of which lay mainly in Judea. With the beginning of the ministry in Galilee, however, with which alone the Synoptic Gospels concern themselves, incidents become numerous. Capernaum now becomes Jesus' home for almost two full years; and no less than eight periods of sojourn there with intervening circuits going out from it as a center can be traced. When the object of this ministry had been accomplished Jesus finally withdraws from Galilee and addresses Himself to the preparation of his followers for the death He had come into the world to accomplish; and this He then brings about in the manner which best subserves His purpose.

Into the substance of Jesus' ministry it is not possible to enter here. Let it only be observed that it is properly called a ministry. He Himself testified that He came not to be ministered unto but to minister, and He added that this ministry was fulfilled in His giving His life as a ransom for many. In other words, the main object of His work was to lay the foundations of the kingdom of God in His blood. Subsidiary to this was His purpose to make vitally known to men the true nature of the kingdom of God, to prepare the way for its advent in their hearts, and above all, to attach them by faith to His person as the founder and consummator of the kingdom. His ministry involved, therefore, a constant presentation of Himself to the people as the promised One, in and by whom the kingdom of God was to be established, a steady "campaign of instruction" as to the nature of the kingdom which He came to found, and a watchful control of the forces which were making for His destruction, until, His work of preparation being ended, He was ready to complete it by offering Himself up. The progress of His ministry is governed by the interplay of these motives. It has been broadly distributed into a year of obscurity, a year of popular favor, and a year of opposition; and if these designations are understood to have only a relative applicability, they may be accepted as generally describing from the outside the development of the ministry. Beginning first in Judea Jesus spent some ten months in attaching to Himself His first disciples, and with apparent fruitlessness proclaiming the kingdom at the center of national life. Then, moving north to Galilee, He quickly won the ear of the people and carried them to the height of their present receptivity; whereupon, breaking from them, He devoted Himself to the more precise instruction of the chosen band He had gathered about Him to be the nucleus of His Church. The Galilean ministry thus divides into two parts, marked respectively by more popular and more intimate teaching. The line

of division falls at the miracle of the feeding of the five thousand, which, as marking a crisis in the ministry, is recorded by all four Evangelists, and is the only miracle which has received this fourfold record. Prior to this point, Jesus' work had been one of gathering disciples; subsequently to it, it was a work of instructing and sifting the disciples whom He had gathered. The end of the Galilean ministry is marked by the confession of Peter and the transfiguration, and after it nothing remained but the preparation of the chosen disciples for the death, which was to close His work; and the consummation of His mission in His death and rising again.

The instruments by which Jesus carried out his ministry were two, teaching and miracles. In both alike He manifested His deity. Wherever He went the supernatural was present in word and deed. His teaching was with authority. In its insight and foresight it was as supernatural as the miracles themselves; the hearts of men and the future lay as open before Him as the forces of nature lay under His control; all that the Father knows He knew also, and He alone was the channel of the revelation of it to men. The power of His "But I say unto you" was as manifest as that of His compelling "Arise and walk." The theme of His teaching was the kingdom of God and Himself as its divine founder and king. Its form ran all the way from crisp gnomic sayings and brief comparisons to elaborate parables and profound spiritual discussions in which the deep things of God are laid bare in simple, searching words. The purport of His miracles was that the kingdom of God was already present in its King. Their number is perhaps usually greatly underestimated. It is true that only about thirty or forty are actually recorded. But these are recorded only as specimens, and as such they represent all classes. Miracles of healing form the preponderant class; but there are also exorcisms, nature-miracles, raisings of the dead. Besides these recorded miracles, however, there are frequent general statements of abounding miraculous manifestations. For a time disease and death must have been almost banished from the land. The country was thoroughly aroused and filled with wonder. In the midst of this universal excitement when the people were ready to take Him by force and make Him King He withdrew Himself from them, and throwing His circuits far afield, beyond the bruit and uproar, addressed Himself to preparing His chosen companions for His great sacrifice first leading them in the so-called "later Galilean ministry" (from the feeding of the 5,000 to the confession at Caesarea Philippi) to a better apprehension of the majesty of His person as the Son of God, and of the character of the kingdom He came to found, as consisting not in meat and drink but in righteousness; and then, in the so-called "Peraean ministry" (from the confession at Caesarea Philippi to the final arrival at Jerusalem) specifically preparing them for His death and resurrection. Thus He walked straightforward in the path He had chosen, and His choice of which is already made clear in the account of His temptation, set at the beginning of His public career; and in His own good time and way in the end forcing the hand of His opponents to secure that he should die at the Passover shed His blood as the blood of the new covenant sacrifice for the remission of sins. Having power thus to lay down His life, He had power also to take it again, and in due time He rose again from the dead and ascended to the right hand of the majesty on high, leaving behind Him His promise to come again in His glory, to perfect the kingdom He had inaugurated.

It is appropriate that this miraculous life should be set between the great marvels of the virgin-birth and the resurrection and ascension. These can appear strange only when the intervening life is looked upon as that of a merely human being, endowed, no doubt, not only with unusual qualities, but also with the unusual favor of God, yet after all nothing more than human and therefore presumably entering the world like other human beings, and at the end paying the universal debt of human nature. From the standpoint of the evangelical writers, and of the entirety of primitive Christianity, which looked upon Jesus not as a merely human being but as God himself come into the world on a mission of mercy that involved the

humiliation of a human life and death, it would be this assumed community with common humanity in mode of entrance into and exit from the earthly life which would seem strange and incredible. The entrance of the Lord of Glory into the world could not but be supernatural; His exit from the world, after the work which He had undertaken had been performed, could not fail to bear the stamp of triumph. There is no reason for doubting the trustworthiness of the narratives at these points, beyond the anti-supernaturalistic instinct which strives consciously or unconsciously to naturalize the whole evangelical narrative. The "infancy chapters" of Luke are demonstrably from Luke's own hand, bear evident traces of having been derived from trustworthy sources of information, and possess all the authority which attaches to the communications of a historian who evinces himself sober, careful, and exact, by every historical test. The parallel chapters of Matthew, while obviously independent of those of Luke recording in common with them not a single incident beyond the bare fact of the virgin-birth are thoroughly at one with them in the main fact, and in the incidents they record fit with remarkable completeness into the interstices of Luke's narrative. Similarly, the narratives of the resurrection, full of diversity in details as they are, and raising repeated puzzling questions of order and arrangement, yet not only bear consentient testimony to all the main facts, but fit into one another so as to create a consistent narrative which has moreover the support of the contemporary testimony of Paul. The persistent attempts to explain away the facts so witnessed or to substitute for the account which the New Testament writers give of them some more plausible explanation, as the naturalistic mind estimates plausibility, are all wrecked on the directness, precision, and copiousness of the testimony; and on the great effects which have flowed from this fact in the revolution wrought in the minds and lives of the apostles themselves, and in the revolution wrought through their preaching of the resurrection in the life and history of the world. The entire history of the world for 2,000 years is the warranty of the reality of the resurrection of Christ, by which the forces were let loose which have created it. "Unique spiritual effects," it has been remarked, with great reasonableness, "require a unique spiritual cause; and we shall never understand the full significance of the cause, if we begin by denying or minimizing its uniqueness."

B. B. Warfield

1.14 THE QUEST OF THE HISTORICAL JESUS, ALBERT SCHWEITZER

Albert Schweitzer, 1875-1965, the German Lutheran and Nobel Peace Prize winner in 1952, was a celebrated organist and medical doctor, as well as a missionary and theologian.

Albert Schweitzer, in his famous work, The Quest of the Historical Jesus, *sounded the death-knell for the "Life of Jesus movement" which was rightly criticized because it revealed more about the presuppositions of its authors than it did about the historical figure of Jesus found in the Gospels.*

CHAPTER 20
Results

Those who are fond of talking about negative theology can find their account here. There is nothing more negative than the result of the critical study of the Life of Jesus.

The Jesus of Nazareth who came forward publicly as the Messiah, who preached the ethic of the Kingdom of God, who founded the Kingdom of Heaven upon earth, and died to give His work its final consecration, never had any existence. He is a figure designed by rationalism, endowed with life by liberalism, and clothed by modern theology in an historical garb.

This image has not been destroyed from without, it has fallen to pieces, cleft and disintegrated by the concrete historical problems which came to the surface one after another, and in spite of all the artifice, art, artificiality, and violence which was applied to them, refused to be planed down to fit the design on which the Jesus of the theology of the last hundred and thirty years had been constructed, and were no sooner covered over than they appeared again in a new form. The thoroughgoing skeptical and the thoroughgoing eschatological school have only completed the work of destruction by linking the problems into a system which undertook to solve each of them separately, that is, in a less difficult form. Henceforth it is no longer permissible to take one problem out of the series and dispose of it by itself, since the weight of the whole hangs upon each.

Whatever the ultimate solution may be, the historical Jesus of whom the criticism of the future, taking as its starting-point the problems which have been recognized and admitted, will draw the portrait, can never render modern theology the services which it claimed from its own half-historical, half-modern, Jesus. He will be a Jesus, who was Messiah, and lived as such, either on the ground of a literary fiction of the earliest Evangelist, or on the ground of a purely eschatological Messianic conception.

In either case, He will not be a Jesus Christ to whom the religion of the present can ascribe, according to its long-cherished custom, its own thoughts and ideas, as it did with the Jesus of its own making. Nor will He be a figure which can be made by a popular historical treatment so sympathetic and universally intelligible to the multitude. The historical Jesus will be to our time a stranger and an enigma.

The study of the Life of Jesus has had a curious history. It set out in quest of the historical Jesus, believing that when it had found Him it could bring Him straight into our time as a Teacher and Savior. It loosed the bands by which He had been riveted for centuries to the stony rocks of ecclesiastical doctrine, and rejoiced to see life and movement coming into the figure once more, and the historical Jesus advancing, as it seemed, to meet it. But He does not stay; He passes by our time and returns to His own. What surprised and dismayed the theology of the last forty years was that, despite all forced and arbitrary interpretations, it could not keep Him in our time, but had to let Him go. He returned to His own time, not owing to the application of any historical ingenuity, but by the same inevitable necessity by which the liberated pendulum returns to its original position.

The historical foundation of Christianity as built up by rationalistic, by liberal, and by modern theology no longer exists; but that does not mean that Christianity has lost its historical foundation. The work which historical theology thought itself bound to carry out, and which fell to pieces just as it was nearing completion, was only the brick facing of the real immovable historical foundation which is independent of any historical confirmation or justification.

Jesus means something to our world because a mighty spiritual force streams forth from Him and flows through our time also. This fact can neither be shaken nor confirmed by any historical discovery. It is the solid foundation of Christianity.

The mistake was to suppose that Jesus could come to mean more to our time by entering into it as a man like ourselves. That is not possible. First because such a Jesus never existed. Secondly because, although historical knowledge can no doubt introduce greater clearness into an existing spiritual life, it cannot call spiritual life into existence. History can destroy the present; it can reconcile the present with the past; can even to a certain extent transport the present into the past; but to contribute to the making of the present is not given unto it.

But it is impossible to over-estimate the value of what German research upon the Life of Jesus has accomplished. It is a uniquely great expression of sincerity, one of the most significant events in the whole mental and spiritual life of humanity. What has been done for the religious life of the present and the immediate future by scholars such as P. W. Schmidt, Bousset, Weinel, Wernle and the others who have been called to the task of bringing to the knowledge of wider circles, in a form which is popular without being superficial, the results of religious-historical study, only becomes evident when one examines the literature and social culture of the Latin nations, who have been scarcely if at all touched by the influence of these thinkers.

And yet the time of doubt was bound to come. We modern theologians are too proud of our historical method, too proud of our historical Jesus, too confident in our belief in the spiritual gains which our historical theology can bring to the world. The thought that we could build up by the increase of historical knowledge a new and vigorous Christianity and set free new spiritual forces, rules us like a fixed idea, and prevents us from seeing that the task which we have grappled with and in some measure discharged is only one of the intellectual preliminaries of the great religious task. We thought that it was for us to lead our time by a roundabout way through the historical Jesus, as we understood Him, in order to bring it to the Jesus who is a spiritual power in the present. This roundabout way has now been closed by genuine history.

There was a danger of our thrusting ourselves between men and the Gospels, and refusing to leave the individual man alone with the sayings of Jesus.

There was a danger that we should offer them a Jesus who was too small, because we had forced Him into conformity with our human standards and human psychology. To see that, one need only read the Lives of Jesus written since the sixties, and notice what they have made of the great imperious sayings of the Lord, how they have weakened down His imperative world-contemning demands upon individuals, that He might not come into conflict with our ethical ideals, and might tune His denial of the world to our acceptance of it. Many of the greatest sayings are found lying in a corner like explosive shells from which the charges have been removed. No small portion of elemental religious power needed to be drawn off from His sayings to prevent them from conflicting with our system of religious world-acceptance. We have made Jesus hold another language with our time from that which He really held.

In the process we ourselves have been enfeebled, and have robbed our own thoughts of their vigor in order to project them back into history and make them speak to us out of the past. It is nothing less than a misfortune for modern theology that it mixes history with everything and ends by being proud of the skill with which it finds its own thoughts—even to its beggarly pseudo-metaphysic with which it has banished genuine speculative metaphysic from the sphere of religion—in Jesus, and represents Him as expressing them. It had almost deserved the reproach: "he who putteth his hand to the plough, and looketh back, is not fit for the Kingdom of God."

It was no small matter, therefore, that in the course of the critical study of the Life of Jesus, after a resistance lasting for two generations, during which first one expedient was tried and then another, theology was forced by genuine history to begin to doubt the artificial history with which it had thought to give new life to our Christianity, and to yield to the facts, which, as Wrede strikingly said, are sometimes the most radical critics of all. History will force it to find a way to transcend history, and to fight for the lordship and rule of Jesus over this world with weapons tempered in a different forge.

We are experiencing what Paul experienced. In the very moment when we were coming nearer to the historical Jesus than men had ever come before, and were already stretching out our hands to draw Him into our own time, we have been obliged to give up the attempt and acknowledge our failure in that paradoxical saying: "If we have known Christ after the flesh yet henceforth know we Him no more." And further we must be prepared to find that the historical knowledge of the personality and life of Jesus will not be a help, but perhaps even an offence to religion.

But the truth is, it is not Jesus as historically known, but Jesus as spiritually arisen within men, who is significant for our time and can help it. Not the historical Jesus, but the spirit which goes forth from Him and in the spirits of men strives for new influence and rule, is that which overcomes the world.

It is not given to history to disengage that which is abiding and eternal in the being of Jesus from the historical forms in which it worked itself out, and to introduce it into our world as a living influence. It has toiled in vain at this undertaking. As a water-plant is beautiful so long as it is growing in the water, but once torn from its roots, withers and becomes unrecognizable, so it is with the historical Jesus when He is wrenched loose from the soil of eschatology, and the attempt is made to conceive Him "historically" as a Being not subject to temporal conditions. The abiding and eternal in Jesus is absolutely independent of historical knowledge and can only be understood by contact with His spirit which is still at work in the world. In proportion as we have the Spirit of Jesus we have the true knowledge of Jesus.

Jesus as a concrete historical personality remains a stranger to our time, but His spirit, which lies hidden in His words, is known in simplicity, and its influence is direct. Every saying contains in its own way the whole Jesus. The very strangeness and unconditionedness in which He stands before us makes it easier for individuals to find their own personal standpoint in regard to Him. Men feared that to admit the claims of eschatology would abolish the significance of His words for our time; and hence there was a feverish eagerness to discover in them any elements that might be considered not eschatologically conditioned. When any sayings were found of which the wording did not absolutely imply an eschatological connection there was a great jubilation—these at least had been saved uninjured from the coming debacle.

But in reality that which is eternal in the words of Jesus is due to the very fact that they are based on an eschatological worldview, and contain the expression of a mind for which the contemporary world with its historical and social circumstances no longer had any existence. They are appropriate, therefore, to any world, for in every world they raise the man who dares to meet their challenge, and does not turn and twist them into meaninglessness, above his world and his time, making him inwardly free, so that he is fitted to be, in his own world and in his own time, a simple channel of the power of Jesus.

Modern Lives of Jesus are too general in their scope. They aim at influencing, by giving a complete impression of the life of Jesus, a whole community. But the historical Jesus, as He is depicted in the Gospels, influenced individuals by the individual word. They understood Him so far as it was necessary for them to understand, without forming any conception of His life as a whole, since this in its ultimate aims remained a mystery even for the disciples.

Because it is thus preoccupied with the general, the universal, modern theology is determined to find its world-accepting ethic in the teaching of Jesus. Therein lies its weakness. The world affirms itself automatically; the modern spirit cannot but affirm it. But why on that account abolish the conflict between modern life, with the world-affirming spirit which inspires it as a whole, and the world-negating spirit of Jesus? Why spare the spirit of the individual man its appointed task of fighting its way through the world-negation of Jesus, of contending with Him at every step over the value of material and intellectual goods—a conflict in which it may never rest? For the general, for the institutions of society, the rule is: affirmation of the world, in conscious opposition to the view of Jesus, on the ground that the world has affirmed itself! This general affirmation of the world, however, if it is to be Christian, must in the individual spirit be Christianized and transfigured by the personal rejection of the world which is preached in the sayings of Jesus. It is only by means of the tension thus set up that religious energy can be communicated to our time. There was a danger that modern theology, for the sake of peace, would deny the world-negation in the sayings of Jesus, with which Protestantism was out of sympathy, and thus unstring the bow and make Protestantism a mere sociological instead of a religious force. There was perhaps also a danger of inward insincerity in the fact that it refused to admit to itself and others that it maintained its affirmation of the world in opposition to the sayings of Jesus, simply because it could not do otherwise.

For that reason it is a good thing that the true historical Jesus should overthrow the modern Jesus, should rise up against the modern spirit and send upon earth, not peace, but a sword. He was not teacher, not a casuist; He was an imperious ruler. It was because He was so in His inmost being that He could think of Himself as the Son of Man. That was only the temporally conditioned expression of the fact that He was an authoritative ruler. The names in which men expressed their recognition of Him as such, Messiah, Son of Man, Son of God, have become for us historical parables. We can find no designation which expresses what He is for us.

He comes to us as One unknown, without a name, as of old, by the lake-side, He came to those men who knew Him not. He speaks to us the same word: "Follow thou me!" and sets us to the tasks which He has to fulfill for our time. He commands. And to those who obey Him, whether they be wise or simple, He will reveal Himself in the toils, the conflicts, the sufferings which they shall pass through in His fellowship, and, as an ineffable mystery, they shall learn in their own experience Who He is.

Albert Schweitzer
The Quest of the Historical Jesus,
A. & C. Black, 1910

1.15 TIMELINES

The timelines shows important dates and events in Jesus' life. The dates are guidelines, as it is not always possible to give exact dates.

1. Timeline of Jesus' life
2. Timeline of Jesus' last week
3. Timeline after Jesus' resurrection

1. TIMELINE OF JESUS' LIFE

6-5 BC
Birth of Jesus
Visit by shepherds
Presentation in the Temple
5-4 BC
Escape to Egypt
Slaughter of babies and children by Herod
4 BC
Herod the Great dies
2 BC
Return to Nazareth
A.D. 7-8
Jesus visits the Temple in Jerusalem as a twelve-year-old
A.D. 27
Jesus' ministry begins. He is baptized in the River Jordan
A.D. 30
Jesus dies

2. TIMELINE OF JESUS' LAST WEEK

Palm Sunday
Jesus enters Jerusalem, Matt. 21:1-11
Monday
Jesus curses the fig-tree, Matt. 21:18, 19
Jesus cleanses the Temple, Matt. 21:12, 13
Tuesday
Jesus' authority questioned, Matt. 21:23-27
Jesus teaches in the Temple, Matt. 21:28-23:39
Jesus anointed, Matt. 26:6-13

Wednesday
The plot against Jesus, Matt. 26:14-16
Maundy Thursday
The Last Supper, Matt. 26:17-29
Jesus comforts his disciples, John 14:1-16, 33
Gethsemane, Matt. 26:36-46
Good Friday
Jesus' arrest (Thursday night) and trial, Matt. 26:47-27:26
Jesus' crucifixion and death at Golgotha, Matt. 27:27-56
The burial of Jesus in Joseph's tomb, Matt. 27:57-66

3. TIMELINE AFTER JESUS' RESURRECTION

Sunday
The empty tomb discovered, Matt. 28:1-10
Mary Magdalene sees Jesus in the garden, Mark 16:9-11
Jesus appears to the two going to Emmaus, Luke 24:13-35
Jesus appears to ten disciples, without Thomas, in Jerusalem, Luke 24:36-43
One week later
Jesus appears to the eleven disciples, including Thomas, in Jerusalem, John 20:26-31
Jesus talks with seven of his disciples on the shore of the Sea of Galilee, John 21:1-25
40 days after the resurrection
Jesus ascends to his Father in heaven from the Mount of Olives, Matt. 28:16-20

4
COMPARING MODERN VIEWPOINTS ON THE PERSON OF JESUS

1.16 BILLY GRAHAM

THE SINLESS SON

All the days of His life on earth He never once committed a sin. He is the only man who ever lived who was sinless. He could stand in front of men and ask, "Can any of you prove me guilty of sin?" (John 8:46). He was hounded by the enemy day and night, but they never found any sin in Him. He was without spot or blemish.

Jesus lived a humble life. He made Himself of no reputation. He received no honor of men. He was born in a stable. He was reared in the insignificant village of Nazareth. He was a carpenter. He gathered around Him a humble group of fishermen as His followers. He walked among men as a man. he was one of the people. He humbled Himself as no other man has ever humbled himself.

Jesus taught with such authority that the people of His day said, "No one ever spoke the way this man does" (John 7:46). Every word that He spoke was historically true. Every word that He spoke was scientifically true. Every word that He spoke was ethically true. There were no loopholes in the moral conceptions and statements of Jesus Christ. His ethical vision was wholly correct, correct in the age in which He lived and correct in every age that has followed it.

The words of this blessed person were prophetically true. He prophesied many things that are even yet in the future. Lawyers tried to catch Him with test questions, but they could never confuse Him. His answers to His opponents were clear and clean-cut. There were no question marks about His statements, no deception in His meaning, no hesitancy in His words.

Billy Graham
Peace With God, *Word Publishing, 1955*

1.17 C. S. LEWIS

JESUS' CLAIM TO BE GOD

. . . people often say about Him: "I'm ready to accept Jesus as a great moral teacher, but I don't accept His claim to be God." That is the one thing we must not say. A man who was merely a man and said the sort of things Jesus said would not be a great moral teacher. He would either be a lunatic—on a level with the man who says he is a poached egg—or else he would be the Devil of Hell. You must make your choice. Either this man was, and is, the Son of God: or else a madman or something worse. You can shut Him up for a fool, you can spit at Him and kill Him as a demon; or you can fall at His feet and call Him Lord and God. But let us not come with any patronizing nonsense about His being a great human teacher. He has not left that open to us. He did not intend to.

C. S. Lewis
Mere Christianity, New York: Macmillan, 1952

DIVINE LIFE . . . HUMAN CONDITIONS

Our model is the Jesus, not only of Calvary, but of the workshop, the roads, the crowds, the clamorous demands and surly oppositions, the lack of all peace and privacy, the interruptions. For this, so strangely unlike anything we can attribute to the divine life in itself, is apparently not only like, but is, the divine life operating under human conditions.

C. S. Lewis
The Four Loves, *London: Fontana, 1960*

1.18 M. LLOYD-JONES

CLAIMS OF DIVINITY

The Bible makes many claims to the effect that Christ is divine; it asserts and teaches His divinity or, still more accurately, His deity. The first evidence is that certain names are ascribed to Him, each of which clearly implies His deity. Here are some of them. He is described as the "Son of God" forty times; He is referred to as "his Son" (God's Son); God refers to Him audibly as "my Son." So there, in various forms, is that title "Son," "Son of God."

Then five times He is also referred to as the "only begotten Son of God." [See] John 1:18, and the wicked husbandman, when God says, "They will reverence my son" (Matthew 21:37). The teaching there is perfectly clear, the words are uttered by our Lord Himself.

He is described in Revelation as "the first and the last," and in verse 11 of the same chapter as the "Alpha and Omega," the beginning and the end. These are obviously terms of deity; there is nothing before the beginning and nothing after the end. Then Peter, preaching in Jerusalem—you will find it recorded in Acts 3:14—refers to Him as the "Holy One": "But ye denied the Holy One and the Just." Again, these are terms of deity.

Then He is actually referred to as "God"; Thomas says, "My Lord and my God" (John 20:28). He is also described as "Emmanuel . . . God with us" in Matthew 1:23; and there is a most remarkable statement in Titus 2:13 where He is referred to as our "great God and Savior Jesus Christ." So there you have a number of names which are ascribed to Him, all of which are divine names.

M. Lloyd-Jones
God the Father, God the Son, Great Doctrines of the Bible
Crossway Books, Wheaton, 1996

JESUS' RELATIONSHIP TO THE FATHER

Our Lord claims that He is in a unique relationship to God in the matter of His knowledge of God. "No man," He says, "knoweth the Son but the Father; neither knoweth any man the Father save the Son." In other words, He looked at these people and said, "You see me but you do not really know me. The only one who really knows me is God and I am the one, the only one, who really knows God. You pray, you speak to God, but do not know God as I do." Nobody "hath seen God at any time," nor seen His shape. But He said that He had seen Him and He claimed, as the Jews realized, an equality with God the Father. He put Himself side by side with God. Occasionally He withdrew the veil and gave a glimpse of that eternal, mystical relationship between the Father and Himself, and He claimed that He was in such an intimate relationship with God that all men were outside it.

He stands there and tells these people, "Do you know that the whole of this world, the while of time, the whole of history, heaven and earth and hell and all things, have been handed over to me by God the Father?" That is His claim: a unique sonship, a unique relationship to God and a unique relationship to this world. He stands there and says quietly that the whole world is in His hands. Never has the world seen or heard anyone who has claimed so much. Who is He, this babe of Bethlehem, this boy of Nazareth, this carpenter, this artisan, who claims that He is indeed the Son of God?

M. Lloyd-Jones
The Heart of the Gospel, Crossway, 1996

1.19 C. F. D. MOULE

FIRMLY-DRAWN PORTRAIT

It is difficult enough for anyone, even a consummate master of imaginative writing, to create a picture of a deeply pure, good person, moving . . . in an impure environment, without making Him a . . . prude or a sort of plaster saint. How is it that, through all the Gospel traditions [we find a] . . . firmly-drawn portrait of an attractive young man moving freely among women of all sorts, including the decidedly disreputable, without a trace of sentimentality, unnaturalness, or prudery and yet, at every point, maintaining a simple integrity of character?

C. F. D. Moule
The Phenomenon of the New Testament,
SCM Press, 1967

1.20 J. I. PACKER

JESUS' IDENTITY

The Incarnation, this mysterious miracle at the heart of historic Christianity, is central in the New Testament witness. That Jews should ever have come to such a belief is amazing. Eight of the nine New Testament writers, like Jesus' original disciples, were Jews, drilled in the Jewish axiom that there is only one God and that no human is divine. They all teach, however, that Jesus is God's Messiah, the Spirit-anointed son of David promised in the Old Testament (e.g., Is. 11:1-5; *Christos*, "Christ," is Greek for Messiah). They all present him in a threefold role as teacher, sin-bearer, and ruler—prophet, priest, and king. And in other words, they all insist that Jesus the Messiah should be personally worshiped and trusted—which is to say that he is God no less than he is man. Observe how the four most masterful New Testament theologians (John, Paul, the writer of Hebrews, and Peter) speak to this.

John's Gospel frames its eyewitness narratives (John 1:14; 19:35; 21:24) with the declarations of its prologue (1:1-18): that Jesus is the eternal divine Logos (Word), agent of Creation and source of all life and light (vv. 1-5, 9), who through becoming "flesh" was revealed as Son of God and source of grace and truth, indeed as "God the only begotten" (vv. 14, 18; NIV text notes). The Gospel is punctuated with "I am" statements that have special significance because I am (Greek: *ego eimi*) was used to render God's name in the Greek translation of Exodus 3:14; whenever John reports Jesus as saying ego eimi, a claim to deity is implicit. . . . Climactically, Thomas worships Jesus as "my Lord and my God"

(20:28). Jesus then pronounces a blessing on all who share Thomas's faith and John urges his readers to join their number (20:29-31).

J. I. Packer
Concise Theology: A Guide To Historic Christian Beliefs
Wheaton, IL: Tyndale House Publishers, Inc., 1993

THE FATHER'S AGENT

If Jesus had been no more than a very remarkable, godly man, the difficulties in believing what the New Testament tells us about his life and work would be truly mountainous. But if Jesus was the same person as the eternal Word, the Father's agent in creation, "through whom also He made the worlds" (Hebrews 1:2, RV), it is no wonder if fresh acts of creative power marked His coming into this world, and His life in it, and His exit from it. It is not strange that He, the author of life, should rise from the dead. If He was truly God the Son, it is much more startling that He should die than He should rise again. "'Tis mystery all! The Immortal dies," wrote Wesley; but there is no comparable mystery in the Immortal's resurrection. And if the immortal Son of God did really submit to taste death, it is not strange that such a death should have saving significance for a doomed race. Once we grant that Jesus was divine, it becomes unreasonable to find difficulty in any of this; it is all of a piece, and hangs together completely. The incarnation is in itself an unfathomable mystery, but it makes sense of everything else that the New Testament contains.

J. I. Packer
Knowing God, *Downers Grove: InterVarsity Press, 1973*

1.21 JOHN STOTT

JESUS' SELF-CENTERED TEACHING

The most striking feature of the teaching of Jesus is that he was constantly talking about himself. It is true that he spoke much about the fatherhood of God and the kingdom of God. But then he added that he was the Father's "Son," and that he had come to inaugurate the kingdom. Entry into the kingdom depended on men's response to him. He even did not hesitate to call the kingdom of God "my kingdom."

This self-centeredness of the teaching of Jesus immediately sets him apart from the other great religious teachers of the world. They were self-effacing. He was self-advancing. They pointed men away from themselves, saying, "That is the truth, so far as I perceive it; follow that." Jesus said, "I am the truth; follow me." The founder of none of the ethnic religions ever dared to say such a thing. The personal pronoun forces itself repeatedly on our attention as we read his words. For example:

I am the bread of life; he who comes to me shall not hunger, and he who believes in me shall never thirst.

I am the light of the world; he who follows me will not walk in darkness, but will have the light of life.

I am the resurrection and the life; he who believes in me, though he die, yet shall he live, and whoever lives and believes in me shall never die.

I am the way, and the truth, and the life; no one comes to the Father, but by me. . . . John 6:35; 8:12; 11:25, 26; 14:6; (see also Matthew 11:28, 29)

. . . With such an opinion of himself, it is not surprising that he called people to himself.

John Stott
Basic Christianity, *Grand Rapids: Eerdmans, 1972*

THE PERSON OF CHRIST

1.22 WAS JESUS ONLY MAN IN APPEARANCE? IGNATIUS OF ANTIOCH

Ignatius writes against the background of an early form of the docetic heresy which claimed that Jesus was not really a human being, but only appeared to be one.

CHAPTER 9

Be ye deaf therefore, when any man speaketh to you apart from Jesus Christ, who was of the race of David, who was the Son of Mary, who was truly born and ate and drank, was truly persecuted under Pontius Pilate, was truly crucified and died in the sight of those in heaven and those on earth and those under the earth; who moreover was truly raised from the dead, His Father having raised Him, who in the like fashion will so raise us also who believe on Him—His Father, I say, will raise us—in

Christ Jesus, apart from whom we have not true life.

CHAPTER 10

But if it were as certain persons who are godless, that is unbelievers, say, that He suffered only in semblance, being themselves mere semblance, why am I in bonds? And why also do I desire to fight with wild beasts? So I die in vain. Truly then I lie against the Lord.

Ignatius of Antioch, Ignatius to the Trallians, *translated by J. B. Lightfoot*

1.23 THE PERSON OF CHRIST, IRENAEUS

With regard to Christ, the law and the prophets and the evangelists have proclaimed that He was born of a virgin, that He suffered upon a beam of wood, and that He appeared from the dead; that He also ascended to the heavens, and was glorified by the Father, and is the Eternal King; that He is the perfect Intelligence, the Word of God, who was begotten before the light; that He was the Founder of the universe, along with it (light), and the Maker of man; that He is All in all: Patriarch among the patriarchs; Law in the laws; Chief Priest among priests; Ruler among kings; the Prophet among prophets; the Angel

among angels; the Man among men; Son in the Father; God in God; King to all eternity. For it is He who sailed [in the ark] along with Noah. . . . , He was sold with Joseph, and He guided Abraham; was bound along with Isaac, and wandered with Jacob; with Moses He was Leader, and, respecting the people, Legislator. He preached in the prophets; was incarnate of a virgin; born in Bethlehem; received by John, and baptized in Jordan; was tempted in the desert, and proved to be the Lord. He gathered the apostles together, and preached the kingdom of heaven; gave light to the blind, and raised the dead; was seen in the temple, but was not held by the people as worthy of credit; was arrested by the priests, conducted before Herod, and condemned in the presence of Pilate; He manifested Himself in the body, was suspended upon a beam of wood, and raised from the dead; shown to the apostles, and, having been carried up to heaven, sitteth on the right hand of the Father, and has been glorified by Him as the Resurrection of the dead. Moreover, He is the Salvation of the lost, the Light to those dwelling in darkness, and Redemption to those who have been born; the Shepherd of the saved, and the Bridegroom of the Church; the Charioteer of the cherubim, the Leader of the angelic host; God of God; Jesus Christ our Savior.

Irenaeus,
Fragments from the Lost Writings of Irenaeus

1.24 JESUS' INCARNATION, TERTULLIAN

Tertullian opposes the heretical suggestion, found in the teachings of Praxeas, that Jesus' nature (being fully God and fully human) was like an amalgam to two metals, such as electrum, which is a naturally occurring amalgam of gold and silver.

CHAPTER 27

The distinction of the Father and the Son, thus established, he now proves the distinction of the two natures, which were, without confusion, united in the person of the Son. The subterfuges of Praxeas thus exposed.

But why should I linger over matters which are so evident, when I ought to be attacking points on which they seek to obscure the plainest proof? For, confuted on all sides on the distinction between the Father and the Son, which we maintain without destroying their inseparable union—as (by the examples) of the sun and the ray, and the fountain and the river—yet, by help of (their conceit) an indivisible number, (with issues) of two and three, they endeavor to interpret this distinction in a way which shall nevertheless tally with their own opinions: so that, all in one Person, they distinguish two, Father and Son, understanding the Son to be flesh, that is man, that is Jesus; and the Father to be spirit, that is God, that is Christ. Thus they, while contending that the Father and the Son are one and the same, do in fact begin by dividing them rather than uniting them. For if Jesus is one, and Christ is another, then the Son will be different from the Father, because the Son is Jesus, and the Father is Christ. Such a monarchy as this they learnt, I suppose, in the school of Valentinus, making two—Jesus and Christ. But this conception of theirs has been, in fact, already confuted in what we have previously advanced, because the Word of God or the Spirit of God is also called the power of the Highest, whom they make the Father; whereas these relations are not themselves the same as He whose relations they are said to be, but they proceed from Him and appertain to Him. However, another refutation awaits them on this point of their heresy. See, say they, it was announced by the angel: "Therefore that Holy Thing which shall be born of you shall be called the Son of God." Therefore, (they argue,) as it was the flesh that was born, it must be the flesh that is the Son of God. Nay, (I answer,) this is spoken concerning the Spirit of God. For it was certainly of the Holy Spirit that the virgin conceived; and that which He conceived, she brought forth. That, therefore, had to be born which was conceived and was to be brought forth; that is to say, the Spirit, whose "name should be called Emmanuel which, being interpreted, is, God with us." Besides, the flesh is not God, so that it could not have been said concerning it, "That Holy Thing shall be called the Son of God," but only that Divine Being who was born in the flesh, of whom the psalm also says, "Since God became man in the midst of it, and established it by the will of the Father." Now what Divine Person was born in it? The Word, and the Spirit which became incarnate with the Word by the will of the Father. The Word, therefore, is incarnate; and this must be the point of our inquiry: How the Word became flesh—whether it was by having been transfigured, as it were, in the flesh, or by having really clothed Himself in flesh. Certainly it was by a real clothing of Himself in flesh. For the rest, we must needs believe God to be unchangeable, and incapable of form, as being eternal. But transfiguration is the destruction of that which previously existed. For whatsoever is transfigured into some other thing ceases to be that which it had been, and begins to be that which it previously was not. God, however, neither ceases to be what He was, nor can He be any other thing than what He is. The Word is God, and "the Word of the Lord remains for ever,"—even by holding on unchangeably in His own proper form. Now, if He admits not of being transfigured, it must follow that He be understood in this sense to have become flesh, when He comes to be in the flesh, and is manifested, and is seen, and is handled by means of the flesh; since all the other points likewise require to be thus understood. For if the Word became flesh by a transfiguration and change of substance, it follows at once that Jesus must be a substance compounded of two substances—of flesh and spirit—a kind of mixture, like electrum, composed of gold and silver; and it begins to be neither gold (that is to say, spirit) nor silver (that is to say, flesh)— the one being changed by the other, and a third substance produced. Jesus, therefore,

cannot at this rate be God for He has ceased to be the Word, which was made flesh; nor can He be Man incarnate for He is not properly flesh, and it was flesh which the Word became. Being compounded, therefore, of both, He actually is neither; He is rather some third substance, very different from either. But the truth is, we find that He is expressly set forth as both God and Man; the very psalm which we have quoted intimating (of the flesh), that "God became Man in the midst of it, He therefore established it by the will of the Father,"—certainly in all respects as the Son of God and the Son of Man, being God and Man, differing no doubt according to each substance in its own especial property, inasmuch as the Word is nothing else but God, and the flesh nothing else but Man. Thus does the apostle also teach respecting His two substances, saying, "who was made of the seed of David;" in which words He will be Man and Son of Man. "Who was declared to be the Son of God, according to the Spirit;" in which words He will be God, and the Word— the Son of God. We see plainly the twofold state, which is not confounded, but conjoined in One Person—Jesus, God and Man. Concerning Christ, indeed, I defer what I have to say. (I remark here), that the property of each nature is so wholly preserved, that the Spirit on the one hand did all things in Jesus suitable to Itself, such as miracles, and mighty deeds, and wonders; and the Flesh, on the other hand, exhibited the affections which belong to it. It was hungry under the devil's temptation, thirsty with the Samaritan woman, wept over Lazarus, was troubled even to death, and at last actually died.

Tertullian
Against Praxeas

1.25 Nicene Creed

This brief statement of the Christian faith is the most widely accepted and most widely used of the Christian creeds.

I believe in one Lord Jesus Christ, the only begotten Son of God, Begotten of his Father before all worlds, God of God, Light of Light, Very God of very God, Begotten, not made, Being of one substance with the Father, By whom all things were made: Who for us men, and for our salvation came down from heaven, And was incarnate by the Holy Ghost of the Virgin Mary, And was made man, And was crucified also for us under Pontius Pilate. He suffered and was buried, And the third day he rose again according to the Scriptures, And Ascended into heaven, And sitteth on the right hand of the Father. And he shall come again with glory to judge both the quick and the dead: Whose kingdom shall have no end.

Nicene Creed, Council of Nicea, June 325

1.26 The Two Natures of Jesus, Leo the Great

Pope Leo the Great wrote to Flavian, the Patriarch of Constantinople, on June 13, 449. His letter is known as the "Tome of Leo" and is regarded as one of the early classic orthodox statements on Christology.

3. Without detriment, therefore, to the properties of either nature and substance (the divine and the human), which then came together in one person, majesty took on humility, strength weakness, eternity mortality, and for the payment of the debt belonging to our condition inviolable nature was united with suffering nature, so that, as suited the needs of our case, one and the same Mediator between God and men, the Man Jesus Christ, could both die with the one and not die with the other. Thus in the whole and perfect nature of true man was true God born, complete in what was his own, complete in what was ours . . . .

4. There enters then these lower parts of the world the Son of God, descending from his heavenly home and yet not quitting His Father's glory, begotten in a new order by a new birthing. In a new order, because being invisible in His own nature, He became visible in ours, and He whom nothing could contain was content to be contained. Abiding before all time, He began to be in time; the Lord of all things He obscured His immeasurable majesty and took on Him the form of a servant. Being God who cannot suffer, He did not disdain to be man that can and, immortal as He is, to subject Himself to the laws of death. The Lord assumed His mother's nature without faultiness, nor in the Lord Jesus Christ, born of the Virgin's womb, does the marvel of His birth make his nature unlike ours. For He who is true God is also true man, and in this union there is no deceit, since the humility of manhood and the loftiness of the Godhead both meet there. For as God is not changed by the showing of pity, so man is not swallowed up in the dignity . . . . To be hungry and thirsty, to be weary and to sleep is clearly human, but to satisfy five

thousand men with five loaves, to bestow on the woman of Samaria living water, draughts of which can secure the drinker from thirsting ever again, to walk upon the surface of the water with feet that do not sink and to quell the risings of the waves by rebuking the winds is without any doubt divine. Just as also—to pass over many other instances—it is not part of the same nature to be moved to tears of pity for a dead friend and, when the stone that closed the four-days grave was removed, to raise that same friend to life with a voice of command; or to hang on the cross, and to turn day into night to make all the elements tremble; or to be pierced with nails and then to open the gates of paradise to the robber's faith. So it is not part of the same nature to say: "I and the Father are one," and to say: "The Father is greater than I"! For although in the Lord Jesus Christ God and man is one person, yet the source of the degradation which is shared by both is one, and the source of the glory which is shared by both is another. For his manhood, which is less than the Father, comes from our side; His Godhead, which is equal to the Father, comes from the Father.

Leo the Great, Letter 28 to Flavian

1.27 THE CHRISTIAN FAITH DEFINED, COUNCIL OF CHALCEDON

On October 22, A.D. 451, Christian leaders agreed on the Church's teaching concerning the two natures of Christ. From that time on, the Christian Church has embraced this confession of faith, which cogently expresses the biblical teaching on the incarnation of God in Jesus of Nazareth. It is regarded by Christian Churches in both the East and the West as the classic orthodox statement on the humanity and divinity of Jesus.

Therefore, following the holy fathers, we all with one accord teach men to acknowledge one and the same Son, our Lord Jesus Christ, at once complete in Godhead and complete in manhood, truly God and truly man, consisting also of a reasonable soul and body; of one substance [*homoousious*] with the Father as regards his Godhead, and at the same time of one substance with us as regards his manhood; like us in all respects, apart from sin; as regards his Godhead, begotten of the Father before the ages, but yet as regards his manhood begotten, for us men and for our salvation, of Mary the Virgin, the God-bearer; one and the same Christ, Son, Lord, Only-begotten, recognized in two natures, without confusion, without change, without division, without separation; the distinction of natures being in no way annulled by the union, but rather the characteristics of each nature being preserved and coming together to form one person and subsistence, not as parted or separated into two persons, but one and the same Son and Only-begotten God the Word, Lord Jesus Christ; even as the prophets from earliest times spoke of him, and our Lord Jesus Christ himself taught us, and the creed of the fathers has handed down to us.

The Council of Chalcedon, 451

1.28 THE PERSON OF CHRIST, A. A. HODGE

A. A. Hodge, 1823—1886, named after Archibald Alexander, was son of Charles Hodge and his successor as the theology professor at Princeton where he carried on the tradition and work of his renowned father.

A. A. Hodge was a Reformed Princeton theologian who defended inerrancy and covenant theology and opposed evolution. Hodge urged his students to shun pride and traditionalism, and not to insist on doctrines beyond their biblical warrant. His most well known titles are: Assurance and Humility; Justification; The Life of Charles Hodge; Outlines of Theology; Sola Scriptura.

It is the grand distinction of Christianity that all its doctrines and all its forces center in the Person of its Founder and Teacher. In the case of all the other founders of philosophical sects and religions, the entire interest of their mission centers in the doctrines they teach, the opinions they disseminate. This was obviously true in the case of Zoroaster, Confucius, and Buddha, of Plato, Aristotle, and Cicero, of Moses and Paul. In the case of each of them the question was not what they were, but what they taught. But in the case of Christianity, the entire system, from foundation to superstructure, rests upon and derives its life from the Person of its Founder. The question of questions is what he was, rather than what he taught.

This can be proved:

(1) From an examination of each of the doctrines of Christianity separately. All that the Scriptures teach of the Mosaic dispensation and its typical character; of the burden of all the prophets; of the new birth; of repentance and faith; of justification and sanctification; of holy living and of the Christian Church; of the state of the soul after death; of the resurrection from the dead; of the general judgment; and of heaven itself—takes its meaning and force from its relation to the person, offices, and work of Christ.

(2) From the experience of Christians. We believe Moses and Paul, but we believe in Christ. To be a Christian is to be in Jesus. To live a Christian is to have fellowship with the Father and the Son. To die a Christian is to sleep in Jesus.

(3) The same is proved, in the third place, from the present attitude of the great controversy between Christianity and its opponents. In this age, in which secular philosophy oscillates between materialism and pantheism, when advanced thinkers disdain all the old questions of theology, natural or revealed, even the most inveterate skeptics acknowledge the necessity of presenting some solution of that miracle of all ages, the Person of Jesus of Nazareth. It is impossible to explain that unique phenomenon which emerged on the hills and valleys of Judea eighteen hundred years ago, whose life, character, and works are truly inexplicable unless we accept the account of his nature and his origin which is given to us in the Word of God. The press groans with Ecce Homos and Lives of Christ, and with new versions of rationalistic theories, mystical and legendary. Thus the infidel is constrained to unite with the believer in bearing testimony to the greatness of that mystery of godliness, God manifest in the flesh.

And here, in the very heart of our religion, all true Christians agree. The entire historical Church, in all its ages and in all its branches—Greek and Roman, Lutheran and Reformed, Calvinist and Arminian—are here entirely at one.

While this is true, as far as the public faith of the Church is concerned, as expressed in its great confessions, liturgies, and hymns, a great variety of opinion and diversity of speculation and definition have prevailed at different times among the various schools of theology. This diversity of speculation naturally arose from the following facts:

(1) The Person of the incarnate God is unique. His birth has had no precedents and his existence no analogy. He cannot be explained by being referred to a class, nor can he be illustrated by an example.

(2) The Scriptures, while clearly and fully revealing all the elements of his Person, yet never present in one formula an exhaustive definition of that Person, nor a connected statement of the elements which constitute it and their mutual relations. The impression is all the more vivid because it is made, as in a picture, by an exhibition of his Person in action—an exhibition in which the divinity and humanity are alike immediately demonstrated by the self-revelation of their attributes in action; and:

(3) This unique personality, as it surpasses all analogy, also transcends all understanding. The proud intellect of man is constantly aspiring to remove all mysteries and to subject the whole sphere of existence to the daylight of rational explanation. Such attempts are constantly ending in the most grotesque failure. Even in the material world it is true that *omnia, exeunt in myseterium*. If we cannot explain the relation which the immaterial soul sustains to the organized body in the person of man, why should we be surprised to find that all attempts to explain the intimate relations which the eternal Word and the human soul and body sustain to each other in the Person of Christ have miserably failed?

Before proceeding to the historical illustration of this doctrine, I call your attention to the following general remarks:

1. The doctrine of the Person of Christ is intimately associated with the doctrine of the Trinity.

It is obviously impossible to hold the orthodox view with respect to the divine-human constitution of our Lord unless we first believe the orthodox doctrine that the one God exists as three eternal Persons, Father, Son, and Holy Ghost. At the same time, few hold the true doctrine as to the tri-personal constitution of the Trinity without at the same time holding the corresponding catholic doctrine as to the Person of the God-man.

Indeed, I happen to know that the great objection which the most able and influential Unitarians entertain to the Trinitarian system is not originated by their difficulty with the Trinity, considered by itself, but because they regard the doctrine of the Trinity to be inseparable from that of the Person of Christ as held by the Church, which to them appears impossible to believe.

And undoubtedly we freely admit just here that in the constitution of the Person of the God-man lies the, to us, absolutely insoluble mystery of godliness. How is it possible that the same Person can be at the same time infinite and finite, ignorant and omniscient, omnipotent and helpless? How can two complete spirits coalesce in one Person? How can two consciousnesses, two understandings, two memories, two imaginations, two wills, constitute one Person? All this is involved in the scriptural and Church doctrine of the Person of Christ. Yet no one can explain it. The numerous attempts made to explain or to expel this mystery have only filled the Church with heresies and obscured the faith of Christians.

2. The Scriptures do not in any one place, or by the means of distinct, comprehensive formulae, give us complete definitions either of the doctrine of the Trinity or of that of the Person of Christ.

They do give us, most explicitly and repeatedly, all the elements of both doctrines, and then leave us to put all the several teachings relating to the same subject together, and so to construct the entire doctrine by the synthesis of the elements.

Thus (1) as to the Doctrine of The Trinity. The Scriptures tell us, first, that there is but one God. Then we would naturally conclude that if there is but one God, there can be but one divine Person. But, again, the Scriptures teach us that Father, Son, and Holy Ghost are that one God. Then, again, we would naturally conclude that the terms Father, Son, and Holy Ghost are only different names, qualitative or official, of one Person. But yet again the Scriptures prevent us, and teach us that these names designate different subjects and agents. The Father is objective to the Son, and the Son to the Father, and both to the Spirit. They love each other and are loved. They converse, using to and of each other the personal pronouns I, thou, he. The Father sends the Son, and the Father and Son send the Spirit, and they, in that order, act as agents, proceed from and return to, and report.

The Scriptures also teach that there is an eternal constitutional relation of order and origin between three Persons. The Father is the fountain of Godhead. He eternally begets the Son (the process is without beginning, or end, or succession), and the Father and Son eternally give origin to the Spirit.

(2) In the very same manner the Scriptures teach us all we know of the Person of Christ. Pointing to that unique phenomenon exhibited biographically in the four Gospels, the Scriptures affirm "He is God." Then we would naturally say, if he is God, he cannot be man; if he is infinite, he cannot be finite. But the Scriptures proceed to affirm, pointing to the same historical subject, "He is man." Then, again, we would naturally say, if that phenomenon is both God and man, he must be two Persons in reality, and one Person only in appearance. But yet again the Scriptures prevent us, In every possible way they set him before us as one Person. His divinity is never objective to his humanity, nor his humanity to his divinity. His divinity never loves, speaks to, nor sends his humanity, but both divinity and humanity act together as the common energies of one Person. All the attributes and all the acts of both natures are referred to the one Person. The same " I " possessed glory with the Father before the world was, and laid down his life for his sheep. Sometimes in a single proposition the title is taken from the divine side of his Person, while the predicate is true only of his human side, as when it is said, "The Church of God, which he hath purchased with his own blood." The same Person is called God because of his divinity, while it is affirmed that he shed his human blood for his Church. Again: while standing among his disciples on the earth, he says, "The Son of man, which is in heaven."

Here the same Person, who is called Son of man because of his humanity, is declared to be omnipresent—that is, at the same time on earth and in heaven—as to his divine nature. This, of course, implies absolute singleness of Person, including at once divine and human attributes.

Again: the Scriptures teach us that this amazing personality does not center in his humanity, and that it is not a composite one originated by the power of the Spirit when he brought the two natures together in the womb of the Virgin Mary. It was not made by adding manhood to Godhead. The Trinity is eternal and unchangeable. A new Person is not substituted for the second Person of the Trinity, neither is a fourth Person added to the Trinity. But the Person of Christ is just the one eternal Word, the second Person of the Trinity, which in time, by the power of the Holy Ghost, through the instrumentality of the womb of the Virgin, took a human nature (not a man, but the seed of man, humanity in the germ) into personal union with himself. The Person is eternal and divine. The humanity is introduced into it. The center of the personality always continues in the eternal personal Word or Son of God.

Let me illustrate this by your personality and mine. We consist of soul and body, two distinct substances, but one person. This personality, however, is not composed of the union of soul and body at birth. The personality from the first to the last centers in the soul, and is only shared in by the body.

By soul we mean only one thing—that is, an incarnate spirit, a spirit with a body. Thus we never speak of the souls of angels. They are pure spirits, having no bodies. Put a spirit in a body, and the spirit becomes a soul, and the body is quickened into life and becomes a part of the person of the soul. Separate soul and body, as death does, and the soul becomes a ghost and the body becomes a corpse. When death takes place the body passes out of the personality, is called "it," and is placed in the grave; while the soul, still continuing the person, goes at once to be judged of God. At the resurrection the same personal soul will return and take up the same body once discarded, and, receiving it again into its personality, will stand before God a complete man.

So the divine Word, which from eternity was the second Person of the Trinity, did eighteen hundred years ago take, not a human person, but a human nature into his eternal personality, which ever continues, not a human person nor a divine-human person, but the eternal second Person of the Trinity, with a human nature embraced in it as its personal organ.

3. There is one obvious respect in which the doctrines of the Trinity and of the Person of Christ agree, and one in which they no less obviously differ.

They agree in that both alike utterly transcend all experience, all analogy, and all adequate grasp of human reason. But they differ in that, while the mystery of the Trinity is that one Spirit should exist eternally as three distinct Persons, the mystery of the Person of Christ is that two distinct spirits should for evermore constitute but one Person.

4. If you give due attention to the difficulties involved in each of these divinely revealed doctrines, you would be able a priori to anticipate all possible heresies which have been evolved in the course of history.

All truth is catholic; it embraces many elements, wide horizons, and therefore involves endless difficulties and apparent inconsistencies. The mind of man seeks for unity, and tends prematurely to force a unity in the sphere of his imperfect knowledge by sacrificing one element of the truth or other to the rest. This is eminently true of all rationalists. They are clear and logical at the expense of being superficial and half-orbed. Heresy means an act of choice, and hence division, the picking and choosing a part, instead of comprehensively embracing the whole of the truth. Almost all heresies are partial truths—true in what they affirm, but false in what they deny.

Take, for instance, the doctrine of the Trinity. One eternal Spirit exists eternally as Father, Son, and Holy Ghost, three distinct Persons. This the rationalists cannot understand, and therefore will not believe.

They proceed, therefore, to deny one or other element of the whole truth, and try to hold the dead fragment remaining.

Thus—(1) they attempted to cut the knot by denying the divinity of Christ, and had pure, lifeless Mohammedan Unitarianism left;

(2) they pressed the unity so close that they had but one Person as well as one God, and the terms " Father," " Son," and " Holy Ghost " became different descriptive or official titles of the same Person: as Grant while in office was one person, and yet at the same time was husband and father, commander-in-chief of the army and navy, and President of the United States, so the Sabellians say Father, Son, and Holy Ghost are different titles of the same Person in different characters and functions;

(3) or, lastly, they ran to the other side of the enclosure and pressed the distinction of Persons to such a degree that they had three Gods instead of the mystery of one God in three Persons.

Take, for another instance, in like manner, the doctrine of the Person of Christ. The mystery is that two spirits—one divine, the other human—two minds, two wills, are so united that without confusion or change or absorption of one in the other they constitute but one Person. Scrutinize this, and you can predict beforehand all the possible heresies or one-sided half-truths. (1) The Unitarian cuts the knot by denying half the facts of the case and leaving out the divinity. (2) The Gnostics held that a man Jesus was temporarily possessed by the supernatural Aeon or Angel Christ. (3) The Docetae cut the knot by denying the other half of the truth, that Christ was a man, holding that the reality was a simple divinity and the humanity a mere appearance. (4) The Eutychians pressed the unity of the Person to such an extent that they confounded the natures, holding that the human was absorbed in the divine. (5) The Nestorians went to the other extreme of emphasizing the integrity of the several natures after their union so very far as to dissolve the unity of the Person, and to set forth Christ, not as a God-man, but as a God and a man intimately united. These, if they do not cover, at least indicate the direction and spirit of all possible heresies relating to these two fundamental doctrines of Christianity.

Let us proceed to the historical development of the doctrine in the consciousness of the Church.

1. In the Council of Nice, A.D. 325, there were three parties.

The Arians, led by Arius, maintained that the superhuman element in the Person of Christ was *heteroousion*—of a different substance from God the Father. The semi-Arians, led by the two bishops Eusebius, held that the superhuman element was *homoiousion*—of a like substance to that of the Father. The Orthodox, led by Athanasius, held that the divine nature of Christ was *homoousion*—of identically the same numerical substance with that of the Father. This last doctrine was embodied in the creed of that council, which, in the form afterward perfected at the end of the fourth century, is received by all Christians, Catholic and Protestant. From this time the doctrine of the Trinity and that of the absolute divinity of Christ have been universally held in the Church.

2. But from that time forth men began to question how the substance of God could be united in one Person with the substance of humanity.

Apollinaris, bishop of Laodicea, in all sincerity attempted, about A.D. 370, to maintain the truth by the following explanation, which really sacrifices an essential part of it. He supposed that the Scripture, (1 Thess. 5:23) and true philosophy teach that every natural human person is composed of three distinct elements—*soma*, body; *psyche*, soul; and *pneuma*, spirit; that the *psyche* is the seat of the animal life and *appetites* and the emotions and logical understanding, and the pneuma is the seat of the reason, the will, and the moral and spiritual nature. These three put in personal union make one complete human person. He held that in the Person of Christ the soma and psyche are human and the *pneuma* is divine.

But this view secures the unity and simplicity of Christ's Person at the expense of the integrity of his humanity. If Christ does not take a human pneuma—that is, a complete human nature—he cannot be our Savior, our High Priest, who feels with us in all our infirmities, having been tempted like us. Indeed, the view of Apollinaris degrades the doctrine by maintaining that the eternal Word took not a complete human nature, but an irrational human animal into personal union with himself.

3. During the fourth and early part of the fifth centuries, theological speculation in the Eastern Church revolved around two great centers, Alexandria in Egypt and Antioch in Syria.

The tendency of the Alexandrian school from Origen to Cyril and Eutychius was mystical and theosophical. With this school the divinity of Christ was everything, and into it the humanity was represented as absorbed. The tendency of the school of Antioch, whose great representatives were Theodore of Mopsuestia and Nestorius, patriarch of Constantinople, was to rationalistic clearness—to the emphasis of moral duties and of the distinctness and independence of the human will. The Alexandrian party generated Eutychianism, which absorbed the humanity in the divinity, in order to maintain the unity of the Person and absoluteness of the divinity; while the Antiochian party generated Nestorianism, in which the unity of the Person is sacrificed to the separate integrity of the natures, and especially of the human nature. Nestorianism was condemned by the ecumenical council held at Ephesus, A.D. 431, and Eutychianism was condemned by the council which met at Chalcedon, A.D. 451.

4. In these decisions the whole Church, Eastern and Western, concurred.

The advocates of Eutychianism endeavored for a time to maintain, as a compromise position, that although the two natures in Christ remain entire and distinct, nevertheless that as they coalesce in Christ in one single Person, so that Person can possess but one will, divine-human, and not a divine and a human will combined in one personality. This party was then known as the Monothelite, the one-will party. After this heresy was condemned at the sixth ecumenical council, held in Constantinople in 681, the controversy was closed, and the faith of the Church remained as represented by the old definitions until the time of the Reformation.

5. After the Reformation the Lutherans, in order to establish their doctrine of the ubiquity of Christ's human nature in the Lord's Supper, introduced a new view as to his Person.

The Eutychians taught that the humanity of Christ was absorbed in his divinity. The Lutherans taught that his humanity was exalted to an equality with the divinity. This they attempted to explain by the *Communicatio Idiomatum*—that is, the communication of attributes from one nature to the other, or the communion of one nature in the attributes of the other. The Lutherans held the formula *Communicatio idiomatum utriusque nature ad naturam*—that is, the communication of the attributes of each nature to the other nature. The Reformed Churches, on the other hand, admitted that the attributes of each nature are communicated only to the one Person, which was common to both natures. The Lutherans thus held that at the moment of the incarnation, in virtue of the union between the divine and human natures, the human nature of Christ became omniscient, omnipotent, and omnipresent.

This doctrine is evidently not supported in Scripture—is not consistent with the integrity of Christ's human nature; for that which is omniscient, omnipotent, and omnipresent is divine and not human, and is plainly inconsistent with all the facts related in the Gospels as to our Lord's earthly life. He is there represented in all respects, as to knowledge, power, and space, as literally finite as other babes and men.

This theory originated in the desire to lay a foundation for their doctrine that the body and blood of Christ are always present in, with, and under the bread and wine in the sacrament of the Lord's Supper. But it is evident that this foundation, instead of supporting, invalidates the sacramental presence. If his body and blood are omnipresent, then they are in, with, and under all food and drink, and indeed in and under all material forms of every kind in all worlds. What they needed was not essential, constant, universal omnipresence, but "voluntary multi-presence"—that is, the power upon Christ's part of rendering his body and blood present at many places at the same time at his own good pleasure.

To reconcile their doctrine with these facts, one school of Lutheran theologians— namely, that of Tubingen, led by John Brentius—held that while on earth the human nature of Christ was really omnipotent and omnipresent, only that he hid the use of these attributes from man, like a king traveling incognito. Another school, that of Chemnitz, held that the use of these divine attributes of Christ's humanity was dependent upon his human will—that in his estate of humiliation on earth he voluntarily abstained from their use.

This speculation of the Lutherans was the latest and most elaborate attempt ever made by theologians to explain how the two natures of Christ can coalesce in one person.

6. The Eutychians

The Eutychians held that the human nature was absorbed in the divine; the Lutherans, that the human nature was exalted to equality with the divine; the Reformed held that the eternal divine Person humbled himself to be united with humanity; the advocates of the modern German doctrine of Kenosis hold that the eternal Word himself became man— that Christ was and is both God and man, but that he is but one single nature as one single Person. They build on such texts as John 1:14 and Phil. 2:7, "He emptied himself." Kenosis means the act of emptying or the state of being emptied. They start with the orthodox doctrine that the Person of the Word, or Son, is eternally generated of his own substance by the Father. This generation makes the Son partaker of all the fullness of the divine nature, and is, they say, dependent upon the will of the Son, his voluntary act conspiring with the act of the Father. At the incarnation the eternal Son, of his voluntary act, emptied his person of the divine fullness, and became an unconscious human germ in the womb of the Virgin. From that point, and under the ordinary conditions of human birth and life, this divine germ developed through all the stages of human experience—infantine, youthful, and mature. After his death and resurrection, this same nature, the self-emptied Word, the divine germ, developed as a man, again expands into infinity, and fills all things as God. His nature hence is one, because from first to last it is the divine substance communicated by the Father to the Son, who in turn voluntarily empties himself of all except the merest point of existence, which after his glorification expands again into infinity. He is one Person because he is one single nature. He is from first to last God as to substance, but he has become, by passing through the womb of the Virgin Mary, man as to form. Thus he ever continues God in the form of man—always God, because he subsists of the one eternal, self-existent Substance; always man, because retaining the human form and experience acquired on earth.

This, confessedly, rests upon the assumption that the divine nature is capable of taking upon itself humanity, and that the human nature is capable of receiving the properties of divinity. Hence it is evidently of a pure pantheistic descent. God is immutable, incapable of becoming unconscious and of passing through the limitations of the finite. To be man is to be finite and dependent; to be God is to be infinite and self-existent. Christ was both at the same time, because his Person embraced two distinct natures, the divine and the human.

7. The common doctrine of the Church, then, is as follows:

1. As to the incarnation.

(1) Substance is that which has objective existence, permanence, and power. Attributes are the active powers of their respective substances, and are inseparable from them. Only a divine substance can have divine attributes; only a human substance can have human attributes. In the Godhead the one infinite divine Substance eternally exists in the form of three equal Persons.

(2) In the incarnation the second Person of this Trinity established a personal union between itself and a human soul and body. These substances remain distinct, and their properties or active powers are inseparable from each substance respectively.

(3) The union between them is not mechanical, as that between oxygen and nitrogen in our air; neither is it chemical, as that between oxygen and hydrogen when water is formed; neither is it organic, as that subsisting between our hearts and our brains: but it is a union more intimate, more profound, and more mysterious than any of these. It is personal. If we cannot understand the nature of the simpler unions, why should we complain because we cannot understand the nature of the most profound of all unions?

2. As to the effects of the incarnation.

(1) The attributes of both natures belong to the one Person, which includes both.

(2) The acts of both natures are the acts of the one Person.

(3) The human nature is greatly exalted, and shares in the love, adoration, and glory of the divine nature. It all belongs to the one Person.

(4) The human attributes of our Redeemer are the organ of his divine Person, and are, through the divinity, rendered virtually inexhaustible and ubiquitously available for us. When you put your babe to bed and leave him, to go your own way to a distant place, you say, "Love, fear not; Jesus well be with you while I am gone." You know Jesus will be with you also at the same time, and with all believers. By this you do not mean simply that Christ's divinity will be with you and the babe. You mean that the Person who is very man as well as very God will be with you both. You want his human love and sympathy as well as his divine benevolence. If he were a mere man, he could be only at one place at one time, and his attention and sympathy would soon be overwhelmed by our demands. But he is at once God and man, and as such, in the wholeness and fullness of both natures, he is inexhaustible and accessible by all believers in heaven and on earth at once and for ever.

The best illustration of this mystery is afforded by the union of soul and body in the unity of our own persons. The body is matter, the soul is spirit. Matter and spirit are incompatible—as far as we understand as incompatible as divinity and humanity. Matter is inert, extended, and the vehicle of force; spirit is spontaneous, unextended, and the generator of force. Yet they form in us, under certain circumstances, one person. This is the person of the soul, not of the body, as shown before. The soul by this union is virtually confined to and extended in space, for wherever the body is, there the soul lives and feels through their union. The body, which is of itself inert and dead, is through its union with the soul palpitating with life, throbbing with feelings, and instinct with energy.

Every act of each nature is also the act of the one person, and both natures concur in our actions, organic and voluntary. Even digestion is possible to the body only through the indwelling of the soul. But in all our higher actions, when the orator speaks or when the singer pours forth his soul in melody, both soul and body penetrating each other, yet distinct, constituting one person, yet unconfused—both soul and body act together inseparably. As human voice and instrument blend in one harmony, as human soul and body blend in each act of feeling, thought, or speech, so, as far as we can know, divinity and humanity act together in the thought and heart and act of the one Christ.

I adore a Christ who is absolutely one— who is at the same time pure, unmixed, unchanged God, and pure, unmixed, unchanged man—and whose Person, in its wholeness and its fullness, is available throughout all space and throughout all time to those who trust him and love his appearing.

A. A. Hodge

1.29 OUR LORD AS A BELIEVING MAN, ALEXANDER WHYTE

The workings of our Lord's human mind, the affections and the emotions of our Lord's human heart, and all the spiritual experiences of our Lord's human life-take Jesus Christ in all these things, and He is the most absorbing, the most satisfying, and the most sanctifying study in all the universe. There is no other doctrine in heaven or on earth for one moment to compare with the doctrine of God in Christ and Christ in God: the Word made flesh, and the flesh made God.

Alexander Whyte
Jesus Christ our Lord
Grand Rapids: Zondervan, 1953

6

THE DEITY OF CHRIST

1.30 THE DEITY OF CHRIST, MARTIN LUTHER

Martin Luther, 1483-1546, German theologian, professor, pastor, and church reformer, sparked off the Protestant Reformation with the publication of his Ninety-Five Theses *on October 31, 1517. In the* Ninety-Five Theses *he attacked the Church's sale of indulgences. He advocated a theology that rested on God's gracious activity in Jesus Christ, rather than in human works. Nearly all Protestants trace their history back to Luther in one way or another.*

The chief lesson and study in divinity is, that we learn well and rightly to know Christ, who is therein very graciously pictured forth unto us. We take pains to conciliate the good will and friendship of men, that so they may show us a favorable countenance; how much the more ought we to conciliate our Lord Jesus, that so he may be gracious unto us. St Peter says: "Grow up in the knowledge of Jesus Christ," of that compassionate Lord and Master, whom all should learn to know him only out of the Scriptures, where he says: "Search the Scriptures, for they do testify of me." St John says: "In the beginning was the Word, and the Word was with God, and the Word was God," etc. The apostle Thomas also calls Christ, God; were he says: "My Lord and my God." In like manner St Paul, Rom. 9:5, speaks of Christ, that he is God; where he says: "Who is God over all, blessed forever, Amen." And Col. 2:9, "In Christ dwelleth all the fullness of the Godhead bodily;" that is, substantially.

Christ must needs be true God, seeing he, through himself, fulfilled and overcame the law; for most certain it is, that no one else could have vanquished the law, angel or human creature, but Christ only, so that it cannot hurt those that believe in him; therefore, most certainly he is the Son of God, and natural God. Now if we comprehend Christ in this manner, as the Holy Scripture

displays him before us, then certain it is, that we can neither err nor be put to confusion; and may then easily judge what is right to be held of all manner of divine qualities, religions, and worship, that are used and practiced in the universal world. Were this picturing of Christ removed out of our sight, or darkened in us, undeniably there must needs follow utter disorder. For human and natural religion, wisdom, and understanding, cannot judge aright or truly the laws of God; therein has been and still is exhausted the art of all philosophers, all the learned and worldly-wise among the children of men. For the law rules and governs mankind; therefore the law judges mankind, and not mankind the law.

If Christ be not God, then neither the Father nor the Holy Ghost is God; for our article of faith speaks thus: "Christ is God, with the Father and the Holy Ghost." Many there are who talk much of the Godhead of Christ, but they discourse thereof as a blind man speaks of colors. Therefore, when I hear Christ speak, and say: "Come to me, all ye that are weary and heavy laden, and I will give you rest," then do I believe steadfastly that the whole Godhead speaks in an undivided and unseparated substance. Wherefore he that preaches a God to me that died not for me the death on the cross, that God will I not receive.

He that has this article, has the chief and principal article of faith, though to the world it seems unmeaning and ridiculous. Christ says: The Comforter which I will send, shall not depart from you, but will remain with you, and will make you able to endure all manner of tribulations and evil. When Christ says: I will pray to the Father, then he speaks as a human creature, or as very man; but when he says: I will do this, or that, as before he said, I will send the Comforter, then he speaks as very God. In this manner do I learn my article, "That Christ is both God and man."

I, out of my own experience, am able to witness, that Jesus Christ is true God; I know full well and have found what the name of Jesus had done for me. I have often been so near death, that I thought verily now must I die, because I teach his Word to the wicked world, and acknowledge him; but always he mercifully put life into me, refreshed and comforted me. Therefore, let us use diligence only to keep him, and then all is safe, although the devil were ever so wicked and crafty, and the world ever so evil and false. Let whatsoever will or can befall me, I will surely cleave by my sweet Savior Christ Jesus, for in him am I baptized; I can neither do nor know anything but only what he has taught me.

The Holy Scriptures, especially St Paul, everywhere ascribe unto Christ that which he gives to the Father, namely, the divine almighty power; so that he can give grace, and peace of conscience, forgiveness of sins, life, victory over sin, and death, and the devil. Now, unless St Paul would rob God of his honor, and give it to another that is not God, he dared not ascribe such properties and attributes to Christ, if he were not true God; and God himself says, Is.

42:8, "I will not give my glory to another." And, indeed, no man can give that to another which he has not himself; but, seeing Christ gives grace and peace, the Holy Ghost also, and redeems from the power of the devil, sin and death, so is it most sure that he has an endless, immeasurable, almighty power, equal with the Father.

Christ brings also peace, but not as the apostles brought it, through preaching; he gives it as a Creator, as his own proper creature. The Father creates and gives life, grace, and peace; and even so gives the Son the same gifts. Now, to give grace, peace, everlasting life, forgiveness of sins, to justify, to save, to deliver from death and hell, surely these are not the works of any creature, but of the sole majesty of God, things which the angels themselves can neither create nor give. Therefore, such works pertain to the high majesty, honor, and glory of God, who is the only and true Creator of all things. We must think of no other God than Christ; that God which speaks not out of Christ's mouth, is not God. God, in the Old Testament, bound himself to the throne of grace; there was the place where he would hear, so long as the policy and government of Moses stood and flourished. In like manner, he will still hear no man or human creature, but only through Christ. As number of the Jews ran to and fro burning incense, and offerings here and there, and seeking God in various places, not regarding the tabernacle, so it goes now; we seek God everywhere; but not seeking him in Christ, we find him nowhere.

Martin Luther, Table Talk, 182

1.31 JESUS CHRIST THE SON OF GOD, THEODORE BEZA

Theodore Beza was born in 1519 at Vézelay in France, and died in 1605 in Geneva. As author, translator, educator, and theologian he assisted and later succeeded John Calvin as a leader of the Protestant Reformation centered at Geneva.

The following extract first appeared in 1558 in a book called Confession De Foi Du Chretien, The Christian Faith. *It was a best-seller during the Protestant Reformation.*

HOW GOD HAS TURNED THE SIN OF MAN TO HIS GLORY

There would remain nothing more for the whole world, except to go to its ruin (Rom. 3:19). But God, being not only very righteous, but also very merciful, had according to His infinite wisdom, eternally established a way to turn all the evils to His great glory: to the greater manifestation of His infinite goodness (Rom. 3:21-25), towards those whom He has chosen eternally so as to be glorified in their salvation (Rom. 8:29; 9:23). And, on the other side, He has turned the sin of man to the manifestation of His sovereign power and His wrath, by the just condemnation of the vessels of wrath prepared for destruction (Rom. 9:22; Ex. 9:6).

As St. Augustine well says; "If all were saved, the wages of sin demanded by justice would be hidden. If none were saved, no-one would see what grace bestows."

JESUS CHRIST IS THE SOLE MEDIATOR CHOSEN AND PROMISED BY GOD

This sole and unique way is the mystery of the Incarnation of the Son of God with all which flows from it. Bit by bit this was promised from Adam to John the Baptist, published and preached by the patriarchs and the prophets, and also typified in various ways under the Law (Gen. 3:15; 12:3; 18:18; 22:18; Deut. 18:15-18; 2 Sam. 7:12; Rom. 1:2-3 etc.) Thus, the Son is fully contained in the books of the Old Testament, so that the men of those times were saved by faith in Jesus Christ who was to come.

THE SIMILARITY AND THE DIFFERENCE BETWEEN THE OLD

AND THE NEW TESTAMENT

Therefore there has never been and there never shall be but one covenant of salvation between God and men (Heb. 13:8; Rom. 3:25; 1 Tim. 2:5-6; 1 Cor. 10:1-11; Eph. 1:7-10; see the whole Epistle to the Hebrews). The substance of this covenant is Jesus Christ. But, having regard to the circumstances, there are two Testaments or "Covenants." We have the authentic titles and contents of them; which we call "Holy Scripture" and the "Word of God." One is called "Old" and the other "New" (Jer. 31:31, 32; Heb. 8:6). The second is much better than the first, for the first did declare Jesus Christ, but from afar off, and hidden under the shadows and images which vanished at His coming; He Himself is the Sun of Righteousness (John 4:23, 24).

WHY IT WAS NECESSARY THAT JESUS CHRIST BE TRUE MAN IN NATURE, IN HIS BODY AND IN HIS SOUL, BUT WITHOUT ANY SIN

It was necessary that the Mediator of this covenant and this reconciliation be true man, but without any stain of original sin or any other, for the following reasons:

Firstly, since God is very righteous and man is the object of His wrath, because of natural corruption (1 Tim. 2:5; John 1:14; Rom. 1:3; Gal. 4:4; Rom. 8:2-4; 1 Cor. 1:30), it was necessary in order to reconcile men with God, that there be a true man in whom the ruins caused by this corruption would be totally repaired.

Secondly, man is compelled to fulfill all the righteousness which God demands from him in order to be glorified (Matt. 3:15; Rom. 5:18; 2 Cor. 5:21). It was therefore necessary that there be a man who would perfectly fulfill all righteousness in order to please God.

Thirdly, all men are covered with an infinite number of sins, as much internal as external; that is why they are liable to the curse of God (Rom. 3:23-26; Is. 53:11, etc). It was therefore necessary that there be a man who would fully satisfy the justice of God in order to pacify Him.

Finally, no corrupt man would have been able, in any way, to even begin to fulfill the least of these actions. He would first of all have had need of a Redeemer for himself (Rom. 8:2; 2 Cor. 5:21; Heb. 4:15; 1 Pet. 2:22; 3:18; 1 John 2:1-2). So much was necessary for himself before he could buy back the others, or could do anything pleasing or satisfying to God (Rom. 14:23; Heb. 11:6). It was therefore necessary that the Mediator and Redeemer of men be true man in his body and in his soul, and that he be, nevertheless, entirely pure and free from all sin.

WHY IT WAS NECESSARY THAT JESUS CHRIST BE TRUE GOD

It was necessary that this same Mediator be true God and not only man (John 1:14, etc); at the very least for the following reasons:

Firstly, if He was not true God, He would not be Savior at all, but would himself have need of a Savior (Is. 43:11; Hos. 13:4; Jer. 17:5-8).

Secondly, it is necessary, from the justice of God, that there be a relationship between the crime and its punishment. The crime is infinite, for it is committed against One whose majesty is infinite. Therefore there is here need of an infinite satisfaction; for the same reason, it was necessary that the One who would accomplish it as true man be also infinite, that is to say, true God.

Thirdly, the wrath of God being infinite, there was no human or angelic strength known which could bear such a weight without being crushed (John 14:10, 12, 31; 16:32; 2 Cor. 5:19). He who was to live again, after having conquered the devil, sin, the world and death united to the wrath of God, had to be therefore not only perfect man, but also true God.

Lastly, in order to better manifest this incomprehensible goodness, God did not wish that His grace should only equal our crime; He willed that where sin abounds, grace super abounds (Rom. 5:15-21). For this reason, while he was created in the image of God, the first Adam, author of our sin, was earthly, as his frailty showed well (1 Cor. 15:45-47). Jesus Christ, on the contrary, the second Adam, through whom we are saved, while being true and perfect man, is nevertheless the Lord come from Heaven, that is to say, the true God. For, in essence, all the fullness of divinity dwells in Him (Col. 2:9). If the disobedience of Adam made us fall, the righteousness of Jesus Christ gives us more security than we had previously. We hope for life procured by Jesus Christ, better than that which we lost in Adam; even more so as Jesus Christ surpasses Adam.

HOW THE MYSTERY OF OUR SALVATION HAS BEEN ACCOMPLISHED IN JESUS CHRIST

Therefore we confess that, in order to fulfill the covenant promised to the ancient fathers and predicted by the mouth of the prophets (Is. 7:14; Luke 1:31, 35, 55, 70) the true, unique and eternal Son of God the Father (Rom. 1:3; John 17:5; 16:28; Phil 2:6-7) took, at the time appointed by the Father, the form of a servant. Being conceived in the womb of the blessed virgin Mary, by the power of the Holy Spirit, and without any operation of man (Matt. 1:20; Luke 1:28, 35), He took human nature with all its infirmities, sin excepted (Heb. 4:15; 5:2). The two natures, that of God and that of man, have been united in one Person since the moment of the conception of the flesh of Christ.

We confess that, from the moment of this conception, the Person of the Son has been inseparably united to the human nature (Matt. 1:20; Luke 1:31, 32, 35, 42, 43). There are not two Sons of God, or two Jesus Christs: but One alone is properly Son of God, Jesus Christ. At all times the properties of each of the two natures remain entire and distinct. For the divinity separated from the humanity, or the humanity disjoined from the divinity, or the one being confounded with the other, would profit us nothing.

Jesus Christ is therefore true God and true man (Matt. 1:21-23, Luke 1:35). He has a true human soul, and a true human body formed from the substance of the virgin Mary, and by the power of the Holy Spirit. By this means, he was conceived and born of this virgin Mary, virgin, I say, before and after the birth. And all this was accomplished for our redemption.

SUMMARY OF THE ACCOMPLISHMENT OF OUR SALVATION IN JESUS CHRIST

He therefore descended to earth to draw us up to Heaven. (Eph. 2:6). From the moment of His conception until His resurrection, He bore the punishment of our sins in order to unburden us of them (Matt. 11:28; 1 Pet. 2:24; 3:18; Is. 53:11). He perfectly fulfilled all righteousness so as to cover our unrighteousness (Rom. 5:19; Matt. 3:15). He has revealed to us the whole will of God His Father, by His words and by the example of His life, so as to show us the true way of salvation (John 15:15; Acts 1:1-2).

Finally, to crown the satisfaction for our sins which He took upon Himself (Is. 53:4-5), He was captured in order to release us, condemned so that we might be acquitted. He suffered infinite reproach in order to place us beyond all shame. He was nailed to the cross for our sins to be nailed there (Col. 2:14). He died bearing the curse which we deserved, so as to appease for ever the wrath of God through the accomplishment of His unique sacrifice (Gal. 3:13; 2 Cor. 5:21; Heb. 10:10, 14). He was entombed to show the truth of His death, and to vanquish death even in its own house, that is to say even in the grave; He experienced no corruption there, to show that, even while dead, he had conquered death (Acts 2:31). He was raised again victorious so that, all our corruption being dead and buried, we might be renewed in new, spiritual and eternal life (Rom. 6; and nearly everywhere in St. Paul). By this means, the first death is no longer to us a punishment for sin and an entrance into the second death, but, on the contrary, is the ending of our corruption and an entrance into life eternal. Lastly, being raised again and then having

spoken throughout forty days here below to give evidence of His resurrection (Acts 1:3, 9-11), He ascended visibly and really far above all heavens, where He sat down at the right hand of God His Father (John 14:2). Having taken possession for us of His eternal kingdom, He is, for us also, the sole Mediator and Advocate (1 Tim. 2:5; Heb. 1:3; 9:24), and governs His Church by His Holy Spirit, until the number of the elect of God, His Father, is completed (Matt. 28:20, etc).

HOW JESUS CHRIST, HAVING WITHDRAWN INTO HEAVEN, IS NEVERTHELESS HERE BELOW WITH HIS OWN

We understand that glorification brought immortality to the body of Jesus Christ, besides sovereign glory; but this did by no means change the nature of His true body, a body confined to one certain space and having bounds (Luke 24:39; John 20:25; Acts 1:3). For this reason, He took away into Heaven, from our midst, His human nature, His true body (Acts 1:9-11; 3:21). There He shall remain until He comes to judge the living and the dead.

But, with regard to the efficacy of His Holy Spirit, as to His Divinity, (by which we are made partakers not only of half of Christ, but of all of Him and all His goods, as will be said soon), we acknowledge that He is and shall be with His own until the end of the world (Matt. 28:20; John 16:13; Eph. 4:8). This is what Jesus Christ said regarding Himself-, "The poor you will have always with you, but Me you will not have always." (Matt. 26:11); again, after His Ascension, the angels say to the Apostles: "Jesus who was taken up from you into heaven shall so come as you saw Him go away into Heaven." (Acts 1:11). And St Peter says to the Jews that Heaven must hold Him until the time of the restoration of all things. (Acts 3:21). For the same reason, St Augustine, following Scripture, has well said that it is necessary to guard oneself from stressing the Divinity to the point of coming to deny the truth of the body; the body is in God, but it is not necessary to draw the conclusion that it is everywhere, as God is everywhere.

THERE CAN BE NO OTHER TRUE RELIGION

In this mystery of our redemption, incomprehensible to human reason, God has revealed Himself as true God, that is to say, perfectly just and perfectly merciful.

Perfectly just, firstly, for He has punished all our sins with full severity (Rom. 3:25; 2 Cor. 5:21), in the Person of Him who made Himself surety and security in our place, that is to say, in Jesus Christ (1 Tim. 2:6; 1 Pet. 2:24). In the next place, He receives us and acknowledges us as His if we are covered and clothed with the innocence, sanctification and perfect righteousness of Jesus Christ (2 Cor. 5:21; Rom. 5:19; Col. 2:14).

On the other side, He has revealed Himself as perfectly merciful, for, finding in us only ground for damnation, He willed that His Son take our nature in order to find in Him the remedy which would appease His justice (Rom. 5:8; 1 Cor. 1:30). Freely communicating Him to us, with all the treasures which He possesses (Rom. 8:32), He makes us partakers of eternal life, solely by His goodness and mercy, on condition that we take hold of Jesus Christ by faith; which we will develop a little later.

But, on the contrary, any religion which opposes to the wrath of God anything other than the sole innocence, righteousness and satisfaction of Jesus Christ, received by faith, strips God of His perfect justice and His mercy. For this reason, such a religion (e.g. Romanism) must be regarded as false and deceptive.

Theodore Beza, The Christian Faith

1.32 THE ETERNAL SONSHIP OF CHRIST, JOHN GILL

A DISSERTATION CONCERNING THE ETERNAL SONSHIP OF CHRIST, SHOWING BY WHOM IT HAS BEEN DENIED AND OPPOSED, AND BY WHOM ASSERTED AND DEFENDED IN ALL AGES OF CHRISTIANITY

The eternal Sonship of Christ, or that he is the Son of God by eternal generation, or that he was the Son of God before he was the son of Mary, even from all eternity, which is denied by the Socinians, and others akin, to them, was known by the saints under the Old Testament; by David (Ps. 2:7, 12); by Solomon (Prov. 8:22, 30), by the prophet Micah, chapter 2, verse 2. His Sonship was known by Daniel, from whom it is probable Nebuchadnezzar had it (Dan. 3:25), from which it appears he was, and was known to be, the Son of God before he was born of the virgin, or before his incarnation, and therefore not called so on that account. This truth is written as with a sun-beam in the New Testament. . . .

All the sound and orthodox writers have unanimously declared for the eternal generation and Sonship of Christ in all ages, and that those only of an unsound mind and judgment, and corrupt in other things as well as this, and many of them men of impure lives and vile principles, have declared against it, such must be guilty of great temerity and rashness to join in an opposition with the one against the other; and to oppose a doctrine the Church of God has always held, and especially being what the scriptures abundantly bear testimony unto, and is a matter of such moment and importance, being a fundamental doctrine of the Christian religion, and indeed what distinguishes it from all other religions, from those of Pagans, Jews and Mahometans, who all believe in God, and generally in one God, but none of them believe in the Son of God: that is peculiar to the Christian religion.

John Gill

1.33 JESUS—GOD AND MAN, WOLFHART PANNENBERG

Christology, the question about Jesus himself, about his person, as he lived on earth in the time of Emperor Tiberius, must remain prior to all questions about his significance, to all soteriology. Soteriology must follow from Christology, not vice versa. Otherwise, faith in salvation loses any real foundation.

Wolfhart Pannenberg
Jesus—God and Man, *Philadelphia:*
Westminster Press, 1968

7

THE CHARACTER/ATTRIBUTES OF JESUS

1.34 JESUS OUR TRUE MOTHER, JULIAN OF NORWICH

Julian of Norwich, 1342—c. 1416, was the most important English mystic of the 14th century. Her spirituality is strongly Trinitarian and in her Revelations of Divine Love *Julian relates that in May 1373, when she was 30 years old, she suffered a serious illness. She received sixteen revelations within the span of a few hours. When she wrote her* Revelations, *she was a recluse at Norwich, living in anchorite seclusion. A woman of little formal education—she calls herself "unlettered"—Julian writes in a beautifully simple style and shows a solid grasp of traditional theology.*

GOD IS AS TRULY OUR MOTHER AS HE IS OUR FATHER

Our great Father, almighty God, who is being, knew and loved us before time began. In that knowledge, out of his wonderful deep love, and with the foresight and counsel of the blessed Trinity, he willed that the second person become our Mother.

Our Father willed it, our Mother accomplished it, our good Lord the Holy Spirit established it. So we must love our God in whom we have our being. We must reverently thank and praise him for our creation, fervently ask our Mother for mercy and compassion, and our Lord for Holy Spirit for help and grace.

From nature, mercy and grace from these three comes our life. From them we have humility and gentleness and pity. From them, too, we get our hatred of sin and wickedness, for it is in the nature of virtue to hate these.

So Jesus is our true Mother in nature because of our first creation, and he is our true Mother in grace because he took our created nature. In the second person there is all the loving service and sweet spontaneous care that belongs to beloved motherhood, and in him our will for God is always whose and safe, both naturally and by grace, because of his own innate goodness.

I saw that the motherhood of God can be looked at in three ways. The first is his creation of our human nature; the second his assumption of nature from which stems the motherhood of grace; and the third is the practical outworking of motherhood, as a result of which, and by that same grace, it spreads out in endless height, breadth, length, and depth. And all is one here.

Julian of Norwich,
Revelations of Divine Love

1.35 JESUS AS LOVER, THOMAS À KEMPIS

Thomas à Kempis (1380—1471) was a medieval Christian monk and author of one of the most well-known Christian books on devotion, The Imitation of Christ.

He was born at Kempen, Germany (40 miles northwest of Cologne) in 1380 and died near Zwolle (52 miles east-north-east of Amsterdam) in 1471. His paternal name was Hemerken or Hammerlein, "little hammer."

Blessed is he who appreciates what it is to love Jesus and who despises himself for the sake of Jesus. Give up all other love for His, since He wishes to be loved alone above all things.

Affection for creatures is deceitful and inconstant, but the love of Jesus is true and enduring. He who clings to a creature will fall with its frailty, but he who gives himself to Jesus will ever be strengthened.

Love Him, then; keep Him as a friend. He will not leave you as others do, or let you suffer lasting death. Sometime, whether you will or not, you will have to part with everything. Cling, therefore, to Jesus in life and death; trust yourself to the glory of Him who alone can help you when all others fail.

Jesus is a lover who tolerates no rivals. He wants your heart for Himself alone, to be enthroned therein as King in His own right. If you but knew how to free yourself entirely from all creatures, Jesus would gladly dwell within you.

Thomas à Kempis, Imitation of Christ, *2.7*

1.36 CHRIST OUR HIGH PRIEST, MARTIN LUTHER

"But Christ being come an high priest of good things to come, by a greater and more perfect tabernacle, not made with hands, that is to say, not of this building; Neither by the blood of goats and calves, but by his own blood he entered in once into the holy place, having obtained eternal redemption for us. For if the blood of bulls and of goats, and the ashes of an heifer sprinkling the unclean, sanctifieth to the purifying of the flesh: How much more shall the blood of Christ, who through the eternal Spirit offered himself without spot to God, purge your conscience from dead works to serve the living God? And for this cause he is the mediator of the new testament, that by means of death, for the redemption of the transgressions that were under the first testament, they which are called might receive the promise of eternal inheritance."Hebrews 9:11-15

1. An understanding of practically all of the Epistle to the Hebrews is necessary before we can hope to make this text clear to ourselves. Briefly, the epistle treats of a twofold priesthood. The former priesthood was a material one, with material adornment, tabernacle, sacrifices and with pardon couched in ritual; material were all its appointments. The new order is a spiritual priesthood, with spiritual adornments, spiritual tabernacle and sacrifices—spiritual in all that pertains to it. Christ, in the exercise of his priestly office, in the sacrifice on the cross, was not adorned with silk and gold and precious stones, but with divine love, wisdom, patience, obedience and all virtues. His adornment was apparent to none but God and possessors, of the Spirit, for it was spiritual.

2. Christ sacrificed not goats nor calves nor birds; not bread; not blood nor flesh, as did Aaron and his posterity: he offered his own body and blood, and the manner of the sacrifice was spiritual; for it took place through the Holy Spirit, as here stated. Though the body and blood of Christ were visible the same as any other material object, the fact that he offered them as a sacrifice was not apparent. It was not a visible sacrifice, as in the case of offerings at the hands of Aaron. Then the goat or calf, the flesh and blood, were material sacrifices visibly offered, and recognized as sacrifices. But Christ offered himself in the heart before God. His sacrifice was perceptible to no mortal. Therefore, his bodily flesh and blood becomes a spiritual sacrifice. Similarly, we Christians, the posterity of Christ our Aaron, offer up our own bodies (Rom. 12:1). And our offering is likewise a spiritual sacrifice, or, as Paul has it, a "reasonable service;" for we make it in spirit, and it is beheld of God alone.

3. Again, in the new order, the tabernacle or house is spiritual; for it is heaven, or the presence of God. Christ hung upon a cross; he was not offered in a temple. He was offered before the eyes of God, and there he still abides. The cross is an altar in a spiritual sense. The material cross was indeed visible, but none knew it as Christ's altar. Again, his prayer, his sprinkled blood, his burnt incense, were all spiritual, for it was all wrought through his spirit.

4. Accordingly, the fruit and blessing of his office and sacrifice, the forgiveness of our sins and our justification, are likewise spiritual. In the Old Covenant, the priest with his sacrifices and sprinklings of blood effected merely as it were an external absolution, or pardon, corresponding to the childhood stage of the people. The recipient was permitted to move publicly among the people; he was externally holy and as one restored from excommunication. He who failed to obtain absolution from the priest was unholy, being denied membership in the congregation and enjoyment of its privileges; in all respects he was separated like those in the ban today.

5. But such absolution rendered no one inwardly holy and just before God.

Something beyond that was necessary to secure true forgiveness. It was the same principle which governs church discipline today. He who has received no more than the remission, or absolution, of the ecclesiastical judge will surely remain forever out of heaven. On the other hand, he who is in the ban of the Church is hellward bound only when the sentence is confirmed at a higher tribunal. I can make no better comparison than to say that it was the same in the old Jewish priesthood as now in the Papal priesthood, which, with its loosing and binding, can prohibit or permit only external communion among Christians. It is true, God required such measures in the time of the Jewish dispensation, that he might restrain by fear; just as now he sanctions church discipline when rightly employed, in order to punish and restrain the evil-doer, though it has no power in itself to raise people to holiness or to push them into wickedness.

6. But with the priesthood of Christ is true spiritual remission, sanctification and absolution. These avail before God—God grant that it be true of us—whether we be outwardly excommunicated, or holy, or not. Christ's blood has obtained for us pardon forever acceptable with God. God will forgive our sins for the sake of that blood so long as its power shall last and its intercession for grace in our behalf, which is forever. Therefore, we are forever holy and blessed before God. This is the substance of the text. Now that we shall find it easy to understand, we will briefly consider it.

"But Christ having come a high priest of the good things to come."

7. The adornment of Aaron and his descendants, the high priests, was of a material nature, and they obtained for the people a merely formal remission of sins, performing their office in a perishable temple, or tabernacle. It was evident to men that their absolution and sanctification before the congregation was a temporal blessing confined to the present. But when Christ came upon the cross no one beheld him as he went before God in the Holy Spirit, adorned with every grace and virtue, a true High Priest. The blessings wrought by him are not

temporal—a merely formal pardon—but the "blessings to come"; namely, blessings which are spiritual and eternal. Paul speaks of them as blessings to come, not that we are to await the life to come before we can have forgiveness and all the blessings of divine grace, but because now we possess them only in faith. They are as yet hidden, to be revealed in the future life. Again, the blessings we have in Christ were, from the standpoint of the Old Testament priesthood, blessings to come.

"Through the greater and more perfect tabernacle, not made with hands, that is to say, not of this creation."

8. The apostle does not name the tabernacle he mentions; nor can he, so strange its nature! It exists only in the sight of God, and is ours in faith, to be revealed hereafter. It is not made with hands, like the Jewish tabernacle; in other words, not of "this building." The old tabernacle, like all buildings of its nature, necessarily was made of wood and other temporal materials created by God. God says in Isaiah 66:1-2: "What manner of house will ye build unto me?. . . For all these things hath my hand made, and so all these things came to be." But that greater tabernacle has not yet form; it is not yet finished. God is building it and he shall reveal it. Christ's words are (John 14:3), "And if I go and prepare a place for you."

"Nor yet through the blood of goats and calves, but through his own blood, entered in once for all into the holy place, having obtained eternal redemption."

9. According to Leviticus 16, the high priest must once a year enter into the holy place with the blood of rams and other offerings, and with these make formal reconciliation for the people. This ceremony typified that Christ, the true Priest, should once die for us, to obtain for us the true atonement. But the former sacrifice, having to be repeated every year, was but a temporary and imperfect atonement; it did not eternally suffice, as does the atonement of Christ. For though we fall and sin repeatedly, we have confidence that the blood of Christ does not

fall, or sin; it remains steadfast before God, and the expiation is perpetual and eternal. Under its sway grace is perpetually renewed, without work or merit on our part, provided we do not stand aloof in unbelief.

"For if the blood of goats and bulls, and the ashes of a heifer," etc.

10. Concerning the water of separation and the ashes of the red heifer, read Numbers 19; and concerning the blood of bulls and goats, Leviticus 16:14-15. According to Paul, these were formal and temporal purifications, as I stated above. But Christ, in God's sight, purifies the conscience of dead works; that is, of sins meriting death, and of works performed in sin and therefore dead. Christ purifies from these, that we may serve the living God by living works.

"And for this cause he is the mediator of a new covenant [testament]," etc.

11. Under the old law, which provided only for formal, or ritualistic pardon, and restored to human fellowship, sin and transgressions remained, burdening the conscience. It—the old law—did not benefit the soul at all, inasmuch as God did not institute it to purify and safeguard the conscience, nor to bestow the Spirit. It existed merely for the purpose of outward discipline, restraint and correction. So Paul teaches that under the Old Testament dispensation man's transgressions remained, but now Christ is our Mediator through his blood; by it our conscience, is freed from sin in the sight of God, inasmuch as God promises the Spirit through the blood of Christ. All, however, do not receive him. Only those called to be heirs eternal, the elect, receive the Spirit.

12. We find, then, in this excellent lesson, the comforting doctrine taught that Christ is he whom we should know as the Priest and Bishop of our souls; that no sin is forgiven, nor the Holy Spirit given, by reason of works or merit on our part, but alone through the blood of Christ, and that to those for whom God has ordained it.

Martin Luther

1.37 CHRIST AS REDEEMER, JOHN CALVIN

CHAPTER 16

How Christ performed the office of redeemer in procuring our salvation. The death, resurrection, and ascension of Christ.

This chapter contains four leading heads:

I. A general consideration of the whole subject, including a discussion of a necessary question concerning the justice of God and his mercy in Christ, sections 1-4.

II. How Christ fulfilled the office of Redeemer in each of its parts, sections 5-17. His death, burial, descent to hell, resurrection, ascension to heaven, seat at the right hand of the Father, and return to judgment.

III. A great part of the Creed being here expounded, a statement is given of the view which ought to be taken of the Creed commonly ascribed to the Apostles, section 18.

IV. Conclusion, setting forth the doctrine of Christ the Redeemer, and the use of the doctrine, section 19.

SECTIONS

1. Every thing needful for us exists in Christ. How it is to be obtained.

2. Question as to the mode of reconciling the justice with the mercy of God. Modes of expression used in Scripture to teach us how miserable our condition is without Christ.

3. Not used improperly; for God finds in us ground both of hatred and love.

4. This confirmed from passages of Scripture and from Augustine.

5. The second part of the chapter, treating of our redemption by Christ. First generally. Redemption extends to the whole course of our Savior's obedience, but is specially ascribed to his death. The voluntary subjection of Christ. His agony. His condemnation before Pilate. Two things observable in his condemnation. 1. That he was numbered among transgressors. 2. That he was declared innocent by the judge. Use to be made of this.

6. Why Christ was crucified. This hidden doctrine typified in the Law, and completed by the Apostles and Prophets. In what sense Christ was made a curse for us. The cross of Christ connected with the shedding of his blood.

7. Of the death of Christ. Why he died. Advantages from his death. Of the burial of Christ. Advantages.

8. Of the descent into hell. This article gradually introduced into the Church. Must not be rejected, nor confounded with the previous article respecting burial.

9. Absurd exposition concerning the *Limbus Patrum*. This fable refuted.

10. The article of the descent to hell more accurately expounded. A great ground of comfort.

11. Confirmation of this exposition from passages of Scripture and the works of ancient Theologians. An objection refuted. Advantages of the doctrine.

12. Another objection that Christ is insulted, and despair ascribed to him in its being said that he feared. Answer, from the statements of the Evangelists, that he did fear, was troubled in spirit, amazed, and tempted in all respects as we are, yet without sin. Why Christ was pleased to become weak. His fear without sin. Refutation of another objection, with an answer to the question, Did Christ fear death, and why? When did Christ descend to hell, and how? What has been said refutes the heresy of Apollinaris and of the Monothelites.

13. Of the resurrection of Christ. The many advantages from it.

    1. Our righteousness in the sight of God renewed and restored.

    2. His life the basis of our life and hope, also the efficacious cause of new life in us.

    3. The pledge of our future resurrection.

14. Of the ascension of Christ. Why he ascended. Advantages derived from it.

15. Of Christ's seat at the Father's right hand. What meant by it.

16. Many advantages from the ascension

of Christ. 1. He gives access to the kingdom which Adam had shut up. 2. He intercedes for us with the Father. 3. His virtue being thence transfused into us, he works effectually in us for salvation.

17. Of the return of Christ to judgment. Its nature. The quick and dead who are to be judged. Passages apparently contradictory reconciled. Mode of judgment.

18. Advantages of the doctrine of Christ's return to judgment. Third part of the chapter, explaining the view to be taken of the Apostles' Creed. Summary of the Apostles' Creed.

19. Conclusion of the whole chapter, showing that in Christ the salvation of the elect in all its parts is comprehended.

1. All that we have hitherto said of Christ leads to this one result, that condemned, dead, and lost in ourselves, we must in him seek righteousness, deliverance, life and salvation, as we are taught by the celebrated words of Peter, "Neither is there salvation in any other: for there is none other name under heaven given among men whereby we must be saved," (Acts 4:12). The name of Jesus was not given him at random, or fortuitously, or by the will of man, but was brought from heaven by an angel, as the herald of the supreme decree; the reason also being added, "for he shall save his people from their sins," (Matt. 1:21). In these words attention should be paid to what we have elsewhere observed, that the office of Redeemer was assigned him in order that he might be our Savior. Still, however, redemption would be defective if it did not conduct us by an uninterrupted progression to the final goal of safety. Therefore, the moment we turn aside from him in the minutest degree, salvation, which resides entirely in him, gradually disappears; so that all who do not rest in him voluntarily deprive themselves of all grace. The observation of Bernard well deserves to be remembered: "The name of Jesus is not only light but food also, yea, oil, without which all the food of the soul is dry; salt, without which as a condiment whatever is set before us is insipid; in fine, honey in the mouth, melody in the ear, joy in the heart, and, at the same time, medicine;

every discourse where this name is not heard is absurd"(Bernard in *Cantica.*, Sermon 15). But here it is necessary diligently to consider in what way we obtain salvation from him, that we may not only be persuaded that he is the author of it, but having embraced whatever is sufficient as a sure foundation of our faith, may eschew all that might make us waver. For seeing no man can descend into himself, and seriously consider what he is, without feeling that God is angry and at enmity with him, and therefore anxiously longing for the means of regaining his favor (this cannot be without satisfaction), the certainty here required is of no ordinary description,—sinners, until freed from guilt, being always liable to the wrath and curse of God, who, as he is a just judge, cannot permit his law to be violated with impunity, but is armed for vengeance.

2. But before we proceed farther, we must see in passing, how can it be said that God, who prevents us with his mercy, was our enemy until he was reconciled to us by Christ. For how could he have given us in his only-begotten Son a singular pledge of his love, if he had not previously embraced us with free favor? As there thus arises some appearance of contradiction, I will explain the difficulty. The mode in which the Spirit usually speaks in Scripture is, that God was the enemy of men until they were restored to favor by the death of Christ (Rom. 5:10); that they were cursed until their iniquity was expiated by the sacrifice of Christ (Gal. 3:10, 13); that they were separated from God, until by means of Christ's body they were received into union (Col. 1:21, 22). Such modes of expression are accommodated to our capacity, that we may the better understand how miserable and calamitous our condition is without Christ. For were it not said in clear terms, that Divine wrath, and vengeance, and eternal death, lay upon us, we should be less sensible of our wretchedness without the mercy of God, and less disposed to value the blessing of deliverance. For example, let a person be told, Had God at the time you were a sinner hated you, and cast you off as you deserved, horrible destruction must have been your doom; but spontaneously and of free indulgence he

retained you in his favor, not suffering you to be estranged from him, and in this way rescued you from danger,—the person will indeed be affected, and made sensible in some degree how much he owes to the mercy of God. But again, let him be told, as Scripture teaches, that he was estranged from God by sin, an heir of wrath, exposed to the curse of eternal death, excluded from all hope of salvation, a complete alien from the blessing of God, the slave of Satan, captive under the yoke of sin; in fine, doomed to horrible destruction, and already involved in it; that then Christ interposed, took the punishment upon himself and bore what by the just judgment of God was impending over sinners; with his own blood expiated the sins which rendered them hateful to God, by this expiation satisfied and duly propitiated God the Father, by this intercession appeased his anger, on this basis founded peace between God and men, and by this tie secured the Divine benevolence toward them; will not these considerations move him the more deeply, the more strikingly they represent the greatness of the calamity from which he was delivered? In short, since our mind cannot lay hold of life through the mercy of God with sufficient eagerness, or receive it with becoming gratitude, unless previously impressed with fear of the Divine anger, and dismayed at the thought of eternal death, we are so instructed by divine truth, as to perceive that without Christ God is in a manner hostile to us, and has his arm raised for our destruction. Thus taught, we look to Christ alone for divine favor and paternal love.

3. Though this is said in accommodation to the weakness of our capacity, it is not said falsely. For God, who is perfect righteousness, cannot love the iniquity which he sees in all. All of us, therefore, have that within which deserves the hatred of God. Hence, in respect, first, of our corrupt nature; and, secondly, of the depraved conduct following upon it, we are all offensive to God, guilty in his sight, and by nature the children of hell. But as the Lord wills not to destroy in us that which is his own, he still finds something in us which in kindness he can love. For though it is by our own fault that we are sinners, we are still

his creatures; though we have brought death upon ourselves he had created us for life. Thus, mere gratuitous love prompts him to receive us into favor. But if there is a perpetual and irreconcilable repugnance between righteousness and iniquity, so long as we remain sinners we cannot be completely received. Therefore, in order that all ground of offence may be removed, and he may completely reconcile us to himself, he, by means of the expiation set forth in the death of Christ, abolishes all the evil that is in us, so that we, formerly impure and unclean, now appear in his sight just and holy. Accordingly, God the Father, by his love, prevents and anticipates our reconciliation in Christ. Nay, it is because he first loves us, that he afterwards reconciles us to himself. But because the iniquity, which deserves the indignation of God, remains in us until the death of Christ comes to our aid, and that iniquity is in his sight accursed and condemned, we are not admitted to full and sure communion with God, unless, in so far as Christ unites us. And, therefore, if we would indulge the hope of having God propitious to us, we must fix our eyes and minds on Christ alone, as it is to him alone it is owing that our sins, which necessarily provoked the wrath of God, are not imputed to us.

4. For this reason Paul says, that God "has blessed us with all spiritual blessings in heavenly places in Christ: according as he has chosen us in him before the foundation of the world," (Eph. 1:3, 4). These things are clear and conformable to Scripture, and admirably reconcile the passages in which it is said, that "God so loved the world, that he gave his only begotten Son," (John 3:16); and yet that it was "when we were enemies we were reconciled to God by the death of his Son," (Rom. 5:10). But to give additional assurance to those who require the authority of the ancient Church, I will quote a passage of Augustine to the same effect: "Incomprehensible and immutable is the love of God. For it was not after we were reconciled to him by the blood of his Son that he began to love us, but he loved us before the foundation of the world, that with his only begotten Son we too might be sons of God before we were any

thing at all. Our being reconciled by the death of Christ must not be understood as if the Son reconciled us, in order that the Father, then hating, might begin to love us, but that we were reconciled to him already, loving, though at enmity with us because of sin. To the truth of both propositions we have the attestation of the Apostle,God commendeth his love toward us, in that while we were yet sinners, Christ died for us,' (Rom. 5:8). Therefore he had this love towards us even when, exercising enmity towards him, we were the workers of iniquity. Accordingly in a manner wondrous and divine, he loved even when he hated us. For he hated us when we were such as he had not made us, and yet because our iniquity had not destroyed his work in every respect, he knew in regard to each one of us, both to hate what we had made, and love what he had made." Such are the words of Augustine (Tract in Jo. 110).

5. When it is asked then how Christ, by abolishing sin, removed the enmity between God and us, and purchased a righteousness which made him favorable and kind to us, it may be answered generally, that he accomplished this by the whole course of his obedience. This is proved by the testimony of Paul, "As by one man's disobedience many were made sinners, so by the obedience of one shall many be made righteous," (Rom. 5:19). And indeed he elsewhere extends the ground of pardon which exempts from the curse of the law to the whole life of Christ, "When the fullness of the time was come, God sent forth his Son, made of a woman, made under the law, to redeem them that were under the law," (Gal. 4:4, 5). Thus even at his baptism he declared that a part of righteousness was fulfilled by his yielding obedience to the command of the Father. In short, from the moment when he assumed the form of a servant, he began, in order to redeem us, to pay the price of deliverance. Scripture, however, the more certainly to define the mode of salvation, ascribes it peculiarly and specially to the death of Christ. He himself declares that he gave his life a ransom for many (Matt. 20:28). Paul teaches that he died for our sins (Rom. 4:25). John Baptist exclaimed, "Behold the Lamb of God, which

taketh away the sin of the world," (John 1:29). Paul in another passage declares, "that we are justified freely by his grace, through the redemption that is in Christ Jesus: whom God has set forth to be a propitiation through faith in his blood," (Rom. 3:25). "Again, being justified by his blood, we shall be saved from wrath through him" (Rom. 5:9). Again "He has made him to be sin for us, who knew no sin; that we might be made the righteousness of God in him," (2 Cor. 5:21). I will not search out all the passages, for the list would be endless, and many are afterwards to be quoted in their order. In the Confession of Faith, called the Apostles' Creed, the transition is admirably made from the birth of Christ to his death and resurrection, in which the completion of a perfect salvation consists. Still there is no exclusion of the other part of obedience which he performed in life. Thus Paul comprehends, from the beginning even to the end, his having assumed the form of a servant, humbled himself, and become obedient to death, even the death of the cross (Phil. 2:7). And, indeed, the first step in obedience was his voluntary subjection; for the sacrifice would have been unavailing to justification if not offered spontaneously. Hence our Lord, after testifying, "I lay down my life for the sheep," distinctly adds, "No man taketh it from me," (John 10:15, 18). In the same sense Isaiah says, " Like a sheep before her shearers is dumb, so he opened not his mouth," (Is. 53:7). The Gospel History relates that he came forth to meet the soldiers; and in presence of Pilate, instead of defending himself, stood to receive judgment. This, indeed, he did not without a struggle, for he had assumed our infirmities also, and in this way it behoved him to prove that he was yielding obedience to his Father. It was no ordinary example of incomparable love towards us to struggle with dire terrors, and amid fearful tortures to cast away all care of himself that he might provide for us. We must bear in minds that Christ could not duly propitiate God without renouncing his own feelings and subjecting himself entirely to his Father's will. To this effect the Apostle appositely quotes a passage from the Psalms, "Lo, I come (in the volume of the book it is written of me) to do thy will, O God," (Heb. 10:5; Ps. 40:7, 8). Thus, as trembling consciences find no rest without sacrifice and ablution by which sins are expiated, we are properly directed thither, the source of our life being placed in the death of Christ. Moreover, as the curse consequent upon guilt remained for the final judgment of God, one principal point in the narrative is his condemnation before Pontius Pilate, the governor of Judea, to teach us, that the punishment to which we were liable was inflicted on that Just One. We could not escape the fearful judgment of God; and Christ, that he might rescue us from it, submitted to be condemned by a mortal, nay, by a wicked and profane man. For the name of Governor is mentioned not only to support the credibility of the narrative, but to remind us of what Isaiah says, that "the chastisement of our peace was upon him;" and that "with his stripes we are healed," (Is. 53:5). For, in order to remove our condemnation, it was not sufficient to endure any kind of death. To satisfy our ransom, it was necessary to select a mode of death in which he might deliver us, both by giving himself up to condemnations and undertaking our expiation. Had he been cut off by assassins, or slain in a seditious tumult, there could have been no kind of satisfaction in such a death. But when he is placed as a criminal at the bar, where witnesses are brought to give evidence against him, and the mouth of the judge condemns him to die, we see him sustaining the character of an offender and evil-doer. Here we must attend to two points which had both been foretold by the prophets, and tend admirably to comfort and confirm our faith. When we read that Christ was led away from the judgment-seat to execution, and was crucified between thieves, we have a fulfillment of the prophecy which is quoted by the Evangelist, "He was numbered with the transgressors," (Is. 53:12; Mark 15:28). Why was it so? That he might bear the character of a sinner, not of a just or innocent person, inasmuch as he met death on account not of innocence, but of sin. On the other hand, when we read that he was acquitted by the same lips that condemned him (for Pilate was forced once and again to bear public testimony to his innocence), let us

call to mind what is said by another prophet, "I restored that which I took not away," (Ps. 69:4). Thus we perceive Christ representing the character of a sinner and a criminal, while, at the same time, his innocence shines forth, and it becomes manifest that he suffers for another's and not for his own crime. He therefore suffered under Pontius Pilate, being thus, by the formal sentence of the judge, ranked among criminals, and yet he is declared innocent by the same judge, when he affirms that he finds no cause of death in him. Our acquittal is in this that the guilt which made us liable to punishment was transferred to the head of the Son of God (Is. 53:12). We must specially remember this substitution in order that we may not be all our lives in trepidation and anxiety, as if the just vengeance which the Son of God transferred to himself, were still impending over us.

6. The very form of the death embodies a striking truth. The cross was cursed not only in the opinion of men, but by the enactment of the Divine Law. Hence Christ, while suspended on it, subjects himself to the curse. And thus it behoved to be done, in order that the whole curse, which on account of our iniquities awaited us, or rather lay upon us, might be taken from us by being transferred to him. This was also shadowed in the Law, since the word by which sin itself is properly designated was applied to the sacrifices and expiations offered for sin. By this application of the term, the Spirit intended to intimate, that they were a kind of purifications, bearing, by substitutions the curse due to sin. But that which was represented figuratively in the Mosaic sacrifices is exhibited in Christ the archetype. Wherefore, in order to accomplish a full expiation, he made his soul a propitiatory victim for sin (as the prophet says, Is. 53:5, 10), on which the guilt and penalty being in a manner laid, ceases to be imputed to us. The Apostle declares this more plainly when he says, that "he made him to be sin for us, who knew no sin; that we might be made the righteousness of God in him," (2 Cor. 5:21). For the Son of God, though spotlessly pure, took upon him the disgrace and ignominy of our iniquities, and in return clothed us with his purity. To the same thing

he seems to refer, when he says, that he "condemned sin in the flesh," (Rom. 8:3), the Father having destroyed the power of sin when it was transferred to the flesh of Christ. This term, therefore, indicates that Christ, in his death, was offered to the Father as a propitiatory victim; that, expiation being made by his sacrifice, we might cease to tremble at the divine wrath. It is now clear what the prophet means when he says, that "the Lord has laid upon him the iniquity of us all," (Is. 53:6); namely, that as he was to wash away the pollution of sins, they were transferred to him by imputation. Of this the cross to which he was nailed was a symbol, as the Apostle declares, "Christ has redeemed us from the curse of the law, being made a curse for us: for it is written, Cursed is every one that hangeth on a tree: that the blessing of Abraham might come on the Gentiles through Jesus Christ," (Gal. 3:13, 14). In the same way Peter says, that he "bare our sins in his own body on the tree," (1 Peter 2:24), inasmuch as from the very symbol of the curse, we perceive more clearly that the burden with which we were oppressed was laid upon him. Nor are we to understand that by the curse which he endured he was himself overwhelmed, but rather that by enduring it he repressed, broke, annihilated all its force. Accordingly, faith apprehends acquittal in the condemnation of Christ, and blessing in his curse. Hence it is not without cause that Paul magnificently celebrates the triumph which Christ obtained upon the cross, as if the cross, the symbol of ignominy, had been converted into a triumphal chariot. For he says, that he blotted out the handwriting of ordinances that was against us, which was contrary to us, and took it out of the way, nailing it to his cross: that "having spoiled principalities and powers he made a show of them openly, triumphing over them in it," (Col. 2:14, 15). Nor is this to be wondered at; for, as another Apostle declares, Christ, "through the eternal Spirit, offered himself without spot to God," (Heb. 9:14), and hence that transformation of the cross which were otherwise against its nature. But that these things may take deep root and have their seat in our inmost hearts, we must never lose sight of sacrifice and

ablution. For, were not Christ a victim, we could have no sure conviction of his being our substitute-ransom and propitiation. And hence mention is always made of blood whenever scripture explains the mode of redemption: although the shedding of Christ's blood was available not only for propitiation, but also acted as a laver to purge our defilements.

7. The Creed next mentions that he "was dead and buried." Here again it is necessary to consider how he substituted himself in order to pay the price of our redemption. Death held us under its yoke, but he in our place delivered himself into its power, that he might exempt us from it. This the Apostle means when he says, "that he tasted death for every man," (Heb. 2:9). By dying he prevented us from dying; or (which is the same thing) he by his death purchased life for us. But in this he differed from us, that in permitting himself to be overcome of death, it was not so as to be engulfed in its abyss but rather to annihilate it, as it must otherwise have annihilated us; he did not allow himself to be so subdued by it as to be crushed by its power; he rather laid it prostrate, when it was impending over us, and exulting over us as already overcome. In fine, his object was, "that through death he might destroy him that had the power of death, that is, the devil, and deliver them who through fear of death were all their lifetime subject to bondage," (Heb. 2:14, 15). This is the first fruit which his death produced to us. Another is, that by fellowship with him he mortifies our earthly members that they may not afterwards exert themselves in action, and kill the old man, that he may not hereafter be in vigor and bring forth fruit. An effect of his burial moreover is that we as his fellows are buried to sin. For when the Apostle says, that we are engrafted into the likeness of Christ's death and that we are buried with him unto sin, that by his cross the world is crucified unto us and we unto the world, and that we are dead with him, he not only exhorts us to manifest an example of his death, but declares that there is an efficacy in it which should appear in all Christians, if they would not render his death unfruitful and useless. Accordingly in the death and burial of Christ

a twofold blessing is set before us—viz. deliverance from death, to which we were enslaved, and the mortification of our flesh (Rom. 6:5; Gal. 2:19, 6:14; Col. 3:3).

8. Here we must not omit the descent to hell, which was of no little importance to the accomplishment of redemption. For although it is apparent from the writings of the ancient Fathers, that the clause which now stands in the Creed was not formerly so much used in the churches, still, in giving a summary of doctrine, a place must be assigned to it, as containing a matter of great importance which ought not by any means to be disregarded. Indeed, some of the ancient Fathers do not omit it, and hence we may conjecture, that having been inserted in the Creed after a considerable lapse of time, it came into use in the Church not immediately but by degrees. This much is uncontroverted, that it was in accordance with the general sentiment of all believers, since there is none of the Fathers who does not mention Christ's descent into hell, though they have various modes of explaining it. But it is of little consequence by whom and at what time it was introduced. The chief thing to be attended to in the Creed is, that it furnishes us with a full and every way complete summary of faith, containing nothing but what has been derived from the infallible word of God. But should any still scruple to give it admission into the Creed, it will shortly be made plain, that the place which it holds in a summary of our redemption is so important, that the omission of it greatly detracts from the benefit of Christ's death. There are some again who think that the article contains nothing new, but is merely a repetition in different words of what was previously said respecting burial, the word Hell being often used in Scripture for sepulcher. I admit the truth of what they allege with regard to the not infrequent use of the term infernos for sepulcher; but I cannot adopt their opinion, for two obvious reasons.

First, What folly would it have been, after explaining a matter attended with no difficulty in clear and unambiguous terms, afterwards to involve rather than illustrate it by clothing it in obscure phraseology? When two expressions having the same meaning are placed together, the latter ought to be explanatory of the former. But what kind of explanation would it be to say, the expression, "Christ was buried," means, that "he descended into hell"?

My second reason is the improbability that a superfluous tautology of this description should have crept into this compendium, in which the principal articles of faith are set down summarily in the fewest possible number of words. I have no doubt that all who weigh the matter with some degree of care will here agree with me.

9. Others interpret differently—viz. That Christ descended to the souls of the Patriarchs who died under the law, to announce his accomplished redemption, and bring them out of the prison in which they were confined. To this effect they wrest the passage in the Psalms "He hath broken the gates of brass, and cut the bars of iron in sunder." (Ps. 107:16); and also the passage in Zechariah, "I have sent forth thy prisoners out of the pit wherein is no water," (Zech. 9:11). But since the psalm foretells the deliverance of those who were held captive in distant lands, and Zechariah comparing the Babylonian disaster into which the people had been plunged to a deep dry well or abyss, at the same time declares, that the salvation of the whole Church was an escape from a profound pit, I know not how it comes to pass, that posterity imagined it to be a subterraneous cavern, to which they gave the name of Limbus. Though this fable has the countenance of great authors, and is now also seriously defended by many as truth, it is nothing but a fable. To conclude from it that the souls of the dead are in prison is childish. And what occasion was there that the soul of Christ should go down thither to set them at liberty? I readily admit that Christ illumined them by the power of his Spirit, enabling them to perceive that the grace of which they had only had a foretaste was then manifested to the world. And to this not improbably the passage of Peter may be applied, wherein he says, that Christ "went and preached to the spirits that were in prison," (or rather "a watch-tower") (I Pet. 3:19). The purport of the context is, that believers who had died before that time were

partakers of the same grace with ourselves: for he celebrates the power of Christ's death, in that he penetrated even to the dead, pious souls obtaining an immediate view of that visitation for which they had anxiously waited; while, on the other hand, the reprobate were more clearly convinced that they were completely excluded from salvation. Although the passage in Peter is not perfectly definite, we must not interpret as if he made no distinction between the righteous and the wicked: he only means to intimate, that the death of Christ was made known to both.

10. But, apart from the Creed, we must seek for a surer exposition of Christ's descent to hell: and the word of God furnishes us with one not only pious and holy, but replete with excellent consolation. Nothing had been done if Christ had only endured corporeal death. In order to interpose between us and God's anger, and satisfy his righteous judgment, it was necessary that he should feel the weight of divine vengeance. Whence also it was necessary that he should engage, as it were, at close quarters with the powers of hell and the horrors of eternal death. We lately quoted from the Prophet, that the "chastisement of our peace was laid upon him" that he "was bruised for our iniquities" that he "bore our infirmities;" expressions which intimate, that, like a sponsor and surety for the guilty, and, as it were, subjected to condemnation, he undertook and paid all the penalties which must have been exacted from them, the only exception being, that the pains of death could not hold him. Hence there is nothing strange in its being said that he descended to hell, seeing he endured the death which is inflicted on the wicked by an angry God. It is frivolous and ridiculous to object that in this way the order is perverted, it being absurd that an event which preceded burial should be placed after it. But after explaining what Christ endured in the sight of man, the Creed appropriately adds the invisible and incomprehensible judgment which he endured before God, to teach us that not only was the body of Christ given up as the price of redemption, but that there was a greater and more excellent price—that he bore in his soul the tortures of condemned and ruined man.

11. In this sense, Peter says that God raised up Christ, "having loosed the pains of death: because it was not possible he should be holden of it," (Acts 2:24). He does not mention death simply, but says that the Son of God endured the pains produced by the curse and wrath of God, the source of death. How small a matter had it been to come forth securely, and as it were in sport to undergo death. Herein was a true proof of boundless mercy, that he shunned not the death he so greatly dreaded. And there can be no doubt that, in the Epistle to the Hebrews, the Apostle means to teach the same thing, when he says that he "was heard in that he feared," (Heb. 5:7). Some instead of "feared," use a term meaning reverence or piety, but how inappropriately, is apparent both from the nature of the thing and the form of expression. Christ then praying in a loud voice, and with tears, is heard in that he feared, not so as to be exempted from death, but so as not to be swallowed up of it like a sinner, though standing as our representative. And certainly no abyss can be imagined more dreadful than to feel that you are abandoned and forsaken of God, and not heard when you invoke him, just as if he had conspired your destruction. To such a degree was Christ dejected, that in the depth of his agony he was forced to exclaim, "My God, my God, why hast thou forsaken me?" The view taken by some, that he here expressed the opinion of others rather than his own conviction, is most improbable; for it is evident that the expression was wrung from the anguish of his inmost soul. We do not, however, insinuate that God was ever hostile to him or angry with him. How could he be angry with the beloved Son, with whom his soul was well pleased? or how could he have appeased the Father by his intercession for others if He were hostile to himself? But this we say, that he bore the weight of the divine anger, that, smitten and afflicted, he experienced all the signs of an angry and avenging God. Hence Hilary argues, that to this descent we owe our exemption from death. Nor does he dissent from this view in other passages, as when he says, "The cross, death, hell, are our life." And again, "The Son of God is in hell, but man is

brought back to heaven." And why do I quote the testimony of a private writer, when an Apostle asserts the same thing, stating it as one fruit of his victory that he delivered "them who through fear of death were all their lifetime subject to bondage?" (Heb. 2:15). He behoved therefore, to conquer the fear which incessantly vexes and agitates the breasts of all mortals; and this he could not do without a contest. Moreover it will shortly appear with greater clearness that his was no common sorrow, was not the result of a trivial cause. Thus by engaging with the power of the devil, the fear of death, and the pains of hell, he gained the victory, and achieved a triumph, so that we now fear not in death those things which our Prince has destroyed.

12. Here some miserable creatures, who, though unlearned, are however impelled more by malice than ignorance, cry out that I am offering an atrocious insult to Christ, because it were most incongruous to hold that he feared for the safety of his soul. And then in harsher terms they urge the calumnious charge that I attribute despair to the Son of God, a feeling the very opposite of faith. First, they wickedly raise a controversy as to the fear and dread which Christ felt, though these are openly affirmed by the Evangelists. For before the hour of his death arrived, he was troubled in spirit, and affected with grief; and at the very onset began to be exceedingly amazed. To speak of these feelings as merely assumed, is a shameful evasion. It becomes us, therefore (as Ambrose truly teaches), boldly to profess the agony of Christ, if we are not ashamed of the cross. And certainly had not his soul shared in the punishment, he would have been a Redeemer of bodies only. The object of his struggle was to raise up those who were lying prostrate; and so far is this from detracting from his heavenly glory, that his goodness, which can never be sufficiently extolled, becomes more conspicuous in this, that he declined not to bear our infirmities. Hence also that solace to our anxieties and griefs which the Apostle sets before us: "We have not an high priest who cannot be touched with the feeling of our infirmities; but was in all respects tempted like as we are, yet without sin," (Heb. 4:15). These men pretend that a thing in its nature vicious is improperly ascribed to Christ; as if they were wiser than the Spirit of God, who in the same passage reconciles the two things—viz. that he was tempted in all respects like as we are, and yet was without sin. There is no reason, therefore, to take alarm at infirmity in Christ, infirmity to which he submitted not under the constraint of violence and necessity, but merely because he loved and pitied us. Whatever he spontaneously suffered, detracts in no degree from his majesty. One thing which misleads these detractors is, that they do not recognize in Christ an infirmity which was pure and free from every species of taint, inasmuch as it was kept within the limits of obedience. As no moderation can be seen in the depravity of our nature, in which all affections with turbulent impetuosity exceed their due bounds, they improperly apply the same standard to the Son of God. But as he was upright, all his affections were under such restraint as prevented every thing like excess. Hence he could resemble us in grief, fear, and dread, but still with this mark of distinction. Thus refuted, they fly off to another cavil, that although Christ feared death, yet he feared not the curse and wrath of God, from which he knew that he was safe. But let the pious reader consider how far it is honorable to Christ to make him more effeminate and timid than the generality of men. Robbers and other malefactors contumaciously hasten to death, many men magnanimously despise it, others meet it calmly. If the Son of God was amazed and terror-struck at the prospect of it, where was his firmness or magnanimity? We are even told, what in a common death would have been deemed most extraordinary, that in the depth of his agony his sweat was like great drops of blood falling to the ground. Nor was this a spectacle exhibited to the eyes of others, since it was from a secluded spot that he uttered his groans to his Father. And that no doubt may remain, it was necessary that angels should come down from heaven to strengthen him with miraculous consolation. How shamefully effeminate would it have been (as I have observed) to be so excruciated by the fear of an ordinary death as to sweat drops of blood, and not even be revived by the

presence of angels? What? Does not that prayer, thrice repeated, "Father, if it be possible, let this cup pass from me," (Matt. 26:39), a prayer dictated by incredible bitterness of soul, show that Christ had a fiercer and more arduous struggle than with ordinary death?

Hence it appears that these triflers, with whom I am disputing, presume to talk of what they know not, never having seriously considered what is meant and implied by ransoming us from the justice of God. It is of consequence to understand aright how much our salvation cost the Son of God. If any one now ask, Did Christ descend to hell at the time when he deprecated death? I answer, that this was the commencement, and that from it we may infer how dire and dreadful were the tortures which he endured when he felt himself standing at the bar of God as a criminal in our stead. And although the divine power of the Spirit veiled itself for a moment, that it might give place to the infirmity of the flesh, we must understand that the trial arising from feelings of grief and fear was such as not to be at variance with faith. And in this was fulfilled what is said in Peter's sermon as to having been loosed from the pains of death, because "it was not possible he could be holden of it," (Acts 2:24). Though feeling, as it were, forsaken of God, he did not cease in the slightest degree to confide in his goodness. This appears from the celebrated prayer in which, in the depth of his agony, he exclaimed, "My God, my God, why hast thou forsaken me?" (Matt. 27:46). Amid all his agony he ceases not to call upon his God, while exclaiming that he is forsaken by him. This refutes the Apollinarian heresy as well as that of those who are called Monothelites. Apollinaris pretended, that in Christ the eternal Spirit supplied the place of a soul, so that he was only half a man; as if he could have expiated our sins in any other way than by obeying the Father. But where does the feeling or desire of obedience reside but in the soul? And we know that his soul was troubled in order that ours, being free from trepidation, might obtain peace and quiet. Moreover, in opposition to the Monothelites, we see that in his human he felt a repugnance

to what he willed in his divine nature. I say nothing of his subduing the fear of which we have spoken by a contrary affection. This appearance of repugnance is obvious in the words, "Father, save me from this hour: but for this cause came I unto this hour. Father, glorify thy name," (John 12:27, 28). Still, in this perplexity, there was no violent emotion, such as we exhibit while making the strongest endeavors to subdue our own feelings.

13. Next follows the resurrection from the dead, without which all that has hitherto been said would be defective. For seeing that in the cross, death, and burial of Christ, nothing but weakness appears, faith must go beyond all these, in order that it may be provided with full strength. Hence, although in his death we have an effectual completion of salvation, because by it we are reconciled to God, satisfaction is given to his justice, the curse is removed, and the penalty paid; still it is not by his death, but by his resurrection, that we are said to be begotten again to a living hope (1 Pet. 1:3); because, as he, by rising again, became victorious over death, so the victory of our faith consists only in his resurrection. The nature of it is better expressed in the words of Paul, "Who (Christ) was delivered for our offences, and was raised again for our justification," (Rom. 4:25); as if he had said, By his death sin was taken away, by his resurrection righteousness was renewed and restored. For how could he by dying have freed us from death, if he had yielded to its power? how could he have obtained the victory for us, if he had fallen in the contest?

Our salvation may be thus divided between the death and the resurrection of Christ: by the former sin was abolished and death annihilated; by the latter righteousness was restored and life revived, the power and efficacy of the former being still bestowed upon us by means of the latter. Paul accordingly affirms, that he was declared to be the Son of God by his resurrection (Rom. 1:4), because he then fully displayed that heavenly power which is both a bright mirror of his divinity, and a sure support of our faith; as he also elsewhere teaches, that "though he was crucified through weakness, yet he liveth by the power of God," (2 Cor. 13:4). In the same sense, in another passage, treating of perfection, he says, "That I may know him and the power of his resurrection," (Phil. 3:10). Immediately after he adds, "being made conformable unto his death." In perfect accordance with this is the passage in Peter, that God "raised him up from the dead, and gave him glory, that your faith and hope might be in God," (1 Pet. 1:21). Not that faith founded merely on his death is vacillating, but that the divine power by which he maintains our faith is most conspicuous in his resurrection. Let us remember, therefore, that when death only is mentioned, everything peculiar to the resurrection is at the same time included, and that there is a like synecdoche in the term resurrection, as often as it is used apart from death, everything peculiar to death being included. But as, by rising again, he obtained the victory, and became the resurrection and the life, Paul justly argues, "If Christ be not raised, your faith is vain; ye are yet in your sins," (1 Cor. 15:17). Accordingly, in another passage, after exulting in the death of Christ in opposition to the terrors of condemnation, he thus enlarges, "Christ that died, yea rather, that is risen again, who is even at the right hand of God, who also maketh intercession for us," (Rom. 8:34). Then, as we have already explained that the mortification of our flesh depends on communion with the cross, so we must also understand, that a corresponding benefit is derived from his resurrection. For as the Apostle says, "Like as Christ was raised up from the dead by the glory of the Father, even so we also should walk in newness of life," (Rom. 6:4). Accordingly, as in another passage, from our being dead with Christ, he inculcates, "Mortify therefore your members which are upon the earth," (Col. 3:5); so from our being risen with Christ he infers, "seek those things which are above, where Christ sitteth at the right hand of God," (Col. 3:1). In these words we are not only urged by the example of a risen Savior to follow newness of life, but are taught that by his power we are renewed unto righteousness. A third benefit derived from it is, that, like an earnest, it assures us of our own resurrection, of which it is certain that his is the surest representation.

This subject is discussed at length (1 Cor. 15). But it is to be observed, in passing, that when he is said to have "risen from the dead," these terms express the reality both of his death and resurrection, as if it had been said, that he died the same death as other men naturally die, and received immortality in the same mortal flesh which he had assumed.

14. The resurrection is naturally followed by the ascension into heaven. For although Christ, by rising again, began fully to display his glory and virtue, having laid aside the abject and ignoble condition of a mortal life, and the ignominy of the cross, yet it was only by his ascension to heaven that his reign truly commenced. This the Apostle shows, when he says he ascended "that he might fill all things," (Eph. 4:10); thus reminding us, that under the appearance of contradiction, there is a beautiful harmony, inasmuch as though he departed from us, it was that his departure might be more useful to us than that presence which was confined in a humble tabernacle of flesh during his abode on the earth. Hence John, after repeating the celebrated invitation, "If any man thirst, let him come unto me and drink," immediately adds, "the Holy Ghost was not yet given; because that Jesus was not yet glorified," (John 7:37, 39). This our Lord himself also declared to his disciples, "It is expedient for you that I go away: for if I go not away the Comforter will not come unto you," (John 16:7). To console them for his bodily absence, he tells them that he will not leave them comfortless, but will come again to them in a manner invisible indeed, but more to be desired, because they were then taught by a surer experience that the government which he had obtained, and the power which he exercises would enable his faithful followers not only to live well, but also to die happily. And, indeed we see how much more abundantly his Spirit was poured out, how much more gloriously his kingdom was advanced, how much greater power was employed in aiding his followers and discomfiting his enemies. Being raised to heaven, he withdrew his bodily presence from our sight, not that he might cease to be with his followers, who are still pilgrims on the earth, but that he might rule both heaven and

earth more immediately by his power; or rather, the promise which he made to be with us even to the end of the world, he fulfilled by this ascension, by which, as his body has been raised above all heavens, so his power and efficacy have been propagated and diffused beyond all the bounds of heaven and earth. This I prefer to explain in the words of Augustine rather than my own: "Through death Christ was to go to the right hand of the Father, whence he is to come to judge the quick and the dead, and that in corporal presence, according to the sound doctrine and rule of faith. For, in spiritual presence, he was to be with them after his ascension," (August. *Tract. in Joann.* 109). In another passage he is more full and explicit: "In regard to ineffable and invisible grace, is fulfilled what he said, Lo, I am with you alway, even to the end of the world (Matt. 28:20); but in regard to the flesh which the Word assumed in regard to his being born of a Virgin, in regard to his being apprehended by the Jews, nailed to the tree, taken down from the cross, wrapt in linen clothes, laid in the sepulcher, and manifested on his resurrection, it may be said, Me ye have not always with you. Why? because, in bodily presence, he conversed with his disciples forty days, and leading them out where they saw, but followed not, he ascended into heaven, and is not here: for there he sits at the right hand of the Father: and yet he is here, for the presence of his Godhead was not withdrawn. Therefore, as regards his divine presence, we have Christ always: as regards his bodily presence, it was truly said to the disciples, Me ye have not always. For a few days the Church had him bodily present. Now, she apprehends him by faith, but sees him not by the eye," (August. *Tract.* 51).

15. Hence it is immediately added, that he "sitteth at the right hand of God the Father;" a similitude borrowed from princes, who have their assessors to whom they commit the office of ruling and issuing commands. Thus Christ, in whom the Father is pleased to be exalted, and by whose hand he is pleased to reign, is said to have been received up, and seated on his right hand (Mark 16:19); as if it had been said, that he was installed in the government of heaven and earth, and formally admitted to possession of the administration committed to him, and not only admitted for once, but to continue until he descend to judgment. For so the Apostle interprets, when he says, that the Father "set him at his own right hand in the heavenly places, far above all principality, and power, and might, and dominion, and every name that is named not only in this world, but also in that which is to come; and has put all things under his feet, and given him to be the head over all things to the Church." You see to what end he is so seated namely, that all creatures both in heaven and earth should reverence his majesty, be ruled by his hand, do him implicit homage, and submit to his power. All that the Apostles intends when they so often mention his seat at the Father's hand, is to teach, that every thing is placed at his disposal. Those, therefore, are in error, who suppose that his blessedness merely is indicated. We may observe, that there is nothing contrary to this doctrine in the testimony of Stephen, that he saw him standing (Acts 7:56), the subject here considered being not the position of his body, but the majesty of his empire, sitting meaning nothing more than presiding on the judgment-seat of heaven.

16. From this doctrine faith derives manifold advantages. First, it perceives that the Lord, by his ascension to heaven, has opened up the access to the heavenly kingdom, which Adam had shut. For having entered it in our flesh, as it were in our name, it follows, as the Apostle says, that we are in a manner now seated in heavenly places, not entertaining a mere hope of heaven, but possessing it in our head. Secondly, faith perceives that his seat beside the Father is not without great advantage to us. Having entered the temple not made with hands, he constantly appears as our advocate and intercessor in the presence of the Father; directs attention to his own righteousness, so as to turn it away from our sins; so reconciles him to us, as by his intercession to pave for us a way of access to his throne, presenting it to miserable sinners, to whom it would otherwise be an object of dread, as replete with grace and mercy. Thirdly, it discerns his

power, on which depend our strength, might, resources, and triumph over hell, "When he ascended up on high, he led captivity captive," (Eph. 4:8). Spoiling his foes, he gave gifts to his people, and daily loads them with spiritual riches. He thus occupies his exalted seat, that thence transferring his virtue unto us, he may quicken us to spiritual life, sanctify us by his Spirit, and adorn his Church with various graces, by his protection preserve it safe from all harm, and by the strength of his hand curb the enemies raging against his cross and our salvation; in fine, that he may possess all power in heaven and earth, until he have utterly routed all his foes, who are also ours and completed the structure of his Church. Such is the true nature of the kingdom, such the power which the Father has conferred upon him, until he arrive to complete the last act by judging the quick and the dead.

17. Christ, indeed, gives his followers no dubious proofs of present power, but as his kingdom in the world is in a manner veiled by the humiliation of a carnal condition, faith is most properly invited to meditate on the visible presence which he will exhibit on the last day. For he will descend from heaven in visible form, in like manner as he was seen to ascend, and appear to all, with the ineffable majesty of his kingdom, the splendor of immortality, the boundless power of divinity, and an attending company of angels. Hence we are told to wait for the Redeemer against that day on which he will separate the sheep from the goats and the elect from the reprobate, and when not one individual either of the living or the dead shall escape his judgment. From the extremities of the universe shall be heard the clang of the trumpet summoning all to his tribunal; both those whom that day shall find alive, and those whom death shall previously have removed from the society of the living. There are some who take the words, quick and dead, in a different sense; and, indeed, some ancient writers appear to have hesitated as to the exposition of them; but our meaning being plain and clear, is much more accordant with the Creed which was certainly written for popular use. There is nothing contrary to it in

the Apostle's declaration, that it is appointed unto all men once to die. For though those who are surviving at the last day shall not die after a natural manner, yet the change which they are to undergo, as it shall resemble, is not improperly called, death (Heb. 9:27). "We shall not all sleep, but we shall all be changed," (1 Cor. 15:51). What does this mean? Their mortal life shall perish and be swallowed up in one moment, and be transformed into an entirely new nature. Though no one can deny that that destruction of the flesh will be death, it still remains true that the quick and the dead shall be summoned to judgment (1 Thess. 4:16); for "the dead in Christ shall rise first; then we which are alive and remain shall be caught up together with them in the clouds to meet the lord in the air." Indeed, it is probable, that these words in the Creed were taken from Peter's sermon as related by Luke (Acts 10:42), and from the solemn charge of Paul to Timothy (2 Tim. 4:1).

18. It is most consolatory to think, that judgment is vested in him who has already destined us to share with him in the honor of judgment (Matt. 19:28); so far is it from being true, that he will ascend the judgment-seat for our condemnation. How could a most merciful prince destroy his own people? how could the head disperse its own members? how could the advocate condemn his clients? For if the Apostle, when contemplating the interposition of Christ, is bold to exclaim, "Who is he that condemneth?" (Rom. 8:33), much more certain is it that Christ, the intercessor, will not condemn those whom he has admitted to his protection. It certainly gives no small security, that we shall be present at no other tribunal than that of our Redeemer, from whom salvation is to be expected; and that he who in the Gospel now promises eternal blessedness, will then as judge ratify his promise. The end for which the Father has honored the Son by committing all judgment to him (John 5:22), was to pacify the consciences of his people when alarmed at the thought of judgment. Hitherto I have followed the order of the Apostles' Creed, because it states the leading articles of redemption in a few words, and

may thus serve as a tablet in which the points of Christian doctrine, most deserving of attention, are brought separately and distinctly before us. I call it the Apostles' Creed, though I am by no means solicitous as to its authorship. The general consent of ancient writers certainly does ascribe it to the Apostles, either because they imagined it was written and published by them for common use, or because they thought it right to give the sanction of such authority to a compendium faithfully drawn up from the doctrine delivered by their hands. I have no doubt, that, from the very commencement of the Church, and, therefore, in the very days of the Apostles, it held the place of a public and universally received confession, whatever be the quarter from which it originally proceeded. It is not probable that it was written by some private individual, since it is certain that, from time immemorial, it was deemed of sacred authority by all Christians. The only point of consequence we hold to be incontrovertible—viz. that it gives, in clear and succinct order, a full statement of our faith, and in every thing which it contains is sanctioned by the sure testimony of Scripture. This being understood, it were to no purpose to labor anxiously, or quarrel with any one as to the authorship, unless, indeed, we think it not enough to possess the sure truth of the Holy Spirit, without, at the same time, knowing by whose mouth it was pronounced, or by whose hand it was written.

19. When we see that the whole sum of our salvation, and every single part of it, are comprehended in Christ, we must beware of deriving even the minutest portion of it from any other quarter. If we seek salvation, we are taught by the very name of Jesus that he possesses it; if we seek any other gifts of the Spirit, we shall find them in his unction; strength in his government; purity in his conception; indulgence in his nativity, in which he was made like us in all respects, in order that he might learn to sympathize with us: if we seek redemption, we shall find it in his passion; acquittal in his condemnation; remission of the curse in his cross; satisfaction in his sacrifice; purification in his blood; reconciliation in his descent to hell; mortification of the flesh in his sepulcher; newness of life in his resurrection; immortality also in his resurrection; the inheritance of a celestial kingdom in his entrance into heaven; protection, security, and the abundant supply of all blessings, in his kingdom; secure anticipation of judgment in the power of judging committed to him. In fine, since in him all kinds of blessings are treasured up, let us draw a full supply from him, and none from any other quarter. Those who, not satisfied with him alone, entertain various hopes from others, though they may continue to look to him chiefly, deviate from the right path by the simple fact, that some portion of their thought takes a different direction. No distrust of this description can arise when once the abundance of his blessings is properly known.

John Calvin
Institutes of Christian Religion, Book 2,
Chapter 16
Henry Beveridge translation

1.38 CHRIST ALTOGETHER LOVELY, JOHN FLAVEL

John Flavel, 1628-1691, the English Nonconformist divine, went to University College, Oxford, and then was ordained as a Presbyterian at Salisbury in 1650 and ministered mainly in Dartmouth, Devonshire. He was one of the ministers who were ejected from his ministerial work in 1662. He was then forced to preach from his own home for ten years. He was instrumental in promoting the union of Presbyterians and Congregationalists in 1682.

HOW CHRIST IS "ALTOGETHER LOVELY" (SONG 5:16)

He is lovely in His person

First, He is altogether lovely in his person: he is Deity dwelling in flesh, John 1:14. The wonderful, perfect union of the divine and human nature in Christ renders him an object of admiration and adoration to both angels and men, 1 Tim. 3:16. God never presented to the world such a vision of glory before. Consider how the human nature of our Lord Jesus Christ is overflowing with all the graces of the Spirit, in such a way as never any of the saints was filled. O what a lovely picture does this paint of him! John 3:34, "God gives the Spirit [to him] without limit." This makes him "the most excellent of men and [his] lips have been anointed with grace," Psalm 45:2. If a small measure of grace in the saints makes them sweet and desirable companions, what must the riches of the Spirit of grace filling Jesus Christ without measure make him in the eyes of believers? O what a glory must it fix upon him!

He is lovely in His offices

Secondly, He is altogether lovely in his offices: let us consider for a moment the suitability, fullness, and comforting nature of them.

First, the suitability of the offices of Christ to the miseries of men. We cannot but adore the infinite wisdom of his receiving them. We are, by nature, blind and ignorant, at best but groping in the dim light of nature after God, Acts 17:27. Jesus Christ is a light to lighten the Gentiles, Is. 49:6. When this great prophet came into the world, then did the day-spring from on high visit us, Luke 1:78. By nature we are alienated from, and at enmity against God; Christ comes into the world to be an atoning sacrifice, making peace by the blood of his cross, Col. 1:20. All the world, by nature, is in bondage and captivity to Satan, a miserable slavery. Christ comes with kingly power, to rescue sinners, as a prey from the mouth of the terrible one.

Secondly, let the fullness of his offices be also considered, which make him able "to save to the uttermost, all that come to God by him," Heb. 7:25. The three offices, comprising in them all that our souls do need, become a universal relief to all our distresses; and therefore,

Thirdly, Unspeakably comforting must the offices of Christ be to the souls of sinners. If light be pleasant to our eyes, how pleasant is that light of life springing from the Sun of righteousness! Mal. 4:2. If a pardon be sweet to a condemned criminal, how sweet must the sprinkling the blood of Jesus be to the trembling conscience of a law-condemned sinner? If a rescue from a cruel tyrant is sweet to a poor captive, how sweet must it be to the ears of enslaved sinners, to hear the voice of liberty and deliverance proclaimed by Jesus Christ? Out of the several offices of Christ, as out of so many fountains, all the promises of the new covenant flow, as so many soul-refreshing streams of peace and joy.

All the promises of illumination, counsel and direction flow out of Christ's prophetic office.

All the promises of reconciliation, peace, pardon, and acceptation flow out of his priestly office, with the sweet streams of joy and spiritual comforts which accompany it.

All the promises of converting, increasing, defending, directing, and supplying grace, flow out of the kingly office of Christ; indeed, all promises may be reduced to these three offices, so that Jesus Christ must be altogether lovely in his offices.

He is lovely in His relations

First, He is a lovely Redeemer, Is. 61:1. He came to open the prison-doors to them that are bound. Needs must this Redeemer be a lovely one, if we consider the depth of misery from which he redeemed us, even "from the wrath to come," 1 Thess. 1:10. Consider the numbers redeemed, and the means of their redemption. Rev. 5:9, "And they sang a new song, saying, You are worthy to take the book, and to open the seals thereof: for you were slain, and have redeemed us to God by your blood, out of every kindred and tongue, and people and nation.'" He redeemed us not with silver and gold, but with his own precious blood, by way of price, 1 Pet. 1:18, 19, with his out-stretched and glorious arm, by way of power, Col. 1:13. He redeemed us freely, Eph. 1:7, fully Rom. 8:1, at the right time, Gal. 4:4, and out of special and particular love, John 17:9. In a word, he has redeemed us for ever, never more to come into bondage, 1 Pet. 1:5, John 10:28. O how lovely is Jesus Christ in the relation of a Redeemer to God's elect!

Secondly, He is a lovely bridegroom to all that he betroths to himself. How does the church glory in him, in the words following my text; "this is my Beloved, and this is my Friend, O ye daughters of Jerusalem!" Heaven and earth cannot show anyone like him, which needs no fuller proof than the following particulars:

1. That he betroths to himself, in mercy and in loving kindness, such deformed, defiled, and altogether unworthy souls as we are. We have no beauty, no goodness to make us desirable in his eyes; all the origins of his love to us are in his own breast, Deut. 7:7. He chooses us, not because we were, but in order that he might make us lovely, Eph. 5:27. He came to us when we lay in our blood, and said unto us, "Live"; and that was the time of love, Ezek. 16:5.

2. He expects no restitution from us, and yet gives himself, and all that he has, to us. Our poverty cannot enrich him, but he made himself poor to enrich us, 2 Cor. 8:9; 1 Cor. 3:22.

3. No husband loves the wife of his bosom, as much as Christ loved his people, Eph. 5:25. He loved the church and gave himself for it.

4. No one bears with weaknesses and provocations as Christ does; the church is called "the Lamb's wife," Rev. 19:9.

5. No husband is so undying and everlasting a husband as Christ is; death separates all other relations, but the soul's union with Christ is not dissolved in the grave. Indeed, the day of a believer's death is his marriage day, the day of his fullest enjoyment of Christ. No husband can say to his wife, what Christ says to the believer, "I will never leave you, nor forsake you," Heb. 8:5.

6. No bridegroom enriches his bride with such honors by marriage, as Christ does; he makes them related to God as their father, and from that day the mighty and glorious angels think it no dishonor to be their servants, Heb. 1:14. The angels will admire the beauty and glory of the spouse of Christ, Rev. 21:9.

7. No marriage was ever consummated with such triumphal proceedings as the marriage of Christ and believers shall be in heaven, Psalm 14:14, 15. "She shall be brought to the king in raiment of needlework, the virgins, her companions that follow her, shall be brought unto thee; with gladness and rejoicing shall they be brought; they shall enter into the king's palace." Among the Jews, the marriage-house was called the house of praise; there was joy upon all hands, but nothing like the joy that will be in heaven when believers, the spouse of Christ, shall be brought there. God the Father will rejoice to behold the blessed accomplishment and confirmation of those glorious plans of his love. Jesus Christ, the Bridegroom will rejoice to see the travail of his soul, the blessed birth and product of all his bitter pains and agonies, Is. 53:11. The Holy Spirit will rejoice to see the completion and perfection of that sanctifying design which was committed to his hand, 2 Cor. 5:5, to see those souls whom he once found as rough stones, now to shine as the bright, polished stones of the spiritual

temple. Angels will rejoice: great was the joy when the foundation of this design was laid, in the incarnation of Christ, Luke 2:13. Great therefore must their joy be, when the top-stone is set up with shouting, crying, "Grace, grace." The saints themselves shall rejoice unspeakably, when they shall enter into the King's palace, and be forever with the Lord, 1 Thess. 4:17. Indeed there will be joy on all hands, except among the devils and damned, who shall gnash their teeth with envy at the everlasting advancement and glory of believers. Thus Christ is altogether lovely, in the relation of a Bridegroom.

Thirdly, Christ is altogether lovely, in the relation of an Advocate. 1 John 2:1, "If any man sin, we have an advocate with the Father, Jesus Christ the righteous, and he is the Propitiation." It is he that pleads the cause of believers in heaven. He appears for them in the presence of God, to prevent any new alienation, and to continue the state of friendship and peace between God and us. In this relation Christ is altogether lovely. For,

1. He makes our cause his own, and acts for us in heaven, as if for himself, Heb. 4:15. He is touched with a most tender understanding of our troubles and dangers, and is not only one with us by way of representation, but also one with us in respect of sympathy and affection.

2. Christ our Advocate tracks our cause and business in heaven, as his great and primary design and business. For this reason in Hebrews 7:25, he is said to "live for ever to make intercession for us." It is as if our concerns were so attended to by him there, that all the glory and honor which is paid him in heaven would not divert him one moment from our business.

3. He pleads the cause of believers by his blood. Unlike other advocates, it is not enough for him to lay out only words, which is a cheaper way of pleading; but he pleads for us by the voice of his own blood, as in Heb. 12:24, where we are said to be come "to the blood of sprinkling, that speaketh better things than that of Abel." Every wound he received for us on earth is a mouth opened to plead with God on our behalf in heaven. And hence it is, that in Rev. 5:6 he is represented

standing before God, as a lamb that had been slain; as it were exhibiting and revealing in heaven those deadly wounds received on earth from the justice of God, on our account. Other advocates spend their breath, Christ spends his blood.

4. He pleads the cause of believers freely. Other advocates plead for reward, and empty the purses, while they plead the causes of their clients.

5. In a word, he obtains for us all the mercies for which he pleads. No cause miscarries in his hand, which he undertakes, Rom. 8:33, 34. What a lovely Advocate is Christ for believers!

Fourthly, Christ is altogether lovely in the relation of a friend, for in this relation he is pleased to acknowledge his people, Luke 12:4, 5. There are certain things in which one friend manifests his affection and friendship to another, but there is not one like Christ. For,

1. No friend is so open-hearted to his friend as Christ is to his people: he reveals the very counsels and secrets of his heart to them. John 15:15, "Henceforth I call you not servants, for the servant knows not what his Lord does; but I have called you friends; for all things that I have heard of my Father, I have made known unto you."

2. No friend in the world is so generous and bountiful to his friend, as Jesus Christ is to believers; he parts with his very blood for them; "Greater love (he says) has no man than this, that a man lay down his life for his friends," John 15:13. He has exhausted the precious treasures of his invaluable blood to pay our debts. O what a lovely friend is Jesus Christ to believers!

3. No friend sympathizes so tenderly with his friend in affliction, as Jesus Christ does with his friends: "In all our afflictions he is afflicted," Heb. 4:15. He feels all our sorrows, needs and burdens as his own. This is why it is said that the sufferings of believers are called the sufferings of Christ, Col. 1:24.

4. No friend in the world takes that contentment in his friends, as Jesus Christ does in believers. Song 4:9, "You have ravished my heart, (he says to the spouse) you have ravished my heart with one of your eyes, with one chain of your neck." The Hebrew,

here rendered "ravished," signifies to puff up, or to make one proud: how the Lord Jesus is pleased to glory in his people! How he is taken and delighted with those gracious ornaments which himself bestows upon them! There is no friend so lovely as Christ.

5. No friend in the world loves his friend with as impassioned and strong affection as Jesus Christ loves believers. Jacob loved Rachel, and endured for her sake the parching heat of summer and cold of winter; but Christ endured the storms of the wrath of God, the heat of his indignation, for our sakes. David manifested his love to Absalom, in wishing, "O that I had died for you!" Christ manifested his love to us, not in wishes that he had died, but in death itself, in our stead, and for our sakes.

6. No friend in the world is so constant and unchangeable in friendship as Christ is.

John 13:1, "Having loved his own which were in the world, he loved them unto the end." He bears with millions of provocations and wrongs, and yet will not break friendship with his people. Peter denied him, yet he will not disown him; but after his resurrection he says, "Go, tell the disciples, and tell Peter." Let him not think he has forfeited by that sin of his, his interest in me. Though he denied me, I will not disown him, Mark 16:7. How lovely is Christ in the relation of a friend!

I might further show you the loveliness of Christ in his ordinances and in his providences, in his communion with us and communications to us, but there is no end of the account of Christ's loveliness: I will rather choose to press believers to their duties towards this altogether lovely Christ.

John Flavel

1.39 CHRIST'S HUMILIATION, THE WESTMINSTER SHORTER CATECHISM

The Westminster Confession and Catechisms were written between 1642 and 1647.

B. B. Warfield, referring to The Westminster Shorter Catechism, *once wrote: "It is worth while to be a Shorter Catechism boy. They grow to be men. And better than that, they are exceedingly apt to grow to be men of God."*

QUESTION 27: WHEREIN DID CONSIST CHRIST'S HUMILIATION?

ANSWER: Christ's humiliation consisted in his being born, and that in a low condition, made under the law, undergoing the miseries of this life, the wrath of God, and the cursed death of the cross; in being buried, and continuing under the power of death for a time.

Luke 2:7. And she brought forth her firstborn son, and wrapped him in swaddling clothes, and laid him in a manger; because there was no room for them in the inn.

Philippians 2:6-8. Who, being in the form of God, thought it not robbery to be equal with God: but made himself of no reputation, and took upon him the form of a servant, and was made in the likeness of men:

and being found in fashion as a man, he humbled himself, and became obedient unto death, even the death of the cross.

2 Corinthians 8:9. For ye know the grace of our Lord Jesus Christ, that, though he was rich, yet for your sakes he became poor, that ye through his poverty might be rich.

Galatians 4:4. Who gave himself for our sins, that he might deliver us from this present evil world, according to the will of God and our Father.

Isaiah 53:3. He is despised and rejected of men; a man of sorrows, and acquainted with grief: and we hid as it were our faces from him; he was despised, and we esteemed him not.

Matthew 27:46. And about the ninth hour Jesus cried with a loud voice, saying, *Eli, Eli, lama sabachthani?* that is to say, My God, my God, why hast thou forsaken me?

Luke 22:41-44. And he was withdrawn from them about a stone's cast, and kneeled down, and prayed, saying, Father, if thou be willing, remove this cup from me: nevertheless not my will, but thine, be done. And there appeared an angel unto him from heaven, strengthening him. And being in an agony he prayed more earnestly: and his sweat was as it were great drops of blood falling down to the ground.

Galatians 3:13. Christ hath redeemed us from the curse of the law, being made a curse for us: for it is written, Cursed is every one that hangeth on a tree.

Philippians 2:8. And being found in fashion as a man, he humbled himself, and became obedient unto death, even the death of the cross.

1 Corinthians 15:3-4 For I delivered unto you first of all that which I also received, how that Christ died for our sins according to the scriptures; and that he was buried, and that he rose again the third day according to the scriptures.

The Westminster Shorter Catechism

1.40 CHRIST'S HUMILIATION, MATTHEW HENRY

Matthew Henry, 1662-1714, was a Welsh-born, English nonconformist minister and Bible commentator. He is remembered for his practical and devotional multi-volume Exposition of the Old and New Testaments that has been in print since its original publication.

1. DID JESUS CHRIST HUMBLE HIMSELF?

Yes: for being in the form of God, he made himself of no reputation, Phil. 2:6, 7. Was it a deep humiliation? Yes for he said, I am a worm, and no man, Ps. 22:6. Was it requisite he should humble himself? Yes : for thus it is written, and thus it behoved Christ to suffer, Luke 24:46. And was that a proper expedient to atone for our sin? Yes: for the sinner had said, I will be like the Most High, Is. 14:14.

2. DID CHRIST HUMBLE HIMSELF IN HIS BIRTH?

Yes: for he who thought it not robbery to be equal with God, was made in the likeness of men, Phil. 2:6, 7. Was he born of that which was then a poor family? Yes: he was a root of dry ground, Is. 53:2. Was he born of a poor woman? Yes: for she offered for her cleansing only a pair of turtle doves, or two young pigeons, Luke 2:24. Compare Lev. 12:8. Was his supposed father a poor man? Yes: they said, Is not this the carpenter's son, Matt. 13:55. Was he born in a poor place?

Yes: Bethlehem was little among the thousands of Judah, Mic. 5:2. Was he born in poor circumstances? Yes: in the stable of an inn, and laid in a manger, Luke 2:7. Had he respect paid him that was due to an incarnate Deity? No: for he was in the world, and the world knew him not, John 1:10. Was he respected by his countrymen? No: he came to his own, but his own received him not, v. 11. Was he born honorably? No: for he took upon him the form of a servant, Phil. 2:7. Was he born wealthy? No: though he was rich yet for our sakes he became poor, 2 Cor. 8:9.

3. WAS CHRIST MADE UNDER THE LAW?

Yes: God sent forth his Son, made of a woman, made under the law, Gal. 4:4. Was he circumcised? Yes: when eight days were accomplished, Luke 2:21. Was he presented in the temple? Yes: they brought him to Jerusalem to present him to the Lord, ver. 22. Did he keep the Passover? Yes: when he was twelve years old, he went up to Jerusalem, after the custom of the feast, ver. 42. Was he obedient to his parents? Yes: he went down with them to Nazareth, and was subject to them, ver. 51. Did he pay tribute? Yes: that give for me and thee, Matt. 17:24, 27. Did he fulfill all righteousness? Yes: thus it becometh us to fulfill all righteousness, Matt. 3:15. Did he submit to the law of the mediatorship? Yes: thy law is within my heart, Ps. 40:8.

4. WAS HIS EDUCATION MEAN?

Yes: for they said, Is not this the carpenter? Mark 6:3. Was the place of his abode despicable? Yes: can any good thing come out of Nazareth? John 1:46. Did he live in honor? No: for he was despised and rejected of men, Is. 53:3. Was he attended by great folks? No: have any of the rulers, or of the Pharisees believed on him? John 7:48. Were his followers mean? Yes: for they were fishers, Matt. 4:18. Did he live in mirth and pleasure? No: he was a man of sorrows, and acquainted with grief, Is. 53:3. Was the sin of sinners a grief to him? Yes: he was grieved for the hardness of their hearts, Mark 3:5. Were the sorrows of his friends a grief to him? Yes: Jesus wept, John 11:35. Had he a house of his own? No: foxes have holes, and the birds of the air have nests, but the Son of man hath not where to lay his head, Luke 11:58. Was he fed with the finest of the wheat? No: he had barley-loaves, John 6:9. Did he live upon alms? Yes: for certain women ministered to him of their substance, Luke 8:3. Had he a stately place to preach in? No: he taught the people out of the ship, Luke 5:8.

5. WAS HE TEMPTED OF SATAN?

Yes: he was in the wilderness forty days tempted of Satan, Mark 1:13. Was that a part of his sufferings? Yes: for he suffered, being tempted, Heb. 2:18. Was he persecuted betimes? Yes: Herod sought the young child to destroy him, Matt. 2:13. Was he slandered and reproached? Yes: they said of him, Behold a gluttonous man, and a wine-bibber, a friend of publicans and sinners, Luke 7:34. Was he represented as a madman? Yes: they said, He hath a devil, and is mad, John 10:20. And as one that is in league with the devil? Yes: they said, He casteth out devils by Beelzebub the prince of the devils, Matt. 12:24. Did they cavil at his preaching? Yes: he endured the contradiction of sinners against himself, Heb. 12:3. Did he bear all this patiently? Yes: when he was reviled, he reviled not again, 1 Pet. 2:23.

6. BUT NOTWITHSTANDING THIS, HAD HE HONOR DONE HIM IN HIS HUMILIATION?

Yes: for it was said of him, He shall be great, Luke 1:82. Did God put honor upon him? Yes: he received from God the Father honor and glory, 2 Pet. 1:17. Did angels do him honor? Yes: behold, angels came and ministered to him, Matt. 4:11. Did foreigners do him honor? Yes: Wise men of the east came to worship him, Matt. 2:2. Did the common report of the people do him honor? Yes: for some said he was Elias, others Jeremiah, or one of the prophets, Matt. 16:14. Did those that saw his miracles do him honor? Yes: for they said, it was never so seen in Israel, Matt. 9:83. Did inferior creatures do him honor? Yes: even the winds and the seas obeyed him, Matt. 8:27. Were devils themselves compelled to acknowledge him? Yes: for they said, We know thee who thou art, the Holy One of God, Mark 1:24.

7. DID HE HUMBLE HIMSELF UNTO DEATH?

Yes: he humbled himself, and became obedient to death, Phil. 2:8. Did he die for us? Yes: he was delivered for our offences, Rom. 4:25. Was this according to the counsels of God? Yes he was delivered by the determinate counsel and foreknowledge of God, Acts 2:23. Did he suffer in his soul? Yes: for he said, Now is my soul troubled, John 12:27. Did he suffer from his Father? Yes: he was stricken, smitten of God, and afflicted, Is. 53:4. Did he suffer in soul from his Father? Yes: for he put him to grief, ver. 10. Did this put him into an agony? Yes: he began to be sorrowful, and very heavy, Matt. 26:37. Did he suffer this for us? Yes: for he made him sin for us who knew no sin, 2 Cor. 5:21. And yet did the Father love him even when he bruised him? Yes: therefore doth my Father love me, because I lay down my life, John 10:17.

8. DID HE SUFFER FROM SATAN?

Yes: thou shall bruise his heel, Gen. 3:15. Did Satan set upon him? Yes: the prince of this world cometh, John 14:30. But did Satan conquer him? No: he hath nothing in me, John 14:30. Did he suffer from the Jews? Yes: for they cried, Crucify him, crucify him, Luke 23:21. Did he suffer from the chief of the Jews? Yes: he was the stone which the builders refused, Ps. 118:29. Did he suffer from the Romans? Yes: the princes of this world crucified the Lord of glory, 1 Cor. 2:8. Was he betrayed by Judas? Yes: they put it into the heart of Judas Iscariot to betray him, John 13:2. Was he sold for thirty pieces of silver? Yes: A goodly price that I was prized at, Zech. 11:13. Was he forsaken by his own disciples? Yes: all his disciples forsook him, and fled, Matt. 26:56.

9. WAS HE FALSELY ACCUSED?

Yes: they sought false witnesses against him to put him to death, Matt. 26:59. Was he basely abused? Yes: he hid not his face from shame and spitting, Is. 1:6. Was he condemned as a blasphemer? Yes: they said, He hath spoken blasphemy, Matt. 25:65. Was he condemned as a traitor? Yes: for they said he perverted the nation, forbidding to give tribute to Caesar, Luke 23:2. Was he scourged? Yes: for by his stripes we are healed, Is. 53:5. Was he exposed to contempt? Yes: he was a reproach of men, and despised of the people, Ps. 22:6. Did they scoff at him as a prophet? Yes: they said, Prophesy who smote thee, Matt. 26:68. Did they scoff at him as a King? Yes: they said, Hail, King of the Jews, Matt. 27:29. Did they scoff at him as a Priest and Savior? Yes: they said, He saved others, himself he cannot save, Matt. 27:42.

10. WAS HE SENTENCED TO THE CROSS?

Yes: Pilate delivered him to be crucified, Matt. 27:26. Was he crucified between two thieves? Yes: he was numbered with the transgressors, Is. 53:12. Did he die a bloody death? Yes: for the life of the flesh is in the blood, and it is the blood that makes atonement for the soul, Lev. 17:11. Did he die a painful death? Yes: they pierced his hands and feet, Ps. 22:16. And a shameful death? Yes: he endured the cross, despising the shame, Heb. 12:2. And accursed

death? Yes: for he that is hanged is accursed of God, Deut, 21:23, Gal. 3:13. Did God seem to withdraw from him in his sufferings? Yes: he cried with a loud voice, My God, my God, why hast thou forsaken me? Matt. 27:46.

11. DID CHRIST DIE TO GLORIFY GOD?

Yes: For this cause came I to this hour. Father, glorify thy name, John 12:27, 28. Did he die to satisfy for our sins? Yes: it was to finish transgression, and to make an end of sins, to make reconciliation for iniquity, and bring in everlasting righteousness, Dan 9:14. Did he die to conquer Satan? Yes: he spoiled principalities and powers, triumphing over them in his cross, Col. 2:15. Did he die to save us from sin? Yes: he gave himself for us, that he might redeem us from all iniquity, Titus 2:14. Did he die to purchase heaven for us? Yes: for it is the purchased possession, Eph. 1:14, Heb. 9:15. Was he in his death made a curse for us? Yes: for Christ hath redeemed us from the curse of the law, being made a curse for us, Gal. 3:13. Did Christ sweat for us? Yes: his sweat was, as it were, great drops of blood, Luke 22:44. And thorns being also a fruit of the curse, did Christ wear them for us? Yes: they platted a crown of thorns and put it upon his head, Matt. 27:29.

12. DID CHRIST DO ALL THAT WAS TO BE DONE IN HIS SUFFERINGS FOR US?

Yes: he said, It is finished, John 19:30. Did the events answer the predictions? Yes: for the Scriptures must be fulfilled, Mark 14:49. Are we sure that Christ was truly dead? Yes: for one of the soldiers with a spear pierced his side, and forthwith came thereout blood and water, and he that saw it bare record, John 19:34, 35. Did Christ die as a martyr? Yes: for before Pontius Pilate he witnessed a good confession, 1 Tim. 6:13. Did he die as a testator? Yes: for where a testament is, there must needs be the death of the testator, Heb. 9:16. Did he die as a sacrifice? Yes: Christ our Passover is sacrificed for us, 1 Cor. 5:7.

13. WAS THERE HONOR DONE TO CHRIST EVEN IN HIS SUFFERINGS?

Yes: the earth did quake, and the rocks rent, and the graves were opened, Matt. 27:51. And were some thereby convinced? Yes: they feared greatly, saying, Truly this was the Son of God, Matt. 27:54. Is the cross of Christ then a reproach to us? No: God forbid that I should glory, save in the cross of our Lord Jesus Christ, Gal. 6:14. Is it what we should all be acquainted with? Yes: I determined to know nothing but Jesus Christ, and him crucified, 1 Cor. 2:12. And ought we to celebrate the praises of our crucified Savior? Yes: Worthy is the Lamb that was slain to receive honor, and glory, and blessing, Rev. 5:12.

14. WHEN CHRIST WAS DEAD, WAS HE BURIED?

Yes: they took him down from the tree, and laid him in a sepulcher, Acts 13:29. Was he buried according to the custom? Yes: as the manner of the Jews is to bury, John 19:40. Did he continue under the power of death for a time? Yes: for as Jonas was three days and three nights in the whale's belly, so shall the Son of man be three days and three nights in the heart of the earth, Matt. 12:40. Was this his descent into hell? Yes: he descended into the lower parts of the earth, Eph. 4:9. Did his separate soul go to paradise? Yes: This day shalt thou be with me in paradise, Luke 23:43. Did his body see corruption? No: Thou wilt not leave my soul in hell, neither wilt thou suffer thine Holy One to see corruption, Acts 2:27.

Matthew Henry
A Scripture Catechism in the method of the Assembly's

1.41 CHRIST'S EXALTATION, THE WESTMINSTER SHORTER CATECHISM

QUESTION 28: WHEREIN CONSISTS CHRIST'S EXALTATION?

ANSWER: Christ's exaltation consisteth in his rising again from the dead on the third day, in ascending up into heaven, in sitting at the right hand of God the Father, and in coming to judge the world at the last day.

1 Corinthians 15:3-4. For I delivered unto you first of all that which I also received, how that Christ died for our sins according to the scriptures; and that he was buried, and that he rose again the third day according to the scriptures.

Acts 1:9. And when he had spoken these things, while they beheld, he was taken up; and a cloud received him out of their sight.

Ephesians 1:19-20. And what is the exceeding greatness of his power to us-ward who believe, according to the working of his mighty power, which he wrought in Christ, when he raised him from the dead, and set him at his own right hand in the heavenly places.

Acts 1:11. Which also said, Ye men of Galilee, why stand ye gazing up into heaven? this same Jesus, which is taken up from you into heaven, shall so come in like manner as ye have seen him go into heaven.

Acts 17:31. Because he hath appointed a day, in the which he will judge the world in righteousness by that man whom he hath ordained; whereof he hath given assurance unto all men, in that he hath raised him from the dead.

The Westminster Shorter Catechism

1.42 CHRIST'S EXALTATION, MATTHEW HENRY

1. IS JESUS CHRIST EXALTED?

Yes: because he humbled himself, therefore God also hath highly exalted him, Phil. 2:9. Was his humiliation the way to exaltation? Yes: he suffered these things, and so entered into his glory, Luke 24:26. Was his exaltation the reward of his humiliation? Yes: I have glorified thee on the earth, and now O Father, glorify thou me, John 17:5. Had he it in his eye in his sufferings? Yes: for the joy that was set before him, he endured the cross, Heb. 12:2.

2. WAS HIS RESURRECTION THE FIRST STEP OF HIS EXALTATION?

Yes: he was buried, and rose again the third day according to the Scriptures, 1 Cor. 15:4. Did he continue always in the hands of death? No: for it was impossible he should be holden of them, Acts 2:24. Did he rise to life? Yes: he both rose and revived, Rom. 14:9. Did the same body rise? Yes: Behold my hands and my feet, that it is I myself, Luke 24:39. Is he the same Jesus still? Yes: I am he that liveth, and was dead, Rev. 1:18. Did he lie in the grave all the Jewish Sabbath? Yes: for he rose in the end of the Sabbath, Matt. 28:1. Did he rise the same day of the week? Yes: as it began to dawn towards the first day of the week, Matt. 28:1. Have we sufficient proof of his resurrection? Yes: he showed himself alive, by many infallible proofs, Acts 1:3. Did he rise to die no more? Yes: Death hath no more dominion over him, Rom. 6:9.

3. DID CHRIST RISE BY HIS OWN POWER?

Yes: Destroy this temple, and in three days I will raise it up, John 2:19. and 10:18. Was that a divine power? Yes: for he was crucified through weakness, but he lived by the power of God, 2 Cor. 13:4. Was it the great proof of his being the Son of God? Yes: he was declared to be the Son of God with power by the resurrection from the dead, Rom. 1:4. Was it the will of the Father he should rise? Yes: for the angel of the Lord descended from heaven, and came, and rolled back the stone, Matt.

28:2. Did the Father raise him? Yes: God raised him from the dead, Acts 13:30. Was this an evidence of the acceptance of his satisfaction? Yes: for he was raised again for our justification, Rom. 4:25. And we may plead it? Yes: it is Christ that died, yea, rather, that is risen again, Rom. 8:34.

4. DID CHRIST RISE AS A PUBLIC PERSON?

Yes: for since by man came death, by man came also the resurrection of the dead, 1 Cor. 15:21. Are true believers raised with him to a spiritual life? Yes: he hath quickened us together with Christ, Eph. 2:5. And shall they be shortly raised to eternal life? Yes: Christ the first-fruits, afterward they that are Christ's at his coming, 1 Cor. 15:23. Is the resurrection of Christ one of the great foundations of Christianity? Yes: if Christ be not risen, our faith is vain, ver. 14.

5. DID CHRIST STAY ON EARTH FORTY DAYS AFTER HIS RESURRECTION?

Yes: he was seen of them forty days, Acts 1:3. Did he then ascend up into heaven? Yes: while he blessed them he was parted from them, and carried up into heaven, Luke 24:51. Did he ascend in a cloud? Yes: a cloud received him out of their sight, Acts 1:9. Was he welcome in heaven? Yes: when the Son of man came with the clouds of heaven, he came to the Ancient of days, and they brought him near before him, Dan. 7:13.

6. WAS IT FOR OUR ADVANTAGE THAT HE ASCENDED UP INTO HEAVEN?

Yes: It is expedient for you that I go away, John 16:7. Did he ascend as a conqueror? Yes: when he ascended on high, he led captivity captive, Eph. 4:8. Did he ascend as our forerunner? Yes: as the forerunner he is for us entered, Heb. 6:20. Is he gone to prepare a place for us? Yes: I go to prepare a place for you, John 14:2. Did he enter as our High Priest, within the veil? Yes: by his own blood he entered in once into the holy place, Heb. 9:12.

7. DID HE SIT AT THE RIGHT HAND OF GOD?

Yes: he is seated on the right hand of the throne of the Majesty in the heavens, Heb. 8:1. Has he authority to sit there? Yes: the Lord said unto my Lord, Sit thou on my right hand, Ps. 110:1. Is he there now? Yes: he is even at the right hand of God, Rom. 8:34. Has he been seen there? Yes: Stephen said, I see the heavens opened, and the Son of man standing on the right hand of God, Acts 7:56. Will he continue there? Yes: the heavens must receive him till the restitution of all things, Acts 3:21. Has he the highest honor there? Yes: God hath given him a name above every name, Phil. 2:9. Has he the sovereign power there? Yes: for angels, authorities, and powers are made subject to him, 1 Pet. 3:22. Is he Lord of all there? Yes: Thou crownedst him with glory and honor, and didst set him over the works of thy hands, Heb. 2:7. Ought we therefore to have our hearts in heaven? Yes: Seek those things which are above, where Christ sits on the right hand of God, Col. 3:1.

8. WILL CHRIST COME AGAIN?

Yes: If I go to prepare a place for you, I will come again, John 14:3. Are you sure he will come again? Yes: for he said, Surely I come quickly, Rev. 22:20. Will he come in glory? Yes: he shall come in the clouds of heaven with power and great glory, Matt. 24:30. Will his angels attend him? Yes: he shall come in his glory, and all the holy angels with him, Matt. 25:31. Will he come publicly? Yes: Behold he comes in the clouds, and every eye shall see him, Rev. 1:7.

9. WILL CHRIST COME TO JUDGE THE WORLD?

Yes: God hath appointed a day in which he will judge the world in righteousness by that Man whom he hath ordained, Acts 17:31. Will he come to the terror of all his enemies? Yes: they also which pierced him shall wail because of him, Rev. 1:7. Will he come to the comfort of all his faithful followers? Yes: to them that look for him, he will appear the second time unto salvation, Heb. 9:28. Will this be at the last day? Yes: I will raise him up at the last day, John 6:39. Ought we to wait for that day? Yes: looking for the blessed hope, and the glorious appearance of the great God and our Savior Jesus Christ, Titus 2:18.

Matthew Henry
A Scripture Catechism in the method of the Assembly's

1.43 THE EXCELLENCY OF CHRIST, JONATHAN EDWARDS

Jonathan Edwards, (October 5, 1703—March 22, 1758), saint and metaphysician, revivalist and theologian, stands out as the one figure of real greatness in the intellectual life of colonial America.

Edwards was no "mute, inglorious Milton," but the most articulate of men. His ontological speculations, on which his title to recognition as a metaphysician mainly rests, belong to his extreme youth, and had been definitely put behind him at an age when most men first begin to probe such problems. It was to theology that he gave his mature years and his most prolonged and searching thought, especially to the problems of sin and salvation. F. J. E. Woodbridge has written of him:

"He was distinctly a great man. He did not merely express the thought of his time, or face it simply in the spirit of his traditions. He stemmed it and molded it. New England thought was already making toward that colorless theology which marked it later. That he checked. It was decidedly Arminian. He made it Calvinistic... His time does not explain him."

Edwards had a remarkable philosophical bent; but he had an even more remarkable sense and taste for divine things and, therefore, as Woodbridge concludes, "we remember him, not as the greatest of American philosophers, but as the greatest of American Calvinists."

Benjamin B. Warfield, Encyclopedia of Religion and Ethics, 1912

"And one of the elders saith unto me, Weep not: behold, the Lion of the tribe of Judah, the Root of David, hath prevailed to open the book, and to loose the seven seals thereof. And I beheld, and, lo, in the midst of the throne, and of the four beasts, and in the midst of the elders, stood a Lamb as it had been slain."

Revelation 5:5-6

INTRODUCTION

The visions and revelations the apostle John had of the future events of God's providence, are here introduced with a vision of the book of God's decrees, by which those events were fore-ordained. This is represented (Revelation 5:1) as a book in the right hand of him who sat on the throne, "written within and on the back side, and sealed with seven seals." Books, in the form in which they were wont of old to be made, were broad leaves of parchment or paper, or something of that nature, joined together at one edge, and so rolled up together, and then sealed, or some way fastened together, to prevent their unfolding and opening. Hence we read of the roll of a book, Jer. 36:2. It seems to have been such a book that John had a vision of here; and therefore it is said to be "written within and on the back side," i.e. on the inside pages, and also on one of the outside pages, namely, that which it was rolled in, in rolling the book up

together. And it is said to be "sealed with seven seals," to signify that what was written in it was perfectly hidden and secret; or that God's decrees of future events are sealed, and shut up from all possibility of being discovered by creatures, till God is pleased to make them known. We find that seven is often used in Scripture as the number of perfection, to signify the superlative or most perfect degree of anything, which probably arose from this, that on the seventh day God beheld the works of creation finished, and rested and rejoiced in them, as being complete and perfect.

When John saw this book, he tells us, he "saw a strong angel proclaiming with a loud voice, Who is worthy to open the book, and to loose the seals thereof? And no man in heaven, nor in earth, neither under the earth, was able to open the book, neither to look thereon." And that he wept much, because "no man was found worthy to open and read the book, neither to look thereon." And then tells us how his tears were dried up, namely, that "one of the elders said unto him, "Weep not, Behold the Lion of the tribe of Judah hath prevailed" etc. as in the text. Though no man nor angel, nor any mere creature, was found either able to loose the seals, or worthy to be admitted to the privilege of reading the book, yet this was declared, for the comfort of this beloved disciple, that Christ was found both able and worthy. And we have an account in the succeeding chapters how he actually did it, opening the seals in order, first one, and then another, revealing what God had decreed should come to pass hereafter. And we have an account in this chapter, of his coming and taking the book out of the right hand of him that sat on the throne, and of the joyful praises that were sung to him in heaven and earth on that occasion.

Many things might be observed in the words of the text; but it is to my present purpose only to take notice of the two distinct appellations here given to Christ.

He is called a Lion. Behold, the Lion of the tribe of Judah. He seems to be called the Lion of the tribe of Judah, in allusion to what Jacob said in his blessing of the tribe on his death-bed; who, when he came to bless Judah, compares him to a lion, Gen. 49:9. "Judah is a lion's whelp; from the prey, my son, thou art gone up: he stooped down, he couched as a lion, and as an old lion; who shall rouse him up?" And also to the standard of the camp of Judah in the wilderness on which was displayed a lion, according to the ancient tradition of the Jews. It is much on account of the valiant acts of David that the tribe of Judah, of which David was, is in Jacob's prophetical blessing compared to a lion; but more especially with an eye to Jesus Christ, who also was of that tribe, and was descended of David, and is in our text called "the Root of David"; and therefore Christ is here called "the Lion of the tribe of Judah."

He is called a Lamb. John was told of a Lion that had prevailed to open the book, and probably expected to see a lion in his vision; but while he is expecting, behold a Lamb appears to open the book, an exceeding diverse kind of creature from a lion. A lion is a devourer, one that is wont to make terrible slaughter of others; and no creature more easily falls a prey to him than a lamb. And Christ is here represented not only as a Lamb, a creature very liable to be slain, but a "Lamb as it had been slain," that is, with the marks of its deadly wounds appearing on it. That which I would observe from the words, for the subject of my present discourse, is this, namely—There is an admirable conjunction of diverse excellencies in Jesus Christ.

The lion and the lamb, though very diverse kinds of creatures, yet have each their peculiar excellencies. The lion excels in strength, and in the majesty of his appearance and voice: the lamb excels in meekness and patience, besides the excellent nature of the creature as good for food, and yielding that which is fit for our clothing and being suitable to be offered in sacrifice to God. But we see that Christ is in the text compared to both, because the diverse excellencies of both wonderfully meet in him—In handling this subject I would

First, Show wherein there is an admirable conjunction of diverse excellencies in Christ.

Second, Show how this admirable conjunction of excellencies appear in Christ's acts.

Third, make application.

PART ONE

First, I would show wherein there is an admirable conjunction of diverse excellencies in Jesus Christ. which appears in three things:

A) There is a conjunction of such excellencies in Christ, as, in our manner of conceiving, are very diverse one from another.

B) There is in him a conjunction of such really diverse excellencies, as otherwise would have seemed to us utterly incompatible in the same subject.

C) Such diverse excellencies are exercised in him towards men that otherwise would have seemed impossible to be exercised towards the same object.

A) There is a conjunction of such excellencies in Christ, as, in our manner of conceiving, are very diverse one from another. Such are the various divine perfections and excellencies that Christ is possessed of. Christ is a divine person, and therefore has all the attributes of God. The difference between these is chiefly relative, and in our manner of conceiving them. And those which, in this sense, are most diverse, meet in the person of Christ. I shall mention two instances.

There do meet in Jesus Christ infinite highness and infinite condescension.

Christ, as he is God, is infinitely great and high above all. He is higher than the kings of the earth; for he is King of kings, and Lord of lords. He is higher than the heavens, and higher than the highest angels of heaven. So great is he, that all men, all kings and princes, are as worms of the dust before him; all nations are as the drop of the bucket, and the light dust of the balance; yea, and angels themselves are as nothing before him. He is so high, that he is infinitely above any need of us; above our reach, that we cannot be profitable to him; and above our conceptions, that we cannot comprehend him. Prov. 30:4, "What is his name, and what is his Son's name, if thou canst tell?" Our understandings, if we stretch them never so far, cannot reach up to his divine glory. Job 11:8, "It is high as heaven, what canst thou do?" Christ is the Creator and great Possessor of heaven and earth. He is sovereign Lord of all. He rules over the whole universe, and doth whatsoever pleaseth him. His knowledge is without bound. His wisdom is perfect, and what none can circumvent. His power is infinite, and none can resist Him. His riches are immense and inexhaustible. His majesty is infinitely awful.

And yet he is one of infinite condescension. None are so low or inferior, but Christ's condescension is sufficient to take a gracious notice of them. He condescends not only to the angels, humbling himself to behold the things that are done in heaven, but he also condescends to such poor creatures as men; and that not only so as to take notice of princes and great men, but of those that are of meanest rank and degree, "the poor of the world," James 2:5. Such as are commonly despised by their fellow creatures, Christ does not despise. 1 Cor. 1:28, "Base things of the world, and things that are despised, hath God chosen." Christ condescends to take notice of

beggars (Luke 16:22) and people of the most despised nations. In Christ Jesus is neither "Barbarian, Scythian, bond nor free" (Col. 3:11). He that is thus high condescends to take a gracious notice of little children. Matt. 19:14, "Suffer little children to come unto me." Yea, which is more, his condescension is sufficient to take a gracious notice of the most unworthy, sinful creatures, those that have no good deservings, and those that have infinite ill deservings.

Yea, so great is his condescension, that it is not only sufficient to take some gracious notice of such as these, but sufficient for every thing that is an act of condescension. His condescension is great enough to become their friend, to become their companion, to unite their souls to him in spiritual marriage. It is enough to take their nature upon him, to become one of them, that he may be one with them. Yea, it is great enough to abase himself yet lower for them, even to expose himself to shame and spitting; yea, to yield up himself to an ignominious death for them. And what act of condescension can be conceived of greater? Yet such an act as this, has his condescension yielded to, for those that are so low and mean, despicable and unworthy!

Such a conjunction of infinite highness and low condescension, in the same person, is admirable. We see, by manifold instances, what a tendency a high station has in men, to make them to be of a quite contrary disposition. If one worm be a little exalted above another, by having more dust, or a bigger dunghill, how much does he make of himself! What a distance does he keep from those that are below him! And a little condescension is what he expects should be made much of, and greatly acknowledged. Christ condescends to wash our feet; but how would great men, (or rather the bigger worms,) account themselves debased by acts of far less condescension!

There meet in Jesus Christ, infinite justice and infinite grace.

As Christ is a divine person, he is infinitely holy and just, hating sin, and disposed to execute condign punishment for sin. He is the Judge of the world, and the infinitely just Judge of it, and will not at all acquit the wicked, or by any means clear the guilty.

And yet he is infinitely gracious and merciful. Though his justice be so strict with respect to all sin, and every breach of the law, yet he has grace sufficient for every sinner, and even the chief of sinners. And it is not only sufficient for the most unworthy to show them mercy, and bestow some good upon them, but to bestow the greatest good; yea, it is sufficient to bestow all good upon them, and to do all things for them. There is no benefit or blessing that they can receive, so great but the grace of Christ is sufficient to bestow it on the greatest sinner that ever lived. And not only so, but so great is his grace, that nothing is too much as the means of this good. It is sufficient not only to do great things, but also to suffer in order to do it, and not only to suffer, but to suffer most extremely even unto death, the most terrible of natural evils; and not only death, but the most ignominious and tormenting, and every way the most terrible that men could inflict; yea, and greater sufferings than men could inflict, who could only torment the body. He had sufferings in his soul, that were the more immediate fruits of the wrath of God against the sins of those he undertakes for.

B) There do meet in the person of Christ such really diverse excellencies, which otherwise would have been thought utterly incompatible in the same subject; such as are conjoined in no other person whatever, either divine, human, or angelical; and such as neither men nor angels would ever have imagined could have met together in the same person, had it not been seen in the person of Christ. I would give some instances.

In the person of Christ do meet together infinite glory and lowest humility.

Infinite glory, and the virtue of humility, meet in no other person but Christ. They meet in no created person; for no created person has infinite glory, and they meet in no other divine person but Christ. For though the divine nature be infinitely abhorrent to pride, yet humility is not properly predicable of God the Father, and the Holy Ghost, that exist only in the divine nature; because it is a

proper excellency only of a created nature; for it consists radically in a sense of a comparative lowness and littleness before God, or the great distance between God and the subject of this virtue; but it would be a contradiction to suppose any such thing in God. But in Jesus Christ, who is both God and man, those two diverse excellencies are sweetly united. He is a person infinitely exalted in glory and dignity. Phil. 2:6, "Being in the form of God, he thought it not robbery to be equal with God" There is equal honor due to him with the Father. John 5:23, "That all men should honor the Son, even as they honor the Father." God himself says to him, "thy throne, O God, is for ever and ever," Heb. 1:8. And there is the same supreme respect and divine worship paid to him by the angels of heaven, as to God the Father, ver. 6. "Let all the angels of God worship him."

But however he is thus above all, yet he is lowest of all in humility. There never was so great an instance of this virtue among either men or angels, as Jesus. None ever was so sensible of the distance between God and him, or had a heart so lowly before God, as the man Christ Jesus, Matt. 11:29. What a wonderful spirit of humility appeared in him, when he was here upon earth, in all his behavior! In his contentment in his mean outward condition, contentedly living in the family of Joseph the carpenter, and Mary his mother, for thirty years together, and afterwards choosing outward meanness, poverty, and contempt, rather than earthly greatness; in his washing his disciples' feet, and in all his speeches and deportment towards them; in his cheerfully sustaining the form of a servant through his whole life, and submitting to such immense humiliation at death!

In the person of Christ do meet together infinite majesty and transcendent meekness.

These again are two qualifications that meet together in no other person but Christ. Meekness, properly so called, is a virtue proper only to the creature: we scarcely ever find meekness mentioned as a divine attribute in Scripture; at least not in the New Testament; for thereby seems to be signified, a calmness and quietness of spirit, arising from humility in mutable beings that are naturally liable to be put into a ruffle by the assaults of a tempestuous and injurious world. But Christ, being both God and man, hath both infinite majesty and superlative meekness. Christ was a person of infinite majesty. It is he that is spoken of, Psalm 45:3. "Gird thy sword upon thy thigh, O most mighty, with thy glory and thy majesty." It is he that is mighty, that rideth on the heavens, and his excellency on the sky. It is he that is terrible out of his holy places; who is mightier than the noise of many waters, yea, than the mighty waves of the sea: before whom a fire goeth, and burneth up his enemies round about; at whose presence the earth quakes, and the hills melt; who sitteth on the circle of the earth, and all the inhabitants thereof are as grasshoppers, who rebukes the sea, and maketh it dry and drieth up the rivers, whose eyes are as a flame of fire, from whose presence, and from the glory of whose power, the wicked shall be punished with everlasting destruction; who is the blessed and only Potentate, the King of kings, and Lord of lords, who hath heaven for his throne, and the earth for his footstool, and is the high and lofty One who inhabits eternity, whose kingdom is an everlasting kingdom, and of whose dominion there is no end.

And yet he was the most marvelous instance of meekness, and humble quietness of spirit, that ever was; agreeable to the prophecies of him, Matthew 21:4f. "All this was done, that it might be fulfilled which was spoken by the prophet, saying, Tell ye the daughter of Sion, Behold, thy King cometh unto thee, meek, and sitting upon an ass, and a colt the foal of an ass." And, agreeable to what Christ declares of himself, Matt. 11:29, "I am meek and lowly in heart." And agreeable to what was manifest in his behavior: for there never was such an instance seen on earth, of a meek behavior, under injuries and reproaches, and towards enemies; who, when he was reviled, reviled not again. He had a wonderful spirit of forgiveness, was ready to forgive his worst enemies, and prayed for them with fervent and effectual prayers. With what meekness did he appear in the ring of soldiers that were contemning and

mocking him; he was silent, and opened not his mouth, but went as a lamb to the slaughter. Thus is Christ a Lion in majesty and a Lamb in meekness.

There meet in the person of Christ the deepest reverence towards God and equality with God.

Christ, when on earth, appeared full of holy reverence towards the Father. He paid the most reverential worship to him, praying to him with postures of reverence. Thus we read of his "kneeling down and praying," Luke 22:41. This became Christ, as one who had taken on him the human nature, but at the same time he existed in the divine nature; whereby his person was in all respects equal to the person of the Father. God the Father hath no attribute or perfection that the Son hath not, in equal degree, and equal glory. These things meet in no other person but Jesus Christ.

There are conjoined in the person of Christ infinite worthiness of good, and the greatest patience under sufferings of evil.

He was perfectly innocent, and deserved no suffering. He deserved nothing from God by any guilt of his own, and he deserved no ill from men. Yea, he was not only harmless and undeserving of suffering, but he was infinitely worthy; worthy of the infinite love of the Father, worthy of infinite and eternal happiness, and infinitely worthy of all possible esteem, love, and service from all men.

And yet he was perfectly patient under the greatest sufferings that ever were endured in this world. Heb. 12:2, "He endured the cross, despising the shame." He suffered not from his Father for his faults, but ours; and he suffered from men not for his faults but for those things on account of which he was infinitely worthy of their love and honor, which made his patience the more wonderful and the more glorious. 1 Pet. 2:20, "For what glory is it, if when ye be buffeted for your faults, ye shall take it patiently, but if when ye do well, and suffer for it, ye take it patiently; this is acceptable with God. For even hereunto were ye called; because Christ also suffered for us, leaving us an example, that we should follow his steps: who did no sin, neither was guile found in his mouth: who when he was reviled, reviled not again, when he suffered, he threatened not, but committed himself to him that judgeth righteously: who his own self bare our sins in his own body on the tree, that we being dead to sin, should live unto righteousness: by whose stripes ye were healed." There is no such conjunction of innocence, worthiness, and patience under sufferings, as in the person of Christ.

In the person of Christ are conjoined an exceeding spirit of obedience, with supreme dominion over heaven and earth.

Christ is the Lord of all things in two respects: he is so, as God-man and Mediator, and thus his dominion is appointed, and given him of the Father. Having it by delegation from God, he is as it were the Father's vicegerent. But he is Lord of all things in another respect, namely, as he is (by his original nature) God; and so he is by natural right the Lord of all, and supreme over all as much as the Father. Thus, he has dominion over the world, not by delegation, but in his own right. He is not an under God, as the Arians suppose, but to all intents and purposes supreme God.

And yet in the same person is found the greatest spirit of obedience to the commands and laws of God that ever was in the universe; which was manifest in his obedience here in this world. John 14:31, "As the Father gave me commandment, even so I do." John 15:10, "Even as I have kept my Father's commandments, and abide in his love." The greatness of his obedience appears in its perfection, and in his obeying commands of such exceeding difficulty. Never any one received commands from God of such difficulty, and that were so great a trial of obedience, as Jesus Christ. One of God's commands to him was, that he should yield himself to those dreadful sufferings that he underwent. See John 10:18. "No man taketh it from me, but I lay it down of myself." "This commandment received I of my Father." And Christ was thoroughly obedient to this command of God. Heb. 5:8, "Though he were a Son, yet he learned obedience by the things that he suffered." Philip. 2:8, "He humbled himself, and became obedient unto death, even the death of the cross." Never was

there such an instance of obedience in man or angel as this, though he was at the same time supreme Lord of both angels and men.

In the person of Christ are conjoined absolute sovereignty and perfect resignation.

This is another unparalleled conjunction. Christ, as he is God, is the absolute sovereign of the world, the sovereign disposer of all events. The decrees of God are all his sovereign decrees; and the work of creation, and all God's works of providence, are his sovereign works. It is he that worketh all things according to the counsel of his own will. Col. 1:16, "By him, and through him, and to him, are all things." John 5:17, "The Father worketh hitherto, and I work." Matt. 8:3, "I will, be thou clean."

But yet Christ was the most wonderful instance of resignation that ever appeared in the world. He was absolutely and perfectly resigned when he had a near and immediate prospect of his terrible sufferings, and the dreadful cup that he was to drink. The idea and expectation of this made his soul exceeding sorrowful even unto death, and put him into such an agony, that his sweat was as it were great drops or clots of blood, falling down to the ground. But in such circumstances he was wholly resigned to the will of God. Matt. 26:39, "O my Father, if it be possible, let this cup pass from me: nevertheless, not as I will, but as thou wilt." Verse 42, "O my Father, if this cup may not pass from me, except I drink it, thy will be done."

In Christ do meet together self-sufficiency, and an entire trust and reliance on God, which is another conjunction peculiar to the person of Christ.

As he is a divine person, he is self-sufficient, standing in need of nothing. All creatures are dependent on him, but he is dependent on none, but is absolutely independent. His proceeding from the Father, in his eternal generation, argues no proper dependence on the will of the Father; for that proceeding was natural and necessary, and not arbitrary.

But yet Christ entirely trusted in God:— his enemies say that of him, "He trusted in God that he would deliver him," Matt. 27:43.

And the apostle testifies, I Pet. 2:23, "That he committed himself God."

C) Such diverse excellencies are expressed in him towards men, that otherwise would have seemed impossible to be exercised towards the same object; as particularly these three, justice, mercy, and truth. The same that are mentioned in Psalm 85:10. "Mercy and truth are met together, righteousness and peace have kissed each other."

The strict justice of God, and even his revenging justice, and that against the sins of men, never was so gloriously manifested as in Christ. He manifested an infinite regard to the attribute of God's justice, in that, when he had a mind to save sinners, he was willing to undergo such extreme sufferings, rather than that their salvation should be to the injury of the honor of that attribute. And as he is the Judge of the world, he doth himself exercise strict justice, he will not clear the guilty, nor at all acquit the wicked in judgment.

Yet how wonderfully is infinite mercy towards sinners displayed in him! And what glorious and ineffable grace and love have been and are exercised by him, towards sinful men! Though he be the just Judge of a sinful world, yet he is also the Savior of the world. Though he be a consuming fire to sin, yet he is the light and life of sinners. Rom. 3:25-26, "Whom God hath set forth to be a propitiation, through faith in his blood, to declare his righteousness for the remission of sins that are past, through the forbearance of God; to declare, I say, at this time his righteousness, that he might be just, and the justifier of him which believeth in Jesus."

So the immutable truth of God, in the threatenings of his law against the sins of men, was never so manifested as it is in Jesus Christ, for there never was any other so great a trial of the unalterableness of the truth of God in those threatenings, as when sin came to be imputed to his own Son. And then in Christ has been seen already an actual complete accomplishment of those threatenings, which never has been nor will be seen in any other instance; because the eternity that will be taken up in fulfilling those threatenings on others, never will be finished. Christ

manifested an infinite regard to this truth of God in his sufferings. And, in his judging the world, he makes the covenant of works, that contains those dreadful threatenings, his rule of judgment. He will see to it, that it is not infringed in the least jot or tittle: he will do nothing contrary to the threatenings of the law, and their complete fulfillment. And yet in him we have many great and precious promises, promises of perfect deliverance from the penalty of the law. And this is the promise that he hath promised us, even eternal life. And in him are all the promises of God yea, and Amen.

PART TWO

Having thus shown wherein there is an admirable conjunction of excellencies in Jesus Christ, I now proceed, secondly, to show how this admirable conjunction of excellencies appears in Christ's acts:

A) in his taking of human nature,

B) in his earthly life,

C) in his sacrificial death,

D) in his exaltation in heaven,

E) in his final subduing of all evil when he returns in glory.

A) It appears in what Christ did in taking on him our nature.

In this act, his infinite condescension wonderfully appeared, That he who was God should become man; that the word should be made flesh, and should take on him a nature infinitely below his original nature! And it appears yet more remarkably in the low circumstances of his incarnation: he was conceived in the womb of a poor young woman, whose poverty appeared in this, when she came to offer sacrifices of her purification, she brought what was allowed of in the law only in case of poverty, as Luke 2:24. "According to what is said in the law of the Lord, a pair of turtle-doves, or two young pigeons." This was allowed only in case the person was so poor that she was not able to offer a lamb, Lev. 12:8.

And though his infinite condescension thus appeared in the manner of his incarnation, yet his divine dignity also appeared in it; for though he was conceived in the womb of a poor virgin, yet he was conceived there by the power of the Holy Ghost. And his divine dignity also appeared in the holiness of his conception and birth. Though he was conceived in the womb of one of the corrupt race of mankind, yet he was conceived and born without sin; as the angel said to the blessed Virgin, Luke 1:35. "The Holy Ghost shall come upon thee, and the power of the Highest shall overshadow thee, therefore also that holy thing which shall be born of thee, shall be called the Son of God."

His infinite condescension marvelously appeared in the manner of his birth. He was brought forth in a stable because there was no room for them in the inn. The inn was taken up by others, that were looked upon as persons of greater account. The Blessed Virgin, being poor and despised, was turned or shut out. Though she was in such necessitous circumstances, yet those that counted themselves her betters would not give place to her; and therefore, in the time of her travail, she was forced to betake herself to a stable; and when the child was born, it was wrapped in swaddling clothes, and laid in a manger. There Christ lay a little infant, and there he eminently appeared as a lamb.

But yet this feeble infant, born thus in a stable, and laid in a manger, was born to conquer and triumph over Satan, that roaring lion. He came to subdue the mighty powers of darkness, and make a show of them openly, and so to restore peace on earth, and to manifest God's good-will towards men, and to bring glory to God in the highest, according as the end of his birth was declared by the joyful songs of the glorious hosts of angels appearing to the shepherds at the same time that the infant lay in the manger; whereby his divine dignity was manifested.

B) This admirable conjunction of excellencies appears in the acts and various passages of Christ's life.

Though Christ dwelt in mean outward circumstances, whereby his condescension and humility especially appeared, and his majesty was veiled; yet his divine divinity and glory did in many of his acts shine through the veil, and it illustriously appeared, that he was not only the Son of man, but the great God.

Thus, in the circumstances of his infancy, his outward meanness appeared; yet there was something then to show forth his divine dignity, in the wise men's being stirred up to come from the east to give honor to him their being led by a miraculous star, and coming and falling down and worshipping him, and presenting him with gold, frankincense, and myrrh. His humility and meekness wonderfully appeared in his subjection to his mother and reputed father when he was a child. Herein he appeared as a lamb. But his divine glory broke forth and shone when, at twelve years old, he disputed with doctors in the temple. In that he appeared, in some measure, as the Lion of the tribe of Judah.

And so, after he entered on his public ministry, his marvelous humility and meekness was manifested in his choosing to appear in such mean outward circumstances; and in being contented in them, when he was so poor that he had not where to lay his head, and depended on the charity of some of his followers for his subsistence, as appears by Luke 8, at the beginning. How meek, condescending, and familiar his treatment of his disciples; his discourses with them, treating them as a father his children, yea, as friends and companions. How patient, bearing such affliction and reproach, and so many injuries from the scribes and Pharisees, and others. In these things he appeared as a Lamb.

And yet he at the same time did in many ways show forth his divine majesty and glory, particularly in the miracles he wrought, which were evidently divine works, and manifested omnipotent power, and so declared him to be the Lion of the tribe of Judah. His wonderful and miraculous works plainly showed him to be the God of nature; in that it appeared by them that he had all nature in his hands, and could lay an arrest upon it, and stop and change its course as he pleased. In healing the sick, and opening the eyes of the blind, and unstopping the ears of the deaf, and healing the lame, he showed that he was the God that framed the eye, and created the ear, and was the author of the frame of man's body. By the dead rising at his command, it appeared that he was the author and fountain of life, and that "God the Lord, to whom belong the issues from death." By his walking on the sea in a storm, when the waves were raised, he showed himself to be that God spoken of in Job 9:8. "That treadeth on the waves of the sea." By his stilling the storm, and calming the rage of the sea, by his powerful command, saying, "Peace, be still," he showed that he has the command of the universe, and that he is that God who brings things to pass by the word of his power, who speaks and it is done, who commands and it stands fast; Psalm 115:7. "Who stilleth the noise of the seas, the noise of their waves." And Psalm 107:29, "That maketh the storm a calm, so that the waves thereof are still." And Psalm 89:8, 9, "O Lord God of hosts, who is a strong Lord like unto thee, or to thy faithfulness round about thee? Thou rulest the raging of the sea: when the waves thereof arise, thou stillest them." Christ, by casting out devils, remarkably appeared as the Lion of the tribe of Judah, and showed that he was stronger than the roaring lion, that seizes whom he may devour. He commanded them to come out, and they were forced to obey. They were terribly afraid of him; they fall down before him, and beseech him not so torment them. He forces a whole legion of them to forsake their hold, by his powerful word; and they could not so much as enter into the swine without his leave. He showed the glory of his omniscience, by telling the thoughts of men; as we have often an account. Herein he appeared to be that God spoken of, Amos 4:13. "That declareth unto man what is his thought." Thus, in the midst of his meanness and humiliation, his divine glory appeared in his miracles, John 2:11. "This beginning of miracles did Jesus in Cana of Galilee, and manifested forth his glory."

And though Christ ordinarily appeared without outward glory, and in great obscurity, yet at a certain time he threw off the veil, and appeared in his divine majesty, so far as it could be outwardly manifested to men in this frail state, when he was transfigured in the mount. The apostle Peter, 2 Pet. 1:16, 17, was an "eye-witness of his majesty, when he received from God the Father honor and glory, when there came such a voice to him from the excellent glory, This is my beloved Son, in whom I am well pleased; which voice that came from heaven they heard, when they were with him in the holy mount."

And at the same time that Christ was wont to appear in such meekness, condescension, and humility, in his familiar discourses with his disciples, appearing therein as the Lamb of God; he was also wont to appear as The Lion of the tribe of Judah, with divine authority and majesty, in his so sharply rebuking the scribes and Pharisees, and other hypocrites.

C) This admirable conjunction of excellencies remarkably appears in his offering up himself a sacrifice for sinners in his last sufferings.

As this was the greatest thing in all the works of redemption, the greatest act of Christ in that work; so in this act especially does there appear that admirable conjunction of excellencies that has been spoken of. Christ never so much appeared as a lamb, as when he was slain: "He came like a lamb to the slaughter," Isaiah 53:7. Then he was offered up to God as a lamb without blemish, and without spot: then especially did he appear to be the anti-type of the lamb of the Passover: 1 Cor 5:7. "Christ our Passover sacrificed for us." And yet in that act he did in an especial manner appear as the Lion of the tribe of Judah; yea, in this above all other acts, in many respects, as may appear in the following things.

Then was Christ in the greatest degree of his humiliation, and yet by that, above all other things, his divine glory appears. Christ's humiliation was great, in being born in such a low condition, of a poor virgin, and in a stable. His humiliation was great, in being subject to Joseph the carpenter, and Mary his mother, and afterwards living in poverty, so as not to have where to lay his head; and in suffering such manifold and bitter reproaches as he suffered, while he went about preaching and working miracles. But his humiliation was never so great as it was, in his last sufferings, beginning with his agony in the garden, till he expired on the cross. Never was he subject to such ignominy as then, never did he suffer so much pain in his body, or so much sorrow in his soul; never was he in so great an exercise of his condescension, humility, meekness, and patience, as he was in these last sufferings; never was his divine glory and majesty covered with so thick and dark a veil; never did he so empty himself and make himself of no reputation, as at this time.

And yet, never was his divine glory so manifested, by any act of his, as in yielding himself up to these sufferings. When the fruit of it came to appear, and the mystery and ends of it to be unfolded in its issue, then did the glory of it appear, then did it appear as the most glorious act of Christ that ever he exercised towards the creature. This act of his is celebrated by the angels and hosts of heaven with peculiar praises, as that which is above all others glorious, as you may see in the context, (Revelation 5:9-12) "And they sang a new song, saying, Thou art worthy to take the book, and to open the seals thereof: for thou wast slain and hast redeemed us to God by thy blood, out of every kindred, and tongue, and people, and nation; and hast made us unto our God kings and priests: and we shall reign on the earth. And I beheld, and I heard the voice of many angels round about the throne, and the beasts, and the elders: and the number of them was ten thousand times ten thousand, and thousands of thousands, saying with a loud voice Worthy is the Lamb that was slain, to receive power, and riches, and wisdom, and strength, and honor, and glory, and blessing."

He never in any act gave so great a manifestation of love to God, and yet never so manifested his love to those that were enemies to God, as in that act. Christ never did any thing whereby his love to the Father was so eminently manifested, as in his laying down his life, under such inexpressible sufferings, in obedience to his command and for the vindication of the honor of his authority and majesty; nor did ever any mere creature give such a testimony of love to God as that was.

And yet this was the greatest expression of his love to sinful men who were enemies to God; Rom. 5:10. "When we were enemies, we were reconciled to God, by the death of his Son." The greatness of Christ's love to such, appears in nothing so much as in its being dying love. That blood of Christ which fell in great drops to the ground, in his agony, was shed from love to God's enemies, and his own. That shame and spitting, that torment of body, and that exceeding sorrow, even unto death, which he endured in his soul, was what he underwent from love to rebels against God to save them from hell, and to purchase for them eternal glory. Never did Christ so eminently show his regard to God's honor, as in offering up himself a victim to Justice. And yet in this above all, he manifested his love to them who dishonored God, so as to bring such guilt on themselves, that nothing less than his blood could atone for it.

Christ never so eminently appeared for divine justice, and yet never suffered so much from divine Justice, as when he offered up himself a sacrifice for our sins. In Christ's great sufferings did his infinite regard to the honor of God's justice distinguishingly appear, for it was from regard to that that he thus humbled himself.

And yet in these sufferings, Christ was the target of the vindictive expressions of that very justice of God. Revenging justice then spent all its force upon him, on account of our guilt; which made him sweat blood, and cry out upon the cross, and probably rent his vitals— broke his heart, the fountain of blood, or some other blood vessels—and by the violent fermentation turned his blood to water. For the blood and water that issued out of his side, when pierced by the spear, seems to have been extravasated blood, and so there might be a kind of literal fulfillment of Psalm 22:14, "I am poured out like water, and all my bones are out of joint: my heart is like wax, it is melted in the midst of my bowels." And this was the way and means by which Christ stood up for the honor of God's justice, namely, by thus suffering its terrible executions. For when he had undertaken for sinners, and had substituted himself in their room, divine justice could have its due honor no other way than by his suffering its revenges.

In this the diverse excellencies that met in the person of Christ appeared, namely, his infinite regard to God's justice, and such love to those that have exposed themselves to it, as induced him thus to yield himself a sacrifice to it.

Christ's holiness never so illustriously shone forth as it did in his last sufferings, and yet he never was to such a degree treated as guilty. Christ's holiness never had such a trial as it had then, and therefore never had so great a manifestation. When it was tried in this furnace it came forth as gold, or as silver purified seven times. His holiness then above all appeared in his steadfast pursuit of the honor of God, and in his obedience to him. For his yielding himself unto death was transcendently the greatest act of obedience that ever was paid to God by any one since the foundation of the world.

And yet then Christ was in the greatest degree treated as a wicked person would have been. He was apprehended and bound as a malefactor. His accusers represented him as a most wicked wretch. In his sufferings before his crucifixion, he was treated as if he had been the worst and vilest of mankind, and then, he was put to a kind of death, that none but the worst sort of malefactors were wont to suffer, those that were most abject in their persons, and guilty of the blackest crimes. And he suffered as though guilty from God himself, by reason of our guilt imputed to him; for he who knew no sin, was made sin for us; he was made subject to wrath, as if he had been sinful himself. He was made a curse for us.

Christ never so greatly manifested his hatred of sin, as against God, as in his dying to take away the dishonor that sin had done to God; and yet never was he to such a degree subject to the terrible effects of God's hatred of sin, and wrath against it, as he was then. in this appears those diverse excellencies meeting in Christ, namely, love to God, and grace to sinners.

He never was so dealt with, as unworthy, as in his last sufferings, and yet it is chiefly on account of them that he is accounted worthy. He was therein dealt with as if he had not been worthy to live: they cry out, "Away with him! away with him! Crucify him." John 19:15. And they prefer Barabbas before him. And he suffered from the Father, as one whose demerits were infinite, by reason of our demerits that were laid upon him.

And yet it was especially by that act of his subjecting himself to those sufferings that he merited, and on the account of which chiefly he was accounted worthy of the glory of his exaltation. Philip. 2:8, 9, "He humbled himself, and became obedient unto death; wherefore God hath highly exalted him." And we see that it is on this account chiefly, that he is extolled as worthy by saints and angels in the context: "Worthy," say they, "is the Lamb that was slain." This shows an admirable conjunction in him of infinite dignity, and infinite condescension and love to the infinitely unworthy.

Christ in his last sufferings suffered most extremely from those towards whom he was then manifesting his greatest act of love. He never suffered so much from his Father, (though not from any hatred to him, but from hatred to our sins,) for he then forsook him, or took away the comforts of his presence; and then "it pleased the Lord to bruise him, and put him to grief," as Isaiah 53:10. And yet he never gave so great a manifestation of love to God as then, as has been already observed.

So Christ never suffered so much from the hands of men as he did then; and yet never was in so high an exercise of love to men. He never was so ill treated by his disciples; who were so unconcerned about his sufferings, that they would not watch with him one hour, in his agony; and when he was apprehended, all forsook him and fled, except Peter, who denied him with oaths and curses. And yet then he was suffering, shedding his blood, and pouring out his soul unto death for them. Yea, he probably was then shedding his blood for some of them that shed his blood, for whom he prayed while they were crucifying him; and who were probably afterwards brought home to Christ by Peter's preaching. (Compare Luke 23:34; Acts 2:23, 36, 37, 41. and chap. 3:17, and chap. 4.) This shows an admirable meeting of justice and grace in the redemption of Christ.

It was in Christ's last sufferings, above all, that he was delivered up to the power of his enemies; and yet by these, above all, he obtained victory over his enemies. Christ never was so in his enemies' hands, as in the time of his last sufferings. They sought his life before; but from time to time they were restrained, and Christ escaped out of their hands, and this reason is given for it, that his time was not yet come. But now they were suffered to work their will upon him, he was in a great degree delivered up to the malice and cruelty of both wicked men and devils. And therefore when Christ's enemies came to apprehend him, he says to them, Luke 22:53. "When I was daily with you in the temple ye stretched forth no hand against me: but this is your hour, and the power of darkness."

And yet it was principally by means of those sufferings that he conquered and overthrew his enemies. Christ never so effectually bruised Satan's head, as when Satan bruised his heel. The weapon with which Christ warred against the devil, and obtained a most complete victory and glorious triumph over him, was the cross, the instrument and weapon with which he thought he had overthrown Christ, and brought on him shameful destruction. Col. 2:14, 15, "Blotting out the handwriting of ordinances,—nailing it to his cross: and having spoiled principalities and powers, he made a show of them openly, triumphing over them in it." In his last sufferings, Christ sapped the very foundations of Satan's kingdom, he conquered his enemies in their own territories, and beat them with their own weapons as David cut off Goliath's head with his own sword. The devil had, as it were, swallowed up Christ, as the whale did Jonah—but it was deadly poison to him, he gave him a mortal wound in his own bowels. He was soon sick of his morsel, and was forced to do by him as the whale did by Jonah. To this day he is heart-sick of what he then swallowed as his prey. In those sufferings of Christ was laid the foundation of all that glorious victory he has already obtained over Satan, in the overthrow of his heathenish kingdom in the Roman empire, and all the success the gospel has had since; and also of all his future and still more glorious victory that is to be obtained in the earth. Thus Samson's riddle is most eminently fulfilled, Judges 14:14. "Out of the eater came forth meat, and out of the strong came forth sweetness." And

thus the true Samson does more towards the destruction of his enemies at his death than in his life, in yielding up himself to death, he pulls down the temple of Dagon, and destroys many thousands of his enemies, even while they are making themselves sport in his sufferings—and so he whose type was the ark, pulls down Dagon, and breaks off his head and hands in his own temple, even while he is brought in there as Dagon's captive. (1 Samuel 5:1-4)

Thus Christ appeared at the same time, and in the same act, as both a lion and a lamb. He appeared as a lamb in the hands of his cruel enemies; as a lamb in the paws, and between the devouring jaws, of a roaring lion; yea, he was a lamb actually slain by this lion: and yet at the same time, as the Lion of the tribe of Judah, he conquers and triumphs over Satan; destroying his own destroyer; as Samson did the lion that roared upon him, when he rent him as he would a kid. And in nothing has Christ appeared so much as a lion, in glorious strength destroying his enemies, as when he was brought as a lamb to the slaughter. In his greatest weakness he was most strong; and when he suffered most from his enemies, he brought the greatest confusion on his enemies.

Thus this admirable conjunction of diverse excellencies was manifest in Christ, in his offering up himself to God in his last sufferings.

D) It is still manifest in his acts, in his present state of exaltation in heaven.

Indeed, in his exalted state, he most eminently appears in manifestation of those excellencies, on the account of which he is compared to a lion; but still he appears as a lamb; Rev. 14:1. "And I looked, and lo, a Lamb stood on mount Sion;" as in his state of humiliation he chiefly appeared as a lamb, and yet did not appear without manifestation of his divine majesty and power, as the Lion of the tribe of Judah. Though Christ be now at the right-hand of God, exalted as King of heaven, and Lord of the universe; yet as he still is in the human nature, he still excels in humility. Though the man Christ Jesus be the highest of all creatures in heaven, yet he as much excels them all in humility as he doth in glory and dignity, for none sees so much of the distance between God and him as he does. And though he now appears in such glorious majesty and dominion in heaven, yet he appears as a lamb in his condescending, mild, and sweet treatment of his saints there, for he is a Lamb still, even amidst the throne of his exaltation, and he that is the Shepherd of the whole flock is himself a Lamb, and goes before them in heaven as such. Rev. 7:17, "For the Lamb, which is in the midst of the throne, shall feed them, and shall lead them unto living fountains of waters, and God shall wipe away all tears from their eyes." Though in heaven every knee bows to him, and though the angels fall down before him adoring him, yet he treats his saints with infinite condescension, mildness, and endearment. And in his acts towards the saints on earth, he still appears as a lamb, manifesting exceeding love and tenderness in his intercession for them, as one that has had experience of affliction and temptation. He has not forgot what these things are, nor has he forgot how to pity those that are subject to them. And he still manifests his lamb-like excellencies, in his dealings with his saints on earth, in admirable forbearance, love, gentleness, and compassion. Behold him instructing, supplying, supporting, and comforting them; often coming to them, and manifesting himself to them by his Spirit, that he may sup with them, and they with him. Behold him admitting them to sweet communion, enabling them with boldness and confidence to come to him, and solacing their hearts. And in heaven Christ still appears, as it were, with the marks of his wounds upon him, and so appears as a Lamb as it had been slain, as he was represented in vision to St John, in the text, when he appeared to open the book sealed with seven seals, which is part of the glory of his exaltation.

E) And lastly, this admirable conjunction of excellencies will be manifest in Christ's acts at the last judgment.

He then, above all other times, will appear as the Lion of the tribe of Judah in infinite greatness and majesty, when he shall come in the glory of his Father, with all the holy angels, and the earth shall tremble before him, and the hills shall melt. This is he (Rev. 20:11) "that shall sit on a great white throne, before whose face the earth and heaven shall flee away." He will then appear in the most dreadful and amazing manner to the wicked. The devils tremble at the thought of that appearance, and when it shall be, the kings, and the great men, and the rich men, and the chief captains and the mighty men, and every bond-man and every free-man, shall hide themselves in the dens, and in the rocks of the mountains, and shall cry to the mountains and rocks to fall on them, to hide them from the face and wrath of the Lamb. And none can declare or conceive of the amazing manifestations of wrath in which he will then appear towards these, or the trembling and astonishment the shrieking and gnashing of teeth, with which they shall stand before his judgment-seat, and receive the terrible sentence of his wrath.

And yet he will at the same time appear as a Lamb to his saints; he will receive them as friends and brethren, treating them with infinite mildness and love. There shall be nothing in him terrible to them, but towards them he will clothe himself wholly with sweetness and endearment. The church shall be then admitted to him as his bride; that shall be her wedding-day. The saints shall all be sweetly invited to come with him to inherit the kingdom, and reign in it with him to all eternity.

PART THREE

I would now show how the aforesaid teaching is of benefit to us, in that:

A) it gives us insight into the names of Christ in Scripture,

B) it encourages us to accept him as our Savior,

C) it encourages us to accept him as our Friend.

A) From this doctrine we may learn one reason why Christ is called by such a variety of names, and held forth under such a variety of representations, in Scripture. It is the better to signify and exhibit to us that variety of excellencies that meet together and are conjoined in him. Many appellations are mentioned together in one verse, Isaiah 9:6. "For unto us a Child is born, unto us a Son is given, and the government shall be upon his shoulder: and his name shall be called Wonderful, Counselor, the mighty God, the everlasting Father, the Prince of Peace." It shows a wonderful conjunction of excellencies, that the same person should be a Son, born and given, and yet be the everlasting Father, without beginning or end, that he should be a Child, and yet be he whose name is Counselor, and the mighty God; and well may his name, in whom such things are conjoined, be called wonderful.

By reason of the same wonderful conjunction, Christ is represented by a great variety of sensible things, that are on some account excellent. Thus in some places he is called a Sun, as Mal. 4:2, in others a Star, Num. 24:17. And he is especially represented by the Morning star, as being that which excels all other stars in brightness, and is the forerunner of the day, Rev. 22:16. And, as in our text, he is compared to a lion in one verse, and a lamb in the next, so sometimes he is compared to a roe or young hart, another creature most diverse from a lion. So in some places he is called a rock, in others he is compared to a pearl. In some places he is called a man of war, and the Captain of our Salvation, in other places he is represented as a bridegroom. In the second chapter of Canticles, the first verse, he is compared to a rose and a lily, that are sweet and beautiful flowers; in the next verse but one, he is compared to a tree bearing sweet fruit. In Isaiah 53:2 he is called a Root out of a dry ground; but elsewhere, instead of that, he is called the Tree of Life, that grows (not in a dry or barren ground, but) "in the midst of the paradise of God," Rev. 2:7.

B) Let the consideration of this wonderful meeting of diverse excellencies in Christ induce you to accept of him, and close with him as your Savior. As all manner of excellencies meet in him, so there are concurring in him all manner of arguments and motives, to move you to choose him for your Savior, and every thing that tends to encourage poor sinners to come and put their trust in him: his fullness and all-sufficiency as a Savior gloriously appear in that variety of excellencies that has been spoken of.

Fallen man is in a state of exceeding great misery, and is helpless in it; he is a poor weak creature, like an infant cast out in its blood in the day that it is born. But Christ is the lion of the tribe of Judah; he is strong, though we are weak; he hath prevailed to do that for us which no creature else could do. Fallen man is a mean despicable creature, a contemptible worm; but Christ, who has undertaken for us, is infinitely honorable and worthy. Fallen man is polluted, but Christ is infinitely holy; fallen man is hateful, but Christ is infinitely lovely; fallen man is the object of God's indignation, but Christ is infinitely dear to him. We have dreadfully provoked God, but Christ has performed that righteousness which is infinitely precious in God's eyes.

And here is not only infinite strength and infinite worthiness, but infinite condescension, and love and mercy, as great as power and dignity. If you are a poor, distressed sinner, whose heart is ready to sink for fear that God never will have mercy on you, you need not be afraid to go to Christ, for fear that he is either unable or unwilling to help you. Here is a strong foundation, and an inexhaustible treasure, to answer the necessities of your poor soul, and here is infinite grace and gentleness to invite and embolden a poor, unworthy, fearful soul to come to it. If Christ accepts of you, you need not fear but that you will be safe, for he is a strong Lion for your defense. And if you come, you need not fear but that you shall be accepted; for he is like a Lamb to all that come to him, and receives then with infinite grace and tenderness. It is true he has awful majesty, he is the great God, and infinitely high above you; but there is this to encourage and embolden the poor sinner, that Christ is man as well as God; he is a creature, as well as the Creator, and he is the most humble and lowly in heart of any creature in heaven or earth. This may well make the poor unworthy creature bold in coming to him. You need not hesitate one moment; but may run to him, and cast yourself upon him. You will certainly be graciously and meekly received by him. Though he is a lion, he will only be a lion to your enemies, but he will be a lamb to you. It could not have been conceived, had it not been so in the person of Christ, that there could have been so much in any Savior, that is inviting and tending to encourage sinners to trust in him. Whatever your circumstances are, you need not be afraid to come to such a Savior as this. Be you never so wicked a creature, here is worthiness enough; be you never so poor, and mean, and ignorant a creature, there is no danger of being despised, for though he be so much greater than you, he is also immensely more humble than you. Any one of you that is a father or mother, will not despise one of your own children that comes to you in distress: much less danger is there of Christ's despising you, if you in your heart come to him.

Here let me a little expostulate with the poor, burdened, distressed soul.

What are you afraid of, that you dare not venture your soul upon Christ? Are you afraid that he cannot save you, that he is not strong enough to conquer the enemies of your soul? But how can you desire one stronger than "the almighty God"? as Christ is called, Is. 9:6. Is there need of greater than infinite strength? Are you afraid that he will not be willing to stoop so low as to take any gracious notice of you? But then, look on him, as he stood in the ring of soldiers, exposing his blessed face to be buffeted and spit upon by them! Behold him bound with his back uncovered to those that smote him! And behold him hanging on the cross! Do you think that he that had condescension enough to stoop to these things, and that for his crucifiers, will be unwilling to accept of you, if you come to him? Or, are you afraid that if he does accept you, that God the Father will not accept of him for you? But consider, will God reject his own Son, in whom his infinite delight is, and has been, from all eternity, and who is so united to him, that if he should reject him he would reject himself? What is there that you can desire should be in a Savior, that is not in Christ? Or, wherein should you desire a Savior should be otherwise than Christ is? What excellency is there wanting? What is there that

is great or good; what is there that is venerable or winning; what is there that is adorable or endearing; or, what can you think of that would be encouraging, which is not to be found in the person of Christ? Would you have your Savior to be great and honorable, because you are not willing to be beholden to a mean person? And, is not Christ a person honorable enough to be worthy that you should be dependent on him? Is he not a person high enough to be appointed to so honorable a work as your salvation? Would you not only have a Savior of high degree, but would you have him, notwithstanding his exaltation and dignity, to be made also of low degree, that he might have experience of afflictions and trials, that he might learn by the things that he has suffered, to pity them that suffer and are tempted? And has not Christ been made low enough for you? and has he not suffered enough? Would you not only have him possess experience of the afflictions you now suffer, but also of that amazing wrath that you fear hereafter, that he may know how to pity those that are in danger, and afraid of it? This Christ has had experience of, which experience gave him a greater sense of it, a thousand times, than you have, or any man living has. Would you have your Savior to be one who is near to God, that so his mediation might be prevalent with him? And can you desire him to be nearer to God than Christ is, who is his only-begotten Son, of the same essence with the Father? And would you not only have him near to God, but also near to you, that you may have free access to him? And would you have him nearer to you than to be in the same nature, united to you by a spiritual union, so close as to be fitly represented by the union of the wife to the husband, of the branch to the vine, of the member to the head; yea, so as to be one spirit? For so he will be united to you, if you accept of him. Would you have a Savior that has given some great and extraordinary testimony of mercy and love to sinners, by something that he has done, as well as by what he says? And can you think or conceive of greater things than Christ has done? Was it not a great thing for him, who was God, to take upon him human nature: to be not only

God, but man thenceforward to all eternity? But would you look upon suffering for sinners to be a yet greater testimony of love to sinners, than merely doing, though it be ever so extraordinary a thing that he has done? And would you desire that a Savior should suffer more than Christ has suffered for sinners? What is there wanting, or what would you add if you could, to make him more fit to be your Savior?

But further, to induce you to accept of Christ as your Savior, consider two things particularly. How much Christ appears as the Lamb of God in his invitations to you to come to him and trust in him. With what sweet grace and kindness does he, from time to time, call and invite you, as Prov. 8:4. "Unto you, O men, I call, and my voice is to the sons of men." And Isaiah 55:1-3, "Ho, every one that thirsteth, come ye to the waters, and he that hath no money, come ye, buy and eat—yea come, buy wine and milk without money, and without price." How gracious is he here in inviting every one that thirsts, and in so repeating his invitation over and over, "Come ye to the waters, come, buy and eat yea come!" Mark the excellency of that entertainment which he invites you to accept of; "Come, buy wine and milk!" Your poverty, having nothing to pay for it, shall be no objection, "Come, he that hath no money, come without money, and without price!" What gracious arguments and expostulations he uses with you! " Wherefore do ye spend money for that which is not bread? and your labor for that which satisfieth not? Hearken diligently unto me, and eat ye that which is good, and let your soul delight itself in fatness." As much as to say, It is altogether needless for you to continue laboring and toiling for that which can never serve your turn, seeking rest in the world, and in your own righteousness—I have made abundant provision for you, of that which is really good, and will fully satisfy your desires, and answer your end, and I stand ready to accept of you: you need not be afraid; If you will come to me, I will engage to see all your wants supplied, and you made a happy creature. As he promises in the third verse, "Incline your ear, and come unto me: Hear, and your soul

shall live, and I will make an everlasting covenant with you, even the sure mercies of David." And so Prov. 9 at the beginning. How gracious and sweet is the invitation there! "Whoso is simple, let him turn in hither." Let you be never so poor, ignorant, and blind a creature, you shall be welcome. And in the following words Christ sets forth the provision that he has made for you, "Come, eat of my bread, and drink of the wine which I have mingled." You are in a poor famishing state, and have nothing wherewith to feed your perishing soul; you have been seeking something, but yet remain destitute. Hearken, how Christ calls you to eat of his bread, and to drink of the wine that he hath mingled! And how much like a lamb does Christ appear in Matt. 9:28-30. "Come unto me, all ye that labor and are heavy laden, and I will give you rest. Take my yoke upon you, and learn of me, for I am meek and lowly in heart, and ye shall find rest to your souls. For my yoke is easy, and my burden is light." O thou poor distressed soul! whoever thou art, consider that Christ mentions thy very case when he calls to them who labor and are heavy laden! How he repeatedly promises you rest if you come to him! In the 28th verse he says, " I will give you rest." And in the 29th verse, "Ye shall find rest to your souls." This is what you want. This is the thing you have been so long in vain seeking after. O how sweet would rest be to you, if you could but obtain it! Come to Christ, and you shall obtain it. And hear how Christ, to encourage you, represents himself as a lamb! He tells you, that he is meek and lowly in heart, and are you afraid to come to such a one! And again, Rev. 3:20, "Behold, I stand at the door and knock: if any man hear my voice, and open the door, I will come in to him, and I will sup with him and he with me." Christ condescends not only to call you to him, but he comes to you; he comes to your door, and there knocks. He might send an officer and seize you as a rebel and vile malefactor, but instead of that, he comes and knocks at your door, and seeks that you would receive him into your house, as your Friend and Savior. And he not only knocks at your door, but he stands there waiting, while you are backward and unwilling. And not only so, but he makes promises what he will do for you, if you will admit him, what privileges he will admit you to; he will sup with you, and you with him. And again, Rev. 22:16, 17, "I am the root and the offspring of David, and the bright and morning star. And the Spirit and the bride say, Come. And let him that heareth, say, Come. And let him that is athirst come. And whosoever will let him take of the water of life freely." How does Christ here graciously set before you his own winning attractive excellency! And how does he condescend to declare to you not only his own invitation, but the invitation of the Spirit and the bride, if by any means he might encourage you to come! And how does he invite every one that will, that they may "take of the water of life freely," that they may take it as a free gift, however precious it be, and though it be the Water of life.

If you do come to Christ, he will appear as a Lion, in his glorious power and dominion, to defend you. All those excellencies of his, in which he appears as a lion, shall be yours, and shall be employed for you in your defense, for your safety, and to promote your glory, he will be as a lion to fight against your enemies. He that touches you, or offends you, will provoke his wrath, as he that stirs up a lion. Unless your enemies can conquer this Lion, they shall not be able to destroy or hurt you; unless they are stronger than he, they shall not be able to hinder your happiness. Isaiah 31:4, "For thus hath the Lord spoken unto me, Like as the lion and the young lion roaring on his prey, when a multitude of shepherds is called forth against him, he will not be afraid of their voice, nor abase himself for the noise of them; so shall the Lord of hosts come down to fight for mount Zion, and for the hill thereof."

C) Let what has been said be improved to induce you to love the Lord Jesus Christ, and choose him for your friend and portion. As there is such an admirable meeting of diverse excellencies in Christ, so there is every thing in him to render him worthy of your love and choice, and to win and engage it. Whatsoever there is or can be desirable in a friend, is in Christ, and that to the highest degree that can be desired.

Would you choose for a friend a person of great dignity? It is a thing taking with men to have those for their friends who are much above them; because they look upon themselves honored by the friendship of such. Thus, how taking would it be with an inferior maid to be the object of the dear love of some great and excellent prince. But Christ is infinitely above you, and above all the princes of the earth; for he is the King of kings. So honorable a person as this offers himself to you, in the nearest and dearest friendship.

And would you choose to have a friend not only great but good? In Christ infinite greatness and infinite goodness meet together, and receive luster and glory one from another. His greatness is rendered lovely by his goodness. The greater any one is without goodness, so much the greater evil; but when infinite goodness is joined with greatness, it renders it a glorious and adorable greatness. So, on the other hand, his infinite goodness receives luster from his greatness. He that is of great understanding and ability, and is withal of a good and excellent disposition, is deservedly more esteemed than a lower and lesser being with the same kind inclination and good will. Indeed goodness is excellent in whatever subject it be found; it is beauty and excellency itself, and renders all excellent that are possessed of it; and yet most excellent when joined with greatness. The very same excellent qualities of gold render the body in which they are inherent more precious, and of greater value, when joined with greater than when with lesser dimensions. And how glorious is the sight, to see him who is the great Creator and supreme Lord of heaven and earth, full of condescension, tender pity and mercy, towards the mean and unworthy! His almighty power, and infinite majesty and self-sufficiency, render his exceeding love and grace the more surprising And how do his condescension and compassion endear his majesty, power, and dominion, and render those attributes pleasant, that would otherwise be only terrible! Would you not desire that your friend, though great and honorable, should be of such condescension and grace, and so to have the way opened to free access to him, that his exaltation above you might not hinder your free enjoyment of his friendship?—And would you choose not only that the infinite greatness and majesty of your friend should be, as it were, mollified and sweetened with condescension and grace; but would you also desire to have your friend brought nearer to you? Would you choose a friend far above you, and yet as it were upon a level with you too? Though it be taking with men to have a near and dear friend of superior dignity, yet there is also an inclination in them to have their friend a sharer with them in circumstances. Thus is Christ. Though he be the great God, yet he has, as it were, brought himself down to be upon a level with you, so as to become man as you are that he might not only be your Lord, but your brother, and that he might be the more fit to be a companion for such a worm of the dust. This is one end of Christ's taking upon him man's nature, that his people might be under advantages for a more familiar converse with him than the infinite distance of the divine nature would allow of. And upon this account the church longed for Christ's incarnation, Cant. 8:1. "O that thou wert my brother that sucked the breast of my mother! when I should find thee without, I would kiss thee, yea, I should not be despised." One design of God in the gospel is to bring us to make God the object of our undivided respect, that he may engross our regard every way, that whatever natural inclination there is in our souls, he may be the center of it; that God may be all in all. But there is an inclination in the creature, not only to the adoration of a Lord and Sovereign, but to complacence in some one as a friend, to love and delight in some one that may be conversed with as a companion. And virtue and holiness do not destroy or weaken this inclination of our nature. But so hath God contrived in the affair of our redemption, that a divine person may be the object even of this inclination of our nature. And in order hereto, such a one is come down to us, and has taken our nature, and is become one of us, and calls himself our friend, brother, and companion. Psalm 122:8, "For my brethren and companions' sake, will I now say, Peace be within thee."

But is it not enough in order to invite and encourage you to free access to a friend so great and high, that he is one of infinite condescending grace, and also has taken your own nature, and is become man? But would you, further to embolden and win you, have him a man of wonderful meekness and humility? Why, such a one is Christ! He is not only become man for you, but far the meekest and most humble of all men, the greatest instance of these sweet virtues that ever was, or will be. And besides these, he has all other human excellencies in the highest perfection. These, indeed, are no proper addition to his divine excellencies. Christ has no more excellency in his person, since his incarnation, than he had before; for divine excellency is infinite, and cannot be added to. Yet his human excellencies are additional manifestations of his glory and excellency to us, and are additional recommendations of him to our esteem and love, who are of finite comprehension. Though his human excellencies are but communications and reflections of his divine, and though this light, as reflected, falls infinitely short of the divine fountain of light in its immediate glory; yet the reflection shines not without its proper advantages, as presented to our view and affection. The glory of Christ in the qualifications of his human nature, appears to us in excellencies that are of our own kind, and are exercised in our own way and manner, and so, in some respect, are peculiarly fitted to invite our acquaintance and draw our affection. The glory of Christ as it appears in his divinity, though far brighter, more dazzles our eyes, and exceeds the strength of our sight or our comprehension; but, as it shines in the human excellencies of Christ, it is brought more to a level with our conceptions, and suitableness to our nature and manner, yet retaining a semblance of the same divine beauty, and a savor of the same divine sweetness. But as both divine and human excellencies meet together in Christ, they set off and recommend each other to us. It tends to endear the divine majesty and holiness of Christ to us, that these are attributes of one in our nature, one of us, who is become our brother, and is the meekest and humblest of men. It encourages us to look upon these divine perfections, however high and great; since we have some near concern in and liberty freely to enjoy them. And on the other hand, how much more glorious and surprising do the meekness, the humility, obedience, resignation, and other human excellencies of Christ appear, when we consider that they are in so great a person, as the eternal Son of God, the Lord of heaven and earth!

By your choosing Christ for your friend and portion, you will obtain these two infinite benefits.

Christ will give himself to you, with all those various excellencies that meet in him, to your full and everlasting enjoyment. He will ever after treat you as his dear friend; and you shall ere long be where he is, and shall behold his glory, and dwell with him, in most free and intimate communion and enjoyment. When the saints get to heaven, they shall not merely see Christ, and have to do with him as subjects and servants with a glorious and gracious Lord and Sovereign, but Christ will entertain them as friends and brethren. This we may learn from the manner of Christ's conversing with his disciples here on earth: though he was their Sovereign Lord, and did not refuse, but required, their supreme respect and adoration, yet he did not treat them as earthly sovereigns are wont to do their subjects. He did not keep them at an awful distance, but all along conversed with them with the most friendly familiarity, as a father amongst a company of children, yea, as with brethren. So he did with the twelve, and so he did with Mary, Martha, and Lazarus. He told his disciples, that he did not call them servants, but friends, and we read of one of them that leaned on his bosom: and doubtless he will not treat his disciples with less freedom and endearment in heaven. He will not keep them at a greater distance for his being in a state of exaltation; but he will rather take them into a state of exaltation with him. This will be the improvement Christ will make of his own glory, to make his beloved friends partakers with him, to glorify them in his glory, as he says to his Father, John 17:22, 23. "And the glory which thou hast given me, have I given them, that they may be one, even

as we are one I in them" etc. We are to consider, that though Christ is greatly exalted, yet he is exalted, not as a private person for himself only, but as his people's head; he is exalted in their name, and upon their account, as the first fruits, and as representing the whole harvest. He is not exalted that he may be at a greater distance from them, but that they may be exalted with him. The exaltation and honor of the head is not to make a greater distance between the head and the members, but the members have the same relation and union with the head they had before, and are honored with the head; and instead of the distance being greater, the union shall be nearer and more perfect. When believers get to heaven, Christ will conform them to himself, as he is set down in his Father's throne, so they shall sit down with him on his throne, and shall in their measure be made like him.

When Christ was going to heaven, he comforted his disciples with the thought, that after a while, he would come again and take them to himself, that they might be with him. And we are not to suppose that when the disciples got to heaven, they found him keeping a greater distance than he used to do. No, doubtless, be embraced them as friends, and welcomed them to his and their Father's house, and to his and their glory. They who had been his friends in this world, who had been together with him here, and had together partaken of sorrows and troubles, are now welcomed by him to rest, and to partake of glory with him. He took them and led them into his chambers, and showed them all his glory; as he prayed, John 17:24. "Father, I will that they also whom thou hast given me, be with me, that they may behold the glory which thou hast given me." And he led them to his living fountains of waters, and made them partake of his delights, as he prays John 17:13. "That my joy may be fulfilled in themselves," and set them down with him at his table in his kingdom, and made them partake with him of his dainties, according to his promise, Luke 22:30, and led them into his banqueting house, and made them to drink new wine with him in the kingdom of his heavenly Father, as he foretold them when he instituted the Lord's supper, Matt. 26:29.

Yea the saints' conversation with Christ in heaven shall not only be as intimate, and their access to him as free, as of the disciples on earth, but in many respects much more so; for in heaven, that vital union shall be perfect, which is exceeding imperfect here. While the saints are in this world, there are great remains of sin and darkness to separate or disunite them from Christ, which shall then all be removed. This is not a time for that full acquaintance, and those glorious manifestations of love, which Christ designs for his people hereafter; which seems to be signified by his speech to Mary Magdalene, when ready to embrace him, when she met him after his resurrection; John 20:17. "Jesus saith unto her, Touch me not; for I am not yet ascended to my Father."

When the saints shall see Christ's glory and exaltation in heaven, it will indeed possess their hearts with the greater admiration and adoring respect, but it will not awe them into any separation, but will serve only to heighten their surprise and joy, when they find Christ condescending to admit them to such intimate access, and so freely and fully communicating himself to them. So that if we choose Christ for our friend and portion, we shall hereafter be so received to him, that there shall be nothing to hinder the fullest enjoyment of him, to the satisfying the utmost cravings of our souls. We may take our full swing at gratifying our spiritual appetite after these holy pleasures. Christ will then say, as in Cant. 5:1, "Eat, O friends, drink, yea, drink abundantly O beloved." And this shall be our entertainment to all eternity! There shall never be any end of this happiness, or any thing to interrupt our enjoyment of it, or in the least to molest us in it!

By your being united to Christ, you will have a more glorious union with and enjoyment of God the Father, than otherwise could be. For hereby the saints' relation to God becomes much nearer; they are the children of God in a higher manner than otherwise could be. For, being members of God's own Son, they are in a sort partakers of his relation to the Father: they are not only sons of God by regeneration, but by a kind of

communion in the sonship of the eternal Son. This seems to be intended, Gal. 4:4-6. "God sent forth his Son, made of a woman, made under the law, to redeem them that are under the law, that we might receive the adoption of sons. And because ye are sons, God hath sent forth the Spirit of his Son into your hearts, crying, Abba, Father." The church is the daughter of God not only as he hath begotten her by his word and Spirit but as she is the spouse of his eternal Son. So we being members of the Son, are partakers in our measure of the Father's love to the Son, and complacence in him. John 17:23, "I in them, and thou in me,—Thou hast loved them as thou hast loved me." And ver. 26, "That the love wherewith thou hast loved me may be in them." And chap. 16:27, "The Father himself loveth you, because ye have loved me, and have believed that I came out from God. " So we shall, according to our capacities, be partakers of the Son's enjoyment of God, and have his joy fulfilled in ourselves, John 17:13. And by this means we shall come to an immensely higher, more intimate and full enjoyment of God, than otherwise could have been. For there is doubtless an infinite intimacy between the Father and the Son which is expressed by his being in the bosom of the Father. And saints being in him, shall, in their measure and manner, partake with him in it, and of the blessedness of it.

And thus is the affair of our redemption ordered, that thereby we are brought to an immensely more exalted kind of union with God, and enjoyment of him, both the Father and the Son, than otherwise could have been. For Christ being united to the human nature, we have advantage for a more free and full enjoyment of him, than we could have had if he had remained only in the divine nature. So again, we being united to a divine person, as his members, can have a more intimate union and intercourse with God the Father, who is only in the divine nature, than otherwise could be. Christ, who is a divine person, by taking on him our nature, descends from the infinite distance and height above us, and is brought nigh to us; whereby we have advantage for the full enjoyment of him. And, on the other hand, we, by being in Christ a divine person, do as it were ascend up to God, through the infinite distance, and have hereby advantage for the full enjoyment of him also.

This was the design of Christ, that he, and his Father, and his people, might all be united in one. John 17:21 23, "That they all may be one, as thou, Father, art in me, and I in thee— that they also may be one in us; that the world may believe that thou hast sent me. And the glory which thou hast given me, I have given

them, that they may be one, even as we are one; I in them and thou in me, that they may be made perfect in one." Christ has brought it to pass, that those whom the Father has given him should be brought into the household of God, that he and his Father, and his people, should be as one society, one family; that the church should be as it were admitted into the society of the blessed Trinity.

Jonathan Edwards

1.44 JESUS THE CONQUEROR, PHILIP SCHAFF

This Jesus of Nazareth, without money and arms, conquered more millions than Alexander, Caesar, Mohammed, and Napoleon; without science and learning, he shed more light on matters human and divine than all philosophers and scholars combined; without the eloquence of schools, he spoke such words of life as were never spoken before or since and produced effects which lie beyond the reach of orator or poet; without

writing a single line, he set more pens in motion, and furnished themes for more sermons, orations, discussions, learned volumes, works of art, and songs of praise than the whole army of great men of ancient and modern times.

Philip Schaff
The Life and Character of Jesus
New York: American Tract Society, 1913

1.45 CHRIST'S FRIENDSHIP, ANDREW MURRAY

Andrew Murray was one of four children born to Pastor Andrew, Sr., and Maria Murray. He was raised in what was considered to be the most remote corner of the world—Graaff-Reinet, South Africa. Educated in Scotland and Holland, in 1848 Andrew, Jr., returned to South Africa as a missionary and minister with the Dutch Reformed Church. His first appointment was to Bloemfontein, a territory of nearly 50,000 square miles and 12,000 people.

Andrew and his brother John had been in close contact with a revival movement in Scotland, an evangelical extension of the ongoing Second Great Awakening in America. He prayed for the same sort of awakening for the church in South Africa and wrote,

"My prayer is for revival, but I am held back by the increasing sense of my own unfitness for the work. I lament the awful pride and self complacency that have till now ruled my heart. O that I may be more and more a minister of the Spirit."

J. du Plessis, The Life of Andrew Murray

In 1860, revival did come to the churches of Cape Town, South Africa, and subsequently spread to surrounding towns and villages. Even remote farms and plantations felt the impact as lives were changed. Where once the churches had not been able to find one man ready to be a leader for God, the revival raised up 50 in Murray's Cape Town parish alone. There were more conversions in one month in that parish than in the whole course of its previous history.

Greatly concerned for the spiritual guidance of new converts and renewed Christians, Andrew Murray wrote over 240 books. His writings reflect his own longing for a deeper life in Christ and his prayer that others would long for and experience that life as well.

CHRIST'S FRIENDSHIP: ITS ORIGIN

"Greater love hath no man than this, that a man lay down his life for his friends."
John 15:13

In the three following verses our Lord speaks of His relation to His disciples under a new aspect—that of friendship. He points us to the love in which on His side has its origin (v. 13), to the obedience on our part by which it is maintained (v. 14); and then to the holy intimacy to which it leads (v. 15).

Our relation to Christ is one of love. In speaking of this previously, He showed us what His love was in its heavenly glory; the same love with which the Father had loved Him. Here we have it in its earthly manifestation—lay down His life for us. "Greater love hath no man than this, that a man lay down his life for his friends." Christ does indeed long to have us know that the secret root and strength of all He is and does for us as the Vine is love. As we learn to believe this, we shall feel that here is something which we not only need to think and know about, but a living power, a divine life which we need to receive within us. Christ and His love are inseparable; they are identical. God is love, and Christ is love. God and Christ and the divine love can only be known by having them, by their life and power working within us. "This is eternal life, that they know thee"; there is no knowing God but by having the life; the life working in us alone gives the knowledge. And even so the love; if we would know it, we must drink of its living stream, we must have it shed forth by the Holy Spirit in us.

"Greater love hath no man than this, that a man give his life for his friends." The life is the most precious thing a man has; the life is all he is; the life is himself. This is the highest measure of love: when a man gives his life, he hold nothing back, he gives all he has and is. It is this our Lord Jesus wants to make clear to us concerning His mystery of the Vine; with all He has He has placed Himself at our disposal. He wants us to count Him our very own; He wants to be wholly our possession, that we may be wholly His possession. He gave His life for us in death not merely as a passing act, that when accomplished was done with; no, but as a making Himself ours for eternity. Life for life; He gave His life for us to possess that we might give our life for Him to possess. This is what is taught by the parable of the Vine and the branch, in their wonderful identification, in their perfect union.

It is as we know something of this, not by reason or imagination, but deep down in the heart and life, that we shall begin to see what ought to be our life as branches of the heavenly Vine. He gave Himself to death; He lost Himself, that we might find life in Him. This is the true Vine, who only lives to live in us. This is the beginning and the root of that holy friendship to which Christ invites us.

Great is the mystery of godliness! Let us confess our ignorance and unbelief. Let us cease from our own understanding and our own efforts to master it. Let us wait for the Holy Spirit who dwells within us to reveal it. Let us trust His infinite love, which gave its life for us, to take possession and rejoice in making us wholly its own.

His life for His friends. How wonderful the lessons of the Vine, giving its very life to its branches! And Jesus gave His life for His friends. And that love gives itself to them and in them. My heavenly Vine, oh, teach me how wholly Thou longest to live in me!

CHRIST'S FRIENDSHIP: ITS EVIDENCE

"Ye are my friends, if ye do the things which I command you." John 15:14

Our Lord has said what He gave as proof of His friendship: He gave His life for us. He now tells us what our part is to be—to do the things which He commands. He gave His life to secure a place for His love in our hearts to rule us; the response His love calls us to, and empowers us for, is that we do what He commands us. As we know the dying love, we shall joyfully obey its commands. As we obey the commands, we shall know the love more fully. Christ had already said: "If ye keep my commandments, ye shall abide in my love." He counts it needful to repeat the truth again: the one proof of our faith in His love, the one way to abide in it, the one mark of being true branches is—to do the things which He commands us. He began with absolute surrender of His life for us. He can ask nothing less from us. This alone is a life in His friendship.

This truth, of the imperative necessity of obedience, doing all that Christ commands us, has not the place in our Christian teaching and living that Christ meant it to have. We have given a far higher place to privilege than to duty. We have not considered implicit obedience as a condition of true discipleship. The secret thought that it is impossible to do the things He commands us, and that therefore it cannot be expected of us, and a subtle and unconscious feeling that sinning is a necessity have frequently robbed both precepts and promises of their power. The whole relation to Christ has become clouded and lowered, the waiting on His teaching, the power to hear and obey His voice, and through obedience to enjoy His love and friendship, have been enfeebled by the terrible mistake. Do let us try to return to the true position, take Christ's words as most literally true, and make nothing less the law of our life: "Ye are my friends, if ye do the things that I command you." Surely our Lord asks nothing less than that we heartily and truthfully say: "Yea, Lord, what Thou dost command, that will I do."

These commands are to be done as a proof of friendship. The power to do them rests entirely in the personal relationship to Jesus. For a friend I could do what I would not for another. The friendship of Jesus is so heavenly and wonderful, it comes to us so as the power of a divine love entering in and taking possession, the unbroken fellowship with Himself is so essential to it, that it implies and imparts a joy and a love which make the obedience a delight. The liberty to claim the friendship of Jesus, the power to enjoy it, the grace to prove it in all its blessedness—all come as we do the things He commands us.

Is not the one thing needful for us that we ask our Lord to reveal Himself to us in the dying love in which He proved Himself our friend, and then listen as He says to us: "Ye are My friends." As we see what our Friend has done for us, and what as unspeakable blessedness it is to have Him call us friends, the doing His commands will become the natural fruit of our life in his love. We shall not fear to say: "Yea, Lord, we are Thy friends, and do what Thou dost command us."

If ye do. Yes, it is in doing that we are blessed, that we abide in His love, that we enjoy His friendship. "If ye do what I command you!" O my Lord, let Thy holy friendship lead me into the love of all Thy commands, and let the doing of Thy commands lead me ever deeper into Thy friendship.

CHRIST'S FRIENDSHIP: ITS INTIMACY

"No longer do I call you servants; for the servant knoweth not what his lord doeth: but I have called you friends; for all things that I heard from my Father, I have made known unto you." John 15:15

The highest proof of true friendship, and one great source of its blessedness, is the intimacy that holds nothing back, and admits the friend to share our inmost secrets. It is a blessed thing to be Christ's servant; His redeemed ones delight to call themselves His slaves. Christ had often spoken of the disciples as His servants. In His great love our Lord now says: "No longer do I call you servants"; with the coming of the Holy Spirit a new era was to be inaugurated. "The servant knoweth not what his Lord doeth"—he has to obey without being consulted or admitted into the secret of all his master's plans. "But, I have called you friends, for all things I heard from my Father I have made known unto you." Christ's friends share with Him in all the secrets the Father has entrusted to Him.

Let us think what this means. When Christ spoke of keeping His Father's commandments, He did not mean merely what was written in Holy Scripture, but those special commandments which were communicated to Him day by day, and from hour to hour. It was of these He said: "The Father loveth the Son, and showeth him all things that he doeth, and he will show him greater things." All that Christ did was God's working. God showed it to Christ, so that He carried out the Father's will and purpose, not, as man often does, blindly and unintelligently, but with full understanding and approval. As one who stood in God's counsel, He knew God's plan.

And this now is the blessedness of being Christ's friends, that we do not, as servants, do His will without much spiritual insight into its meaning and aim, but are admitted, as an inner circle, into some knowledge of God's more secret thoughts. From the Day of Pentecost on, by the Holy Spirit, Christ was to lead His disciples into the spiritual apprehension of the mysteries of the kingdom, of which He had hitherto spoken only by parables.

Friendship delights in fellowship. Friends hold council. Friends dare trust to each other what they would not for anything have others know. What is it that gives a Christian access to this holy intimacy with Jesus? That gives him the spiritual capacity for receiving the communications Christ has to make of what the Father has shown Him? "Ye are my friends if ye do what I command you." It is loving obedience that purifies the soul. That refers not only to the commandments of the Word, but to that blessed application of the Word to our daily life, which none but our Lord Himself can give. But as these are waited for in dependence and humility, and faithfully obeyed, the soul becomes fitted for ever closer fellowship, and the daily life may become a continual experience: "I have called you friends; for all things I have heard from my Father, I have made known unto you."

I have called you friends. What an unspeakable honor! What a heavenly privilege! O Savior, speak the word with power into my soul: "I have called you My friend, whom I love, whom I trust, to whom I make known all that passes between my Father and Me."

Andrew Murray
The True Vine: Meditations for a month
on John 15:1-16
Chicago, IL: Moody Press

1.46 CHRIST JESUS, C. H. SPURGEON

Charles H. Spurgeon, 1834-1892, was an English Baptist preacher—the most famous and popular of his day, as well as an author, and editor. He was pastor at the Metropolitan Tabernacle, London, from 1861 until his death. He also founded a pastors' college (1856), an orphanage (1867), and edited the monthly The Sword and the Trowel *magazine. His most famous writings are his seven-volume commentary on the Psalms, called the* Treasury of David. *Spurgeon's first sermon in the new Metropolitan Tabernacle, preached on March 25, 1861, follows.*

I do not know whether there are any persons here present who can contrive to put themselves into my present position, and to feel my present feelings. If they can effect that, they will give me credit for meaning what I say, when I declare that I feel totally unable to preach. And, indeed, I think I shall scarcely attempt a sermon, but rather give a sort of declaration of the truths from which future sermons shall be made. I will give you bullion rather than coin; the block from the quarry, and not the statue from the chisel. It appears that the one subject upon which men preached in the apostolic age was *Jesus Christ.* The tendency of man, if left alone, is continually to go further and further from God, and the Church of God itself is no exception to the general rule. For the first few years, during and after the apostolic era, Christ Jesus was preached, but gradually the Church departed from the central point, and began rather to preach ceremonials and church offices than the person of their Lord. So has it been in these modern times: we also have fallen into the same error, at least to a degree, and have gone from preaching Christ to preaching doctrines about Christ, inferences which may be drawn from his life, or definitions which may be gathered from his discourses. We are not content to stand like angels *in* the sun; our fancies disturb our rest and must needs fly on the sunbeams, further and further from the glorious source of light. In the days of Paul it was not difficult at once, in one word, to give the sum and substance of the current theology. It was Christ Jesus. Had you asked anyone of those disciples what he believed, he would have replied, "I believe Christ." If you had requested him to show you his Body of Divinity, he would have pointed upward, reminding you that divinity never had but one body, the suffering and crucified human frame of Jesus Christ, who ascended up on high. To them, Christ was not a notion refined, but unsubstantial; not an historical personage who had left only the savor of his character behind, but whose person was dead; to them he was not a set of ideas, not a creed, nor an incarnation of an abstract theory; but he was a person, one whom some of them had seen, whose hands they had handled, nay, one of whose flesh they had all been made to eat, and of whose blood they had spiritually been made to drink. Christ was substance to them, I fear he is too often but shadow to us. He was a reality to their minds; to us—though, perhaps, we would scarcely allow it in so many words—rather a myth than a man; rather a person who was, than he who was, and is, and is to come—the Almighty.

I would propose (and O may the Lord grant us grace to carry out that proposition, from which no Christian can dissent), I would propose that the subject of the ministry of this house, as long as this platform shall stand, and as long as this house shall be frequented by worshippers, shall be the person of Jesus Christ. I am never ashamed to avow myself a Calvinist, although I claim to be rather a Calvinist according to Calvin, than after the modern debased fashion. I do not hesitate to take the name of Baptist. You have there [pointing to the baptistery] substantial evidence that I am not ashamed of that ordinance of our Lord Jesus Christ; but if I am asked to say what is my creed, I think I must reply: "It is Jesus Christ." My venerable predecessor, Dr. Gill, has left a body of divinity admirable and excellent in its way; but the body of divinity to which I would pin and bind myself for ever, God helping me, is not his system of divinity or any other human treatise, but Christ Jesus, who is the sum and substance of the gospel; who is in himself all theology, the incarnation of every precious truth, the all-glorious personal embodiment of the way, the truth, and the life.

This afternoon I will try to describe *the subject, Christ Jesus;* then, secondly, to speak for a little while upon its *comprehensiveness;* then to enlarge upon sundry of *its excellencies;* and conclude by testing *its power.*

1. FIRST, THEN, THE SUBJECT

They continued both to teach and preach *Jesus Christ.*

To preach Jesus Christ aright we must preach him in his *infinite and indisputable Godhead.* We may be attacked by philosophers, who will either make him no God at all, or one constituted temporarily and, I must add, absurdly a God for a season. We shall have at once upon us those who view Christ as a prophet, as a great man, as an admirable exemplar; we shall be assailed on all sides by those who choose rather to draw their divinity from their own addled brains than from the simplicity of Holy Writ; but what mattereth this? We must reiterate again and again the absolute and proper deity of Christ; for without this we are in the position of those described by the prophet:—"Their tacklings are loosed, they could not well strengthen their mast" and soon will our enemies prevail against us, and the prey of a great spoil shall be taken. Take away the divinity of Christ from the gospel, and you have nothing whatever left upon which the anxious soul can rest. Remove the Word who was in the beginning with God, and who was God, and the Jachin and Boaz of the temple are overturned. Without a divine Savior, your gospel is a rope of sand; a bubble; a something less substantial than a dream. If Christ were not God, he was the basest of impostors. He was either one of two things, very God of very God, or else an arch-deceiver of the souls of men, for he made many of them believe he was God, and brought upon himself the consequences of what they called blasphemy; so that if he were not God, he was the greatest deceiver that ever lived. But God he is; and here, in this house, we must and will adore him. With the multitude of his redeemed we *will* sing:

> "Jesus is worthy to receive,
> Honor and power *divine,*
> And blessings more, than we can give
> Be *Lord* for ever thine."

To preach Christ, however, we must also preach *his true humanity.* We must never make him to be less manlike because he was perfectly divine. I love that hymn of Hart which begins—

> "A man there was—a real man,
> Who once on Calvary died."

"Real man!" I think we do not often realize that manhood of Christ; we do not see that he was bone of our bone, and flesh of our flesh; feeling, thinking, acting, suffering, doing, just like ourselves—one of our fellows, and only above us because he is "exalted with the oil of gladness above his fellows." We must have a human Christ, and we must have one of real flesh and blood too; not of shadows or filmy fancies. We must have one to whom we can talk, one with whom we can walk, one

> "Who in his measure feels afresh
> What every member bears;"

who is so intimately connected with us in ties of blood, that he is as with us one, the head of the family, first-born among many brethren. I am never more glad than when I am preaching a *personal* Christ. A doctrinal Christ, a practical Christ, or an experimental Christ, as some good men make him to be according to the temper of their minds, I do not feel to be sufficient for the people of God. We want a *personal* Christ. This has been a power to the Romish church—a power which they have used for ill, but always a power; they have had a personal Christ, but then it has either been a baby Christ in his mother's arms, or else a dead Christ upon the cross. They never reached the force of a real full-grown Christ, one who not only lived and suffered, but who died and rose again, and sits at the right hand of God, the Head of the Church, the one ruler of men. Oh! we must bring out more and more clearly each day the real personality of the Redeemer in his complex person. Whatever we fail to preach, we must preach *him.* If we are wrong in many points, if we be but right here, this will save our ministry from the flames; but if we be wrong here, however orthodox we may pretend to be, we cannot be right in the rest unless we think rightly of him.

But, further, to preach Christ Jesus, it is absolutely necessary we should preach him as *the only mediator between God and man.* Admitting the efficacy of the intercession of living saints for sinners, never for a moment denying that every man is bound to make supplication for all ranks and conditions of men, yet must we have it that the only mediator in the heavens, and the only direct intercessor with God, is the man Christ Jesus. Nay, we must not be content with making him the only mediator; we must set aside all approach to God in any way whatever, except by him. We must not only have him for the priest, but we must have him for the altar, the victim, and the offerer too. We must learn in full the meaning of that precious text— "Christ is all." We must not see a part of the types here and a part there, but all gathered up in him, the one door of heaven, the one crimson way by which our souls approach to God. We must not allow that approaches can be made in human strength, by human learning, or by human effort; but in him and through him, and by him, and in dependence upon him, must all be done between God and man. We have no wings, my brethren, with which to fly to heaven; our journey thither must be on the rounds [rungs] of Jacob's ladder. We cannot approach God by anything we have, or know, or do. Christ crucified, and he alone, must lift us up to God.

And more, we must preach Christ in the solitariness of his redemption work. We must not permit for a moment the fair white linen of his righteousness to be stained by the patch-work of our filthy rags. We must not submit that the precious blood of his veins should be diluted by any offering of ours co-acting therewith, for our salvation. He hath, by one sacrifice, for ever put away sin. We shall never preach Christ unless we have a real atonement. There be certain people nowadays who are making the atonement, first a sort of compromise, and the next step is to make the atonement a display of what ought to have been, instead of the thing which should have been. Then, next, there are some who make it to be a mere picture, an exhibition, a shadow—a shadow, the substance of which they have not seen. And the day will come, and there are sundry traces of it here and there, in which in some churches the atonement shall be utterly denied, and yet men shall call themselves Christians, while they have broken themselves against the corner-stone of the entire system. I have no kith nor kin, nor friendship, nor Christian amity, with any man whatever who claims to be a Christian and yet denies the atonement. There is a limit to the charity of Christians, and there can be none whatever entertained to the man who is dishonest enough to occupy a Christian pulpit and to deny Christ. It is only in the Christian church that such a thing can be tolerated. I appeal to you. Was there ever known a Buddhist acknowledged in the temple of Buddha who denied the basic doctrine of the sect? Was there ever known a Mahomadan Imaum who was sanctioned in the mosque while he cried down the Prophet? It remains for Christian churches only to have in their midst men who can bear the name of

Christian, who can even venture to be Christian teachers, while they slander the Deity of him who is the Christian's God, and speak lightly of the efficacy of his blood who is the Christian's atonement. May this deadly cancer be cut out root and branch; and whatever tearing of the flesh there may be, better cut it out with a jagged knife than suffer to exist because no lancet is to be found to do it daintily. We must have, then, Christ in the efficacy of his precious blood as the only Redeemer of the souls of men, and as the only mediator, who, without assistance of ours, has brought us to God and made reconciliation through his blood.

Our ministry will scarcely be complete unless we preach *Christ as the only lawgiver and Rabbi of the Church.* When you put it down as a canon of your faith that the church has right and power to decree rites and ceremonies, you have robbed Christ at once of his proper position as the only teacher of the church. Or when you claim the office of controlling other men's consciences by the decree of the church, or the vote of a synod, apart from the authority of Christ, you have taken away from Christ that chair which he occupies in the Christian church, as the teacher in the great Christian school, as the Rabbi, and the only Rabbi, of our faith. God forbid that we should hold a single truth except on his authority. Let not our faith stand in the wisdom of man, but in the power of God. You refer me to the writings of Doctor this and Doctor the other: what are these? The words of Christ, these are truth, and these are wisdom. You bring me authority from the practice of a church three or four centuries removed from the crucifixion as the proof of the existence of a certain ceremony and the righteousness of certain ecclesiastical offices. What is your proof worth? If Christ hath not specially ordained it, and if he hath not commanded his people to obey it, of what value is any rite whatever? We acknowledge Christ as ordaining all things for his church, and presenting that church with a finished code of laws, from which any deviation is a sin, and to which any addition is a high crime. Any church officer who is not ordained of Christ occupies an office which he ought to resign. Any person who practices a ceremony for which he has not scriptural authority should renounce it; and any man who preaches a doctrine for which he has not Christ as his certifier, should not demand for it the faith of men.

But I fear there are times coming when the minister will not be true to his duty unless he goes further, and preaches Christ as *the sole King of the Church*. There has been a disposition on the part of the state, especially with regard to the Free Church of Scotland, to exercise power and judgment over church decrees. No king, no queen that ever lived, or can live, has any authority whatever over the church of Christ. The church has none to govern and rule over her but her Lord and her King. The church can suffer, but she cannot yield; you may break her confessors alive upon the wheel, but she, in her uprightness, will neither bend nor bow. From the sentence of our church there is no appeal whatever on earth. To the court of heaven a man may appeal if the sentence of the church be wrong, but to Caesar never. Neither the best nor the worst of kings or queens may ever dare to put their finger upon the prerogative of Christ as the head of the church. Up, church of God! If once there be any laws of man passed to govern thee, up, dash them in pieces! Let us each catch up the war cry, and uplift the lion standard of the tribe of Judah; let us challenge the kings of the earth and say, *"Who shall rouse him up?"* The church is queen above all queens, and Christ her only King. None have jurisdiction or power in the church of Christ save Jesus Christ himself. If any of our acts violate the civil laws, we are men and citizens, and we acknowledge the right of a state to govern us as individuals. None of us wish to be less subjects of the realm because we are kings and priests unto God. But as members of Christian churches we maintain that the excommunication of a Christian church can never be reversed by the civil power, or by any state act, nor are its censures to be examined, much less to be removed, mitigated, or even judged. We must have, as Christ's church, a full recognition of his imperial rights, and the day will come when the state will not only tolerate us as a mere society, but admit that as we profess to be the church of Christ, we

have a right by that very fact to be self-governing, and never to be interfered with in any sense whatever, so far as our ecclesiastical affairs are concerned.

Christ must be preached, then, and exalted in all these respects, or else we have not preached a full Christ; but I go one step further. We have not yet mounted to the full height of our ministry unless we learn to preach *Christ as the King of kings*. He has an absolute right to the entire dominion of this world. The Christian minister, as ordained of God to preach, has a perfect right in God's name to preach upon any subject touching the Lord's kingdom, and to rebuke and exhort even the greatest of men. Sometimes I have heard it said, when we have canvassed the acts of an emperor or senator, "These are politics;" but Christ is King of politics as well as theology. "Oh! but"—say they—"what have you to do with what the state does?" Why, just this: that Christ is the head of all states, and while the state has no authority over the church, yet Christ himself is King of kings, and Lord of lords. Oh, that the church would put her diadem upon her head, and take her right position! We are not slaves. The church of God is not a groveling corporation bound for ever to sit upon a dunghill; never queen was so fair as she, and never robe so rich as the purple which she wears. Arise, O Church! arise, the earth is thine; claim it. Send out thy missionary, not as a petitioner to creep at the feet of princes, but as an ambassador for God to make peace between God and man. Send him out to claim the possession which belongs to thee, and which God has given to thee to be thine for ever and ever, by a right which kings may dispute, but which one day every one of them shall acknowledge.

The fact is, we must bring *Christ himself* back into camp once more. It is of little use having our true Jerusalem swords, and the shields, and the banners, and the trumpets, and the drums; we want the King himself in the midst of us. More and more of a personal Christ is the great lack of the time. I would not wish for less doctrine, less experience, or less practice, but more of all this put into Christ, and Christ preached as the sum and substance of it all.

2. BUT, SECONDLY, I AM NOW TO SPEAK, FOR A SHORT TIME, UPON THE COMPREHENSIVENESS OF THE SUBJECT WHICH THE TEXT ANNOUNCES

It is an old and trite saying that the ministers of the gospel may be divided into three kinds—the doctrinal, the experimental, and the practical. The saying is so often repeated that very few would contradict it. But it betrays at once, if it be true, the absence and lack of a something essentially necessary for the church's success. Where is the preacher of *Christ* out of these? I propound this, that if a man be found a preacher of Christ, he is doctrinal, experimental, and practical. The *doctrinal* preacher generally has a limited range. He is useful, exceedingly useful; God constitutes him a barrier against the innovations of the times: he preaches upon his subjects so frequently that he is well versed in them, and becomes one of the armed men about the bed of Solomon. But suppose the doctrinal preacher should have it all his own way, and there should be none others at all, what would be the effect? See it in our Baptist churches about one hundred and fifty years ago. They were all *sound* and sound asleep. Those doctrines had preached them into a lethargy, and had is not been for some few who started up and proposed the missions for the heathen, and who found but little sympathy at first, the church would have been utterly inactive. Now, I would not be hard with any, but there are some brethren still whose preaching might justly be summed up as being doctrinal, nothing more than doctrinal, and what is the effect of their ministry? Bitterness. They learn to contend not only earnestly for the faith, but savagely for it. Certainly we admire their earnestness, and we thank God for their soundness, but we wish there were mingled with their doctrine a somewhat else which might tone down their severity and make them seek rather the unity and fellowship of the saints than the division and discord which they labor to create.

Again, I will refer you to the next class of preachers, the *experimental*. How delightful it is to sit under an experimental preacher! Perhaps of all ministries this one is the most useful, he who preaches the doubts, the fears, the joys, the ecstasies of the people of God. How often do the saints see the footsteps of the flock, and then they find the shepherd under an experimental minister! But do you know the effect of an experimental minister, purely so, I mean, when all else is put aside to make room for experience? There is one school of divines always preaching the corruption of the human heart. This is their style; "Except thou be flayed alive by the law; except thou art daily feeling the utter rottenness of thine heart; except than art a stranger to full assurance, and dost always doubt and fear; except thou abidest on the dunghill and dost scrape thyself with a potsherd, thou art no child of God." Who told you that? This has been the preaching of some experimental preachers, and the effect has been just this. Men have come to think the deformities of God's people to be their beauty. They are like certain courtiers of the reign of Richard III, who is said by history to have had a hump upon his back and his admirers stuffed their backs that they might have a graceful hump too. And there be many who, because a minister preaches of doubts and fears, feel they must doubt and fear too; and then that which is both uncomfortable to themselves and dishonoring to God comes to be the very mark of God's people. This is the tendency of experimental preaching, however judiciously managed, when ministers harp on that string and on that alone; the tendency is either to preach the people into a soft and savory state, in which there is not a bit of manliness or might, or else into that dead and rotten state in which corruption outswells communion, and the savor is not the perfume of the king's ointments, but the stench of a corrupt and filthy heart.

Take also the *practical* preacher; who would say a word against this good man? He stirs the people up, excites the children of God to holy duties, promotes every excellent object, and is in his way an admirable supplement to the two other kinds of ministers. But sit under the practical preacher; sit under him all the year round and listen to his people as they come out. There is one who says, *"the same thing over again—Do, do, do, nothing but do."* There is a poor sinner yonder just gone down the front steps. Follow him, "Oh," says he, "I came here to find out what *Christ* could do for me, and I have only been told what *I* must do for myself" Now this it a great evil, and persons who sit under such a ministry become lean, starveling things. I would that practical preachers would listen to our farmers, who always say it is better to put the whip in the manger than upon the horse's back. Let them feed the people with food convenient for them, and they will be practical enough; but all practice and no promise, all exhortation and no sound doctrine, will never make the man of God perfect and zealous for good works.

But what am I driving at in bringing up these three sorts of ministers? Why just this: to show you that there is one minister who can preach all this, without the dangers of any one of the others, but with the excellencies of the whole. And who is he? Why, any man in the world who preaches Christ. If he preaches Christ's person he must preach *doctrine*. If I preach Christ I must preach him as the covenant head of his people, and how far am I then from the doctrine of election? If I preach Christ I must preach the efficacy of his blood, and how far am I removed then from the great doctrine of an effectual atonement? If I preach Christ I *must* preach the love of his heart, and how can I deny the final perseverance of the saints? If I preach the Lord Jesus as the great Head and King, how far am I removed from divine Sovereignty? Must I not, if I preach Christ personally, preach his doctrines? I believe they are nothing but the natural outgrowth of that great root thought, or root substance rather, the person of the Lord Jesus Christ. He who will preach Christ fully will never be lax in doctrine. And what better *experience* can you preach than in preaching Christ? Would you preach the sufferings of the saints, preach *his* agony and bloody sweat, his cross and passion; for the true sufferings of the saints are in fellowship with him. If you would preach their joys, preach *his* resurrection, his ascension, and his advent; you are never far from the joys of the saints when you are near to the joys of Christ; for did not he say, *"My* joy shall be in them

that their joy may be full"? And what better *practice* can be preached than preaching Christ? Of every virtue he is the pattern; of the perfection of human character he is the very mirror; of everything that is holy and of good report, he is the abiding incarnation. He cannot fail, then, to be a good doctrinal, experimental, practical preacher, who preaches Christ. Did you ever know a congregation grow less spiritual by a minister preaching Christ? Did you ever know them get full of doubts and fears by preaching Christ? Did you ever hear of their getting lax in sentiment by his preaching Christ? Did you ever hear a whisper that men became unholy in their lives because they heard too much about Christ? I think that all the excellencies of all ministers may be gathered up into the teaching of the man who can preach Christ every day in the week, while there will not be any of the evils connected with the other forms of preaching.

3. I SHALL NOW PASS ONTO NOTICE SOME OF THE SURPASSING EXCELLENCIES OF THE SUBJECT

First, he will always have a *blessed variety* in his preaching. In Australia I have heard that the only change for the backwoodsmen is to have one day damper [unleavened cake baked in wood ashes], tea, and bread; the next day, bread, damper, and tea; and the next day, tea, bread, and damper. The only variety some ministers give, is one Sunday to have depravity, election, and perseverance, and the next Sunday, election, perseverance, and depravity. There are many strings to the harp of the gospel. There are some brethren who are so rightly charmed with five of the strings, which certainly have very rich music in them, that they never meddle with any of the other strings; the cobwebs hang on the rest, while these five are pretty well worn out. It is always pretty much the same thing from the first of January to the last of December. Their organ has very few keys, and upon these they may make a very blessed variety, but I think not a very extensive one. Any man who preaches Christ will ensure variety in his preaching. *He* is all manner of precious perfume, myrrh, and aloes, and cassia. He is all sorts of music, he is everything that is sweet to the ear; he is all manner of fruits; there is not one dainty in him but many. This tree of life bears twelve manner of fruits. He is all manner of raiment; he is golden raiment for beauty, he is the warm raiment for comfort, he is the stout raiment for harness in the day of battle. There are all things in Christ, and he that hath Christ will have as great a variety as there is to be found in the scenery of the world where are no two rocks alike, and no two rivers wind in precisely the same manner, and no two trees grow in precisely the same form. Any other subject you may preach upon till your hearers feel satiety; but with Christ for a subject, you may go on, and on, and on, till the sermon swells into the eternal song, and you begin to sing, "Unto him that loved us and washed us from our sins in his own blood."

There is yet another excellence about this subject, namely, *that it suits all sorts of people.* Are there rebels present? Preach Christ; it will suit them. Are there pardoned sinners present? What is better, to melt their hearts than the blood of the Lord Jesus. Are there doubting Christians? What can cheer them better than the name of Christ. Are there strong believers? What is stronger meat than Jesus crucified? Are there learned, polite, intellectual hearers? If they are not satisfied with Christ, they ought to be. Are there poor, ignorant, unlettered men? Jesus Christ is just the thing to preach to them—a naked Christ to their simple ears. Jesus Christ is a topic that will keep in all climates. Land in New Zealand in the midst of uncivilized men, move off to another post and stand in the midst of poetical Persia or fickle France, the cross is adapted to all. We need not inquire into the doctrinal opinion of our hearers. If they are high, I am sure Christ will suit them. If they are low, if they be true believers, I am sure Christ Jesus will suit *them.* No Christians will reject such meat as this; only prepare it, and with a hot heart serve it up on the table, and they will be satisfied and feed to the full. So that there is adaptation as well as variety in this subject.

4. BUT MORE THAN THIS, I MUST ADD, AND THIS WILL BRING ME TO

MY LAST POINT, FOR MY TIME FLIES—THERE IS A POWER ABOUT THIS SUBJECT WHEN IT IS PREACHED WITH THE DEMONSTRATION OF THE SPIRIT, WHICH IS NOT FOUND IN ANY OTHER. MY BRETHREN, WHAT POWER THERE IS IN THIS SUBJECT TO PROMOTE *THE UNION* OF THE PEOPLE OF GOD!

There is a man there, he is almost a Puseyite. "I do not like him," says one. Stop till I tell you something more about him, and you will. There is another man there, a Presbyterian—true blue; he cannot bear Independency, or anything but Presbytery—a covenant man. "Well," says one, "I like him a little better; but I do not suppose we shall get on very well." Stop! I will tell you some more about him. There is another man down there; he is a very strong Calvinist. "Humph," says one, "I shall not admire *him.*" Stop, stop! Now, here are these three men; let us hear what they say of each other. If they know nothing of each other except what I have stated, the first time they meet there will be a magnificent quarrel. There is yonder clergyman—he will have little fraternity whatever with the ultra-Evangelical; while the Presbyterian will reject them both, for he abhors black prelacy. But, my dear brethren, all three of you, we of this congregation will approve of you all, and you will approve of one another when I have stated your true character. That man yonder, whom I called almost a Puseyite, was George Herbert. How he loved the doornails of the church! I think he would scarce have had a spider killed that had once crept across the church aisles. He was a thorough churchman, to the very center of the marrow of his bones; but what a Christian! What a lover of his sweet Lord Jesus! You know that hymn of his which I have so often quoted, and mean to quote a hundred times more: "How sweetly doth my Master's sound," and so forth. I hear a knock at the door. "Who is that?" "Why, it is a very strong churchman." "Do not show him in; I am at prayer; I cannot pray with him." "Oh, but it is George Herbert!" "Oh, let him in, let him in! No man could I pray better with than Mr. Herbert. Walk in, Mr.

Herbert; we are right glad to see you; you are our dear companion; your hymns have made us glad."

But who was that second man, the Presbyterian, who would not have liked George Herbert at all? Why, that was Samuel Rutherford. What a seraphic spirit! What splendid metaphors he uses about his sweet Lord Jesus! He has written all Solomon's Song over without knowing it. He felt and proved it to be divine. The Spirit in him re-dictated the song. Well now, I think, we will introduce Mr. Rutherford and Mr. Herbert together, and I am persuaded when they begin to speak about their Master they will find each other next of kin; and I feel sure that, by this time, Samuel Rutherford and George Herbert have found each other out in heaven, and are sitting side by side. Well, but then we mentioned another; who was that high Calvinist? He was the man who was called the Leviathan of Antinomians. That he was a leviathan I will grant, but that he was an Antinomian is false. It was Dr. Hawker. Now, I am sure, George Herbert would not have liked Dr. Hawker, and I am certain that Dr. Hawker would not have liked George Herbert, and I do not suppose that Samuel Rutherford would have had anything to do with either of them. "No, no," he would say, "your black prelacy I hate." But look at Hawker, there is a sweet spirit; he cannot take up his pen but he dips it in Christ, and begins to write about his Lord at once "Precious Immanuel—precious Jesus." Those words in his morning and evening portions are repeated again and again, and again. I recollect hearing of Mr. Rowland Hill, that he said to a young man who was at tea with him one night when he was about to go:—"Where are you going to?" "Oh!" said he, "I am going to hear Dr. Hawker, at St. George's in the Borough." "Oh, go and hear him," he said; "he is a right good man, worth hearing. But there is this difference between him and me; my preaching is something like a pudding, with here and there a plum; but Dr. Hawker's is all plum." And that was very near the mark, because Dr. Hawker was all Christ. He was constantly preaching of his Master; and even if he gave an invitation to a sinner, it was generally put in this way: "What sayest thou?

Wilt thou go with *this man,* and be married and espoused unto *him?*" It was the preaching of a personal Christ that made his ministry so full of marrow and fatness.

My dear friends, let a man stand up and exalt Christ, and we are all agreed. I see before me this afternoon members of all Christian denominations; but if Christ Jesus is not the topic that suits you, why then I think we may question your Christianity. The more Christ is preached, the more will the Church prove, and exhibit, and assert, and maintain her unity; but the less Christ is preached, and the more of Paul, and Apollos, and Cephas, the more of strife and division, and the less of true Christian fellowship.

We will only mention the power of the preaching of Christ *upon the heart of sinners.* There is a person, now a member of my church, whose conversion was owing to the reading of that hymn: "Jesus, lover of my soul."

"Ah," said he, "does Jesus love my soul? Then how vile I have been to neglect him." There are scores whose conversion is distinctly and directly traceable, not to doctrine— though that is often useful—nor experience, nor practice, though these are fruitful, but to the preaching of Christ. I think you will find the most fertile sermons have always been the most Christly sermons. This is a seed which seldom rots under the clod. One may fall upon the stony ground, but it oftener happens that the seed breaks the stone when it falls, and as Christ is a root out of a dry ground, so this finds root for itself even in dry, hard, stony hearts. We ought to preach the law, we ought to thunder out the threatenings of God, but they must never be the main topic. Christ, Christ, Christ, if we would have men converted. Do you want to convince yonder careless one? Tell him the story of the cross. Under God it will arrest his attention and awaken his thoughts. Would you subdue the carnal affections of yonder profligate? Preach the love of Christ, and that new love shall uproot the old. Would you bind up yonder broken heart? Bring forth Christ, for in him there is a cordial for every fear. Christ is preached and we do rejoice, yea, and will rejoice "for he is the power of God unto salvation unto every one that believeth." Judge not, my dear brethren, any man's ministry. The world has too often condemned the man whom God intended to honor. Say not of such an one, "He can do no good, for his language is rough and rude." Say not of another that his style is too often marred with flippancy. Say not of a third that he is too erudite or soars too high. Every man in his own order. If that man preach Christ, whether he be Paul, or Apollos, or Cephas, we wish him God speed; for God will bless the Christ he preaches, and forgive the error which mingled with his ministry. I must even frankly admit the truth of many a criticism that has been uttered on my ministry, but I know it has been successful, and under God it has been, because I *have* sought to preach Christ. I say that without boasting or egotism, because if I had not done so I had no right so be a minister of Christ at all, and as I claim to be God's minister, I will and must declare it, whatever I have not preached, *I have preached Christ,* and into whatever mistakes I have fallen, I have sought to point to his cross, and say, "Behold the way to God." And if ye see others preaching Christ, be not you their foe. Pray for them; bear them in your arms before God; their errors may yet be outgrown, if they preach Christ; but if not, I care not what their excellency may be, the excellency shall die and expire like sparks that go out in darkness. They have not the fuel of the flame, for they have not Christ Jesus as the substance of their ministry.

May I entreat, in closing, your earnest prayer, each one of you, that in this house as well as in all the places of worship round about, Christ may evermore be preached, and I may add my own sincere desire that this place may become a hissing and the abode of dragons, and this pulpit be burned with fire, or ever any other gospel be preached here than that which we have received of the holy apostles of God; and of which Jesus Christ himself is the chief corner stone. Let me have your incessant prayers. May God speed every minister of Christ. But where there is so large a field of labor may I claim your earnest and constant intercessions, that where Christ is lifted up, men may be drawn to hear, and afterwards drawn to believe, that they may find Christ the Savior of our souls. "He that believeth, and is baptized, shall be saved; he that believeth not shall be damned." "Repent and be converted, every one of you," said Peter. Yet again said Paul to the jailer, "Believe in the Lord Jesus, and thou shalt be saved, and thy house."

God give us grace to believe, and unto him be glory for ever and ever. Amen.

C. H. Spurgeon

CHECK-LISTS

1.47 BIBLE STUDY ON THE ATTRIBUTES/CHARACTER OF JESUS, ORVILLE J. NAVE

Nave's Topics was produced by Orville J. Nave while he served as a U.S. Army chaplain after years of "delightful and untiring study of the Word of God."

Billy Graham said of Nave's Topical Bible, *"Outside of the Bible, this is the book I depend on more than any other." Nave's* Topical Bible *is an encyclopedia of Bible passages, containing over 20,000 topics and sub-topics and over 100,000 scripture references.*

CONTENTS

Anointed with the Holy Spirit
Reveals God
Declared his doctrine to be that of the
Father
Foretold things to come
Faithful
Abounded in wisdom
Mighty in deed and word
Unostentatious in his teaching
God commands us to hear
God will severely punish those who reject
him
Jesus is received
Instances of Jesus being received
By Matthew
By Peter and other disciples
By Zacchaeus
By Philip
By Nathanael
By three thousand people on the day
of Pentecost
By the Ethiopian eunuch
Rejection of Jesus
Jesus' relation to the Father
Jesus' resurrection
Revelations made by Jesus
Concerning his kingdom
His betrayal
Crucifixion
Judgments upon the Jews
The destruction of the temple, and
Jerusalem
The destruction of Capernaum
Concerning persecutions of Christians
His being forsaken by his disciples
Concerning Lazarus
Concerning Peter
Fame of the woman who anointed his
head
Antichrist
Concerning His death and resurrection
His ascension
Jesus as Savior
Jesus' second coming
Jesus as the true Shepherd
Foretold
The chief
The good
The great
His sheep he knows
He calls

He gathers
He guides
He feeds
He cherishes tenderly
He protects and preserves
He laid down his life for
He gives eternal life to
Typified: David
Jesus the Son of God
Sufferings of Jesus
Prophecies about the sufferings of Jesus
Jesus as Teacher
The temptations of Jesus
Jesus as unchangeable
Worship of Jesus
Zeal of Jesus

BIBLE STUDIES

The compassion of Jesus
Isaiah 40:11; 42:3; 53:4; 63:7-9; Matthew 8:3,
16, 17; 9:36; 14:14; 15:32; 18:11-13; 20:34;
23:37; Mark 6:34; 8:2, 3; Luke 7:13; 19:41,
42; John 11:34-38; 18:8, 9; 2 Corinthians 8:9;
Hebrews 4:15

Jesus as Creator
John 1:3, 10; 1 Corinthians 8:6; Ephesians
3:9; Colossians 1:16, 17; Hebrews 1:2, 10;
Revelation 3:14

Jesus' divinity
As Jehovah
Isaiah 40:3; Matthew 3:3
  Jehovah of glory
  Psalms 24:7, 10; 1
  Corinthians 2:8; James 2:1
  Jehovah our righteousness
  Jeremiah 23:5, 6; 1 Corinthians 1:30
  Jehovah above all
  Psalms 97:9; John 3:31
  Jehovah the first and the last
  Isaiah 44:6; Revelation 1:17; Isaiah
  48:12-16; Revelation 22:13
  Jehovah's fellow and equal
  Zechariah 13:7; Philippians 2:6
  Jehovah of hosts
  Isaiah 6:1-3; John 12:41; Isaiah 8:13,
  14; 1 Peter 2:8
  Jehovah
  Psalms 110:1; Matthew 22:42-45

Jehovah the shepherd
Isaiah 40:10, 11; Hebrews 13:20
Jehovah, for whose glory all things were created
Proverbs 16:4; Colossians 1:16
Jehovah the messenger of the covenant
Malachi 3:1; Luke 2:27
Invoked as Jehovah
Joel 2:32; 1 Corinthians 1:2
As the eternal God and Creator
Psalms 102:24-27; Hebrews 1:8, 10-12
The mighty God
Isaiah 9:6
The Great God and Savior
Hosea 1:7; Titus 2:13
God over all
Romans 9:5
God the Judge
Ecclesiastes 12:14; 1 Corinthians 4:5; 2 Corinthians 5:10; 2 Timothy 4:1
Emmanuel
Isaiah 7:14; Matthew 1:23
King of kings and Lord of lords
Daniel 10:17; Revelation 1:5; 17:14
The Holy One
1 Samuel 2:2; Acts 3:14
The Lord from heaven
1 Corinthians 15:47
Lord of the Sabbath
Genesis 2:3; Matthew 12:8
Lord of all
Acts 10:36; Romans 10:11-13
Son of God
Matthew 26:63-67
The one and only Son of the Father
John 1:14, 18; 3:16, 18; 1 John 4:9
His blood is called the blood of God
Acts 20:28
One with the Father
John 10:30, 38; 12:45; 14:7-10; 17:10
As sending the Spirit equally with the Father
John 14:16; 15:26
As unsearchable equally with the Father
Proverbs 30:4; Matthew 11:27
As Creator of all things
Isaiah 40:28; John 1:3; Colossians 1:16
Supporter and preserver of all things

Nehemiah 9:6; Colossians 1:17; Hebrews 1:3
Acknowledged by Old Testament saints
Genesis 17:1; 48:15, 16; 32:24-30; Hosea 12:3-5; Judges 6:22-24; 13:21, 22; Job 19:25-27
Unclassified Scriptures relating to Jesus' divinity
Genesis 1:1-14; Exodus 23:20, 21; Numbers 21:6; Psalms 45:6, 7; 102:24-27; 110:1; Isaiah 6:1; 7:14; 8:13, 14; 9:6; 40:3, 9, 10; Malachi 3:1; Matthew 1:23; 3:3; 8:29; 9:6; 11:10; 22:43-45; 28:17, 18; Mark 5:6, 7; Luke 4:12, 33, 34; 8:28; 9:43, 44; John 1:1, 2; 5:17, 18, 21-23; 10:30-33; 12:41, 45; 20:28; Acts 7:37-39; 20:28; Romans 1:7; 1 Corinthians 1:3; 2:8; 8:6; 10:9; 15:47; 2 Corinthians 1:2; Galatians 1:1, 2; Ephesians 1:2; 6:23, 24; Philippians 1:2; Colossians 1:2; 1 Thessalonians 1:1; 3:11; 2 Thessalonians 1:1, 2; 2:16, 17; 1 Timothy 3:16; 2 Timothy 1:2; Titus 2:13; Hebrews 1:8, 10; 1 Peter 2:8; 1 John 5:20

Jesus, eternity of

Psalms 102:24-27; Proverbs 8:22-25; Isaiah 9:6; Micah 5:2; Mark 12:36, 37; John 1:1, 2, 4, 15; 6:62; 8:23, 58; 12:41; 17:5, 24, 25; Ephesians 3:21; 4:10; Colossians 1:17; 2 Timothy 1:9; Hebrews 1:10-12; 6:20; 7:16, 24, 25; 13:8; 1 Peter 1:20; 1 John 1:1, 2; 2:13, 14; Revelation 1:8, 11, 17, 18; 5:13, 14
See also below: Jesus' pre-existence

Exaltation of Jesus

Psalms 2:8, 9; 24:7-10; 68:18; Mark 16:19; Luke 22:69; 24:26; John 7:39; 13:31, 32; 17:5; Acts 2:33, 34; 3:20, 21; 5:31; 7:55, 56; Romans 8:17, 34; Ephesians 1:20; 4:8, 10; Philippians 2:9-11; Colossians 2:15; 3:1; 1 Timothy 3:16; Hebrews 1:3; 2:9; 4:10, 14; 6:20; 7:26; 8:1; 9:12, 24; 10:12, 13; 12:2; 1 Peter 3:22

Example of Jesus

Matthew 11:29; 20:28; Mark 10:43-45; Luke 22:26, 27; John 10:4; 13:13-15, 34; 17:14, 18, 21, 22; Romans 8:29; 13:14; 15:2, 3, 5, 7;

2 Corinthians 4:10; 8:9; 10:1; Galatians 3:27; 6:2; Ephesians 4:13, 15, 24, 32; 5:2; 6:9; Philippians 2:5-8; Colossians 3:10, 11, 13; 1 Thessalonians 1:6; Hebrews 3:1; 12:2-4; 1 Peter 1:15, 16; 2:21-24; 3:17, 18; 1 John 2:6; 3:1-3, 16; 4:17; Revelation 3:21; 14:4

Holiness of Jesus

Psalms 45:7; 89:19; Isaiah 11:4, 5; 32:1; 42:21; 49:7; 50:5; 53:9; 59:17; Jeremiah 23:5; Zechariah 9:9; Mark 1:24; Luke 1:35; 4:34; 23:40, 41, 47; John 5:30; 7:18; 8:46; 14:30; 16:10; Acts 3:14; 4:27, 30; 13:28, 35; 2 Corinthians 4:4; 5:21; Hebrews 1:9; 4:15; 7:26-28; 9:14; 1 Peter 1:19; 2:22; 1 John 2:29; 3:5; Revelation 3:7

Humanity of Jesus

Genesis 3:15; Deuteronomy 18:15-19; Psalms 22:22; Isaiah 8:18; 9:6; Daniel 7:13; Matthew 16:27, 28; 18:11; 20:28, 30, 31; 21:9; 26:2, 26-28, 36-45, 64; Mark 2:28; 9:9, 12; 10:33, 45; 14:21, 34, 42, 62; Luke 2:11-14; 5:24; 17:22, 24; 18:31; 19:10; 21:36; 22:48, 69; John 1:14; 5:27; 12:34; 13:31; Acts 7:56; 17:31; Galatians 4:4; Philippians 2:7, 8; 1 Timothy 2:5; Hebrews 2:9, 10, 14-18; 10:12; 1 John 4:2, 3; 2 John 1:7; Revelation 1:13; 14:14

Humility of Jesus

Zechariah 9:9; Matthew 9:10; 21:5; Mark 2:14; Luke 5:27, 28; 22:27; John 13:5, 14; Acts 8:32, 33; 2 Corinthians 8:9; 10:1; Philippians 2:7, 8

Incarnation of Jesus

Genesis 3:15; 12:3; 17:7; 22:18; Deuteronomy 18:15-19; 2 Samuel 7:12; 1 Chronicles 5:2; Psalms 2:7; 40:7, 8; 80:17; 89:19, 35, 36; Isaiah 7:14-16; 9:6; 11:1; 32:2; 49:1, 5; Jeremiah 23:5; Micah 5:2, 3; Matthew 1:1, 16-18, 23; 2:5, 6; 8:20; 13:55, 56; 22:45; Luke 1:26-35, 38-56; 2:1-21; 3:23-38; 24:39; John 1:14; 7:42; 20:27; Acts 2:30; 3:22; 13:23, 33; Romans 1:3; 8:3; 9:5; 1 Corinthians 15:47; 2 Corinthians 5:16; Galatians 3:16; 4:4; Philippians 2:7, 8; Colossians 1:15; 1 Timothy 3:16; Hebrews 1:3, 6; 2:9-17; 7:14; 10:5; 1 John 1:1-3; 4:2, 3; 2 John 1:7; Revelation 22:16

Jesus as Judge

Psalms 72:2, 4; 75:2; 96:13; 110:6; Isaiah 2:4; 11:3, 4; Micah 4:3; 5:1; Matthew 3:2, 3, 12; 19:28; 25:31-34; Luke 3:17; Acts 10:42; 17:31; Romans 2:16; 10:12; 14:10; 1 Corinthians 4:4, 5; 2 Corinthians 5:10; 2 Timothy 4:1, 8; James 5:9; Revelation 2:23

Justice of Jesus

2 Samuel 23:3; Zechariah 9:9; Matthew 27:19; John 5:30; Acts 3:14; 22:14

Jesus as King

Genesis 49:10; Numbers 24:17; 1 Samuel 2:10; Psalms 2:6; 18:43, 44; 24:7-10; 45:3-7; 72:5, 8, 11; 89:3, 4, 19-21, 23, 27, 29, 36, 37; 110:1, 2; 132:11, 17, 18; Solomon 1:4, 12; Isaiah 6:1-3; 9:6, 7; 11:10; 22:22; 32:1; 33:17; 40:10; 52:7, 13; Jeremiah 23:5, 6; 30:9; 33:17; Ezekiel 37:24, 25; Daniel 2:35, 44; 7:13, 14; 8:23, 25; 9:25; Hosea 3:5; Micah 5:2, 4; Zechariah 6:13; 9:9, 10; Matthew 2:2, 6; 3:12; 11:27; 12:6; 13:41; 19:28; 21:5; 25:31-34; 26:64; 27:11; 28:18; Mark 14:62; Luke 1:32, 33; 2:11; 3:17; 10:22; 19:27, 38; 22:29, 30, 69; 23:42; John 1:49; 3:31; 12:13, 15, 41; 13:3; 18:36, 37; 19:19; Acts 2:30; 3:15; 5:31; 10:36; Romans 9:5; 14:9; 1 Corinthians 15:23-28; Ephesians 1:20-22; Philippians 2:9-11; 1 Timothy 6:15, 16; 2 Timothy 4:8; Hebrews 2:7, 8; 10:12, 13; 1 Peter 3:22; Revelation 1:5-7, 18; 3:7, 14, 21; 5:5, 12; 6:2, 15-17; 11:15; 12:10; 14:14; 17:14; 19:11, 12, 15, 16; 20:4, 6

Jesus' kingdom
Its nature
Matthew 13:24-51; 18:3, 4; Luke 17:21; John 8:23; 18:36, 37; 2 Corinthians 5:16, 17; 10:3-5
Prophecies about the universality of Jesus' kingdom
Genesis 12:3; 49:10; Deuteronomy 32:21; Psalms 2:8; 22:27-31; 47:8; 65:2; 66:4; 68:31, 32; 72:5, 8-11, 16, 17, 19; 85:10-12; 86:9; 87:1-5; 89:1-37; 96:1-13; 102:13-15; 110:1-6; 113:3; 138:4, 5; 145:10, 11; Isaiah 2:2-5; 4:2, 3; 9:1-7; 11:1-10; 24:16; 25:6-8; 29:18, 19; 32:15-17; 35:1, 2; 40:4-11; 42:3; 45:8, 23, 24; 49:1-26; 51:6,

8; 53:10-12; 54:1-3; 55:5, 10-13; 56:3-8; 59:19-21; 60:1-5, 7-9; 66:7-23; Jeremiah 3:17; 4:2; 16:19-21; 31:34; 33:22; Ezekiel 17:22, 23; 47:1-12; Daniel 2:35, 44; 7:13, 14, 18, 22, 27; 12:4; Joel 2:28, 29; Micah 4:1-4; Habakkuk 2:14; Zephaniah 2:11; 3:9; Haggai 2:7-9; Zechariah 2:10, 11; 4:10; 6:15; 8:20-23; 9:1, 10; 14:8, 9, 16, 20, 21; Malachi 1:11; Matthew 8:11; 13:31-33; Mark 13:10; Luke 1:33; 2:10; John 3:30; 10:16; 12:31, 32; Acts 2:34, 35; 1 Corinthians 15:24-28; Ephesians 1:10; Philippians 2:10, 11; Hebrews 8:11; 10:13; 12:23, 24, 27, 28; Revelation 5:9, 10, 13, 14; 6:2; 11:15; 12:10; 14:6; 15:4; 17:14; 19:6, 11-21; 20:1-3

Unclassified prophecies about the kingdom of Jesus

Genesis 22:18; 49:10; Psalms 2:9; 46:9; 67:1-7; 72:12; Isaiah 2:2-4; 9:5; 11:1-13; 25:6; 35:1-10; 42:1-7, 18-21; 45:14; 49:5, 18-23; 55:1-13; 62:11; 65:17-25; 66:19; Jeremiah 3:14-19; Daniel 2:44; 7:9-14, 27; Hosea 2:18, 23; Amos 9:11, 12; Micah 4:1-7; Zechariah 8:20-23; 9:9; 11:12, 13; 13:7; Malachi 3:1; Matthew 11:10, 15; 12:18-21, 29; 16:28; 21:4, 5; 26:15, 31; 27:3-10; 28:18; Luke 1:32, 33; 22:29, 30; Hebrews 1:8; 2 Peter 1:11

Jesus' love

Psalms 69:9; 72:14; Proverbs 8:17, 31; Isaiah 40:11; 42:3; 53:4; 63:7-9; Micah 5:4; Matthew 8:17; 9:36; 12:49, 50; 14:14; 15:32; 18:2-6, 10-13; 19:13-15; 23:37; 28:10; Mark 3:31-35; 9:36, 37, 42; 10:13, 14, 16, 21; Luke 7:13; 8:19-21; 9:48; 18:15, 16; 22:31, 32; 23:28; 24:38-40; John 10:3, 4, 11, 14-16; 11:5, 33-36; 13:1, 23, 34; 14:1-3, 18, 21, 27; 15:9-13, 15; 17:12, 15, 19; 18:8, 9; 19:26, 27; 20:17, 27; 21:15-17; Acts 9:4, 5; 10:38; Romans 8:35, 37-39; 15:3; 2 Corinthians 5:13, 14; 8:9; Galatians 2:20; Ephesians 3:17-19; 5:2, 25, 29, 30; 2 Thessalonians 2:13; Hebrews 2:11, 18; 4:15; 1 John 3:16; Revelation 1:5; 3:9, 19

See also above: The compassion of Jesus

Jesus' meekness

Psalms 45:4; Isaiah 42:2; 50:5, 6; 52:13; 53:7; Matthew 11:29; 12:19, 20; 21:5; 26:49-63; 27:12-14; Mark 2:6-11; Luke 22:27; 23:34; John 8:48-50; 13:5, 14; Acts 8:32; 2 Corinthians 10:1; Philippians 2:7, 8; Hebrews 12:2, 3; 1 Peter 2:23

Jesus the Messiah

Messianic psalms

Psalms 2:1-12; 16:7-11; 67:1-7; 68:28-35; 69:1-36; 72:1-19; 93:1-5; 96:1-13; 97:1-12; 98:1-9; 99:1-9; 110:1-7; 118:19-29

Other Scriptures relating to Jesus as Messiah

Psalms 2:2; Daniel 9:25, 26; Matthew 11:3-6; 16:15, 16; 22:42-45; 26:63, 64; Mark 12:35-37; Luke 2:28-32, 38; 20:41-44; 24:25-27; John 1:41, 45; 4:25, 26, 29, 42; 5:33, 36, 37, 39, 46; 6:27; 8:14, 17, 18, 25, 28, 56; 13:19; Acts 3:18, 20, 24; 4:26, 27; 9:22; 13:27; 17:2, 3; 26:6, 7, 22, 23; 28:23; Romans 1:1-3; 1 Corinthians 15:3; 1 Peter 1:10, 11; 2 Peter 1:16-18; 1 John 5:6-9

Jesus' obedience

Psalms 40:8; Isaiah 11:5; 42:21; 50:5, 6; Matthew 3:15; 26:39, 42; Mark 14:36; Luke 2:49; 22:42; John 4:34; 5:30, 36; 6:38; 7:18; 8:29, 46, 55; 9:4; 14:31; 15:10; 17:4; 19:30; Philippians 2:8; Hebrews 5:8; 10:7-9

Jesus' omnipotence

Psalms 45:3-5; 110:3; Isaiah 9:6; 40:10; 50:2, 4; 63:1; Matthew 8:3, 16, 27; 10:1; 12:13, 28, 29; 28:18; Mark 3:27; 6:7; Luke 5:17; 9:1; 11:20-22; John 2:19; 5:21, 28, 29; 10:17, 18, 28; 17:1, 2; Philippians 3:20, 21; Colossians 1:17; 2 Thessalonians 1:9; 1 Timothy 6:16; Hebrews 1:3; 7:25; 2 Peter 1:16; Revelation 1:8; 3:7; 5:12

Jesus' omnipresence

Matthew 18:20; 28:20; John 3:13; Ephesians 1:23

Jesus' omniscience

Proverbs 8:1-16; Isaiah 11:2, 3; 50:4; Matthew 9:4; 11:27; 12:25; 13:54; 22:18;

24:25; 26:46; Mark 2:8; 5:30; 14:13-15, 42; Luke 2:40, 47, 52; 5:22; 6:8; 9:46-48; 22:10-13; John 1:48; 2:24, 25; 3:32; 4:16-19, 28, 29; 5:30, 42; 6:64; 8:16; 13:1, 2, 10, 11; 16:30, 32; 17:1; 18:4; 21:17; Acts 1:24; Colossians 2:3; Revelation 2:18, 23; 5:5, 12

Jesus' power to forgive sins
Matthew 9:2, 6; Mark 2:5, 10; Luke 5:20, 24; 7:47-50; Acts 5:31; Colossians 3:13

Jesus' prayers
Matthew 11:25, 26; 14:23; 15:36; 19:13; 26:26, 27, 36, 39, 42, 44; 27:46; Mark 1:35; 6:41, 46; 14:32-39; Luke 3:21; 5:16; 6:12; 9:18, 28, 29; 11:1; 22:32, 41-44; 23:34; John 11:41, 42; 12:27, 28; 17:1-26; 1 Corinthians 11:24; Hebrews 5:7

Jesus' pre-existence
Genesis 1:26; Psalms 102:25-27; Proverbs 8:22-36; John 1:1-3; 6:62; 8:56-58; 17:5; Romans 11:36; 1 Corinthians 8:6; Philippians 2:5-7; Colossians 1:15-17; Hebrews 1:1, 2, 8-12; 2:9, 14-16; 4:8; Revelation 4:11

Jesus' priesthood
Appointed and called by God
Hebrews 3:1, 2; 5:4, 5
After the order of Melchizedek
Psalms 110:4; Hebrews 5:6; 6:20; 7:15, 17
Superior to Aaron and the Levitical priests
Hebrews 7:11, 16, 22; 8:1, 2, 6
Consecrated with an oath
Hebrews 7:20, 21
Has an unchangeable priesthood
Hebrews 7:23, 28
Is of unblemished purity
Hebrews 7:26, 28
Faithful
Hebrews 3:2
Needed no sacrifice for himself
Hebrews 7:27
Offered himself as a sacrifice
Hebrews 9:14, 26
His sacrifice superior to all others
Hebrews 9:13, 14, 23
Offered sacrifice only once
Hebrews 7:27
Made reconciliation
Hebrews 2:17
Obtained redemption for us
Hebrews 9:12
Entered into heaven
Hebrews 4:14; 10:12
Sympathizes with saints
Hebrews 2:18; 4:15
Intercedes
Hebrews 7:25; 9:24
Blesses
Numbers 6:23-26; Acts 3:26
On his throne
Zechariah 6:13
Appointment of, an encouragement to steadfastness
Hebrews 4:14
Typified
Melchizedek
Genesis 14:18-20
Aaron and his sons
Exodus 40:12-15

Jesus' prophetic promises
Matthew 19:28, 29; Mark 10:29, 30; Luke 18:29, 30; 22:29, 30; 23:43; 24:49; John 5:25-29; 6:54, 57, 58; 7:39; 12:25, 26; 14:16, 26; 15:26, 27; 16:7-16, 20-26, 33; Acts 1:4-8

Promises about Jesus' coming
Genesis 3:15; 12:3; 49:10; Deuteronomy 32:18; 1 Samuel 2:10; Job 19:25; Psalms 21:5-7; 40:6-10; 68:18; 118:22-24, 26; Isaiah 11:1-16; 28:16; 40:3, 11; 42:1-4; 49:1-26; 55:3-5; 56:1; 59:16-18, 20; 62:10, 11; Jeremiah 23:5, 6; 33:15-18; Daniel 7:13, 14; 9:24-27; Haggai 2:7; Zechariah 3:8; 9:9; 13:1; Malachi 3:1-3; 4:2; Matthew 1:20-23; Luke 1:26-37, 41-45; 2:26, 31, 32, 34, 35, 38; 3:4; John 8:56; Acts 3:22-24; Romans 1:2, 3; 15:12; Hebrews 7:16; 10:9

Prophecies about the future glory and power of Jesus
Isaiah 22:22; Mark 14:62; 1 Peter 3:22; Jude 1:14, 15; Revelation 1:5-7, 18; 2:23; 3:7, 14, 21; 5:5, 12; 6:16, 17; 7:9-17; 11:15; 12:10; 14:14; 17:14; 19:11, 12, 15, 16; 20:4, 6

Jesus as prophet

Foretold
Isaiah 52:7; Nahum 1:15

Anointed with the Holy Spirit
Isaiah 42:1; 61:1; Luke 4:18; John 3:34

Reveals God
Matthew 11:27; John 3:2, 13, 34; 17:6, 14, 26; Hebrews 1:1, 2

Declared his doctrine to be that of the Father
John 8:26, 28; 12:49, 50; 14:10, 24; 15:15; 17:8, 26

Foretold things to come
Matthew 24:3-35; Luke 19:41-44

Faithful
Luke 4:43; John 17:8; Hebrews 3:2; Revelation 1:5; 3:14

Abounded in wisdom
Luke 2:40, 47, 52; Colossians 2:3

Mighty in deed and word
Matthew 13:54; Mark 1:27; Luke 4:32; John 7:46

Unostentatious in his teaching
Isaiah 42:2; Matthew 12:17-20

God commands us to hear
Deuteronomy 18:15; Acts 3:22

God will severely punish those who reject him
Deuteronomy 18:10; Acts 3:23; Hebrews 2:3; Deuteronomy 18:15; Acts 3:22, 23; 7:37; Matthew 21:11, 46; Luke 7:16, 39; 13:33; 24:19; John 3:2; 4:19; 6:14; 7:40; 9:17

Jesus is received
Matthew 4:24, 25; 7:28, 29; 8:1; 9:8, 27, 33; 12:23, 38; 13:2, 54; 14:13, 33, 35; 15:31; 16:1, 14; 19:1, 2; 21:8-11, 15; 27:54; Mark 1:22, 27, 33, 37, 45; 2:2, 12, 15; 3:7, 20, 21; 4:1; 5:21, 42; 6:2, 33, 51, 52, 55, 56; 7:37; 8:11, 28; 10:1; 11:8-10, 18; 12:37; 15:39; Luke 4:14, 15, 22, 32, 36, 37, 42; 5:1, 17, 19, 26; 6:17-19; 7:16-18; 8:56; 9:11, 19; 11:16; 12:1; 13:17; 18:43; 19:36-38, 47, 48; 21:38; 23:27, 47; John 2:11, 23; 6:2; 7:31, 40-44, 46; 8:2, 30; 9:17, 24, 25, 29, 30, 33; 10:41, 42; 11:37, 45-48; 12:9, 11, 12, 13, 18-21, 34, 42

Instances of Jesus being received
By Matthew

Matthew 9:9, 10
By Peter and other disciples
Mark 1:16-20; Luke 5:3-11
By Zacchaeus
Luke 19:1-10
By Philip
John 1:43, 45
By Nathanael
John 1:45-50
By three thousand people on the day of Pentecost
Acts 2:41; 4:4
By the Ethiopian eunuch
Acts 8:37

Rejection of Jesus
Psalms 2:1-3; 118:22; Isaiah 6:9, 10; 8:14; 49:4; 50:1-11; 53:1-4; Matthew 7:26, 27; 8:12, 34; 10:14, 15, 33; 11:16-19; 12:38-45; 13:3-14, 58; 17:17; 21:32, 38-45; 22:2-13; 26:31-35, 69-75; Mark 5:17; 6:3-6; 12:1-12; 14:27-31, 66-72; 16:16; Luke 6:46-49; 7:30-35; 8:37; 10:16; 11:23-26; 13:34; 14:16-24; 17:25; 19:42; 20:9-18; 22:31-34, 54-62, 67; 24:11, 15-25, 37-39; John 1:11; 3:11, 12, 18, 19, 32; 5:38, 40, 43; 6:36, 60-68; 7:3-5, 12, 13, 15, 25-27; 8:13, 21, 22, 24-30, 45-47, 53; 9:16, 17, 24; 10:20, 21, 24, 33; 11:46-48; 12:37, 48; 15:18, 20, 24; 18:15-27; Acts 13:46; 18:5, 6; 22:18; 28:24, 25, 27; Romans 3:3; 9:31, 32; 10:16, 21; 1 Corinthians 1:18, 23; 2 Timothy 2:12; Hebrews 6:6; 10:29; 1 Peter 2:4, 7, 8; 2 Peter 2:1; 1 John 2:22, 23; 2 John 1:7; Jude 1:4

Jesus' relation to the Father
Psalms 110:1; Isaiah 42:1; 49:5, 6; 61:1; Micah 5:4; Matthew 20:23; 26:39; Mark 10:40; 13:32; John 1:1, 2, 14; 3:34, 35; 4:34; 5:19-31, 37, 45; 6:32, 33, 38-40, 44-46; 7:16, 28, 29, 33; 8:16, 19, 28, 29, 38, 40, 42; 49, 54, 55; 9:4; 10:15, 18, 25, 29, 30, 32, 33, 36-38; 11:41, 42; 12:44, 49, 50; 14:7, 9-14, 20, 24, 28, 31; 15:9, 10, 15, 23-26; 16:5, 10, 15, 23, 25, 27, 28, 32; 17:1-26; Acts 2:33, 36; 10:38; 13:37; Romans 1:4; 8:32; 1 Corinthians 1:30; 3:23; 11:3; 15:24, 27, 28; 2 Corinthians 4:4, 6; Ephesians 1:17, 20-22; Philippians 2:6, 11; Colossians 1:15, 19; 1 Thessalonians 5:18; Hebrews 1:2, 3; 2:9; 3:2; 5:5-10; 1 Peter 1:21; 2:4, 23; 2 Peter

1:17; 1 John 4:9, 10, 14; Revelation 2:27; 3:12, 21

Jesus' resurrection

Psalms 2:7; 16:9, 10; Isaiah 26:19; Matthew 12:40; 16:4, 21; 17:23; 20:19; 26:32; 27:52, 53, 63; 28:6, 7; Mark 8:31; 9:9, 10; 10:34; 14:28, 58; 16:6, 7; Luke 9:22, 31; 18:33; 24:5-7, 46; John 2:19, 21, 22; 12:23; 16:16, 22; 20:1-18; Acts 1:3, 22; 2:24, 31, 32; 3:15; 4:10, 33; 5:30-32; 10:40, 41; 13:30-34; 17:2, 3, 31; 26:23, 26; Romans 1:4; 4:24, 25; 5:10; 6:4, 5, 9, 10; 8:11, 34; 10:9; 1 Corinthians 6:14; 15:3-8, 12-23; 2 Corinthians 4:10, 11, 14; 5:15; 13:4; Galatians 1:1; Ephesians 1:20; Philippians 3:10; Colossians 1:18; 2:12; 1 Thessalonians 1:10; 4:14; 2 Timothy 2:8; Hebrews 13:20; 1 Peter 1:3, 21; 3:18, 21; Revelation 1:5, 18

Revelations made by Jesus

Concerning his kingdom

Matthew 8:11, 12; Luke 13:28, 29; Matthew 10:23, 34; 13:24-50; 16:18, 28; Mark 9:1; Luke 9:27; Matthew 21:43, 44; 24:14; Mark 16:17, 18; Luke 12:40-53; 13:24-35; 17:20-37; John 4:21, 23; 5:25, 29; 6:39, 54; 12:35; 13:19; 14:29; 16:4

His rejection by the Jews

Matthew 21:33-44; Luke 17:25

His betrayal

Matthew 26:21, 23-25

Crucifixion

John 3:14; 8:28; 12:32

Judgments upon the Jews

Matthew 23:37-39; 25; Mark 11:12-14

The destruction of the Temple, and Jerusalem

Matthew 24; Mark 13; Luke 19:41-48

The destruction of Capernaum

Matthew 11:23; Luke 10:15

Concerning persecutions of Christians

Matthew 23:34-36

His being forsaken by his disciples

John 16:32

Concerning Lazarus

John 11:4, 11, 23, 40

Concerning Peter

John 21:18-23

Fame of the woman who anointed his head

Matthew 26:13; Mark 14:8, 9

Antichrist

Matthew 24:4, 5, 23-26; Mark 13:5, 6, 21-23; Luke 17:23, 24; 21:8; Acts 5:36, 37

Concerning His death and resurrection

Matthew 12:39, 40; 16:21; 17:22, 23; 20:18, 19; 26:2, 21, 23, 24, 45, 46; Mark 8:31; 9:31; 10:32-34; Luke 9:22-24; 18:31-33; John 2:19; 12:7, 23; 13:18-27, 36-38; 16:32

His ascension

John 7:33, 34; 8:21; 12:8; 13:33; 16:10, 16

Jesus as Savior

Genesis 12:3; 49:18; 2 Samuel 23:6, 7; Job 33:23, 24; Psalms 14:7; 72:4, 12-14, 17; 80:17; 89:19; Isaiah 8:14; 28:16; 32:2; 40:10, 11; 42:6, 7; 49:6, 8, 9; 50:2, 8, 9; 53:10, 11; 59:16, 17, 20; 61:1-3; 62:11; 63:1, 5, 8, 9; Jeremiah 23:5, 6; 33:15, 16; Ezekiel 34:23; Haggai 2:7; Zechariah 4:7; 9:9; Malachi 4:2; Matthew 1:21; 9:12, 13; 15:24; 18:11-13; Luke 1:68-77; 2:11, 31, 32, 34; 5:31, 32; 9:56; 15:1-10; 19:10; John 1:9, 29; 3:16, 17; 4:14, 42; 5:26, 33, 34, 40; 6:27, 32, 33, 35, 37, 39, 51, 53-58, 68; 7:37-39; 8:12; 9:5, 39; 10:7, 9-11, 14-16, 27, 28; 11:25-27; 12:47; 14:6, 19; 16:33; 17:2, 3; Acts 3:26; 4:12; 5:31; 13:23, 38, 39, 47; 15:11; 16:31; Romans 3:24-26; 4:25; 5:1, 6, 8-11, 15, 17-19, 21; 6:23; 8:2; 10:9, 11; 15:7, 9; 1 Corinthians 1:30; 3:11; 6:11; 10:3, 4; 15:17, 57; 2 Corinthians 5:18, 19, 21; Galatians 1:3, 4; 2:20; 4:7; Ephesians 1:10, 11; 2:7, 13-18, 20; 4:8; 5:2, 14, 23, 25, 26; Philippians 3:20; Colossians 1:12-14, 27, 28; 2:8, 10; 3:3, 4, 11; 1 Thessalonians 1:10; 5:9, 10; 2 Thessalonians 1:12; 1 Timothy 1:1, 15; 2 Timothy 1:1, 9, 10, 12; 2:10; 3:15; Titus 1:4; 2:13, 14; Hebrews 2:3, 17; 5:9; 7:22, 25; 13:10, 20; 1 Peter 1:3, 18, 19; 2:4-7, 25; 3:18, 21; 5:10; 2 Peter 1:3, 11; 2:20; 1 John 3:5, 8; 4:9, 10, 14; 5:11-13, 20; Jude 1:1; Revelation 2:7; 3:18; 5:5-14; 7:10; 14:4; 21:27; 22:1, 2

Jesus' second coming

Job 19:25, 26; Matthew 16:27, 28; 23:39; 24:1-51; 25:1-13, 19, 31-46; 26:64; Mark 8:38; 9:1; 13:1-37; 14:62; Luke 9:26, 27; 12:37-40; 17:22-37; 18:8; 19:12, 13, 15; 21:5-36; John 14:3, 18, 28, 29; Acts 1:11; 3:20, 21; 1 Corinthians 1:7, 8; 4:5; 11:26; 15:23; Philippians 3:20, 21; 4:5; Colossians 3:4; 1 Thessalonians 1:10; 2:19; 3:13; 4:15-17; 5:2, 3, 23; 2 Thessalonians 1:7-10; 2:1-3, 5, 8; 3:5; 1 Timothy 6:14, 15; 2 Timothy 4:1, 8; Titus 2:13; Hebrews 9:28; James 5:7-9; 1 Peter 1:7, 13; 4:13; 5:4; 2 Peter 1:16; 3:3, 4, 8-14; 1 John 2:28; 3:2; Jude 1:14, 15; Revelation 1:7; 3:11; 16:15; 22:12, 20

Jesus as the true Shepherd

Foretold
Genesis 49:24; Isaiah 40:11; Ezekiel 34:23; 37:24

The chief
1 Peter 5:4

The good
John 10:11, 14

The great
Micah 5:4; Hebrews 13:20

His sheep he knows
John 10:14, 27

He calls
John 10:3

He gathers
Isaiah 40:11; John 10:16

He guides
Psalms 23:3; John 10:3, 4

He feeds
Psalms 23:1, 2; John 10:9

He cherishes tenderly
Isaiah 40:11

He protects and preserves
Jeremiah 31:10; Ezekiel 34:10; Zechariah 9:16; John 10:28

He laid down his life for
Zechariah 13:7; Matthew 26:31; John 10:11, 15; Acts 20:28

He gives eternal life to
John 10:28

Typified: David
1 Samuel 16:11

Jesus the Son of God

Psalms 2:7; 89:26, 27; Matthew 3:17; 4:3, 6;

10:40; 11:27; 14:33; 15:13; 16:15-17; 17:5; 18:10, 19; 20:23; 21:37; 26:53, 63, 64; 27:43, 54; Mark 1:1, 11; 3:11; 5:7; 9:7; 14:61, 62; 15:39; Luke 1:32, 35; 3:22; 4:3, 9, 41; 8:28; 9:35; 10:22; 20:13; 22:29, 70; John 1:1, 2, 14, 18, 34, 49, 50; 3:16-18, 34-36; 5:19-21, 23, 26, 27, 30, 32, 36, 37; 6:27, 38, 40, 46, 57, 69; 7:16, 28, 29; 8:16, 19, 26-29, 38, 40, 42, 49, 54; 9:35-37; 10:15, 17, 18, 29, 30, 36-38; 11:4, 27, 41; 12:49, 50; 13:3; 14:7, 9-11, 13, 16, 20, 24, 28, 31; 15:1, 8-10, 23, 24; 16:5, 15, 27, 28, 32; 17:1-26; 19:7; 20:17, 21, 31; Acts 3:13; 13:33; Romans 1:3, 4, 9; 8:3, 29, 32; 1 Corinthians 1:9; 15:24, 27, 28; 2 Corinthians 1:3, 19; Galatians 1:16; 4:4; Ephesians 1:3; 3:14; Colossians 1:3, 15, 19; 3:17; 1 Thessalonians 1:10; Hebrews 1:1-3, 5; 4:14; 5:5, 8, 10; 6:6; 7:3; 10:29; 2 Peter 1:17; 1 John 1:7; 2:22-24; 3:8, 23; 4:9, 10, 14; 5:5, 9, 10, 13, 20; 2 John 1:3; Revelation 2:18

Jesus the Son of Man

See also above, Humanity of Jesus

Sufferings of Jesus

Matthew 26:38-45; 27:24-50; Mark 14:15; 15:34; Luke 2:34; 4:28, 29; 22:23, 44; 24:46; John 4:6; 11:33, 35; 12:27; 18:11, 19; 19:28; Acts 3:18; 17:3; 2 Corinthians 1:5; Philippians 2:7, 8; 3:10; Hebrews 2:9; 4:15; 5:7, 8; 12:2, 3; 1 Peter 1:11; 2:21-23; 4:1; Revelation 5:6; 19:13

Prophecies about the sufferings of Jesus
Psalms 22:6-8, 11-13, 17-21; 69:7-9, 20; 109:25; Isaiah 50:6; 52:13, 14; 53:1-12; Micah 5:1; Zechariah 11:12, 13; 13:6, 7; Matthew 16:21; 17:12, 22, 23; 20:17-19; 27:35; Mark 8:31; 10:32-34; 15:24; Luke 2:34, 35; 9:22; 18:31-33; 22:37; 23:34; John 12:38; 19:23; 1 Peter 1:11

Jesus as Teacher

Matthew 4:23; 5:1; 7:29; 11:1; 21:23; 22:16; 23:8; 26:55; Mark 4:1; 12:14; Luke 4:15; 6:6; 20:21; 23:5; John 3:2; Acts 1:1

The temptations of Jesus

Isaiah 7:16; Matthew 4:1-11; Mark 1:12, 13;

Luke 4:1-13; 22:28; John 14:30; Hebrews 4:15

Jesus as unchangeable
Hebrews 13:8

Worship of Jesus
Joshua 5:14, 15; Psalms 45:11, 17; 72:15; Matthew 2:2, 11; 9:18; 14:33; 15:25; 20:20; 21:9; 28:9, 16, 17; Mark 3:11; 5:6, 7; 11:9, 10; Luke 4:41; 5:8; 23:42; 24:52; John 5:23; 9:38; 12:13; Acts 1:24; 7:59, 60; 1 Corinthians 1:2; 2 Corinthians 12:8, 9; Philippians 2:10, 11; 1 Timothy 1:12;

Hebrews 1:6; 2 Peter 3:18; Revelation 5:8, 9, 12-14; 7:10

Zeal of Jesus
Psalms 69:9; Isaiah 59:17; Matthew 4:23; 9:35; Mark 1:38; 3:20, 21; 6:6; Luke 2:49; 4:43; 8:1; 9:51; 12:50; 13:32, 33; John 2:17; 4:32, 34; 9:4; Acts 10:38; Romans 15:3; 1 Timothy 6:13

Orville J. Nave
Topical Bible

1.48 BIBLE STUDY ON JESUS' NAMES AND TITLES

The following entry lists the names and titles given specifically to Jesus.

ADAM: (1 Corinthians 15:45) And so it is written, The first man Adam was made a living soul; the last Adam was made a quickening spirit.

ADVOCATE: (1 John 2:1) My little children, these things write I unto you, that ye sin not. And if any man sin, we have an advocate with the Father, Jesus Christ the righteous:

ALMIGHTY: (Revelation 1:8) I am Alpha and Omega, the beginning and the ending, saith the Lord, which is, and which was, and which is to come, the Almighty.

ALPHA AND OMEGA: (Revelation 1:8) I am Alpha and Omega, the beginning and the ending, saith the Lord, which is, and which was, and which is to come, the Almighty.

AMEN: (Revelation 3:14) And unto the angel of the church of the Laodiceans write; These things saith the Amen, the faithful and true witness, the beginning of the creation of God;

APOSTLE OF OUR PROFESSION: (Hebrews 3:1) Wherefore, holy brethren, partakers of the heavenly calling, consider the Apostle and High Priest of our profession, Christ Jesus;

ARM OF THE LORD: (Isaiah 51:9) Awake, awake, put on strength, O arm of the LORD; awake, as in the ancient days, in the generations of old. Art thou not it that hath cut Rahab, and wounded the dragon?

(Isaiah 53:1) Who hath believed our report? and to whom is the arm of the LORD revealed?

AUTHOR AND FINISHER OF OUR FAITH: (Hebrews 12:2) Looking unto Jesus the author and finisher of our faith; who for the joy that was set before him endured the cross, despising the shame, and is set down at the right hand of the throne of God.

AUTHOR OF ETERNAL SALVATION: (Hebrews 5:9) And being made perfect, he became the author of eternal salvation unto all them that obey him;

BEGINNING OF CREATION OF GOD: (Revelation 3:14) And unto the angel of the church of the Laodiceans write; These things saith the Amen, the faithful and true witness, the beginning of the creation of God;

BELOVED: (Matthew 12:18) Behold my servant, whom I have chosen; my beloved, in whom my soul is well pleased: I will put my spirit upon him, and he shall show judgment to the Gentiles.

BLESSED AND ONLY POTENTATE: (1 Timothy 6:15) Which in his times he shall show, who is the blessed and only Potentate, the King of kings, and Lord of lords;

BRANCH: (Isaiah 4:2) In that day shall the branch of the LORD be beautiful and glorious, and the fruit of the earth shall be excellent and comely for them that are escaped of Israel.

BREAD OF LIFE: (John 6:32) Then Jesus said unto them, Verily, verily, I say unto you, Moses gave you not that bread from heaven; but my Father giveth you the true bread from heaven.

CAPTAIN OF SALVATION: (Hebrews 2:10) For it became him, for whom are all things, and by whom are all things, in bringing many sons unto glory, to make the captain of their salvation perfect through sufferings.

CHIEF SHEPHERD: (1 Peter 5:4) And when the chief Shepherd shall appear, ye shall receive a crown of glory that fadeth not away.

CHRIST OF GOD: (Luke 9:20) He said unto them, But whom say ye that I am? Peter answering said, The Christ of God.

CONSOLATION OF ISRAEL: (Luke 2:25) And, behold, there was a man in Jerusalem, whose name was Simeon; and the same man was just and devout, waiting for the consolation of Israel: and the Holy Ghost was upon him.

CORNERSTONE: (Psalm 118:22) The stone which the builders refused is become the head stone of the corner.

COUNSELLOR: (Isaiah 9:6) For unto us a child is born, unto us a son is given: and the government shall be upon his shoulder: and his name shall be called Wonderful, Counselor, The mighty God, The everlasting Father, The Prince of Peace.

CREATOR: (John 1:3) All things were made by him; and without him was not any thing made that was made.

DAYSPRING: (Luke 1:78) Through the tender mercy of our God; whereby the dayspring from on high hath visited us,

DELIVERER: (Romans 11:26) And so all Israel shall be saved: as it is written, There shall come out of Zion the Deliverer, and shall turn away ungodliness from Jacob:

DESIRE OF THE NATIONS: (Haggai 2:7) And I will shake all nations, and the desire of all nations shall come: and I will fill this house with glory, saith the LORD of hosts.

DOOR: (John 10:7) Then said Jesus unto them again, Verily, verily, I say unto you, I am the door of the sheep.

ELECT OF GOD: (Isaiah 42:1) Behold my servant, whom I uphold; mine elect, in whom my soul delighteth; I have put my spirit upon him: he shall bring forth judgment to the Gentiles.

EVERLASTING FATHER: (Isaiah 9:6) For unto us a child is born, unto us a son is given: and the government shall be upon his shoulder: and his name shall be called Wonderful, Counselor, The mighty God, The everlasting Father, The Prince of Peace.

FAITHFUL WITNESS: (Revelation 1:5) And from Jesus Christ, who is the faithful witness, and the first begotten of the dead, and the prince of the kings of the earth. Unto him that loved us, and washed us from our sins in his own blood,

FIRST AND LAST: (Revelation 1:17) And when I saw him, I fell at his feet as dead. And he laid his right hand upon me, saying unto me, Fear not; I am the first and the last:

FIRST BEGOTTEN: (Revelation 1:5) And from Jesus Christ, who is the faithful witness, and the first begotten of the dead, and the prince of the kings of the earth. Unto him that loved us, and washed us from our sins in his own blood,

FORERUNNER: (Hebrews 6:20) Whither the forerunner is for us entered, even Jesus, made an high priest for ever after the order of Melchisedec.

GLORY OF THE LORD: (Isaiah 40:5) And the glory of the LORD shall be revealed, and all flesh shall see it together: for the mouth of the LORD hath spoken it.

GOD: (Isaiah 40:3) The voice of him that crieth in the wilderness, Prepare ye the way of the LORD, make straight in the desert a highway for our God.

GOD BLESSED: (Romans 9:5) Whose are the fathers, and of whom as concerning the flesh Christ came, who is over all, God blessed for ever. Amen.

GOOD SHEPHERD: (John 10:11) I am the good shepherd: the good shepherd giveth his life for the sheep.

GOVERNOR: (Matthew 2:6) And thou Bethlehem, in the land of Juda, art not the least among the princes of Juda: for out of thee shall come a Governor, that shall rule my people Israel.

GREAT HIGH PRIEST: (Hebrews 4:14) Seeing then that we have a great high priest, that is passed into the heavens, Jesus the Son of God, let us hold fast our profession.

HEAD OF THE CHURCH: (Ephesians 1:22) And hath put all things under his feet, and gave him to be the head over all things to the church,

HEIR OF ALL THINGS: (Hebrews 1:2) Hath in these last days spoken unto us by his Son, whom he hath appointed heir of all things, by whom also he made the worlds;

HOLY CHILD: (Acts 4:27) For of a truth against thy holy child Jesus, whom thou hast anointed, both Herod, and Pontius Pilate, with the Gentiles, and the people of Israel, were gathered together,

HOLY ONE: (Acts 3:14) But ye denied the Holy One and the Just, and desired a murderer to be granted unto you;

HOLY ONE OF GOD: (Mark 1:24) Saying, Let us alone; what have we to do with thee, thou Jesus of Nazareth? art thou come to destroy us? I know thee who thou art, the Holy One of God.

HOLY ONE OF ISRAEL: (Isaiah 41:14) Fear not, thou worm Jacob, and ye men of Israel; I will help thee, saith the LORD, and thy redeemer, the Holy One of Israel.

HORN OF SALVATION: (Luke 1:69) And hath raised up an horn of salvation for us in the house of his servant David;

I AM: (John 8:58) Jesus said unto them, Verily, verily, I say unto you, Before Abraham was, I am.

IMAGE OF GOD: (2 Corinthians 4:4) In whom the god of this world hath blinded the minds of them which believe not, lest the light of the glorious gospel of Christ, who is the image of God, should shine unto them.

IMMANUEL: (Isaiah 7:14) Therefore the Lord himself shall give you a sign; Behold, a virgin shall conceive, and bear a son, and shall call his name Immanuel.

JEHOVAH: (Isaiah 26:4) Trust ye in the LORD for ever: for in the LORD JEHOVAH is everlasting strength:

JESUS: (Matthew 1:21) And she shall bring forth a son, and thou shalt call his name

JESUS, for he shall save his people from their sins.

JESUS OF NAZARETH: (Matthew 21:11) And the multitude said, This is Jesus the prophet of Nazareth of Galilee.

JUDGE OF ISRAEL: (Micah 5:1) Now gather thyself in troops, O daughter of troops: he hath laid siege against us: they shall smite the judge of Israel with a rod upon the cheek.

THE JUST ONE: (Acts 7:52) Which of the prophets have not your fathers persecuted? and they have slain them which showed before of the coming of the Just One; of whom ye have been now the betrayers and murderers:

KING: (Zechariah 9:9) Rejoice greatly, O daughter of Zion; shout, O daughter of Jerusalem: behold, thy King cometh unto thee: he is just, and having salvation; lowly, and riding upon an ass, and upon a colt the foal of an ass.

KING OF THE AGES: (1 Timothy 1:17) Now unto the King eternal, immortal, invisible, the only wise God, be honor and glory for ever and ever. Amen.

KING OF THE JEWS: (Matthew 2:2) Saying, Where is he that is born King of the Jews? for we have seen his star in the east, and are come to worship him.

KING OF KINGS: (1 Timothy 6:15) Which in his times he shall show, who is the blessed and only Potentate, the King of kings, and Lord of lords;

KING OF SAINTS: (Revelation 15:3) And they sing the song of Moses the servant of God, and the song of the Lamb, saying, Great and marvelous are thy works, Lord God Almighty; just and true are thy ways, thou King of saints.

LAWGIVER: (Isaiah 33:22) For the LORD is our judge, the LORD is our lawgiver, the LORD is our king; he will save us.

LAMB: (Revelation 13:8) And all that dwell upon the earth shall worship him, whose names are not written in the book of life of the Lamb slain from the foundation of the world.

LAMB OF GOD: (John 1:29) The next day John seeth Jesus coming unto him, and saith, Behold the Lamb of God, which taketh away the sin of the world.

LEADER AND COMMANDER: (Isaiah 55:4) Behold, I have given him for a witness to the people, a leader and commander to the people.

THE LIFE: (John 14:6) Jesus saith unto him, I am the way, the truth, and the life: no man cometh unto the Father, but by me.

LIGHT OF THE WORLD: (John 8:12) Then spake Jesus again unto them, saying, I am the light of the world: he that followeth me shall not walk in darkness, but shall have the light of life.

LION OF THE TRIBE OF JUDAH: (Revelation 5:5) And one of the elders saith unto me, Weep not: behold, the Lion of the tribe of Juda, the Root of David, hath prevailed to open the book, and to loose the seven seals thereof.

LORD OF ALL: (Acts 10:36) The word which God sent unto the children of Israel, preaching peace by Jesus Christ: (he is Lord of all:)

LORD OF GLORY: (1 Corinthians 2:8) Which none of the princes of this world knew: for had they known it, they would not have crucified the Lord of glory.

LORD OF LORDS: (1 Timothy 6:15) Which in his times he shall show, who is the blessed and only Potentate, the King of kings, and Lord of lords;

LORD OF OUR RIGHTEOUSNESS: (Jeremiah 23:6) In his days Judah shall be saved, and Israel shall dwell safely: and this is his name whereby he shall be called, THE LORD OUR RIGHTEOUSNESS.

MAN OF SORROWS: (Isaiah 53:3) He is despised and rejected of men; a man of sorrows, and acquainted with grief: and we hid as it were our faces from him; he was despised, and we esteemed him not.

MEDIATOR: (1 Timothy 2:5) For there is one God, and one mediator between God and men, the man Christ Jesus;

MESSENGER OF THE COVENANT: (Malachi 3:1) Behold, I will send my messenger, and he shall prepare the way before me: and the Lord, whom ye seek, shall suddenly come to his temple, even the messenger of the covenant, whom ye delight in: behold, he shall come, saith the LORD of hosts.

MESSIAH: (Daniel 9:25) Know therefore and understand, that from the going forth of the commandment to restore and to build Jerusalem unto the Messiah the Prince shall be seven weeks, and threescore and two weeks: the street shall be built again, and the wall, even in troublous times.

(John 1:41) He first findeth his own brother Simon, and saith unto him, We have found the Messiah, which is, being interpreted, the Christ.

MIGHTY GOD: (Isaiah 9:6) For unto us a child is born, unto us a son is given: and the government shall be upon his shoulder: and his name shall be called Wonderful, Counselor, The mighty God, The everlasting Father, The Prince of Peace.

MIGHTY ONE: (Isaiah 60:16) Thou shalt also suck the milk of the Gentiles, and shalt suck the breast of kings: and thou shalt know that I the LORD am thy Savior and thy Redeemer, the mighty One of Jacob.

MORNING STAR: (Revelation 22:16) I Jesus have sent mine angel to testify unto you these things in the churches. I am the root and

the offspring of David, and the bright and morning star.

NAZARENE: (Matthew 2:23) And he came and dwelt in a city called Nazareth: that it might be fulfilled which was spoken by the prophets, He shall be called a Nazarene.

ONLY BEGOTTEN SON: (John 1:18) No man hath seen God at any time; the only begotten Son, which is in the bosom of the Father, he hath declared him.

OUR PASSOVER: (1 Corinthians 5:7) Purge out therefore the old leaven, that ye may be a new lump, as ye are unleavened. For even Christ our Passover is sacrificed for us:

PRINCE OF LIFE: (Acts 3:15) And killed the Prince of life, whom God hath raised from the dead; whereof we are witnesses.

PRINCE OF KINGS: (Revelation 1:5) And from Jesus Christ, who is the faithful witness, and the first begotten of the dead, and the prince of the kings of the earth. Unto him that loved us, and washed us from our sins in his own blood,

PRINCE OF PEACE: (Isaiah 9:6) For unto us a child is born, unto us a son is given: and the government shall be upon his shoulder: and his name shall be called Wonderful, Counselor, The mighty God, The everlasting Father, The Prince of Peace.

PROPHET: (Luke 24:19) And he said unto them, What things? And they said unto him, Concerning Jesus of Nazareth, which was a prophet mighty in deed and word before God and all the people:

(Acts 3:22) For Moses truly said unto the fathers, A prophet shall the Lord your God raise up unto you of your brethren, like unto me; him shall ye hear in all things whatsoever he shall say unto you.

REDEEMER: (Job 19:25) For I know that my redeemer liveth, and that he shall stand at the latter day upon the earth:

RESURRECTION AND LIFE: (John 11:25) Jesus said unto her, I am the resurrection, and the life: he that believeth in me, though he were dead, yet shall he live:

ROCK: (1 Corinthians 10:4) And did all drink the same spiritual drink: for they drank of that spiritual Rock that followed them: and that Rock was Christ.

ROOT OF DAVID: (Revelation 22:16) I Jesus have sent mine angel to testify unto you these things in the churches. I am the root and the offspring of David, and the bright and morning star.

ROSE OF SHARON: (Song 2:1) I am the rose of Sharon, and the lily of the valleys.

SAVIOR: (Luke 2:11) For unto you is born this day in the city of David a Savior, which is Christ the Lord.

SEED OF WOMAN: (Genesis 3:15) And I will put enmity between thee and the woman, and between thy seed and her seed; it shall bruise thy head, and thou shalt bruise his heel.

SHEPHERD AND BISHOP OF SOULS: (1 Peter 2:25) For ye were as sheep going astray; but are now returned unto the Shepherd and Bishop of your souls.

SHILOH: (Genesis 49:10) The scepter shall not depart from Judah, nor a lawgiver from between his feet, until Shiloh come; and unto him shall the gathering of the people be.

SON OF THE BLESSED: (Mark 14:61) But he held his peace, and answered nothing. Again the high priest asked him, and said unto him, Art thou the Christ, the Son of the Blessed?

SON OF DAVID: (Matthew 1:1) The book of the generation of Jesus Christ, the son of David, the son of Abraham.

SON OF GOD: (Matthew 2:15) And was there until the death of Herod: that it might be fulfilled which was spoken of the Lord by the prophet, saying, Out of Egypt have I called my son.

SON OF THE HIGHEST: (Luke 1:32) He shall be great, and shall be called the Son of the Highest: and the Lord God shall give unto him the throne of his father David:

SUN OF RIGHTEOUSNESS: (Malachi 4:2) But unto you that fear my name shall the Sun of righteousness arise with healing in his wings; and ye shall go forth, and grow up as calves of the stall.

TRUE LIGHT: (John 1:9) That was the true Light, which lighteth every man that cometh into the world.

TRUE VINE: (John 15:1) I am the true vine, and my Father is the husbandman.

TRUTH: (John 1:14) And the Word was made flesh, and dwelt among us, (and we beheld his glory, the glory as of the only begotten of the Father,) full of grace and truth.

WITNESS: (Isaiah 55:4) Behold, I have given him for a witness to the people, a leader and commander to the people.

WORD: (John 1:1) In the beginning was the Word, and the Word was with God, and the Word was God.

WORD OF GOD: (Revelation 19:13) And he was clothed with a vesture dipped in blood: and his name is called The Word of God.

8

JESUS AND THE NEW TESTAMENT

1.49 THE DIVINITY OF CHRIST, CHARLES HODGE

Charles Hodge, 1797-1878, was the principal of Princeton Theological Seminary between 1851 and 1878. He was one of the greatest exponents and defenders of historical Calvinism in America during the 19th century.

Hodge is famed for being a Reformed theologian. His well-known three-volume work Systematic Theology *(1871) became one of the most influential works among Reformed Christians in 19th and early 20th centuries. He also wrote important commentaries on the Epistle to the Romans, the Epistle to the Ephesians, and the First and Second Epistles to the Corinthians.*

PARTICULAR PASSAGES WHICH TEACH THE DIVINITY OF CHRIST
A. The writings of John
John 1:1-14

Why the higher nature of Christ is called "the Word" and why John used that designation, are different questions. As the word *logos* does not occur in Scripture in the sense of reason, it should be taken in its ordinary meaning. The question why the Son is called "The Word" may be answered by saying that the term expresses both his nature and his office. The word is that which reveals. The Son is the image and the radiance of God's glory, and therefore his word. It is his office to make God known to his creatures. No man hath seen God at any time; the only begotten Son who is in the bosom of the Father, He hath declared Him. The Son, therefore, as the revealer of God, is the Word. The reason why John selected this designation of the divine nature of Christ, is not so easy to determine. It may indeed be said that there is ground for the use of the term in the usage of the Old Testament and of the Jews who were contemporaries with the Apostle. In the Hebrew Scriptures the manifested Jehovah is called the Word of God, and to Him individual subsistence and divine perfections are ascribed. (Ps. 33:6; 119:89; Is.

40:8; Ps. 107:20; 147:18.) This is more frequently done in the apocryphal books and in the Targums. It was not therefore an unusual or unknown term introduced by the Apostle John. Still as he only, of the New Testament writers, thus employs the word, there must have been some special reason for his doing so. That reason may have been to counteract the erroneous views concerning the nature of God and his Word, which had begun to prevail, and which had some support from the doctrines of Philo and other Alexandrian Jews. It is, however, of less importance to determine why John calls the Son *logos*, than to ascertain what he teaches concerning Him. He does teach

(1) That He is eternal. He was in the beginning; i.e., was before the creation; before the foundation of the world; before the world was. Compare Prov. 8:23; John 17:5, 24; Eph. 1:4. These are all Scriptural forms of expressing the idea of eternity.

(2) The eternal Word existed in intimate union with God. "The Word was with God"; as Wisdom is said to have been with Him in the beginning. (Prov. 8:30; John 1:18.)

(3) He was God. *Theos* without the article occurs frequently in the New Testament when it refers to the supreme God.

(4) The *logos* is the creator of all things. All things were made by Him. The Father operates through the Son and the Son through the Spirit. All that the preposition indicates is subordination as to the mode of operation, which is elsewhere taught in relation to the persons of the Trinity. That all creatures owe their being to the Word, is made the more prominent by saying, "Without him was not anything made that was made." He therefore cannot be a creature. He was not only before all creatures, but everything created was by Him caused to be.

(5) The *logos* is self-existent. He is underived. "In him was life." This is true only of God. The Godhead subsisting in the Father, Word, and Spirit, alone is self-existent, having life in itself.

(6) The life of the Word "is the light of men." Having life in Himself, the Word is the source of life in all that lives, and especially of the intellectual and spiritual life of man; and therefore He is said to be the light of men; i.e., the source of intellectual life and knowledge in all their forms.

(7) The *logos*, as the true or real light, shineth in darkness in the midst of a world alienated from God. The men of the world, the children of darkness, do not comprehend the light; they do not recognize the Word as God, the creator of all things, and the source of life and knowledge. To those who do thus recognize Him, He gives power to become the sons of God, that is, He raises them to the dignity and blessedness of God's children.

(8) This Word became flesh that is, became a man. This use of the word flesh is explained by such passages as 1 Tim. 3:16; Heb. 2:14; Rom. 8:3, in connection with Luke 1:35; Gal. 4:4; Phil. 2:7. As to the glory of the incarnate *logos*, the Apostle says of himself and of his fellow disciples, "We beheld his glory, the glory as of the only begotten of the Father"; such as could belong to none other than to Him who is the eternal Son of God, consubstantial with the Father.

Other passages in John's Gospel

This introduction, which thus unmistakably sets forth the divine nature of Christ, is the key-note of John's Gospel, and of all his other writings. His main object is to convince men that Jesus is God manifest in the flesh, and that the acknowledgment of Him as such is necessary to salvation. In verse 18 of this chapter he says that the Son alone has the knowledge of God, and is the source of that knowledge to others. He showed Nathanael that He knew his character, being the searcher of hearts. In his discourse with Nicodemus, He spoke with divine authority; revealing the things of heaven, because He came from heaven and was even then in heaven. His coming into the world was the highest evidence of divine love, and the salvation of all men depends on faith in Him; that is, on their believing that He is what He declared Himself to be, and trusting Him and obeying Him accordingly. When the Jews censured Him for healing a lame man on the Sabbath, He defended Himself by saying that God worked on the Sabbath; that He and the Father were one; that He did whatever God did; that He could give life to whom He willed; that all judgment was committed to Him, and that He was entitled to the same honor as the Father. In the sixth chapter He sets Himself forth as the source of life, first under the figure of bread, and then under that of a sacrifice. In the eighth chapter He declares Himself to be the light of the world. "He that followeth me shall not walk in darkness, but shall have the light of life." He alone could give true freedom, freedom from the condemnation and power of sin. He had been the only Savior from the beginning as He was the object of faith to Abraham, who saw his day, and rejoiced, for he says, "Before Abraham was I am," thereby asserting not only his preexistence, but his eternity, as He declares himself to be the "I am," that is, the self-existing and immutable Jehovah.

In chapter 10, under the character of a shepherd, He represents Himself as the head of all God's people, whose voice they hear, whose steps they follow, and in whose care they trust. For them He lays down his life, and takes it again. To them He gives eternal life, and their salvation is certain, for no one is able to pluck them out of his hands; and He and the Father are one. The eleventh chapter contains the history of the resurrection of Lazarus, on which it maybe remarked,

(1) That his disciples had full confidence that Christ could deliver from death whom He pleased.

(2) That He claims to be the resurrection and the life. To all that believe on Him He is the source of spiritual life to the soul, and of a resurrection to the body.

(3) In illustration and proof of his divine power, He called Lazarus from the grave.

Our Lord's last discourse

The discourse recorded in the 14th, 15th, and 16th, and the prayer recorded in the 17th chapter, are the words of God to men. No created being could speak as Christ here speaks. He begins by exhorting his disciples to have the same faith in Him which they had in God. He went to prepare heaven for them, and would return and take them to Himself. The knowledge of Him is the knowledge of God. He who had seen Him had seen the Father also; for He and the Father are one. He promised to send them the Holy Ghost to abide with them permanently; and that He would manifest Himself to them as God manifests Himself to the saints, revealing to them his glory and love, and making them sensible of his presence. He would continue to be to his Church the source of life; union with Him is as necessary as the union of a branch to the vine. The Holy Spirit sent by Him would reveal the things of Christ, rendering the Apostles infallible as teachers, and giving divine illumination to all believers. It was necessary that He should leave them in order to send the Spirit, who would convince the world of the sin of not believing Him to be all He claimed to be; of the righteousness of his assumption to be the Son of God and Savior of the world, of which his going to the Father (i.e. resurrection) was the decisive proof; and also of the certainty of a future judgment, inasmuch as the prince of this world was already judged. The Spirit was to glorify Christ, i.e., to reveal Him as possessing all divine perfections, for whatsoever the Father hath the Son hath likewise. His intercessory prayer could proceed from the lips of none but a divine person. He speaks as one who had

power over all flesh, and who could give eternal life to all whom God the Father had given Him. Eternal life consists in the knowledge of God, and of Him whom God had sent. He prays that He, clothed in our nature, might be glorified with the glory which He had before the foundation of the world; that his people might be sanctified; that they might be one by his dwelling in them, and that they might be made partakers of his glory.

He was condemned by the Jews for claiming to be the Son of God, and by Pilate for claiming to be a king. When He was crucified the heavens were darkened, the earth trembled, the dead arose, and the vail of the temple was rent. By his resurrection his claim to be the Son of God and Savior of men was authenticated. Thomas, not being present at the first interview between Christ and his disciples, doubted the fact of his resurrection; but when he saw Him he was fully convinced, and owned Him as his Lord and God. (John 20:28.)

The epistles of John

In his epistles the Apostle John presents the divinity of Christ with equal prominence. The great design of those epistles was to establish the faith of believers in the midst of the errors which had begun to prevail. The chief of those errors was denial, in some form, of the incarnation of the Son of God. Hence the Apostle not only insists so strenuously on the acknowledgment that Jesus Christ had come in the flesh, but makes that the one great fundamental doctrine of the gospel. "Whosoever shall confess that Jesus is the Son of God, God dwelleth in him, and he in God." He begins his epistles by reminding his readers that the Apostles had enjoyed the clearest possible evidence that He who has life and gives life was manifest in the flesh. They had seen, looked upon, and handled Him. John gave believers this assurance in order that they might have fellowship with God and with his Son Jesus Christ. Many had already apostatized and denied the doctrine of the incarnation. To deny that doctrine, however, was to deny God; for whosoever denies the Son, rejects the Father also. He exhorts them, therefore, to abide in the Son as the only means of abiding in God and attaining eternal life. The tests by which they were to try those who professed to be inspired teachers, were,

(1) Whether they acknowledged the doctrine of the incarnation, i.e., of the true divinity and humanity of Christ. (4:2, 3, 15.)

(2) Conformity of doctrine with the teachings of the Apostles.

(3) Love to God, founded on his redeeming love to us, and love to the brethren, springing from this love to God. In chapter 5 he tells his readers that the great truth to be believed is that Jesus is the Son of God. This is the faith which overcomes the world. This great truth is established by the testimony of God, both external and internal, for he that believeth on the Son of God hath the witness in himself; he that believeth not this testimony makes God a liar, because he believeth not the record which God has given of his Son. In Him is eternal life, so that he that hath the Son, hath life. He closes his epistle by saying: "We know that the Son of God is come, and hath given us an understanding, that we may know Him that is true (i.e., that we may know the true God); and we are in Him that is true (i.e., the true God), even in his Son Jesus Christ. This (i.e., this person Jesus Christ) is the true God and eternal life."

That this passage is to be referred to Christ, is plain.

(1) Because He is the subject of discourse in the context, and throughout the epistle. The great design of the Apostle is to tell us who and what Christ is.

(2) In the immediately preceding clauses he had called Him the true, "we are in Him that is true," even in Jesus Christ. "The true" and "the true God," are used as convertible expressions.

(3) Christ is repeatedly called "eternal life," by this Apostle, and "eternal life" is said to be in Him, which language is not used of God as such, nor of the Father.

(4) This has been the received interpretation in the Church, at least since the Arian controversy; and the objections urged against it are mainly theological, rather than exegetical.

The Apocalypse

The Book of Revelation is one continued hymn of praise to Christ, setting forth the glory of his person and the triumph of his kingdom; representing Him as the ground of confidence to his people, and the object of worship to all the inhabitants of heaven. He is declared to be the ruler of the kings of the earth. He has made us kings and priests unto God. He is the First and the Last, language never used but of God, and true of Him alone. Compare Is. 44:6. In the epistles to the seven churches, Christ assumes the titles and prerogatives of God. He calls Himself, He who holds the seven stars in his right hand; the First and the Last; He who has the sharp sword and eyes of fire, from which nothing can be hid. He has the seven spirits. He is the Holy and the True. He has the keys of David; He opens and no man shuts, and shuts and no man opens; his decision on the destiny of men admits of no appeal. He is the supreme arbiter; the faithful and true witness; the principle, i.e., both the head and source, of the whole creation. He reproves the churches for their sins, or praises them for their fidelity, as their moral ruler against whom sin is committed and to whom obedience is rendered. He threatens punishments and promises blessings which God alone can inflict or bestow. In chapter 5 the Apostle represents all the inhabitants of heaven as prostrate at the feet of Christ, ascribing blessings and honor and glory and power to Him that sitteth upon the throne and unto the Lamb forever and ever. The New Jerusalem is the seat of his kingdom. He is its light, glory, and blessedness. He again and again declares himself to be the Alpha and Omega, the First and the Last (i.e., the immutable and eternal), the Beginning and the End, for whose second coming the whole Church is in earnest expectation.

B. The epistles of St. Paul

In the epistles of Paul, the same exalted exhibition is made of the person and work of Christ. In the Epistle to the Romans, Christ is declared to be the Son of God, the object of faith, the judge of the world, the God of providence, the giver of the Holy Spirit, and what in the Old Testament is said of Jehovah, the Apostle applies to Christ. In chapter 9:5, He is expressly declared to be "over all, God blessed forever." The text here is beyond dispute. It was universally agreed that this referred to Christ in the ancient Church, by all the Reformers, by all the older theologians, and by almost all of the modern interpreters who believe in the divinity of Christ. This uniformity of assent is itself a decisive proof that the common interpretation is the natural one. We are bound to take every passage of Scripture in its obvious and natural sense, unless the plainer declarations of the Word of God show that a less obvious meaning must be the true one.

The epistles to the Corinthians

In the epistles to the Corinthians, Christ is represented,

(1) As the proper object of religious homage. All believers are represented as his worshippers. (1 Cor. 1:2.)

(2) As the source of spiritual life. (1 Cor. 1:4-9, 30, 31.)

(3) As the Lord of all Christians and the Lord of glory. (1 Cor. 2:8.)

(4) As creator of the universe. (1 Cor. 8:6.)

(5) As the Jehovah of the Old Testament, who led the Israelites through the wilderness. (1 Cor. 10:1-13.)

(6) As the giver of spiritual gifts. (1 Cor. 12.)

(7) As the Lord from heaven to whom the universe is subject. (1 Cor. 15:25.)

(8) A life-giving Spirit i.e., a Spirit having life in Himself and a source of life to others. (1 Cor. 15:45.)

(9) The proper object of supreme love, whom not to love, justly subjects the soul to eternal death. (1 Cor. 16:22.)

(10) The object of prayer (1 Cor. 16:23), from whom grace is to be sought.

(11) He gives success in preaching the gospel, causing his ministers to triumph. (2 Cor. 2:14.)

(12) The vision of his glory transforms the soul into his likeness. (2 Cor. 3:17, 18.)

(13) In his face is the glory of God, to which those only are blind who are lost. (2 Cor. 4:3-6.)

(14) His presence, or being with Him, constitutes the believers heaven. (2 Cor. 5:1-8.)

(15) Before his judgment-seat all men are to be arraigned. (2 Cor. 5:10.)

(16) His love is the highest motive to action. (2 Cor. 5:14.)

Galatians

In Galatians:

(1) Paul says that he was an Apostle not by the will of man, but by Jesus Christ. (1:1.)

(2) The conversion of the soul is effected by the knowledge of Christ as the Son of God. (2:16.)

(3) Spiritual life is maintained by faith of which Christ is the object. (2:20, 21.)

(4) Christ lives in us, as God is said to dwell in his people. (2:20.)

(5) He was the object of Abraham's faith. (3:6-9.)

(6) He was Abraham's seed in whom all nations are blessed. (3:16.)

(7) By faith in Him we become the sons of God. (3:26.)

(8) The Holy Ghost is the Spirit of Christ. (4:6.)

(9) His will is our law. (6:2.)

(10) His grace or favor the source of all good. (6:18.)

Ephesians

In Ephesians the apostle Paul states:

(1) In Christ and under Him all the objects of God's redeeming love are to be united in one harmonious whole. (1:10.)

(2) In Him we have eternal life, or are made the heirs of God. (1:11-14.)

(3) He is exalted above all principality, and power, and might, and dominion, i.e., above all rational creatures. (1:21.)

(4) In Him we are quickened, or raised from the death of sin, made partakers of spiritual life, and exalted to heaven. (2:1-6.)

(5) In 3:9, God is said to have created all things by Jesus Christ. (The text, however, in that passage is somewhat doubtful.)

(6) He fills the universe. (1:. 23, and 4:10.)

(7) He is the head of the Church, from whom it derives its life. (4:16.)

(8) He sanctifies the Church. (v. 26.)

(9) The discharge of all social duties is enforced by the consideration of the authority of Christ. We are to serve men as doing service to Him. (6:1-9.)

Philippians

In Philippians, besides the usual recognition of Christ as the source and giver of grace and peace, which comprehend all spiritual blessings, and the acknowledgment of Him as the end of our being (1:21, 22), we have in 2:6-11 the clearest declaration of the divinity of Christ. It is said,

(1) That He "was (or existed,) in the form of God," i.e., was God both as to nature and manifestation. He could not be the one without being the other. He who existed in the form of God, took upon Him the form of a servant i.e., the real condition of a servant.

(2) He is declared to be equal with God. This he did not consider as an act of robbery, or an unjust assumption. He was fully entitled to claim equality with God.

(3) This truly divine person assumed the fashion of a man, which is explained by saying He was found "in the likeness of men." He appeared in form, carriage, language, mode of thinking, speaking, feeling, and acting, like other men. He was not a mere man, but "God incarnate," God manifest in the flesh.

(4) This divine person, clothed in man's nature, humbled Himself even unto death, even to the death of the cross.

(5) Therefore He is exalted above every name that is named, "that at the name of Jesus, (as it is He as a divine person clothed in the nature of man, who is the object of worship,) every knee should bow, of things in heaven, and things in earth, and things under the earth." This is an exhaustive amplification. It includes the whole rational creation, from the highest archangel to the weakest saint; all, all that have life acknowledge Christ to be what God alone can be, their supreme and absolute Lord. It is because Christ is and has done what is represented, that the Apostle says, in the following chapter, that He counted all things as nothing for the knowledge of Christ, and that his only desire was to be found in Him and clothed in his righteousness. This divine Redeemer is to come again, and "shall change our vile body, that it may be fashioned like unto his glorious body, according to the working whereby He is able even to subdue all things unto Himself." (3:21.)

Colossians

Colossians 1:15-20, is expressly designed to set forth the true Godhead of Christ in opposition to the errors springing from the emanation theory, which had already begun to prevail in the churches of Asia Minor. This passage sets forth the relation of Christ, first to God, and secondly to the universe, and thirdly to the Church.

The relation of Christ to God, in this passage is expressed,

(1) By the words just quoted, "He is the image of the invisible God." He is so related to God that He reveals what God is, so that those who see Him, see God, those who know Him, know God, and those who hear Him, hear God. He is the brightness of God's glory, and his express image.

(2) His relation to God is also expressed by saying that He is begotten from eternity, or the only begotten Son.

Secondly, the relation of Christ to the universe is expressed in this passage by saying,

(1) That He is the Creator of all things. This is amplified, as the all things are declared to include all that are in heaven and earth, visible and invisible, rational and irrational, however exalted, even thrones, dominions, principalities, and powers; that is, the whole hierarchy of the spiritual world.

(2) He is not only the author but the end of the creation, for all things were not only created by Him, but for Him.

(3) He upholds all things; by Him all things consist, i.e., are preserved in being, life, and order.

Thirdly, Christ is the head of the Church, the source of life and grace to all its members. For in Him "all fullness," the plenitude of divine blessings dwells. In chapter 2:3, all the treasures of wisdom and knowledge (i.e., all knowledge or omniscience) are said to dwell in Christ; and in 2:9, that He is filled with "the fullness of the Godhead." The entire plenitude of the divine essence (not a mere emanation of that essence as the rising sect of the Gnostics taught), dwells (permanently abides, it is no transient manifestation) in Him bodily, invested with a body. The Godhead in its fullness is incarnate in Christ. More than Paul says cannot be said.

The pastoral epistles

In Paul's pastoral epistles to Timothy and Titus, besides the ordinary recognition of the divinity of Christ found in almost every page of the New Testament, there are four passages in which, at least according to the comnnon text and the most natural interpretation, he is directly called God. Even 1 Tim. 1:1, may be naturally rendered, "according to the command of God our Savior, even our Lord Jesus Christ." This is in accordance with the parallel passages in Titus 1:3, "according to the commandment of God our Savior;" and Titus 2:13, "of the great God our Savior Jesus Christ." In this latter passage there is no reason, as Winer and De Wette acknowledge, for questioning that Christ is called the great God, except what they regard as the Christology of the New Testament. They do not admit that Christ is the great God according to the doctrine of Paul, and therefore they are unwilling to admit that this passage contains that declaration. But if, as we have seen, and as the whole Church believes, not only Paul but all the Apostles and prophets, abundantly teach that the Messiah is truly God as well as truly man, there is no force in this objection. The fair meaning of the words is, "The Great God who is our Savior Jesus Christ." This interpretation is also demanded,

(1) By the context. Jesus Christ is the subject of discourse. Of Him it is said that He is the great God our Savior, who gave Himself for us.

(2) Because the appearance (here in reference to the second advent), is repeatedly used in the New Testament of Christ, but never of God as such, or of God the Father. See 2 Tim. 1:10; 2 Thess. 2:8; 1 Tim. 6:14; 2 Tim. 4:1, 8.

The most important passage, however, in these pastoral epistles, is 1 Tim. 3:16. With regard to that passage it may be remarked,

(1) That it admits of two interpretations. According to the one the Church is declared to be the pillar and ground of truth, according to the other, the pillar and ground of truth is the great mystery of godliness. The latter is greatly to be preferred as equally consistent with the grammatical structure of the passage, and as far more in harmony with the analogy of Scripture. The pillar and ground of truth, the great fundamental doctrine of the Gospel, is often elsewhere declared to be the doctrine of the manifestation of God in the flesh. On this doctrine all our hopes of salvation rest.

(2) The passage must refer to Christ. He it was who was manifest in the flesh, justified by the Spirit, and received up into glory.

(3) Whatever reading be adopted, the passage assumes or asserts the divinity of our Lord. With the apostolic writers, the doctrine of the incarnation is expressed by saying, that the *logos* "became flesh" (John 1:14); or, "Christ is come in the flesh" (1 John 4:2); or, "He who is the brightness of Gods glory" took part of flesh and blood (Heb. 2:14); or, He that was "equal with God" was "found in fashion as a man." (Phil. 2:8.) The same truth, therefore, is expressed, whether we say, "God was manifest in the flesh"; or, "He who was manifest in the flesh"; or, that "the mystery of godliness was manifest in the flesh."

(4) The internal evidence, so far as the perspicuity of the passage and the analogy of Scripture are concerned, are decidedly in favor of the common text. There is something remarkable in the passage; it is brought in apparently as a quotation from a hymn, as some think, or from a confession of faith, as others suppose, at least, as a familiar formula in which the leading truths concerning the manifestation of Christ are concisely stated. (1) He is God. (2) He was manifest in the flesh, or became man. (3) He was justified, i.e., his claims to be regarded as God manifest in the flesh were proved to be just, by the Spirit. (4) He was seen of angels. They recognized and served Him. (5) He was preached unto the Gentiles, as He came to be the Savior of all men, and not of the Jews only. (6) He was believed upon as God and Savior; and (7) He was received up into glory, where He now lives, reigns, and intercedes.

Epistle to the Hebrews

The doctrines of the Bible are generally stated with authority; announced as facts to be received on the testimony of God. It is seldom that the sacred writers undertake to prove what they teach. The first chapter of the Epistle to the Hebrews is an exception to this general rule. The divinity of Christ is here formally proved. As the design of the Apostle was to persuade the Hebrew Christians to adhere to the gospel, and to guard them from the fatal sin of apostatizing to Judaism, he sets before them the immeasurable superiority of the gospel to the Mosaic economy. The first point of that superiority, and that on which all the others depend, is the superior dignity of Christ as a divine person, to Moses and all the prophets. To set forth that superiority, he first asserts that Christ, the Son of God, is the possessor of all things; that through Him God made the world; that He is the brightness of God's glory, the express image of his nature, upholding all things by the word of his power; and that because He has by Himself made purification for sin, He is now, as the *Theanthropos*, set down at the right hand of the majesty on high. The true divinity of Christ being thus asserted, the Apostle proceeds to prove that this is the doctrine of the Scriptures.

(1) Because He is in the Bible called the Son of God, a title which cannot be given in its true sense to any creature. Christ, therefore, is higher than the angels; and as the word angels in the Bible includes all intelligent creatures higher than man, Christ is higher than all creatures, and therefore cannot Himself be a creature. He belongs to a different category of being.

(2) All angels (i.e., all the higher intelligences) are commanded to worship Him (i.e., to prostrate themselves before Him).

(3) While the angels are addressed as mere instruments by which God effects his purposes, the Son is addressed as God. "Thy throne O God is for ever and ever."

(4) He laid the foundations of the earth, and the heavens are the work of his hands.

(5) They are mutable, but He is immutable and eternal.

(6) He is associated with God in glory and dominion. On this great truth, thus established, the Apostle grounds all the duties and doctrines which he urges on the faith and obedience of his readers. It is on this ground that there is no escape for those who reject the salvation which He has provided. (2:1-5.) It is on this ground also that He has a dominion never granted to angels, all things being made subject to Him. (2:5-10.) As it was a divine person, the eternal Son of God, who assumed our nature, and became a high priest for us, his sacrifice is efficacious, and need not be repeated; and He is a perpetual priest, higher than the heavens, who can save to the uttermost all who come unto God by Him. This Savior is the same yesterday, to-day, and forever. Faith in Him will enable us to overcome the world, as faith in the promises concerning Christ enabled the ancient worthies to witness a good confession under the greatest trials and sufferings.

The other sacred writers of the New Testament

The same testimony to the divinity of our Lord is borne by the Apostles James and Peter. The former calls Him the Lord of glory, the latter in his First Epistle represents Him as the proper object of supreme love. Faith in Him secures salvation. His spirit dwelt in the ancient prophets. He is the foundation of the Church. (2:6.) Having suffered the just for the unjust to bring us unto God, He is now exalted at the right hand of God, the whole universe of intelligent creatures being subject to Him. (3:18.) In his Second Epistle he speaks of the knowledge of Christ as the source of grace and peace (1:2), and of holiness (ver. 8). At death believers enter into his everlasting kingdom (ver. 11). Peter was an eyewitness of his divine majesty when he was with Him in the holy mount. Lord and Savior, equivalent in the lips of a Jew, to Jehovah Savior, is his common designation of Christ. True religion, according to this Apostle, consists in the knowledge of Christ as the Son of God, to whom, therefore, he ascribes eternal glory.

Imperfect and unsatisfactory as this survey necessarily is, it is enough to prove not only that the Scriptures teach the divinity of Christ, but that Christianity as a religion consists in the love, worship, and service of the Lord Jesus, whose creatures we are, and to whom we belong by the still dearer relation of those whom He hath purchased with his own precious blood.

Charles Hodge
Systematic Theology
New York: Charles Scribner's Son, 1887

1.50 THE CHRIST THAT PAUL PREACHED, B. B. WARFIELD

"The monumental Introduction of the Epistle to the Romans"—it is thus that W. Bousset speaks of the seven opening verses of the Epistle—is, from the formal point of view, merely the Address of the Epistle. In primary purpose and fundamental structure it does not differ from the Addresses of Paul's other Epistles. But even in the Addresses of his Epistles Paul does not confine himself to the simple repetition of a formula. Here too he writes at his ease and shows himself very much the master of his form.

It is Paul's custom to expand one or another of the essential elements of the Address of his Epistles as circumstances suggested, and thus to impart to it in each several instance a specific character. The Address of the Epistle to the Romans is the extreme example of this expansion. Paul is approaching in it a church which he had not visited, and to which he apparently felt himself somewhat of a stranger. He naturally begins with some words adapted to justify his writing to it, especially as an authoritative teacher of Christian truth. In doing this he is led to describe briefly the Gospel which had been committed to him, and that particularly with regard to its contents.

There is very strikingly illustrated here a peculiarity of Paul's style, which has been called "going off at a word." His particular purpose is to represent himself as one authoritatively appointed to teach the Gospel of God. But he is more interested in the Gospel than he is in himself; and he no sooner mentions the Gospel than off he goes on a tangent to describe it. In describing it, he naturally tells us particularly what its contents

are. Its contents, however, were for him summed up in Christ. No sooner does he mention Christ than off he goes again on a tangent to describe Christ. Thus it comes about that this passage, formally only the Address of the Epistle, becomes actually a great Christological deliverance, one of the chief sources of our knowledge of Paul's conception of Christ. It presents itself to our view like one of those nests of Chinese boxes; the outer encasement is the Address of the Epistle; within that fits neatly Paul's justification of his addressing the Romans as an authoritative teacher of the Gospel; within that a description of the Gospel committed to him; and within that a great declaration of who and what Jesus Christ is, as the contents of this Gospel.

The manner in which Paul approaches this great declaration concerning Christ lends it a very special interest. What we are given is not merely how Paul thought of Christ, but how Paul preached Christ. It is the content of "the Gospel of God," the Gospel to which he as "a called apostle" had been "separated," which he outlines in these pregnant words. This is how Paul preached Christ to the faith of men as he went up and down the world "serving God in his spirit in the Gospel of His Son." We have no abstract *theologoumena* here, categories of speculative thought appropriate only to the closet. We have the great facts about Jesus which made the Gospel that Paul preached the power of God unto salvation to every one that believed. Nowhere else do we get a more direct description of specifically the Christ that Paul preached.

The direct description of the Christ that Paul preached is given us, of course, in the third and fourth verses. But the wider setting in which these verses are embedded cannot be neglected in seeking to get at their significance. In this wider setting the particular aspect in which Christ is presented is that of "Lord." It is as "Lord" that Paul is thinking of Jesus when he describes himself in the opening words of the Address—in the very first item of his commendation of himself to the Romans—as "the slave of Christ Jesus." "Slave" is the correlate of "Lord," and the relation must be taken at its height. When Paul calls himself the slave of Christ Jesus, he is calling Christ Jesus his Lord in the most complete sense which can be ascribed to that word (cf. Rom. 1:1, Col. 3:4). He is declaring that he recognizes in Christ Jesus one over against whom he has no rights, whose property he is, body and soul, to be disposed of as He will. This is not because he abases himself. It is because he exalts Christ. It is because Christ is thought of by him as one whose right it is to rule, and to rule with no limit to His right.

How Paul thought of Christ as Lord comes out, however, with most startling clearness in the closing words of the Address. There he couples "the Lord Jesus Christ" with "God our Father" as the common source from which he seeks in prayer the divine gifts of grace and peace for the Romans. We must renounce enervating glossing here too. Paul is not thinking of the Lord Jesus Christ as only the channel through which grace and peace come from God our Father to men; nor is he thinking of the Lord Jesus Christ as only the channel through which his prayer finds its way to God our Father. His prayer for these blessings for the Romans is offered up to God our Father and the Lord Jesus Christ together, as the conjoint object addressed in his petition. So far as this Bousset's remark is just: "Prayer to God in Christ is for Pauline Christianity, too, a false formula; adoration of the Kyrios stands in the Pauline communities side by side with adoration of God in unreconciled reality."

Only, we must go further. Paul couples God our Father and the Lord Jesus Christ in his prayer on a complete equality. They are, for the purposes of the prayer, for the purposes of the bestowment of grace and peace, one to him. Christ is so highly exalted in his sight that, looking up to Him through the immense stretches which separate Him from the plane of human life, "the forms of God and Christ," as Bousset puts it, are brought to the eye of faith into close conjunction." He should have said that they completely coalesce. It is only half the truth—though it is half the truth—to say that, with Paul, "the object of religious faith, as of religious worship, presents itself in a singular, thoroughgoing dualism." The other half of the truth is that this dualism resolves itself into a complete unity. The two, God our Father and the Lord Jesus Christ, are steadily recognized as two, and are spoken of by the distinguishing designations of "God" and "Lord." But they are equally steadily envisaged as one, and are combined as the common object of every religious aspiration and the common source of every spiritual blessing. It is no accident that they are united in our present passage under the government of the single preposition, "from,"—"Grace to you and peace from God our Father and the Lord Jesus Christ." This is normal with Paul. God our Father and the Lord Jesus Christ are not to him two objects of worship, two sources of blessing, but one object of worship, one source of blessing. Does he not tell us plainly that we who have one God the Father and one Lord Jesus Christ yet know perfectly well that there is no God but one (1 Cor. 8:4, 6)?

Paul is writing the Address of his Epistle to the Romans, then, with his mind fixed on the divine dignity of Christ. It is this divine Christ who, he must be understood to be telling his readers, constitutes the substance of his Gospel-proclamation. He does not leave us, however, merely to infer this. He openly declares it. The Gospel he preaches, he says, concerns precisely "the Son of God . . . Jesus Christ our Lord." He expressly says, then, that he presents Christ in his preaching as our Lord." It was the divine Christ that he preached, the Christ that the eye of faith could not distinguish from God, who was addressed in common with God in prayer, and was looked to in common with God as the source of all spiritual blessings. Paul does not speak of Christ here, however, merely as "our Lord." He gives Him the two designations: "the Son of God, Jesus Christ our Lord." The second designation obviously is explanatory of the first. Not as if it were the more current or the more intelligible designation. It may, or it may not, have been both the one and the other; but that is not the point here. The point here is that it is the more intimate, the more appealing designation. It is the designation which tells what Christ is to us. He is our Lord, He to whom we go in prayer, He to whom we look for blessings, He to whom all our religious emotions turn, on whom all our hopes are set—for this life and for that to come. Paul tells the Romans that this is the Christ that he preaches, their and his Lord whom both they and he reverence and worship and love and trust in. This is, of course, what he mainly wishes to say to them; and it is up to this that all else that he says of the Christ that he preaches leads.

The other designation—"the Son of God"—which Paul prefixes to this in his fundamental declaration concerning the Christ that he preached, supplies the basis for this. It does not tell us what Christ is to us, but what Christ is in Himself. In Himself He is the Son of God; and it is only because He is the Son of God in Himself, that He can be and is our Lord. The Lordship of Christ is rooted by Paul, in other words, not in any adventitious circumstances connected with His historical manifestation; not in any powers or dignities conferred on Him or acquired by Him; but fundamentally in His metaphysical nature. The designation "Son of God" is a metaphysical designation and tells us what He is in His being of being. And what it tells us that Christ is in His being of being is that He is just what God is. It is undeniable—and Bousset, for example, does not deny it,—that, from the earliest days of Christianity on, (in Bousset's words) "Son of God was equivalent simply to equal with God" (Mark 14:61-63; John 10:31-39).

That Paul meant scarcely so much as this, Bousset to be sure would fain have us believe. He does not dream, of course, of supposing

Paul to mean nothing more than that Jesus had been elevated into the relation of Sonship to God because of His moral uniqueness, or of His community of will with God. He is compelled to allow that "the Son of God appears in Paul as a supramundane Being standing in close metaphysical relation with God." But he would have us understand that, however close He stands to God, He is not, in Paul's view, quite equal with God. Paul, he suggests, has seized on this term to help him through the frightful problem of conceiving of this second Divine Being consistently with his monotheism. Christ is not quite God to him, but only the Son of God. Of such refinements, however, Paul knows nothing. With him too the maxim rules that whatever the father is, that the son is also: every father begets his son in his own likeness. The Son of God is necessarily to him just God, and he does not scruple to declare this Son of God all that God is (Phil. 2:6; Col. 2:9) and even to give him the supreme name of "God over all" (Rom. 9:5).

This is fundamentally, then, how Paul preached Christ—as the Son of God in this supereminent sense, and therefore our divine Lord on whom we absolutely depend and to whom we owe absolute obedience. But this was not all that he was accustomed to preach concerning Christ. Paul preached the historical Jesus as well as the eternal Son of God. And between these two designations— Son of God, our Lord Jesus Christ—he inserts two clauses which tell us how he preached the historical Jesus. All that he taught about Christ was thrown up against the background of His deity: He is the Son of God, our Lord. But who is this that is thus so fervently declared to be the Son of God and our Lord? It is in the two clauses which are now to occupy our attention that Paul tells us.

If we reduce what he tells us to its lowest terms it amounts just to this: Paul preached the historical Christ as the promised Messiah and as the very Son of God. But he declares Christ to be the promised Messiah and the very Son of God in language so pregnant, so packed with implications, as to carry us into the heart of the great problem of the two-natured person of Christ. The exact terms in which he describes Christ as the promised Messiah and the very Son of God are these: "Who became of the seed of David according to the flesh, who was marked out as the Son of God in power according to the Spirit of holiness by the resurrection of the dead." This in brief is the account which Paul gives of the historical Christ whom he preached.

Of course there is a temporal succession suggested in the declarations of the two clauses They so far give us not only a description of the historical Christ, but the life-history of the Christ that Paul preached. Jesus Christ became of the seed of David at His birth and by His birth. He was marked out as the Son of God in power only at His resurrection and by His resurrection. But it was not to indicate this temporal succession that Paul sets the two declarations side by side. It emerges merely as the incidental, or we may say even the accidental, result of their collocation. The relation in which Paul sets the two declarations to one another is a logical rather than a temporal one: it is the relation of climax. His purpose is to exalt Jesus Christ. He wishes to say the great things about Him. And the two greatest things he has to say about Him in His historical manifestation are these-that He became of the seed of David according to the flesh, that He was marked out, as the Son of God in power according to the Spirit of holiness by the resurrection of the dead.

Both of these declarations, we say, are made for the purpose of extolling Christ: the former just as truly as the latter. That Christ came as the Messiah belongs to His glory: and the particular terms in which His Messiahship is intimated are chosen in order to enhance His glory. The word "came," "became" is correlated with the "promised afore" of the preceding verse. This is He, Paul says, whom all the prophets did before signify, and who at length came—even as they signified—of the seed of David. There is doubtless an intimation of the preexistence of Christ here also, as J. B. Lightfoot properly instructs us: He who was always the Son of God now "became" of the seed of David. But this lies somewhat apart from the main current of thought. The heart of the declaration resides in the great words, "Of the seed of David." For these are great words. In declaring the Messiahship of Jesus Paul adduces His royal dignity. And he adduces it because he is thinking of the majesty of the Messiahship. We must beware, then, of reading this clause depreciatingly, as if Paul were making a concession in it: "He came, no doubt, . . . He came, indeed, . . . of the seed of David, but . . ." Paul never for an instant thought of the Messiahship of Jesus as a thing to be apologized for. The relation of the second clause to the first is not that of opposition, but of climax; and it contains only so much of contrast as is intrinsic in a climax. The connection would be better expressed by an "and" than by a "but"; or, if by a "but," not by an "indeed . . . but," but by a "not only . . . but." Even the Messiahship, inexpressibly glorious as it is, does not exhaust the glory of Christ. He had a glory greater than even this. This was but the beginning of His glory. But it was the beginning of His glory. He came into the world as the promised Messiah, and He went out of the world as the demonstrated Son of God. In these two things is summed up the majesty of His historical manifestation.

It is not intended to say that when He went out of the world, He left His Messiahship behind Him. The relation of the second clause to the first is not that of supersession but that of superposition. Paul passes from one glory to another, but he is as far as possible from suggesting that the one glory extinguished the other. The resurrection of Christ had no tendency to abolish His Messiahship, and the exalted Christ remains "of the seed of David." There is no reason to doubt that Paul would have exhorted his readers when he wrote these words with all the fervor with which he did later to "remember Jesus Christ, risen from the dead, of the seed of David" (2 Tim. 2:8). "According to my Gospel," he adds there, as an intimation that it was as "of the seed of David" that he was accustomed to preach Jesus Christ, whether as on earth as here, or as in heaven as there. It is the exalted Jesus that proclaims Himself in the Apocalypse "the root and the offspring of David" (Rev. 22:16, 5:5), and in whose hands "the key of David" is found (3:7).

And as it is not intimated that Christ ceased to be "of the seed of David" when He rose from the dead, neither is it intimated that He then first became the Son of God. He was already the Son of God when and before He became of the seed of David: and He did not cease to be the Son of God on and by becoming of the seed of David. It was rather just because He was the Son of God that He became of the seed of David, to become which, in the great sense of the prophetic announcements and of His own accomplishment, He was qualified only by being the Son of God. Therefore Paul does not say He was made the Son of God by the resurrection of the dead. He says he was defined, marked out, as the Son of God by the resurrection of the dead. His resurrection from the dead was well adapted to mark Him out as the Son of God: scarcely to make Him the Son of God. Consider but what the Son of God in Paul's usage means; and precisely what the resurrection was and did. It was a thing which was quite appropriate to happen to the Son of God; and, happening, could bear strong witness to Him as such: but how could it make one the Son of God?

We might possibly say, no doubt, with a tolerable meaning, that Christ was installed, even constituted, "Son of God in power" by the resurrection of the dead—if we could see our way to construe the words "in power" thus directly with "the Son of God." That too would imply that He was already the Son of God before He rose from the dead,—only then in weakness; what He had been all along in weakness He now was constituted in power. This construction, however, though not impossible, is hardly natural. And it imposes a sense on the preceding clause of which it itself gives no suggestion, and which it is reluctant to receive. To say, "of the seed of David" is not to say weakness; it is to say majesty. It is quite certain, indeed, that the assertion "who was made of the seed of David" cannot be read concessively, preparing the way for the celebration of Christ's glory in the succeeding clause. It stands rather in parallelism with the clause that follows it, asserting with it the supreme glory of Christ.

In any case the two clauses do not express two essentially different modes of being

through which Christ successively passed. We could think at most only of two successive stages of manifestation of the Son of God. At most we could see in it a declaration that He who always was and continues always to be the Son of God was manifested to men first as the Son of David, and then, after His resurrection, as also the exalted Lord. He always was in the essence of His being the Son of God; this Son of God became of the seed of David and was installed as—what He always was—the Son of God, though now in His proper power, by the resurrection of the dead. It is assuredly wrong, however, to press even so far the idea of temporal succession. Temporal succession was not what it was in Paul's mind to emphasize, and is not the ruling idea of his assertion. The ruling idea of his assertion is the celebration of the glory of Christ. We think of temporal succession only because of the mention of the resurrection, which, in point of fact, cuts our Lord's life-manifestation into two sections. But Paul is not adducing the resurrection because it cuts our Lord's life-manifestation into two sections; but because of the demonstration it brought of the dignity of His person. It is quite indifferent to his declaration when the resurrection took place. He is not adducing it as the producing cause of a change in our Lord's mode of being. In point of fact it did not produce a change in our Lord's mode of being, although it stood at the opening of a new stage of His life-history. What it did, and what Paul adduces it here as doing, was that it brought out into plain view who and what Christ really was. This, says Paul, is the Christ I preach—He who came of the seed of David, He who was marked out in power as the Son of God, by the resurrection of the dead. His thought of Christ runs in the two molds—His Messiahship, His resurrection. But he is not particularly concerned here with the temporal relations of these two facts.

Paul does not, however, say of Christ merely that He became of the seed of David and was marked out as the Son of God in power by the resurrection of the dead. He introduces a qualifying phrase into each clause. He says that He became of the seed of David "according to the flesh," and that He was marked out as the Son of God in power "according to the Spirit of holiness" by the resurrection of the dead. What is the nature of the qualifications made by these phrases?

It is obvious at once that they are not temporal qualifications. Paul does not mean to say, in effect, that our Lord was Messiah only during His earthly manifestation, and became the Son of God only on and by means of His resurrection. It has already appeared that Paul did not think of the Messiahship of our Lord only in connection with His earthly manifestation, or of His Sonship to God only in connection with His post-resurrection existence. And the qualifying phrases themselves are ill-adapted to express this temporal distinction. Even if we could twist the phrase "according to the flesh" into meaning "according to His human manifestation" and violently make that do duty as a temporal definition, the parallel phrase "according to the Spirit of holiness" utterly refuses to yield to any treatment which could make it mean, "according to His heavenly manifestation." And nothing could be more monstrous than to represent precisely the resurrection as in the case of Christ the producing cause of—the source out of which proceeds—a condition of existence which could be properly characterized as distinctively "spiritual." Exactly what the resurrection did was to bring it about that His subsequent mode of existence should continue to be, like the precedent, "fleshly"; to assimilate His post-resurrection to His pre-resurrection mode of existence in the matter of the constitution of His person. And if we fall back on the ethical contrast of the terms, that could only mean that Christ should be supposed to be represented as imperfectly holy in His earthly stage of existence, and as only on His resurrection attaining to complete holiness (cf. 1 Cor. 15:44, 46). It is very certain that Paul did not mean that (2 Cor. 5:21).

It is clear enough, then, that Paul cannot by any possibility have intended to represent Christ as in His pre-resurrection and His post-resurrection modes of being differing in any way which can be naturally expressed by the contrasting terms "flesh" and "spirit." Least of all can he be supposed to have intended this distinction in the sense of the ethical contrast between these terms. But a further word may be pardoned as to this. That it is precisely this ethical contrast that Paul intends has been insisted on under cover of the adjunct "of holiness" attached here to "spirit." The contrast, it is said, is not between "flesh" and "spirit," but between "flesh" and "spirit of holiness"; and what is intended is to represent Christ, who on earth was merely "Christ according to the flesh"—the "flesh of sin" of course, it is added, that is "the flesh which was in the grasp of sin"—to have been, "after and in consequence of the resurrection," "set free" from "the likeness of (weak and sinful) flesh." Through the resurrection, in other words, Christ has for the first time become the holy Son of God, free from entanglement with sin-cursed flesh; and having thus saved Himself, is qualified, we suppose, now to save others, by bringing them through the same experience of resurrection to the same holiness. We have obviously wandered here sufficiently far from the declarations of the Apostle; and we have landed in a *reductio ad absurdum* of this whole system of interpretation. Paul is not here distinguishing times and contrasting two successive modes of our Lord's being. He is distinguishing elements in the constitution of our Lord's person, by virtue of which He is at one and the same time both the Messiah and the Son of God. He became of the seed of David with respect to the flesh, and by the resurrection of the dead was mightily proven to be also the Son of God with respect to the Spirit of holiness.

It ought to go without saying that by these two elements in the constitution of our Lord's person, the flesh and the spirit of holiness, by virtue of which He is at once of the seed of David and the Son of God, are not intended the two constituent elements, flesh and spirit, which go to make up common humanity. It is impossible that Paul should have represented our Lord as the Messiah only by virtue of His bodily nature; and it is absurd to suppose him to suggest that His Sonship to God was proved by His resurrection to reside in His mental nature or even in His ethical purity—to say nothing now of supposing him to assert that He was made by the resurrection into the Son of God, or into "the Son of God in power" with respect to His mental nature here described as holy. How the resurrection—which was in itself just the resumption of the body—of all things, could be thought of as constituting our Lord's mental nature the Son of God passes imagination; and if it be conceivable that it might at least prove that He was the Son of God, it remains hidden how it could be so emphatically asserted that it was only with reference to His mental nature, in sharp contrast with His bodily, thus recovered to Him, that this was proved concerning Him precisely by His resurrection. Is Paul's real purpose here to guard men from supposing that our Lord's bodily nature, though recovered to Him in this great act, the resurrection entered into His Sonship to God? There is no reason discoverable in the context why this distinction between our Lord's bodily and mental natures should be so strongly stressed here. It is clearly an artificial distinction imposed on the passage.

When Paul tells us of the Christ which he preached that He was made of the seed of David "according to the flesh," he quite certainly has the whole of His humanity in mind. And in introducing this limitation, "according to the flesh," into his declaration that Christ was "made of the seed of David," he intimates not obscurely that there was another side—not aspect but element—of His being besides His humanity, in which He was not made of the seed of David, but was something other and higher. If he had said nothing more than just these words: "He was made of the seed of David according to the flesh," this intimation would still have been express; though we might have been left to speculation to determine what other element could have entered into His being, and what He must have been according to that element. He has not left us, however, to this speculation, but has plainly told us that the Christ he preached was not merely made of the seed of David according to the flesh, but was also marked out as the Son of God, in power, according to the Spirit of holiness by the resurrection of the dead. Since the "according to the flesh" includes all His

humanity, the "according to the Spirit of holiness" which is set in contrast with it, and according to which He is declared to be the Son of God, must be sought outside of His humanity. What the nature of this element of His being in which He is superior to humanity is, is already clear from the fact that according to it He is the Son of God. "Son of God" is, as we have already seen, a metaphysical designation asserting equality with God. It is a divine name. To say that Christ is, according to the Spirit of holiness, the Son of God, is to say that the Spirit of holiness is a designation of His divine nature. Paul's whole assertion therefore amounts to saying that, in one element of His being, the Christ that he preached was man, in another God. Looked at from the point of view of His human nature He was the Messiah—"of the seed of David." Looked at from the point of view of His divine nature, He was the Son of God. Looked at in His composite personality, He was both the Messiah and the Son of God, because in Him were united both He that came of the seed of David according to the flesh and He who was marked out as the Son of God in power according to the Spirit of holiness by the resurrection of the dead.

We may be somewhat puzzled by the designation of the divine nature of Christ as "the Spirit of holiness." But not only is it plain from its relation to its contrast, "the flesh," and to its correlate, "the Son of God," that it is His divine nature which is so designated, but this is made superabundantly clear from the closely parallel passage, Rom. 9:5. There, in enumerating the glories of Israel, the Apostle comes to his climax in this great declaration,—that from Israel Christ came. But there, no more than here, will he allow that it was the whole Christ who came-as said there from the stock of Israel, as said here from the seed of David. He adds there too at once the limitation, "as concerns the flesh,"—just as he adds it here. Thus he intimates with emphasis that something more is to be said, if we are to give a complete account of Christ's being; there was something about Him in which He did not come from Israel, and in which He is more than "flesh." What this something is, Paul adds in the great words,

"God over all." He who was from Israel according to the flesh is, on the other side of His being, in which He is not from Israel and not "flesh," nothing other than "God over all." In our present passage, the phrase, "Spirit of holiness" takes the place of "God over all" in the other. Clearly Paul means the same thing by them both.

This being very clear, what interests us most is the emphasis which Paul throws on holiness in his designation of the divine nature of Christ. The simple word "Spirit" might have been ambiguous: when "the Spirit of holiness" is spoken of, the divine nature is expressly named. No doubt, Paul might have used the adjective, "holy," instead of the genitive of the substantive, "of holiness"; and have said "the Holy Spirit." Had he done so, he would have as expressly intimated deity as in his actual phrase. But he would have left open the possibility of being misunderstood as speaking of that distinct Holy Spirit to which this designation is commonly applied. The relation in which the divine nature which he attributes to Christ stands to the Holy Spirit was in Paul's mind no doubt very close; as close as the relation between "God" and "Lord" whom he constantly treats as, though two, yet also one. Not only does he identify the activities of the two (e. g., Rom. 8:9 ff.); but also, in some high sense, he identifies them themselves. He can make use, for example, of such a startling expression as "the Lord is the Spirit" (2 Cor. 3:17). Nevertheless it is perfectly clear that "the Lord" and "the Spirit" are not one person to Paul, and the distinguishing employment of the designations "the Spirit," "the Holy Spirit" is spread broadcast over his pages. Even in immediate connection with his declaration that "the Lord is the Spirit," he can speak with the utmost naturalness not only of "the Spirit of the Lord," but also of "the Lord of the Spirit" (2 Cor. 3:17 f.). What is of especial importance to note in our present connection is that he is not speaking of an endowment of Christ either from or with the Holy Spirit; although he would be the last to doubt that He who was made of the seed of David according to the flesh was plenarily endowed both from and with the Spirit. He is speaking of that divine Spirit which is the complement in the constitution of Christ's person of the human nature according to which He was the Messiah, and by virtue of which He was not merely the Messiah, but also the very Son of God. This Spirit he calls distinguishingly the Spirit of holiness, the Spirit the very characteristic of which is holiness. He is speaking not of an acquired holiness but of an intrinsic holiness; not, then, of a holiness which had been conferred at the time of or attained by means of the resurrection from the dead; but of a holiness which had always been the very quality of Christ's being. He is not representing Christ as having first been after a fleshly fashion the son of David and afterwards becoming by or at the resurrection from the dead, after a spiritual fashion, the holy Son of God. He is representing Him as being in his very nature essentially and therefore always and in every mode of His manifestation holy. Bousset is quite right when he declares that there is no reference in the phrase "Spirit of holiness" to the preservation of His holiness by Christ in His earthly manifestation, but that it is a metaphysical designation describing according to its intrinsic quality an element in the constitution of Christ's person from the beginning. This is the characteristic of the Christ Paul preached; as truly His characteristic as that He was the Messiah. Evidently in Paul's thought of deity holiness held a prominent place. When he wishes to distinguish Spirit from spirit, it is enough for him that he may designate Spirit as divine, to define it as that Spirit the fundamental characteristic of which is that it is holy.

It belongs to the very essence of the conception of Christ as Paul preached Him, therefore, that He was of two natures, human and divine. He could not preach Him at once as of the seed of David and as the Son of God without so preaching Him. It never entered Paul's mind that the Son of God could become a mere man, or that a mere man could become the Son of God. We may say that the conception of the two natures is unthinkable to us. That is our own concern. That a single nature could be at once or successively God and man, man and God, was what was unthinkable to Paul. In his view, when we say

God and man we say two natures; when we put a hyphen between them and say God-man, we do not merge them one in the other but join the two together. That this was Paul's mode of thinking of Jesus, Bousset, for example, does not dream of denying. What Bousset is unwilling to admit is that the divine element in his two-natured Christ was conceived by Paul as completely divine. Two metaphysical entities, he says, combined themselves for Paul in the person of Christ: one of these was a human, the other a divine nature: and Paul, along with the whole Christian community of his day, worshipped this two-natured Christ, though he (not they) ranked Him in his thought of His higher nature below the God over all.

The trouble with this construction is that Paul himself gives a different account of the matter. The point of Paul's designation of Christ as the Son of God is, not to subordinate Him to God, as Bousset affirms, but to equalize Him with God. He knows no difference in dignity between his God and his Lord; to both alike, or rather to both in common, he offers his prayers; from both alike and both together he expects all spiritual blessings (Rom. 1:7). He roundly calls Christ, by virtue of His higher nature, by the supreme name of "God over all" (Rom. 9:5). These things cannot be obscured by pointing to expressions in which he ascribes to the Divine-human Christ a relation of subordination to God in His saving work. Paul does not fail to distinguish between what Christ is in the higher element of His being, and what He became when, becoming poor that we might be made rich, He assumed for His work's sake the position of a servant in the world. Nor

does he permit the one set of facts to crowd the other out of his mind. It is no accident that all that he says about the historical two-natured Christ in our present passage is inserted between His two divine designations of the Son of God and Lord; that the Christ that he preached he describes precisely as "the Son of God—who was made of the seed of David according to the flesh, who was marked out as the Son of God in power according to the Spirit of holiness by the resurrection of the dead—Jesus Christ our Lord." He who is defined as on the human side of David, on the divine side the Son of God, this two-natured person, is declared to be from the point of view of God, His own Son, and—as all sons are—like Him in essential nature; from the point of view of man, our supreme Lord, whose we are and whom we obey. Ascription of proper deity could not be made more complete; whether we look at Him from the point of view of God or from the point of view of man, He is God. But what Paul preached concerning this divine Being belonged to His earthly manifestation; He was made of the seed of David, He was marked out as God's Son. The conception of the two natures is not with Paul a negligible speculation attached to his Gospel. He preached Jesus. And he preached of Jesus that He was the Messiah. But the Messiah that he preached was no merely human Messiah. He was the Son of God who was made of the seed of David. And He was demonstrated to be what He really was by His resurrection from the dead.

This was the Jesus that Paul preached: this and none other.

B. B. Warfield

1.51 THE PERSON OF CHRIST ACCORDING TO THE NEW TESTAMENT, B. B. WARFIELD

It is the purpose of this article to make as clear as possible the conception of the Person of Christ, in the technical sense of that term, which lies on—or, if we prefer to say so, beneath—the pages of the New Testament. Were it its purpose to trace out the process by which this great mystery has been revealed to men, a beginning would need to be taken from the intimations as to the nature of the person of the Messiah in Old Testament prophecy, and an attempt would require to be made to discriminate the exact contribution of each organ of revelation to our knowledge. And were there added to this a desire to ascertain the progress of the apprehension of this mystery by men, there would be demanded a further inquiry into the exact degree of understanding which was brought to the truth revealed at each stage of its revelation. The magnitudes with which such investigations deal, however, are very minute; and the profit to be derived from them is not, in a case like the present, very great. It is, of course, of importance to know how the person of the Messiah was represented in the predictions of the Old Testament; and it is a matter at least of interest to note, for example, the difficulty experienced by Our Lord's immediate disciples in comprehending all that was involved in His manifestation. But, after all, the constitution of Our Lord's person is a matter of revelation, not of human thought; and it is preeminently a revelation of the New Testament, not of the Old Testament. And the New Testament is all the product of a single movement, at a single stage of its development, and therefore presents in its fundamental teaching a common character. The whole of the New Testament was written within the limits of about half a century; or, if we except the writings of John, within the narrow bounds of a couple of decades; and the entire body of writings which enter into it are so much of a piece that it may be plausibly represented that they all bear the stamp of a single mind. In its fundamental teaching, the New Testament lends itself, therefore, more readily to what is called dogmatic than to what is called genetic treatment; and we shall penetrate most surely into its essential meaning if we take our start from its clearest and fullest statements, and permit their light to be thrown upon its more incidental allusions. This is peculiarly the case with such a matter as the person of Christ, which is dealt with chiefly incidentally, as a thing already understood by all, and needing only to be alluded to rather than formally expounded. That we may interpret these allusions aright, it is requisite that we should recover from the first the common conception which underlies them all.

I. THE TEACHING OF PAUL

We begin, then, with the most didactic of the New Testament writers, the apostle Paul, and with one of the passages in which he most fully intimates his conception of the person of his Lord, Phil. 2:5-9. Even here, however, Paul is not formally expounding the doctrine of the Person of Christ; he is only alluding to certain facts concerning His person and action perfectly well known to his readers, in order that he may give point to an adduction of Christ's example. He is exhorting his readers to unselfishness, such unselfishness as esteems others better than ourselves, and looks not only on our own things but also on those of others. Precisely this unselfishness, he declares, was exemplified by Our Lord. He did not look upon His own things but the things of others; that is to say, He did not stand upon His rights, but was willing to forego all that He might justly have claimed for Himself for the good of others. For, says Paul, though, as we all know, in His intrinsic nature He was nothing other than God, yet He did not, as we all know right well, look greedily on His condition of equality with God, but made no account of Himself, taking the form of a servant, being made in the likeness of men; and, being found in fashion as a man, humbled Himself, becoming obedient up to death itself, and that, the death of the cross. The statement is thrown into historical form; it tells the story of Christ's life on earth. But it presents His life on earth as a life in all its elements alien to His intrinsic nature, and assumed only in the performance of an unselfish purpose. On earth He lived as a man, and subjected Himself to the common lot of men. But He was not by nature a man, nor was He in His own nature subject to the fortunes of human life. By nature He was God; and He would have naturally lived as became God—'on an equality with God.' He became man by a voluntary act, taking no account of Himself,' and, having become man, He voluntarily lived out His human life under the conditions which the fulfillment of His unselfish purpose imposed on Him.

The terms in which these great affirmations are made deserve the most careful attention. The language in which Our Lord's intrinsic Deity is expressed, for example, is probably as strong as any that could be devised. Paul does not say simply, "He was God." He says, "He was in the form of God," employing a turn of speech which throws emphasis upon Our Lord's possession of the specific quality of God. "Form" is a term which expresses the sum of those characterizing qualities which make a thing the precise thing that it is. Thus, the "form" of a sword (in this case mostly matters of external configuration) is all that makes a given piece of metal specifically a sword, rather than, say, a spade. And "the form of God" is the sum of the characteristics which make the being we call "God," specifically God, rather than some other being—an angel, say, or a man. When Our Lord is said to be in "the form of God," therefore, He is declared, in the most express manner possible, to be all that God is, to possess the whole fullness of attributes which make God God. Paul chooses this manner of expressing himself here instinctively, because, in adducing Our Lord as our example of self-abnegation, his mind is naturally resting, not on the bare fact that He is God, but on the richness and fullness of His being as God. He

was all this, yet He did not look on His own things but on those of others.

It should be carefully observed also that in making this great affirmation concerning Our Lord, Paul does not throw it distinctively into the past, as if he were describing a mode of being formerly Our Lord's, indeed, but no longer His because of the action by which He became our example of unselfishness. Our Lord, he says, "being," "existing," "subsisting" "in the form of God"—as it is variously rendered. The rendering proposed by the Revised Version margin, "being originally," while right in substance, is somewhat misleading. The verb employed means strictly "to be beforehand," "to be already so and so," "to be there and ready," and intimates the existing circumstances, disposition of mind, or, as here, mode of subsistence in which the action to be described takes place. It contains no intimation, however, of the cessation of these circumstances or disposition, or mode of subsistence; and that, the less in a case like the present, where it is cast in a tense (the imperfect) which in no way suggests that the mode of subsistence intimated came to an end in the action described by the succeeding verb (cf. the parallels, Luke 16:14, 28; 23:50; Acts 2:80; 3:2; 2 Cor. 8:17; 12:16; Gal. 1:14). Paul is not telling us here, then, what Our Lord was once, but rather what He already was, or, better, what in His intrinsic nature He is; he is not describing a past mode of existence of Our Lord, before the action he is adducing as an example took place—although the mode of existence he describes was Our Lord's mode of existence before this action—so much as painting in the background upon which the action adduced may be thrown up into prominence. He is telling us who and what He is who did these things for us, that we may appreciate how great the things He did for us are.

And here it is important to observe that the whole of the action adduced is thrown up thus against this background—not only its negative description to the effect that Our Lord (although all that God is) did not look greedily on His (consequent) being on an equality with God; but its positive description as well, introduced by the "but. . . ." and that in both of its elements, not merely that to the effect (ver. 7) that he took no account of himself (rendered not badly by the Authorized Version, He "made himself of no reputation"; but quite misleading by the Revised Version, He "emptied himself"), but equally that to the effect (ver. 8) that "he humbled himself." It is the whole of what Our Lord is described as doing in vs. 6-8, that He is described as doing despite His "subsistence in the form of God." So far is Paul from intimating, therefore, that Our Lord laid aside His Deity in entering upon His life on earth, that he rather asserts that He retained His Deity throughout His life on earth, and in the whole course of His humiliation, up to death itself, was consciously ever exercising self-abnegation, living a life which did not by nature belong to Him, which stood in fact in direct contradiction to the life which was naturally His. It is this underlying implication which determines the whole choice of the language in which Our Lord's earthly life is described. It is because it is kept in mind that He still was "in the form of God," that is, that He still had in possession all that body of characterizing qualities by which God is made God, for example, that He is said to have been made, not man, but "in the likeness of man," to have been found, not man, but "in fashion as a man"; and that the wonder of His servant-hood and obedience, the mark of servant-hood, is thought of as so great. Though He was truly man, He was much more than man; and Paul would not have his readers imagine that He had become merely man. In other words, Paul does not teach that Our Lord was once God but had become instead man; he teaches that though He was God, He had become also man.

An impression that Paul means to imply, that in entering upon His earthly life Our Lord had laid aside His Deity, may be created by a very prevalent misinterpretation of the central clause of his statement—a misinterpretation unfortunately given currency by the rendering of the English Revised Version: "counted it not a prize to be on an equality with God, but emptied himself," varied without improvement in the American Revised Version to: "counted not

the being on an equality with God a thing to be grasped, but emptied himself." The former (negative) member of this clause means just: He did not look greedily upon His being on an equality with God; did not "set supreme store" by it (see Lightfoot on the clause). The latter (positive) member of it, however, cannot mean in antithesis to this, that He therefore "emptied himself," divested Himself of this, His being on an equality with God, much less that He "emptied himself," divested Himself of His Deity ("form of God") itself, of which His being on an equality with God is the manifested consequence. The verb here rendered "emptied" is in constant use in a metaphorical sense (so only in the New Testament: Rom. 4:14; 1 Cor. 1:17; 9:15; 2 Cor. 9:3) and cannot here be taken literally. This is already apparent from the definition of the manner in which the "emptying" is said to have been accomplished, supplied by the modal clause which is at once attached: by "taking the form of a servant." You cannot "empty" by "taking"—adding. It is equally apparent, however, from the strength of the emphasis which, by its position, is thrown upon the "himself." We may speak of Our Lord as "emptying Himself" of something else, but scarcely, with this strength of emphasis, of His "emptying Himself" of something else. This emphatic "Himself," interposed between the preceding clause and the verb rendered "emptied," builds a barrier over which we cannot climb backward in search of that of which Our Lord emptied Himself. The whole thought is necessarily contained in the two words, "emptied Himself," in which the word "emptied" must therefore be taken in a sense analogous to that which it bears in the other passages in the New Testament where it occurs. Paul, in a word, says here nothing more than that Our Lord, who did not look with greedy eyes upon His estate of equality with God, emptied Himself, if the language may be pardoned, of Himself; that is to say, in precise accordance with the exhortation for the enhancement of which His example is adduced, that He did not look on His own things. He made no account of Himself, we may fairly paraphrase the clause; and thus all question of what He emptied Himself of falls away. What Our Lord actually did, according to Paul, is expressed in the following clauses; those now before us express more the moral character of His act. He took "the form of a servant," and so was "made in the likeness of men." But His doing this showed that He did not set overweening store by His state of equality with God, and did not account Himself the sufficient object of all the efforts. He was not self-regarding: He had regard for others. Thus He becomes our supreme example of self-abnegating conduct.

The language in which the act by which Our Lord showed that He was self-abnegating is described, requires to be taken in its complete meaning. He took "the form of a servant, being made in the likeness of men," says Paul. The term "form" here, of course, bears the same full meaning as in the preceding instance of its occurrence in the phrase "the form of God." It imparts the specific quality, the whole body of characteristics, by which a servant is made what we know as a servant. Our Lord assumed, then, according to Paul, not the mere state or condition or outward appearance of a servant, but the reality; He became an actual "servant" in the world. The act by which He did this is described as a "taking," or, as it has become customary from this description of it to phrase it, as an assumption. What is meant is that Our Lord took up into His personality a human nature; and therefore it is immediately explained that He took the form of a servant by "being made in the likeness of men." That the apostle does not say, shortly, that He assumed a human nature, is due to the engagement of his mind with the contrast which he wishes to bring out forcibly for the enhancement of his appeal to Our Lord's example, between what Our Lord is by nature and what He was willing to become, not looking on His own things but also on the things of others. This contrast is, no doubt, embodied in the simple opposition of God and man; it is much more pungently expressed in the quantitative terms, "form of God" and "form of a servant." The Lord of the world became a servant in the world; He

whose right it was to rule took obedience as His life-characteristic. Naturally therefore Paul employs here a word of quality rather than a word of mere nature; and then defines his meaning in this word of quality by a further exegetical clause. This further clause—"being made in the likeness of men"—does not throw doubt on the reality of the human nature that was assumed, in contradiction to the emphasis on its reality in the phrase "the form of a servant." It, along with the succeeding clause—"and being found in fashion as a man"—owes its peculiar form, as has already been pointed out, to the vividness of the apostle's consciousness, that he is speaking of one who, though really man, possessing all that makes a man a man, is yet, at the same time, infinitely more than a man, no less than God Himself, in possession of all that makes God God. Christ Jesus is in his view, therefore (as in the view of his readers, for he is not instructing his readers here as to the nature of Christ's person, but reminding them of certain elements in it for the purposes of his exhortation), both God and man, God who has "assumed" man into personal union with Himself, and has in this His assumed manhood lived out a human life on earth.

The elements of Paul's conception of the person of Christ are brought before us in this suggestive passage with unwonted fullness. But they all receive endless illustration from his occasional allusions to them, one or another, throughout his Epistles. The leading motive of this passage, for example, reappears quite perfectly in 2 Cor. 8:9, where we are exhorted to imitate the graciousness of Our Lord Jesus Christ, who became for our sakes (emphatic) poor—He who was (again an imperfect participle, and therefore without suggestion of the cessation of the condition described) rich—that we might by His (very emphatic) poverty be made rich. Here the change in Our Lord's condition at a point of time perfectly understood between the writer and his readers is adverted to and assigned to its motive, but no further definition is given of the nature of either condition referred to. We are brought closer to the precise nature of the act by which the change was wrought by such a passage as Gal. 4:4. We read that

"When the fullness of the time came, God sent forth his Son, born of a woman, born under the law, that he might redeem them that were under the law." The whole transaction is referred to the Father in fulfillment of His eternal plan of redemption, and it is described specifically as an incarnation: the Son of God is born of a woman—He who is in His own nature the Son of God, abiding with God, is sent forth from God in such a manner as to be born a human being, subject to law. The primary implications are that this was not the beginning of His being; but that before this He was neither a man nor subject to law. But there is no suggestion that on becoming man and subject to law, He ceased to be the Son of God or lost anything intimated by that high designation. The uniqueness of His relation to God as His Son is emphasized in a kindred passage (Rom. 8:3) by the heightening of the designation to that of God's "own Son," and His distinction from other men is intimated in the same passage by the declaration that God sent Him, not in sinful flesh, but only "in the likeness of sinful flesh." The reality of Our Lord's flesh is not thrown into doubt by this turn of speech, but His freedom from the sin which is associated with flesh as it exists in lost humanity is asserted (cf. 2 Cor. 5:21). Though true man, therefore (1 Cor. 15:21; Rom. 5:21; Acts 17:31), He is not without differences from other men; and these differences do not concern merely the condition (as sinful) in which men presently find themselves; but also their very origin: they are from below, He from above—'the first man is from the earth, earthy; the second man is from heaven' (1 Cor. 15:47). This is His peculiarity: He was born of a woman like other men; yet He descended from Heaven (cf. Eph. 4:9; John 3:13). It is not meant, of course, that already in heaven He was a man; what is meant is that even though man He derives His origin in an exceptional sense from heaven. Paul describes what He Was in heaven (but not alone in heaven)—that is to say before He was sent in the likeness of sinful flesh (though not alone before this)—in the great terms of "God's Son," "God's Own Son," "the form of God," or yet again in

words whose import cannot be mistaken, 'God over all' (Rom. 9:5). In the last cited passage, together with its parallel earlier in the same epistle (Rom. 1:3), the two sides or elements of Our Lord's person are brought into collocation after a fashion that can leave no doubt of Paul's conception of His twofold nature. In the earlier of these passages he tells us that Jesus Christ was born, indeed, of the seed of David according to the flesh, that is, so far as the human side of His being is concerned, but was powerfully marked out as the Son of God according to the Spirit of Holiness, that is, with respect to His higher nature, by the resurrection of the dead, which in a true sense began in His own rising from the dead. In the later of them, he tells us that Christ sprang indeed, as concerns the flesh, that is on the human side of His being, from Israel, but that, despite this earthly origin of His human nature, He yet is and abides (present participle) nothing less than the Supreme God, "God over all [emphatic], blessed forever." Thus Paul teaches us that by His coming forth from God to be born of woman, Our Lord, assuming a human nature to Himself, has, while remaining the Supreme God, become also true and perfect man. Accordingly, in a context in which the resources of language are strained to the utmost to make the exaltation of Our Lord's being clear—in which He is described as the image of the invisible God, whose being antedates all that is created, in whom, through whom and to whom all things have been created, and in whom they all subsist—we are told not only that (naturally) in Him all the fullness dwells (Col. 1:19), but, with complete explication, that all the fullness of the Godhead dwells in him bodily (Col. 2:9); that is to say, the very Deity of God, that which makes God God, in all its completeness, has its permanent home in Our Lord, and that in a "bodily fashion," that is, it is in Him clothed with a body. He who looks upon Jesus Christ sees, no doubt, a body and a man; but as he sees the man clothed with the body, so he sees God Himself, in all the fullness of His Deity, clothed with the humanity. Jesus Christ is therefore God "manifested in the flesh" (1 Tim. 3:16), and His appearance on earth is an "epiphany" (2 Tim. 1:10), which is the technical term for manifestations on earth of a God. Though truly man, He is nevertheless also our "great God" (Titus 2:13).

II. TEACHING OF THE EPISTLE TO THE HEBREWS

The conception of the person of Christ which underlies and finds expression in the Epistle to the Hebrews is indistinguishable from that which governs all the allusions to Our Lord in the Epistles of Paul. To the author of this epistle Our Lord is above all else the Son of God in the most eminent sense of that word; and it is the Divine dignity and majesty belonging to Him from His very nature which forms the fundamental feature of the image of Christ which stands before his mind. And yet it is this author who, perhaps above all others of the New Testament writers, emphasizes the truth of the humanity of Christ, and dwells with most particularity upon the elements of His human nature and experience.

The great Christological passage which fills chap. 2 of the Epistle to the Hebrews rivals in its richness and fullness of detail, and its breadth of implication, that of Phil. 2. It is thrown up against the background of the remarkable exposition of the Divine dignity of the Son which occupies chap. 1 (notice the "therefore" of 2:1). There the Son had been declared to be "the effulgence of his (God's) glory, and the very image of his substance, through whom the universe has been created and by the word of whose power all things are held in being"; and His exaltation above the angels, by means of whom the Old Covenant had been inaugurated, is measured by the difference between the designations "ministering spirits" proper to the one, and the Son of God, nay, God itself (1:8, 9), proper to the other. The purpose of the succeeding statement is to enhance in the thought of the Jewish readers of the epistle the value of the salvation wrought by this Divine Savior, by removing from their minds the offence they were in danger of taking at His lowly life and shameful death on earth. This earthly humiliation finds its abundant justification, we are told, in the greatness of the end which it sought and attained. By it

Our Lord has, with His strong feet, broken out a pathway along which, in Him, sinful man may at length climb up to the high destiny which was promised him when it was declared he should have dominion over all creation. Jesus Christ stooped only to conquer, and He stooped to conquer not for Himself (for He was in His own person no less than God), but for us.

The language in which the humiliation of the Son of God is in the first instance described is derived from the context. The establishment of His Divine majesty in chap. 1 had taken the form of an exposition of His infinite exaltation above the angels, the highest of all creatures. His humiliation is described here therefore as being "made a little lower than the angels" (2:9). What is meant is simply that He became man; the phraseology is derived from Ps. 8, Authorized Version, from which had just been cited the declaration that God has made man (despite his insignificance) "but a little lower than the angels," thus crowning him with glory and honor. The adoption of the language of the psalm to describe Our Lord's humiliation has the secondary effect, accordingly, of greatly enlarging the reader's sense of the immensity of the humiliation of the Son of God in becoming man: He descended an infinite distance to reach man's highest conceivable exaltation. As, however, the primary purpose of the adoption of the language is merely to declare that the Son of God became man, so it is shortly afterward explained (2:14) as an entering into participation in the blood and flesh which are common to men: "Since then the children are sharers in flesh and blood, he also himself in like manner partook of the same." The voluntariness, the reality, the completeness of the assumption of humanity by the Son of God, are all here emphasized.

The proximate end of Our Lord's assumption of humanity is declared to be that He might die; He was "made a little lower than the angels . . . because of the suffering of death" (2:9); He took part in blood and flesh in order "that through death . . ." (2:14). The Son of God as such could not die; to Him belongs by nature an "indissoluble life" (7:16). If he was to die, therefore, He must take to Himself another nature to which the experience of death were not impossible (2:17). Of course it is not meant that death was desired by Him for its own sake. The purpose of our passage is to save its Jewish readers from the offence of the death of Christ. What they are bidden to observe is, therefore, Jesus, who was made a little lower than the angels because of the suffering of death, crowned with glory and honor, that by the grace of God the bitterness of death which he tasted might redound to the benefit of every man (2:9), and the argument is immediately pressed home that it was eminently suitable for God Almighty, in bringing many sons into glory, to make the Captain of their salvation perfect (as a Savior) by means of suffering. The meaning is that it was only through suffering that these men, being sinners, could be brought into glory. And therefore in the plainer statement of verse 14 we read that Our Lord took part in flesh and blood in order "that through death he might bring to nought him that has the power of death, that is, the devil; and might deliver all them who through fear of death were all their lifetime subject to bondage"; and in the still plainer statement of verse 17 that the ultimate object of His assimilation to men was that He might "make propitiation for the sins of the people." It is for the salvation of sinners that Our Lord has come into the world; but, as that salvation can be wrought only by suffering and death, the proximate end of His assumption of humanity remains that He might die; whatever is more than this gathers around this.

The completeness of Our Lord's assumption of humanity and of His identification of Himself with it receives strong emphasis in this passage. He took part in the flesh and blood which is the common heritage of men, after the same fashion that other men participate in it (2:14); and, having thus become a man among men, He shared with other men the ordinary circumstances and fortunes of life, "in all things" (2:17). The stress is laid on trials, sufferings, death; but this is due to the actual course in which His life ran—and that it might run in which He became man—and is not exclusive of Other

human experiences. What is intended is that He became truly a man, and lived a truly human life, subject to all the experiences natural to a man in the particular circumstances in which He lived.

It is not implied, however, that during this human life—"the days of his flesh" (v. 7)—He had ceased to be God, or to have at His disposal the attributes which belonged to Him as God. That is already excluded by the representations of chap. 1. The glory of this dispensation consists precisely in the bringing of its revelations directly by the Divine Son rather than by mere prophets (1:1), and it was as the effulgence of God's glory and the express image of His substance, upholding the universe by the word of His power, that this Son made purification of sins (1:3). Indeed, we are expressly told that even in the days of the flesh, He continued still a Son (v. 8), and that it was precisely in this that the wonder lay: that though He was and remained (imperfect participle) a Son, He yet learned the obedience He had set Himself to (cf. Phil. 2:8) by the things which He suffered. Similarly, we are told not only that, though an Israelite of the tribe of Judah, He possessed "the power of an indissoluble life" (7:16), but, describing that higher nature which gave Him this power as an "eternal Spirit" (cf. "spirit of holiness," Rom. 1:4), that it was through this eternal Spirit that He could offer Himself without blemish unto God, a real and sufficing sacrifice, in contrast with the shadows of the Old Covenant (9:14). Though a man, therefore, and truly man, sprung out of Judah (7:14), touched with the feeling of human infirmities (4:15), and tempted like as we are, He was not altogether like other men. For one thing, He was "without sin" (4:15; 7:26), and, by this characteristic, He was, in every sense of the words, separated from sinners. Despite the completeness of His identification with men, He remained, therefore, even in the days of His flesh different from them and above them.

III. TEACHING OF OTHER EPISTLES

It is only as we carry this conception of the person of Our Lord with us—the conception of Him as at once our Supreme Lord, to whom our adoration is due, and our fellow in the experiences of a human life—that unity is induced in the multiform allusions to Him throughout, whether the Epistles of Paul or the Epistle to the Hebrews, or, indeed, the other epistolary literature of the New Testament. For in this matter there is no difference between those and these. There are no doubt a few passages in these other letters in which a plurality of the elements of the person of Christ are brought together and given detailed mention. In I Pet. 3:18, for instance, the two constitutive elements of His person are spoken of in the contrast, familiar from Paul, of the "flesh" and the "spirit." But ordinarily we meet only with references to this or that element separately. Everywhere Our Lord is spoken of as having lived out His life as a man; but everywhere also He is spoken of with the supreme reverence which is due to God alone, and the very name of God is not withheld from Him. In I Pet. 1:11 His preexistence is taken for granted; in James 2:1 He is identified with the Shekinah, the manifested Jehovah—"our Lord Jesus Christ, the Glory"; in Jude verse 4 "He is our only Master and Lord"; over and over again He is the Divine Lord who is Jehovah (e. g., I Pet. 2:3, 13; II Pet. 3:2, 18); in II Pet. 1:1, He is roundly called "our God and Savior." There is nowhere formal inculcation of the entire doctrine of the person of Christ. But everywhere its elements, now one and now another, are presupposed as the common property of writer and readers. It is only in the Epistles of John that this easy and unstudied presupposition of them gives way to pointed insistence upon them.

IV. TEACHING OF JOHN

In the circumstances in which he wrote, John found it necessary to insist upon the elements of the person of Our Lord—His true Deity, His true humanity and the unity of His person—in a manner which is more didactic in form than anything we find in the other writings of the New Testament. The great depository of his teaching on the subject is, of course, the prologue to his Gospel. But it is not merely in this prologue, nor in the Gospel to which it forms a fitting introduction, that these didactic statements are found. The full emphasis of John's witness to the twofold nature of the Lord is brought out, indeed, only by combining what he says in the Gospel and in the Epistles. "In the Gospel," remarks Westcott (on John 20:31), "the evangelist shows step by step that the historic Jesus was the Christ, the Son of God (opposed to mere flesh); in the Epistle he re-affirms that the Christ, the Son of God, was true man (opposed to mere spirit; 1 John 4:2)." What John is concerned to show throughout is that it was "the true God" (1 John 5:20) who was "made flesh" (John 1:14); and that this "only God" (John 1:18, Revised Version, margin "God only begotten") has truly come in . . . flesh" (1 John 4:2). In all the universe there is no other being of whom it can be said that He is God come in flesh (cf. 2 John ver. 7, He that "cometh in the flesh," whose characteristic this is). And of all the marvels which have ever occurred in the marvelous history of the universe, this is the greatest—thatwhat was from the beginning' (1 John 2:13, 14) has been heard and gazed upon, seen and handled by men (1 John 1:1).

From the point of view from which we now approach it, the prologue to the Gospel of John may be said to fall into three parts. In the first of these, the nature of the Being who became incarnate in the person we know as Jesus Christ is described; in the second, the general nature of the act we call the incarnation; and in the third, the nature of the incarnated person. John here calls the person who became incarnate by a name peculiar to himself in the New Testament—the "Logos" orWord." According to the predicates which he here applies to Him, he can mean by the "Word" nothing else but God Himself, "considered in His creative, operative, self-revealing, and communicating character," the sum total of what is Divine (C. F. Schmid). In three crisp sentences he declares at the outset His eternal subsistence, His eternal intercommunion with God, His eternal identity with God: "In the beginning the Word was; and the Word was with God; and the Word was God" (John 1:1). "In the beginning," at that point of time when things first began to be (Gen. 1:1), the Word already "was." He antedates the beginning of all things. And He not merely antedates them, but it is immediately added that He is Himself the creator of all that is: "All things were made by him, and apart from him was not made one thing that hath been made" (1:3). Thus He is taken out of the category of creatures altogether. Accordingly, what is said of Him is not that He was the first of existences to come into being—that "in the beginning He already had come into being"—but that "in the beginning, when things began to come into being, He already was." It is express eternity of being that is asserted: "the imperfect tense of the original suggests in this relation, as far as human language can do so, the notion of absolute, supra-temporal existence" (Westcott). This, His eternal subsistence, was not, however, in isolation: "And the Word was with God." The language is pregnant. It is not merely coexistence with God that is asserted, as of two beings standing side by side, united in a local relation, or even in a common conception. What is suggested is an active relation of intercourse. The distinct personality of the Word is therefore not obscurely intimated. From all eternity the Word has been with God as a fellow: He who in the very beginning already "was," "was" also in communion with God. Though He was thus in some sense a second along with God, He was nevertheless not a separate being from God: "And the Word was"—still the eternal. In some sense distinguishable from God, He was in an equally true sense identical with God. There is but one eternal God; this eternal God, the Word is; in whatever sense we may distinguish Him from the God whom He is "with," He is yet not another than this God, but Himself is this God. The predicate "God" occupies the position of emphasis in this great declaration, and is so placed in the sentence as to be thrown up in sharp contrast with the phrase "with God," as if to prevent inadequate inferences as to the nature of the Word being drawn even momentarily from that phrase. John would have us realize that what the Word was in eternity was not merely God's coeternal fellow, but the eternal God's self.

Now, John tells us that it was this Word, eternal in His subsistence, God's eternal fellow, the eternal God's self, that, as "come in the flesh," was Jesus Christ (1 John 4:2). "And the Word became flesh" (John 1:14), he says. The terms he employs here are not terms of substance, but of personality. The meaning is not that the substance of God was transmuted into that substance which we call "flesh." "The Word" is a personal name of the eternal God; "flesh" is an appropriate designation of humanity in its entirety, with the implications of dependence and weakness. The meaning, then, is simply that He who had just been described as the eternal God became, by a voluntary act in time, a man. The exact nature of the act by which He "became" man lies outside the statement; it was matter of common knowledge between the writer and the reader. The language employed intimates merely that it was a definite act, and that it involved a change in the life-history of the eternal God, here designated "the Word." The whole emphasis falls on the nature of this change in His life-history. He became flesh. That is to say, He entered upon a mode of existence in which the experiences that belong to human beings would also be His. The dependence, the weakness, which constitute the very idea of flesh, in contrast with God, would now enter into His personal experience. And it is precisely because these are the connotations of the term "flesh" that John chooses that term here, instead of the more simply denotative term "man." What he means is merely that the eternal God became man. But he elects to say this in the language which throws best up to view what it is to become man. The contrast between the Word as the eternal God and the human nature which He assumed as flesh, is the hinge of the statement. Had the evangelist said (as he does in 1 John 4:2) that the Word came in flesh, it would have been the continuity through the change which would have been most emphasized. When he says rather that the Word became flesh, while the continuity of the personal subject is, of course, intimated, it is the reality and the completeness of the humanity assumed which is made most prominent.

That in becoming flesh the Word did not cease to be what He was before entering upon this new sphere of experiences, the evangelist does not leave, however, to mere suggestion. The glory of the Word was so far from quenched, in his view, by His becoming flesh, that he gives us at once to understand that it was rather as "trailing clouds of glory" that He came. "And the Word became flesh," he says, and immediately adds: "and dwelt among us (and we beheld his glory, glory as of the only begotten from the Father), full of grace and truth" (1:14). The language is colored by reminiscences from the Tabernacle, in which the Glory of God, the Shekinah, dwelt. The flesh of Our Lord became, on its assumption by the Word, the Temple of God on earth (cf. John 2:19), and the glory of the Lord filled the house of the Lord. John tells us expressly that this glory was visible, that it was precisely what was appropriate to the Son of God as such. "And we beheld his glory," he says; not divined it, or inferred it, but perceived it. It was open to sight, and the actual object of observation. Jesus Christ was obviously more than man; He was obviously God. His actually observed glory, John tells us further, was a "glory as of the only begotten from the Father." It was unique; nothing like it was ever seen in another, And its uniqueness consisted precisely in its consonance with what the unique Son of God, sent forth from the Father, would naturally have; men recognized and could not but recognize in Jesus Christ the unique Son of God. When this unique Son of God is further described as "full of grace and truth," the elements of His manifested glory are not to be supposed to be exhausted by this description (cf. 2:11). Certain items of it only are singled out for particular mention. The visible glory of the incarnated Word was such a glory as the unique Son of God, sent forth from the Father, who was full of grace and truth, would naturally manifest.

That nothing should be lacking to the declaration of the continuity of all that belongs to the Word as such into this new sphere of existence, and its full manifestation through the veil of His flesh, John adds at the close of his exposition the remarkable sentence: "As for God, no one has even yet seen him; God only begotten, who is in the bosom of the Father—He hath declared him" (1:18 in.). It is the incarnate Word which is here called "only begotten God." The absence of the article with this designation is doubtless due to its parallelism with the word "God" which stands at the head of the corresponding clause. The effect of its absence is to throw up into emphasis the quality rather than the mere individuality of the person so designated. The adjective "only begotten" conveys the idea, not of derivation and subordination, but of uniqueness and consubstantiality: Jesus is all that God is, and He alone is this. Of this "only begotten God" it is now declared that He "is"—not "was," the state is not one which has been left behind at the incarnation, but one which continues uninterrupted and unmodified—"into "—not merely "in"—"the bosom of the Father"—that is to say, He continues in the most intimate and complete communion with the Father. Though now incarnate, He is still "with God" in the full sense of the external relation intimated in 1:1. This being true, He has much more than seen God, and is fully able to "interpret" God to men. Though no one has ever yet seen God, yet he who has seen Jesus Christ, "God only begotten," has seen the Father (cf. 14:9; 12:45). In this remarkable sentence there is asserted in the most direct manner the full Deity of the incarnate Word, and the continuity of His life as such in His incarnate life; thus He is fitted to be the absolute revelation of God to man.

This condensed statement of the whole doctrine of the incarnation is only the prologue to a historical treatise. The historical treatise which it introduces, naturally, is written from the point of view of its prologue. Its object is to present Jesus Christ in His historical manifestation, as obviously the Son of God in flesh. "These are written," the Gospel testifies, "that ye may believe that Jesus is the Christ, the Son of God" (20:31); that Jesus who came as a man (1:30) was thoroughly known in His human origin (7:27), confessed Himself man (8:40), and died as a man dies (19:5), was, nevertheless, not only the Messiah, the Sent of God, the fulfiller of all the Divine promises of redemption, but also the very Son of God, that God only begotten, who, abiding in the bosom of the Father, is His sole adequate interpreter. From the beginning of the Gospel onward, this purpose is pursued: Jesus is pictured as ever, while truly man, yet manifesting Himself as equally truly God, until the veil which covered the eyes of His followers was wholly lifted, and He is greeted as both Lord and God (20:28). But though it is the prime purpose of this Gospel to exhibit the Divinity of the man Jesus, no obscuration of His manhood is involved. It is the Deity of the man Jesus which is insisted on, but the true manhood of Jesus is as prominent in the representation as in any other portion of the New Testament. Nor is any effacement of the humiliation of His earthly life involved. For the Son of man to come from heaven was a descent (3:13), and the mission which He came to fulfill was a mission of contest and conflict, of suffering and death. He brought His glory with Him (1:14), but the glory that was His on earth (17:22) was not all the glory which He had had with the Father before the world was, and to which, after His work was done, He should return (17:5). Here too the glory of the celestial is one and the glory of the terrestrial is another. In any event, John has no difficulty in presenting the life of Our Lord on earth as the life of God in flesh, and in insisting at once on the glory that belongs to Him as God and on the humiliation which is brought to Him by the flesh. It is distinctly a duplex life which he ascribes to Christ, and he attributes to Him without embarrassment all the powers and modes of activity appropriate on the one hand to Deity and on the other to sinless (John 7:46; cf. 14:30; 1 John 3:5) human nature. In a true sense his portrait of Our Lord is a dramatization of the God-man which he presents to our contemplation in his prologue.

V. TEACHING OF THE SYNOPTIC GOSPELS

The same may be said of the other Gospels. They are all dramatizations of the God-man set forth in theoretical exposition in the prologue to John's Gospel. The Gospel of Luke, written by a known companion of Paul, gives us in a living narrative the same Jesus who is presupposed in all Paul's allusions to Him. That of Mark, who was also a companion of Paul, as also of Peter, is, as truly as the Gospel of John itself, a presentation of facts in the life of Jesus with a view to making it plain that this was the life of no mere man, human as it was, but of the Son of God Himself. Matthew's Gospel differs from its fellows mainly in the greater richness of Jesus' own testimony to His Deity which it records. What is characteristic of all three is the inextricable interlacing in their narratives of the human and Divine traits which alike marked the life they are depicting. It is possible, by neglecting one series of their representations and attending only to the other, to sift out from them at will the portrait of either a purely Divine or a purely human Jesus. It is impossible to derive from them the portrait of any other than a Divine-human Jesus if we surrender ourselves to their guidance and take off of their pages the portrait they have endeavored to draw. As in their narratives they cursorily suggest now the fullness of His Deity and now the completeness of His humanity and everywhere the unity of His person, they present as real and as forcible a testimony to the constitution of Our Lord's person as uniting in one personal life a truly Divine and a truly human nature, as if they announced this fact in analytical statement. Only on the assumption of this conception of Our Lord's person as underlying and determining their presentation, can unity be given to their representations; while, on this supposition, all their representations fall into their places as elements in one consistent whole. Within the limits of their common presupposition, each Gospel has no doubt its own peculiarities in the distribution of its emphasis. Mark lays particular stress on the Divine power of the man Jesus, as evidence of His supernatural being; and on the irresistible impression of a veritable Son of God, a Divine being walking the earth as a man, which He made upon all with whom He came into contact. Luke places his Gospel by the side of the Epistle to the Hebrews in the prominence it gives to the human development of the Divine being whose life on earth it is depicting and to the range of temptation to which He was subjected. Matthew's Gospel is notable chiefly for the heights of the Divine self-consciousness which it uncovers in its report of the words of Him whom it represents as nevertheless the Son of David, the Son of Abraham; heights of Divine self-consciousness which fall in nothing short of those attained in the great utterances preserved for us by John. But amid whatever variety there may exist in the aspects on which each lays his particular emphasis, it is the same Jesus Christ which all three bring before us, a Jesus Christ who is at once God and man and one individual person. If that be not recognized, the whole narrative of the Synoptic Gospels is thrown into confusion; their portrait of Christ becomes an insoluble puzzle; and the mass of details which they present of His life-experiences is transmuted into a mere set of crass contradictions.

VI. TEACHING OF JESUS
1. The Johannine Jesus
The Gospel narratives not only present us, however, with dramatizations of the God-man, according to their authors' conception of His composite person. They preserve for us also a considerable body of the utterances of Jesus Himself, and this enables us to observe the conception of His person which underlay and found expression in Our Lord's own teaching. The discourses of Our Lord which have been selected for record by John have been chosen (among other reasons) expressly for the reason that they bear witness to His essential Deity. They are accordingly peculiarly rich in material for forming a judgment of Our Lord's conception of His higher nature. This conception, it is needless to say, is precisely that which John, taught by it, has announced in the prologue to his Gospel, and has illustrated by his Gospel itself, compacted as it is of these discourses. It will not be necessary to present the evidence for this in its fullness. It will be enough to point to a few characteristic passages, in which Our Lord's conception of His higher nature finds especially clear expression.

That He was of higher than earthly origin and nature, He repeatedly asserts. "Ye are from beneath," he says to the Jews (8:23), "I am from above: ye are of this world; I am not of this world" (cf. 17:16). Therefore, He taught that He, the Son of Man, had "descended out of heaven" (3:13), where was His true abode. This carried with it, of course, an assertion of preexistence; and this preexistence is explicitly affirmed: "What then," He asks, "if ye should behold the Son of man ascending where he was before?" (6:62). It is not merely preexistence, however, but eternal preexistence which He claims for Himself: "And now, Father," He prays (17:5), "glorify thou me with thine own self with the glory which I had with thee before the world was" (cf. ver. 24); and again, as the most impressive language possible, He declares (8:58 A.V.): "Verily, verily, I say unto you, Before Abraham was, I am," where He claims for Himself the timeless present of eternity as His mode of existence. In the former of these two last-cited passages, the character of His preexistent life is intimated; in it He shared the Father's glory from all eternity ("before the world was"); He stood by the Father's side as a companion in His glory. He came forth, when He descended to earth, therefore, not from heaven only, but from the very side of God (8:42; 17:8). Even this, however, does not express the whole truth; He came forth not only from the Father's side where He had shared in the Father's glory; He came forth out of the Father's very being—"I came out from the Father, and am come into the world" (16:28; cf. 8:42). "The connection described is internal and essential, and not that of presence or external fellowship" (Westcott). This prepares us for the great assertion: "I and the Father are one" (10:30), from which it is a mere corollary that "He that hath seen me hath seen the Father" (14:9; cf. 8:19; 12:45).

In all these declarations the subject of the affirmation is the actual person speaking: it is of Himself who stood before men and spoke to them that Our Lord makes these immense assertions. Accordingly, when He majestically declared, "I and the Father are" (plurality of persons) "one" (neuter singular, and accordingly singleness of being), the Jews naturally understood Him to be making Himself, the person then speaking to them, God (10:33; cf. 5:18; 19:7). The continued sameness of the person who has been, from all eternity down to this hour, one with God, is therefore fully safeguarded. His earthly life is, however, distinctly represented as a humiliation. Though even on earth He is one with the Father, yet He "descended" to earth; He had come out from the Father and out of God; a glory had been left behind which was yet to be returned to, and His sojourn on earth was therefore to that extent an obscuration of His proper glory. There was a sense, then, in which, because He had "descended," He was no longer equal with the Father. It was in order to justify an assertion of equality with the Father in power (10:25, 29) that He was led to declare: "I and my Father are one" (10:30). But He can also declare "The Father is greater than I" (14:28). Obviously this means that there was a sense in which He had ceased to be equal with the Father, because of the humiliation of His present condition, and in so far as this humiliation involved entrance into a status lower than that which belonged to Him by nature. Precisely in what this humiliation consisted can be gathered only from the general implication of many statements. In it He was "a man who hath told you the truth, which I have heard from God" (8:40), where the contrast with "God" throws the assertion of humanity into emphasis (cf. 10:33). The truth of His human nature is, however, everywhere assumed and endlessly illustrated, rather than explicitly asserted. He possessed a human soul (12:27) and bodily parts (flesh and blood, 6:53; hands and side, 20:27); and was subject alike to physical affections (weariness, 4:6, and thirst, 19:28, suffering and death), and to all the common human emotions—not merely the love of compassion (13:34; 14:21; 15:8-13), but the love of simple affection which we pour out on "friends" (11:11; cf. 15:14, 15), indignation (11:33, 38) and joy (15:11; 17:13). He felt the perturbation produced by strong excitement (11:33; 12:27; 13:21), the sympathy with suffering which shows itself in tears (11:35), the thankfulness which fills the grateful heart (6:11, 23; 11:41). Only one human characteristic was alien to Him: He was without sin: "the prince of the world," He declared, "hath nothing in me" (14:30; cf. 8:46). Clearly our Lord, as reported by John, knew Himself to be true God and true man in one indivisible person, the common subject of the qualities which belong to each.

2. The Synoptic Jesus
(a) Mark 13:32

The same is true of His self-consciousness as revealed in His sayings recorded by the Synoptics. Perhaps no more striking illustration of this could be adduced than the remarkable declaration recorded in Mark 13:82 (cf. Matt. 24:36) "But of that day or that hour knoweth no one, not even the angels in heaven, nor yet the Son, but the Father." Here Jesus places Himself, in an ascending scale of being, above "the angels in heaven," that is to say, the highest of all creatures, significantly marked here as super-mundane. Accordingly, He presents Himself elsewhere as the Lord of the angels, whose requests they obey: "The Son of man shall send forth his angels, and they shall gather out of his kingdom all things that cause stumbling, and them that do iniquity" (Matt. 13:41), "And he shall send forth his angels with a great sound of a trumpet, and they shall gather together his elect from the four winds, from one end of heaven to the other" (Matt. 24:31; cf. 13:49; 25:31; Mark 8:38). Thus the "angels of God" (Luke 12:8, 9; 15:10) Christ designates as His angels, the "kingdom of God" (Matt. 12:28; 19:24; 21:31, 43; Mark and Luke often) as His Kingdom, the "elect of God" (Mark 13:20; Luke 18:7; cf. Rom. 8:33; Gal. 3:12; Titus 1:1) as His elect. He is obviously speaking in Mark 13:22 out of a Divine self-consciousness: "Only a Divine being can be exalted above angels" (B. Weiss). He therefore designates Himself by His Divine name, "the Son," that is to say, the unique Son of God (9:7; 1:11), to claim to be whom would for a man be blasphemy (Mark 14:61, 64). But though He designates Himself by this Divine name, He is not speaking of what He once was, but of what at the moment of speaking

He is: the action of the verb is present, "knoweth." He is claiming, in other words, the supreme designation of "the Son," with all that is involved in it, for His present self, as He moved among men: He is, not merely was, "the Son." Nevertheless, what He affirms of Himself cannot be affirmed of Himself distinctively as "the Son." For what He affirms of Himself is ignorance—not even the Son knows it; and ignorance does not belong to the Divine nature which the term "the Son" connotes. An extreme appearance of contradiction accordingly arises from the use of this terminology, just as it arises when Paul says that the Jews "crucified the Lord of glory" (1 Cor. 2:8), or exhorts the Ephesian elders to "feed the church of God which he purchased with his own blood" (Acts 20:28); or John Keble praises Our Lord for "the blood of souls by Thee redeemed." It was not the Lord of Glory as such who was nailed to the tree, nor have either "God" or "souls" blood to shed.

We know how this apparently contradictory mode of speech has arisen in Keble's case. He is speaking of men who are composite beings, consisting of souls and bodies, and these men come to be designated from one element of their composite personalities, though what is affirmed by them belongs rather to the other; we may speak, therefore, of the "blood of souls" meaning that these "souls," while not having blood as such, yet designate persons who have bodies and therefore blood. We know equally how to account for Paul's apparent contradictions. We know that he conceived of Our Lord as a composite person, uniting in Himself a Divine and a human nature. In Paul's view, therefore, though God as such has no blood, yet Jesus Christ who is God has blood because He is also man. He can justly speak, therefore, when speaking of Jesus Christ, of His blood as the blood of God. When precisely the same phenomenon meets us in Our Lord's speech of Himself, we must presume that it is the outgrowth of precisely the same state of things. When He speaks of "the Son" (who is God) as ignorant, we must understand that He is designating Himself as "the Son" because of His higher nature, and

yet has in mind the ignorance of His lower nature; what He means is that the person properly designated "the Son" is ignorant, that is to say with respect to the human nature which is as intimate an element of His personality as is His Deity.

When our Lord says, then, that "the Son knows not," He becomes as express a witness to the two natures which constitute His person as Paul is when he speaks of the blood of God, or as Keble is a witness to the twofold constitution of a human being when he speaks of souls shedding blood. In this short sentence, thus, Our Lord bears witness to His Divine nature with its supremacy above all creatures, to His human nature with its creaturely limitations, and to the unity of the subject possessed of these two natures.

b) Other passages: Son of Man and Son of God

All these elements of His personality find severally repeated assertions in other utterances of Our Lord recorded in the Synoptics. There is no need to insist here on the elevation of Himself above the kings and prophets of the Old Covenant (Matt. 12:41), above the temple itself (Matt. 12:6), and the ordinances of the Divine Law (Matt. 12:8); or on His accent of authority in both His teaching and action, His great "I say unto you (Matt. 5:21, 22), "I will; be cleansed" (Mark 1:41; 2:5; Luke 7:14); or on His separation of Himself from men in His relation to God, never including them with Himself in an "Our Father," but consistently speaking distinctively of "my Father" (e.g., Luke 24:49) and "your Father" (e.g., Matt. 5:16); or on His intimation that He is not merely David's Son but David's Lord, and that a Lord sitting on the right hand of God (Matt. 22:44); or on His parabolic discrimination of Himself a Son and Heir from all "servants" (Matt. 21:33); or even on His ascription to Himself of the purely Divine functions of the forgiveness of sins (Mark 2:8) and judgment of the world (Matt. 25:31), or of the purely Divine powers of reading the heart (Mark 2:8; Luke 9:47), omnipotence (Matt. 24:30; Mark 14:62) and omnipresence (Matt. 18:20; 28:10). These things illustrate His constant assumption of the possession of Divine dignity and attributes; the claim itself is more directly made in the two great designations which He currently gave Himself, the Son of Man and the Son of God. The former of these is His favorite self-designation. Derived from Dan. 7:13, 14, it intimates on every occasion of its employment Our Lord's consciousness of being a super-mundane being, who has entered into a sphere of earthly life on a high mission, on the accomplishment of which

He is to return to His heavenly sphere, whence He shall in due season come back to earth, now, however, in His proper majesty, to gather up the fruits of His work and consummate all things. It is a designation, thus, which implies at once a heavenly preexistence, a present humiliation, and a future glory; and He proclaims Himself in this future glory no less than the universal King seated on the throne of judgment for quick and dead (Mark 8:31; Matt. 25:31). The implication of Deity imbedded in the designation, Son of Man, is perhaps more plainly spoken out in the companion designation, Son of God, which Our Lord not only accepts at the hands of others, accepting with it the implication of blasphemy in permitting its application to Himself (Matt. 26:63, 65; Mark 14:61, 64; Luke 22:29, 30), but persistently claims for Himself both, in His constant designation of God as His Father in a distinctive sense, and in His less frequent but more pregnant designation of Himself as, by way of eminence, "the Son." That His consciousness of the peculiar relation to God expressed by this designation was not an attainment of His mature spiritual development, but was part of His most intimate consciousness from the beginning, is suggested by the sole glimpse which is given us into His mind as a child (Luke 2:49). The high significance which the designation bore to Him is revealed to us in two remarkable utterances preserved, the one by both Matthew (11:27) and Luke (10:22), and the other by Matthew (28:19).

(c) Matt. 11:27; 28:19

In the former of these utterances, Our Lord, speaking in the most solemn manner, not only presents Himself, as the Son, as the sole source of knowledge of God and of blessedness for men, but places Himself in a position, not of equality merely, but of absolute reciprocity and interpretation of knowledge with the Father. "No one," He says, "knoweth the Son, save the Father; neither doth any know the Father, save the Son . . ." varied in Luke so as to read: "No one knoweth who the Son is, save the Father; and who the Father is, save the Son . . ." as if the being of the Son were so immense that only God could know it thoroughly; and the knowledge of the Son was so unlimited that He could know God to perfection. The peculiarly pregnant employment here of the terms "Son" and "Father" over against one another is explained to us in the other utterance (Matt. 28:19). It is the resurrected Lord's commission to His disciples. Claiming for Himself all authority in heaven and on earth—which implies the possession of omnipotence—and promising to be with His follower "salway, even to the end of the world"—which adds the implications of omnipresence and omniscience—He commands them to baptize their converts "in the name of the Father and of the Son and of the Holy Ghost." The precise form of the formula must be carefully observed. It does not read: "In the names" (plural)—as if there were three beings enumerated, each with its distinguishing name. Nor yet: "In the name of the Father, Son and Holy Ghost," as if there were one person, going by a threefold name. It reads: "In the name [singular] of the Father, and of the [article repeated] Son, and of the [article repeated] Holy Ghost," carefully distinguishing three persons, though uniting them all under one name. The name of God was to the Jews Jehovah, and to name the name of Jehovah upon them was to make them His. What Jesus did in this great injunction was to command His followers to name the name of God upon their converts, and to announce the name of God which is to be named on their converts in the threefold enumeration of "the Father" and "the Son" and "the Holy Ghost." As it is unquestionable that He intended Himself by "the Son," He here places Himself by the side of the Father and the Spirit, as together with them constituting the one God. It is, of course, the Trinity which He is describing; and that is as much as to say that He announces Himself as one of the persons of the Trinity. This is what Jesus, as reported by the Synoptics, understood Himself to be.

In announcing Himself to be God, however, Jesus does not deny that He is man also. If all His speech of Himself rests on His consciousness of a Divine nature, no less does all His speech manifest His consciousness of a human nature. He easily identifies Himself with men (Matt. 4:4; Luke 4:4), and receives without protest the imputation of humanity (Matt. 11:19; Luke 7:34). He speaks familiarly of His body (Matt. 26:12, 26; Mark 14:8; 14:22; Luke 22:19), and of His bodily parts—His feet and hands (Luke 24:39), His head and feet (Luke 7:44-46), His flesh and bones (Luke 24:39), His blood (Matt. 26:28; Mark 14:24; Luke 22:20). We chance to be given indeed a very express affirmation on His part of the reality of His bodily nature; when His disciples were terrified at His appearing before them after His resurrection, supposing Him to be a spirit, He reassures them with the direct declaration: "See my hands and my feet, that it is I myself: handle me, and see; for a spirit hath not flesh and bones, as ye behold me having" (Luke 24:39). His testimony to His human soul is just as express: "My soul," says He, "is exceeding sorrowful, even unto death" (Matt. 26:38; Mark 14:34). He speaks of the human dread with which He looked forward to His approaching death (Luke 12:50), and expresses in a poignant cry His sense of desolation on the cross (Matt. 27:46; Mark 15:34). He speaks also of His pity for the weary and hungering people (Matt. 15:32; Mark 8:2), and of a strong human desire which He felt (Luke 22:15). Nothing that is human is alien to Him except sin. He never ascribes imperfection to Himself and never betrays consciousness of sin. He recognizes the evil of those about Him (Luke 11:13; Matt. 11; 12:34, 39; Luke 11:29), but never identifies Himself with it. It is those who do the will of God with whom He feels kinship (Matt. 12:50), and He offers Himself to the morally sick as a physician (Matt. 9:12). He

proposes Himself as an example of the highest virtues (Matt. 11:28) and pronounces him blessed who shall find no occasion of stumbling in Him (Matt. 11:6).

These manifestations of a human and Divine consciousness simply stand side by side in the records of Our Lord's self-expression. Neither is suppressed or even qualified by the other. If we attend only to the one class we might suppose Him to proclaim Himself wholly Divine; if only to the other we might equally easily imagine Him to be representing Himself as wholly human. With both together before us we perceive Him alternately speaking out of a Divine and out of a human consciousness; manifesting Himself as all that God is and as all that man is; yet with the most marked unity of consciousness. He, the one Jesus Christ, was to His own apprehension true God and complete man in a unitary personal life.

VII. THE TWO NATURES EVERYWHERE PRESUPPOSED

There underlies, thus, the entire literature of the New Testament a single, unvarying conception of the constitution of Our Lord's person. From Matthew where He is presented as one of the persons of the Holy Trinity (28:19)—or if we prefer the chronological order of books, from the Epistle of James where He is spoken of as the Glory of God, the Shekinah—to the Apocalypse where He is represented as declaring that He is the Alpha and the Omega, the First and the Last, the Beginning and the End (1:8, 17; 22:13), He is consistently thought of as in His fundamental being just God. At the same time from the Synoptic Gospels, in which He is dramatized as a man walking among men, His human descent carefully recorded, and His sense of dependence on God so emphasized that prayer becomes almost His most characteristic action, to the Epistles of John in which it is made the note of a Christian that He confesses that Jesus Christ has come in flesh (1 John 4:2) and the Apocalypse in which His birth in the tribe of Judah and the house of David (v. 5; 22:16), His exemplary life of conflict and victory (3:21), His death on the cross (11:8) are noted, He is equally consistently thought of as true man. Nevertheless, from the beginning to the end of the whole series of books, while first one and then the other of His two natures comes into repeated prominence, there is never a question of conflict between the two, never any confusion in their relations, never any schism in His unitary personal action; but He is obviously considered and presented as one, composite indeed, but undivided personality. In this state of the case not only may evidence of the constitution of Our Lord's person properly be drawn indifferently from every part of the New Testament, and passage justly be cited to support and explain passage without reference to the portion of the New Testament in which it is found, but we should be without justification if we did not employ this common presupposition of the whole body of this literature to illustrate and explain the varied representations which meet us cursorily in its pages, representations which might easily be made to appear mutually contradictory were they not brought into harmony by their relation as natural component parts of this one unitary conception which underlies and gives consistency to them all. There can scarcely be imagined a better proof of the truth of a doctrine than its power completely to harmonize a multitude of statements which without it would present to our view only a mass of confused inconsistencies. A key which perfectly fits a lock of very complicated wards can scarcely fail to be the true key.

VIII. FORMULATION OF THE DOCTRINE

Meanwhile the wards remain complicated. Even in the case of our own composite structure, of soul and body, familiar as we are with it from our daily experience, the mutual relations of elements so disparate in a single personality remain an unplumbed mystery, and give rise to paradoxical modes of speech, which would be misleading, were not their source in our duplex nature well understood. We may read, in careful writers, of souls being left dead on battlefields, and of everybody's immortality. The mysteries of the relations in which the constituent elements in the more

complex personality of Our Lord stand to one another are immeasurably greater than in our simpler case. We can never hope to comprehend how the infinite God and a finite humanity can be united in a single person; and it is very easy to go fatally astray in attempting to explain the interactions in the unitary person of natures so diverse from one another. It is not surprising, therefore, that so soon as serious efforts began to be made to give systematic explanations of the Biblical facts as to Our Lord's person, many one-sided and incomplete statements were formulated which required correction and complementing before at length a mode of statement was devised which did full justice to the Biblical data. It was accordingly only after more than a century of controversy, during which nearly every conceivable method of construing and misconstruing the Biblical facts had been proposed and tested, that a formula was framed which successfully guarded the essential data supplied by the Scriptures from destructive misconception. This formula, put together by the Council of Chalcedon, A.D. 451, declares it to have always been the doctrine of the church, derived from the Scriptures and Our Lord Himself, that Our Lord Jesus Christ is "truly God and truly man, of a reasonable soul and body; consubstantial with the Father according to the Godhead, and consubstantial with us according to the manhood; in all things like unto us, without sin; begotten before all ages of the Father according to the Godhead, and in these latter days, for us and for our salvation, born of the Virgin Mary, the Mother of God, according to the manhood; one and the same Christ, Son, Lord, Only-begotten, to be acknowledged in two natures unconfusedly, unchangeably, indivisibly, inseparably; the distinction of natures being by no means taken away by the union, but rather the property of each nature being preserved, and concurring in one Person and one subsistence, not parted or divided into two persons, but one and the same Son, Only-begotten, God, the Word, the Lord Jesus Christ." There is nothing here but a careful statement in systematic form of the pure teaching of the Scriptures; and therefore this statement has stood ever since as the norm of thought and teaching as to the person of the Lord. As such, it has been incorporated, in one form or another, into the creeds of all the great branches of the church; it underlies and gives their form to all the allusions to Christ in the great mass of preaching and song which has accumulated during the centuries; and it has supplied the background of the devotions of the untold multitudes who through the Christian ages have been worshippers of Christ.

B. B. Warfield

1.52 THE PLACE OF CHRIST IN NEW TESTAMENT FAITH, JAMES DENNEY

James Denney (1856-1917) was a prominent New Testament scholar and theologian of the United Free Church, Scotland. He wrote The Death of Christ *and* Studies In Theology.

When we open the New Testament we find ourselves in presence of a glowing religious life. There is nothing in the world which offers any real parallel either to this life, or to the collection of books which attests it. The soul, which in contemporary literature is bound in shallows and in miseries, is here raised as on a great tidal wave of spiritual blessing. Nothing that belongs to a complete religious life is wanting, neither convictions nor motives, neither penitence nor ideals, neither vocation nor the assurance of victory. And from beginning to end, in all its parts and aspects and elements, this religious life is determined by Christ. It owes its character at every point to Him. Its convictions are convictions about Him. Its hopes are hopes which He has inspired and which it is for Him to fulfill. Its ideals are born of His teaching, and His life. Its strength is the strength of His spirit. If we sum it up in the one word faith, it is faith in God through Him—a faith which owes to Him all that is characteristic in it, all that distinguishes it from what is elsewhere known among men by that name.

This, at least, is the prima facie impression which the New Testament makes upon a reader brought up in the Christian Church. The simplest way to express it is to say that Christianity as it is represented in the New Testament is the life of faith in Jesus Christ. It is a life in which faith is directed to Him as its object, and in which everything depends upon the fact that the believer can be sure of his Lord. Christ so conceived is a person of transcendent greatness, but He is a real person, a historical person, and the representations of His greatness are true. They reproduce the reality which He is, and they justify that attitude of the soul to Him which the early Christians called faith, and which was the spring of all their Christian experiences. This, we repeat, is the impression which the New Testament makes on the ordinary Christian reader, but it is possible to react against it. In point of fact, the reaction has taken place, and has been profound and far-reaching. Two main questions have been raised by it which it is the object of the present work to examine. The first is, How far is the description just given of the New Testament correct? Is it the case that the Christian religious life, as the New Testament exhibits it, really puts Jesus into the place indicated, and that everything in this life, and everything especially in the relations of God and man, is determined by Him? In other words, is it the case that from the very beginning Christianity has existed only in the form of a faith which has Christ as its object, and not at all in the form of a faith which has had Christ simply as its living pattern? The second question is of importance to those who accept what seems at a glance the only possible answer to the first. It is this: Can the Christian religion, as the New Testament exhibits it, justify itself by appeal to Jesus? Granting that the spiritual phenomenon is what it is said to be, are the underlying historical facts sufficient to sustain it? In particular, it may be said, is the mind of Christians about Christ supported by the mind of Christ about Himself? Is that which has come to be known in the world as Christian faith-known, let us admit, in the apostolic age and ever since-such faith as Jesus lived and died to produce? Did He take for Himself the extraordinary place which He fills in the mind and the world even of primitive Christians, or was this greatness thrust upon Him without His knowledge, against His will, and in inconsistency with His true place and nature? We are familiar with the idea that we can appeal to Christ against any phenomenon of our own age which claims to be Christian; is it not conceivable that we may have to appeal to Him even against the earliest forms which Christianity assumed?

No one who is familiar with the currents of thought whether within or without the Church can doubt that these questions are of present and urgent interest. To some, indeed, it may seem that there are questions more fundamental, and that when men are discussing whether Jesus ever lived, or whether we know anything about Him, it is trifling to ask whether the apostolic faith in Him is justified by the facts of His history. No serious person, however, doubts that Jesus existed, and the second of our two questions has been stated in the most searching form conceivable. It raises in all its dimensions the problem of the life and mind of Jesus, and in answering it we shall have opportunity to examine fully the sources on which our knowledge of Jesus rests. For those who stand outside the Christian Church, this second question is naturally of greater interest than the other, yet even for them it is impossible to ignore the connection of the two. For it is in the Church and through its testimony to Jesus that whatever knowledge we have of Him, even in the purely historical sense, has been preserved. But for those who are within the Church, the first question also has an interest of its own. To ask whether the prima facie impression which the New Testament makes upon us is verified by a closer examination— whether the interpretation of Christ which is current in the Church is that which is really yielded by the primitive witnesses—is to ask in other words whether the Church's faith to-day is continuous with that of apostolic times; and there can be few Christians who are indifferent to the answer. But though the profession of indifference would be absurd, it is not absurd to aim at sincerity and truth. No one can be more anxious to know the truth than the man to whom it means a great deal that the truth should be thus or thus. It we could imagine a person to whom it was a matter of indifference whether the Christian Church of to-day understood rightly or wrongly what the New Testament means by Christian faith, or who did not care in the least whether the historical facts about Jesus justified that faith or not, we should have imagined a person not ideally competent but absolutely incompetent to deal with either the one question or the other. The writer does not wish to disguise the fact that he is vitally interested in both, for he is convinced that on no other condition is there any likelihood of the true answer being found. But he disclaims at the same time any "apologetic" intention. There is no policy in what he has written, either in its manner or its substance. Nothing, so far as he is conscious, is set down for any other reason than that he believes it to be the truth, and nothing is to be discounted or allowed for as though he were mediating or negotiating between the progressive and the stationary elements in a Christian society, and would have said more or less if he had been free to speak without reserve. To the best of his knowledge he speaks without reserve, and has neither more nor less to say. This does not exclude the intention and the hope to say what may be of service to Christian faith and to the Christian Church; all it excludes is the idea that Christian faith or the Christian Church can be served by anything else than simple truth.

The two questions with which we have to deal are in one important respect of very different character. The first is quite simple: Is the conception of the Christian religion which prevails and has always prevailed in the Church borne out by the New Testament? As we know it, and as it has been known in history, the Christian life is the life of faith in Jesus Christ: is this what it was in primitive times? Does the New Testament throughout give that solitary and all-determining place to Jesus which He holds in the later Christian religion? This is a simple question, and no difficulty can be raised about the proper method of answering it. All we have to do is to go to the New Testament and scrutinize its evidence. The laws of interpretation are agreed upon among intelligent people, and no difficulty about "presuppositions" is raised. But the second question is of a different kind. It has to do with what is historically known of Jesus, and here the difficulty about "presuppositions" becomes acute. It is possible to argue that much of what the New Testament records concerning Jesus cannot be historically known—that it transcends the conception of what is historical, and must either be known on other terms than history, or dismissed from the region of knowledge altogether. It is not necessary at this stage to raise the abstract problem; when we

come to the second question it will be considered as far as the case requires. Here the writer would only express his distrust of a priori determinations of what is possible either in the natural or the historical sphere. There is only one universe: nature is not the whole of it, neither is history; and neither nature nor history is a whole apart from it. Nature and history do not exist in isolation; they are caught up into a moral and spiritual system with which they are throughout in vital relations. It is not for anyone to say offhand and a priori what is or is not naturally or historically conceivable in such a system. Its possibilities, in all likelihood, rather transcend than fall short of our anticipations; we need not be too much surprised if experience calls rather for elasticity than for rigidity of mind. If anything is certain, it is that the world is not made to the measure of any science or philosophy, but on a scale which perpetually summons philosophy and science to construct themselves anew; and it is with the undogmatic temper which recognizes this that the problems indicated above are approached in this book.

James Denney
Jesus and the Gospel, *1908*

---

9. QUOTATION COLLECTION ON THE PERSON OF JESUS

Without a cause men hated Christ; without a cause he loves them.

Milton S. Agnew, Salvation Army colonel

They do greatly err who acknowledge that the flesh of man was taken on Himself by Christ, but deny that the affections of man were taken; and they contravene the purpose of the Lord Jesus Himself, since thus they take away from man what constitutes man, for man cannot be man without human affections.

Ambrose

As the print of the seal on the wax is the express image of the seal itself, so Christ is the

express image—the perfect representation of God.

Ambrose

He said that he was in existence before Abraham and that he was "lord" of the Sabbath; he claimed to forgive sins; he continually identified himself, in his work, his person and his glory, with the one he termed his heavenly Father; he accepted men's worship; and he said that he was to be the judge of men at the last day, and that their eternal destiny would depend on their attitude to him.

J. N. D. Anderson

[Christ] was primarily concerned to change men as men rather than the political regime under which they lived; to transform their attitude rather than their circumstances; to treat the sickness of their hearts rather than the problems of their environment.

J. N. D. Anderson

Jesus is either God, or he is not good.

Anselm

I believe in . . . Jesus Christ his only Son our Lord. Who was conceived by the Holy Ghost. Born of the Virgin Mary. Suffered under Pontius Pilate. Was crucified, dead and buried. He descended into hell. the third day he rose again from the dead.

The Apostles' Creed

Jesus whom I know as my Redeemer cannot be less than God.

Athanasius

He became what we are that he might make us what he is.

Athanasius

The uniqueness of the Savior's works marked Him, alone of men, as Son of God.

Athanasius

Christ was a complete man.

Augustine

Christ came when all things were growing old. He made them new.

Augustine

The highest service may be prepared for and done in the humblest surroundings. In silence, in waiting, in obscure, unnoticed offices, in years of uneventful, unrecorded duties, the Son of God grew and waxed strong.

Author unknown, inscription in the Chapel of Stanford University

In Jesus, God wills to be true God not only in the height but also in the depth—in the depth of human creatureliness, sinfulness and mortality.

Karl Barth

Fundamentally, our Lord's message was Himself. He did not come merely to preach a Gospel; He himself is that Gospel.

J. Sidlow Baxter

Christ is the Morning Star who, when the night of this world is past brings to his saints the promise of the light of life and opens everlasting day.

Venerable Bede

If Christ is not divine, every impulse of the Christian world falls to a lower octave, and light and love and hope decline.

Henry Ward Beecher

The virgin birth is important because of its unique and miraculous nature, which therefore points to the uniqueness of Jesus Christ.

J. M. Boice

The good news is that sin has been dealt with; that Jesus has suffered its penalty for us as our representative, so that we might never have to suffer it; and that therefore all who believe in him can look forward to heaven.

J. M. Boice

Alexander, Caesar, Charlemagne, and I founded empires; but upon what did we rest the creations of our genius? Upon force. Jesus Christ alone founded his empire upon love; and at this hour millions of men would die for him.

Napoleon Bonaparte

Everything in Christ astonishes me. His spirit overawes me, and His will confounds me. Between Him and whoever else in the world, there is no possible term of comparison. He is truly a being by Himself.

Napoleon Bonaparte

I know men; and I tell you that Jesus Christ was not a man.

Napoleon Bonaparte

I marvel that whereas the ambitious dreams of myself, Caesar, and Alexander should have vanished into thin air, a Judean peasant Jesus should be able to stretch his hands across the centuries and control the destinies of men and nations.

Napoleon Bonaparte

I search in vain in history to find the similar to Jesus Christ, or anything which can approach the gospel.

Napoleon Bonaparte

If Jesus Christ is not true God, how could he help us? If he is not true man, how could he help us?

Dietrich Bonhoeffer

God is best known in Christ; the sun is not seen but by the light of the sun.

William Bridge

Jesus Christ, the condescension of divinity, and the exaltation of humanity.

Phillips Brooks

The power Jesus exhibited [in his miracles] was a foretaste of the power to be revealed at the end of the age.

Colin Brown

No matter how far back we may press our researches into the roots of the gospel story, no matter how we classify the gospel material, we never arrive at a non-supernatural Jesus.

F. F. Bruce

Whatever else may be thought of the evidence from early Jewish and Gentile writers it does at least establish, for those who refuse the witness of Christian writings, the historical character of Jesus himself.

F. F. Bruce

Some writers may toy with the fancy of a "Christ-myth," but they do not do so on the ground of historical evidence. The historicity of Christ is as axiomatic for an unbiased historian as the historicity of Julius Caesar. It is not historian who propagate the "Christ-myth" theories.

F. F. Bruce

He [Christ] delights most in loving the worst.

John Bunyan

It would be a dangerous error to imagine that the characteristics of an historical religion would be maintained if the Christ of the theologians were divorced from the Jesus of history.

Herbert Butterfield

Let no one object that life or salvation is transfused into Christ by God. For it is said not that he received salvation, but that he himself is salvation.

John Calvin

Those who despoil Christ of either his divinity or his humanity diminish his majesty and glory, and obscure his goodness.

John Calvin

He who was the Son of God became the Son of man, not by confusion of substance, but by unity of person.

John Calvin

Although Christ was God before he became man, he did not therefore begin to be a new God.

John Calvin

As Christ is the end of the Law and the Gospel and has within himself all the treasures of wisdom and understanding, so also is he the mark at which all heretics aim and direct their arrows.

John Calvin

For we affirm His divinity so joined and united with His humanity that each retains its distinctive nature unimpaired, and yet those two natures constitute one Christ.

John Calvin

The Word was eternally begotten by God, and dwelt with him from everlasting. In this way, his true essence, his eternity, and divinity, are established.

John Calvin

Thomas, by addressing Christ as his Lord and God, certainly professes that he was the only God whom he had ever adored (John 20:28).

John Calvin

If apart from God there is no salvation, no righteousness, no life, Christ, having all these in himself, is certainly God.

John Calvin

His full deity and complete humanity are essential to His work on the cross. If He were not man, He could not die; if He were not God, His death would not have had infinite value.

Lewis Sperry Chafer

Our Lord's Life is the exhibition of eternal Life in time.

Oswald Chambers

Never take Jesus Christ as the Representative of God: He is God or there is none.

Oswald Chambers

If Jesus Christ is not God manifest in the flesh, we know nothing whatever about God; we are not only agnostic, but hopeless.

Oswald Chambers

Yea, for it was removal of punishment, and remission of sins, and righteousness, and sanctification, and redemption, and adoption, and an inheritance of Heaven, and a relationship unto the Son of God, which he came declaring unto all; to enemies, to the perverse, to them that were sitting in darkness. What then could ever be equal to these good tidings?

John Chrysostom

The Lord has turned all our sunsets into sunrise.

Clement of Alexandria

Brethren, we ought so to think of Jesus Christ as of God.

2 Clement, the oldest known sermon after the New Testament sermons

A borrowed manger and a borrowed tomb framed his earthly life.

Charles Colson

The full coequal deity of Jesus is nowhere taught in the New Testament.

Don Cupitt and Peter Armstrong

[In the person of Christ] a man has not become God; God has become man.

Cyril of Alexandria

The whole life of Christ was a continual passion. Others die martyrs, but Christ was born a martyr.

John Donne

Christ's Christmas Day and his Good Friday are but the evening and morning of one and the same day.

John Donne

Christ either deceived mankind by conscious fraud, or he was himself deluded, or he was divine. There is no getting out of this trilemma.

George Duncan

For a Jew to speak of a man, Jesus, in terms which showed Him as sharing in the deity of God, was a quite astonishing feature of earliest Christianity.

James D. G. Dunn

That a few simple men should in one generation have invented so powerful and appealing a personality, so lofty an ethic, and so inspiring a vision of human brotherhood, would be a miracle far more incredible than any recorded in the Gospels.

William Durant

As a child I received instruction both in the Bible and in the Talmud. I am a Jew, but I am enthralled by the luminous figure of the Nazarene. . . . No one can read the Gospels without feeling the actual presence of Jesus. His personality pulsates in every word. No myth is filled with such life.

Albert Einstein

Jesus became as like us as God can be.

Donald English

Earth grows into heaven, as we come to live and breathe in the atmosphere of the incarnation. Jesus makes heaven wherever He is.

F. W. Faber

The state of Christ, from his conception to his resurrection, was a state of deep debasement and humiliation.

John Flavel

I cannot say that Jesus was uniquely divine. He was as much God as Krishna, or Rama, or Mohammed, or Zoroaster.

Mahatma Gandhi

In Christ God has come into this world, truly human and yet without sin and still God.

Paul D. Gardner

The Jesus Christ of the Gospels could not possibly have been a real person. He is a combination of impossible elements.

Marshall J. Gauvin

It is one thing to claim deity and quite another to have the credentials to support that claim. Christ did both. He offered three unique and miraculous facts as evidence of his claim: the fulfillment of prophecy, a uniquely miraculous life, and the resurrection from the dead. All of these are historically provable and unique to Jesus of Nazareth. We argue, therefore, that Jesus alone claims to be and proves to be God.

Norman Geisler

The Godhead of Christ is that which stamps value upon His sufferings and renders the whole of His obedience, in life and in death, infinitely meritorious and effectual.

John Gill

Jesus is God lived by man.

F. Godet

Jesus is the exact revelation of what is on the mind and heart and in the will of God!

Anne Graham Lotz

Once disprove the historicity of Jesus Christ, and Christianity will collapse like a pack of cards.

Michael Green

The man who can read the first three Gospels … without being sensible that a mighty personality is at work in them—a personality swaying the hearts of men and far beyond the power of men to invent—must be denied the capacity to distinguish between fiction and the documentary evidence to a historical and personal life.

Adolf Harnack

No founder of any religion has dared to claim for himself one fraction of the assertions made by the Lord Jesus Christ about himself.

Henry J. Heydt

Christ is both God and man, in two distinct natures, and one person forever.

Charles Hodge

The simple, sublime, saving Christology of the Bible and the Church universal is: That the eternal Son of God became man by taking to Himself a true body and a reasonable soul, and so was and continues to be God and man in two distinct natures and one person forever.

Charles Hodge

God has revealed himself in his Son Jesus Christ, who is his Word issuing from the silence.

Ignatius of Antioch

After 1900 years, Jesus Christ still counts for more in human life than any other man that ever lived.

Dean Inge

For I have shown from the scriptures, that no one of the sons of Adam is as to everything, and absolutely, called God, or named Lord. But that He is Himself in His own right, beyond all men who ever lived, God, and Lord, and King Eternal, and the Incarnate Word, proclaimed by all the prophets, the apostles, and by the Spirit Himself, may be seen by all who have attained to even a small portion of the truth. Now, the scriptures would not have testified these things of Him, if, like others, He had been a mere man.

Irenaeus

Christ is a substitute for everything, but nothing is a substitute for Christ.

H. A. Ironside

Ignorance of scripture is ignorance of Christ.

Jerome

Jesus Christ has had an enormous impact—more than anybody else—on history. Whatever Jesus touched or whatever He did transformed that aspect of human life.

D. James Kennedy

Jesus Christ was an extremist for love, truth and goodness.

Martin Luther King, Jr.

No one else holds or has held the place in the heart of the world which Jesus holds. Other gods have been as devoutly worshipped; no other man has been so devoutly loved.

John Knox

After the fall of so many gods in this century, this person [Jesus], broken at the hands of his opponents and constantly betrayed through the ages by his adherents, is obviously still for innumerable people the most moving figure in the long history of mankind.

Hans Küng

He was made both Son of God in the spirit and Son of man in the flesh that is, both God and man.

Lactantius, third century Christian apologist

If Shakespeare should come into this room, we would all rise; but if Jesus Christ should come in, we would all kneel.

Charles Lamb

There has only ever been one perfect man, the Lord Jesus, and we killed him. I only missed a putt.

Bernhard Langer

You must make your choice. Either this man was, and is, the Son of God: or else a madman or something worse. You can shut him up for a fool; you can spit at him and kill him for a demon; or you can fall at his feet and call him Lord and God. But let us not come with any patronizing nonsense about his being a great human teacher. He has not left that open to us. He did not intend to.

C. S. Lewis

This man was, and is, the Son of God, or else a madman or something worse.

C. S. Lewis

The only Christ for whom there is a shred of evidence is a miraculous figure making stupendous claims.

C. S. Lewis

Christians believe that Jesus Christ is the Son of God because He said so. The other evidence about Him has convinced them that He was neither a lunatic nor a quack.

C. S. Lewis

Either this man [Jesus] was, and is, the son of God, or else a madman or something worse.

C. S. Lewis

Either He was a raving lunatic of an unusually abominable type, or else, He was, and is, precisely what He said [he was].

C. S. Lewis

Through Christ alone . . . salvation comes to us.

Franz Liszt

God had only one Son, and he was a missionary and a physician.

David Livingstone

Christ is the fulfillment of all the Old Testament prophecies and promises.

D. Martyn Lloyd-Jones

What God has done in Christ exhausts all that God has to do for us.

R. C. Lucas

He [Christ, our Sin-bearer] is not like Moses who only shows sin, but rather like Aaron who bears sin.

Martin Luther

Jesus became the greatest liar, perjurer, thief, adulterer and murderer than mankind has ever known—not because he committed these sins but because he was actually made sin for us.

Martin Luther

It is not a shame that we are always afraid of Christ, whereas there was never in heaven or earth a more loving, familiar, or milder man, in words, works and demeanor, especially towards the poor, sorrowful and tormented consciences?

Martin Luther

In his life Christ is an example, showing us how to live;
In his death he is a sacrifice, satisfying for our sins;
In his resurrection, a conqueror;
In his ascension, a king;
In his intercession, a high priest.

Martin Luther

He ate, drank, slept, walked, was weary, sorrowful, rejoicing, he wept and laughed; he knew hunger and thirst and sweat; he talked, he toiled, he prayed . . . so that there was no difference between him and other men, save only this, that he was God and had no sin.

Martin Luther

Take hold of Christ as a man and you will discover he is God.

Martin Luther

Anything that one imagines of God apart from Christ is only useless thinking and vain idolatry.

Martin Luther

To the two questions: What does God offer to man? and What does God require of man? the New Testament returns one answer: the life of Christ.

T. W. Manson

In the Scriptures there is a portrait of God, but in Christ there is God himself. A coin bears the image of Caesar, but Caesar's son is his own lively resemblance. Christ is the living Bible.

Thomas Manton

Christ is the great hidden mystery, the blessed goal, the purpose for which everything was created.

Maximus the Confessor,
Byzantine theologian (580-662)

We may not like the Jesus of the historical documents; but like him or not, we meet him there as a divine being on whom our personal destiny depends.

John Warwick Montgomery

With one accord the New Testament writers insist that Jesus must be thought of as God in the fullest sense.

Leon Morris

[All the New Testament authors find their unity in] devotion to the person of Jesus Christ—the historical Jesus acknowledged as continuous with the one now acknowledged as the transcendent Lord.

C. F. D. Moule

The one really distinctive thing for which the Christians stood was their declaration that Jesus had been raised from the dead according to God's design, and the consequent estimate of him as in a unique sense Son of God and representative man, and the resulting conception of the way to reconciliation.

C. F. D. Moule

Jesus was man in guise, not in disguise.

Handley C. G. Moule

Christ is the humility of God embodied in human nature, which redeems us from pride.

Andrew Murray

God will answer all our questions in one way and one way only. Namely, by showing us more of his Son.

Watchman Nee

Jesus' life, his method, and his message do not make sense, unless they are interpreted in the light of his own conviction that he was in fact the final and decisive word of God to men.

Stephen Neill

No one in the Islamic world has ever dreamed of according to Muhammad divine honors— he would have been the first to reject any such suggestion.

Stephen Neill

There is power here [in Jesus] but there is no violence. There is authority, but it is the authority of one who has taken upon himself the form of a servant.

Stephen Neill

Every passage in the history of our Lord and Savior is of unfathomable depth and affords inexhaustible matter for contemplation.

J. H. Newman

For Scripture as much announces Christ as also God, as it announces God Himself as man. It has as much described Jesus Christ to be man, as moreover it has also described Christ the Lord to be God. Let them, therefore, who read that Jesus Christ the Son of man is man, read also that this same Jesus is called also God and the Son of God.

Novatian

Although Christ was God, he took flesh; and having been made man, he remained what he was, God.

Origen

The Bible presents Jesus as King, as Lord, as the maximum authority. Jesus is at the very center.

Juan Carlos Ortiz

This Word was made flesh, not by any change of his own nature or essence, not by a transubstantiation of the divine nature into the human, not by ceasing to be what he was, but by becoming what he was not, in taking our nature to his own, to be his own, whereby he dwelt among us.

John Owen

The impression of Jesus which the Gospels give is not so much one of deity reduced as of divine capacities restrained.

J. I. Packer

Christianity isn't just a message it's centered in a person. You can have Confucianism without Confucius, Buddhism without Buddha, and Judaism without Abraham or Moses. You can even have Islam without Muhammad.

Luis Palau

Jesus Christ's claim of divinity is the most serious claim anyone ever made. Everything about Christianity hinges on His incarnation, crucifixion, and resurrection. That's what Christmas, Good Friday, and Easter are all about.

Luis Palau

It takes a Newton to forge a Newton. What man could have fabricated a Jesus? None but a Jesus.

Theodore Parker

The Incarnation shows man the greatness of his misery by the greatness of the remedy which is required.

Blaize Pascal

Regardless of what anyone may personally think or believe about him, Jesus of Nazareth has been the dominant figure in the history of western culture for almost twenty centuries.

Jaroslav Pelikan

Though our Savior's passion is over, his compassion is not.

William Penn

Christ—was never in a hurry, never impressed by numbers, never a slave to the clock.

J. B. Phillips

The reason why I take my stand within the Christian community lies in certain events which took place in Palestine nearly two thousand years ago.

Dr. John Polkinghorne, theoretical physicist

Oh what a mystery! I see his wonderful deeds and so proclaim his divinity; I contemplate his sufferings, and so cannot deny his humanity.

Proclus of Constantinople

Liberals cannot preach the ethics of Jesus while leaving aside his person and work.

Vic Reasoner

Jesus was the greatest religious genius that ever lived. His beauty is eternal and his reign will never end. He is in every respect unique and nothing can be compared with him.

Joseph Ernest Renan

All history is incomprehensible without Christ.

Joseph Ernest Renan

The divinity of Jesus is not a dispensable extra that has no significance for our salvation. On the contrary, our salvation depends on it. We can be saved only by God Himself.

K. Runia

I fear the personality of our Lord is sadly lost sight of by many professors in the present day. There talk is more about salvation, than about the Savior; more about redemption, than about the Redeemer; more about redemption, than about the Redeemer; more about justification, than about Jesus; more about Christ's work, than about Christ's person.

J. C. Ryle

The person of Christ is to me the greatest and surest of all facts.

Philip Schaff

The life and character of Jesus Christ is the holy of holies in the history of the world.

Philip Schaff

In vain do we look through the entire biography of Jesus for a single stain or the slightest shadow of his moral character. There never lived a more harmless being on earth. He injured nobody, he took advantage of nobody. He never wrote an improper word. He never committed a wrong action.

Philip Schaff

If you take Christ out of Christianity, Christianity is dead.

C. H. Spurgeon

Christ is in all believers, and all believers are in Christ.

C. H. Spurgeon

Remember, Christ was not a deified man, neither was he a humanized God. He was perfectly God and at the same time perfectly man.

C. H. Spurgeon

Christ was not half a God and half a man; he was perfectly God and perfectly man.

James Stalker

Jesus of Nazareth was not mere man, excelling others in purity of life and conduct and in sincerity of purpose, simply distinguished from other teachers by the fullness of His knowledge. He is the God-man.

John Stott

Jesus was extremely self-centered in his words, but absolutely unself-centered in his deeds. . . . This combination of egocentricity and humility has no parallel in the history of the world. The only way to resolve it is to acknowledge that Jesus of Nazareth was and is the Son of God.

John Stott

Jesus was sinless because he was selfless. Such selflessness is love. And God is love.

John Stott

So close was Christ's connection with God that he equated a man's attitude to himself with the man's attitude to God.

John Stott

His humanity is traced to the human mother who bore him, his sinlessness and deity to the Holy Spirit who overshadowed her.

John R. W. Stott

Nothing is more offensive than to claim the uniqueness of Jesus Christ.

John Stott

. . . [we] pay our tribute to the original Jesus, the Jesus of the New Testament witness, who is the incomparable Christ.

John Stott

He whom God gave to the church to be its head was already the head of the universe. Thus both the universe and church have in Jesus Christ the same head.

John Stott

There is nobody like him [Jesus]; there never has been, and there never will be.

John Stott

Christ's character was more wonderful than the greatest miracle.

Alfred Lord Tennyson

They should have known that he was God. His patience should have proved that to them.

Tertullian

There was never a moment in the life of the Lord Jesus that was without divine significance.

W. Ian Thomas

Christ said, "I am the Truth;" he did not say, "I am the custom."

St. Toribio

In Jesus Christ and in the Holy Spirit God freely gives to us in such a way that the Gift and the Giver are one and the same in the wholeness and indivisibility of His grace.

Thomas F. Torrance

In nature, we see God, as it were, like the sun in a picture; in the law, as the sun in a cloud; in Christ we see Him in His beams; He being "the brightness of His glory, and the exact image of His person."

Thomas Watson

His holy life was a perfect commentary upon the law of God.

Thomas Watson

Christ hath ended his passion but not his compassion.

Thomas Watson

Christ is the most tender-hearted physician. He hath ended his passion but not his compassion. He is not more full of skill than sympathy, "He healed the broken in heart, and bindeth up their wounds" (Psalm 147:3). Every groan of the patient goes to the heart of the physician.

Thomas Watson

Christ heals with more ease than any other. Christ makes the devil go out with a word (Mark 9:25). Nay, he can cure with a look: Christ's look melted Peter into repentance; it

was a healing look. If Christ doth but cast a look upon the soul he can recover it.

Thomas Watson

I am an historian, I am not a believer, but I must confess as a historian that this penniless preacher from Nazareth is irrevocably the very center of history. Jesus Christ is easily the most dominant figure in all history.

H. G. Wells

He was God and man in one person, that God and man might be happy together again.

George Whitefield

Only once did God choose a completely sinless preacher.

Alexander Whyte

It is the view of many competent scholars today that all the fragments of Christian tradition which we possess in the New Testament bear witness with singular unanimity to one single historical figure, unlike any other that has ever walked among the sons of men.

N. T. Wright

Unlike any other leader in history, Jesus displayed a perfectly flawless, perfectly trustworthy character.

Rivi Zacharias

Christology is the subject of theology. More precisely put, Jesus Christ is the subject of theology.

Paul F. M. Zahl

Do you think it was self-denial for the Lord Jesus to come down from heaven to rescue a world: Was it self-denial? No, it was love— love that swallows up everything, and first of all self.

Nikolaus Ludwig von Zinzendorf to John Wesley

Christ is the only mediator between God and man.

Huldrych Zwingli

Christ is the only way to salvation.

Huldrych Zwingli

Part Two

THE LIFE OF JESUS

INTRODUCTION

Christians have always believed that the four Gospels were given so that we might understand and appreciate the life of Jesus. In Part Two, the first section, "Jesus and the Gospels," explores this belief. A. W. Pink's *Why Four Gospels?* contain what amounts to four mini-commentaries on the Gospels.

John Calvin wrote commentaries on every book of the New Testament except for 1 and 2 John and the book of Revelation. However, when he came to write his commentary on the first three Gospels, he did not write one on Matthew's Gospel, one on Mark's Gospel, and one on Luke's Gospel. Rather he wrote his *Harmony of the Gospels.* The complete outline of this book, together with the first and last entries of the accompanying commentary are included in this first section.

The following sections trace the life of Jesus from his birth to the time he spent in Gethsemane, on the eve of his death.

In addition to the numerous writings by leading theologians, two extracts from the fiction of Lew Wallace are included: from *Ben-Hur,* "Christ is born," and, "The wise find the child."

Thomas Linacre, 1460-1524, a man highly educated in medicine, and in classical Greek and Latin, had an illustrious career. He was tutor to Prince Arthur, teacher of both Erasmus and Thomas More, and was also founder of the British Royal College of Surgeons and adviser and physician to King Henry VIII of England. Towards the end of his life, he began to study, for the first time, the Gospels and their accounts of the life of Jesus. He was astonished by what he discovered there, and exclaimed, "Either this is not the Gospel, or we are not Christians!"

1
JESUS AND THE GOSPELS

2.1 HISTORIES OF CHRIST, MARTIN LUTHER

We should consider the histories of Christ in three ways;
first, as a history of acts;
secondly, as a gift or a present;
thirdly, as an example, which we should believe and follow.

Martin Luther, Table Talk, *239*

2.2 HARMONY OF THE GOSPELS, JOHN CALVIN

Bible scholars have often commented on the similarities between the Gospels, especially between Matthew, Mark, and Luke. When Calvin came to write his commentaries on the Gospels he wrote a separate commentary on John's Gospel. But he did not write separate commentaries on Matthew, Mark and Luke. Instead he wrote one combined commentary on the Synoptics, called the Harmony of the Gospels.

In this commentary Calvin grouped together similar material in the first three Gospels. One way to read the life of Jesus is to read the three Synoptic Gospels as arranged in Calvin's Harmony of the Gospels, *which is set out below.*

Luke 1:1-4

Luke 1:5-13

Luke 1:14-17

Luke 1:18-20

Luke 1:21-25

Luke 1:26-33

Luke 1:34-38

Luke 1:39-45

Luke 1:46-50

Luke 1:51-55

Luke 1:56-66

Luke 1:67-75

Luke 1:76-80

Matthew 1:1-17; Luke 3:23-38

Matthew 1:18-25

Luke 2:1-7

Luke 2:8-14

Luke 2:15-21

Matthew 2:1-6

Matthew 2:7-12

Luke 2:22-32

Luke 2:33-39

Matthew 2:13-18

Matthew 2:19-23

Luke 2:40-47

Luke 2:48-52

Matthew 3:1-6; Mark 1:1-6; Luke 3:1-6

Matthew 3:7-10; Luke 3:7-14

Matthew 3:11-12; Mark 1:7-8; Luke 3:15-18

Matthew 3:13-17; Mark 1:9-11; Luke 3:21-23

Matthew 4:1-4; Mark 1:12-13a; Luke 4:1-4

Matthew 4:5-11; Mark 1:13b; Luke 4:5-13

Matthew 4:12, 17; Mark 1:14-15; Luke 3:19-20; 4:14-15

Luke 4:16-22
Luke 4:23-30
Matthew 4:13-16
Matthew 4:18-25; Mark 1:16-20; Luke 5:1-11
Mark 1:21-28; Luke 4:31-37
Matthew 8:14-18; Mark 1:29-39; Luke 4:38-44
Mark 3:13-19; Luke 6:12-19
Matthew 5:1-12; Luke 6:20-26
Matthew 5:13-16; Mark 9:49-50; 4:21; Luke 14:34-35; 8:16; 11:33
Matthew 5:17-19; Luke 16:16-17
Matthew 5:20-22
Matthew 5:23-26; Luke 12:58-59
Matthew 5:27-30
Matthew 5:31-32; Luke 16:18
Matthew 5:33-37
Matthew 5:38-41; Luke 6:29-30
Matthew 5:42; Luke 6:34-35a
Matthew 5:43-48; Luke 6:27-28, 32-33, 35b-36
Matthew 6:1-4
Matthew 6:5-8
Matthew 6:9-13; Luke 11:1-4
Matthew 6:14-15; Mark 11:25-26
Matthew 6:16-18
Matthew 6:19-21; Luke 12:33-34
Matthew 6:22-24; Luke 11:34-36; 16:13
Matthew 6:25-30; Luke 12:22-28
Matthew 6:31-34; Luke 12:29-32
Matthew 7:1-5; Mark 4:24; Luke 6:37-42
Matthew 7:6
Matthew 7:7-11; Luke 11:5-13
Matthew 7:12-14; Luke 6:31
Luke 13:23-24
Luke 13:25-30
Matthew 7:15-20; Luke 6:43-45
Matthew 7:21-23; Luke 6:46
Matthew 7:24-29; Luke 6:47-49
Matthew 8:1-4; Mark 1:40-45; Luke 5:12-16
Matthew 8:5-13; Luke 7:1-10
Luke 7:11-17
Matthew 8:19-22; Luke 9:57-62
Matthew 9:1-8; Mark 2:1-12; Luke 5:17-26
Matthew 9:9-13; Mark 2:13-17; Luke 5:27-32
Matthew 9:14-17; Mark 2:18-22; Luke 5:33-39
Matthew 9:18-22; Mark 5:21-34; Luke 8:40-48
Matthew 9:23-26; Mark 5:35-43; Luke 8:49-56
Matthew 9:27-34
Matthew 9:35-38
Matthew 8:23-27; Mark 4:35-41; Luke 8:22-25
Matthew 8:28-34; Mark 5:1-20; Luke 8:26-39

Matthew 10:1-8; Mark 6:7; Luke 9:1-2
Matthew 10:9-15; Mark 6:8-11; Luke 9:3-5
Matthew 10:16-20; Luke 12:11-12
Matthew 10:21-25; Luke 6:40
Matthew 10:26-31; Mark 4:22-23; Luke 8:17; 12:2-7
Matthew 10:32-36; Mark 8:38; Luke 9:26; 12:8-9, 51-53
Matthew 10:37-42; Mark 9:41; Luke 14:25-33
Mark 6:12-13; Luke 9:6
Matthew 11:1-6; Luke 7:18-23
Matthew 11:7-15; Luke 7:24-28
Matthew 11:16-19; Luke 7:29-35
Luke 10:1-12
Matthew 11:20-24; Luke 10:13-16
Luke 10:17-20
Matthew 11:25-30; Luke 10:21-22
Matthew 12:1-8; Mark 2:23-28; Luke 6:1-5
Matthew 12:9-13; Mark 3:1-5; Luke 6:6-10
Matthew 12:14-21; Mark 3:6-12; Luke 6:11
Matthew 12:22-24; Mark 3:20-22; Luke 11:14-15
Matthew 12:25-32; Mark 3:23-30; Luke 11:16-23; 12:10
Matthew 12:33-37
Matthew 12:43-45; Luke 11:24-26
Matthew 12:46-50; Mark 3:31-35; Luke 11:27-28; 8:19-21
Matthew 12:38-42; Luke 11:29-32
Matthew 13:1-17; Mark 4:1-12, 25; Luke 8:1-10, 18; 10:23-24
Matthew 13:18-23; Mark 4:13-20; Luke 8:11-15
Matthew 13:24-30, 36-43
Matthew 13:31-35; Mark 4:26-34; Luke 13:18-22
Matthew 13:44-52
Luke 7:36-50
Luke 10:38-42
Luke 12:13-21
Luke 13:1-9
Luke 13:10-17
Luke 13:31-33
Luke 11:37-41
Luke 14:1-6
Luke 14:7-14
Matthew 22:1-24; Luke 14:15-24
Luke 16:1-15
Luke 16:19-31
Luke 17:7-10
Luke 18:1-8

Luke 18:9-14
Luke 17:11-21
Matthew 13:53-58; Mark 6:1-6
Matthew 14:1-2; Mark 6:14-16; Luke 9:7-9
Matthew 14:3-12; Mark 6:17-29
Matthew 14:13-21; Mark 6:30-44; Luke 9:10-17
Matthew 14:22-33; Mark 6:45-52
Matthew 14:34-36; Mark 6:53-56
Matthew 15:1-9; Mark 7:1-13
Matthew 15:10-20; Mark 7:14-23
Matthew 15:21-28; Mark 7:24-30
Matthew 15:29-39; Mark 7:31-37, 8:1-10
Matthew 16:1-4; Mark 8:11-13; Luke 12:54-57
Matthew 16:5-12; Mark 8:14-21; Luke 12:1
Mark 8:22-26
Matthew 16:13-19; Mark 8:27-29; Luke 9:18-20
Matthew 16:20-28; Mark 8:30-37, 9:1; Luke 9:21-27
Matthew 17:1-8; Mark 9:2-8; Luke 9:28-36a
Matthew 17:9-13; Mark9:9-13; Luke 9:36b
Matthew 17:14-18; Mark 9:14-27; Luke 9:37-43a
Matthew 17:19-21; Mark 9:28-29; Luke 17:5-6
Matthew 17:22-23, 18:1-5; Mark 9:30-37; Luke 9:43b-48
Matthew 18:6-10; Mark 9:42-48; Luke 17:1-2
Matthew 18:11-14; Luke 15:1-10
Luke 15:11-24
Luke 15:25-32
Matthew 18:15-20; Luke 17:3
Matthew 18:21-35 Luke 17:4
Matthew 17:24-27
Matthew 19:1-2; Mark 9:38-40, 10:1; Luke 9:49-56
Matthew 19:3-9; Mark 10:2-12
Matthew 19:10-12
Matthew 19:13-15; Mark 10:13-16; Luke 18:15-17
Matthew 19:16-22; Mark 10:17-22; Luke 18:18-23
Matthew 19:23-26; Mark 10:23-27; Luke 18:24-27
Matthew 19:27-30; Mark 10:28-31; Luke 18:28-30; 22:28-30
Matthew 20:1-16
Matthew 20:17-19; Mark 10:32-34; Luke 18:31-34

Matthew 20:20-23; Mark 10:35-40
Matthew 20:24-28; Mark 10:41-45; Luke 22:24-27
Matthew 20:29-34; Mark 10:46-52; Luke 18:35-43
Luke 19:1-10
Matthew 25:14-30; Luke 19:11-28
Matthew 21:1-9; Mark 11:1-10; Luke 19:29-38
Luke 19:41-44
Matthew 21:10-22; Mark 11:11-24; Luke 19:39-48
Matthew 21:23-27; Mark 11:27-33; Luke 20:1-8
Matthew 21:28-32
Matthew 21:33-46; Mark 12:1-12; Luke 20:9-19
Matthew 22:15-22; Mark 12:13-17; Luke 20:20-26
Matthew 22:23-33; Mark 12:18-27; Luke 20:27-40
Matthew 22:34-40; Mark 12:28-34; Luke 10:25-37
Matthew 22:41-46; Mark 12:35-37; Luke 20:41-44
Matthew 23:1-12; Mark 12:38-39; Luke 11:43, 45-46; 20:45-46
Matthew 23:13-15; Mark 12:40 Luke 11:52; 20:47
Matthew 23:16-22
Matthew 23:23-28; Luke 11:42, 44
Matthew 23:29-39; Luke 11:47-51; 13:34-35; 11:53-54
Mark 12:41-44; Luke 21:1-4
Matthew 24:1-8; Mark 13:1-8; Luke 21:5-11
Matthew 24:9-14; Mark 13:9-13; Luke 21:12-19
Matthew 24:15-28; Mark 13:14-23; Luke 21:20-24; 17:22-25
Matthew 24:29-31; Mark 13:24-27; Luke 21:25-28
Matthew 24:32-36; Mark 13:28-32; Luke 21:29-33
Matthew 24:37-42; Mark 13:33; Luke 17:26-37; 21:34-36
Matthew 24:43-51; Mark 13:34-37; Luke 12:35-50
Matthew 25:1-13
Matthew 25:31-46; Luke 21:37-38
Matthew 26:1-13; Mark 14:1-9; Luke 22:1-2
Matthew 26:14-20; Mark 14:10-17; Luke 22:3-14

Matthew 26:21-25; Mark 14:18-21; Luke 22:15-16, 21-23

Matthew 26:26-30; Mark 14:22-26; Luke 22:17-20

Matthew 26:31-35; Mark 14:27-31; Luke 22:31-34

Luke 22:35-38

Matthew 26:36-44; Mark 14:32-40; Luke 22:39-46

Matthew 26:45-50; Mark 14:41-46; Luke 22:47-48

Matthew 26:51-56; Mark 14:47-52; Luke 22:49-53

Matthew 26:57-61; Mark 14:53-59; Luke 22:54

Matthew 26:62-68; Mark 14:60-65; Luke 22:63-71

Matthew 26:69-75; Mark 14:66-72; Luke 22:55-62

Matthew 27:1-10; Mark 15:1; Luke 23:1

Matthew 27:11-14; Mark 15:2-5; Luke 23:2-12

Matthew 27:15-23; Mark 15:6-14; Luke 23:13-23

Matthew 27:24-32; Mark 15:15-21; Luke 23:24-32

Matthew 27:33-38; Mark 15:22-28; Luke 23:33-34, 38

Matthew 27:39-44; Mark 15:29-32; Luke 23:35-37, 39-43

Matthew 27:45-56; Mark 15:33-41; Luke 23:44-49

Matthew 27:57-61; Mark 15:42-47; Luke 23:50-56

Matthew 27:62-66

Matthew 28:1-7; Mark 16:1-7; Luke 24:1-8

Matthew 28:8-10; Mark 16:8-11; Luke 24:9-12

Matthew 28:11-15

Mark 16:12; Luke 24:13-30

Mark 16:13, 14 Luke 24:31-40

Luke 24:41-49

Matthew 28:16-20; Mark 16:15-18

Mark 16:19-20; Luke 24:50-53

Calvin's own commentary on the first and last entries in his Harmony of the Gospels *read as follows:*

Luke 1:1-4

Luke is the only Evangelist who makes a preface to his Gospel, for the purpose of explaining briefly the motive which induced

him to write. By addressing a single individual he may appear to have acted foolishly, instead of sounding the trumpet aloud, as was his duty, and inviting all men to believe. It appears, therefore, to be unsuitable that the doctrine which does not peculiarly belong to one person or to another, but is common to all, should be privately sent to his friend Theophilus. Hence some have been led to think that Theophilus is an appellative noun, and is applied to all godly people on account of their love of God; but the epithet which is joined to it is inconsistent with that opinion. Nor is there any reason for dreading the absurdity which drove them to adopt such an expedient. For it is not less true that Paul's doctrine belongs to all, though some of his Epistles were addressed to certain cities, and others to certain men.

Nay, we must acknowledge, if we take into account the state of those times, that Luke adopted a conscientious and prudent course. There were tyrants on every hand who, by terror and alarm, were prepared to obstruct the progress of sound doctrine. This gave occasion to Satan and his ministers for spreading abroad the clouds of error, by which the pure light would be obscured. Now, as the great body of men cared little about maintaining the purity of the Gospel, and few considered attentively the inventions of Satan or the amount of danger that lurked under such disguises, every one who excelled others by uncommon faith, or by extraordinary gifts of the Spirit, was the more strongly bound to do his utmost, by care and industry, for preserving the doctrine of godliness pure and uncontaminated from every corruption. Such persons were chosen by God to be the sacred keepers of the law, by whom the heavenly doctrine committed to them should be honestly handed down to posterity. With this view therefore, Luke dedicates his Gospel to Theophilus, that he might undertake the faithful preservation of it; and the same duty Paul enjoins and recommends to Timothy, (2 Timothy 1:14; 3:14.)

Luke 1:1

Forasmuch as many He assigns a reason for writing which, one would think, ought rather to have dissuaded him from writing. To compose a history, which had already employed many authors, was unnecessary labor, at least if they had faithfully discharged their duty. But no accusation of imposture, or carelessness, or any other fault, is in the slightest degree insinuated. It looks, therefore, as if he were expressing a resolution to do what had been already done. I reply, though he deals gently with those who had written before him, he does not altogether approve of their labors. He does not expressly say that they had written on matters with which they were imperfectly acquainted, but by laying claim to certainty as to the facts, he modestly denies their title to full and unshaken confidence. It may be objected that, if they made false statements, they ought rather to have been severely censured. I reply again, they may not have been deeply in fault; they may have erred more from want of consideration than from malice; and, consequently, there would be no necessity for greater fierceness of attack. And certainly there is reason to believe that these were little more than historical sketches which, though comparatively harmless at the time, would afterwards, if they had not been promptly counteracted, have done serious injury to the faith. But it is worthy of remark that, in applying this remedy through Luke to unnecessary writings, God had a wonderful design in view of obtaining, by universal consent, the rejection of others, and thus securing undivided credit to those which reflect brightly his adorable majesty. There is the less excuse for those silly people, by whom disgusting stories, under the name of Nicodemus, or some other person, are, at the present day, palmed upon the world.

Are most surely believed among us The participle *peplērophorēmena*, which Luke employs, denotes things fully ascertained, and which do not admit of doubt. The old translator has repeatedly fallen into mistakes about this word, and through that ignorance has given us a corrupted sense of some very beautiful passages. One of these occurs in the writings of Paul, where he enjoins every man to be fully persuaded in his own mind, (Romans 14:5,) that conscience may not hesitate and

waver, tossed to and fro (Ephesians 4:14) by doubtful opinions. Hence, too, is derived the word *plērophoria*, which he erroneously renders fullness, while it denotes that strong conviction springing from faith, in which godly minds safely rest. There is still, as I have said, an implied contrast; for, by claiming for himself the authority of a faithful witness, he destroys the credit of others who give contrary statements.

Among us has the same meaning as with us. He appears to make faith rest on a weak foundation, its relation to men, while it ought to rest on the Word of God only; and certainly the full assurance (*plērophoria*) of faith is ascribed to the sealing of the Spirit, (1 Thessalonians 1:5; Hebrews 10:22.) I reply, if the Word of God does not hold the first rank, faith will not be satisfied with any human testimonies, but, where the inward confirmation of the Spirit has already taken place, it allows them some weight in the historical knowledge of facts. By historical knowledge I mean that knowledge which we obtain respecting events, either by our own observation or by the statement of others. For, with respect to the visible works of God, it is equally proper to listen to eyewitnesses as to rely on experience. Besides, those whom Luke follows were not private authors, but were also ministers of the Word By this commendation he exalts them above the rank of human authority; for he intimates that the persons from whom he received his information had been divinely authorized to preach the Gospel. Hence, too, that security which he shortly afterwards mentions, and which, if it does not rest upon God, may soon be disturbed. There is great weight in his denominating those from whom he received his Gospel ministers of the Word; for on that ground believers conclude that the witnesses are beyond all exception, as the Lawyers express it, and cannot lawfully be set aside.

Erasmus, who has borrowed from Virgil a phrase used in his version, did not sufficiently consider the estimation and weight due to a Divine calling. Luke does not talk in a profane style, but enjoins us in the person of his friend Theophilus to keep in view the command of

Christ, and to hear with reverence the Son of God speaking through his Apostles. It is a great matter that he affirms them to have been eyewitnesses, but, by calling them ministers, he takes them out of the common order of men, that our faith may have its support in heaven and not in earth. In short, Luke's meaning is this: "that, since thou now hast those things committed faithfully to writing which thou hadst formerly learned by oral statements, thou mayest place a stronger reliance on the received doctrine." It is thus evident that God has employed every method to prevent our faith from being suspended on the doubtful and shifting opinions of men. There is the less room for excusing the ingratitude of the world, which, as if it openly preferred the uncertainty arising out of vague and unfounded reports, turns from so great a Divine favor with loathing. But let us attend to the remarkable distinction which our Lord has laid down, that foolish credulity may not insinuate itself under the name of faith. Meanwhile, let us allow the world to be allured, as it deserves, by the deceitful baits of foolish curiosity, and even to surrender itself willingly to the delusions of Satan.

Luke 1:3
Having carefully examined all things The old translator has it, having followed out all things; and the Greek verb *parakolouthein* is taken metaphorically from those who tread in the footsteps of others, that nothing may escape them. So that Luke intended to express his close and laborious investigation, just as Demosthenes employs the same word, when, in examining an embassy against which he brings an accusation, he boasts of his diligence to have been such, that he perceived every thing that had been done as well as if he had been a spectator.

Mark 16:19-20; Luke 24:50-53

Mark 16:19
And after the Lord had thus spoken to them The Evangelist Matthew, having extolled in magnificent language the reign of Christ over the whole world, says nothing about his ascension to heaven. Mark, too, takes no notice of the place and the manner, both of which are described by Luke; for he says that **the disciples were led out to Bethany**, that from the Mount of Olives, (Matthew 24:3,) whence he had descended to undergo the ignominy of the cross, he might ascend the heavenly throne. Now as he did not, after his resurrection, appear indiscriminately to all, so he did not permit all to be the witnesses of his ascension to heaven; for he intended that this mystery of faith should be known by the preaching of the gospel rather than beheld by the eyes.

Luke 24:50
And lifted up his hands, and blessed them; by which he showed that the office of blessing, which was enjoined on the priests under the law, belonged truly and properly to himself. When men bless one another it is nothing else than praying in behalf of their brethren; but with God it is otherwise, for he does not merely befriend us by wishes, but by a simple act of his will grants what is desirable for us. But while He is the only Author of all blessing, yet that men might obtain a familiar view of his grace, he chose that at first the priests should bless in his name as mediators. Thus Melchizedek blessed Abraham, (Genesis 14:19,) and in Numbers 6:23-27, a perpetual law is laid down in reference to this matter. To this purport also is what we read in Psalm 118:26, We bless you out of the house of the Lord. In short, the apostle has told us that to bless others is a Mark of superiority; for the less, he says, is blessed by the greater, (Hebrews 7:7.) Now when Christ, the true Melchizedek and eternal Priest, was manifested, it was necessary that in him should be fulfilled what had been shadowed out by the figures of the law; as Paul also shows that we are blessed in him by God the Father, that we may be rich in all heavenly blessings, (Ephesians 1:3.) Openly and solemnly he once blessed the apostles, that believers may go direct to himself, if they desire to be partakers of his grace. In the **lifting up of the hands** is described an ancient ceremony which, we know, was previously used by the priests.

Luke 24:52

And having worshipped him, they returned By the word **worship**, Luke means, first, that the apostles were relieved from all doubt, because at that time the majesty of Christ shone on all sides, so that there was no longer any room for doubting of his resurrection; and, secondly, that for the same reason they began to honor him with greater reverence than when they enjoyed his society on earth. For the worship which is here mentioned was rendered to him not only as Master or Prophet, nor even as the Messiah, whose character had been but half known, but as the King of glory and the Judge of the world. Now as Luke intended to give a longer narrative, he only states briefly what the apostles did during ten days. The amount of what is said is, that through the fervor of their joy they broke out openly into the praises of God, and were continually in the temple; not that they remained there by day and by night, but that they attended the public assemblies, and were present at the ordinary and stated hours to render thanksgiving to God. This joy is contrasted with the fear which formerly kept them retired and concealed at home.

Mark 16:19.

And sat down at the right hand of God. In other passages I have explained what is meant by this expression, namely, that Christ was raised on high, that he might be exalted above angels and all creatures; that by his agency the Father might govern the world, and, in short, that before him every knee might bow, (Philippians 2:10.) It is the same as if he were called God's Deputy, to represent the person of God; and, therefore, we must not imagine to ourselves any one place, since the right hand is a metaphor which denotes the power that is next to God. This was purposely added by Mark, in order to inform us that Christ was taken up into heaven, not to enjoy blessed rest at a distance from us, but to govern the world for the salvation of all believers.

Mark 16:20

And they went out and preached. Mark here notices briefly those events of which Luke continues the history in his second book

[That inspired book which is now generally known by the name of The Acts of the Apostles, was often called "Second Luke", by older writers,] that the voice of a small and dispersed body of men resounded even to the extremities of the world. For exactly in proportion as the fact was less credible, so much the more manifestly was there displayed in it a miracle of heavenly power. Every person would have thought that, by the death of the cross, Christ would either be altogether extinguished, or so completely overwhelmed, that he would never be again mentioned but with shame and loathing. The apostles, whom he had chosen to be his witnesses, had basely deserted him, and had betaken themselves to darkness and concealment. Such was their ignorance and want of education, and such was the contempt in which they were held, that they hardly ventured to utter a word in public. Was it to be expected that men who were unlearned, and were held in no esteem, and had even deserted their Master, should, by the sound of their voice, reduce so many scattered nations into subjection to him who had been crucified? There is great emphasis, therefore, in the words, they went out and preached everywhere—men who but lately shut themselves up, trembling and silent, in their prison. For it was impossible that so sudden a change should be accomplished in a moment by human power; and therefore Mark adds,

The Lord working with them; by which he means that this was truly a divine work. And yet by this mode of expression he does not represent them as sharing their work or labor with the grace of God, as if they contributed any thing to it of themselves; but simply means that they were assisted by God, because, according to the flesh, they would in vain have attempted what was actually performed by them. The ministers of the word, I acknowledge, are called fellow-workers with God, (1 Corinthians 3:9,) because he makes use of their agency; but we ought to understand that they have no power beyond what he bestows, and that by planting and watering they do no good, unless the increase come from the secret efficacy of the Spirit.

And confirming the word. Here, in my opinion, Mark points out a particular instance of what he had just now stated in general terms; for there were other methods by which the Lord wrought with them, that the preaching of the gospel might not be fruitless; but this was a striking proof of his assistance, that he confirmed their doctrine by miracles. Now this passage shows what use we ought to make of miracles, if we do not choose to apply them to perverse corruptions; namely, that they aid the gospel. Hence it follows that God's holy order is subverted, if miracles are separated from the word of God, to which they are appendages; and if they are employed to adorn wicked doctrines, or to disguise corrupt modes of worship.

John Calvin, Harmony of the Gospels

2.3 WHY FOUR GOSPELS?, A. W. PINK

A. W. Pink, 1886-1952, was a Reformed evangelical, noted for being an eloquent and prolific English Baptist preacher and theologian. He was highly evangelistic and produced many tracts focusing on repentance. He wrote: The Attributes of God; The Divine Inspiration of the Bible; The Sovereignty of God; Spiritual Growth; Spiritual Union and Communion; *and the Gleanings commentary series.*

INTRODUCTION

It seems strange that such a question needs to be asked at this late date. The New Testament has now been in the hands of the Lord's people for almost two thousand years, and yet, comparatively few seem to grasp the character and scope of its first four books. No part of the Scriptures has been studied more widely than have the four Gospels: innumerable sermons have been preached from them, and every two or three years sections from one of the Gospels is assigned as the course for study in our Sunday Schools. Yet, the fact remains, that the peculiar design and character of Matthew, Mark, Luke, and John, is rarely perceived even by those most familiar with their contents.

Why four Gospels? It does not seem to have occurred to the minds of many to ask such a question. That we have four Gospels which treat of the earthly ministry of Christ is universally accepted, but as to why we have them, as to what they are severally designed to teach, as to their peculiar characteristics, as to their distinctive beauties—these are little discerned and even less appreciated. It is true that each of the four Gospels has much in common to all: each of them deals with the same period of history, each sets forth the teaching and miracles of the Savior, each describes His death and resurrection. But while the four Evangelists have much in common, each has much that is peculiar to himself, and it is in noting their variations that we are brought to see their true meaning and scope and to appreciate their perfections. Just as a course in architecture enables the student to discern the subtle distinctions between the Ionic, the Gothic, and the Corinthian styles—distinctions which are lost upon the uninstructed; or, just as a musical training fits one to appreciate the grandeur of a master-production, the loftiness of its theme, the beauty of its chords, the variety of its parts, or its rendition—all lost upon uninitiated; so the exquisite perfections of the four Gospels are unnoticed and unknown by those who see in them nothing more than four biographies of Christ.

In carefully reading through the four Gospels it soon becomes apparent to any reflecting mind that in none of them, nor in the four together, do we have anything approaching a complete biography of our

Savior's earthly ministry. There are great gaps in His life which none of the Evangelists profess to fill in. After the record of His infancy, nothing whatever is told us about Him till He had reached the age of twelve, and after the brief record which Luke gives of Christ as a boy in the Temple at Jerusalem, followed by the statement that His parents went to Nazareth and that there He was "subject unto them" (Luke 2), nothing further is told us about Him until He had reached the age of thirty. Even when we come to the accounts of His public ministry it is clear that the records are but fragmentary; the Evangelists select only portions of His teachings and describe in detail but a few of His miracles. Concerning the full scope of all that was crowded into His wonderful life, John gives us some idea when he says, "And there are also many other things which Jesus did, the which, if they should be written every one, I suppose that even the world itself could not contain the books that should be written" (John 21:25).

If then the Gospels are not complete biographies of Christ, what are they? The first answer must be, Four books inspired, fully inspired, of God; four books written by men moved by the Holy Spirit; books that are true, flawless, perfect. The second answer is that, the four Gospels are so many books, each complete in itself, each of which is written with a distinctive design, and that which is included in its pages, and all that is left out, is strictly subordinated to that design, according to a principle of selection. In other words, nothing whatever is brought into any one of the Gospels save that which was strictly relevant and pertinent to its peculiar theme and subject, and all that was irrelevant and failed to illustrate and exemplify its theme was excluded. The same plan of selection is noticeable in every section of the Holy Scriptures.

Take Genesis as an example. Why is it that the first two thousand years of history are briefly outlined in its first eleven chapters, and that the next three hundred years is spread out over thirty-nine chapters? Why is it that so very little is said about the men who lived before the Flood, whereas the lives of

Abraham and Isaac, Jacob and Joseph are described in such fullness of detail? Why is it that the Holy Spirit has seen well to depict at greater length the experiences of Joseph in Egypt than He devoted to the Account of Creation? Take, again, the later historical books. A great deal is given us concerning the varied experiences of Abraham's descendants, but little notice is taken of the mighty Nations which were contemporaneous with them. Why is it that Israel's history is described at such length, and that of the Egyptians, the Hittites, the Babylonians, the Persians, and the Greeks, is almost entirely ignored? The answer to all of these questions is that, the Holy Spirit selected only that which served the purpose before Him. The purpose of Genesis is to explain to us the origin of that Nation which occupies so prominent a place in the Old Testament Scriptures, hence, the Holy Spirit hurries over, as it were, the centuries before Abraham was born, and then proceeds to describe in detail the lives of the fathers from which the Chosen Nation sprang. The same principle obtains in the other books of the Old Testament. Because the Holy Spirit is there setting forth the dealings of God with Israel, the other great nations of antiquity are largely ignored, and only come into view at all as they directly concerned the Twelve-Tribed people. So it is in the four Gospels: each of the Evangelists was guided by the Spirit to record only that which served to set forth Christ in the particular character in which He was there to be viewed, and that which was not in keeping with that particular character was left out. Our meaning will become clearer as the reader proceeds.

Why four Gospels? Because one or two was not sufficient to give a perfect presentation of the varied glories of our blessed Lord. Just as no one of the Old Testament typical personages (such as Isaac or Joseph, Moses or David) give an exhaustive foreshadowment of our Lord, so, no one of the four Gospels presents a complete portrayal of Christ's manifold excellencies. Just as no one or two of the five great offerings appointed by God for Israel (see Lev. 1-6) could, by itself, represent the many-sided sacrifice of Christ, so no one, or two, of the Gospels could, by itself, display fully the varied relationships which the Lord Jesus sustained when He was here upon earth. In a word, the four Gospels set Christ before us as filling four distinct offices. We might illustrate it thus. Suppose I was to visit a strange town in which there was an imposing city-hall, and that I was anxious to convey to my friends at home the best possible idea of it. What would I do? I would use my camera to take four different pictures of it, one from each side, and thus my friends would be able to obtain a complete conception of its structure and beauty. Now that is exactly what we have in the four Gospels. Speaking reverently, we may say that the Holy Spirit has photographed the Lord Jesus from four different angles, viewing Him in four different relationships, displaying Him as perfectly discharging the responsibilities of four different offices. And it is impossible to read the Gospels intelligently, to understand their variations, to appreciate their details, to get out of them what we ought, until the reader learns exactly from which angle each separate Gospel is viewing Christ, which particular relationship Matthew or Mark shows Him to be discharging, which office Luke or John shows Him to be filling.

The four Gospels alike present to us the person and work of our blessed Savior, but each one views Him in a distinct relationship, and only that which served to illustrate the separate design which each Evangelist had before him found a place in his Gospel; everything else which was not strictly germane to his immediate purpose was omitted. To make this still more simple we will use another illustration. Suppose that today four men should undertake to write a "life" of ex-president Roosevelt, and that each one designed to present him in a different character. Suppose that the first should treat of his private and domestic life, the second deal with him as a sportsman and hunter of big game, the third depict his military prowess and the fourth traced his political and presidential career. Now it will be seen at once that these four biographers while writing of the life of the same man would, nevertheless, view him in four entirely different relationships. Moreover, it will be evident that these biographers would

be governed in the selection of their material by the particular purpose each one had before him: each would include only that which was germane to his own specific viewpoint, and for the same reason each would omit that which was irrelevant. For instance: suppose it was known that Mr. Roosevelt, as a boy, had excelled in gymnastics and athletics which of his biographers would mention this fact? Clearly, the second one, who was depicting him as a sportsman. Suppose that as a boy Mr. Roosevelt had frequently engaged in fistic encounters, which one would make mention of it? Evidently, the one who was depicting his military career, for it would serve to illustrate his fighting qualities. Again, suppose that when a college-student Mr. R. had displayed an aptitude for debating, which biographer would refer to it? The fourth, who was treating of his political and presidential life. Finally, suppose that from youth upwards, Mr. R. had manifested a marked fondness for children, which of his biographers would refer to it? The first, for he is treating of the ex-president's private and domestic life.

The above example may serve to illustrate what we have in the four Gospels. In Matthew, Christ is presented as the Son of David, the King of the Jews, and everything in his narrative centers around this truth. This explains why the first Gospel opens with a setting forth of Christ's royal genealogy, and why in the second chapter mention is made of the journey of the wise men from the East, who came to Jerusalem inquiring "Where is He that is born King of the Jews?", and why in chapters five to seven we have what is known as "The Sermon on the Mount" but which, in reality, is the Manifesto of the King, containing an enunciation of the Laws of His Kingdom.

In Mark, Christ is depicted as the Servant of Jehovah, as the One who through equal with God made Himself of no reputation and "took upon Him the form of a servant." Everything in this second Gospel contributes to this central theme, and everything foreign to it is rigidly excluded. This explains why there is no genealogy recorded in Mark, why Christ is introduced at the beginning of His public ministry (nothing whatever being told us here of His earlier life), and why there are more miracles (deeds of service) detailed here than in any of the other Gospels.

In Luke, Christ is set forth as the Son of Man, as connected with but contrasted from the sons of men, and everything in the narrative serves to bring this out. This explains why the third Gospel traces His genealogy back to Adam, the first man, (instead of to Abraham only, as in Matthew), why as the perfect Man He is seen here so frequently in prayer, and why the angels are seen ministering to Him, instead of commanded by Him as they are in Matthew.

In John, Christ is revealed as the Son of God, and everything in this fourth Gospel is made to illustrate and demonstrate this Divine relationship. This explains why in the opening verse we are carried back to a point before time began, and we are shown Christ as the Word "in the beginning," with God, and Himself expressly declared to be God; why we get here so many of His Divine titles, as "The only begotten of the Father," the "Lamb of God," the "Light of the world" etc.; why we are told here that prayer should be made in His Name, and why the Holy Spirit is here said to be sent from the Son as well as from the Father.

It is a remarkable fact that this fourfold presentation of Christ in the Gospels was specifically indicated through the Old Testament seers. Conspicuous among the many prophecies of the Old Testament are those which spoke of the coming Messiah under the title of "the Branch." From these we may select four which correspond exactly with the manner in which the Lord Jesus is looked at, respectively, in each of the four Gospels:—

In Jeremiah 23:5 we read, "Behold, the days come, saith the Lord, that I will raise unto DAVID a righteous Branch, and a King shall reign and prosper, and shall execute judgment and justice in the earth." These words fit the first Gospel as glove fits hand.

In Zechariah 3:8 we read, "Behold, I will bring forth My Servant the Branch." These words might well be taken as a title for the second Gospel.

In Zechariah 6:12 we read, "Behold the Man whose name is the Branch." How

accurately this corresponds with Luke's delineation of Christ needs not to be pointed out.

In Isaiah 4:2 we read, "In that day shall the Branch of the Lord be beautiful and glorious." Thus, this last quoted of these Messianic predictions, which spoke of the Coming One under the figure of "the Branch," tallies exactly with the fourth Gospel, which portrays our Savior as the Son of God.

But, not only did Old Testament prophecy anticipate the four chief relationships which Christ sustained on earth, the Old Testament types also foreshadowed this fourfold division. In Genesis 2:10 we read "And a river went out of Eden to water the garden; and from thence it was parted, and became into four heads." Note carefully the words "from thence." In Eden itself "the river" was one, but "from thence" it "was parted" and became into four heads. There must be some deeply hidden meaning to this, for why tell us how many "heads" this river had? The mere historical fact is without interest or value for us, and that the Holy Spirit has condescended to record this detail prepares us to look beneath the surface and seek for some mystical meaning. And surely that is not far to seek. "Eden" suggests to us the Paradise above: the "river" which "watered" it, tells of Christ who is the Light and Joy of Heaven. Interpreting this mystic figure, then, we learn that in Heaven Christ was seen in one character only—"The Lord of Glory"—but just as when the "river" left Eden it was parted and became "four heads" and as such thus watered the earth, so, too, the earthly ministry of the Lord Jesus has been, by the Holy Spirit, "parted into four heads" in the Four Gospels.

Another Old Testament type which anticipated the fourfold division of Christ's ministry as recorded in the four Gospels may be seen in Exodus 26:31, 32, "And thou shalt make a veil of blue, and purple, and scarlet, and fine twined linen of cunning work: with cherubim shall it be made. And thou shalt hang it upon four pillars of shittim wood overlaid with gold: their hooks shall be of gold, upon the four sockets of silver." From Hebrews 10:19, 20 we learn that the "veil" foreshadowed the Incarnation, God manifest in flesh—"through the veil, that is to say, His flesh." It is surely significant that this "veil" was hung upon "four pillars of shittim wood overlaid with gold:" the wood, again, speaking of His humanity, and the gold of His Deity. Just as these "four pillars" served to display the beautiful veil, so in the four Gospels we have made manifest the perfections of the only-begotten of the Father tabernacling among men.

In connection with the Scripture last quoted, we may observe one other feature—"with cherubim shall it be made." The veil was ornamented, apparently, with the "cherubim" embroidered upon it in colors of blue, purple, and scarlet. In Ezekiel 10:15, 17, etc. the cherubim are termed "the living creature:" this enables us to identify the "four beasts" of Revelation 4:6 for rendered literally the Greek reads "four living creatures." These "living creatures" or "cherubim" are also four in number, and from the description which is furnished of them in Revelation 4:7 it will be found that they correspond, most remarkably with the various characters in which the Lord Jesus Christ is set forth in Matthew, Mark, Luke and John.

"And the first living creature was like a lion, and the second living creature like a calf, and the third living creature had a face as a man, and the fourth living creature was like a flying eagle" (Rev. 4:7). The first cherubim, then, was like "a lion" which reminds us at once of the titles which are used of Christ in Revelation 5:5—"The Lion of the Tribe of Judah, the Root of David." The lion, which is the king among the beasts is an apt symbol for portraying Christ as He is presented in Matthew's Gospel. Note also that the Lion of the Tribe of Judah is here termed "the Root of David." Thus the description given in Revelation 4:7 of the first "cherubim" corresponds exactly with the character in which Christ is set forth in the first Gospel, viz., as "the Son of David," the "King of the Jews." The second cherubim was "like a calf" or "young ox." The young ox aptly symbolizes Christ as He is presented in Mark's Gospel, for just as the ox was the chief animal of service in Israel, so in the second Gospel we

have Christ presented in lowliness as the perfect "Servant of Jehovah." The third cherubim "had a face as a man," which corresponds with the third Gospel where our Lord's Humanity is in view. The fourth cherubim was "like a flying eagle:" how significant! The first three—the lion, young ox, and man,—all belong to the earth, just as each of the first three Gospels each set forth Christ in an earthly relationship; but this fourth cherubim lifts us up above the earth, and brings the heavens into view! The eagle is the bird that soars the highest and symbolizes the character in which Christ is seen in John's Gospel, viz., as the Son of God. Incidentally we may observe how this description of the four cherubim in Revelation 4:7 authenticates the arrangement of the four Gospels as we have them in our Bibles, evidencing the fact that their present order is of Divine arrangement as Revelation 4:7 confirms!

We would call attention to one other feature ere closing this Introduction and turning to the Gospels themselves. Behold the wisdom of God displayed in the selection of the four men whom He employed to write the Gospels. In each one we may discern a peculiar suitability and fitness for his task.

The instrumental selection by God to write this first Gospel was singularly fitted for the task before him. Matthew is the only one of the four Evangelists who presents Christ in an official relationship, namely, as the Messiah and King of Israel, and Matthew himself was the only one of the four who filled an official position; for, unlike Luke, who was by profession a physician, or John who was a fisherman, Matthew was a tax-gatherer in the employ of the Romans. Again; Matthew presents Christ in Kingdom connections, as the One who possessed the title to reign over Israel; how fitting, then, that Matthew, who was an officer of and accustomed to look out over a vast empire, should be the one selected for this task. Again; Matthew was a publican. The Romans appointed officials whose duty it was to collect the Jewish taxes. The tax-gatherers were hated by the Jews more bitterly than the Romans themselves. Such a man was Matthew. How feelingly, then, could he write of the One who was "hated without a cause"!

and set forth the Messiah-Savior, as "despised and rejected" by His own nation. Finally, in God appointing this man, who by calling was connected with the Romans, we have a striking anticipation of the grace of God reaching out to the despised Gentiles.

Mark's Gospel sets before us the Servant of Jehovah, God's perfect Workman. And the instrument chosen to write this second Gospel seems to have held an unique position which well fitted him for his task. He was not himself one of the apostles, but was rather a servant of an apostle. In 2 Timothy 4:11 we have a scripture which brings this out in a striking manner—"Take Mark, and bring him with thee: for he is profitable to me for the ministry." Thus the one who wrote of our Lord as the Servant of God, was himself one who ministered to others!

Luke's Gospel deals with our Lord's Humanity, and presents Him as the Son of Man related to but contrasted from the sons of men. Luke's Gospel is the one which gives us the fullest account of the virgin-birth. Luke's Gospel also reveals more fully than any of the others the fallen and depraved state of human nature. Again; Luke's Gospel is far more international in its scope than the other three, and is more Gentilish than Jewish— evidences of this will be presented when we come to examine his Gospel in detail. Now observe the appropriateness of the selection of Luke to write this Gospel. Who was he? He was neither a fisherman nor a tax-gatherer, but a "physician" (see Col. 4:14), and as such, a student of human nature and a diagnostician of the human frame. Moreover, there is good reason to believe that Luke himself was not a Jew but a Gentile, and hence it was peculiarly fitting that he should present Christ not as "the Son of David" but as "The Son of Man."

John's Gospel presents Christ in the loftiest character of all, setting Him forth in Divine relationship, showing that He was the Son of God. This was a task that called for a man of high spirituality, one who was intimate with our Lord in a special manner, one who was gifted with unusual spiritual discernment. And surely John, who was nearer to the Savior than any of the twelve, surely John "the disciple whom Jesus loved,"

was well chosen. How fitting that the one who leaned on the Master's bosom should be the instrument to portray Christ as "The only-begotten Son, which is in the bosom of the Father"! Thus may we discern and admire the manifold wisdom of God in equipping the four "Evangelists" for their honorous work.

Ere closing this Introduction we would return once more to our opening query— Why four Gospels? This time we shall give the question a different emphasis. Thus far, we have considered, "Why four Gospels? And we have seen that the answer is, In order to present the person of Christ in four different characters. But we would now ask, Why four Gospels? Why not have reduced them to two or three? Or, why not have added a fifth? Why four? God has a wise reason for everything, and we may be assured there is a Divine fitness in the number of the Gospels.

In seeking to answer the question, Why four Gospels, we are not left to the uncertainties of speculation or imagination. Scripture is its own interpreter. A study of God's Word reveals the fact (as pointed out by others before us), that in it the numerals are used with definite precision and meaning. "Four" is the number of the earth. It is, therefore, also, the world number. We subjoin a few illustrations of this. There are four points to earth's compass—nor the, east, south, and west. There are four seasons to earth's year—spring, summer, autumn, and winter. There are four elements connected with our world—earth, air, fire, and water. There have been four, and only four, great world-empires—the Babylonian, the Medo-Persian, the Grecian, and the Roman. Scripture divides earth's inhabitants into four classes—"kindred, and tongue, and people, and nation" (Rev. 5:9 etc.). In the Parable of the Sower, our Lord divided the field into four kinds of soil, and later He said, "the field is the world." The fourth commandment has to do with rest from all earth's labors. The fourth clause in what is known as the Lord's prayer is, "Thy will be done on earth." And so we might go on. Four is thus the earth number. How fitting, then, that the Holy Spirit should have given us four Gospels in which to set forth the earthly ministry of the Heavenly One.

1. THE GOSPEL OF MATTHEW

Matthew's Gospel breaks the long silence that followed the ministry of Malachi the last of the Old Testament prophets. This silence extended for four hundred years, and during that time God was hid from Israel's view. Throughout this period there were no angelic manifestations, no prophet spake for Jehovah, and, though the Chosen People were sorely pressed, yet were there no Divine interpositions on their behalf. For four centuries God shut His people up to His written Word. Again and again had God promised to send the Messiah, and from Malachi's time and onwards the saints of the Lord anxiously awaited the appearing of the predicted One. It is at this point Matthew's Gospel is to present Christ as the Fulfiller of the promises made to Israel and the prophecies which related to their Messiah. This is why the word "fulfilled" occurs in Matthew fifteen times, and why there are more quotations from the Old Testament in this first Gospel than in the remaining three put together.

The position which Matthew's Gospel occupies in the Sacred Canon indicates its scope: it follows immediately after the Old Testament, and stands at the beginning of the New. It is therefore a connecting link between them. Hence it is transitional in its character, and more Jewish than any other book in the New Testament. Matthew reveals God appealing to and dealing with His Old Testament people; presents the Lord Jesus as occupying a distinctively Jewish relationship; and, is the only one of the four Evangelists that records Messiah's express declaration, "I am not sent but unto the lost sheep of the House of Israel" (15:24). The numerical position given to Matthew's Gospel in the Divine library confirms what has been said, for, being the fortieth book it shows us Israel in the place of probation, tested by the presence of Messiah in their midst.

Matthew presents the Lord Jesus as Israel's Messiah and King, as well as the One who shall save His people from their sins. The opening sentence gives the key to the book— "The book of the generation of Jesus Christ, the Son of David, the Son of Abraham."

Seven times the Lord Jesus is addressed as "Son of David" in the Gospel, and ten times, altogether, is this title found there. "Son of David" connects the Savior with Israel's throne, "Son of Abraham" linking Him with Israel's land—Abraham being the one to whom Jehovah first gave the land. But nowhere after the opening verse is this title "Son of Abraham" applied to Christ, for the restoration of the land to Israel is consequent upon their acceptance of Him as their Savior—King, and that which is made prominent in this first Gospel is the presentation of Christ as King—twelve times over is this title here applied to Christ.

Matthew is essentially the dispensational Gospel and it is impossible to over-estimate its importance and value. Matthew shows us Christ offered to the Jews, and the consequences of their rejection of Him, namely, the setting aside of Israel, and God turning in grace to the Gentiles. Rom. 15:8, 9 summarizes the scope of Matthew's Gospel— "Jesus Christ was a minister of the circumcision for the truth of God, to confirm the promises made unto the fathers; And that the Gentiles might glorify God for His mercy." Christ was not only born of the Jews, but He was born, first, to the Jews, so that in the language of their prophet they could exclaim, "Unto us a Child is born, unto us a Son is given" (Is. 9:6). Matthew's Gospel explains why Israel, in their later books of the New Testament, is seen temporally cast off by God, and why He is now taking out from the Gentiles a people for His name; in other words, it makes known why, in the present dispensation, the Church has superseded the Jewish theocracy. It supplies the key to God's dealings with the earth in this Age: without a workable knowledge of this first Gospel it is well-nigh impossible to understand the remaining portions of the New Testament. We turn now to consider some of the outstanding features and peculiar characteristics of Matthew's Gospel.

The first thing which arrests our attention is the opening verse. God, in His tender grace, has hung the key right over the entrance. The opening verse is that which unlocks the contents of this Gospel—"The book of the generation of Jesus Christ the Son of David, the Son of Abraham." The first five English words here are but two in the Greek—"*Biblos geneseos.*" These two words indicate the peculiarly Jewish character of the earlier portions of this Gospel, for it is an Old Testament expression. It is noteworthy that this expression which commences the New Testament is found almost at the beginning of the first book in the Old Testament, for in Gen. 5:1 we read, "This is the book of the generations of Adam." We need hardly say that this word "generation" signifies "the history of." These two "books"—the book of the generation of Adam, and the book of the generation of Jesus Christ—might well be termed the Book of Death and the Book of Life. Not only does the whole Bible center around these two books, but the sum of human destiny also. How strikingly this expression, found at the beginning of Genesis and the beginning of Matthew, brings out the Unity of the two Testaments!

In the book of Genesis we have eleven different "generations" or histories enumerated, beginning with the "generations of the heavens and the earth," and closing with the "generations of Jacob"—see 2:4; 5:1; 6:9; 11:10; 11:27; 25:12; 25:19; 36:1; 36:9; 37:2—thus dividing the first book of the Bible into twelve sections, twelve being the number of Divine government, which is what is before us in Genesis—God in sovereign government. From Exodus to Daniel we find government entrusted, instrumentally, to Israel, and from Daniel onwards it is in the hands of the Gentiles; but in Genesis we antedate the Jewish theocracy, and there government is found directly in the hands of God, hence its twelve-fold division. Twice more, namely, in Numbers 3:1 and Ruth 4:18, do we get this expression "the generation of," making in the Old Testament thirteen in all, which is the number of apostasy, for that is all the Law revealed! But, as we have seen, this expression occurs once more (and there for the last time in Holy Writ) in the opening verse of the New Testament, thus making fourteen in all, and the fourteenth is "the book of the generation of Jesus Christ." How profoundly significant

and suggestive this is! Fourteen is 2 x 7, and two signifies (among its other meanings) contrast or difference, and seven is the number of perfection and completeness—and what a complete difference the Coming of Jesus Christ made!

"The book of the generation of Jesus Christ, the Son of David, the Son of Abraham" (Matt. 1:1). These titles of our Savior have, at least, a threefold significance. In the first place, both of them connect Him with Israel: "Son of David" linking Him with Israel's Throne, and "Son of Abraham" with Israel's Land. In the second place, "Son of David" limits Him to Israel, whereas "Son of Abraham" is wider in its scope, reaching forth to the Gentiles, for God's original promise was that in Abraham "shall all the families of the earth be blessed" (Gen. 12:3). In the third place, as Dr. W. L. Tucker has pointed out, these titles correspond exactly with the twofold (structural) division of Matthew's Gospel. Up to 4:16 all is Introductory, and 4:17 opens the first division of the book, reading, "From that time Jesus began to preach, and to say, Repent: for the Kingdom of heaven is at hand." This section treats of the Official ministry of Christ and presents Him as "the Son of David." The second section commences at 16:21 and reads, "From that time forth Jesus began to show unto His disciples, how that He must go unto Jerusalem, and suffer many things of the elders and chief priests and scribes, and be killed, and be raised again the third day." This section treats, primarily, of the Sacrificial work of Christ, and views Him as "the Son of Abraham," typified, of old, by Isaac—laid on the altar.

Having dwelt at some length on the opening verse of our Gospel, we may next notice that the remainder of the chapter down to the end of verse 17 is occupied with the Genealogy of Jesus Christ. The prime significance of this is worthy of our closest attention, for it fixes with certainty the character and dominant theme of this Gospel. The very first book of the New Testament opens a long list of names! What a proof that no uninspired man composed it! But God's thoughts and ways are ever different from ours, and ever perfect too. The reason for this Genealogy is not far to seek. As we have seen, the opening sentence of Matthew contains the key to the book, intimating plainly that Christ is here viewed, first, in a Jewish relationship, fully entitled to sit on David's Throne. How then is His title established? By showing that, according to the flesh, He belonged to the royal tribe: by setting forth His Kingly line of descent. A King's title to occupy the throne depends not on the public ballot, but lies in his blood rights. Therefore, the first thing which the Holy Spirit does in this Gospel is to give us the Royal Genealogy of the Messiah, showing that as a lineal descendant of David He was fully entitled to Israel's Throne.

The Genealogy recorded in Matthew 1 gives us not merely the human ancestry of Christ, but, particularly, His royal line of descent, this being one of the essential features which differentiates it from the Genealogy recorded in Luke 3. The fundamental design of Matthew 1:1-17 is to prove Christ's right to reign as King of the Jews. This is why the genealogy is traced no further back than Abraham, he being the father of the Hebrew people. This is why, in the opening verse, the order is "Jesus Christ, the Son of David, the Son of Abraham," instead of "the Son of Abraham, the Son of David" as might be expected from the order which immediately follows, for there we start with Abraham and work up to David. Why, then, is this order reversed in the opening verse? The answer must be that David comes first because it is the Kingly line which is here being emphasized! This also explains why, in verse 2 we read "Abraham begat Isaac; and Isaac begat Jacob, and Jacob begat Judah and his brethren." Why should Judah alone be here singled out for mention from the twelve sons of Jacob? Why not have said "Jacob begat Reuben and his brethren"? for he was Jacob's firstborn. If it be objected that the birthright was transferred from Reuben to Joseph, then we ask, why not have said "Jacob begat Joseph"? especially as Joseph was his favorite son. The answer is, Because Judah was the royal tribe, and it is the Kingly line which is here before us. Again: in verse 6 we read, "And Jesse begat David the King: and David the

king begat Solomon of her that had been the wife of Uriah." Of all those who reigned over Israel whose names are here recorded in Matthew 1, David is the only one that is denominated "King," and he, twice over in the same verse! Why is this, except to bring David into special prominence, and thus show us the significance of the title given to our Lord in the opening verse—"the Son of David."

There are many interesting features of this Genealogy which we must now pass over, but its numerical arrangement calls for a few brief comments. The Genealogy is divided into three parts: the first section, running from Abraham to David, may be termed the period of Preparation; the second section running from Solomon to the Babylonian captivity, may be called the period of Degeneration; while the third period, running from the Babylonian captivity till the Birth of Christ, may be named the period of Expectation. The numeral three signifies, in Scripture, manifestation, and how appropriate this arrangement was here, for not until Christ appears is God's purpose concerning Abraham and his seed fully manifested. Each of these three sections in the Royal Genealogy contains fourteen generations, which is 2×7, two signifying (among its slightly varied meanings) testimony or competent witness, and seven standing for perfection. Again we may note these numerals in this genealogy of Christ, for only in Him do we get perfect testimony—the "Faithful and True Witness." Finally, be it observed, that 14×3 gives us 42 generations in all from Abraham to Christ, or 7×6, seven signifying perfection, and six being the number of man, so that Christ—the forty-second from Abraham—brings us to the Perfect Man!! How microscopically perfect is the Word of God!

"And Jacob begat Joseph the husband of Mary, of whom was born Jesus, who is called Christ" (Matt. 1:16). Matthew does not connect Joseph and Jesus as father and son, but departs from the usual phraseology of the genealogy so as to indicate the peculiarity, the uniqueness, of the Savior's birth. Abraham might begat Isaac, and Isaac begat Jacob, but Joseph the husband of Mary did not begat

Jesus, instead, we read, "Now the birth of Jesus Christ was on this wise: when as His mother Mary was espoused to Joseph, before they came together, she was found with child of the Holy Spirit" (1:18). As Isaiah had foretold (7:14) seven hundred years before, Messiah was to be born of "the virgin." But a virgin had no right to Israel's throne, but Joseph had this right, being a direct descendant of David, and so through Joseph, His legal father (for be it remembered that betrothal was as binding with the Jews as marriage is with us) the Lord Jesus secured His rights, according to the flesh, to be King of the Jews.

Coming now to Matthew 2 we may observe that we have in this chapter an incident recorded which is entirely passed over by the other Evangelists, but which is peculiarly appropriate in this first Gospel. This incident is the visit of the wise men who came from the East to honor and worship the Christ Child. The details which the Holy Spirit gives us of this visit strikingly illustrate the distinctive character and scope of Matthew's Gospel. This chapter opens as follows, "Now when Jesus was born in Bethlehem of Judea in the days of Herod the King, behold, there came wise men from the east to Jerusalem, Saying, Where is He that is born King of the Jews? for we have seen His star in the east, and are come to worship Him." Notice, these wise men came not inquiring, "Where is He that is born the Savior of the world?", nor, "Where is the Word now incarnate?", but instead, "Where is He that is born King of the Jews?" The fact that Mark, Luke and John are entirely silent about this, and the fact that Matthew's Gospel does record it, is surely proof positive that this First Gospel presents Christ in a distinctively Jewish relationship. The evidence for this is cumulative: there is first the peculiar expression with which Matthew opens—"the book of the generation of," which is an Old Testament expression, and met with nowhere else in the New Testament; there is the first title which is given to Christ in this Gospel—"Son of David"; there is the Royal Genealogy which immediately follows; and now there is the record of the visit of the wise men, saying,

"Where is He that is born King of the Jews?" Thus has the Spirit of God made so plain and prominent the peculiarly Jewish character of the opening chapters of Matthew's Gospel that none save those who are blinded by prejudice can fail to see its true dispensational place. Thus, too, has He rendered excuseless the foolish agitation which is now, in certain quarters, being raised, and which tends only to confuse and confound.

But there is far more in Matthew 2 than the recognition of Christ as the rightful King of the Jews. The incident therein narrated contains a foreshadowment of the reception which Christ was to meet with here in the world, anticipating the end from the beginning. What we find here in Matthew 2 is really a prophetic outline of the whole course of Matthew's Gospel. First, we have the affirmation that the Lord Jesus was born "King of the Jews"; then we have the fact that Christ is found not in Jerusalem, the royal city, but outside of it; then we have the blindness and indifference of the Jews to the presence of David's Son in their midst—seen in the fact that, first, His own people were unaware that the Messiah was now there among them, and second, in their failure to accompany the wise men as they left Jerusalem seeking the young Child; then we are shown strangers from a far-distant land with a heart for the Savior, seeking Him out and worshipping Him; finally, we learn of the civil ruler filled with hatred and seeking His life. Thus, the incident as a whole marvelously foreshadowed Christ's rejection by the Jews and His acceptance by the Gentiles. Thus do we find epitomized here the whole burden of Matthew's Gospel, the special purpose of which is to show Christ presenting Himself to Israel, Israel's rejection of Him, with the consequent result of God setting Israel aside for a season, and reaching out in grace to the despised Gentiles.

Next we read, "And when they were departed, behold the angel of the Lord appeareth to Joseph in a dream, saying, Arise and take the young Child and His mother, and flee into Egypt, and be thou there until I bring thee word: for Herod will seek the young Child to destroy Him" (2:13). Observe that it is Joseph and not Mary that figures so prominently in the first two chapters of Matthew, for it was not through His mother, but through His legal father that the Lord Jesus acquired His title to David's throne—compare Matthew 1:20, where Joseph is termed "son of David"! It should also be pointed out that Matthew is, again, the only one of the four Evangelists to record this journey into Egypt, and the subsequent return to Palestine. This is profoundly suggestive, and strikingly in accord with the special design of this First Gospel, for it shows how Israel's Messiah took the very same place as where Israel's history as a Nation began!

"But when Herod was dead, behold, an angel of the Lord appeareth in a dream to Joseph in Egypt, Saying, Arise, and take the young Child and His mother, and go into the land of Israel: for they are dead which sought the young Child's life. And he arose, and took the young Child and His mother, and came into the land of Israel" (2:19-21). Once more we discover another line which brings out the peculiarly Jewish character of Matthew's delineation of Christ. This is the only place in the New Testament where Palestine is termed "the land of Israel," and it is significantly proclaimed as such here in connection with Israel's King, for it is not until He shall set up His Throne in Jerusalem that Palestine shall become in fact, as it has so long been in promise, "the land of Israel." Yet how tragically suggestive is the statement that immediately follows here, and which closes Matthew 2. No sooner do we read of "the land of Israel" than we find "But" as the very next word, and in Scripture, "but" almost always points a contrast. Here we read, "But when he heard that Archelaus did reign in Judea in the room of his father Herod, he was afraid to go thither: notwithstanding, being warned of God in a dream, he turned aside into the parts of Galilee:

And he came and dwelt in a city called Nazareth: that it might be fulfilled which was spoken by the prophets, He shall be called a Nazarene" (2:21-23). Nazareth was the most despised place in that despised province of Galilee, and thus we see how early the Messiah took the place of the despised One,

again foreshadowing His rejection by the Jews—but mention of "Nazareth" follows, be it observed, mention of "the land of Israel."

Matthew 3 opens by bringing before us a most striking character: "In those days"—that is, while the Lord Jesus still dwelt in despised Nazareth of Galilee—"came John the Baptist, preaching in the wilderness of Judea." He was the predicted forerunner of Israel's Messiah. He was the one of whom Isaiah had said should prepare the way for the Lord, and this by preparing a people to receive Him by such time as He should appear to the public view. He came "in the spirit and power of Elijah" (Luke 1:17), to do a work similar in character to that of the yet future mission of the Tishbite (Matt. 4:5, 6).

John addressed himself to the Covenant people, and restricted himself to the land of Judea. He preached not in Jerusalem but in the wilderness. The reason for this is obvious: God would not own the degenerate system of Judaism, but stationed His messenger outside all the religious circles of that day. The "wilderness" but symbolized the barrenness and desolation of Israel's spiritual condition.

The message of John was simple and to the point—"Repent ye." It was a call for Israel to judge themselves. It was a word which demanded that the Jews take their proper place before God, confessing their sins. Only thus could a people be made ready for the Lord, the Messiah. The Call to Repentance was enforced by a timely warning—"Repent ye, for the Kingdom of Heaven is at hand." Observe, "Repent ye" not because "the Savior is at hand," not because "God incarnate is now in your midst," and not because "A new Dispensation has dawned"; but because "the Kingdom of Heaven" was "at hand." What would John's hearers understand by this expression? What meaning could those Jews attach to his words? Surely the Baptist did not employ language which, in the nature of the case, it was impossible for them to grasp. And yet we are asked to believe that John was here introducing Christianity! A wilder and more ridiculous theory it would be hard to imagine. If by the "Kingdom of Heaven" John signified the Christian dispensation, then he addressed those Jewish hearers in an unknown tongue.

We say it with calm deliberation, that if John bade his auditors repent because the Christian dispensation was then being inaugurated, he mocked them, by employing a term which not only must have been entirely unintelligible to them, but utterly misleading. To charge God's messenger with doing that is perilously near committing a sin which we shrink from naming.

What then, we ask again, would John's hearers understand him to mean when he said, "Repent ye, for the Kingdom of Heaven is at hand"? Addressing, as he was, a people who were familiar with the Old Testament Scriptures, they could place but one meaning upon his words, namely, that he was referring to the Kingdom spoken of again and again by their prophets—the Messianic Kingdom. That which should distinguish Messiah's Kingdom from all the kingdoms that have preceded it, is this: all the kingdoms of this world have been ruled over by Satan and his hosts, whereas, when Messiah's Kingdom is established, it shall be a rule of the Heavens over the earth.

The question has been raised as to why Israel refused the Kingdom on which their hearts were set. Did not the establishing of Messiah's Kingdom mean an end of the Roman dominion? and was not that the one thing they desired above all others? In reply to such questions several things must be insisted upon. In the first place, it is a mistake to say that Israel "refused" the Kingdom, for, in strict accuracy of language, the Kingdom was never "offered" to them—rather was the Kingdom heralded or proclaimed. The Kingdom was "at hand" because the Heir to David's throne was about to present Himself to them. In the second place, before the Kingdom could be set up, Israel must first "Repent," but this, as is well known, is just what they, as a nation, steadily refused to do. As we are expressly told in Luke 7:29, 30. "And all the people that heard him, and the publicans, justified God, being baptized with the baptism of John. But the Pharisees and lawyers rejected the counsel of God against themselves, being not baptized of him." In the third place, the reader will, perhaps, see our meaning clearer if we illustrate by an analogy:

the world today is eagerly longing for the Golden Age. A millennium of peace and rest is the great desideratum among diplomats and politicians. But they want it on their own terms. They desire to bring it about by their own efforts. They have no desire for a Millennium brought about by the personal return to earth of the Lord Jesus Christ. Exactly so was it with Israel in the days of John the Baptist. True, they desired to be delivered from the Roman dominion. True, they wished to be freed for ever from the Gentile yoke. True, they longed for a millennium of undisturbed prosperity in a restored Palestine, but they did not want it in GOD'S terms.

The ministry of John the Baptist is referred to at greater or shorter length in each of the four Gospels, but Matthew is the only one who records this utterance "Repent ye, for the Kingdom of heaven is at hand." To ignore this fact is to fail in "rightly dividing the Word of truth." It is to lose sight of the characteristic distinctions which the Holy Spirit has been pleased to make in the four Gospels. It is to reduce those four independent delineations of Christ's person and ministry to a meaningless jumble. It is to lay bare the incompetence of a would-be-teacher of Scripture as one who is not a "scribe who is instructed unto the Kingdom of heaven" (Matt. 13:52).

John's baptism confirmed his preaching. He baptized "unto repentance," and in Jordan, the river of death. Those who were baptized "confessed their sins" (Mark 1:5), of which death was the just due, the "wages" earned. But Christian baptism is entirely different from this: there, we take not the place of those who deserve death, but of those who show forth the fact that they have, already, died with Christ.

It is beyond our present purpose to attempt a detailed exposition of this entire Gospel, rather shall we single out those features which are characteristic of and peculiar to this first Gospel. Accordingly, we may notice an expression found in 3:11, and which occurs nowhere else in the New Testament outside of the four Gospels, and this is the more remarkable because a portion of this very verse is quoted in the Acts.

Speaking to the Pharisees and Sadducees who had "come to his baptism," but whom the Lord's forerunner quickly discerned were not in any condition to be baptized; who had been warned to flee from the wrath to come, and therefore were in urgent need of bringing forth "fruit meet for repentance" (in their case, humbling themselves before God, abandoning their lofty pretensions and self righteousness, and taking their place as genuine self-confessed sinners), and to whom John had said, "Think not to say within yourselves, We have Abraham to our father: for I say unto you, that God is able of these stones to raise up children unto (not God, be it noted, but) Abraham" (v. 9); to them John announced: "but he that cometh after me is mightier than I, whose shoes I am not worthy to bear: He shall baptize you with the Spirit and fire."

In Acts 1, where we behold the risen Lord in the midst of His disciples, we read, "And, being assembled together with them, commended them that they should not depart from Jerusalem, but wait for the promise of the Father, which, saith He, ye have heard of Me. For John truly baptized with water: but ye shall be baptized with the Holy Spirit not many days hence" (vv. 4, 5). His forerunner had declared that Christ should baptize Israel with "the Holy Spirit and fire," yet, here, the Lord speaks only of the disciples being baptized with the Holy Spirit. Why is this? Why did the Lord Jesus omit the words "and fire"? The simple answer is that in Scripture "fire" is, invariably, connected with Divine judgment. Thus, the reason is obvious why the Lord omits "and fire" from His utterance recorded in Acts 1. He was about to deal, not in judgment but, in grace! It is equally evident why the words "and fire" are recorded by Matthew, for his Gospel, deals, essentially with Dispensational relationships, and makes known much concerning End-time conditions. God is yet to "baptize" recreant Israel "with fire," the reference being to the tribulation judgments, during the time of "Jacob's Trouble." Then will the winnowing fan be held by the hand of the rejected Messiah, and then "He will thoroughly purge His floor, and gather His wheat into the

darner: but He will burn up the chaff with unquenchable fire" (Matt. 3:12). How manifestly do the words last quoted define for us the baptism of "fire"!

The silence of the risen Lord as to the "fire" when speaking to the disciples about "the baptism of the Spirit," has added force and significance when we find that Mark's Gospel gives the substance of what Matthew records of the Baptist's utterance, while omitting the words "and fire"—"There cometh One mightier than I after me, the latchet of whose shoes I am not worthy to stoop down and unloose. I indeed have baptized you with water: but He shall baptize you with the Holy Spirit" (Mark 1:7, 8). Why is this? Because, as we have pointed out, "fire" is the well-known symbol of God's judgment (often displayed in literal fire), and Mark, who is presenting Christ as the Servant of Jehovah, was most obviously led of the Spirit to leave out the words "and fire," for as Servant He does not execute judgment. The words "and with fire" are found, though, in Luke, and this, again, is most significant. For, Luke is presenting Christ as "The Son of Man," and in John 5 we read, "And hath given Him authority to execute judgment also because He is the Son of Man" (v. 27). How strikingly, then, does the inclusion of the words "and fire" in Matthew and Luke, and their omission in Mark, bring out the verbal inspiration of Scripture over the instruments He employed in the writing of God's Word!

The closing verses of Matthew 3 show us the Lord Jesus, in marvelous grace, taking His place with the believing remnant of Israel: "Then cometh Jesus from Galilee to Jordan unto John, to be baptized of him" (3:13). John was so startled that, at first, he refused to baptize Him—so little do the best of men enter into the meaning of the things of God— "But John forbad Him, saying, I have need to be baptized by Thee, and comest Thou to me?" (3:14). Observe once—more, that Matthew is the only one of the Evangelists which mentions this shrinking of the Baptist from baptizing the Lord Jesus. Appropriately does it find a place here, for it brings out the royal dignity and majesty of Israel's Messiah. As to the meaning and significance of the

Savior's baptism we do not now enter at length, suffice it here to say that it revealed Christ as the One who had come down from heaven to act as the Substitute of His people, to die in their stead, and thus at the beginning of His public ministry He identifies Himself with those whom He represented, taking His place alongside of them in that which spoke of death. The descent of the Holy Spirit upon Him attested Him, indeed, as the true Messiah, the Anointed One (see Acts 10:38), and the audible testimony of the Father witnessed to His perfections, and fitness for the Work He was to do.

The first half of Matthew 4 records our Lord's Temptation, into which we do not now enter. The next thing we are told is, "Now when Jesus had heard that John was cast into prison, He departed into Galilee; And leaving Nazareth, He came and dwelt in Capernaum, which is upon the sea coast, in the borders of Zebulon and Naphtali" (4:12, 13), and this in order that a prophecy of Isaiah's might be fulfilled. And then we read, "From that time Jesus began to preach, and to say, Repent: for the Kingdom of heaven is at hand" (4:17). It would seem that the words "from that time" refer to the casting of the Baptist into prison. John's message had been, "Repent ye, for the Kingdom of heaven is at hand" (3:2), and now that His forerunner had been incarcerated, the Messiah Himself takes up identically the same message—the proclamation of the Kingdom. In keeping with this, we read, "And Jesus went about all Galilee teaching in their synagogues, and preaching the Gospel (not, be it noted, the "Gospel of the Grace of God"—Acts 20:24; nor "the Gospel of Peace"—Eph. 6:15; but "the Gospel") of the Kingdom, and healing all manner of sickness and all manner of disease among the people" (4:23).

Our Lord's miracles of healing were not simply exhibitions of power, or manifestations of mercy, they were also a supplement of His preaching and teaching, and their prime value was evidential. These miracles, which are frequently termed "signs," formed an essential part of Messiahs credentials. This is established, unequivocally, by what we read in Matthew 11. When John the Baptist was cast into prison, his faith as to the Messiahship of Jesus wavered, and so he sent two of His disciples unto Him, asking, "Art Thou He that should come, or do we look for another?" (11:2). Notice, carefully, the Lord's reply, "Go and show John again those things which ye do hear and see: The blind receive their sight, and the lame walk, the lepers are cleansed, and the deaf hear, the dead are raised up, and the poor have the Gospel preached to them" (11:4, 5). Appeal was made to two things: His teaching and His miracles of healing. The two are linked together, again, in 9:35—"And Jesus went about all the cities and villages, teaching in their synagogues, and preaching the Gospel of the Kingdom, and healing every sickness, and every disease among the people." And, again, when the Lord sent forth, the Twelve, "But go rather to the lost sheep of the House of Israel. And as ye go, preach, saying, The Kingdom of heaven is at hand. Heal the sick, raise the dead, cast out demons; freely ye have received, freely give" (10:6-8). Miracles of healing, then, were inseparably connected with the Kingdom testimony. They were among the most important of "The Signs of the times" concerning which the Messiah reproached the Pharisees and Sadducees for their failure to discern (see Matt. 16:1-3). Similar miracles of healing shall be repeated when the Messiah returns to the earth, for we read in Is. 35:4-6, "Say to them that are of a fearful heart, Be strong, fear not: behold, your God will come with vengeance, even God with a recompense; He will come and save you (i.e., the godly Jewish remnant of the tribulation period). Then the eyes of the blind shall be opened, and the ears of the deaf shall be unstopped. Then shall the lame man leap as a hart, and the tongue of the dumb sing." It should be diligently observed that Matthew, once more, is the only one of the four Evangelists that makes mention of the Lord Jesus going forth and preaching "The Gospel of the Kingdom," as he is the only one that informs us of the Twelve being sent out with the message to the lost sheep of the House of Israel, "The Kingdom of heaven is at hand." How significant this is! and how it indicates, again, the peculiarly Jewish character of these opening chapters of the New Testament!

As the result of these miracles of healing Messiah's fame went abroad throughout the length and breadth of the Land, and great multitudes followed Him. It is at this stage, we read, "And seeing the multitudes, He went up into a mountain: and when He was set, His disciples came unto Him: and He opened His mouth, and taught them" (5:1, 2). We are tempted to pause here, and enter into a detailed examination of this important, but much misunderstood portion of Scripture—the "Sermon on the Mount." But we must not depart from the central design of this book, hence a few words by way of summary is all we shall now attempt.

The first thing to be remarked is that "the Sermon on the Mount" recorded in Matthew 5 to 7 is peculiar to this first Gospel, no mention of it being made in the other three. This, together with the fact that in Matthew the "Sermon on the Mount" is found in the first section of the book, is sufficient to indicate its dispensational bearings. Secondly, the place from whence this "Sermon" was delivered affords another key to its scope. It was delivered from a "mountain." When the Savior ascended the mount He was elevated above the common level, and did, in symbolic action, take His place upon the Throne. With Matthew 5:1 should be compared 17:1—it was upon a mountain that the Messiah was "transfigured," and in that wonderous scene we behold a miniature and spectacular setting forth of "the Son of Man coming in His Kingdom" (see 16:28). Again, in 24:3, we find that it was upon a mountain that Christ gave that wondrous prophecy (recorded in 24 and 25) which describes the conditions which are to prevail just before the Kingdom of Christ is set up, and which goes on to tell of what shall transpire when He sits upon the Throne of His glory. With these passages should be compared two others in the Old Testament which clinch what we have just said. In Zech. 14:4 we read, "And His feet shall stand in that day upon the mount of Olives," the reference being to the return of Christ to the earth to set up His Kingdom. Again, in Psalm 2 we read that God shall yet say, in reply to the concerted attempt of earth's rulers to prevent it, "Yet have I set My King upon My holy Hill of Zion."

The "Sermon on the Mount" sets forth the Manifesto of the King. It contains the "Constitution" of His Kingdom. It defines the character of those who shall enter into it. It tells of the experiences through which they pass while being fitted for that Kingdom. It enunciates the laws which are to govern their conduct. The authority of the King is evidences by His "I say unto you," repeated no less than fourteen times in this "Sermon." The effect this had upon those who heard Him is apparent from the closing verses, "And it came to pass, when Jesus had ended these sayings, the people were astonished at His doctrine: for He taught them as One having authority, and not as the scribes" (7:28, 29).

Another line of evidence which brings out Christ's authority (ever the most prominent characteristic in connection with a King), which is very pronounced in this Gospel, is seen in His command over the angels. One thing found in connection with kings is the many servants they have to wait upon them and do their bidding. So we find here in connection with "the Son of David." In Matthew 13:41 we read, "The Son of man shall send forth His angels, and they shall gather out of His Kingdom all things that offend, and them which do iniquity." Observe that here these celestial servants are termed not "the angels," but, specifically, "His angels," that is, Messiah's angels, and that they are sent forth in connection with "His Kingdom." Again, in 24:30, 31 we read, "And they shall see the Son of Man coming in the clouds of heaven with power and great glory (this, at His return to earth to establish His Kingdom). And He shall send His angels with a great sound of a trumpet, and they shall gather together His elect from the four winds, from one end of heaven to the other." And, again in 26:53, "Thinkest thou that I cannot now pray to (better, "ask") My Father, and He shall presently (immediately) give Me more than twelve legions of angels?" Matthew, be it particularly noted, is the only one that brings out this feature.

Still another line of evidence of the Kingly majesty of Christ should be pointed out. As it is well known, kings are honored by the homage paid them by their subjects. We need not be surprised, then, to find in this Gospel, which depicts the Savior as "the Son of David," that Christ is frequently seen as the One before whom men prostrated themselves. Only once each in Mark, Luke, and John, do we read of Him receiving worship, but here in Matthew no less than ten times! See 2:2, 8, 11; 8:2; 9:18; 14:33; 15:25; 20:20; 28:9, 17.

Coming now to Matthew 10 (in 8 and 9 we have the Authentication of the King by the special miracles which He wrought), in the opening verses we have an incident which is recorded in each of the first three Gospels, namely, the selection and sending forth of the Twelve. But in Matthew's account there are several characteristic lines found nowhere else. For instance, only here do we learn that when the Lord sent them forth, He commanded them, saying, "Go not into the way of the Gentiles, and into any city of the Samaritans enter ye not: But go rather to the lost sheep of the House of Israel" (10:5, 6). Perfectly appropriate is this here, but it would have been altogether out of place in any of the others. Notice, also, that the Lord added, "And as ye go, preach, saying, The Kingdom of heaven is at hand." How the connection in which this expression is found defines for us its dispensational scope! It was only to "the lost sheep of the House of Israel" they were to say "The Kingdom of heaven is at hand"!

In Matthew 12 we have recorded the most remarkable miracle the Messiah performed before His break with Israel. It was the healing of a man possessed of a demon, and who, in addition, was both dumb and blind. Luke, also, records the same miracle, but in describing the effects this wonder had upon the people who witnessed it, Matthew mentions something which Luke omits, something which strikingly illustrates the special design of his Gospel. In the parallel passage in Luke 11:14 we read, "And He was casting out a demon, and it was dumb. And it came to pass, when the demon was gone out, the dumb spake; and the people wondered," and there the beloved physician stops. But Matthew says, "And all the people were amazed, and said, Is not this the Son of

David?" (12:23). Thus we see, again, how that the bringing out of the Kingship of Christ is the particular object which Matthew, under the Holy Spirit, had before him.

In Matthew 13 we find the seven parables of the Kingdom (in its "mystery" form), the first of which is the well known parable of the Sower, the Seed, and the Soils. Both Mark and Luke also record it, but with characteristic differences of detail. We call attention to one point in Christ's interpretation of it. Mark reads, "The Sower soweth the Word" (4:14). Luke says, "Now the parable is this: the Seed is the Word of God" (8:11). But Matthew, in harmony with his theme says, "Hear ye therefore the parable of the Sower. When anyone heareth the Word of the Kingdom" etc. (13:18, 19). This is but a minor point, but how it brings out the perfections of the Holy Writ, down to the minutest detail! How evident it is that no mere man, or number of men, composed this Book of books! Well many we sing, "How firm a foundation, ye saints of the Lord, is laid for your faith in His excellent Word."

In Matthew 15 we have the well known incident of the Canaanitish woman coming to Christ on the behalf of her demon-distressed daughter. Mark also mentions the same, but omits several of the distinguishing features noted by Matthew. We quote first Mark's account, and then Matthew's, placing in italics the expressions which show forth the special design of his Gospel. "A certain woman whose young daughter had an unclean spirit, heard of Him, and came and fell at His feet. The woman was a Greek, a Syrophenician by nation; and she besought Him that He would cast forth the demon out of her daughter. But Jesus said unto her, Let the children first be filled: for it is not meet to take the children's bread, and to cast it unto the dogs. And she answered and said unto Him, Yes, Lord; yet the dogs under the table eat of the children's crumbs. And He said unto her, For this saying go thy way: the demon is gone out of thy daughter" (Mark 7:25-29). "Behold, a woman of Canaan came out of the same coasts, and cried unto Him saying, Have mercy on me, O Lord, Thou Son of David: my daughter is grievously vexed with a demon. But He answered her not a word (for, as a Gentile, she had no claim upon Him as the "Son of David"). And His disciples came and besought Him, saying, Send her away; for she crieth after us. But He answered and said, I am not sent but unto the lost sheep of the House of Israel. Then came she and worshipped Him, saying Lord, help me. But He answered and said, It is not meet to take the children's bread, and to cast it to dogs. And she said, Truth, Lord; yet the dogs eat of the crumbs, which fall from their master's table. Then Jesus answered and said unto her, O woman great is thy faith: be it unto thee even as thou wilt" (Matt. 15:22-28).

In the opening verse of Matthew 16 we read of how the Pharisees and Sadducees came to Christ tempting Him, and desiring that He would show them a sign from heaven. Mark and Luke both refer to this, but neither of them record that part of our Lord's reply which is found here in verse 2 and 3—"He answered and said unto them, When it is evening, ye say, It will be fair weather: for the sky is red. And in the morning, It will be foul weather to day: for the sky is red and lowering. O ye hypocrites, ye can discern the face of the sky; but can ye not discern the Signs of the Times?" The "signs of the times" were the fulfillment of the Old Testament predictions concerning the Messiah. Every proof had been given to Israel that He was, indeed, the promised One. He had been born of a "virgin," in Bethlehem, the appointed place; a forerunner had prepared His way, exactly as Isaiah had foretold; and, in addition, there had been His mighty works, just as prophecy had fore-announced. But the Jews were blinded by their pride and self-righteousness. That Matthew alone makes mention of the Messiah's reference to these "Signs of the Times" is still another evidence of the distinctively Jewish character of his Gospel.

In Matthew 16:18 and 18:17 the "church" is twice referred to, and Matthew is the only one of the four Evangelists which makes any direct mention of it. This has puzzled many, but the explanation is quite simple. As previously pointed out, the great purpose of this first Gospel is to show how

Christ presented Himself to the Jews, how they rejected Him as their Messiah, and what were the consequences of this, namely, the setting aside of Israel by God for a season, and His visiting the Gentiles in sovereign grace to take out of them a people for His name. Thus, are we here shown how that, and why, the Church has, in this dispensation, superseded the Jewish theocracy.

In Matthew 20 we have recorded the parable of the Householder, who went out and hired laborers for His vineyard, agreeing to pay them one penny for the day. Matthew is the only of the Evangelists that refers to this parable, and the pertinency of its place in his Gospel is clear on the surface. It brings out a characteristic of the Kingdom of Christ. The parable tells of how, at the end of the day, when the workers came to receive their wages, there was complaining among them, because those hired at the eleventh hour received the same as those who had toiled all through the day—verily, there is nothing new under the sun, the dissatisfaction of Labor being seen here in the first century! The Owner of the vineyard vindicated Himself by reminding the discontented workers that He paid to each what they had agreed to accept, and then inquired, "Is it not lawful for Me to do what I will with Mine own?" Thus did He, as Sovereign, insist on His rights to pay what He pleased, no one being wronged thereby.

In Matthew 22 we have the parable of the wedding feast of the King's Son. A parable that is very similar to this one is found in Luke's Gospel, and while there are many points of resemblance between them, yet are there some striking variations. In Luke 14:16 we read, "Then said He unto him, A certain man made a great supper, and bade many." Whereas, in Matthew 22:2 we are told, "The Kingdom of heaven is like unto a certain King, which made a marriage for His Son." At the close of this parable in Matthew there is something which finds no parallel whatever in Luke. Here we read, "And when the King came in to see the guests, He saw there a guest which had not on a wedding garment: And He saith unto him, Friend, how comest thou in hither not having a wedding garment? And he was speechless. Then said the King to His servants, Bind him hand and foot, and take him away, and cast him into outer darkness: there shall be weeping, and gnashing of teeth" (22:11-13). How this brings out the authority of the King needs scarcely to be pointed out.

The whole of Matthew 25 is peculiar to this first Gospel. We cannot now dwell upon the contents of this interesting chapter, but would call attention to what is recorded in verses 31 to 46. That the contents of these verses is found nowhere else in the four Gospels, and its presence here is another proof of the design and scope of Matthew's. These verses portray the Son of man seated upon the throne of His glory, and before Him are gathered all nations, these being divided into two classes, and stationed on His right and left hand, respectively. In addressing each class we read, "Then shall the King say" etc. (see verses 34 and 40).

There are a number of items concerning the Passion of the Lord Jesus recorded only by Matthew. In 26:59, 60 we read, "Now the chief priests, and elders, and all the council, sought false witnesses against Jesus, to put Him to death. But found none. At the last came two false witnesses"—two, because that was the minimum number required by the law, in order that the truth might be established. It is interesting to note how frequently the two witnesses are found in Matthew. In 8:28 we read, "And when He was come to the other side into the country of the Gergesenes, there met Him two possessed with demons"—compare Mark 5:1, 2, where only one of these men is referred to. Again in 9:27 we read, "And when Jesus departed thence two blind men followed Him" etc.—compare Mark 10:46. In 11:2 we are told, "When John had heard in the prison the works of Christ, he sent two of his disciples." Finally, in 27:24 we find Pilate's testimony to the fact that Christ was a "just man," but in 27:19 we also read, "His wife sent unto him, saying, Have thou nothing to do with that just man." And this, as well as the others cited above, is found only in Matthew. Again, in 26:63, 64 we find a characteristic word omitted "and said unto Him, I adjure thee by the living God, that Thou tell us whether Thou be the Christ, the Son of God. Jesus

said unto him, Thou hast said: nevertheless I say unto you, Hereafter shall ye see the Son of man sitting on the right hand of power, and coming in the clouds of heaven." Here only are we told that the guilty Jews cried, "His blood be on us, and on our children" (27:25). And again, Matthew is the only one that informs us of the enmity of Israel pursuing their Messiah even after His death—see 27:62-64.

The closing chapter of this Gospel is equally striking. No mention is made by Matthew of the Ascension of Christ. This, too, is in perfect accord with the theme and scope of this Gospel. The curtain falls here with the Messiah still on earth, for it is on earth, and not in heaven, that the Son of David shall yet reign in glory. Here only is recorded the Lord's word, "All power is given unto Me in heaven and in earth" (28:18)—for "power" is the outstanding mark of a king. Finally, the closing verses form a fitting conclusion, for they view Christ, on a "mountain," commanding and commissioning His servants to go forth and disciple the nations, ending with the comforting assurance, "Lo, I am with you alway, even unto the end of the Age."

2. THE GOSPEL OF MARK

Mark's Gospel differs widely from Matthew's, both in character and scope. The contrasts between them are marked and many. Matthew has twenty-eight chapters, Mark but sixteen. Matthew abounds in parables, Mark records but few. Matthew portrays Christ as the Son of David, Mark delineates Him as the humble but perfect Servant of Jehovah. Matthew is designed particularly (not exclusively) for the Jew, whereas Mark is specially appropriate for Christian workers. Matthew sets forth the Kingly dignity and authority of Christ, Mark views Him in His lowliness and meekness. Matthew depicts Him as testing Israel, Marks shows Him ministering to the Chosen People. This is one reason why, no doubt, that Mark's Gospel is the second book in the New Testament—like Matthew's, it views Him in connection with the Old Testament people of God. Luke's Gospel, has a wider scope, looking at Christ in relation to the human race. While in John, He is shown to be the Son of God, spiritually related to the household of faith.

In turning now to look at the contents of this second Gospel in some detail, we would notice,

I. Things omitted from Mark's Gospel

a. Just as the skill of a master artist is discovered in the objects which he leaves out of his picture (the amateur crowding in everything on to the canvass for which he can find room), so the discerning eye at once detects the handiwork of the Holy Spirit in the various things which are included and omitted from different parts of the Word. Notably is this the case with Mark's Gospel. Here we find no Genealogy at the commencement, as in Matthew; the miraculous Conception is omitted, and there is no mention made of His birth. Fancy a whole Gospel written and yet no reference to the Savior's birth in it! At first glance this is puzzling, but a little reflection assures one of the Divine wisdom which directed Mark to say nothing about it. Once we see what is the special design of each separate Gospel, we are the better enabled to appreciate their individual perfections. The birth of Christ did not fall within the compass of this second Gospel, nor did the record of His genealogy. Mark is presenting Christ as the Servant of Jehovah, and in connection with a servant a genealogy or particulars of birth are scarcely points of interest or importance. But how this demonstrates the Divine Authorship of the books of the Bible! Suppose the Genealogy had been omitted by Matthew, and inserted by Mark, then, the unity of each Gospel would have been destroyed. But just as the Creator placed each organ of the body in the wisest possible place, so the Holy Spirit guided in the placing of each book in the Bible (each member in this Living Organism), and each detail of each book. For the same reason as the Genealogy is omitted, nothing is said by Mark of the visit of the wise men, for a "servant" is not one that receives homage! Mark also passes over what Luke tells us of Christ as a boy of twelve in the temple of Jerusalem, and His subsequent return to Nazareth, where He continued in subjection

to His parents, for, while these are points of interest in connection with His humanity, they were irrelevant to a setting forth of His Servanthood.

b. In Mark's Gospel we find no Sermon on the Mount. Matthew devotes three whole chapters to it, but Mark records it not, though some of its teachings are found in other connections in this second Gospel. Why, then, we may ask, is this important utterance of Christ omitted by Mark? The answer must be sought in the character and design of the "Sermon." As we have pointed out, the Sermon on the Mount contains the King's Manifesto. It sets forth the laws of His Kingdom, and describes the character of those who are to be its subjects. But Mark is presenting Christ as the perfect Workman of God, and a servant has no "Kingdom," and frames no "laws." Hence the appropriateness of the "Sermon" in Matthew, and the Divine wisdom in its exclusion from Mark.

c. Mark records fewer Parables than Matthew. In Mark there are but four all told, whereas in Matthew there are at least fourteen. Mark says nothing about the Householder hiring laborers for His vineyard, claiming the right to do as He wills with that which is His own; for, as God's Servant, He is seen in the place of the Laborer, instead of in the position where He hires others. Mark omits all reference to the parable of the Marriage of the King's Son, at the close of which He is seen giving orders for the man without the wedding-garment to be bound and cast into the outer darkness—such is not the prerogative of a Servant. All reference to the parable of the Talents is omitted by Mark, for as God's Servant He neither gives talents nor rewards for the use of them. Each of these parables, and many others all found in Matthew, are excluded by Mark, and their omission only serves to bring out the minute perfections of each Gospel.

d. In Mark nothing whatever is said of Christ's command over angels, and His right to send them forth to do His bidding; instead we find here "the angels ministered unto Him" (1:13).

e. Here there is no arraignment of Israel, and no sentence is passed upon Jerusalem as in the other Gospels. Again, in Matthew 23 the "Son of David" utters a most solemn sevenfold "Woe"—"Woe unto you scribes and Pharisees, hypocrites," "Woe unto you, ye blind guides" etc., He says there; but not a word of this is found in Mark. The reason for this is obvious. It is not the part of the Servant to pass judgment on others, but "to be gentle unto all, apt to teach, patient" (2 Tim. 2:24). We have another striking illustration of this same characteristic in connection with our Lord cleansing the Temple. In Matthew 21:12 we read, "And Jesus went into the temple of God, and cast out all them that sold and bought in the temple, and overthrew the tables of the money changers, and the seats of them that sold doves," and immediately following this we are told, "And He left them, and went out of the city into Bethany; and He lodged there" (21:17). But in Mark it is simply said, "And Jesus entered into Jerusalem, and into the temple: and when He had looked round about upon all things, and now the eventide was come, He went out unto Bethany with the twelve" (11:11). Mark is clearly writing of the same incident. He refers to the Lord entering the temple, but says nothing about Him casting out those who bought and sold there, nor of Him overthrowing the tables. How striking is this omission. As the Messiah and King it was fitting that He should cleanse the defiled Temple, but in His character of Servant it would have been incongruous!

f. The omission of so many of the Divine titles from this second Gospel is most significant. In Mark, He is never owned as "King" save in derision. In Mark, we do not read, as in Matthew, "They shall call His name Emmanuel, which being interpreted is, God with us," and only once is He here termed "the Son of David." It is very striking to observe how the Holy Spirit has avoided this in the second Gospel. In connection with the "Triumphant Entry into Jerusalem," when recording the acclamations of the people, Matthew says, "And the multitudes that went before, and that followed, cried, saying, Hosanna to the Son of David: Blessed is He that cometh in the name of the Lord; Hosanna in the highest" (21:9). But in Mark's

account we read, "And they that went before, and they that followed, cried, saying, Hosanna: Blessed is He that cometh in the name of the Lord: Blessed be the Kingdom of our father David, that cometh in the name of the Lord: Hosanna in the highest" (11:9, 10). Thus it will be seen that the Servant of God was not hailed here as "the Son of David." Side by side with this, should be placed the words used by our Lord when announcing, a week beforehand, His "transfiguration." In Matthew's account, we read that He told His disciples, "Verily I say unto you, There be some standing here, which shall not taste of death, till they see the Son of Man coming in His Kingdom." But, here in Mark, we are told that He said to the disciples, "Verily I say unto you, That there be some of them that stand here, which shall not taste of death, till they have seen the Kingdom of God come with power" (9:1). How significant this is! Here it is simply the "Kingdom of God" that is spoken of, instead of Christ's own Kingdom!

But that which is most noteworthy here in connection with the titles of Christ, is the fact that He is so frequently addressed as "Master," when, in the parallel passages in the other Gospels, He is owned as "Lord." For example: in Matthew 8:25 we read, "And His disciples came to Him, and awoke Him, saying Lord, save us; we perish"; but in Mark, "And they awake Him, and say unto Him, Master, carest Thou not that we perish?" (4:38). Following the announcement of His coming death, Matthew tells us, "Then Peter took Him, and began to rebuke Him, saying, Be it far from Thee, Lord: this shall not be unto Thee" (16:22). But in Mark it reads, "And Peter took Him, and began to rebuke Him" (8:32), and there it stops. On the Mount of Transfiguration, Peter said, "Lord, it is good for us to be here" (17:4); but Mark says, "And Peter answered and said to Jesus, Master, it is good for us to be here" (9:5). When the Savior announced that one of the Twelve would betray Him, Matthew tells us, "And they were exceeding sorrowful, and began every one of them to say unto Him, Lord, is it I?" (26:22); but Mark tells us, "And they began to be sorrowful, and to say unto Him, one by one, "Is it I?" (14:19). These are but a few of the examples which might be adduced, but sufficient have been given to bring out this striking and most appropriate feature of Mark's Gospel.

g. It is deeply interesting and instructive to note the various circumstances and events connected with our Lord's sufferings which are omitted from Mark. Here, as He entered the awful darkness of Gethsemane, He says to the three disciples, "Tarry ye here, and watch" (14:34), not "watch with Me," as in Matthew, for as the Servant He turns only to God for comfort; and here, nothing is said at the close, of an angel from Heaven appearing and "strengthening" Him, for as Servant He draws strength from God alone. No mention is made by Mark of Pilate's "I find no fault in Him," nor are we told of Pilate's wife counseling her husband to have nothing to do with "this Just Man," nor do we read here of Judas returning to the priests, and saying, "I have betrayed innocent blood"; all of these are omitted by Mark, for the Servant must look to God alone for vindication. Nothing is said in Mark of the women following Christ as He was led to the place of execution, "bewailing and lamenting Him" (Luke 23:27), for sometimes the suffering Servant of God is denied the sympathy of others. The words of the dying thief, "Lord, remember me when Thou comest into Thy Kingdom" are here omitted, for in this Gospel, Christ is neither presented as "Lord" nor as One having a "Kingdom." The Savior's triumphant cry from the Cross, "It is finished" is also omitted. At first sight this seems strange, but a little reflection will discover the Divine wisdom for its exclusion. It is not for the Servant to say when his work is finished—that is for God to decide! We pass on now to notice

II. Things which are characteristic of Mark.

a. Mark's Gospel opens in a manner quite different from the others. In Matthew, Luke and John, there is what may be termed a lengthy Introduction, but in Mark it is quite otherwise. Matthew records Christ's genealogy, His birth, the visit and homage of the wise men, the flight into Egypt, and subsequent return and sojourn in Nazareth; describes at length both His baptism and temptation, and

not till we reach the end of the fourth chapter do we arrive at His public ministry. Luke opens with some interesting details concerning the parentage of John the Baptist, describes at length the interview between the angel and the Savior's mother previous to His birth, records her beautiful Song, tells of the angelic visitation to the Bethlehem shepherds at Christ's birth, pictures the presentation of the Child in the temple, and refers to many other things; and not until we reach the fourth chapter do we come to the public ministry of the Redeemer. So, too, in John. There is first a lengthy Prologue, in which is set forth the Divine glories of the One who became flesh; then follows the testimony of His forerunner to the Divine dignity of the One he had come to herald; then we have described a visit to John of a delegation sent from Jerusalem to inquire as to who he was; finally, there is the witness of the Baptist to Christ as the Lamb of God: and all this before we here read of Him calling His first disciples. But how entirely different is the opening of the second Gospel. Here there is but a brief notice of the Baptist and his testimony, a few words concerning Christ's baptism and His temptation, and then, in the fourteenth verse of the first chapter we read, "Now after that John was put in prison, Jesus came into Galilee, preaching the gospel of the Kingdom of God." The first thirty years of His life here on earth are passed over in silence, and Mark at once introduces Christ at the beginning of His public ministry. Mark presents Christ actually serving.

b. The opening verse of Mark is very striking: "The beginning of the Gospel of Jesus Christ, the Son of God." Observe, it is not here "the Gospel of the Kingdom" (as in Matthew), but "the Gospel of Jesus Christ." How significant that it is added "the Gospel of Jesus Christ, the Son of God." Thus has the Holy Spirit guarded His Divine glory in the very place where His lowliness as the "Servant" is set forth. It is also to be remarked that this word "Gospel" is found much more frequently in Mark than in any of the other Gospels. The term "Gospel" occurs twelve times in all in Matthew, Mark, Luke, and John, and no less than eight of these are found in Mark, so that the word "Gospel" is found twice as often in Mark as in the other three added together! The reason for this is obvious: as the Servant of Jehovah, the Lord Jesus was the Bearer of good news, the Herald of glad tidings! What a lesson to be taken to heart by all of the servants of God to-day!

c. Another characteristic term which occurs with even greater frequency in this second Gospel is the Greek word "Eutheos," which is variously translated "forthwith, straightway, immediately" etc. Notice a few of the occurrences of this word in the first chapter alone: "And straightway coming up out of the water, He saw the heavens opened, and the Spirit like a dove descending upon Him" (v. 10). "And immediately the Spirit driveth Him into the wilderness" (v. 12). "And when He had gone a little further thence, He saw James the son of Zebedee, and John his brother, who also were in the ship mending their nets, And straightway He called them" (vv. 19, 20). "And they went into Capernaum; and straightway on the Sabbath day He entered into the synagogue, and taught" (v. 21). "And forthwith when they were come out of the synagogue, they entered into the house of Simon" (v. 29). "And He came and took her by the hand, and lifted her up, and immediately the fever left her" (v. 31). "And He straightly charged him, and forthwith sent him away" (v. 43). In all, this word is found no less than forty times in Mark's Gospel. It is a most suggestive and expressive term, bringing out the perfections of God's Servant by showing us how He served. There was no tardiness about Christ's service, but "straightway" He was ever about His "Father's business." There was no delay, but "forthwith" He performed the work given Him to do. This word tells of the promptitude of His service and the urgency of His mission. There was no holding back, no reluctance, no slackness, but a blessed "immediateness" about all His work. Well may we learn from this perfect example which He has left us.

d. The way in which so many of the chapters open in this second Gospel is worthy of our close attention. Turn to the first verse of chapter 2, "And again He entered into Capernaum after some days." Again, the first verse of chapter 3, "And He entered again into the synagogue." So in 4:1, "And He began again to teach by the seaside." So in 5:1, "And they came over unto the other side of the sea." This is seemingly a trivial point, and yet, how unique! It is now more than ten years since the writer first observed this feature of Mark's Gospel, and since then, many hundreds of books, of various sorts, have been read by him, but never once has he seen a single book of human authorship which had in it one chapter that commenced with the word "And." Test this, reader, by your own library. Yet here in Mark's Gospel no less than twelve of its chapters begun with "And"!

"And," as we know, is a conjunction joining together two other parts of speech; it is that which links two or more things together. The service of Christ, then, was characterized by that which "And" signifies. In other words, His service was one complete and perfect whole, with no breaks in it. Ah, how unlike ours! Yours and mine is so disjointed. We serve God for a time, and then there comes a slackening up, a pause, a break, which is followed by a period of inactivity, before we begin again. But not so with Christ. His service was a series of perfect acts, fitly joined together, without a break or blemish. "And," then as characterizing the service of Christ, tells of ceaseless activity. It speaks of the continuity of His labors. It shows us how He was "instant in season and out of season." It reveals how He never grew weary of well doing. May God's grace cause the "And" to have a more prominent place in our service for Him.

e. In the former section we have pointed out how that Mark records fewer parables than Matthew, and we may add, fewer than Luke too. But, on the other hand, Mark describes more miracles. This, also, is in keeping with the design and scope of this second Gospel. Parables contained our Lord's teachings, whereas the miracles were a part of His active ministry. Service consists more of deeds than teaching, doing rather than speaking. How often our service is more with our lips than our hands. We are big talkers and little doers!

Mark records just four parables, and it is a most significant thing that each of them has to do, directly, with service. The first is the parable of the Sower, and this views the Savior as going forth with the Word (4:3-20). The second parable is that of the Seed cast into the ground, which sprang up and grew, and brought forth first the blade, then the ear, after that the full corn in the ear, and finally was harvested (4:26-29). The third parable is that of the Mustard-seed (4:30-32). The fourth is that of the Wicked Husbandmen who mistreated the Owner's servants, and ended by killing His well-beloved Son (12:1-9). Thus it will be seen, that each has to do with ministry or service: the first three with sowing Seed, and the last with the Servant going forth "that He might receive of the husbandman of the fruit of the vineyard."

f. In Mark's Gospel, the hand of Christ is frequently mentioned, and this is peculiarly appropriate in the Gospel which treats of His service. It might well be termed, the Ministry of the Hand. How prominent this feature is here may be seen by consulting the following passages. "And He came and took her by the hand, and lifted her up; and immediately the fever left her" (1:31). "And Jesus, moved with compassion, put forth His hand, and touched him, and saith unto him, I will; be thou clean" (1:41). "And He took the damsel by the hand, and said unto her, *Talitha cumi*: which is, being interpreted, Damsel, I say unto thee, arise" (5:41). "And they bring unto Him one that was deaf, and had an impediment in his speech; and they beseech Him to put His hand upon him" (7:32). How beautiful is this. Divinely enlightened, these people had learned of the tenderness and virtue of His hand. Again we read, "And He cometh to Bethsaida; and they bring a blind man unto Him, and besought Him to touch him" (8:22). They, too, had discovered the blessedness and power of His touch. "And He took the blind man by the hand, and led him out of the town. After that He put His hands again upon his eyes, and made him look up: and he was restored, and saw every man clearly" (8:23, 25). Once more we read, "But Jesus took him by the hand, and lifted him up; and he arose" (9:27). How blessed for every believer to know that he is safely held in that same blessed Hand (John 10:28).

g. The Holy Spirit has also called special attention in this Gospel to the eyes of the perfect Servant. "And when He had looked round about on them with anger, being grieved for the hardness of their hearts" (3:5). How those Holy eyes must have flashed upon those who would condemn Him for healing on the Sabbath day the man with the withered hand! "And He looked round about on them which sat about Him, and said, Behold My mother and My brethren! For whosoever shall do the will of God, the same is My brother, and My sister, and My mother" (3:34, 35). This time the Savior's eyes turned upon His disciples, and what love must have appeared in them as He turned and beheld those who had forsaken all to follow Him! "But when He had turned about and looked on His disciples, He rebuked Peter, saying, Get thee behind Me, Satan" (8:33). What a touch in the picture is this—before He rebuked Peter, He, first, turned, and "looked" on His disciples! Concerning the rich young ruler who came to Him, we read here (and here only)," Then Jesus beholding him, loved him" (10:21). What Divine pity and compassion must have shone in His eyes at that moment! So again in 11:11 we read, "And Jesus entered into Jerusalem, and into the temple, and when He had looked round upon all things, and now the eventide was come, He went out into Bethany with the twelve." How those eyes must have blazed with righteous indignation, as He beheld the desecration of the Father's house! These passages which mention the Savior "looking" and "beholding," tell us of His thoughtfulness, His attention to detail, His thoroughness. Next we will notice,

III. The manner in which Christ served

In order to discover the manner in which Christ served, we must examine closely the details of what the Holy Spirit has recorded here for our learning and profit, and for the benefit of our readers we shall classify those under suitable headings.

a. Christ served with marked unostentation

"And Simon and they that were with him followed after Him. And when they had found Him, they said unto Him, All men seek for Thee. And He said unto them, Let us go into the next towns, that I may preach there also: for therefore came I forth" (Mark 1:36-38). This incident occurred near the beginning of our Lord's public ministry. He had wrought some mighty works, many of the sick had been healed, and His fame had gone abroad. In consequence, great throngs of people sought for Him. He was, for a brief season, the popular Idol of the hour. But what was His response? Instead of remaining where He was to receive the plaudits of a fickle crowd, He moves away to preach in other towns. How unlike many of us today! When we are well received, when we become the center of an admiring crowd, our desire is to remain there. Such a reception is pleasing to the flesh; it panders to our pride. We like to boast of the crowds that attend our ministry. But the perfect Servant of God never courted popularity, He shunned it! And when His disciples came and told Him—no doubt with pleasurable pride— "All men seek for Thee," His immediate response was, "Let us go"!

At the close of Mark 1 we read of a leper being cleansed by the great Physician, and, dismissing him, He said, "See thou say nothing to any man: but go thy way, shew thyself to the priest, and offer for thy cleansing those things which Moses commanded, for a testimony unto them." How utterly unlike many of His servants to day, who spare no pains or expense to advertise themselves! How entirely different we are from the One who said, "I receive not honor from men" (John 5:41)! No; He ever wrought with an eye single to God's glory. Notice, farther, how this comes out again in the sequel to the above miracle. The healed leper heeded not the admonition of his Benefactor, instead, we read, "But he went out, and began to publish it much, and to blaze abroad the matter." How gratifying this would have been to most of us! But not so with Him who sought only the Father's glory. Instead of following the man who had been healed, to become the Object of the admiring gaze and flattering remarks of the leper's friends and neighbors, we read, that "Jesus could no more openly enter into the city, but

was without in desert places"! Are we not to learn from this, that when people begin to "blaze abroad" what God has wrought through us, it is time for us to move on, lest we receive the honor and glory which is due Him alone!

In full harmony with what has just been before us in the closing verses of Mark 1, we read in the first verses of the next chapter, "And again He entered into Capernaum, after some days, and it was noised that He was in the house," for, evidently, the healed leper belonged to that highly favored town. Hence it was that we here find Him seeking the privacy and quietude of the "house." So again in 3:19 we read, "And they (Christ and the apostles) went into an house." His reason for doing this, here, was to escape from the crowd, as is evident from the words which immediately follow, "And the multitude cometh together again." Again in 7:17 we are told, "And when He was entered into the house from the people." His life was not lived before the footlights, but quietly and unobtrusively He went about doing the Father's will. What a word is this—"And when He was entered into the house from the people"! And how different from some of His servants today, whose one great aim seems to be the seeking of the patronage of "the people," and the soliciting of their favors! So, again in 9:28 we read, "And when He was come into the house, His disciples asked Him privately, Why could not we cast him out?" (9:28). And once more in 9:33, we read "And He came to Capernaum: and being in the house He asked them, What was it that ye disputed among yourselves by the way?" Mark, we may add, is the only one of the four Evangelists that makes this repeated reference to "the house." It is just one of the smaller lines in the picture that serves to bring out the Unostentation of the perfect Servant.

In the closing verses of Mark 7 we have recorded the miracle of Christ restoring one that was deaf and had an impediment in his speech. And in chapter eight is recorded the healing of the blind man, who, at the first touch of the Lord's hands saw men as trees walking, but who, at the second touch, "saw every man clearly." Mark is the only one that records either of these miracles. One reason for their inclusion here, is seen in a feature that is common to them both. In 7:36 we are told, "And He charged them that they should tell no man: but the more He charged them, so much the more a great deal they published it." Concerning the latter we read, "And He sent him away to his house, saying, Neither go into the town, nor tell it to any in the town" (8:26). What a lesson for all of us: perfect service is rendered to God alone, and often is unseen, unappreciated, unthanked by man. The Servant of Jehovah threw a veil over His gracious acts.

b. Christ served with great tenderness

This comes out so often in this second Gospel. We single out four examples, and the better to appreciate them, we quote first the parallel references in the other Gospels, before noticing Mark's account. "And Simon's wife's mother was taken with a great fever; and they besought Him for her. And He stood over her, and rebuked the fever; and it left her; and immediately she arose and ministered unto them" (Luke 4:38, 39). "But Simon's wife's mother lay sick of a fever, and anon they tell Him of her. And He came and took her by the hand, and lifted her up; and immediately the fever left her, and she ministered unto them" (Mark 1:30, 31). What a beautiful line in the picture is this! How it shows us that Christ's service was no mere perfunctory one, performed with mechanical indifference, but that He came near to those to whom He ministered and entered, sympathetically, into their condition.

In Luke 9 we read of the father who sought out the Lord Jesus on behalf of his demon-possessed son, and in healing him we read, "And Jesus rebuked the unclean spirit, and healed the child, and delivered him again to his father" (9:42). But Mark brings into his picture a characteristic line which Luke omitted, "But Jesus took him by the hand, and lifted him up, and he arose" (9:27). There was no aloofness about the perfect Servant. How this rebukes the assumed self-superiority of those who think it beneath their dignity to shake hands with those to whom they have ministered the Word! To take some people "by

the hand" is to get nearer their hearts. Let us seek to serve as Christ did.

In Matthew 18:2 we read, "And Jesus called a little child unto Him, and set him in the midst of them; and when He had taken him in His arms, He said unto them" (9:36). Again, in Matthew 19:13-15 we are told, "Then were there brought unto Him little children, that He should put His hands on them, and pray: and the disciples rebuked them. But Jesus said, Suffer little children, and forbid them not, to come unto Me, for of such is the kingdom of heaven. And He laid His hands on them, and departed thence." But once more we may observe how that Mark adds a line all his own, "And they brought young children to Him, that He should touch them: and His disciples rebuked those that brought them. But when Jesus saw it, He was much displeased, and said unto them, Suffer the little children to come unto Me, and forbid them not: for of such is the kingdom of God. Verily I say unto you, Whosoever shall not receive the kingdom of God as a little child, he shall not enter therein. And He took them up in His arms, put His hands upon them, and blessed them" (10:13-16). What tenderness do these acts display! And what an example He has left us!

c. Christ served encountering great opposition

Here we shall take a rapid review of Mark's reference to this feature of his theme, instead of commenting on each passage, though a remark here and there will, perhaps, not be out of place.

"But there were certain of the scribes sitting there, and reasoning in their hearts (there are usually a few such in most congregations), Why does this man thus speak blasphemies?" (2:6, 7). "And when the scribes and Pharisees saw Him eat with publicans and sinners, they said unto His disciples, How is it that He eateth and drinketh with publicans and sinners?" (2:16). "And the Pharisees said unto Him, behold why do they on the Sabbath day that which is not lawful?" (2:24). The servant of God must expect to be misunderstood and encounter criticism and opposition. "And they watched Him whether

He would heal him on the Sabbath day" (3:2). And the servant of God is still watched by unfriendly eyes! "And the Pharisees went forth, and straightway took counsel with the Herodians against Him, how they might destroy Him" (3:6). Every faction of the peoples was "against" Him. "And the scribes which came down from Jerusalem said, He hath Beelzebub, and by the prince of the demons casteth He out demons" (3:22). The servant may expect to be called hard names. "And they began to pray Him to depart out of their coasts" (5:17). Christ was not wanted. His testimony condemned His hearers. So will it be now with every servant of God that is faithful. "And they laughed Him to scorn" (5:40). To be sneered and jeered at, then, is nothing new: sufficient for the disciple to suffer what his Master did before him. "And they were offended at Him" (6:3). The Christ of God did not suit everybody; far from it. But let us see to it that we give none other occasion for "offense" than He did! "And He could there do no mighty work, save that He laid His hands upon a few sick folk, and healed them" (6:5). The servant of God will come to some places which are unfavorable for effective ministry, and where the unbelief of the professed people of the Lord will hinder the Spirit of God. "Then came together unto Him the Pharisees, and certain of the scribes, which came from Jerusalem. And when they saw some of His disciples eat bread with defiled, that is to say, with unwashen hands, they found fault" (7:1, 2). Nevertheless, the Lord Jesus declined to respect their "traditions," refusing to allow His disciples to be brought into bondage thus. Well for God's servants now if they disregard the "touch not, taste not, handle not" of men, yet must they be prepared to be "found fault" with as the result. "And the Pharisees came forth, and began to question with Him, seeking of Him a sign from heaven, tempting Him" (8:11). So, too, will the emissaries of the Enemy seek now to entangle and ensnare the servants of God. Compare Mark 10:2. "And the scribes and chief priests heard it, and sought how they might destroy Him: for they feared Him, because all the people was astonished at His doctrine" (11:18). They were jealous of His influence.

And human nature has not changed since then! "And they come again to Jerusalem: and as He was walking in the temple, there came to Him the chief priests and the scribes, and the elders. And say unto Him, By what authority doest Thou these things? and who gave Thee this authority?" (11:27, 28). How history repeats itself! From what College have you graduated? and in which Seminary were you trained? are the modern form of this query. "And they sent unto Him certain of the Pharisees, and of the Herodians, to catch Him in His words" (12:13). And some of their descendants still survive, and woe be to the man who fails to pronounce their shibboleths! What a list this is! and we have by no means exhausted it; see further 12:18; 12:28; 14:1, etc. All the way through, the perfect Servant of God was dogged by His enemies; at every step He encountered opposition and persecution in some form. And these things are all recorded for our instruction. The Enemy is not dead. God's servants today are called to tread a similar path.

d. Christ served with much self-sacrifice

"And the multitude cometh together again, so that they could not so much as eat bread" (3:20). So thoroughly was He at the disposal of others. How completely did He know what it was to spend and be spent!

"And the same day, when the even was come, He saith unto them, Let us pass over into the other side. And when they had sent away the multitude, they took Him, even as He was into the ship" (4:35, 36). How touching is this! A study of the context, with the parallel passages in the other Gospel, shows this evening here was the close of a busy and crowded day. From early morn till sunset, the Master had been ministering to others, and now He is so weary and worn from His labors He had to be "taken"—led and lifted—into the ship! "Even as He was"—how much do these words cover? Ah, Christian worker, next time you come to the close of a full day of service for God, and your mind is tired and your nerves are quivering, remember that thy Lord, before thee, knew what it was to lay down (see 4:38) so tired that even the storm awoke Him not!

"And He said unto them, Come ye yourselves apart into a desert place and rest a while: for there were many coming and going, and they had NO leisure so much as to eat" (6:31). That is how the perfect Workman of God served. Ever intent in being about His Father's business: no rest, no leisure, at times so thronged that He went without His meals.

Christ's service cost Him something. Note how this comes out in the next quotations. "And when He had looked round about on them with anger, being grieved for the hardness of their hearts" (3:5). He was no frigid Stoic. "And looking up to heaven He sighed, and saith unto him, *Ephphatha*, that is, Be opened" (7:34). Christ's service was not rendered formally and perfunctorily; but He entered, sympathetically, into the condition of the sufferer. "And He sighed deeply in His spirit, and saith, Why doth this generation seek after a sign?" (8:12). Thus did He take to heart the sad unbelief of those to whom He ministered. He suffered inwardly as well as outwardly.

"And the multitude cometh together again, so that they could not so much as eat bread. And when His friends heard of it, they went out to lay hold on Him: for they said, He is beside Himself" (3:20, 21). So incapable were they of entering into the thoughts of God. They sought to check Him in the accomplishing of God's will. Their purpose was well meant, no doubt, but it was a zeal "without knowledge." What a warning is this for all of God's servants. Watch out for well intentioned "friends" who, lacking in discernment, may seek to hinder the one who is completely yielded to God, and who, like the apostle Paul, "counts not his life dear unto himself" (Acts 20:24).

e. Christ served in an orderly manner

This comes out, in an incidental way, in several statements which are found only in Mark. We single out but two. In 6:7 we read, "And He called unto Him the twelve, and began to send them forth by two and two." Again; when about to feed the hungering multitude, we are told, "And He commanded them to make them all sit down by companies upon the green grass. And they sat down in ranks, by hundreds, and by fifties" (6:39, 40). What attention to details was this! And how it rebukes much of our slipshod work! If Scripture enjoins, "Whatsoever thine hand findeth to do, do it with thy might," then, surely our service for God calls for our most careful and prayerful attention! God is never the author of "confusion," as Christ's example here plainly shows.

f. Christ's service was prompted by love

"And Jesus, moved with compassion, put forth His hand, and touched him. (the leper), and said unto him, I will; be thou clean" (1:41). "And Jesus, when He came out, saw much people, and was moved with compassion toward them, because they were as sheep not having a shepherd; and He began to teach them many things" (6:34). "I have compassion on the multitude, because they have now been with Me three days, and have nothing to eat" (8:1). Mark is the only one of the Evangelists that brings this lovely and touching line into the picture. And O how it rebukes the writer for his hardness of heart, and cold indifference to the perishing all around! How little real "compassion" one finds today! "Then Jesus beholding him (the rich young man) loved him" (Mark 10:21). Mark is the only one who tells us this, as though to show that without "love" service is barren.

g. Christ's service was preceded by prayer

"And in the morning, rising up a great while before day, He went out, and departed into a solitary place, and there prayed" (1:35). Mark is the only one that records this. And how significant that this statement is placed in his first chapter, as though to let us into the secret of the uniqueness and perfection of Christ's service!

There is much more that is peculiar to this second Gospel which we now pass over. In closing here we would call attention to the manner in which Mark concludes:—"And they (the apostles) went forth, and preached everywhere, the Lord working with them, and confirming the Word with signs following. Amen" (16:20). How significant and appropriate! The last view we have here of

God's perfect Servant, He is still "working," now, not alone, but "with them" His servants.

Our study of this lovely view of Christ will have been in vain, unless it has brought home to our hearts with new power the admonition of God through His apostle, "Therefore, my beloved brethren, be ye steadfast, unmovable, always abounding in the work of the Lord, forasmuch as ye know that your labor is not in vain in the Lord" (1 Cor. 15:58).

3. THE GOSPEL OF LUKE

The numerical position which Luke occupies in the Sacred Canon, supplies a sure key to its interpretation. It is the third book in the New Testament, and the forty-second in the Bible as a whole. Each of these numbers are profoundly significant and suggestive in this connection. Three is the number of manifestation, and particularly, the manifestation of God and His activities. It is in the Three Persons of the Blessed Trinity that the one true and living God is fully revealed. Hence, also, three is the number of resurrection, for resurrection is when life is fully manifested. Appropriately, then, is Luke's Gospel the third book of the New Testament, for here it is we are shown, as nowhere else so fully, God manifest in flesh. But Luke's Gospel is also the forty-second book in the Bible as a whole, and this is, if possible, even more significant, for 42 is 7 x 6, and seven stands for perfection while six is the number of man: putting the two together we get the Perfect Man! And this is precisely what the Holy Spirit brings before us in this forty-second book of the Bible. What an evidence this is, not only of the Divine inspiration of Scripture but, that God has unmistakably superintended the placing of the different books in the Sacred Canon just as we now have them!

Luke's Gospel is concerned with the Humanity of our Lord. In Matthew, Christ is seen testing Israel, and that is why his Gospel has the first place in the New Testament, as being the necessary link with the Old. In Mark, Christ appears as serving Israel, and that is why his Gospel is given the second place. But in Luke, the writer's scope is enlarged: here Christ is seen in racial connections as the Son of Man, contrasted from the sons of men. In John, Christ's highest glory is revealed, for there He is viewed as the Son of God, and, as connected not with Israel, not with men as men, but with believers. Thus we may admire the Divine wisdom in the arrangement of the four Gospels, and see the beautiful gradation in their order. Matthew is designed specially for the Jews; Mark is peculiarly suited to God's servants; Luke is adapted to men as men—all men; while John's is the one wherein the Church has found its chief delight.

Luke's Gospel, then, is the Gospel of Christ's Manhood. It shows us God manifest in flesh. It presents Christ as "The Son of Man." It views the Lord of glory as having come down to our level, entering into our conditions (sin excepted), subject to our circumstances, and living His life on the same plane as ours is lived. Yet, while He is here seen mingling with men, at every point He appears in sharp contrast from them. There was as great a difference between Christ as the Son of Man, and any one of us as a son of man, as there is now between Him as the Son of God, and any believer as a son of God. That difference was not merely relative, but absolute; not simply incidental, but essential; not one of degree, but of kind. "The Son of Man" predicts the uniqueness of His humanity. The humanity of our Lord was miraculously begotten, it was intrinsically holy in its nature, and therefore, saw not corruption in death. As The Son of Man, He was born as none other ever was, He lived as none other did, and He died as none other ever could.

The humanity of Christ, like everything else connected with His peerless person, needs to be discussed with profound reverence and care. Speculation concerning it is profane. Rash conjectures about it must not be allowed for a moment. All that we can know about it is what has been revealed in the Scriptures. Had some of our theologians adhered more rigidly to what the Holy Spirit has said on the subject, had they exercised more care in "holding fast the form of sound words," much that has been so dishonoring to our Lord had never been written. The person of the God-

Man is not presented to our view for intellectual analysis, but for the worship of our hearts. It is not without good reason that we have been expressly warned, "great is the Mystery of Godliness. God was manifest in flesh" (1 Tim. 3:16).

As we prayerfully examine the written word it will be found that Divine care has been taken to guard the perfections of our Lord's humanity, and to bring out its holy character. This appears not only in connection with the more direct references to His person, but also in the types and prophecies of the Old Testament. The "lamb," which portrayed Him as the appointed Sacrifice for sin, must be "without spot and blemish," and the very houses wherein the lamb was eaten, must have all leaven (emblem of evil) carefully excluded from them. The "manna," which spoke of Christ as the Food for God's people, is described as being "white" in color (Ex. 16:31). The Meal offering, which directly pointed to the Humanity of Christ, was to be only of "fine flour" (Lev. 2:1), that is, flour without any grit or unevenness; moreover, it was to be presented to the Lord accompanied with "oil" and "frankincense," which were emblems of the Holy Spirit, and the fragrance of Christ's person. Joseph, the most striking of all the personal types of the Lord Jesus, was, we are told, "A goodly person, and well favored" (Gen. 39:6).

This same feature is noticeable in the prophecies which referred to the humanity of the Coming One. It was a "virgin" in whose womb He should be conceived (Is. 7:14). As the Incarnate One, God spake of Him thus: "Behold My Servant, whom I uphold; Mine Elect, in whom My soul delighteth; I have put My Spirit upon Him" (Is. 42:1). Touching the personal excellencies of the Son of Man, the Spirit of prophecy exclaimed, "Thou art fairer than the children of men: grace is poured into Thy lips: therefore God hath blessed Thee for ever" (Ps. 45:2). Concerning the Sinlessness of Him who was cut off out of the land of the living, it was affirmed, "He hath done no violence, neither was any deceit found in His mouth" (Is. 53:9). Looking forward to the time when His humanity should pass through death without corruption, it was said, "His

leaf also shall not wither" (or, "fade," margin), Psalm 1:3—contrast with this, "We all do fade as a leaf" (Is. 64:6).

Coming now to the New Testament, we may observe how carefully God has distinguished the Man Christ Jesus from all other men. In 1 Timothy 3:16 we read, "Great is the mystery of godliness: God was manifest in the flesh." It is remarkable that in the Greek there is no definite article here: what the Holy Spirit really says is, "God was manifest in flesh." Manifest in "flesh" He was, but not in the flesh, for that would point to fallen human nature, shared by all the depraved descendants of Adam. Not in the flesh, but in flesh, sinless and holy flesh, was God "manifest." O the marvelous minute accuracy of Scripture! In like manner we read again concerning the humanity of Christ, "What the law could not do in that it was weak through the flesh, God sending His own Son in the likeness of sin's flesh (Greek)," Romans 8:3. The spotless and perfect humanity of the Savior was not sinful like ours, but only after its "likeness" or outward form. As Hebrews 7:26 declares He was "holy, harmless, undefiled, separate from sinners." Separate from sinners He was, both in the perfect life He lived here. He "knew no sin" (2 Cor. 5:21); He "did not sin" (1 Pet. 2:22); He was "without sin" (Heb. 4:15); therefore could He say, "The prince of this world (Satan) cometh and hath nothing in Me" (John 14:30).

In keeping with the theme of Luke's Gospel, it is here we have the fullest particulars concerning the miraculous birth of the Lord Jesus. Here we read, "In the sixth month (how significant is this number here, for six is the number of man) the angel Gabriel was sent from God unto a city of Galilee, called Nazareth, To a virgin espoused to a man whose name was Joseph, of the house of David; and the virgin's name was Mary" (Luke 1:26, 27). Twice over is it here recorded that Mary was a "virgin." Continuing, we read, "And the angel came in unto her, and said, Hail, thou art highly favored, the Lord is with thee: blessed art thou among women." This troubled Mary, for she wondered at this strange salutation. The angel continued, "Fear not, Mary, for thou hast found favor with God. And, behold, thou shalt conceive in thy womb, and bring forth a son, and shalt call His name Jesus." In reply, Mary asked, "How shall this be, seeing I know not a man?" And the angel answered, "The Holy Spirit shall come upon thee, and the power of the Highest shall overshadow thee: therefore also that holy thing which shall be born of thee shall be called the Son of God" (Luke 1:35).

The coming of the Holy Spirit "upon" a person is always, in Scripture, to effect a supernatural, a Divine work. The promise of the angel to Mary that the power of the Highest should "overshadow" her, suggests a double thought: she should be protected by God Himself, and how this promise was fulfilled Matthew 1:19, 20 informs us; while it is also a warning that the modus operandi of this miracle is hidden from us. The words of the angel to Mary "that holy thing which shall be born of thee," have been a sore puzzle to the commentators. Yet the meaning of this expression is very simple. It refers not, concretely, to our Lord's person, but instead, abstractly, to His humanity. It calls attention to the uniqueness of His humanity. It is in pointed contrast from ours. Put these words of Luke 1:35 over against another expression in Isaiah 64:6 and their meaning will be clear—"We are all as an unclean thing." Our human nature, looked at abstractly, (that is, apart from its personnel acts) is, essentially, "unclean," whereas that which the Son of God took unto Himself, when He became incarnate, was incapable of sinning (which is merely a negative affirmation), but it was inherently and positively "holy." Therein the humanity of Christ differed from that of Adam. Adam, in his unfallen state, was merely innocent (a negative quality again), but Christ was holy. Perhaps it may be well for us to offer a few remarks at this point concerning the Savior's "temptation."

We are frequently hearing of preachers making the statement that our Lord could have yielded to the solicitations of Satan, and that to affirm He could not is to rob the account of His conflict with the Devil of all meaning. But this is not only a mistake, it is a serious error. It dishonors the person of our blessed Lord. It denies His impeccability. It impeaches His own declaration that Satan had "nothing" in Him—nothing to which he could appeal. If there had been a possibility of the Savior yielding to the Devil that season in the wilderness, then for forty days the salvation of all God's elect (to say nothing of the outworking of God's eternal purpose) was in jeopardy; and surely that is unthinkable. But, it is asked, If there was no possibility of Christ yielding, wherein lay the force of the Temptation? If He could not sin, was it not a meaningless performance to allow Satan to tempt Christ at all? Such questions only betray the deplorable ignorance of those who ask them.

It ought to be well understood that the word "tempt" has a double significance, a primary and secondary meaning, and it is the application of the secondary meaning of the term as it is used in Matthew 4 and the parallel passages, which had led so many into error on this point. The word "tempt" literally means "to stretch out" so as to try the strength of anything. It comes from the Latin word "*tendo*"—to stretch. Our English word attempt, meaning to try, brings out its significance. "Tempt," then, primarily signifies "to try, test, put to the proof." It is only in its secondary meaning that it has come to signify "to solicit to evil." In Genesis 22:1 we read, "And it came to pass after these things, that God did tempt Abraham." But God did not solicit Abraham to evil, for, "God cannot be tempted with evil, neither tempteth He (in this sense) any man" (James 1:13). So, too, we read, "Then was Jesus led up of the Spirit into the wilderness to be tempted of the Devil" (Matt. 4:1). The purpose of this Temptation was not to discover whether or not the Savior would yield to Satan, but to demonstrate that He could not. Its design was to display His impeccability, to show forth the fact that there was "nothing" in Him to which Satan could appeal. It was in order that Christ might be tried and proven: just as the more you crush a rose, the more its fragrance is evidenced, so the assaults of the Devil upon the God-Man only served the more to bring out His perfections, and thus reveal Him as fully qualified to be the Savior of sinners.

That the Savior could not sin, does not rob the Temptation of its meaning, it only helps us discern its true meaning. It is because He was the Holy One of God that He felt the force of Satan's fiery darts as no sinful man ever could. It is impossible to find an analogy in the human realm for the Lord Jesus was absolutely unique. But let us attempt to illustrate the principle which is here involved. Is it true that in proportion as a man is weak morally that he feels the force of a temptation? Surely not. It is the man who is strong morally that feels the force of it. A man who is weakened in his moral fiber by sin, is weakened in his sensitiveness in the presence of temptation. Why does the young believer ask, "How is it that since I became a Christian I am tempted to do wrong a hundred times more than I was formerly?" The correct answer is, he is not; but the life of Christ within him has made him keener, quicker, more sensitive to the force of temptation. The illustration fails, we know; but seek to elevate the principle to an infinite height, and apply it to Christ, and then instead of saying that because He had no sin and could not sin His temptation, therefore, was meaningless, you will perhaps discover a far deeper meaning in it, and appreciate as never before the force of the words, "He Himself hath suffered, being tempted" (Heb. 2:18). Should it be asked further: But does not this rob the Savior of the capacity to sympathize with me when I am tempted? The answer is, A thousand times No! But it is to be feared that this last question is really an evasion. Does not the questioner, deep down in his heart, really mean, Can Christ sympathize with me when I yield to temptation? The question has only to be stated thus to answer it. Being holy, Christ never sympathizes with sin or sinning. Here then is the vital difference: when Christ was tempted He "suffered," but when we are drawn away by temptation we enjoy it. If, however, we seek grace to sustain us while we are under temptation, and are not drawn away by it, then shall we suffer too, but then we also have a merciful and faithful High Priest who is able, not only to sympathize with us but to, "succor them that are tempted" (Heb. 2:18). Our digression has been rather a lengthy one,

but necessary, perhaps, in a consideration of the Humanity of Christ, one postulate of which is His impeccability.

As previously stated, Luke's Gospel is wider in its range than either of the two which precede it, in both of which Christ is viewed in connection with Israel. But here there are no national limitations. The "Son of David" of the first Gospel, widens out into the "Son of Man" in the third Gospel. As "Son of Man" He is the Catholic Man. He is linked with, though separated from, the whole human race. Luke's Gospel, therefore, is in a special sense the Gentile Gospel, as Matthew's is the Jewish Gospel. It is not surprising to find, then, that the writer of it was himself, in all probability, a Gentile—the only one in all the Bible. It is generally conceded by scholars that Luke is an abbreviation of the Latin "Lucanus" or "Lucius." His name is twice found in the Pauline Epistles in a list of Gentile names, see 2 Timothy 4:10-12 and Philemon 24. It is also noteworthy that this third Gospel is addressed, not to a Jew, but to a Gentile, by name "Theophilus," which means "Beloved of God." It is in this Gentile Gospel, and nowhere else, that Christ is presented as the good "Samaritan." Obviously, this would have been quite out of place in Matthew's Gospel, but how thoroughly accordant is it here! So, too, it is only here that we are told that "Jerusalem shall be trodden down of the Gentiles, until the times of the Gentiles be fulfilled" (Luke 21:24). And again, it is in this Gospel that, in describing End-time conditions, we learn that Christ spake to His disciples this parable: "Behold the fig tree, and all the trees" (21:29). Matthew mentions the former (24:32), as the "fig tree" is the well known symbol of Israel, but Luke, alone, adds "and all the trees," thus bringing out the international scope of his Gospel. Other illustrations of this same feature will be discovered by the careful student.

Returning to the central theme of this Gospel, we may observe that "the Son of Man" links Christ with the earth. It is the title by which Christ most frequently referred to Himself. Not once did any one else ever address Him by this name. The first occurrence of this title is found in the Old Testament, in the 8th Psalm, where we read, "What is man that Thou art mindful of Him? and the Son of Man that Thou visitest him? For Thou hast made him a little lower than the angels, and hast crowned him with glory and honor. Thou madest him to have dominion over the works of Thy hands; Thou hast put all things under his feet" (vv. 4-6). The immediate reference is to Adam, in his unfallen condition, and refers to his Headship over all the lower orders of creation. It speaks of earthly dominion, for "Have dominion over the fish of the sea, and over the fowl of the air, and over every living thing that moveth upon the earth" (Gen. 1:28), is what God said to our first parent in the day that he was created. But from this position of "dominion" Adam fell, and it was (among other things, to recover the dominion that Adam had lost, that our Lord became incarnate. Thus the eighth Psalm, as is evident from its quotation in Hebrews 2, finds its ultimate fulfillment in "the Second Man." But, before this Second Man could be "crowned with glory and honor," He must first humble Himself and pass through the portals of death. Thus the "Son of Man" title speaks first of humiliation, and ultimately of dominion and glory.

"The Son of Man" occurs 88 times in the New Testament (which is a very significant number, for 8 signifies a new beginning, and it is by the Second Man the beginning of the new "Dominion" will be established), and it is deeply interesting and instructive to trace out the connections in which it occurs. It is found for the first time in the New Testament in Matthew 8:20, where the Savior says, "The foxes have holes, and the birds of the air have nests; but the Son of Man hath not where to lay His head." Here attention is called to the depths of humiliation into which the Beloved of the Father had entered: the One who shall yet have complete dominion over all the earth, when here before, was but a homeless Stranger. The second occurrence of this title helps to define its scope—"The Son of Man hath power on earth to forgive sins" (Matt. 9:6). The last time it is found in Matthew's Gospel is in 26:64—"Hereafter shall ye see

the Son of Man sitting on the right hand of power, and coming in the clouds of heaven." Here we are carried forward to the time when the Lord Jesus shall return to these scenes, not in weakness and humiliation, but in power and glory. In John 3:13 there is a statement made which proves that the Son of Man was God as well, "And no man hath ascended up to Heaven, but He that came down from Heaven, even the Son of Man which is in Heaven." Nowhere in the Epistles (save in Heb. 2 where Ps. 8 is quoted) is this title found, for the Church has a heavenly calling and destiny, and is linked to the Son of God in Heaven, and not to the Son of Man as He is related to the earth. The last time this title occurs in Scripture is in Revelation 14:14, where we read, "And I looked, and behold a white cloud, and upon the cloud One sat like unto the Son of Man, having on His head a golden crown." What a contrast is this from the first mention of this title in the New Testament where we read of Him not having where to lay "His head"!

It is now high time for us to turn from these generalizations and consider some features of Luke's Gospel in more detail. To begin with, we may observe, as others have noticed, how distinctive and characteristic is the Preface to this third Gospel: "For as much as many have taken in hand to set forth in order a declaration of those things which are most surely believed among us, even as they delivered them unto us, which from the beginning were eyewitnesses, and ministers of the Word: It seemed good to me also, having had perfect understanding of all things from the very first to write unto thee, in order, most excellent Theophilus, that thou mightest know the certainty of those things, wherein thou hast been instructed" (1:1-4).

What a contrast is this from what we have at the commencement of the other Gospels. Here more pronouncedly than elsewhere, we see the human element in the communication of God's revelation to us. The human instrument is brought plainly before us. Luke speaks of his personal knowledge of that of which he is about to treat. He refers to what others had done before him in this direction, but feels the need of a more orderly and full setting forth of those things which were most surely believed. But apparently he was quite unconscious of the fact, as he sat down to write to his friend Theophilus, that he was being "moved" (better, "borne along") by the Holy Spirit, or that he was about to communicate that which should be of lasting value to the whole Church of God. Instead, the Divine Inspirer is hidden here, and only the human penman is seen. Strikingly appropriate is this in the Gospel which treats not of the official glories of Christ, nor of His Deity, but of His Manhood. There is a marvelous analogy between the written Word of God and the Incarnate Word, the details of which are capable of being extended indefinitely. Just as Christ was the God-Man, Divine yet human, so the Holy Scriptures though given "by inspiration of God" were, nevertheless, communicated through human channels; but, just as Christ in becoming Man did so without being contaminated by sin, so God's revelation has come to us through human medium without being defiled by any of their imperfections. Moreover, just as it is here in Luke's Gospel that our Lord's humanity is brought so prominently before us, so it is here that the human element in the giving of the Holy Scriptures is most plainly to be seen.

There are many other things of interest and importance to be found in this first chapter of Luke which we cannot now consider in detail, but we would point out, in passing, how the human element prevails throughout. We may notice, for instance, how that here God is seen on more intimate terms with those whom He addresses than in Matthew 1. There, when communicating with Joseph, He did so in "dreams," but here, when sending a message to Zacharias, it is by an angel, who speaks to the father of the Baptist face to face. Still more intimate is God's communication to Mary, for here the angel speaks not to the mother of our Lord in the temple, but more familiarly, in the home—an intimation of how near God was about to come to men in His marvelous grace. Again; far more is told us of Mary here than elsewhere, and Luke is the only one who records her song of joy which followed the great Annunciation, as he alone records the prophecy of Zacharias, uttered on the occasion of the naming of his illustrious son. Thus, the emotions of the human heart are here manifested as they were expressed in song and praise.

The opening verses of Luke 2 are equally characteristic and distinctive. Here we are told, "And it came to pass in those days, that there went out a decree from Caesar Augustus, that all the world should be taxed. And this taxing was first made when Cyrenius was governor of Syria. And all went to be taxed, every one into his own city. And Joseph also went up from Galilee, out of the city of Nazareth, into Judea, unto the city of David, which is called Bethlehem; because he was of the house and lineage of David: to be taxed with Mary his espoused wife" (Luke 2:1-5). We shall look in vain for anything like this in the other Gospels. Here the Lord of glory is contemplated not as the One who had come to reign, but instead, as One who had descended to the level of other men, as One whose mother and legal father were subject to the common taxation. This would have been altogether out of keeping with the theme and scope of Matthew's Gospel, and a point of no interest in Mark, but how thoroughly in accord with the character of Luke's Gospel!

"And she brought forth her firstborn son, and wrapped Him in swaddling clothes, and laid Him in a manger; because there was no room for them in the inn" (Luke 2:7). Luke is the only one of the four evangelists who tells us of this—a point of touching interest concerning His humanity, and one that is worthy of our reverent contemplation. Why was it the Father suffered His blessed Son, now incarnate, to be born in a stable? Why were the cattle of the field His first companions? What spiritual lessons are we intended to learn from His being placed in a manger? Weighty questions are these admitting, perhaps, of at least a sevenfold answer.

a. He was laid in a manger because there was no room in the inn. How solemnly this brings out the world's estimate of the Christ of God. There was no appreciation of His amazing condescension. He was not wanted. It is so still. There is no room for Him in the schools, in society, in the business world, among the great throngs of pleasure seekers, in the political realm, in the newspapers, nor in many of the churches. It is only history repeating itself. All that the world gave the Savior, was a stable for His cradle, a cross on which to die, and a borrowed grave to receive His murdered body.

b. He was laid in a manger to demonstrate the extent of His poverty. "For ye know the grace of our Lord Jesus Christ, that, though He was rich, yet for your sakes He became poor, that ye through His poverty might be rich" (2 Cor. 8:9). How "poor" He became, was thus manifested at the beginning. The One who, afterwards, had not where to lay His head, who had to ask for a penny when He would reply to His critics about the question of tribute, and who had to use another man's house when instituting the Holy Supper, was, from the first, a homeless Stranger here. And the "manger" was the earliest evidence of this.

c. He was laid in a manger in order to be Accessible to all. Had He been in a palace, or in some room in the Temple, few could have reached Him without the formality of first gaining permission from those who would have been in attendance at such places. But none would have any difficulty in obtaining access to a stable; there He would be within easy reach of poor and rich alike. Thus, from the beginning, He was easy to approach. No intermediaries had first to be passed in order to reach Him. No priest had to be interviewed before entree could be obtained to His presence. Thus it was then; and so it is now, thank God.

d. He was laid in a manger so as to foreshadow the Character of those among whom He had come. The stable was the place for beasts of the field, and it was into their midst the newly-born Savior came. And how well did they symbolize the moral character of men! The beasts of the field are devoid of any spiritual life, and so have no knowledge of God. Such, too, was the condition of both Jews and Gentiles. And how beast-like in character were those into whose midst the Savior came: stupid and stubborn as the ass or mule, cunning and cruel as the fox, groveling and filthy as the swine, and ever thirsting for His blood as the more savage of the animals. Fittingly, then, was He placed amid the beasts of the field at His birth.

e. He was laid in a manger to show His contempt for Worldly riches and pomp. We had thought it more fitting for the Christ of God to be born in a palace, and laid in a cradle of gold, lined with costly silks. Ah, but as He Himself reminds us in this same Gospel, "that which is highly esteemed among men, is abomination in the sight of God" (Luke 16:15). And what an exemplification of this truth was given when the infant Savior was placed, not in a cradle of gold but, in an humble manger.

f. He was laid in a manger to mark His identification with human suffering and wretchedness. The One born was "The Son of Man." He had left the heights of Heaven's glory and had descended to our level, and here we behold Him entering the human lot at its lowest point. Adam was first placed in a garden, surrounded by the exquisite beauties of Nature as it left the hands of the Creator. But sin had come in, and with sin all its sad consequences of suffering and wretchedness. Therefore, does the One who had come here to recover and restore what the first man lost, appear first, in surroundings which spoke of abject need and wretchedness; just as a little later we find Him taken down into Egypt, in order that God might call His Son from the same place as where His people Israel commenced their national history in misery and wretchedness. Thus did the Man of Sorrows identify Himself with human suffering.

g. He was laid in a manger because such was the place of Sacrifice. The manger was the place where vegetable life was sacrificed to sustain animal life. Fitting place was this, then, for Him who had come to be the great Sacrifice, laying down His life for His people, that we might through His death be made alive. Remarkably suggestive, therefore, and full of emblematic design, was the place appointed by God to receive the infant body of the incarnate Savior.

It is only in Luke's Gospel that we read of the shepherds who kept watch over their flocks by night, and to whom the angel of the Lord appeared, saying, "Fear not: for, behold, I bring you good tidings of great joy, which shall be to all people. For unto you is born this day in the city of David a Savior, which is Christ the Lord" (2:10, 11). Note that the One born is here spoken of not as "The King of the Jews," but as "a Savior, which is Christ the Lord"—titles which reach out beyond the confines of Israel, and take in the Gentiles too.

Again, it is only here in Luke that we behold the Savior as a Boy of twelve going up to Jerusalem, and being found in the Temple "sitting in the midst of the doctors, both hearing them, and asking them questions" (2:46). How intensely human is this! Yet side by side with it there is a strong hint given that he was more than human, for we read, "And all that heard Him were astonished at His understanding and answers." So, too, it is only here that we are told, "And He went down with them (His parents), and was subject unto them" (2:51). How this brings out the excellencies of His humanity, perfectly discharging the responsibilities of every relationship which He sustained to men as well as to God! And how strikingly appropriate is the closing verse of this chapter—"And Jesus increased in wisdom and stature and in favor with God and man"! There is nothing like this in any of the other Gospels; but Luke's would have been incomplete without it. What proofs are these that Luke, as the others, was guided by the Spirit of God in the selection of his materials!

Luke 3 opens by presenting to us the person and mission of John the Baptist. Matthew and Mark have both referred to this, but Luke adds to the picture his own characteristic lines. Only here do we read that it was "in the fifteenth year of the reign of Tiberius Caesar, Pontius Pilate being governor of Judea, and Herod being tetrarch of Galilee, and his brother Philip tetrarch of Iturea and of the region of Trachonitis, and Lysanias the tetrarch of Abilena, Annas and Caiaphas being the high priests, the Word of God came unto John, the son of Zacharias in the wilderness" (3:1, 2)—points of historic interest in connection with these human relationships. So, too, it is only here that we read of other human relationships of "the people" who asked John "What shall we do?" (3:10), of the "publicans" who asked him the same question (3:12), and of "the soldiers" is also to be noted, that only here is the Lord Jesus directly linked with "all the people" when He was baptized, for we read, "Now when all the people were baptized, it came to pass that Jesus also being baptized" (3:21), thus showing Him as the One who had come down to the common level. And again, it is only here we are told of the age of the Savior when He entered upon His public ministry (3:23), this being another point of interest in connection with His humanity.

Luke 3 closes with a record of the Genealogy of the Son of Man, and noticeable are the differences between what we have here, and what is found in Matthew 1. There, it is the royal genealogy of the Son of David, here it is His strictly personal genealogy. There, it is His line of descent through Joseph which is given, here it is His ancestry through Mary. There, His genealogy is traced forwards from Abraham, here it is followed backwards to Adam. This is very striking, and brings out in an unmistakable manner the respective character and scope of each Gospel. Matthew is showing Christ's relation to Israel, and therefore he goes back no farther than to Abraham, the father of the Jewish people; but here, it is His connection with the human race that is before us, and hence his genealogy in Luke is traced right back to Adam, the father of the human family. But notice, particularly, that at the close it is said, "Adam was the son of God" (3:38). Thus the humanity of Christ is here traced not merely back to Adam, but through Adam directly to God Himself. How marvelously this agrees with the words of the Lord Jesus as found in Heb. 10:5—"A body hast Thou prepared Me"!

Luke 4 opens by telling us "And Jesus being full of the Holy Spirit returned from Jordan, and was led by the Spirit into the wilderness, being tempted forty days of the Devil." Only here do we learn that the Savior was "full of the Holy Spirit" as He returned from the Jordan. Then follows the account of the Temptation. It will be observed by the close student that between Matthew and Luke there is a difference in the order of mention of Satan's three attacks upon Christ. In Matthew the order is, first the asking of the Lord Jesus to turn the stones into bread, second the bidding Him cast Himself down from the pinnacle of the Temple, and third the offer to Him of all the kingdoms of this world on the condition of worshipping Satan. But here in Luke we have first the request to make the stones into bread, second the offer of the kingdoms of the world, and third the challenge for Him to cast Himself down from the pinnacle of the temple. The reason for this variation is not hard to find. In Matthew, the order is arranged climactically, so as to make Rulership over all the kingdoms of the world the final bait which the Devil dangled before the Son of David. But in Luke we have, no doubt, the chronological order, the order in which they actually occurred, and these correspond with the order of temptation of the first man and his wife in Eden, where the appeal was made, as here in Luke, to the lust of the flesh, the lust of the eyes, and the pride of life—see 1 John 2:16 and compare Genesis 3:6. We may also note that Luke is the only one to tell us that "Jesus returned in the power of the Spirit into Galilee" (4:14), showing that the old Serpent had utterly failed to disturb the perfect fellowship which existed between the incarnate Son of God upon earth and His Father in Heaven. After the horrible conflict was over, the Lord Jesus returned to Galilee in the unabated "power of the Spirit."

Following the account of the Temptation, Luke next tells us, "And He came to Nazareth, where He had been brought up: and, as His custom was, He went into the synagogue on the Sabbath day, and stood up for to read" (4:16). Luke again, is the only one that mentions this, it being another point of interest in connection with our Lord's Manhood, informing us, as it does, of the place where He had been "brought up," and showing us how He had there been wont to occupy Himself on each Sabbath day. In the words that follow there is a small line in the picture which is very significant and suggestive: "And there was delivered unto Him the book of the prophet Isaiah. And when He had opened the book, He found the place where it was written, The Spirit of the Lord is upon Me" etc. The book, be it noted, did not open magically at the page He desired to read from, but, like any other, the Son of Man turned the pages until He had "found the place" required!

Others have called attention to another thing which occurred on this occasion and which was profoundly suggestive. There in the synagogue at Nazareth the Savior read from the opening words of Isaiah 61, and it will be found by comparing the record of the prophet with the Lord's reading as recorded in Luke 4, that He stopped at a most significant point. Isaiah says the Spirit of the Lord was upon Him to "preach good tidings unto the meek to proclaim the acceptable year of the Lord, and the day of vengeance of our God"; but in Luke 4 we find the Savior read that the Spirit of the Lord was upon Him to "preach" the gospel to the poor to proclaim the acceptable year of the Lord," and there He stopped, for immediately following we are told, "He closed the book." He ceased His reading from Isaiah in the midst of a sentence; He concluded at a comma! Why was it that He did not complete the verse, and add, "The Day of Vengeance of our God"? The answer is, Because such did not fall within the scope of His mission at His first Advent. The "Day of Vengeance" is yet future. The Lord Jesus was setting us an example of "rightly dividing the Word of Truth" (2 Tim. 2:15). As the Savior closed the book that day in Nazareth's synagogue, He declared, "This day is this Scripture fulfilled in your ears" (Luke 4:21), and that which was then "fulfilled" was the portion He had read to them from Isaiah 61:1, 2; the remainder of Isaiah 61:2 was not then fulfilled, for it has to do with that which is yet future: hence, He read it not. It should be added that the next time we find the Lord Jesus with a "book" in His hands is in Revelation 5:7, and there we read of Him opening it—see Revelation 6:1 etc.—and the striking thing is that when the Lord opens that book the Day of God's Vengeance, so long delayed, then commences! These points have been brought out by others before us, but we have not seen it intimated that Luke is the only one of the four Evangelists to refer to this incident. Not only was there a dispensational reason why the Lord Jesus read not the whole of Isaiah 61:2 in the Nazareth synagogue that day, but it was peculiarly fitting that the one whose happy task it was to present the human perfections of Christ, should note our Lord's silence concerning the Day of God "vengeance"!

It is beyond our present purpose to attempt even a running exposition of each chapter of this third Evangel. We are not seeking to be exhaustive, but simply suggestive, calling attention to some of the more outstanding features of Luke's Gospel. There is so much here that is not found in the other three Gospels, that to examine in detail every distinctive feature would call for a large volume. As this would defeat our object, we shall be content to single out a few things here and there.

Luke 7 records the raising of the widow of Nain's son. None of the others mention this. There are several lines in this picture which serve to bring out that which is central in Luke's Gospel, namely, human need, human relationships, and human sympathies. Thus we may note that the one here raised by Christ was "the only son of his mother" and that she was a "widow"; that when the Lord saw her "weep not"; that before He commanded the dead to "Arise," He first "came and touched the bier," and that after the dead one was restored to life, the Savior "delivered him to his mother."

In Luke 8:2, 3 we are told, "And certain women which had been healed of evil spirits and infirmities, Mary called Magdalene, out of whom went seven demons, and Joanna the wife of Chuza, Herod's steward, and Susanna, and many others, which ministered unto Him of their substance." How this shows us the place which our blessed Lord had taken as the Son of Man! Nothing like this is found in the other Gospels, and that for a very good reason. It would have been beneath the dignity of the King of the Jews to be "ministered unto" with the substance of women; it would be out of place in Mark's Gospel, for there the Holy Spirit shows us that the Servant must look to God only for the

supply of His every need; while John, of course, would not mention it, for he sets forth the Divine glories of our Lord. But it is perfectly appropriate, and illuminative too, in the Gospel which treats of Christ's humanity.

Above we have noted that Luke informs us the one raised from death by Christ at Nain was a widow's "only son," and we may now notice two other examples from this Gospel where the same feature is mentioned. The first is in connection with the daughter of Jairus. Matthew says, "While He spake these things unto them, behold, there came a certain ruler, and worshipped Him saying, My daughter is even now dead" (9:18). Mark tells us, "Behold, there cometh one of the rulers of the synagogue, Jairus by name; and when he saw Him, saying, My little daughter lieth at the point of death" (5:22, 23). But Luke gives additional information, "And, behold, there came a man named Jairus, and he was a ruler of the synagogue: and he fell down at Jesus' feet, and besought Him that He would come into his house: for he had one only daughter, about twelve years of age, and she lay a dying" (8:41, 42). The second example is in connection with the demon possessed child, whose father sought relief at the hands of Christ's disciples. Matthew says, "And when they were come to the multitude, there came to Him a certain man, kneeling down to Him, and saying, Lord, have mercy on my son: for he is lunatic, and sore vexed: for oft-times he falleth into the fire, and oft into the water. And I brought him to Thy disciples, and they could not cure him" (17:14-16). But Luke tells us, "And, behold, a man of the company cried out, saying, Master, I beseech Thee, look upon my son: for he is mine only child. And, lo, a spirit taketh him, and he suddenly crieth out; and it teareth him that he foameth again; and bruising him hardly departeth from him. And I besought Thy disciples to cast him out; and they could not" (9:38-40). Thus in each case Luke calls attention to the fact that it was an "only child" that was healed, thereby appealing to human sympathies.

Luke is the only one who records the exquisite story of the Good Samaritan ministering to the wounded traveler, and there are many lines in the picture of this incident which bring out, strikingly, the distinctive character of this third Gospel. First, we are shown the traveler himself falling among thieves, who strip him of his raiment, wound him, and depart, leaving him half dead. How this brings out the lawlessness, the avarice, the brutality, and the heartlessness of fallen human nature! Next, we hear of the priest who saw the pitiable state of the wounded traveller, lying helpless by the road, yet did he "pass by on the other side." The priest was followed by a Levite who, though he "came and looked on" on the poor man that was in such sore need of help, also "passed by on the other side." Thus we behold the selfishness, the callousness, the cruel indifference of even religious men toward one who had such a claim upon their sympathies. In blessed contrast from these, we are shown the grace of the Savior who, under the figure of a "Samaritan," is here seen moved "with compassion" as He came to where the poor traveler lay. Instead of passing by on the other side, He goes to him, binds up his wounds, sets him on His own beast, and brings him to an inn, where full provision is made for him. So does this incident, summarize as it were, the scope of this entire Gospel, by showing the infinite contrast that existed between the perfect Son of Man and the fallen and depraved sons of men.

In Luke 11 we read of the unclean spirit who goes out of a man, and later, returns to his house, to find it "swept and garnished." Then, we are told, this unclean spirit takes with him seven other spirits more wicked than himself, and they "enter in and dwell there; and the last state of that man is worse than the first" (11:24-26). Matthew also refers to this in 12:43-45 in almost identical language, but it is very significant to observe that Luke omits a sentence with which Matthew closes his narrative. There in Matthew 12 we find the Lord applied the incident to the Jewish nation by saying, "Even so shall it be also unto this wicked generation" (or "race"). This was the dispensational application, which limits it to Israel. But appropriately does Luke omit these qualifying words, for in his Gospel this incident has a wider application, a moral application, representing the condition of a more extensive class, namely, those who hear the Gospel, and reform, but who are never regenerated. Such may clean up their houses, but though they are "swept and garnished," yet they are still empty—the Spirit of God does not indwell them! They are like the foolish virgins, who, though they mingled with the wise virgins and carried the lamp of public profession, yet had they no oil (emblem of the Holy Spirit) in their vessels. Such cases of reformation though at first they appear to be genuine instances of regeneration, ultimately prove to be but counterfeits, and at the last their condition is worse than it was at the beginning—they have been deceived by their own treacherous hearts and deluded and blinded by Satan, and in consequence, are far harder to reach with the Truth of God.

In Luke 12 we have an incident recorded which is similar in principle to Luke's notice of our Lord's omission of the closing words of Isaiah 61:2 when reading from this scripture in the synagogue at Nazareth. Here we find that a certain man came to Christ and said, "Master, speak to my brother, that he divide the inheritance with me" (12:13). But the Master refused to grant this request and said, "Man, who made Me a judge or a divider over you?" The reason why Luke is the only one to mention this is easily seen. It would have been incongruous for Matthew to have referred to an incident wherein the Lord Jesus declined to occupy the place of authority and act as the administrator, of an inheritance; as it would have been equally out of place for Mark to have noticed this case where one should have asked the Servant to officiate as "judge and divider." But it is fitting it should have found a place in this Third Gospel, for the words of Christ on this occasion, "Who made Me a judge or a divider over you?" only show us, once more, the lowly place which He had taken as "The Son of Man."

In Luke 14 there is recorded a parable which is found nowhere else: "And He put forth a parable to those which were bidden, when He marked how they chose out the chief rooms; saying unto them, When thou art bidden of any man to a wedding, sit not down in the highest room, lest a more honorable man than thou be bidden of him;

And he that bade thee and him come and say to thee, Give this man place; and thou begin with shame to take the lowest room. But when thou art bidden, go and sit down in the lowest room; that when he that bade thee cometh, he may say unto thee, Friend, go up higher: then shalt thou have worship (or "glory") in the presence of them that sit at meat with thee. For whosoever exalteth himself shall be abased; and he that humbleth himself shall be exalted" (vv. 7-11). How thoroughly is this parable in accord with the character and scope of Luke's Gospel! First, it ministers a much needed rebuke upon the general tendency of fallen human nature to seek out the best places and aim at positions of honor and glory. Secondly, it inculcates the spirit of meekness and modesty, admonishing us to take the lowly place. And thirdly, it is an obvious shadowing forth of that which the Lord of glory had done Himself, leaving as He had, the position of dignity and glory in Heaven, and taking the "lowest" place of all down here.

In accordance with the fact that Luke's Gospel is the third book of the New Testament (the number which stands for manifestation), we may notice that in the fifteenth chapter we have a parable which reveals to us the Three Persons of the Godhead, each actively engaged in the salvation of a sinner. It is very striking that it is one parable in three parts which, taken together, makes fully manifest the One true God in the Person of the Father, the Son, and the Holy Spirit.

Luke 15 may well be entitled, God seeking and saving the lost. In the third part of this parable, which deals with the "prodigal Son," we are shown the sinner actually coming into the presence of the Father, and there receiving a cordial welcome, being suitably clothed, and given a place at His table in happy fellowship. In what precedes we learn of that which was necessary on the part of God before the sinner could thus be reconciled. The second part of the parable brings before us the work of the Holy Spirit, going after the one dead in sins and illuminating him, and this under the figure of a woman who, with a light in her hand (emblematic of the Lamp of God's Word),

seeks diligently till she finds that which was lost. Notice, particularly, that her work was inside the house, just as the Holy Spirit works within the sinner. In the first part of the parable we are shown that which preceded the present work of God's Spirit. The ministry of the Spirit is the complement to the Work of Christ, hence, at the beginning of the chapter, the Savior Himself is before us, under the figure of the Shepherd, who went forth to seek and to save the sheep that was lost. Thus, the first part of the parable tells of God's Work for us, as the second tells of God's work in us, the third part making known the blessed result and happy sequel. So, in this one parable in three parts, we have revealed the One God in the Three Persons of the Holy Trinity, fully manifested in the work of seeking and saving the lost.

In full accord with what has just been before us in Luke 15, though in marked and solemn contrast, we find that in the next chapter the Lord Jesus makes fully manifest the state of the lost after death. Nowhere else in the four Gospels do we find, as here, the lifting of the veil which separates and hides from us the condition of those who have passed into the next world. Here the Lord gives us a specimen case of the present torments of the lost, in the experiences of the "rich man" after death. We read "In hell he lift up his eyes, being in torments, and seeth Abraham afar off, and Lazarus in his bosom. And he cried and said, Father Abraham, have mercy on me, and send Lazarus that he may dip the tip of his finger in water, and cool my tongue; for I am tormented in this flame. But Abraham said, Son, remember that thou in thy lifetime receivest thy good things, and Lazarus evil things: but now he is comforted, and thou art tormented. And beside all this, between us and you there is a great gulf fixed: so that they which would pass from hence to you cannot; neither can they pass to us, that would come from thence" (vv. 23-26). Here we learn that the damned, even now, are in a place of suffering; that they are "in torments; "that the misery of their awful lot is accentuated by being enabled to "see" the happy portion of the redeemed; that there is, however, an impassible gulf fixed between the saved and the lost, which makes it impossible for the one to go to the other; that memory is still active in those that are in Hell, so that they are reminded of the opportunities wasted, while they were upon earth; that they cry for mercy and beg for water to allay their fiery sufferings, but that this is denied them. Unspeakably solemn is this, and a most pointed warning to all still upon earth to "flee from the wrath to come" and to take refuge in the only One who can deliver from it.

Passing on now to the nineteenth chapter we may observe how Luke there records something that is absent from the other Gospels. "And when He was come near, He beheld the city, and weep over it, Saying, If thou hadst known, which belong unto thy peace! but now they are hid from thine eyes" (vv. 41, 42). How this brings out the human sympathies of the Savior! As He looked upon Jerusalem, and foresaw the miseries which were shortly to be its portion, the Son of Man wept. He was no stoic, but One whose heart was full of compassion for the sufferers of earth.

In drawing to a close, we would notice seven features which are particularly prominent in this Gospel, and which are in striking accord with its particular theme and scope:—

1. The full description here given of fallen human nature.

Luke's is the Gospel of our Lord's Manhood, and, as He is the true Light shining amid the darkness, it is here also that the characteristics of our corrupt human nature are shown up as nowhere else. Luke's special design is to present the Lord Jesus as the Son of Man contrasted from the sons of men. Hence it is that the depravity, the impotency, the degradation and the spiritual deadness of all the members of Adam's fallen race is brought out here with such fullness and clearness. It is here, and here only, we read that, until the miracle-working power of God intervened, the mother of John the Baptist was barren— apt symbol of fallen human nature with its total absence of spiritual fruit; and that his father, though a priest, was filled with unbelief when God's messenger announced

to him the forth-coming miracle. It is only here that we read of all the world being "taxed" (Luke 2:1), which tells, in suggestive symbol, of the burdens imposed by Satan on his captive subjects. It is only here that we read that when Mary brought forth her Son, there was "no room for them in the inn," signifying the world's rejection of the Savior from the beginning. It is only here we are told that when the Lord Jesus came to Nazareth and read in the synagogue from the prophet Isaiah, adding a comment of His own, that "All they in the synagogue, when they heard these things, were filled with wrath, And rose up, and thrust Him out of the city, and led Him unto the brow of the hill whereon their city was built, that they might cast Him down headlong" (4:28, 29): thus did those who ought to have known Him the best, manifest the terrible enmity of the carnal mind against God and His Christ. It is only here that we read, "And it came to pass, when He was in a certain city, behold a man full of leprosy: who seeing Jesus fell on his face, and besought Him, saying Lord, if Thou wilt, Thou canst make me clean" (5:12). In the other Gospels reference is made to this same incident, but Luke alone tells us that the subject of this miracle was full of leprosy. "Leprosy" is the well known figure of sin, and it is only in Luke that man's total depravity is fully revealed. It is only in Luke that we hear of the disciples of Christ asking permission to call down fire from Heaven to consume those who received not the Savior (9:51-55). It is only here that Christ, in the well known parable of the Good Samaritan, portrays the abject condition of the natural man, under the figure of the one who, having fallen among thieves, had been stripped of his raiment, sorely wounded, and left by the wayside half dead. It is only here that we read of the Rich Fool who declared, "I will say to my soul, Soul, thou hast much goods laid up for many years; take thine ease, eat, drink, and be merry" (12:19), for such is the invariable tendency of the boastful human heart. So, too, it is only here that in Luke 15 the sinner is likened unto a lost sheep—an animal so senseless that once it is lost, it only continues to stray farther and farther away from the fold. It is only here that we find the Savior drawing that matchless picture of the Prodigal Son, who so accurately depicts the sinner away from God, having wasted his substance in riotous living, and who, reduced to want, finds nothing in the far country to feed upon, except the husks which the swine did eat. It is only here that we learn of the heartless indifference of the rich man who neglected the poor wretch that lay at his gate full of sores. It is only here that the self-righteousness of man is fully disclosed in the person of the Pharisee in the Temple (Luke 18). And so we might go on. But sufficient has been said to prove our statement at the head of this paragraph.

2. The manner in which Luke introduces his parables, etc.

In perfect accord with the character and scope of His Gospel, we find that Luke introduces most of his parables, also various incidents narrated by him, as well as certain portions of our Lord's teachings, in a way quite peculiar to himself. By comparing the parallel passages in the other Gospels, and by noting the words we now place in italics, this will be apparent to the reader.

In Luke 5:12, we are told, that "a man full of leprosy" came to Christ to be healed, whereas Matthew, when describing the same incident, merely says, "there came a leper" to Him (8:2). Again, in 8:27 we read, "When He went forth to land, there met Him out of the city, a certain man, which had demons a long time, and ware no clothes, neither abode in any house, but in the tombs"; whereas Matthew 8:28 reads, "And when He was come to the other side into the country of the Gergessenes, there met Him (not "two men," but) two possessed with demons coming out of the tombs" etc. Again, in 8:41 we read, "There came a man named Jairus, and he was a ruler of the synagogue: and he fell down at Jesus' feet," whereas Mark 5:22 says, "There cometh one of the rulers of the synagogue, Jairus by name; and when he saw Him, he fell at His feet." In Luke 9:57 we read, "And it came to pass, that, as they went in the way, a certain man said unto Him, Lord, I will follow Thee whithersoever Thou goest,"

whereas Matthew 8:19 reads, "And a certain scribe came, and said unto Him, Master, I will follow Thee whithersoever Thou goest." In Luke 9:62 we find that the Lord said, "No man (not "disciple," be it noted), having put his hand to the plough, and looking back, is fit for the kingdom of God." In 19:35 we read, "As He was come nigh unto Jericho, a certain blind man sat by the wayside begging," but in Mark 10:46 we are told, "As He went out of Jericho with His disciples and a great number of people, blinded Bartimaeus, the son of Timaeus, sat by the wayside begging."

Coming now to the parables, note the striking way in which they are introduced here: "And He spake also a parable unto them: No man putteth a piece of a new garment upon an old" etc. (5:36). "A certain man went down from Jerusalem to Jericho, and fell among thieves" etc. (10:30). "And He spake a parable unto them, saying, The ground of a certain rich man brought forth plentifully" etc. (12:16). "He spake also this parable: A certain man had a fig tree planted in his vineyard" etc. (13:6). "Then said He unto him, A certain man made a great supper" etc. (14:16). "And He spake this parable unto them, saying, What man of you, having a hundred sheep" etc. (15:3, 4). "And He said, A certain man had two sons" etc. (15:11). "And He said also unto His disciples, There was a certain rich man, which had a steward" etc. (16:1). "There was a certain rich man, which was clothed in purple and fine linen" etc. (16:19). "And He spake a parable to them to this end, that men (not "believers") ought always to pray, and not to faint" etc. (18:1). "Then began He to speak to the people of this parable; A certain man planted a vineyard" etc. (20:9). "And He spake also this parable unto certain which trusted in themselves that they were righteous, and despised others. Two men went up into the Temple to pray" etc. (18:9, 10). Thus we see how the human element is emphasized here.

3. The references to Christ as "The Son of Man."

It is only in this Gospel we read that the Savior said to the Pharisees, "The days will come, when ye shall desire to see one of the days of the Son of Man, and ye shall not see it" (17:22). It is only in this Gospel we find that the Savior put the question, "When the Son of Man cometh, shall He find faith on the earth?" (18:8). It is only in this Gospel we find that the Savior said to His followers, "Watch ye therefore, and pray always, that ye may be accounted worthy to escape all these things that shall come to pass, and to stand before the Son of Man" (21:36). And it is only in this Gospel we find that the Savior said to Judas in the garden, "Betrayest thou the Son of Man with a kiss?" (22:14).

It is, perhaps even more striking to notice that Luke records a number of instances where our Lord referred to Himself as "The Son of Man" where, in the parallel passages in the other Gospels this title is omitted. For example, in Matthew 16:21 we read, "From that time forth began Jesus to show unto His disciples, how that He must go unto Jerusalem, and suffer many things of the elders and chief priests and scribes, and be killed, and be raised again the third day;" whereas, in Luke 9:22 we learn that He said unto His disciples, "The Son of Man must suffer many things, and be rejected of the elders and chief priests and scribes, and be slain, and be raised the third day." Again; in Matthew 5:11 the Lord said to His disciples, "Blessed are ye, when men shall revile you, and persecute you, and shall say all manner of evil against you falsely, for My sake;" whereas, in the parallel passage in Luke we read, "Blessed are ye, when men shall hate you, and when they shall separate you from their company, and shall reproach you, and cast out your name as evil, for the Son of Man's sake" (6:22). Again; in Matthew 10:32 we read, "But whosoever shall confess Me before men, him will I confess before My Father which is in Heaven;" whereas in Luke 12:8 we are told, "Whosoever shall confess Me before men, him shall the Son of Man confess before the angels of God." Once more; in John 3:17 we are told, "For God sent not His Son into the world to condemn the world; but that the world through Him might be saved;" whereas, in Luke 9:56 we read, "For the Son of Man is not come to destroy men's lives, but to save

them." How these examples bring out the verbal perfections of Holy Writ!

4. The Lord is referred to as "the Friend" of publicans and sinners.

It is only Luke who tells us, "And Levi made Him a great feast in his own house: and there was a great company of publicans and of others that sat down with them" (5:29). It is only here we learn that Christ said to the querulous Jews, "For John the Baptist came neither eating bread nor drinking wine, and ye say, He hath a demon. The Son of Man is come eating and drinking; and ye say, Behold a gluttonous man, and a winebibber, a Friend of publicans and sinners!" (7:33, 34). It is only in this Gospel we find that the Savior's critics openly murmured, and said, "This Man receiveth sinners, and eateth with them" (15:2). And it is only here we are told that because Zaccheus had joyfully received the Savior into his house "they all murmured, saying, That He was gone to be guest with a man that is a sinner" (19:7).

It is beautiful to notice the graduation pointed by the Holy Spirit in the last three passages quoted above. In 7:34 Christ is simply "The Friend of publicans and sinners." In 15:2 it was said, "This Man receiveth sinners and eateth with them." But in 19:7 we are told, "He was gone to be guest with a man that is a sinner"! Thus did God make even the wrath of man to praise Him.

5. The Lord is here portrayed as a man of prayer.

It is indeed striking to see how often the Savior is seen engaged in prayer in this Gospel. The following passages bring this out: "Now when all the people were baptized, it came to pass that Jesus also being baptized, and praying, the heaven was opened" (3:21). "And He withdrew Himself into the wilderness, and prayed" (5:16). "And it came to pass in those days, that He went out into a mountain to pray, and continued all night in prayer to God" (6:12). "And it came to pass about an eight days after these sayings, He took Peter and John and James, and went up into a mountain to pray. And as He prayed, the fashion of His countenance was altered"

(9:28, 29). "And it came to pass, that, as He was praying in a certain place, when He ceased, one of His disciples said unto Him, Lord, teach us to pray" (11:1). "And the Lord said, Simon, Simon, behold, Satan hath desired to have you, that he may sift you as wheat: But I have prayed for thee, that thy faith fail not" (22:31, 32). "And He was withdrawn from them about a stone's cast, and kneeled down, and prayed. And being in an agony He prayed more earnestly" (22:41, 44). "Then said Jesus, Father, forgive them for they know not what they do" (23:34): only here do we find Him praying thus for His murderers. Add to these examples the fact that Luke alone records our Lord's teaching on Prayer which is found in 11:5-8, that he only tells us of His parable on Importunity in prayer (18:1-7), and that he alone tells us of the two men who went up to the Temple to pray, and it will be seen what a prominent place prayer has in Luke's Gospel.

6. Christ is frequently seen here eating food.

"And one of the Pharisees desired Him that He would eat with him. And He went into the Pharisee's house and sat down to meat" (7:36). "And as He spake, a certain Pharisee besought Him to dine with him: and He went in, and sat down to meat" (11:37). "And it came to pass, as He went into the house of one of the chief Pharisees to eat bread on the Sabbath day, they watched Him" (14:1). "And when they say it, they all murmured, saying, That He was gone to be guest with a man that is a sinner" (19:7). "And it came to pass, as He sat at meat with them, He took bread, and blessed it, and brake, and gave to them" (24:30). "And they gave Him a piece of a broiled fish, and of an honeycomb. And He took it, and did eat before them" (24:42, 43). It scarcely needs to be pointed out that these examples demonstrated the reality of His Manhood.

7. The circumstances connected with his death and resurrection.

The awful hour spent in Gethsemane is described in this third Gospel with a fullness of detail which is not found in the others.

Luke is the only one that tells us, "And there appeared an angel unto Him from heaven, strengthening Him"; as he is the only one to say, "And being in agony He prayed more earnestly: and His sweat was as it were great drops of blood falling down to the ground" (22:43, 44). Then followed the Arrest, and as they were all leaving the Garden, we read, "And one of them smote the servant of the high priest, and cut off his ear. And Jesus answered and said, Suffer ye thus far, and He touched his ear, and healed him" (22:50, 51). The other Evangelists record this incident of the smiting of the high priest's servant, but only Luke shows us the tenderness of the Savior, full of compassion toward the suffering of others, right to the last.

Luke is the only one to tell us, "And there followed Him a great company of people, and of women, which also bewailed and lamented Him. But Jesus turning unto them said, Daughters of Jerusalem, weep not for Me, but weep for yourselves, and for your children" (23:27, 28). Appropriately, does this find a place here, bringing out, as it does, human emotions and sympathies. Luke is the only one to designate the place where the Savior was crucified by its Gentile name—"And when they were come to the place, which is called Calvary, there they crucified Him" (23:33). And, again, Luke tells us, "A superscription also was written over Him in letters of Greek, and Latin, and Hebrew, This is the King of the Jews" (23:38). How this hints at the international scope of this third Gospel! Matthew and Mark give no hint of the "superscription" being written in the world-languages of the day; though John does, for he, again, presents Christ in connection with "the world." Luke is the only one to describe the conversion of the dying robber, and to record his witness to the Human perfections of the Lord Jesus: "This Man hath done nothing amiss" (23:41). So, too, it is only here we find a similar testimony borne by the Roman centurion: "Now when the centurion saw what was done, he glorified God, saying, Certainly this was a righteous Man" (23:47).

After His resurrection from the dead, it is only Luke who mentions that long walk of the

Savior with the two disciples, and of the familiar intercourse which they had together as they journeyed to Emmaus. And Luke is the only one who presents the Lord to our view as eating food after He had risen in triumph from the grave.

It only remains to add a brief word concerning the characteristic manner in which this third Gospel closes. Luke alone tells us, "And He led them out as far as to Bethany, and He lifted up His hands, and blessed them" (24:50)—a beautiful touch is this! Then we are told, "And it came to pass, while He blessed them, He was parted from them, and carried up into Heaven" (24:51). Note, particularly, that Luke says that the Son of Man was "carried up into Heaven," not that He ascended! And then the curtain falls to the strains of the expressions of human joy and praise: "And they worshipped Him, and returned to Jerusalem with great joy: and were continually in the Temple, praising and blessing God. Amen" (24:52, 53).

4. THE GOSPEL OF JOHN

As we turn to the fourth Gospel we come to entirely different ground from that which we have traversed in the other three. True, the period of time which is covered by it, is the same as in the others; true, that some of the incidents that have already been looked at will here come before us again; and true it is that he who has occupied the central position in the narratives of the first three Evangelists, is the same One that is made preeminent by John; but otherwise, everything here is entirely new. The fourth Gospel is more elevated in its tone, its viewpoint is more exalted, its contents bring before us spiritual relationships rather than human ties, and higher glories are revealed as touching the peerless person of the Savior. In each of the first three Gospels, Christ is viewed in human connections, but no so in the fourth. Matthew presents Him as the Son of David; Mark, as the perfect Workman of God; Luke, as the Son of Man; but John unveils His Divine glories. Again; Matthew writes, particularly, for the Jews; Mark, is specially adapted to God's servants; Luke's is written for men as men; but John's Gospel is concerned with the Family of God.

John's Gospel is the fourth book of the New Testament, and four is 3+1. The numerals of Scripture are not employed fortuitously, but are used with Divine discrimination and significance. The reverent student is not left free to juggle with them at his own caprice, nor may he give to them an arbitrary meaning, so as to fit in with any private interpretations of his own. If he is honest, he will gather his definitions from the manner in which they are employed in Scripture itself. Thus, whether our statement that four is 3+1 is an arbitrary assertion or not, must be determined by its support, or lack of it, in the Word. The numeral four is used two ways in the Bible. First, its meaning as a whole number, and second, its meaning as a distributive number. In its first usage, four is the world number, the number of the earth and all things therein, the number of the creature, as such; and hence, it comes to signify, Universality. But in its second usage, the distributive, when employed in connection with a series, it is frequently divided into three and one. Four is rarely, if ever an intensified two; that is, its significance does not represent 2x2.

The last paragraph sounds somewhat academic, we fear, but its force may become more apparent as we apply its principles to our present subject. The four Gospels form a series, and the character of their contents obviously divide them into a three and a one, just as in the four kinds of soil in the parable of the Sower, representing four classes of hearers of the Word, are a series, and similarly divided—three barren and one fruitful. As we have seen, the first three Gospels have that in common which, necessarily, binds them together—each looking at Christ in human connections. But the fourth is clearly distinguished from the others by presenting Christ in a Divine relationship, and therefore it stands separated from the others. This conclusion is established beyond all doubt, when we observe that the character of its contents is in perfect accord with the significance of the numeral one. One speaks, primarily, of God: "Hear, O Israel: the Lord our God is one Lord" (Deut. 6:4). And again: "And the Lord shall be King over all the earth:

in that day shall there be one Lord, and His name one" (Zech. 14:9). In all languages one is the symbol of unity: it excludes all others. The first of the ten commandments, therefore, was:

"Thou shalt have no other gods before Me" (Ex. 20:3). So in John's Gospel, the one following the other three, it is the Godhead of Christ which is in view.

Each book in the Bible has a prominent and dominant theme which is peculiar to itself. Just as each member in the human body has its own particular function, so every book in the living Body of Divine Truth has its own special purpose and mission. The theme of John's Gospel is the Deity of Christ. Here, as nowhere else so fully, the Godhead of the Lord Jesus is presented to our view. That which is outstanding in this fourth Gospel is the Divine Sonship of our Savior. In this Gospel we are shown that the One born at Bethlehem, who walked this earth for over thirty years, who was crucified at Calvary, and who forty-three days later departed from these scenes, was none other than "the Only-Begotten of the Father." The evidence presented for this is overwhelming, the proofs almost without number, and the effect of contemplating them must be to bow our hearts in worship before "The great God, and our Savior Jesus Christ" (Titus 2:13).

Here is a theme worthy of our most reverent and prayerful attention. If such Divine care was taken, as we saw in the previous chapter, to guard the perfections of our Lord's humanity, equally so, has the Holy Spirit seen to it that there should be no uncertainty concerning the affirmation of the absolute Deity of our Savior. Just as the Old Testament prophets made known that the Coming One should be a Man, and a perfect Man, so did Messianic prediction also give plain intimation that He would be more than a Man. Through Isaiah, God foretold that unto Israel a Child should be born, and unto them a Son should be given, and that "the government shall be upon His shoulder: and His name shall be called Wonderful, Counselor, The mighty God, the Father of the ages (Heb.), the Prince of Peace" (9:6). Through Micah, He declared, "But thou,

Bethlehem Ephratah, though thou be little among the thousands of Judah, yet out of thee shall He come forth unto Me that is to be Ruler in Israel: whose goings forth have been from the days of eternity"—marginal rendering (5:2)! Through Zechariah, He said "Awake, O Sword, against My Shepherd, and against the Man that is My Fellow, saith the Lord of hosts" (13:7). Through the Psalmist, He announced, "The Lord said unto my Lord, Sit Thou at My right hand, until I make Thine enemies Thy footstool" (110:1). And again, when looking forward to the time of the second Advent, "The Lord hath said unto Me, Thou art My Son; this day have I begotten Thee" (or, "brought Thee forth") 2:7.

Coming now to the New Testament we may single out two or three of the most explicit witnesses to the Deity of Christ. In Romans 9, where the apostle is enumerating the peculiar privileges of Israel, he says in verse 5, "Whose are the fathers, and of whom as concerning the flesh Christ came, who is over all, God blessed for ever. Amen." In 1 Corinthians 15 we are told, "And the first man is of the earth, earthy, but the second Man is the Lord from Heaven" (v. 47). In Colossians 1:16 we read, "For by Him were all things created, that are in heaven, and that are in earth, visible and invisible, whether they be thrones, or dominions, or principalities or powers: all things were created by Him and for Him;" and again, in 2:9, "For in Him dwelleth all the fullness of the Godhead bodily." In Hebrews 1 we learn that "God, who at sundry times and in divers manners spake in time past unto the fathers by the prophets, Hath in these last days spoken unto us by His Son, whom He hath appointed Heir of all things, by whom also He made the worlds; Who being the Brightness of His glory, and the express Image of His person, and upholding all things by the Word of His power, when He had by Himself purged our sins, sat down on the right hand of the Majesty on high" (Heb. 1:1-3). While in Revelation 19:16 we are informed that when He comes back to earth again, "He hath on His vesture and on His thigh a name written, King of Kings, and Lord of lords." A more emphatic, positive, and unequivocal testimony to the absolute Deity of Christ could not be borne.

In these days of widespread departure from the Truth, it cannot be insisted upon too strongly or too frequently that the Lord Jesus Christ is none other than the Second Person in the Holy Trinity. Vicious but specious are the attacks now being made upon this cardinal article in the faith once for all delivered to the saints. Satan, who poses as an angel of light, is now sending forth his ministers "transformed as the ministers of righteousness." Men who are loudly trumpeting their faith in the verbal inspiration of Scripture, and who even profess to believe in the vicarious Sacrifice of Christ are, nevertheless, denying the absolute Godhood of Him whom they claim to be serving: they repudiate His essential Deity, they deny His Eternality, and reduce Him to the level of a mere creature. It was concerning men of this class that the Holy Spirit said, "For such are false apostles, deceitful workers, transforming themselves into the apostles of Christ" (2 Cor. 11:13).

In keeping with the special theme of the fourth Gospel, it is here that we have the fullest unveiling of Christ's Divine glories. It is here we behold Him dwelling "with God" before time began and before ever a creature was formed (1:1, 2). It is here that He is denominated "the Only Begotten of the Father' (1:14). It is here John the Baptist bears record that "this is the Son of God" (1:34). It is here we read, "This beginning of miracles did Jesus in Cana of Galilee, and manifested forth His glory" (2:11). It is here we are told that the Savior said, "Destroy this temple, and in three days I will raise it up" (2:19). It is here we read that God sent His Son into the world, not to condemn but to save (3:17). It is here we learn that Christ declared, "For as the Father raiseth up the dead, and quickeneth them; even so the Son quickeneth whom He will. For the Father judgeth no man, but hath committed all judgment unto the Son: That all men should honor the Son, even as they honor the Father. He that honoreth not the Son honoreth not the Father which hath sent Him" (5:21-23). It is here that we find Him affirming, "For the Bread of God is He which

cometh down from Heaven, and giveth life unto the world" (6:35). It is here we find Him saying, "Before Abraham was, I am" (8:58). It is here that we find Him declaring, "I and Father are One" (10:30). It is here we hear Him saying, "He that hath seen Me, hath seen the Father" (14:9). It is here He promises "Whatsoever ye shall ask in My name, that will I do, that the Father may glorified in the Son" (14:13). It is here that He asks, "And now, O Father, glorify Thou Me with Thine own Self with the glory which I had with Thee before the world was" (17:5).

Before we take up John's Gospel in detail, and examine some of the more prominent lines in his delineation of Christ's person and ministry, a few words should be said concerning the dispensational scope and bearings of this Gospel. It should be evident at once that this one is quite different from the other Gospels. There, Christ is seen in a human relationship, and as connected with an earthly people; but here, He is viewed in a Divine relationship, and as connected with a heavenly people. It is true that the mystery of the one Body is not unfolded here, rather is it the family of God which is in view. It is also true that the Heavenly Calling is not fully disclosed, yet are there plain intimations of it—what else can be said, for example of the Lord's words which are found in 14:2, 3?—"In My Father's House are many mansions: if it were not so, I would have told you. I go to prepare a place for you. And if I go and prepare a place for you, I will come again, and receive you unto Myself; that where I am, there ye may be also."

In the first three Gospels, Christ is seen connected with the Jews, proclaiming the Messianic kingdom, a proclamation which ceased, however, as soon as it became evident that the Nation had rejected Him. But here, in John's Gospel, His rejection is announced at the beginning, for in the very first chapter we are told, "He came unto His own, and His own received Him not." It is, therefore, most significant to note that John's Gospel, which instead of presenting Christ in connection with Israel, views Him as related to believers by spiritual ties, was not written until after A.D. 70, when the Temple was destroyed, and the Jews dispersed throughout the world!

The dispensational limitations which attach to much that is found in the first three Gospels, do not hold good with John's Gospel, for as Son of God, He can be known only by believers as such. On this plane the Jew has no priority. The Jews claim upon Christ was purely a fleshy one, whereas believers are related to the Son of God by spiritual union. The Son of David, and the Son of Man titles link Christ to the earth, but the "Son of God" connects Him with the Father in Heaven; hence, in this fourth Gospel, the earthly kingdom is almost entirely ignored. In harmony with these facts we may observe, that it is only here in John's Gospel we hear of Christ saying, "And other sheep I have, which are not of this (i.e., the Jewish) fold. Them also I must bring, and they shall hear My voice; and there shall be one fold (i.e., the Christian fold), and one Shepherd" (10:16). It is only here in John we learn of the wider scope of God's purpose in the Death of His Son, "Being high priest that year, he prophesied that Jesus should die for that nation; And not for that nation only, but that also He should gather together in one the children of God that were scattered abroad" (11:51, 52). It is only here in John that we have fully unfolded the relation of the Holy Spirit to believers. And it is only here in John that we have recorded our Lord's High Priestly prayer, which gives a sample of His present intercession on high. These considerations, then, should make it abundantly clear that the dispensational bearings of John's Gospel are entirely different from the other three.

Coming now to a closer view of this fourth Gospel we may observe how striking are its opening verses: "In the beginning was the Word, and the Word was with God, and the Word was God. The same was in the beginning with God. All things were made by Him; and without Him was not anything made that was made" (1:1-3). How entirely different is this from what we find in the introductory statements in the other Gospels! John starts, immediately, by presenting Christ as the Son of God, not as the Son of David, or the Son of Man. John takes up back to the beginning, and shows that our Lord had no beginning, for He was in the beginning. John goes right back behind creation, and shows that Christ was Himself the Creator.

Every clause in these opening verses is worthy of our closest attention. First, the Lord Jesus is here termed, "The Word." The significance of this title may, perhaps, be most easily grasped by comparing with it what is said in verse 18 of this first chapter of John. Here we are told: "No man hath seen God at any time; the Only Begotten Son, which is in the bosom of the Father, He hath declared Him," or "told Him out." Christ is the One who came here to tell out God. He came here to make God intelligible to men. As we read in Hebrews 1: "God, who at sundry times and in divers manners spake in time past unto the fathers by the prophets, Hath in these last days spoken unto us by His Son." Christ is the final Spokesman of God. Again; the force of this title of Christ, "the Word," may be discovered by comparing it with the name given to the Bible—the Word of God. What are the Scriptures? They are, the Word of God. And what does that mean? This: that the Scriptures reveal God's mind, express His will, make known His perfections, and lay bare His heart. This is precisely what the Lord Jesus Christ has done for the Father. But let us enter a little more into detail:

a. A "word" is a medium of manifestation. I have in my mind a thought, but others know not its nature. But the moment I clothe that thought in words, it becomes cognizable. Words, then, make objective, unseen thoughts. This is precisely what the Lord Jesus has done, as the "Word" Christ has made manifest the invisible God. Christ is God clothed in perfect humanity.

b. A "word" is a means of communication. By means of words I transmit information to others. By words I express myself, make known my will, and impart knowledge. So, Christ as the "Word," is the Divine Transmitter, communicating to us the Life and Love of God.

c. A "word" is a method of revelation. By his words a speaker reveals both his intellectual caliber and his moral character. It is by our words we shall be justified, and by our words we shall be condemned. And

Christ, as the "Word," fully reveals the attributes and the character of God. How fully He has revealed God! He has displayed His power: He has manifested His wisdom: He has exhibited His holiness: He has made known His grace: He has unveiled His heart. In Christ, and nowhere else, is God fully and finally revealed.

But was not God fully revealed in Nature? "Revealed," yes; but "fully revealed," no. Nature conceals as well as reveals. Nature is under the Curse, and is far different now from what it was in the day that it left the hands of the Creator. Nature is imperfect to day, and how can that which is imperfect be a perfect medium for manifesting the infinite perfections of God. The ancients had Nature before them, and what did they learn of God? Let that altar, which the apostle beheld in one of the great centers of ancient culture and learning, make answer—"To the unknown God," is what he found inscribed thereon. No; in Christ, and in and by Him alone, is God fully and finally revealed.

But lest this figurative expression—"the Word"—should convey to us an inadequate conception of the Divine person of the Lord Jesus, the Holy Spirit goes on to say, in the opening verse of this Gospel, "And the Word was with God." This denotes His separate Personality, and also indicates His essential relation to the Godhead. He was not "in God." And, as though this were not strong enough, the Spirit expressly adds, "And the Word was God." Not an emanation from God, but none other than God. Not merely a manifestation of God, but God Himself made manifest. Not only the Revealer of God, but God Himself revealed. A more unequivocal affirmation of the essential Deity of the Lord Jesus Christ it is impossible to imagine. Granted, that we are in the realm of mystery, yet, the force of what is here affirmed of the absolute Godhead of Christ cannot be honestly evaded. As to how Christ can be the Revealer of God, and yet God Himself revealed; as to how He can be "with God," and yet be God, are high mysteries that our finite minds are no more capable of fathoming than we can understand how that God can be without beginning. What is here

stated in John 1:1, is to be received by simple, unquestioning faith.

Next we read, "All things were made by Him; and without Him (apart from Him) was not anything made that was made" (1:3). Here, again, the absolute Deity of Christ is emphatically affirmed, for creation is ascribed to Him, and none but God can create. Man, despite all his proud boasts and lofty pretensions, is utterly unable to create even a blade of grass. If, then, Christ is the Creator, He must be God. Observe, too, that the whole of Creation is here attributed to the Son of God—"all things were made by Him." This would not be true, if He were Himself a creature, even though the first and highest. But nothing is excepted—"all things were made by Him." Just as He was Eternal— before all things—so was He the Originator of all things.

Again we are told, "In Him was life; and the life was the Light of men." This follows, necessarily, from what has been said in the previous verse. If Christ created all things, He must be the Fount of life. He is the Life-Giver. But more: "The Life was the light of men." What this means is made clear in the verses that follow. "There was a man (in contrast from "the Word," who is God) sent from God, whose name was John," and he, "Came for a witness, to bear witness of the Light, that all through him might believe" (1:6, 7). Compare with these words what we are told in 1 John 1:5, "God is Light, and in Him is no darkness at all." The conclusion, then, is irresistible, that the Lord Jesus is none other than God, the Second Person in the Holy Trinity.

But we pass now to the fourteenth verse of this opening chapter of John. Having shown the relation of our Lord to Time—without beginning; having declared His relation to the Godhead—a separate Person of the Trinity, but Himself also God; having defined His relation to the Universe—the Creator of it, and the great Life-Giver; having stated His relation to Men—the One who is their God, their "Light," having announced that the Baptist bore witness to Him as the Light; and having described the reception which He met with here upon earth—unknown by the world, rejected by Israel, but received by a people who were "born of God," the Holy Spirit goes on to say, "And the Word was made (better, "became") flesh, and dwelt (tabernacled) among us, and we beheld His glory, the glory as of the Only Begotten of the Father, full of grace and truth." This verse announces the Divine incarnation, and brings out, once more, the Divine glories of the One born of Mary.

"The Word became flesh." He became what He was not previously. He did not cease to be God, but He became Man. becoming Man, He "tabernacled" among men. He pitched His tent here for thirty-three years. And then we are told that the testimony of those whose eyes Divine power had opened, was, "We beheld His glory." The language of this verse takes us back in thought to the Tabernacle which was pitched in the wilderness, of old. The Tabernacle was the place of Jehovah's abode in the midst of Israel. It was here that He made His dwelling-place. The Tabernacle was where God met with His people, hence was it termed "the Tent of Meeting." There, within the Holy of Holies was the Shekinah Glory manifested. The Lord Jesus Christ was the Anti-type. He was, in His own person, the Meeting-place between God and men. And just as the Shekinah—the visible and glorious manifestation of Jehovah—was seen in the Holy of Holies, so those who came near to Christ, in faith, "beheld His glory." The Lord Jesus was God manifest in the flesh, displaying "the glory as of the Only Begotten of the Father." For, as the 18th verse goes on to say, "No man hath seen God at any time; the Only Begotten Son, which is in the bosom of the Father, He hath declared Him." Thus, the essential Deity of the One born at Bethlehem is, once more, expressly affirmed.

Next we have the witness of John the Baptist. This is quite different from what we find in the other Gospels. Here there is no Call to Repentance, there is no announcement of "The kingdom of heaven" being at hand, and there is no mention of Christ Himself being baptized by His forerunner. Instead of these things, here we find John saying, "Behold the Lamb of God, which taketh away the sin of the world" (1:29). And again he says, "And I saw, and bare record that this is the Son of God" (1:34). It is also to be noted that when referring to the anointing of Christ with the Holy Spirit, a word is used which is not found in the other Gospels: "And John bare record, saying, I saw the Spirit descending from Heaven like a dove, and it abode upon Him" (1:32). The Spirit did not come upon Him and then leave again, as with the prophets of old: it "abode," a characteristic and prominent word in John's Gospel (see particularly chapter 15), having to do with the Divine side of things, and speaking of Fellowship. We have the same word again in 14:10—"Believest thou not that I am in the Father, and the Father in Me? the words that I speak unto you I speak not of Myself: but the Father that dwelleth ("abideth," it should be) in Me, He doeth the works."

The first chapter closes by describing the personal Call (not the ministerial call in the other Gospels) of the first disciples of the Lord. Here only do we read of Christ saying to Nathaniel, "Before that Philip called thee, when thou wast under the fig tree, I saw thee" (1:48): thus manifesting His Omniscience. Here only do we find recorded Nathaniel's witness to Christ. "Rabbi, Thou art the Son of God; Thou art the King of Israel" (1:49). And here only did Christ tell His disciples that, in the coming Day they should "see Heaven open, and the angels of God ascending and descending on the Son of Man" (1:51).

Coming now to the second chapter, we find described there the first miracle performed by the Lord Jesus, namely, the turning of the water into wine. John alone records this, for only God can fill the human heart with that Divine joy, of which the wine was here the emblem. In this miracle we are shown the "Word" at work. He, Himself, did nothing. He simply told the servants what to do, and at His word the wonder was performed. The special point in connection with this miracle is stated in verse 11, "This beginning of miracles did Jesus in Cana of Galilee, and manifested forth His glory; and his disciples believed on Him."

In the remainder of this chapter we witness Christ cleansing the Temple. Here, again, John brings into the picture his own distinctive lines. Here only do we find the Lord terming the Temple "My Father's house" (v. 16). Here only do we find Him saying, in reply to the challenge of His critics for a sign, "Destroy this temple (meaning His body), and in three days I will raise it up" (v. 19). And, here only do we read, "Now when He was in Jerusalem at the Passover, in the feast, many believed in His name, when they saw the miracles which He did. But Jesus did not commit Himself unto them, because He knew all, and needed not that any should testify of man: for He knew what was in man" (vv. 23-25). What a proof was this of His Deity! Only He "knew what was in man." Compare with this the words of 1 Kings 8:39—"Hear Thou in Heaven Thy dwelling place, and forgive, and do, and give to every man according to his ways, whose heart Thou knowest—for Thou, even Thou only, knowest the hearts of all the children of men." In thus reading the hearts of men, what a demonstration did the Savior give, that He was God manifest in flesh!

John 3 records the interview of Nicodemus with Christ—something not found in the other three Gospels. In full accord with the scope of this Gospel, we find the Savior here speaking to Nicodemus not of faith or repentance, but of the New Birth, which is the Divine side in salvation, declaring that, "Except a man be born again, he cannot see the kingdom of God." And only here in the four Gospels do we read, "God so loved the world, that He gave his Only Begotten Son, that whosoever believeth in Him should not perish, but have everlasting life" (3:16).

In John 4 we find another incident that is not described elsewhere, namely, the Lord's dealings with the poor Samaritan adulteress. And here, once more, we behold flashes of His Divine glory shining forth. He tells her, "Whosoever drinketh of the water that I shall give him shall never thirst; but the water that I shall give him shall be in him a well of water springing up into everlasting life" (v. 14). He manifests His omniscience by declaring, "Thou hast had five husbands; and he whom thou now hast is not thy husband" (v. 18). He

speaks to her of worshipping the Father "in spirit and in truth." He reveals Himself to her as the great "I am" (v. 26). He brings her from death unto life, and out of darkness into His own marvelous light. Finally, He proved His oneness with the Father by affirming, "My meat is to do the will of Him that sent Me, and to finish His work" (4:34).

John 5 opens by recording the healing of the impotent man who had an infirmity thirty-eight years. None of the other Evangelists make mention of it. This miracle evidenced "the Word" at work again. He does nothing to the poor sufferer, not even laying hands upon him. He simply speaks the authoritative and healing word, "Rise, take up thy bed, and walk," and "immediately," we read, "the man was made whole, and took up his bed, and walked" (v. 9). The miracle was performed on the Sabbath day, and the Lord's enemies used this as an occasion of criticism. Not only so, but we read, "Therefore did the Jews persecute Jesus, and sought to slay Him, because He had done these things on the Sabbath day" (v. 16). We also read in the other Gospels, of Christ being condemned because He transgressed the Jews' traditions respecting the Sabbath. But there, we find a very different reply from Him than what is recorded here. There, He insisted on the right of performing works of mercy on the Sabbath. There, too, He appealed to the priests carrying out their Temple duties on the Sabbath. But here He takes higher ground. Here, He says, "My Father worketh hitherto, and I work" (v. 17). The meaning of these words could not be mistaken. Christ reminded His critics, how that His "Father" worked on the Sabbath day, worked in connection with His government of the universe, in maintaining the orderly course of Nature, in sending rain, and so on. And because He was one with "the Father," He insisted that what was right for the Father to do, was equally right for Him to do. That this was the force of His reply, is clear from the next verse, "Therefore the Jews sought the more to kill Him, because He not only had broken the Sabbath, but said also that God was His Father, making Himself equal with God" (5:18). In the remaining verses of the chapter we find that Christ continued to affirm His absolute equality with the Father.

The sixth chapter opens by describing a miracle, which is narrated by each of the other Evangelists, the Feeding of the five thousand. But, here, it is followed by a lengthy discourse which is not recorded elsewhere. Here the Lord presents Himself as "The Bread of God," which had come down from Heaven to give life unto the world. He here declares that He alone can satisfy the needy soul of man: "And Jesus said unto them, I am the Bread of Life: he that cometh to Me shall never hunger; and he that believeth on Me shall never thirst" (v. 35). We cannot now follow the details of this wonderful chapter, but it will be evident to the student that it is the Divine side of things which is here dwelt upon. For example: it is here we are told that the Savior said, "No man can come to Me, except the Father which hath sent Me draw him" (v. 44). It is here we are told that "Jesus knew from the beginning who they were that believed not, and who should betray him" (v. 64). And it is here we learn that when many of the disciples "went back and walked no more with Him," and He said to the twelve, "Will ye also go away?" that Peter replied, "Lord, to whom shall we go? Thou hast the words of eternal life" (v. 68).

The seventh chapter brings before us Christ at Jerusalem during the feast of tabernacles. There is much here that is of deepest interest, but it is beside our present purpose to give a complete exposition. We are not here writing a brief commentary on John, rather are we attempting to point out that which is distinctive and characteristic in this fourth Gospel. Notice, then, one or two lines in this scene which serve to emphasize the Divine glories of Christ. We are told that, about the middle of the feast, "Jesus went up into the Temple, and taught." His teaching must have been exceedingly impressive, for we read, "And the Jews marveled, saying, How knoweth this man letters, having never learned" (v. 15). But, arresting as was His manner of delivery, what He said only served to bring out the enmity of those who heard Him: "Then they sought to take Him: but no

man laid hands on Him, because His hour was not yet come" (v. 30). How striking this is, and how thoroughly in accord with the central theme of John's Gospel! bringing out, as it does, the Divine side, by showing us God's complete control over the enemies of His Son. Next, we read "In the last day, that great day of the feast, Jesus stood and cried, saying, If any man thirst, let him come unto Me, and drink. He that believeth on Me, as the Scripture hath said, out of his belly shall flow rivers of living water" (vv. 37, 38). How this brings out the Divine sufficiency of Christ! None but God could make such a claim as that. Finally, we may observe here, that when the Pharisees heard that many of the people believed on Him, they "sent officers to take Him" (vv. 31, 32). How striking was the sequel: "Then came the officers to the chief priests and Pharisees; and they said unto them, Why have ye not brought Him? The officers answered, Never man spake like this Man" (vv. 45, 46).

John 8 opens by recording the incident of the woman taken in adultery, brought to Christ by the scribes and Pharisees. Their motive in doing this was an evil one. It was not that they were zealous of upholding the claims of God's law, but that they sought to ensnare God's Son. They set a trap for Him. They reminded Him that Moses had given commandment that such as this woman should be stoned—"but what sayest Thou?" they asked. He had declared that, "God sent not His Son into the world to condemn the world; but that the world through Him might be saved" (John 3:17). Would He, then, suffer this guilty adulteress to escape the penalty of the Law? If so, what became of His other claim, "Think not that I am come to destroy, but to fulfill" (Matt. 5:17)? It seemed as though He was caught on the horns of a dilemma. If He gave the word for her to be stoned, where was grace? On the other hand, if He allowed her to go free, where was righteousness? Ah, how blessedly did His Divine wisdom appear, in the masterly manner in which He dealt with the situation. Said He to them that sought to trap Him, "He that is without sin among you, let him first cast a stone at her." It was "the Word" at work again, the Divine Word, for we read, "And they which heard Him, being convicted by their conscience, went out one by one, beginning at the eldest, even unto the last: and Jesus was left alone, and the woman standing in the midst" (v. 9). The way was now open for Him to display His mercy. The Law required two "witnesses" at least; but none were left. To the woman He said, "Where are those thine accusers? hath no man condemned thee?" And she answered, "No man, Lord." And then, to manifest His holiness He said, "Neither do I condemn thee: go, and sin no more" (v. 11). Thus, do we here behold His glory, "the glory as of the Only Begotten of the Father, full of grace and truth." Then followed that lovely discourse in which Christ proclaimed Himself as "The Light of the world," saying, "he that followeth Me shall not walk in darkness, but shall have the light of life" (v. 12). This was peculiarly appropriate to the occasion, for He had just given proof that He was such, by turning the searching Light of God upon the conscience of those who accused the adulteress.

What follows in the next chapter is closely linked to that which has just been before us. Here Christ gives sight to a man who had been blind from his birth, and immediately before He gives light to the darkened eyes of this man, He uses the occasion to say, again, "As long as I am in the world, I am the light of the world" (9:5). The sequel to this miracle had both its pathetic and its blessed sides. The one who had had his eyes opened was brought to the Pharisees, and after a lengthy examination they excommunicated him, because of the bold testimony he had borne to his Benefactor. But we are told, "Jesus heard that they had cast him out; and when He had found Him, He said unto him, Dost thou believe on the Son of God? And he answered and said, Who is he, Lord, that I might believe on Him? And Jesus said unto him, Thou hast both seen Him, and He it is that talketh with thee. And he said, Lord, I believe. And he worshipped Him" (vv. 35-37). Thus did Christ graciously evidence that when God begins a good work in a soul, He ceases not until it has been perfected. The chapter closes with a most solemn word against those who opposed Christ, in which

we behold the Light blinding: "And Jesus said, For judgment I am come into this world, that they which see not might see; and that they which see might be made blind" (v. 39).

John 10 is the chapter in which Christ is revealed as the Good Shepherd, and there is much in it which brings out His Divine glories. Here He presents Himself as the Owner of the fold, and makes it known that believers, under the figure of sheep, belong to Him. They are His property, as well as the objects of His tender solicitude. They know Him, and they are known of Him. His, is the Voice they follow, and the voice of strangers they heed not. For the sheep He will lay down His life. But, be it carefully noted, the Savior declares, "No man taketh it from Me, but I lay it down of Myself. I have power to lay it down, and I have power to take it again" (v. 18). No mere man could have made good such a claim as this. Nor could any mere human teacher say to his disciples, "And I give unto them eternal life; and they shall never perish, neither shall any pluck them out of My hand" (v. 28). That He was more than Man, that He was God the Son, incarnate, is expressly affirmed in the words with which the Savior here closed His discourse—"I and Father are one" (v. 30).

John 11 brings us to what, perhaps, was the most wonderful miracle that our Lord performed, while here on earth, namely, the Raising of Lazarus. Record of this was, appropriately, reserved for the fourth Gospel. The others tell us of the raising of the daughter of Jairus, just dead; and Luke mentions the raising of the widow of Nain's son, as his body was on the way to the cemetery; but John only records the raising of Lazarus, who had been in the grave four days, and whose body had already begun to corrupt. Signally did the performance of this miracle demonstrate Christ to be the Son of God. Here, too, we behold "the Word" at work. The daughter of Jairus He took by the hand; concerning the widow's son, we read, "He touched the bier;" but here He did nothing but speak: first, to the spectators to remove the stone which lay over the entrance to the grave, and then to Lazarus, He cried, "Come forth."

John 12 brings us to the close of our Lord's public ministry as it is followed in this Gospel. The chapter opens with a scene which has won the hearts of all who have gazed by faith upon it. The Savior is seen in a Bethany home, where deep gratitude made Him a supper, and Lazarus is also one of the guests. After the meal was over, Mary anointed His feet with fragrant ointment that was "very costly," and wiped His feet with her hair. It is very striking to notice the differences between Matthew's account of this incident and what is recorded here. It is only John who tells us that Lazarus sat at the table with the Lord; it is only John who says that "Martha served," and it is only John who gives the name of this devoted woman who expressed such love for Christ: here everything is "made manifest" by the Light. Moreover, note particularly, that Matthew says the woman poured the ointment "on His head" (26:7), but here in John, we are told, she "anointed the feet of Jesus" (12:3). The two accounts are not contradictory, but supplementary. Both are true, but we see the hand of the Holy Spirit controlling each Evangelist to record only that which was in keeping with his theme. In Matthew it is the King who is before us, hence it is His "head" that is anointed; but in John we are shown the Son of God, and therefore does Mary here take her place at His "feet"!

John 13 is in striking contrast with what is found at the beginning of the previous chapter. There, we behold the feet of the Lord; here we see the feet of His disciples. There, we saw His feet anointed; here, the feet of the disciples are washed. There, the feet of Christ were anointed with fragrant and costly ointment; here the feet of the disciples are washed with water. There, the feet of the feet of the Lord was washed by another; but here, the feet of the disciples are washed by none other than the Son of God Himself. And observe that the anointing of His feet comes before the washing of the disciples' feet, for in all things He must have the preeminence. And what a contrast is here presented! The "feet" speak of the walk. The feet of the disciples were soiled: their walk needed to be cleansed. Not so with the Lord of glory: His walk emitted nought but a sweet fragrance to the Father.

At first sight it appears strange that this lowly task of washing the disciples feet should be recorded by John. And yet the very fact that it is recorded here supplies the surest key to the interpretation of its significance. The act itself only brought out the amazing condescension of the Son of God, who would stoop so low as to perform the common duties of a slave. But the mention of this incident by John indicates there is a spiritual meaning to the act. And such, indeed, there was. The "feet," as we have seen, point to the walk, and "water" is the well known emblem of the written Word. Spiritually, the act spoke of Christ maintaining the walk of His disciples, removing the defilements which unfit them for communion with a holy God. It was members of His Church that were here being cleansed by the Head "with the washing of water by the Word" (Eph. 5:26). How fitting, then, that this should have found a place in this fourth Gospel, for who but a Divine Person is capable of cleansing the walk of believers and maintaining their fellowship with the Father!

In the remainder of John 13 and to the end of chapter 16 we have what is known as the Lord's "Pascal discourse." This, too, is peculiar to John, and almost everything in it brings out the Divine glories of the Savior. It is here that He says to the disciples, "Ye call Me Master and Lord: and ye say well; for so I am" (13:13). It is here that Christ said, anticipating the Cross, "Now is the Son of Man glorified, and God is glorified in Him" (13:31). It is here that He speaks of going away to "prepare a place" for His people (14:2, 3). It is here He invites His disciples to pray in His name (14:13). It is here He says, "Peace I leave with you, My peace I give unto you: not as the world giveth, give I unto you" (14:27). It is here that He says so much about fruit-bearing, under the beautiful figure of the Vine. It is here that He speaks of "The Comforter whom I will send unto you from the Father" (15:26). And it is here that He declares of the Holy Spirit, "He shall glorify Me: for He shall receive of Mine, and shall show it unto you" (16:14).

John 17 contains what is known as the High Priestly prayer of Christ. Nothing like it is found in the other Gospels. It gives us a specimen of His present ministry on High. Here we find the Savior saying, "Father, the hour is come; glorify Thy Son, that Thy Son also may glorify Thee" (v. 1). Here He speaks of Himself as the One given "power over all flesh" (v. 2). Here He is inseparably linked with "the only true God" (v. 3). Here He speaks (by way of anticipation) of having "finished" the work given Him to do (v. 4). Here He asks, "O Father, glorify Thou Me with Thine own self with the glory which I had with Thee before the world was" (v. 5). Here He prays for His own beloved people: for their preservation from evil, for the supply of their every need, for their sanctification and unification. His perfect equality with the Father is evidenced when He says, "Father, I will that they also, whom Thou hast given Me, be with Me where I am; that they may behold My glory, which Thou hast given Me: for Thou lovest Me before the foundation of the world" (v. 24).

The remaining chapters will be considered in another connection, so we pass on now to notice some of the general features which characterize this Gospel in its parts and as a whole.

I. Things omitted from John's Gospel.

While examining the second Gospel, we dwelt at some length upon the different things of which Mark took no notice, and saw that the items excluded made manifest the perfections of his particular portrayal of Christ. Here, too, a similar line of thought may be followed out at even greater length. Much that is found in the first three Gospels is omitted by John, as being irrelevant to his special theme. Some of the more outstanding of these we shall now consider:

a. In John's Gospel there is no genealogy, neither His legal through Joseph, nor his personal through Mary. Nor is there any account of His birth. Instead, as we have seen, He was "In the beginning." For a similar reason, John is silent about Herod's attempt to slay the Christ Child, about the flight into Egypt, and subsequent return to Galilee. Nothing is said about the Lord Jesus as a Boy of twelve, in the midst of the doctors in the Temple. No reference is made to the years spent at Nazareth, and no hint is given of Christ working at the carpenter's bench before He began His public ministry. All these are passed over as not being germane.

b. Here, there is no description of His baptism. Mark refers to the Lord Jesus being baptized by his forerunner, and Matthew and Luke each describe at length the attendant circumstances. John's reason for saying nothing about this is obvious. In His baptism, Christ, in condescending grace, took His place alongside of His needy people, saying to the one who baptized Him, "Thus it becometh us to fulfill all righteousness" (Matt. 3:15).

c. John says nothing about the Temptation. Here, again, we may observe the superintending hand of the Holy Spirit, guiding the different Evangelists in the selection of their material. Each of the first three Gospels make mention of the season spent by Christ in the wilderness, where He was tempted for forty days of the Devil. But John is silent about it. And why? Because John is presenting Christ as God the Son, and "God cannot be tempted" (James 1:13).

d. There is no account of His transfiguration. At first sight this seems strange, but a little attention to details will reveal the reason for this. The wonderful scene witnessed by the three disciples upon the holy mount, was not an unveiling of His Divine glories, but a miniature representation, a spectacular showing forth of the Son of Man coming in His kingdom (see Matt. 16:28 etc.). But the earthly kingdom does not fall within the scope of this Gospel. Here, it is spiritual and heavenly relationships which are made most prominent.

e. Here there is no Appointing of the Apostles. In the other Gospels we find the Lord Jesus selecting, equipping, and sending forth the Twelve, to preach, and to heal; and in Luke we also read of Him sending out the Seventy. But here, in harmony with the character of this Gospel, all ministry and miracle working is left entirely in the hands of the Son of God.

f. Never once is Christ here seen praying. This does not come out so clearly in our English translation as it does in the original Greek. In John's Gospel we never find the word associated with Christ which signifies taking the place of a supplicant; instead, the word "*erotos*" is used, and this word denotes "speaking" as to an equal. It is very striking to compare what each Evangelist records following the miracle of the Feeding of the five thousand: Matthew says, "And when He had sent the multitudes away, He went up into a mountain apart to pray" (14:23). Mark says, "When He had sent them away, He departed into a mountain to pray" (6:46). Luke also follows his narration of this miracle with the words, "And it came to pass, as He was alone praying" (9:8). But when we come to the fourth Gospel, we read, "He departed again to a mountain Himself alone" (6:15), and there John stops! The contents of John 17 may seem to contradict what we have just said above, but really it is not so. At the beginning of the chapter we read, "Jesus lifted up His eyes to Heaven, and said, Father, the hour is come; glorify Thy Son, that Thy Son also may glorify Thee" (v. 1). And at its close we read that He said, "Father I will that they also, whom Thou hast given Me, be with Me where I am" (v. 24). Thus He spoke to the Father as to an Equal.

g. We never read in John's Gospel of "The Coming of the Son of Man," and for the same reason as this, He is never addressed as "The Son of David" here. The Coming of the Son of Man always has reference to His return to the earth itself, coming back to His earthly people. But here we read, not of a restored Palestine, but of the "Father's House" and its "many mansions," of Christ going on High to prepare a place "for His heavenly people, and of Him coming back to receive them unto Himself, that there may they be also.

h. We never find the word "Repent" in John. In the other Gospels this is a term of frequent occurrence; what, then, is the reason for its absence here? In the other Gospels the sinner is viewed as guilty, and needing, therefore, to "repent." But here, the sinner is looked upon as spiritually dead, and therefore, in sore need of that which only God can

impart—"life"! It is here we read of man needing to be "born again" (3:7), needing to be "quickened" (5:21), and needing to be "drawn" (6:44).

i. Neither is the word "Forgive" found in John. This, too, is a word often met with in the other Gospels. Why, then, its omission here? In Matthew 9:6 we read, "The Son of Man hath power on earth to forgive sins." As Son of Man He "forgives;" as Son of God He bestows "eternal life."

j. No Parables are found in John's Gospel. This is a very notable omission. The key to it is found in Matthew 13: "And the disciples came, and said unto Him, Why speakest Thou unto them in parables? He answered and said unto them, Because it is given unto you to know the mysteries of the kingdom of heaven, but to them it is not given. Therefore speak I to them in parables: because they seeing see not; and hearing they hear not, neither do they understand" (vv. 10-13). Here we learn why that Christ, in the later stages of His ministry, taught in "parables." It was to conceal from those who had rejected Him, what was comprehensible only to those who had spiritual discernment. But here in John, Christ is not concealing, but revealing—revealing God. It is to be deplored that the rationale of our Lord's parabolic form of teaching should be known to so few. The popular definition of Christ's parables is that they were earthly stories with a heavenly meaning. How man gets things upside down! The truth is, that His parables were heavenly stories with an earthly meaning, having to do with His earthly people, in earthly connections. This is another reason why none are found in John—the word in 10:6 is "proverb."

k. In John's Gospel no mention is made of the Demons. Why this is we do not know. To say that no reference is here made to them, was, because mention of them would be incompatible with the Divine glories of Christ, hardly seems satisfactory; for, Satan himself is referred to here, again and again. It is, in fact, only here, that the Devil is spoken of three times over as "The prince of this world;" and, Judas, too, as the son of Perdition, occupies a more prominent position here than in the other Gospels. Should it be revealed to any of our readers why the "demons" are excluded from this Gospel, we shall be very glad to hear from them.

1. There is no account of Christ's Ascension in this fourth Gospel. This is very striking, and by implication brings out clearly the Deity of the Lord Jesus. As God the Son He was omnipresent, and so, needed not to ascend. As God the Son He fills both heaven and earth. We turn now to,

II. Positive features of John's Gospel.
a. The titles of Christ are very significant.
Only here (in the four Gospels) is the Lord Jesus revealed as "the Word" (1:1). Only here is He declared to be the Creator of all things (1:3). Only here is He spoken of as "The Only Begotten of the Father" (1:14). Only here was He hailed as "The Lamb of God" (1:29). Only here is He revealed as the great "I am." When Jehovah appeared to Moses at the burning bush, and commissioned him to go down into Egypt and demand from Pharaoh the release of His people Israel, Moses said, Who shall I say hath sent me? And God answered, "Thus shalt thou say unto the Children of Israel, I am hath sent me unto you" (Ex. 3:14). And here in John's Gospel Christ takes this most sacred title of Deity and appropriates it unto Himself, filling it out with sevenfold fullness: "I am the Bread of Life" (6:35); "I am the Light of the world" (9:5); "I am the Door" (10:7); "I am the Good Shepherd" (10:11); "I am the Resurrection and the Life" (11:25); "I am the Way, the Truth, and the Life" (14:6); "I am the true Vine" (15:1).

b. The deity of Christ is prominently revealed here.
Christ Himself expressly affirmed it: "Verily, verily, I say unto you, The hour is coming, and now is, when the dead shall hear the voice of the Son of God: and they that hear shall live" (5:25). Again; "Jesus heard that they had cast him out; and when He had found him, he said unto him, Dost thou believe on the Son of God? He answered and said, Who is He, Lord, that I might believe on Him? And Jesus said unto him, Thou hast

both seen Him, and it is He that talketh with thee" (9:35-37). Once more. "His sisters sent unto Him, saying, Lord, behold, he whom Thou lovest is sick. When Jesus heard that, He said, This sickness is not unto death, but for the glory of God, that the Son of God might be glorified thereby" (11:3, 4). Thirty-five times in this Gospel we find the Lord Jesus speaking of God as "My Father." Twenty-five times He here says "Verily, verily" (of a truth, of a truth)—nowhere else found in this intensified form.

Including His own affirmation of it, seven different ones avow His Deity in this Gospel. First, John the Baptist: "And I saw and bare record that this is the Son of God" (1:34). Second, Nathaniel, "Rabbi, Thou art the Son of God" (1:49). Third, Peter, "And we believe and are sure that Thou art that Christ, the Son of the living God" (6:69). The Lord Himself, "Say ye of Him, whom the Father hath sanctified, and sent into the world, Thou blasphemest; because I said, I am the Son of God" (10:36). Fifth, Martha, "She saith unto Him, Yea, Lord, I believe that Thou art the Christ, the Son of God, which should come into the world" (11:27). Sixth, Thomas, "And Thomas answered and said unto Him, My Lord and my God" (20:28). Seventh, the writer of this fourth Gospel, "These are written, that ye might believe that Jesus is the Christ, the Son of God; and that believing ye might have life through His name" (20:31).

c. There is a remarkable series of sevens here.
It is striking to discover how frequently this numeral is found here, and when we remember the significance of this numeral it is even more arresting. Seven is the number of perfection, and absolute perfection is not found until we reach God Himself. How wonderful, then, that in this Gospel which sets forth the Deity of Christ, the number seven meets us at every turn!

By seven different persons is the Deity of Christ confessed here, and, as we have seen seven times does He fill out the ineffable "I am" title. John records seven miracles performed by our Lord during His public ministry, no more and no less. Seven times do we read, "These things have I spoken unto you." Seven times did Christ address the woman at the well. Seven times, in John 6, did Christ speak of Himself as "The Bread of Life."

Seven things we read of the Good Shepherd doing for His sheep, and seven things Christ says about His sheep in John 10. Seven times does Christ make reference to "the hour" which was to see the accomplishment of the Work given Him to do. Seven times did He bid His disciples pray "in His name." Seven times is the word "hate" found in John 15. There are seven things enumerated in John 16:13, 14 which the Holy Spirit is to do for believers. There were seven things which Christ asked the Father for believers in John 17, and seven times over does He there refer to them as the Father's "gift" to Him. Seven times in this Gospel do we read that Christ declared He spoke only the Word of the Father—7:16; 8:28; 8:47; 12:49; 14:10; 14:24; 17:8. Seven times does the writer of this Gospel refer to himself, without directly mentioning his own name. There are seven important things found in John which are common to all four Gospels. And so we might continue. Let the reader search carefully for himself and he will find many other examples.

d. Man's futile attempts on His life.
Not only was the Christ of God "despised and rejected of men," not only was He "hated without a cause," but His enemies repeatedly sought His life. This feature is noticed, briefly, by the other writers, but John is the only one that tells us why their efforts were futile. For example, in John 7:30 we read, "Then they sought to take Him: but no man laid hands on Him, because His hour was not yet come." And again, in 8:20 we read, "These words spake Jesus in the treasury, as He taught in the Temple: and no man laid hands on Him; for His hour was not yet come." These Scriptures, in accord with the special character of this fourth Gospel, bring before us the Divine side of things. They tell us that the events of earth transpire only according to the appointment of Heaven. They show that God is working all things

after the counsel of His own will and according to His eternal purpose. They teach us that nothing is left to chance, but that when God's "hour" arrives that which has been decreed by His sovereign will, is performed. They reveal the fact that even His enemies are entirely subject to God's immediate control, and that they cannot make a single move without His direct permission.

The Lord Jesus Christ was not the helpless Victim of an angry mob. What He suffered, He endured voluntarily. The enemy might roar against Him, and His emissaries might thirst for His blood, but not a thing could they do without His consent. It is in this Gospel we hear Him saying, "Therefore doth My Father love Me, because I lay down My life, that I might take it again. No man taketh it from Me, but I lay it down of Myself. I have power to lay it down, and I have power to take it again" (10:17. 18). While He hung upon the Cross, His enemies said, "He saved others; let Him save Himself, if He be Christ, the Chosen of God" (Luke 23:35). And He accepted their challenge! He saved Himself not from death, but out of it; not from the Cross, but the Tomb.

e. The purpose and scope of this Gospel.
The key to it is hung right under the door. The opening verse intimates that the Deity of Christ is the special theme of this Gospel. The order of its contents is defined in 16:28: (1.) "I came forth from the Father:" this may be taken as the heading for the Introductory portion, the first eighteen verses of the opening chapter; (2.) "And am come into the world:" this may be taken as the heading for the first main section of this Gospel, running from 1:19 to the end of chapter 12. (3.) "Again, I leave the world:" this may be taken as the heading for the second great section of the Gospel, comprising chapter 13 to 17 inclusive, where the Lord is seen apart from "the world," alone with His beloved disciples. (4.) "And go to the Father:" this may be taken as the heading for the closing section of this Gospel, made up of its last four chapters, which give us the final scenes, preparatory to the Lord's return to His Father.

The closing verses of John 20 tell us the purpose of this Gospel: "And many other signs truly did Jesus in the presence of His disciples, which are not written in this book. But these are written, that ye might believe that Jesus is the Christ, the Son of God; and that believing ye might have life through His name." John's Gospel, then, is peculiarly suited to the unsaved. But this does not exhaust its scope. It is equally fitted for and written to believers; in fact, the opening chapter intimates it is designed specially for the saved, for in 1:16 we read, "And of His fullness have all we received, and grace for grace."

f. The account of His Passion is remarkable.

Here there is no glimpse given us of the Savior's agony in Gethsemane: there is no crying, "If it be possible let this cup pass from Me," there is no bloody sweat, no angel appearing to strengthen Him. Here there is no seeking of companionship from His disciples in the Garden; instead, he knows them only as needing His protection (see 18:8). Here there is no compelling of Simon to bear His cross. Here there is no mention of the three hours of darkness, nor is reference made to the awful cry, "My God, My God, why hast Thou forsaken Me?" Here there is nothing said of the spectators taunting the dying Savior, and no mention is made of the insulting challenge of the rulers for Him to descend from the Cross and they would believe in Him. And here there is no word said of the Rending of the Veil, as the Redeemer breathed His last. How striking is this, for in John's Gospel God is unveiled throughout; no need, then, for the veil to be rent here! John says nothing about Him eating food after the resurrection, for as Son of God, He needed it not!

g. Christ's dignity and majesty comes out here amid His humiliation.

John is the only one that tells us that when the Lord's enemies came to arrest Him in the Garden that when He asked them "Whom seek ye?", and they replied, "Jesus of Nazareth," and he then pronounced the sacred "I am," they "went backward and fell to the ground" (18:6). What a demonstration of His Godhead was this! How easily could He have walked away unmolested had He so pleased!

John is the only one to speak of His coat "without seam" which the soldiers would not rend (19:24). John is the only one to show us how completely the Savior was master of Himself—"Jesus knowing that all things were now accomplished" (19:28). His mind was not beclouded, nor was His memory impaired. No; even at the close of all His sufferings, the whole scheme of Messianic prediction stood out clearly before Him.

John is the only one of the four Evangelists to record the Savior's triumphant cry, "It is finished" (19:30), as he is the only one to say that after He had expired the soldier's "brake not His legs" (19:33). John is the only one to tell us of Love's race to the sepulcher (20:3, 4). And John is the only one to say that the risen Savior "breathed" on the disciples, and said, "Receive ye the Holy Spirit" (20:22).

The closing verse of this Gospel is in perfect keeping with its character and scope. Here, and here only, we are told, "And there are also many other things which Jesus did, the which, if they should be written every one, I suppose that even the world itself could not contain the books that should be written. Amen" (21:25). Thus, the last note here sounded is that of infinity!

CONCLUSION

On our somewhat brief examination of the four Gospels it has been the writer's design to bring before the reader that which is characteristic in each one, pointing out the various connections in which the different Evangelists view our Lord and Savior. It is evident that each of the Gospels contemplates Him in a distinct relationship—Matthew as King, Mark as Servant, Luke as Son of Man, and John as Son of God. But while each Evangelist portrays the Lord Jesus in an entirely different viewpoint from the others, yet he does not altogether exclude that which is found in the remaining three. God knew that where the Scriptures would be translated into heathen tongues, before the whole Bible or even the complete New Testament was given to different peoples, oftentimes only a single Gospel would be translated as a beginning, and therefore has the Holy Spirit seen to it that each Gospel presents a more or less complete setting forth of the manifold glories of His Son. In other words, He caused each writer to combine in his own Evangel the various lines of Truth found in the others, though making these subordinate to that which was central and peculiar to himself.

That which is dominant in Matthew's delineation of the Lord Jesus is the presentation of Him as the Son of David, the Heir of Israel's throne, the Messiah and King of the Jews. Yet, while this is the outstanding feature of the first Gospel, nevertheless, a careful study of it will discover traces therein of the other offices that Christ filled. Even in Matthew the Servant character of our Lord comes into view, though, in an incidental manner. It is Matthew who tells us that when the sons of Zebedee came requesting of Him that they might sit on His right hand and on His left in His kingdom, and that when the other ten apostles were moved with indignation against them, He said, "Ye know that the princes of the Gentiles exercise dominion over them, and that they that are great exercise authority upon them. But it shall not be so among you: but whosoever will be great among you, let him be your minister; and whosoever will be chief among you, let him be your servant: Even as the Son of Man came not to be ministered unto, but to minister, and to give His life a ransom for many" (20:25-28); and it is from this Gospel we learn that when He sent forth the Twelve, He warned them, "The disciple is not above his Master, nor the servant above his Lord. It is enough for the disciple that he be as his Master, and the servant as his Lord. If they have called the Master of the house Beelzebub, how much more shall they call them of His household" (10:24, 25).

Again; Matthew's Gospel does not hide from us the lowly place the Lord took as the Son of Man, for it is here we have recorded His word, "The foxes have holes, and the birds of the air have nests; but the Son of Man hath not where to lay His head" (8:20): as it is here we are told that when they that received

tribute came to Peter and asked, "Doth your Master pay tribute?" that the Lord said to His disciple, "What thinkest thou, Simon? of whom do the kings of the earth take custom or tribute? of their own children, or of strangers? Peter said unto Him, Of strangers. Jesus said unto him, Then are the children (i.e. of kings) free. Notwithstanding, lest we should offend them, to thou to the sea, and cast an hook, and take up the fish that first cometh up; and when thou hast opened his mouth, thou shalt find a piece of money: that take, and give unto them, for Me and thee" (17:25-27).

So, too, do the Divine glories of Christ shine forth on the pages of this first Gospel. It is here that we are told, "Behold, a virgin shall be with Child, and shall bring forth a Son, and they shall call His name Emmanuel, which being interpreted is, God with us" (1:23). And it is here we have recorded most fully Peter's notable confession, "Thou art the Christ, the Son of the living God" (16:16).

Mark's central purpose is to present Christ as God's perfect Workman yet, here and there, he gives hints that the Servant of Jehovah possessed other and higher glories. This second Gospel, as well as the first and third, record His Transfiguration upon the holy mount (9:2), and Mark also tells us of the Triumphal Entry into Jerusalem (11:7-10). It is here we are told that when the high priest asked Him, "Art Thou the Christ, the Son of the Blessed?" that He answered, "I am: and ye shall see the Son of Man sitting on the right hand of power, and coming in the clouds of Heaven" (14:62). Thus did He bear witness to His Messianic and Kingly glory.

Mark is also careful to tell us in the opening verse of his Gospel that Jesus Christ was "the Son of God," as he also informs us that the demon-possessed man from the tombs cried and said, "What have I to do with Thee, Jesus, Thou Son of the most high God?" (5:7). These things do not detract from that which is central in this second Gospel, but guard the Divine glories of Him that "took upon Him the form of a servant."

Luke describes the Humanity of the Savior, pictures Him as the Son of Man, and shows us the lowly place which He took. But while this is the central theme of the third Gospel, references are also made, here, to His higher glories. It is here we read that the Savior told the people, "Behold a greater than Solomon is here" (11:31), as it is here we also find Him owned as "The Son of David" (18:38). Luke also refers to the Transfiguration and the Triumphal Entry into Jerusalem.

This third Gospel reveals the fact that the Savior was more than Man. It is here we are told that the angel of the Lord said unto Mary, "That Holy Thing which shall be born of thee shall be called the Son of God" (1:35); as it is here also read of the demon-possessed man crying, "What have we to do with Thee Jesus, Thou Son of God most high" (8:28)!

So it is with the fourth Gospel. The outstanding feature there is the setting forth of the Deity of Christ, yet a careful reading of John will also reveal His Kingship as well as His Human lowliness. It is here we read of Andrew telling his brother Simon, "We have found the Messiah, which is, being interpreted, the Christ" (1:41). It is here that we are told Nathaniel owned our Lord as, "The King of Israel" (1:49). It is in this forth Gospel we hear the Samaritans saying unto the converted adulteress, "Now we believe, not because of thy saying: for we have heard Him ourselves, and know that this is indeed the Christ (i.e., the Messiah), the Savior of the world" (4:42). And it is here also we learn that when entering Jerusalem, the people "took branches of palm trees, and went forth to meet Him, and cried, Hosanna, Blessed is The King of Israel that cometh in the name of the Lord" (12:13).

In like manner, we find in John illustrations of our Lord's lowliness. It is in this fourth Gospel that we read, "Jesus therefore, being wearied with his journey, sat thus on the well" (4:6). It is here we find recorded the pathetic fact, that, "every man went unto his own house—Jesus went unto the mount of Olives" (7:53; 8:1). Every "man" had his "own house" to which he retired at night, but the Beloved of the Father was a homeless Stranger here! So, again, it is John who tells us, "And it was winter, and (being cold out on the mountain) Jesus walked in the Temple in Solomon's porch" (10:22, 23). Once more: it is

John who shows us the Lord, as the perfect Man, making provision for His widowed mother, providing her a home with His beloved disciple (19:26, 27).

Returning now to our central design in this book, we would take a look at two or three incidents found in all four Gospels, and comparing them carefully, would notice the characteristic and distinctive lines in each one. First, let us observe the reference which each Evangelist makes to John the Baptist. Matthew alone tells us that he cried, "Repent ye: for the kingdom of heaven is at hand" (3:3), for Matthew is the one who presents the Lord Jesus as Israel's King and Messiah. Mark is the only one to tell us that those who were baptized by our Lord's forerunner "confessed their sins" (1:5), this being in accord with the ministerial character of this second Gospel. Luke, who dwells on human relationships, is the only writer that tells us about the parentage of the Baptist (chap. 1), as he is the only one to describe in detail the various classes of people who came to him at the Jordan. All of these things are significantly omitted by John, for in this fourth Gospel the emphasis is placed not upon the Baptist, but upon the One he was sent to herald. Here only are we told that he "came to bear witness of the Light" (1:7); that Christ existed before him (1:15), though as a Child He was born three months after him; and that he testified Christ was both God's "Lamb" (1:29) and God's Son" (1:34).

Again; let us note what each Evangelist has said about the Feeding of the five thousand, and particularly the way in which this miracle is introduced. Matthew says, "And Jesus went forth, and saw a great multitude, and was moved with compassion toward them, and He healed their sick. And when it was evening, His disciples came to Him, saying, This is a desert place, and the time is now past; send the multitude away, that they may go into the villages, and buy themselves victuals. But Jesus said unto them, They need not depart; give ye them to eat" (14:14-16). Thus, Matthew prefaces his account of this miracle by speaking of Christ "healing the sick," for this was one of the Messianic signs. Mark says: "And Jesus, when He came out, saw much people, and was moved with compassion toward them, because they were as sheep not having a shepherd: and He began to teach them many things. And when the day was now far spent, His disciples came unto Him, and said, This is a desert place, and now the time is far passed: Send them away, that they may go into the country round about, and into the villages, and buy themselves bread: for they have nothing to eat. He answered and said unto them, Give them to eat" (6:34-37). Instead of mentioning the "healing of the sick," Mark brings a beautiful ministerial touch into his picture by telling us the Savior was moved with compassion toward the people because they were "as sheep not having a shepherd," and then makes known how the perfect Servant "began to teach them many things," thus ministering to them the Word of God. Luke tells us, "And the people, when they knew it, followed Him: and He received them, and spake unto them of the kingdom of God, and healed them that had need of healing. And when the day began to wear away, then came the twelve, and said unto Him, Send the multitude away, that they may go into the towns and country round about, and lodge, and get victuals: for we are here in a desert place. But He said unto them, Give ye them to eat" (Luke 9:11-13). Here we find Human sympathy and human want brought out, for Luke presents the great Physician healing, not as a Messianic sign, but healing those "that had need of healing." Now, observe, how entirely different is John's method of introducing this miracle. He says nothing about the Messianic sign of healing, nothing about the Servant of God "teaching" the people, and nothing of the Son of Man ministering to the "need" of the sick; instead, he tells us, "When Jesus then lifted up his eyes, and saw a great company come unto Him, He saith unto Philip, Whence shall we buy bread, that these may eat? And He said this to prove him: for He himself *knew* what He would do" (6:5, 6). Thus the fourth Gospel, again, brings out the Deity of Christ, by revealing His Omniscience.

As another example of the characteristic differences of each of the four Evangelists when recording the same or a similar incident, let us take the Sabbath criticisms which the Savior met with. Each of the Gospels make mention of Christ being condemned for transgressing the traditions of the elders with which the Jews had cumbered the Sabbath, and each tells us the reply which He made to His objectors, and the arguments He used to vindicate Himself. In Matthew 12:2, 3 we read, "At that time Jesus went on the Sabbath day through the corn; and His disciples were an hungered, and began to pluck the ears of corn, and to eat. But when the Pharisees saw it, they said unto him, Behold, Thy disciples do that which is not lawful to do upon the Sabbath day." To this our Lord made answer by reminding the Pharisees how that David, when he was an hungered, entered the house of God and did eat the shewbread, sharing it also with those that were with him. Then He went on to say, "Have ye not read in the Law, how that on the Sabbath days the priests in the temple profane the Sabbath, and are blameless? But I say unto you, That in this place is One greater than the Temple" (Matt. 12:5, 6). Mark also refers to this same incident, and records part of the reply which the Savior made on this occasion (see 2:23-28), but it is very striking to observe that he omits the Lord's statement that He was "Greater than the Temple." In Luke's Gospel there is a miracle recorded which is not found elsewhere—the healing of the woman who had an infirmity for eighteen years (Luke 13:11-13). As the sequel to this we are told, "And the ruler of the synagogue answered with indignation because that Jesus had healed on the Sabbath day, and said unto the people, There are six days in which men ought to work: in them therefore come and be healed, and not on the Sabbath" (11:14). But on this occasion we find Christ employed an argument to vindicate Himself, which was thoroughly in keeping with the scope of this third Gospel. "The Lord then answered him, and said, Thou hypocrite, doth not each one of you on the Sabbath loose his ox or his ass from the stall, and lead him away to watering? And ought not this woman, being a daughter of Abraham, whom Satan hath bound, lo, these eighteen years, be loosed from this bond on the Sabbath day?" (13:15, 16). Here the appeal was not to the Old Testament scriptures, nor to His own Greatness, but to human sympathies. John records another miracle, not mentioned by the others, which also met with a similar rebuke from the Lord's foes. But here, in answering His critics, the Lord Jesus vindicated Himself by using an entirely different argument from those employed on other occasions, as noted by other Evangelists. Here we find Him replying: "My Father worketh hitherto, and I work" (5:17). Thus, we see again, the principle of selection determining what each Evangelist recorded.

One more example must suffice. Let us observe what each Gospel says about the Arrest in the Garden. Matthew tells us, "And while He yet spake, lo, Judas, one of the twelve, came, and with him a great multitude with swords and staves, from the chief priests and elders of the people. Now he that betrayed Him gave them a sign, saying, Whomsoever I shall kiss, that same is He: hold Him fast. And forthwith he came to Jesus, and said, Hail, Master; and kissed Him. And Jesus said unto him, Friend, wherefore art thou come? Then came they, and laid hands on Jesus, and took Him. And, behold, one of them which was with Jesus stretched out his hand, and drew his sword, and struck a servant of the high priest's and smote off his ear. Then said Jesus unto him, Put up thy sword again unto his place: for all they that take the sword shall perish with the sword. Thinkest thou that I cannot now pray to My Father, and He shall presently give Me more than twelve legions of angels? But how then shall the Scriptures be fulfilled, that thus it must be?" (26:47-54). Mark says: "And immediately, while He spake, cometh Judas, one of the twelve, and with him a great multitude with swords and staves, from the chief priests and the scribes and the elders. And he that betrayed Him had given them a token, saying, Whomsoever I shall kiss, that same is He; take Him and lead Him away safely. And as soon as he was come, he goeth straightway to Him, and saith, Master, Master; and kissed Him. And they laid their hands on Him, and took Him. And one of them that stood by drew a sword, and smote a servant of the high priest, and cut off his ear.

And Jesus answered and said unto them, Are ye come out as against a thief, with swords and with staves to take Me? I was daily with you in the Temple teaching, and ye took Me not: but the Scriptures must be fulfilled" (14:43-49). It will be observed that Mark omits the fact that Christ addressed the traitor as "Friend" (see Ps. 41:9—Messianic prophecy), as he also says nothing about His right to ask the Father for twelve legions of angels. In Luke we read, "And while He yet spake, behold a multitude, and he that was called Judas, one of the twelve, went before them, and drew near unto Jesus to kiss Him. But Jesus said unto him, Judas, betrayest thou the Son of Man with a kiss? When they that were about Him, saw what would follow, they said unto Him, Lord, shall we smite with the sword? and one of them smote the servant of the high priest, and cut off his right ear. Then Jesus answered and said, Suffer ye thus far. And He touched his ear, and healed him. Then Jesus said unto the chief priests, and captains of the temple, and the elders, which were come unto Him, Be ye come out, as against a thief, with swords, and staves? When I was daily with you in the Temple, ye stretched forth no hands against Me, but this is your hour, and the power of darkness" (Luke 22:47-53). Luke is the only one to record Christ's touching but searching question to Judas, as he is the only one to tell us of Christ healing the ear of the high priest's servant. Entirely different is John's account. In 18:3 we read, "Judas then, having received a band of men and officers from the chief priests and Pharisees, cometh thither with lanterns and torches and weapons." But here only is it added, "Jesus therefore, knowing all things that should come upon Him, went forth, and said unto them, Whom seek ye. They answered Him, Jesus of Nazareth." Here only are we told, "Jesus said unto them, I am. And Judas also, which betrayed Him, stood with them. As soon then as He had said unto them, I am, they went backward, and fell to the ground" (18:5, 6). Here only do we read, "If therefore ye seek Me, let these go their way: that the saying might be fulfilled, which he spoke, Of them which Thou gavest Me have I lost none" (18:8, 9). And here only are we told that the Lord said to the disciple who had cut off the ear of the priest's servant, "Put up thy sword into the sheath: the cup which My Father hath given Me, shall I not drink it?" (John 18:11).

In closing, we would call attention to one other feature of the Gospels, that has often been noticed by others, and that is, what is found in the closing portions of the respective Gospels. There is a striking and climatic order observed. At the close of Matthew's Gospel, we read of the Resurrection of Christ (28:1-8).

At the close of Mark's Gospel, we read of the Ascension of Christ (16:19). At the close of Luke's Gospel, we hear of the Coming of the Holy Spirit (24:49). While at the close of John's Gospel, reference is made to the Return of Christ (21:21-23)! May that Day soon dawn when He shall come again to receive us unto Himself, and in the little interval that yet awaits, may we study His Word more diligently and obey its precepts more carefully.

A. W. Pink, Why Four Gospels? *1921*

2.4 THE GOSPELS, M. G. EASTON

The only reliable sources of information regarding the life of Christ on earth are the Gospels, which present in historical detail the words and the work of Christ in so many different aspects.

M. G. Easton, Easton Illustrated Dictionary

2.5 HISTORICITY OF THE GOSPELS, J. B. PHILLIPS

I have heard professing Christians of our own day speak as though the historicity of the Gospels does not matter—all that matters is the contemporary Spirit of Christ. I contend that the historicity does matter, and I do not see why we, who live nearly two thousand years later, should call into question an Event for which there were many eye-witnesses still living at the time when most of the New Testament was written. It was no "cunningly devised fable" but an historic irruption of God into human history which gave birth to a young church so sturdy that the pagan world could not stifle or destroy it.

J. B. Phillips
Ring of Truth
Wheaton, Illinois: Harold Shaw Publishers, 1967

2.6 THE STORY OF THE BIRTH OF JESUS, MARTIN LUTHER

Sermon preached on Christmas Day, from Luke 2:1-14, at Wartburg Church Postil, 1521

I. THE BIRTH OF JESUS

1. It is written in Haggai 2:6-7, that God says, "I will shake the heavens; and the precious things of all nations shall come." This is fulfilled today, for the heavens were shaken, that is, the angels in the heavens sang praises to God. And the earth was shaken, that is, the people on the earth were agitated; one journeying to this city, another to that throughout the whole land, as the Gospel tells us. It was not a violent, bloody uprising, but rather a peaceful one brought about by God who is the God of peace.

2. This taxing, enrollment, or census, says Luke, was the first; but in the Gospel according to Matthew 17:24, and at other places we read that it was continued from time to time, that they even demanded tribute of Christ, and tempted him with the tribute money, Matt. 22:17. This taxing was nothing other than a common decree throughout the whole empire that every individual should annually pay a penny, and the officers who collected the tribute were called publicans, who in German are wrongly interpreted "notorious sinners."

3. Observe how exact the Evangelist is in his statement that the birth of Christ occurred in the time of Caesar Augustus, and when Quirinius was governor of Syria, of which the land of Judea was a part, just as Austria is a part of the German land. This being the very first taxing, it appears that this tribute was never before paid until just at the time when Christ was to be born. By this Jesus shows that his kingdom was not to be of an earthly character nor to exercise worldly power and lordship, but that he, together with his parents, is subject to the powers that be. Since he comes at the time of the very first enrollment, he leaves no doubt with respect to this, for had he desired to leave it in doubt, he might have willed to be born under another enrollment, so that it might have been said it just happened so, without any divine intent.

4. And had he not willed to be submissive, he might have been born before there was any enrollment decreed. Since now all the deeds of Jesus provide valuable lessons, this fact must be interpreted to mean that he by divine counsel and purpose will not exercise any worldly authority; but will be subject to it.

5. This Gospel is so clear that it requires very little explanation, but it should be well considered and taken deeply to heart; and no one will receive more benefit from it than those who, with a calm, quiet heart, banish everything else from their mind, and diligently look into it. It is just as the sun which is reflected in calm water and gives out vigorous warmth, but which cannot be so readily seen nor can it give out such warmth in water that is in disturbed and fast-moving.

Therefore, if you would be enlightened and warmed, if you would see the wonders of divine grace and have your heart aglow and enlightened, devout and joyful, go where you can silently meditate and lay hold of this picture deep in your heart, and you will see miracle upon miracle.

6. First, note how things that appear to be very ordinary to us are viewed very differently in heaven.

On earth the event is viewed as follows: Here is a poor young woman, Mary of Nazareth, not highly esteemed, but the humblest citizen of the village. No one is conscious of the great baby she will bear. She is silent, keeps her own counsel, and thinks of herself as the least significant in the town. She sets out with her husband Joseph. They most probably had no servant, so Joseph had to do the work of master and servant, and Mary the work of mistress and maid.

7. Now it is seems likely that they owned a donkey, on which Mary rode, although the Gospel does not mention it, and it is possible that she traveled on foot with Joseph. Imagine how she was despised at the inns and stopping places along the way, although she was worthy of riding in state in a chariot of gold.

8. There were, no doubt, many wives and daughters of prominent men at that time, who lived in fine apartments and great splendor, while the mother of God takes a journey in mid-winter under most trying circumstances. It was more than a day's journey from Nazareth in Galilee to Bethlehem. They had to journey either by or through Jerusalem, for Bethlehem is south of Jerusalem while Nazareth is north.

9. The Evangelist shows how, when they arrived in Bethlehem, they were the most insignificant and despised of people. They were obliged to take refuge in a stable, to share a room with the cattle. No one noticed what God was doing in that stable. O what a dark night this was for Bethlehem, that was not conscious of that glorious light! See how God shows that he utterly disregards what the world is, has or desires; and furthermore, that the world shows how little it knows or notices what God is, has and does.

10. See, this is the first picture with which Christ puts the world to shame and exposes all it does and knows. It shows that the world's greatest wisdom is foolishness, her best actions are wrong and her greatest treasures are misfortunes. What had Bethlehem when it did not have Christ?

11. Some have commented on the word "*diversorium*," as if it meant an open archway, through which every body could pass, where some asses stood, and that Mary could not get

to a lodging place. This is not right. The Evangelist desires to show that Joseph and Mary had to occupy a stable, because there was no room for her in the inn, in the place where the pilgrim guests generally lodged. All the guests were cared for in the inn or caravansary, with room, food and bed, except these poor people who had to creep into a stable where it was customary to house cattle. They had neither money nor influence to secure a room in the inn, hence they were obliged to stay in a stable. O world, how stupid! O man, how blind thou art!

12. But the birth itself is still more pitiful. There was no one to take pity on this young wife who was for the first time to give birth to a child; no one to take to heart her condition that she, a stranger, did not have the least thing a mother needs as she gives birth. . . .

13. Some argue about how this birth took place, as if Jesus was born while Mary was praying and rejoicing, without any pain, and before she was conscious of it. While I do not altogether discard that pious supposition, it was evidently invented for the sake of simple minded people. But we must abide by the Gospel, that he was born of the virgin Mary. There is no deception here, for the Word clearly states that it was an actual birth.

14. It is well known what is meant by giving birth. Mary's experience was not different from that of other women, so that the birth of Christ was a real natural birth, Mary being his natural mother and he being her natural son. Therefore her body performed its functions of giving birth, which naturally belonged to it, except that she brought forth without sin, without shame, without pain and without injury, just as she had conceived without sin. The curse of Eve did not come on her, where God said: "In pain thou shalt bring forth children," Gen. 3:16; otherwise it was the same with her in every detail as with every woman who gives birth to a child.

15. Grace does not interfere with nature and her work, but rather improves and promotes it. Likewise Mary, without doubt, also nourished the child with milk from her breast. I mention this that we may be grounded in the faith and know that Jesus was

a natural man in every respect just as we, the only difference being in his relationship to sin and grace. Jesus did not have a sinful nature. In him and in his mother nature was pure. Here God bestowed special honor upon nature and its work.

It is a great comfort to us that Jesus took upon himself our nature and flesh. Therefore we are not to take away from him or his mother anything that is not in conflict with grace, for the text clearly says that "she brought him forth," and the angels said, "unto you he is born."

16. How could God have shown his goodness in a more sublime way than by humbling himself to partake of flesh and blood? In no way could he have given us stronger, more forcible and purer pictures of chastity than in this birth. When we look at this birth, and reflect upon how the sublime Majesty moves with great earnestness and inexpressible love and goodness upon the flesh and blood of this virgin, we see how here all evil lust and every evil thought is banished.

17. No woman can inspire such pure thoughts in a man as this virgin; nor can any man inspire such pure thought in a woman as this child. If in reflecting on this birth we recognize the work of God that is embodied in it, only chastity and purity spring from it.

18. But what happens in heaven concerning this birth? As much as it is despised on earth, so much and a thousand times more is it honored in heaven. If an angel from heaven came and praised you and your work, would you not regard it of greater value than all the praise and honor the world could give you, and for which you would be willing to bear the greatest humility and reproach? What exalted honor is that when all the angels in heaven cannot restrain themselves from rejoicing, so that even poor shepherds in the fields hear them preach, praise God, sing and pour out their joy?

19. Note how richly God honors those who are despised by men. Here you see that God's eyes look into the depths of humility, as is written, "He sitteth above the cherubim" and looketh into the depths. Nor could the angels find princes or valiant men to whom to communicate the good news; but only

uneducated laymen, the most humble people upon earth. Could they not have addressed the high priests, who it was assumed knew so much concerning God and the angels? No, God chose poor shepherds, who, though they were held in low esteem in the sight of men, were in heaven regarded as worthy of such great grace and honor. . . .

22. We must adapt ourselves to God, he will not adapt himself to us. Moreover, he who will not regard his word, nor the manner in which he works to bring comfort to men, has assuredly no good evidence of being saved. In what more lovely manner could he have shown his grace to the humble and despised of earth, than through this birth in poverty, over which the angels rejoice, and make it known to no one but to the poor shepherds?

23. Let us now look at the mysteries set before us in this history. Two things are especially emphasized: the Gospel and faith: that is, what is to be preached and what is to be believed; who are to be the preachers, and who are to be the believers. This we will now consider.

II. THE SPIRITUAL MEANING OF THE BIRTH OF JESUS
a. The teaching concerning faith

24. Faith is first. There is no point in only believing that this history is true as it is written; for all sinners, even those condemned, believe that. The Scripture, God's Word, does not teach that faith is a natural work, or that it can happen without grace. The kind of faith which God demands is that you firmly believe that Christ is born for you, and that this birth took place for your welfare. The Gospel teaches that Christ was born, and that he did and suffered everything in our behalf, as is here declared by the angel: "Behold, I bring you good tidings of great joy which shall be to all the people; for there is born to you this day a Savior, who is Christ the Lord." In these words you clearly see that he is born for us.

25. He does not simply say, Christ is born, but "to you" he is born, neither does he say, I bring glad tidings, but "to you" I bring glad tidings of great joy. Furthermore, this joy was not to remain in Christ, but it shall be to

all the people. This faith no condemned or wicked man has, nor can he have it; for the right basis of salvation which unites Christ and the believing heart is that they have all things in common.

26. Christ has a pure, innocent, and holy birth. Man has an unclean, sinful, condemned birth; as David says, Ps. 51:5, "Behold I was brought forth in iniquity; and in sin did my mother conceive me." Nothing can help this unholy birth except the pure birth of Christ. The effect of Christ's birth is imparted spiritually, through the Word, as the angel says, it is given to all who firmly believe so that no harm will come to them because of their impure birth. This it the way in which we are to be cleansed from the miserable birth we have from Adam. For this purpose Christ willed to be born, that through him we might be born again, as he says in John 3:3, that it takes place through faith. James says the same in James 1:18.

27. We see here how Christ, as it were, takes our birth from us and absorbs it in his birth, and grants us his, that in it we might become pure and holy, as if it were our own, so that every Christian may rejoice and glory in Christ's birth as much as if he had himself been born of Mary as was Christ. Whoever does not believe this, or doubts, is no Christian.

28. O, this is the great joy of which the angel speaks. This is the comfort and exceeding goodness of God that, if a person believes this, he can boast of the treasure that Mary is his rightful mother, Christ his brother, and God his father. For these things actually occurred and are true, but we must believe. This is the principal thing and the principal treasure in every Gospel, before any doctrine of good works can be taken out of it. Christ must above all things become our own and we become his, before we can do good works.

But this cannot occur except through the faith that teaches us rightly to understand the Gospel and properly to lay hold of it. This is the only way in which Christ can be rightly known so that the conscience is satisfied and made to rejoice. Out of this grow love and praise to God who in Christ has bestowed

upon us such unspeakable gifts. This gives courage to do or leave undone, and living or dying, to suffer everything that is well pleasing to God. This is what is meant by Isaiah 9:6, "Unto us a child is born, unto us a son is given," to us, to us, to us is born, and to us is given this child.

29. Therefore see to it that you do not find pleasure in the Gospel only as a history, for that is only transient; neither regard it only as an example, for it is of no value without faith; but see to it that you make this birth your own and that Christ is born in you. This will be the case if you believe, then you will repose in the lap of the virgin Mary and be her dear child. But you must exercise this faith and pray while you live, you cannot establish it too firmly. This is our foundation and inheritance, upon which good works must be built. . . .

b. The spiritual meaning of the doctrine of this Gospel

34. The other mystery, or spiritual teaching, is that in the churches the Gospel only should be preached and nothing more. Now it is evident that the Gospel teaches nothing but the following two things, Christ and his example and two kinds of good works, the one belonging to Christ by which we are saved through faith, the other belonging to us by which our neighbor receives help. Whosoever therefore teaches any thing different from the Gospel leads people astray; and whosoever does not teach the Gospel in these two parts, leads people all the more astray and is worse than the former who teaches without the Gospel, because he abuses and corrupts God's Word, as St. Paul complains concerning some. 2 Cor. 2:17.

35. Now it is clear that nature could not have discovered such a doctrine, nor could all the ingenuity, reason and wisdom of the world have thought it up. Who would be able to discover by means of his own efforts, that faith in Christ makes us one with Christ and gives us for our own all that is Christ's? Who would be able to discover that no works are of any value except those intended to benefit our neighbor? Nature teaches no more than that which is wrought by the law. Therefore it falls

back upon its own work, so that this one thinks he fulfills the commandment by founding some institution or order, that one by fasting, this one by the kind of clothes he wears, that one by going on pilgrimages; this one in this manner, that one in that manner; and yet all their works are worthless, for no one is helped by them. Such is the case at the present time in which the whole world is blinded and is going astray through the doctrines and works of men, so that faith and love along with the Gospel have perished.

36. Therefore the Gospel properly apprehended, is a supernatural sermon and light which makes known Christ only. This is pointed out first of all by the fact that it was not a man that made it known to others, but that an angel came down from heaven and made known to the shepherds the birth of Jesus, while no human being knew any thing about it.

37. In the second place it is pointed out by the fact that Christ was born at midnight, by which he indicates that all the world is in darkness as to its future and that Christ can not be known by mere reason, but that knowledge concerning him must be revealed from heaven.

38. In the third place, it is shown by the light that shined around the shepherds, which teaches that here there must be an entirely different light than that of human reason. Moreover, when Luke says, *Gloria Dei*, the glory of God, shone around them, he calls that light a brightness, or the glory of God. Why does he say that? In order to call attention to the mystery and reveal the character of the Gospel. For while the Gospel is a heavenly light that teaches nothing more than Christ, in whom God's grace is given to us and all human merit is entirely cast aside, it exalts only the glory of God, so that henceforth no one may be able to boast of his own power; but must give God the glory, that it is of his love and goodness alone that we are saved through Christ.

See, the divine honor, the divine glory, is the light in the Gospel, which shines around us from heaven through the apostles and their followers who preach the Gospel. The angel here was in the place of all the preachers of the Gospel, and the shepherds in the place of all the hearers, as we shall see. For this reason the Gospel can tolerate no other teaching besides its own; for the teaching of men is earthly light and human glory; it exalts the honor and praise of men, and makes souls to glory in their own works; while the Gospel glories in Christ, in God's grace and goodness, and teaches us to boast of and confide in Christ.

39. In the fourth place this is represented by the name Judea and Bethlehem, where Christ chose to be born. Judea is interpreted, confession or thanksgiving; as when we confess, praise and thank God, acknowledging that all we possess are his gifts. One who so confesses and praises is called Judaeus. Such a king of the Jews is Christ, as the expression is: "*Jesus Nazarenus Rex Judaeorum*," Jesus the Nazarene, the king of the Jews, of those confessing God. By this is shown that no teaching whatever can make such a confession except the Gospel, which teaches Christ.

40. Beth means house; Lehem means bread, Bethlehem, a house of bread. The city had that name because it was situated in a good, fruitful country, rich in grain; so that it was the granary for the neighboring towns, or as we would call it, a fertile country. In olden times the name of the city was Ephrata, which means fruitful. Both names imply that the city was in a fruitful and rich land. By this is represented that without the Gospel this earth is a wilderness and there is no confession of God nor thanksgiving.

41. Moreover where Christ and the Gospel are there is the fruitful Bethlehem and the thankful Judea. There every one has enough in Christ, and overflows with thanksgiving for the divine grace. But while men are thankful for human teachings, they can not satisfy, but leave a barren land and deadly hunger. No heart can ever be satisfied unless it bears Christ rightly proclaimed in the Gospel. In this a man comes to Bethlehem and finds him, he also comes to and remains in Judea and thanks his God eternally; here he is satisfied, here God receives his praise and confession, while outside of the Gospel there is nothing but thanklessness and starvation.

42. But the angel shows most clearly that nothing is to be preached in Christendom

except the Gospel, he takes upon himself the office of a preacher of the Gospel. He does not say, I preach to you, but "glad tidings I bring to you." I am an Evangelist and my word is an evangel, good news. The meaning of the word Gospel is, a good, joyful message, that is preached in the New Testament. Of what does the Gospel testify? Listen! the angel says: "I bring you glad tidings of great joy," my Gospel speaks of great joy. Where is it? Hear again: "For there is born to you this day in the city of David a Savior, who is Christ the Lord."

43. Behold here what the Gospel is, namely, a joyful sermon concerning Christ, our Savior. Whoever preaches him rightly, preaches the Gospel of pure joy. How is it possible for man to hear of greater joy than that Christ has given to him as his own? He does not only say Christ is born, but he makes his birth our own by saying, to you a Savior.

44. Therefore the Gospel does not only teach the history concerning Christ; but it enables all who believe it to receive it as their own, which is the way the Gospel operates, as has just been set forth. Of what benefit would it be to me if Christ had been born a thousand times, and it would daily be sung into my ears in a most lovely manner, if I were never to hear that he was born for me and was to be my very own? If the voice gives forth this pleasant sound, even if it be in homely phrase, my heart listens with joy for it is a lovely sound which penetrates the soul. If now there were any thing else to be preached, the evangelical angel and the angelic evangelist would certainly have touched upon it.

c. The spiritual meaning of the signs, the angel and the shepherds

45. The angel says further: "And this is the sign unto you; Ye shall find the babe wrapped in swaddling clothes, and lying in a manger." The clothes are nothing else than the holy Scriptures, in which the Christian truth lies wrapped, in which the faith is described. For the Old Testament contains nothing else than Christ as he is preached in the Gospel. Therefore we see how the apostles appeal to the testimony of the Scriptures and with them prove every thing that is to be preached and

believed concerning Christ. Thus St. Paul says, Rom. 3:21, That the faith of Christ through which we become righteous is witnessed by the law and the prophets. And Christ himself, after his resurrection, opened to them the Scriptures, which speak of him. Luke 24:27.

46. When he was transfigured on the mount, Matt. 17:3, Moses and Elijah stood by him; that means, the law and the prophets as his two witnesses, which are signs pointing to him. Therefore the angel says, the sign by which he is recognized is the swaddling clothes, for there is no other testimony on earth concerning Christian truth than the holy Scriptures. . . .

47. From this we see that the law and the prophets can not be rightly preached and known unless we see Christ wrapped up in them. It is true that Christ does not seem to be in them, nor do the Jews find him there. They appear to be insignificant and unimportant clothes, simple words, which seem to speak of unimportant external matters, the import of which is not recognized; but the New Testament, the Gospel, must open it, throw its light upon it and reveal it, as has been said.

48. First of all then the Gospel must be heard, and the appearance and the voice of the angel must be believed. Had the shepherds not heard from the angel that Christ lay there, they might have seen him ten thousand times without ever knowing that the child was Christ. Accordingly St. Paul says, 2 Cor. 3:16, that the law remains dark and covered up for the Jews until they are converted to Christ.

Christ must first be heard in the Gospel, then it will be seen how beautiful and lovely the whole Old Testament is in harmony with him, so that a man cannot help giving himself in submission to faith and be enabled to recognize the truth of what Christ says in John 5:46, "For if ye believed Moses, ye would believe me, for he wrote of me."

49. Therefore let us beware of all teaching that does not set forth Christ. What more would you know? What more do you need, if indeed you know Christ, as above set forth, if you walk by faith In God, and by love to your neighbor, doing to your fellow man as Christ

has done to you. This is indeed the whole Scripture in its briefest form, that no more words or books are necessary, but only life and action.

50. He lies in the manger. Notice here that nothing but Christ is to be preached throughout the whole world. What is the manger but the congregations of Christians in the churches to hear the preaching? We are the beasts before this manger; and Christ is laid before us upon whom we are to feed our souls. Whosoever goes to hear the preaching, goes to this manger; but it must be the preaching of Christ. Not all mangers have Christ neither do all sermons teach the true faith. There was but one manger in Bethlehem in which this treasure lay, and besides it was an empty and despised manger in which there was no fodder.

Therefore the preaching of the Gospel is divorced from all other things, it has and teaches nothing besides Christ; should any thing else be taught, then it is no more the manger of Christ, but the manger of war horses full of temporal things and of fodder for the body.

51. But in order to show that Christ in swaddling clothes represents the faith in the Old Testaments, we will here give several examples. We read in Matt. 8:4, when Christ cleansed the leper, that he said to him: "Go, show thyself to the priest, and offer the gift that Moses commanded, for a testimony unto them." Here you perceive that the law of Moses was given to the Jews for a testimony, or sign, as the angel also here says, namely, that such law represents something different from itself. What? Christ is the priest, all men are spiritual lepers because of unbelief; but when we come to faith in him he touches us With his hand, gives and lays upon us his merit and we become clean and whole without any merit on our part whatever. We are therefore to show our gratitude to him and acknowledge that we have not become pious by our own works, but through his grace, then our course will be right before God. In addition we are to offer our gifts, that is, give of our own to help our fellow man, to do good to him as Christ has done to us. Thus Christ is served and an offering is brought to the rightful priest, for it is done for his sake, in order to love and praise him.

Do you here see how, figuratively speaking, Christ and the faith are wrapped up in the plain Scriptures? It is here made evident how Moses in the law gave only testimony and an interpretation of Christ. The whole Old Testament should be understood in this manner, and should be taken to be the swaddling clothes as a sign pointing out and making Christ known.

52. Again, it was commanded that the Sabbath should be strictly observed and no work should be done, which shows that not our works but Christ's works should dwell in us; for it is written that we are not saved by our works but by the works of Christ. Now these works of Christ are twofold, as shown before. On the one hand, those that Christ has done personally without us, which are the most important and in which we believe. The others, those he performs in us, in our love to our neighbor. The first may be called the evening works and the second the morning works, so that evening and morning make one day, as it is written in Gen. 1:5, for the Scriptures begin the day in the evening and end in the morning, that is, the evening with the night is the first half, the morning with the day is the second half of the whole natural day. Now as the first half is dark and the second half is light, so the first works of Christ are concealed in our faith, but the others, the works of love, are to appear, to be openly shown toward our fellow man. Here then you see how the whole Sabbath is observed and hallowed. . . .

53. Do you see how beautifully Christ lies in these swaddling clothes? How beautifully the Old Testament reveals the faith and love of Christ and of his Christians? Now, swaddling clothes are as a rule of two kinds, the outside of coarse woolen cloth, the inner of linen. The outer or coarse woolen cloth represents the testimony of the law, but the linen are the words of the prophets. As Isaiah says in 7:14, "Behold, a virgin shall conceive, and bear a son, and shall call his name Immanuel," and similar passages which would not be understood of Christ, had the Gospel not revealed it and shown that Christ is in them.

54. Here then we have these two, the faith and the Gospel, that these and nothing else are to be preached throughout Christendom. Let us now see who are to be the preachers and who the learners. The preachers are to be angels, that is, God's messengers, who are to lead a heavenly life, are to be constantly engaged with God's Word that they under no circumstances preach the doctrine of men. It is a most incongruous thing to be God's messenger and not to further God's message. Angelus means a messenger, and Luke calls him God's messenger. The message also is of more importance than the messenger's life. If he leads a wicked life he only injures himself, but if he brings a false message in the place of God's message, he leads astray and injures every one that hears him, and causes idolatry among the people in that they accept lies for the truth, honor men instead of God, and pray to the devil instead of to God.

55. There is no more terrible plague, misfortune or cause for distress upon earth than a preacher who does not preach God's Word; of whom, alas, the world today is full; and yet they think they are pious and do good when indeed their whole work is nothing but murdering souls, blaspheming God and setting up idolatry, so that it would be much better for them if they were robbers, murderers, and the worst scoundrels, for then they would know that they are doing wickedly. . . .

56. The learners are shepherds, poor people out in the fields. Here Jesus does what he says, Matt. 11:5, "And the poor have good tidings preached to them", and Matt. 5:8, "Blessed are the poor in spirit; for theirs is the kingdom of heaven." Here are no learned, no rich, no mighty ones, for such people do not as a rule accept the Gospel. The Gospel is a heavenly treasure, which will not tolerate any other treasure, and will not agree with any earthly guest in the heart. Therefore whoever loves the one must let go the other, as Christ says, Matt. 6:24, "You cannot serve God and mammon."

This is shown by the shepherds in that they were in the field, under the canopy of heaven, and not in houses, showing that they do not hold fast and cling to temporal things; and besides they are in the fields by night, despised by and unknown to the world which sleeps in the night, and by day delights so to walk that it may be noticed; but the poor shepherds go about their work at night. They represent all the lowly who live on earth, often despised and unnoticed but dwell only under the protection of heaven; they eagerly desire the Gospel.

57. That there were shepherds, means that no one is to hear the Gospel for himself alone, but every one is to tell it to others who are not acquainted with it. For he who believes for himself has enough and should endeavor to bring others to such faith and knowledge, so that one may be a shepherd of the other, to wait upon and lead him into the pasture of the Gospel in this world, during the night time of this earthly life.

At first the shepherds were sore afraid because of the angel; for human nature is shocked when it first hears in the Gospel that all our works are nothing and are condemned before God, for it does not easily give up its prejudices and presumptions.

58. Now let every one examine himself in the light of the Gospel and see how far he is from Christ, what is the character of his faith and love. There are many who are enkindled with dreamy devotion, when they hear of such poverty of Christ, are almost angry with the citizens of Bethlehem, denounce their blindness and ingratitude, and think, if they had been there, they would have shown the Lord and his mother a more becoming service, and would not have permitted them to be treated so miserably. But they do not look by their side to see how many of their fellow men need their help, and which they let go on in their misery unaided. Who is there upon earth that has no poor, miserable, sick, erring ones, or sinful people around him? Why does he not exercise his love to those? Why does he not do to them as Christ has done to him?

59. It is altogether false to think that you have done much for Christ, if you do nothing for those needy ones. Had you been at Bethlehem you would have paid as little attention to Christ as they did; but since it is now made known who Christ is, you profess

to serve him. Should he come now and lay himself in a manger, and would send you word that it was he, of whom you now know so much, you might do something for him, but you would not have done it before. Had it been positively made known to the rich man in the Gospel, to what high position Lazarus would be exalted, and he would have been convinced of the fact, he would not have left him lie and perish as he did.

60. Therefore, if your neighbor were now what he shall be in the future, and lay before you, you would surely give him attention. But now, since it is not so, you beat the air and do not recognize the Lord in your neighbor, you do not do to him as he has done to you. Therefore God permits you to be blinded, and deceived by . . . false preachers, so that you squander on wood, stone, paper, and wax that with which you might help your fellow man.

III. EXPLANATION OF THE ANGELS' SONG OF PRAISE

61. Finally we must also treat of the angels' song, which we use daily in our service: *Gloria in excelcis Deo.* There are three things to be considered in this song, the glory to God, the peace to the earth, and the good will to mankind. The good will might be understood as the divine good will God has toward men through Christ. But we will admit it to mean the good will which is granted unto men through this birth, as it is set forth in the words thus, *en anthropis eudokia, hominibus beneplacitum.*

62. The first is the glory to God. Thus we should also begin, so that in all things the praise and glory be given to God as the one who does, gives and possesses all things, that no one ascribe any thing to himself or claim any merit for himself. For the glory belongs to no one but to God alone, it does not permit of being made common by being shared by any person.

63. Adam stole the glory through the evil spirit and appropriated it to himself, so that all men with him have come into disgrace, which evil is so deeply rooted in all mankind that there is no vice in them as great as vanity. Every one is well pleased with himself and no one wants to be nothing, and they desire

nothing, which spirit of vanity is the cause of all distress, strife and war upon earth.

64. Christ has again brought back the glory to God, in that he has taught us how all we have or can do is nothing but wrath and displeasure before God, so that we may not be boastful and self-satisfied, but rather be filled with fear and shame, so that in this manner our glory and self-satisfaction may be crushed, and we be glad to be rid of it, in order that we may be found and preserved in Christ.

65. The second is the peace on earth. For just as strife must exist where God's glory is not found, as Solomon says, Prov. 13:10, "By pride cometh only contention"; so also, where God's glory is there must be peace. Why should they quarrel when they know that nothing is their own, but that all they are, have and can desire is from God; they leave everything in his hands and are content that they have such a gracious God. He knows that all he may have, is nothing before God, he does not seek his own honor, but thinks of him who is something before God, namely Christ.

66. From this it follows that where there are true Christians, there is no strife, contention, or discord; as Isaiah says in 2:4, "And they shall beat their swords into plow shears, and their spears into pruning hooks; nation shall not lift up sword against nation, neither shall they learn war any more."

67. Therefore our Lord Christ is called a king of peace, and is represented by king Solomon, whose name implies, rich in peace, that inwardly he may give us peace in our conscience toward God through faith; and outwardly, that we may exercise love to our fellow men, so that through him there may be everywhere peace on earth.

68. The third is good will toward men. By good will is not meant the will that does good works, but the good will and peace of heart, which is equally submissive in every thing that may betide, be it good or evil. The angels knew very well that the peace, of which they sang, does not extend farther than to the Christians who truly believe, such have certainly peace among themselves. But the world and the devil have no reproof, they do not permit them to have peace but persecute

them to death; as Christ says, John 16:33, "In me ye may have peace. In the world ye have tribulation."

69. Hence it was not enough for the angels to sing peace on earth, they added to it the good will toward men, that they take pleasure in all that God does, regard all God's dealing with them as wise and good, and praise and thank him for it. They do not murmur, but willingly submit to God's will. Moreover since they know that God, whom they have received by faith in Christ as a gracious Father, can do all things, they exult and rejoice even under persecution as St. Paul says, Rom. 5:3, "We also rejoice in our tribulations." They regard all that happens to them as for the best, out of the abundant satisfaction they have in Christ.

70. Behold, it is such a good will, pleasure, good opinion in all things whether good or evil, that the angels wish to express in their song; for where there is no good will, peace will not long exist. The unbelieving put the worst construction on every thing, always magnify the evil and double every mishap. Therefore God's dealings with them does not please them, they would have it different, and that which is written in Psalm 18:25-26 is fulfilled: "With the merciful thou wilt show thyself merciful, with the perfect man thou wilt show thyself perfect; with the pure thou wilt show thyself pure," that is, whoever has such pleasure in all things which thou doest. In him thou, and all thine, will also have pleasure, and with the perverse thou wilt show thyself froward, that is, as thou and all thou doest, does not please him, so he is not well pleasing to thee and all that are thine.

71. Concerning the good will St. Paul says: 1 Cor. 10:33, "Even as I also please all men in all things." How does he do that? If you are content and satisfied with every thing, you will in turn please everybody. It is a short rule: If you will please no one, be pleased with no one; if you will please every one, be pleased with every one; in so far, however, that you do not violate God's Word, for in that case all pleasing and displeasing ceases. But what may be omitted without doing violence to God's Word, may be omitted, that you may please every one and at the same time be faithful to

God, then you have this good will of which the angels sing.

72. From this song we may learn what kind of creatures the angels are. Don't consider what the great masters of art dream about them, here they are all painted in such a manner that their heart and their own thoughts may be recognized. In the first place, in that they joyfully sing, ascribing the glory to God, they show how full of his light and fire they are, not praising themselves, but recognizing that all things belong to God alone, so that with great earnestness they ascribe the glory to him to whom it belongs. Therefore if you would think of a humble, pure, obedient and joyful heart, praising God, think of the angels. This is their first step, that by which they serve God.

73. The second is their love to us as has been shown. Here you see what great and gracious friends we have in them, that they favor us no less than themselves; rejoice in our welfare quite as much as they do in their own, so much so that in this song they give us a most comforting inducement to regard them as the best of friends. In this way you rightly understand the angels, not according to their being, which the masters of art attempt fearlessly to portray, but according to their inner heart, spirit and sense, that though I know not what they are, I know what their chief desire and constant work is; by this you look into their heart. This is enough concerning this Gospel. What is meant by Mary, Joseph, Nazareth will be explained in Luke 1.

IV. THE ARMOR OF THIS GOSPEL

74. In this Gospel is the foundation of the article of our faith when we say: "I believe in Jesus Christ, born of the virgin Mary." Although the same article is founded on different passages of Scripture, yet on none so clearly as on this one. Mark says no more than that Christ has a mother, the same is also the case with John, neither saying any thing of his birth. Matthew says he is born of Mary in Bethlehem, but lets it remain at that, without gloriously proclaiming the virginity of Mary. But Luke describes it clearly and diligently.

75. In olden times it was also proclaimed by patriarchs and prophets; as when God says to Abraham, Gen. 22:17, "And in thy seed shall all the nations of the earth be blessed." Again he says to David, Ps. 89:4, and 132:11, "Jehovah hath sworn unto David in truth; he will not return from it; of the fruit of thy body will I set upon thy throne." But those are obscure words compared with the Gospel.

76. Again it is also represented in many figures, as in the rod of Aaron which budded in a supernatural manner, although a dry piece of wood, Num. 7:5. So also Mary, exempt from all natural generation, brought forth, in a supernatural manner, really and truly a natural son, just as the rod bore natural almonds, and still remained a natural rod. Again by Gideon's fleece, Judges 6:37, which was wet by the dew of heaven, while the land around it remained dry, and many like figures which it is not necessary to enumerate. Nor do these figures conflict with faith, they rather adorn it; for it must at first be firmly believed before I can believe that the figure serves to illustrate it.

77. There is a great deal in this article, of which, in time of temptation, we would not be deprived, for the evil spirit attacks nothing so severely as our faith. Therefore it is of the greatest importance for us to know where in God's Word this faith is set forth, and in time of temptation point to that, for the evil spirit can not stand against God's Word.

78. There are also many ethical teachings in the Gospel, as for example, meekness, patience, poverty and the like; but these are touched upon enough and are not points of controversy, for they are fruits of faith and good works.

Martin Luther

2.7 A DAILY CELEBRATION, ST. PAUL OF THE CROSS

Celebrate the feast of Christmas every day, even every moment in the interior temple of your spirit, remaining like a baby in the bosom of the heavenly Father, where you will be reborn each moment in the Divine Word, Jesus Christ.

St. Paul of the Cross

2.8 A REFLECTION ON THE INCARNATION, ST. ALPHONSUS LIGUORI

St Alphonsus Liguori, 1696–1787, Italian churchman, and Doctor of the Church, he was originally named Alfonso Maria de' Liguori. In 1732 he founded the Congregation of the Most Holy Redeemer (the Redemptorists) for religious work among the poor, especially in the country. He refused the archiepiscopal see of Palermo, accepting instead (1762) the poor country diocese of Sant'Agata dei Goti. He labored incessantly until 1775, when sickness forced him to resign. He worked for his order under great difficulties caused by an anticlerical government and overzealous monks.

"A child is born to us, and a son is given to us," Isaiah 9:6.

Consider that after so many centuries, after so many prayers and sighs, the Messiah, whom the holy patriarchs and prophets were not worthy to see, whom the nations sighed for, "the desire of the everlasting hills," our Savior, has come; he is already born, and has given himself entirely to us: "A child is born to us, and a son is given to us."

The Son of God has made himself little, in order to make us great.

He has given himself to us, in order that we may give ourselves to him.

He has come to show us his love, in order that we may respond to it by giving him ours.

Let us, therefore, receive him with affection. Let us love him, and have recourse to him in all our necessities.

"A child gives easily," says St. Bernard; children readily give anything, that is asked of them. Jesus came into the world as a child in order to show himself ready and willing to give us all good gifts: "The Father hath given all things into his hands."

If we wish for light, he has come on purpose to enlighten us.

If we wish for strength to resist our enemies, he has come to give us comfort.

If we wish for pardon and salvation, he has come to pardon and save us.

If, in short, we desire the sovereign gift of divine love, he has come to inflame our hearts with it; and, above all, for this very purpose, he has become a child, and has chosen to show himself to us worthy of our love, in proportion as he was poor and humble, in order to take away from us all fear, and to gain our affections.

"So," said St. Peter Chrysologus, "should he come who willed to drive away fear, and seek for love." And Jesus has chosen to come as a little child to make us love him, not only with an appreciative but even a tender love. All infants attract the tender affection of those who behold them; but who will not love, with all the tenderness of which they are capable, a God whom they behold as a little child, in need of milk to nourish him, trembling with cold, poor, abased, and forsaken, weeping and crying in a manger, and lying on straw?

It was this that made the loving St. Francis exclaim: "Let us love the child of Bethlehem, let us love the child of Bethlehem. Come, souls, and love a God who has become a child, and poor, who is so lovable, and who has come down from heaven to give himself entirely to you."

St. Alphonsus Liguori

2.9 CHRIST'S HUMILIATION IN HIS INCARNATION, THOMAS WATSON

Thomas Watson, 1620-86. "Thomas Watson's Body of Practical Divinity *is one of the most precious of the peerless works of the Puritans; and those best acquainted with it prize it most. Watson was one of the most concise, racy, illustrative, and suggestive of those eminent divines who made the Puritan age the Augustan period of evangelical literature. There is a happy union of sound doctrine, heart-searching experience and practical wisdom throughout all his works, and his* Body of Divinity *is, beyond all the rest, useful to the student and the minister. Although Thomas Watson issued several most valuable books, comparatively little is known of him—even the dates of his birth and death are unknown. His writings are his best memorial; perhaps he needed no other, and therefore providence forbade the superfluity. We shall not attempt to discover his pedigree, and, after the manner of antiquarians, derive his family from a certain famous Wat, whose son distinguished himself in the Crusades, or in some other insane enterprise; whether blue blood was in his veins or no is of small consequence, since we know that he was the seed-royal of the redeemed of the Lord. Some men are their own ancestors, and, for aught we know, Thomas Watson's genealogy reflected no fame upon him, but derived all its luster from his achievements." C. H. Spurgeon*

"Great is the mystery of godliness, God manifest in the flesh." 1 Timothy 3:13.

QUESTION 27
Wherein did Christ's humiliation consist?

ANSWER
In his being born, and that in a low condition, made under the law, exposed to the miseries of this life, the wrath of God, and the cursed death of the cross.

Christ's humiliation consisted in his incarnation, his taking flesh, and being born. It was real flesh that Christ took; not the image of a body (as the Manichees erroneously hold), but a true body; therefore he is said to be "made of a woman." Galatians 5:4. As bread is made of wheat, and wine is made of the grape; so Christ is made of a woman: his body was part of the flesh and substance of the virgin. This is a glorious mystery, "God manifest in the flesh." In the creation, man was made in God's image; in the incarnation God was made in man's image.

QUESTION
How came Christ to be made flesh?

ANSWER
It was by his Father's special designation. "God sent forth his Son, made of a woman." Galatians 4:4. God the Father in a special manner appointed Christ to be incarnate; which shows how needful a call is to any business of weight and importance: to act without a call, is to act without a blessing. Christ would not be incarnate, and take upon him the work of a mediator till he had a call. "God sent forth his Son, made of a woman."

QUESTION
But was there no other way for the restoring of fallen man but that God should take flesh?

ANSWER
We must not ask a reason of God's will; it is dangerous to pry into God's ark; we are not to dispute but adore. The wise God saw it to be the best way for our redemption, that Christ should be incarnate. It was not fit for any to satisfy God's justice but man; none could do it but God; therefore, Christ being both God and man, is the fittest to undertake this work of redemption.

QUESTION
Why was Christ born of a woman?

ANSWER
1. That God might fulfill that promise in Genesis 3:15, "The seed of the woman shall break the serpent's head."

2. Christ was born of a woman, that he might roll away that reproach from the woman, which she had contracted by being seduced by the serpent. Christ, in taking his flesh from the woman, has honored her sex; that as at the first the woman had made man a sinner; so now, to make him amends, she should bring him a savior.

QUESTION
Why was Christ born of a virgin?

ANSWER
1. For decency. It became not God to have any mother but a maid, and it became not a maid to have any other son but a God.

2. For necessity. Christ was to be a high priest, most pure and holy. Had he been born after the ordinary course of nature he had been defiled, since all that spring out of Adam's loins have a tincture of sin, but, that "Christ's substance might remain pure and immaculate," he was born of a virgin.

3. To answer the type. Melchizedec was a type of Christ, who is said to be "without father and without mother." Christ being born of a virgin, answered the type; he was without father and without mother; without

mother as he was God, without father as he was man.

QUESTION

How could Christ be made of the flesh and blood of a virgin, and yet be without sin? The purest virgin is stained with original sin.

ANSWER

This knot the Scripture unties. "The Holy Ghost shall come upon thee, and overshadow thee: therefore that holy thing, which shall be born of thee, shall be called the Son of God," Luke 1:35. "The Holy Ghost shall come upon thee," that is, the Holy Ghost did consecrate and purify that part of the virgin's flesh whereof Christ was made. As the alchemist extracts and draws away the dross from the gold, so the Holy Ghost refines and clarifies that part of the virgin's flesh, separating it from sin. Though the Virgin Mary herself had sin, yet that part of her flesh, whereof Christ was made, was without sin; otherwise it must have been an impure conception.

QUESTION

What is meant by the power of the Holy Ghost overshadowing the virgin?

ANSWER

Basil says, "It was the Holy Ghost's blessing that flesh of the virgin whereof Christ was formed." But there is a further mystery in it; the Holy Ghost having framed Christ in the virgin's womb, did, in a wonderful manner, unite Christ's human nature to his divine, and so of both made one person. This is a mystery, which the angels pry into with adoration.

QUESTION

Why was Christ incarnate?

ANSWER

In the fullness of time. "When the fullness of time was come, God sent forth his Son, made of a woman." Galatians 4:4. By the fullness of time we must understand, *tempus a patre praefinitum*; so Ambrose, Luther, Corn. a Lap. the determinate time that God had set. More particularly, this fullness of time was when all the prophecies of the coming of the Messiah

were accomplished; and all legal shadows and figures, whereby he was typified, were abrogated. This may comfort us, in regard to the church of God, that though at present we do not see that peace and purity in the church which we could desire, yet in the fullness of time, when God's time is come and mercy is ripe, then shall deliverance spring up, and God will come riding upon the chariots of salvation.

QUESTION

Why was Jesus Christ made flesh?

ANSWER

1. The *causa prima*, and impulsive cause, was free grace. It was love in God the Father to send Christ, and love in Christ that he came to be incarnate. Love was the intrinsic motive. Christ is God-man, because he is a lover of man. Christ came out of pity and indulgence to us: *non merita nostra, sed misera nostra*. Aug. Not our deserts, but our misery made Christ take flesh. Christ's taking flesh was a plot of free grace, and a pure design of love. God himself, though Almighty, was overcome with love. Christ incarnate is nothing but love covered with flesh. As Christ's assuming our human nature was a masterpiece of wisdom, so it was a monument of free grace.

2. Christ took our flesh upon him, that he might take our sins upon him. He was, says Luther, *maximus peccator*, the greatest sinner, having the weight of the sins of the whole world lying upon him. He took our flesh that he might take our sins, and so appease God's wrath.

3. Christ took our flesh that he might make the human nature appear lovely to God, and the divine nature appear lovely to man.

a. That he might make the human nature lovely to God. Upon our fall from God, our nature became odious to him; no vermin is so odious to us as the human nature was to God. When once our virgin nature was become sinful, it was like flesh running into sores, loathsome to behold. He was so odious to God that he could not endure to look upon us. Christ taking our flesh, makes this human nature appear lovely to God. As when the sun shines on the glass it casts a bright luster, so Christ being clad with our flesh makes the human nature shine, and appear amiable in God's eyes.

b. As Christ being clothed with our flesh makes the human nature appear lovely to God, so he makes the divine nature appear lovely to man. The pure Godhead is terrible to behold, we could not see it and live; but Christ clothing himself with our flesh, makes the divine nature more amiable and delightful to us. We need not be afraid to look upon God through Christ's human nature. It was a custom of old among shepherds to clothe themselves with sheepskins, to be more pleasing to the sheep; so Christ clothed himself with our flesh, that the divine nature may be more pleasing to us. The human nature is a glass, through which we may see the love and wisdom and glory of God clearly represented to us. Through the lantern of Christ's humanity we may behold the light of the Deity. Christ being incarnate makes the sight of the Deity not formidable, but delightful to us.

4. Jesus Christ united himself to man, "that man might be drawn nearer to God." God before was an enemy to us by reason of sin; but Christ having taken our flesh, mediates for us, and brings us into favor with God. As when a king is angry with a subject, the kings son marries his daughter, and so mediates for the subject, and brings him into favor with the king, again; so when God the Father was angry with us, Christ married himself to our nature, and now mediates for us with his Father, and brings us to be friends again, and God looks upon us with a favorable aspect. As Joab pleaded for Absalom, and brought him to King David, and David kissed him; so Jesus Christ ingratiates us into the love and favor of God. Therefore he may well be called a peacemaker, having taken our flesh upon him, and so made peace between us and his Father.

Use 1. Of instruction

1. See here, as in a glass, the infinite love of God the Father; that when we had lost ourselves by sin, God, in the riches of his grace, sent forth his Son, made of a woman, to redeem us. And behold the infinite love of Christ, in that he was willing thus to condescend to take our flesh. Surely the angels would have disdained to have taken our flesh; it would have been a disparagement to them. What king would be willing to wear sackcloth over his cloth of gold? but Christ did not disdain to take our flesh. Oh the love of Christ! Had not Christ been made flesh, we had been made a curse; had he not been incarnate, we had been incarcerate, and had been for ever in prison. Well might an angel be the herald to proclaim this joyful news of Christ's incarnation: "Behold, I bring you good tidings of great joy; for unto you is born this. day in the city of David a Savior, which is Christ the Lord." The love of Christ, in being incarcerated, will the more appear if we consider,

a. Whence Christ came, He came from heaven, and from the richest place in heaven, his Father's bosom, that hive of sweetness.

b. To whom Christ came. Was it to his friends? No; he came to sinful man. Man that had defaced his image, and abused his love; man who was turned rebel; yet he came to man, resolving to conquer obstinacy with kindness. If he would come to any, why not to the angels that fell? "He took not on him the nature. of angels." Hebrews 2:16. The angels are of a more noble origin, more intelligent creatures, more able for service; ay, but behold the love of Christ, he came not to the fallen angels, but to mankind. Among the several wonders of the loadstone it is not the least, that it will not draw gold or pearl, but despising these, it draws the iron to it, one of the most inferior metals: thus Christ leaves angels, those noble spirits, the gold and the pearl, and comes to poor sinful man, and draws him into his embraces.

c. In what manner he came. He came not in the majesty of a king, attended with his life-guard, but he came poor; not like the heir of heaven, but like one of an inferior descent. The place he was born in was poor; not the royal city Jerusalem, but Bethlehem, a poor obscure place. He was born in an inn, and a manger was his cradle, the cobwebs his curtains, the beasts his Companions; he descended of poor parents. One would have thought, if Christ would have come into the world, he would have made choice of some queen or personage of honor to have descended from; but he comes of mean obscure parents, for that they were poor appears by their offering. "A pair of turtledoves," Luke 2:24, which was the usual offering of the poor. Leviticus 12:8. Christ was so poor, that when he wanted money he was fain to work a miracle for it. Matthew 17:27. When he died he made no will. He came into the world poor.

d. Why he came. That he might take our flesh, and redeem us; that he might instate us, into a kingdom. He was poor, that he might make us rich. 2 Corinthians 8:3. He was born of a virgin, that we might be born of God. He took our flesh, that he might give us his Spirit. He lay in the manger that we might lie in paradise. He came down, from heaven, that he might bring us to heaven. And what was all this but love? If our hearts be not rocks, this love of Christ should affect us. Behold love that passeth knowledge! Ephesians 3:19.

2. See here the wonderful humility of Christ. Christ was made flesh.

That Christ should clothe himself with our flesh, a piece of that earth which we tread upon; oh infinite humility! Christ's taking our flesh was one of the lowest steps of his humiliation. He humbled himself more in lying in the virgin's womb than in hanging upon the cross. It was not so much for man to die, but for God to become man was the wonder of humility. "He was made in the likeness of men." Philippians 2:7. For Christ to be made flesh was more humility than for the angels to be made worms. Christ's flesh is called a veil in Hebrews 10:20. "Through the veil," that is, his flesh. Christ's wearing our flesh veiled. his glory. For him to be made flesh, who was equal with God, oh what humility! "Who being in the form of God thought it not robbery to. be equal with God." Philippians 2:6. He stood upon even ground with God, he was co-essential and con-substantial with his Father, as Austin and Cyril, and the Council of Nice express it; yet for all that he takes flash. He stripped himself of the robes of his glory, and covered himself with the rags of our humanity. If Solomon wondered that God should dwell in the temple which was enriched and hung with gold, how my we wonder that God should dwell in man's weak and frail nature! Nay, which is yet more humility, Christ not only took our flesh, but took it when it was at the worst, under disgrace; as if a servant should wear a nobleman's livery when he is impeached of high treason. Besides all this he took all the infirmities of our flesh. There are two sorts of infirmities such as are sinful without pain, and such as are painful without sin. The first of these infirmities Christ did not take upon him; as sinful infirmities, to be covetous or ambitious. But he took upon him painful infirmities; as, 1. Hunger. "He came to the fig-tree, and would have eaten." Matthew 21:18. 2. Weariness. As when he sat on Jacob's well to rest him. John 4:6. 3. Sorrow. "My soul is exceeding sorrowful, even unto death." Matthew 26:38. It was a sorrow guilded with reason, not disturbed with passion. 4. Fear. "He was heard in that he feared." Heb. 5:7. A further degree of Christ's humility was, that he not only was made flesh, but in the likeness of sinful flesh. "He knew no sin, yet he was made sin." 2 Corinthians 5:21. He was like a sinner; he had all sin laid upon him, but no sin lived in him. "He was numbered among transgressors." Isaiah 53:12. He who was numbered among the persons of the Trinity is said to bear the "sins of many." Hebrews 9:28. Now, this was the lowest degree of Christ's humiliation; for Christ to be reputed as a sinner was the greatest pattern of humility. That Christ, who would not endure sin in the angels, should himself endure to have sin imputed to him is the most amazing humility that ever was.

From all this learn to be humble. Dost thou see Christ humbling himself, and art thou proud? It is the humble saint that is Christ's picture. Christians, be not proud of fine feathers.

a. Hast thou an estate? Be not proud. The earth thou treadest on is richer than thou. It has mines of gold and silver in its bowls.

b. Hast thou beauty? Be not proud. It is but air and dust mingled.

c. Hast thou skill and parts? Be humble. Lucifer has more knowledge than thou.

d. Hast thou grace? Be humble. Thou hast it not of thy own growth; it is borrowed.

Were it not folly to be proud of a ring that is lent? 1 Corinthians 4:7. Thou hast more sin than grace, more spots than beauty. Oh look on Christ, this rare pattern, and be humbled! It is an unseemly sight to see God humbling himself and man exalting himself; to see a humble Savior and a proud sinner. God hates the very semblance of pride. Leviticus 2:11. He would have no honey in the sacrifice. Indeed, leaven is sour; but why no honey? Because, when honey is mingled with meal or flour, it makes the meal to rise and swell; therefore no honey. God hates the resemblance of the sin of pride; better want parts, and the comfort of the Spirit, than humility. "If God," says Austin, "spared not the angels, when they grew proud, will he spare thee, who art but dust and rottenness?"

3. Behold here a sacred riddle or paradox— "God manifest in the flesh." That man should be made in God's image was a wonder, but that God should be made in mans image is a granter wonder. That the Ancient of Days should be born, that he who thunders in the heavens should cry in the cradle; that he who rules the stars should suck the breast; that a virgin should conceive; that Christ should be made of a woman, and of that woman which himself made; that the branch should bear the vine; that the mother should be younger than the child she bare, and the child in the womb bigger than the mother; that the human nature should not be God, yet one with God; this was not only *mirum but miraculum*. Christ taking flesh is a mystery we shall never fully understand till we come to heaven, when our light shall be clear, as well as our love perfect.

4. From hence, "God manifest in the flesh, Christ born of a virgin," a thing not only strange in nature, but impossible, learn, that there were no impossibilities with God. God can bring about things which are not within the sphere of nature to produce; as that iron should swim, that the rock should gush out water, and that the fire should lick up the water in the trenches. 1 Kings 18:38. It is natural for water to quench fire, but for fire to consume water is impossible in the course of nature; but God can bring about all this. "There is nothing too hard for thee." Jeremiah 32:27. "If it be marvelous in your eyes, should it be marvelous in my eyes? sayeth the Lord." Zechariah 8:6. How should God be united to our flesh? It is impossible to us, but not with God; he can do what transcends reason, and exceeds faith. He would not be our God if he could not do more than we can think. Ephesians 3:20. He can reconcile contraries. How apt are we to be discouraged with seeming impossibilities? How do our hearts die within us when things go cross to sense and reason? We are apt to say as that prince in 2 Kings 7:1, 2, "If the Lord would make windows in heaven, might this thing be?" It was a time of famine, and now that a measure of wheat, which was a good part of a bushel, should be sold for a shekel, half an ounce of silver, how can this be? So, when things are cross, or strange, God's own people are apt to question, how they should be brought about with success? Moses, who was a man of God, and one of the brightest stars that ever shone in the firmament of God's church, was apt to be discouraged with seeming impossibilities. "And Moses said, The people among whom I am are six hundred thousand footmen; and thou hast said, I will give them flesh, that they may eat a whole month. Shall the flocks and the herds be slain for them, to suffice them? or shall all the fish of the sea be gathered together for them, to suffice them?" Numbers 11:21. As if he had said, in plain language, he did not see how the people of Israel, being so numerous, could be fed for a month. "And the Lord said, Is the Lord's hand waxed short?" verse 23. That God who brought Isaac out of a dead womb, and the Messiah out of a virgin's womb, what cannot he do? Oh let us rest upon the arm of God's power, and believe in him, in the midst of seeming impossibilities! Remember, "there are no impossibilities with God." He can subdue a proud heart. He can raise a dying church. Christ born of a virgin! The wonder-working God that wrought this can bring to pass the greatest seeming impossibility.

Use 2. Of exhortation

1. Seeing Christ took our flesh and was born of a virgin, let us labor that he may be spiritually born in our hearts. What will it profit us, that Christ was born into the world, unless he be born in our hearts, that he was united to our persons? Marvel not. that I say unto you, Christ must be born in your hearts. "Till Christ be formed in you." Galatians 4:19.

Now, then, try if Christ be born in your hearts.

QUESTION

How shall we know that?

ANSWER

1. Are there pangs before the birth? So before Christ is born in the heart, there are spiritual pangs; pangs of conscience, and deep convictions. "They were pricked at their heart." Acts 2:37. I grant in the new birth all have not the same pangs of sorrow and humiliation, yet all have pangs. If Christ be born in thy heart, thou hast been deeply afflicted for sin. Christ is never born in the heart without pangs. Many thank God they never had any trouble of spirit, they were always quiet; a sign Christ is not yet formed in them.

ANSWER

2. When Christ was born into the world, he was made flesh; so, if he be born in thy heart, he makes thy heart a heart of flesh. Ezekiel 36:26. Is thy heart flesh? Before it was a rocky heart, and would not yield to God, or take the impressions of the word; now it is fleshy and tender like melted wax, to take any stamp of the Spirit. It is a sign Christ is, born in our hearts when they are hearts of flesh, when they melt in tears and in love. What is it the better that Christ was made flesh, unless he has given thee a heart of flesh?

ANSWER

3. As Christ was conceived in the womb of a virgin; so, if he be born in thee, thy heart is a virgin-heart, in respect of sincerity and sanctity. Art thou purified from the love of sin? If Christ be born in thy heart, it is a Sanctum Sanctorum, a holy of holies. If thy heart be polluted with the predominant love of sin, never think Christ is born there, Christ will never lie any more in a stable. If he be born in thy heart, it is consecrated by the Holy Ghost.

ANSWER

4. If Christ be born in thy heart, then it is with thee as in a birth.

a. There is life. Faith is *principum vivens*, it is the vital organ of the soul. "The life that I live in the flesh is by the faith of the Son of God." Galatians 2:20.

b. There is appetite. "As new-born babes, desire the sincere milk of the word." 1 Peter 2:23. The word is like breast-milk, pure, sweet, nourishing; and the soul in which Christ is formed desires this breast-milk. Bernard, in one of his soliloquies, comforts himself with this, that he surely had the new birth in him, because he found in his heart such strong breathings and thirstings after God.

c. Motion. After Christ is born in the heart, there is a violent motion; there is a striving to enter in at the strait gate, and offering, violence to the kingdom of heaven. Matthew 11:12. By this we may know Christ is formed in us. This is the only comfort, that as Christ was born into the world, so he is born in our hearts; as he was united to our flesh, so he is united to our person

2. As Christ was made in our image, let us labor to be made in his image. Christ being incarnate was made like us, let us labor to be made like him. There are five things in which we should labor to be like Christ.

a. In disposition. He was of a most sweet disposition. He invites sinners to come to him. He has bowels to pity us, breasts to feed us, wings to cover us. He would not break our heart but with mercy. Was Christ made in our likeness? Let us be like him in sweetness of disposition; be not of a morose spirit. It was said of Nabal, "he is such a son of Belial that a man cannot speak to him." 1 Samuel 25:25. Some are so barbarous, as if they were akin to the ostrich, they are fired with rage, and breathe forth nothing but revenge, or like those two men in the gospel, "Possessed with devils, coming out of the tombs, exceeding fierce." Matthew 8:28. Let us be like Christ in mildness and sweetness. Let us pray for our enemies, and conquer them, by love. David's kindness melted Saul's heart. 1 Samuel 24:16. A frozen heart will be thawed with the fire of love.

b. Be like Christ in grace. He was like us in having our flesh, Let us be like him in having his grace. In three graces we should labor to be like Christ. 1. In humility, "He humbled himself." Philippians 2:8. He left the bright robes of his glory to be clothed with the rags of our humanity: a wonder to humility! Humility, says Bernard, is a contempt of self-excellence, a kind of a self-annihilation. This is the glory of a Christian. We are never so comely in God's eyes as when we are black in our own. In this let us be like Christ. True religion is, to imitate Christ.

And indeed, what cause have we to be humble, if we look within us, below us, above us!

If we look *intra nos*, within us, here we see our sins represented to us in the glass of conscience; lust, envy, passion. Our sins are like vermin crawling in our souls. "How many are my iniquities?" Job 13:23. Our sins are as the sands of the sea for number, as the rocks of the sea for weight. Austin cries out, My heart, which is God's temple, is polluted with sin.

If we look *juxta nos*, about us, there is that may humble us. We may see other Christians outshining us in gifts and graces, as the sun outshines the lesser planets. Others are laden with fruit, perhaps we have but here and there an olive-berry growing, to show that we are of the right kind. Isaiah 17:6.

If we look *infra nos*, below us; there is that may humble us. We may see the mother earth, out of which we came. The earth is the most ignoble element: "Thou art viler than the earth." Job 30:8. Thou that dost set up thy escutcheon, and blaze thy coat of arms, behold thy pedigree; thou art but *pulvis animalus*, walking ashes: and wilt thou be proud? What is Adam? The Son of dust. And what is dust? The son of nothing.

If we look *supra nos*, above us; there is that may humble us. If we look to heaven, there we may see God resisting the proud. The proud man is the mark which God shoots at, and he never misses the mark. He threw proud Lucifer out of heaven; he thrust proud Nebuchadnezzar out of his throne, and turned him to eat grass. Daniel 4:25. Oh then be like Christ in humility!

c. Did Christ take our flesh? Was he made like to us? let us be made like him in zeal. "The zeal of thy house hath eaten me up." John 2:14. He was zealous when his Father was dishonored. In this let us be like Christ, zealous for God's wrath and glory, which are the two orient pearls of the crown of heaven. Zeal is as needful for a Christian as salt for the sacrifice or fire on the altar. Zeal without prudence is rashness; prudence without zeal is cowardliness. Without zeal, our duties are not acceptable to God. Zeal is like rosin to the bow-strings, without which the lute makes no music.

d. Be like Christ, in the contempt of the world. When Christ took our flesh, he came not in the pride of flesh, he did not descend immediately from kings and nobles, but was of mean parentage. Christ was not ambitious of titles or of honor. He declined worldly dignity and greatness as much as others seek it. When they would have made him a king, he refused it; he chose rather to ride upon the foal of an ass, than be drawn in a chariot; and to hang upon a wooden cross, than to wear a golden crown. He scorned the pomp and glory of the world. He waved secular affairs. "Who made me a judge?" Luke 12:14. His work was not to arbitrate matters of law; he came not into the world to be a magistrate, but a Redeemer. He was like a star in a higher orb, he minded nothing but heaven. Was Christ made like us? Let us be made like him, in heavenliness and contempt of the world. Let us not be ambitious of the honors and preferments of the world. Let us not purchase the world with the loss of a good conscience. What wise man would damn himself to grow rich? or pull down his soul, to build up an estate? Be like Christ in a holy contempt of the world.

e. Be like Christ in conversation. Was Christ incarnate? Was he made like us? Let us be like him in holiness of life. No temptation could fasten upon him. "The prince of this world cometh, and hath nothing in me." John 14:30. Temptation to Christ was like a spark of fire, upon a marble pillar, which glides off. Christ's life, says Chrysostom, was brighter than the sunbeams. Let us be like him in this. "Be ye holy in all manner of conversation." 1 Peter 1:15. We are not, says Austin, to be like Christ in working miracles, but in a holy life. A Christian should be both a loadstone and a diamond; a loadstone, in drawing others to Christ; a diamond, in casting a sparkling luster of holiness in his life. Oh let us be so just in our dealings, so true in our promises, so devout in our worship, so unblameable in our lives, that we may be the walking pictures of Christ. Thus as Christ was made in our likeness, let us labor to be made in his.

3. If Jesus Christ was so abased for us; took our flesh, which was a disparagement to him; mingling dust with gold; if he abased himself so for us, let us be willing to be abased for him. If the world reproach us for Christ's sake, and cast dust on our name, let us bear it with patience. The apostles departed from the council, "rejoicing that they were counted worthy to suffer shame for Christ's name," Acts 5:41: that they were graced to be disgraced for Christ. That is a good saying of Austin, *Quid sui detrahit famoe, addet mercedi*

sua; they who take away from a saint's name, shall add to his reward; and while they make his credit weigh lighter, will make his crown weigh heavier. Oh, was Christ content to be humbled and abased for us, to take our flesh, and to take it when it was in disgrace? Let us not think much to be abased for Christ. Say as David, "If this be to be vile, I will yet be more vile." 2 Samuel 6:22. If to serve my Lord Christ, if to keep my conscience pure, if this be to be vile, I will yet be more vile.

Use 3. Of comfort

Jesus Christ, having taken our flesh, has ennobled our nature. Our nature is now invested with greater royalties and privileges than in time of innocence. Before, in innocence, we were made in the image of God; but now, Christ having assumed our nature, we are made one with God; our nature is ennobled above the angelic nature. Christ taking our flesh, has made us nearer to himself than the angels. The angels are his friends, believers are flesh of his flesh, his members. Ephesians 5:30. and chap. 1:28. The same glory which is put upon Christ's human nature, shall be put upon believers.

Thomas Watson,
A Body Of Practical Divinity, 1692

2.10 Christ is born, Lew Wallace

Lew Wallace, 1827-1905, was a lawyer, soldier, politician, diplomat, and author. He served in both the War with Mexico and as a Major General during the Civil War. He served Indiana as a state senator, was appointed territorial Governor of New Mexico, and Minister to Turkey. He wrote the novel Ben Hur, *one of the most popular novels of the 19th century.*

A mile and a half, it may be two miles, southeast of Bethlehem, there is a plain separated from the town by an intervening swell of the mountain. Besides being well sheltered from the north winds, the vale was covered with a growth of sycamore, dwarf-oak, and pine trees, while in the glens and ravines adjoining

there were thickets of olive and mulberry; all at this season of the year invaluable for the support of sheep, goats, and cattle, of which the wandering flocks consisted.

At the side farthest from the town, close under a bluff, there was an extensive *marah*, or sheepcot, ages old. In some long-forgotten foray the building had been unroofed and almost demolished. The enclosure attached to it remained intact, however, and that was of more importance to the shepherds who drove their charges thither than the house itself. The stone wall around the lot was high as a man's head, yet not so high but that sometimes a panther or a lion, hungering from the wilderness, leaped boldly in. On the inside of the wall, and as an additional security against the constant danger a hedge of the rhamnus had been planted, an invention so successful that now a sparrow could hardly penetrate the overtopping branches, armed as they were with great clusters of thorns hard as spikes.

The day of the occurrences which occupy the preceding chapters, a number of shepherds, seeking fresh walks for their flocks, led them up to this plain; and from early morning the groves had been made ring with calls, and the blows of axes, the bleating of sheep and goats, the tinkling of bells, the lowing of cattle, and the barking of dogs. When the sun went down, they led the way to the marah, and by nightfall had everything safe in the field; then they kindled a fire down by the gate, partook of their humble supper, and sat down to rest and talk, leaving one on watch.

There were six of these men, omitting the watchman; and after a while they assembled in a group near the fire, some sitting, some lying prone. As they went bareheaded habitually, their hair stood out in thick, coarse, sunburnt shocks; their beard covered their throats, and fell in mats down the breast; mantles of the skin of kids and lambs, with the fleece on, wrapped them from neck to knee, leaving the arms exposed; broad belts girthed the rude garments to their waists; their sandals were of the coarsest quality; from their right shoulders hung scrips containing food and selected stones for slings, with which they were armed; on the ground near each one lay his crook, a symbol of his calling and a weapon of offence.

Such were the shepherds of Judea! In appearance, rough and savage as the gaunt dogs sitting with them around the blaze; in fact, simple-minded, tender-hearted; effects due, in part, to the primitive life they led, but chiefly to their constant care of things lovable and helpless.

They rested and talked; and their talk was all about their flocks-a dull theme to the world, yet a theme which was all the world to them. If in narrative they dwelt long upon affairs of trifling moment; if one of them omitted nothing of detail in recounting the loss of a lamb, the relation between him and the unfortunate should be remembered: at birth it became his charge, his to keep all its days, to help over the floods, to carry down the hollows, to name and train; it was to be his companion, his object of thought and interest, the subject of his will; it was to enliven and share his wanderings; in its defense he might be called on to face the lion or robber-to die.

MOTHER OF HUR

The great events, such as blotted out nations and changed the mastery of the world, were trifles to them, if perchance they came to their knowledge. Of what Herod was doing in this city or that, building palaces and gymnasia, and indulging forbidden practices, they occasionally heard. As was her habit in those days, Rome did not wait for people slow to inquire about her; she came to them. Over the hills along which he was leading his lagging herd, or in the fastnesses in which he was hiding them, not infrequently the shepherd was startled by the blare of trumpets, and, peering out beheld a cohort, sometimes a legion, in march; and when the glittering crests were gone, and the excitement incident to the intrusion over, he bent himself to evolve the meaning of the eagle and gilded globes of the soldiery, and the charm of a life so the opposite of his own.

Yet these men, rude and simple as they were, had a knowledge and a wisdom of their own. On Sabbaths they were accustomed to purify themselves, and go up into the synagogues, and sit on the benches farthest from the ark. When the chazzan bore the Torah round, none kissed it with greater zest; when the sheliach read the text, none listened to the interpreter with more absolute faith; and none took away with them more of the elder's sermon, or gave it more thought afterwards. In a verse of the Shema they found all the learning and all the law of their simple lives-that their Lord was One God, and that they must love Him with all their souls. And they loved Him, and such was their wisdom, surpassing that of kings.

While they talked, and before the first watch was over, one by one the shepherds went to sleep, each lying where he had sat.

The night, like most nights of the winter season in the hill country, was clear, crisp, and sparkling with stars. There was no wind. The atmosphere seemed never so pure, and the stillness was more than silence; it was a holy hush, a warning that heaven was stooping low to whisper some good thing to the listening earth.

By the gate, hugging his mantle close, the watchman walked; at times he stopped, attracted by a stir among the sleeping herds, or by a Jackal's cry off on the mountain-side. The midnight was slow coming to him; but at last it came. His task was done; now for the dreamless sleep with which labor blesses its wearied children! He moved towards the fire, but paused; a light was breaking around him, soft and white, like the moon's. He waited breathlessly. The light, deepened; things before invisible came to view; he saw the whole field, and all it sheltered. A chill sharper than that of the frosty air-a chill of fear-smote him. He looked up; the stars were gone; the light was dropping as from a window in the sky; as he looked, it became a splendor; then, in terror he cried:

"Awake, awake!"

Up sprang the dogs, and, howling, ran away. The herds rushed together bewildered.

The men clambered to their feet, weapons in hand.

"What is it?" they asked, in one voice.

"See!" cried the watchman, "the sky is on fire!"

Suddenly the light became intolerably bright, and they covered their eyes, and dropped upon their knees; then, as their souls shrank with fear, they fell upon their faces blind and fainting, and would have died had not a voice said to them-

"Fear not!"

And they listened.

"Fear not: for behold, I bring you good tidings of great joy, which shall be to all people."

The voice, in sweetness and soothing more than human, and low and clear, penetrated all their being, and filled them with assurance. They rose upon their knees, and, looking worshipfully, beheld in the center of a great glory the appearance of a man, clad in a robe intensely white; above its shoulders towered the tops of wings shining and folded; a star over its forehead glowed with steady luster, brilliant as Hesperus; its hands were stretched towards them in blessing; its face was serene and divinely beautiful.

They had often heard, and in their simple way talked, of angels; and they doubted not now, but said, in their hearts, The glory of God is about us, and this is he who of old came to the prophet by the river of Ulai.

Directly the angel continued-

"For unto you is born this day, in the city of David, a Savior which is Christ the Lord!"

Again there was a rest, while the words sank into their minds.

"And this shall be a sign unto you," the enunciator said next. "Ye shall find the babe, wrapped in swaddling-clothes, lying in a manger."

The herald spoke not again; his good tidings were told; yet he stayed awhile. Suddenly the light, of which he seemed the center, turned roseate and began to tremble; then up, far as the men could see, there was flashing of white wings, and coming and going of radiant forms, and voices as of a multitude chanting in unison-

"Glory to God in the highest, and on earth peace, good-will towards men!"

Not once the praise, but many times.

Then the herald raised his eyes as seeking approval of one far off; his wings stirred, and spread slowly and majestically, on their upper side white as snow, in the shadow tinted, like mother-of-pearl; when they were expanded many cubits beyond his stature, he rose lightly, and, without effort, floated out of view, taking the light up with him. Long after he was gone, down from the sky fell the refrain in measure mellowed by distance, "Glory to God in the highest, and on earth peace, good-will towards men."

When the shepherds came fully to their senses, they stared at each other stupidly, until one of them said, "It was Gabriel, the Lord's messenger unto men."

None answered.

"Christ the Lord is born; said he not so?"

Then another recovered his voice, and replied, "That is what he said."

"And did he not also say, in the city of David, which is our Bethlehem yonder. And that we should find Him a babe in swaddling clothes?"

"And lying in a manger."

The first speaker gazed into the fire thoughtfully, but at length said, like one possessed of a sudden resolve, "There is but one place in Bethlehem where there are mangers; but one, and that is in the cave near the old khan. Brethren, let us go see this thing which has come to pass. The priests and doctors have been a long time looking for the Christ. Now He is born, and the Lord has given us a sign by which to know Him. Let us go and worship Him."

"But the flocks!"

"The Lord will take care of them. Let us make haste."

Then they all arose and left the marah.

Around the mountain and through the town they passed, and came to the gate of the khan, where there was a man on watch.

"What would you have?" he asked.

"We have seen and heard great things to-night," they replied.

"Well, we, too, have seen great things, but heard nothing. What did you hear?"

"Let us go down to the cave in the enclosure, that we may be sure; then we will tell you all. Come with us, and see for yourself."

"It is a fool's errand."

"No, the Christ is born."

"The Christ! How do you know?"

"Let us go and see first."

The man laughed scornfully.

"The Christ indeed! How are you to know Him?"

"He was born this night, and is now lying in a manger, so we were told; and there is but one place in Bethlehem with mangers."

"The cave?"

"Yes. Come with us."

They went through the court-yard without notice, although there were some up even then talking about the wonderful light. The door of the cavern was open. A lantern was burning within, and they entered unceremoniously.

"I give you peace," the watchman said to Joseph and the Beth-Dagonite. "Here are people looking for a child born this night, whom they are to know by finding Him in swaddling-clothes and lying in a manger."

For a moment the face of the stolid Nazarene was moved; turning away, he said, "The child is here."

They were led to one of the mangers, and there the child was. The lantern was brought, and the shepherds stood by mute. The little one made no sign; it was as others just born.

"Where is the mother?" asked the watchman.

One of the women took the baby, and went to Mary, lying near, and put it in her arms. Then the bystanders collected about the two.

"It is the Christ!" said a shepherd at last.

"The Christ!" they all repeated, falling upon their knees in worship. One of them repeated several times over-

"It is the Lord, and His glory is above the earth and heaven."

And the simple men, never doubting, kissed the hem of the mother's robe, and with joyful faces departed. In the khan, to all the people aroused and pressing about them, they told their story; and through the town, and all the way back to the marah, they chanted the refrain of the angels, "Glory to God in the highest, and on earth peace, good-will towards men!"

The story went abroad, confirmed by the light so generally seen; and the next day, and for days thereafter, the cave was visited by curious crowds, of whom some believed, though the greater part laughed and mocked.

Lew Wallace
Ben-Hur, a tale of the Christ, *"Christ is born," 1880*

2.11 THE WISE FIND THE CHILD, LEW WALLACE

It was now the beginning of the third watch, and at Bethlehem the morning was breaking over the mountains in the east, but so feebly that it was yet night in the valley. The watchman on the roof of the old khan, shivering in the chilly air, was listening for the first distinguishable sounds with which life, awakening, greets the dawn, when a light came moving up the hill towards the house. He thought it a torch in some one's hand; next moment he thought it a meteor; the brilliance grew, however, until it became a star. Sore afraid, he cried out, and brought everybody within the walls to the roof. The phenomenon, in eccentric motion, continued to approach; the rocks, trees, and roadway under it shone as in a glare of lightning; directly its brightness became blinding. The more timid of the beholders fell upon their knees, and prayed, with their faces hidden; the boldest, covering their eyes, crouched, and now and then snatched glances fearfully. After a while the khan and everything thereabout lay under the intolerable radiance. Such as dared look beheld the star standing still directly over the house in front of the cave where the Child had been born.

In the height of this scene the wise men came up, and at the gate dismounted from their camels, and shouted for admission. When the steward so far mastered his terror as to give them heed, he drew the bars and opened to them. The camels looked spectral in the unnatural light, and, besides their outlandishness, there were in the faces and manner of the three visitors an eagerness and exaltation which still further excited the keeper's fears and fancy; he fell back, and for a time could not answer the question they put to him.

"Is not this Bethlehem of Judea?"

But others came, and by their presence gave him assurance.

"No, this is but the khan; the town lies farther on."

"Is there not here a child newly born?"

The bystanders turned to each other marveling, though some of them answered, "Yes, yes."

"Show us to him!" said the Greek, impatiently.

"Show us to him!" cried Balthasar, breaking through his gravity; "for we have seen his star, even that which ye behold over the house, and are come to worship him."

The Hindu clasped his hands, exclaiming, "God indeed lives! Make haste, make haste! The Savior is found. Blessed, blessed are we above men!"

The people from the roof came down and followed the strangers as they were taken through the court and out into the enclosure; at sight of the star yet above the cave, though less candescent than before, some turned back afraid; the greater part went on. As the strangers neared the house, the orb arose; when they were at the door, it was high up overhead vanishing; when they entered, it went out, lost to sight. And to the witnesses of what then took place came a conviction that there was a divine relation between the star and the strangers, which extended also to at least some of the occupants of the cave. When the door was opened, they crowded in.

The apartment was lighted by a lantern enough to enable the strangers to find the mother, and the child awake in her lap.

"Is the child thine?" asked Balthasar of Mary.

And she, who had kept all the things in the least affecting the little one, and pondered them in her heart, held it up in the light, saying:

"He is my son!"

And they fell down and worshipped him.

They saw the child was as other children: about its head was neither nimbus nor material crown; its lips opened not in speech; if it heard their expressions of joy, their invocations, their prayers, it made no sign whatever, but, baby-like, looked longer at the flame in the lantern than at them.

In a little while they arose, and, returning to the camels, brought gifts of gold, frankincense, and myrrh, and laid them before the child, abating nothing of their worshipful speeches; of which no part is given, for the thoughtful know that the pure worship of the pure heart was then what it is now, and has always been, an inspired song.

And this was the Savior they had come so far to find!

Yet they worshipped without a doubt.

Why?

Their faith rested upon the signs sent them by him whom we have since come to know as the Father: and they were of the kind to whom his promises were so all-sufficient that they asked nothing about his ways. Few there were who had seen the signs and heard the promises-the Mother and Joseph, the shepherds, and the Three-yet they all believed alike; that is to say, in this period of the plan of salvation, God was all and the Child nothing. But look forward, O reader! A time will come when the signs will all proceed from the Son. Happy they who then believe in him!

Let us wait that period.

Lew Wallace
Ben-Hur, a tale of the Christ, *"The wise find the child," 1880*

2.12 THE NATIVITY, F. W. FARRAR

Frederic W. Farrar, 1831-1903, was Chaplain to Queen Victoria, 1871-1876, Headmaster of Marlborough College, Canon of Westminster Abbey, Rector of St. Margaret's, Westminster, Archdeacon of Westminster, and Dean of Canterbury.

He published a number of works including Eric, or Little by Little *(1858),* Julian Home: a Tale of College Life *(18th ed., 1905),* An Essay on the Origin of Language: based on Modern Researches and especially on the Works of M. Renan *(1860), and* Families of Speech *(1890). In 1866, Farrar was elected a fellow of the Royal Society in recognition for his work as a philologist. He composed a card of "Greek Grammar Rule"" and published* A Brief Greek Syntax *(1867). In 1870, he visited Palestine with Walter Leaf to finish research for his* Life of Christ *(1874). He also completed the* Life of St. Paul *(1879) and* The Early Days of Christianity *(1882).*

One mile from Bethlehem is a little plain, in which, under a grove of olives, stands the bare and neglected chapel known by the name of "the Angel to the Shepherds." It is built over the traditional site of the fields where, in the beautiful language of Luke—more exquisite than any idyll to Christian ears—"there were shepherds keeping watch over their flock by night, when, lo, the angel of the Lord came upon them, and, the glory of the Lord shone round about them," and to their happy ears were uttered the good tidings of great joy, that unto them was born that day in the city of David a Savior, which was Christ the Lord.

The associations of our Lord's nativity were all of the humblest character, and the very scenery of His birthplace was connected with memories of poverty and toil. On that night, indeed, it seemed as though the heavens must burst to disclose their radiant minstrelsies; and the stars, and the feeding sheep, and the "light and sound in the darkness and stillness," and the rapture of faithful hearts, combine to furnish us with a picture painted in the colors of heaven. But in the brief and thrilling verses of the Evangelist we are not told that those angel songs were heard by any except the wakeful shepherds of an obscure village;—and these shepherds, amid the chill dews of a winter night, were guarding their flocks from the wolf and the robber, in fields where Ruth, their Savior's ancestress, had gleaned, sick at heart, amid the alien corn, and David, the despised and youngest son of a numerous family, had followed the ewes great with young.

"And suddenly," adds the sole Evangelist who has narrated the circumstances of that memorable night in which Jesus was born, amid the indifference of a world unconscious of its Deliverer, "there was with the angel a multitude of the heavenly host, praising God, and saying, Glory to God in the highest, and on earth peace among men of good will."

It might have been expected that Christian piety would have marked the spot by splendid memorials, and enshrined the rude grotto of the shepherds in the marbles and mosaics of some stately church. But, instead of this, the Chapel of the Herald Angel is a mere rude crypt; and as the traveler descends down the broken steps which lead from the olive-grove into its dim recess, he can hardly persuade himself that he is in a consecrated place. Yet a half-unconscious sense of fitness has, perhaps, contributed to this apparent neglect. The poverty of the chapel harmonizes well with the humble toil of those whose radiant vision it is intended to commemorate.

"Come now! let us go unto Bethlehem, and see this thing which has come to pass, which the Lord made known to us," said the shepherds, when those angel songs had ceased to break the starry silence. Their way would lead them up the terraced hill, and through the moonlit gardens of Bethlehem, until they reached the summit of the gray ridge on which the little town is built. On that summit stood the village inn. The khan (or caravanserai) of a Syrian village, at that day, was probably identical, in its appearance and accommodation, with those which still exist in modern Palestine. A khan is a low structure, built of rough stones, and generally only a single story in height. It consists for the most part of a square enclosure, in which the cattle can be tied up in safety for the night, and an arched recess for the accommodation of travelers. The *leewan*, or paved floor of the recess, is raised a foot or two above the level of the court-yard. A large khan—such, for instance, as that of which the ruins may still be

seen at Khan Minyeh, on the shore of the Sea of Galilee—might contain a series of such recesses, which are, in fact, low small rooms with no front wall to them. They are, of course, perfectly public; everything that takes place in them is visible to every person in the khan. They are also totally devoid of even the most ordinary furniture. The traveler may bring his own carpet if he likes, may sit cross-legged upon it for his meals, and may lie upon it at night. As a rule, too, he must bring his own food, attend to his own cattle, and draw his own water from the neighboring spring. He would neither expect nor require attendance, and would pay only the merest trifle for the advantage of shelter, safety, and a floor on which to lie. But if he chanced to arrive late, and the *leewans* were all occupied by earlier guests, he would have no choice but to be content with such accommodation as he could find in the court-yard below, and secure for himself and his family such small amount of cleanliness and decency as are compatible with an unoccupied corner on the filthy area, which must he shared with horses, mules, and camels. The litter, the closeness, the unpleasant smell of the crowded animals, the unwelcome intrusion of the pariah dogs, the necessary society of the very lowest hangers-on of the caravanserai, are adjuncts to such a position which can only be realized by any traveler in the East who happens to have been placed in similar circumstances.

In Palestine it not infrequently happens that the entire khan, or at any rate the portion of it in which the animals are housed, is one of those innumerable caves which abound in the limestone rocks of its central hills. Such seems to have been the case at the little town of Bethlehem-Ephratah, in the land of Judah. Justin Martyr, the Apologist, who, from his birth at Shechem, was familiar with Palestine, and who lived less than a century after the time of our Lord, places the scene of the nativity in a cave. This is, indeed, the ancient and constant tradition both of the Eastern and the Western Churches, and it is one of the few to which, though unrecorded in the Gospel history, we may attach a reasonable probability. Over this cave has risen the Church and Convent of the

Nativity, and it was in a cave close beside it that one of the most learned, eloquent, and holy of the Fathers of the Church—that great St. Jerome to whom we owe the received Latin translation of the Bible—spent thirty of his declining years in study, and fast, and prayer.

From their northern home at Nazareth, in the mountains of Zabulon, Joseph, the village carpenter, had made his way along the wintry roads with Mary his espoused wife, being great with child. Fallen as were their fortunes, they were both of the house and lineage of David, and they were traversing a journey of eighty miles to the village which had been the home of their great ancestor while he was still a ruddy shepherd lad, tending his flocks upon the lonely hills. The object of that toilsome journey, which could not but be disagreeable to the settled habits of Oriental life, was to enroll their names as members of the house of David in a census which had been ordered by the Emperor Augustus. In the political condition of the Roman Empire, of which Judea then formed a part, a single whisper of the Emperor was sufficiently powerful to secure the execution of his mandates in the remotest corners of the civilized world. Great as are the historic difficulties in which the census is involved, there seems to be good independent grounds for believing that it may have been originally ordered by Sentius Saturninus, that it was begun by Publius Sulpicius Quirinus, when he was for the first time legate of Syria, and that it was completed during his second term of office. In deference to Jewish prejudices, any infringement of which was the certain signal for violent tumults and insurrection, it was not carried out in the ordinary Roman manner, at each person's place of residence, but according to Jewish custom, at the town to which their family originally belonged. The Jews still clung to their genealogies and to the memory of long-extinct tribal relations; and though the journey was a weary and distasteful one, the mind of Joseph may well have been consoled by the remembrance of that heroic descent which would now be authoritatively recognized, and by the glow of those Messianic hopes to which the marvelous

circumstances of which he was almost the sole depositary would give a tenfold intensity.

Traveling in the East is a very slow and leisurely affair, and was likely to be still more so if, as is probable, the country was at that time agitated by political animosities. Beeroth, which is fifteen miles distant from Bethlehem, or possibly even Jerusalem, which is only six miles off, may have been the resting-place of Mary and Joseph before this last stage of their journey. But the heavy languor, or even the commencing pangs of travail, must necessarily have retarded the progress of the maiden-mother. Others who were traveling on the same errand, would easily have passed them on the road, and when, after toiling up the steep hill-side, by David's well, they arrived at the khan— probably the very one which had been known for centuries as the House of Chimham, and if so, covering perhaps the very ground on which, one thousand years before, had stood the hereditary house of Boaz, of Jesse, and of David—every leewan was occupied. The enrolment had drawn so many strangers to the little town, that "there was no room for them in the inn." In the rude limestone grotto attached to it as a stable, among the hay and straw spread for the food and rest of the cattle, weary with their day's journey, far from home, in the midst of strangers, in the chilly winter night—in circumstances so devoid of all earthly comfort or splendor that it is impossible to imagine a humbler nativity— Christ was born.

Distant but a few miles, on the plateau of the abrupt and singular hill now called Jebel Fureidis, or "Little Paradise Mountain," towered the palace fortress of the Great Herod. The magnificent houses of his friends and courtiers crowded around its base. The humble wayfarers, as they passed near it, might have heard the hired and voluptuous minstrelsy with which its feasts were celebrated, or the shouting of the rough mercenaries whose arms enforced obedience to its despotic lord. But the true King of the Jews—the rightful Lord of the Universe—was not to be found in palace or fortress. They who wear soft clothing are in king's houses. The cattle-stables of the lowly caravanserai were a more fitting birthplace for Him who came to reveal that the soul of the greatest monarch was no dearer or greater in God's sight than the soul of his meanest slave; for him who had not where to lay His head; for him who, from His cross of shame, was to rule the world.

Guided by the lamp which usually swings from the center of a rope hung across the entrance of the khan, the shepherds made their way to the inn of Bethlehem, and found Mary, and Joseph, and the Babe lying in the manger. The fancy of poet and painter has reveled in the imaginary glories of the scene. They have sung of the "bright harnessed angels" who hovered there, and of the stars lingering beyond their time to shed their sweet influences upon that smiling infancy. They have painted the radiation of light from his manger-cradle, illuminating all the place till the bystanders are forced to shade their eyes from that heavenly splendor. But all this is wide of the reality. Such glories as the simple shepherds saw were seen only by the eye of faith; and all which met their gaze was a peasant of Galilee, already beyond the prime of life, and a young mother, of whom they could not know that she was wedded maid and virgin wife, with an Infant Child, whom, since there were none to help her, her own hands had wrapped in swaddling-clothes. The light that shined in the darkness was no physical, but a spiritual beam; the Dayspring from on high, which had now visited mankind, dawned only in a few faithful and humble hearts.

And the Gospels, always truthful and bearing on every page that simplicity which is the stamp of honest narrative, indicate this fact without comment. There is in them nothing of the exuberance of marvel, and mystery, and miracle, which appears alike in the Jewish imaginations about their coming Messiah, and in the apocryphal narratives about the Infant Christ. There is no more decisive criterion of their absolute credibility as simple histories, than the marked and violent contrast which they offer to all the spurious gospels of the early centuries, and all the imaginative legends which have clustered about them. Had our Gospels been unauthentic, they too must

inevitably have partaken of the characteristics which mark, without exception, every early fiction about the Savior's life. To the unilluminated fancy it would have seemed incredible that the most stupendous event in the world's history should have taken place without convulsions and catastrophes. In the Gospel of St. James there is a really striking chapter, describing how, at the awful moment of the nativity, the pole of the heaven stood motionless, and the birds were still, and there were workmen lying on the earth with their hands in a vessel, "and those who handled did not handle it, and those who took did not lift, and those who presented it to their mouth did not present it, but the faces of all were looking up; and I saw the sheep scattered and the sheep stood, and the shepherd lifted up his hand to strike, and his hand remained up; and I looked at the stream of the river, and the mouths of the kids were down, and were not drinking; and everything which was being propelled forward was intercepted in its course." But of this sudden hush and pause of awe-struck nature, of the mysterious splendors which blazed in many places of the world, of the painless childbirth, of the perpetual virginity, of the ox and the ass kneeling to worship Him in the manger, of the voice with which immediately after His birth He told his mother that He was the Son of God, and of many another wonder which rooted itself in the earliest traditions, there is no trace whatever in the New Testament. The inventions of man differ wholly from the dealings of God. In His designs there is no haste, no rest, no weariness, no discontinuity; all things are done by him in the majesty of silence, and they are seen under a light that shineth quietly in the darkness, "showing all things in the slow history of their ripening." "The unfathomable depths of the Divine counsels," it has been said, "were moved; the fountains of the great deep were broken up; the healing of the nations was issuing forth; but nothing was seen on the surface of human society but this slight rippling of the water; the course of human things went on as usual, while each was taken up with little projects of his own."

How long the Virgin Mother and her holy Child stayed in this cave, or cattle-enclosure, we cannot tell, but probably it was not for long. The word rendered "manger" in Luke 2:7, is of very uncertain meaning, nor can we discover more about it than that it means a place where animals were fed. It is probable that the crowd in the khan would not be permanent, and common humanity would have dictated an early removal of the mother and her child to some more appropriate resting-place. The Magi, as we see from Matthew, visited Mary in "the house." But on all these minor incidents the Gospels do not dwell. The fullest of them is Luke, and the singular sweetness of his narrative, its almost idyllic grace, its sweet calm tone of noble reticence, seem clearly to indicate that he derived it, though but in fragmentary notices, from the lips of Mary herself. It is, indeed, difficult to imagine from whom else it could have come, for mothers are the natural historians of infant years; but it is interesting to find, in the actual style, that "coloring of a woman's memory and a woman's view," which we should naturally have expected in confirmation of a conjecture so obvious and so interesting. To one who was giving the reins to his imagination, the minutest incidents would have claimed a description; to Mary they would have seemed trivial and irrelevant. Others might wonder, but in her all wonder was lost in the one overwhelming revelation—the one absorbing consciousness. Of such things she could not lightly speak; "she kept all these things, and pondered them in her heart." The very depth and sacredness of that reticence is the natural and probable explanation of the fact, that some of the details of the Savior's infancy are fully recorded by Luke alone.

F. W. Farrar
The Life of Christ, *New York: AL Burt Company*

2.13 THE GRAND MIRACLE, C. S. LEWIS

C. S. Lewis called the incarnation, "the grand miracle" of Christianity.

The central miracle asserted by Christians is the Incarnation. . . . Every other miracle prepares for this, or exhibits this, or results from this. . . . It was the central event in the history of the Earth—the very thing that the whole story has been about. . . . He comes down; down from the heights of absolute being into time and space, down into humanity; down further still . . . (to) the womb . . . down to the very roots and sea-bed of the Nature He has created. But He goes down to come up again and bring the whole ruined world up with Him."

C. S. Lewis
Miracles, *New York: Macmillan, 1960*

2.14 He came down, Helmut Thielicke

Jesus Christ did not remain at base headquarters, receiving reports of the world's suffering from below and shouting a few encouraging words to us from a safe distance. No, He . . . came down where we live in the front line trenches . . . where we contend with our anxieties and the feeling of emptiness and futility, where we sin and suffer guilt, and where we must finally die. There is nothing that he did not endure with us. He understands everything.

Helmut Thielicke
Theological Ethics, *Grand Rapids, MI:*
Eerdmans, 1966

3

POEMS, HYMNS, MEDITATIONS, AND PRAYERS ON JESUS' BIRTH

2.15 AUGUSTINE, MAKER OF THE SUN

Maker of the sun,
He is made under the sun.
Disposer of all ages
in the bosom of the Father,
He consecrates this day
in the womb of His mother.
In Him He remains,
from her He goes forth.
Creator of heaven and earth,
He was made on earth under Heaven.

Unspeakably wise,
He is wisely speechless;
Filling the world,
He lies in a manger;
Ruler of the stars,
He nurses at His mother's bosom.
He is both great in the nature of God
and small in the form of a servant.

Augustine

2.16 A CHRISTMAS DEDICATION, LANCELOT ANDREWES

Lord Jesus,
I give you my hands to do your work,
I give you my feet to go your way,
I give you my eyes to see as you do.
I give you my tongue to speak your words,
I give you my mind that you may think in me,
I give you my spirit that you may pray in me.
Above all, I give you my heart that you may
love in me, your Father, and all mankind.

I give you my whole self that you may grow in
me, so that it is you, Lord Jesus, who live and
work and pray in me.
I hand over to your care, Lord, my soul and
body, my mind and thoughts, my prayers and
hopes, my health and my work, my life and
my death, my parents and my family, my
friends and my neighbors, my country and all
men. Today and always.

Lancelot Andrewes, Private Prayers

2.17 HARK! THE HERALD ANGELS SING, CHARLES WESLEY

Hark! The herald angels sing,
"Glory to the newborn King;
Peace on earth, and mercy mild,
God and sinners reconciled!"
Joyful, all ye nations rise,
Join the triumph of the skies;
With th'angelic host proclaim,
"Christ is born in Bethlehem!"

Refrain
Hark! the herald angels sing,
"Glory to the newborn King!"

Christ, by highest Heav'n adored;
Christ the everlasting Lord;
Late in time, behold Him come,
Offspring of a virgin's womb.

Veiled in flesh the Godhead see;
Hail th'incarnate Deity,
Pleased with us in flesh to dwell,
Jesus our Emmanuel.

Refrain

Hail the heav'nly Prince of Peace!
Hail the Sun of Righteousness!
Light and life to all He brings,
Ris'n with healing in His wings.
Mild He lays His glory by,
Born that man no more may die.
Born to raise the sons of earth,
Born to give them second birth.

Refrain

Charles Wesley

2.18 ANGELS FROM THE REALMS OF GLORY, JAMES MONTGOMERY

Angels from the realms of glory,
Wing your flight o'er all the earth;
Ye who sang creation's story
Now proclaim Messiah's birth.

Refrain
Come and worship, come and worship,
Worship Christ, the newborn King.

Shepherds, in the field abiding,
Watching o'er your flocks by night,
God with us is now residing;
Yonder shines the infant light:

Refrain

Sages, leave your contemplations,
Brighter visions beam afar;
Seek the great Desire of nations;
Ye have seen His natal star.

Refrain

Saints, before the altar bending,
Watching long in hope and fear;

Suddenly the Lord, descending,
In His temple shall appear.

Refrain

Sinners, wrung with true repentance,
Doomed for guilt to endless pains,
Justice now revokes the sentence,
Mercy calls you; break your chains.

Refrain

Though an Infant now we view Him,
He shall fill His Father's throne,
Gather all the nations to Him;
Every knee shall then bow down:

Refrain

All creation, join in praising
God, the Father, Spirit, Son,
Evermore your voices raising
To th'eternal Three in One.

Refrain

James Montgomery

2.19 IN THE BLEAK MIDWINTER, CHRISTINA ROSSETTI

In the bleak midwinter
Frosty wind made moan,
Earth stood hard as iron,
Water like a stone;
Snow had fallen, snow on snow,
Snow on snow,
In the bleak midwinter
Long ago.

Our God, Heaven cannot hold Him,
Nor earth sustain;
Heaven and earth shall flee away
When He comes to reign:
In the bleak midwinter
A stableplace sufficed
The Lord God Almighty
Jesus Christ.

Enough for Him whom cherubim
Worship night and day,
A breastful of milk
And a mangerful of hay;
Enough for Him whom angels

Fall down before,
The ox and ass and camel
Which adore.

Angels and archangels
May have gathered there,
Cherubim and seraphim
Throng'd the air,
But only His mother
In her maiden bliss
Worshipped the Beloved
With a kiss.

What can I give Him,
Poor as I am?
If I were a shepherd
I would bring a lamb,
If I were a wise man
I would do my part,
Yet what I can I give Him;
Give my heart.

Christina Rossetti

2.20 AWAY IN A MANGER, JAMES R. MURRAY

Away in a manger, no crib for a bed,
The little Lord Jesus laid down His sweet head.
The stars in the sky looked down where He lay,
The little Lord Jesus, asleep on the hay.

The cattle are lowing, the Baby awakes,
But little Lord Jesus, no crying He makes;

I love Thee, Lord Jesus, look down from the sky
And stay by my cradle til morning is nigh.

Be near me, Lord Jesus, I ask Thee to stay
Close by me forever, and love me, I pray;
Bless all the dear children in Thy tender care,
And fit us for Heaven to live with Thee there.

James R. Murray

JESUS' HIDDEN YEARS

2.21 JESUS' HOME LIFE, ALFRED EDERSHEIM

Alfred Edersheim, 1825-1889, was an Anglican biblical scholar. His writings included, Sketches of Jewish Social Life, Temple—Its Ministry and Services, *and* Life and Times of Jesus the Messiah.

Once only is the great silence, which lies on the history of Christ's early life, broken. It is to record what took place on His first visit to the Temple. What this meant, even to an ordinary devout Jew, may easily be imagined. Where life and religion were so intertwined, and both in such organic connection with the Temple and the people of Israel, every thoughtful Israelite must have felt as if his real life were not in what was around, but ran up into the grand unity of the people of God, and were compassed by the halo of its sanctity. To him it would be true in the deepest sense, that, so to speak, each Israelite was born in Zion, as, assuredly, all the wellsprings of his life were there. It was, therefore, not merely the natural eagerness to see the City of their God and of their fathers, glorious Jerusalem; nor yet the lawful enthusiasm, national or religious, which would kindle at the thought of "our feet" standing within those gates, through which priests, prophets, and kings had passed; but far deeper feelings which would make glad, when it was said: "Let us go into the house of Jehovah." They were not ruins to which precious memories clung, nor did the great hope seem to lie afar off, behind the evening-mist. But "glorious things were spoken of Zion, the City of God," in the past, and in the near future "the thrones of David" were to be set within her walls, and amidst her palaces.

With His return to Nazareth began Jesus' Life of youth and early manhood, with all of inward and outward development, of

heavenly and earthly approbation which it carried. Whether or not He went to Jerusalem on recurring Feasts, we know not, and need not inquire. For only once during that period, on His first visit to the Temple, and in the awakening of His Youth-Life, could there have been such outward forth-bursting of His real Being and Mission. Other influences were at their silent work to weld His inward and outward development, and to determine the manner of His later Manifesting of Himself. We assume that the School-education of Jesus must have ceased soon after His return to Nazareth. Henceforth the Nazareth-influences on the Life and Thinking of Jesus may be grouped, and progressively as He advanced from youth to manhood, under these particulars:

Home,

Nature, and

Prevailing ideas.

1. HOME

Jewish home-life, especially in the country, was of the simplest. Even in luxurious Alexandria it seems often to have been such, alike as regarded the furnishing of the house, and the provisions of the table. The morning and midday meal must have been of the plainest, and even the larger evening meal of the simplest, in the home at Nazareth. Only the Sabbath and festivals, whether domestic or public, brought what of the best lay within reach. But Nazareth was not the city of the wealthy or influential, and such festive evening-entertainments, with elaborate ceremoniousness of reception, arranging of guests according to rank, and rich spread of board, would but rarely, if ever, be witnessed in those quiet homes. The same simplicity would prevail in dress and manners. But close and loving were the bonds which drew together the members of a family, and deep the influence which they exercised on each other. We cannot here discuss the vexed question whether "the brothers and sisters" of Jesus were such in the real sense, or step-brothers and sisters, or else cousins, though it seems to us as if the primary meaning of the terms would scarcely have been called in question, but for a theory of false asceticism, and an undervaluing of the sanctity of the married estate. [See St. Matt. 1:24; Luke 2:7; St. Matt. 12:46; 13:55, 56; Mark 3:31; 6:3; Acts 1:14; 1 Cor. 9:5; Gal. 1:19.] But, whatever the precise relationship between Jesus and these "brothers and sisters," it must, on any theory, have been of the closest, and exercised its influence upon Him.

. . . We turn to what is certain in connection with His Family-Life and its influences. From Mark 6:3, we may infer with great probability, though not with absolute certainty, [see St. Matt. 13:55; John 6:42.] that He had adopted the trade of Joseph. Among the Jews the contempt for manual labor, which was one of the painful characteristics of heathenism, did not exist. On the contrary, it was deemed a religious duty, frequently and most earnestly insisted upon, to learn some trade, provided it did not minister to luxury, nor tend to lead away from personal observance of the Law. There was not such separation between rich and poor as with us, and while wealth might confer social distinction, the absence of it in no way implied social inferiority. Nor could it be otherwise where wants were so few, life was so simple, and its highest aim so ever present to the mind.

The love of parents to children, appearing even in the curse which was felt to attach to childlessness; the reverence towards parents, as a duty higher than any of outward observance; and the love of brethren, which Jesus had learned in His home, form, so to speak, the natural basis of many of the teachings of Jesus. They give us also an insight into the family-life of Nazareth. And yet there is nothing somber nor morose about it; and even the joyous games of children, as well as festive gatherings of families, find their record in the words and the life of Christ. This also is characteristic of His past. And so are His deep sympathy with all sorrow and suffering, and His love for the family circle, as evidenced in the home of Lazarus. That He spoke Hebrew, and used and quoted the Scriptures in the original, has already been shown, although, no doubt, He understood Greek, possibly also Latin.

2. NATURE AND EVERY-DAY LIFE

The most superficial perusal of the teaching of Christ must convince how deeply sympathetic He was with nature, and how keenly observant of man. Here there is no contrast between love of the country and the habits of city life; the two are found side by side. On His lonely walks He must have had an eye for the beauty of the lilies of the field, and thought of it, how the birds of the air received their food from an Unseen Hand, and with what maternal affection the hen gathered her chickens under her wing. He had watched the sower or the vinedresser as he went forth to his labor, and read the teaching of the tares which sprang up among the wheat. To Him the vocation of the shepherd must have been full of meaning, as he led, and fed, and watched his flock, spoke to his sheep with well-known voice, brought them to the fold, or followed, and tenderly carried back, those that had strayed, ever ready to defend them, even at the cost of his own life. Nay, He even seems to have watched the habits of the fox in its secret lair. But he also equally knew the joys, the sorrows, the wants and sufferings of the busy multitude. The play in the market, the marriage processions, the funeral rites, the wrongs of injustice and oppression, the urgent harshness of the creditor, the bonds and prison of the debtor, the palaces and luxury of princes and courtiers, the self-indulgence of the rich, the avarice of the covetous, the exactions of the tax-gatherer, and the oppression of the widow by unjust judges, had all made an indelible impression on His mind. And yet this evil world was not one which He hated, and from which He would withdraw Himself with His disciples, though ever and again He felt the need of periods of meditation and prayer. On the contrary, while He confronted all the evil in it, He would fain pervade the mass with the new leaven; not cast it away, but renew it. He recognized the good and the hopeful, even in those who seemed most lost. He quenched not the dimly burning flax, nor brake the bruised reed. It was not contempt of the world, but sadness over it; not condemnation of man, but drawing him to His Heavenly Father; not despising of the little and the poor, whether outwardly or inwardly such, but encouragement and adoption of them, together with keen insight into the real under the mask of the apparent, and withering denunciation and unsparing exposure of all that was evil, mean, and unreal, wherever it might appear. Such were some of the results gathered from His past life, as presented in His teaching.

3. PREVAILING IDEAS
Of the prevailing ideas around, with which He was brought in contact, some have already been mentioned. Surely, the earnestness of His Shammaite brother, if such we may venture to designate him; the idea of the Kingdom suggested by the Nationalists, only in its purest and most spiritual form, as not of this world, and as truly realizing the sovereignty of God in the individual, whoever he might be; even the dreamy thoughts of the prophetic literature of those times, which sought to read the mysteries of the coming Kingdom; as well as the prophet-like asceticism of His forerunner and kinsman, formed at least so many points of contact for His teaching. Thus, Christ was in sympathy with all the highest tendencies of His people and time. Above all, there was His intimate converse with the Scriptures of the Old Testament. If, in the Synagogue, He saw much to show the hollowness, self-seeking, pride, and literalism which a mere external observance of the Law fostered, He would ever turn from what man or devils said to what He read, to what was "written." Not one dot or hook of it could fall to the ground, all must be established and fulfilled. The Law of Moses in all its bearings, the utterances of the prophets, Isaiah, Jeremiah, Ezekiel, Daniel, Hosea, Micah, Zechhariah, Malachi, and the hopes and consolations of the Psalms, were all to Him literally true, and cast their light upon the building which Moses had reared. It was all one, a grand unity; not an aggregation of different parts, but the unfolding of a living organism. Chiefest of all, it was the thought of the Messianic bearing of all Scripture to its unity, the idea of the Kingdom of God and the King of Zion, which was the life and light of all. Beyond this, into the mystery of His inner converse with God, the unfolding of His spiritual receptiveness, and the increasing communication from above, we dare not enter. Even what His bodily appearance may have been, we scarcely venture to imagine. It could not but be that His outer man in some measure bodied forth His "inner being." Yet we dread gathering around our thoughts of Him the artificial flowers of legend. What His manner and mode of receiving and dealing with men were, we can portray to ourselves from His life. And so it is best to remain content with the simple account of the evangelic narrative: "Jesus increased in favor with God and Man."

Alfred Edersheim,
Life and Times of Jesus the Messiah, *10, 1886*

2.22 The silent years at Nazareth, James M. Stalker

Rev James M. Stalker, DD, 1848-1927, Scottish Presbyterian pastor, scholar, professor and author was, according to Roy Greenhill, Sr., "without peer, as a singular figure in the history of Christianity."

He was minister at St. Brycedale, Kirkcaldy, and St. Matthew's, Glasgow and was more widely known in America than any other Scottish preacher of his day.

Dr. George Jackson said of Stalker's Life of Christ: *"The ease, the lucidity, the crystalline clearness with which the familiar story is retold are the last result of years of patient study and deep meditation. Dr. Stalker writes clearly because he sees clearly. The dead past has lived again before him; and it lives still for us in these graphic, vivid pages. Yet, throughout, the imagination works under wise restraints. The small canvas is never overcrowded. The leading facts of the history are seized and fixed with a master hand; the rest is forgotten. In nothing is the touch of the true literary artist more clearly seen than in the skill with which the writer has first selected and then grasped his materials. His book is a miracle of condensation, a miniature masterpiece."*

The records which we possess up to this point are comparatively full. But with the settlement at Nazareth, after the return from Egypt, our information comes to a sudden stop, and over the rest of the life of Jesus, till His public ministry begins, a thick covering is drawn, which is only lifted once. We should have wished the narrative to continue with the same fullness through the years of His boyhood and youth. In the modern biographies there are few parts more interesting than the anecdotes which they furnish of the childhood of their subjects, for in these we can often see, in miniature and in charming simplicity, the character and the plan of the future life. What would we not give to know the habits, the friendships, the thoughts, the words and the actions of Jesus during so many years? Only one flower of anecdote has been thrown over the wall of the hidden garden, and it is so exquisite as to fill us with intense longing to see the garden itself. But it has pleased God, whose silence is no less wonderful than His words, to keep it shut.

APOCRYPHAL GOSPELS

It was natural that, where God was silent and curiosity was strong, the fancy of man should attempt to fill up the blank. Accordingly, in the early Church there appeared Apocryphal Gospels, pretending to give full details where the inspired Gospels were silent. They were particularly full of the sayings and doings of the childhood of Jesus. But they only show how unequal the human imagination was to such a theme, and bring out by the contrast of glitter and caricature the solidity and truthfulness of the Scripture narrative. They make Him a worker of frivolous and useless marvels, who molded birds of clay and made them fly, changed His playmates into kids, and so forth. In short, they are compilations of worthless and often blasphemous fables.

These grotesque failures warn us not to intrude with the suggestions of fancy into the hallowed enclosure. It is enough to know that He grew in wisdom and stature, and in favor with God and Man. He was a real child and youth, and passed through all the stages of natural development. Body and mind grew together, the one expanding to manly vigor, and the other acquiring more and more knowledge and power. His opening character exhibited a grace that made everyone who saw it wonder and love its goodness and purity.

But, though we are forbidden to let the fancy loose here, we are not prohibited, but, on the contrary, it is our duty, to make use of such authentic materials as are supplied by the manners and customs of the time, or by incidents of His later life which refer back to His earlier years, in order to connect the infancy with the period when the narrative of the Gospels again takes up the thread of biography. It is possible in this way to gain, at least in some degree, a true conception of what He was as a boy and a young man, and what were the influences amidst which His development proceeded through so many silent years.

HIS HOME LIFE

We know amidst what kind of home influences He was brought up. His home was one of those which were the glory of His country, as they are of our own—the abodes of the godly and intelligent working class. Joseph, its head, was a man saintly and wise; but the fact that he is not mentioned in Christ's afterlife has generally been believed to indicate that he died during the youth of Jesus, perhaps leaving the care of the household on His shoulders. His mother probably exercised the most decisive of all external influences on His development. What she was may be inferred from the fact that she was chosen from all the women of the world to be crowned with the supreme honor of womanhood. The song which she poured forth on the subject of her own great destiny shows her to have been a woman religious, fervently poetical and patriotic; a student of Scripture, and especially of its great women, for it is saturated with Old Testament ideas, and molded on Hannah's song; a spirit exquisitely humble, yet capable of thoroughly appreciating the honor conferred upon her. She was no miraculous queen of heaven, as superstition has caricatured her, but a woman exquisitely pure, saintly, loving and high-souled. This is aureole enough. Jesus grew up in her love and passionately returned it.

There were other inmates of the household. He had brothers and sisters. From two of them, James and Jude, we have epistles in Holy Scripture, in which we may read what their character was. Perhaps it is not irreverent to infer from the severe tone of their epistles, that, in their unbelieving state, they may have been somewhat harsh and unsympathetic men. At all events, they never believed on Him during His lifetime, and it is not likely that they were close companions to Him in Nazareth. He was probably much alone; and the pathos of His saying, that a prophet is not without honor save in his own country and in his own house, probably reached back into the years before His ministry began.

EDUCATIONAL INFLUENCES

He received His education at home, or from a scribe attached to the village synagogue. It was only, however, a poor man's education. As the scribes contemptuously said, He had never learned, or, as we should say, He was not college-bred. No; but the love of knowledge was early awake within Him. He daily knew the joy of deep and happy thought; He had the best of all keys to knowledge—the open mind and the loving heart; and the three great books lay ever open before Him—the Bible, Man and Nature.

It is easy to understand with what fervent enthusiasm He would devote Himself to the Old Testament; and His sayings, which are full of quotations from it, afford abundant proof of how constantly it formed the food of His mind and the comfort of His soul. His youthful study of it was the secret of the marvelous facility with which He made use of it afterwards in order to enrich His preaching and enforce His doctrine, to repel the assaults of opponents and overcome the temptations of the Evil One. His quotations also show that He read it in the original Hebrew, and not in the Greek translation, which was then in general use. The Hebrew was a dead language even in Palestine, just as Latin now is in Italy; but He would naturally long to read it in the very words in which it was written. Those who have not enjoyed a liberal education, but amidst many difficulties have mastered Greek in order to read their New Testament in the original, will perhaps best understand how, in a country village, He made Himself master of the ancient tongue, and with what delight He was wont, in the rolls of the synagogue or in such manuscripts as he may have Himself possessed, to pore over the sacred page. The language in which He thought and spoke familiarly was Aramaic, a branch of the same stem to which the Hebrew belongs. We have fragments of it in some recorded sayings of His, such as "*Talitha, cumi,*" and "*Eloi, Eloi, lama sabachtani.*" He would have the same chance of learning Greek as a boy born in the Scottish Highlands has of learning English, "Galilee of the Gentiles" being then full of Greek-speaking inhabitants. Thus He was probably master of three languages, one of them the grand religious language of the world, in whose literature He was deeply versed; another the most perfect means of expressing secular thought which has ever existed, although there is no evidence that He had any acquaintance with the masterpieces of Greek literature; and the third the language the common people, to whom His preaching was to be specially addressed.

HIS COUNTRY VILLAGE

There are few places where human nature can be better studied than in a country village; for there one sees the whole of each individual life and knows all one's neighbors thoroughly. In a city far more people are seen, but far fewer known; it is only the outside of life that is visible. In a village the view outwards is circumscribed; but the view downwards is deep, and the view upwards unimpeded. Nazareth was a notoriously wicked town, as we learn from the proverbial question, Can any good thing come out of Nazareth? Jesus had no acquaintance with sin in His own soul, but in the town he had a full exhibition of the awful problem with which it was to be His life-work to deal. He was still further brought into contact with human nature by His trade. That he worked as a carpenter in Joseph' shop there can be no doubt. Who could know better than His own townsmen, who asked, in their astonishment at His preaching, Is not this the carpenter? It would be difficult to exhaust the significance of the fact that God chose for His Son, when He dwelt among men, out of all the possible positions in which He might have placed Him, the lot of a working man. It stamped men's common toils with everlasting honor. It acquainted Jesus with the feelings of the

multitude, and helped Him to know what was in man. It was afterwards said that He knew this so well that He needed not that any man should teach Him.

THE SPOT WHERE HE GREW UP

Travelers tell us that the spot where He grew up is one of the most beautiful on the face of the earth. Nazareth is situated in a secluded, cup-like valley amid the mountains of Zebulon, just where they dip down in to the plain of Esdraelon, with which it is connected by a steep and rocky path. Its white houses, with vines clinging to their walls, are embowered amidst gardens and groves of olive, fig, orange and pomegranate trees. The fields are divided by hedges of cactus, and enameled with innumerable flowers of every hue. Behind the village rises a hill five hundred feet in height, from whose summit there is seen one of the most wonderful views in the world—the mountains of Galilee, with snowy Hermon towering above them, to the north; the ridge of Carmel, the coast of Tyre and the sparkling waters of the Mediterranean, to the west; a few miles to the east, the wooded, cone-like bulk of Tabor; and to the south, the plain of Esdraelon, with the mountains of Ephraim beyond. The preaching of Jesus shows how deeply He had drunk into the essence of natural beauty and reveled in the changing aspects of the seasons. It was when wandering as a lad in these fields that He gathered the images of beauty which he poured out in his parables and addresses. It was on that hill that he acquired the habit of His after-life of retreating to the mountain-tops to spend the night in solitary prayer. The doctrines of His preaching were not thought out on the spur of the moment. They were poured out in a living stream when the occasion came, but the water had been gathering into the hidden well for many years before. In the fields and on the mountainside He had thought them out during the years of happy and undisturbed meditation and prayer.

James M. Stalker
The Life of Jesus Christ, *Revell, 1896*

2.23 The human development of Jesus, B. B. Warfield

It is Luke's distinction among the evangelists that he has given us a narrative, founded, as he tells us, on an investigation which "traced the coarse of all things accurately from the first" (Luke 1:3). We note the careful exactness with which he records the performance by our Lord's parents of "all things that were according to the law of the Lord"—the circumcision of their marvelous child, "when eight days were fulfilled for circumcising him" (Luke 2:21); his presentation in the Temple, "when the days of their purification according to the law of Moses were fulfilled" (Luke 2:22); the annual visit to Jerusalem at the feast of the Passover (2:41); and the like. Luke marks for us with careful precision, the stages of the growth of the child. He does not indeed distinguish all the eight stadia of development for which the sweet homeliness of Jewish speech provided separate designations." but with some pointedness he brings Jesus before us successively as "infant" (Luke 2:16), as "child" (vs. 40), as "boy" (vs. 43) in his progress to man's estate, and all this within the compass of a single chapter. The second chapter of Luke may fairly be looked upon, accordingly, as an express history of the development of the man, Christ Jesus; and it puts in what almost amounts to a direct claim to be such by formally summing up in two comprehensive verses his entire growth from childhood to boyhood and from boyhood to manhood, "And the child grew," we read, "and waxed strong, becoming (more and more) filled with wisdom: and the grace of God was upon him" (vs. 40). "And Jesus advanced in wisdom and stature, and in favor with God and man" (vs. 52).

It would seem absurd to question that there is attributed to Jesus here what may in the fullest sense of the word be called a normal human development, The language is charged, indeed, with suggestions that this was an extraordinary child: whose growth we are witnessing, and his development was an extraordinary development. Attention is called alike to his physical, intellectual and moral or spiritual progress; and in all alike it seems to be implied that his advance was steady, unbroken, rapid and remarkable. Those who looked on him in the cradle would see that, even beyond the infant Moses of old, this was "a goodly child" (Heb. 11:23), and day by day he grew and waxed strong: and as he increased in stature, he advanced also in wisdom. Not in knowledge only, but in that instinctive skill in the practical use of knowledge, that moral and spiritual insight, which we call wisdom.

"And the grace of God was upon him," and he advanced with equal steps "in favor with God." As he grew, "becoming more and more filled with wisdom," he became more and more filled also with grace. Not only man, but God looked upon his developing powers and character with ever increasing favor. The goodly child grew steadily into the goodly youth, and the goodly youth into the good man. With every accession of stature and strength there was the accompanying increase of wisdom; and with every increase of wisdom there was the accompanying advance in moral and spiritual power. In a word, Jesus grew as steadily and rapidly in character and in holiness as he grew in wisdom, and as steadily and rapidly in wisdom as he grew in stature. The promise of the goodly child passed without jar and without break into the fruitage of the perfect manhood; and those who looked on the babe with admiration could not but look on the youth with marveling (Luke 2:47) and (for "he advanced in favor with men") on the man with reverence. This is, therefore, no ordinary human development that Luke pictures to us here but it is none the less—say rather, all the more—a normal human development, the only strictly normal human development, from birth to manhood, the world has ever seen. For this child is the only child who has ever been born into the world without the fatal entail of sin and the only child that has ever grown into manhood without having his walk and speech marred at every step by the destructive influences of sin and error.

We may well account it one of the gains that we derive from the picture which Luke draws for us of the growth of Jesus from infancy to manhood, that thus we are given the sight of one normally developing human being. This is how men ought to grow up; how, were men not sinners, men would grow up. It is a great thing for the world to have seen one such instance. As an example, it may seem indeed set too high for us; our wings are clipped and we feel that we cannot soar into these elevated regions of doing and living. But, as an ideal realized in life, it must stand ever before us as an incitement and an inspiration. When we observe this perfect human development of Jesus, issuing into the perfect life of the man, we discern in it a model for every age and for every condition of man of quite inestimable alluring power. "He came to save all by means of himself," says Irenaeus—"all, I say, who through him are born again unto God—infants, and children and boys and youths and old men. He therefore passed through every age, becoming an infant for infants, thus sanctifying infants; a child for children, thus sanctifying those who are of this age, being at the same time made to them an example of piety, righteousness and submission; a youth for youths, becoming an example to youths, and thus sanctifying them for the Lord."

Quite the most fundamental gain we derive, however, from Luke's picture of the human development of Jesus is the assurance it gives us of the truth and reality of our Lord's humanity. It is this, indeed, that Irenaeus has in mind in the passage we have just quoted from him. The immediately preceding words run: "He did not seem one thing while he was another, as those affirm who describe him as being a man only in appearance; but what he was that also he appeared to be. Being a Master, therefore, he also possessed the age of a Master, not despising or evading any condition of humanity, nor setting aside in himself that law which he had appointed for the human race, but sanctifying every age by that period corresponding to it which belonged to himself." It would appear to be impossible to read Luke's language and doubt the real humanity of the child whose advance into manhood he is describing—advance along every element of his being—physical, intellectual and spiritual—alike. And this attribution of a complete and real humanity to Jesus is continued throughout the whole gospel narrative, and that in all the Gospels alike. Everywhere the man Christ Jesus is kept before our eyes, and every characteristic that belongs to a complete and perfect manhood is exhibited in his life as dramatized in the gospel story. All the limitations of humanity, therefore, remained his throughout. One fresh from reading the gospel narrative will certainly fail to understand the attitude of those, who we are told exist, who for example, "admit his growth in knowledge during childhood," "yet deny as intolerable the hypothesis of a limitation of his knowledge during his ministry." Surely Jesus himself has told us that he was ignorant of the time of the day of judgment (Mark 13:32); he repeatedly is represented as seeking knowledge through questions, which undoubtedly were not asked only to give the appearance of a dependence on information from without that was not real with him: he is made to express surprise; and to make trial of new circumstances; and the like. There are no human traits lacking to the picture that is drawn of him: he was open to temptation; he was conscious of dependence on God; he was a man of prayer; he knew a "will" within him that might conceivably be opposed to the will of God; he exercised faith; he learned obedience by the things that he suffered. It was not merely the mind of a man that was in him, but the heart of a man as well, and the spirit of a man. In a word, he was all that a man—a man without error and sin—is, and must be conceived to have grown, as it is proper for a man to grow, not only during his youth, but continuously through life, not alone in knowledge, but in wisdom, and not alone in wisdom, but "in reverence and charity"—in moral strength and in beauty of holiness alike. Indeed, we find it insufficient to say, as the writer whom we have just quoted says, Luke places no limit to the statement that he increased in wisdom; and it seems, therefore, to be allowable to believe that it continued until the great "It is finished" on the cross. Of course; and even beyond that "It is finished": and that not only with reference to his wisdom, but also with reference to all the traits of his blessed humanity. For Christ, just because he is the risen Christ, is man and true man—all that man is, with all that is involved in being man—through all the ages and into the eternity of the eternities.

We need not fear, therefore, that we may emphasize too strongly the true, the complete humanity of Christ. It is gain and nothing but gain, that we should realize it with an acuteness that may bear the term of poignant. All that man as man is, that Christ is to eternity. The Reformed theology which it is our happiness to inherit, has never hesitated to face the fact and rejoice in it, with all its implications. With regard to knowledge, for example, it has not shrunk from recognizing that Christ, as man, had a finite knowledge and must continue to have a finite knowledge forever. Human nature is ever finite, it declares, and is no more capable of infinite charismata, than of the infinite idiomata or attributes of the divine nature; so that it is certain that the knowledge of Christ's human nature is not and can never be the infinite wisdom of God itself. The Reformed Theology has no reserves, therefore, in confessing the limitations of the knowledge of Christ as man, and no fear of overstating the perfection and completeness of his humanity. No danger can possibly arise, of course, from our accepting in the fullest meaning that can be given to them the accounts of our Lord's early development that Luke gives us, and the descriptions of his human traits provided for us by all the evangelists. It is, as we have said, gain and nothing but gain, to realize in all its fullness that our Lord was man even as we are men, made "in all things like unto his brethren" (Heb. 2:17).

Where danger and evil enter in, is when, in order to realize the completeness of Jesus' humanity, we begin to attenuate, [thin] or put out of view, or even mayhap to push out of recognition his deity. For though the Scriptures represent Christ as all that man is, and attribute to him all that is predicable of humanity, they are far from representing him as only what man is, and as possessing nothing that cannot, in one way or another, be predicated of humanity. Alongside of these clear declarations and rich indications of his true and complete humanity, there runs an equally pervasive attribution to him of all that belongs to deity. If for example, he is represented as not knowing this or that matter of fact (Mark 13:32), he is equally represented as knowing all thing's (John 20:17; 16:30). If he is represented as acquiring information from without, asking questions and expressing surprise, he is equally represented as knowing without human information all that occurs or has occurred—the secret prayer of Nathaniel (John 1:47), the whole life of the Samaritan woman (John 4:29), the very thoughts of his enemies (Matt. 9:4), all that is in man (John 2:25). Nor are these two classes of facts kept separate; they are rather interlaced in the most amazing manner. If it is by human informants that he is told of Lazarus' sickness (John 11:3, 6), it is on no human information that he knows him to be dead (John 11:11, 14); if he asks "Where have ye laid him?" and weeps with the sorrowing sister, he knows from the beginning (John 11:11) what his might should accomplish for the assuagement of this grief. Everywhere, in a word, we see a double life unveiled before us in the dramatization of the actions of Jesus among men; not, indeed, in the sense that he is represented as acting inconsistently, or is inconsistently represented as acting now in one order and now in another; but rather in the sense that a duplex life is attributed to him as his constant possession. If all that man is is attributed to him, no less is all that God is attributed to him, and the one attribution is no more pervasive than the other. With reference to his knowledge, for example—a topic very much under discussion nowadays—we do not think any simple reader of the Gospels will hesitate to set his seal to the following representation, drawn from a recent German writer, whose own solution of the problem of Christ's double knowledge is, however, far from that of the Bible itself.

The Scriptures presuppose the Son's omniscience as self-evident. If Jesus calls himself the Truth, he must first know all things, before he could say it; if he is the

Light, he must not only see all things but he must see all things only in his light (Ps. 36:9); and in fine, if he calls himself the life, no man can breathe and no angel can think without his living in them, and so filling and knowing all heaven and earth, so that in him are hidden all the treasures of wisdom and knowledge, and without him there is no knowing. As, therefore, his disciples already in his lifetime (John 10:30), as also Peter after his resurrection (John 21:17), say "Thou knowest all things"—so we rightly conclude from his divine Being also his divine knowing, and that he has known all things even as man—already as child—yea in the womb—and therefore, at all times.

That this conjoint humanity and deity, within the limits of a single personality, presents serious problems to the human intellect, in its attempts to comprehend it, in itself or in its activities, goes without saying. Small wonder that many errors have been committed in the necessary effort which men have made rightly to conceive it. The short and easy method of dealing with it, is to grasp firmly the one series of representations and simply neglect or openly discard the other. This has been the procedure in all ages of those who would fain see in Jesus only a human Messiah; and it is a pitfall into which we easily stumble if we do not carefully keep in mind the whole double series of representations concerning him. In our vivid realization of the complete humanity attributed to him, it is distressingly easy to forget the equally complete deity attributed. to him. Others seek to pare down both series of representations until, out of the trimmed fragments that remain, they can succeed in fitting together for themselves the portrait of some middle being—neither man nor God— which they call Jesus. Thus violence is done to both series of representations alike: and the result is a fair reproduction of no single declaration of the Bible. Others still would seek to distinguish between the essential nature of Jesus and his earthly manifestations; or even between the two kinds of knowledge in him, intuitive and experimental, in the hope of thus finding a key to unlock the puzzle. All equally in vain; the Biblical facts require us to recognize in the constant possession and use of the God-man a double series of qualities—the one essentially divine and the other essentially human; and in doing so, they impose on us the recognition in him of two natures—so that he is perfect in his deity and perfect in his humanity—subsisting in one person, without conversion, without confusion, eternally and inseparably.

In these words is enunciated, it need hardly be said, the doctrine of the Person of Christ which has been since the Council of Chalcedon (held in A.D. 451) the common heritage of the Christian Churches. It was not arrived at easily or without long and searching study of the Scripture material, and long and sharp controversy among conflicting constructions. Every other solution was tried and found wanting; in this solution the Church found at last rest, and in it she has rested until our own day. In it alone, it is not too much to say, can the varied representations of the Bible find each full justice, and all harmonious adjustment. If it be true, then all that is true of God may be attributed to Christ, and equally all that is true of man. Full account is taken of all the phenomena; violence is done to none. If it be not true, it is safe to say that the puzzle remains insoluble. No doubt it is difficult to conceive of two complete and perfect natures united in one person; but that once conceived all that the Scriptures say of Jesus follows as a matter of course. He within whom dwells both an infinite an a finite mind, both at every moment of time knows all things and is throughout all time advancing in knowledge. There is mystery enough attaching to the conception; but it is the simple and pure mystery of the Incarnation—without which a real Incarnation would be inconceivable. The glory of the Incarnation is that it presents to our adoring gaze, not a humanized God or a deified man, but a true God-man—one who is all that God is and at the same time all that man is: on whose almighty arm we can rest, and to whose human sympathy we can appeal. We cannot afford to lose either the God in the man or the man in the God; our hearts cry out for the complete God-man whom the Scriptures offer us. It may be much to say that it is because he is man that he is capable of growth in wisdom, and because he is God that he is from the beginning Wisdom Itself. It is more to say that because he is man he is able to pour out his blood, and because he is God his blood is of infinite value to save; and that it is only because he is both God and Man in one person, that we can speak of God purchasing his Church with his own blood (Acts 20:28).

And unless God has purchased his Church with his own blood, in what shall his Church find a ground for its hope?

B. B. Warfield,
The human development of Jesus

4

JESUS' MINISTRY

2.24 THE COMPASSION OF JESUS, C. H. SPURGEON

This sermon was preached by Spurgeon at the Metropolitan Tabernacle, Newington, London, and first published on Thursday, December 24th, 1914.

"He was moved with compassion." Matthew 9:36

This is said of Christ Jesus several times in the New Testament. The original word is a very remarkable one. It is not found in classic Greek. It is not found in the Septuagint. The fact is, it was a word coined by the evangelists themselves. They did not find one in the whole Greek language that suited their purpose, and therefore they had to make one. It is expressive of the deepest emotion; a striving of the bowels—a yearning of the innermost nature with pity. I suppose that when our Savior looked upon certain sights, those who watched him closely perceived that his internal agitation was very great, his emotions were very deep, and then his face betrayed it, his eyes gushed like founts with tears, and you saw that his big heart was ready to burst with pity for the sorrow upon which his eyes were gazing. He was moved with compassion. His whole nature was agitated with commiseration for the sufferers before him.

Now, although this word is not used many times even by the evangelists, yet it may be taken as a clue to the Savior's whole life, and I intend thus to apply it to him. If you would sum up the whole character of Christ in reference to ourselves, it might be gathered into this one sentence, "He was moved with compassion." Upon this one point we shall try to insist now, and may God grant that good practical result may come of it.

First, I shall lead your meditations to the great transactions of our Savior's life;

secondly, to the special instances in which this expression is used by the evangelists;

thirdly, to the forethought which he took on our behalf; and

fourthly to the personal testimony which one's own recollections can furnish.

Let us take a rapid survey of:

1. THE GREAT LIFE OF CHRIST

The great life of Christ, just touching, as with a swallow's wing, the evidence it bears from the beginning. Before ever the earth was framed; before the foundations of the everlasting hills were laid, when as yet the stars had not begun their shining, it was known to God that his creature man would sin; that the whole race would fall from its pure original state in the first Adam, the covenant head as well as the common parent of the entire human family; and that in consequence of that one man's disobedience every soul born of his lineage would become a sinner too. Then, as the Creator knew that his creatures would rebel against him, he saw that it would become necessary, eventually, to avenge his injured law. Therefore, it was purposed, in the eternal plan, ere the stream of time had commenced its course, or ages had began to accumulate their voluminous records, that there should be an interposer—one ordained to come and re-head the race, to be a second Adam, a federal Chief; to restore the breach, and repair the mischief of the first Adam; to be a Surety to answer for the sons of men on whom God's love did light; that their sins should be laid upon him, and that he should save them with an everlasting salvation. No angel could venture to intrude into those divine counsels and decrees, or to offer himself as the surety and sponsor for that new covenant. Yet there was one—and he none other than Jehovah's self—of whom he said, Let all the angels of God worship him, the Son, the well beloved of the Father, of whom it is written in the Word, "When he prepared the heavens I was there, when he set a compass upon the face of the depth, when he established the clouds above, when he strengthened the fountain of the deep"; then, "I was by him as one brought up with him, and I was daily his delight, rejoicing always before him; rejoicing in the habitable parts of the earth; and my delights were with the sons of men." He it is of whom the Apostle John speaks as the Word who was God, and was in the beginning with God. Was he not moved with compassion when he entered into a covenant with his father on our behalf, even on the behalf of all his chosen—a covenant in which he was to be the sufferer, and they the gainers—in which he was to bear the shame that he might bring them into his own glory? Yes, verily, he was even then moved with compassion, for his delights even then were with the sons of men. Nor did his compassion peer forth in the prospect of an emergency presently to diminish and disappear as the rebellion took a more active form, and the ruin assumed more palpable proportions. It was no transient feeling. He continued still to pity men. He saw the fall of man; he marked the subtle serpent's mortal sting; he watched the trail as the slime of the serpent passed over the fair glades of Eden; he observed man in his evil progress, adding sin to sin through generation after generation, fouling every page of history until God's patience had been tried to the uttermost; and then, according as it was written in the volume of the Book that he must appear, Jesus Christ came himself into this stricken world. Came how? O, be astonished, ye angels, that ye were witnesses of it, and ye men that ye beheld it. The Infinite came down to earth in the form of an infant; he who spans the heavens and holds the ocean in the hollow of his hand, condescended to

hang upon a woman's breast—the King eternal became a little child. Let Bethlehem tell that he had compassion. There was no way of saving us but by stooping to us. To bring earth up to heaven, he must bring heaven down to earth. Therefore, in the incarnation, he must bring heaven down to earth. Therefore, in the incarnation, he had compassion, for he took upon himself our infirmities, and was made like unto ourselves. Matchless pity, indeed, was this!

Then, while he tarried in the world, a man among men, and we beheld his glory, the glory as of the Only Begotten of the Father, full of grace and truth, he was constantly moved with compassion; for he felt all the griefs of mankind in himself. He took our sicknesses and carried our sorrows: he proved himself a true brother, with quick, human sensibilities. A tear brought a tear into his eye; a cry made him pause to ask what help he could render. So generous was his soul, that he gave all he had for the help of those that had not. The fox had its hole, and the bird its nest, but he had no dwelling-place. Stripped even of his garments, he hung upon the cross to die. Never one so indigent in death as he, without a friend, without even a tomb, except such as a loan could find him. He gave up all the comforts of life—he gave his life itself; he gave his very self to prove that he was moved with compassion. Most of all do we see how he was moved with compassion in his terrible death. Oft and oft again have I told this story, yet these lips shall be dumb ere they cease to reiterate the old, old tidings. God must punish sin, or else he would relinquish the government of the universe. He could not let iniquity go unchastened without compromising the purity of his administration. Therefore, the law must be honored, justice must be vindicated, righteousness must be upheld, crime must be expiated by suffering. Who, then, shall endure the penance or make the reparation? Shall the dread sentence fall upon all mankind? How far shall vengeance proceed before equity is satisfied? After what manner shall the sword do homage to the scepter? Must the elect of God be condemned for their sins? No; Jesus is moved with compassion. He steps in, he takes upon himself the uplifted lash, and his shoulders run with gore; he bares his bosom to the furbished sword, and it smites the Shepherd that the sheep may escape. "He looked, and there was no man, and wondered that there was no intercessor; therefore, his arm brought salvation." He trod the wine-press alone, and "bore, that we might never bear, his Father's righteous ire."

Are ye asked what means the crucifixion of a perfect man upon a felon's cross, ye may reply, "He was moved with compassion." "He saved others; himself he could not save." He was so moved with compassion, that compassion, as it were, did eat him up. He could save nothing from the general conflagration: he was utterly consumed with love, and died in the flame of ardent love towards the sons of men. And after he had died and slept a little while in the grave, he rose again. He has gone into his glory; he is living at the right hand of the Father; but this is just as true of him, "He is moved with compassion." Is proof wanted? Let faith pass within the veil, and let your spirits for a moment stand upon that sea of glass mingled with fire where stand the harpers tuning their never-ceasing melodies. What see you there conspicuous in the very midst of heaven but One who looks like a lamb that has been slain, and wears his priesthood still? What is his occupation there in heaven? He has no bloody sacrifice to offer, for he has perfected for ever those that were set apart. That work is done, but what is he doing now? He is pleading for his people; he is their perpetual Advocate, their continual Intercessor; he never rests until they come to their rest; he never holds his peace for them, but pleads the merit of his blood, and will do so till all whom the Father gave him shall be with him where he is. Well indeed does our hymn express it:

"Now, though he reigns exalted high,
His love is still as great;
Well he remembers Calvary,
Nor will his saints forget."

His tender heart pities all the griefs of his dear people. There is not a pang they have but the head feels it, feels it for all the members. Still doth he look upon their imperfections and their infirmities, yet not with anger, not with loss of patience, but with gentleness and sympathy, "He is moved with compassion." Having thus briefly sketched the life of Christ, I want you to turn to:

2. THOSE PASSAGES OF THE EVANGELISTS IN WHICH THEY TESTIFY THAT HE WAS MOVED WITH COMPASSION

You will find one case in Matthew 20:31: "Two blind men sat by the wayside begging, and when they heard that Jesus passed by, they said, O Lord, thou Son of David, have mercy on us.'" Jesus stood still, called them, questioned them, and they seem to have had full conviction that he both could and would restore their sight, so Jesus had compassion on them, touched their eyes, and immediately they received sight.

Yes, and what a lesson this is for any here present who have a like conviction. Do you believe that Christ can heal you? Do you believe that he is willing to heal you? Then let me assure you that a channel of communication is opened between him and you, for he is moved with compassion towards you, and already I hear him command you to come to him. He is ready to heal you now. The sad condition of a blind man should always move pity in the breast of the humane, but a glance at these two poor men—I do not know that there was anything strange or uncommon about their appearance—touched the Savior's sensibility. And when he heard them say that they did believe he could heal them, he seemed to perceive that they had inward sight, and to account it a pity that they should not have outward sight too. So at once he put his fingers upon their eyes, and they received the power of seeing. O soul, if thou believest Christ can save thee, and if you wilt now trust in him to save thee, be of good cheer, thou art saved; that faith of thine hath saved thee. The very fact that thou believest that Jesus is the Christ, and doth rely upon him, may stand as evidence to thee that thou art forgiven, that thou art saved. There is no let or bar to thy full redemption. Go thy way and rejoice in thy Lord. He hath compassion on thee.

The next case I shall cite is that of the leper, Mark 1:41. This poor man was covered with a sad and foul disease, when he said to

Jesus, "Lord, if thou wilt, thou canst make me clean." He had full faith in Christ's ability, but he had some doubts as to Christ's willingness. Our Savior looked at him, and though he might very well have rebuked him that he should doubt his willingness, he merely said, "I will, be thou clean," and straightway he was made whole of that loathsome plague. If there is in this assembly one grievously defiled or openly disgraced by sin, seest thou the leprosy upon thyself, and dost thou say, "I believe he could save me if he would"? Hast thou some lingering doubt about the Savior's willingness? Yet I beseech you breathe this prayer, "Lord, I believe, I believe thy power. Help thou mine unbelief which lingers round thy willingness." Then little as thy faith is, it shall save thee. Jesus, full of compassion, will pity even thine unbelief, and accept what is faith, and forgive what is unbelief. There is a second instance.

The third I will give you is from Mark 5:19. It was the demoniac. There met Christ a man so possessed with a devil as to be mad, and instead of belief in Christ or asking for healing, this spirit within the man compelled him to say, "Wilt thou torment us before the time?"—and rather to stand against Christ healing him than to ask for it; but Christ was moved with compassion, and he bade the evil spirit come out of the evil man. Oh! I am so glad of this instance of his being moved with compassion. I do not so much wonder that he has pity on those that believe in him, neither do I so much marvel that he has pity even on weak faith; but here was a case in which there was no faith, no desire, nor anything that could commend him to our Lord's sympathy. Is there no such case among the crowds gathered together here? You do not know why you have come into this assembly. You scarcely feel at home in this place. Though you have led a very sad life, you do not want to be converted—not you. You almost shun the thought. Yet it is written, "He will have compassion on whom he will have compassion." Well we have known it in this house, and I hope we shall know it again and again that the Lord has laid violent hands of love upon unprepared souls. They have been smitten down with repentance, renewed in heart, and saved from their sins. Saul of Tarsus

had no thought that he should ever be an apostle of Christ, but the Lord stopped the persecutor, and changed him into a preacher; so that ever afterwards he propagated the faith which once he destroyed. May the Lord have compassion on you tonight. Well may we offer that prayer; for what will be your fate if you die as you are? What will be your doom eternally if you pass out of this world, as soon you must, without being sprinkled with the blood of Christ, and forgiven your iniquities? Jesus knows the terrors of the world to come. He describes the torments of hell. He sees your danger; he warns you; he pities you; he sends his messengers to counsel you; he bids me say to the very chief of sinners, "Come unto me, and I will give you rest." "Only return unto me and confess thine iniquity, and I will have mercy upon thee," saith the Lord. May God grant that the compassion of Christ may be seen in thy case.

As I turned over the Greek concordance to find out where this word is repeated again and again, I found one instance in Luke 7:13. It refers to the widow at the gates of Nain. Her son was being carried out—her only son. He was dead, and she was desolate. The widow's only son was to her her sole stay; the succor as well as the solace of her old age. He was dead and laid upon the bier, and when Jesus saw the disconsolate mother, he was moved with compassion, and he restored her son. Oh! is there not refreshment here for you mothers that are weeping for your boys; you that have ungodly sons, unconverted daughters, the Lord Jesus sees your tears. You weep alone sometimes, and when you are sitting and enjoying the Word, you think, "Oh! that my Absalom were renewed; oh! that Ishmael might live before thee." Jesus knows about it. He was always tender to his own mother, and he will be so to you. And you that are mourning over those that have been lately taken from you, Jesus pities you. Jesus wept, he sympathizes with your tears. He will dry them and give you consolation. "He was moved with compassion."

Still the occasions on which we find this expression most frequently used in the Evangelists are when crowds of people were assembled. At the sight of the great congregations that gathered to hear him, our Lord was often moved with compassion. Sometimes it was because that they were hungry and faint, and in the fullness of his sympathy he multiplied the loaves and fishes to feed them. At the same time he showed his disciples that it is a good work to feed the poor. He would not have them so spiritually-minded as to forget that the poor have flesh and blood that require sustenance, and they need to eat and to drink, to be housed and clothed: the Christian's charity must not lie in words only, but in deeds. Our Lord was moved with compassion, it is said, when he saw the number of sick people in the throng, for they made a hospital of his preaching place. Wherever he paused or even passed by, they laid the sick in the streets; he could not stand or walk without the spectacle of their pallets to harrow his feelings. And he healed their impotent folk, as if to show that the Christian does well to minister to the sick— that the patient watcher by the bedside may be serving the Lord, and following his example, as well as the most diligent teacher or the most earnest preacher of the glorious gospel. All means that can be used to mitigate human suffering are Christlike, and they ought to be carried out in his name, and carried to the utmost perfection possible. Christ is the patron of the hospital: he is the president of all places where men's bodies are cared for. But we are also told that the multitude excited his compassion because they were like sheep without a shepherd. So he taught them as a guide that showed the path by leading the way; and he looked after their welfare as a Shepherd who regarded the health of their bodies as well as the good estate of their souls. Surely, brethren and sisters, if you love him, and wish to be like him, you cannot look on this congregation without pity. You cannot go out into the streets of London and stand in the high roads among the surging masses for half an hour without saying, "Whither away these souls? Which road are they traveling? Will they all meet in heaven?" What! live ye in London, move ye about in this great metropolis, and do ye never have the heartache, never feel your soul ready to burst with pity? Then shame upon you! Ask

yourself whether ye have the spirit of Christ at all. In this congregation, were we all moved with pity as we should be, I should not have to complain, as I sometimes must, that persons come in and out here in want of someone to speak with them, to condole, to console, or to commune with them in their loneliness, and they find no helper. Time was when such a thing never occurred, but, in conversing with enquirers lately, I have met with several cases in which persons in a distressed state of mind have said that they would have given anything for half an hour's conversation with any Christian to whom they might have opened their hearts. They came from the country, attended the Tabernacle, and no one spoke to them. I am sorry it should be so. You used to watch for souls, most of you. Very careful were you to speak to those whom you saw again and again. I do pray you mend that matter. If you have any bowels of mercy, you should be looking out for opportunities to do good. Oh! never let a poor wounded soul faint for want of the balm. You know the balm. It has healed yourselves. Use it wherever the arrows of God have smitten a soul. Enough; I must leave this point; I have given you, I think, every case in which it is said that Jesus was moved with compassion. Very briefly let me notice:

3. SOME OF THE FORESIGHTS OF HIS COMPASSION

The Lord has gone from us, but as he knew what would happen while he was away, he has, with blessed forethought, provided for our wants. Well he knew that we should never be able to preserve the truth pure by tradition. That is a stream that always muddies and defiles everything. So in tender forethought he has given us the consolidated testimony, the unchangeable truth in his own Book; for he was moved with compassion. He knew the priests would not preach the gospel; he knew that no order of men could be trusted to hold fast sound doctrine from generation to generation; he knew there would be hirelings that dare not be faithful to their conscience lest they should lose their pay; while there would be others who love to tickle men's ears and flatter their vanity rather than to tell out plainly and distinctly the whole counsel of God. Therefore, he has put it here, so that if you live where there is no preacher of the gospel, you have the old Book to go to. He is moved with compassion for you. For where a man cannot go, the Book can go, and where in silence no voice is heard, the still clear voice of this blessed Book can reach the heart. Because he knew the people would require this sacred teaching, and could not have it otherwise, he was moved with compassion towards us all, and gave us the blessed Book of inspired God-breathed Scripture.

But then, since he knew that some would not read the Bible, and others might read and not understand it, he has sent his ministers forth to do the work of evangelists. He raises up men, saved themselves from great sin, trophies of redeeming grace, who feel a sympathy with their fellow-men who are reveling in sin, reckless of their danger. These servants of his the Lord enables to preach his truth, some with more, some with less ability than others; still, there are, thank God, throughout this happy realm, and in other favored lands, men everywhere, who, because sinners will not come to Christ of themselves, go after them and persuade them, plead with them, and entreat them to believe and turn to the Lord. This cometh of Christ's tender gentleness. He was moved with compassion, and therefore he sent his servants to call sinners to repentance.

But since the minister, though he may call as he may, will not bring souls to Christ of himself, the Lord Jesus, moved with compassion, has sent his Spirit. The Holy Ghost is here. We have not to say:—

"Come Holy Spirit, heavenly dove."

He is here. He dwells in his Church, and he moves over the congregation, and he touches men's hearts, and he subtly inclines them to believe in Christ. Oh! this is great mercy when a Prince spreads a feast and gives an invitation. That is all you can expect him to do. But if he keeps a host of footmen and says, "Go and fetch them one by one till they do come," that is more gracious still. But if he goes himself and with sacred violence compels them to come in—oh! this is more than we could have thought he would have done; but

he is moved with compassion, and he does that. Furthermore, brethren, the Lord Jesus knew that after we were saved from the damning power of sin, we should always be full of wants, and therefore he was moved with compassion, and he sets up the throne of grace, the mercy-seat, to which we may always come, and from which we may always obtain grace to help in time of need. Helped by his Spirit, we can bring what petitions we will, and they shall be heard. And then, since he knew we could not pray as we ought, he was moved with compassion when he sent the Holy Spirit to help our infirmities, to teach us how to pray. Now I do not know a single infirmity that I have or that you have, my Christian brother, but what Christ Jesus has been moved with compassion about it, and has provided for it. He has not left one single weak point of which we have to say, "There I shall fail, because he will not help there"; but he has looked us over and over from head to foot, and said, "You will have an infirmity there: I will provide for it. You will have a weakness there: I will provide for it." And oh! how his promises meet every case! Did you ever get into a corner where there was not a promise in the corner too? Had you ever to pass through a river but there was a promise about his being in the river with you? Were you ever on the sick bed without a promise like this, "I will make thy bed in thy sickness?" In the midst of pestilence have not you found a promise that "he shall cover thee with his feathers, and under his wings shalt thou trust?" The Lord's great compassion has met the wants of all his servants to the end. If our children should ever need much patience to be exercised towards them as Christ needs to exercise towards us, I am sure there would be none of us able to bear the house. They have their infirmities, and they full often vex and grieve us, it may be, but oh! we ought to have much compassion for the infirmities of our children—ay, and of our brethren and sisters, and neighbors—for what compassion has the Lord had with us? I do believe none but God could bear with such untoward children as we ourselves are. He sees our faults, you know, when we do not see them, and he knows what those faults are more thoroughly than we do.

Yet still he never smites in anger. He cuts us not off, but he still continues to show us abounding mercies. Oh! what a guardian Savior is the Lord Jesus Christ to us, and how we ought to bless his name at all times, and how his praise should be continually in our mouth. One thought strikes me that I must put in here: he knew that we should be very forgetful; and he was moved with compassion with our forgetfulness when he instituted the blessed Supper, and we can sit around the table and break bread, and pour forth the wine in remembrance of him. Surely this is another instance of how he is moved with compassion, and not with indignation, towards our weaknesses. And now let me close with:

4. PERSONAL RECOLLECTIONS OF THE COMPASSION OF CHRIST

I shall only recall my own experience in order to stir up your pure minds by way of remembrance, my brethren and sisters. I do well remember when I was under conviction of sin, and smarted bitterly under the rod of God, that when I was most heavy and depressed there would sometimes come something like hope across my spirit. I knew what it was to say, "My soul chooseth strangling rather than life," yet when I was at the lowest ebb and most ready to despair, though I could not quite lay hold of Christ, I used to get a touch of the promise now and then, till I half hoped that, after all, I might prove to be God's prisoner, and he might yet set me free. I do remember well, when my sins compassed me about like bees, and I thought it was all over with me, and I must be destroyed by them, it was at that moment when Jesus revealed himself to me. Had he waited a little longer, I had died of despair, but that was no desire of his. On swift wings of love he came and manifested his dear wounded self to my heart. I looked to him and was lightened, and my peace flowed like a river. I rejoiced in him. Yes, he was moved with compassion. He would not let the pangs of conviction be too severe; neither would he suffer them to be protracted too long for the spirit of man to fail before him. It is not his wont to break a leaf that is driven by the tempest. "He will not quench the smoking flax." Yea, and I do remember since I first saw him and began to love him many sharp and severe troubles, dark and heavy trials, yet have I noted this, that they have never reached that pitch of severity which I was unable to bear. When all gates seemed closed, there has still been with the trial a way of escape, and I have noted again that in deeper depressions of spirits through which I have passed, and horrible despondencies that have crushed me down, I have had some gleams of love, and hope, and faith at the last moment; for he was moved with compassion. If he withdrew his face, it was only till my heart broke for him, and then he showed me the light of his countenance again. If he laid the rod upon me, yet when my soul cried under his chastening he could not bear it, but he put back the rod, and he said, "My child, I will comfort thee." Oh! the comforts that he gives on a sick bed! Oh! the consolations of Christ! when you are very low. If there is anything dainty to the taste in the Word of God, you get it then; if there be any bowels of mercy, you hear them sounding for you then. When you are in the saddest plight, Christ comes to your aid with the sweetest manifestations; for he is moved with compassion. How frequently have I noticed, and I tell it to his praise, for though it shows my weakness, it proves his compassion, that sometimes, after preaching the gospel, I have been so filled with self-reproach, that I could hardly sleep through the night because I had not preached as I desired. I have sat me down and cried over some sermons, as though I knew that I had missed the mark and lost the opportunity. Not once nor twice, but many a time has it happened, that within a few days someone has come to tell me that he found the Lord through that very sermon, the shortcoming of which I had deplored. Glory be to Jesus; it was his gentleness that did it. He did not want his servant to be too much bowed down with a sense of infirmity, and so he had compassion on him and comforted him. Have not you noticed, some of you, that after doing your best to serve the Lord, when somebody has sneered at you, or you have met with such a rebuff as made you half-inclined to give up the work, an unexpected success has been given you, so that you have not played the Jonah and ran away to Tarshish, but kept to your work? Ah! how many times in your life, if you could read it all, you would have to stop and write between the lines, "He was moved with compassion." Many and many a time, when no other compassion could help, when all the sympathy of friends would be unavailing, he has been moved with compassion towards us, has said to us, "Be of good cheer," banished our fears with the magic of his voice, and filled our souls to overflowing with gratitude. When we have been misrepresented, traduced, and slandered, we have found in the sympathy of Christ our richest support, till we could sing with rapture the verse—I cannot help quoting it now, though I have often quoted it before:—

"If on my face for thy dear name
Shame and reproach shall be,
I'll hail reproach and welcome shame,
Since thou rememberest me."

The compassion of the Master making up for all the abuses of his enemies. And, believe me, there is nothing sweeter to a forlorn and broken spirit than the fact that Jesus has compassion. Are any of you sad and lonely? Have any of you been cruelly wronged? Have you lost the goodwill of some you esteemed? Do you seem as if you had the cold shoulder even from good people? Do not say, in the anguish of your spirit, "I am lost," and give up. He hath compassion on you. Nay, poor fallen woman, seek not the dark river and the cold stream—he has compassion. He who looks down with the bright eyes of yonder stars and watches thee is thy friend. He yet can help thee. Though thou hast gone so far from the path of virtue, throw not thyself away in blank despair, for he hath compassion. And thou, broken down in health and broken down in fortune, scarcely with shoe to thy feet, thou art welcome in the house of God, welcome as the most honored guest in the assembly of the saints. Let not the weighty grief that overhangs thy soul tempt thee to think that hopeless darkness has settled thy fate and foreclosed thy doom. Though thy sin may have beggared thee, Christ can enrich thee with better riches. He hath compassion. "Ah!" say you, "they will pass me on the stairs; they will give me a broad pathway, and if they see me in the street they will not speak to me—even his disciples will not." Be it so; but better than his disciples, tenderer by far, is Jesus. Is there a man here, whom to associate with were a scandal from which the pure and pious would shrink?; the holy, harmless, undefiled one will not disdain even him—for this man receiveth sinners—he is a friend of publicans and sinners. He is never happier than when he is relieving and retrieving the forlorn, the abject, and the outcast. He despises not any that confess their sins and seek his mercy. No pride nestles in his dear heart, no sarcastic word rolls off his gracious tongue, no bitter expression falls from his blessed lips. He still receives the guilty. Pray to him now. Now let the silent prayer go up, "My Savior, have pity upon me; be moved with compassion towards me, for if misery be any qualification for mercy, I am a fit object for thy compassion. Oh! save me for thy mercy's sake!" Amen.

C. H. Spurgeon

2.25 THREE YEARS OF MINISTRY, JAMES M. STALKER

Each of these years had features of its own.

The first year may be called the year of obscurity, both because the records of it which we possess are very scanty, and because he seems during it to have been only slowly emerging into public notice. It was spent for the most part in Judea.

The second year was the year of public favor, during which the country had become thoroughly aware of him; his activity was incessant, and his fame rang through the length and breadth of the land. It was almost wholly passed in Galilee.

The third was the year of opposition, when the public favor ebbed away. His enemies multiplied and assailed him with more and more pertinacity, and at last he fell a victim to their hatred. The first six months of this final year were passed in Galilee, and the last six in other parts of the land.

James M. Stalker, The Life of Jesus Christ, Revell, 1896

---

6. JESUS' MIRACLES
2.26 CHRONOLOGICAL TABLE OF THE MIRACLES OF CHRIST, DAVID BROWN

David Brown, together with Robert Jamieson, and A. R. Faussett is most well-known for writing a one volume commentary on the Bible entitled A Commentary, Critical, Explanatory, and Practical, on the Old and New Testament, *which was first published in 1871.*

On the order of some of our Lord's miracles and parables, the data being scanty, considerable difference obtains.

Miracles	*Where performed*	*Where Recorded*
Water made wine	Cana	John 2:1-11.
Traders cast out of the temple	Jerusalem	John 2:13-17.
Nobleman's son healed	Cana	John 4:46-54.
First miraculous draught of fishes	Sea of Galilee	Luke 5:1-11.
Leper healed	Capernaum	Matt. 8:2-4; Mark 1:40-45; Luke 5:12-15.
Centurion's servant healed	Capernaum	Matt. 8:5-13; Luke 7:1-10.
Widow's son raised to life	Nain	Luke 7:11-17.
Demoniac healed	Capernaum	Mark 1:21-28; Luke 4:31-37.
Peter's mother-in-law healed	Capernaum	Matt. 8:14, 15; Mark 1:29-31; Luke 4:38, 39.
Paralytic healed	Capernaum	Matt. 9:2-8; Mark 2:1-12; Luke 5:17-26.

Miracles	Where performed	Where Recorded
Impotent man healed	Jerusalem	John 5:1-16.
Man with withered hand healed	Galilee	Matt. 12:10-14; Mark3:1-6; Luke 6:6-11.
Blind and dumb demoniac healed	Galilee	Matt. 12:22-24; Luke 11:14.
Tempest stilled	Sea of Galilee	Matt. 8:23-27; Mark 4:35-41; Luke 8:22-25.
Demoniacs dispossessed	Gadara	Matt. 8:28-34; Mark 5:1-20.
Jairus' daughter raised to life	Capernaum	Matt. 9:18-26; Mark 5:22-24; Luke 8:41-56.
Issue of blood healed	Near Capernaum	Matt. 9:18-26; Mark 5:22-24; Luke 8:41-56.
Two blind men restored to sight	Capernaum	Matt. 9:27-31.
Dumb demoniac healed	Capernaum	Matt. 9:32-34.
Five thousand miraculously fed	Decapolis	Matt. 14:13-21; Mark 6:31-44; Luke 9:10-17; John 6:5-14.
Jesus walks on the sea	Sea of Galilee	Matt. 14:22-33; Mark 6:45-52; John 6:15-21.
Syrophœnician's daughter healed	Coasts of Tyre and Sidon	Matt. 15:21-28; Mark 7:24-30.
Deaf and dumb man healed	Decapolis	Mark 7:31-37.
Four thousand fed	Decapolis	Matt. 15:32-39; Mark 8:1-9.
Blind man restored to sight	Bethsaida	Mark 8:22-26.
Demoniac and lunatic boy healed	Near Caesarea Philippi	Matt. 17:14-21; Mark 9:14-29; Luke 9:37-43.
Miraculous provision of tribute	Capernaum	Matt. 17:24-27.
The eyes of one born blind opened	Jerusalem	John 9:1-41.
Woman of eighteen years' infirmity healed	Perea	Luke 13:10-17.
Dropsical man healed	Perea	Luke 14:1-6.
Ten lepers cleansed	Borders of Samaria	Luke 17:11-19.
Lazarus raised to life	Bethany	John 11:1-46.
Two blind beggars restored to sight	Jericho	Matt. 20:29-34;52; Mark 10:46-52; Luke 18:35-43 Mark 10:46-52; Luke 18:35-43.
Barren fig tree blighted	Bethany	Matt. 21:12, 13, 18, 19; Mark, 11:12-24.
Buyers and sellers again cast out	Jerusalem	Luke 19:45, 46.

Miracles	Where performed	Where Recorded
Malchus' ear healed	Gethsemane	Matt. 26:51-54; Mark 14:47-49; Luke 22:50-51; John 18:10-11.
Second draught of fishes	Sea of Galilee	John 21:1-14.

David Brown
Commentary Critical and Explanatory on the Whole Bible, *1871*

2.27 MIRACLES IN JOHN'S GOSPEL, R. C. TRENCH

They are called signs because they are no idle spectacles, but are designed to teach. Prodigies (wonders), because by their unwontedness they should rouse and strike. Powers or virtues (miracles), because they are greater indications of divine power than the things which are seen in the ordinary course of nature.

R. C. Trench, Miracles, *1846*

2.28 THE PROPER EVIDENCE OF MIRACLES, H. P. LIDDON

H. P. Liddon, 1829-1890, did more than any other writer in his day and country to reassert Christ's true historical relation to the Christian Church. The influential Harry Parry Liddon was Canon of St. Paul's Cathedral, London, and a powerful preacher who attracted large audiences. His enduring legacy seems to have been his Bampton lectures on the divinity of Christ. For Liddon, the attacks on the Old Testament—for instance the denial of the Mosaic origin and authority of the Pentateuch—were a heretical attack on the infallibility of Christ Himself (considering the references to Moses recorded in the Gospels). For Liddon, every attack on the Faith was ultimately an attack on the Incarnation.

But if the miracles of Jesus be admitted in the block, as by a "rational" believer in the resurrection they must be admitted they do point, as I have said, to the Catholic [universal] belief, as distinct from any lower conceptions respecting the Person of Jesus Christ. They differ from the miracles of prophets and apostles in that, instead of being answers to prayer, granted by a Higher Power, they manifestly flow forth from the majestic life resident in the Worker. John accordingly calls them Christ's "works," meaning that they were just such acts as might be expected from Him, being such as He was. For our Lord's miracles are something more than evidences that He was the organ of a Divine revelation. They do not merely secure a deferential attention to His disclosures respecting the nature of God, the duty and destiny of man, His own Person, mission, and work. Certainly they have this properly evidential force; He Himself appealed to them as having it. But it would be difficult altogether to account for their form, or for their varieties, or for the times at which they were wrought, or for the motives which were actually assigned for working them, on the supposition that their value was only evidential. They are like the kind deeds of the wealthy, or the good advice of the wise; they are like that debt of charity which is due from the possessors of great endowments to suffering humanity. Christ as Man owed this tribute of mercy which His Godhead had rendered it possible for Him to pay to those whom (such was His love) He was not ashamed to call His brethren. But besides this, Christ s miracles are physical and symbolic representations of His redemptive action as tile Divine Savior of mankind. Their form is carefully adapted to express this action. By healing the palsied, the blind, the lame, Christ clothed with a visible form His plenary power to cure spiritual diseases, such as the weakness, the darkness, the deadly torpor of the soul. By casting out devils from the possessed He pointed to His victory over the principalities and powers of evil, whereby man would be freed from their thraldom and restored to moral liberty. By raising Lazarus from the corruption of the grave He proclaimed Himself not merely a Revealer of the resurrection, but the Resurrection and the Life itself.

THEY MANIFEST HIS MEDIATORIAL GLORY

In our Lord's miracles then we have before us something more than a set of credentials, since they manifest forth His mediatorial glory. They exhibit various aspects of that redemptive power whereby He designed to save lost man from sin and death; and they lead us to study, from many separate points of view, Christ's majestic personality as the source of the various wonders which radiate from it. And assuredly such a study can have but one result for those who honestly believe in the literal reality of the wonders described; it must force upon them a conviction of the Divinity of the Worker.

A MIRACLE AT ENTRY AND EXIT OF CHRIST

But the miracles which especially point to the Catholic doctrine as their justification, and

which are simply incumbrances blocking up the way of a humanitarian theorist, are those of which our Lord's Manhood is itself the subject. According to the Gospel narrative Jesus enters this world by one miracle and He leaves it by another. His human manifestation centers in that miracle of miracles, His resurrection from the grave after death. The resurrection is the central fact up to which all leads, and from which all radiates. Such wonders as Christ's birth of a virgin mother, His resurrection from the tomb, and His ascension into Heaven are not merely the credentials of our redemption they are distinct stages and processes of the redemptive work itself. Taken in their entirety they interpose a measureless interval between the life of Jesus and the lives of the greatest of prophets or of apostles, even of those to whom it was given to still the elements and to raise the dead. To expel these miracles from the life of Jesus is to destroy the identity of the Christ of the Gospels; it is to substitute a new christ for the Christ of Christendom. Who would recognize the true Christ in the natural son of a human father, or in the crucified prophet whose body has rotted in an earthly grave? Yet on the other hand, who will not admit that He who was conceived of the Holy Ghost and born of a virgin mother, who, after being crucified, dead, and buried, rose again the third day from the dead and then went up into Heaven before the eyes of His apostles, must needs be an altogether superhuman being? The Catholic doctrine then is at home among the facts of the Gospel narrative by the mere fact of its proclaiming a superhuman Christ, while the modern Humanitarian theories are ill at ease among those facts. The four evangelists, amid their distinguishing peculiarities, concur in representing a Christ whose life is encased in a setting of miracles. The Catholic doctrine meets these representations more than half way; they are in sympathy with, if they are not admitted to anticipate, its assertion. The Gospel miracles point at the very least to a Christ who is altogether above the range of human experience, and the creeds recognize and confirm this indication by saying that He is God. Thus

THE CHRIST OF DOGMA IS THE CHRIST OF HISTORY

He is the Christ of the only extant history which describes the Founder of Christendom at all. A neutral attitude towards the miraculous element in the Gospel history is impossible. The claim to work miracles is not the least prominent element of our Lord's teaching, nor are the miracles which are said to have been wrought by Him a fanciful or ornamental appendage to His action. The miraculous is inextricably interwoven with the whole life of Christ. The ethical beauty, nay, the moral integrity of our Lord's character is dependent, whether we will it or not, upon the reality of His miracles. It may be very desirable to defer as far as possible to the mental prepossessions of our time; but it is not practicable to put asunder two things which God has joined together, namely, the beauty of Christ's character and the bona fide reality of the miracles which He professed to work.

H. P. Liddon
The Divinity of Our Lord and Savior Jesus
Christ, *1866*

2.29 JESUS AND DEMON-POSSESSION, C. S. LEWIS

There are two equal and opposite errors into which our race can fall about the devils. One is to disbelieve in their existence. The other is to believe, and to feel an excessive and unhealthy interest in them. They themselves are equally pleased by both errors, and hail a materialist or a magician with the same delight.

C. S. Lewis,
The Screwtape Letters, *New York:*
The Macmillan Co., 1971

Jesus' Teaching

2.30 Christ's Sermon on the Mount, John Bunyan

MATTHEW, CHAPTER 5

And Jesus, seeing the multitudes, ascended
Up to a mount, where sitting, and attended
By his disciples, he began to preach;
And on this manner following did them
teach.
Blessed are all such as are poor in spirit,
For they the heavenly kingdom do inherit.
Blessed are they that mourn; for in the stead
Thereof shall comfort be administered.
Blessed are they, whose meekness doth excel:
For on the earth their portion is to dwell.
Blessed are they, who after righteousness
Hunger and thirst; for they shall it possess.
Blessed are they, for they shall mercy find,
Who to do mercifully are inclin'd.
Blessed are all such as are pure in heart;
For God his presence shall to them impart.
Blessed are they that do make peace; for why?
They shall be call'd the sons of the Most High.
Blessed are they which suffer for the sake
Of righteousness: for they of heav'n partake.
Blessed are ye, when men shall falsely speak
All kind of ill against you for my sake,
And shall revile, and persecute you sore;
Rejoice, and be exceeding glad therefore:
For your reward in heav'n will be great:
For thus of old they did the prophets treat.
Ye are the salt o' th' earth; but wherewith must
The earth be season'd when the savour's lost?
It is from thenceforth good for nothing, but
To be cast out, and trodd'n under foot.
Ye are the light o' th' world; a city set
Upon an hill cannot be hid; nor yet
Do men a candle with a bushel cover,
But set it where it lights the whole house over.
So shine your light, your good works seen
thereby
Men may your heavenly Father glorify.

Think not that to destroy the law I came,
Or prophets; no, but to fulfill the same.
For till the heav'n and earth shall pass away,
One jot or tittle from the law, I say,
Shall never pass, till all shall be complete.
Whoso therefore presumes to violate,
One of these least commands, and teacheth
so,
Shall in God's kingdom be accounted low.
But he that doth, and teacheth them likewise,
Shall in God's kingdom have great dignities.
For I declare unto you, that unless
You shall exceed the scribe and pharisees
In righteousness; you shall on no condition,
Into the heavenly kingdom gain admission.
Ye've heard twas said of old, Thou shalt not
kill.'
And he incurs the judgment who shall spill
His brother's blood: but I to you declare,
That he that's wroth without a cause, shall
bear
The judgment. Likewise of the council he
That sayeth racha shall in danger be.
But whosoe'er shall say, Thou fool, the same
Shall be in danger of eternal flame.
When therefore to the altar thou dost bring
Thy gift, and there rememb'rest any thing
Thy brother hath against thee: leave it there
Before the altar, and come thou not near,
Till thou hast first made reconciliation,
Then may'st thou come and offer thine
oblation.
Make an agreement with thine adversary
Whilst thou art in the way, and do not tarry;
Lest he at any time deliver thee
Unto the judge, and by the judge thou be
Unto the officer forthwith resign'd,
And in imprisonment thou be confin'd;
I do affirm thou shalt not be enlarg'd,

Till thou the utmost farthing hast discharg'd.
Ye've heard that they of old did testify,
That men should not commit adultery:
But I pronounce him an adulterer,
Who views a woman to lust after her.
And if thy right eye shall offensive be,
Pluck thou it out and cast the same from thee;
For it is better lose one, than that all
Thy members should into hell torments fall.
And if thy right hand doth offend, cut off it,
And cast it from thee, for it will thee profit
Much rather that one of thy members fell,
Than that they should be all condemned to
hell.
It hath been said, whoso away shall force
His wife, shall give her a bill of divorce:
But whosoe'er shall put his wife away,
Except for fornication's sake, I say,
Makes her adult'ress, and who marries her,
So put away, is an adulterer.
Again: Ye've heard, Thou shalt not be
forsworn,
Was ancient doctrine, but thou shalt perform
Unto the Lord thine oaths: But I declare,
That thou shalt not at all presume to swear;
Neither by heaven, for it is God's throne;
Nor by the earth, for his foot stands thereon:
Neither swear by Jerusalem, for why?
It is the city of the King Most High:
Nor swear thou by thine head, for thou canst
make
No hair thereof to be or white or black:
But let yea, yea; nay, nay, in speech suffice,
For what is more from evil doth arise.
Ye've heard, it hath been said; Eye for an eye,
And tooth for tooth: But I do testify,
That you shall not resist; but let him smite
Thy left cheek also, who assaults thy right.
And if that any by a lawsuit shall
Demand thy coat, let them have cloak and all.
And whosoe'er compelleth thee to go
A mile, refuse not to go with him two.
Give him that asketh, and from him that may
Have need to borrow, turn not thou away.
Ye've heard, twas said: That thou shalt love thy
friend
And hate thy foe: But let your love extend
Unto your enemies: thus I declare,
Bless them that curse, do good to them that
bear
Ill will, and for your persecutors pray,

And them that do reproach you; that you may
Be children of your Father that's in heaven;
For he on good and bad alike hath given
His sun to rise, and in like manner doth
Send rain upon the just and unjust both
For what is your reward, if you love them
That love you? Do not publicans the same?
And if your brethren only you salute,
What more than they do ye? They also do't.
I will therefore that you be perfect, ev'n
As is your Father perfect that's in heaven.

MATTHEW, CHAPTER 6

Take heed you do not your alms-deed bestow
Before men, purposely to make a shew;
For then there will no recompence be given
Unto you of your Father that's in heaven:
With sound of trumpet do not thou therefore
Proclaim what thou art giving to the poor;
As is the manner of the hypocrites
To do in th' synagogues, and in the streets;
That men may give them praises. Verily
They have their recompence, I testify.
But when thou dost alms, let thy left hand
know
Not what thy right hand is about to do:
That giving secretly, thy Father may,
Who sees in secret, openly repay.
And when thou pray'st be not as hypocrites;
For they love in the corners of the streets,
And in the synagogues to stand and pray,
There to be seen: they've their reward I say.
But thou, when thou dost make thy pray'r, go
thee
Into thy closet, shut thy door unto thee,
And there in secret to thy Father cry,
Who seeing thee shall reward thee openly.
But when ye pray use not vain repetitions,
As heathens do, for they think their petitions
Prevail; when they the same do multiply:
Be ye not like to them therefore; for why;
Your Father knows what things you need
before
You ask him, on this wise pray ye therefore.

Our Father which art in heav'n, thy name
alone
Be hallowed. Thy glorious kingdom come.
Thy will be done on earth astis in heaven.
Give us this day our daily bread. And ev'n
As we remit our debtors, grant remission

To us. And lead us not into temptation,
But from all evil do thou us deliver;
For th' kingdom, power and glory's thine for
ever.
Amen.

For if you do forgive men that offend,
Your heavenly Father will to you extend
Forgiveness; but if not, nor will he spare,
At any time when you offenders are.
Moreover when you fast beware lest you
Look sad, as hypocrites are wont to do;
For they disguise their faces, that they may
Appear to fast: they've their reward I say.
But thou, when thou dost fast, anoint thine
head
And wash thy face, that undiscovered
Thy fasting may be unto men, but rather
That thou be seen in secret of thy Father:
And then thy Father, who in secrecy
Beholds thee, shall reward thee openly.
Lay not up treasure for yourselves in store
Upon the earth, where moth and rust devour,
And where by thieves you may be quite
bereaven.
But lay up treasure for yourselves in heaven,
Where neither moth, nor rust, nor thieves can
enter:
For where's your treasure there your hearts will
center.
The eye's the light o' th' body, which if right
Then thy whole body will be full of light:
But if thine eye be evil, then there will
A total darkness thy whole body fill.
If therefore all the light that is in thee
Be darkness, how great must that darkness be?
No man can serve two masters, either he
Will hate one, and love t'other, or will be
Faithful to one, and t'other will forego.
Ye cannot serve both God and mammon too.
Take no thought therefore for your life, I say,
What you shall eat or drink; or how you may
Your bodies clothe. Is not the life much more
Than meat; Is not the body far before
The clothes thereof? Behold the fowls o' th'
air,
Nor sow nor reap, nor take they any care;
How they provision into barns may gather;
Yet they are nourish'd by your heavenly Father:
Are ye not worth much more? Which of you
can

By taking thought add to his height one span?
And why for raiment are ye taking thought?
See how the lilies grow; they labor not,
Nor do they spin; yet Solomon, I say,
In all his pomp, had no such gay array.
If in the field God so doth clothe the grass,
Which is to-day, and doth to-morrow pass
Into the oven, shall he not therefore
O ye of little faith, clothe you much more?
Take no thought therefore, saying, What shall
we eat,
Or drink, or where shall we our raiment get:
(For thus the heathen people use to do)
For that you need them doth your Father
know.
But seek God's kingdom, and his
righteousness
First, and then all these things you shall
possess.
Be not then exercis'd with care and sorrow,
In making preparation for the morrow;
The morrow shall things for itself prepare:
Sufficient to the day is each day's care.

MATTHEW, CHAPTER 7

Judge not that you may not be judg'd; for even
As you pass judgment, judgment shall be
giv'n:
And with such measure as you mete to men,
It shall be measured unto you again.
And why dost thou take notice of the mote
That's in thy brother's eye; but dost not note
The beam that's in thine own? How wilt thou
say
Unto thy brother, let me take away
The mote that's in thine eye, when yet tis
plain
The beam that's in thine own doth still
remain?
First cast away the beam, thou hypocrite,
From thine own eye, so shall thy clearer sight
The better be enabled to descry,
And pluck the mote out of thy brother's eye.
Give not to dogs the things that are divine,
Neither cast ye your pearls before the swine
Lest that they should their feet them trample
under,
And turn upon you, and rend you asunder.
Ask, and obtain; seek, and ye shall find; do ye
Knock, and it shall be opened unto ye:
For he that seeks, shall find; that asks, obtain,

And he that knocks, shall an admittance gain.
Or what man is there of you, if his son
Shall ask him bread, will he give him a stone?
Or if he ask a fish, will he bestow
A serpent? If then ye being evil know
To give your children good gifts, how much rather
To them that ask him shall your heav'nly Father.
Then what you wou'd men shou'd to you, so do
To them: for that's the law and prophets too.
Enter in at the strait gate, for the road
That doth unto destruction lead, is broad;
And wide the gate; and many there be that
Enter therein: because strait is the gate,
And narrow is the way that is inclin'd
To life, and which there are but few that find.
False prophets shun, who in sheep's clothes appear,
But inwardly devouring wolves they are:
Ye by their fruits shall know them. Do men either
Pluck grapes of thorns, or figs or thistles gather?
Even so each good tree good fruit will produce;
But a corrupt tree fruit unfit for use:
A good tree cannot bring forth evil food,
Nor can an evil tree bear fruit that's good:
Each tree that bears not good fruit's hewn down
And burnt, thus by their fruits they shall be known.

Not every one that saith Lord, Lord, but he
That doth my heav'nly Father's will shall be
An heir of heaven: many in that day
Will call Lord, Lord, and thus to me will say;
Have we not prophesied in thy name?
Cast devils out, done wonders in the same?
And then will I profess I know you not;
Depart from me ye that have evil wrought.
Whoso therefore these sayings of mine doth hear,
And doth them, to a wise man I'll compare,
The which upon a rock his building founded,
The rain descended and the floods surrounded,
The winds arose, and gave it many a shock,
And it fell not, being founded on a rock.
And ev'ry one that hears these sayings of mine,
And not to do them doth his heart incline,
Unto a foolish man shall be compar'd;
Who his foundation on the sand prepar'd:
The rain descended and the floods were great,
The winds did blow, and vehemently beat
Against that house; and down the building came,
And mighty was the downfall of the same.
And now when Jesus thus had finished
His sayings, the people were astonished
Thereat: for not as do the scribes taught he
Them, but as one that had authority.

John Bunyan
Scriptural poems; being several portions of
scripture digested into English verse

2.31 LESSONS OF PRAYER, A. B. BRUCE

Alexander Balmain Bruce, was born on a Perthshire farm and educated in an Edinburgh college in the 19th century. He ministered in Scottish country parishes and taught in a Glasgow seminary. His most famous book was The Training of the Twelve.

Matt. 6:5-13; 7:7-11; Luke 11:1-13; 18:1-5.

It would have been matter for surprise if, among the manifold subjects on which Jesus gave instruction to His disciples, prayer had not occupied a prominent place. Prayer is a necessity of spiritual life, and all who earnestly try to pray soon feel the need of teaching how to do it. And what theme more likely to engage the thoughts of a Master who was Himself emphatically a man of prayer, spending occasionally whole nights in prayerful communion with His heavenly Father?

We find, accordingly, that prayer was a subject on which Jesus often spoke in the hearing of His disciples. In the Sermon on the Mount, for example, He devoted a paragraph to that topic, in which He cautioned His hearers against pharisaic ostentation and heathenish repetition, and recited a form of devotion as a model of simplicity, comprehensiveness, and brevity. At other times He directed attention to the necessity, in order to acceptable and prevailing prayer, of perseverance, concord, strong faith, and large expectation.

The passage cited from the eleventh chapter of Luke's Gospel gives an account of what may be regarded as the most complete and comprehensive of all the lessons communicated by Jesus to His disciples on the important subject to which it relates. The circumstances in which this lesson was given are interesting. The lesson on prayer was itself an answer to prayer. A disciple, in all probability one of the twelve, after hearing Jesus pray, made the request: "Lord, teach us to pray, as John also taught his disciples." The request and its occasion taken together convey to us incidentally two pieces of information. From the latter we learn that Jesus, besides praying much alone, also prayed in company with His disciples, practising family prayer as the head of a household, as well as secret prayer in personal fellowship with God His Father. From the former we learn that the social prayers of Jesus were most impressive. Disciples hearing them were made painfully conscious of their own incapacity, and after the Amen were ready instinctively to proffer the request, "Lord, teach us to pray," as if ashamed any more to attempt the exercise in their own feeble, vague, stammering words.

When this lesson was given we know not, for Luke introduces his narrative of it in the most indefinite manner, without noting either time or place. The reference to John in the past tense might seem to indicate a date subsequent to his death; but the mode of expression would

be sufficiently explained by the supposition that the disciple who made the request had previously been a disciple of the Baptist. Nor can any certain inference be drawn from the contents of the lesson. It is a lesson which might have been given to the twelve at any time during their disciplehood, so far as their spiritual necessities were concerned. It is a lesson for children, for spiritual minors, for Christians in the crude stage of the divine life, afflicted with confusion of mind, dumbness, dejection, unable to pray for want of clear thought, apt words, and above all, of faith that knows how to wait in hope; and it meets the wants of such by suggesting topics, supplying forms of language, and furnishing their weak faith with the props of cogent arguments for perseverance. Now such was the state of the twelve during all the time they were with Jesus; till He ascended to heaven, and power descended from heaven on them, bringing with it a loosed tongue and an enlarged heart. During the whole period of their discipleship, they needed prompting in prayer such as a mother gives her child, and exhortations to perseverance in the habit of praying, even as do the humblest followers of Christ. Far from being exempt from such infirmities, the twelve may even have experienced them in a superlative degree. The heights correspond to the depths in religious experience. Men who are destined to be apostles must, as disciples, know more than most of the chaotic, speechless condition, and of the great, irksome, but most salutary business of Waiting on God for light, and truth, and grace, earnestly desired but long withheld.

It was well for the church that her first ministers needed this lesson on prayer; for the time comes in the case of most, if not all, who are spiritually earnest, when its teaching is very seasonable. In the spring of the divine life, the beautiful blossom-time of piety, Christians may be able to pray with fluency and fervor, unembarrassed by want of words, thoughts, and feelings of a certain kind. But that happy stage soon passes, and is succeeded by one in which prayer often becomes a helpless struggle, an inarticulate groan, a silent, distressed, despondent waiting on God, on the part of men who are tempted to doubt whether God be indeed the hearer of prayer, whether prayer be not altogether idle and useless. The three wants contemplated and provided for in this lesson—the want of ideas, of words, and of faith—are as common as they are grievous. How long it takes most to fill even the simple petitions of the Lord's Prayer with definite meanings! the second petition, e.g., "Thy kingdom come," which can be presented with perfect intelligence only by such as have formed for themselves a clear conception of the ideal spiritual republic or commonwealth. How difficult, and therefore how rare, to find out acceptable words for precious thoughts slowly reached! How many, who have never got any thing on which their hearts were set without needing to ask for it often, and to wait for it long (no uncommon experience), have been tempted by the delay to give up asking in despair! And no wonder; for delay is hard to bear in all cases, especially in connection with spiritual blessings, which are in fact, and are by Christ here assumed to be, the principal object of a Christian man's desires. Devout souls would not be utterly confounded by delay, or even refusal, in connection with mere temporal goods; for they know that such things as health, wealth, wife, children, home, position, are not unconditionally good, and that it may be well sometimes not to obtain them, or not easily and too soon. But it is most confounding to desire with all one's heart the Holy Ghost, and yet seem to be denied the priceless boon; to pray for light, and to get instead deeper darkness; for faith, and to be tormented with doubts which shake cherished convictions to their foundations; for sanctity, and to have the mud of corruption stirred up by temptation from the bottom of the well of eternal life in the heart. Yet all this, as every experienced Christian knows, is part of the discipline through which scholars in Christ's school have to pass ere the desire of their heart be fulfilled.

The lesson on prayer taught by Christ, in answer to request, consists of two parts, in one of which thoughts and words are put into the mouths of immature disciples, while the other provides aids to faith in God as the answerer of prayer. There is first a form of prayer, and then an argument enforcing perseverance in prayer.

The form of prayer commonly called the Lord's Prayer, which appears in the Sermon on the Mount as a sample of the right kind of prayer, is given here as a summary of the general heads under which all special petitions may be comprehended. We may call this form the alphabet of all possible prayer. It embraces the elements of all spiritual desire, summed up in a few choice sentences, for the benefit of those who may not be able to bring their struggling aspirations to birth in articulate language. It contains in all six petitions, of which three—the first three, as was meet— refer to God's glory, and the remaining three to man's good. We are taught to pray, first for the advent of the divine kingdom, in the form of universal reverence for the divine name, and universal obedience to the divine will; and then, in the second place, for daily bread, pardon, and protection from evil for ourselves. The whole is addressed to God as Father, and is supposed to proceed from such as realize their fellowship one with another as members of a divine family, and therefore say, "Our Father." The prayer does not end, as our prayers now commonly do, with the formula, "for Christ's sake"; nor could it, consistently with the supposition that it proceeded from Jesus. No prayer given by Him for the present use of His disciples, before His death, could have such an ending, because the plea it contains was not intelligible to them previous to that event. The twelve did not yet know what Christ's sake (*sache*) meant, nor would they till after their Lord had ascended, and the Spirit had descended and revealed to them the true meaning of the facts of Christ's earthly history. Hence we find Jesus, on the eve of His passion, telling His disciples that up to that time they had asked nothing in His name, and representing the use of His name as a plea to be heard, as one of the privileges awaiting them in the future. "Hitherto," He said, "have ye asked nothing in my name; ask, and ye shall receive, that your joy may be full." And in another part of His discourse: "Whatsoever ye shall ask in my name, that will I do, that the Father may be glorified in the Son."

To what extent the disciples afterwards made use of this beautifully simple yet profoundly significant form, we do not know; but it may be assumed that they were in the habit of repeating it as the disciples of the Baptist might repeat the forms taught them by their master. There is, however, no reason to think that the "Lord's Prayer," though of permanent value as a part of Christ's teaching, was designed to be a stereotyped, binding method of addressing the Father in heaven. It was meant to be an aid to inexperienced disciples, not a rule imposed upon apostles. Even after they had attained to spiritual maturity, the twelve might use this form if they pleased, and possibly they did occasionally use it; but Jesus expected that by the time they came to be teachers in the church they should have outgrown the need of it as an aid to devotion. Filled with the Spirit, enlarged in heart, mature in spiritual understanding, they should then be able to pray as their Lord had prayed when He was with them; and while the six petitions of the model prayer would still enter into all their supplications at the throne of grace, they would do so only as the alphabet of a language enters into the most extended and eloquent utterances of a speaker, who never thinks of the letters of which the words he utters are composed.

In maintaining the provisional, pro tempore character of the Lord's Prayer, so far as the twelve were concerned, we lay no stress on the fact already adverted to, that it does not end with the phrase, "for Christ's sake." That defect could easily be supplied afterwards mentally or orally, and therefore was no valid reason for disuse. The same remark applies to our use of the prayer in question. To allow this form to fall into desuetude merely because the customary concluding plea is wanting, is as weak on one side as the too frequent repetition of it is on the other. The Lord's Prayer is neither a piece of Deism unworthy of a Christian, nor a magic charm like the "Pater noster" of Roman Catholic devotion. The most advanced believer will often find relief and rest to his spirit in falling back on its simple, sublime sentences, while mentally realizing the manifold particulars which each of them

includes; and he is but a tyro in the art of praying, and in the divine life generally, whose devotions consist exclusively, or even mainly, in repeating the words which Jesus put into the mouths of immature disciples.

The view now advocated regarding the purpose of the Lord's Prayer is in harmony with the spirit of Christ's whole teaching. Liturgical forms and religious methodism in general were much more congenial to the strict ascetic school of the Baptist than to the free school of Jesus. Our Lord evidently attached little importance to forms of prayer, any more than to fixed periodic fasts, else He would not have waited till He was asked for a form, but would have made systematic provision for the wants of His followers, even as the Baptist did, by, so to speak, compiling a book of devotion or composing a liturgy. It is evident, even from the present instructions on the subject of praying, that Jesus considered the form He supplied of quite subordinate importance: a mere temporary remedy for a minor evil, the want of utterance, till the greater evil, the want of faith, should be cured; for the larger portion of the lesson is devoted to the purpose of supplying an antidote to unbelief.

The second part of this lesson on prayer is intended to convey the same moral as that which is prefixed to the parable of the unjust judge—"that men ought always to pray, and not to faint." The supposed cause of fainting is also the same, even delay on the part of God in answering our prayers. This is not, indeed, made so obvious in the earlier lesson as in the later. The parable of the ungenerous neighbor is not adapted to convey the idea of long delay: for the favor asked, if granted at all, must be granted in a very few minutes. But the lapse of time between the presenting and the granting of our requests is implied and presupposed as a matter of course. It is by delay that God seems to say to us what the ungenerous neighbor said to his friend, and that we are tempted to think that we pray to no purpose.

Both the parables spoken by Christ to inculcate perseverance in prayer seek to effect their purpose by showing the power of importunity in the most unpromising circumstances. The characters appealed to are both bad—one in ungenerous, and the other unjust; and from neither is any thing to be gained except by working on his selfishness. And the point of the parable in either case is, that importunity has a power of annoyance which enables it to gain its object.

It is important again to observe what is supposed to be the leading subject of prayer in connection with the argument now to be considered. The thing upon which Christ assumes His disciples to have set their hearts is personal sanctification. This appears from the concluding sentence of the discourse: "How much more shall your heavenly Father give the Holy Spirit to them that ask Him!" Jesus takes for granted that the persons to whom He addresses Himself here seek first the kingdom of God and His righteousness. Therefore, though He inserted a petition for daily bread in the form of prayer, He drops that object out of view in the latter part of His discourse; both because it is by hypothesis not the chief object of desire, and also because, for all who truly give God's kingdom the first place in their regards, food and raiment are thrown into the bargain.

To such as do not desire the Holy Spirit above all things, Jesus has nothing to say. He does not encourage them to hope that they shall receive any thing of the Lord; least of all, the righteousness of the kingdom, personal sanctification. He regards the prayers of a double-minded man, who has two chief ends in view, as a hollow mockery—mere words, which never reach Heaven's ear.

The supposed cause of fainting being delay, and the supposed object of desire being the Holy Spirit, the spiritual situation contemplated in the argument is definitely determined. The Teacher's aim is to succor and encourage those who feel that the work of grace goes slowly on within them, and wonder why it does so, and sadly sigh because it does so. Such we conceive to have been the state of the twelve when this lesson was given them. They had been made painfully conscious of incapacity to perform aright their devotional duties, and they took that incapacity to be an index of their general spiritual condition, and were much depressed in consequence.

The argument by which Jesus sought to inspire His discouraged disciples with hope and confidence as to the ultimate fulfillment of their desires, is characterized by boldness, geniality, wisdom, and logical force. Its boldness is evinced in the choice of illustrations. Jesus has such confidence in the goodness of His cause, that He states the case as disadvantageously for Himself as possible, by selecting for illustration not good samples of men, but persons rather below than above the ordinary standard of human virtue. A man who, on being applied to at any hour of the night by a neighbor for help in a real emergency, such as that supposed in the parable, or in a case of sudden sickness, should put him off with such an answer as this, "Trouble me not, the door is now shut, and my children are with me in bed; I cannot rise and give thee," would justly incur the contempt of his acquaintances, and become a byword among them for all that is ungenerous and heartless. The same readiness to take an extreme case is observable in the second argument, drawn from the conduct of fathers towards their children. "If a son shall ask bread of any of you"—so it begins. Jesus does not care what father may be selected; He is willing to take any one they please: He will take the very worst as readily as the best; nay, more readily, for the argument turns not on the goodness of the parent, but rather on his want of goodness, as it aims to show that no special goodness is required to keep all parents from doing what would be an outrage on natural affection, and revolting to the feelings of all mankind.

The genial, kindly character of the argument is manifest from the insight and sympathy displayed therein. Jesus divines what hard thoughts men think of God under the burden of unfulfilled desire; how they doubt His goodness, and deem Him indifferent, heartless, unjust. He shows His intimate knowledge of their secret imaginations by the cases He puts; for the unkind friend and unnatural father, and we may add, the unjust judge, are pictures not indeed of what God is, or of what He would have us believe God to be, but certainly of what even pious men sometimes think Him to be. And

He cannot only divine, but sympathize. He does not, like Job's friends, find fault with those who harbor doubting and apparently profane thoughts, nor chide them for impatience, distrust, and despondency. He deals with them as men compassed with infirmity, and needing sympathy, counsel, and help. And in supplying these, He comes down to their level of feeling, and tries to show that, even if things were as they seem, there is no cause for despair. He argues from their own thoughts of God, that they should still hope in Him. "Suppose," He says in effect, "God to be what you fancy, indifferent and heartless, still pray on; see, in the case I put, what perseverance can effect. Ask as the man who wanted loaves asked, and ye shall also receive from Him who seems at present deaf to your petitions. Appearances, I grant, may be very unfavorable, but they cannot be more so in your case than in that of the petitioner in the parable; and yet you observe how he fared through not being too easily disheartened."

Jesus displays His wisdom in dealing with the doubts of His disciples, by avoiding all elaborate explanations of the causes or reasons of delay in the answering of prayer, and using only arguments adapted to the capacity of persons weak in faith and in spiritual understanding. He does not attempt to show why sanctification is a slow, tedious work, not a momentary act: why the Spirit is given gradually and in limited measure, not at once and without measure. He simply urges His hearers to persevere in seeking the Holy Spirit, assuring them that, in spite of trying delay, their desires will be fulfilled in the end. He teaches them no philosophy of waiting on God, but only tells them that they shall not wait in vain.

This method the Teacher followed not from necessity, but from choice. For though no attempt was made at explaining divine delays in providence and grace, it was not because explanation was impossible. There were many things which Christ might have said to His disciples at this time if they could have borne them; some of which they afterwards said themselves, when the Spirit of Truth had come, and guided them into all truth, and made them acquainted with the secret of God's way. He might have pointed out to them, e.g., that the delays of which they complained were according to the analogy of nature, in which gradual growth is the universal law; that time was needed for the production of the ripe fruits of the Spirit, just in the same way as for the production of the ripe fruits of the field or of the orchard; that it was not to be wondered at if the spiritual fruits were peculiarly slow in ripening, as it was a law of growth that the higher the product in the scale of being, the slower the process by which it is produced; that a momentary sanctification, though not impossible, would be as much a miracle in the sense of a departure from law, as was the immediate transformation of water into wine at the marriage in Cana; that if instantaneous sanctification were the rule instead of the rare exception, the kingdom of grace would become too like the imaginary worlds of children's dreams, in which trees, fruits, and palaces spring into being full-grown, ripe, and furnished, in a moment as by enchantment, and too unlike the real, actual world with which men are conversant, in which delay, growth, and fixed law are invariable characteristics.

Jesus might further have sought to reconcile His disciples to delay by descanting on the virtue of patience. Much could be said on that topic. It could be shown that a character cannot be perfect in which the virtue of patience has no place, and that the gradual method of sanctification is best adapted for its development, as affording abundant scope for its exercise. It might be pointed out how much the ultimate enjoyment of any good thing is enhanced by its having to be waited for; how in proportion to the trial is the triumph of faith; how, in the quaint words of one who was taught wisdom in this matter by his own experience, and by the times in which he lived, "It is fit we see and feel the shaping and sewing of every piece of the wedding garment, and the framing and moulding and fitting of the crown of glory for the head of the citizen of heaven;" how "the repeated sense and frequent experience of grace in the ups and downs in the way, the falls and risings again of the traveler, the revolutions and changes of the spiritual condition, the new moon, the darkened moon, the full moon in the Spirit's ebbing and flowing, raiseth in the heart of saints on their way to the country a sweet smell of the fairest rose and lily of Sharon;" how, "as travelers at night talk of their foul ways, and of the praises of their guide, and battle being ended, soldiers number their wounds, extol the valor, skill, and courage of their leader and captain," so "it is meet that the glorified soldiers may take loads of experience of free grace to heaven with them, and there speak of their way and their country, and the praises of Him that hath redeemed them out of all nations, tongues, and languages."

Such considerations, however just, would have been wasted on men in the spiritual condition of the disciples. Children have no sympathy with growth in any world, whether of nature or of grace. Nothing pleases them but that an acorn should become an oak at once, and that immediately after the blossom should come the ripe fruit. Then it is idle to speak of the uses of patience to the inexperienced; for the moral value of the discipline of trial cannot be appreciated till the trial is past. Therefore, as before stated, Jesus abstained entirely from reflections of the kind suggested, and adopted a simple, popular style of reasoning which even a child could understand.

The reasoning of Jesus, while very simple, is very cogent and conclusive. The first argument—that contained in the parable of the ungenerous neighbor—is fitted to inspire hope in God, even in the darkest hour, when He appears indifferent to our cry, or positively unwilling to help, and so to induce us to persevere in asking. "As the man who wanted the loaves knocked on louder and louder, with an importunity that knew no shame, and would take no refusal, and thereby gained his object, the selfish friend being glad at last to get up and serve him out of sheer regard to his own comfort, it being simply impossible to sleep with such a noise; so (such is the drift of the argument), so continue thou knocking at the door of heaven, and thou shalt obtain thy desire if it were only to be rid of thee. See in this parable what a power importunity has,

even at a most unpromising time—midnight—and with a most unpromising person, who prefers his own comfort to a neighbor's good: ask, therefore, persistently, and it shall be given unto you also; seek, and ye shall find; knock, and it shall be opened unto you."

At one point, indeed, this most pathetic and sympathetic argument seems to be weak. The petitioner in the parable had the selfish friend in his power by being able to annoy him and keep him from sleeping. Now, the tried desponding disciple whom Jesus would comfort may rejoin: "What power have I to annoy God, who dwelleth on high, far beyond my reach, in imperturbable felicity? Oh that I knew where I might find Him, that I might come even to His seat! But, behold, I go forward, but He is not there; and backward, but I cannot perceive Him: on the left hand, where He doth work, but I cannot behold Him: He hideth Himself on the right hand, that I cannot see Him." The objection is one which can hardly fail to occur to the subtle spirit of despondency, and it must be admitted that it is not frivolous. There is really a failure of the analogy at this point. We can annoy a man, like the ungenerous neighbor in bed, or the unjust judge, but we cannot annoy God. The parable does not suggest the true explanation of divine delay, or of the ultimate success of importunity. It merely proves, by a homely instance, that delay, apparent refusal, from whatever cause it may arise, is not necessarily final, and therefore can be no good reason for giving up asking.

This is a real if not a great service rendered. But the doubting disciple, besides discovering with characteristic acuteness what the parable fails to prove, may not be able to extract any comfort from what it does prove. What is he to do then? Fall back on the strong asseveration with which Jesus follows up the parable: "And I say unto you." Here, doubter, is an oracular dictum from One who can speak with authority; One who has been in the bosom of the eternal God, and has come forth to reveal His inmost heart to men groping in the darkness of nature after Him, if haply they might find Him. When He addresses you in such emphatic, solemn terms as these, "I say unto you, Ask, and it shall be given you; seek, and ye shall find; knock, and it shall be opened unto you," you may take the matter on His word, at least pro tempore. Even those who doubt the reasonableness of prayer, because of the constancy of nature's laws and the unchangeableness of divine purposes, might take Christ's word for it that prayer is not vain, even in relation to daily bread, not to speak of higher matters, until they arrive at greater certainty on the subject than they can at present pretend to. Such may, if they choose, despise the parable as childish, or as conveying crude anthropopathic ideas of the Divine Being, but they cannot despise the deliberate declarations of One whom even they regard as the wisest and best of men.

The second argument employed by Jesus to urge perseverance in prayer is of the nature of a reductio ad absurdum, ending with a conclusion [hungarumlaut] fortiori. "If," it is reasoned, "God refused to hear His children's prayers, or, worse still, if He mocked them by giving them something bearing a superficial resemblance to the things asked, only to cause bitter disappointment when the deception was discovered, then were He not only as bad as, but far worse than, even the most depraved of mankind. For, take fathers at random, which of them, if a son were to ask bread, would give him a stone? or if he asked a fish, would give him a serpent? or if he asked an egg, would offer him a scorpion? The very supposition is monstrous. Human nature is largely vitiated by moral evil; there is, in particular, an evil spirit of selfishness in the heart which comes into conflict with the generous affections, and leads men ofttimes to do base and unnatural things. But men taken at the average are not diabolic; and nothing short of a diabolic spirit of mischief could prompt a father to mock a child's misery, or deliberately to give him things fraught with deadly harm. If, then, earthly parents, though evil in many of their dispositions, give good, and, so far as they know, only good, gifts to their children, and would shrink with horror from any other mode of treatment, is it to be credited that the Divine Being, that Providence, can do what only devils would

think of doing? On the contrary, what is only barely possible for man is for God altogether impossible, and what all but monsters of iniquity will not fail to do God will do much more. He will most surely give good gifts, and only good gifts, to His asking children; most especially will He give His best gift, which His true children desire above all things, even the Holy Spirit, the enlightener and the sanctifier. Therefore again I say unto you: Ask, and ye shall receive; seek, and ye shall find; knock, and it shall be opened."

Yet it is implied in the very fact that Christ puts such cases as a stone given for bread, a serpent for a fish, or a scorpion for an egg, that God seems at least sometimes so to treat His children. The time came when the twelve thought they had been so treated in reference to the very subject in which they were most deeply interested, after their own personal sanctification, viz., the restoration of the kingdom to Israel. But their experience illustrates the general truth, that when the Hearer of prayer seems to deal unnaturally with His servants, it is because they have made a mistake about the nature of good, and have not known what they asked. They have asked for a stone, thinking it bread, and hence the true bread seems a stone; for a shadow, thinking it a substance, and hence the substance seems a shadow. The kingdom for which the twelve prayed was a shadow, hence their disappointment and despair when Jesus was put to death: the egg of hope, which their fond imagination had been hatching, brought forth the scorpion of the cross, and they fancied that God had mocked and deceived them. But they lived to see that God was true and good, and that they had deceived themselves, and that all which Christ had told them had been fulfilled. And all who wait on God ultimately make a similar discovery, and unite in testifying that "the Lord is good unto them that wait for Him, to the soul that seeketh Him."

For these reasons should all men pray, and not faint. Prayer is rational, even if the Divine Being were like men in the average, not indisposed to do good when self-interest does not stand in the way—the creed of heathenism. It is still more manifestly rational if, as Christ taught and Christians believe, God be better than the best of men—the one supremely good Being—the Father in heaven. Only in either of two cases would prayer really be irrational: if God were no living being at all,—the creed of atheists, with whom Christ holds no argument; or if He were a being capable of doing things from which even bad men would start back in horror, i.e., a being of diabolic nature,—the creed, it is to be hoped, of no human being.

A. B. Bruce, The Training of the Twelve, *1871*

2.32 THE KINGDOM OF GOD, ALFRED EDERSHEIM

An analysis of 119 passages in the New Testament where the expression "Kingdom" occurs, shows that it means the rule of God; which was manifested in and through Christ; is apparent in the Church; gradually develops amidst hindrances; is triumphant at the second coming of Christ ("the end"); and, finally perfected in the world to come.

Alfred Edersheim, The Life and Times of Jesus the Messiah, *1886*

2.33 BORN AGAIN, M. LLOYD-JONES

"Jesus answered and said unto him, Verily, verily, I say unto thee, Except a man be born again, he cannot see the kingdom of God. . . . Verily, verily, I say unto thee, Except a man be born of water and of the Spirit, he cannot enter into the kingdom of God" (John 3:3, 5).

When our Lord says, "Ye must be born again", He throws down the gauntlet. He says, in effect, "It is all right; I know what you are going to say, but you need not say it, it is all wrong, you must be born again. Verily, verily'—'truly, truly.'" Whenever He uses that formula He is always saying something of unusual seriousness and of deep import. He says, "Verily, verily, I say unto thee, Except [unless] a man be born again, he cannot see the kingdom of God."

This is the crucial phrase, the key phrase of Christianity: "Born again"! Some people say it should be translated "born from above." Others say it should be translated "born anew." I think that they are probably nearest to the truth who say that undoubtedly our Lord was speaking to Nicodemus in Aramaic, that the Greek is a translation from the Aramaic, and that then our English is a translation from the Greek. But the original was probably Aramaic, and there it means "except a man has another birth, he will never see the kingdom of God." It is the same thing. "Born again," "another birth," "born from above," "born of the Spirit"—take any of the terms you like.

This is the great New Testament doctrine and what it means, negatively, is that Christianity is not just an addition to something you have already got. Christianity, in other words, is not something that you and I, as we are, can take up; all that is contradicted here. Before we can be come Christians we need an entirely new start.

M. Lloyd-Jones
The Kingdom of God, *Wheaton, Crossway Books, 1992*

PARABLES

2.34 PARABLES, COLIN BROWN

It has been estimated that roughly one third of the recorded teaching of Jesus consists of parables and parabolic statements, and that there are some forty of the former and twenty of the latter (A. M. Hunter, *Interpreting the Parables,* 1960). In its broadest sense a parable is a form of speech used to illustrate and persuade by the help of a picture. In ancient writing, including the Bible, the use of figurative speech was widespread in giving concrete, pictorial and challenging expression to religious ideas for which there were no corresponding abstract concepts. Figurative speech is still part and parcel of every day life. On a philosophical and theoretical level religious language is interpreted in terms of abstractions and concepts relative to a contemporary world view. But this is merely to translate one set of thought forms from one conceptual scheme into those of another. In so doing care must be taken to avoid losing the original content of the picture and also the challenge which was an essential feature of the language. In discussing the character of the parable, scholars distinguish the parable proper from figurative language in general, metaphors, similes and similitudes, parabolic stories, illustrative stories, and allegories.

Colin Brown, Ed.
The New International Dictionary of New
Testament Theology
Grand Rapids: Zondervan, 1976

2.35 CHRONOLOGICAL TABLE OF THE PARABLES OF CHRIST, DAVID BROWN

Name of parable	*Where spoken*	*Where recorded*
The two debtors	Capernaum	Luke 7:40-43.
The strong man armed	Galilee	Matt. 12:29; Mark 3:27; Luke 11:21, 22.
The unclean spirit	Galilee	Matt. 12:43-45; Luke 11:24-26.
The sower	Seashore of Galilee	Matt. 13:3-9, 18-23; Mark 4:3-9, 14-20; Luke 8:5-8, 11-15.
The tares and wheat	Seashore of Galilee	Matt. 13:24-30, 36-43.
The mustard seed	Seashore of Galilee	Matt. 13:31, 32; Mark 4:30-32; Luke 13:18-19.
The seed growing secretly	Seashore of Galilee	Mark 4:26-29.
The leaven	Seashore of Galilee	Matt. 13:33; Luke 13:20, 21.
The hid treasure	Seashore of Galilee	Matt. 13:44.
The pearl of great price	Seashore of Galilee	Matt. 13:45, 46.
The draw net	Seashore of Galilee	Matt. 13:47-50.
The unmerciful servant	Capernaum	Matt. 18:21-35.
The good Samaritan	Near Jerusalem	Luke 10:29-37.
The friend at midnight	Near Jerusalem	Luke 11:5-8.

Name of parable	Where spoken	Where recorded
The rich fool	Galilee	Luke 12:16-21.
The barren fig tree	Galilee	Luke 13:6-9.
The great supper	Perea	Luke 14:15-24.
The lost sheep	Perea	Matt. 18:12-14; Luke 15:3-7.
The lost piece of money	Perea	Luke 15:8-10.
The prodigal son	Perea	Luke 15:11-32.
The good shepherd	Jerusalem	John 10:1-18.
The unjust steward	Perea	Luke 16:1-8.
The rich man and Lazarus	Perea	Luke 16:19-31.
The profitable servants	Perea	Luke 17:7-10.
The importunate widow	Perea	Luke 18:1-8.
The Pharisees and publicans	Perea	Luke 18:9-14.
The laborers in the vineyard	Perea	Matt. 20:1-16.
The pounds	Jericho	Luke 19:11-27.
The two sons	Jerusalem	Matt. 21:28-32.
The wicked husbandmen	Jerusalem	Matt. 21:33-44; Mark 12:1-12; Luke 20:9-18.
The marriage of the king's son	Jerusalem	Matt. 22:1-14.
The ten virgins	Mount of Olives	Matt. 25:1-13.
The talents	Mount of Olives	Matt. 25:14-30.

David Brown
Commentary Critical and Explanatory on the Whole Bible, *1871*

2.36 ON THE INTERPRETATION OF PARABLES, R. C. TRENCH

R. C. Trench, 1807–1886, was archbishop of Dublin and professor of divinity at King's College, London and later Dean of Westminster Seminary.

The parables, fair in their outward form, are yet fairer within, "apples of gold in network of silver"; each one of them like a casket, itself of exquisite workmanship, but in which jewels yet richer than itself are laid up; or as fruit, which, however lovely to look upon, is yet in its inner sweetness more delectable still. To find, then, the golden key for this casket, at whose touch it shall reveal its treasures; so to open this fruit, that nothing of its hidden kernel shall be missed or lost, has naturally been regarded ever as a matter of high concern. In this, the interpretation of the parable there is one question of more importance than any other—one so constantly presenting itself anew, that it will naturally claim to be the first and most fully considered. It is this, How much of them is to be taken as significant? To this question answers the most different have been returned. There are those who lay themselves out for the tracing a general correspondence between the sign and the thing signified, and this having done refuse to advance any further; while others aim at running out the interpretation into the minutest details; with those who occupy every intermediate stage between these extremes. Some have gone far in saying, This is merely drapery and ornament, and not the vehicle of essential truth; this was introduced either to give liveliness and a general air of verisimilitude to the narrative, or as actually necessary to make the story, the vehicle of the truth, a consistent whole, without which consistency the hearer would have been perplexed or offended; or else to hold together and connect the different parts,—just as in the most splendid house there must be passages, not for their own sake, but to lead from one room to another. They have used often the illustration of the knife, which is not all edge; of the harp, which is not all strings; urging that much in the knife, which does not cut, the handle for example, is yet of prime necessity,—much, in the musical instrument, which is never intended to give sound, must yet not be wanting: or, to use another comparison, that many circumstances "in Christ's parables are like the feathers which wing our arrows, which, though they pierce not like the head, but seem slight things and of a different matter from the rest, are yet requisite to make the shaft to pierce, and do both convey it to and penetrate the mark."

To this school Chrysostom belongs. He continually warns against pressing too anxiously all the circumstances of a parable, and often cuts his own interpretation somewhat short in language like this, "Be not over-busy about the rest." It is the same with the interpreters who habitually follow him, Theophylact and others, though not always faithful to their own principles. So also with Origen, who illustrates his meaning by a comparison of much beauty: "For as the likenesses which are given in pictures and statues are not perfect resemblances of those things for whose sake they are made—but for instance the image which is painted in wax on a plain surface of wood, contains a resemblance of the superficies and colors, but does not also preserve the depressions and prominences, but only a representation of them—while a statue, again, seeks to preserve the likeness which consists in prominences and depressions, but not as well that which is in colors—but should the statue be of wax, it seeks to retain both, I mean the colors, and also the depressions and prominences, but is not an image of those things which are within—in the same manner, of the parables

which are contained in the Gospels so account, that the kingdom of heaven, when it is likened to anything, is not likened to it according to all the things which are contained in that with which the comparison is instituted, but according to certain qualities which the matter in hand requires." Exactly thus Tillotson has said that the parable and its interpretation are not to be contemplated as two planes, touching one another at every point, but oftentimes rather as a plane and a globe, which, though brought into contact, yet touch each other only at one.

On the other hand, Augustine, though himself sometimes laying down the same canon, frequently extends the interpretation through all the branches and minutest fibres of the narrative; and Origen no less, despite the passage which I have just quoted. And in modern times, the followers of Cocceius have been particularly earnest in affirming all parts of a parable to be significant. There is a noble passage in the writings of Edward Irving, in which he describes the long and laborious care which he took to master the literal meaning of every word in the parables, being confident of the riches of inward truth which every one of those words contained; he goes on to say: "Of all which my feeling and progress in studying the parables of our Lord, I have found no similitude worthy to convey the impression, save that of sailing through between the Pillars of Hercules into the Mediterranean Sea, where you have to pass between armed rocks, in a strait, and under a current—all requiring careful and skilful seamanship—but, being passed, opening into such a large, expansive, and serene ocean of truth, so engirdled round with rich and fertile lands, so inlaid with beautiful and verdant islands, and full of rich colonies and populous cities, that unspeakable is the delight and the reward it yieldeth to the voyager." He and others have protested against that shallow spirit which is ever ready to empty Scripture of its deeper significance, to exclaim, "This means nothing; this circumstance is not to be pressed"; which, satisfying itself with sayings like these, fails to draw out from the word of God all the rich treasures contained in it for us, or to recognize the manifold wisdom with which its type is often constructed to correspond with the antitype. They bid us to observe that of those who start with the principle of setting aside so much as non-essential, scarcely any two, when it comes to the application of their principle, are agreed concerning what actually is to be set aside; what one rejects, another regains, and the contrary: and further, that the more this scheme is carried out, the more the peculiar beauty of the parable disappears, and the interest of it is lost. For example, when Calvin will not allow the oil in the vessels of the wise Virgins (Matt. 25:4) to mean anything, nor the vessels themselves, nor the lamps; or when Storr, who, perhaps more than any other, would leave the parables bare trunks, stripped of all their foliage and branches, of everything that made for beauty and ornament, denies that the Prodigal leaving his father's house has any direct reference to man's departure from the presence of his heavenly Father, it is at once evident of how much not merely of pleasure, but of instruction, they would deprive us. It is urged, too, in opposition to this interpretation of the parables merely in the gross, that when our Lord Himself interpreted the two first which He delivered, namely, that of the Sower and of the Tares, He most probably intended to furnish us with a rule for the interpretation of all. These explanations, therefore, are most important, not merely for their own sakes, but as supplying principles and canons of interpretation to be applied throughout. Now, in these the moral application descends to some of the minutest details: thus, the birds which snatch away the seed sown, are explained as Satan who takes the good word out of the heart (Matt. 13:19), the thorns which choke the good seed correspond to the cares and pleasures of life (Matt. 13:22), with much more of the same kind.

On a review of the whole controversy it may safely be said, that there have been exaggerations upon both sides. The advocates of interpretation in the gross and not in detail have been too easily satisfied with their favourite maxim, "Every comparison must halt somewhere"; since one may fairly demand, "Where is the necessity?" There is no

force in the rejoinder, that unless it did so, it would not be an illustration of the thing, but the thing itself. Such is not the fact. Two lines do not cease to be two, nor become one and the same, because they run parallel through their whole course. Doubtless in the opposite extreme of interpretation there lies the danger of an ingenious trifling with the word of God; a danger, too, lest the interpreter's delight in the exercise of this ingenuity, with the admiration of it on the part of others, may not put somewhat out of sight that the sanctification of the heart through the truth is the main purpose of all Scripture: even as we shall presently note the manner in which heretics, through this pressing of all parts of a parable to the uttermost, have been able to extort from it almost any meaning that they pleased.

After all has been urged on the one side and on the other, it must be confessed that no absolute rule can be laid down beforehand to guide the expositor how far he shall proceed. Much must be left to good sense, to spiritual tact, to that reverence for the word of God, which will show itself sometimes in refusing curiosities of interpretation, no less than at other times in demanding a distinct spiritual meaning for the words which are before it. The nearest approach, perhaps, to a canon of interpretation on the matter is that which Tholuck lays down:—"It must be allowed," he says, "that a similitude is perfect in proportion as it is on all sides rich in applications; and hence, in treating the parables of Christ, the expositor must proceed on the presumption that there is import in every single point and only desist from seeking it when either it does not result without forcing, or when we can clearly show that this or that circumstance was merely added for the sake of giving intuitiveness to the narrative. We should not assume anything to be non-essential, except when by holding it fast as essential, the unity of the whole is marred and troubled." For, to follow up these words of his,—in the same manner as a statue is the more perfect in the measure that the life, the idea that was in the sculptor's mind, breathes out of and looks through every feature and limb, so much the greater being the triumph of spirit, penetrating through and glorifying the matter which it has assumed; so the more translucent a parable is in all parts with the divine truth which it embodies, the more the garment with which that is arrayed, is a garment of light, pierced through, as was once the raiment of Christ, with the brightness within—illuminating it in all its recesses and corners, and leaving no dark place in it—by so much the more beautiful and perfect it must be esteemed.

It will much help us in this determining of what is essential and what not, if, before we attempt to explain the particular parts, we obtain a firm grasp of the central truth which the ramble would set forth, and distinguish it in the mind as sharply and accurately as we can from all cognate truths which border upon it; for only seen from that middle point will the different parts appear in their true light. "One may compare," says a late writer on the parables, "the entire parable with a circle, of which the middle point is the spiritual truth or doctrine, and of which the radii are the several circumstances of the narration; so long as one has not placed oneself in the center, neither the circle itself appears in its perfect shape, nor will the beautiful unity with which the radii converge to a single point be perceived, but this is all observed as soon as the eye looks forth from the center. Even so in the Parable; if we have recognized its middle point, its main doctrine, in full light, then will the proportion and right signification of all particular circumstances be clear unto us, and we shall lay stress upon them only so far as the main truth is thereby more vividly set forth."

There is another rule which it is important to observe, one so simple and obvious, that were it not continually neglected, one would be content to leave it to the common sense of every interpreter. It is this, that as, in the explanation of the fable, the introduction (*promuthion*) and application (*epimuthion*) claim to be most carefully attended to, so here what some have entitled the pro-parabola and epi-parabola, though the other terms would have done sufficiently well; which are invariably the finger-posts pointing to the direction in which we are to look for the meaning—the key to the whole matter. The neglect of these often involves in the most untenable explanations; for instance, how many interpretations which have been elaborately worked out of the Laborers in the Vineyard, could never have been so much as once proposed, if heed had been paid to the context, or the necessity been acknowledged of bringing the interpretation into harmony with the saying which introduces and winds up the parable. These helps to interpretation, though rarely or never lacking, are yet given in no Lord or formal manner; sometimes they are supplied by the Lord Himself (Matt. 22:14; 25:18); sometimes by the inspired narrators of his words (Luke 15:1, 2; 18:1); sometimes, as the prologue, they precede the parable (Luke 18:9; 19:11); sometimes, as the epilogue, they follow (Matt. 25:18; Luke 16:9). Occasionally a parable is furnished with these helps to assist understanding both at the opening and the close; as is that of the Unmerciful Servant (Matt. 18:23-34), which is suggested by the question which Peter asks (ver. 21), and wound up by the application which the Lord Himself makes (ver. 35). So again the parable at Matt. 20:1-15 begins and finishes with the same saying, and Luke 12:16-20 is supplied with the same amount of help for its right understanding.

Again, we may observe that a correct interpretation, besides being thus in accordance with its context, must be so without any very violent means being necessary to bring it into such agreement; even as, generally, the interpretation must be easy—if not always easy to discover, yet, being discovered, easy. For it is here as with the laws of nature; the proleptic mind of genius may be needful to discover the law, but, once discovered, it throws back light on itself, and commends itself unto all. And there is this other point of similarity also; it is a proof that we have found the law, when it explains alt the phenomena, and not merely some; if, sooner or later, they all marshal themselves in order under it; so it is good evidence that we have discovered the right interpretation of a parable, if it leave none of the main circumstances unexplained. A false interpretation will inevitably betray itself, since it will "invariably paralyze and render nugatory some important member of an entire account." If we have the right key in our hand, not merely some of the wards, but all, will have their parts corresponding; the key too will turn without grating or over-much forcing; and if we have the right interpretation, it will scarcely need to be defended and made plausible with great appliance of learning, to be propped up by remote allusions to Rabbinical or profane literature, by illustrations drawn from the recesses of antiquity.

Once more: the parables may not be made primary sources of doctrine, and seats of this. Doctrines otherwise and already established may be illustrated, or indeed further confirmed by them; but it is not allowable to constitute doctrine first by their aid. They may be the outer ornamental fringe, but not the main texture, of the proof. For from the literal to the figurative, from the clearer to the more obscure, has been ever recognized as the order of Scripture interpretation. This rule, however, has been often forgotten, and controversialists, looking round for arguments with which to sustain some weak position, for which they can find no other support in Scripture, often invent for themselves supports in these. Thus Bellarmine presses the parable of the Good Samaritan, and the circumstance that in that the thieves are said first to have stripped the traveler, and afterwards to have inflicted wounds on him (Luke 10:80), as proving certain views upon which the Roman Church sets a high value, on the order of man's fall, the succession and sequence in which, first losing heavenly gifts, the robe of a divine righteousness, he afterwards, and as a consequence, endured actual hurts in his soul. And in the same way Faustus Socinus argues from the parable of the Unmerciful Servant, that as the king pardoned his servant merely on his petition (Matt. 18:32), and not on tho score of any satisfaction made, or any mediator intervening, we may from this conclude, that in the same way, and without requiring sacrifice or intercessor, God will pardon sinners simply on the ground of their prayers.

But by much the worst offenders against this rule were the Gnostics and Manichaeans in old time, and especially the former. Their whole scheme was one, which however it may have been a result of the Gospel, inasmuch as that set the religious speculation of the world vigorously at work, was yet of independent growth; and they only came to the Scripture to find a varnish, an outer Christian coloring, for a system essentially antichristian;—they came, not to learn its language, but to see if they could not compel it to speak theirs; with no desire to draw out of Scripture its meaning, but only to thrust into Scripture their own. When they fell thus to picking and choosing what in it they might best turn to their ends, the parables naturally invited them almost more than any other portions of Scripture. In the literal portions of Scripture they could find no color for their scheme; their only refuge therefore was in the figurative, in those which might receive more interpretations than one; such, perhaps, they might bend or compel to their purposes. Accordingly, we find them claiming continually the parables for their own; with no joy, indeed, in their simplicity, or practical depth, or ethical beauty; for they seem to have had no sense or feeling of these; but delighted to superinduce upon them their own capricious and extravagant fancies. Irenaeus is continually compelled to rescue the parables from the extreme abuse to which these submitted them; for, indeed, they not merely warped and drew them a little aside, but made them tell wholly a different tale from that which they were intended to tell. Against these Gnostics he lays down that canon, namely, that the parables cannot be in any case the primary, much less the exclusive, foundations of any doctrine, but must be themselves interpreted according to the analogy of faith; since, if every subtle solution of one of these might raise itself at once to the dignity and authority of a Christian doctrine, the rule of faith would be nowhere. So to build, as he shows, were to build not on the rock, but on the sand.

Tertullian has the same conflict to maintain. The whole scheme of the Gnostics, as he observes, was a great floating cloud-palace, the figment of their own brain, with no counterpart in the world of spiritual realities. They could therefore mould it as they would; and thus they found no difficulty in forcing the parables to seem to be upon their side, shaping, as they had no scruple in doing, their doctrine according to the leadings and suggestions of these, till they brought the two into apparent agreement with one another. There was nothing to hinder them here; their creed was not a fixed body of divine truth, which they could neither add to nor diminish; which was given them from above, and in which they could only acquiesce; but an invention of their own, which they could therefore fashion, modify, and alter as best suited the purpose they had in hand. We, as Tertullian often urges, are kept within limits in the exposition of the parables, accepting, as we do, the other Scriptures as the rule of truth, as the rule, therefore, of their interpretation. It is otherwise with these heretics; their doctrine is their own; they can first dexterously adapt it to the parables, and then bring forward the conformity between the two as a testimony of its truth.

As it was with the Gnostics of the early Church, exactly so was it with the sects which, in a later day, were their spiritual successors, the Cathari and Bogomili. They, too, found in the parables no teaching about sin and grace and redemption, no truths of the kingdom, but fitted to the parables the speculations about the creation, the origin of evil, the fall of angels, which were uppermost in their own minds; which they had not drawn from Scripture; but which having themselves framed, they afterwards turned to Scripture, endeavouring to find there that which they could compel to fall into their scheme. Thus, the apostasy of Satan and his drawing after him a part of the host of heaven, they found set forth by the parable of the Unjust Steward. Satan was the chief steward over God's house, who being deposed from his place of highest trust, drew after him the other angels, with the suggestion of lighter tasks and relief from the burden of their imposed duties.

But to come to more modern times. Though not testifying to evils at all so grave in the devisers of the scheme, nor leading altogether out of the region of Christian truth, yet sufficiently injurious to the sober interpretation of the parables is such a theory concerning them as that entertained, and in actual exposition carried out, by Cocceius and his followers of what we may call the historico-prophetical school. By the parables, they say, and so far they have right, are declared the mysteries of the kingdom of God. But then, ascribing to those words, "kingdom of God," a far too narrow sense, they are resolved to find in every one of the parables a part of the history of that kingdom's progressive development in the world to the latest time. They will not allow any to be merely ethical, but affirm all to be historico-prophetical. Thus, to let one of them speak for himself, in the remarkable words of Krummacher: "The parables of Jesus have not primarily a moral, but a politico-religious, or theocratic purpose. To use a comparison, we may consider the kingdom of God carried forward under his guidance, as the action, gradually unfolding itself, of an Epos, of which the first germ lay prepared long beforehand in the Jewish economy of the Old Testament, but which through Him began to unfold itself, and will continue to do so to the end of time. The name and superscription of the Epos is, THE KINGDOM OF GOD. The parables belong essentially to the Gospel of the kingdom, not merely as containing its doctrine, but its progressive development. They connect themselves with certain fixed periods of that development, and, as soon as these periods are completed, lose themselves in the very completion; that is, considered as independent portions of the Epos, remaining for us only in the image and external letter." He must mean, of course, in the same manner and degree as all other fulfilled prophecy; in the light of such accomplished prophecy, he would say, they must henceforth be regarded.

Boyle gives some, though a very moderate, countenance to the same opinion: "some, if not most, do, like those oysters that, besides the meat they afford us, contain pearls, not only include excellent moralities, but comprise important prophecies"; and, having adduced the Mustard-seed and the Wicked Husbandmen as plainly containing such prophecies, he goes on, "I despair not to see unheeded prophecies disclosed in others of them." Vitringa's Elucidation of the Parables is a practical application of this scheme of interpretation, and one which will scarcely win many supporters for it. Thus, the servant owing the ten thousand talents (Matt. 18:8, 9), is the Pope or line of Popes, placed in highest trust in the Church, but who, misusing the powers committed to them, were warned by the invasion of Goths, Lombards, and other barbarians, of judgment at the door, and indeed seemed given into their hands for doom; but being mercifully delivered from this fear of imminent destruction by the Frankish kings, so far from repenting and amending, on the contrary now more than ever oppressed and maltreated the true servants of God, and who therefore should be delivered over to an irreversible doom. He gives a yet more marvelous explanation of the Merchant seeking goodly pearls, this pearl of price being the Church of Geneva and the doctrine of Calvin, opposed to the abortive pearls, that is, to all the other Reformed Churches. Other examples may be found in Cocceius—an interpretation, for

instance, of the Ten Virgins, after this same fashion. Deyling has an interesting essay on this school of interpreters, and passes a severe, though not undeserved, condemnation on them. Prophetical, no doubt, many of the parables are; for they declare how the new element of life, which the Lord was bringing into the world, would work—the future influences and results of his doctrine—that the little mustard-seed would grow to a great tree—that the leaven would continue working till it had leavened the whole lump. But they declare not so much the facts as the laws of the kingdom. Historico-prophetical are only a few; as that of the Wicked Husbandmen, which Boyle adduced, in which there is a clear prophecy of the death of Christ; as that of the Marriage of the King's Son, in which there is an equally clear announcement of the destruction of Jerusalem, and the transfer of the kingdom of God from the Jews to the Gentiles.

R. C. Trench, Notes on the Parables, *1841*

2.37 INTERPRETING PARABLES, WILLIAM SMITH

In interpreting parables note—(1) The analogies must be real, not arbitrary; (2) The parables are to be considered as parts of a whole, and the interpretation of one is not to override or encroach upon the lessons taught by others; (3) The direct teaching of Christ presents the standard to which all our interpretations are to be referred, and by which they are to be measured.

William Smith, Smith's Bible Dictionary, *1884*

2.38 PARABLE, G. H. SCHODDE

PARABLE
(par'-a-b'-l)

1. Name
2. Historical data
3. Christ's use of parables.
4. Purpose of Christ in using parables
5. Interpretation of the parables
6. Doctrinal value of the parables

1. NAME
Etymologically the word "parable" (*paraballo*) signifies a placing of two or more objects together, usually for the purpose of a comparison. In this widest sense of the term there is practically no difference between parable and simile (see Thayer, Dictionary of New Testament Greek, under the word). This is also what substantially some of Christ's parables amount to, which consist of only one comparison and in a single verse (compare Matthew 13:33, 44-46). In the more usual and technical sense of the word, "parable" ordinarily signifies an imaginary story, yet one that in its details could have actually transpired, the purpose of the story being to illustrate and inculcate some higher spiritual truth. These features differentiate it from other and similar figurative narratives as also from actual history. The similarity between the last-mentioned and a parable is sometimes so small that exegetes have differed in the interpretation of certain pericopes. A characteristic example of this uncertainty is the story of Dives and Lazarus in Luke 16:19-31. The problem is of a serious nature, as those who regard this as actual history are compelled to interpret each and every statement, including too the close proximity of heaven and hell and the possibility of speaking from one place to the other, while those who regard it as a parable can restrict their interpretation to the features that constitute the substance of the story. It differs again from the fable, in so far as the latter is a story that could not actually have occurred (e.g. Judges 9:8; 2 Kings 14:9; Ezekiel 17:2 f).

The parable is often described as an extended metaphor.

2. HISTORICAL DATA
Although Christ employed the parable as a means of inculcating His message more extensively and more effectively than any other teacher, He did not invent the parable. It was His custom in general to take over from the religious and linguistic world of thought in His own day the materials that He employed to convey the higher and deeper truths of His gospels, giving them a world of meaning they had never before possessed. Thus, e.g. every petition of the Lord's Prayer can be duplicated in the Jewish liturgies of the times, yet on Christ's lips these petitions have a significance they never had or could have for the Jews. The term "Word" for the second person in the Godhead is an adaptation from the Logos-idea in contemporaneous religious thought, though not specifically of Philo's. Baptism, regeneration, and kindred expressions of fundamental thoughts in the Christian system, are terms not absolutely new. The parable was employed both in the Old Testament and in contemporaneous Jewish literature (compare e.g. 2 Samuel 12:1-4; Isaiah 5:1-6; 28:24-28).

3. CHRIST'S USE OF PARABLES
The one and only teacher of parables in the New Testament is Christ Himself. The Epistles, although they often employ rhetorical allegories and similes, make absolutely no use of the parable, so common in Christ's pedagogical methods. The distribution of these in the Canonical Gospels is unequal, and they are strictly confined to the three Synoptic Gospels. Mark again has only one peculiar to this book, namely, the Seed Growing in Secret (Mark 4:26), and he gives only three others that are found also in Matt. and Luke, namely the Sower, the Mustard Seed, and the Wicked Husbandman, so that the bulk of the parables are found in the First and the Third Gospels. Two are

common to Matthew and Luke, namely the Leaven (Matthew 13:33; Luke 13:21) and the Lost Sheep (Matthew 18:12; Luke 15:3). Of the remaining parables, 18 are found only in Luke and 10 only in Matt. Luke's 18 include some of the finest, namely, the Two Debtors, the Good Samaritan, the Friend at Midnight, the Rich Fool, the Watchful Servants, the Barren Fig Tree, the Chief Seats, the Great Supper, the Rash Builder, the Rash King, the Lost Coin, the Lost Son, the Unrighteous Steward, the Rich Man and Lazarus, the Unprofitable Servants, the Unrighteous Judge, the Pharisee and Publican, and the Pounds. The 10 peculiar to Matthew are the Tares, the Hidden Treasure, the Pearl of Great Price, the Draw Net, the Unmerciful Servant, the Laborers in the Vineyard, the Two Sons, the Marriage of the King's Son, the Ten Virgins, and the Talents. There is some uncertainty as to the exact number of parables we have from Christ, as the Marriage of the King's Son is sometimes regarded as a different recension of the Great Supper, and the Talents of the Pounds.

4. PURPOSE OF CHRIST IN USING PARABLES

It is evident from such passages as Matthew 13:10 (compare Mark 4:10; Luke 8:9) that Christ did not in the beginning of His career employ the parable as a method of teaching, but introduced it later. This took place evidently during the 2nd year of His public ministry, and is closely connected with the changes which about that time He made in His attitude toward the people in general. It evidently was Christ's purpose at the outset to win over, if possible, the nation as a whole to His cause and to the gospel; when it appeared that the leaders and the great bulk of the people would not accept Him for what He wanted to be and clung tenaciously to their carnal Messianic ideas and ideals, Christ ceased largely to appeal to the masses, and, by confining His instructions chiefly to His disciples and special friends, saw the necessity of organizing an ecclesiola in ecclesia, which was eventually to develop into the world-conquering church. One part of this general withdrawal of Christ from a proclamation of

His gospel to the whole nation was this change in His method of teaching and the adoption of the parable. On that subject He leaves no doubt, according to Matthew 13:11; Mark 4:12; Luke 8:10. The purpose of the parable is both to reveal and to conceal the truth. It was to serve the first purpose in the case of the disciples, the second in the case of the undeserving Jews. Psychologically this difference, notwithstanding the acknowledged inferiority in the training and education of the disciples, especially as compared with the scribes and lawyers, is not hard to understand. A simple-minded Christian, who has some understanding of the truth, can readily understand figurative illustrations of this truth, which would be absolute enigmas even to an educated Hindu or Chinaman. The theological problem involved is more difficult. Yet it is evident that we are not dealing with those who have committed the sin against the Holy Ghost, for whom there is no possibility of a return to grace, according to Hebrews 6:4-10; 10:26 (compare Matthew 12:31, 32; Mark 3:28-30), and who accordingly could no longer be influenced by an appeal of the gospel, and we have rather before us those from whom Christ has determined to withdraw the offer of redemption—whether temporarily or definitely and finally, remaining an open question—according to His policy of not casting pearls before the swine. The proper sense of these passages can be ascertained only when we remember that in Mark 4:12 and Luke 8:10, the hina, need not express purpose, but that this particle is used here to express mere result only, as is clear too from the passage in Matthew 13:13, where the hoti, is found. The word is to be withheld from these people, so that this preaching would not bring about the ordinary results of conversion and forgiveness of sins. Hence, Christ now adopts a method of teaching that will hide the truth from all those who have not yet been imbued by it, and this new method is that of the parable.

5. INTERPRETATION OF THE PARABLES

The principles for the interpretation of the parables, which are all intended primarily and in the first place for the disciples, are furnished by the nature of the parable itself and by Christ's own method of interpreting some of them. The first and foremost thing to be discovered is the scope or the particular spiritual truth which the parable is intended to convey. Just what this scope is may be stated in so many words, as is done, e.g., by the introductory words to that of the Pharisee and the Publican. Again the scope may be learned from the occasion of the parable, as the question of Peter in Matthew 18:21 gives the scope of the following parable, and the real purpose of the Prodigal Son parable in Luke 15:11 is not the story of this young man himself, but is set over against the murmuring of the Pharisees because Christ received publicans and sinners, in 15:1 and 2, to exemplify the all-forgiving love of the Father. Not the Son but the Father is in the foreground in this parable, which fact is also the connecting link between the two parts. Sometimes the scope can be learned only from an examination of the details of the parable itself and then may be all the more uncertain.

A second principle of the interpretation of the parables is that a sharp distinction must be made between what the older interpreters called the body (*corpus*) and the soul (*anima*) of the story; or, to use other expressions, between the shell or bark (*cortex*) and the marrow (*medulla*). Whatever serves only the purpose of the story is the "ornamentation" of the parable, and does not belong to the substance. The former does not call for interpretation or higher spiritual lesson; the latter does. This distinction between those parts of the parable that are intended to convey spiritual meanings and those which are to be ignored in the interpretation is based on Christ's own interpretation of the so-called *parabolae perfectae*. Christ Himself, in Matthew 13:18, interprets the parable of the Sower, yet a number of data, such as the fact that there are four, and not more or fewer kinds of land, and others, are discarded in this explanation as without meaning. Again in His interpretation of the Tares among the Wheat in Matthew 13:36, a number of details of the original parable are discarded as meaningless.

Just which details are significant and which are meaningless in a parable is often hard, sometimes impossible to determine, as the history of their exegesis amply shows. In general it can be laid down as a rule, that those features which illustrate the scope of the parable belong to its substance, and those which do not, belong to the ornamentation. But even with this rule there remain many exegetical cruces or difficulties. Certain, too, it is that not all of the details are capable of interpretation. Some are added of a nature that indeed illustrate the story as a story, but, from the standpoint of Christian morals, are more than objectionable. The Unjust Steward in using his authority to make the bills of the debtors of his master smaller may be a model, in the shrewd use of this world's goods for his purpose, that the Christian may follow in making use of his goods for his purposes, but the action of the steward itself is incapable of defense. Again, the man who finds in somebody else's property a pearl of great price but conceals this fact from the owner of the land and quietly buys this ground may serve as an example to show how much the kingdom of God is worth, but from an ethical standpoint his action cannot be sanctioned. In general, the parable, like all other forms of figurative expression, has a meaning only as far as the tertium comparationis goes, that is, the third thing which is common to the two things compared. But all this still leaves a large debatable ground in many parables. In the Laborers in the Vineyard does the "penny" mean anything, or is it an ornament? The history of the debate on this subject is long. In the Prodigal Son do all the details of his sufferings, such as eating the husks intended for swine, have a spiritual meaning?

6. DOCTRINAL VALUE OF THE PARABLES

The interpreters of former generations laid down the rule, *theologia parabolica non eat argumentativa*, i.e. the parables, very rich in mission thoughts, do not furnish a basis for doctrinal argument. Like all figurative expressions and forms of thought, the parables too contain elements of doubt as far as their interpretation is concerned. They illustrate truth but they do not prove or demonstrate truth. *Omnia aimilia claudicunt,* "all comparisons limp," is applicable here also. No point of doctrine can be established on figurative passages of Scripture, as then all elements of doubt would not be eliminated, this doubt being based on the nature of language itself. The argumentative or doctrinal value of parables is found in this, that they may, in accordance with the analogy of Scripture, illustrate truth already clearly expressed elsewhere.

G. H. Schodde
International Standard Bible Encyclopedia,
General Editor, James Orr, 1915

INDIVIDUAL PARABLES

2.39 THE PARABLE OF THE SOWER, MARTIN LUTHER

THE DISCIPLES AND THE FRUITS OF GOD'S WORD

And when much people were gathered together, and were come to him out of every city, he spake by a parable: A sower went out to sow his seed: and as he sowed, some fell by the way side; and it was trodden down, and the fowls of the air devoured it. And some fell upon a rock; and as soon as it was sprung up, it withered away, because it lacked moisture. And some fell among thorns; and the thorns sprang up with it, and choked it. And other fell on good ground, and sprang up, and bare fruit an hundredfold. And when he had said these things, he cried, He that hath ears to hear, let him hear. And his disciples asked him, saying, What might this parable be? And he said, Unto you it is given to know the mysteries of the kingdom of God: but to others in parables; that seeing they might not see, and hearing they might not understand. Now the parable is this: The seed is the word of God. Those by the way side are they that hear; then cometh the devil, and taketh away the word out of their hearts, lest they should believe and be saved. They on the rock are they, which, when they hear, receive the word with joy; and these have no root, which for a while believe, and in time of temptation fall away. And that which fell among thorns are they, which, when they have heard, go forth, and are choked with cares and riches and pleasures of this life, and bring no fruit to perfection. But that on the good ground are they, which in an honest and good heart, having heard the word, keep it, and bring forth fruit with patience. Luke 8:4-15

I. THE NATURE OF THE WORD SPOKEN HERE

1. This Gospel treats of the disciples and the fruits, which the Word of God develops in the world. It does not speak of the law nor of human institutions; but, as Christ himself says, of the Word of God, which he himself the sower preaches, for the law bears no fruit, just as little as do the institutions of men. Christ however sets forth here four kinds of disciples of the divine Word.

II. THE DISCIPLES OF THIS WORD

2. The first class of disciples are those who hear the Word but neither understand nor esteem it. And these are not the mean people in the world, but the greatest, wisest and the most saintly, in short they are the greatest part of mankind; for Christ does not speak here of those who persecute the Word nor of those who fail to give their ear to it, but of those who hear it and are students of it, who also wish to be called true Christians and to live in Christian fellowship with Christians and are partakers of baptism and the Lord's Supper. But they are of a carnal heart, and remain so, failing to appropriate the Word of God to themselves, it goes in one ear and out the other. Just like the seed along the wayside did

not fall into the earth, but remained lying on the ground in the wayside, because the road was tramped hard by the feet of man and beast and it could not take root.

3. Therefore Christ says the devil cometh and taketh away the Word from their heart, that they may not believe and be saved. What power of Satan this alone reveals, that hearts, hardened through a worldly mind and life, lose the Word and let it go, so that they never understand or confess it; but instead of the Word of God Satan sends false teachers to tread it under foot by the doctrines of men. For it stands here written both that it was trodden under foot, and the birds of the heaven devoured it. The birds Christ himself interprets as the messengers of the devil, who snatch away the Word and devour it, which is done when he turns and blinds their hearts so that they neither understand nor esteem it, as St. Paul says in 2 Tim. 4:4: "They will turn away their ears from the truth, and turn aside unto fables." By the treading under foot of men Christ means the teachings of men, that rule in our hearts, as he says in Matt. 5:13 also of the salt that has lost its savor, it is cast out and trodden under foot, of men; that is, as St. Paul says in 2 Thess. 2:11, they must believe a lie because they have not been obedient to the truth.

4. Thus all heretics, fanatics and sects belong to this number, who understand the Gospel in a carnal way and explain it as they please, to suit their own ideas, all of whom hear the Gospel and yet they bear no fruit, yea, more, they are governed by Satan and are harder oppressed by human institutions than they were before they heard the Word. For it is a dreadful utterance that Christ here gives that the devil taketh away the Word from their hearts, by which he clearly proves that the devil rules mightily in their hearts, notwithstanding they are called Christians and hear the Word. Likewise it sounds terribly that they are to be trodden under foot, and must be subject unto men and to their ruinous teachings, by which under the appearance and name of the Gospel the devil takes the Word from them, so that they may never believe and be saved, but must be lost forever; as the fanatical spirits of our day do in all lands. For where this Word is not, there is no salvation, and great works or holy

lives avail nothing, for it is with this, that he says: "They shall not be saved," since they have not the Word, he shows forcibly enough, that not their works but their faith in the Word alone saves, as Paul says to the Romans: "It is, the power of God unto salvation to every one that believeth" (Rom. 1:16).

5. The second class of hearers are those who receive the Word with joy, but they do not persevere. These are also a large multitude who understand the Word correctly and lay hold of it in its purity without any spirit of sect, division or fanaticism, they rejoice also in that they know the real truth, and are able to know how they may be saved without works through faith. They also know that they are free from the bondage of the law, of their conscience and of human teachings; but when it comes to the test that they must suffer harm, disgrace and loss of life or property, then they fall and deny it; for they have not root enough, and are not planted deep enough in the soil. Hence they are like the growth on a rock, which springs forth fresh and green, that it is a pleasure to behold it and it awakens bright hopes. But when the sun shines hot it withers, because it has no soil and moisture, and only rock is there. So these do; in times of persecution they deny or keep silence about the Word, and work, speak and suffer all that their persecutors mention or wish, who formerly went forth and spoke, and confessed with a fresh and joyful spirit the same, while there was still peace and no heat, so that there was hope they would bear much fruit and serve the people. For these fruits are not only the works, but more the confession, preaching and spreading of the Word, so that many others may thereby be converted and the kingdom of God be developed.

6. The third class are those who hear and understand the Word, but still it falls on the other side of the road, among the pleasures and cares of this life, so that they also do nothing with the Word. And there is quite a large multitude of these; for although they do not start heresies, like the first, but always possess the absolutely pure Word, they are also, not attacked on the left as the others with opposition and persecution; yet they fall on the right side, and it is their ruin that they enjoy peace and good days. Therefore they do

not earnestly give themselves to the Word, but become indifferent and sink in the cares, riches and pleasures of this life, so that they are of no benefit to any one. Therefore they are like the seed that fell among the thorns. Although it is not rocky but good soil; not wayside but deeply plowed soil; yet, the thorns will not let it spring up, they choke it. Thus these have all in the Word that is needed for their salvation, but they do not make any use of it, and they rot in this life in carnal pleasures. To these belong those who hear the Word but do not bring under subjection their flesh. They know their duty but do it not, they teach but do not practice what they teach, and are this year as they were last.

7. The fourth class are those who lay hold of and keep the Word in a good and honest heart, and bring forth fruit with patience, those who hear the Word and steadfastly retain it, meditate upon it and act in harmony with it. The devil does not snatch it away, nor are they thereby led astray, moreover the heat of persecution does not rob them of it, and the thorns of pleasure and the avarice of the times do not hinder its growth; but they bear fruit by teaching others and by developing the kingdom of God, hence they also do good to their neighbor in love; and therefore Christ adds, "they bring forth fruit with patience." For these must suffer much on account of the Word, shame and disgrace from fanatics and heretics, hatred and jealousy with injury to body and property from their persecutors, not to mention what the thorns and the temptations of their own flesh do, so that it may well be called the Word of the cross; for he who would keep it must bear the cross and misfortune, and triumph.

8. He says: "In honest and good hearts." Like a field that is without a thorn or brush, cleared and spacious, as a beautiful clean place: so a heart is also cleared and clean, broad and spacious, that is without cares and avarice as to temporal needs, so that the Word of God truly finds lodgment there. But the field is good, not only when it lies there cleared and level, but when it is also rich and fruitful, possesses soil and is productive, and not like a stony and gravelly field. Just so is the heart that has good soil and with a full

spirit is strong, fertile and good to keep the Word and bring forth fruit with patience.

9. Here we see why it is no wonder there are so few true Christians, for all the seed does not fall into good ground, but only the fourth and small part; and that they are not to be trusted who boast they are Christians and praise the teaching of the Gospel; like Demas, a disciple of St. Paul, who forsook him at last (2 Tim. 4:10); like the disciples of Jesus, who turned their backs to him (John 6:66). For Christ himself cries out here: "He that hath ears to hear, let him hear," as if he should say: O, how few true Christians there are; one dare not believe all to be Christians who are called Christians and hear the Gospel, more is required than that.

10. All this is spoken for our instruction, that we may not go astray, since so many misuse the Gospel and few lay hold of it aright. True it is unpleasant to preach to those who treat the Gospel so shamefully and even oppose it. For preaching is to become so universal that the Gospel is to be proclaimed to all creatures, as Christ says in Mark 16:15: "Preach the Gospel to the whole creation," and Ps. 19:4: "Their line is gone out through all the earth, and their words to the end of the world." What business is it of mine that many do not esteem it? It must be that many are called but few are chosen. For the sake of the good ground that brings forth fruit with patience, the seed must also fall fruitless by the wayside, on the rock and among the thorns; inasmuch as we are assured that the Word of God does not go forth without bearing some fruit, but it always finds also good ground; as Christ says here, some seed of the sower falls also into good ground, and not only by the wayside, among the thorns and on stony ground. For wherever the Gospel goes you will find Christians. "My word shall not return unto me void" (Is. 55:11).

IV. WHY CHRIST CALLS THE DOCTRINE CONCERNING THE DISCIPLES AND THE FRUITS OF THE WORD A MYSTERY.

19. But what does it mean when he says: "Unto you it is given to know the mysteries of

the kingdom of God", etc.? What are the mysteries? Shall one not know them, why then are they preached? A "mystery" is a hidden secret, that is not known: and the "mysteries of the kingdom of God" are the things in the kingdom of God, as for example Christ with all his grace, which he manifests to us, as Paul describes him; for he who knows Christ aright understands what God's kingdom is, and what is in it. And it is called a mystery because it is spiritual and secret, and indeed it remains so, where the spirit does not reveal it. For although there are many who see and hear it, yet they do not understand it, just as there are many who preach and hear Christ, how he offered himself for us; but all that is only upon their tongue and not in their heart; for they themselves do not believe it, they do not experience it, as Paul in 1 Cor. 2:14 says: "The natural man receiveth not the things of the Spirit of God!" Therefore Christ says here: "Unto you it is given," the Spirit gives it to you that you not only hear and see it, but acknowledge and believe it with your heart. Therefore it is now no longer a mystery to you. But to the others who hear it as well as you, and have no faith in their heart, they see and understand it not; to them it is a mystery and it will continue unknown to them, and all that they hear is only like one hearing a parable or a dark saying. This is also proved by the fanatics of our day, who know so much to preach about Christ; but as they themselves do not experience it in their heart, they rush ahead and pass by the true foundation of the mystery and tramp around with questions and rare foundlings, and when it comes to the test they do not know the least thing about trusting in God and finding in Christ the forgiveness of their sins.

20. But Mark says (4:33), "Christ spake therefore to the people with parables, that they might understand, each according to his ability." How does that agree with what Matthew says, 13:13-14: "He spake therefore unto them in parables, because they did not understand?" It must surely be that Mark wishes to say that parables serve to the end that they may get a hold of coarse, rough people, although they do not indeed understand them, yet later, they may be taught and then they know: for parables are naturally pleasing to the common people, and they easily remember them since they are taken from common every day affairs, in the midst of which the people live. But Matthew means to say that these parables are of the nature that no one can understand them, they may grasp and hear them as often as they will, unless the Spirit makes them known and reveals them. Not that they should preach that we shall not understand them; but it naturally follows that wherever the Spirit does not reveal them, no one understands them. However, Christ took these words from Is. 6:9-10, where the high meaning of the divine foreknowledge is referred to, that God conceals and reveals to whom he will and whom he had in mind from eternity.

Martin Luther

2.40 THE PRODIGAL SON, B. B. WARFIELD

This sermon was preached in the Chapel of Princeton Seminary between 1910-1913.

I wish to speak to you to-day of the parable of the prodigal son, Luke 15:11-32, or, as it is becoming very common to call it, perhaps with greater exactness, the parable of the lost son. . . . Probably no passage of the Scriptures is more widely known or more universally admired. The conversation and literature of devotion are full of allusions to it. And in the conversation and literature of the world it has far from an unhonoured place.

It owes the high appreciation it has won, no doubt, in large part to the exquisiteness of its literary form. From this point of view it fully deserves not only the, measured praise of a Grotius, but the enthusiastic exclamations of a Trench. It is "the finest of Christ's parables, filled with true feeling, and painted in the most beautiful colors." It is "the pearl and crown of all the parables of Scripture." Nothing could exceed the chaste perfection of the narrative, the picturesque truth of its portraiture, the psychological delicacy of its analysis. Here is a gem of story-telling, which must be pronounced nothing less than artistically perfect, whether viewed in its general impression, or in the elaboration of its details. We must add to its literary beauty, however, the preciousness of the lesson it conveys before we account for the place it has won for itself in the hearts of men. In this setting of fretted gold, a marvel of the artificer, there lies a priceless jewel; and this jewel is displayed to such advantage by its setting that men cannot choose but see and admire.

Indeed, we may even say that the universal admiration the parable commands has finished by becoming in some quarters a little excessive. The message which the parable brings us is certainly a great one. To lost sinners like you and me, assuredly few messages could appeal with more overwhelming force. Our hearts are wrung within us as we are made to realize that our Father in heaven will receive our wandering souls back with the joy with which this father in the parable received back his errant son. But it is an exaggeration to represent this message as all the Gospel, or even as the core of the Gospel; and to speak of this parable therefore, as it has become widely common to speak of it, as "the Gospel in the Gospel," or even as the summation of the Gospel. It is not that. There are many truths which it has no power to teach us that are essential to the integrity of the Gospel: nay, the very heart of the Gospel is not in it. And, therefore, precious as this parable is to us, and priceless as is its message, there are many other passages of Scripture more precious still, because their message enters more deeply into the substance of the Gospel. Take this passage for example: "For God so loved the world, that He gave His only begotten Son, that whosoever believeth on Him should not perish, but have

ever lasting life." Or this passage: "God, being rich in mercy, for His great love wherewith He loved us, even when we were dead through our trespasses, quickened us together with Christ (by grace have ye been saved), and raised us up with Him and made us sit with Him in the heavenly places with Christ Jesus." Or even this short passage: "For the Son of Man came to seek and to save that which was lost." All these are more precious passages than the parable of the lost son, not merely because they tell us more fully what is contained in the Gospel, but because they uncover to us, as it does not, what lies at the heart of the Gospel.

It is important that we should recognize this. For the exaggerated estimate which has been put upon this parable has borne bitter fruit in the world. Beginning with an effort to read into it all the Gospel, or at least the essence of the Gospel, it has ended by reading out of the Gospel all that is not in the parable. And thus this parable, the vehicle of a priceless message, has been transformed into the instrument of a great wrong. The worst things are often the corruption of the best: and the attempt to make the parable of the lost son the norm of the Gospel has resulted, I will not say merely in the curtailment of the Gospel,— I will say rather in the evisceration of the Gospel. On this platform there take their stand today a growing multitude the entire tendency and effect of all of whose efforts it is to eliminate from Christianity all that gives it value in the world, all that makes it that religion which has saved the world, and to reduce it to the level of a merely natural religion. "The Christianity of the prodigal son is enough for us," they declare: and they declare this with gusto because, to put it briefly, they do not like the Christianity of the Bible or the Christianity of Christ, and are happy not to find them in the parable of the lost son.

Now, let us recognize frankly at the outset, that the reason why these new teachers of an unchristian Christianity do not find Christianity in the parable of the lost son is, briefly, because this parable does not set forth Christianity, but only a small fragment of Christian teaching. The turn they have given to affairs is therefore merely the nemesis that treads on the heels of the mistaken attempts to read a full Christianity into this parable. The parable was not given to teach us Christianity, in its essence or its sum. It was given to teach us one single truth: a truth of the utmost value, not only full of emotional power, but, when placed in its relation to other truths, of the highest doctrinal significance; but not in itself sufficient to constitute Christianity, or even to embody its essence. How little what this parable teaches us can be conceived as of itself Christianity may easily be made plain by simply enumerating some of the fundamental elements of Christianity which receive no expression in it: and this negative task seems to be made incumbent on us at the outset of any study of the parable by the circumstance of its perversion to the uses of the propaganda of unbelief.

We observe, then, in the first place, that there is no atonement in this parable. And indeed it is precisely because there is no atonement in this parable that it has been seized upon by the modern tendency to which we have alluded, as the norm of the only Christianity it will profess. For nothing is more characteristic of this new type of Christianity than that it knows and will know nothing of an atonement. The old Socinians were quick to perceive this feature of the parable, and to make use of it in their assault upon the doctrine of Christ's satisfaction for sin. See, they cried, the father in the parable asks no satisfaction before he will receive back his son: he rather sees him afar off and runs to meet him and gives him a free and royal welcome. The response is no doubt just that other Scriptures clearly teach the atonement of which no hint is given here; and that we have no "right to expect that every passage in Scripture, and least of all these parables, which exist under necessary limitations in their power of setting forth the truth, shall contain the whole circle of Christian doctrine." This answer is sufficient against the Socinian who appealed to Scripture as a whole and required to be reminded that we "must consider not what one Scripture says, but what all." But it scarcely avails against our modern enthusiast who either professedly or

practically would fain make this parable the embodiment of all the Christianity he will profess. For him, Christianity must do without an atonement, because it is quite obvious that there is no atonement in this parable.

Nor is that more than the beginning of the matter. It must do without a Christ as well. For, we must observe, the parable has as little of Christ in it as it has of an atonement. The Socinians neglected to take note of this. In their zeal to point out that there is no trace in the parable of a satisfaction offered to the Father by which alone He might be enabled to receive back the sinner, they failed to note that neither is there trace in it of any mission of a Son at all-even merely to plead with the wanderer, make known the Father's continued love to him, and win him back to his right relation to the Father. That much of a mission of Christ they themselves confessed. But it is as absent from the parable as is the expiating Christ of the Evangelicals. In truth, there is in the parable no trace whatsoever of a Christ, in any form of mission. From all that appears from the narrative, the errant son was left absolutely alone in his sin, until, wholly of his own motion, he conceived the idea of returning to the Father. If its teaching is to be the one exclusive source of our Christianity we must content ourselves therefore with a Christianity without Christ.

Nor is even this by any means all. For, as has no doubt been noted already, there is as little trace of the saving work of the Holy Spirit in the parable as of that of Christ. The old Pelagians were as quick to see this as were the Socinians later to observe the absence of any hint of a sacrificial atonement. See, they said, the prodigal moves wholly of his own power: there is no efficient grace here, no effectual calling, no regeneration of the Spirit. And there is not. If this parable is to constitute our Christianity, then our Christianity must do without these things.

And doing without these things, it must do without a Holy Spirit altogether. For there is not the slightest hint of a Holy Spirit in any conceivable activity he may be thought to employ in the whole parable. Reduce the mode and effect of His operation to the most attenuated possible. Allow Him merely to plead with men from without the penetralium of their personality, to exercise influences upon them only of the nature of persuasion, such as men can exercise upon one another—still there is no hint of such influences here. From all that appears, the prodigal suo motu turned to the Father and owed to no one so much as a suggestion, much less assistance, in his resolve or its execution. If our Christianity is to be derived from this parable only, we shall have to get along without any Holy Spirit.

And even this is only the beginning. We shall have to get along also without any God the Father. What you say,—the whole parable concerns the father But what a father is this? It is certainly not the Father of the Christian revelation and not the Father of the Christian heart. He permits his son to depart from him without apparent emotion; and so far as appears he endures the absence of his son without a pang,—making not the slightest endeavor to establish or maintain communication with him or to recover him either to good or to himself. If he manifests joy at the happy return of the son after so many days, there is not the least evidence that in all the intervening time he had expended upon him so much as a single message, much less brought to bear upon him the smallest inducement to return. In other words, what we know as the "seeking love of God" is absolutely absent from the dealing of the father with the son as here depicted: that is, the love of God which most nearly concerns you and me as sinners is conspicuous only by its absence. In this respect the parable stands in its suggestions below the companion parables of the lost sheep and the lost coin. When the shepherd lost his sheep, he left the ninety and nine in the wilderness and went after the lost one until he found it. When the woman lost her coin, she lit a candle and swept the house and sought diligently until she found it. But in the parable of the lost son, the father is not pictured as doing anything of the sort. The son leaves him and the son returns to him; and meanwhile the father, so far as appears, goes about his own affairs and leaves the son to go about his. So clear is it

that this parable was not intended to embody the whole Gospel and does not contain even its essence. For what is the essence of the Gospel if it is not the seeking love of God?

The commentators, of course, have not left it so. Determined to get the Gospel out of the parable, they diligently go to work first to put it in. Thus one, in depicting the father's state of mind, grows eloquent in his description of his yearning love. "He has not forgotten his son, though he has forgotten him. He has been thinking of him during the long period of his absence. Probably he often cast glances along the road to see if perchance the erring one was returning, thinking he saw him in every stranger who made his appearance. He has continued looking, longing, till hope deferred has made the heart sick and weary to despair." Now no doubt the father felt all this.

Only the parable does not tell us so. And it would not have omitted to tell us so, if this state of mind on the father's part entered into the essence of its teaching. The fact is that this commentator is rewriting the parable. He is not expounding the parable we have, but composing another parable, a different parable with different lessons. Our Lord, with His exquisitely nice adjustment of every detail of this parable to His purpose, we may be sure, has omitted nothing needed for the most poignant conveyance of the meaning He intended it to convey. That the expositor feels it necessary to insert all this merely proves that he is bent on making the parable teach something foreign to it as it stands. What he has especially in mind to make it teach proves, as we read on, to be the autonomy of the human will. The lost thing, in the case of this parable, is a man: and because he is a man, and no lifeless thing nor an unthinking beast, we are told, he cannot, like the coin and the sheep, be sought. He must be left alone, to return, if return he ever does, wholly of his own motion and accord. Therefore, for sooth, the father's solicitude can only take the form of a waiting! Seeking love can be expended on a coin or a sheep, but not, it seems, on a man. In the case of a man, waiting love is all that is in place, or is possible. Is this the Gospel? Is this the Gospel even of these three parables?

When we were told of the shepherd seeking his sheep, of the woman searching for her coin, was it of sheep and coins that the Master would have His hearers think? Does God care for oxen, or was it not altogether for our sakes that these parables too were spoken?

Into such self-contradictions, to say nothing of oppositions to the very coy cordis of the Gospel, do we fall when we refuse to be led by the text and begin to twist it like a nose of wax to the teaching of our own lessons. The fact is, the parable teaches us none of these things and we must not bend or break it in a vain effort to make it teach them. Even when another commentator more modestly tells us that the two earlier parables-those of the lost sheep and the lost coin-set forth mainly the seeking love of God; while the third-that of the lost son—"describes rather the rise and growth, responsive to that love, of repentance in—the heart of man"; he has gone far beyond his warrant. Why say this parable teaches the "rise and growth of repentance responsive to the seeking love of God"? There is no seeking love of God in the parable's picture of the relation of the father to the lost son, as indeed had just been allowed, in the assignment of the teaching as to that to the preceding parables. But why say even that it describes "the rise and growth of repentance"? It does of course describe the path which one repentant sinner's feet trod as he returned to his father: and so far as the case of one may be the case of all, we may therefore be said to have here, so far as the narrative goes, a typical instance. But there is no evidence that this description was intended as normative, and certainly no ground for finding in this the purpose of the parable. That purpose the text itself places elsewhere; and our wisdom certainly lies in refusing to turn the parable into allegory, reading into it all sorts of lessons which we fancy we may see lurking in its language here and there. We are safest in strictly confining ourselves to reading out of it the lesson it was designed to teach. This lesson was certainly not "the growth and course of sin" and "the growth and course of repentance"; but simply that "there is joy in heaven over one sinner that repenteth." The exquisite surety of our Lord's touch as He paints the career of the

unhappy man whose fortunes He employs to point His moral may tempt us to look upon the vivid picture He draws as the normative instance of sin and repentance: and surely there is no reason why we should not recognize that the picture thus brought before us corresponds with remarkable closeness to the great drama of human sin and repentance. But one must be on his guard against being led astray here. After all, the descriptions and analyses in the parable are determined directly by the requirements of the story, not by those of the history of the sinful soul over against its God; and we must beware of treating the parable as if its details belonged less to the picture than to something else which it seems to us adapted to illustrate. The only safe course is strictly to confine ourselves to the lesson the parable was framed to teach.

This is not to say, however, that this lesson is so single and simple that we can derive no teaching from the parable beyond what is compressible into a single proposition. It undoubtedly has its main lesson; but it could not well teach that lesson without teaching along with it certain subsidiary ones, closely connected with it as corollaries and supports, or at least implicated in the manner in which it is taught. Only, we must be very wary that we do not either on the one hand confuse these subsidiary things with the main lesson of the parable, or on the other read into it lessons of our own, fancifully derived from its mere forms of expression. We may perhaps illustrate what we mean and at the same time gather the teaching we may legitimately derive from the parable by asking ourselves now seriously what we do really learn from it.

And here, beginning at the extreme circumference of what we may really affirm we learn from this parable, I think we may say that we may derive from it, in the first place,—in its context, in the way it is introduced and in its relation to the fellow-parables coupled with it—one of those subtle, evidences of the deity of our Lord which are strewn through the Synoptic Gospels. Although it leads us away from our main course, it behoves us to pause and take note of this, in view of the tendency lingering in some quarters to deny to the Synoptic Gospels a doctrine of the deity of Christ, and especially to the Jesus of the Synoptics any real divine consciousness. It would seem impossible for the unprejudiced reader to glance over these parables in their setting without feeling that both the evangelist and the Master as reported by him speak here out of an underlying consciousness of His divine claims and estate. For, note the occasion out of which these parables arose and the immediate end to which they are directed. The publicans and sinners were flocking to the gracious preaching of Jesus, and Jesus was so far from repelling them, that He welcomed them to Him and mixed in intimate intercourse with them. This the Pharisees and Scribes made the subject of unpleasant remark among themselves. And our Lord spoke these parables in defense of Himself against their attack. But now note how He defends Himself. By parables of a good shepherd seeking his lost sheep; of a distressed woman seeking her lost coin; of a deserted father receiving back his wayward child. We surely do not need to argue that the good shepherd, the distressed woman, the deserted father stands in each instance for God. Jesus Himself tells us this in His application: "I say unto you" (and we must not miss here the slight but majestic intimation of the dignity of His person) "that there shall be joy in heaven" ;"Likewise, I say unto you there is joy before the angels of God." Yet these parables are spoken to vindicate not God's, but Jesus' reception of sinners. The underlying assumption that Jesus' action and God's action are one and the same thing is unmistakable: and no reader fails tacitly to recognize Jesus Himself under the good shepherd and the distressed woman and the deserted father. In Him and His action men may see how things are looked upon in heaven. The lost, when they come to Him, are received because this is heaven's way; and since this is heaven's way, how could He do otherwise? This is not a mere appeal, as some have supposed, to the sympathy of heaven: as if He would say to the objector, "I have not your sympathy in this, but heaven is on my side!" Nor is it a mere appeal to a future vindication: as if He would say, "Now you

condemn, but you will see it differently after a while." It is a defense of His conduct by reference of it to its true category. These publicans and sinners-why, they are His lost ones: and does not in every sphere of life he who loses what he values welcome its recovery with joy? Throughout the whole discussion there throbs thus the open implication that He bears the same relation to these sinners that the shepherd does to the sheep lost from the flock, the woman does to a coin lost from her store, the father does to a wandering child. And what is this but an equally open implication that He is in some mysterious way that Divine Being against whom all sin is committed, away from whose smile all sinners have turned, and back to whom they come when, repenting of their sin, they are recovered to good and to God?

In these parables, then, we see Jesus teaching with authority. And His divine voice is heard in them also rebuking sin. For the next thing, perhaps, which it behoves us to take notice of is the rebuke that sounds in them of the sin of spiritual pride and jealousy. This rebuke of course culminates in the portrait of the elder son and his unsympathetic attitude towards the rejoicing over his brother's return home, which occupies the latter part of the parable of the lost son. This episode has given the expositors much trouble; but this has been occasioned solely by their failure to apprehend aright the purpose of the parable. It is in truth an integral part of the parable, without which the parable would be incomplete.

In the former two parables-those of the lost sheep and the lost coin-Jesus was directly justifying Himself for "receiving sinners and eating with them." His justification is, shortly, that it is precisely the lost who require His attention: He came to seek and to save the lost. But these parables run up into a higher declaration: the declaration that there is joy in heaven over one sinner that repents rather than over ninety and nine just persons who need no repentance. This high note then becomes the dominant note of the discourse: and it is to illustrate it and to give it vividness and force in the consciousness of His hearers that the third parable-that of the lost son-is spoken. This third parable has not precisely the same direct apologetic purpose, therefore, which dominates the other two. It becomes more didactic and as such more of a mirror to reflect the entire situation and to carry home to the questioners the whole involved truth. Its incidents are drawn from a higher plane of experience and the action becomes more complex, by which a more varied play of emotion is allowed and a more complicated series of lessons is suggested. It is, therefore, not content, like the former parables, merely to illustrate the bare fact that joy accompanies the finding of the lost, with the implication that as sinners are what is lost to God, it is their recovery which causes Him joy. It undertakes to take up this fact, already established by the preceding parables, and to fix it in the heart as well as in the mind by summoning to its support the deepest emotions of the human soul, relieving at the same time the free play of these emotions from all interference from the side of a scrupulous sense of justice.

It is this latter function which the episode of the elder brother subserves; and it appears therefore not as an excrescence upon the parable, but as an essential element in it. Its object is to hold up the mirror of fact to the Pharisaic objectors that they may see their conduct and attitude of mind in their true light. Their moving principle was not, as they fancied, a zeal for righteousness which would not have sin condoned, but just a mean-spirited jealousy which was incapable of the natural response of the human spirit in the presence of a great blessing. They are like some crusty elder brother, says our Lord, who, when the long-lost wanderer comes contritely home, is filled with bitter jealousy of the joyful reception he receives rather than with the generous delight that moves all human hearts at the recovery of the lost.

The effect, you see, is to place the Pharisaic objectors themselves in the category of sinners, side by side with the outcasts they had despised; to probe their hard hearts until they recognized their lost estate also; and so to bring them as themselves prodigals back in repentance to the Father's house. That they came back the parable does not say. It leaves them in the midst of bitter controversy with the Father because He is good. And here emerges a wonderful thing. That "seeking love" which is not signalized in the parable with reference to the lost—the confessedly lost—son, is brought before us in all its beautiful appeal with reference to these yet unrepentant elder brothers. For, you will observe, the father does not wait for the elder brother to come into the house to him; he goes out to him. He speaks soothing words to him in response to his outpouring of bitterness and disrespect. When, in outrageous words, this son celebrates his own righteousness and accuses the father of hardness and neglect, refusing indeed in his wrath to recognize his relationship either with him or his: the father responds with mild entreaties, addressing him tenderly as "child," proffering unbroken intercourse with him, endowing him with all his possessions,—in a word, pleading with him as only a loving father can. Did the elder son hearken to these soft reproofs and yield to this endearing appeal? It was for the Pharisees to answer that question. Our Lord leaves it there. And the effect of the whole is to show them that, contrary to their assumption, the Father in heaven has no righteous children on earth; that His grace is needed for all, and most of all for those who dream they have no need of it. By thus skillfully dissecting, under the cover of the sour elder brother, the state of mind of the Pharisaic objectors, our Lord breaks down the artificial distinction by which they had separated themselves from their sinful brethren, and in doing so breaks down also the barriers which held their sympathies back and opens the way to full appreciation by them of the joy He would have them feel in the recovery of the lost. Was there one among them with heart yet open to the appeal of the seeking God, surely he smote his breast as he heard these poignant closing words of the parable and cried, no longer in the voice of a Pharisee, but in the voice of the publican, "God be merciful to me a sinner!" Surely, like one of their own number only a few years later, the scales fell from his eyes and he confessed himself not only a sinner, but even the chief of sinners.

It would not be quite exact perhaps to say that the parable rebukes spiritual pride and jealousy as well as proclaims the joy in heaven over the recovery of the lost. Its lesson is one; and its one lesson is only thrown into a clearer light by the revelation of the dreadfulness of its contrast in jealousy of the good fortune of the saved. Men all are in equal need of salvation, where is there room for censorious complaint of the goodness of God? This leveling effect of the parable raises the question whether there is not contained in it some hint of the universalism of the Gospel. Surely through and through its structure sounds the note of, "For there is no difference!" No difference between the publicans and sinners on the one side, and the Pharisees and the Scribes on the other. The Pharisees themselves being judges, this were equivalent to no difference between Jew and Gentile. Were not the publicans to them as heathen men? And was not "sinners" just the name by which they designated the Gentiles? If their scrupulous attention to the law did not raise them above all commerce or comparison with sinners, what profit was there in being a Jew? We certainly do not purpose to say with some that Jesus was teaching a universal religion without knowing it: and we certainly do not discover here the germ of a universal religion in this—that Jesus meant to teach that nothing lies between the sinner and his recovery to God but an act of the sinner's own will, an act to which every sinner is ever competent, at all times and in all circumstances. And yet it seems not improper to perceive in the leveling effect of the implied inclusion of the Pharisees themselves—in the one great class of sinners a hint of that universalism which Jesus gave His Gospel when He proclaimed Himself the Savior of all who believe on Him.

But, however this may be, we approach nearer to the great lesson of the parable when we note that there is certainly imbedded in its teaching that great and inexpressibly moving truth that there is no depth of degradation, return from which will not be welcomed by God. A sinner may be too vile for any and every thing else; but he cannot be too vile for salvation. We observe at any rate that our

Lord does not hold His hand when He comes to paint the degradation of sinners, through His picture of the degradation into which the lost son had sunk. No depths are left beneath the depths which He here portrays for us. This man had dealt with his inheritance with the utmost recklessness. He had wasted the whole of it until he was left stripped bare of all that he had brought from his father's house. Nor was there anything to take its place. The country in which he had elected to dwell was smitten, throughout its whole extent, with a biting famine. In all its length and breadth there was nothing on which a man might live. The prodigal was reduced to bend and pray and fawn at the feet of a certain citizen of that dread land and was sent by him out into the barren fields—to feed swine! To a Jew, degradation could not be more poignantly depicted. Yes, it could: there was one stage worse and that stage was reached. The lost son not only herded the swine; he herded with them. "He was fain to fill his belly from the husks that the swine did eat." Not with the same quality of food, observe, but from the swine's own store—for "no man gave unto him." In this terrible description of extreme degradation there may be a side glance at the actual state of the publicans, our Lord's reception of and association with whom was such an offence to the Jewish consciousness. For did not they not merely serve against their own people those swines of Gentiles but actually feed themselves at their trough? But however this may be, it is clear that our Lord means to paint degradation in its depths. He does not spare the sinners with whom He consorted. His defense for receiving them does not turn upon any failure to recognize or feel their true quality; any representation of them as not so bad after all; as if they had been painted blacker than they were, and were nice enough people to associate with if only we were not so fastidious. He says rather that they are bad past expression and past belief. His defense is that they can be saved; and that He is here to save them. Lost? Yes, they are lost; and there is no reason why we should not take the word at the top—or rather at the bottom- of its meaning: this is the parable of the lost son. But Jesus is the Savior of the lost; and there is none so lost that he may not be found by Him, and, being found by Him, be also found in Him. Oh, no! Jesus does not rejoice in sinners: it is not sin He loves nor sinners as sinners. What He rejoices in is the rescue of sinners from their sin. And the deeper the sin the greater the rescue and the greater the joy. "I say unto you, there is joy before the angels of God over one sinner that repenteth." "I say unto you, there shall be joy in heaven over one sinner that repenteth, rather than over ninety and nine just persons, such as have no need of repentance."

It is in this great declaration that the real purport of the parable is expressed. This parable was spoken to teach us, to put it briefly, that God in heaven rejoices over the repentance of every sinner that repents. It is a commentary therefore on those great passages which tell us that God would have no man perish, but all to come to Him and live; and it is more than a commentary on these passages, inasmuch as it throws the emphasis upon the positive side and tells us of the joy that God feels at the repentance of every sinner who repents. To the carrying of this great message home to our hearts all the art of the parable is directed, and it is our wisdom to read it simply to this end. We need not puzzle ourselves over the significance, then, of this detail or that, as if we were bound or indeed permitted to discover, allegorically, some spiritual meaning in each turn of the story. The most of these find their account in the demands of the story itself and enter into its lesson only as contributory details, adding vividness and truth to the illustration.

Thus, for instance, if we ask why there are only two sons in the parable, while there were ten pieces of silver in the preceding one, and a hundred sheep in the first one; the answer is that just two sons were needed to serve Jesus' purpose of illustrating the contrast between the Pharisees and Scribes on the one side and the publicans and sinners on the other; his purpose not being at all to indicate proportion of numbers, but difference in status and conduct. In the former parables the suggestion of comparative insignificance was requisite to bring out the full lesson; in this, the contrast of character serves His purpose. If

again it is asked why it is the younger son who becomes a prodigal, the answer is that the propriety of the story demands it. It would be inconceivable that the older son, who according to custom was the co-possessor and heir of the fundamental estate, should have asked or received an inheritance apart from it. But the thing was not unnatural, and doubtless not unusual, in a younger son, who was to be portioned off in any event in the end, and was only asking that he might not wait on his father's death, but might be permitted to "set up for himself" at once. We cannot therefore with confidence discover the beginnings of the prodigal's downfall in his request that his inheritance might be told off to him, or wonder overmuch why the father so readily granted this request. It is tempting, no doubt, to see in the wish of the son to "set up for himself" a hint of a heart already little at one with the law and custom of the father's house. But such allegorizing is dangerous, especially when not suggested by any hint in the language of the narrative or necessarily contained in the situation depicted. It is customary to speak of the younger son as a young man. It may be so. But the narrative does not say so. He may have been in middle life; and it may well have seemed to all concerned that a desire on his part to begin to build up his own house was altogether right and fitting. The separation of his goods from his father's at all events appears in the parable only as the precedent condition of his spending them, not as the beginning of his downfall.

We need not go further, however, into detail. Enough that the story has a single point. And that point is the joy of the father at the return of the son, a joy which is the expression, not of the natural love of the father for a son, but of the overwhelming emotion of mingled relief and thankfulness and over mastering rapture which fills the heart of a father on the recovery of a lost son. The point of the narrative is not, then, that this prodigal is a son, though that underlies and gives its verisimilitude to the picture. The point is that this son is a prodigal. It is because he has been lost and is now found that the joy of the father is so great. The elder son is a son too; and the father loves him also. Let him who doubts it read again the exquisite narrative of the father's tender and patient dealings with him. There is not in all literature a more beautiful picture of parental affection pleading with unfilial passion. This father knew perfectly how to fulfill the injunction later laid down by the apostle Paul: "And ye fathers, provoke not your children to wrath; but nurture them in the chastening and admonition of the Lord." From this point of view that soothing admonition, "Child, thou" (the emphasis on the "thou" must not be neglected) "art always with me; and all that is mine is thine; but it was meet to make merry and be glad, because this thy brother was dead and is alive, and was lost and is found"—is simply perfect. So clear is it that the lesson of the parable does not turn on the prodigal's being a son, but on this son being a prodigal.

In other words, its lesson is not that God loves His children, but that God loves sinners. And thus this parable is seen ranging with the preceding ones. The lost sheep, the lost coin, the lost son, have only this one thing in common, that they are lost; and the three parables unite in commending the one common lesson to us, that as men rejoice in the recovery of what is lost, so God rejoices in the recovery of sinners since sinners are the things that to Him are lost. We must not, then, use this parable to prove that God is a father, or draw inferences from it as if that were its fundamental teaching. It does not teach that. What it teaches is that God will receive the returning sinner with the same joy that the father in the parable received the returning prodigal; because as this son was to that father's heart above all other things that he had lost, his lost one, and his return was therefore above all other things that might have been returned to him his recovery; so sinners are above all else that God has lost in the world His lost ones, and their return to Him above all other restorations that may be made to Him His recovery. The vivid picture of the father not staying to receive the returning son, but, moved with compassion as he spied him yet a great way off, running out to meet him and falling on his neck and kissing him in his ecstasy again and again;

cutting short his words of confession with the command that the best robe be brought to clothe him, and shoes for his blistered feet, and a ring for his finger, and the order that the fatted calf be killed and the feast be spread, and the music and the dance be prepared because, as he says, "This my son was dead and is alive, was lost and is found "—all this in the picture is meant to quicken our hearts to some apprehension of the joy that fills God's heart at the return of sinners to Him.

O brethren, our minds are dulled with much repetition, and refuse to take the impression our Lord would make on them. But even we-can we fail to be moved with wonder to-day at this great message, that God in heaven rejoices—exults in joy like this human father receiving back his son-when sinners repent and turn to Him? On less assurance than that of Jesus Christ Himself the thing were perhaps incredible. But on that assurance shall we not take its comfort to our hearts? We are sinners. And our only hope is in one who loves sinners; and has come into the world to die for sinners. Marvel, marvel beyond our conception; but, blessed be God, as true as marvelous. And when we know Him better, perhaps it may more and more cease to be a marvel. At least, one of those who have known Him best and served Him most richly in our generation, has taught us to sing thus of His wondrous death for us:

That He should leave His place on high,
And come for sinful man to die,
You count it strange?—so do not I,
Since I have known my Savior.

Nay, had there been in all this wide
Wide world no other soul beside
But only mine, then He had died
That He might be its Savior;

Then had He left His Father's throne,
The joy untold, the love unknown,
And for that soul had given His own,
That He might be its Savior!

Is that too high a flight for us—that passion of appropriation by which the love of Jesus for me—my own personal soul—is appreciated so fully that it seems natural to us that He, moved by that great love that was in

Him for me—even me—should leave His throne that He might die for me,—just me,—even were there none else beside? At least we may assent to the dispassionate recognition that in the depths of our parable is hidden the revelation of that fundamental characteristic of Jesus Christ by virtue of which He did become the Savior at least of sinners. And seeing this and knowing ourselves to be sinners, we may acknowledge Him afresh today as our Savior, and at least gratefully join in our passionate sinner's prayer:

And oh! that He fulfilled may see
The travail of His soul in me,
And with His work contented be,
As I am with my Savior!

Yea, living, dying, let me bring
My strength, my solace from this spring,
That He who lives to be my King,
Once died to be my Savior!

B. B. Warfield

---

8. QUOTATION COLLECTION ON THE TEACHING OF JESUS

Jesus . . . endorsed the authority of those Old Testament prophets who vehemently rebuked social injustice; and he consistently identified himself with the poor and weak, with social outcasts and those who were regarded as morally disreputable.

J. N. D. Anderson

I have read Plato and Cicero sayings that are very wise and beautiful; but I never read in either of them: "Come unto me all ye that labor and are heavy laden and I will give thee rest."

Augustine

If we are to accept the teaching of Jesus at all, then the only test of the reality of a man's religion is his attitude to his fellow men. The only possible proof that a man loves God is the demonstrated fact that he loves his fellow men.

William Barclay

Jesus does not give recipes that show the way to God as other teachers of religion do. He is himself the way.

Karl Barth

The Fourfold Gospel is the central portion of Divine Revelation. Into it, as a Reservoir, all

the foregoing revelations pour their full tide and out of it, as a Fountain, flow all subsequent revelations.

David Brown

[There is] not one shred of evidence that the early church ever concocted sayings of Jesus in order to settle any of its problems.

George B. Caird

The four Gospels all had the same purpose: to point out Christ. The first three Gospels show his body, so to speak, but John shows his soul.

John Calvin

The summing up of the life of faith is the teaching of Jesus in the Sermon on the Mount.

Oswald Chambers

The gospel of Jesus Christ must be the bad news of the conviction of sin before it can be the Good News of redemption.

Charles Colson

The most radical social teaching of Jesus was his total reversal of the contemporary notion of greatness.

Richard Foster

The gospel is so simple that small children can understand it, and it is so profound that studies by the wisest theologians will never exhaust its riches.

Charles Hodge

The gospel was not good advice but good news.

W. R. Inge

Had the doctrines of Jesus been preached always as pure as they came from his lips, the whole civilized world would now have been Christian.

Thomas Jefferson

Many teachers of the world have tried to explain everything—they have changed little or nothing. Jesus explained little and changed everything.

E. Stanley Jones

Christ taught the purest and sublimest system of ethics . . . one which throws the moral precepts and maxims of the wisest men in history far into the shade.

Joseph Klausner, Jewish scholar

If we once accept the doctrine of the Incarnation, we must surely be very cautious in suggesting that any circumstance in the culture of first-century Palestine was a hampering or distorting influence upon His teaching.

C. S. Lewis

The Gospels were written in order that the truth concerning the Lord Jesus Christ might be known exactly.

D. Martyn Lloyd-Jones

Any attempt to equate the teaching of the New Testament with any one of the political parties, or any other party, is to do violence to the teaching of Christ.

D. Martyn Lloyd-Jones

The gospel of Jesus Christ openly and uncompromisingly announces itself as being something with a narrow entrance, a strait gate.

D. Martyn Lloyd-Jones

The gospel of Jesus Christ does not so much take the Christian out of the world, as take the world out of the Christian.

D. Martyn Lloyd-Jones

When Jesus Christ utters a word, He opens His mouth so wide that it embraces all Heaven and earth, even though that word be but in a whisper.

Martin Luther

The Son of God is the teacher of men, giving to them of His Spirit—that Spirit which manifests the deep things of God, being to a man the mind of Christ.

George MacDonald

The gospel is not speculation but fact. It is truth, because it is the record of a person who is the Truth.

Alexander Maclaren

The beginning of the gospel is nothing but the whole Old Testament.

Origen

The gospel of Jesus is autobasilea, the kingdom himself.

Origen

After reading the doctrines of Plato, Socrates or Aristotle, we feel the specific difference between their words and Christ's is the difference between an inquiry and a revelation.

Joseph Parker

I would very earnestly ask you to check your conception of Christ, the image of Him which as a Christian you hold in your mind, with the actual revealed Person who can be seen and studied in action in the pages of the Gospels.

J. B. Phillips

In the teaching of that man, Jesus Christ, we find repeated again and again, an insistence on love to God and love to men being inseparably linked.

J. B. Phillips

The gospel is in essence the good news of Christ crucified.

John Stott

If Mark's is the Gospel of Christ the suffering Servant, and Luke's the Gospel of Christ the universal Savior, Matthew's is the Gospel of Christ the ruling King.

John Stott

Look into the preaching Jesus did and you will find it was aimed straight at the big sinners on the front seats.

William Ashley (Billy) Sunday

The teaching of Christ is more excellent than all the advice of the saints, and he who has His spirit will find in it a hidden manna.

Thomas à Kempis

Whenever you read the Gospel, Christ himself is speaking to you.

Tikhon of Zadonsk

To Christ the Bible is true, authoritative, inspired, to him the God of the Bible is the living God, and the teaching of the Bible is the teaching of the living God. To him what Scripture says, God says.

John W. Wenham

The only weapon that will ever effectively win the war against disease, hunger, injustice and poverty in Asia is the Gospel of Jesus Christ.

K. P. Yohannan

INCIDENTS IN JESUS' LIFE

2.41 JESUS THROWING OUT THE MONEY-CHANGERS, MARTIN LUTHER

Many say that Christ having by force driven the buyers and sellers out of the temple, we also may use force against the popish bishops and enemies of God's Word, as Munzer and other seducers. But Christ did many things which we neither may nor can do after him. He walked upon the water, he fasted forty days and forty nights, he raised Lazarus from death, after he had lain four days in the grave, etc.; such and the like we must leave undone. Much less will Christ consent that we by force assail the enemies of the truth; he commands the contrary: "Love your enemies, pray for them that vex and persecute you"; "Be merciful, as your Father is merciful"; "Take my yoke upon you and learn of me, for I am meek and humble in heart"; "He that will follow me, let him deny himself, take up his cross, and follow me."

Martin Luther, Table Talk, *219*

2.42 JESUS' OPPONENTS, ALFRED EDERSHEIM

THE DEPUTATION FROM JERUSALEM—THE THREE SECTS OF THE PHARISEES, SADDUCEES, AND ESSENES—EXAMINATION OF THEIR DISTINCTIVE DOCTRINES. JOHN 1:19-24.

Apart from the repulsively carnal form which it had taken, there is something absolutely sublime in the continuance and intensity of the Jewish expectation of the Messiah. It outlived not only the delay of long centuries, but the persecutions and scattering of the people; it continued under the disappointment of the Maccabees, the rule of a Herod, the administration of a corrupt and contemptible Priesthood, and, finally, the government of Rome as represented by a Pilate; nay, it grew in intensity almost in proportion as it seemed unlikely of realization. These are facts which show that

the doctrine of the Kingdom, as the sum and substance of Old Testament teaching, was the very heart of Jewish religious life; while, at the same time, they evidence a moral elevation which placed abstract religious conviction far beyond the reach of passing events, and clung to it with a tenacity which nothing could loosen.

Tidings of what these many months had occurred by the banks of the Jordan must have early reached Jerusalem, and ultimately stirred to the depths its religious society, whatever its preoccupation with ritual questions or political matters. For it was not an ordinary movement, nor in connection with any of the existing parties, religious or political. An extraordinary preacher, of extraordinary appearance and habits, not aiming, like others, after renewed zeal in legal observances, or increased Levitical purity, but preaching repentance and moral renovation in preparation for the coming

Kingdom, and sealing this novel doctrine with an equally novel rite, had drawn from town and country multitudes of all classes—inquirers, penitents and novices. The great and burning question seemed, what the real character and meaning of it was? or rather, whence did it issue, and whither did it tend? The religious leaders of the people proposed to answer this by instituting an inquiry through a trust-worthy deputation. In the account of this by John certain points seem clearly implied; on others only suggestions can be ventured.

That the interview referred to occurred after the Baptism of Jesus, appears from the whole context. Similarly, the statement that the deputation which came to John was "sent from Jerusalem" by "the Jews," implies that it proceeded from authority, even if it did not bear more than a semi-official character. For, although the expression "Jews" in the fourth Gospel generally conveys the idea of contrast to the disciples of Christ (for example John 7:15), yet it refers to the people in their corporate capacity, that is, as represented by their constituted religious authorities. On the other hand, although the term "scribes and elders" does not occur in the Gospel of John, it by no means follows thatthe Priests and Levites' sent from the capital either represented the two great divisions of the Sanhedrin, or, indeed, that the deputation issued from the Great Sanhedrin itself. The former suggestion is entirely ungrounded; the latter at least problematic. It seems a legitimate inference that, considering their own tendencies, and the political dangers connected with such a step, the Sanhedrin of Jerusalem would not have come to the formal resolution of sending a regular deputation on such an inquiry. Moreover, a measure like this would have been entirely outside their recognized mode of procedure. The Sanhedrin did not, and could not, originate charges. It only investigated those brought before it. It is quite true that judgment upon false prophets and religious seducers lay with it; but the Baptist had not as yet said or done anything to lay him open to such an accusation. He had in no way infringed the Law by word or deed, nor had he even claimed to be a prophet. If, nevertheless, it

seems most probable that the "Priests and Levites" came from the Sanhedrin, we are led to the conclusion that theirs was an informal mission, rather privately arranged than publicly determined upon.

And with this the character of the deputies agrees. "Priests and Levites"—the colleagues of John the Priest—would be selected for such an errand, rather than leading Rabbinic authorities. The presence of the latter would, indeed, have given to the movement an importance, if not a sanction, which the Sanhedrin could not have wished. The only other authority in Jerusalem from which such a deputation could have issued was the so-called "Council of the Temple," "Judicature of the Priests," or "Elders of the Priesthood," which consisted of the fourteen chief officers of the Temple. But although they may afterwards have taken their full part in the condemnation of Jesus, ordinarily their duty was only connected with the services of the Sanctuary, and not with criminal questions or doctrinal investigations. It would be too much to suppose, that they would take the initiative in such a matter on the ground that the Baptist was a member of the Priesthood. Finally, it seems quite natural that such an informal inquiry, set on foot most probably by the Sanhedrists, should have been entrusted exclusively to the Pharisaic party. It would in no way have interested the Sadducees; and what members of that party had seen of John must have convinced them that his views and aims lay entirely beyond their horizon.

The origin of the two great parties of Pharisees and Sadducees has already been traced. They mark, not sects, but mental directions, such as in their principles are natural and universal, and, indeed, appear in connection with all metaphysical questions. They are the different modes in which the human mind views supersensuous problems, and which afterwards, when one-sidedly followed out, harden into diverging schools of thought. If Pharisees and Sadducess were not "sects" in the sense of separation from the unity of the Jewish ecclesiastical community, neither were theirs "heresies" in the conventional, but only in the original sense of tendency, direction, or, at most, views, differing from those commonly entertained. Our sources of information here are: the New Testament, Josephus, and Rabbinic writings. The New Testament only marks, in broad outlines and popularly, the peculiarities of each party; but from the absence of bias it may safely be regarded as the most trustworthy authority on the matter. The inferences which we derive from the statements of Josephus, though always to be qualified by our general estimate of his animus, accord with those from the New Testament. In regard to Rabbinic writings, we have to bear in mind the admittedly unhistorical character of most of their notices, the strong party-bias which colored almost all their statements regarding opponents, and their constant tendency to trace later views and practices to earlier times.

Without entering on the principles and supposed practices of "the fraternity" or "association" (Chebher, Chabhurah, Chab-hurta) of Pharisees, which was comparatively small, numbering only about 6,000 members, the following particulars may be of interest. The object of the association was twofold: to observe in the strictest manner, and according to traditional law, all the ordinances concerning Levitical purity, and to be extremely punctilious in all connected with religious dues (tithes and all other dues). A person might undertake only the second, without the first of these obligations. In that case he was simply a Neeman, an "accredited one" with whom one might enter freely into commerce, as he was supposed to have paid all dues. But a person could not undertake the vow of Levitical purity without also taking the obligation of all religious dues. If he undertook both vows he was a Chabher, or associate. Here there were four degrees, marking an ascending scale of Levitical purity, or separation from all that was profane. In opposition to these was the Am ha-arets, or "country people" (the people which knew not, or cared not for the Law, and were regarded as "cursed"). But it must not be thought that every Chabher was either a learned Scribe, or that every Scribe was a Chabher. On the contrary, as a man might be a Chabher

without being either a Scribe or an elder, so there must have been sages, and even teachers, who did not belong to the association, since special rules are laid down for the reception of such. Candidates had to be formally admitted into the "fraternity" in the presence of three members. But every accredited public "teacher" was, unless anything was known to the contrary, supposed to have taken upon him the obligations referred to. The family of a Chabher belonged, as a matter of course, to the community; but this ordinance was afterwards altered. The Neeman undertook these four obligations: to tithe what he ate, what he sold, and what he bought, and not to be a guest with an Am ha-arets. The full Chabher undertook not to sell to an "Am ha-arets" any fluid or dry substance (nutriment or fruit), not to buy from him any such fluid, not to be a guest with him, not to entertain him as a guest in his own clothes (on account of their possible impurity)—to which one authority adds other particulars, which, however, were not recognized by the Rabbis generally as of primary importance.

These two great obligations of the "official" Pharisee, or "Associate" are pointedly referred to by Christ—both that in regard to tithing (the vow of the Neeman); and that in regard to Levitical purity (the special vow of the Chabher). In both cases they are associated with a want of corresponding inward reality, and with hypocrisy. These charges cannot have come upon the people by surprise, and they may account for the circumstance that so many of the learned kept aloof from the "Association" as such. Indeed, the sayings of some of the Rabbis in regard to Pharisaism and the professional Pharisee are more withering than any in the New Testament. It is not necessary here to repeat the well-known description, both in the Jerusalem and the Babylon Talmud, of the seven kinds of Pharisees, of whom six (the "Shechemite," the "stumbling," the "bleeding," the "mortar," the "I want to know what is incumbent on me," and "the Pharisee from fear") mark various kinds of unreality, and only one is "the Pharisee from love." Such an expression as "the plague of Pharisaism" is not uncommon; and a silly pietist, a clever sinner, and a female Pharisee, are ranked among the troubles of life. "Shall we then explain a verse according to the opinions of the Pharisees?" asks a Rabbi, in supreme contempt for the arrogance of the fraternity. "It is as a tradition among the pharisees to torment themselves in this world, and yet they will gain nothing by it in the next." The Sadducees had some reason for the taunt, that "the Pharisees would by-and-by subject the globe of the sun itself to their purifications," the more so that their assertions of purity were sometimes conjoined with Epicurean maxims, betokening a very different state of mind, such as, "Make haste to eat and drink, for the world which we quit resembles a wedding feast;" or this: "My son, if thou possess anything, enjoy thyself, for there is no pleasure in Hades, and death grants no respite. But if thou sayest, What then would I leave to my sons and daughters? Who will thank thee for this appointment in Hades?" Maxims these to which, alas! too many of their recorded stories and deeds form a painful commentary.

But it would be grossly unjust to identify Pharisaism, as a religious direction, with such embodiments of it or even with the official "fraternity." While it may be granted that the tendency and logical sequence of their views and practices were such, their system, as opposed to Sadduceeism, had very serious bearings: dogmatic, ritual, and legal. It is, however, erroneous to suppose, either that their system represented traditionalism itself, or that Scribes and Pharisees are convertible terms, while the Sadducees represented the civil and political element. The Pharisees represented only the prevailing system of, not traditionalism itself; while the Sadducees also numbered among them many learned men. They were able to enter into controversy, often protracted and fierce, with their opponents, and they acted as members of the Sanhedrin, although they had diverging traditions of their own, and even, as it would appear, at one time a complete code of canon-law. Moreover, the admitted fact, that when in office the Sadducees conformed to the principles and practices of the Pharisees, proves at least that they must have been acquainted with the ordinances of traditionalism. Lastly, there were certain traditional ordinances on which both parties were at one. Thus it seems Sadduceeism was in a sense rather a speculative than a practical system, starting from simple and well-defined principles, but wide-reaching in its possible consequences. Perhaps it may best be described as a general reaction against the extremes of Pharisaism, springing from moderate and rationalistic tendencies; intended to secure a footing within the recognized bounds of Judaism; and seeking to defend its principles by a strict literalism of interpretation and application. If so, these interpretations would be intended rather for defensive than offensive purposes, and the great aim of the party would be after rational freedom—or, it might be, free rationality. Practically, the party would, of course, tend in broad, and often grossly unorthodox, directions.

The fundamental dogmatic differences between the Pharisees and Sadducees concerned: the rule of faith and practice; the "after death;" the existence of angels and spirits; and free will and pre-destination. In regard to the first of these points, it has already been stated that the Sadducees did not lay down the principle of absolute rejection of all traditions as such, but that they were opposed to traditionalism as represented and carried out by the Pharisees. When put down by sheer weight of authority, they would probably carry the controversy further, and retort on their opponents by an appeal to Scripture as against their traditions, perhaps ultimately even by an attack on traditionalism; but always as represented by the Pharisees. A careful examination of the statements of Josephus on this subject will show that they convey no more than this. The Pharisaic view of this aspect of the controversy appears, perhaps, most satisfactorily because indirectly, in certain sayings of the Mishnah, which attribute all national calamities to those persons, whom they adjudge to eternal perdition, who interpret Scripture "not as does the Halakhah," or established Pharisaic rule. In this respect, then, the commonly received idea concerning the Pharisees and Sadducees will require to be seriously modified. As regards the practice of the Pharisees, as distinguished from that of the Sadducees, we may safely treat the statements of Josephus as the exaggerated representations of a partisan, who wishes to place his party in the best light. It is, indeed, true that the Pharisees, "interpreting the legal ordinances with rigour," imposed on themselves the necessity of much self-denial, especially in regard to food, but that their practice was under the guidance of reason, as Josephus asserts, is one of those bold mis-statements with which he has too often to be credited. His vindication of their special reverence for age and authority must refer to the honors paid by the party to "the Elders," not to the old. And that there was sufficient ground for Sadducean opposition to Pharisaic traditionalism, alike in principle and in practice, will appear from the following quotation, to which we add, by way of explanation, that the wearing of phylacteries was deemed by that party of Scriptural obligation, and that the phylactery for the head was to consist (according to tradition) of four compartments. "Against the words of the Scribes is more punishable than against the words of Scripture. He who says, No phylacteries, so as to transgress the words of Scripture, is not guilty (free); five compartments—to add to the words of the Scribes—he is guilty."

The second doctrinal difference between Pharisees and Sadducees concerned the "after death." According to the New Testament, the Sadducees denied the resurrection of the dead, while Josephus, going further, imputes to them denial of reward or punishment after death, and even the doctrine that the soul perishes with the body. The latter statement may be dismissed as among those inferences which theological controversialists are too fond of imputing to their opponents. This is fully borne out by the account of a later work, to the effect, that by successive misunderstandings of the saying of Antigonus of Socho, that men were to serve God without regard to reward, his later pupils had arrived at the inference that there was no other world—which, however, might only refer to the Pharisaic ideal of "the world to come," not to the denial of the immortality of the soul—and no resurrection

of the dead. We may therefore credit Josephus with merely reporting the common inference of his party. But it is otherwise in regard to their denial of the resurrection of the dead. Not only Josephus, but the New Testament and Rabbinic writings attest this. The Mishnah expressly states that the formula "from age to age," or rather "from world to world," had been introduced as a protest against the opposite theory; while the Talmud, which records disputations between Gamaliel and the Sadducees on the subject of the resurrection, expressly imputes the denial of this doctrine to the "Scribes of the Sadducees." In fairness it is perhaps only right to add that, in the discussion, the Sadducees seem only to have actually denied that there was proof for this doctrine in the Pentateuch, and that they ultimately professed themselves convinced by the reasoning of Gamaliel. Still the concurrent testimony of the New Testament and of Josephus leaves no doubt, that in this instance their views had not been misrepresented. Whether or not their opposition to the doctrine of the Resurrection arose in the first instance from, or was prompted by, Rationalistic views, which they endeavored to support by an appeal to the letter of the Pentateuch, as the source of traditionalism, it deserves notice that in His controversy with the Sadducees Christ appealed to the Pentateuch in proof of His teaching.

Connected with this was the equally Rationalistic opposition to belief in Angels and Spirits. It is only mentioned in the New Testament, but seems almost to follow as a corollary. Remembering what the Jewish Angelology was, one can scarcely wonder that in controversy the Sadducees should have been led to the opposite extreme.

The last dogmatic difference between the two "sects" concerned that problem which has at all times engaged religious thinkers: man's free will and God's pre-ordination, or rather their compatibility. Josephus—or the reviser whom he employed—indeed, uses the purely heathen expression "fate" to designate the Jewish idea of the pre-ordination of God. But, properly understood, the real difference between the Pharisees and Sadducees seems to have amounted to this: that the former accentuated God's preordination, the latter man's free will; and that, while the Pharisees admitted only a partial influence of the human element on what happened, or the co-operation of the human with the Divine, the Sadducees denied all absolute pre-ordination, and made man's choice of evil or good, with its consequences of misery or happiness, to depend entirely on the exercise of free will and self-determination. And in this, like many opponents of "Predestinarianism," they seem to have started from the principle, that it was impossible for God "either to commit or to foresee [in the sense of fore-ordaining] anything evil." The mutual misunderstanding here was that common in all such controversies. Although Josephus writes as if, according to the Pharisees, the chief part in every good action depended upon fate [pre-ordination] rather than on man's doing, yet in another place he disclaims for them the notion that the will of man was destitute of spontaneous activity, and speaks somewhat confusedly—for he is by no means a good reasoner—of "a mixture" of the Divine and human elements, in which the human will, with its sequence of virtue or wickedness, is subject to the will of fate. A yet further modification of this statement occurs in another place, where we are told that, according to the Pharisees, some things depended upon fate, and more on man himself. Manifestly, there is not a very wide difference between this and the fundamental principle of the Sadducees in what we may suppose its primitive form.

But something more will have to be said as illustrative of Pharisaic teaching on this subject. No one who has entered into the spirit of the Old Testament can doubt that its outcome was faith, in its twofold aspect of acknowledgment of the absolute Rule, and simple submission to the Will, of God. What distinguished this so widely from fatalism was what may be termed Jehovahism—that is, the moral element in its thoughts of God, and that He was ever presented as in paternal relationship to men. But the Pharisees carried their accentuation of the Divine to the verge of fatalism. Even the idea that God had created man with two impulses, the one to good, the other to evil; and that the latter was absolutely necessary for the continuance of this world, would in some measure trace the causation of moral evil to the Divine Being. The absolute and unalterable pre-ordination of every event, to its minutest details, is frequently insisted upon. Adam had been shown all the generations that were to spring from him. Every incident in the history of Israel had been foreordained, and the actors in it—for good or for evil—were only instruments for carrying out the Divine Will. What were ever Moses and Aaron? God would have delivered Israel out of Egypt, and given them the Law, had there been no such persons. Similarly was it in regard to Solomon, to Esther, to Nebuchadnezzar, and others. Nay, it was because man was predestined to die that the serpent came to seduce our first parents. And as regarded the history of each individual: all that concerned his mental and physical capacity, or that would betide him, was prearranged. His name, place, position, circumstances, the very name of her whom he was to wed, were proclaimed in heaven, just as the hour of his death was foreordered. There might be seven years of pestilence in the land, and yet no one died before his time. Even if a man inflicted a cut on his finger, he might be sure that this also had been preordered. Nay, "wheresoever a man was destined to die, thither would his feet carry him." We can well understand how the Sadducees would oppose notions like these, and all such coarse expressions of fatalism. And it is significant of the exaggeration of Josephus, that neither the New Testament, nor Rabbinic writings, bring the charge of the denial of God's prevision against the Sadducees.

But there is another aspect of this question also. While the Pharisees thus held the doctrine of absolute preordination, side by side with it they were anxious to insist on man's freedom of choice, his personal responsibility, and moral obligation. Although every event depended upon God, whether a man served God or not was entirely in his own choice. As a logical sequence of this, fate had no influence as regarded Israel, since all depended on prayer, repentance, and good works. Indeed, otherwise that repentance, on which Rabbinism so largely insists, would have had no meaning. Moreover, it seems as if it had been intended to convey that, while our evil actions were entirely our own choice, if a man sought to amend his ways, he would be helped of God. It was, indeed, true that God had created the evil impulse in us; but He had also given the remedy in the Law. This is parabolically represented under the figure of a man seated at the parting of two ways, who warned all passers that if they chose one road it would lead them among the thorns, while on the other brief difficulties would end in a plain path (joy). Or, to put it in the language of the great Akiba: "Everything is foreseen; free determination is accorded to man; and the world is judged in goodness." With this simple juxtaposition of two propositions equally true, but incapable of metaphysical combination, as are most things in which the empirically cognisable and uncognisable are joined together, we are content to leave the matter.

The other differences between the Pharisees and Sadducees can be easily and briefly summed up. They concern ceremonial, ritual, and juridical questions. In regard to the first, the opposition of the Sadducees to the excessive scruples of the Pharisees on the subject of Levitical defilements led to frequent controversy. Four points in dispute are mentioned, of which, however, three read more like ironical comments than serious divergences. Thus, the Sadducees taunted their opponents with their many lustrations, including that of the Golden Candlestick in the Temple. Two other similar instances are mentioned. By way of guarding against the possibility of profanation, the Pharisees enacted, that the touch of any thing sacred "defiled" the hands. The Sadducees, on the other hand, ridiculed the idea that the Holy Scriptures "defiled" the hands, but not such a book as Homer. In the same spirit, the Sadducees would ask the Pharisees how it came, that water pouring from a clean into an unclean vessel did not lose its purity and purifying power. If these represent no serious controversies, on another ceremonial question there was real difference, though its existence

shows how far party-spirit could lead the Pharisees. No ceremony was surrounded with greater care to prevent defilement than that of preparing the ashes of the Red Heifer. What seem the original ordinances, directed that, for seven days previous to the burning of the Red Heifer, the priest was to be kept in separation in the Temple, sprinkled with the ashes of all sin-offerings, and kept from the touch of his brother-priests, with even greater rigor than the High-Priest in his preparation for the Day of Atonement. The Sadducees insisted that, as "till sundown" was the rule in all purification, the priest must be in cleanliness till then, before burning the Red Heifer. But, apparently for the sake of opposition, and in contravention to their own principles, the Pharisees would actually "defile" the priest on his way to the place of burning, and then immediately make him take a bath of purification which had been prepared, so as to show that the Sadducees were in error. In the same spirit, the Sadducees seem to have prohibited the use of anything made from animals which were either interdicted as food, or by reason of their not having been properly slaughtered; while the Pharisees allowed it, and, in the case of Levitically clean animals which had died or been torn, even made their skin into parchment, which might be used for sacred purposes.

These may seem trifling distinctions, but they sufficed to kindle the passions. Even greater importance attached to differences on ritual questions, although the controversy here was purely theoretical. For, the Sadducees, when in office, always conformed to the prevailing Pharisaic practices. Thus the Sadducees would have interpreted Lev. 23:11, 15, 16, as meaning that the wave-sheaf (or, rather, the Omer) was to be offered on "the morrow after the weekly Sabbath"—that is, on the Sunday in Easter week—which would have brought the Feast of Pentecost always on a Sunday; while the Pharisees understood the term "Sabbath" of the festive Paschal day. Connected with this were disputes about the examination of the witnesses who testified to the appearance of the new moon, and whom the Pharisees accused of having been suborned by their opponents.

The Sadducean objection to pouring the water of libation upon the altar on the Feast of Tabernacles, led to riot and bloody reprisals on the only occasion on which it seems to have been carried into practice. Similarly, the Sadducees objected to the beating off the willow-branches after the procession round the altar on the last day of the Feast of Tabernacles, if it were a Sabbath. Again, the Sadducees would have had the High-Priest, on the Day of Atonement, kindle the incense before entering the Most Holy Place; the Pharisees after he had entered the Sanctuary. Lastly, the Pharisees contended that the cost of the daily Sacrifices should be discharged from the general Temple treasury, while the Sadducees would have paid it from free-will offerings. Other differences, which seem not so well established, need not here be discussed.

Among the divergences on juridical questions, reference has already been made to that in regard to marriage with the "betrothed," or else actually espoused widow of a deceased, childless brother. Josephus, indeed, charges the Sadducees with extreme severity in criminal matters; but this must refer to the fact that the ingenuity or punctiliousness of the Pharisees would afford to most offenders a loophole of escape. On the other hand, such of the diverging juridical principles of the Sadducees, as are attested on trustworthy authority, seem more in accordance with justice than those of the Pharisees. They concerned (besides the Levirate marriage) chiefly three points. According to the Sadducees, the punishment against false witnesses was only to be executed if the innocent person, condemned on their testimony, had actually suffered punishment, while the Pharisees held that this was to be done if the sentence had been actually pronounced, although not carried out. Again, according to Jewish law, only a son, but not a daughter, inherited the father's property. From this the Pharisees argued, that if, at the time of his father's decease, that son were dead, leaving only a daughter, this granddaughter would (as representative of the son) be the heir, while the daughter would be excluded. On the other hand, the Sadducees held that,

in such a case, daughter and granddaughter should share alike. Lastly, the Sadducees argued that if, according to Exodus 21:28, 29, a man was responsible for damage done by his cattle, he was equally, if not more, responsible for damage done by his slave, while the Pharisees refused to recognize any responsibility on the latter score.

For the sake of completeness it has been necessary to enter into details, which may not posses a general interest. This, however, will be marked, that, with the exception of dogmatic differences, the controversy turned on questions of "canon-law." Josephus tells us that the Pharisees commanded the masses, and especially the female world, while the Sadducees attached to their ranks only a minority, and that belonging to the highest class. The leading priests in Jerusalem formed, of course, part of that highest class of society; and from the New Testament and Josephus we learn that the High-Priestly families belonged to the Sadducean party. But to conclude from this, either that the Sadducees represented the civil and political aspect of society, and the Pharisees the religious; or, that the Sadducees were the priest-party, in opposition to the popular and democratic Pharisees, are inferences not only unsupported, but opposed to historical facts. For, not a few of the Pharisaic leaders were actually priests, while the Pharisaic ordinances make more than ample recognition of the privileges and rights of the Priesthood. This would certainly not have been the case if, as some have maintained, Sadducean and priest-party had been convertible terms. Even as regards the deputation to the Baptist of "Priests and Levites" from Jerusalem, we are expressly told that they "were of the Pharisees."

This bold hypothesis seems, indeed, to have been invented chiefly for the sake of another, still more unhistorical. The derivation of the name "Sadducee" has always been in dispite. According to a Jewish legend of about the seventh century of our era, the name was derived from one Tsadoq (Zadok), a disciple of Antigonus of Socho, whose principle of not serving God for reward had been gradually misinterpreted into Sadduceeism. But, apart from the objection that in such case the party should rather have taken the name of Antigonites, the story itself receives no support either from Josephus or from early Jewish writings. Accordingly modern critics have adopted another hypothesis, which seems at least equally untenable. On the supposition that the Sadducees were the "priest-party," the name of the sect is derived from Zadok (Tsadoq), the High-Priest in the time of Solomon. But the objections to this are insuperable. Not to speak of the linguistic difficulty of deriving Tsadduqim (Zaddukim, Sadducees) from Tsadoq (Zadok), neither Josephus nor the Rabbis know anything of such a connection between Tsadoq and the Sadducees, of which, indeed, the rationale would be difficult to perceive. Besides, is it likely that a party would have gone back so many centuries for a name, which had no connection with their distinctive principles? The name of a party is, if self-chosen (which is rarely the case), derived from its founder or place of origin, or else from what it claims as distinctive principles or practices. Opponents might either pervert such a name, or else give a designation, generally opprobrious, which would express their own relation to the party, or to some of its supposed peculiarities. But on none of these principles can the origin of the name of Sadducees from Tsadoq be accounted for. Lastly, on the supposition mentioned, the Sadducees must have given the name to their party, since it cannot be imagined that the Pharisees would have connected their opponents with the honored name of the High-Priest Tsadoq.

If it is highly improbable that the Sadducees, who, of course, professed to be the right interpreters of Scripture, would choose any party-name, thereby stamping themselves as sectaries, this derivation of their name is also contrary to historical analogy. For even the name Pharisees, "Perushim," "separated ones," was not taken by the party itself, but given to it by their opponents. From 1 Macc. 2:42; 7:13; 2 Macc. 14:6, it appears that originally they had taken the sacred name of Chasidim, or "the pious." This, no doubt, on the ground that they were truly those who, according to the directions of Ezra, had separated themselves (become nibhdalim) "from the filthiness of the heathen" (all heathen defilement) by carrying out the traditional ordinances. In fact, Ezra marked the beginning of the "later," in contradistinction to the "earlier," or Scripture-Chasidim. If we are correct in supposing that their opponents had called them Perushim, instead of the Scriptural designation of Nibhdalim, the inference is at hand, that, while the "Pharisees" would arrogate to themselves the Scriptural name of Chasidim, or "the pious," their opponents would retort that they were satisfied to be Tsaddiqim, or "righteous." Thus the name of Tsaddiqim would become that of the party opposing the Pharisees, that is, of the Sadducees. Such mode of giving a "by-name" to a party or government is, at least, not irrational, nor is it uncommon.

While the Pharisees and Sadducees were parties within the Synagogue, the Essenes were, although strict Jews, yet separatists, and, alike in doctrine, worship, and practice, outside the Jewish body ecclesiastic. Their numbers amounted to only about 4,000. They are not mentioned in the New Testament, and only very indirectly referred to in Rabbinic writings, perhaps without clear knowledge on the part of the Rabbis. If the conclusion concerning them, which we shall by-and-by indicate, be correct, we can scarcely wonder at this. Indeed, their entire separation from all who did not belong to their sect, the terrible oaths by which they bound themselves to secrecy about their doctrines, and which would prevent any free religious discussion, as well as the character of what is known of their views, would account for the scanty notices about them. Josephus and Philo, who speak of them in the most sympathetic manner, had, no doubt, taken special pains to ascertain all that could be learned. For this Josephus seems to have enjoyed special opportunities. Still, the secrecy of their doctrines renders us dependent on writers, of whom at least one (Josephus) lies open to the suspicion of coloring and exaggeration. But of one thing we may feel certain: neither John the Baptist, and his Baptism, nor the teaching of Christianity, had any connection with

Essenism. It were utterly unhistorical to infer such from a few points of contact—and these only of similarity, not identity—when the differences between them are so fundamental. That an Essene would have preached repentance and the Kingdom of God to multitudes, baptized the uninitiated, and given supreme testimony to One like Jesus, are assertions only less extravagant than this, that One Who mingled with society as Jesus did, and Whose teaching, alike in that respect, and in all its tendencies, was so utterly Non-, and even Anti-Essenic, had derived any part of His doctrine from Essenism. Besides, when we remember the views of the Essenes on purification, and on Sabbath observance, and their denial of the Resurrection, we feel that, whatever points of resemblance critical ingenuity may emphasise, the teaching of Christianity was in a direction opposite from that of Essenism.

We posses no data for the history of the origin and development (if such there was) of Essenism. We may admit a certain connection between Pharisaism and Essenism, though it has been greatly exaggerated by modern Jewish writers. Both directions originated from a desire after "purity," though there seems a fundamental difference between them, alike in the idea of what constituted purity, and in the means for attaining it. To the Pharisee it was Levitical and legal purity, secured by the hedge of ordinances which they drew around themselves. To the Essene it was absolute purity in separation from the "material," which in itself was defiling. The Pharisee attained in this manner the distinctive merit of a saint; the Essene obtained a higher fellowship with the Divine, "inward" purity, and not only freedom from the detracting, degrading influence of matter, but command over matter and nature. As the result of this higher fellowship with the Divine, the adept possessed the power of prediction; as the result of his freedom from, and command over matter, the power of miraculous cures. That their purifications, strictest Sabbath observance, and other practices, would form points of contact with Pharisaism, follows as a matter of course; and a little reflection will show, that such

observances would naturally be adopted by the Essenes, since they were within the lines of Judaism, although separatists from its body ecclesiastic. On the other hand, their fundamental tendency was quite other than that of Pharisaism, and strongly tinged with Eastern (Parsee) elements. After this the inquiry as to the precise date of its origin, and whether Essenism was an offshoot from the original (ancient) Assideans or Chasidim, seems needless. Certain it is that we find its first mention about 150 B.C., and that we meet the first Essence in the reign of Aristobulus I.

Before stating our conclusions as to its relation to Judaism and the meaning of the name, we shall put together what information may be derived of the sect from the writings of Josephus, Philo, and Pliny. Even its outward organization and the mode of life must have made as deep, and, considering the habits and circumstances of the time, even deeper impression than does the strictest asceticism on the part of any modern monastic order, without the unnatural and repulsive characteristics of the latter. There were no vows of absolute silence, broken only by weird chant of prayer or "memento mori;" no penances, nor self-chastisement. But the person who had entered the "order" was as effectually separated from all outside as if he had lived in another world. Avoiding the large cities as the centers of immorality, they chose for their settlements chiefly villages, one of their largest colonies being by the shore of the Dead Sea. At the same time they had also "houses" inmost, if not all the cities of Palestine, notably in Jerusalem, where, indeed, one of the gates was named after them. In these "houses" they lived in common, under officials of their own. The affairs of "the order" were administered by a tribunal of at least a hundred members, wore a common dress, engaged in common labor, united in common prayers, partook of common meals, and devoted themselves to works of charity, for which each had liberty to draw from the common treasury at his own discretion, except in the case of relatives. It scarcely needs mention that they extended fullest hospitality to strangers belonging to the order; in fact, a special official was appointed for this purpose in every city. Everything was of the simplest character, and intended to purify the soul by the greatest possible avoidance, not only of what was sinful, but of what was material. Rising at dawn, no profane word was spoken till they had offered their prayers. These were addressed towards, if not to, the rising sun—probably, as they would have explained it, as the emblem of the Divine Light, but implying invocation, if not adoration, of the sun. After that they were dismissed by their officers to common work. The morning meal was preceded by a lustration, or bath. Then they put on their "festive" linen garments, and entered, purified, the common hall as their Sanctuary. For each meal was sacrificial, in fact, the only sacrifices which they acknowledged. The "baker," who was really their priest—and naturally so, since he prepared the sacrifice—set before each bread, and the cook a mess of vegetables. The meal began with prayer by the presiding priest, for those who presided at these "sacrifices" were also "priests," although in neither case probably of Aaronic descent, but consecrated by themselves. The sacrificial meal was again concluded by prayer, when they put off their sacred dress, and returned to their labor. The evening meal was of exactly the same description, and partaken of with the same rites as that of the morning.

Although the Essenes, who, with the exception of a small party among them, repudiated marriage, adopted children to train them in the principles of their sect, yet admission to the order was only granted to adults, and after a novitiate which lasted three years. On entering, the novice received the three symbols of purity: an axe, or rather a spade, with which to dig a pit, a foot deep, to cover up the excrements; an apron, to bind round the loins in bathing; and a white dress, which was always worn, the festive garment at meals being of linen. At the end of the first year the novice was admitted to the lustrations. He had now entered on the second grade, in which he remained for another year. After its lapse, he was advanced to the third grade, but still continued a novice, until, at the close of the third year of his probation, he was admitted to the fourth grade—that of full member, when, for the first time, he was admitted to the sacrifice of the common meals. The mere touch of one of a lower grade in the order defiled the Essene, and necessitated the lustration of a bath. Before admission to full membership, a terrible oath was taken. As, among other things, it bound to the most absolute secrecy, we can scarcely suppose that its form, as given by Josephus, contains much beyond what was generally allowed to transpire. Thus the long list given by the Jewish historian of moral obligations which the Essenes undertook, is probably only a rhetorical enlargement of some simple formula. More credit attaches to the alleged undertaking of avoidance of all vanity, falsehood, dishonesty, and unlawful gains. The last parts of the oath alone indicate the peculiar vows of the sect, that is, so far as they could be learned by the outside world, probably chiefly through the practice of the Essenes. They bound each member not to conceal anything from his own sect, nor, even on peril of death, to disclose their doctrines to others; to hand down their doctrines exactly as they had received them; to abstain from robbery; and to guard the books belonging to their sect, and the names of the Angels.

It is evident that, while all else was intended as safeguards of a rigorous sect of purists, and with the view of strictly keeping it a secret order, the last-mentioned particulars furnish significant indications of their peculiar doctrines. Some of these may be regarded as only exaggerations of Judaism, though not of the Pharisaic kind. Among them we reckon the extravagant reverence for the name of their legislator (presumably Moses), whom to blaspheme was a capital offence; their rigid abstinence from all prohibited food; and their exaggerated Sabbath-observance, when, not only no food was prepared, but not a vessel moved, nay, not even nature eased. But this latter was connected with their fundamental idea of inherent impurity in the body, and, indeed, in all that is material. Hence, also, their asceticism, their repudiation of marriage, and their frequent lustrations in clean water, not only before their sacrificial meals, but upon contact even with an Essene of a lower grade, and after attending to the calls of nature. Their undoubted denial of the resurrection of the body seems only the logical sequence from it. If the soul was a substance of the subtlest ether, drawn by certain natural enticement into the body, which was its prison, a state of perfectness could not have consisted in the restoration of that which, being material, was in itself impure. And, indeed, what we have called the exaggerated Judaism of the sect—its rigid abstinence from all forbidden food, and peculiar Sabbath-observance—may all have had the same object, that of tending towards an external purism, which the Divine legislator would have introduced, but the "carnally-minded" could not receive. Hence, also, the strict separation of the order, its grades, its rigorous discipline, as well as its abstinence from wine, meat, and all ointments—from every luxury, even from trades which would encourage this, or any vice. This aim after external purity explains many of their outward arrangements, such as that their labor was of the simplest kind, and the commonality of all property in the order; perhaps, also, what may seem more ethical ordinances, such as the repudiation of slavery, their refusal to take an oath, and even their scrupulous care of truth. The white garments, which they always wore, seem to have been but a symbol of that purity which they sought. For this purpose they submitted, not only to strict asceticism, but to a discipline which gave the officials authority to expel all offenders, even though in so doing they virtually condemned them to death by starvation, since the most terrible oaths had bound all entrants into the order not to partake of any food other than that prepared by their "priests."

In such a system there would, of course, be no place for either an Aaronic priesthood, or bloody sacrifices. In fact, they repudiated both. Without formally rejecting the Temple and its services, there was no room in their system for such ordinances. They sent, indeed, thank offerings to the Temple, but what part had they in bloody sacrifices and an Aaronic ministry, which constituted the main business of the Temple? Their "priests" were their bakers and presidents; their sacrifices those of fellowship, their sacred meals of purity. It is

quite in accordance with this tendency when we learn from Philo that, in their diligent study of the Scriptures, they chiefly adopted the allegorical mode of interpretation.

We can scarcely wonder that such Jews as Josephus and Philo, and such heathens as Pliny, were attracted by such an unworldly and lofty sect. Here were about 4,000 men, who deliberately separated themselves, not only from all that made life pleasant, but from all around; who, after passing a long and strict novitiate, were content to live under the most rigid rule, obedient to their superiors; who gave up all their possessions, as well as the earnings of their daily toil in the fields, or of their simple trades; who held all things for the common benefit, entertained strangers, nursed their sick, and tended their aged as if their own parents, and were charitable to all men; who renounced all animal passions, eschewed anger, ate and drank in strictest moderation, accumulated neither wealth nor possessions, wore the simplest white dress till it was no longer fit for use; repudiated slavery, oaths, marriage; abstained from meat and wine, even from the common Eastern anointing with oil; used mystic lustrations, had mystic rites and mystic prayers, an esoteric literature and doctrines; whose every meal was a sacrifice, and every act one of self-denial; who, besides, were strictly truthful, honest, upright, virtuous, chaste, and charitable, in short, whose life meant, positively and negatively, a continual purification of the soul by mortification of the body. To the astonished onlookers this mode of life was rendered even more sacred by doctrines, a literature, and magic power known only to the initiated. Their mysterious conditions made them cognisant of the names of Angels, by which we are, no doubt, to understand a theosophic knowledge, fellowship with the Angelic world, and the power of employing its ministry. Their constant purifications, and the study of their prophetic writings, gave them the power of prediction; the same mystic writings revealed the secret remedies of plants and stones for the healing of the body, as well as what was needed for the cure of souls.

It deserves special notice that this intercourse with Angels, this secret traditional literature, and its teaching concerning mysterious remedies in plants and stones, are not infrequently referred to in that Apocalyptic literature known as the "Pseudepigraphic Writings." Confining ourselves to undoubtedly Jewish and pre-Christian documents, we know what development the doctrine of Angels received both in the Book of Enoch and in the Book of Jubilees, and how the "seers" received Angelic instruction and revelations. The distinctively Rabbinic teaching on these subjects is fully set forth in another part of this work. Here we would only specially notice that in the Book of Jubilees Angels are represented as teaching Noah all "herbal remedies" for diseases, while in the later Pirqé de R. Eliezer this instruction is said to have been given to Moses. These two points seem to connect the secret writings of the Essenes with that "outside" literature which in Rabbinic writings is known as Sepharim haChitsonim, "outside writings." The point is of greatest importance, as will presently appear.

It needs no demonstration, that a system which proceeded from a contempt of the body and of all that is material; in some manner identified the Divine manifestation with the Sun; denied the Resurrection, the Temple-priesthood, and sacrifices; preached abstinence from meats and from marriage; decreed such entire separation from all around that their very contact defiled, and that its adherents would have perished of hunger rather than join in the meals of the outside world; which, moreover, contained not a trace of Messianic elements—indeed, had no room for them—could have had no internal connection with the origin of Christianity. Equally certain is it that, in respect of doctrine, life, and worship, it really stood outside Judaism, as represented by either Pharisees or Sadducees. The question whence the foreign elements were derived, which were its distinctive characteristics, has of late been so learnedly discussed, that only the conclusions arrived at require to be stated. Of the two theories, of which the one traces Essenism to Neo-Pythagorean, the other to Persian sources, the latter seems fully established—without, however, wholly denying at least the possibility of Neo-

Pythagorean influences. To the grounds which have been so conclusively urged in support of the Eastern origin of Essenism, in its distinctive features, may be added this, that Jewish Angelology, which played so great a part in the system, was derived from Chaldee and Persian sources, and perhaps also the curious notion, that the knowledge of medicaments, originally derived by Noah from the angels, came to the Egyptians chiefly through the magic books of the Chaldees.

It is only at the conclusion of these investigations that we are prepared to enter on the question of the origin and meaning of the name Essenes, important as this inquiry is, not only in itself, but in regard to the relation of the sect to orthodox Judaism. The eighteen or nineteen proposed explanations of a term, which must undoubtedly be of Hebrew etymology, all proceed on the idea of its derivation from something which implied praise of the sect, the two least objectionable explaining the name as equivalent either to "the pious," or else to "the silent ones." But against all such derivations there is the obvious objection, that the Pharisees, who had the moulding of the theological language, and who were in the habit of giving the hardest names to those who differed from them, would certainly not have bestowed a title implying encomium on a sect which, in principle and practices, stood so entirely outside, not only of their own views, but even of the Synagogue itself. Again, if they had given a name of encomium to the sect, it is only reasonable to suppose that they would not have kept, in regard to their doctrines and practices, a silence which is only broken by dim and indirect allusions. Yet, as we examine it, the origin and meaning of the name seem implied in their very position towards the Synagogue. They were the only real sect, strictly outsiders, and their name Essenes seems the Greek equivalent for Chitsonim, "the outsiders." Even the circumstance that the axe, or rather spade, which every novice received, has for its Rabbinic equivalent the word Chatsina, is here not without significance.

This derivation of the name Essenes, which strictly expresses the character and standing of the sect relatively to orthodox Judaism, and, indeed, is the Greek form of the

Hebrew term foroutsiders,' is also otherwise confirmed. It has already been said, that no direct statement concerning the Essenes occurs in Rabbinic writings. Nor need this surprise us, when we remember the general reluctance of the Rabbis to refer to their opponents, except in actual controversy; and, that, when traditionalism was reduced to writing, Essenism, as a Jewish sect, had ceased to exist. Some of its elements had passed into the Synagogue, influencing its general teaching, and greatly contributing to that mystic direction which afterwards found expression in what is now known as the Kabbalah. But the general movement had passed beyond the bounds of Judaism, and appeared in some forms of the Gnostic heresy. But still there are Rabbinic references to the Chitsonim, which seem to identify them with the sect of the Essenes. Thus, in one passage certain practices of the Sadducees and of the Chitsonim are mentioned together, and it is difficult to see who could be meant by the latter if not the Essenes. Besides, the practices there referred to seem to contain covert allusions to those of the Essenes. Thus, the Mishnah begins by prohibiting the public reading of the Law by those who would not appear in a colored, but only in a white dress. Again, the curious statement is made that the manner of the Chitsonim was to cover the phylacteries with gold—a statement unexplained in the Gemara, and inexplicable,

unless we see in it an allusion to the Essene practice of facing the rising Sun in their morning prayers.

On one point, at least, our inquiry into the three "parties" can leave no doubt. The Essenes could never have been drawn either to the person, or the preaching of John the Baptist. Similarly, the Sadducees would, after they knew its real character and goal, turn contemptuously from a movement which would awaken no sympathy in them, and could only become of interest when it threatened to endanger their class by awakening popular enthusiasm, and so rousing the suspicions of the Romans. To the Pharisees there were questions of dogmatic, ritual, and even national importance involved, which made the barest possibility of what John announced a question of supreme moment. And, although we judge that the report which the earliest Pharisaic hearers of John brought to Jerusalem—no doubt, detailed and accurate—and which led to the despatch of the deputation, would entirely predispose them against the Baptist, yet it behooved them, as leaders of public opinion, to take such cognisance of it, as would not only finally determine their own relation to the movement, but enable them effectually to direct that of others also.

Alfred Edersheim, Life and Times of Jesus the Messiah, *1886*

10

JESUS' TRANSFIGURATION

2.43 CHRIST'S TRANSFIGURATION, GEORGE WHITEFIELD

George Whitefield was a minister in the Church of England and one of the leaders of the Methodist movement. He was born on December 16, 1714 at the Bell Inn, Gloucester, and died in Newburyport, Connecticut on September 30, 1770. In contemporary accounts, he, not John Wesley, is sometimes spoken of as the supreme figure in Methodism. He was famous for his preaching in America where his sermons played a significant part in the Great Awakening movement of Christian revival.

"And it came to pass about an eight days after these sayings, he took Peter and John and James, and went up into a mountain to pray. And as he prayed, the fashion of his countenance was altered, and his raiment white [and] glistering. And, behold, there talked with him two men, which were Moses and Elias: Who appeared in glory, and spake of his decease which he should accomplish at Jerusalem. But Peter and they that were with him were heavy with sleep: and when they were awake, they saw his glory, and the two men that stood with him. And it came to pass, as they departed from him, Peter said unto Jesus, Master, it is good for us to be here: and let us make three tabernacles; one for thee, and one for Moses, and one for Elias: not knowing what he said. While he thus spake, there came a cloud, and overshadowed them: and they feared as they entered into the cloud. And there came a voice out of the cloud, saying, This is my beloved Son: hear him. And when the voice was past, Jesus was found alone. And they kept [it] close, and told no man in those days any of those things which they had seen." Luke 9:28-36

When the angel was sent to the Redeemer's beloved disciple John, we are told that the angel said unto him, "Come up hither." He was to be exalted, to be brought nearer heaven, that his mind might be better prepared for those great manifestations, which an infinitely great and condescending God intended to vouchsafe him. And on reading the verse that you have just now heard, when I also see such a great and serious assembly convened in the presence of God, I think I must address you, as the angel addressed John, and say unto you, "Come up hither"; leave your worldly thoughts, for a time forget the earth. And as it is the Lord's day, a time in which we ought more particularly to think of heaven, I must desire

you to pray to God, that ye may get up on Pisgah's mount, and take a view of the promised land. It is true, indeed, eye hath not seen, ear hath not heard, nor hath it entered into the heart of any man to conceive the great and good things, which God hath prepared for his people here; much less, those infinitely greater and more glorious things, that he hath laid up for them that fear him, in the eternal world: but, blessed be God! Though we are not yet in heaven, unless to be in Christ may properly be termed heaven, and then all real Christians are there already; yet, but blessed Jesus has been pleased to leave upon record some account of himself, of what happened to him in the days of his flesh, and of some manifestations he was pleased to grant to a few of his disciples; that from what happened to them here below, we may form some faint, though but a faint idea of that happiness that awaits his people in his kingdom above. If any of you inquire, in what part of our Lord's life those instances are recorded, I have an answer ready: One of these instances, and that a very remarkable one, is recorded in the verses that I have now chosen for the subject of your meditation.

The verses give us an account of what is generally called our Lord's Transfiguration; his being wonderfully changed, and his being wonderfully owned by his Father upon the mount. Some think that this was done upon a Sabbath-day; and the particular occasion of our blessed Lord's condescending to let his servants have such a sight as this, we may gather from the 27th verse. It seems our blessed Lord had been promising a great reward to those who should not be ashamed of him: "Whosoever shall be ashamed of me and of my words, of him shall the Son of Man be ashamed, when he shall come in his own glory, and of his Father, and of the holy angels." In this threatening is implied, a reward to those who should not be ashamed of him: "But, (adds he) I tell you of a truth, there be some standing here, who shall not taste of death, till they see the kingdom of God." As much as to say, There will be a day, when I will come in the glory of my Father and of his holy angels; but I tell you there are some of my favorites; I tell you of a truth, though you may think it too good news, there are some of you that shall not taste of death, till ye shall see the kingdom of God. Some divines think, that this promise has reference to our Lord's creating a gospel church; and if we take it in this sense, it means that the Apostles, who were then present, some of them at least, should not die, till they saw Satan's kingdom in a great measure pulled down, and the Redeemer's gospel kingdom erected. Some think it has a peculiar reference to John, who it seems survived all the other Apostles, and lived till Christ came; that is, till he came to destroy Jerusalem. But it is the opinion of Mr. Henry, of Bishop Hall, of Burkit, and others, who have written upon this passage, that our blessed Lord has a peculiar reference to the transfiguration upon the mount: "There be some of you here, that shall not taste of death, till ye see my transfiguration upon the mount; till ye see some glorified saint come down from heaven and pay me a visit, and consequently see a little of that kingdom of God, which ye shall have a full sight of when ye come to glory." This seems to be the right interpretation. If you will look to the margin of your Bibles, you will see the parallel place in Matthew, where the account of our Lord's transfiguration is given, and there you will find it immediately follows upon this promise of our Lord.

Well, as Christ had told them, that they should not taste of death, till they had seen the kingdom of God, why the Evangelist, at the 28th verse, tells us, "It came to pass about an eight days after these sayings, he took Peter, and John, and James, and went up into a mountain to pray." About an eight days; that is, as Bishop Hall thinks, upon the Sabbath-day; or, according to some, the first day of the week, which was hereafter to be the Christian Sabbath; our blessed Lord takes Peter, John, and James: Why did not the Lord Jesus Christ take more of his disciples? Why three, and these three? And why three only? Our blessed Lord was pleased to take three and no more, to show us that he is a sovereign agent; to show us, that though he loved all his disciples, yet there are some to whom he is pleased to allow peculiar visits. He loved Peter, and all the other disciples; yet John was the disciple that he peculiarly loved. And he took three rather than one, because three were sufficient to testify the truth of his being transfigured: "Out of the mouth of two or three witnesses every word shall be established." And he took no more than three, because these three were enough. And he took these three, Peter, John, and James, in particular, because these very persons that were not to see Christ transfigured, were hereafter to see him agonizing in the garden, sweating great drops of blood falling unto the ground. And had not these three disciples seen Christ upon the mount, the seeing him afterwards in the garden, might have staggered them exceedingly: they might have doubted whether it was possible for the Son of God to be in such doleful circumstances. Well, our Lord takes these three "up into a mountain." Why so? Because Christ Jesus was to be like Moses, who was taken up into a mountain, when God intended to deliver unto him the moral law: And our blessed Lord went up into a mountain, because a mountain befriended devotion. When he had a mind to retire to pray to his Father, he went to such places where he could be most secret, and give the greatest vent to his heart. Thus we are told, that once when Peter prayed, it was upon the house-top. And if we have a mind to be near God, we should choose such places as are freest from ostentation, and that most befriend our communion with God. And what doth Christ, when he got up into a mountain? We are told, he went up into a mountain "to pray." Christ had no corruption to confess, and he had but few wants of his own to be relieved; yet we hear of Christ being much in prayer; we hear of his going up to a mountain to pray; of his rising up a great while before it was day to pray; and of his spending a whole night in prayer to God.

In the 20th verse, you have an account of the effect of our Lord's praying: "As he prayed, the fashion of his countenance was altered, and his raiment was white and glittering." I would have you take notice, that our Lord was not changed in respect of his body, while he was going up to the mount, but when he got upon the mount, and while engaged in prayer. It is sufficient that way for our souls to be transformed: the time we are more particularly to expect the influences of God's Spirit, is, when we are engaged in prayer. There seems to be a very great propriety in our Lord's being transfigured or changed upon the mount. I hope I need inform none of you, that when Moses went up to the mount of God, God was pleased to speak to him face to face; and when he came down from the mount, the people of Israel observed that Moses' face shone so, that he was obliged to have a veil put upon his face. Now the shining of Moses' face, was a proof to the people, that Moses had been conversing with God. And Moses told the people, "That the Lord would raise up unto them a prophet like unto him,

whom the people were to hear." God the Father, in order to give his Son (considering him as man) a testimony that he was a prophet, was pleased not only to let his face glitter or shine; but to show that he was a prophet far superior to Moses, he was pleased to let his garment be white and glittering, and "his countenance(as we are told by another Evangelist) did shine as the sun." What change was here! What a sight! Methinks I see Peter, James, and John surprised; and, indeed, well might the Evangelist, considering what happened, usher in the following part of the story with the word Behold; "Behold, there talked with him two men, Moses and Elias:" And in the 31st verse, you have an account of their dress, "They appeared in glory"; and of their discourse, "They spake of his decease which he should accomplish at Jerusalem."

"Behold, two men, which were Moses and Elias"; these were two very proper persons to come upon this embassy to the Son of God. Moses was the great lawgiver, Elias was the great restorer of the law: The body of Moses was hidden and never found, Elias' body was translated immediately, and carried up in a fiery chariot to heaven: And it may be that this was done particularly, because these two were hereafter to have the honor of waiting upon the Son of God. "They appeared in glory"; that is, their bodies were not in that glorious habit, in which the bodies of believers are to be at the morning of the resurrection. Christ was, as it were, now fitting in his royal robes; and as it is usual for ambassadors, when they are to be admitted into the king's presence, on bringing a message from one king to another, to appear in all their grandeur, to make the message more solemn; so here, these heavenly messengers being to wait upon the Lord Jesus Christ, are invested as with royal dignity, they appeared in glory, and "they spake of his decease which he should accomplish at Jerusalem," they came to tell the Redeemer of his sufferings, and of the place of his sufferings, and to acquaint him, that his sufferings, however great, however bitter, were to be accomplished; that there was o be an end put to them, as our Lord himself speaks, "The things concerning me are to have an end." What other particulars they spoke to our Lord, we are not told. But what effect this had upon the disciples, you may learn from the 32nd verse, "Peter, and they that were with him, were heavy with sleep."

We are not to suppose, that Peter, James and John, were now asleep in a literal sense; no, if we compare this, with another passage of holy writ, I mean the account given us of Daniel's being impressed and overcome, when he saw the angel of the Lord, you will find that this sleep implies what we call a swoon. They were overcome with the sight of the glory of Christ's garments, the glittering of his body, and the glory in Moses and Elias appeared: these quite overcame them, sunk them down, and, like the Queen of Sheba, when she saw Solomon's glory, they had no life in them. But they recovered themselves: "when they were awake," that is, when they had recovered their strength, when God had put strength into them, as the angel put strength into Daniel, "they saw his glory, and the two men that stood with him." And how do you think they gazed upon Christ? How may we suppose they fixed their eyes upon Moses and Elias? Peter, who was always the first speaker, out of the abundance of his heart, spoke upon this occasion. Verse 33, "And it came to pass as they departed from him, Peter said unto Jesus, Master, it is good for us to be here; and let us make three tabernacles, one for thee, and one for Moses, and one for Elias, not knowing what he said." Peter, when he had drank a little of Christ's new wine, speaks like a person intoxicated; he was overpowered with the brightness of the manifestation. "Let us make three tabernacles, one for thee, and one for Moses, and one for Elias." It is well added, "not knowing what he said." That he should cry out, "Master, it is good for us to be here," in such good company, and in so glorious a condition, is no wonder; which of us all would not have been apt to have done the same? But to talk of building tabernacles, and one for Christ, and one for Moses, and one for Elias, was saying something for which Peter himself must stand reproved. Surely, Peter, thou wast not quite awake! Thou talkest like one I a dream: If thy Lord had taken thee at thy word, what a poor

tabernacle wouldst thou have had, in comparison of that house not made with hands, eternal in the heavens, in which thou hast long since dwelt, now the earthly house of the tabernacle of thy body is dissolved? What! Build tabernacles below, and have the crown, before thou hast borne the cross? O Peter, Peter! "Master, spare thyself," sticks too too closely to thee: And why so selfish, Peter? Carest thou not for thy fellow disciples that are below, who came not up with thee to the mount? Carest thou not for the precious souls, that are as sheep having no shepherd, and must perish for ever, unless thy Master descends from the mount to teach, and to die for them? Wouldst thou thus eat thy spiritual morsels alone? Besides, if thou art for building tabernacles, why must there be three of them, one for Christ, and one for Moses, and one for Elias? Are Christ and the prophets divided? Do they not sweetly harmonize and agree in one? Did they not prophesy concerning the sufferings of thy Lord, as well as of the glory that should follow? Alas, how unlike is their conversation to thine? Moses and Elias came down to talk of suffering, and thou are dreaming of building I know not what tabernacles. Surely, Peter, thou art so high upon the mount, that thy head runs giddy.

However, in the midst of these infirmities, there was something that bespoke the honesty and integrity of his heart. Though he knew not very well what he said, yet he was not so stupid as his pretended successor at Rome. He does not fall down and worship these two departed saints, neither do I hear him say to either, *Ora prosobis*; he had not so learnt Christ; no, he applies himself directly to the head, he said unto Jesus, "Master, it is good for us to be here." And though he was for building, yet he would not build without his Master's leave. "Master, let us build," or, as Mark words it, "wilt thou that we build three tabernacles, one for thee, and one for Moses, and one for Elias?" I do not hear him add, and one for James, and one for John, and one for Peter. No, he would willingly stay out with them upon the mount, though it was in the cold and dark night, so that Christ and his heavenly attendants were taken care of. The sweetness of such a heavenly vision, would more than compensate for any bodily suffering that might be the consequence of their longer abode there: nay farther, he does not desire that either Christ, or Moses, or Elias, should have any trouble in building; neither does he say, let my curates, James and John, build, whilst I sit idle and lord it over my brethren; but he says, "let us build"; he will work as hard, if not harder than either of them, and desire to be distinguished only by his activity, enduring hardness, and his zeal to promote the welfare of their common Lord and Master.

Doubtless, Peter had read how the glory of the Lord filled the tabernacle, and the temple of old; and now Jesus is transfigured, and Moses and Elias appear in glory, he thinks it right that new tabernacles shall be erected for them. Such a mixture of nature and grace, of short-sightedness and infirmity, is there in the most ardent and well-meant zeal of the very best of men, when nearest the throne of grace, or even upon the mount with God. Perfection in any grace must be looked for, or expected, only among the spirits of just men made perfect in heaven. Those who talk of any such thing on earth, like Peter, they know not what they say.

But how came Peter so readily to distinguish which was Moses, and which was Elias? He seems to speak without the least hesitation, "Let us build three tabernacles, one for thee, and one for Moses, and one for Elias," as though he was very well acquainted with them, whereas they had both been dead, long, long before Peter was born. Was there, do you imagine, any thing distinguishing in their apparel? Or any thing in their conversation that discovered them? Or rather, did he not know them here on the mount, as we may from hence infer, that departed saints do, and will know each other in heaven, even by intuition and immediate revelation? But alas! how transient are our views of heaven, during our sojourning here on earth: Verse 34, "Whilst he thus spake," whilst Peter was talking of building tabernacles, whilst he was saying, "it is good for us to be here," whilst he was dreaming that his mountain was s strong that it never could be moved, "there came a cloud and overshadowed them." Matthew observes, it was a bright cloud,

not dark like that on mount Sinai, but bright, because the gospel opens to us a far more bright dispensation than that of the law. This overshadowed, and thereby not only filled them with an holy awe, but also screened them, in some measure, from the brightness of that glory with which they were now surrounded, and which otherwise would have been insupportable. This cloud was like the veil thrown on the face of Moses, and prepared them for the voice which they were soon to hear coming out of it. I am not much surprised at being informed by Matthew, that they feared as they entered into the cloud, or by Mark that "they were sore afraid." For since the fall, there is such a consciousness in us all of deserved wrath, that we cannot help fearing when we enter into a cloud, even though Jesus Christ himself be in the midst of it. Ah Peter, where is thy talk of building tabernacles now? Is thy strong mountain so quickly removed? What, come down so soon? why do we not now hear thee saying, "It is good for us to be here?" Alas! he and his fellow disciples are quite struck dumb; see how they tremble, and, like Moses upon another occasion, exceedingly quake and fear. But how quickly are those fears dispelled, how soon is the tumult of their minds hushed and calmed, with that soul-reviving voice that came from the excellent glory, verse 35, "This is my beloved Son, hear him."

Mark and Matthew add "in whom I am well pleased." The same testimony that God the Father gave to the blessed Jesus at his baptism, before he entered upon his temptation, is now repeated, in order to strengthen and prepare him for his impending agony in the garden. Probably, it was a small still though articulate voice, attended neither with thunder nor lightning, nor the sound of a trumpet, but, agreeable to the blessed news which it contained, ushered in with tokens of unspeakable complacency and love. God the Father, hereby gives Moses and Elias a solemn discharge, as though they were sent from heaven on purpose to give up their commission to their rightful Lord, and like the morning star, disappear when the Sun of Righteousness himself arises to bring in a gospel day. "This is my beloved Son, hear Him." But the emphasis upon the word

THIS; this Son of Man, this Jesus, whom you are shortly to see in a bloody sweat, blindfolded, spit upon, buffeted, scourged, and at length hanging upon a tree, I am not ashamed to own to be my Son, my only begotten Son, who was with me before the heavens were made, or the foundations of the earth were laid; my beloved Son, in whom I am well pleased, in whom my soul delighteth, and whom I do by these presents, publicly constitute and appoint to be the king, priest, and prophet of the church. "Hear ye Him." No longer look to Moses or Elias, no longer expect to be saved by the works of the law; but by the preaching and application of the ever-blessed gospel. Hear ye him, so as to believe on, love, serve, obey, and, if needs be, to die and lay down your very lives for him. "Hear him"; hear what he hath to say, for he comes with a commission from above. Hear his doctrine; hear him, so as to obey him; hear him, so as to put in practice his precepts, and copy after his good example.

In the 36th verse, we have the close of his heavenly feast; "When the voice was past, Jesus was found alone; and they kept it close, and told no man in those days, any of those things which they had seen." If we compare this, with the account which the other Evangelists give of our blessed Lord's transfiguration, you will find this was done by Christ's order: Peter, James, and John, would otherwise have gone down and told the whole world, that they had seen the Lord Christ upon the mount of transfiguration; but our Lord ordered them to keep it silent. Why so? If they had gone down from the mount, and told it to the other disciples, it might have raised ill blood in the others; they might have said, Why did our Master single our Peter, James, and John? Why might not we have had the privilege of going up to the mount as well as they? Had they said, that their Lord was transfigured, people would not have believed them; they would have thought, that Peter, James, and John were only enthusiasts; but if they kept it till after his resurrection, and he had broken the gates of death, for them then to say, that they saw him upon the mount transfigured, would corroborate the evidence.

I have thus paraphrased the words for your better understanding the account the Evangelist gives of our blessed Lord's transfiguration; but I have not yet done; I have been speaking to your heads; the practical part is yet to come. O that God may reach your hearts! And though, according to order, I ought to begin with the practical inferences that might be drawn from the first part; yet, I think it best to show you, who are the people of God, especially you young converts, that have honesty, but not much prudence, what instructions our Lord would here have you to learn.

"When the voice was past, Jesus was found alone, and they kept it close, and told no man in those days any of those things which they had seen." There is nothing more common, when God vouchsafes communications to a poor soul, than for the person that enjoys them, to go and tell all that he has seen and felt, and often at improper seasons and to improper persons. I remember that Mr. Henry observes, "Joseph had more honesty than he had policy, or else he would never have told his brethren of his dreams." Young Christians are too apt to blunder thus: I am sure it is a fault of which I have been exceedingly guilty, speaking of things, which, perhaps, had better been concealed; which is a fault God's people are too apt to fall into. Though it is good for those that have seen Christ, and that have felt his love, to tell others what God hath done for their souls; yet, however you may think of it now, when you come down from the mount, and know yourselves a little, ye will find reason often to hold your tongue. Young Christians are like children, to whom if you give a little money in their pocket, they cannot be quiet till they have spent it upon something or other: young Christians, when they get a little of God, are ready to talk too much of it. They should therefore beware, and know when to speak, and when to be silent.

But, my dear friends, did our Lord Jesus Christ take Peter, James, and John into a mountain to pray? Are any of you fathers, mothers, masters and mistresses of families? Learn then from hence to take your children, your servants, and those that belong to you, from the world, at certain times, and not only pray for them, but pray with them. If Christ did thus, who had few wants of his own to be supplied, and nothing to confess and lament over; if Christ was such a lover of prayer, surely, you and I, who have so many wants to be supplied, so many corruptions to mourn over; you and I should spend much time in prayer. I do not say that you are to lock yourselves up in your closets, and not mind your shops or farms, or worldly business; I only say, that you should take care to husband all your time: and if you are God's children, you will frequently retire from the world, and seek a visit from your God.

Was the Lord Jesus transformed or transfigured, while he was praying? Learn hence, to be much in spiritual prayer. The way to have the soul transformed, changed into, and make like unto God, is frequently to converse with God. We say, a man is as his company. Persons by conversing together, frequently catch each others tempers: and if you have a mind to imbibe the divine temper, pray much. And as Christ's garments became white and glittering, so shall your souls get a little of God's light to shine upon them.

Did Moses and Elias appear in glory? Are there any old saints here? I doubt not but there are a considerable number. And are any of you afraid of death? Do any of you carry about with you a body that weighs down your immortal soul? I am sure a poor creature is preaching to you, that every day drags a crazy load along. But come, believers, come, ye children of God, come, ye aged decrepit saints, come and trample upon that monster death. As thou goest over yonder church-yard, do as I know an old excellent Christian in Maryland did; go, sit upon the grave, and meditate on thine own dissolution. Thou mayest, perhaps, have a natural fear of dying: the body and the soul do not care to part without a little sympathy and a groan; but O look yonder, loon up to heaven, see there thy Jesus, thy Redeemer, and learn, that thy body is to be fashioned here-after like unto Christ's most glorious body; that poor body which is not subject to gout and gravel, and that thou canst scarce drag along; that poor body, which hinders thee so much in the spiritual life, will

ere long hinder thee no more; it shall be put into the grave; but though it be sown in corruption, it shall be raised in incorruption; though it is sown in dishonor, it shall be raised again in glory. This consideration made blessed Paul to cry out, "O death, where is thy sting! O grave, where is thy victory!" Thy soul and body shall be united together again, and thou shalt be "forever with the Lord." Those knees of thine, which perhaps are hard by kneeling in prayer; that tongue of thine, which hath sung hymns to Christ; those hands of thine, which have wrought for God; those feet, which have ran to Christ's ordinances; shall all, in the twinkling of an eye, be changed; and thou shalt be able to stand under an exceeding and an eternal weight of glory. Come then, ye believers in Christ, look beyond the grave; come, ye dear children of God, and however weak and sickly ye are now, say, Blessed be God, I shall soon have a body strong, full of vigor and of glory.

But as this speaks comfort to saints, it speaks terror to sinners, to all persons that live and die out of Christ. It is the opinion of Archbishop Usher, that as the bodies of the saints shall be glorified, so the bodies of the damned shall be deformed. And if this be true, alas! what a poor figure will the fine ladies cut, who die without a Christ! What a poor figure will the fine gentleman cut in the morning of the resurrection, that now dresses up his body, and at the same time neglects to secure an interest in Christ and eternal happiness! It is the opinion, likewise of Archbishop Usher, that damned souls will lose all the good tempers they had here; so that though God gave unregenerate people a constitutional meekness, good nature, and courage, for the benefit of the common-wealth; yet, the use of those blessings being over, and they having died without Christ, and it being impossible there will be an appearance of good in hell, their good tempers will be forever lost. If this be so, it is an awful consideration; and I think persons who love their bodies, should also hence take care to secure the welfare of their souls.

Did Peter know which was Moses and which Elias? Then I think, and God be praised for it, it is plain from this and other passages of scripture, that we shall know one another when we come to heaven. Dives knew Lazarus: "Father Abraham, send Lazarus:" And we are told, "he saw Lazarus sitting in Abraham's bosom." Adam knew his wife Eve; though cast into a deep sleep when God made her out of his rib, yes, by a kind of intuition he says, "This is bone of my bone, and flesh of my flesh." And it is on this account, that the Apostle, speaking to the Philippians, says, "Ye are my joy and crown of rejoicing, in the day of the Lord." What comfort will this be to a spiritual father! Says one, Here is the man, O Lord Jesus, that brought my soul to taste of thy love; says another, This is the man, that at such a time, and with such words, struck my heart: thou, O Lord knowest it. Then the spiritual father will rejoice over his children. You that have met and have prayed together, sighted and sympathized together, and told your temptations to one another, shall be forever with the Lord and with each other. There we shall see Abraham, Isaac, and Jacob sitting, with all the redeemed company; and we shall know the names of every one mentioned in the book of God. O blessed prospect! O blessed time! Who that thinks of this, of seeing the Lamb sitting upon the throne, with all God's people about him, but must desire to go to heaven, and be forever, forever with the Lord. And if there is such comfort for believers to know one another in heaven, with what comfort may any of you, that have lost fathers, mothers, or friends, think of them: we are parted for a little while, but we shall see them again. My father died in Christ, my mother died in the Lord, my husband, my wife, was a follower of Jesus; I shall see them, though not now; I shall go to them, but they shall not return to me! This may keep you from sorrowing as persons without hope; and keep you from being so cruel, as to wish them to come down to this evil world.

But O what a dreadful consideration is this for damned souls! I believe, that as glorified spirits will know one another, so will damned souls know one another too. And as the company of the blessed increases the happiness of heaven, so the company of the damned will increase their torments. What made Dives to put up that petition? "I have five brethren; send somebody to my father's house to testify unto them, lest they also come into this place of torment." One would imagine at first reading, that hell had made Dives charitable, and that though he was ill natured on earth, yet he had acquired some good nature in hell. No, no, there is not a spark of good nature in the place of torment. But Dives knew, if his five brethren came there, they might say, We may thank you, next to an evil heart, for coming hither; you made us drink healths, till we were drunk; you taught us to game, to curse, to swear, &c. He knew very well, that his five brethren being brought to hell by his example, hell would be heated five times hotter to torment his soul. One will cry out, Cursed be the day that ever I was companions with such an one in sin; cursed be the day that ever we hearkened to one another's advice, and were allured by each others example to sin against God!

But did a cloud overshadow Peter, James, and John? Were heavenly and divine visits here but short? Then wonder not, ye people of God, if ye are upon the mount one hour, and down in the valley of the shadow of death the next. There is nothing in the world more common, after you have been in a good frame, than for a cloud to overshadow you. We generally say, "It is good to be here," and often make a Christ of our graces; and therefore the Lord sends a cloud to overshadow us. But never fear; God shall speak to you out of the cloud; God will reveal himself to you; this cloud shall soon be gone; ere long we shall be in heaven, and in that glory where no cloud can possibly reach us.

I can now only mention one thing more, and that is, Did the Father say, "This is my beloved Son, hear him?" then let every one of our hearts echo to this testimony give of Christ, "This is my beloved Savior." Did God so love the world, as to send his only begotten Son, his well beloved Son to preach to us? Then, my dear friends, HEAR HIM. What God said seventeen hundred years ago, immediately by a voice from heaven, concerning his Son upon the mount, that same thing God says to you immediately by his word, "Hear him." If ye never heard him before, hear him now. Hear him so as to take him to be your prophet, priest, and your king; hear him, so as to take him to be your God and your all. Hear him today, ye youth, while it is called today; hear him now, lest God should cut you off before you have another invitation to hear him; hear him while he cries, "Come unto me"; hear him while he opens his hand and his heart; hear him while he knocks at the door of your souls, lest you should hear him saying, "Depart, depart, ye cursed, into everlasting fire, prepared for the devil and his angels." Hear him, ye old and gray-headed, hear him, ye that have one foot in the grave; hear him, I say; and if ye are dull of hearing, beg of God to open the ears of your hearts, and your blind eyes; beg of God that you may have an enlarged and a believing heart, and that ye may know what the Lord God saith concerning you. God will resent it, he will avenge himself on his adversaries, if you do not hear a blessed Savior. He is God's son, he is God's beloved son; he came upon a great errand, even to shed his precious blood for sinners; he came to cleanse you from all sin, and to save you with an everlasting salvation. Ye who have heard him, hear him again; still go on, believe in and obey him, and by-and-by you shall hear him saying, "Come, ye blessed of my Father, receive the kingdom prepared for you from the foundation of the world." May God grant it to you all, for the Lord Jesus Christ's sake. Amen, and Amen.

George Whitefield

2.44 TRANSFIGURATION, A. B. BRUCE

Matt. 17:1-13; Mark 9:2-13; Luke 9:28-36

The transfiguration is one of those passages in the Savior's earthly history which an expositor would rather pass over in reverent silence. For such silence the same apology might be pleaded which is so kindly made in the Gospel narrative for Peter's foolish speech concerning the three tabernacles: "He wist not what to say." Who does know what to say any more than he? Who is able fully to speak of that wondrous night-scene among the mountains, during which heaven was for a few brief moments let down to earth, and the mortal body of Jesus being transfigured shone with celestial brightness, and the spirits of just men made perfect appeared and held converse with Him respecting His approaching passion, and a voice came forth from the excellent glory, pronouncing Him to be God's well-beloved Son? It is too high for us, this august spectacle, we cannot attain unto it; its grandeur oppresses and stupefies; its mystery surpasses our comprehension; its glory is ineffable. Therefore, avoiding all speculation, curious questioning, theological disquisition, and ambitious word-picturing in connection with the remarkable occurrence here recorded, we confine ourselves in this chapter to the humble task of explaining briefly its significance for Jesus Himself, and its lesson for His disciples.

The "transfiguration," to be understood, must be viewed in connection with the announcement made by Jesus shortly before it happened, concerning His death. This it evident from the simple fact, that the three evangelists who relate the event so carefully note the time of its occurrence with reference to that announcement, and the conversation which accompanied it. All tell how, within six or eight days thereafter, Jesus took three of His disciples, Peter, James, and John, and brought them into an high mountain apart, and was transfigured before them. The Gospel historians are not wont to be so careful in their indications of time, and their minute accuracy here signifies in effect: "While the foregoing communications and discourses concerning the cross were fresh in the thoughts of all the parties, the wondrous events we are now to relate took place." The relative date, in fact, is a finger post pointing back to the conversation on the passion, and saying: "If you desire to understand what follows, remember what went before."

This inference from the note of time given by all the evangelists is fully borne out by a statement made by Luke alone, respecting the subject of the conversation on the holy mount between Jesus and His celestial visitants. "And," we read, "behold, there talked with Him two men, which were Moses and Elias; who appeared in glory, and spake of His decease (or exodus) which He should accomplish at Jerusalem." That exit, so different from their own in its circumstances and consequences, was the theme of their taLuke They had appeared to Jesus to converse with Him thereon; and when they ceased speaking concerning it, they took their departure for the abodes of the blessed. How long the conference lasted we know not, but the subject was sufficiently suggestive of interesting topics of conversation. There was, e.g, the surprising contrast between the death of Moses, immediate and painless, while his eye was not dim nor his natural force abated, and the painful and ignominious death to be endured by Jesus. Then there was the not less remarkable contrast between the manner of Elijah's departure from the earth—translated to heaven without tasting death at all, making a triumphant exit out of the world in a chariot of fire, and the way by which Jesus should enter into glory—the via dolorosa of the cross. Whence this privilege of exemption from death, or from its bitterness, granted to the representatives of the law and the prophets, and wherefore denied to Him who was the end both of law and of prophecy? On these points, and others of kindred nature, the two celestial messengers, enlightened by the clear light of heaven, may have held intelligent and sympathetic converse with the Son of man, to the refreshment of His weary, saddened, solitary soul.

The same evangelist who specifies the subject of conversation on the holy mount further records that, previous to His transfiguration, Jesus had been engaged in prayer. We may therefore see, in the honor and glory conferred on Him there, the Father's answer to His Son's supplications; and from the nature of the answer we may infer the subject of prayer. It was the same as afterwards in the garden of Gethsemane. The cup of death was present to the mind of Jesus now, as then; the cross was visible to His spiritual eye; and He prayed for nerve to drink, for courage to endure. The attendance of the three confidential disciples, Peter, James, and John, significantly hints at the similarity of the two occasions. The Master took these disciples with Him into the mount, as He afterwards took them into the garden, that He might not be altogether destitute of company and kindly sympathy as He walked through the valley of the shadow of death, and felt the horror and the loneliness of the situation.

It is now clear how we must view the transfiguration scene in relation to Jesus. It was an aid to faith and patience, specially vouchsafed to the meek and lowly Son of man, in answer to His prayers, to cheer Him on His sorrowful path towards Jerusalem and Calvary. Three distinct aids to His faith were supplied in the experiences of that wondrous night. The first was a foretaste of the glory with which He should be rewarded after His passion, for His voluntary humiliation and obedience unto death. For the moment He was, as it were, rapt up into heaven, where He had been before He came into the world; for His face shone like the sun, and His raiment was white as the pure untrodden snow on the high alpine summits of Herman. "Be of good cheer," said that sudden flood of celestial light: "the suffering will soon be past, and Thou shalt enter into Thine eternal joy!"

A second source of comfort to Jesus in the experiences on the mount, was the assurance that the mystery of the cross was understood and appreciated by saints in heaven, if not by the darkened minds of sinful men on earth. He greatly needed such comfort; for among the men then living, not excepting His chosen disciples, there was not one to whom He could speak on that theme with any hope of eliciting an intelligent and sympathetic response. Only a few days ago, He had ascertained by painful experience the utter incapacity of the twelve, even of the most quick-witted and warm-hearted among them, to comprehend the mystery of His passion, or even to believe in it as a certain fact. Verily the Son of man was most lonely as He passed through the dark valley! the very presence of stupid, unsympathetic companions serving only to enhance the sense of solitariness. When He wanted company that could understand His passion thoughts, He was obliged to hold converse with spirits of just men made perfect; for, as far as mortal men were concerned, He had to be content to finish His great work without the comfort of being understood until it was accomplished.

The talk of the great lawgiver and of the great prophet of Israel on the subject of His death was doubtless a real solace to the spirit of Jesus. We know how He comforted Himself at other times with the thought of being understood in heaven if not on earth. When heartless Pharisees called in question His conduct in receiving sinners, He sought at once His defense and His consolation in the blessed fact that there was joy in heaven at least, whatever there might be among them, over one penitent sinner, more than over ninety and nine just persons that needed no repentance. When He thought how "little ones," the weak and helpless, were despised and trampled under foot in this proud inhuman world, He reflected with unspeakable satisfaction that in heaven their angels did always behold the face of His Father; yea, that in heaven there were angels who made the care of little ones their special business, and were therefore fully able to appreciate the doctrine of humility and kindness which He strove to inculcate on ambitious and quarrelsome disciples. Surely, then, we may believe that when He looked forward to His own decease—the crowning evidence of His love for sinners—it was a comfort to His heart to think: "Up yonder they know that I am to suffer, and comprehend the reason why, and watch with eager interest to see how I move on with unfaltering step, with my face steadfastly set to go to Jerusalem." And would it not be specially comforting to have sensible evidence of this, in an actual visit from two denizens of the upper world, deputed as it were and commissioned to express the general mind of the whole community of glorified saints, who understood that their presence in heaven was due to the merits of that sacrifice which He was about to offer up in His own person on the hill of Calvary?

A third, and the chief solace to the heart of Jesus, was the approving voice of His heavenly Father: "This is my beloved Son, in whom I am well pleased." That voice, uttered then, meant: "Go on Thy present way, self-devoted to death, and shrinking not from the cross. I am pleased with Thee, because Thou pleasest not Thyself. Pleased with Thee at all times, I am most emphatically delighted with Thee when, in a signal manner, as lately in the announcement made to Thy disciples, Thou dost show it to be Thy fixed purpose to save others, and not to save Thyself."

This voice from the excellent glory was one of three uttered by the divine Father in the hearing of His Son during His life on earth. The first was uttered by the Jordan, after the baptism of Jesus, and was the same as the present, save that it was spoken to Him, not concerning Him, to others. The last was uttered at Jerusalem shortly before the crucifixion, and was of similar import with the two preceding, but different in form. The soul of Jesus being troubled with the near prospect of death, He prayed: "Father, save me from this hour; but for this cause came I unto this hour. Father, glorify Thy name." Then, we read, came there a voice from heaven, saying: "I have both glorified it (by Thy life), and will glorify it again" (more signally by Thy death). All three voices served one end. Elicited at crises in Christ's history, when He manifested in peculiar intensity His devotion to the work for which He had come into the world, and His determination to finish it, however irksome the task might be to flesh and blood, these voices expressed, for His encouragement and strengthening, the complacency with which His Father regarded His self-humiliation and obedience unto death. At His baptism, He, so to speak, confessed the sins of the whole world; and by submitting to the rite, expressed His purpose to fulfill all righteousness as the Redeemer from sin. Therefore the Father then, for the first time, pronounced Him His beloved Son. Shortly before the transfiguration He had energetically repelled the suggestion of an affectionate disciple, that He should save Himself from His anticipated doom, as a temptation of the devil; therefore the Father renewed the declaration, changing the second person into the third, for the sake of those disciples who were present, and specially of Peter, who had listened to the voice of his own heart rather than to his Master's words. Finally, a few days before His death, He overcame a temptation of the same nature as that to which Peter had subjected Him, springing this time out of the sinless infirmity of His own human nature. Beginning His prayer with the expression of a wish to be saved from the dark hour, He ended it with the petition, "Glorify Thy name." Therefore the Father once more repeated the expression of His approval, declaring in effect His satisfaction with the way in which His Son had glorified His name hitherto, and His confidence that He would not fail to crown His career of obedience by a God-glorifying death.

Such being the meaning of the vision on the mount for Jesus, we have now to consider what lesson it taught the disciples who were present, and through them their brethren and all Christians.

The main point in this connection is the injunction appended to the heavenly voice: "Hear Him." This command refers specially to the doctrine of the cross preached by Jesus to the twelve, and so ill received by them. It was meant to be a solemn, deliberate endorsement of all that He had said then concerning His own sufferings, and concerning the obligation to bear their cross lying on all His followers. Peter, James, and John were, as it were, invited to recall all that had fallen from their Master's lips on the unwelcome topic, and assured that it was wholly true and in accordance with the divine mind. Nay, as these disciples had received the doctrine with murmurs of disapprobation, the voice from heaven addressed to them was a stern word of rebuke, which said: "Murmur not, but devoutly and obediently hear."

This rebuke was all the more needful, that the disciples had just shown that they were still of the same mind as they had been six days ago. Peter at least was as yet in no cross-bearing humor. When, on wakening up to clear consciousness from the drowsy fit which had fallen on him, that disciple observed the two strangers in the act of departing, he exclaimed: "Master, it is good for us to be here, and let us make three tabernacles; one for Thee, and one for Moses, and one for Elias." He was minded, we perceive, to enjoy the felicities of heaven without any preliminary process of cross-bearing. He thought to himself: "How much better to abide up here with the saints than down below amidst unbelieving captious Pharisees and miserable human beings, enduring the contradiction of sinners, and battling with the manifold ills wherewith the earth is cursed! Stay here, my Master, and you may bid good-by to all those dark forebodings of coming sufferings, and will be beyond the reach of malevolent priests, elders, and scribes. Stay here, on this sun-lit, heaven-kissing hill; go no more down into the depressing, somber valley of humiliation. Farewell, earth and the cross: welcome, heaven and the crown!"

We do not forget, while thus paraphrasing Peter's foolish speech, that when he uttered it he was dazed with sleep and the splendors of the midnight scene. Yet, when due allowance has been made for this, it remains true that the idle suggestion was an index of the disciple's present mind. Peter was drunken, though not with wine; but what men say, even when drunken, is characteristic. There was a sober meaning in his senseless speech about the tabernacle. He really meant that the celestial visitants should remain, and not go away, as they were in the act of doing when he spoke. This appears from the conversation which took place between Jesus and the three disciples while descending the mountain. Peter and his two companions asked their Master: "Why then say the scribes that Elias must first come?" The question referred, we think, not to the injunction laid on the disciples by Jesus just before, "Tell the vision to no man until the Son of man be risen again from the dead," but rather to the fugitive, fleeting character of the whole scene on the mountain. The three brethren were not only disappointed, but perplexed, that the two celestials had been so like angels in the shortness of their stay and the suddenness of their departure. They had accepted the current notion about the advent of Elias before, and in order to, the restoration of the kingdom; and they fondly hoped that this was he come at last in company with Moses, heralding the approaching glory, as the advent of swallows from tropical climes is a sign that summer is nigh, and that winter with its storms and rigors is over and gone. In truth, while their Master was preaching the cross they had been dreaming of crowns. We shall find them continuing so to dream till the very end.

"Hear ye Him:"—this voice was not meant for the three disciples alone, or even for the twelve, but for all professed followers of Christ as well as for them. It says to every Christian: "Hear Jesus, and strive to understand Him while He speaks of the mystery of His sufferings and the glory that should follow—those themes which even angels desire to look into. Hear Him when He proclaims cross-bearing as a duty incumbent on all disciples, and listen not to self-indulgent suggestions of flesh and blood, or the temptations of Satan counseling thee to make self-interest or self-preservation thy chief end. Hear Him, yet again, and weary not of the world, nor seek to lay down thy burden before the time. Dream not of tabernacles where thou mayest dwell secure, like a hermit in the wild, having no share in all that is done beneath the circuit of the sun. Do thy part manfully, and in due season thou shalt have, not a tent, but a temple to dwell in: an house not made with hands, eternal in the heavens."

It is true, indeed, that we who are in this tabernacle of the body, in this world of sorrow, cannot but groan now and then, being burdened. This is our infirmity, and in itself it is not sinful; neither is it wrong to heave an occasional sigh, and utter a passing wish that the time of cross-bearing were over. Even the holy Jesus felt at times this weariness of life. An expression of something like impatience escaped His lips at this very season. When He came down from the mount and learned what was going on at its base, He exclaimed, with reference at once to the unbelief of the scribes who were present, to the weak faith of the disciples, and to the miseries of mankind suffering the consequences of the curse: "O faithless and perverse generation, how long shall I be with you? how long shall I suffer you?" Even the loving Redeemer of man felt tempted to be weary in well-doing—weary of encountering the contradiction of sinners and of bearing with the spiritual weakness of disciples. Such weariness therefore, as a momentary feeling, is not necessarily sinful: it may rather be a part of our cross. But it must not be indulged in or yielded to. Jesus did not give Himself up to the feeling. Though He complained of the generation amidst which He lived, He did not cease from His labors of love for its benefit. Having relieved His heart by this utterance of a reproachful exclamation, He gave orders that the poor lunatic should be brought to Him that he might be healed. Then, when He had wrought this new miracle of mercy, He patiently explained to His own disciples the cause of their impotence to cope successfully with the maladies of men, and taught them how they might attain the power of casting out all sorts of devils, even those whose hold of their victims was most obstinate, viz. by faith and prayer. So He continued laboring in helping the miserable and instructing the ignorant, till the hour came when He could truly say, "It is finished."

A. B. Bruce, The Training of the Twelve, *1871*

11

THE LAST SUPPER

2.45 THE LORD'S SUPPER IS . . . , J. I. PACKER

The Lord's Supper is an act of worship taking the form of a ceremonial meal, in which Christ's servants share bread and wine in memory of their crucified Lord and in celebration of the new covenant relationship with God through Christ's death.

J. I. Packer
Concise Theology: A Guide To Historic Christian Beliefs
Wheaton, IL: Tyndale House Publishers, Inc., 1993

2.46 SHORT TREATY ON THE SUPPER OF OUR LORD, JOHN CALVIN

Theodore Beza called this article, "a little golden Treatise on the Lord's Supper for the use of his countrymen in French." Beza believed that it made such a contribution to a correct understanding of the meaning of the Lord's Supper that "a termination of those most unhappy controversies, in which all the learned and all the good deservedly acquiesced, is chiefly to be ascribed under God to that treatise."

IN WHICH IS SHOWN ITS TRUE INSTITUTION, BENEFIT, AND UTILITY.

1. Reason why many weak consciences remain in suspense as to the true doctrine of the Supper

As the holy sacrament of the Supper of our Lord Jesus Christ has long been the subject of several important errors, and in these past years been anew enveloped in diverse opinions and contentious disputes, it is no wonder if many weak consciences cannot fairly resolve what view they ought to take of it, but remain in doubt and perplexity, waiting till all contention being laid aside, the servants of God come to some agreement upon it. However, as it is a very perilous thing to have no certainty on an ordinance, the understanding of which is so requisite for our salvation, I have thought it might be a very useful labor to treat briefly and, nevertheless, clearly deduce a summary of what is necessary to be known of it. I may add that I have been requested to do so by some worthy persons, whom I could not refuse without neglecting my duty. In order to rid ourselves of all difficulty, it is expedient to attend to the order which I have determined to follow.

2. The order to be observed in this treatise

First, then, we will explain to what end and for what reason our Lord instituted this holy sacrament.

Secondly, What fruit and utility we receive from it, when it will likewise be shown how the body of Jesus Christ is given to us.

Thirdly, What is the legitimate use of it.

Fourthly, We will detail the errors and superstitions with which it has been contaminated, when it will be shown how the servants of God ought to differ from the Papists.

Lastly, We will mention what has been the source of the discussion which has been so keenly carried on, even among those who have, in our time, brought back the light of the gospel, and employed themselves in rightly edifying the Church in sound doctrine.

3. At baptism God receives us into his church as members of his family

In regard to the first article—Since it has pleased our good God to receive us by baptism into his Church, which is his house, which he desires to maintain and govern, and since he has received us to keep us not merely as domestics, but as his own children, it remains that, in order to do the office of a good father, he nourish and provide us with every thing necessary for our life. In regard to corporal nourishment, as it is common to all, and the bad share in it as well as the good, it is not peculiar to his family. It is very true that we have an evidence of his paternal goodness in maintaining our bodies, seeing that we partake in all the good things which he gives us with his blessing. But as the life into which he has begotten us again is spiritual, so must the food, in order to preserve and strengthen us, be spiritual also. For we should understand, that not only has he called us one day to possess his heavenly inheritance, but that by hope he has already in some measure installed us in possession; that not only has he promised us life, but already transported us into it, delivering us from death, when by adopting us as his children, he begot us again by immortal seed, namely, his word imprinted on our hearts by the Holy Spirit.

4. The virtue and office of the Word of God in regard to our souls

To maintain us in this spiritual life, the thing requisite is not to feed our bodies with fading and corruptible food, but to nourish our souls on the best and most precious diet. Now all Scripture tells us, that the spiritual food by which our souls are maintained is that same word by which the Lord has regenerated us; but it frequently adds the reason, viz., that in it Jesus Christ, our only life, is given and administered to us. For we must not imagine that there is life any where than in God. But just as God has placed all fullness of life in Jesus, in order to communicate it to us by his means, so he ordained his word as the instrument by which Jesus Christ, with all his graces, is dispensed to us. Still it always remains true, that our souls have no other pasture than Jesus Christ. Our heavenly Father, therefore, in his care to nourish us, gives us no other, but rather recommends us to take our fill there, as a refreshment amply sufficient, with which we cannot dispense, and beyond which no other can be found.

5. Jesus Christ the only spiritual nourishment of our souls

We have already seen that Jesus Christ is the only food by which our souls are nourished; but as it is distributed to us by the word of the Lord, which he has appointed an instrument for that purpose, that word is also called bread and water. Now what is said of the word applies as well to the sacrament of the Supper, by means of which the Lord leads us to communion with Jesus Christ. For seeing we are so weak that we cannot receive him with true heartfelt trust, when he is presented to us by simple doctrine and preaching, the Father of mercy, disdaining not to condescend in this matter to our infirmity, has been pleased to add to his word a visible sign, by which he might represent the substance of his promises, to confirm and fortify us by delivering us from all doubt and uncertainty. Since, then, there is something so mysterious and incomprehensible in saying that we have communion with the body and the blood of Jesus Christ, and we on our part are so rude and gross that we cannot understand the least things of God, it was of importance that we should be given to understand it as far as our capacity could admit.

6. Why our Lord instituted the Supper

Our Lord, therefore, instituted the Supper, first, in order to sign and seal in our consciences the promises contained in his gospel concerning our being made partakers of his body and blood, and to give us certainty and assurance that therein lies our trio spiritual nourishment, and that having such an earnest, we may entertain a right reliance on salvation. Secondly, in order to exercise us in recognizing his great goodness toward us, and thus lead us to laud and magnify him more fully. Thirdly, in order to exhort us to all holiness and innocence, inasmuch as we are members of Jesus Christ; and specially to exhort us to union and brotherly charity, as we are expressly commanded. When we shall have well considered these three reasons, to which the Lord had respect in ordaining his Supper, we shall be able to understand, both what benefit accrues to us from it, and what is our duty in order to use it. properly.

7. The means of knowing the great benefit of the Supper

It is now time to come to the second point, viz., to show how the Lord's Supper is profitable to us, provided we use it profitably. Now we shall know its utility by reflecting on the indigence which it is meant to succor. We must necessarily be under great trouble and torment of conscience, when we consider who we are, and examine what is in us. For not one of us can find one particle of righteousness in himself, but on the contrary we are all full of sins and iniquities, so much so that no other party is required to accuse us than our own conscience, no other judge to condemn us. It follows that the wrath of God is kindled against us, and that none can escape eternal death. If we are not asleep and stupified, this horrible thought must be a kind of perpetual hell to vex and torment us. For the judgment of God cannot come into our remembrance without letting us see that our condemnation follows as a consequence.

8. The misery of humankind

We are then already in the gulf, if God does not in mercy draw us out of it. Moreover, what hope of resurrection can we have while considering our flesh, which is only rottenness and corruption? Thus in regard to the soul, as well as the body, we are more than miserable if we remain within ourselves, and this misery cannot but produce great sadness and anguish of soul. Now our heavenly Father, to succor us in this, gives us the Supper as a mirror, in which we may contemplate our Lord Jesus Christ, crucified to take away our faults and offences, and raised again to deliver us from corruption and death, restoring us to a celestial immortality.

9. The Supper invites us to the promises of salvation

Here, then, is the singular consolation which we derive from the Supper. It directs and leads us to the cross of Jesus Christ and to his resurrection, to certify us that whatever iniquity there may be in us, the Lord nevertheless recognizes and accepts us as righteous—whatever materials of death may be in us, he nevertheless gives us life—whatever misery may be in us, he nevertheless fills us with all felicity. Or to explain the matter more simply—as in ourselves we are devoid of all good, and have not one particle of what might help to procure salvation, the Supper is an attestation that, having been made partakers of the death and passion of Jesus Christ, we have every thing that is useful and salutary to us.

10. All the treasures of spiritual grace presented in the supper

We can therefore say, that in it the Lord displays to us all the treasures of his spiritual grace, inasmuch as he associates us in all the blessings and riches of our Lord Jesus. Let us recollect, then, that the Supper is given us as a mirror in which we may contemplate Jesus Christ crucified in order to deliver us from condemnation, and raised again in order to procure for us righteousness and eternal life. It is indeed true that this same grace is offered us by the gospel, yet as in the Supper we have more ample certainty, and fuller enjoyment of it, with good cause do we recognize this fruit as coming from it.

11. Jesus Christ is the substance of the sacraments

But as the blessings of Jesus Christ do not belong to us at all, unless he be previously ours, it is necessary, first of all, that he be given us in the Supper, in order that the things which we have mentioned may be truly accomplished in us. For this reason I am wont to say, that the substance of the sacraments is the Lord Jesus, and the efficacy of them the graces and blessings which we have by his means. Now the efficacy of the Supper is to confirm to us the reconciliation which we have with God through our Savior's death and passion; the washing of our souls which we have in the shedding of his blood; the righteousness which we have in his obedience; in short, the hope of salvation which we have in all that he has done for us. It is necessary, then, that the substance should be conjoined with these, otherwise nothing would be firm or certain. Hence we conclude that two things are presented to us in the Supper, viz., Jesus Christ as the source and substance of all good; and, secondly, the fruit and efficacy of his death and passion. This is implied in the words which were used. For after commanding us to eat his body and drink his blood, he adds that his body was delivered for us, and his blood shed for the remission of our sins. Hereby he intimates, first, that we ought not simply to communicate in his body and blood, without any other consideration, but in order to receive the fruit derived to us from his death and passion; secondly, that we can attain the enjoyment of such fruit only by participating in his body and blood, from which it is derived.

12. How the bread is called the body, and the wine the blood of Christ

We begin now to enter on the question so much debated, both anciently and at the present time—how we are to understand the words in which the bread is called the body of Christ, and the wine his blood. This may be disposed of without much difficulty, if we carefully observe the principle which I lately laid down, viz., that all the benefit which we should seek in the Supper is annihilated if Jesus Christ be not there given to us as the substance and foundation of all. That being fixed, we will confess, without doubt, that to deny that a true communication of Jesus Christ is presented to us in the Supper, is to

render this holy sacrament frivolous and useless—an execrable blasphemy unfit to be listened to.

13. What is requisite in order to live in Jesus Christ

Moreover, if the reason for communicating with Jesus Christ is to have part and portion in all the graces which he purchased for us by his death, the thing requisite must be not only to be partakers of his Spirit, but also to participate in his humanity, in which he rendered all obedience to God his Father, in order to satisfy our debts, although, properly speaking, the one cannot be without the other; for when he gives himself to us, it is in order that we may possess him entirely. Hence, as it is said that his Spirit is our life, so he himself, with his own lips, declares that his flesh is meat indeed, and his blood drink indeed. (John 6:55.) If these words are not to go for nothing, it follows that in order to have our life in Christ our souls must feed on his body and blood as their proper food. This, then, is expressly attested in the Supper, when of the bread it is said to us that we are to take it and eat it, and that it is his body, and of the cup that we are to drink it, and that it is his blood. This is expressly spoken of the body and blood, in order that we may learn to seek there the substance of our spiritual life.

14. How the bread and wine are the body of Jesus Christ

Now, if it be asked whether the bread is the body of Christ and the wine his blood, we answer, that the bread and the wine are visible signs, which represent to us the body and blood, but that this name and title of body and blood is given to them because they are as it were instruments by which the Lord distributes them to us. This form and manner of speaking is very appropriate. For as the communion which we have with the body of Christ is a thing incomprehensible, not only to the eye but to our natural sense, it is there visibly demonstrated to us. Of this we have a striking example in an analogous case. Our Lord, wishing to give a visible appearance to his Spirit at the baptism of Christ, presented him under the form of a dove. St. John the

Baptist, narrating the fact, says, that he saw the Spirit of God descending. If we look more closely, we shall find that he saw nothing but the dove, in respect that the Holy Spirit is in his essence invisible. Still, knowing that this vision was not an empty phantom, but a sure sign of the presence of the Holy Spirit, he doubts not to say that he saw it, (John 1:32,) because it was represented to him according to his capacity.

16. The sacrament is represented by visible signs

Thus it is with the communion which we have in the body and blood of the Lord Jesus. It is a spiritual mystery which can neither be seen by the eye nor comprehended by the human understanding. It is therefore figured to us by visible signs, according as our weakness requires, in such manner, nevertheless, that it is not a bare figure but is combined with the reality and substance. It is with good reason then that the bread is called the body, since it not only represents but also presents it to us. Hence we indeed infer that the name of the body of Jesus Christ is transferred to the bread, inasmuch as it is the sacrament and figure of it. But we likewise add, that the sacraments of the Lord should not and cannot be at all separated from their reality and substance. To distinguish, in order to guard against confounding them, is not only good and reasonable, but altogether necessary; but to divide them, so as to make the one exist without the other, is absurd.

16. The proper body and blood of Jesus Christ received only by faith

Hence when we see the visible sign we must consider what it represents, and by whom it has been given us. The bread is given us to figure the body of Jesus Christ, with command to eat it, and it is given us of God, who is certain and immutable truth. If God cannot deceive or lie, it follows that it accomplishes all which it signifies. We must then truly receive in the Supper the body and blood of Jesus Christ, since the Lord there represents to us the communion of both. Were it otherwise, what could be meant by saying, that we eat the bread and drink the

wine as a sign that his body is our meat and his blood our drink? If he gave us only bread and wine, leaving the spiritual reality behind, would it not be under false colors that this ordinance had been instituted?

17. The internal substance is conjoined with the visible signs

We must confess, then, that if the representation which God gives us in the Supper is true, the internal substance of the sacrament is conjoined with the visible signs; and as the bread is distributed to us by the hand, so the body of Christ is communicated to us in order that we may be made partakers of it. Though there should be nothing more, we have good cause to be satisfied, when we understand that Jesus Christ gives us in the Supper the proper substance of his body and blood, in order that we may possess it fully, and possessing it have part in all his blessings. For seeing we have him, all the riches of God which are comprehended in him are exhibited to us, in order that they may be ours. Thus, as a brief definition of this utility of the Supper, we may say, that Jesus Christ is there offered to us in order that we may possess him, and in him all the fullness of grace which we can desire, and that herein we have a good aid to confirm our consciences in the faith which we ought to have in him.

18. In the Supper we are reminded of our duty towards God

The second benefit of the Supper is, that it admonishes and incites us more strongly to recognize the blessings which we have received, and receive daily from the Lord Jesus, in order that we may ascribe to him the praise which is due. For in ourselves we are so negligent that we rarely think of the goodness of God, if he do not arouse us from our indolence, and urge us to our duty. Now there cannot be a spur which can pierce us more to the quick than when he makes us, so to speak, see with the eye, touch with the hand, and distinctly perceive this inestimable blessing of feeding on his own substance. This he means to intimate when he commands us to show forth his death till he come. (1 Cor. 11:26.) If it is then so essential to salvation not to overlook the gifts which God has given us, but diligently to keep them in mind, and extol them to others for mutual edification; we see another singular advantage of the Supper in this, that it draws us off from ingratitude, and allows us not to forget the benefit which our Lord Jesus bestowed upon us in dying for us, but induces us to render him thanks, and, as it were, publicly protest how much we are indebted to him.

19. The sacrament a strong inducement to holy living and brotherly love

The third advantage of the Sacrament consists in furnishing a most powerful incitement to live holily, and especially observe charity and brotherly love toward all. For seeing we have been made members of Jesus Christ, being incorporated into him, and united with him as our head, it is most reasonable that we should become conformable to him in purity and innocence, and especially that we should cultivate charity and concord together as becomes members of the same body. But to understand this advantage properly, we must not suppose that our Lord warns, incites, and inflames our hearts by the external sign merely; for the principal point is, that he operates in us inwardly by his Holy Spirit, in order to give efficacy to his ordinance, which he has destined for that purpose, as an instrument by which he wishes to do his work in us. Wherefore, inasmuch as the virtue of the Holy Spirit is conjoined with the sacraments when we duly receive them, we have reason to hope they will prove a good mean and aid to make us grow and advance in holiness of life, and specially in charity.

20. What it is to pollute the holy supper—the great guilt of so doing

Let us come to the third point which we proposed at the commencement of this treatise, viz., the legitimate use, which consists in reverently observing our Lord's institution. Whoever approaches the sacrament with contempt or indifference, not caring much about following when the Lord calls him, perversely abuses, and in abusing pollutes it. Now to pollute and contaminate what God has so highly sanctified, is intolerable

blasphemy. Not without cause then does St. Paul denounce such heavy condemnation on all who take it unworthily. (1 Cor. 11:29.) For if there is nothing in heaven nor on earth of greater price and dignity than the body and blood of the Lord, it is no slight fault to take it inconsiderately and without being well prepared. Hence he exhorts us to examine ourselves carefully, in order to make the proper use of it. When we understand what this examination should be, we shall know the use after which we are inquiring.

21. The manner of examining ourselves

Here it is necessary to be well on our guard. For as we cannot be too diligent in examining ourselves as the Lord enjoins, so, on the other hand, sophistical doctors have brought poor consciences into perilous perplexity, or rather into a horrible Gehenna, requiring I know not what examination, which it is not possible for any man to make. To rid ourselves of all these perplexities, we must reduce the whole, as I have already said, to the ordinance of the Lord, as the rule which, if we follow it, will not allow us to err. In following it, we have to examine whether we have true repentance in ourselves, and true faith in our Lord Jesus Christ. These two things are so conjoined, that the one cannot subsist without the other.

22. To participate in the blessings of Christ, we must renounce all that is our own.

If we consider our life to be placed in Christ, we must acknowledge that we are dead in ourselves. If we seek our strength in him, we must understand that in ourselves we are weak. If we think that all our felicity is in his grace, we must understand how miserable we are without it. If we have our rest in him, we must feel within ourselves only disquietude and torment. Now such feelings cannot exist, without producing, first, dissatisfaction with our whole life; secondly, anxiety and fear; lastly, a desire and love of righteousness. For he who knows the turpitude of his sin and the wretchedness of his state and condition while alienated from God, is so ashamed that he is constrained to be dissatisfied with himself, to condemn himself, to sigh and groan in great sadness. Moreover, the justice of God immediately presents itself and oppresses the wretched conscience with keen anguish, from not seeing any means of escape, or having any thing to answer in defense. When under such a conviction of our misery we get a taste of the goodness of God, it is then we would wish to regulate our conduct by his will, and renounce all our bygone life, in order to be made new creatures in him.

23. The requisites of worthy communion

Hence if we would worthily communicate in the Lord's Supper, we must with firm heartfelt reliance regard the Lord Jesus as our only righteousness, life, and salvation, receiving and accepting the promises which are given us by him as sure and certain, and renouncing all other confidence, so that distrusting ourselves and all creatures, we may rest fully in him, and be contented with his grace alone. Now as that cannot be until we know how necessary it is that he come to our aid, it is of importance to have a deep-seated conviction of our own misery, which will make us hunger and thirst after him. And, in fact, what mockery would it be to go in search of food when we have no appetite? Now to have a good appetite it is not enough that the stomach be empty, it must also be in good order and capable of receiving its food. Hence it follows that our souls must be pressed with famine and have a desire and ardent longing to be fed, in order to find their proper nourishment in the Lord's Supper.

24. Self-denial necessary

Moreover, it is to be observed that we cannot desire Jesus Christ without aspiring to the righteousness of God, which consists in renouncing ourselves and obeying his will. For it is preposterous to pretend that we are of the body of Christ, while abandoning ourselves to all licentiousness, and leading a dissolute life. Since in Christ is naught but chastity, benignity, sobriety, truth, humility, and such like virtues, if we would be his members, all uncleanness, intemperance, falsehood, pride, and similar vices must be put from us. For we cannot intermingle these things with him without offering him great dishonor and insult. We ought always to remember that there is no more agreement between him and

iniquity than between light and darkness. If we would come then to true repentance, we must endeavor to make our whole life conformable to the example of Jesus Christ.

25. Charity especially necessary

And while this must be general in every part of our life, it must be specially so in respect of charity, which is, above all other virtues, recommended to us in this sacrament: for which reason it is called the bond of charity. For as the bread which is there sanctified for the common use of all is composed of several grains so mixed together that they cannot be distinguished from each other, so ought we to be united together in indissoluble friendship. Moreover, we all receive there one body of Christ. If then we have strife and discord among ourselves, it is not owing to us that Christ Jesus is not rent in pieces, and we are therefore guilty of sacrilege, as if we had done it. We must not, then, on any account, presume to approach if we bear hatred or rancor against any man living, and especially any Christian who is in the unity of the Church. In order fully to comply with our Lord's injunction, there is another disposition which we must bring. It is to confess with the mouth and testify how much we are indebted to our Savior, and return him thanks, not only that his name may be glorified in us, but also to edify others, and instruct them, by our example, what they ought to do.

26. All people are imperfect and blameworthy

But as not a man will be found upon the earth who has made such progress in faith and holiness, as not to be still very defective in both, there might be a danger that several good consciences might be troubled by what has been said, did we not obviate it by tempering the injunctions which we have given in regard both to faith and repentance. It is a perilous mode of teaching which some adopt, when they require perfect reliance of heart and perfect penitence, and exclude all who have them not. For in so doing they exclude all without excepting one. Where is the man who can boast that he is not stained by some spot of distrust? that he is not subject to some vice or infirmity? Assuredly the faith which the children of God have is such that they have ever occasion to pray,—Lord, help our unbelief. For it is a malady so rooted in our nature, that we are never completely cured until we are delivered from the prison of the body. Moreover, the purity of life in which they walk is only such that they have occasion daily to pray, as well for remission of sins as for grace to make greater progress. Although some are more and others less imperfect, still there is none who does not fail in many respects. Hence the Supper would be not only useless, but pernicious to all, if it were necessary to bring a faith or integrity, as to which there would be nothing to gainsay. This would be contrary to the intention of our Lord, as there is nothing which he has given to his Church that is more salutary.

27. Imperfection must not make us cease to hope for salvation

Therefore, although we feel our faith to be imperfect, and our conscience not so pure that it does not accuse us of many vices, that ought not to hinder us from presenting ourselves at the Lord's holy table, provided that amid this infirmity we feel in our heart that without hypocrisy and dissimulation we hope for salvation in Christ, and desire to live according to the rule of the gospel. I say expressly, provided there be no hypocrisy. For there are many who deceive themselves by vain flattery, making themselves believe that it is enough if they condemn their vices, though they continue to persist in them, or rather, if they give them up for a time, to return to them immediately after. True repentance is firm and constant, and makes us war with the evil that is in us, not for a day or a week, but without end and without intermission.

28. The imperfections of believers should rather incline them to use the Supper.

When we feel within ourselves a strong dislike and hatred of all sin, proceeding from the fear of God, and a desire to live well in order to please our Lord, we are fit to partake of the Supper, notwithstanding of the remains of infirmity which we carry in our flesh. Nay, if we were not weak, subject to distrust and an imperfect life, the sacrament would be of no use to us, and it would have been superfluous to institute it. Seeing, then, it is a remedy which God has given us to help our weakness, to strengthen our faith, increase our charity, and advance us in all holiness of life, the use becomes the more necessary the more we feel pressed by the disease; so far ought that to be from making us abstain. For if we allege as an excuse for not coming to the Supper, that we are still weak in faith or integrity of life, it is as if a man were to excuse himself from taking medicine because he was sick. See then how the weakness of faith which we feel in our heart, and the imperfections which are in our life, should admonish us to come to the Supper, as a special remedy to correct them. Only let us not come devoid of faith and repentance. The former is hidden in, the heart, and therefore conscience must be its witness before God. The latter is manifested by works, and must therefore be apparent in our life.

29. Times of using the Supper—propriety of frequent communion

As to the time of using it, no certain rule can be prescribed for all. For there are sometimes special circumstances which excuse a man for abstaining; and, moreover, we have no express command to constrain all Christians to use a specified day. However, if we duly consider the end which our Lord has in view, we shall perceive that the use should be more frequent than many make it: for the more infirmity presses, the more necessary is it frequently to have recourse to what may and will serve to confirm our faith, and advance us in purity of life; and, therefore, the practice of all well ordered churches should be to celebrate the Supper frequently, so far as the capacity of the people will admit. And each individual in his own place should prepare himself to receive whenever it is administered in the holy assembly, provided there is not some great impediment which constrains him to abstain. Although we have no express commandment specifying the time and the day, it should suffice us to know the intention of our Lord to be, that we should use it often, if we would fully experience the benefit which accrues from it.

30. Impropriety of abstaining on frivolous grounds—pretended unworthiness in ourselves

The excuses alleged are very frivolous. Some say that they do not feel themselves to be worthy, and, under this pretext, abstain for a whole year. Others, not contented with looking to their own unworthiness, pretend that they cannot communicate with persons whom they see coming without being duly prepared. Some also think that it is superfluous to use it frequently, because if we have once received Jesus Christ, there is no occasion to return so often after to receive him. I ask the first who make a cloak of their unworthiness, how their conscience can allow them to remain more than a year in so poor a state, that they dare not invoke God directly? They will acknowledge that it is presumption to invoke God as our Father, if we are not members of Jesus Christ. This we cannot be, without having the reality and substance of the Supper accomplished in us. Now, if we have the reality, we are by stronger reason capable of receiving the sign. We see then that he who would exempt himself from receiving the Supper on account of unworthiness, must hold himself unfit to pray to God. I mean not to force consciences which are tormented with certain scruples which suggest themselves, they scarcely know how, but counsel them to wait till the Lord deliver them. Likewise, if there is a legitimate cause of hindrance, I deny not that it is lawful to delay. Only I wish to show that no one ought long to rest satisfied with abstaining on the ground of unworthiness, seeing that in so doing he deprives himself of the communion of the Church, in which all our wellbeing consists. Let him rather contend against all the impediments which the devil throws in his way, and not be excluded from so great a benefit, and from all the graces consequent thereupon.

31. Abstaining because of pretended unworthiness in others

The second class have some plausibility. The argument they use is, that it is not lawful to eat common bread with those who call themselves brethren, and lead a dissolute life—a fortiori,

we must abstain from communicating with them in the Lord's bread, which is sanctified in order to represent and dispense to us the body of Christ., But the answer is not very difficult. It is not the office of each individual to judge and discern, to admit or debar whom he pleases; seeing that this prerogative belongs to all the Church in general, or rather to the pastor, with the elders, whom he ought to have to assist him in the government of the Church. St. Paul does not command us to examine others, but each to examine himself. It is very true that it is our duty to admonish those whom we see walking disorderly, and if they will not listen to us, to give notice to the pastor, in order that he may proceed by ecclesiastical authority. But the proper method of withdrawing from the company of the wicked, is not to quit the communion of the Church. More-ever, it will most frequently happen, that sins are not so notorious as to justify proceeding to excommunication; for though the pastor may in his heart judge some man to be unworthy, he has not the power of pronouncing him such, and interdicting him from the Supper, if he cannot prove the unworthiness by an ecclesiastical judgment. In such case we have no other remedy than to pray God that he would more and more deliver his Church from all scandals, and wait for the last day, when the chaff will be completely separated from the good grain.

32. Excuse, that having already received Christ, it is unnecessary to return often to receive him

The third class have no semblance of plausibility. The spiritual bread is not given us to eat our fill of it all at once, but rather, that having had some taste of its sweetness, we may long for it the more, and use it when it is offered to us. This we explained above. So long as we remain in this mortal life, Jesus Christ is never communicated in such a way as to satiate our souls, but wills to be our constant nourishment.

33. Fourth general division.—errors on the Supper

We come to the fourth principal point. The devil knowing that our Lord has left nothing to his Church more useful than the holy sacrament, has after his usual manner laboured from the beginning to contaminate it by errors and superstitions, in order to corrupt and destroy the benefit of it, and has never ceased to pursue this course, until he has as it were completely reversed the ordinance of the Lord, and converted it into falsehood and vanity. My intention is not to point out at what time each abuse took its rise and at what time it was augmented; it will be sufficient to notice articulately the errors which the devil has introduced, and against which we must guard if we would have the Lord's Supper in its integrity.

34. First error

The first error is this—While the Lord gave us the Supper that it might be distributed amongst us to testify to us that in communicating in his body we have part in the sacrifice which he offered on the cross to God his Father, for the expiation and satisfaction of our sins—men have out of their own head invented, on the contrary, that it is a sacrifice by which we obtain the forgiveness of our sins before God. This is a blasphemy which it is impossible to bear. For if we do not recognize the death of the Lord Jesus, and regard it as our only sacrifice by which he has reconciled us to the Father, effacing all the faults for which we were accountable to his justice, we destroy its virtue. If we do not acknowledge Jesus Christ to be the only sacrifice, or, as we commonly call it, priest, by whose intercession we are restored to the Father's favor, we rob him of his honor and do him high injustice.

35. The sacrament not a sacrifice

The opinion that the Supper is a sacrifice derogates from that of Christ, and must therefore be condemned as devilish. That it does so derogate is notorious. For how can we reconcile the two things, that Jesus Christ in dying offered a sacrifice to his Father by which he has once for all purchased forgiveness and pardon for all our faults, and that it is every day necessary to sacrifice in order to obtain that which we ought to seek in his death only? This error was not at first so extreme, but

increased by little and little, until it came to what it now is. It appears that the ancient fathers called the Supper a sacrifice; but the reason they give is, because the death of Christ is represented in it. Hence their view comes to this—that this name is given it merely because it is a memorial, of the one sacrifice, at which we ought entirely to stop. And yet I cannot altogether excuse the custom of the early Church. By gestures and modes of acting they figured a species of sacrifice, with a ceremony resembling that which existed under the Old Testament, excepting that instead of a beast they used bread as the host. As that approaches too near to Judaism, and does not correspond to our Lord's institution, I approve it not. For under the Old Testament, during the time of figures, the Lord ordained such ceremonies, until the sacrifice should be made in the person of his well-beloved Son, which was the fulfillment of them. Since it was finished, it now only remains for us to receive the communication of it. It is superfluous, therefore, to exhibit it any longer under figure.

36. The bread in the supper ordained to be eaten, not sacrificed.—errors of the mass

And such is the import of the injunction which Jesus Christ has left. It is not that we are to offer or immolate, but to take and eat what has been offered and immolated. However, though there was some weakness in such observance, there was not such impiety as afterwards supervened. For to the Mass has been wholly transferred what was proper to the death of Christ, viz., to satisfy God for our sins, and so reconcile us to him. Moreover, the office of Christ has been transferred to those whom they name priests, viz., persons to sacrifice to God, and in sacrificing, intercede to obtain for us grace, and the pardon of our offences.

37. Attempted defense of the sacrifice of the mass

I wish not to keep back the explanations which the enemies of the truth here offer. They say that the Mass is not a new sacrifice but only an application of the sacrifice of which we have spoken. Although they color their abomination somewhat by so saying, still it is a mere quibble. For it is not merely said that the sacrifice of Christ is one, but that it is not to be repeated, because its efficacy endures for ever. It is not said that Christ once offered himself to the Father, in order that others might afterwards make the same oblation, and so apply to us the virtue of his intercession. As to applying to us the merit of his death, that we may perceive the benefit of it, that is done not in the way in. which the Popish Church has supposed, but when we receive the message of the gospel, according as it is testified to us by the ministers whom God has appointed as his ambassadors, and is sealed by the sacraments.

38. Errors connected with the abomination of the mass

The common opinion approved by all their doctors and prelates is, that by hearing Mass, and causing it to be said, they perform a service meriting grace and righteousness before God. We say, that to derive benefit from the Supper, it is not necessary to bring any thing of our own in order to merit what we ask. We have only to receive in faith the grace which is there presented to us, and which resides not in the sacrament, but refers us to the cross of Jesus Christ as proceeding therefrom. Hence there is nothing more contrary to the true meaning of the Supper, than to make a sacrifice of it. The effect of so doing is to lead us off from recognizing the death of Christ as the only sacrifice, whose virtue endures for ever. This being well understood, it will be apparent that all masses in which there is no such communion as the Lord enjoined, are only an abomination. The Lord did not order that a single priest, after making his sacrifice, should keep himself apart, but that the sacrament should be distributed in the assembly after the manner of the first Supper, which he made with his apostles. But after this cursed opinion was forged, out of it, as an abyss, came forth the unhappy custom by which the people, contenting themselves with being present to partake in the merit of what is done, abstain from communicating, because the priest gives out that he offers his host for all, and specially

for those present. I speak not of abuses, which are so absurd, that they deserve not to be noticed, such as giving each saint his mass, and transferring what is said of the Lord's Supper to St. William and St. Walter, and making an ordinary fair of masses, buying and selling them with the other abominations which the word sacrifice has engendered.

39. Transubstantiation

The second error which the devil has sown to corrupt this holy ordinance, is in forging and inventing that after the words are pronounced with an intention to consecrate, the bread is transubstantiated into the body of Christ, and the wine into his blood. First of all, this falsehood has no foundation in Scripture, and no countenance from the Primitive Church, and what is more, cannot be reconciled or consist with the word of God. When Jesus Christ, pointing to the bread, calls it his body, is it not a very forced construction to say, that the substance of the bread is annihilated, and the body of Christ substituted in its stead? But there is no cause to discuss the thing as a doubtful matter, seeing the truth is sufficiently clear to refute the absurdity. I leave out innumerable passages of Scripture and quotations from the Fathers, in which the sacrament is called bread. I only say that the nature of the sacrament requires, that the material bread remain as a visible sign of the body.

40. From the nature of a sacrament the substance of the visible sign must remain

It is a general rule in all sacraments that the signs which we see must have some correspondence with the spiritual thing which is figured. Thus, as in baptism, we are assured of the internal washing of our souls when water is given us as an attestation, its property being to cleanse corporal pollution; so in the Supper, there must be material bread to testify to us that the body of Christ is our food. For otherwise how could the mere color of white give us such, a figure? We thus clearly see how the whole representation, which the Lord was pleased to give us in condescension to our weakness, would be lost if the bread did not truly remain. The words which our Lord uses imply as much as if he had said: Just as man is supported and maintained in his body by eating bread, so my flesh is the spiritual nourishment by which souls are vivified. Moreover, what would become of the other similitude which St. Paul employs? As several grains of corn are mixed together to form one bread, so must we together be one, because we partake of one bread. If there were whiteness only without the substance, would it not be mockery to speak thus? Therefore we conclude, without doubt, that this transubstantiation is an invention forged by the devil to corrupt the true nature of the Supper.

41. False opinion of the bodily presence of Christ in the Supper

Out of this fantasy several other follies have sprung. Would to God they were only follies, and not gross abominations. They have imagined I know not what local presence and thought, that Jesus Christ in his divinity and humanity was attached to this whiteness, without paying regard to all the absurdities which follow from it. Although the old doctors of Sorbonne dispute more subtilely how the body and blood are conjoined with the signs, still it cannot be denied that this opinion has been received by great and small in the Popish Church, and that it is cruelly maintained in the present day by fire and sword, that Jesus Christ is contained under these signs, and that there we must seek him. Now to maintain that, it must be confessed either that the body of Christ is without limit, or that it may be in different places. In saying this we are brought at last to the point, that it is a mere phantom. To wish then to establish such a presence as is to enclose the body within the sign, or to be joined to it locally, is not only a reverie, but a damnable error, derogatory to the glory of Christ, and destructive of what we ought to hold in regard to his human nature. For Scripture everywhere teaches us, that as the Lord on earth took our humanity, so he has exalted it to heaven, withdrawing it from mortal condition, but not changing its nature.

42. The body of our Savior in heaven the same as that which he had on earth

We have two things to consider when we speak of our Lord's humanity. We must neither destroy the reality of the nature, nor derogate in any respect from his state of glory. To do so we must always raise our thoughts on high, and there seek our Redeemer. For if we would place him under the corruptible elements of this world, besides subverting what Scripture tells us in regard to his human nature, we annihilate the glory of his ascension. As several others have treated this subject at large, I refrain from going farther. I only wished to observe, in passing, that to fancy Jesus Christ enclosed under the bread and wine, or so to conjoin him with it as to amuse our understanding there without looking up to heaven, is a diabolical reverie. We will touch on this in another place.

43. Other abuses arising out of an imaginary bodily presence

This perverse opinion, after it was once received, engendered numerous other superstitions. First of all comes that carnal adoration which is mere idolatry. For to prostrate ourselves before the bread of the Supper, and worship Jesus Christ as if he were contained in it, is to make an idol of it rather than a sacrament. The command given us is not to adore, but to take and eat. That, therefore, ought not to have been presumptuously attempted. Moreover, the practice always observed by the early Church, when about to celebrate the Supper, was solemnly to exhort the people to raise their hearts on high, to intimate, that if we would adore Christ aright, we must not stop at the visible sign. But there is no need to contend long on this point when the presence and conjunction of the reality with the sign (of which we have spoken, and will again speak) is well understood. From the same source have proceeded other superstitious practices, as carrying the sacrament in procession through the streets once a year; at another time making a tabernacle for it, and keeping it to the year's end in a cupboard to amuse the people with it, as if it were a god. As all that has not only been invented without authority from the word of God, but is also directly opposed to the institution of the Supper, it ought to be rejected by Christians.

44. Reason why the papists communicate only once a year

We have shown the origin of the calamity which befell the Popish Church—I mean that of abstaining from communicating in the Supper for the whole period of a year. It is because they regard the Supper as a sacrifice which is offered by one in the name of all. But even while thus used only once a year, it is sadly wasted and as it were torn to pieces. For instead of distributing the sacrament of blood to the people, as our Lord's command bears, they are made to believe that they ought to be contented with the other half. Thus poor believers are defrauded of the gift which the Lord Jesus had given them. For if it is no small benefit to have communion in the blood of the Lord as our nourishment, it is great cruelty to rob those of it to whom it belongs. In this we may see with what boldness and audacity the Pope has tyrannized over the Church after he had once usurped domination.

45. The pope has made exceptions to the general rules laid down by our Lord

Our Lord having commanded his disciples to eat the bread sanctified in his body, when he comes to the cup, does not say simply, "drink," but he adds expressly, that all are to drink. Would we have any thing clearer than this? He says that we are to eat the bread without using an universal term. He says that we are all to drink of the cup. Whence this difference, but just that he was pleased by anticipation to meet this wickedness of the devil? And yet such is the pride of the Pope that he dares to say, Let not all drink. And to show that he is wiser than God, he alleges it to be very reasonable that the priest should have some privilege beyond the people, in honor of the sacerdotal dignity; as if our Lord had not duly considered what distinction should be made between them. Moreover, he objects dangers which might happen if the cup were given in common to all. Some drop of it might occasionally be spilt; as if our Lord had not foreseen that. Is not this to accuse God quite openly of having confounded the order which he ought to have observed, and exposed his people to danger without cause?

46. Frivolous reasons for withholding the cup

To show that there is no great inconvenience in this change, they argue, that under one species the whole is comprised, inasmuch as the body cannot be separated from the blood: as if our Lord had without reason distinguished the one from the other. For if we can leave one of the parts behind as superfluous, what folly must it have been to recommend them separately. Some of his supporters, seeing that it was impudence to maintain this abomination, have wished to give it a different color, viz., that Jesus Christ, in instituting, spoke only to his apostles whom he had raised to the sacerdotal order. But how will they answer what St. Paul said, when he delivered to all the people what he had received of the Lord—that each should eat of this bread and drink of this cup? Besides, who told them that our Lord gave the Supper to his apostles as priests? The words import the opposite, when he commands them to do after his example. (Luke 22:19.) Therefore he delivers the rule which he wishes to be always observed in his Church; and so it was anciently observed until Antichrist, having gained the upper hand, openly raised his horns against God and his truth to destroy it totally. We see then that it is an intolerable perversion thus to divide and rend the sacrament, separating the parts which God has joined.

47. The buffoonery of the pope in regard to the supper

To get to an end, we shall embrace under one head what might otherwise have been considered separately. This head is, that the devil has introduced the fashion of celebrating the Supper without any doctrine, and for doctrine has substituted ceremonies partly inept and of no utility, and partly dangerous, having proved the cause of much mischief. To such an extent has this been done, that the Mass, which in the Popish Church is held to be the Supper, is, when well explained, nothing but pure apishness and buffoonery. I call it apishness, because they there counterfeit the Lord's Supper without reason, just as an ape at random and without discernment imitates what he sees done.

48. The Word ought always to accompany the sacraments

The principal thing recommended by our Lord is to celebrate the ordinance with true understanding. From this it follows that the essential part lies in the doctrine. This being taken away, it is only a frigid unavailing ceremony. This is not only shown by Scripture, but attested by the canons of the Pope, (Can. Detrahe. i. 4, 1,) in a passage quoted from St. Augustine, (Tract 80, in Joan.) in which he asks—"What is the water of baptism without the word but just a corruptible element? The word (he immediately adds) not as pronounced, but as understood." By this he means, that the sacraments derive their virtue from the word when it is preached intelligibly. Without this they deserve not the name of sacraments. Now so far is there from being any intelligible doctrine in the Mass, that, on the contrary, the whole mystery is considered spoiled if every thing be not said and done in whispers, so that nothing is understood. Hence their consecration is only a species of sorcery, seeing that by muttering and gesticulating like sorcerers, they think to constrain Jesus to come down into their hands. We thus see how the Mass, being thus arranged, is an evident profanation of the Supper of Christ, rather than an observance of it, as the proper and principal substance of the Supper is wanting, viz., full explanation of the ordinance and clear statement of the promises, instead of the priest standing apart and muttering to himself without sense or reason. I call it buffoonery, also, because of mimicry and gestures, better adapted to a farce than to such an ordinance as the sacred Supper of our Lord.

49. The ceremonies of the ancient law, why appointed—those of the papists censurable

It is true, indeed, that the sacrifices under the Old Testament were performed with many ornaments and ceremonies, but because there was a good meaning under them, and the whole was proper to instruct and exercise the people in piety, they are very far from being

like those which are now used, and serve no purpose but to amuse the people without doing them any good. As these gentry allege the example of the Old Testament in defense of their ceremonies, we have to observe what difference there is between what they do, and what God commanded the people of Israel. Were there only this single point, that what was then observed was founded on the commandment of the Lord, whereas all those frivolities have no foundation, even then the difference would be large. But we have much more to censure in them.

50. The Jewish ceremonies having served their purpose, the imitation of them absurd

With good cause our Lord ordained the Jewish form for a time, intending that it should one day come to an end and be abrogated. Not having then given such clearness of doctrine, he was pleased that the people should be more exercised in figures to compensate for the defect. But since Jesus Christ has been manifested in the flesh, doctrine having been much more clearly delivered, ceremonies have diminished. As we have now the body, we should leave off shadows. To return to the ceremonies which are abolished, is to repair the veil of the temple which Jesus Christ rent by his death, and so far obscure the brightness of his gospel. Hence we see, that such a multitude of ceremonies in the Mass is a form of Judaism quite contrary to Christianity. I mean not to condemn the ceremonies which are subservient to decency and public order, and increase the reverence for the sacrament, provided they are sober and suitable. But such an abyss without end or limit is not at all tolerable, seeing that it has engendered a thousand superstitions, and has in a manner stupified the people without yielding any edification.

51. The death and passion of our Lord the perfect and only sacrifice

Hence also we see how those to whom God has given the knowledge of his truth should differ from the Papists. First, they cannot doubt that it is abominable blasphemy to regard the Mass as a sacrifice by which the forgiveness of sins is purchased for us; or rather, that the priest is a kind of mediator to apply the merit of Christ's passion and death to those who purchase his mass, or are present at it, or feel devotion for it. On the contrary, they must hold decidedly that the death and suffering of the Lord is the only sacrifice by which the anger of God has been satisfied, and eternal righteousness procured for us; and, likewise, that the Lord Jesus has entered into the heavenly sanctuary in order to appear there for us, and intercede in virtue of his sacrifice. Moreover, they will readily grant, that the benefit of his death is communicated to us in the Supper, not by the merit of the act, but because of the promises which are given us, provided we receive them in faith. Secondly, they should on no account grant that the bread is transubstantiated into the body of Jesus Christ, nor the wine into his blood, but should persist in holding that the visible signs retain their true substance, in order to represent the spiritual reality of which we have spoken. Thirdly, they ought also to hold for certain, that the Lord gives us in the Supper that which he signifies by it, and, consequently, that we truly receive the body and blood of Jesus Christ. Nevertheless they will not seek him as if he were enclosed under the bread, or attached locally to the visible sign. So far from adoring the sacrament, they will rather raise their understandings and their hearts on high, as well to receive Jesus Christ, as to adore him.

52. View of enlightened Christians in regard to the Supper

Hence they will despise and condemn as idolatrous all those superstitious practices of carrying about the sacrament in pomp and procession, and building tabernacles in which to adore it. For the promises of our Lord extend only to the uses which he has authorized. Next, they will hold that to deprive the people of one of the parts of the sacrament, viz., the cup, is to violate and corrupt the ordinance of the Lord, and that to observe it properly it must be administered in all its integrity. Lastly, they will regard it as a superfluity, not only useless but dangerous, and not at all suitable to Christianity, to use so many ceremonies taken from the Jews contrary to the simplicity which the Apostles left us, and that it is still more perverse to celebrate the Supper with mimicry and buffoonery, while no doctrine is stated, or rather all doctrine is buried, as if the Supper were a kind of magical trick. . . .

John Calvin, 1540

2.47 AN OVERVIEW OF THE LORD'S SUPPER, CHARLES HODGE

In the Lord's Supper we are said to receive Christ and the benefits of His redemption to our spiritual nourishment and growth in grace. As our natural food imparts life and strength to our bodies, so this sacrament is one of the divinely appointed means to strengthen the principle of life in the soul of the believer and to confirm his faith in the promises of the gospel. By partaking of the bread and wine, the symbols of Christ's body and blood given for us, we are united to Him as our head, our life. He then works in us to will and to do of His own good pleasure. He works in us according to the laws of our nature in the production of everything that is good, so that it is from Him that all holy desires, all good counsels, and all just works proceed. It is not, therefore, we that live, but Christ that liveth in us.

What our Lord said to the apostles He says in the most impressive manner in this ordinance to every believing communicant: "This is my body, broken for you . . . this is my blood shed for you." These words when received by faith fill the heart with joy, confidence, gratitude, love, and devotion, so that the believer rises from the Lord's table refreshed by the infusion of a new life.

The efficacy of this sacrament, according to the Reformed doctrine, is not to be referred to any virtue in the ordinance itself, whether in its elements or actions; much less to any virtue in the administrator; nor to the mere power of the truths which it signifies; nor to the inherent divine power in the word or promise by which it is attended; nor to the real presence of the material body and blood of Christ (i.e., of the body born of the Virgin), whether by the way of transubstantiation, consubstantiation or impanation; but only to the blessing of Christ and the working of His Spirit in them that receive the sacrament of His body and blood.

To summarize the Reformed position: The Lord's Supper is a holy ordinance instituted by Christ as a memorial of His death wherein, under the symbols of bread and wine, His body as broken and His blood as shed for the remission of sins are signified and, by the power of the Holy Ghost. sealed and applied to believers. Thereby their union with Christ and their mutual fellowship are set forth and confirmed, their faith strengthened, and their souls nourished unto eternal life.

In this sacrament Christ is present not bodily, but spiritually—not in the sense of local nearness, but of efficacious operation. His people receive Him not with the mouth, but by faith; they do not receive His flesh and blood as material particles, but His body as broken and His blood as shed. The union thus signified and effected is not a corporeal union, not a mixture of substances, but a spiritual and mystical union due to the indwelling of the Holy Spirit. The efficacy of this sacrament as a means of grace is not in the signs, nor in the service, nor in the minister, nor in the word, but in the attending influence of the Holy Ghost.

Charles Hodge,
Systematic Theology, *New York: Charles Scribner's Son, 1887*

2.48 "THIS DO IN REMEMBRANCE OF ME," ROBERT MURRAY M'CHEYNE

Robert Murray M'Cheyne (1813–1843) was a minister in the Church of Scotland from 1835 to 1843. He first served as an assistant to John Bonar in the parish of Larbert and Dunipace from 1835 to 1838. Thereafter he became forever associated with St. Peter's Church in Dundee, where he served as minister until his untimely death at the age of 29 during an epidemic of typhus.

Not long after his death, his friend Andrew Alexander Bonar edited his biography. This was published with some of his manuscripts as The Memoir and Remains of the Rev. Robert Murray M'Cheyne. *The book went into many editions. It has had a lasting influence on Evangelical Christianity world-wide.*

In 1839, M'Cheyne and Bonar, together with two older ministers, Dr. Alexander Black and Dr. Alexander Keith, were sent to Palestine on a mission of inquiry to the condition of the Jews. Upon their return, their official report for the Board of Mission of the Church of Scotland was published as Narrative of a Visit to the Holy Land and Mission of Inquiry to the Jews. This led subsequently to the establishment of missions to the Jews by the

Church of Scotland and by the Free Church of Scotland.

M'Cheyne was a preacher, a pastor, a poet, and wrote many letters. He was also a man of deep piety and a man of prayer. He never married.

THE LORD'S SUPPER IS THE SWEETEST OF ALL ORDINANCES:

1. Because of the time when it was instituted.

"The Lord Jesus, the same night in which He was betrayed, took bread." It was the darkest night that ever was in this world, and yet the brightest—the night when His love of the sinners was put to the severest test. How amazing that He should remember our comfort at such a time!

2. Because it is the believer's ordinance.

It is the duty of all men to pray. God hears the ravens when they cry, and so He often hears the prayers of the unconverted men (Psalm 107; Acts 8:22). It is the duty of all men to hear the preached gospel. "Unto you, O men, I call, and my voice is to the sons of men." But the Lord's Supper is the children's bread; it is intended only for those who know and love the Lord Jesus.

3. Because Christ is the beginning, middle, and end of it.

"This do in remembrance of Me." "Ye do show the Lord's death till He come." There are many sermons in which Christ is not from beginning to end; many books where you cannot find the fragrance of His name: but there cannot be a sacrament where Christ is not from beginning to end. Christ is the Alpha and Omega of the Lord's Supper; it is all Christ and Him crucified. These things give a peculiar sweetness to the broken bread and poured-out wine.

I fear the Lord's Supper is profaned in a dreadful manner among you. Many come who are living in positive sins, or in the neglect of positive duties. Many come who know that they were never converted; many who in their hearts ridicule the very thoughts of conversion. Unworthy communicating is a fearful sin; on account of it God is greatly provoked to withdraw His Spirit from you, to visit you with frowns of providence, and to seal you to the day of perdition. Am I become your enemy because I tell you the truth? Deal honestly with your soul, and pray over what I am now writing; and He who opened the heart of Lydia open your heart while I explain.

THE ACTIONS OF THE COMMUNICANT

1. He takes the bread and the wine.

When the minister offers the bread and wine to those at the table, this represents Christ freely offered to sinners, even the chief. The receiving of the bread and wine means—I do thankfully receive the broken, bleeding Savior as my Surety. The act of taking that bread and wine is an appropriating act; it is saying before God, and angels, and men, and devils, "I do flee to the Lord Jesus Christ as my refuge." Noah entering into the ark was an appropriating act. Let others fly to the tops of their houses, to their castles and towers, to the rugged rocks, to the summits of the highest mountains,—as for me, I believe the word of God, and flee to the ark as my only refuge (Heb. 11:7). When the manslayer fled into the city of refuge, it was an appropriating act. As he entered breathless at gates of the Hebron, his friends might cry to him, Flee unto the wilderness! or Flee beyond Jordan! But no, he would say, I believe the word of God, that I shall be safe only within these walls; this is my only refuge city, here only will I hide! (Joshua 20). When the Israelite brought an offering of the herd or of the flock, when the priest had bound it with cords to the horns of the altar, the offerer laid his hands upon the head of the lamb: this was an appropriating act, as much as to say, I take this lamb as dying for me. The world might say, How will this save you? mend your life, give alms to the poor. I believe the word of God, he would say; I do not wish to bear my own sins, I lay them on the Lamb of God (Lev. 1:4). When the woman, trembling, came behind Jesus and touched the hem of His garment, this also was an appropriating act. Her friends might say to her, Come and try some more physicians, or wait till you are somewhat better. No, said she, "If I may but touch His garment, I shall be made whole" (Mark 5:28). In the 42nd Psalm, David's enemies said to him continually, "Where is thy

God?" This made tears his meat night and day. It was like a sword in his bones. But in the 43rd Psalm he gathers courage, and says, "I will go unto the altar of God," where the lamb was slain; and then he says, " Unto God, my exceeding joy." You say, I have no God: behold, I take this lamb as slain for me, and therefore God is my God. In the Song of Solomon, when the bride found Him whom her soul loved, she says, "I held Him, and would not let Him go." This was true appropriating faith. The world might say to her, " Come this way, and we will show thee other beloveds, fairer than thy beloved." Nay, saith she, "I held Him, and would not let Him go. This is my beloved, and this is my friend" (Song 3:4).

Just such, beloved, is the meaning of receiving broken bread and poured-out wine at the Lord's table. It is the most solemn appropriating act of all your lives. It is declaring by signs, "I do enter into the ark; I flee into the city of refuge; I lay my hand on the head of the Lamb; I do touch the hem of His garment; I do take Jesus to be my Lord and my God; I hold Him, and by grace I will never let Him go." It is a deliberate closing with Christ, by means of signs, in the presence of witnesses. When a bride accepts the right hand in marriage before many witnesses, it is a solemn declaration to all the world that she does accept the bridegroom to be her only husband. So, in the Lord's Supper, when you receive that bread and wine, you solemnly declare that, forsaking all others, you heartily do receive the Lord Jesus as your only Lord and Savior.

If these things be true, should not many stay from this holy table? Many of you know that a work of grace has never been begun in your heart; you never were made to tremble for your soul; you never were made to pray, "God be merciful to me a sinner"; you never were brought to "rejoice, believing in God." Oh, beloved, let me say it with all tenderness, this table is not for you. Many of you know you are not in the state you would do to die in. You say, "I hope to turn yet before I die." Does not this show that your sins are not covered—that you are not born again—that you are not fled to the hope set before you?

This table is not for you. Some of you know well that you have had convictions of sin, but they passed away. The walls of the house of God have seen you trembling on the brink of eternity, but you were never brought to "peace in believing"—to "peace with God." You have drowned your anxieties in the whirl of business or of pleasure. You have drawn back. Your goodness is like the "morning cloud and early dew, it goeth away." This table is not for you. I speak to your sense of honor and common honesty. In worldly things, would you tell a lie either by word or by signs? And is it a light matter to tell a lie in eternal things? Will you deliberately declare, by taking the broken bread and poured-out wine, what you know to be a lie? Oh, pray over the story of Ananias and Sapphira, and tremble (Acts 5:1-11). May it not be said in heaven of many, "Thou hast not lied unto men, but unto God?"

A word to trembling, believing souls. This feast is spread for you. "Eat, O friends; drink, yea, drink abundantly, O beloved." If you have faith as a grain of mustard seed, come. If you are "weak in the faith," ministers are commanded to receive you. If on the morning of the communion Sabbath, even for the first time in your life, Christ appeared full and free to you, so that you cannot but believe on Him, do not hesitate to come. Come to the table, leaning on the Beloved, and you will have John's place there. You will lean peacefully upon His breast.

2. He eats the bread and drinks the wine.

"Take, eat"—"Drink ye all of it." Eating and drinking in this ordinance imply feeding upon Christ. It is said of bread that it "strengtheth man's heart," and of wine, that it "maketh glad the heart of man." Bread is the staff of life, and wine is very reviving to those who, like Timothy, have often infirmities. They are the greatest nutritive blessings which man possesses. To feed on them in the Lord's Supper is as much as to say, I do feed on Jesus, as my strength; "in the Lord have I righteousness and strength." To take the bread into the hand is by saying, "He is made of God unto me righteousness." To feed upon it is saying, "He is made unto me sanctification."

When Israel fed on manna for forty years, and drank water from the rock, they were strengthened for their journey through the howling wilderness. This was a picture of believers journeying through this world. They feed every day on Christ their strength; He is their daily manna; He is the rock that follows them. When the bride sat under the shadow of the apple-tree, she says, "His fruit was sweet to my taste"; and again, "Stay me with flagons, comfort me with apples, for I am sick of love." Believers, this is a picture of you. No sooner are you sheltered by the Savior, than you are nourished and renewed by Him. He comforts your hearts, and stablishes you in every good word and work. In the 36th Psalm, when David speaks of men trusting under the wings of the Lord Jesus, he adds, "They shall be abundantly satisfied with the fatness of thy house, and Thou shalt make them drink of the river of Thy pleasures." Little children, you know by experience what this means. When you were brought to believe on the Son of God, you were adopted into His family, fed with the children's bread, and your heart filled with the holy pleasures of God. The same thing is represented in feeding on the bread and wine. It is a solemn declaration in the sight of the whole world, that you have been put into the clefts of the smitten rock, and that you are feeding on the honey treasured there. It is declaring that you have sat down under Christ's shadow, and you are comforted and nourished by the fruit of that tree of life. It is saying, "I have come to trust under the shadow of His wings, and now I drink of the river of His pleasures." It is a sweet declaration of your own helplessness and weakness, and that Christ is all your strength—all your life.

If this be true, should not many stay away from the Lord's table? Many of you know that you were never really grafted into the true vine—that you never received and nourishment from Christ—that you never received the Holy Spirit. Many of you know that you are dead branches—that you only seem to be united to the vine—that you are the branches that bear no fruit, which He taketh away. Why should you feed on that bread and wine? Some of you may know that you are dead in sins, unconverted, unborn again—that you never experienced any change of heart like that spoken of in Ezek. 36:26. This bread and wine are not for you. Some of you know that you are living in under the power of sins that you could name: some of you, perhaps, in secret profanation of the holy Sabbath, "doing your own ways, finding your own pleasures, speaking your own words." Some, perhaps, in secret swearing, or lying, or dishonesty, or drinking, or uncleanness! Ah! why should you feed on this bread and wine? It will do you no good. Can you for a moment doubt that you will eat and drink unworthily? Dare you do this? Pray over these awful words and tremble: "He that eateth and drinketh unworthily, eateth and drinketh damnation to himself."

All who are really "looking unto Jesus" are invited to come to the Lord's table. Some feel like a sick person recovering from a fever: you are without strength, you cannot lift your hand or your head. Yet you look unto Jesus as your strength: He died for sinners, and He lives for them. You look to Him day by day. You say, He is my bread, He is my wine; I have no strength but what comes from Him. Come you and feed at the Lord's table, and welcome. Some feel like a traveler when he arrives at an inn, faint and weary: you have no strength to go farther, you cannot take another step; but you lean on Jesus as your strength; you believe that word: "Because I live, ye shall live also." Come you and feed on this bread and wine, with your staff in your hand and shoes on your feet, and will "go on your way rejoicing." Feeble branches need most nourishment. The more you feel your weakness, the amazing depravity of your heart, the power of Satan, and the hatred of the world, the more need have you to lean on Jesus, to feed on this bread and wine—you are all the more welcome.

3. He shares the bread and wine with others.

The Lord's table is not a selfish, solitary meal. To eat bread and wine alone is not the Lord's Supper. It is a family meal of that family spoken of in Eph. 3:15. You do not eat and drink alone by yourself; you share the bread and wine with all at the same table. Jesus said, "Drink ye all of it."

This expresses love to the brethren,—a sweet feeling of oneness with "all those who love the Lord Jesus in sincerity,"—a heart-filling desire that all should have the same peace, the same joy, the same spirit, the same holiness, the same heaven with yourself. You remember the golden candlestick in the temple, with its seven lamps. It was fed out of one golden bowl on the top of it, which was constantly full of oil. The oil ran down the shaft of the candlestick, and was distributed to each lamp by seven golden pipes or branches. All the lamps shared the same oil. It passed from branch to branch. None of the lamps kept the oil to itself; it was shared among them all. So it is in the vine-tree. The sap ascends from the root, and fills all the branches. When one branch is satisfied, it lets the streams pass on to the next; nay, it carries the rich juice to the smaller twigs and tendrils, that all may have their share—that all may bear their precious fruit. So it is with the body. The blood comes from the heart in full and nourishing streams,—it flows to all members,—one member conducts it to another, that all may be kept alive, and all may grow.

So it is in the Lord's Supper. The bread and wine are passed from hand to hand, to show that we are members one of another. "For we being many, are one bread and one body, for we are all partakers of that one bread" (I Cor. 10:17). It is a solemn declaration that you are one with all true Christians, one in peace, one in feeling, one in holiness; and that if one member suffer, you will suffer with it, or if one member be honored, you will rejoice with it. You thereby declare that you are branches of the true Vine, and are vitally united to all the branches—that you wish the same Holy Spirit to pervade every bosom. You declare that you are lamps of the same golden candlestick, and that you wish the same golden oil to keep you and them burning and shining as lights in a dark world. Learn, once more, that most should stay away from this table. Some of you know that you have not a spark of love to the Christians. You persecute them, or despise them. Your tongue is like a sharp razor against them; you ridicule their notions of grace, and conversion, and the work of the Spirit. You hate their conversation; you call it cant and

hypocrisy. When they are speaking on divine things with a full heart, and you come in, they are obliged to stop because you dislike it. Why should you come to this holy table? What is hypocrisy, if this is not? You put on a serious face and air; you press eagerly in to the table; you sit down, and look deeply solemnized; you take the bread into your hand, pretending to declare that you have been converted, and brought to accept of a crucified Christ. You then eat of the broken bread and drink of that cup with evident marks of emotion, pretending that you are one of those who live upon Jesus, who are filled with the Spirit. You then pass the bread and wine to others, pretending that you love the Christians,—that you wish all to be partakers with you in the grace of the Lord Jesus; and yet all the while you hate and detest them, their thoughts, their ways, their company. You would not for the world become a man of prayer. Beloved souls, what is hypocrisy, if this is not? I solemnly declare that I had rather see you "breathing out threatenings and slaughter against the disciples of the Lord," than come to be a wolf in sheep's clothing. Are you not afraid lest, while you are sitting at the table, you should hear the voice of the Lord Jesus saying, "Judas, betrayest thou the Son of man with a kiss?"

Dear believer, you "know that you are passed from death unto life, because you love the brethren." This pure and holy life is one of the first feelings in the converted bosom. It is divine and imperishable. You are a companion of all that fear God. It would be hell to you to spend eternity with wicked men. Come and show this love at the feast of love. The table in the upper room at Jerusalem was but a type and earnest of the table in the upper room of glory. Soon we shall exchange the table below for the table above, where we shall give full expression to our love to all eternity. There no betrayers can come—"no unclean thing can enter." Jesus shall be at the head of the table, and God shall wipe away all tears from our eyes.

Questions addressed to young communicants, to be answered in secret to God

1. Is it to please your father or mother, or any one on earth, that you think of coming to the Lord's table?

2. Is it because it is the custom, and your friends and companions are coming?

3. Is it because you have come to a certain time of life?

4. What are your real motives for wishing to come to the Lord's table? Is it to thank God for saving your soul?—(Ps. 116:12-13); to remember Jesus?—(Luke 22:19); to get near to Christ?—(John 13:23); or is it for worldly character? to gain a name? to gain money?—(Matt. 26:15).

5. Who do you think should come to the Lord's table? who should stay away?

6. Do you think any should come but those who are truly converted? and what is it to be converted?

7. Would you come if you knew yourself to be unconverted?

8. Should those come who have had deep concern about their soul, but are not come to Christ?

9. Do you think you have been awakened by the Holy Spirit? brought to Christ? born again? What makes you think so?

10. What is the meaning of the broken bread and poured-out wine?

11. What is the meaning of taking the bread and wine into your hand? Have you as truly received the Lord Jesus Christ?

12. What is the meaning of feeding upon them? Are you as truly living upon Christ?

13. What is the meaning of giving the bread and wine to those at the same table as you? Do you as truly love the brethren?

Scriptures to be meditated on at a communion season

Ex. 12; Pss. 22, 51, 69, 116; Song of Solomon; Is. 53; Matt. 22:1-14; 26, 27; Mark 14, 15; Luke 22, 23; John 13, 14, 15, 16, 17; 1 Cor. 11:23-34.

Robert Murray M'Cheyne,
St. Peter's Church, Dundee, October 1841

2.49 THE LAST SUPPER, F. W. FARRAR

On the Tuesday evening in Passion week Jesus had spoken of the Passover as the season of His death. If the customs enjoined by the Law had been capable of rigid and exact fulfillment, the Paschal lamb for the use of Himself and His disciples would have been set apart on the previous Sunday evening; but although, since the days of the exile, the Passover had been observed, it is probable that the changed circumstances of the nation had introduced many natural and perfectly justifiable changes in the old regulations. It would have been a simple impossibility for the myriads of pilgrims to provide themselves beforehand with a Paschal lamb.

It was on the morning of Thursday—Green Thursday, as it used to be called during the Middle Ages—that some conversation took place between Jesus and his disciples about the Paschal feast. They asked him where He wished the preparation for it to be made. As He had now withdrawn from all public teaching, and was spending this Thursday, as He had spent the previous day, in complete seclusion, they probably expected that He would eat the Passover at Bethany, which for such purposes had been decided by rabbinical authority to be within the limits of Jerusalem. But His plans were otherwise. He, the true Paschal Lamb, was to be sacrificed once and for ever in the Holy City, where it is probable that in that very Passover, and on the very same day, some 260,000 of those lambs of which He was the antitype were destined to be slain.

Accordingly He sent Peter and John to Jerusalem, and appointing for them a sign both mysterious and secret, told them that on entering the gate they would meet a servant carrying a pitcher of water from one of the fountains for evening use; following him they would reach a house, to the owner of which they were to intimate the intention of the Master to eat the Passover there with His disciples; and this householder—conjectured by some to have been Joseph of Arimathea, by others John Mark—would at once place at their disposal a furnished upper room, ready provided with the requisite table and couches. They found all as Jesus had said, and there "made ready the Passover." There are ample reasons for believing that this was not the ordinary Jewish Passover, but a meal eaten by our Lord and his Apostles on the previous evening, Thursday, Nisan 13, to which a quasi-Paschal character was given, but which was intended to supersede the Jewish festival by one of far deeper and diviner significance.

It was towards the evening, probably when the gathering dusk would prevent all needless observation, that Jesus and His disciples walked from Bethany, by that old familiar road over the Mount of Olives, which His sacred feet were never again destined to traverse until after death. How far they attracted attention, or how it was that He whose person was known to so many—and who, as the great central figure of such great counter agitations, had, four days before, been accompanied with shouts of triumph, as He would be, on the following day, with yells of insult—could now enter Jerusalem unnoticed with His followers, we cannot tell. We catch no glimpse of the little company till we find them assembled in that "large upper room"— perhaps the very room where three days afterwards the sorrow-stricken Apostles first saw their risen Savior—perhaps the very room where, amid the sound of a rushing mighty wind, each meek brow was first mitred with Pentecostal flame.

When they arrived, the meal was ready, the table spread, the triclinia laid with cushions for the guests. Imagination loves to reproduce all the probable details of that deeply moving and eternally sacred scene; and if we compare the notices of ancient Jewish custom, with the immemorial fashions still existing in the changeless East, we can feel but little doubt as to the general nature of the arrangements. They were totally unlike those with which the genius of Leonardo da Vinci, and other great painters, has made us so familiar. The room probably had white walls, and was bare of all except the most necessary furniture and adornment. The couches or cushions, each large enough to hold three persons, were placed around three sides of one or more low tables of gaily painted wood, each scarcely higher than stools. The seat of honor was the central one of the central triclinium, or mat. This was, of course, occupied by the Lord. Each guest reclined at full length, leaning on his left elbow, that his right hand might be free. At the right hand of Jesus reclined the beloved disciple, whose head therefore could, at any moment, be placed upon the breast of his friend and Lord.

It may be that the very act of taking their seats at the table had, once more, stirred up in the minds of the Apostles those disputes about precedence which, on previous occasions, our Lord had so tenderly and beautifully rebuked. The mere question of a place at table might seem a matter too infinitesimal and unimportant to ruffle the feelings of good and self-denying men at an hour so supreme and solemn; but that love for "the chief seats" at feasts and elsewhere, which Jesus had denounced in the Pharisees, is not only innate in the human heart, but is even so powerful that it has at times caused the most terrific tragedies. But at this moment, when the soul of Jesus was full of such sublime purpose— when He was breathing the pure unmingled air of Eternity, and the Eternal was to Him, in spite of His mortal investiture, not only the present but the seen—a strife of this kind must have been more than ever painful. It showed how little, as yet, even these His chosen followers had entered into the meaning of His life. It showed that the evil spirits of pride and selfishness were not yet exorcised from their struggling souls. It showed that, even now, they had wholly failed to understand His many and earnest warnings as to the nature of His kingdom, and the certainty of His fate. That some great crisis was at hand—that their Master was to suffer and be slain—they must have partially realized: but they seem to have regarded this as a mere temporary obscuration, to be followed by an immediate divulgence of His splendor, and the setting up on earth of His Messianic throne.

In pained silence Jesus had heard their murmured jealousies, while they were arranging their places at the feast. Not by mere verbal reproof, but by an act more profoundly significant and touching, He determined to teach to them, and to all who love Him, a nobler lesson.

Every Eastern room, if it belongs to any but the very poorest, has the central part of the floor covered with mats, and as a person enters, he lays aside his sandals at the door of the room, mainly in order not to defile the clean white mats with the dust and dirt of the road or streets, and also (at any rate among Mahometans) because the mat is hallowed by being knelt upon in prayer. Before they reclined at the table, the disciples had doubtless conformed to this cleanly and reasonable custom; but another customary and pleasant habit, which we know that Jesus appreciated, had been neglected. Their feet must have been covered with dust from their walk along the hot and much frequented road from Bethany to Jerusalem, and under such circumstances they would have been refreshed for the festival by washing their feet after putting off their sandals. But to wash the feet was the work of slaves; and since no one had offered to perform the kindly office, Jesus Himself, in His eternal humility and self-denial, rose from His place at the meal to do the menial service which none of His disciples had offered to do for Him. Well may the amazement of the beloved disciple show itself in his narrative, as he dwells on every particular of that solemn scene. "Though He knew that the Father had given all things into His hands, and that He came from God and was going to God, He arose from the supper and laid aside His garments, and taking a towel, girded Himself." It is probable that in the utterness of self-abnegation, He entirely stripped His upper limbs, laying aside both the *simchah* and the *cetôneth*, as though He had been the meanest slave, and wrapping the towel round His waist. Then pouring water into the large copper basin with which an Oriental house is always provided, He began without a word to wash His disciples' feet, and wipe them dry with the towel which served Him as a girdle. Awe and shame kept them silent until He came to Peter, whose irrepressible emotions found vent in the surprised, half-indignant question, "Lord, dost Thou seek to wash my feet?" Then, the Son of God, the King of Israel, who hast the words of eternal life—Thou, whose feet Oriental kings should anoint with their costliest spikenard, and penitents bathe in precious tears—dost Thou wash Peter's feet? It was the old dread and self-depreciation which, more than three years before, had prompted the cry of the rude fisherman of Galilee, "Depart from me, for I am a sinful man, O Lord"; it was the old self-will which, a year before, had expressed itself in the self-confident dissuasion of the elated Man of Rock—"That be far from Thee, Lord; this shall not happen unto Thee." Gently recognizing what was good in His impetuous follower's ejaculation, Jesus calmly tells him that as yet he is too immature to understand the meaning of His actions, though the day should come when their significance should dawn upon him. But Peter, obstinate and rash—as though he felt, even more than his Lord, the greatness of Him that ministered, and the meanness of him to whom the service would he done—persisted in his opposition: "Never, never, till the end of time," he impetuously exclaims; "shalt Thou wash my feet? "But then Jesus revealed to him the dangerous self-assertion which lurked in this false humility. "If I wash thee not, thou hast no share with me." Alike, thy self-conceit and thy self-disgust must be laid aside if thou wouldest be mine. My follower must accept my will, even when he least can comprehend it, even when it seems to violate his own conceptions of what I am. That calm word changed the whole current of thought and feeling in the warm-hearted passionate disciple. "No share with Thee? oh, forbid it, Heaven! Lord, not my feet only, but also my hands and my head!" But no: once more he must accept what Christ wills, not in his own way, but in Christ's way. This total washing was not needed. The baptism of his initiation was over; in that laver of regeneration he had been already dipped. Nothing more was needed than the daily cleansing from minor and freshly-contracted stains. The feet soiled with the clinging dust of daily sins, these must be washed in daily renovation; but the heart and being of the man, these were already washed, were cleansed, were sanctified. Jesus saith to him, "He that is bathed hath no need save to wash his feet, but is clean every whit. And ye are clean;" and then He was forced to add with a deep sigh, "but not all." The last words were an allusion to His consciousness of one traitorous presence; for He knew, what as yet they knew not, that the hands of the Lord of Life had just washed the traitor's feet. Oh, strange unfathomable depth of human infatuation and ingratitude; that traitor, with all the black and accursed treachery in his false heart, had seen, had known, had suffered it; had felt the touch of those kind and gentle hands, had been refreshed by the cleansing water, had seen that sacred head bent over his feet, stained as they yet were with the hurried secret walk which had taken him into the throng of sanctimonious murderers over the shoulder of Olivet. But for him there had been no purification in that lustral water; neither was the devil within him exorcised by that gentle voice, nor the leprosy of his heart healed by that miracle-producing touch.

The other Apostles did not at the moment notice that grievous exception—"but not all." It may be that their consciences gave to all, even to the most faithful, too sad a cause to echo the words, with something of misgiving, to his own soul. Then Jesus, after having washed their feet, resumed His garments, and once more reclined at the meal. As he leaned there on His left elbow, John lay at his right, with His head quite close to Jesus' breast. Next to John, and at the top of the next mat or cushion, would probably be his brother James; and—as we infer from the few details of the meal—at the left of Jesus lay the Man of Kerioth, who may either have thrust himself into that position, or who, as the holder of the common purse, occupied a place of some prominence among the little band. It seems probable that Peter's place was at the top of the next mat, and at the left of Judas. And as the meal began, Jesus taught them what His act had meant. Rightly, and with proper respect, they called Him "Master" and "Lord," for so He was; yet, though the Lord is greater than the slave, the Sender greater than His Apostle, He their Lord and Master had washed their feet. It was a kind and gracious task, and such ought to be the nature of all their dealings with each other. He had done it to teach them humility, to teach them self-denial, to teach them love: blessed they if they learnt the lesson! blessed if they learnt that the struggles for precedence, the assertions of claims, the standings upon dignity, the fondness for the mere exercise of authority, marked the tyrannies and immaturities of heathendom, and that the greatest Christian is ever the humblest. He should be chief among them who, for the sake of others, gladly laid on himself the lowliest burdens, and sought for himself the humblest services. Again and again He warned them that they were not to look for earthly reward or earthly prosperity; the throne, and the table, and the kingdom, and the many mansions were not of earth.

And then again the trouble of His spirit broke forth. He was speaking of those whom He had chosen; He was not speaking of them all. Among the blessed company sat one who even then was drawing on his own head, a curse. It had been so with David, whose nearest friend had become his bitterest foe; it was foreordained that it should be so likewise with David's Son. Soon should they know with what full foreknowledge He had gone to all that awaited Him; soon should they be able to judge that, just as the man who receives in Christ's name His humblest servant receiveth Him, so the rejection of Him is the rejection of His Father, and that this rejection of the Living God was the crime which at this moment was being committed, and committed in their very midst.

There, next but one to Him, hearing all these words unmoved, full of spite and hatred, utterly hardening his heart, and leaning the whole weight of his demoniac possession against that door of mercy which even now and even here His Savior would have opened to him, sat Judas, the false smile of hypocrisy on his face, but rage, and shame, and greed, and anguish, and treachery in his heart. The near presence of that black iniquity, the failure of even his pathetic lowliness to move or touch the man's hideous purpose, troubled the human heart of Jesus to its inmost depths—wrung from Him His agony of yet plainer prediction, "Verily, verily, I say unto you, that one of you shall betray me!" That night all, even the best beloved, were to forsake Him, but it was not that; that night even the boldest-hearted was to deny Him with oaths, but it was not that; nay, but one of them was to betray Him. Their hearts misgave them as they listened. Already a deep unspeakable sadness had fallen over the sacred meal. Like the somber and threatening crimson that intermingles with the colors of sunset, a dark omen seemed to be overshadowing them—a shapeless presentiment of evil—an unspoken sense of dread. If all their hopes were to be thus blighted—if at this very Passover, He for whom they had given up all, and who had been to them all in all, was indeed to be betrayed by one of themselves to an unpitied and ignominious end—if this were possible, anything seemed possible. Their hearts were troubled. All their want of nobility, all their failure in love, all the depth of their selfishness, all the weakness of their faith—

"Every evil thought they ever thought,
And every evil word they ever said,
And every evil thing they ever did,"

all crowded upon their memories, and made their consciences afraid. None of them seemed safe from anything, and each read his own self-distrust in his brother-disciple's eye. And hence, at that moment of supreme sadness and almost despair, it was with lips that faltered and cheeks that paled, that each asked the humble question, "Lord, is it I?" Better always that question than "Is it he?"—better the penitent watchfulness of a self-condemning humility than the haughty Pharisaism of censorious pride. The very horror that breathed through their question, the very trustfulness which prompted it, involved their acquittal. Jesus only remained silent, in order that even then, if it were

possible, there might be time for Judas to repent. But Peter was unable to restrain his sorrow and his impatience. Eager to know and to prevent the treachery—unseen by Jesus, whose back was turned to him as He reclined at the meal—he made a signal to John to ask "who it was." The head of John was close to Jesus, and laying it with affectionate trustfulness on his Master's breast, he said in a whisper, "Lord, who is it?" The reply, given in a tone equally low, was heard by John alone, and confirmed the suspicions with which it is evident that the repellent nature of Judas had already inspired him. At Eastern meals all the guests eat with their fingers out of a common dish, and it is common for one at times to dip into the dish a piece of the thin flexible cake of bread which is placed by each, and taking up with it a portion of the meat or rice in the dish, to hand it to another guest. So ordinary an incident of any daily meal would attract no notice whatever. Jesus handed to the traitor Apostle a "sop" of this kind, and this, as He told John, was the sign which should indicate to him, and possibly through him to St. Peter, which was the guilty member of the little band. And then He added aloud, in words which can have but one significance, in words the most awful and crushing that ever passed His lips, "The Son of Man goeth indeed, as it is written of Him: but woe unto that man by whom the Son of Man is betrayed! It were good for that man if he had not been born!" "Words," it has been well said, "of immeasurable ruin, words of immeasurable woe"—and the more terrible because uttered by the lips of immeasurable Love: words capable, if any were capable, of revealing to the lost soul of the traitor all the black gulf of horror that was yawning before his feet. He must have known something of what had passed; he may well have overheard some fragment of the conversation, or at least have had a dim consciousness that in some way it referred to him. He may even have been aware that when his hand met the hand of Jesus over the dish there was some meaning in the action. When the others were questioning among themselves "which was the traitor?" he had remained silent in the defiant hardness of contempt or the sullen gloom of guilt; but now—stung, it may be, by some sense of the shuddering horror with which the mere possibility of his guilt was regarded—he nerved himself for the shameful and shameless question. After all the rest had sunk into silence, there grated upon the Savior's ear that hoarse untimely whisper, in all the bitterness of its defiant mockery—not asking, as the rest had asked, in loving reverence, "Lord, is it I?" but with the cold formal title, "Rabbi, is it I?" Then that low unreproachful answer, "Thou hast said," sealed his guilt. The rest did not hear it; it was probably caught by Peter and John alone; and Judas ate the sop which Jesus had given him, and after the sop Satan entered into him. As all the winds, on some night of storm, riot and howl through the rent walls of some desecrated shrine, so through the ruined life of Judas envy and avarice, and hatred and ingratitude, were rushing all at once. In that bewildering chaos of a soul spotted with mortal guilt, the Satanic had triumphed over the human; in that dark heart earth and hell were thenceforth at one; in that lost soul sin had conceived and brought forth death. "What thou art doing, do more quickly," said Jesus to him aloud. He knew what the words implied, he knew that they meant, "Thy fell purpose is matured, carry it out with no more of these futile hypocrisies and meaningless delays." Judas rose from the feast. The innocent-hearted Apostles thought that Jesus had bidden him go out and make purchases for to-morrow's Passover, or give something out of the common store which should enable the poor to buy their Paschal lamb. And so from the lighted room, from the holy banquet, from the blessed company, from the presence of his Lord, he went immediately out, and—as the beloved disciple adds, with a shudder of dread significance letting the curtain of darkness fall for ever on that appalling figure—"and it was night."

We cannot tell with any certainty whether this took place before or after the institution of the Lord's Supper—whether Judas partook or not of those hallowed symbols. Nor can we tell whether at all, or, if at all, to what extent, our Lord conformed the minor details of His last supper to the half-joyous, half-mournful customs of the Paschal feast; nor, again, can

we tell how far the customs of the Passover in that day resembled those detailed to us in the Rabbinic writings. Nothing could have been simpler than the ancient method of their commemorating their deliverance from Egypt and from the destroying angel. The central custom of the feast was the hasty eating of the Paschal lamb, with unleavened bread and bitter herbs, in a standing attitude, with loins girt and shoes upon the feet, as they had eaten hastily on the night of their deliverance. In this way the Passover is still yearly eaten by the Samaritans at the summit of Gerizim, and there to this day they will hand to the stranger the little olive-shaped morsel of unleavened bread, enclosing a green fragment of wild endive or some other bitter herb, which may perhaps resemble, except that it is not dipped in the dish, the very psomíon which Judas received at the hands of Christ. But even if the Last Supper was a Passover, we are told that the Jews had long ceased to eat it standing, or to observe the rule which forbade any guest to leave the house till morning. They made, in fact, many radical distinctions between the Egyptian and the permanent Passover which was subsequently observed. The latter meal began by filling each guest a cup of wine, over which the head of the family pronounced a benediction. After this the hands were washed in a bason of water, and a table was brought in, on which were placed the bitter herbs, the unleavened bread, the charoseth, (a dish made of dates, raisins, and vinegar), the Paschal lamb, and the flesh of the chagigah. The father dipped a piece of herb in the charoseth, ate it, with a benediction, and distributed a similar morsel to all. A second cup of wine was then poured out; the youngest present inquired the meaning of the Paschal night; the father replied with a full account of the observance; the first part of the Hallel (Ps. 107-114:) was then sung, a blessing repeated, a third cup of wine was drunk, grace was said, a fourth cup poured out, the rest of the Hallel (Ps. 115-118) sung, and the ceremony ended by the blessing of the song. Some, no doubt, of the facts mentioned at the Last Supper may be brought into comparison with parts of this ceremony. It appears, for instance, that the supper began with a benediction, and the passing of a cup of wine, which Jesus bade them divide among themselves, saying that he would not drink of the fruit of the vine until the kingdom of God should come. The other cup—passed round after supper—has been identified by some with the third cup, the "cup of blessing" of the Jewish ceremonial (1 Cor. 10:16); and the hymn which was sung before the departure of the little company to Gethsemane has, with much probability, been supposed to be the second part of the great Hallel.

The relation of these incidents of the meal to the various Paschal observances which we have detailed is, however, doubtful. What is not doubtful, and what has the deepest interest for all Christians, is the establishment at this last supper of the Sacrament of the Eucharist. Of this we have no fewer than four accounts—the brief description of St. Paul agreeing in almost verbal exactness with those of the Synoptists. In each account we clearly recognize the main facts which St. Paul expressly tells us that "he had received of the Lord"—viz., "that the Lord Jesus, on the same night in which He was betrayed, took bread; and when He had given thanks, He brake it, and said, Take, eat; this is my body which is broken for you; this do in remembrance of me. After the same manner also He took the cup when He had supped, saying, This cup is the New Testament in my blood; this do ye, as oft as ye drink it, in remembrance of me" (1 Cor. 11:23-25). Never since that memorable evening has the Church ceased to observe the commandment of her Lord; ever since that day, from age to age, has this blessed and holy Sacrament been a memorial of the death of Christ, and a strengthening and refreshing of the soul by the body and blood, as the body is refreshed and strengthened by the bread and wine.

F. W. Farrar, The Life of Christ, New York: AL Burt Company

12

JESUS IN GETHSEMANE

2.50 CHRIST'S AGONY, JONATHAN EDWARDS

"And being in an agony he prayed more earnestly, and his sweat was as it were great drops of blood falling down to the ground." Luke 22:44

Our Lord Jesus Christ, in his original nature, was infinitely above all suffering, for he was "God over all, blessed for evermore;" but, when he became man, he was not only capable of suffering, but partook of that nature that is remarkably feeble and exposed to suffering. The human nature, on account of its weakness, is in Scripture compared to the grass of the field, which easily withers and decays. So it is compared to a leaf; and to the dry stubble; and to a blast of wind: and the nature of feeble man is said to be but dust and ashes, to have its foundation in the dust, and to be crushed before the moth. It was this nature, with all its weakness and exposedness to sufferings, which Christ, who is the Lord God omnipotent, took upon him. He did not take the human nature on him in its first, most perfect and vigorous state, but in that feeble forlorn state which it is in since the fall; and therefore Christ is called "a tender plant," and "a root out of a dry ground." Is. 53:2. "For he shall grow up before him as a tender plant, and as a root out of a dry ground: he hath no form nor comeliness; and when we shall see him, there is no beauty that we should desire him." Thus, as Christ's principal errand into the world was suffering, so, agreeably to that errand, he came with such a nature and in such circumstances, as most made way for his suffering; so his whole life was filled up with suffering, he began to suffer in his infancy, but his suffering increased the more he drew near to the close of his life. His suffering after his public ministry began, was probably much greater than before; and the latter part of the

time of his public ministry seems to have been distinguished by suffering. The longer Christ lived in the world, the more men saw and heard of him, the more they hated him. His enemies were more and more enraged by the continuance of the opposition that he made to their lusts; and the devil having been often baffled by him, grew more and more enraged, and strengthened the battle more and more against him: so that the cloud over Christ's head grew darker and darker, as long as he lived in the world, till it was in its greatest blackness when he hung upon the cross and cried out, My God, my God, why hast thou forsaken me! Before this, it was exceedingly dark, in the time of his agony in the garden; of which we have an account in the words now read; and which I propose to make the subject of my present discourse. The word agony properly signifies an earnest strife, such as is witnessed in wrestling, running, or fighting. And therefore in Luke 13:24. "Strive to enter in at the strait gate: for many, I say unto you, will seek to enter in, and shall not be able"; the word in the original, translated strive, is ἀγωνίζεσθε. "Agonize, to enter in at the strait gate." The word is especially used for that sort of strife, which in those days was exhibited in the Olympic games, in which men strove for the mastery in running, wrestling, and other such kinds of exercises; and a prize was set up that was bestowed on the conqueror. Those, who thus contended, were, in the language then in use, said to agonize. Thus the apostle in his epistle to the Christians of Corinth, a city of Greece, where such games were annually exhibited, says in allusion to the strivings of the combatants, "And every man that striveth for the mastery," in the original, every one that agonizeth, "is temperate in all things." The place where those games were held was called Αγων, or the place of agony; and the word is particularly used in Scripture for that striving in earnest prayer wherein persons wrestle with God: they are said to agonize, or to be in agony, in prayer. So the word is used Rom. 15:30. "Now I beseech you, brethren, for the Lord Jesus Christ's sake, and for the love of the Spirit, that ye strive together with me in your prayers to God for me"; in the original συναγωνίσασθαί μοι, that ye agonize together with me. So Col. 4:12. "Always laboring fervently for you in prayer, that ye may stand perfect and complete in all the will of God"; in the original ἀγωνιζόμενος agonizing for you. So that when it is said in the text that Christ was in an agony, the meaning is, that his soul was in a great and earnest strife and conflict. It was so in two respects:

1. As his soul was in a great and sore conflict with those terrible and amazing views and apprehensions which he then had.

2. As he was at the same time in great labor and earnest strife with God in prayer.

I propose therefore, in discoursing on the subject of Christ's agony, distinctly to unfold it, under these two propositions,

I. That the soul of Christ in his agony in the garden had a sore conflict with those terrible and amazing views and apprehensions, of which he was then the subject.

II. That the soul of Christ in his agony in the garden had a great and earnest labor and struggle with God in prayer.

I. THE SOUL OF CHRIST IN HIS AGONY IN THE GARDEN HAD A SORE CONFLICT WITH THOSE TERRIBLE AMAZING VIEWS AND APPREHENSIONS, OF WHICH HE WAS THEN THE SUBJECT.

In illustrating this proposition I shall endeavor to show,

1. What those views and apprehensions were.

2. That the conflict or agony of Christ's soul was occasioned by those views and apprehensions.

3. That this conflict was peculiarly great and distressing; and,

4. What we may suppose to be the special design of God in giving Christ those terrible views and apprehensions, and causing him to suffer that dreadful conflict, before he was crucified.

I propose to show,

First, What were those terrible views and amazing apprehensions which Christ had in his agony. This may be explained by considering,

1. The cause of those views and apprehensions; and,

2. The manner in which they were then experienced.

1. The cause of those views and apprehensions, which Christ had in his agony in the garden, was the bitter cup which he was soon after to drink on the cross. The sufferings which Christ underwent in his agony in the garden, were not his greatest sufferings; though they were so very great. But his last sufferings upon the cross were his principal sufferings; and therefore they are called "the cup that he had to drink." The sufferings of the cross, under which he was slain, are always in the Scriptures represented as the main sufferings of Christ; those in which especially "he bare our sins in his own body," and made atonement for sin. His enduring the cross, his humbling himself, and becoming obedient unto death, even the death of the cross, is spoken of as the main thing wherein his sufferings appeared. This is the cup that Christ had set before him in his agony. It is manifest that Christ had this in view at this time, from the prayers which he then offered. According to Matthew, Christ made three prayers that evening while in the garden of Gethsemane, and all on this one subject, the bitter cup that he was to drink. Of the first, we have an account in Matt. 26:39.

"And he went a little farther, and fell on his face and prayed, saying, O my Father, if it be possible, let this cup pass from me; nevertheless, not as I will but as thou wilt"; of the second in the 42d verse, "He went away again the second time and prayed, saying, O my Father, if this cup may not pass from me, except I drink it, thy will be done"; and of the third in the 44th verse, "And he left them, and went away again, and prayed the third time, saying the same words." From this it plainly appears what it was of which Christ had such terrible views and apprehensions at that time. What he thus insists on in his prayers, shows on what his mind was so deeply intent. It was his sufferings on the cross, which were to be endured the next day, when there should be darkness over all the earth, and at the same time a deeper darkness over the soul of Christ, of which he had now such lively views and distressing apprehensions.

2. The manner in which this bitter cup was now set in Christ's view.

(1) He had a lively apprehension of it impressed at that time on his mind. He had an apprehension of the cup that he was to drink before. His principal errand into the the world was to drink that cup, and he therefore was never unthoughtful of it, but always bore it in his mind, and often spoke of it to his disciples. Thus Matt. 16:21. "From that time forth began Jesus to show unto his disciples how that he must go unto Jerusalem, and suffer many things of the elders, and chief priests, and scribes, and be killed, and be raised again the third day ." Again ch. 20:17, 18, 19. "And Jesus going up to Jerusalem, took the twelve disciples apart in the way, and said unto them, Behold, we go up to Jerusalem; and the Son of man shall be betrayed unto the chief priests, and unto the scribes, and they shall condemn him to death. And shall deliver him to the Gentiles to mock, and to scourge, and to crucify him: and the third day he shall rise again." The same thing was the subject of conversation on the mount with Moses and Elias when he was transfigured. So he speaks of his bloody baptism, Luke 12:50. "But I have a baptism to be baptized with; and how am I straitened till it be accomplished!" He speaks

of it again to Zebedee's children, Matt. 20:22. "Are ye able to drink of the cup that I shall drink of, and to be baptized with the baptism that I am baptized with? They say unto him, We are able." He spake of his being lifted up. John 8:28. "Then said Jesus unto them, When ye have lifted up the Son of man, then shall ye know that I am he, and that I do nothing of myself; but as my Father hath taught me, I speak these things ." John 12:34. "The people answered him, We have heard out of the law that Christ abideth for ever: and how sayest thou, The Son of man must be lifted up? Who is this Son of man?" So he spake of destroying the temple of his body, John 2:19. "Jesus answered and said unto them, Destroy this temple, and in three days I will raise it up." And he was very much in speaking of it a little before his agony, in his dying counsels to his disciples in the 12th and 13th ch. of John. Thus this was not the first time that Christ had this bitter cup in his view. On the contrary, he seems always to have had it in view. But it seems that at this time God gave him an extraordinary view of it. A sense of that wrath that was to be poured out upon him, and of those amazing sufferings that he was to undergo, was strongly impressed on his mind by the immediate power of God; so that he had far more full and lively apprehensions of the bitterness of the cup which he was to drink than he ever had before, and these apprehensions were so terrible, that his feeble human nature shrunk at the sight, and was ready to sink.

(2) The cup of bitterness was now represented as just at hand. He had not only a more clear and lively view of it than before; but it was now set directly before him, that he might without delay take it up and drink it; for then, within that same hour, Judas was to come with his band of men, and he was then to deliver up himself into their hands to the end that he might drink this cup the next day; unless indeed he refused to take it, and so made his escape from that place where Judas would come; which he had opportunity enough to do if he had been so minded. Having thus shown what those terrible views and apprehensions were which Christ had in the time of his agony; I shall endeavor to show,

II. That the conflict which the soul of Christ then endured was occasioned by those views and apprehensions.

The sorrow and distress which his soul then suffered, arose from that lively, and full, and immediate view which he had then given him of that cup of wrath; by which God the Father did as it were set the cup down before him, for him to take it and drink it. Some have inquired, what was the occasion of that distress and agony, and many speculations there have been about it, but the account which the Scripture itself gives us is sufficiently full in this matter, and does not leave room for speculation or doubt. The thing that Christ's mind was so full of at that time was, without doubt, the same with that which his mouth was so full of: it was the dread which his feeble human nature had of that dreadful cup, which was vastly more terrible than Nebuchadnezzar's fiery furnace. He had then a near view of that furnace of wrath, into which he was to be cast; he was brought to the mouth of the furnace that he might look into it, and stand and view its raging flames, and see the glowings of its heat, that he might know where he was going and what he was about to suffer. This was the thing that filled his soul with sorrow and darkness, this terrible sight as it were overwhelmed him. For what was that human nature of Christ to such mighty wrath as this? it was in itself, without the supports of God, but a feeble worm of the dust, a thing that was crushed before the moth, none of God's children ever had such a cup set before them, as this first being of every creature had. But not to dwell any longer on this, I hasten to show,

III. That the conflict in Christ's soul, in this view of his last sufferings, was dreadful, beyond all expression or conception. This will appear,

1. From what is said of its dreadfulness in the history. By one evangelist we are told, (Matt. 26:37) "He began to be sorrowful and very heavy; and by another, (Mark 14:33) "And he taketh with him Peter, and James, and John, and began to be sore amazed, and to be very heavy." These expressions hold forth the intense and overwhelming distress that his soul was in. Luke's expression in the text of his being in an agony, according to the signification of that word in the original, implies no common degree of sorrow, but such extreme distress that his nature had a most violent conflict with it, as a man that wrestles with all his might with a strong man, who labors and exerts his utmost strength to gain a conquest over him.

2. From what Christ himself says of it, who was not wont to magnify things beyond the truth. He says, "My soul is exceeding sorrowful even unto death." Matt. 26:38. What language can more strongly express the most extreme degree of sorrow? His soul was not only "sorrowful," but "exceeding sorrowful"; and not only so, but because that did not fully express the degree of his sorrow, he adds, "even unto death"; which seems to intimate that the very pains and sorrows of hell, of eternal death, had got hold upon him. The Hebrews were wont to express the utmost degree of sorrow that any creature could be liable to by the phrase, the shadow of death. Christ had now, as it were, the shadow of death brought over his soul by the near view which he had of that bitter cup that was now set before him.

3. From the effect which it had on his body, in causing that bloody sweat that we read of in the text. In our translation it is said, that "his sweat was, as it were, great drops of blood, falling down to the ground." The word rendered great drops, is in the original θρόμβοι, which properly signifies lumps or clots; for we may suppose that the blood that was pressed out through the pores of his skin by the violence of that inward struggle and conflict that there was, when it came to be exposed to the cool air of the night, congealed and stiffened, as is the nature of blood, and so fell off from him not in drops, but in clots. If the suffering of Christ had occasioned merely a violent sweat, it would have shown that he was in great agony; for it must be an extraordinary grief and exercise of mind that causes the body to be all of a sweat abroad in the open air, in a cold night as that was, as is evident from John 18:18. "And the servants and officers stood there, who had made a fire

of coals, (for it was cold,) and they warmed themselves; and Peter stood with them, and warmed himself." This was the same night in which Christ had his agony in the garden. But Christ's inward distress and grief was not merely such as caused him to be in a violent and universal sweat, but such as caused him to sweat blood. The distress and anguish of his mind was so unspeakably extreme as to force his blood through the pores of his skin, and that so plentifully as to fall in great clots or drops from his body to the ground. I come now to show,

IV. What may be supposed to be the special end of God's giving Christ beforehand these terrible views of his last sufferings; in other words, why it was needful that he should have a more full and extraordinary view of the cup that he was to drink, a little before he drank it, than ever he had before; or why he must have such a foretaste of the wrath of God to be endured on the cross, before the time came that he was actually to endure it.

Answer. It was needful, in order that he might take the cup and drink it, as knowing what he did. Unless the human nature of Christ had had an extraordinary view given him beforehand of what he was to suffer, he could not, as man, fully know beforehand what he was going to suffer, and therefore could not, as man, know what he did when he took the cup to drink it, because he would not fully have known what the cup was—it being a cup that he never drank before. If Christ had plunged himself into those dreadful sufferings, without being fully sensible beforehand of their bitterness and dreadfulness, he must have done he knew not what. As man, he would have plunged himself into sufferings of the amount of which he was ignorant, and so have acted blindfold; and of course his taking upon him these sufferings could not have been so fully his own act. Christ, as God, perfectly knew what these sufferings were; but it was more needful also that he should know as man; for he was to suffer as man, and the act of Christ in taking that cup was the act of Christ as God man. But the man Christ Jesus hitherto never had had experience of any such sufferings as he was now to endure on the cross; and therefore he could

not fully know what they were beforehand, but by having an extraordinary view of them set before him, and an extraordinary sense of them impressed on his mind. We have heard of tortures that others have undergone, but we do not fully know what they were, because we never experienced them; and it is impossible that we should fully know what they were but in one of these two ways, either by experiencing them, or by having a view given of them, or a sense of them impressed in an extraordinary way. Such a sense was impressed on the mind of the man Christ Jesus, in the garden of Gethsemane, of his last sufferings, and that caused his agony. When he had a full sight given him what that wrath of God was that he was to suffer, the sight was overwhelming to him; it made his soul exceeding sorrowful, even unto death. Christ was going to be cast into a dreadful furnace of wrath, and it was not proper that he should plunge himself into it blindfold, as not knowing how dreadful the furnace was. Therefore that he might not do so, God first brought him and set him at the mouth of the furnace, that he might look in, and stand and view its fierce and raging flames, and might see where he was going, and might voluntarily enter into it and bear it for sinners, as knowing what it was. This view Christ had in his agony. Then God brought the cup that he was to drink, and set it down before him, that he might have a full view of it, and see what it was before he took it and drank it. If Christ had not fully known what the dreadfulness of these sufferings was, before he took them upon him, his taking them upon him could not have been fully his own act as man; there could have been no explicit act of his will about that which he was ignorant of; there could have been no proper trial, whether he would be willing to undergo such dreadful sufferings or not, unless he had known beforehand how dreadful they were; but when he had seen what they were, by having an extraordinary view given him of them, and then undertaken to endure them afterwards; then he acted as knowing what he did; then his taking that cup, and bearing such dreadful sufferings, was properly his own act by an explicit choice; and so his love to sinners, in that choice of his, was the more wonderful, as also his obedience to God in it. And it was necessary that this extraordinary view that Christ had of the cup he was to drink should be given at that time, just before he was apprehended. This was the most proper season for it, just before he took the cup, and while he yet had opportunity to refuse the cup; for before he was apprehended by the company led by Judas, he had opportunity to make his escape at pleasure. For the place where he was, was without the city, where he was not at all confined, and was a lonesome, solitary place; and it was the night season; so that he might have gone from that place where he would, and his enemies not have known where to have found him. This view that he had of the bitter cup was given him while he was yet fully at liberty, before he was given into the hands of his enemies. Christ's delivering himself up into the hands of his enemies, as he did when Judas came, which was just after his agony, was properly his act of taking the cup in order to drink; for Christ knew that the issue of that would be his crucifixion the next day. These things may show us the end of Christ's agony, and the necessity there was of such an agony before his last sufferings.

Application

I. Hence we may learn how dreadful Christ's last sufferings were. We learn it from the dreadful effect which the bare foresight of them had upon him in his agony. His last sufferings were so dreadful, that the view which Christ had of them before overwhelmed him and amazed him, as it is said he began to be sore amazed. The very sight of these last sufferings was so very dreadful as to sink his soul down into the dark shadow of death; yea, so dreadful was it, that in the sore conflict which his nature had with it, he was all in a sweat of blood, his body all over was covered with clotted blood, and not only his body, but the very ground under him with the blood that fell from him, which had been forced through his pores through the violence of his agony. And if only the foresight of the cup was so dreadful, how dreadful was the cup itself, how far beyond all that can be uttered or conceived! Many of the martyrs have endured extreme tortures, but from what

has been said, there is all reason to think those all were a mere nothing to the last sufferings of Christ on the cross. And what has been said affords a convincing argument that the sufferings which Christ endured in his body on the cross, though they were very dreadful, were yet the least part of his last sufferings; and that beside those, he endured sufferings in his soul which were vastly greater. For if it had been only the sufferings which he endured in his body, though they were very dreadful, we cannot conceive that the mere anticipation of them would have such an effect on Christ. Many of the martyrs, for aught we know, have endured as severe tortures in their bodies as Christ did. Many of the martyrs have been crucified, as Christ was; and yet their souls have not been so overwhelmed. There has been no appearance of such amazing sorrow and distress of mind either at the anticipation of their sufferings, or in the actual enduring of them.

First inference

From what has been said, we may see the wonderful strength of the love of Christ to sinners. What has been said shows the strength of Christ's love two ways.

1. That it was so strong as to carry him through that agony that he was then in. The suffering that he then was actually subject to, was dreadful and amazing, as has been shown; and how wonderful was his love that lasted and was upheld still! The love of any mere man or angel would doubtless have sunk under such a weight, and never would have endured such a conflict in such a bloody sweat as that of Jesus Christ. The anguish of Christ's soul at that time was so strong as to cause that wonderful effect on his body. But his love to his enemies, poor and unworthy as they were, was stronger still. The heart of Christ at that time was full of distress, but it was fuller of love to vile worms: his sorrows abounded, but his love did much more abound. Christ's soul was overwhelmed with a deluge of grief, but this was from a deluge of love to sinners in his heart sufficient to overflow the world, and overwhelm the highest mountains of its sins. Those great drops of blood that fell down to the ground were a manifestation of an ocean of love in Christ's heart.

2. The strength of Christ's love more especially appears in this, that when he had such a full view of the dreadfulness of the cup that he was to drink, that so amazed him, he would notwithstanding even then take it up, and drink it. Then seems to have been the greatest and most peculiar trial of the strength of the love of Christ, when God set down the bitter portion before him, and let him see what he had to drink, if he persisted in his love to sinners; and brought him to the mouth of the furnace that he might see its fierceness, and have a full view of it, and have time then to consider whether he would go in and suffer the flames of this furnace for such unworthy creatures, or not. This was as it were proposing it to Christ's last consideration what he would do; as much as if it had then been said to him, Here is the cup that you are to drink, unless you will give up your undertaking for sinners, and even leave them to perish as they deserve. Will you take this cup, and drink it for them, or not? There is the furnace into which you are to be cast, if they are to be saved; either they must perish, or you must endure this for them. There you see how terrible the heat of the furnace is; you see what pain and anguish you must endure on the morrow, unless you give up the cause of sinners. What will you do? is your love such that you will go on? Will you cast yourself into this dreadful furnace of wrath? Christ's soul was overwhelmed with the thought; his feeble human nature shrunk at the dismal sight. It put him into this dreadful agony which you have heard described; but his love to sinners held out. Christ would not undergo these sufferings needlessly, if sinners could be saved without. If there was not an absolute necessity of his suffering them in order to their salvation, he desired that the cup might pass from him. But if sinners, on whom he had set his love, could not, agreeably to the will of God, be saved without his drinking it, he chose that the will of God should be done. He chose to go on and endure the suffering, awful as it appeared to him. And this was his final conclusion, after the dismal conflict of his poor feeble human nature, after he had had the cup in view, and for at least the space of one hour, had seen how amazing it was.

Still he finally resolved that he would bear it, rather than those poor sinners whom he had loved from all eternity should perish. When the dreadful cup was before him, he did not say within himself, why should I, who am so great and glorious a person, infinitely more honorable than all the angels of heaven, Why should I go to plunge myself into such dreadful, amazing torments for worthless wretched worms that cannot be profitable to God, or me, and that deserve to be hated by me, and not to be loved? Why should I, who have been living from all eternity in the enjoyment of the Father's love, go to cast myself into such a furnace for them that never can requite me for it? Why should I yield myself to be thus crushed by the weight of divine wrath, for them who have no love to me, and are my enemies? they do not deserve any union with me, and never did, and never will do, any thing to recommend themselves to me. What shall I be the richer for having saved a number of miserable haters of God and me, who deserve to have divine justice glorified in their destruction? Such, however, was not the language of Christ's heart, in these circumstances; but on the contrary, his love held out, and he resolved even then, in the midst of his agony, to yield himself up to the will of God, and to take the cup and drink it. He would not flee to get out of the way of Judas and those that were with him, though he knew they were coming, but that same hour delivered himself voluntarily into their hands. When they came with swords and staves to apprehend him, and he could have called upon his Father, who would immediately have sent many legions of angels to repel his enemies, and have delivered him, he would not do it; and when his disciples would have made resistance, he would not suffer them, as you may see in Matt. 26:51, and onward: "And, behold, one of them which were with Jesus stretched out his hand, and drew his sword, and struck a servant of the high priest's, and smote off his ear. Then said Jesus unto him, Put up again thy sword into its place: for all they that take the sword shall perish with the sword. Thinkest thou that I cannot now pray to my Father, and he will presently give me more than twelve legions of angels? But how then shall the scriptures be fulfilled, that thus it must be? In that same hour said Jesus to the multitudes, Are ye come out as against a thief, with swords and staves for to take me? I sat daily with you teaching in the temple, and ye laid no hold on me. But all this was done that the scriptures of the prophets might be fulfilled." And Christ, instead of hiding himself from Judas and the soldiers, told them, when they seemed to be at a loss whether he was the person whom they sought; and when they seemed still somewhat to hesitate, being seized with some terror in their minds, he told them so again, and so yielded himself up into their hands, to be bound by them, after he had shown them that he could easily resist them if he pleased, when a single word spoken by him, threw them backwards to the ground, as you may see in John 18:3, etc. "Judas then, having received a band of men and officers from the chief priests and Pharisees, cometh thither with lanterns, and torches, and weapons. Jesus therefore, knowing all things that should come upon him, went forth, and said unto them, Whom seek ye? They answered him, Jesus of Nazareth. Jesus said unto them, I am he. As soon then as he had said unto them, I am he, they went backward and fell to the ground." Thus powerful, constant, and violent was the love of Christ; and the special trial of his love above all others in his whole life seems to have been in the time of his agony. For though his sufferings were greater afterwards, when he was on the cross, yet he saw clearly what those sufferings were to be, in the time of his agony; and that seems to have been the first time that ever Christ Jesus had a clear view what these sufferings were; and after this the trial was not so great, because the conflict was over. His human nature had been in a struggle with his love to sinners, but his love had got the victory. The thing, upon a full view of his sufferings, had been resolved on and concluded; and accordingly, when the moment arrived, he actually went through with those sufferings.

Second inference

But there are two circumstances of Christ's agony that do still make the strength and constancy of his love to sinners the more conspicuous.

1. That at the same time that he had such a view of the dreadfulness of his sufferings, he had also an extraordinary view of the hatefulness of the wickedness of those for whom those sufferings were to make atonement. There are two things that render Christ's love wonderful:

a. That he should be willing to endure sufferings that were so great; and

b. That he should be willing to endure them to make atonement for wickedness that was so great.

But in order to its being properly said, Christ of his own act and choice endured sufferings that were so great, to make atonement for wickedness that was so great, two things were necessary.

a. That he should have an extraordinary sense how great these sufferings were to be, before he endured them. This was given in his agony.

And b. That he should also at the same time have an extraordinary sense how great and hateful was the wickedness of men for which he suffered to make atonement; or how unworthy those were for whom he died. And both these were given at the same time. When Christ had such an extraordinary sense how bitter his cup was to be, he had much to make him sensible how unworthy and hateful that wickedness of mankind was for which he suffered; because the hateful and malignant nature of that corruption never appeared more fully than in the spite and cruelty of men in these sufferings; and yet his love was such that he went on notwithstanding to suffer for them who were full of such hateful corruption.

It was the corruption and wickedness of men that contrived and effected his death; it was the wickedness of men that agreed with Judas, it was the wickedness of men that betrayed him, and that apprehended him, and bound him, and led him away like a malefactor; it was by men's corruption and wickedness that he was arraigned, and falsely accused, and unjustly judged. It was by men's wickedness that he was reproached, mocked, buffeted, and spit upon. It was by men's wickedness that Barabbas was preferred before him. It was men's wickedness that laid the cross upon him to bear, and that nailed him to it, and put him to so cruel and ignominious a death. This tended to give Christ an extraordinary sense of the greatness and hatefulness of the depravity of mankind.

a. Because hereby in the time of his sufferings he had that depravity set before him as it is, without disguise. When it killed Christ, it appeared in its proper colors. Here Christ saw it in its true nature, which is the utmost hatred and contempt of God; in its ultimate tendency and desire, which is to kill God; and in its greatest aggravation and highest act, which is killing a person that was God.

b. Because in these sufferings he felt the fruits of that wickedness. It was then directly leveled against himself, and exerted itself against him to work his reproach and torment, which tended to impress a stronger sense of its hatefulness on the human nature of Christ. But yet at the same time, so wonderful was the love of Christ to those who exhibited this hateful corruption, that he endured those very sufferings to deliver them from the punishment of that very corruption. The wonderfulness of Christ's dying love appears partly in that he died for those that were so unworthy in themselves, as all mankind have the same kind of corruptions in their hearts, and partly in that he died for those who were not only so wicked, but whose wickedness consists in being enemies to him; so that he did not only die for the wicked, but for his own enemies; and partly in that he was willing to die for his enemies at the same time that he was feeling the fruits of their enmity, while he felt the utmost effects and exertions of their spite against him in the greatest possible contempt and cruelty towards him in his own greatest ignominy, torments, and death; and partly in that he was willing to atone for their being his enemies in these very sufferings, and by that very ignominy, torment, and death that was the fruit of it.

The sin and wickedness of men, for which Christ suffered to make atonement, was, as it were, set before Christ in his view.

a. In that this wickedness was but a sample of the wickedness of mankind; for the corruption of all mankind is of the same nature, and the wickedness that is in one man's heart is of the same nature and tendency as in another's. As in water, face answereth to face, so the heart of man to man.

b. It is probable that Christ died to make atonement for that individual actual wickedness that wrought his sufferings, that reproached, mocked, buffeted, and crucified him. Some of his crucifiers, for whom he prayed that they might be forgiven, while they were in the very act of crucifying him, were afterwards, in answer to his prayer, converted, by the preaching of Peter; as we have an account of in the 2d chapter of Acts.

2. Another circumstance of Christ's agony that shows the strength of his love, is the ungrateful carriage of his disciples at that time. Christ's disciples were among those for whom he endured this agony, and among those for whom he was going to endure those last sufferings, of which he now had such dreadful apprehensions. Yet Christ had already given them an interest in the benefits of those sufferings. Their sins had already been forgiven them through that blood that he was going to shed, and they had been infinite gainers already by that dying pity and love which he had to them, and had through his sufferings been distinguished from all the world besides. Christ had put greater honor upon them than any other, by making them his disciples in a more honorable sense than he had done any other. And yet now, when he had that dreadful cup set before him which he was going to drink for them, and was in such an agony at the sight of it, he saw no return on their part but indifference and ingratitude. When he only desired them to watch with him, that he might be comforted in their company, now at this sorrowful moment they fell asleep; and showed that they had not concern enough about it to induce them to keep awake with him even for one hour, though he desired it of them once and again. But yet this ungrateful treatment of theirs, for whom he was to drink the cup of wrath which God had set before him, did not discourage him from taking it, and drinking it for them. His love held out to them; having loved his

own, he loved them to the end. He did not say within himself when this cup of trembling was before him, Why should I endure so much for those that are so ungrateful; why should I here wrestle with the expectation of the terrible wrath of God to be borne by me to-morrow, for them that in the mean time have not so much concern for me as to keep awake with me when I desire it of them even for one hour? But on the contrary, with tender and fatherly compassions he excuses this ingratitude of his disciples, and says, Matt. 26:41. "Watch and pray, that ye enter not into temptation; the spirit indeed is willing, but the flesh is weak"; and went and was apprehended, and mocked, and scourged, and crucified, and poured out his soul unto death, under the heavy weight of God's dreadful wrath on the cross for them.

Third inference

From what has been said, we may learn the wonderfulness of Christ's submission to the will of God. Christ, as he was a divine person, was the absolute sovereign of heaven and earth, but yet he was the most wonderful instance of submission to God's sovereignty that ever was. When he had such a view of the terribleness of his last sufferings, and prayed if it were possible that that cup might pass from him, i.e. if there was not an absolute necessity of it in order to the salvation of sinners, yet it was with a perfect submission to the will of God. He adds, "Nevertheless, not my will, but thine be done." He chose rather that the inclination of his human nature, which so much dreaded such exquisite torments, should be crossed, than that God's will should not take place. He delighted in the thought of God's will being done; and when he went and prayed the second time, he had nothing else to say but, "O my Father, if this cup may not pass from me except I drink it, thy will be done"; and so the third time. What are such trials of submission as any of us sometimes have in the afflictions that we suffer in comparison of this? If God does but in his providence signify it to be his will that we should part with a child, how hardly are we brought to yield to it, how ready to be unsubmissive and froward! Or if God lays his

hand upon us in some acute pain of body, how ready are we to be discontented and impatient; when the innocent Son of God, who deserved no suffering could quietly submit to sufferings inconceivably great, and say it over and over, God's will be done! When he was brought and set before that dreadful furnace of wrath into which he was to be cast, in order that he might look into it and have a full view of its fierceness, when his flesh shrunk at it, and his nature was in such a conflict, that his body was all covered with a sweat of blood falling in great drops to the ground, yet his soul quietly yielded that the will of God should be done, rather than the will or inclination of his human nature.

Fourth inference

What has been said on this subject also shows us the glory of Christ's obedience. Christ was subject to the moral law as Adam was, and he was also subject to the ceremonial and judicial laws of Moses; but the principal command that he had received of the Father was, that he should lay down his life, that he should voluntarily yield up himself to those terrible sufferings on the cross. To do this was his principal errand into the world; and doubtless the principal command that he received, was about that which was the principal errand on which he was sent. The Father, when he sent him into the world, sent him with commands concerning what he should do in the world; and his chief command of all was about that, which was the errand he was chiefly sent upon, which was to lay down his life. And therefore this command was the principal trial of his obedience. It was the greatest trial of his obedience, because it was by far the most difficult command: all the rest were easy in comparison of this. And the main trial that Christ had, whether he would obey this command, was in the time of his agony; for that was within an hour before he was apprehended in order to his sufferings, when he must either yield himself up to them, or fly from them. And then it was the first time that Christ had a full view of the difficulty of this command; which appeared so great as to cause that bloody sweat. Then was the conflict of weak human nature with the difficulty, then was the sore struggles and wrestling with the heavy trial he had, and then Christ got the victory over the temptation, from the dread of his human nature. His obedience held out through the conflict. Then we may suppose that Satan was especially let loose to set in with the natural dread that the human nature had of such torments, and to strive to his utmost to dissuade Christ from going on to drink the bitter cup; for about that time, towards the close of Christ's life, was he especially delivered up into the hands of Satan to be tempted of him, more than he was immediately after his baptism; for Christ says, speaking of that time, Luke 22:53. "When I was daily with you in the temple, ye stretched forth no hands against me; but this is your hour, and the power of darkness." So that Christ, in the time of his agony, was wrestling not only with overwhelming views of his last sufferings, but he also wrestled, in that bloody sweat, with principalities and powers—he contended at that time with the great leviathan that laboured to his utmost to tempt him to disobedience. So that then Christ had temptations every way to draw him off from obedience to God. He had temptations from his feeble human nature, that exceedingly dreaded such torments; and he had temptations from men, who were his enemies; and he had temptations from the ungrateful carriage of his own disciples; and he had temptations from the devil. He had also an overwhelming trial from the manifestation of God's own wrath; when, in the words of Isaiah, it pleased the Lord to bruise him and put him to grief. But yet he failed not, but got the victory over all, and performed that great act of obedience at that time to that same God that hid himself from him, and was showing his wrath to him for men's sins, which he must presently suffer. Nothing could move him away from his steadfast obedience to God, but he persisted in saying, "Thy will be done": expressing not only his submission, but his obedience; not only his compliance with the disposing will of God, but also with his preceptive will. God had given him this cup to drink, and had commanded him to drink it, and that was reason enough with him to drink it; hence he says, at the conclusion of his

agony, when Judas came with his band, "The cup which my Father giveth me to drink, shall I not drink it?" John 18:11. Christ, at the time of his agony, had an inconceivably greater trial of obedience than any man or any angel ever had. How much was this trial of the obedience of the second Adam beyond the trial of the obedience of the first Adam! How light was our first father's temptation in comparison of this! And yet our first surety failed, and our second failed not, but obtained a glorious victory, and went and became obedient unto death, even the death of the cross. Thus wonderful and glorious was the obedience of Christ, by which he wrought out righteousness for believers, and which obedience is imputed to them. No wonder that it is a sweet penalty sown, and that God stands ready to bestow heaven as its reward on all that believe on him.

Fifth inference

What has been said shows us the sottishness of secure sinners in being so fearless of the wrath of God. If the wrath of God was so dreadful, that, when Christ only expected it, his human nature was nearly overwhelmed with the fear of it, and his soul was amazed, and his body all over in a bloody sweat; then how sottish are sinners, who are under the threatening of the same wrath of God, and are condemned to it, and are every moment exposed to it; and yet, instead of manifesting intense apprehension, are quiet and easy, and unconcerned; instead of being sorrowful and very heavy, go about with a light and careless heart; instead of crying out in bitter agony, are often gay and cheerful, and eat and drink, and sleep quietly, and go on in sin, provoking the wrath of God more and more, without any great matter of concern! How stupid and sottish are such persons! Let such senseless sinners consider, that that misery, of which they are in danger from the wrath of God, is infinitely more terrible than that, the fear of which occasioned in Christ his agony and bloody sweat. It is more terrible, both as it differs both in its nature and degree, and also as it differs in its duration. It is more terrible in its nature and degree. Christ suffered that which, as it upheld the honor of the divine law, was fully equivalent to the misery of the damned; and in some respect it was the same suffering; for it was the wrath of the same God; but yet in other respects it vastly differed. The difference does not arise from the difference in the wrath poured out on one and the other, for it is the same wrath, but from the difference of the subject, which may be best illustrated from Christ's own comparison. Luke 23:31. "For if they do these things in a green tree, what shall be done in the dry?" Here he calls himself the green tree, and wicked men the dry, intimating that the misery that will come on wicked men will be far more dreadful than those sufferings which came on him, and the difference arises from the different nature of the subject. The green tree and the dry are both cast into the fire; but the flames seize and kindle on the dry tree much more fiercely than on the green.

The sufferings that Christ endured differ from the misery of the wicked in hell in nature and degree in the following respects.

1. Christ felt not the gnawings of a guilty, condemning conscience.

2. He felt no torment from the reigning of inward corruptions and lusts as the damned do. The wicked in hell are their own tormentors, their lusts are their tormentors, and being without restraint, (for there is no restraining grace in hell,) their lusts will rage like raging flames in their hearts. They shall be tormented with the unrestrained violence of a spirit of envy and malice against God, and against the angels and saints in heaven, and against one another. Now Christ suffered nothing of this.

3. Christ had not to consider that God hated him. The wicked in hell have this to make their misery perfect, they know that God perfectly hates them without the least pity or regard to them, which will fill their souls with inexpressible misery. But it was not so with Christ. God withdrew his comfortable presence from Christ, and hid his face from him, and so poured out his wrath upon him, as made him feel its terrible effects in his soul; but yet he knew at the same time that God did not hate him, but infinitely loved him. He cried out of God's forsaking him, but yet at the same time calls him "My God, my God!"

knowing that he was his God still, though he had forsaken him. But the wicked in hell will know that he is not their God, but their judge and irreconcilable enemy.

4. Christ did not suffer despair, as the wicked do in hell. He knew that there would be an end to his sufferings in a few hours; and that after that he should enter into eternal glory. But it will be far otherwise with you that are impenitent; if you die in your present condition, you will be in perfect despair. On these accounts, the misery of the wicked in hell will be immensely more dreadful in nature and degree, than those sufferings with the fears of which Christ's soul was so much overwhelmed.

5. It will infinitely differ in duration. Christ's sufferings lasted but a few hours, and there was an eternal end to them, and eternal glory succeeded. But you that are a secure, senseless sinner, are every day exposed to be cast into everlasting misery, a fire that never shall be quenched. If then the Son of God was in such amazement, in the expectation of what he was to suffer for a few hours, how sottish are you who are continually exposed to sufferings, immensely more dreadful in nature and degree, and that are to be without any end, but which must be endured without any rest day or night for ever and ever! If you had a full sense of the greatness of that misery to which you are exposed, and how dreadful your present condition is on that account, it would this moment put you into as dreadful an agony as that which Christ underwent; yea, if your nature could endure it, one much more dreadful. We should now see you fall down in a bloody sweat, wallowing in your gore, and crying out in terrible amazement.

Having thus endeavored to explain and illustrate the former of the two propositions mentioned in the commencement of this discourse, I shall now proceed to show:

II. THAT THE SOUL OF CHRIST IN HIS AGONY IN THE GARDEN WAS IN A GREAT AND EARNEST STRIFE AND CONFLICT IN HIS PRAYER TO GOD.

The labor and striving of Christ's soul in prayer was a part of his agony, and was without doubt a part of what is intended in the text, when it is said that Christ was in an agony; for, as we have shown, the word is especially used in Scripture in other places for striving or wrestling with God in prayer. From this fact, and from the evangelist mentioning his being in agony, and his praying earnestly in the same sentence, we may well understand him as mentioning his striving in prayer as part of his agony. The words of the text seem to hold forth as much as that Christ was in an agony in prayer: "Being in an agony, he prayed more earnestly; and his sweat was, as it were, great drops of blood falling to the ground." This language seems to imply thus much, that the labor and earnestness of Christ's soul was so great in his wrestling with God in prayer, that he was in a mere agony, and all over in a sweat of blood.

What I propose now, in this second proposition, is by the help of God to explain this part of Christ's agony which consisted in the agonizing and wrestling of his soul in prayer; which is the more worthy of a particular inquiry, being that which probably is but little understood; though, as may appear in the sequel, the right understanding of it is of great use and consequence in divinity. It is not as I conceive ordinarily well understood what is meant when it is said in the text that Christ prayed more earnestly; or what was the thing that he wrestled with God for, or what was the subject matter of this earnest prayer, or what was the reason of his being so very earnest in prayer at this time. And therefore, to set this whole matter in a clear light, I would particularly inquire,

1. Of what nature this prayer was;
2. What was the subject matter of this earnest prayer of Christ to the Father;
3. In what capacity Christ offered up this prayer to God;
4. Why he was so earnest in his prayer;
5. What was the success of this his earnest wrestling with God in prayer; and then make some improvement.

1. Of what nature this prayer of Christ was
Addresses that are made to God may be of various kinds. Some are confessions on the part of the individual, or expressions of his sense of his own unworthiness before God, and are thus penitential addresses to God. Others are doxologies or prayers intended to express the sense which the person has of God's greatness and glory. Such are many of the psalms of David. Others are gratulatory addresses, or expressions of thanksgiving and praise for mercies received. Others are submissive addresses, or expressions of submission and resignation to the will of God, whereby he that addresses the Majesty of heaven, expresses the compliance of his will with the sovereign will of God; saying, "Thy will, O Lord, be done!" as David, 2 Sam. 15:26. "But if he thus say, I have no delight in thee; behold, here am I; let him do to me as seemeth good unto him." Others are petitory or supplicatory; whereby the person that prays, begs of God and cries to him for some favor desired of him.

Hence the inquiry is, of which of these kinds was the prayer of Christ, that we read of in the text.

Answer. It was chiefly supplicatory. It was not penitential or confessional; for Christ had no sin or unworthiness to confess. Nor was it a doxology or a thanksgiving or merely an expression of submission; for none of these agree with what is said in the text, viz. that he prayed more earnestly. When any one is said to pray earnestly, it implies an earnest request for some benefit, or favor desired; and not merely a confession, or submission, or gratulation. So what the apostle says of this prayer, in Heb. 5:7. "Who in the days of his flesh, when he had offered up prayers and supplications, with strong crying and tears, unto him that was able to save him from death, and was heard, in that he feared," shows that it was petitory, or an earnest supplication for some desired benefit. They are not confessions, or doxologies, or thanksgivings. or resignations, that are called "supplications" and "strong cyings," but petitions for some benefit earnestly desired. And having thus resolved the first inquiry, and shown that this earnest prayer of Christ was of the nature of a supplication for some benefit or favor which Christ earnestly desired, I come to inquire,

2. What was the subject matter of this supplication; or what favor and benefit that was for which Christ so earnestly supplicated in this prayer of which we have an account in the text. Now the words of the text are not express on this matter. It is said that Christ, "being in an agony, prayed more earnestly"; but yet it is not said what he prayed so earnestly for. And here is the greatest difficulty attending this account: even what that was which Christ so earnestly desired, for which he so wrestled with God at that time. And though we are not expressly told in the text, yet the Scriptures have not left us without sufficient light in this matter. And the more effectually to avoid mistakes, I would answer,

1. Negatively, the thing that Christ so earnestly prayed for at this time, was not that the bitter cup which he had to drink might pass from him. Christ had before prayed for this, as in the next verse but one before the text, saying "Father, if thou be willing, remove this cup from me! nevertheless, not my will, but thine be done!" It is after this that we have an account that Christ being in an agony, prayed more earnestly; but we are not to understand that he prayed more earnestly than he had done before, that the cup might pass from him. That this was not the thing that he so earnestly prayed for in this second prayer, the following things seem to prove:

a. This second prayer was after the angel had appeared to him from heaven, strengthening him, the more cheerfully to take the cup and drink it. The evangelists inform us that when Christ came into the garden, he began to be sorrowful, and very heavy, and that he said his soul was exceeding sorrowful, even unto death, and that then he went and prayed to God, that if it were possible the cup might pass from him. Luke says in the 41st and 42nd verses, "that being withdrawn from his disciples about a stone's cast, he kneeled down and prayed, saying, Father, if thou be willing, remove this cup from me; nevertheless, not my will, but thine be done!" And then, after this, it is said in the next verse, that there appeared an angel from heaven unto him strengthening him. Now this can be understood no otherwise than that the angel appeared to him, strengthening him

and encouraging him to go through his great and difficult work, to take the cup and drink it. Accordingly we must suppose, that now Christ was more strengthened and encouraged to go through with his sufferings: and therefore we cannot suppose that after this he would pray more earnestly than before to be delivered from his sufferings; and of course that it was something else that Christ more earnestly prayed for, after that strengthening of the angel, and not that the cup might pass from him. Though Christ seems to have a greater sight of his sufferings given him after this strengthening of the angel than before, that caused such an agony, yet he was more strengthened to fit him for a greater sight of them, he had greater strength and courage to grapple with these awful apprehensions, than before. His strength to bear sufferings is increased with the sense of his sufferings.

a. Christ, before his second prayer, had had an intimation from the Father, that it was not his will that the cup should pass from him. The angel's coming from heaven to strengthen him must be so understood. Christ first prays, that if it may be the will of the Father, the cup might pass; but not, if it was not his will; and then God immediately upon this sends an angel to strengthen, and encourage him to take the cup, which was a plain intimation to Christ that it was the Father's will that he should take it, and that it should not pass from him. And so Christ received it; as appears from the account which Matthew gives of this second prayer. Matt. 26:42. "He went away again the second time and prayed, saying, O my Father, if this cup may not pass away from me except I drink it, thy will be done." He speaks as one that now had had an intimation, since he prayed before, that it was not the will of God. And Luke tells us how, viz. by God's sending an angel. Matthew informs us, as Luke does, that in his first prayer, he prayed that if it were possible the cup might pass from him; but then God sends an angel to signify that it was not his will, and to encourage him to take it. And then Christ having received this plain intimation that it was not the will of God that the cup should pass from him, yields to the message he had received, and says, O my

Father, if it be so as thou hast now signified, thy will be done. Therefore we may surely conclude that what Christ prayed more earnestly for after this, was not that the cup might pass from him, but something else; for he would not go to pray more earnestly that the cup might pass from him, after God had signified that it was not his will that it should pass from him, than he did before; that would be blasphemous to suppose. And then,

c. The language of the second prayer, as recited by Matthew, "O my Father, if this cup may not pass from me except I drink it, thy will be done," shows that Christ did not then pray that the cup might pass from him. This certainly is not praying more earnestly that the cup might pass: it is rather a yielding that point, and ceasing any more to urge it, and submitting to it as a thing now determined by the will of God, made known by the angel. And,

d. From the apostle's account of this prayer in the 5th ch. of Hebrews, the words of the apostle are these, "Who in the days of his flesh, when he had offered up his prayers and supplications, with strong crying and tears, unto him that was able to save him from death, and was heard in that he feared." The strong crying and tears of which the apostle speaks, are doubtless the same that Luke speaks of in the text, when he says, "he being in an agony, prayed more earnestly"; for this was the sharpest and most earnest crying of Christ, of which we have any where any account. But according to the apostle's account, that which Christ feared, and that for which he so strongly cried to God in this prayer, was something that he was heard in, something that God granted him his request in, and therefore it was not that the cup might pass from him. Having thus shown what it was not that Christ prayed for in this earnest prayer, I proceed to show,

2. What it was that Christ so earnestly sought of God in this prayer.

I answer in one word, it was, That God's will might be done, in what related to his sufferings. Matthew gives this express account of it, in the very language of the prayer which has been recited several times already, "O my

Father, if this cup may not pass from me, except I drink it, thy will be done!" This is a yielding, and an expression of submission; but it is not merely that. Such words, "The will of the Lord be done," as they are most commonly used, are not understood as a supplication or request, but only as an expression of submission. But the words are not always to be understood in that sense in Scripture, but sometimes are to be understood as a request. So they are to be understood in the third petition of the Lord's prayer, "Thy will be done in earth as in heaven." There the words are to be understood both as an expression of submission, and also a request, as they are explained in the Assembly's Catechism, and so the words are to be understood here. The evangelist Mark says that Christ went away again and spake the same words that he had done in his first prayer. Mark 14:39. But then we must understand it as of the same words with the latter part of his first prayer, "nevertheless not my will but thine be done," as Matthew's more full and particular account shows. So that the thing mentioned in the text, for which Christ was wrestling with God in this prayer, was, that God's will might be done in what related to his sufferings.

But then here another inquiry may arise, viz. What is implied in Christ's praying that God's will might be done in what related to his sufferings? To this I answer,

1. This implies a request that he might be strengthened and supported, and enabled to do God's will, by going through with these sufferings. The same as when he says, "Lo, I come, in the volume of the book it is written of me, to do thy will, O God." It was the preceptive will of God that he should take that cup and drink it: it was the Father's command to him. The Father had given him the cup, and as it were set it down before him with the command that he should drink it. This was the greatest act of obedience that Christ was to perform. He prays for strength and help, that his poor feeble human nature might be supported, that he might not fail in this great trial, that he might not sink and be swallowed up, and his strength so overcome that he should not hold out, and finish the

appointed obedience. This was the thing that he feared, of which the apostle speaks in the 5th of Hebrews, when he says,"he was heard in that he feared." When he had such an extraordinary sense of the dreadfulness of his sufferings impressed on his mind, the fearfulness of it amazed him. He was afraid lest his poor feeble strength should be overcome, and that he should fail in so great a trial, that he should be swallowed up by that death that he was to die, and so should not be saved from death; and therefore he offered up strong crying and tears unto him that was able to strengthen him, and support, and save him from death, that the death he was to suffer might not overcome his love and obedience, but that he might overcome death, and so be saved from it. If Christ's courage had failed in the trial, and he had not held out under his dying sufferings, he never would have been saved from death, but he would have sunk in the deep mire; he never would have risen from the dead, for his rising from the dead was a reward of his victory. If his courage had failed, and he had given up, he would have remained from under the power of death, and so we should all have perished, we should have remained yet in our sins. If he had failed, all would have failed. If he had not overcome in that sore conflict, neither he nor we could have been freed from death, we all must have perished together. Therefore this was the saving from death that the apostle speaks of, that Christ feared and prayed for with strong crying and tears. His being overcome of death was the thing that he feared, and so he was heard in that he feared. This Christ prayed, that the will of God might be done in his sufferings, even that he might not fail of obeying God's will in his sufferings; and therefore it follows in the next verse in that passage of Hebrews, "Though he were a Son, yet learned he obedience by the things which he suffered." That it was in this respect that Christ in his agony so earnestly prayed that the will of God might be done, viz. that he might have strength to do his will, and might not sink and fail in such great sufferings; is confirmed from the scriptures of the Old Testament, as particularly from the 69th Psalm. The psalmist represents Christ in that

psalm, as is evident from the fact that the words of that psalm are represented as Christ's words in many places of the New Testament. That psalm is represented as Christ's prayer to God when his soul was overwhelmed with sorrow and amazement, as it was in his agony; as you may see in the 1st and 2nd verses, "Save me, O God, for the waters are come in unto my soul: I sink in deep mire, where there is no standing: I am come into deep waters, where the floods overflow me." But then the thing that is represented as being the thing that he feared, was failing, and being overwhelmed, in this great trial: verses 14 and 15. "Deliver me out of the mire, and let me not sink: let me be delivered from them that hate me, and out of the deep waters. Let not the water-flood overflow me, neither let the deep swallow me up, and let not the pit shut her mouth upon me." So again in the 22d Psalm, which is also represented as the prayer of Christ under his dreadful sorrow and sufferings, verses 19, 20, 21. "But be not thou far from me, O Lord; O my Strength, haste thee to help me. Deliver my soul from the sword; my darling from the power of the dog. Save me from the lion's mouth." It was meet and suitable that Christ, when about to engage in that terrible conflict, should thus earnestly seek help from God to enable him to do his will; for he needed God's help—the strength of his human nature, without divine help, was not sufficient to carry him through. This was, without doubt, that in which the first Adam failed in his first trial, that when the trial came he was not sensible of his own weakness and dependence. If he had been, and had leaned on God, and cried to him for his assistance and strength against the temptation, in all likelihood we should have remained innocent and happy creatures to this day.

2. It implies a request that God's will and purpose might be obtained in the effects and fruits of his sufferings, in the glory to his name, that was his design in them; and particularly in the glory of his grace, in the eternal salvation and happiness of his elect. This is confirmed by John 12:27, 28. "Now is my soul troubled; and what shall I say?— Father, save me from this hour: but for this cause came I unto this hour. Father, glorify

thy name. Then came there a voice from heaven, saying, I have both glorified, and will glorify it again." There the first request is the same with the first request of Christ here in like trouble: "Now is my soul troubled; and what shall I say? Father, save me from this hour." He first prays, as he does here, that he might be saved from his last sufferings. Then, after he was determined within himself that the will of God must be otherwise, that he should not be saved from that hour, "but for this cause," says he, "came I to this hour"; and then his second request after this is, "Father, glorify thy name!" So this is doubtless the purport of the second request in his agony, when he prayed that God's will might be done. It is that God's will might be done in that glory to his own name that he intended in the effects and fruits of his sufferings, that seeing that it was his will that he should suffer, he earnestly prays that the end of his suffering, in the glory of God and the salvation of the elect, may not fail. And these things are what Christ so earnestly wrestled with God for in his prayer, of which we have an account in the text, and we have no reason to think that they were not expressed in prayer as well as implied. It is not reasonable to suppose that the evangelist in his other account of things mentions all the words of Christ's prayer. He only mentions the substance.

3. In what capacity did Christ offer up those earnest prayers to God in his agony?

In answer to this inquiry, I observe that he offered them up not as a private person, but as high priest. The apostle speaks of the strong crying and tears, as what Christ offered up as high priest. Heb. 5:6-7. "As he says also in another place, Thou art a priest for ever, after the order of Melchisedek: who in the days of his flesh, when he had offered up prayers and supplications with strong crying and tears," etc. The things that Christ prayed for in those strong cryings, were things not of a private nature, but of common concern to the whole church of which he was the high priest. That the will of God should be done in his obedience unto death, that his strength and courage should not fail, but that he should hold out, was of common concern; for, if he

had failed, all would have failed and perished for ever. And of course, that God's name should be glorified in the effects and fruits of his sufferings, and in the salvation and glory of all his elect, was a thing of common concern. Christ offered up these strong cries with his flesh in the same manner as the priests of old were wont to offer up prayers with their sacrifices. Christ mixed strong crying and tears with his blood, and so offered up his blood and his prayers together, that the effect and success of his blood might be obtained. Such earnest agonizing prayers were offered with his blood, and his infinitely precious and meritorious blood was offered with his prayers.

4. Why was Christ so earnest in those supplications? Luke speaks of them as very earnest; the apostle speaks of them as strong crying; and his agony partly consisted in this earnestness: and the account that Luke gives us, seems to imply that his bloody sweat was partly at least with the great labor and earnest sense of his soul in wrestling with God in prayer. There were three things that concurred at that time, especially to cause Christ to be thus earnest and engaged.

a. He had then an extraordinary sense how dreadful the consequence would be, if God's will should fail of being done. He had then an extraordinary sense of his own last suffering under the wrath of God, and if he had failed in those sufferings, he knew the consequence must be dreadful. He having now such an extraordinary view of the terribleness of the wrath of God, his love to the elect tended to make him more than ordinarily earnest that they might be delivered from suffering that wrath to all eternity, which could not have been if he had failed of doing God's will, or if the will of God in the effect of his suffering had failed.

b. No wonder that that extraordinary sense that Christ then had of the costliness of the means of sinners' salvation, made him very earnest for the success of those means, as you have already heard.

c. Christ had an extraordinary sense of his dependence on God, and his need of his help to enable him to do God's will in this great trial. Though he was innocent, yet he needed divine help. He was dependent on God, as man, and therefore we read that he trusted in God. Matt. 27:43. "He trusted in God; let him deliver him now, if he will have him: for he said, I am the Son of God." And when he had such an extraordinary sight of the dreadfulness of that wrath he was to suffer, he saw how much it was beyond the strength of his human nature alone.

5. What was the success of this prayer of Christ?

To this I answer, He obtained all his requests. The apostle says, "He was heard in that he feared"; in all that he feared. He obtained strength and help from God, all that he needed, and was carried through. He was enabled to do and to suffer the whole will of God; and he obtained the whole of the end of his sufferings—a full atonement for the sins of the whole world, and the full salvation of every one of those who were given him in the covenant of redemption, and all that glory to the name of God, which his mediation was designed to accomplish, not one jot or tittle hath failed. Herein Christ in his agony was above all others Jacob's antitype, in his wrestling with God for a blessing; which Jacob did, not as a private person, but as the head of his posterity, the nation of Israel, and by which he obtained that commendation of God, "As a prince thou hast power with God"; and therein was a type of him who was the Prince of princes.

Application

Great improvement may be made of the consideration of the strong crying and tears of Christ in the days of his flesh, many ways for our benefit.

1. This may teach us after what manner we should pray to God, not in a cold and careless manner, but with great earnestness and engagedness of spirit, and especially when we are praying to God for those things that are of infinite importance, such as spiritual and eternal blessings. Such were the benefits that Christ prayed for with such strong crying and tears, that he might be enabled to do God's will in that great and difficult work that God

had appointed him, that he might not sink and fail, but might get the victory, and so finally be delivered from death, and that God's will and end might be obtained as the fruit of his sufferings, in the glory of God, and the salvation of the elect.

When we go before God in prayer with a cold, dull heart, and in a lifeless and listless manner pray to him for eternal blessings, and those of infinite import to our souls, we should think of Christ's earnest prayers that he poured out to God, with tears and a bloody sweat. The consideration of it may well make us ashamed of our dull, lifeless prayers to God, wherein, indeed, we rather ask a denial than ask to be heard; for the language of such a manner of praying to God, is, that we do not look upon the benefit that we pray for as of any great importance, that we are indifferent whether God answers us or not. The example of Jacob in wrestling with God for the blessing, should teach us earnestness in our prayers, but more especially the example of Jesus Christ, who wrestled with God in a bloody sweat. If we were sensible as Christ was of the great importance of those benefits that are of eternal consequence, our prayers to God for such benefits would be after another manner than now they are. Our souls also would with earnest labor and strife be engaged in this duty.

There are many benefits that we ask of God in our prayers, which are every whit of as great importance to us as those benefits which Christ asked of God in his agony were to him. It is of as great importance to us that we should be enabled to do the will of God, and perform a sincere, universal, and persevering obedience to his commands, as it was to Christ that he should not fail of doing God's will in his great work. It is of as great importance to us to be saved from death, as it was to Christ that he should get the victory over death, and so be saved from it. It is of as great, and infinitely greater, importance to us, that Christ's redemption should be successful in us, as it was to him that God's will should be done, in the fruits and success of his redemption.

Christ recommended earnest watchfulness and prayerfulness to his disciples, by prayer and example, both at the same time. When Christ was in his agony, and came and found his disciples asleep, he bid them watch and pray, Matt. 26:41. "Watch and pray, that ye enter not into temptation: the spirit indeed is willing, but the flesh is weak." At the same time he set them an example of that which he commanded them, for though they slept he watched, and poured out his soul in those earnest prayers that you have heard of; and Christ has elsewhere taught us to ask those blessings of God that are of infinite importance, as those that will take no denial. We have another example of the great conflicts and engagedness of Christ's spirit in this duty. Luke 6:12. "And it came to pass in those days, that he went out into a mountain to pray, and continued all night in prayer to God." And he was often recommending earnestness in crying to God in prayers. In the parable of the unjust judge, Luke 18 at the beginning; "And he spake a parable unto them to this end, that men ought always to pray, and not to faint; saying There was in a city a judge, which feared not God, neither regarded man; and there was a widow in that city; and she came unto him, saying, Avenge me of mine adversary. And he would not for awhile: but afterwards he saith within himself, Though I fear not God nor regard man, yet because this widow troubleth me, I will avenge her, lest by her continual coming she weary me. And the Lord said, Hear what the unjust judge saith." Luke 6:5, etc. "And he said unto them, Which of you shall have a friend, and shall go unto him at midnight, and say unto him, Friend, lend me three loaves; for a friend of mine in his journey is come to me, and I have nothing to set before him? And he from within shall answer and say, Trouble me not: the door is now shut, and my children are with me in bed; I cannot rise and give thee. I say unto you, though he will not rise and give him because he is his friend, yet because of his importunity, he will rise and give him as many as he needeth." He taught it in his own way of answering prayer, as in answering the woman of Canaan, Matt. 15:22, etc. "And behold a woman of Canaan came out of the coasts, and cried unto him, saying, Have mercy on me, O Lord, thou Son of David; my daughter is grievously vexed with a devil. But he answered her not a word. And his disciples came and besought him, saying, Send her away; for she crieth after us. But he answered and said, I am not sent but unto the lost sheep of the house of Israel. Then came she and worshipped him, saying, Lord, help me. But he answered and said, It is not meet to take the children's bread and cast it to dogs. And she said, Truth, Lord; yet the dogs eat of the crumbs which fall from their master's table. Then Jesus answered and said unto her, O woman, great is thy faith; be it unto thee even as thou wilt. And her daughter was made whole from that very hour." And as Christ prayed in his agony, so I have already mentioned several texts of Scripture wherein we are directed to agonize in our prayers to God.

2. These earnest prayers and strong cries of Christ to the Father in his agony, show the greatness of his love to sinners. For, as has been shown, these strong cries of Jesus Christ were what he offered up to God as a public person, in the capacity of high priest, and in the behalf of those whose priest he was. When he offered up his sacrifice for sinners whom he had loved from eternity, he withal offered up earnest prayers. His strong cries, his tears, and his blood, were all offered up together to God, and they were all offered up for the same end, for the glory of God in the salvation of the elect. They were all offered up for the same persons, viz. for his people. For them he shed his blood and that bloody sweat, when it fell down in clotted lumps to the ground; and for them he so earnestly cried to God at the same time. It was that the will of God might be done in the success of his sufferings, in the success of that blood, in the salvation of those for whom that blood was shed, and therefore this strong crying shows his strong love; it shows how greatly he desired the salvation of sinners. He cried to God that he might not sink and fail in that great undertaking, because if he did so, sinners could not be saved, but all must perish. He prayed that he might get the victory over death, because if he did not get the victory, his people could never obtain that victory, and they can conquer no otherwise than by his conquest. If the Captain of our salvation had not conquered in this sore

conflict, none of us could have conquered, but we must have all sunk with him. He cried to God that he might be saved from death, and if he had not been saved from death in his resurrection, none of us could ever have been saved from death. It was a great sight to see Christ in that great conflict that he was in in his agony, but every thing in it was from love, that strong love that was in his heart. His tears that flowed from his eyes were from love; his great sweat was from love; his blood, his prostrating himself on the ground before the Father, was from love; his earnest crying to God was from the strength and ardency of his love. It is looked upon as one principal way wherein true love and good will is shown in Christian friends one towards another, heartily to pray one for another; and it is one way wherein Christ directs us to show our love to our enemies, even praying for them. Matt. 5:44. "But I say unto you, Love your enemies, bless them that curse you, and pray for them which despitefully use you, and persecute you." But was there ever any prayer that manifested love to enemies to such a degree, as those strong cries and tears of the Son of God for the success of his blood in the salvation of his enemies; the strife and conflict of whose soul in prayer was such as to produce his agony and his bloody sweat?

3. If Christ was thus earnest in prayer to God, that the end of his sufferings might be obtained in the salvation of sinners, then how much ought those sinners to be reproved that do not earnestly seek their own salvation! If Christ offered up such strong cries for sinners as their high priest, that bought their salvation, who stood in no need of sinners, who had been happy from all eternity without them, and could not be made happier by them; then how great is the sottishness of those sinners that seek their own salvation in a dull and lifeless manner; that content themselves with a formal attendance on the duties of religion, with their hearts in the mean time much more earnestly set after other things! They after a sort attend on the duty of social prayer, wherein they pray to God that he would have mercy on them and save them; but after what a poor dull way is it that they do it! they do not apply their heart

unto wisdom, nor incline their ear to understanding; they do not cry after wisdom, nor lift up their voice for understanding; they do not seek it as silver, nor search for it as for hidden treasures. Christ's earnest cries in his agony may convince us that it was not without reason that he insisted upon it, in Luke 13:24 that we should strive to enter in at the strait gate, which, as I have already observed to you, is, in the original, ἀγωνίζεσθε, "Agonize to enter in at the strait gate." If sinners would be in a hopeful way to obtain their salvation, they should agonize in that great concern as men that are taking a city by violence, as Matt. 11:12. "And from the days of John the Baptist until now the kingdom of heaven suffereth violence, and the violent take it by force." When a body of resolute soldiers are attempting to take a strong city in which they meet with great opposition, what violent conflicts are there before the city is taken! How do the soldiers press on against the very mouths of the enemies' cannon, and upon the points of their swords! When the soldiers are scaling the walls, and making their first entrance into the city, what a violent struggle is there between them and their enemies that strive to keep them out! How do they, as it were, agonize with all their strength! So ought we to seek our salvation, if we would be in a likely way to obtain it. How great is the folly then of those who content themselves with seeking with a cold and lifeless frame of spirit, and so continue from month to month, and from year to year, and yet flatter themselves that they shall be successful!

How much more still are they to be reproved, who are not in a way of seeking their salvation at all, but wholly neglect their precious souls, and attend the duties of religion no further than is just necessary to keep up their credit among men; and instead of pressing into the kingdom of God, are rather violently pressing on towards their own destruction and ruin, being hurried on by their many head strong lusts, as the herd of swine were hurried on by the legion of devils, and ran violently down a steep place into the sea, and perished in the waters! Matt. 8:32.

4. From what has been said under this proposition, we may learn after what manner Christians ought to go through the work that is before them. Christ had a great work before him when that took place, of which we have an account in the text. Though it was very near the close of his life, yet he then, when his agony began, had the chief part of the work before him that he came into the world to do; which was to offer up that sacrifice which he offered in his last sufferings, and therein to perform the greatest act of his obedience to God. And so the Christians have a great work to do, a service they are to perform to God, that is attended with great difficulty. They have a race set before them that they have to run, a warfare that is appointed them. Christ was the subject of a very great trial in the time of his agony; so God is wont to exercise his people with great trials. Christ met with great opposition in that work that he had to do; so believers are like to meet with great opposition in running the race that is set before them. Christ, as man, had a feeble nature, that was in itself very insufficient to sustain such a conflict, or to support such a load as was coming upon him. So the saints have the same weak human nature, and beside that, great sinful infirmities that Christ had not, which lay them under great disadvantages, and greatly enhance the difficulty of their work. Those great tribulations and difficulties that were before Christ, were the way in which he was to enter into the kingdom of heaven; so his followers must expect, "through much tribulation to enter into the kingdom of heaven." The cross was to Christ the way to the crown of glory, and so it is to his disciples. The circumstances of Christ and of his followers in those things are alike, their case, therefore, is the same; and therefore Christ's behaviour under those circumstances, was a fit example for them to follow. They should look to their Captain, and observe after what manner he went through his great work, and the great tribulations which he endured. They should observe after what manner he entered into the kingdom of heaven, and obtained the crown of glory, and so they also should run the race that is set before them. "Wherefore, seeing we also are compassed about with so great a cloud of witnesses, let us lay aside every weight, and the sin which doth so easily beset us, and let us run with patience the race that is set before us. Looking unto Jesus, the author and finisher of our faith; who for the joy that was set before him, endured the cross, despising the shame, and is set down at the right hand of the throne of God." Particularly,

a. When others are asleep they should be awake, as it was with Christ. The time of Christ's agony was the night season, the time wherein persons were wont to be asleep: it was the time wherein the disciples that were about Christ were asleep; but Christ then had something else to do than to sleep; he had a great work to do; he kept awake, with his heart engaged in this work. So should it be with the believers of Christ; when the souls of their neighbors are asleep in their sins, and under the power of a lethargic insensibility and sloth, they should watch and pray, and maintain a lively sense of the infinite importance of their spiritual concerns. 1 Thess. 5:6. "Therefore let us not sleep, as do others, but let us watch and be sober."

b. They should go through their work with earnest labor, as Christ did. The time when others were asleep was a time when Christ was about his great work, and was engaged in it with all his might, agonizing in it; conflicting and wrestling, in tears, and in blood. So should Christians with the utmost earnestness improve their time with souls engaged in this work, pushing through the opposition they meet with in it, pushing through all difficulties and sufferings there are in the way, running with patience the race set before them, conflicting with the enemies of their souls with all their might; as those that wrestle not with flesh and blood, but with principalities and powers, and the rulers of the darkness of this world, and spiritual wickedness in high places.

c. This labor and strife should be, that God may be glorified, and their own eternal happiness obtained in a way of doing God's will. Thus it was with Christ: what he so earnestly strove for was, that he might do the will of God, that he might keep his command, his difficult command, without failing in it, and that in this way God's will might be done, in that glory to his ever great name, and that salvation to his elect that he intended by his sufferings. Here is an example for the saints to follow in that holy strife, and race, and warfare, which God has appointed them; they should strive to do the will of their heavenly Father, that they may, as the apostle expresses it, Rom. 12:2. "Prove what is that good, and acceptable, and perfect will of God," and that in this way they may glorify God, and may come at last to be happy for ever in the enjoyment of God.

(4.) In all the great work they have to do, their eye should be to God for his help to enable them to overcome. Thus did the man Christ Jesus: he strove in his work even to such an agony and bloody sweat. But how did he strive? It was not in his own strength, but his eyes were to God, he cries unto him for his help and strength to uphold him, that he might not fail; he watched and prayed, as he desired his disciples to do; he wrestled with his enemies and with his great sufferings, but at the same time wrestled with God to obtain his help, to enable him to get the victory. Thus the saints should use their strength in their Christian course to the utmost, but not as depending on their own strength, but crying mightily to God for his strength to make them conquerors.

(5.) In this way they should hold out to the end as Christ did. Christ in this way was successful, and obtained the victory, and won the prize; he overcame, and is set down with the Father in his throne. So Christians should persevere and hold out in their great work to the end; they should continue to run their race till they have come to the end of it; they should be faithful unto the death as Christ was; and then, when they have overcome, they shall sit down with him in his throne. Rev. 3:21. "To him that overcometh will I grant to sit with me in my throne, even as I also overcame, and am set down with my Father in his throne."

5. Hence burdened and distressed sinners, if any such are here present, may have abundant ground of encouragement to come to Christ for salvation. Here is great encouragement to sinners to come to this high priest that offered up such strong crying and tears with his blood, for the success of his sufferings in the salvation of sinners. For,

1st, Here is great ground of assurance that Christ stands ready to accept of sinners, and bestow salvation upon them; for those strong cries of his that he offered up in the capacity of our high priest, show how earnestly desirous he was of it. If he was not willing that sinners should be saved, be they ever so unworthy of it, then why would he so wrestle with God for it in such a bloody sweat? Would any one so earnestly cry to God with such costly cries, in such great labor and travail of soul, for that, that he did not desire that God should bestow? No, surely! but this shows how greatly his heart was set on the success of his redemption; and therefore since he has by such earnest prayers, and by such a bloody sweat, obtained salvation of the Father to bestow on sinners, he will surely be ready to bestow it upon them, if they come to him for it; otherwise he will frustrate his own design; and he that so earnestly cried to God that his design might not be frustrated, will not, after all, frustrate it himself.

2nd, Here is the strongest ground of assurance that God stands ready to accept of all those that come to him for mercy through Christ, for this is what Christ prayed for in those earnest prayers, whose prayers were always heard, as Christ says, John 11:42. "And I knew that thou hearest me always." And especially may they conclude, that heard their high priest in those strong cries that he offered up with his blood, and that especially on the following account.

(1.) They were the most earnest prayers that ever were made. Jacob was very earnest when he wrestled with God; and many others have wrestled with God with many tears; yea, doubtless, many of the saints have wrestled with God with such inward labor and strife as to produce powerful effects on the body. But so earnest was Christ, so strong was the labor and fervency of his heart, that he cried to God in a sweat of blood; so that if any earnestness and importunity in prayer ever prevailed with God, we may conclude that that prevailed.

(2.) He who then prayed was the most worthy person that ever put up a prayer. He had more worthiness than ever men or angels had in the sight of God, according as by inheritance he has obtained a more excellent name than they; for he was the only-begotten Son of God, infinitely lovely in his sight, the Son in whom he declared once and again he was well-pleased. He was infinitely near and dear to God, and had more worthiness in his eyes ten thousand times than all men and angels put together. And can we suppose any other than that such a person was heard when he cried to God with such earnestness? Did Jacob, a poor sinful man, when he had wrestled with God, obtain of God the name of ISRAEL, and that encomium, that as a prince he had power with God, and prevailed? And did Elijah, who was a man of like passions, and of like corruptions with us, when he prayed, earnestly prevail on God to work such great wonders? And shall not the only-begotten Son of God, when wrestling with God in tears and blood, prevail, and have his request granted him?

Surely there is no room to suppose any such thing; and therefore, there is no room to doubt whether God will bestow salvation on those that believe in him, at his request.

(3.) Christ offered up these earnest prayers with the best plea for an answer that ever was offered to God, viz. his own blood; which was an equivalent for the thing that he asked. He not only offered up strong cries, but he offered them up with a price fully sufficient to purchase the benefit he asked.

(4.) Christ offered this price and those strong cries both together; for at the same time that he was pouring out these earnest requests for the success of his redemption in the salvation of sinners, he also shed his blood. His blood fell down to the ground at the same instant that his cries went up to heaven. Let burdened and distressed sinners, that are ready to doubt of the efficacy of Christ's intercession for such unworthy creatures as they, and to call in question God's readiness to accept them for Christ's sake, consider these things. Go to the garden where the Son of God was in an agony, and where he cried to God so earnestly, and where his sweat was, as it were, great drops of blood, and then see what a conclusion you will draw up from such a wonderful sight.

6. The godly may take great comfort in this, that Christ has as their high priest offered up such strong cries to God. You that have good evidence of your being believers in Christ, and his true followers and servants, may comfort yourselves in this, that Christ Jesus is your high priest, that that blood, which Christ shed in his agony, fell down to the ground for you, and that those earnest cries were sent up to God for you, for the success of his labors and sufferings in all that good you stood in need of in this world, and in your everlasting happiness in the world to come. This may be a comfort to you in all losses, and under all difficulties, that you may encourage your faith, and strengthen your hope, and cause you greatly to rejoice. If you were under any remarkable difficulties, it would be a great comfort to you to have the prayers of some man that you looked upon to be a man of eminent piety, and one that had a great interest at the throne of grace, and especially if you knew that he was very earnest and greatly engaged in prayer for you. But how much more may you be comforted in it, that you have an interest in the prayers and cries of the only-begotten and infinitely worthy Son of God, and that he was so earnest in his prayers for you, as you have heard!

7. Hence we may learn how earnest Christians ought to be in their prayers and endeavors for the salvation of others. Christians are the followers of Christ, and they should follow him in this. We see from what we have heard, how great the labor and travail of Christ's soul was for others' salvation, and what earnest and strong cries to God accompanied his labours. Here he hath set us an example. Herein he hath set an example for ministers, who should as co-workers with Christ travail in birth with them till Christ be found in them. Gal. 4:19. "My little children, of whom I travail in birth again, until Christ be formed in you." They should be willing to spend and be spent for them. They should not only labor for them, and pray earnestly for them, but should, if occasion required, be ready to suffer for them, and to spend not only their strength, but their blood for them. 2 Cor. 12:15. "And I will very

gladly spend and be spent for you, though the more abundantly I love you, the less I be loved." Here is an example for parents, showing how they ought to labor and cry to God for the spiritual good of their children. You see how Christ labored and strove and cried to God for the salvation of his spiritual children; and will not you earnestly seek and cry to God for your natural children?

Here is an example for neighbors one towards another how they should seek and cry for the good of one another's souls, for this is the command of Christ, that they should love one another as Christ loved them. John 15:12. Here is an example for us, showing how we should earnestly seek and pray for the spiritual and eternal good of our enemies, for Christ did all this for his enemies, and when some of those enemies were at that very instant plotting his death, and busily contriving to satiate their malice and cruelty, in his most extreme torments, and most ignominious destruction.

Jonathan Edwards

2.51 GETHSEMANE, ALFRED EDERSHEIM

St. Matt. 26:30-56; Mark 14:26-52; Luke 22:31-53; John 18:1-11.

We turn once more to follow the steps of Christ, now among the last He trod upon earth. The "hymn," with which the Paschal Supper ended, had been sung. Probably we are to understand this of the second portion of the Hallel, sung some time after the third Cup, or else of Psalm 136, which, in the present Ritual, stands near the end of the service. The last Discourses had been spoken, the last Prayer, that of Consecration, had been offered, and Jesus prepared to go forth out of the City, to the Mount of Olives. The streets could scarcely be said to be deserted, for, from many a house shone the festive lamp, and many a company may still have been gathered; and everywhere was the bustle of preparation for going up to the Temple, the gates of which were thrown open at midnight.

Passing out by the gate north of the Temple, we descend into a lonely part of the valley of black Kidron, at that season swelled into a winter torrent. Crossing it, we turn somewhat to the left, where the road leads towards Olivet. Not many steps farther (beyond, and on the other side of the present Church of the Sepulcher of the Virgin) we turn aside from the road to the right, and reach what tradition has since earliest times—and probably correctly—pointed out as "Gethsemane," the "Oil-press." It was a small property enclosed, "a garden" in the Eastern sense, where probably, amidst a variety of fruit trees and flowering shrubs, was a lowly, quiet summer-retreat, connected with, or near by, the "Olive-press." The present Gethsemane is only some seventy steps square, and though its old gnarled olives cannot be those (if such there were) of the time of Jesus, since all trees in that valley—those also which stretched their shadows over Jesus—were hewn down in the Roman siege, they may have sprung from the old roots, or from the odd kernels. But we love to think of this "Garden" as the place where Jesus "often"—not merely on this occasion, but perhaps on previous visits to Jerusalem—gathered with His disciples. It was a quiet resting-place, for retirement, prayer, perhaps sleep, and a trysting-place also where not only the Twelve, but others also, may have been wont to meet the Master. And as such it was known to Judas, and thither he led the armed band, when they found the Upper Chamber no longer occupied by Jesus and His disciples. Whether it had been intended that He should spend part of the night there, before returning to the Temple, and whose that enclosed garden was—the other Eden, in which the Second Adam, the Lord from heaven, bore the penalty of the first, and in obeying gained life—we know not, and perhaps ought not to inquire. It may have belonged to Mark's father. But if otherwise, Jesus had loving disciples even in Jerusalem, and, we rejoice to think, not only a home at Bethany, and an Upper Chamber furnished in the City, but a quiet retreat and trysting-place for His own under the bosom of Olivet, in the shadow of the garden of "the Oil-press."

The sickly light of the moon was falling full on them as they were crossing Kidron. It was here, we imagine, after they had left the City behind them, that the Lord addressed Himself first to the disciples generally. We can scarcely call it either prediction or warning. Rather, as we think of that last Supper, of Christ passing through the streets of the City for the last time into that Garden, and especially of what was now immediately before Him, does what He spake seem natural, even necessary. To them—yes, to them all—He would that night be even a stumbling-block. And so had it been foretold of old, that the Shepherd would be smitten, and the sheep scattered. Did this prophecy of His suffering, in its grand outlines, fill the mind of the Savior as He went forth on His Passion? Such Old Testament thoughts were at any rate present with Him, when, not unconsciously nor of necessity, but as the Lamb of God, He went to the slaughter. A peculiar significance also attaches to His prediction that, after He was risen, He would go before them into Galilee. For, with their scattering upon His Death, it seems to us, the Apostolic circle or College, as such, was for a time broken up. They continued, indeed, to meet together as individual disciples, but the Apostolic bond was temporarily dissolved. This explains many things: the absence of Thomas on the first, and his peculiar position on the second Sunday; the uncertainty of the disciples, as evidenced by the words of those on the way to Emmaus; as well as the seemingly strange movements of the Apostles—all which are quite changed when the Apostolic bond is restored. Similarly, we mark, that only seven of them seem to have

been together by the Lake of Galilee, and that only afterwards the Eleven met Him on the mountain to which He had directed them. It was here that the Apostolic circle or College was once more re-formed, and the Apostolic commission renewed, and thence they returned to Jerusalem, once more sent forth from Galilee, to wait the final events of His Ascension, and the Coming of the Holy Ghost.

But in that night they understood none of these things. While all were staggering under the blow of their predicted scattering, the Lord seems to have turned to Peter individually. What he said, and how He put it, equally demand our attention: "Simon, Simon"—using His old name when referring to the old man in him—"Satan has obtained you, for the purpose of sifting like as wheat. But I have made supplication for thee, that thy faith fail not." The words admit us into two mysteries of heaven. This night seems to have been "the power of darkness," when, left of God, Christ had to meet by himself the whole assault of hell, and to conquer in His own strength as Man's Substitute and Representative. It is a great mystery: but quite consistent with itself. We do not, as others, here see any analogy to the permission given to Satan in the opening chapter of the Book of Job, always supposing that this embodies a real, not an allegorical story. But in that night the fierce wind of hell was allowed to sweep unbroken over the Savior, and even to expend its fury upon those that stood behind in His Shelter. Satan had "out-asked," obtained it—yet not to destroy, nor to cast down, but "to sift," like as wheat is shaken in a sieve to cast out of it what is not grain. Hitherto, and no farther, had Satan obtained it. In that night of Christ's Agony and loneliness, of the utmost conflict between Christ and Satan, this seems almost a necessary element.

This, then, was the first mystery that had passed. And this sifting would affect Peter more than the others. Judas, who loved not Jesus at all, has already fallen; Peter, who loved Him—perhaps not most intensely, but, if the expression be allowed, most extensively—stood next to Judas in danger. In truth, though most widely apart in their direction, the springs of their inner life rose in close proximity. There was the same readiness to kindle into enthusiasm, the same desire to have public opinion with him, the same shrinking from the Cross, the same moral inability or unwillingness to stand alone, in the one as in the other. Peter had abundant courage to sally out, but not to stand out. Viewed in its primal elements (not in its development), Peter's character was, among the disciples, the likest to that of Judas. If this shows what Judas might have become, it also explains how Peter was most in danger that night; and, indeed, the husks of him were cast out of the sieve in his denial of the Christ. But what distinguished Peter from Judas was his "faith" of spirit, soul, and heart—of spirit, when he apprehended the spiritual element in Christ; of soul, when he confessed Him as the Christ; and of heart, when he could ask Him to sound the depths of his inner being, to find there real, personal love to Jesus.

The second mystery of that night was Christ's supplication for Peter. We dare not say, as the High-Priest—and we know not when and where it was offered. But the expression is very strong, as of one who has need of a thing. And that for which He made such supplication was, that Peter's faith should not fail. This, and not that something new might be given him, or the trial removed from Peter. We mark, how Divine grace presupposes, not supersedes, human liberty. And this also explains why Jesus had so prayed for Peter, not for Judas. In the former case there was faith, which only required to be strengthened against failure—an eventuality which, without the intercession of Christ, was possible. To these words of His, Christ added this significant commission: "And thou, when thou hast turned again, confirm thy brethren." And how fully he did this, both in the Apostolic circle and in the Church, history has chronicled. Thus, although such may come in the regular moral order of things, Satan has not even power to "sift" without leave of God; and thus does the Father watch in such terrible sifting over them for whom Christ has prayed. This is the first fulfillment of Christ's Prayer, that the Father would "keep them from the Evil One." Not by any process

from without, but by the preservation of their faith. And thus also may we learn, to our great and unspeakable comfort, that not every sin—not even conscious and willful sin—implies the failure of our faith, very closely though it lead to it; still less, our final rejection. On the contrary, as the fall of Simon was the outcome of the natural elements in him, so would it lead to their being brought to light and removed, thus fitting him the better for confirming his brethren. And so would light come out of darkness. From our human standpoint we might call such teaching needful: in the Divine arrangement it is only the Divine sequent upon the human antecedent.

We can understand the vehement earnestness and sincerity with which Peter protested against of any failure on his part. We mostly deem those sins farthest which are nearest to us; else, much of the power of their temptation would be gone, and temptation changed into conflict. The things which we least anticipate are our falls. In all honesty—and not necessarily with self elevation over the others—he said, that even if all should be offended in Christ, he never could be, but was ready to go with Him into prison and death. And when, to enforce the warning, Christ predicted that before the repeated crowing of the cock ushered in the morning, Peter would thrice deny that he knew Him, Peter not only persisted in his asseverations, but was joined in them by the rest. Yet—and this seems the meaning and object of the words of Christ which follow—they were not aware terribly changed the former relations had become, and what they would have to suffer in consequence. When formerly He had sent forth, both without provision and defense, had they lacked anything? No! But now no helping hand would be extended to them; nay, what seemingly they would need even more than anything else would be "a sword"—defense against attacks, for at the close of His history He was reckoned with transgressors. The Master a crucified Malefactor—what could His followers expect? But once more they understood Him in a grossly realistic manner. These Galileans, after the custom of their countrymen, had provided themselves with short swords, which they concealed under their upper garment. It was natural for men of their disposition, so imperfectly understanding their Master's teaching, to have taken what might seem to them only a needful precaution in coming to Jerusalem. At least two of them—among them Peter—now produced swords. But this was not the time of reason with them, and our Lord simply put it aside. Events would only too soon teach them.

They had now reached the entrance of Gethsemane. It may have been that it led through the building with the oil-press,' and that the eight Apostles, who were not to come nearer to the "Bush burning, but not consumed," were left there. Or they may have been taken within the entrance of the Garden, and left there, while, pointing forward with a gesture of the Hand, He went yonder and prayed According to Luke, He added the parting warning to pray that they might not enter into temptation.

Eight did He leave there. The other three—Peter, James and John—companions before of His glory, both when He raised the daughter of Jairus and on the Mount of Transfiguration—He took with Him farther. If in that last contest His Human Soul craved for the presence of those who stood nearest Him and loved Him best, or if He would have them baptized with His Baptism, and drink of His Cup, these were the three of all others to be chosen. And now of a sudden the cold flood broke over Him. Within these few moments He had passed from the calm of assured victory into the anguish of the contest. Increasingly, with every step forward, He became "sorrowful," full of sorrow, "sore amazed," and "desolate." He told them of the deep sorrow of His Soul even unto death, and bade them tarry there to watch with Him. Himself went forward to enter the contest with prayer. Only the first attitude of the wrestling Savior saw they, only the first words in that Hour of Agony did they hear. For, as in our present state not uncommonly in the deepest emotions of the soul, and as had been the case on the Mount of Transfiguration, irresistible sleep crept over their frame. But what, we may reverently ask, was the cause of

this sorrow unto death of the Lord Jesus Christ? Not fear, either of bodily or mental suffering: but Death. Man's nature, created of God immortal, shrinks (by the law of its nature) from the dissolution of the bond that binds body to soul. Yet to fallen man Death is not by any means fully Death, for he is born with the taste of it in his soul. Not so Christ. It was the Unfallen Man dying; it was He, Who had no experience of it, tasting Death, and that not for Himself but for every man, emptying the cup to its bitter dregs. It was the Christ undergoing Death by man and for man; the Incarnate God, the God-Man, submitting Himself vicariously to the deepest humiliation, and paying the utmost penalty: Death—all Death. No one as He could know what Death was (not dying, which men dread, but Christ dreaded not); no one could taste its bitterness as He. His going into Death was His final conflict with Satan for man, and on his behalf. By submitting to it He took away the power of Death; He disarmed Death by burying his shaft in His own Heart. And beyond this lies the deep, unutterable mystery of Christ bearing the penalty due to our sin, bearing our death, bearing the penalty of the broken Law, the accumulated guilt of humanity, and the holy wrath of the Righteous Judge upon them. And in view of this mystery the heaviness of sleep seems to steal over our apprehension.

Alone, as in His first conflict with the Evil One in the Temptation in the wilderness, must the Savior enter on the last contest. With what agony of soul He took upon Him now and there the sins of the world, and in taking expiated them, we may learn from this account of what passed, when, "with strong crying and tears unto Him that was able to save Him from death," He "offered up prayers and supplications." And—we anticipate it already—with these results: that He was heard; that He learned obedience by the things which He suffered; that He was made perfect; and that He became: to us the Author of Eternal Salvation, and before God, a High-Priest after the order of Melchizedek. Alone—and yet even this being "parted from them," implied sorrow. And now, "on His knees," prostrate on the ground, prostrate on His

Face, began His Agony. His very address bears witness to it. It is the only time, so far as recorded in the Gospels, when He addressed God with the personal pronoun: "My Father." The object of the prayer was, that, "if it were possible, the hour might pass away from Him." The subject of the prayer (as recorded by the three Gospels) was, that the Cup itself might pass away, yet always with the limitation, that not His Will but the Father's might be done. The petition of Christ, therefore, was subject not only to the Will of the Father, but to His own Will that the Father's Will might be done. We are here in full view of the deepest mystery of our faith: the two Natures in One Person. Both Natures spake here, and the "if it be possible" of Matthew and Mark is in Luke "if Thou be willing." In any case, the "possibility" is not physical—for with God all things are possible—but moral: that of inward fitness. Was there, then, any thought or view of "a possibility," that Christ's work could be accomplished without that hour and Cup? Or did it only mark the utmost limit of His endurance and submission? We dare not answer; we only reverently follow what is recorded.

It was in this extreme Agony of Soul almost unto death, that the Angel appeared (as in the Temptation in the wilderness) to "strengthen" and support His Body and Soul. And so the conflict went on, with increasing earnestness of prayer, all that terrible hour. For, the appearance of the Angel must have intimated to Him, that the Cup could not pass away. And at the close of that hour—as we infer from the fact that the disciples must still have seen on His Brow the marks of the Bloody Sweat—His Sweat, mingled with Blood, fell in great drops on the ground. And when the Savior with this mark of His Agony on His Brow returned to the three, He found that deep sleep held them. While He lay in prayer, they lay in sleep; and yet where soul-agony leads not to the one, it often induces the other. His words, primarily addressed to "Simon," roused them, yet not sufficiently to fully carry to their hearts either the loving reproach, the admonition to "Watch and pray" in view of the coming temptation, or

the most seasonable warning about the weakness of the flesh, even where the spirit was willing, ready and ardent.

The conflict had been virtually, though not finally, decided, when the Savior went back to the three sleeping disciples. He now returned to complete it, though both the attitude in which He prayed (no longer prostrate) and the wording of His Prayer—only slightly altered as it was—indicate how near it was to perfect victory. And once more, on His return to them, He found that sleep had weighted their eyes, and they scarce knew what answer to make to Him. Yet a third time He left them to pray as before. And now He returned victorious. After three assaults had the Tempter left Him in the wilderness; after the threefold conflict in the Garden he was vanquished. Christ came forth triumphant. No longer did He bid His disciples watch. They might, nay they should, sleep and take rest, ere the near terrible events of His Betrayal—for, the hour had come when the Son of Man was to be betrayed into the hands of sinners.

A very brief period of rest this, soon broken by the call of Jesus to rise and go to where the other eight had been left, at the entrance of the Garden—to go forward and meet the band which was coming under the guidance of the Betrayer. And while He was speaking, the heavy tramp of many men and the light of lanterns and torches indicated the approach of Judas and his band. During the hours that had passed all had been prepared. When, according to arrangement, he appeared at the High-Priestly Palace, or more probably at that of Annas, who seems to have had the direction of affairs, the Jewish leaders first communicated with the Roman garrison. By their own admission they possessed no longer (for forty years before the destruction of Jerusalem) the power of pronouncing capital sentence. It is difficult to understand how, in view of this fact (so fully confirmed in the New Testament), it could have been imagined (as so generally) that the Sanhedrin had, in regular session, sought formally to pronounce on Jesus what, admittedly, they had not the power to execute. Nor, indeed, did they, when appealing to Pilate, plead that they had pronounced sentence of death, but only that they had a law by which Jesus should die. It was otherwise as regarded civil causes, or even minor offences. The Sanhedrin, not possessing the power of the sword, had, of course, neither soldiery, nor regularly armed band at command. The "Temple-guard" under their officers served merely for purposes of police, and, indeed, were neither regularly armed nor trained. Nor would the Romans have tolerated a regular armed Jewish force in Jerusalem.

We can now understand the progress of events. In the fortress of Antonia, close to the Temple and connected with it by two stairs, lay the Roman garrison. But during the Feast the Temple itself was guarded by an armed Cohort, consisting of from 400 to 600 men, so as to prevent or quell any tumult among the numerous pilgrims. It would be to the captain of this "Cohort" that the Chief Priests and leaders of the Pharisees would, in the first place, apply for an armed guard to effect the arrest of Jesus, on the ground that it might lead to some popular tumult. This, without necessarily having to state the charge that was to be brought against Him, which might have led to other complications. Although John speaks of "the band" by a word which always designates a "Cohort"—in this case "the Cohort," the definite article marking it as that of the Temple—yet there is no reason for believing that the whole Cohort was sent. Still, its commander would scarcely have sent a strong detachment out of the Temple, and on what might lead to a riot, without having first referred to the Procurator, Pontius Pilate. And if further evidence were required, it would be in the fact that the band was led not by a Centurion, but by a Chiliarch, which, as there were no intermediate grades in the Roman army, must represent one of the six tribunes attached to each legion. This also explains not only the apparent preparedness of Pilate to sit in judgment early next morning, but also how Pilate's wife may have been disposed for those dreams about Jesus which so affrighted her.

This Roman detachment, armed with swords and "staves"—with the latter of which Pilate on other occasions also directed his soldiers to attack them who raised a tumult—was accompanied by servants from the High-Priest's Palace, and other Jewish officers, to direct the arrest of Jesus. They bore torches and lamps placed on the top of poles, so as to prevent any possible concealment.

Whether or not this was the "great multitude" mentioned by Matthew and Mark, or the band was swelled by volunteers or curious onlookers, is a matter of no importance. Having received this band, Judas proceeded on his errand. As we believe, their first move was to the house where the Supper had been celebrated. Learning that Jesus had left it with His disciples, perhaps two or three hours before, Judas next directed the band to the spot he knew so well: to Gethsemane. A signal by which to recognize Jesus seemed almost necessary with so large a band, and where escape or resistance might be apprehended. It was—terrible to say—none other than a kiss. As soon as he had so marked Him, the guard were to seize, and lead Him safely away.

Combining the notices in the four Gospels, we thus picture to ourselves the succession of events. As the band reached the Garden, Judas went somewhat in advance of them, and reached Jesus just as He had roused the three and was preparing to go and meet His captors. He saluted Him, "Hail, Rabbi," so as to be heard by the rest, and not only kissed but covered Him with kisses, kissed Him repeatedly, loudly, effusively. The Savior submitted to the indignity, not stopping, but only saying as He passed on: "Friend, that for which thou art here;" and then, perhaps in answer to his questioning gesture: "Judas, with a kiss deliverest thou up the Son of Man?" If Judas had wished, by thus going in advance of the band and saluting the Master with a kiss, even now to act the hypocrite and deceive Jesus and the disciples, as if he had not come with the armed men, perhaps only to warn Him of their approach, what the Lord said must have reached his inmost being. Indeed, it was the first mortal shaft in the soul of Judas. The only time we again see him, till he goes on what ends in his self-destruction, is as he stands, as it were sheltering himself, with the armed men.

It is at this point, as we suppose, that the notices from John's Gospel come in. Leaving the traitor, and ignoring the signal which he had given them, Jesus advanced to the band, and asked them: "Whom seek ye?" To the brief spoken, perhaps somewhat contemptuous, "Jesus the Nazarene," He replied with infinite calmness and majesty: "I am He." The immediate effect of these words was, we shall not say magical, but Divine. They had no doubt been prepared for quite other: either compromise, fear, or resistance. But the appearance and majesty of that calm Christ—heaven in His look and peace on His lips—was too overpowering in its effects on that untutored heathen soldiery, who perhaps cherished in their hearts secret misgivings of the work they had in hand. The foremost of them went backward, and they fell to the ground. But Christ's hour had come. And once more He now asked them the same question as before, and, on repeating their former answer, He said: "I told you that I am He; if therefore ye seek Me, let these go their way,"—the Evangelist seeing in this watchful care over His own the initial fulfillment of the words which the Lord had previously spoken concerning their safe preservation, not only in the sense of their outward preservation, but in that of their being guarded from such temptations as, in their then state, they could not have endured.

The words of Christ about those that were with Him seem to have recalled the leaders of the guard to full consciousness—perhaps awakened in them fears of a possible rising at the incitement of His adherents. Accordingly, it is here that we insert the notice of Matthew, and of Mark, that they laid hands on Jesus and took Him. Then it was that Peter, seeing what was coming, drew the sword which he carried, and putting the question to Jesus, but without awaiting His answer, struck at Malchus, the servant of the High-Priest—perhaps the Jewish leader of the band—cutting off his ear. But Jesus immediately restrained all such violence, and rebuked all self-vindication by outward violence (the taking of the sword that had not been received)—nay, with it all merely outward zeal, pointing to the fact how easily He might, as against this "cohort," have commanded Angelic legions. He had in wrestling Agony received from His Father that Cup to drink, and the Scriptures must in that wise be fulfilled. And so saying, He touched the ear of Malchus, and healed him.

But this faint appearance of resistance was enough for the guard. Their leaders now bound Jesus. It was to this last, most underserved and uncalled-for indignity that Jesus replied by asking them, why they had come against Him as against a robber—one of those wild, murderous Sicarii. Had He not been all that week daily in the Temple, teaching? Why not then seize Him? But this "hour" of theirs that had come, and "the power of darkness"—this also had been foretold in Scripture!

And as the ranks of the armed men now closed around the bound Christ, none dared to stay with Him, lest they also should be bound as resisting authority. So they all forsook Him and fled. But there was one there who joined not in the flight, but remained, a deeply interested onlooker. When the soldiers had come to seek Jesus in the Upper Chamber of his home, Mark, roused from sleep, had hastily cast about him the loose linen garment or wrapper that lay by his bedside, and followed the armed band to see what would come of it. He now lingered in the rear, and followed as they led away Jesus, never imagining that they would attempt to lay hold on him, since he had not been with the disciples nor yet in the Garden. But they, perhaps the Jewish servants of the High-Priest, had noticed him. They attempted to lay hold on him, when, disengaging himself from their grasp, he left his upper garment in their hands, and fled.

So ended the first scene in the terrible drama of that night.

Alfred Edersheim, Life and Times of Jesus the Messiah, *1886*

2.52 GREAT DROPS OF BLOOD, C. H. SPURGEON

Delivered on Sunday morning, February 8th, 1863, at the Metropolitan Tabernacle, Newington, London

"And being in agony He prayed more earnestly: and His sweat was as it were great drops of blood falling down to the ground." Luke 22:44

Our Lord after having eaten the Passover and celebrating the supper with His disciples, went with them to the Mount of Olives, and entered the garden of Gethsemane. What induced Him to select that place to be the scene of His terrible agony? Why there in preference to anywhere else would He be arrested by His enemies? May we not conceive that as in a garden Adam's self-indulgence ruined us, so in another garden the agonies of the second Adam should restore us. Gethsemane supplies the medicine for the ills which followed upon the forbidden fruit of Eden. No flowers which bloomed upon the banks of the four-fold river were ever so precious to our race as the bitter herbs which grew hard by the black and sullen stream of Kedron.

May not our Lord also have thought of David, when on that memorable occasion he fled out of the city from his rebellious son, and it is written, "The king also himself passed over the brook Kedron," and he and his people went up bare-footed and bare-headed, weeping as they went? Behold, the greater David leaves the temple to become desolate, and forsakes the city which had rejected His admonitions, and with a sorrowful heart crosses the foul brook, to find in solitude a solace for His woes. Our Lord Jesus, moreover, meant us to see that our sin changed everything about Him into sorrow, it turned His riches into poverty, His peace into travail, His glory into shame, and so the place of His peaceful retirement, where in hallowed devotion He had been nearest heaven in communication with God, our sin transformed into the focus of His sorrow, the center of His woe. Where He had enjoyed most, there He must be called to suffer most.

Our Lord may also have chosen the garden, because needing every remembrance that could sustain Him in the conflict, He felt refreshed by the memory of former hours which there had passed away so quietly. He had there prayed, and gained strength and comfort. Those gnarled and twisted olives knew Him well; there was scarce a blade of grass in the garden which He had not knelt upon; He had consecrated the spot to fellowship with God. What wonder then that He preferred this favored soil? Just as a man would choose in sickness to lie in his own bed, so Jesus chose to endure His agony in His own oratory, where the recollections of former communings with His Father would come so vividly before Him.

But probably, the chief reason for His resort to Gethsemane was, that it was His well-known haunt, and John tells us, "Judas also knew the place." Our Lord did not wish to conceal Himself, He did not need to be hunted down like a thief, or searched out by spies. He went boldly to the place where His enemies knew that He was accustomed to pray, for He was willing to be taken to suffering and to death. They did not drag Him off to Pilate's hall against His will, but He went with them voluntarily. When the hour was come for Him to be betrayed there was He in a place where the traitor could readily find Him, and when Judas would betray Him with a kiss His cheek was ready to receive the traitorous salutation. The blessed Savior delighted to do the will of the Lord, though it involved obedience to death.

We have thus come to the gate of the garden of Gethsemane, let us now enter; but first let us put off our shoes from our foot, as Moses did, when he also saw the bush which burned with fire, and was not consumed. Surely we may say with Jacob, "How dreadful is this place!" I tremble at the task which lies before me, for how shall my feeble speech describe those agonies, for which strong crying and tears were scarcely an adequate expression? I desire with you to survey the sufferings of our Redeemer, but oh, may the Spirit of God prevent our mind from thinking aught amiss, or our tongue from speaking even one word which would be derogatory to Him either in His immaculate manhood or his glorious Godhead. It is not easy when you are speaking of one who is both God and man to observe the exact line of correct speech; it is so easy to describe the divine side in such a manner as to trench upon the human, or to depict the human at the cost of the divine. Make me not an offender for a word if I should err. A man had need himself to be inspired, or to confine himself to the very words of inspiration, fitly to speak at all times upon the great "mystery of godliness," God manifest in the flesh, and especially when he has to dwell most upon God so manifest in suffering flesh that the weakest traits in manhood become the most conspicuous. O Lord, open Thou my lips that my tongue may utter right words.

Meditating upon the agonizing scene in Gethsemane we are compelled to observe that our Savior there endured a grief unknown to any previous period of His life, and therefore we will commence our discourse by raising the question, WHAT WAS THE CAUSE OF THE PECULIAR GRIEF IN GETHSEMANE? Our Lord was the "man of sorrows and acquainted with grief" throughout His whole life, and yet, though it may sound paradoxical, I scarcely think there existed on the face of the earth a happier man than Jesus of Nazareth, for the griefs which He endured were counterbalanced by the peace of purity, the calm of fellowship with God, and the joy of benevolence. This last every good man knows to be very sweet, and all the sweeter in proportion to the pain which is voluntarily endured for the carrying out of its kind designs. It is always joy to do good, cost what it may. Moreover Jesus dwelt at perfect peace

with God at all times; we know that He did so, for He could bequeath to His disciples, and ere He died He said unto them, "Peace I leave with you, My peace I give unto you." He was meek and lowly of heart, and therefore His soul had rest; He was one of the meek who inherit the earth; one of the peacemakers who are and must be blessed. I think I mistake not when I say that our Lord was far from being an unhappy man. But in Gethsemane all seems changed, His peace is gone, His calm is turned to tempest. After supper our Lord had sung a hymn, but there was no singing in Gethsemane.

Adown the steep bank which led from Jerusalem to the Kedron He talked very cheerfully, saying "I am the vine and ye are the branches," and that wondrous prayer which He prayed with His disciples after that discourse, is very full of majesty: "Father, I will that they also whom Thou hast given me be with Me where I am," is a very different prayer from that inside Gethsemane's walls, where He cries, "If it be possible, let this cup pass from me." Notice that all His life long, you scarcely find Him uttering an expression of grief, and yet here He says, not only by His sighs and by His bloody sweat, but in so many words, "My soul is exceedingly sorrowful even unto death." In the garden the Sufferer could not conceal His grief, and does not appear to have wished to do so. Backward and forward thrice He ran to His disciples, He let them see His sorrow and appealed to them for sympathy; His exclamations were very piteous, and His sighs and groans were I doubt not, very terrible to hear. Chiefly did that sorrow reveal itself in bloody sweat, which is a very unusual phenomenon, although I suppose we must believe those writers who record instances somewhat similar. The old physician Galen gives an instance in which, through extremity of horror, an individual poured forth a discolored sweat, so nearly crimson as at any rate to appear to have been blood. Other cases are given by medical authorities. We do not, however, on any previous occasion observe anything like this in our Lord's life. It was only in the last grim struggle among the olive trees that our Champion resisted unto blood, agonizing against sin. What ailed Thee, O Lord, that Thou shouldst be so sorely troubled just then?

We are clear that His deep sorrow and distress were not occasioned by any bodily pain. Our Savior had doubtless been familiar with weakness and pain, for He took our sickness, but He never in any previous instance complained of physical suffering. Neither at the time when He entered Gethsemane had He been grieved by any bereavement. We know why it is written, "Jesus wept," it was because His friend Lazarus was dead; but here there was no funeral, nor sick bed, nor particular cause of grief in that direction. Nor was it the revived remembrance of any past reproaches which had lain dormant in His mind. Long before this "reproach had broken His heart," and He had known to the full the vexations of contumely and scorn. They had called Him a "drunken man and a wine bibber," they had charged Him with casting out devils by the prince of the devils; they could not say more and yet He had bravely faced it all, it could not be possible that He was now sorrowful unto death for such a cause. There must have been a something sharper than pain, more cutting than reproach, more terrible than bereavement, which now at this time grappled with the Savior, and made Him "exceeding sorrowful, and very heavy."

Do you suppose it was the fear of coming scorn, or the dread of crucifixion? Was it terror at the thought of death? Is not such a supposition impossible? Every man dreads death, and as man Jesus could not shrink from it. When we were originally made we were created for immortality, and therefore to die is strange and uncongenial work to us, and the instincts of self-preservation cause us to start back from it; but surely in our Lord's case that natural cause could not have produced such specially painful results. It does not make even such poor cowards, as we are sweat great drops of blood, why then should it work such terror in Him? It is dishonoring to our Lord to imagine Him less brave than His own disciples, yet we have seen some of the very feeblest of His saints triumphant in the prospect of departing. Read the stories of the martyrs, and you will frequently find them exultant in the near approach of the most cruel sufferings. The joy of the Lord has given such strength to them, that no coward thought has alarmed them for a single moment, but they have gone to the stake, or to the block, with psalms of victory upon their lips. Our Master must not be thought of as inferior to His boldest servant, it cannot be that He should tremble where they were brave. Oh, no; the noblest spirit among yon martyr-band is the Leader Himself, who in suffering and heroism surpassed them all; none could so defy the pangs of death as the Lord Jesus, who, for the joy which was set before Him, endured the cross despising the shame.

I cannot conceive that the pangs of Gethsemane were occasioned by any extraordinary attack from Satan. It is possible that Satan was there, and that his presence may have darkened the shade, but he was not the most prominent cause of that hour of darkness. Thus much is quite clear, that our Lord at the commencement of His ministry engaged in a very severe duel with the prince of darkness, and the wilderness a single syllable as to His soul's being sorrowful, neither do we find that He "was sore amazed and was very heavy," nor is there a solitary hint at anything approaching to bloody sweat. When the Lord of angels condescended to stand foot to foot with the prince of the power of the air, He had no such dread of him as to utter strong cries and tears and fall prostrate on the ground with threefold appeals to the Great Father. Comparatively speaking, to put His foot on the old serpent was an easy task for Christ, and did but cost Him a bruised heel, but this Gethsemane agony wounded His very soul even unto death.

What is it then, think you, that so peculiarly marks off Gethsemane and the griefs thereof? We believe that now the Father put Him to grief for us. It was now that our Lord had to take a certain cup from the Father's hand. Not from the Jews, not from the traitor Judas, not from the sleeping disciples, not from the devil came the trial now, but it was a cup filled by One whom He knew to be His Father, but who nevertheless He understood to have appointed Him a very bitter potion, a cup not to be drunk by His body and to spend its gall upon His flesh, but a cup which specially amazed His soul and troubled His inmost heart. He shrank from it, and therefore be ye sure that it was a draught more dreadful than physical pain, since from that He did not shrink; it was a potion more dreadful than reproach, from that He had not turned aside; more dreadful than Satanic temptation,—that He had overcome: it was a something inconceivably terrible, amazingly full of dread, which came from His Father's hand. This removes all doubt as to what it was, for we read "It pleased the Lord to bruise Him, He hath put Him to grief: when Thou shalt make His soul an offering for sin." "The Lord hath made to meet on Him the iniquity of us all." He hath made Him to be sin for us though He knew no sin. This, then is that which caused the Savior such extraordinary depression. He was now about to "taste death for every man," to bear the curse which was due to sinners, because He stood in the sinner's place and must suffer in the sinner's stead. Here is the secret of those agonies which it is not possible for me to set forth in order before you, so true is it that:

"'Tis to God, and God alone,
That His griefs are fully known."

Yet would I exhort you to consider these griefs awhile, that you may love the Sufferer. He now realized, perhaps for the first time, what it was to be a sin bearer. As God He was perfectly holy and incapable of sin, and as man He was without original taint and spotlessly pure; yet He had to bear sin, to be led forth as the scapegoat bearing the iniquity of Israel upon His head, to be taken and made a sin offering, and as a loathsome thing (for nothing was more loathsome than the sin offering) to be taken without the camp and utterly consumed with the fire of divine wrath. Do you wonder that His infinite purity started back from that? Would He have been what He was if it had not been a very solemn thing for Him to stand before God in the position of a sinner? yea, and as Luther would have said it, to be looked upon by God as if He were all the sinners in the world, and as if

He had committed all the sin that ever had been committed by His people, for it was all laid on Him, and on Him must the vengeance due for it all be poured; He must be the center of all vengeance and bear away upon Himself what ought to have fallen upon the guilty sons of men. To stand in such a position when once it was realized must have been very terrible to the Redeemer's holy soul. Now also the Savior's mind was intently fixed upon the dreadful nature of sin. Sin had always been abhorrent to Him, but now His thoughts were engrossed with it, He saw its worse than deadly nature, its heinous character, and horrible aim.

Probably at this time beyond any former period He had, as man, a view of the wide range and all-pervading evil of sin, and a sense of the blackness of its darkness, and the desperateness of its guilt as being a direct attack upon the throne, yea, and upon the very being of God. He saw in His own person to what lengths sinners would go, how they would sell their Lord like Judas, and seek to destroy Him as did the Jews. The cruel and ungenerous treatment He had Himself received displayed man's hate of God, and, as He saw it, horror took hold upon Him, and His soul was heavy to think that He must bear such an evil and be numbered with such transgressors, to be wounded for their transgressions, and be bruised for their iniquities. Not the wounding nor the bruising distressed Him so much as the sin itself, and that utterly overwhelmed His soul.

Then, too, no doubt the penalty of sin began to be realized by Him in the Garden—first the sin which had put Him in the position of a suffering substitute, and then the penalty which must be borne, because He was in that position. I dread to the last degree that kind of theology which is so common nowadays, which seeks to depreciate and diminish our estimate of the sufferings of our Lord Jesus Christ. Brethren, that was no trifling suffering which made recompense to the justice of God for the sins of men. I am never afraid of exaggeration when I speak of what my Lord endured. All hell was distilled into that cup, of which our God and Savior Jesus Christ was made to drink. It was not eternal suffering, but since He was divine He could in a short time offer unto God a vindication of His justice which sinners in hell could not have offered had they been left to suffer in their own person for ever. The woe that broke over the Savior's spirit, the great and fathomless ocean of inexpressible anguish which dashed over the Savior's soul when He died, is so inconceivable, that I must not venture far, lest I be accused of a vain attempt to express the unutterable; but this I will say, the very spray from that great tempestuous deep, as it fell on Christ, baptized Him in a bloody sweat. He had not yet come to the raging billows as He heard the awful surf breaking at His feet, the shadow of the coming tempest, it was the prelude of the dread desertion which He had to endure, when He stood where we ought to have stood, and from us; it was this which laid Him low. To be treated as a sinner, to be smitten as a sinner, though in Him was no sin,—this it was which caused Him the agony of which our text speaks.

Having thus spoken of the cause of His peculiar grief, I think we shall be able to support our view of the matter, while we lead you to consider, WHAT WAS THE CHARACTER OF THE GRIEF ITSELF? I shall trouble you, as little as possible, with the Greek words used by the evangelists; I have studied each one of them, to try and find out the shades of their meaning, but it will suffice if I give you the results of my careful investigation. What was the grief itself? How was it described? This great sorrow assailed our Lord some four days before He suffered. If you turn to John 22:27, you find that remarkable utterance, "Now is my soul troubled." We never knew Him say that before. This was a foretaste of the great depression of spirit which was so soon to lay Him prostrate in Gethsemane. "Now is My soul troubled; and what shall I say? Father, save Me from this hour; but for this cause came I unto this hour." After that we read of Him in Matthew 26:37, that "He began to be sorrowful and very heavy." The depression had come over Him again. It was not pain, it was not a palpitation of the heart, or an aching of the brow, it was worse than these.

Trouble of spirit is worse than pain of body; pain may bring trouble and be the incidental cause of sorrow, but if the mind is perfectly untroubled, how well a man can bear pain, and when the soul is exhilarated and lifted up with inward joy pain of body is almost forgotten, the soul conquering the body. On the other hand the soul's sorrow will create bodily pain, the lower nature sympathizing with the higher. Our Lord's main suffering lay in His soul—His soul-sufferings were the soul of His sufferings. "A wounded spirit who can bear?" Pain of spirit is the worst of pain, sorrow of heart is the climax of griefs. Let those who have ever know sinking spirits, despondency, and mental gloom, attest the truth of what I say!

This sorrow of heart appears to have led to a very deep depression of our Lord's spirit. In the 26th of Matthew, 37th verse, you find it recorded that He was "very heavy", and that expression is full of meaning,—of more meaning, indeed than it would be easy to explain. The word in the original is a very difficult one to translate. It may signify the abstraction of the mind, and its complete occupation by sorrow, to the exclusion of every thought which might have alleviated the distress. One burning thought consumed His whole soul, and burned up all that might have yielded comfort. For awhile His mind refused to dwell upon the result of His death, the consequent joy which was set before Him. His position as a sin bearer, and the desertion by His Father which was necessitated thereby, engrossed His contemplations and hurried His soul away from all else. Some have seen in the word a measure of distraction and though I will not go far in that direction, yet it does seem as if our Savior's mind underwent perturbations and convulsions widely different from His usual calm, collected spirit. He was tossed to and fro as upon a mighty sea of trouble, which was wrought to tempest, and carried Him away in its fury. "We did esteem Him stricken, smitten of God and afflicted." as the psalmist said, innumerable evils compassed Him about so that His heart failed Him. His heart was melted like wax in the midst of His bowels with sheer dismay. He was "very heavy." Some consider the word to signify at its root, "separated from the people," as if He had become unlike other men, even as one whose mind is staggered by a sudden blow, or pressed with some astounding calamity, is no more as ordinary men are.

Mere onlookers would have thought our Lord to be a man distraught, burdened beyond the wont of men, and borne down by a sorrow unparalleled among men. The learned Thomas Goodwin says, "The word denotes a failing, deficiency, and sinking of spirit, such as happens to men in sickness and wounding." Epaphroditus' sickness, whereby he was brought near to death, is called by the same word; so that we see, that Christ's soul was sick and fainted. Was not His sweat produced by exhaustion? The cold, clammy sweat of dying men comes through faintness of body, but the bloody sweat of Jesus came from an utter faintness and prostration of soul. He was in an awful soul swoon, and suffered an inward death, whose accompaniment was not watery tears from the eyes, but a weeping of blood from the entire man. Many of you, however, know in your measure what it is to be very heavy without my multiplying words in explanation, and if you do not know by personal experience all explanations must be vain. When deep despondency comes on, when you forget everything that would sustain you and your spirit sinks down, down, down, then can you sympathize with your Lord. Others think you foolish, call you nervous, and bid you rally yourself, but they know not your case. Did they understand it, they would not mock you with such admonitions, impossible to those who are sinking beneath inward woe. Our Lord was "very heavy," very sinking, very despondent, overwhelmed with grief.

Mark tells us next, in his fourteenth chapter and thirty-third verse, that our Lord was "sore amazed." The Greek word does not merely import that he was astonished and surprised, but that His amazement went to an extremity of horror, such as men fall into when their hair stands upon end and their flesh trembles. As the delivery of the law made Moses exceedingly fear and quake, and as David said, "My flesh trembleth because of

They judgements," so our Lord was stricken with horror at the sight of the sin which was laid upon Him and the vengeance which was due on account of it. The Savior was first "sorrowful," then depressed, and "heavy," and lastly, sore amazed and filled with amazement; for even He as a man could scarce have known what it was that he had undertaken to bear. He had looked at it calmly and quietly, and felt that whatever it was He would bear it for our sake; but when it actually came to the bearing of sin He was utterly astonished and taken aback at the dreadful position of standing in the sinner's place before God, of having His holy Father look upon Him as the sinner's representative, and of being forsaken by that Father with whom He had lived on terms of amity and delight from old eternity. It staggered His holy, tender, loving nature, and He was "sore amazed" and was "very heavy."

We are further taught that there surrounded encompassed, and overwhelmed Him an ocean of sorrow, for the thirty-eighth verse of the twenty-sixth of Matthew contains the word *perilupos*, which signifies an encompassing around with sorrows. In all ordinary miseries there is generally some loophole of escape, some breathing place for hope. We can generally remind our friends in trouble that their case might be worse, but in our Lord's griefs worse could not be imagined; for He could say with David, "The pains of hell gat hold upon Me." All God's waves and billows went over Him. Above Him, beneath Him, around Him, without Him, and within all, all was anguish neither was there one alleviation or source of consolation. His disciples could not help Him,—they were all but one sleeping, and he who was awake was on the road to betray Him. His spirit cried out in the presence of the Almighty God beneath the crushing burden and unbearable load of His miseries. No griefs could have gone further than Christ's, and He Himself said, "My soul is exceeding sorrowful," or surrounded with sorrow "even unto death." He did not die in the garden, but He suffered as much as if He had died. He endured death intensively, though not extensively. It did not extend to the making His body a corpse, but it went as far in pain as if it had been so. His pangs and anguish went up to the mortal agony, and only paused on the verge of death.

Luke, to crown all, tells us in our text, that our Lord was in an agony. The expression "agony" signifies a conflict, a contest, a wrestling. With whom was the agony? With whom did He wrestle? I believe it was with Himself; the contest here intended was not with His God; no, "not as I will, but as Thou wilt" does not look like wrestling with God; it was not a contest with Satan, for, as we have already seen, He would not have been so sore amazed had that been the conflict, but it was a terrible combat within Himself, an agony within His own soul. Remember that He could have escaped from all this grief with one resolve of His will, and naturally the manhood in Him said, "Do not bear it!" and the purity of His heart said, "Oh do not bear it, do not stand in the place of the sinner": and the delicate sensitiveness of His mysterious nature shrank altogether from any form of connection with sin; yet infinite love said, "Bear it, stoop beneath the load": and so there was agony between the attributes of His nature, a battle on an awful scale in the arena of His soul. The purity which cannot bear to come into contact with sin must have been very mighty in Christ, while the love which would not let His people perish was very mighty too. It was a struggle on a Titanic scale, as if a Hercules had met another Hercules; two tremendous forces strove and fought and agonized within the bleeding heart of Jesus. Nothing causes a man more torture than to be dragged hither and thither with contending emotions; as civil war is the worst and most cruel kind of war, so a war within a man's soul when two great passions in him struggle for the mastery, and both noble passions too, causes a trouble and distress which none but he that feels it can understand. I marvel not that our Lord's sweat was as it were great drops of blood, when such an inward pressure made Him like a cluster trodden in the winepress. I hope I have not presumptuously looked into the ark, or gazed within the veiled holy of holies; God forbid that curiosity or pride should urge me to intrude where the Lord has set a barrier. I have

brought you as far as I can, and must again drop the curtain with the words I used just now,

"'Tis to God, and God alone,
That His griefs are fully known."

Our third question shall be, WHAT WAS OUR LORD'S SOLACE IN ALL THIS?

He sought help in human companionship, and very natural it was that He should do so. God has created in our human nature a craving for sympathy. We do not amiss when we expect our brethren to watch with us in our hour of trial; but our Lord did not find that men were able to assist Him; however willing their spirit might be, their flesh was weak. What, then, did He do? He resorted to prayer, and especially to prayer to God under the character of Father. I have learned by experience that we never know the sweetness of the Fatherhood of God so much as when we are in a very bitter anguish; I can understand why the Savior said, "Abba, Father," it was anguish that brought Him down as a chastened child to appeal plaintively to a Father's love. In the bitterness of my soul I have cried, "If indeed, Thou be my Father, by the bowels of Thy fatherhood have pity on Thy child"; and here Jesus pleads with His Father as we have done, and finds comfort in that pleading. Prayer was the channel of the Redeemer's comfort, earnest, intense, reverent, repeated prayer, and after each time of prayer He seems to have grown quiet, and to have gone to His disciples with a measure of restored peace of mind. The sight of their sleeping helped to bring back His griefs, and therefore He returned to pray again, and each time He was comforted, so that when He had prayed for the third time He was prepared to meet Judas and the soldiers and to go with silent patience to judgment and death. His great comfort was prayer and submission to the divine will, for when He had laid His own will down at His Father's feet the feebleness of His flesh spoke no more complainingly, but in sweet silence, like a sheep dumb before her shearers, He contained His soul in patience and rest. Dear brothers and sisters, if any of you shall have your Gethsemane and your heavy griefs, imitate your Master by resorting to prayer, by crying to your Father, and by learning submission to His will.

I shall conclude by drawing two or three inferences from the whole subject. May the Holy Spirit instruct us.

The first is,—Learn, dear brethren, the real humanity of our Lord Jesus Christ. Do not think of Him as God merely, though He is assuredly divine, but feel Him to be near of kin to you, bone of your bone, flesh of your flesh. How thoroughly can He sympathize with you! He has been burdened with all your burdens and grieved with all you griefs. Are the waters very deep through which you are passing? Yet they are not deep compared with the torrents with which He was buffeted. Never a pang penetrates your spirit to which your covenant Head was a stranger. Jesus can sympathize with you in all your sorrows, for He has suffered far more than you have ever suffered, and is able therefore to succor you in your temptations. Lay hold on Jesus as your familiar friend, your brother born for adversity, and you will have obtained a consolation which will bear you through the uttermost deeps.

Next, see here the intolerable evil of sin. You are a sinner, which Jesus never was, yet even to stand in the sinner's place was so dreadful to Him that He was sorrowful even unto death. What will sin one day be to you if you should be found guilty at the last! Oh, could we tell the horror of sin there is not one among us that would be satisfied to remain in sin for a single moment; I believe there would go up from this house of prayer this morning a weeping and a wailing such as might be heard in the very streets, if men and women here who are living in sin could really know what sin is, and what the wrath of God is that rests upon them, and what the judgements of God will be that will shortly surround them and destroy them. Oh soul, sin must be an awful thing if it so crushed our Lord. If the very imputation of it fetched bloody sweat from the pure and holy Savior, what must sin itself be? Avoid it, pass not by it, turn away from the very appearance of it, walk humbly and carefully with your God that sin may not

harm you, for it is an exceeding plague, an infinite pest.

Learn next, but oh how few minutes have I in which to speak of such a lesson, the matchless love of Jesus, that for your sakes and mine He would not merely suffer in body, but consented even to bear the horror of being accounted a sinner, and coming under the wrath of God because of our sins: though it cost Him suffering unto death and sore amazement, yet sooner than that we shall perish, the Lord smarted as our surety. Can we not cheerfully endure persecution for His sake? Can we not labor earnestly for Him? Are we so ungenerous that His cause shall know a lack while we have the means of helping it? Are we so base that His work shall flag while we have strength to carry it on? I charge you by Gethsemane, my brethren, if you have a part and lot in the passion of your Savior, love Him much who loved you so immeasurably, and spend and be spent for Him.

Again looking at Jesus in the garden, we learn the excellence and completeness of the atonement. How black I am, how filthy, how loathsome in the sight of God,—I feel myself only fit to be cast into the lowest hell, and I wonder that God has not long ago cast me there; but I go into Gethsemane, and I peer under those gnarled olive trees, and I see my Savior. Yes, I see Him wallowing on the ground in anguish, and hear such groans come from Him as never came from human breast before. I look upon the earth and see it red with His blood, while His face is smeared with gory sweat, and I say to myself, "My God, my Savior, what aileth Thee?" I hear Him reply, "I am suffering for thy sin," and then I take comfort, for while I fain would have spared my Lord such an anguish, now that the anguish is over I can understand how Jehovah can spare me, because He smote His Son in my stead. Now I have hope of justification, for I bring before the justice of God and my own conscience the remembrance of my bleeding Savior, and I say, Canst Thou twice demand payment, first at the hand of Thy agonizing Son and then again at mine? Sinner as I am, I stand before the burning throne of the severity of God, and am not afraid of it. Canst thou scorch me, O consuming fire, when Thou hast not only scorched but utterly consumed my substitute? Nay, by faith, my soul sees justice satisfied, the law honored, the moral government of God established and yet my once guilty soul absolved and set free. The fire of avenging justice has spent itself, and the law has exhausted its most rigorous demands upon the person of Him who was made a curse for us, that we might be made the righteousness of God in Him. Oh the sweetness of the comfort which flows from the atoning blood! Obtain that comfort, my brethren, and never leave it. Cling to you Lord's bleeding heart, and drink in abundant consolation.

Last of all, what must be the terror of the punishment which will fall upon those men who reject the atoning blood, and who will have to stand before God in their own proper persons to suffer for their sins. I will tell you, sirs, with pain in my heart as I tell you it, what will happen to those of you who reject my Lord. Jesus Christ my Lord and Master is a sign and prophecy to you of what will happen to you. Not in a garden, but on that bed of yours where you have so often been refreshed, you will be surprised and overtaken, and the pains of death will get hold upon you. With and exceeding sorrow and remorse for your misspent life and for a rejected Savior you will be made very heavy. Then will your darling sin, your favourite lust, like another Judas, betray you with a kiss. While yet your soul lingers on your lips you will be seized and taken off by a body of evil ones, and carried away to the bar of God, just as Jesus was taken to the judgment seat of Caiaphas. There shall be a speedy, personal, and somewhat private judgment, by which you shall be committed to prison where, in darkness and weeping, and wailing you shall spend the night before the great assize of the judgment morning. Then shall the day break and the resurrection morning come, and as our Lord then appeared before Pilate, so will you appear before the highest tribunal, not that of Pilate, but the dread judgment seat of the Son of God, whom you have despised and rejected.

Then will witnesses come against you, not false witnesses, but true, and you will stand speechless, even as Jesus said not a word before His accusers. Then will conscience and despair buffet you, until you will become such a monument of misery, such a spectacle of contempt, as to be fitly noted by another Ecce Homo, and men shall look at you and say, "Behold the man and the suffering which has come upon him, because he despised his God and found pleasure in sin." Then shall you be condemned. "Depart, ye cursed," shall be your sentence, even as "Let Him be crucified" was the doom of Jesus. You shall be taken away by the officers of justice to your doom. Then like the sinner's substitute you will cry, "I thirst," but not a drop of water shall be given you; you shall taste nothing but the gall of bitterness. You shall be executed publicly with your crimes written over your head that all may read and understand that you are justly condemned; and then will you be mocked as Jesus was, especially if you have been a professor of religion and a false one; all that pass by will say "He saved others, he preached to others, but himself he cannot save." God Himself will mock you. Nay, think not I dream, has He not said it: "I also will laugh at your calamity, I will mock when your fear cometh"? Cry unto your gods, that you once trusted in! Get comfort out of the lusts ye once delighted in, O ye that are cast away forever! To your shame, and to the confusion of your nakedness, shall you that have despised the Savior be made a spectacle of the justice of God forever. It is right it should be so, justice rightly demands it. Sin made the Savior suffer an agony, shall it not make you suffer? Moreover, in addition to your sin, you have rejected the Savior; you have said, "He shall not be my trust and confidence." Voluntarily, presumptuously, and against your own conscience you have refused eternal life; and if you die rejecting mercy what can come of it but that first your sin, and secondly your unbelief, shall condemn you to misery without limit or end. Let Gethsemane warn you, let its groans, and tears, and bloody sweat admonish you. Repent of sin, and believe in Jesus. May His Spirit enable you, for Jesus' sake. Amen.

C. H. Spurgeon

13

POEMS, HYMNS, MEDITATIONS, AND PRAYERS ON THE LIFE OF JESUS

2.53 MY DANCING DAY, AUTHOR UNKNOWN

Tomorrow shall be my dancing day:
I would my true love did so chance
To see the legend of my play,
To call my true love to my dance:

Chorus
Sing O my love, O my love, my love, my love;
This have I done for my true love.

Then was I born of a virgin pure,
Of here I took fleshly substance;
Thus was I knit to man's nature,
To call my true love to my dance:

Chorus

In a manger laid and wrapped I was,
So very poor, this was my chance,
Betwixt an ox and a silly poor ass,
To call my true love to my dance:

Chorus

Then afterwards baptized I was;
The Holy Ghost on me did glance,
My Father's voice heard from above,
To call my true love to my dance:

Chorus

Into the desert I was led,
Where I fasted without substance;
The devil bade me make stones my bread,
To call my true love to my dance:

Chorus

The Jews on me they made great suit,
And with me made great variance,

Because they loved darkness rather than light,
To call my true love to my dance:

Chorus

For thirty pence Judas me sold,
His covetousness for to advance;
'Mark whom I kiss, the same do hold,'
The same is he shall lead the dance.

Chorus

Before Pilate the Jews me brought,
Where Barabbas had deliverance;
They scourged me and set me at nought,
Judged me to die to lead the dance:

Chorus

Then on the cross hanged I was,
Where a spear to my heart did glance;
There issued forth both water and blood,
To call my true love to my dance:

Chorus

Then down to hell I took my way
For my true love's deliverance,
And rose again on the third day,
Up to my true love and the dance:

Chorus

Then up to heaven I did ascend,
Where now I dwell in sure substance,
On the right hand of God, that man
May come unto the general dance.

Author unknown, 15th century

2.54 ONE SOLITARY LIFE, AUTHOR UNKNOWN

He was born in an obscure village, the child of a peasant woman. He grew up in another village, where He worked in a carpenter shop until He was thirty. Then for three years He was an itinerant preacher. He never wrote a book. He never held an office. He never had a family or owned a home. He didn't go to college. He never visited a big city. He never traveled two hundred miles from the place where he was born. He did none of the things that usually accompany greatness. He had no credentials but Himself.

He was only thirty-three when the tide of public opinion turned against Him. His friends ran away. One of them denied Him. He was turned over to His enemies and went through the mockery of a trial. He was nailed to a cross between two thieves.

While He was dying, His executioners gambled for His garments, the only property he had on earth. When He was dead, He was laid in a borrowed grave through the pity of a friend. Nineteen centuries have come and gone, and today He is the central figure of the human race.

All the armies that ever marched, all the navies that ever sailed, all the parliaments that ever sat, all the kings that ever reigned, put together, have not affected the life of man on this earth as much as that one solitary life.

Author unknown

2.55 JESUS IN THE BIBLE, AUTHOR UNKNOWN

More than 1, 900 years ago there was a Man born contrary to the laws of life. This Man lived in poverty and was reared in obscurity. He did not travel extensively. Only once did He cross the boundary of the country in which He lived and that was during His exile in childhood.

He possessed neither name, wealth, nor influence. His relatives were inconspicuous, uninfluential, and had neither training nor education.

In infancy He startled a king; in childhood He puzzled the doctors; in manhood He ruled the course of nature, walked upon billows as if pavements, and hushed the sea to sleep.

He healed the multitudes without medicine and made no charge for His service.

He never wrote a book, and yet all the libraries of the country could not hold the books that have been written about Him.

He never wrote a song, and yet He has furnished the theme for more songs than all the songwriters combined.

He never founded a college, but all the schools put together cannot boast of having as many students.

He never practiced medicine, and yet He has healed more broken hearts than all the doctors far and near.

He never marshaled an army, nor drafted a soldier, nor fired a gun, and yet no leader ever had more volunteers who have, under His orders, made more rebels stack arms and surrender without a shot being fired.

He is the Star of astronomy, the Rock of geology, the Lion and Lamb of the zoological kingdom.

He is the Revealer of the snares that lurk in the darkness; and Rebuker of every evil thing that prowls by night; the Quickener of all that is wholesome; the Adorner of all that is beautiful; the Reconciler of all that is contradictory; the Harmonizer of all discords; the Healer of all diseases; and the Savior of all mankind.

He fills the pages of theology and hymnology. Every prayer that goes up to God goes up In His name and is asked to be granted for His sake.

Every seventh day the wheels of commerce cease their turning and multitudes wend their way to worshiping assemblies to pay homage and respect to Him.

The names of the past proud statesmen of Greece and Rome have come and gone. The names of the past scientists, philosophers, and theologians have come and gone; but the name of this Man abounds more and more. Though time has spread 1900 years between the people of this generation.

Abel's lamb was a type of Christ, Abraham offering Isaac on Mount Moriah was a type of God giving Christ, His only Son, on Mount Calvary. The Passover lamb in Egypt was a type of Christ. The brazen serpent in the wilderness was a type of Christ-He told Nicodemus so Himself. The scapegoat typified Him bearing our sins. The scarlet thread that the harlot Rahab hung in the window of her home in Jericho typified Him. Joseph, pictured to us by the Bible without a flaw, was a type of Christ "who did not sin, neither was guile found in his mouth."

In the Old Testament He is spoken of as "the angel of the Lord," and as such He appeared unto men. He was with Adam and Eve in the Garden of Eden. He was with Abel in his death. He walked with Enoch. He rode with Noah in the Ark. He ate with Abraham in his desert tent. He pled with Lot to leave wicked Sodom.

He watched Isaac reopen the wells that his father Abraham had dug. He wrestled with Jacob at Peniel. He strengthened Joseph in his time of temptation, protected him in prison, and exalted him to first place in the kingdom. He watched over Moses in the ark of bulrushes, talked to him from the burning bush, went down into Egypt with him, opened the Red Sea for him, fed him on bread from heaven, protected him with a pillar of fire by night, and after 120 years of such blessed companionship that they left no marks of passing time upon Moses, led him up from the plains of Moab unto the mountain of Nebo, to the top of Pisgah, let him take one long, loving look at the Promised Land, and then kissed him to sleep, folded Moses' hands over his breast, and buried his body in an unmarked grave, to sleep in Jesus till the morning of the great resurrection day.

He was the Captain of the Lord's host to Joshua, led him over the swollen stream of Jordan in flood tide, around Jericho, in conquest of Ai, helped him conquer Canaan, divide the land, and say good-bye to the children of Israel. He was with Gideon and his famous 300. He was with Samuel when he rebuked Saul. He was with David when he wrote the twenty-third psalm. He was with Solomon when he built the first temple. He was with good king Hezekiah when Sennacherib invaded the land. He was with Josiah in his great reformation that brought the people back to the law. He was with Ezekiel and Daniel in Babylon. He was with Jeremiah in Egypt. He was with Ezra when he returned from Babylon, and with Nehemiah when he rebuilt the wall. In fact, He was with all those "who through faith subdued kingdoms, wrought righteousness, obtained promises, stopped the mouths of lions, quenched the violence of fire, escaped the edge of the sword, out of weakness were made strong, waxed valiant in fight, turned to flight the armies of the aliens."

Abraham saw His day and rejoiced. Jacob called Him the "Lawgiver of Judah." Moses called Him the "Prophet that was to come." Job called Him "My Living Redeemer." Daniel called Him the "Ancient of Days." Jeremiah called Him "The Lord our Righteousness." Isaiah called Him "Wonderful Counselor, the Mighty God, the Everlasting Father, the Prince of Peace."

All of this in the Old Testament? Yes, and much more besides. "To Him give all the prophets witness." Micah tells of the place of His birth. Jonah tells of His death, burial, and resurrection. Amos tells of His second coming to build again the tabernacles of David. Joel describes the day of His wrath. Zechariah tells of His coming reign as King over all the earth. Ezekiel gives us a picture of His millennial temple.

In fact, my friends, it matters little where we wander down the aisles, avenues, byways, or highways of the Old Testament. Jesus walks beside us as He walked beside the two disciples on that dusty road to Emmaus on that glorious resurrection day long, long ago.

Its types tell of Him, its sacrifices show Him, its symbols signify Him, its histories are His-stories, its songs are His sentiments, its prophecies are His pictures, its promises are His pledges; and our hearts burn within us as we walk beside Him across its living pages!

When we open the New Testament, the Word which was in the beginning with God becomes flesh and dwells among us, and we behold His glory, the glory as of the only begotten of the Father, full of grace and truth.

There are four personal histories of His earthly life written In the New Testament. One is by Matthew, the redeemed publican, and signifies His lineage; one is by Mark, the unknown servant, which magnifies His service; one is by Luke, "the beloved physician," and tells of His humanity; and one is by John, "whom Jesus loved," and it tells of His deity. He is Christ the King in Matthew, the Servant in Mark, the Man in Luke, and the Incarnate Word in John.

Concerning His royal lineage we learn that He was born in Bethlehem, the Seed of Abraham, the Son of David, the Son of Mary, the Son of God; and was acknowledged as "King of the Jews," "Christ the Lord," "God's Son," "The Savior of Men," by angels, demons, shepherds, and wise men; and that He received tribute of gold, frankincense, and myrrh.

Concerning His service we learn that He labored as a carpenter, opened eyes of the blind, unstopped deaf ears, loosed dumb tongues, cleansed lepers, healed the sick, restored withered hands, fed the hungry, sympathized with the sad, washed the disciples' feet, wept with Mary and Martha, preached the Gospel to the poor, went about doing good, and gave His life as a ransom for many.

Concerning His humanity we learn that He was born of a woman, as a little babe was wrapped in swaddling clothes, grew up and developed as a child in wisdom, stature, and in favor with God and men. He worked with His hands, He grew weary, He hungered, He thirsted, He slept, He felt the surge of anger; knew what it was to be sad, shed tears, sweat drops of blood; was betrayed, went though the mockery of a criminal trial, was scourged, had His hands and feet pierced; wore a crown of thorns, was spit upon, was crucified, was wrapped in a winding sheet, and was buried in a borrowed tomb behind a sealed stone, and was guarded by Roman soldiers in His death.

Concerning His deity we read that He was born of a virgin, lived a sinless life, spoke matchless words, stilled storms, calmed waves, rebuked winds, multiplied loaves, turned water to wine, raised the dead, foretold the future, gave hearing to the deaf, sight to the blind, speech to the dumb, cast out demons, healed diseases, forgave sins, claimed equality with God, arose from the dead, possessed all authority both in heaven and in earth.

He was both God and Man; two individuals united in one personality. "As a man, He thirsted; as God, He gave living water. As a man, He went to a wedding; as God, He turned the water to wine. As man, He slept in a boat; as God, He stilled the storm. As man, He was tempted; as God, He sinned not. As man, He wept; as God, He raised Lazarus from the dead. As man, He prayed; as God, He makes intercession for all men."

This is what Paul means when he writes, "Without controversy great is the mystery of godliness; God was manifest in the flesh, justified in the Spirit, seen of angels, preached unto the Gentiles, believed on in the world, received up into glory." He was made unto us wisdom, righteousness, sanctification, and redemption. He is the Light of this world. He is the Bread of Life. He is the True Vine. He is the Good Shepherd. He is the Way. He is the Life. He is the Door to Heaven.

He is the Faithful Witness, the First Begotten of the dead, the Prince of the kings of the earth, the King of Kings, and the Lord of lords, Alpha and Omega, the first and the last, the beginning and the ending, the Lord who is, who was, and who is to come, the Almighty. "I am He that liveth, and was dead; and behold, I am alive forevermore, and have the keys of hell and of death."

He is Abel's Sacrifice, Noah's Rainbow, Abraham's Ram, Isaac's Wells, Jacob's Ladder, Issachar's Burdens, Jacob's Scepter, Balaam's Shiloh, Moses' Rod, Joshua's Sun and Moon that stood still, Elijah's Mantle, Elisha's Staff, Gideon's Fleece, Samuel's Horn of Oil, David's Slingshot, Isaiah's Fig Poultice, Hezekiah's Sundial, Daniel's Visions, Amos' Burden, and Malachi's Sun of Righteousness.

He is Peter's Shadow, Stephen's Signs and Wonders, Paul's Handkerchiefs and Aprons, and John's Pearly White City.

He is Father to the Orphan, Husband to the Widow, to the traveler in the night He is the Bright and Morning Star, to those who walk in the Lonesome Valley He is the Lily of the Valley, the Rose of Sharon, and Honey in the Rock.

He is the Brightness of God's Glory, the Express Image of His Person, the King of Glory, the Pearl of Great Price, the Rock in a Weary Land, the Cup that runneth over, the Rod and Staff that comfort, and the Government of our life is upon his shoulders.

He is Jesus of Nazareth, the Son of the living God! My Savior, my Companion, my Lord and King!

Author unknown

2.56 *ADORO TE DEVOTE*, THOMAS AQUINAS

Lost, all lost in wonder

Godhead here in hiding, whom I do adore,
Masked by these bare shadows, shape and nothing more,
See, Lord, at thy service low lies here a heart
Lost, all lost in wonder at the God thou art.

Seeing, touching, tasting are in thee deceived:
How says trusty hearing? that shall be believed;
What God's Son has told me, take for truth I do;
Truth himself speaks truly or there's nothing true.

On the cross thy godhead made no sign to men,
Here thy very manhood steals from human ken:
Both are my confession, both are my belief,
And I pray the prayer of the dying thief.

I am not like Thomas, wounds I cannot see,
But can plainly call thee Lord and God as he;
Let me to a deeper faith daily nearer move,
Daily make me harder hope and dearer love.

O thou our reminder of Christ crucified,
Living Bread, the life of us for whom he died,
Lend this life to me then: feed and feast my mind,
There be thou the sweetness man was meant to find.

Bring the tender tale true of the Pelican;
Bathe me, Jesu Lord, in what thy bosom ran—
Blood whereof a single drop has power to win
All the world forgiveness of its world of sin.

Jesu, whom I look at shrouded here below,
I beseech thee send me what I thirst for so,
Some day to gaze on thee face to face in light
And be blest for ever with thy glory's sight.
Amen.

Thomas Aquinas, translated by Gerard Manley Hopkins

2.57 POEMS ABOUT JESUS, GEORGE HERBERT

George Herbert (April 3, 1593–March 1, 1633) was an English poet and orator. Despite living for only 40 years, his stock as a poet has risen and risen. Remarkably, none of his work was published in his lifetime. The poems of his final years, written while as a clergyman at Bemerton near Salisbury, England, are like nothing else in literature. They combine a profound spirituality with a restless experimentation. Their language remains fresh and inspiring today.

After graduating from Trinity College, Cambridge, Herbert took the post of "public orator" of Cambridge, a position to which he was probably appointed because of his poetic skill. In 1624 he became a Member of Parliament. Both jobs indicate an intent to have a career at court; but 1625 witnessed the death of James I, who had shown favor to Herbert, and in the late 1620s, however, two influential patrons of Herbert died. Thus Herbert's choice of a career in the Church of England ——he was ordained in 1630—— was, to some extent, pragmatic.

He took up his duties in a rural parish in Wiltshire, about 75 miles southwest of London. He was an earnest and conscientious minister. In poor health, he died only three years after his ordination. On his deathbed, he gave the manuscript of The Temple, *his collection of poetry, to Nicholas Ferrar, the founder of a semi-monastic Anglican religious community at Little Gidding (a name best known today through the poetry of T. S. Eliot), telling him to publish the poems if he thought they might "turn to the advantage of any dejected poor soul," and otherwise, to burn them. By 1680* The Temple *had gone through thirteen printings.*

The life of Jesus is depicted in the following poems of George Herbert. They all come from his work, The Temple.

The poems include:
The Bag
Christmas
Love-joy
The Call
Mary Magdalene
The Pearl
The Agonie
Redemption
The Sacrifice
Good Friday
Sepulcher
Easter
Easter Song
Easter Wings
The Dawning
Colossians 3:3
Jesu
Sepulchre
Death
Love Bade Me Welcome

THE BAG

Away, despair! my gracious Lord doth hear.
Though winds and waves assault my keel,
He doth preserve it: he doth steer,
Ev'n when the boat seems most to reel.
Storms are the triumph of his art:
Well may he close his eyes, but not his heart.

Hast thou not heard, that my Lord Jesus died?
Then let me tell thee a strange story.
The God of power, as he did ride
In his majestic robes of glory,
Resolved to light; and so one day
He did descend, undressing all the way.

The stars his tire [circle, halo] of light and
rings obtain'd,
The cloud his bow, the fire his spear,
The sky his azure mantle gain'd.
And when they ask'd, what he would wear;
He smil'd, and said as he did go,
He had new clothes a making here below.

When he was come, as travellers are wont,
He did repair unto an inn.
Both then, and after, many a brunt
He did endure to cancel sin:
And having giv'n the rest before,
Here he gave up his life to pay our score.

But as he was returning, there came one
That ran upon him with a spear.
He, who came hither all alone,
Bringing nor man, nor arms, nor fear,
Receiv'd the blow upon his side,
And straight he turn'd, and to his brethren
cried,

If ye have any thing to send or write,
(I have no bag, but here is room:)
Unto my Father's hands and sight,
Believe me, it shall safely come.
That I shall mind, what you impart;
Look, you may put it very near my heart.

Or if hereafter any of my friends
Will use me in this kind, the door
Shall still be open; what he sends
I will present, and somewhat more,
Not to his hurt. Sighs will convey
Any thing to me. Hark Despair, away.
                    George Herbert, The Temple

CHRISTMAS

All after pleasures as I rid one day,
My horse and I, both tir'd, body and mind,
With full cry of affections, quite astray,
I took up in the next Inn I could find,

There when I came, whom found I but my
dear,
My dearest Lord, expecting till the grief
Of pleasures brought me to Him, ready
there
To be all passengers' most sweet relief?

O Thou, whose glorious, yet contracted light,
Wrapt in night's mantle, stole into a manger;
Since my dark soul and brutish is thy right,
To Man of all beasts be not thou a stranger:

Furnish and deck my soul, that thou may'st
have
A better lodging, than a rack, or grave.

The shepherds sing; and shall I silent be?
My God, no hymn for thee?
My soul's a shepherd too: a flock it feeds
Of thoughts, and words, and deeds.
The pasture is thy word; the streams, thy grace
Enriching all the place.

Shepherd and flock shall sing, and all my
powers
Out-sing the daylight hours.
Then we will chide the Sun for letting night
Take up his place and right:
We sing one common Lord; wherefore he
should
Himself the candle hold.

I will go searching, till I find a sun
Shall stay, till we have done;
A willing shiner, that shall shine as gladly,
As frost-nipt Suns look sadly.
Then we will sing, and shine all our own day,
And one another pay:

His beams shall cheer my breast, and both so
twine,
Till ev'n his beams sing, and my music shine.
                    George Herbert, The Temple

LOVE-JOY

As on a window late I cast mine eye,
I saw a vine drop grapes with *J* and *C*
Anneal'd on every bunch. One standing by
Ask'd what it meant. I (who am never loth
To spend my judgment) said, It seem'd to me
To be the body and the letters both
Of *Joy* and *Charity*. Sir, you have not miss'd,
The man replied; It figures, JESUS CHRIST.
                    George Herbert, The Temple

THE CALL

Come, my Way, my Truth, my Life:
Such a Way, as gives us breath:
Such a Truth, as ends all strife:

Such a Life, as killeth death.
Come, my Light, my Feast, my Strength:
Such a Light, as shows a feast:
Such a Feast, as mends in length:
Such a Strength, as makes his guest.

Come, my Joy, my Love, my Heart:
Such a Joy, as none can move:
Such a Love, as none can part:
Such a Heart, as joys in love.

George Herbert, The Temple

MARIE MAGDALEN

When blessed Marie wiped her Saviour's feet,
(Whose precepts she had trampled on before)
And wore them for a Jewel on her head,
Showing his steps should be the street,
Wherein she thenceforth evermore
With pensive humbleness would live and
tread:

She being stain'd her self, why did she strive
To make him clean, who could not be defil'd?
Why kept she not her tears for her own faults,
And not his feet? Though we could dive
In tears like seas, our sins are pil'd
Deeper then they, in words, and works, and
thoughts.

Dear soul, she knew who did vouchsafe and
deign
To bear her filth; and that her sins did dash
Ev'n God himself: wherefore she was not loath,
As she had brought wherewith to stain,
So to bring in wherewith to wash:
And yet in washing one, she washed both.

George Herbert, The Temple

THE PEARL. MATTHEW 13

"Again, the kingdom of heaven is like unto a
merchant man, seeking goodly pearls: Who,
when he had found one pearl of great price, went
and sold all that he had, and bought it."
Matthew 13:45

I Know the ways of Learning; both the head
And Pipes that feed the presse, and make it run;

What Reason hath from Nature borrowed,
Or of it self, like a good houswife, spun
In laws and policy; what the stars conspire,
What willing Nature speaks, what forc'd by
fire;
Both th' old discoveries, and the new-found
seas,

The stock and surplus, cause and history:
All these stand open, or I have the keys:
Yet I love thee.

I know the ways of Honour, what maintains
The quick returns of courtesy and wit:
In vies of favours whether party gains,
When glory swells the heart, and mouldeth it
To all expressions both of hand and eye,
Which on the world a true-love-knot may tie,
And bear the bundle, wheresoe're it goes:
How many drames of spirit there must be
To sell my life unto my friends or foes:
Yet I love thee.

I know the ways of Pleasure, the sweet strains,
The lullings and the relishes of it;
The propositions of hot blood and brains;
What mirth and music mean; what love and
wit
Have done these twenty hundred years, and
more:
I know the projects of unbridled store:
My stuff is flesh, not brass; my senses live,
And grumble oft, that they have more in me
Than he that curbs them, being but one to
five:
Yet I love thee.

I know all these, and have them in my hand:
Therefore not sealed, but with open eyes
I fly to thee, and fully understand
Both the main sale, and the commodities;
And at what rate and price I have thy love;
With all the circumstances that may move:
Yet through the labyrinths, not my grovelling wit,
But thy silk-twist let down from heav'n to me,
Did both conduct and teach me, how by it
To climb to thee.

George Herbert, The Temple

THE AGONY

Philosophers have measured mountains,
Fathom'd the depths of seas, of states, and kings,
Walk'd with a staff to heav'n, and traced fountains:
But there are two vast, spacious things,
The which to measure it doth more behove:
Yet few there are that sound them; Sin and Love.

Who would know Sin, let him repair
Unto Mount Olivet; there shall he see
A man so wrung with pains, that all his hair,
His skin, his garments bloody be.
Sinne is that Press and Vice, which forceth pain
To hunt his cruel food through ev'ry vein.

Who knows not Love, let him assay
And taste that juice, which on the cross a pike
Did set again abroach [to pierce]; then let him say
If ever he did taste the like.
Love in that liquor sweet and most divine,
Which my God feels as blood; but I, as wine.

George Herbert, The Temple

REDEMPTION

Having been tenant long to a rich Lord,
Not thriving, I resolved to be bold,
And make a suit unto him, to afford
A new small-rented lease, and cancel th' old.

In heaven at his manor I him sought:
They told me there, that he was lately gone
About some land, which he had dearly bought
Long since on earth, to take possession.

I straight return'd, and knowing his great birth,
Sought him accordingly in great resorts;
In cities, theatres, gardens, parks, and courts:
At length I heard a ragged noise and mirth

Of thieves and murderers: there I him espied,
Who straight, *Your suit is granted,* said, and died.

George Herbert, The Temple

THE SACRIFICE

O all ye, who passe by, whose eyes and mind
To worldly things are sharp, but to me blind;
To me, who took eyes that I might you find:
    Was ever grief like mine?

The Princes of my people make a head
Against their Maker: they do wish me dead,
Who cannot wish, except I give them bread;
    Was ever grief like mine?

Without me each one, who doth now me brave,
Had to this day been an Egyptian slave.
They use that power against me, which I gave:
    Was ever grief like mine?

Mine own Apostle, who the bag did bear,
Though he had all I had, did not forbear
To sell me also, and to put me there:
    Was ever grief like mine?

For thirty pence he did my death devise,
Who at three hundred did the ointment prize,
Not half so sweet as my sweet sacrifice:
    Was ever grief like mine?

Therefore my soul melts, and my heart's dear treasure
Drops blood (the only beads) my words to measure:
O let this cup pass, if it be thy pleasure:
    Was ever grief like mine?

These drops being temper'd with a sinner's tears
A balsom are for both the Hemispheres:
Curing all wounds, but mine; all, but my fears:
    Was ever grief like mine?

Yet my Disciples sleep; I cannot gain
One hour of watching; but their drowsy brain

Comforts not me, and doth my doctrine stain:
Was ever grief like mine?

Arise, arise, they come! Look how they run!
Alas! what haste they make to be undone!
How with their lanterns do they seek the sun!
Was ever grief like mine?

With clubs and staves they seek me, as a thief,
Who am the Way and Truth, the true relief;
Most true to those, who are my greatest grief:
Was ever grief like mine?

Judas, dost thou betray me with a kiss?
Canst thou find hell about my lips? and miss
Of life, just at the gates of life and bliss?
Was ever grief like mine?

See, they lay hold on me, not with the hands
Of faith, but fury: yet at their commands
I suffer binding, who have loos'd their bands
Was ever grief like mine?

All my Disciples fly; fear puts a bar
Betwixt my friends and me. They leave the star,
That brought the wise men of the East from far.
Was ever grief like mine?

Then from one ruler to another bound
They lead me; urging, that it was not sound
What I taught: Comments would the test confound.
Was ever grief like mine?

The Priest and rulers all false witnesse seek
'Gainst him, who seeks not life, but is the meek
And ready Paschal Lamb of this great week:
Was ever grief like mine?

Then they accuse me of great blasphemy,
That I did thrust into the Deity,
Who never thought that any robbery:
Was ever grief like mine?

Some said, that I the Temple to the floor
In three dayes razed, and raised as before.
Why, he that built the world can do much more:
Was ever grief like mine?

Then they condemn me all with that same breath,
Which I do give them daily, unto death.
Thus Adam my first breathing rendereth:
Was ever grief like mine?

They bind, and lead me unto Herod: he
Sends me to Pilate. This makes them agree;
But yet their friendship is my enmity:
Was ever grief like mine?

Herod and all his bands do set me light,
Who teach all hands to war, fingers to fight,
And only am the Lord of Hosts and might:
Was ever grief like mine?

Herod in judgment sits, while I do stand;
Examines me with a censorious hand:
I him obey, who all things else command:
Was ever grief like mine?

The Jews accuse me with dispitefulness;
And vying malice with my gentleness,
Pick quarrels with their only happiness:
Was ever grief like mine?

I answer nothing, but with patience prove
If stony hearts will melt with gentle love.
But who does hawk at eagles with a dove?
Was ever grief like mine?

My silence rather doth augment their cry;
My dove doth back into my bosom fly,
Because the raging waters still are high:
Was ever grief like mine?

Hark how they cry aloud still, *Crucify:*
It is not fit he live a day, they cry,
Who cannot live less than eternally:
Was ever grief like mine?

Pilate, a stranger, holdeth off; but they,
Mine own dear people, cry, *Away, away,*
With noises confused frighting the day:
Was ever grief like mine?

Yet still they shout, and cry, and stop their ears,
Putting my life among their sins and fears,
And therefore wish *my blood on them and theirs:*
Was ever grief like mine?

See how spite cankers things. These words
aright
Used, and wished, are the whole world's light:
But honey is their gall, brightness their night:
    Was ever grief like mine?

They choose a murderer, and all agree
In him to do themselves a courtesy:
For it was their own cause who killed me:
    Was ever grief like mine?

And a seditious murderer he was:
But I the Prince of peace; peace that doth pass
All understanding, more then heav'n doth
glass:
    Was ever grief like mine?

Why, Caesar is their only King, not I:
He clave the stony rock, when they were dry;
But surely not their hearts, as I well try:
    Was ever grief like mine?

Ah! how they scourge me! yet my tenderness
Doubles each lash: and yet their bitterness
Winds up my grief to a mysteriousness:
    Was ever grief like mine?

They buffet me, and box me as they list,
Who grasp the earth and heaven with my fist,
And never yet, whom he would punish,
miss'd:
    Was ever grief like mine?

Behold, they spit on me in scornful wise,
Who with my spittle gave the blind man eyes,
Leaving his blindness to mine enemies:
    Was ever grief like mine?

My face they cover, though it be divine.
As Moses' face was veiled, so is mine,
Lest on their double-dark souls either shine:
    Was ever grief like mine?

Servants and abjects flout me; they are witty:
Now prophesy who strikes thee, is their ditty.
So they in me deny themselves all pity:
    Was ever grief like mine?

And now I am deliver'd unto death,
Which each one calls for so with utmost
breath,

That he before me well-nigh suffereth:
    Was ever grief like mine?

Weep not, dear friends, since I for both have
wept
When all my tears were blood, the while you slept:
Your tears for your own fortunes should be
kept:
    Was ever grief like mine?

The soldiers lead me to the common hall;
There they deride me, they abuse me all:
Yet for twelve heav'nly legions I could call:
    Was ever grief like mine?

Then with a scarlet robe they me array;
Which shows my blood to be the only way
And cordial left to repair man's decay:
    Was ever grief like mine?

Then on my head a crown of thorns I
wear:
For these are all the grapes Sion doth bear,
Though I my vine planted and watred there:
    Was ever grief like mine?

So sits the earth's great curse in Adam's fall
Upon my head: so I remove it all
From th' earth unto my brows, and bear the
thrall:
    Was ever grief like mine?

Then with the reed they gave to me before,
They strike my head, the rock from thence all
store
Of heav'nly blessings issue evermore:
    Was ever grief like mine?

They bow their knees to me, and cry, *Hail,
King*:
What ever scoffs and scornfulness can bring,
I am the floor, the sink, where they it fling:
    Was ever grief like mine?

Yet since man's sceptres are as frail as reeds,
And thorny all their crowns, bloody their weeds;
I, who am Truth, turn into truth their deeds:
    Was ever grief like mine?

The soldiers also spit upon that face,
Which Angels did desire to have the grace,

And Prophets, once to see, but found no place:
Was ever grief like mine?

Thus trimmed, forth they bring me to the rout,
Who Crucify him, cry with one strong shout.
God holds his peace at man, and man cries out:
Was ever grief like mine?

They lead me in once more, and putting then
Mine own clothes on, they lead me out again.
Whom devils fly, thus is he toss'd of men:
Was ever grief like mine?

And now weary of sport, glad to engross
All spite in one, counting my life their loss,
They carry me to my most bitter cross:
Was ever grief like mine?

My cross I bear myself, until I faint:
Then Simon bears it for me by constraint,
The decreed burden of each mortal saint:
Was ever grief like mine?

O all ye who passe by, behold and see;
Man stole the fruit, but I must climb the
tree;
The tree of life to all, but only me:
Was ever grief like mine?

Lo, here I hang, charg'd with a world of sin,
The greater world o' th' two; for that came in
Bywords, but this by sorrow I must win:
Was ever grief like mine?

Such sorrow as, if sinful man could feel,
Or feel his part, he would not cease to kneel.
Till all were melted, though he were all steel:
Was ever grief like mine?

But, O my God, my God! why leav'st thou me,
The son, in whom thou dost delight to be?
My God, my God———
Never was grief like mine.

Shame tears my soul, my body many a wound;
Sharp nails pierce this, but sharper that confound;
Reproaches, which are free, while I am bound.
Was ever grief like mine?

Now heal thyself, Physician; now come down.
Alas! I did so, when I left my crown

And Father's smile for you, to feel his frown:
Was ever grief like mine?

In healing not myself, there doth consist
All that salvation, which ye now resist;
Your safety in my sickness doth subsist:
Was ever grief like mine?

Betwixt two thieves I spend my utmost breath,
As he that for some robbery suffereth.
Alas! what have I stolen from you? death.
Was ever grief like mine?

A king my title is, prefixt on high;
Yet by my subjects I'm condemn'd to die
A servile death in servile company:
Was ever grief like mine?

They give me vinegar mingled with gall,
But more with malice: yet, when they did call,
With Manna, Angels' food, I fed them all:
Was ever grief like mine?

They part my garments, and by lot dispose
My coat, the type of love, which once cur'd those
Who sought for help, never malicious foes:
Was ever grief like mine?

Nay, after death their spite shall further go;
For they will pierce my side, I full well know;
That as sin came, so Sacraments might flow:
Was ever grief like mine?

But now I die; now all is finished.
My woe, man's weal: and now I bow my head.
Only let others say, when I am dead,
Never was grief like mine.
George Herbert, The Temple

GOOD FRIDAY

O My chief good,
How shall I measure out thy blood?
How shall I count what thee befell,
And each grief tell?

Shall I thy woes
Number according to thy foes?
Or, since one star show'd thy first breath,
Shall all thy death?

Or shall each leaf,
Which falls in Autumn, score a grief?
Or cannot leaves, but fruit, be sign
    Of the true vine?

Then let each hour
Of my whole life one grief devour;
That thy distress through all may run,
    And be my sun.

Or rather let
My several sins their sorrows get;
That, as each beast his cure doth know,
    Each sin may so.

Since blood is fittest, Lord, to write
Thy sorrows in, and bloody fight;
My heart hath store, write there, where in
One box doth lie both ink and sin:

That when sin spies so many foes,
Thy whips, thy nails, thy wounds, thy woes,
All come to lodge there, sin may say,
No room for me, and fly away.

Sin being gone, oh fill the place,
And keep possession with thy grace;
Lest sin take courage and return,
And all the writings blot or burn.
              George Herbert, The Temple

SEPULCHRE

O blessed body! whither art thou thrown?
No lodging for thee, but a cold hard stone?
So many hearts on earth, and yet not one
Receive thee?

Sure there is room within our hearts good
store;
For they can lodge transgressions by the score:
Thousands of toys dwell there, yet out of door
They leave thee.

But that which shows them large, shows them
unfit.
Whatever sin did this pure rock commit,
Which holds thee now? Who hath indited it
Of murder?

Where our hard hearts took up of stones to
brain thee,
And missing this, most falsely did arraign
thee;
Only these stones in quiet entertain thee,
And order.

And as of old, the Law by heavenly art
Was writ in stone; so thou, which also art
The letter of the word, find'st no fit heart
To hold thee.

Yet do we still persist as we began,
And so should perish, but that nothing can,
Though it be cold, hard, foul, from loving
man
Withhold thee.
              George Herbert, The Temple

EASTER

Rise, heart! thy Lord is risen. Sing His
praise
Without delays,
Who takes thee by the hand, that thou
likewise
With Him may'st rise:
That, as His death calcinèd thee to dust,
His life may make thee gold, and much more
just.

Awake, my lute, and struggle for thy part
With all thy art.
The cross taught all wood to resound His
name
Who bore the same.
His stretchèd sinews taught all strings what
key
Is best to celebrate this most high day.

Consort both heart and lute, and twist a song
Pleasant and long:
Or, since all music is but three parts vied
And multiplied,
Oh, let Thy blessed Spirit bear a part,
And make up our defects with His sweet art.
              George Herbert, The Temple

EASTER SONG

I got me flowers to strew Thy way,
I got me boughs off many a tree,
But Thou wast up by break of day,
And brought'st Thy sweets along with Thee

The sun arising in the East,
Though he give light and th' East perfume,
If they should offer to contest
With Thy arising, they presume

Can there be any day but this,
Though many suns to shine endeavor?
We count three hundred, but we miss:
There is but one, and that one ever.
George Herbert, The Temple

EASTER WINGS

LORD, who createdst man in wealth and store,
Though foolishly he lost the same,
Decaying more and more,
Till he became
Most poor :

With thee
O let me rise
As larks, harmoniously,
And sing this day thy victories:
Then shall the fall farther the flight in me.

My tender age
In sorrow did begin:
And still with sicknesses and shame
Thou didst so punish sin,
That I became
Most thin.

With thee
Let me combine,
And feel this day thy victory,
For, if I imp my wing on thine,
Affliction shall advance the flight in me.
George Herbert, The Temple

THE DAWNING

Awake, sad heart, whom sorrow ever drowns;
Take up thine eyes, which feed on earth;

Unfold thy forehead gather'd into frowns:
Thy Saviour comes, and with him mirth:
　　　Awake, awake;
And with a thankful heart his comforts take.
But thou dost still lament, and pine, and cry;
And feel his death, but not his victory.

Arise, sad heart; if thou dost not withstand,
Christ's resurrection thine may be:
Do not by hanging down break from the hand,
Which as it riseth, raiseth thee:
　　　Arise, arise;
And with his burial-linen dry thine eyes:
Christ left his grave-clothes, that we might, when grief
Draws tears, or blood, not want an handkerchief.
George Herbert, The Temple

COLOSSIANS 3:3. OUR LIFE IS HID WITH CHRIST IN GOD

My words and thoughts do both express this notion,
That *Life* hath with the sun a double motion.
The first *Is* straight, and our diurnal friend;
The other *Hid* and doth obliquely bend.
One life is wrapt *In* flesh, and tends to earth:
The other winds toward *Him*, whose happy birth
Taught me to live here so, *That* still one eye
Should aim & shoot at that which *Is* on high:
Quitting with daily labour all *My* pleasure,
To gain at harvest an eternal *Treasure*.

["For ye are dead, and your life is hid with Christ in God." Colossians 3:3]
George Herbert, The Temple

JESU

JESU is in my heart, his sacred name
Is deeply carved there: but th'other week
A great affliction broke the little frame,
Ev'n all to pieces: which I went to seek:

And first I found the corner, where was *J*,
After, where *ES*, and next where *U* was graved,
When I had got these parcels, instantly
I sat me down to spell them, and perceived
That to my broken heart he was *I ease you*,
And to the whole is *J E S U*.
>> *George Herbert*, The Temple

SEPULCHRE

O Blessed body! Whither art thou thrown?
No lodging for thee, but a cold hard stone?
So many hearts on earth, and yet not one
>> Receive thee?

Sure there is room within our hearts good
store;
For they can lodge transgressions by the score:
Thousands of toys dwell there, yet out of door
>> They leave thee.

But that which shows them large, shows them
unfit.
Whatever sin did this pure rock commit,
Which holds thee now? Who hath indited it
>> Of murder?

Where our hard hearts have took up stones to
brain thee,
And missing this, most falsely did arraign thee;
Only these stones in quiet entertain thee,
>> And order.

And as of old, the Law by heav'nly art
Was writ in stone; so thou, which also art
The letter of the word, find'st no fit heart
>> To hold thee.

Yet do we still persist as we began,
And so should perish, but that nothing can,
Though it be cold, hard, foul, from loving
man
>> Withhold thee.
>> *George Herbert*, The Temple

DEATH

Death, thou wast once an uncouth hideous
thing,
Nothing but bones,

The sad effect of sadder groans:
Thy mouth was open, but thou couldst not
sing.

For we consider'd thee as at some six
Or ten years hence,
After the loss of life and sense,
Flesh being turn'd to dust, and bones to sticks.

We look'd on this side of thee, shooting short;
Where we did find
The shells of fledge souls left behind,
Dry dust, which sheds no tears, but may extort.

But since our Saviour's death did put some
blood
Into thy face;
Thou art grown fair and full of grace,
Much in request, much sought for, as a good.

For we do now behold thee gay and glad,
As at doomsday;
When souls shall wear their new array,
And all thy bones with beauty shall be clad.

Therefore we can go die as sleep, and trust
Half that we have
Unto an honest faithful grave;
Making our pillows either down, or dust.
>> *George Herbert*, The Temple

LOVE BADE ME WELCOME

Love bade me welcome, yet my soul drew
back,
Guilty of dust and sin.
But quick-ey'd Love, observing me grow slack
From my first entrance in,
Drew nearer to me, sweetly questioning
If I lack'd anything.

"A guest," I answer'd, "worthy to be here";
Love said, "You shall be he."
"I, the unkind, the ungrateful? ah my dear,
I cannot look on thee."
Love took my hand and smiling did reply,
"Who made the eyes but I?"

"Truth, Lord, but I have marr'd them; let my
shame

Go where it doth deserve."
"And know you not," says Love, "who bore the blame?"
"My dear, then I will serve."

"You must sit down," says Love, "and taste my meat."
So I did sit and eat.

George Herbert, The Temple

2.58 *LA CORONA*, JOHN DONNE

John Donne (pronounced "Dun"; 1572–March 31, 1631) was a major English poet and writer, and perhaps the greatest of the metaphysical poets. His works include love poetry, sermons and religious poems, Latin translations, epigrams, elegies, songs, and sonnets.

Donne was educated at both Oxford and Cambridge universities. However, Catholics such as he were barred from graduating, and he thus could not complete his education. Donne was ordained in 1615. With the death of his wife in 1617 the tone of his poetry deepened, particularly in the "Holy Sonnets."

After his ordination, Donne wrote a number of religious works, such as his Devotions *(1624) and various sermons. Several of these sermons were published during his lifetime. Donne was also regarded as one of the most eloquent preachers of his day. In 1621, Donne was made Dean of St. Paul's, a position he held until his death.*

The story of Donne's death—as Walton tells it, at least—is justly well known. Suffering through the illness that would kill him only days later, in front of an audience many of whom, according to Walton, said that Donne seemed to be preaching his own funeral sermon, he gave an address called Death's Duel, *one of the high points of seventeenth-century English prose. "We have a winding sheet in our mother's womb," he told his listeners, "which grows with us from our conception, and we come into the world wound up in that winding sheet, for we come to seek a grave." He then retired to his quarters, and had a portrait made of himself in his funeral shroud. This portrait he placed near his bedside, where he meditated on it until his death.*

"No man is an island, entire of itself; every man is a piece of the continent, a part of the main. If a clod be washed away by the sea, Europe is the less, as well as if a promontory were, as well as if a manor of thy friend's or of thine own were. Any man's death diminishes me because I am involved in mankind; and therefore never send to know for whom the bell tolls; it tolls for thee." Meditation XVII (also the quote which begins Ernest Hemingway's novel For Whom the Bell Tolls*).*

La Corona, "The Crown," are seven sonnets linked by the repetition of each last line as the first line of the next poem. The crown is closed at the end, the last line of the last sonnet repeating the first line of the first.

> *Deign at my hands this crown of prayer and praise,*
> Weav'd in my low devout melancholy,
> Thou which of good, hast, yea art treasury,
> All changing unchanged Ancient of days,

But do not, with a vile crown of frail bays,
Reward my muse's white sincerity,
But what thy thorny crown gained, that give me,
A crown of Glory, which doth flower always;
The ends crown our works, but thou crown'st our ends,
For at our end begins our endless rest,
The first last end, now zealously possest,
With a strong sober thirst, my soul attends.
'Tis time that heart and voice be lifted high,
Salvation to all that will is nigh.

ANNUNCIATION

Salvation to all that will is nigh,
That All, which always is All everywhere,
Which cannot sin, and yet all sins must bear,
Which cannot die, yet cannot choose but die,
Lo, faithful Virgin, yields himself to lie
In prison, in thy womb; and though he there
Can take no sin, nor thou give, yet he will wear
Taken from thence, flesh, which death's force may try.
Ere by the spheres time was created, thou
Wast in his mind, who is thy Son, and Brother,
Whom thou conceiv'st, conceiv'd; yea thou art now
Thy maker's maker, and thy Father's mother,
Thou hast light in dark; and shutst in little room,
Immensity cloistered in thy dear womb.

NATIVITY

Immensity cloistered in thy dear womb,
Now leaves his welbelov'd imprisonment,
There he hath made himself to his intent
Weak enough, now into our world to come;
But Oh, for thee, for him, hath th'Inne no room?
Yet lay him in this stall, and from the Orient,
Stars, and wisemen will travel to prevent
Th'effect of Herod's jealous general doom;
Seest thou, my Soul, with thy faith's eyes, how he
Which fills all place, yet none holds him, doth lie?
Was not his pity towards thee wondrous high,
That would have need to be pitied by thee?
Kiss him, and with him into Egypt go,
With his kind mother, who partakes thy woe.

TEMPLE

With his kind mother, who partakes thy woe,
Joseph turn back; see where your child doth sit,
Blowing, yea blowing out those sparks of wit,
Which himself on the Doctors did bestow;
The Word but lately could not speak, and lo
It suddenly speaks wonders, whence comes it,
That all which was, and all which should be writ,

A shallow seeming child, should deeply know?
His Godhead was not soul to his manhood,
Nor had time mellow'd him to this ripeness,
But as for one which hath a long task, tis good,
With the Sunn to begin his business,
He in His age's morning thus began
By miracles exceeding power of man.

CRUCIFYING

By miracles exceeding power of man,
He faith in some, envy in some begat,
For, what weak spirits admire, ambitious hate:
In both affections many to him ran,
But Oh! the worst are most, they will and can,
Alas, and do, unto the immaculate,
Whose creature Fate is, now prescribe a Fate,
Measuring self-life's infinity to a span,
Nay to an inch. Lo, where condemned he
Bears his own cross, with pain, yet by and by
When it bears him, he must bear more and die;
Now thou art lifted up, draw me to thee,
And at thy death giving such liberal dole,
Moist, with one drop of thy blood, my dry soul.

RESURRECTION

Moist, with one drop of thy blood, my dry soul
Shall (though she now be in extreme degree
Too stony hard, and yet too fleshly) be
Freed by that drop, from being starved, hard, or foul,
And life, by this death abled, shall control
Death, whom thy death slew; nor shall to me
Fear of first or last death, bring misery,
If in thy little book my name thou enroll,
Flesh in that long sleep is not putrified,
But made that there, of which, and for which twas;
Nor can by other means be glorified.
May then sin's sleep, and death's soon from me pass,
That waked from both, I again risen may
Salute the last, and everlasting day.

ASCENSION

Salute the last, and everlasting day,
Joy at the uprising of this Sun, and Son,
Ye whose just tears, or tribulation

Have purely washed, or burnt your drossy
clay;
Behold the Highest, parting hence away,
Lightens the dark clouds, which he treads
upon,
Nor doth he by ascending, show alone,
But first he, and he first enters the way.
O strong Ram which hast battered heaven for
me,
Mild lamb, which with thy blood, hast
marked the path;
Bright Torch, which shin'st, that I the way
may see,
Oh, with thy own blood quench thy own just
wrath.
And if the holy Spirit, my Muse did raise,
*Deign at my hands this crown of prayer and
praise.*

John Donne, La Corona

2.59 The blasted fig-tree, John Newton

Mark 11:20

One awful word which JESUS spoke,
Against the tree which bore no fruit;
More piercing than the lightning's stroke,
Blasted and dried it to the root.

But could a tree the LORD offend,
To make him show his anger thus?
He surely had a farther end,
To be a warning word to us.

The fig-tree by its leaves was known,
But having not a fig to show;
It brought a heavy sentence down,
"Let none hereafter on thee grow."

Too many, who the gospel hear,
Whom Satan blinds and sin deceives;

We to this fig-tree may compare,
They yield no fruit, but only leaves.

Knowledge, and zeal, and gifts, and talk,
Unless combined with faith and love,
And witnessed by a gospel walk,
Will not a true profession prove.

Without the fruit the LORD expects
Knowledge will make our state the worse;
The barren trees he still rejects,
And soon will blast them with his curse.

O LORD, unite our hearts in prayer!
On each of us thy Spirit send;
That we the fruits of grace may bear,
And find acceptance in the end.

John Newton, Hymn 97

2.60 The centurion, Richard Crashaw

*"I am not worthy that thou shouldest come
under my roof." Matthew 8:8*

Thy God was making haste into thy roof,

Thy humble faith and fear keeps Him aloof :
He'll be thy guest ; because He may not be,
He'll come—into thy house? No, into thee.

Richard Crashaw

2.61 LAZARUS, ALFRED LORD TENNYSON

When Lazarus left his charnel-cave,
And home to Mary's house return'd,
Was this demanded—if he yearn'd
To hear her weeping by his grave?

"Where wert thou, brother, those four days?'"
There lives no record of reply,
Which telling what it is to die
Had surely added praise to praise.

From every house the neighbors met,
The streets were fill'd with joyful sound,
A solemn gladness even crown'd
The purple brows of Olivet.

Behold a man raised up by Christ!
The rest remaineth unreveal'd;

He told it not; or something seal'd
The lips of that Evangelist.
Her eyes are homes of silent prayer,
Nor other thought her mind admits
But, he was dead, and there he sits,
And he that brought him back is there.

Then one deep love doth supersede
All other, when her ardent gaze
Roves from the living brother's face,
And rests upon the Life indeed.

All subtle thought, all curious fears,
Borne down by gladness so complete,
She bows, she bathes the Saviour's feet
With costly spikenard and with tears.

Alfred Lord Tennyson

2.62 BLIND BARTIMEUS, HENRY WADSWORTH LONGFELLOW

Mark 20:46-52

Blind Bartimeus at the gates
Of Jericho in darkness waits;
He hears the crowd;—he hears a breath
Say, "It is Christ of Nazareth!"
And calls, in tones of agony,
"Jesus have mercy on me!"

The thronging multitudes increase;
Blind Bartimeus, hold thy peace!
But still, above the noisy crowd,
The beggar's cry is shrill and loud;
Until they say, "He calleth thee!"
"Fear not, arise, He calleth thee!"

Then saith the Christ, as silent stands
The crowd, "What wilt thou at my hands?"
And he replies, "O give me light!
Rabbi, restore the blind man's sight."
And Jesus answers,
            "Go in peace
Thy faith from blindness gives release!"

Ye that have eyes yet cannot see,
In darkness and in misery,
Recall those mighty Voices Three,
"Jesus have mercy on me!"
"Fear not, arise, He calleth thee!"
"Thy faith from blindness gives release!"

Henry Wadsworth Longfellow

Part Three

THE DEATH OF JESUS

INTRODUCTION

Jesus' death has always been a matter of controversy. Even among Christians the precise meaning of Jesus' death has been a matter of much heated debate. This has been illustrated in the twenty-first century by the contrasting reactions to Mel Gibson's film *The Passion of the Christ*.

Unsurprisingly, some of the secular press attacked the film even before it was released. It was accused of being pornographic, and even branded as a "snuff" film. A. O. Scott wrote: "This film . . . shifts from horror-movie suspense to slasher-film dread." Frank Rich went as far as to claim that: "With its laborious build-up to its orgasmic spurtings of blood and other bodily fluids, the film is constructed like nothing so much as a porn movie." David Edelstein exclaimed that: "This is a two-hour-and six-minute snuff movie—the Jesus Chainsaw Massacre." Christopher Hitchens maintained that "Gibson has made a film that principally appeals to the gay Christian sadomasochistic community. . . . If you like seeing handsome young men stripped and tied up and flayed with whips, *The Passion of the Christ* is the movie for you."

Perhaps a little more surprising has been the wide variation of reactions among Christians to this film. Mel Gibson says, "I want to show the humanity of Christ as well as the divine aspect. It's a rendering that for me is very realistic and as close as possible to what I perceive the truth to be." Many Christians would endorse the Hollywood Film Festival's Board of Advisors' announcement in 2004 that: "This year's festival will honor Oscar-winning producer/director Mel Gibson with its Hollywood Producer of the Year Award."

A host of leading Christians were not slow to make known their enthusiastic reactions about the film.

"Every time I preach or speak about the Cross, the things I saw on the screen will be on my heart and mind," Billy Graham, *Billy Graham Evangelistic Association*.

"*The Passion* tells the story of the twelve hours surrounding the Crucifixion. While The Passion is only the latest in a series of films about Jesus, it stands out for two reasons: First, it is unsparing and unsentimental. In Gibson's opinion, previous cinematic efforts had failed to capture the enormity of Jesus' suffering on our behalf," Chuck Colson, *Break Point*.

"It has been nearly three weeks since I saw the rough cut of *The Passion*. It is still impacting my life. I can't stop thinking about it nor can I stop talking about it. I have never seen a film that has so affected my life," Del Tackett, Executive Vice President, *Focus On The Family*.

"Three words summarize for me: Sobering, Stunning, Haunting. The film speaks for itself. I hope you keep the graphic nature of it complete in the film, because it will cause everyone to reflect on what His death was. The world tends to wash over this directness. The details are very accurate—this is the kind of death our Lord died for me," Dr. Darrell Bock, Research Professor of New Testament, Dallas Theological Seminary.

"It is deeply moving, powerful, and disturbing. A film that must be seen— although the graphic scenes of the scourging of Jesus are emotionally wrenching," James Dobson.

"Mr. Gibson has attempted to painstakingly recreate the crucifixion of Christ, not to assail Jews, but to arouse in people a desire to understand the price paid for their salvation," Jerry Falwell.

"*The Passion* is simply fabulous. It is emotionally wrenching because it is brutally honest about the violence of Jesus' death. Never in my life have I seen any movie that comes even close to depicting what Roman crucifixion was really like. Long familiarity and theological explanation have leached out in our minds the awful brutality of Jesus' trial and death. John's simple words, 'Then Pilate took Jesus and scourged him' feel vastly different as you watch two brutal Roman soldiers go on minute after terrible minute bludgeoning Jesus' near-naked body with flesh-gouging whips. Pious talk about Jesus' death for our sins takes on a whole new meaning," Ron Sider.

"Thank you for allowing our congregation to preview the movie trailer of *The Passion*. In just four short minutes, the images and the authenticity left our members spell bound. The message went right to the heart of those who watched the trailer," Max Lucado.

However, other Christian leaders, while admiring the aim of the film, were critical about certain key features in the film, such as its concentration on violence. Some of its historical accuracy has also been questioned.

Part three of *The Encyclopedia of Jesus' Life and Time* includes a section on "Jesus' physical death" as well as a much longer section on "The meaning of Jesus' death."

1
COMPARING MODERN VIEWPOINTS ON THE DEATH OF JESUS

3.1 BILLY GRAHAM

JESUS THE REDEEMER

Again Jesus said of Himself, "I am Alpha and Omega, the beginning and the end." He, and He alone, had the power and capacity to bring man back to God. But would He? If He did, He would have to come to earth. He would have to take the form of a servant. He would have to humble Himself and become obedient unto death. He would have to grapple with sin. He would have to meet and overcome Satan, the enemy of man's souls. He would have to redeem sinners out of the slave market of sin. He would have to loose the bonds and set the prisoners free by paying a price—that price would be His own life. He would have to be despised and rejected of men, a man of sorrows and acquainted with grief. He would have to be smitten of God and separated from God. He would have to be wounded for the transgressions of men and bruised for their iniquities, His blood shed to atone for man's sin. He would have to reconcile God and man. He would be the great Mediator of history. He would have to be a substitute. He would have to die in the place of sinful man. All this would have to be done—voluntarily.

And that is exactly what happened! . . . Jesus Christ partook of flesh and blood in order that He might die (Hebrews 2:14). "He appeared so that He might take away our sins (1 John 3:5). The very purpose of Christ's coming into the world was that He might offer up His life as a sacrifice for the sins of men. He came to die. The shadow of His death hung like a pall over all of His thirty-three years.

Billy Graham, Peace With God, *Word Publishing, 1955*

THREE THINGS IN THE CROSS

In the cross of Christ I see three things: First, a description of the depth of man's sin. Do not blame the people of that day for hanging Christ on the cross. You and I are just as guilty. It was not the people or the Roman soldiers who put Him to the cross—it was your sins and my sins that made it necessary for Him to volunteer this death.

Second, in the cross I see the overwhelming love of God. If ever you should doubt the love of God, take a long, deep look at the cross, for in the cross you find the expression of God's love.

Third, in the cross is the only way of salvation. Jesus said, "I am the way, the truth and the life: no man comes to the Father but by me" (John 14:6). There is no possibility of being saved from sin and hell, except by identifying yourself with the Christ of the cross. If there had been any other way to save you, He would have found it. If reformation, or living a good moral and ethical life would have saved you, Jesus never would have died. A substitute had to take your place. men do not like to talk about it. They do not like to hear about it because it injures their pride. It takes all self out.

Billy Graham, Peace With God, *Word Publishing, 1955*

3.2 C. S. LEWIS

Why Jesus had to suffer and die

We are told that Christ was killed for us, that His death has washed out our sins, and that by dying He disabled death itself. That is the formula. That is Christianity. That is what has to be believed. Any theories we build up as to how Christ's death did all this are, in my view, quite secondary: mere plans or diagrams to be left alone if they do not help us, and, even if they do help us, not to be confused with the thing itself. All the same, some of these theories are worth looking at.

. . . supposing God became a man— suppose our human nature which can suffer and die was amalgamated with God's nature in one person—then that person could help us. He could surrender His will, and suffer and die, because He was man; and He could do it perfectly because He was God. You and I can go through this process only if God does it in us; but God can do it only if He becomes man. Our attempts at this dying will succeed only if we men share in God's dying, just as our thinking can succeed only because it is a drop out of the ocean of His intelligence: but we cannot share God's dying unless God dies; and he cannot die except by being a man. That is the sense in which He pays our debt, and suffers for us what He Himself need not suffer at all.

C. S. Lewis, Mere Christianity, *New York:*
Macmillan, 1943

3.3 MARTYN LLOYD-JONES

THE CROSS AND JUSTIFICATION

The cross is the door that leads to all blessings. Without it there is nothing. Without the cross and all it means, we have no blessings from God at all. But the cross opens the possibility to all of the endless blessings of the glorious God.

What are they? The apostle Paul never got tires of saying these things. Read what he says in Romans. He puts it like this: "Therefore being justified by faith, we have peace with God through our Lord Jesus Christ" (Romans 5:1). Justified by faith means that the moment you believe in what happened on the cross, and see that that is God's way of reconciling you unto Himself, you are immediately regarded as just, your sins are all forgiven and blotted out, and you are clothed in the righteousness of Christ.

"Therefore," says Paul, "being justified by faith, we have peace with God." That is the first thing that comes out of this belief. There is no more important word in the letter of Paul than the word *therefore*. Note it. He always brings this word "therefore" in at a point of this kind. He has been laying down the doctrine, and especially the doctrine of the cross, and then he says, "therefore"— because of that, this is what follows.

And here is the first thing that follows. Being justified by faith we have peace with God. Do you realize what that means? Do your realize that that is the most important and most wonderful thing that can ever happen to you, that you are given peace and made at peace with God. All our troubles in this life as human beings are due to the fact that we are in the wrong relationship to God. It is as simple as that.

M. Lloyd-Jones, The Cross, *Wheaton,*
Crossway Books, 1986

JUSTIFICATION BY FAITH

Justification is opposed to condemnation, and nobody can bring an accusation because it is God who declares people just.

The whole time justification is legal and forensic, and as you go on with the Scriptures you will find this in other places: "But ye are washed, but ye are sanctified, but ye are justified in the name of the Lord Jesus, and by the Spirit of our God" (1 Corinthians 6:11). And in Galatians 2:16 there is a statement which is parallel to those in Romans: "Knowing that a man is not justified by the works of the law, but by the faith of Jesus Christ, even we have believed in Jesus Christ, that we might be justified by the faith of Christ, and not by the works of the law: for by the works of the law shall no flesh be justified." Galatians is the great epistle that gave Martin Luther his liberty. His famous commentary on the epistle to the Galatians is a book that you should read and the more you go on with it, the more you will enjoy it. Do not be put off by his polemic against the Roman Catholics. He had to do that because you must show what is wrong as well as what is right. People do not like that today, but Luther had to do it, and I think we must do it in our generation.

God makes a legal declaration that all the demands of the law upon us, as a condition of life, are fully satisfied with regard to all who believe on the Lord Jesus Christ. We are no longer in a state of condemnation. Why? Because God has declared it. He is the lawgiver and he says that Christ has satisfied the law, Romans 10:4.

Martyn Lloyd-Jones, God the Holy Spirit,
Wheaton, Crossway Books, 1997

3.4 J. I. PACKER

THE MEANS OF JUSTIFICATION

Justification, said the Reformers, is by faith only. Why so? Not because there are no "good works" in the believer's life (on the contrary, faith works by love untiringly and the knowledge of justification is the supreme ethical dynamic), 15, but because Christ's vicarious righteousness is the only ground of justification, and it is only by faith that we lay hold of Christ, for his righteousness to become ours. Faith is a conscious acknowledgment of our own unrighteousness and ungodliness and on that basis a looking to Christ as our righteousness, a clasping of him as the ring clasps the jewel (so Luther), a receiving of him as an empty vessel receives treasure (so Calvin), and a reverent, resolute reliance on the biblical promise of life through him for all who believe. Faith is our act, but not our work; it is an instrument of reception without being a means of merit; it is the work in us of the Holy Spirit, who both evokes it and through it engrafts us into Christ in such a sense that we know at once the personal relationship of sinner to Savior and disciple to Master and with that the dynamic relationship of resurrection life, communicated through the Spirit's indwelling. So faith takes, and rejoices, and hopes, and loves, and triumphs.

Though the Reformers said much about faith, even to the point of calling their message of justification "the doctrine of faith," their interest was not of the modern kind. It was not subject-centered but object-centered, not psychological but theological, not anthropocentric but Christocentric. The Reformers saw faith as a relationship, not to oneself, as did Tillich, but to the living Christ of the Bible, and they fed faith in themselves and in others by concentrating on that Christ as the Savior and Lord.

J. I. Packer, "Sole Fide: The Reformed
Doctrine of Justification,"
in Soli Deo Gloria, *Philadelphia:*
Presbyterian and Reformed, 1976

JUSTIFICATION

Justification has two sides. On the one hand, it means the pardon, remission, and non-imputation of all sins, reconciliation to God, and the end of his enmity and wrath . . . On the other hand, it means the bestowal of a righteous man's status and a title to all the blessings promised to the just: a thought which Paul amplifies by linking justification with the adoption of believers as God's sons and heirs.

J. I. Packer, "Justification"
in W. A. Elwell, Evangelical Dictionary of
Theology, Marshall Pickering, 1985

DEATH OF DEATH

It is from degenerate faith and preaching of this kind that Owen's book could set us free. If we listen to him, he will teach us both how to believe the Scripture gospel and how to preach it. For the first: he will lead us to bow down before a sovereign Savior Who really saves, and to praise Him for a redeeming death which made it certain that all for whom He died will come to glory. It cannot be overemphasized that we have not seen the full meaning of the Cross till we have seen it as the divines of Dort display it—as the center of the gospel, flanked on the one hand by total inability and unconditional election, and on the other by irresistible grace and final preservation. For the full meaning of the Cross only appears when the atonement is defined in terms of these four truths. Christ died to save a certain company of helpless sinners upon whom God had set His free

saving love. Christ's death ensured the calling and keeping—the present and final salvation—of all whose sins He bore. That is what Calvary meant, and means. The Cross saved; the Cross saves. This is the heart of true evangelical faith; as Cowper sang—

> "Dear dying Lamb, Thy precious blood
> Shall never lose its power,
> Till all the ransomed church of God
> Be saved to sin no more."

This is the triumphant conviction which underlay the old gospel, as it does the whole New Testament.

J. I. Packer, Introductory Essay to John Owen's
The Death of Death in the Death of Christ
Carlisle, PA, The Banner of Truth Trust,
reprinted 1995

SOLE FIDE

The heart of the biblical gospel was to them [Luther and the Reformers] God's free gift of righteousness and justification. Here was the sum and substance of that *sole Fide—sola Gratia—solo Christo—sola Scriptura—soli Deo gloria* which was the sustained theme of their proclamation, polemics, praises and prayers. . . . Justification by faith, by grace, by Christ, through Scripture, to the glory of God was to them a single topic, just as a fugue with several voices is a single piece.

J. I. Packer
"Sole Fide: The Reformed Doctrine of
Justification," in Soli Deo Gloria
Philadelphia: Presbyterian and Reformed,
1976

3.5 JOHN STOTT

THE CROSS

A Christian's rejection of old nature is to be pitiless. Crucifixion in the Graeco-Roman world was not a pleasant form of execution, nor was it administered to nice or refined people; it was reserved for the worst criminals . . . If therefore, we are to crucify' our flesh, it is plain that the flesh (old self) is not something respectable to be treated with courtesy and deference, but something so evil that it deserves no better fate than to be crucified . . . the rejection of our old nature is to be decisive . . . Criminals who were nailed to the cross did not survive . . . We crucified everything we knew to be wrong . . . So, Paul says, if we crucified the flesh, we must leave it there to die. We must renew every day this attitude towards sin of ruthless and uncompromising rejection. . . . if, having nailed our old nature to the cross, we keep wistfully returning to the scene of its execution. We begin to fondle it, to caress it, to long for its release, even to try to take it down again from the cross. We need to learn to leave it there. When some jealous, or proud, or malicious, or impure thought invades our mind we must kick it out at once. It is fatal to begin to examine it and consider whether we are going to give in to it or not. We have declared war on it; we are not going to resume negotiations. . . . Our task is to take time each day to remember these truths about ourselves and to live accordingly. It we have crucified the flesh, then we must leave it securely nailed to the cross, where it deserves to be.

John Stott, The Message Of Galatians, *IVP, Downers Grove, 1968*

STANDING BEFORE THE CROSS

As we stand before the cross, we begin to gain a clear view both of God and of ourselves, especially in relation to each other. Instead of inflicting upon us the judgment we deserved,

God in Christ endured it in our place. Hell is the only alternative. This is the "scandal," the stumbling-block, of the cross. For our proud hearts rebel against it. We cannot bear to acknowledge either the seriousness of our sin and guilt or our utter indebtedness to the cross. Surely, we say, there must be something we can do, or at least contribute, in order to make amends?

. . . The gospel demands . . . an abject self-humbling on our part. As Emil Brunner put it, "All other forms of religion . . . deal with the problem of guilt apart from the intervention of God, and therefore they come to a cheap conclusion. In them man is spared the final humiliation of knowing that the Mediator must bear the punishment instead of him. To this yoke he need not submit. He is not stripped absolutely naked."

But we cannot escape the embarrassment of standing stark naked before God. It is no use our trying to cover up like Adam and Eve in the garden. Our attempts at self-justification are as ineffectual as their fig-leaves. We have to acknowledge our nakedness, see the divine substitute wearing our filthy rags instead of us, and allow him to clothe us with his own righteousness. Nobody has ever put it better than Augustus Toplady in his immortal hymn "Rock of Ages:"

"Nothing in my hand I bring,
Simply to your Cross I cling;
Naked, come to you for dress;
Helpless, look to you for grace;
Foul, I to the fountain fly;
Wash me, Savior, or I die."

John Stott, "Naked Pride," from
The Cross of Christ
IVP, Downers Grove, 1986

2

JESUS' PHYSICAL DEATH

3.6 THE TORTURER'S ART, LEON MORRIS

Goguel quotes A. Reville's description: "It represented the acme of the torturer's art: atrocious physical sufferings, length of torment, ignominy, the effect on the crowd gathered to witness the long agony of the crucified. Nothing could be more horrible than the sight of this living body, breathing, seeing, hearing, still able to feel, and yet reduced to the state of a corpse by forced immobility and absolute helplessness. We cannot even say that the crucified person writhed in agony, for it was impossible for him to move. Stripped of his clothing, unable even to brush away the flies which fell upon his wounded flesh, already lacerated by the preliminary scourging, exposed to the insults and curses of people who can always find some sickening pleasure in sight of the tortures of others, a feeling which is increased and not diminished by the sight of pain—the cross represented miserable humanity reduced to the last degree of impotence, suffering, and degradation. The penalty of crucifixion combined all that the most ardent tormentor could desire: torture, the pillory, degradation, and certain death, distilled slowly drop by drop. It was an ideal form of torture (*The Life of Jesus*, London, 1958, pp. 535f.)."

Leon Morris, The Gospel According to John
Grand Rapids: Eerdmans, 1971

3.7 DEATH BY CRUCIFIXION, WILLIAM BARCLAY

Klauaner, the Jewish writer, writing of crucifixion says, "Crucifixion is the most terrible and cruel death which man has ever devised for taking vengeance on his fellow-men." Cicero called it "the most cruel and the most horrible torture." Tactitus called it, "a torture only fit for slaves." It originated in Persia; and its origin came from the fact that the earth was considered to be sacred to Ormuzd the god, and the criminal was lifted up from it that he might not defile the earth, which was the god's property. From Persia crucifixion passed to Carthage in North Africa; and it was then from Carthage that Rome learned it, although the Romans kept it exclusively for rebels, runaway slaves, and the lowest type of criminal. It was indeed a punishment which it was illegal to inflict on a Roman citizen.

William Barclay, The Gospel of Matthew
Philadelphia: Westminster, 1958

3.8 THE SPEAR, JOHN LYLE CAMERON

[Tasker quotes John Lyle Cameron:] The soldier was a Roman: he would be well trained, proficient, and would know his duty. He would know which part of the body to pierce in order that he might obtain a speedily fatal result or ensure that the victim was undeniably dead. He would thrust through the left side of the chest a little below the center. Here he would penetrate the heart and the great blood vessels at their origin, and also the lung on the side. The soldier, standing below our crucified Lord as He hung on the cross, would thrust upwards under the left ribs. The broad, clean cutting, two-edged spearhead would enter the left side of the upper abdomen, would open the greatly distended stomach, would pierce the diaphragm, would cut, wide open, the heart and great blood vessels, arteries and veins now fully distended with blood, a considerable proportion of all the blood in the body, and would lacerate the lung. The wound would be large enough to permit the open hand to be thrust into it. Blood from the greatly engorged veins, pulmonary vessel and dilated right side of the heart, together with water from the acutely dilated stomach, would flow forth in abundance.

R. V. G. Tasker, The Gospel According to John *Grand Rapids: Eerdmans, 1960*

3.9 THE CROSS, HENRY E. DOSKER

(*stauros,* "a cross," "the crucifixion"; *skolops,* "a stake," "a pole"):

The name is not found in the Old Testament. It is derived from the Latin word *crux.* In the Greek language it is *stauros,* but sometimes we find the word *skolops* used as its Greek equivalent. The historical writers, who transferred the events of Roman history into the Greek language, make use of these two words. No word in human language has become more universally known than this word, and that because all of the history of the world since the death of Christ has been measured by the distance which separates events from it. The symbol and principal content of the Christian religion and of Christian civilization is found in this one word.

1. FORMS OF THE CROSS

The cross occurs in at least four different forms:

(1) the form usually seen in pictures, the *crux immissa,* in which the upright beam projected above the shorter crosspiece; this is most likely the type of cross on which the Savior died, as may be inferred from the inscription which was nailed above His head;

(2) the *crux commissa,* or Anthony's cross, which has the shape of the letter T;

(3) the Greek cross of later date, in which the pieces are equally long;

(4) the *crux decussata,* or Andrew's cross, which has the shape of the letter 10.

2. DISCOVERY OF THE TRUE CROSS

The early church historians Socrates (1, 17), Sozomen (2, 1), Rufinus (1, 7) and Theodoret (1, 18) all make mention of this tradition. The most significant thing is that Eusebius (Vit. Const., 3:26-28), who carries more weight than they all together, wholly omits it.

According to it, Helena, the mother of Constantine the Great, in 325 AD, when she was 79 years old, discovered the true cross of Jesus by an excavation she caused to be made on the traditional spot of His grave. With the cross of the Savior were found the two crosses of the malefactors who were crucified with

Him. A miracle of healing, wrought by touching the true cross, revealed its identity. When found it was intact, even the holy nails of the crucifixion being discovered. The main part of the cross was deposited by Helena in a church erected over the spot. Of the remainder, a portion was inserted into the head of the statue of Constantine, and the balance was placed in a new church, specially erected for it at Rome and named after it Santa Croce. Small fragments of the wood of the true cross were sold, encrusted with gold and jewels, and since many among the wealthy believers were desirous of possessing such priceless relics, the miracle of the "multiplication of the cross" was devised, so that the relic suffered no diminution "et quasi intacta maneret" (Paulinus epistle 11 ad Sev). Fragments of the true cross are thus to be found in many Roman Catholic churches of many countries, all over Christendom. It is said that the East celebrated the staurosimos hemera (Crucifixion Day) on September 14, since the 4th century. The evidence for this fact is late and untrustworthy. It is certain that the West celebrated the Invention of the Cross, on May 3, since the time of Gregory the Great in the 6th century. The finding and publication of the apocryphal "Doctrina Addaei" has made it evident that the entire legend of the discovery of the cross by Helena is but a version of the old Edessa legend, which tells of an identical discovery of the cross, under the very same circumstances, by the wife of the emperor Claudius, who had been converted to Christianity by the preaching of Peter.

3. SYMBOLICAL USES OF THE CROSS
(1) Extra-Scriptural

The sign of the cross was well known in the symbolics of various ancient nations. Among the Egyptians it is said to have been the symbol of divinity and eternal life, and to have been found in the temple of Serapis. It is known either in the form of the Greek cross or in the form of the letter "T". The Spaniards found it to be well known, as a symbol, by the Mexicans and Peruvians, perhaps signifying the four elements, or the four seasons, or the four points of the compass.

(2) Scriptural

The suffering implied in crucifixion naturally made the cross a symbol of pain, distress and burden-bearing. Thus Jesus used it Himself (Matthew 10:38; 16:24). In Paulinic literature the cross stands for the preaching of the doctrine of the Atonement (1 Corinthians 1:18; Galatians 6:14; Philippians 3:18; Colossians 1:20). It expresses the bond of unity between the Jew and the Gentile (Ephesians 2:16), and between the believer and Christ, and also symbolizes sanctification (Galatians 5:24). The cross is the center and circumference of the preaching of the apostles and of the life of the New Testament church.

4. CRUCIFIXION

As an instrument of death the cross was detested by the Jews. "Cursed is everyone that hangeth on a tree" (Galatians 3:13; compare Deuteronomy 21:23), hence, it became a stumbling-block to them, for how could one accursed of God be their Messiah? Nor was the cross differently considered by the Romans. "Let the very name of the cross be far away not only from the body of a Roman citizen, but even from his thoughts, his eyes, his ears" (Cicero Pro Rabirio 5). The earliest mode of crucifixion seems to have been by impalation, the transfixion of the body lengthwise and crosswise by sharpened stakes, a mode of death-punishment still well known among the Mongol race. The usual mode of crucifixion was familiar to the Greeks, the Romans, the Egyptians, Persians and Babylonians (Thuc. 1, 110; Herod. 3:125, 159). Alexander the Great executed two thousand Tyrian captives in this way, after the fall of the city. The Jews received this form of punishment from the Syrians and Romans (Ant., XII, v, 4; XX, vi, 2; BJ, I, iv, 6). The Roman citizen was exempt from this form of death, it being considered the death of a slave (Cicero In Verrem 1:5, 66; Quint. 8:4). The punishment was meted out for such crimes as treason, desertion in the face of the enemy, robbery, piracy, assassination, sedition, etc. It continued in vogue in the Roman empire till the day of Constantine, when it was abolished as an insult to Christianity. Among the Romans crucifixion was preceded by scourging, undoubtedly to hasten impending death. The victim then bore his own cross, or at least the upright beam, to the place of execution. This in itself proves that the structure was less ponderous than is commonly supposed. When he was tied to the cross nothing further was done and he was left to die from starvation. If he was nailed to the cross, at least in Judea, a stupefying drink was given him to deaden the agony. The number of nails used seems to have been indeterminate. A tablet, on which the feet rested or on which the body was partly supported, seems to have been a part of the cross to keep the wounds from tearing through the transfixed members (Iren., Adv. haer., 2:42). The suffering of death by crucifixion was intense, especially in hot climates. Severe local inflammation, coupled with an insignificant bleeding of the jagged wounds, produced traumatic fever, which was aggravated by exposure to the heat of the sun, the strain[ing] of the body and insufferable thirst. The swell[ing] about the rough nails and the torn lacerated tendons and nerves caused excruciating agony. The arteries of the head and stomach were surcharged with blood and a terrific throbbing headache ensued. The mind was confused and filled with anxiety and dread foreboding. The

victim of crucifixion literally died a thousand deaths. Tetanus not rarely supervened and the rigors of the attending convulsions would tear at the wounds and add to the burden of pain, till at last the bodily forces were exhausted and the victim sank to unconsciousness and death. The sufferings were so frightful that "even among the raging passions of war pity was sometimes excited" (BJ, V, xi, 1). The length of this agony was wholly determined by the constitution of the victim, but death rarely ensued before thirty-six hours had elapsed. Instances are on record of victims of the cross who survived their terrible injuries when taken down from the cross after many hours of suspension (Josephus, Vita, 75). Death was sometimes hastened by breaking the legs of the victims and by a hard blow delivered under the armpit before crucifixion. Crura fracta was a well-known Roman term (Cicero Phil. 13:12). The sudden death of Christ evidently was a matter of astonishment (Mark 15:44). The peculiar symptoms mentioned by John (19:34) would seem to point to a rupture of the heart, of which the Savior died, independent of the cross itself, or perhaps hastened by its agony.

Henry E. Dosker, International Standard Bible Encyclopedia
General Editor, James Orr, 1915

3.10 THE CRUCIFIXION, LEW WALLACE

THE CRUCIFIXION

When the party-Balthasar, Simonides, Ben-Hur, Esther, and the two faithful Galileans-reached the place of crucifixion, Ben-Hur was in advance leading them. How they had been able to make way through the great press of excited people, he never knew; no more did he know the road by which they came or the time it took them to come. He had walked in total unconsciousness, neither hearing nor seeing anybody or anything, and without a thought of where he was going, or the ghostliest semblance of a purpose in his mind.

In such condition a little child could have done as much as he to prevent the awful crime he was about to witness. The intentions of God are always strange to us; but not more so than the means by which they are wrought out, and at last made plain to our belief.

Ben-Hur came to a stop; those following him also stopped. As a curtain rises before an audience, the spell holding him in its sleep-awake rose, and he saw with a clear understanding.

There was a space upon the top of a low knoll rounded like a skull, and dry, dusty, and without vegetation, except some scrubby hyssop. The boundary of the space was a living wall of men, with men behind struggling, some to look over, others to look through it. An inner wall of Roman soldiery held the dense outer wall rigidly to its place. A centurion kept eye upon the soldiers. Up to the very line so vigilantly guarded Ben-Hur had been led; at the line he now stood, his face to the north-west. The knoll was the old Aramaic Golgotha-in Latin, Calvaria; anglicized, Calvary; translated, The Skull.

On its slopes, in the low places, on the swells and higher hills, the earth sparkled with a strange enamelling. Look where he would outside the walled space, he saw no patch of brown soil, no rock, no green thing; he saw only thousands of eyes in ruddy faces; off a little way in the perspective only ruddy faced without eyes; off a little farther only a broad, broad circle, which the nearer view instructed him was also of faces. And this was the ensemble of three millions of people; under it three millions of hearts throbbing with passionate interest in what was taking place upon the knoll; indifferent as to the thieves, caring only for the Nazarene, and for him only as he was an object of hate or fear or curiosity-he who loved them all, and was about to die for them.

In the spectacle of a great assemblage of people there are always the bewilderment and fascination one feels while looking over a stretch of sea in agitation, and never had this one been exceeded; yet Ben-Hur gave it but a passing glance, for that which was going on in the space described would permit no division of his interest.

Up on the knoll so high as to be above the living wall, and visible over the heads of an attending company of notables, conspicuous because of his miter and vestments and his haughty air, stood the high-priest. Up the knoll still higher, up quite to the round summit, so as to be seen far and near, was the Nazarene, stooped and suffering, but silent. The wit among the guard had complemented the crown upon his head by putting a reed in his hand for a scepter. Clamors blew upon him like blasts-laughter-execrations-sometimes both together indistinguishably. A man-only a

man, O reader, would have charged the blasts with the remainder of his love for the race, and let it go forever.

All the eyes then looking were fixed upon the Nazarene. It may have been pity with which he was moved; whatever the cause, Ben-Hur was conscious of a change in his feelings. A conception of something better than the best of this life-something so much better that it could serve a weak man with strength to endure agonies of spirit as well as of body; something to make death welcome-perhaps another life purer than this one-perhaps the spirit-life which Balthasar held to so fast, began to dawn upon his mind clearer and clearer, bringing to him a certain sense that, after all, the mission of the Nazarene was that of guide across the boundary for such as loved him; across the boundary to where his kingdom was set up and waiting for him. Then, as something borne through the air out of the almost forgotten, he heard again, or seemed to hear, the saying of the Nazarene-

"I AM THE RESURRECTION AND THE LIFE."

And the words repeated themselves over and over, and took form, and the dawn touched them with its light, and filled them with a new meaning. And as men repeat a question to grasp and fix the meaning, he asked, gazing at the figure on the hill fainting under its crown, Who the Resurrection? and who the Life?

"I AM," the figure seemed to say-and say it for him; for instantly he was sensible of a peace such as he had never known-the peace which is the end of doubt and mystery, and the beginning of faith and love and clear understanding.

From this dreamy state Ben-Hur was aroused by the sound of hammering. On the summit of the knoll he observed then what had escaped him before-some soldiers and workmen preparing the crosses. The holes for planting the trees were ready, and now the transverse beams were being fitted to their places.

"Bid the men make haste," said the high-priest to the centurion. "These"-and he pointed to the Nazarene-"must be dead by the going-down of the sun, and buried, that the land may not be defiled. Such is the Law."

With a better mind, a soldier went to the Nazarene and offered him something to drink, but he refused the cup. Then another went to him and took from his neck the board with the inscription upon it, which he nailed to the tree of the cross-and the preparation was complete.

"The crosses are ready," said the centurion to the pontiff, who received the report with a wave of the hand and the reply-

"Let the blasphemer go first. The Son of God should be able to save himself. We will see."

The people to whom the preparation in its several stages was visible, and who to this time had assailed the hill with incessant cries of impatience, permitted a lull which directly became a universal hush. The part of the infliction most shocking, at least to the thought, was reached-the men were to be nailed to their crosses. When for that purpose the soldiers laid their hands upon the Nazarene first, a shudder passed through the great concourse; the most brutalized shrank with dread. Afterwards there were those who said the air suddenly chilled and made them shiver.

"How very still it is!" Esther said, as she put her arm about her father's neck.

And remembering the torture he himself had suffered, he drew her face down upon his breast, and sat trembling.

"Avoid it, Esther, avoid it!" he said, "I know not but all who stand and see it-the innocent as well as the guilty-may be cursed from this hour."

Balthasar sank upon his knees.

"Son of Hur," said Simonides, with increasing excitement-"son of Hur, if Jehovah stretch not forth his hand, and quickly, Israel is lost-and we are lost."

Ben-Hur answered, calmly, "I have been in a dream, Simonides, and heard in it why all this should be, and why it should go on. It is the will of the Nazarene-it is God's will. Let us do as the Egyptian here-let us hold our peace and pray."

As he looked up on the knoll again, the words were wafted to him through the awful stillness-

"I AM THE RESURRECTION AND THE LIFE."

He bowed reverently as to a person speaking.

Up on the summit meantime the work went on. The guard took the Nazarene's clothes from him; so that he stood before the millions naked. The stripes of the scourging he had received in the early morning were still bloody upon his back; yet he was laid pitilessly down, and stretched upon the cross-first, the arms upon the transverse beam; the spikes were sharp-a few blows, and they were driven through the tender palms; next, they drew his knees up until the soles of the feet rested flat upon the tree; then they placed one foot upon the other, and one spike fixed both of them fast. The dulled sound of the hammering was heard outside the guarded space; and such as could not hear, yet saw the hammer as it fell, shivered with fear. And withal not a groan, or cry, or word of remonstrance from the sufferer: nothing at which an enemy could laugh; nothing a lover could regret.

"Which way wilt thou have him faced?" asked a soldier, bluntly.

"Towards the Temple," the pontiff replied. "In dying I would have him see the holy house hath not suffered by him."

The workmen put their hands to the cross, and carried it, burden and all, to the place of planting. At a word they dropped the tree, into the hole; and the body of the Nazarene also dropped heavily and hung by the bleeding hands. Still no cry of pain-only the exclamation divinest of all recorded exclamations-

"Father, forgive them, for they know not what they do."

The cross, reared now above all other objects, and standing singly out against the sky, was greeted with a burst of delight; and all who could see and read the writing upon the board over the Nazarene's head made haste to decipher it. Soon as read, the legend was adopted by them and communicated, and presently the whole mighty concourse was ringing the salutation from side to side, and repeating it with laughter and groans-

"King of the Jews! Hail, King of the Jews!"

The pontiff, with a clearer idea of the import of the inscription, protested against it, but in vain; so the titled King, looking from the knoll with dying eyes, must have had the city of his fathers at rest below him-she who had so ignominiously cast him out.

The sun was rising rapidly to noon; the hills bared their brown breasts lovingly to it; the more distant mountains rejoiced in the purple with which it so regally dressed them. In the city, the temples, palaces, towers, pinnacles, and all points of beauty and prominence, seemed to lift themselves into the unrivalled brilliance, as if they knew the pride they were giving the many who from time to time turned to look at them. Suddenly a dimness began to fill the sky and cover the earth-at first no more than a scarce perceptible fading of the day; a twilight out of time; an evening gliding in upon the splendors of noon. But it deepened, and directly drew attention; whereat the noise of the shouting and laughter fell off, and men, doubting their senses, gazed at each other curiously: then they looked to the sun again; then at the mountains, getting farther away; at the sky and the near landscape, sinking in shadow; at the hill upon which the tragedy was enacting; and from all these they gazed at each other again, and turned pale, and held their peace.

"It is only a mist or passing cloud," Simonides said soothingly to Esther, who was alarmed. "It will brighten presently."

Ben-Hur did not think so.

"It is not a mist or a cloud," he said. "The spirits who live in the air-the prophets and saints-are at work in mercy to themselves and nature. I say to you, O Simonides, truly as God lives, he who hangs yonder is the Son of God."

And leaving Simonides lost in wonder at such a speech from him, he went where Balthasar was kneeling near by, and laid his hand upon the good man's shoulder.

"O wise Egyptian, hearken! Thou alone wert right-the Nazarene is indeed the Son of God."

Balthasar drew him down to him, and replied, feebly, "I saw him a child in the manger where he was first laid; it is not strange that I knew him sooner than thou; but oh that I should live to see this day! Would I had died with my brethren! Happy Melchior! Happy, happy Gaspar!"

"Comfort thee!" said Ben-Hur. "Doubtless they too are here."

The dimness went on deepening into obscurity, and that into positive darkness, but without deterring the bolder spirits upon the knoll. One after the other the thieves were raised on their crosses, and the crosses planted. The guard was then withdrawn, and the people set free closed in upon the height, and surged up it, like a converging wave. A man might take a look, when a new-comer would push him on, and take his place, to be in turn pushed on-and there were laughter and ribaldry and revilements, all for the Nazarene.

"Ha, ha! If thou be King of the Jews, save thyself," a soldier shouted.

"Ay," said a priest, "if he will come down to us now, we will believe in him."

Others wagged their heads wisely saying, "He would destroy the Temple, and rebuild it in three days, but cannot save himself."

Others still-"He called himself the Son of God; let us see if God will have him."

What all there is in prejudice no one has ever said. The Nazarene had never harmed the people; far the greater part of them had never seen him except in this his hour of calamity; yet-singular contrariety!-they loaded him with their curses, and gave their sympathy to the thieves.

The supernatural night, dropped thus from the heavens, affected Esther as it began to affect thousands of others braver and stronger.

"Let us go home," she prayed-twice, three times-saying, "it is the frown of God, father. What other dreadful things may happen, who can tell? I am afraid."

Simonides was obstinate. He said little, but was plainly under great excitement. Observing, about the end of the first hour, that the violence of the crowding up on the knoll was somewhat abated, at his suggestion the party advanced to take position nearer the crosses. Ben-Hur gave his arm to Balthasar; yet the Egyptian made the ascent with difficulty. From their new stand the Nazarene was imperfectly visible, appearing to them not more than a dark suspended figure. They could hear him, however-hear his sighing, which showed an endurance or exhaustion greater than that of his fellow-sufferers; for they filled every lull in the noises with their groans and entreaties.

The second hour after the suspension passed like the first one. To the Nazarene they were hours of insult, provocation, and slow dying. He spoke but once in the time. Some women came and knelt at the foot of his cross. Among them he recognized his mother with the beloved disciple.

"Woman," he said, raising his voice, "behold thy son!" And to the disciple, "Behold thy mother!"

The third hour came, and still the people surged round the hill, held to it by some strange attraction, with which, in probability, the night in midday had much to do. They were quieter than in the preceding hour; yet at intervals they could be heard off in the darkness shouting to each other, multitude calling unto multitude. It was noticeable, also, that coming now to the Nazarene, they approached his cross in silence, took the look in silence, and so departed. This change extended even to the guard, who so shortly before had cast lots for the clothes of the crucified; they stood with their officers a little apart, more watchful of the one convict than of the throngs coming and going. If he but breathed heavily, or tossed his head in a paroxysm of pain, they were instantly on the alert. Most marvelous of all, however, was the altered behavior of the high-priest and his following, the wise men who had assisted him in the trial in the night, and, in the victim's face, kept place by him with zealous approval. When the darkness began to fall, they began to lose their confidence. There were among them many learned in astronomy, and familiar with the apparitions so terrible in those days to the masses; much of the knowledge was descended to them from their fathers far back; some of it had been brought away at the end of the Captivity; and the necessities of the Temple service kept it all bright. These closed together when the sun commenced to fade before their eyes, and the mountains and hills to recede; they drew together in a group around their pontiff, and debated what they saw. "The moon is at its full," they said, with

truth, "and this cannot be an eclipse." Then, as no one could answer the question common with them all-as no one could account for the darkness, or for its occurrence at that particular time-in their secret hearts they associated it with the Nazarene, and yielded to an alarm which the long continuance of the phenomenon steadily increased. In their place behind the soldiers they noted every word and motion of the Nazarene, and hung with fear upon his sighs, and talked in whispers. The man might be the Messiah, and then-But they would wait and see!

In the meantime Ben-Hur was not once visited by the old spirit. The perfect peace abode with him. He prayed simply that the end might be hastened. He knew the condition of Simonides' mind-that he was hesitating on the verge of belief. He could see the massive face weighed down by solemn reflection. He noticed him casting inquiring glances at the sun, as seeking the cause of the darkness. Nor did he fail to notice the solicitude with which Esther clung to him, smothering her fears to accommodate his wishes.

"Be not afraid," he heard him say to her; "but stay and watch with me. Thou mayst live twice the span of my life, and see nothing of human interest equal to this; and there may be revelations more. Let us stay to the close."

When the third hour was about half gone, some men of the rudest class-wretches from the tombs about the city-came and stopped in front of the center cross.

"This is he, the new King of the Jews," said one of them.

The others cried, with laughter, "Hail, all hail, King of the Jews!"

Receiving no reply, they went closer.

"If thou be King of the Jews, or Son of God, come down," they said, loudly.

At this, one of the thieves quit groaning, and called to the Nazarene, "Yes, if thou be Christ, save thyself and us."

The people laughed and applauded; then, while they were listening for a reply, the other felon was heard to say to the first one, "Dost thou not fear God? We receive the due rewards of our deeds; but this man hath done nothing amiss."

The bystanders were astonished; in the midst of the hush which ensued, the second felon spoke again, but this time to the Nazarene-

"Lord," he said, "remember me when thou comest into thy kingdom."

Simonides gave a great start. "When thou comest into thy kingdom!" It was the very point of doubt in his mind; the point he had so often debated with Balthasar.

"Didst thou hear?" said Ben-Hur to him. "The kingdom cannot be of this world. Yon witness saith the King is but going to his kingdom; and, in effect, I heard the same in my dream."

"Hush!" said Simonides, more imperiously than ever before in speech to Ben-Hur. "Hush, I pray thee. If the Nazarene should answer-"

And as he spoke the Nazarene did answer, in a clear voice, full of confidence-

"Verily I say unto thee, To-day shalt thou be with me in Paradise!"

Simonides waited to hear if that were all; then he folded his hands and said, "No more, no more, Lord! The darkness is gone; I see with other eyes-even as Balthasar, I see with eyes of perfect faith."

The faithful servant had at last his fitting reward. His broken body might never be restored; nor was there riddance of the recollection of his sufferings, or recall of the years imbittered by them; but suddenly a new life was shown him, with assurance that it was for him-a new life lying just beyond this one-and its name was Paradise. There he would find the Kingdom of which he had been dreaming, and the King. A perfect peace fell upon him.

Over the way, in front of the cross, however, there were surprise and consternation. The cunning casuists there put the assumption underlying the question and the admission underlying the answer together. For saying through the land that he was the Messiah, they had brought the Nazarene to the cross; and, lo! on the cross, more confidently than ever, he had not only reasserted himself, but promised enjoyment of his Paradise to a malefactor. They trembled at what they were doing. The pontiff, with all his pride, was afraid. Where

got the man his confidence except from Truth? And what should the Truth be but God? A very little now would put them all to flight.

The breathing of the Nazarene grew harder; his sighs became great gasps. Only three hours upon the cross, and he was dying!

The intelligence was carried from man to man, until every one knew it; and then everything hushed; the breeze faltered and died; a stifling vapor loaded the air; heat was superadded to darkness; nor might any one unknowing the fact have thought that off the hill, out under the overhanging pall, there were three millions of people waiting awestruck what should happen next-they were so still!

Then there went out through the gloom, over the heads of such as were on the hill within hearing of the dying man, a cry of despair, if not reproach-

"My God! my God! why hast thou forsaken me?"

The voice startled all who heard it. One it touched uncontrollably.

The soldiers in coming had brought with them a vessel of wine and water, and set it down a little way from Ben-Hur. With a sponge dipped into the liquor, and put on the end of a stick, they could moisten the tongue of a sufferer at their pleasure. Ben-Hur thought of the draught he had had at the well near Nazareth; an impulse seized him; catching up the sponge, he dipped it into the vessel, and started for the cross.

"Let him be!" the people in the way shouted, angrily. "Let him be!"

Without minding them, he ran on, and put the sponge to the Nazarene's lips. Too late, too late!

The face then plainly seen by Ben-Hur, bruised and black with blood and dust as it was, lighted nevertheless with a sudden glow; the eyes opened wide, and fixed upon some one visible to them alone in the far heavens; and there were content and relief, even triumph, in the shout the victim gave-

"It is finished! It is finished!"

So a hero, dying in the doing a great deed, celebrates his success with a last cheer.

The light in the eyes went out; slowly the crowned head sank upon the laboring breast.

Ben-Hur thought the struggle over; but the fainting soul recollected itself, so that he and those around him caught the other and last words, spoken in a low voice, as if to one listening close by-

"Father, into thy hands I commend my spirit."

A tremor shook the tortured body; there was a scream of fiercest anguish, and the mission and the earthly life were over at once. The heart, with all its love, was broken; for of that, O reader, the man died!

Ben-Hur went back to his friends, saying, simply, "It is over; he is dead."

In a space incredibly short the multitude was informed of the circumstance. No one repeated it aloud; there was a murmur which spread from the knoll in every direction; a murmur that was little more than a whispering, "He is dead! he is dead!" and that was all. The people had their wish; the Nazarene was dead; yet they stared at each other aghast. His blood was upon them! And while they stood staring at each other, the ground commenced to shake; each man took hold of his neighbor to support himself; in a twinkling the darkness disappeared, and the sun came out; and everybody, as with the same glance, beheld the crosses upon the hill all reeling drunken-like in the earthquake. They beheld all three of them; but the one in the center was arbitrary; it alone would be seen; and for that it seemed to extend itself upwards, and lift its burden, and swing it to and fro higher and higher in the blue of the sky. And every man among them who had jeered at the Nazarene; every one who had struck him; every one who had voted to crucify him; every one who had marched in the procession from the city; every one who had in his heart wished him dead, and they were as ten to one, felt that he was in some way individually singled out from the many, and that if he would live he must get away quickly as possible from that menace in the sky. They started to run; they ran with all their might; on horseback, and camels, and in chariots they ran, as well as on foot; but then, as if it were mad at them for what they had done, and had taken up the cause of the unoffending and friendless dead, the

earthquake pursued them, and tossed them about, and flung them down, and terrified them yet more by the horrible noise of great rocks grinding and rending beneath them. They beat their breasts and shrieked with fear. His blood was upon them! The home-bred and the foreign, priest and layman, beggar, Sadducee, Pharisee, were overtaken in the race, and tumbled about indiscriminately. If they called on the Lord, the outraged earth answered for him in fury, and dealt them all alike. It did not even know wherein the high-priest was better than his guilty brethren; overtaking him, it tripped him up also, and smirched the fringing of his robe, and filled the golden bells with sand, and his mouth with dust. He and his people were alike in the one thing at least-the blood of the Nazarene was upon them all!

When the sunlight broke upon the crucifixion, the mother of the Nazarene, the disciple, and the faithful women of Galilee, the centurion and his soldiers, and Ben-Hur and his party, were all who remained upon the hill. These had not time to observe the flight of the multitude; they were too loudly called upon to take care of themselves.

"Seat thyself here," said Ben-Hur to Esther, making a place for her at her father's feet. "Now cover thine eyes, and look not up; but put thy trust in God, and the spirit of yon just man so foully slain."

"Nay," said Simonides, reverently, "Let us henceforth speak of him as the Christ."

"Be it so," said Ben-Hur.

Presently a wave of the earthquake struck the hill. The shrieks of the thieves upon the reeling crosses were terrible to hear. Though giddy with the movements of the ground, Ben-Hur had time to look at Balthasar, and beheld him prostrate and still. He ran to him and called-there was no reply. The good man was dead! Then Ben-Hur remembered to have heard a cry in answer, as it were, to the scream of the Nazarene in his last moment; but he had not looked to see from whom it had proceeded; and ever after he believed the spirit of the Egyptian accompanied that of his Master over the boundary into the kingdom of Paradise. The idea rested not only upon the cry heard, but upon the exceeding fitness of the distinction. If faith were worthy reward in the person of Gaspar, and love in that of Melchior, surely he should have some special mead who through a long life had so excellently illustrated the three virtues in combination-Faith, Love, and Good Works.

The servants of Balthasar had deserted their master; but when all was over, the two Galileans bore the old man in his litter back to the city.

It was a sorrowful procession that entered the south gate of the palace of the Hurs about the set of sun that memorable day. About the same hour the body of the Christ was taken down from the cross.

Lew Wallace, Ben-Hur, a tale of the Christ, *1880*

3

THE MEANING OF JESUS' DEATH

3.11 THE CRUCIFIXION, JULIAN OF NORWICH

As I looked I saw the body bleeding heavily, apparently from the flogging. The smooth skin was gashed and all over his body I saw deep weals in the tender flesh caused by many sharp blows. The blood flowed so hot and thick that neither the wounds nor the skin could be seen: in was all covered in blood. The blood flowed all down his body, but at the point of falling to the ground, it disappeared. The bleeding continued for a while, giving me time to see it and think about it. It was so heavy that I thought that if it had been real the whole bed and everything around would have been soaked in blood.

Then the idea come to me that out of his tender love for us God has created a vast supply of water for us to use to make ourselves comfortable on this earth. Yet he would rather that we make ourselves at home with him by using his holy blood to wash ourselves clean from our sin: for no liquid has been made which he would prefer to give. It is as plentiful as it is precious because it is divine. It is part of us, and is most blissfully ours because of his precious love.

The beloved blood of our Lord Jesus Christ is truly as plentiful as it is precious. Look and see for yourself. It flows over the whole world ready to wash every human being from all sin, present, past and future, if they are willing.

Julian of Norwich, Revelations of Divine Love

3.12 I SAW HIS PASSION, JULIAN OF NORWICH

I saw the red blood trickle down from under the garland of thorns, a stream of hot, fresh blood, just as it was in the time of his Passion when the crown was pressed on to the blessed head of the God-Man who suffered in this way for me. And I saw clearly, powerfully and truly, that it was none other than Jesus himself who showed this vision to me.

In that same vision, the Trinity suddenly filled my heart with the deepest joy, and I knew that all those who go to heaven will experience this joy for ever. For the Trinity is God: God is the Trinity; the Trinity is our Creator and Keeper, the Trinity is our eternal love, joy and bliss, through our Lord Jesus Christ. This was revealed to me in this first vision and indeed in all of them, for it seems to me that wherever Jesus appears the blessed Trinity is also present.

"*Benedicite, Domine!*" ["Welcome, O Lord!"] I cried, and I meant it in all reverence and shouted it at the top of my voice! I was overwhelmed with wonder that he, so holy and awesome, should be so at home with the likes of me—I, who am so sinful, with such a wretched earthly body.

Julian of Norwich, Revelations of Divine Love

3.13 CHRIST'S HOLY SUFFERINGS, MARTIN LUTHER

TRUE AND FALSE VIEWS OF CHRIST'S SUFFERINGS

Section I
The false views of Christ's suffering

1. In the first place, some reflect upon the sufferings of Christ in a way that they become angry at the Jews, sing and lament about poor Judas, and are then satisfied; just like by habit they complain of other persons, and condemn and spend their time with their enemies. Such an exercise may truly be called a meditation not on the sufferings of Christ, but on the wickedness of Judas and the Jews.

2. In the second place, others have pointed out the different benefits and fruits springing from a consideration of Christ's Passion. Here the saying ascribed to Albertus is misleading, that to think once superficially on the sufferings of Christ is better than to fast a whole year or to pray the Psalter every day, etc. The people thus blindly follow him and act contrary to the true fruits of Christ's Passion; for they seek therein their own selfish interests. Therefore they decorate themselves with pictures and booklets, with letters and crucifixes, and some go so far as to imagine that they thus protect themselves against the perils of water, of fire, and of the sword, and all other dangers. In this way the suffering of Christ is to work in them an absence of suffering, which is contrary to its nature and character.

3. A third class so, sympathize with Christ as to weep and lament for him because he was so innocent, like the women who followed Christ from Jerusalem, whom he rebuked, in that they should better weep for themselves and for their children. Such are they who run far away in the midst of the Passion season, and are greatly benefited by the departure of Christ from Bethany and by the pains and sorrows of the Virgin Mary, but they never get farther. Hence they postpone the Passion many hours, and God only knows whether it is devised more for sleeping than for watching. And among these fanatics are those who taught what great blessings come from the holy mass, and in their simple way they think it is enough if they attend mass. To this we are led through the sayings of certain teachers, that the mass *opere operati, non opere operantis*, is acceptable of itself, even without our merit and worthiness, just as if that were enough. Nevertheless the mass was not instituted for the sake of its own worthiness but to prove us, especially for the purpose of meditating upon the sufferings of Christ. For where this is not done, we make a temporal, unfruitful work out of the mass, however good it may be in itself. For what help is it to you, that God is God, if he is not God to you? What benefit is it that eating and drinking are in themselves healthful and good, if they are not healthful for you, and there is fear that we never grow better by reason of our many masses, if we fail to seek the true fruit in them?

Section II
The true view of Christ's sufferings

4. Fourthly, they meditate on the Passion of Christ aright, who so view Christ that they become terror-stricken in heart at the sight, and their conscience at once sinks in despair. This terror-stricken feeling should spring forth, so that you see the severe wrath and the unchangeable earnestness of God in regard to sin and sinners, in that he was unwilling that his only and dearly beloved Son should set sinners free unless he paid the costly ransom for them as is mentioned in Is. 53:8: "For the transgression of my people was he stricken." What happens to the sinner, when the dear child is thus stricken? An earnestness must be present that is inexpressible and unbearable, which a person so immeasurably great goes to meet, and suffers and dies for it; and if you reflect upon it real deeply, that God's Son, the eternal wisdom of the Father, himself suffers, you will indeed be terror-stricken; and the more you reflect the deeper will be the impression.

5. Fifthly, that you deeply believe and never doubt the least, that you are the one who thus martyred Christ. For your sins most

surely did it. Thus St. Peter struck and terrified the Jews as with a thunderbolt in Acts 2:36-37, when he spoke to them all in common: "Him have ye crucified," so that three thousand were terror-stricken the same day and tremblingly cried to the apostles: "O beloved brethren what shall we do?" Therefore, when you view the nails piercing through his hands, firmly believe it is your work. Do you behold his crown of thorns, believe the thorns are your wicked thoughts, etc.

6. Sixthly, now see, where one thorn pierces Christ, there more than a thousand thorns should pierce thee, yea, eternally should they thus and even more painfully pierce thee. Where one nail is driven through his hands and feet, thou shouldest eternally suffer such and even more painful nails; as will be also visited upon those who, let Christ's sufferings be lost and fruitless as far as they are concerned. For this earnest mirror, Christ, will neither lie nor mock; whatever he says must be fully realized.

7. Seventhly, St. Bernard was so terror-stricken by Christ's sufferings that he said: I imagined I was secure and I knew nothing of the eternal judgment passed upon me in heaven, until I saw that the eternal Son of God took mercy upon me, stepped forward and offered himself on my behalf in the same judgment. Ah, it does not become me still to play and remain secure when such earnestness, is behind those sufferings. Hence he commanded the women: "Weep not for me, but weep for yourselves, and for your children." Luke 23:28; and gives in the 31st verse the reason: "For if they do these things in the green tree, what shall be done in the dry?" As if to say: Learn from my martyrdom what you have merited and how you should be rewarded. For here it is true that a little dog was slain in order to terrorize a big one. Likewise the prophet also said: "All generations shall lament and bewail themselves more than him"; it is not said they shall lament him, but themselves rather than him. Likewise were also the apostles terror-stricken in Acts 2:27, as mentioned before, so that they said to the apostles: "O, brethren, what shall we do?" So the church also sings: I will diligently meditate thereon, and thus my soul in me will exhaust itself.

8. Eighthly, one must skillfully exercise himself in this point, for the benefit of Christ's sufferings depends almost entirely upon man coming to a true knowledge of himself, and becoming terror-stricken and slain before himself. And where man does not come to this point, the sufferings of Christ have become of no true benefit to him. For the characteristic, natural work of Christ's sufferings is that they make all men equal and alike, so that as Christ was horribly martyred as to body and soul in our sins, we must also like him be martyred in our consciences by our sins. This does not take place by means of many words, but by means of deep thoughts and a profound realization of our sins. Take an illustration: If an evil-doer were judged because he had slain the child of a prince or king, and you were in safety, and sang and played, as if you were entirely innocent, until one seized you in a horrible manner and convinced you that you had enabled the wicked person to do the act; behold, then you would be in the greatest straits, especially if your conscience also revolted against you. Thus much more anxious you should be, when you consider Christ's sufferings. For the evil doers, the Jews, although they have now judged and banished God, they have still been the servants of your sins, and you are truly the one who strangled and crucified the Son of God through your sins, as has been said.

9. Ninthly, whoever perceives himself to be so hard and sterile that he is not terror-stricken by Christ's sufferings and led to a knowledge of him, he should fear and tremble. For it cannot be otherwise; you must become like the picture and sufferings of Christ, be it realized in life or in hell; you must at the time of death, if not sooner, fall into terror, tremble, quake and experience all Christ suffered on the cross. It is truly terrible to attend to this on your deathbed; therefore you should pray God to soften your heart and permit you fruitfully to meditate upon Christ's Passion. For it is impossible for us profoundly to meditate upon the sufferings of Christ of ourselves, unless God sink them into our hearts. Further, neither this meditation nor any other doctrine is given to you to the end that you should fall fresh upon it of

yourself, to accomplish the same; but you are first to seek and long for the grace of God, that you may accomplish it through God's grace and not through your own power. For in this way it happens that those referred to above never treat the sufferings of Christ aright; for they never call upon God to that end, but devise out of their own ability their own way, and treat those sufferings entirely in a human and an unfruitful manner.

10 Tenthly, whoever meditates thus upon God's sufferings for a day, an hour, yea, for a quarter of an hour, we wish to say freely and publicly, that it is better than if he fasts a whole year, prays the Psalter every day, yea, than if he hears a hundred masses. For such a meditation changes a man's character and almost as in baptism he is born again, anew. Then Christ's suffering accomplishes its true, natural and noble work, it slays the old Adam, banishes all lust, pleasure and security that one may obtain from God's creatures; just like Christ was forsaken by all, even by God.

11. Eleventhly, since then such a work is not in our hands, it happens that sometimes we pray and do not receive it at the time; in spite of this one should not despair nor cease to pray. At times it comes when we are not praying for it, as God knows and wills; for it will be free and unbound: then man is distressed in conscience and is wickedly displeased with his own life, and it may easily happen that he does not know that Christ's Passion is working this very thing in him, of which perhaps he was not aware, just like the others so exclusively meditated on Christ's Passion that in their knowledge of self they could not extricate themselves out of that state of meditation. Among the first the sufferings of Christ are quite and true, among the others a show and false, and according to its nature God often turns the leaf, so that those who do not meditate on the Passion, really do, meditate on it; and those who bear the mass, do not hear it; and those who hear it not, do hear it.

Section III
The comfort of Christ's sufferings

12. Until the present we have been in the Passion week and have celebrated Good Friday in the right way: now we come to Easter and Christ's resurrection. When man perceives his sins in this light and is completely terror-stricken in his conscience, he must be on his guard that his sins do not thus remain in his conscience, and nothing but pure doubt certainly come out of it; but just as the sins flowed out of Christ and we became conscious of them, so should we pour them again upon him and set our conscience free. Therefore see well to it that you act not like perverted people, who bite and devour themselves with their sins in their heart, and run here and there with their good works or their own satisfaction, or even work themselves out of this condition by means of indulgences and become rid of their sins; which is impossible, and, alas, such a false refuge of satisfaction and pilgrimages has spread far and wide.

13. Thirteenthly. Then cast your sins from yourself upon Christ, believe with a festive spirit that your sins are his wounds and sufferings, that he carries them and makes satisfaction for them, as Is. 53:6 says: "Jehovah hath laid on him the iniquity of us all"; and St. Peter in his first Epistle 2:24: "Who his own self bare our sins in his body upon the tree" of the cross; and St. Paul in 2 Cor. 5:21: "Him who knew no sin was made to be sin on our behalf; that we might become the righteousness of God in him." Upon these and like passages you must rely with all your weight, and so much the more the harder your conscience martyrs you. For if you do not take this course, but miss the opportunity of stilling your heart, then you will never secure peace, and must yet finally despair in doubt. For if we deal with our sins in our conscience and let them continue within us and be cherished in our hearts, they become much too strong for us to manage and they will live forever. But when we see that they are laid on Christ and he has triumphed over them by his resurrection and we fearlessly believe it, then they are dead and have become as nothing. For upon Christ they cannot rest, there they are swallowed up by his resurrection, and you see now no wound, no pain, in him, that is, no sign of sin. Thus St. Paul speaks in Rom. 4:25, that he was delivered up for our trespasses and was raised for our justification;

that is, in his sufferings he made known our sins and also crucified them; but by his resurrection he makes us righteous and free from all sin, even if we believe the same differently.

14. Fourteenthly. Now if you are not able to believe, then, as I said before, you should pray to God for faith. For this is a matter in the hands of God that is entirely free, and is also bestowed alike at times knowingly, at times secretly, as was just said on the subject of suffering.

15. But now bestir yourself to the end: first, not to behold Christ's sufferings any longer; for they have already done their work and terrified you; but press through all difficulties and behold his friendly heart, how full of love it is toward you, which love constrained him to bear the heavy load of your conscience and your sin. Thus will your heart be loving and sweet toward him, and the assurance of your faith be strengthened. Then ascend higher through the heart of Christ to the heart of God, and see that Christ would not have been able to love you if God had not willed it in eternal love, to which Christ is obedient in his love toward you; there you will find the divine, good father heart, and, as Christ says, be thus drawn to the Father through Christ. Then will you understand the saying of Christ in John 3:16: "God so loved the world that he gave his only begotten Son," etc. That means to know God aright, if we apprehend him not by his power and wisdom, which terrify us, but by his goodness and love; there our faith and confidence can then stand unmovable and man is truly thus born anew in God.

16. Sixteenthly. When your heart is thus established in Christ, and you are an enemy of sin, out of love and not out of fear of punishment, Christ's sufferings should also be an example for your whole life, and you should meditate on the same in a different way. For hitherto we have considered Christ's Passion as a sacrament that works in us and we suffer; now we consider it, that we also work, namely thus: if a day of sorrow or sickness weighs you down, think, how trifling that is,

compared with the thorns and nails of Christ. If you must do or leave undone what is distasteful to you: think, how Christ was led hither and thither, bound and a captive. Does pride attack you: behold, how your Lord was mocked and disgraced with murderers. Do unchastity and lust thrust themselves against you: think, how bitter it was for Christ to have his tender flesh torn, pierced and beaten again and again. Do hatred and envy war against you, or do you seek vengeance: remember how Christ with many tears and cries prayed for you and all his enemies, who indeed had more reason to seek revenge. If trouble or whatever adversity of body or soul afflict you, strengthen your heart and say: Ah, why then should I not also suffer a little since my Lord sweat blood in the garden because of anxiety and grief? That would be a lazy, disgraceful servant who would wish to lie in his bed while his lord was compelled to battle with the pangs of death.

17. Behold, one can thus find in Christ strength and comfort against all vice and bad habits. That is the right observance of Christ's Passion, and that is the fruit of his suffering, and he who exercises himself thus in the same does better than by hearing the whole Passion or reading all masses. And they are called true Christians who incorporate the life and name of Christ into their own life, as St. Paul says in Gal. 5:24: "And they that are of Christ Jesus have crucified the flesh with the passions and the lusts thereof." For Christ's Passion must be dealt with not in words and a show, but in our lives and in truth. Thus St. Paul admonishes us in Heb. 12:3: "For consider192 him that hath endured such gainsaying of sinners against himself, that ye wax not weary, fainting in your souls;" and St. Peter in his 1st Epistle 4:1: "As Christ suffered in the flesh, arm ye yourselves also with the same mind." But this kind of meditation is now out of use and very rare, although the Epistles of St. Paul and St. Peter are full of it. We have changed the essence into a mere show, and painted the meditation of Christ's sufferings only in letters and on walls.

Martin Luther, Sermon, c. 1520

3.14 Christ's righteousness is the Christian's righteousness, Martin Luther

"For our sake [God] made him to be sin who knew no sin, so that in him we might become the righteousness of God." 2 Corinthians 5:21

This is that mystery which is rich in divine grace to sinners, wherein by a wonderful exchange our sins are no longer ours but Christ's, and the righteousness of Christ is not Christ's but ours. He has emptied himself of his righteousness that he might clothe us with it, and fill us with it; and he has taken our evils upon himself that he might deliver us from them. So that now the righteousness of Christ is ours not only objectively (as they term it) but formally also.

Martin Luther, Commentary on the Psalms

3.15 Penal substitution, Martin Luther

"Christ redeemed us from the curse of the law, having become a curse for us." Galatians 3:13

We are sinners and thieves, and therefore guilty of death and everlasting damnation. But Christ took all our sins upon him, and for them died upon the cross . . . all the prophets did foresee in spirit, that Christ should become the greatest transgressor, murderer, adulterer, thief, rebel, blasphemer, etc. that ever was for he being made a sacrifice, for the sins of the whole world, is now an innocent person and without sins . . . our most merciful Father, seeing us to be oppressed overwhelmed with the curse of the law, and so to be holden under the same that we could never be delivered from it by our own power, sent his only Son into the world and laid upon him all the sins of all men, saying: Be thou Peter that denier; Paul that persecutor, blasphemer and cruel oppressor; David that adulterer; that sinner which did eat the apple in Paradise; that thief which hanged upon the cross; and, briefly, be thou the person which hath committed the sins of all men; see therefore that thou pay and satisfy for them. Here now cometh the law and saith: I find him a sinner, and that such a one as hath taken upon him the sins of all men, and I see no sins but in him; therefore let him die upon the cross. And so he setteth upon him and killeth him. By this means the whole world is purged and cleansed from all sins, and so delivered from death and all evils.

Martin Luther, Galatians

3.16 Our justification, Don Benedetto

The Benefit of Christ Crucified *was arguably the most popular book of the short lived Italian Reformation. It is estimated that 40,000–80,000 copies were printed between 1541-1548, of which very few remain today due to the fact that most were burned once the title was placed on the list of prohibited books during the Inquisition. The treatise was originally published anonymously under the title* Trattato Ultilissimo Del Beneficio Di Geisu Christo Crocifisso, *and was for a few hundred years mistakenly attributed to Aonio Paleario (1503-1570), a martyr for the Reformation cause in Italy.*

That the forgiveness of our sins, our justification, and all our salvation dependeth on Christ.

Forsomuch now as our Lord God hath thus sent that great prophet whom He promised, which is His only-begotten Son, to the intent that he should deliver us from the malediction or curse of the law, and should reconcile us unto God, and make able our will to do good works, healing our freewill, and restoring to us that likeness of God which we had lost by the sin of our first parents; and forsomuch as we know that under heaven there is given none other name to mankind whereby we may be saved besides the name of Jesus Christ, let us therefore run with the paces or steps of our lively faith in him, into his arms that calleth us crying, Come to me, all ye that labor and are laden, and I will ease you. What consolation, what joyfulness of heart in this life, may be compared to his joy and comfort that having felt himself first oppressed with the intolerable weight of his sins, heareth afterward so sweet and pleasant a saying of the Son of God, who promised him so mercifully thoroughly to ease and to deliver him of so great a burden? But all consisteth in this, that we know from whence our sickness and misery cometh: for no man tasteth or truly discerneth that that is good, unless first he have felt that that is evil; and therefore saith Christ, If any man thirst let him come to me and drink; as he might say, except a man know himself a sinner, and thirst for righteousness, he cannot taste how sweet this our Jesus Christ is, nor bow pleasant it is to think and speak of Him, and to follow his most holy life and conversation. If then we know our sickness by the office of the law, behold then Saint John Baptist sheweth with his finger unto us our merciful healer and Savior, saying, Behold the Lamb of God that taketh away the sins of the world. The which (I say) delivered us from the grievous yoke of the law, abrogating and making of none effect the maledictions or cursings, and sharp threatenings thereof; healing all our sicknesses, reforming our freewill, and restoring us unto

our first innocence, and bringing to us again the likeness of God. And therefore, as Saint Paul saith, As by Adam we are all dead, even so by Christ we all are revived. Then let not us believe that the sin of Adam, which we have inherited, is of greater efficacy than the righteousness of Christ, which we have in like manner by faith inherited.

It might have seemed that a man might have been sorry that without his occasion he should be born and conceived in sin, through the iniquity of his parents, whereby death reigned over all men; but now is taken away all lamentation, forasmuch as in the selfsame manner, without our occasion, the righteousness of Christ, and life everlasting by Christ, is come unto us, death being by him slain; Whereupon Saint Paul maketh a very goodly discourse, which I will hereunder write: As by one man sin entered into the world, and death by the means of sin, and so death went over all men, insomuch that all men sinned; for even unto the time of the law was sin in the world, but sin was not regarded as long as there was no law: nevertheless death reigned from Adam to Moses, even over them all that sinned not with like transgression as Adam did, which is the similitude of him that is to come. But the gift is not like as the sin. For if through the sin of one many be dead, much more plenteous upon many was the grace of God and gift by grace, which grace was given by one man, Jesus Christ: and the gift is not over one sin, as death came through one sin of one that sinned; for damnation came of one sin unto condemnation, but the gift came to justify from many sins. For if by the sin of one death reigned by the means of one, much more shall they that receive abundance of grace, and of the gift of righteousness, reign in life by means of one, that is to say, Jesus Christ. Likewise then as by the sin of one condemnation came on all men, even so by the justifying of one cometh the righteousness that bringeth life upon all men. For as by one man's disobedience many became sinners, so by the obedience of one shall many be made righteous. But the law in the meantime entered in, that sin should increase; never the less, where abundance of sin was, there was more plenteousness of grace, that as sin had reigned unto death, even so might grace reign through righteousness unto eternal life, by the help of Jesus Christ.

By these words of Saint Paul we know that is above said, that is to say, that the law was given to the intent that sin might be known, and that thereby we might know that it is not of greater efficacy than is the righteousness of Christ, by the which we are justified before God. Therefore as Christ is of more power than Adam, even so the righteousness of Christ is of more efficacy than the sin of Adam. And if the sin of Adam were sufficient to make us sinners, and the children of wrath, without any sin actually done of us, much more shall be sufficient the righteousness of Christ to make us righteous, and the children of grace, without any of our good works. Neither can they be good except that before we do them we our own selves be made good and righteous by faith, as affirmed in like manner Saint Augustine. Hereby a man may know in how much error they be which for any sin, be it never so great, do despair of the mercy of God, and do think that he is not able to forgive, take away and pardon every sin, be it never so grievous, when he hath in his only-begotten Son already chastened all our faults and iniquities, and therefore consequently hath given a general pardon to all mankind, whereof every one hath benefit and fruition that believeth the gospel, that is to say, the most happy news which the apostles have published throughout the world, saying, We even in Christ's stead pray you that ye be reconciled unto God; for he hath made him which knew no sin to be sin for us, that we by his means might be that righteousness that before God is allowed. And Esay, who evidently setteth forth so well the passion of Jesus Christ and the cause of it, that in the writing of the apostles there is not found a better description or a plainer setting forth; he (I say), foreseeing this great benefit of the mercy of God, writeth this most godly sentence, Who giveth credence unto I our

preaching, or to whom is the arm of the Lord known? he shall grow before the Lord like as a branch, and as a root in a dry ground: he shall have neither beauty nor favor: when we look on him there shall be no fairness, we shall have no lust unto him; he shall be the most simple and despised of all: which yet hath good experience of sorrows and infirmities; we shall reckon him so simple and so vile, that we shall hide our faces from him. Howbeit (of a truth) he taketh only away our infirmity, and beareth our pain, yet we shall judge him as though he were plagued and cast down of God; whereas he (notwithstanding) shall be wounded for our offences and smitten for our wickedness; for the pain of our punishment shall be laid on him, and with his stripes shall we be healed. As for us, we go all astray like sheep, every one turneth his own way; but through him the Lord pardoneth all our sins. He shall be pained and troubled, and shall not open his mouth; he shall be led as a sheep to be slain, yet shall he be still as a lamb before the shearer, and not open his mouth. O great ingratitude and abominable thing it is if we, professing ourselves to be Christians, and knowing that the Son of God hath taken upon him all our sins, and has also cancelled them with his own most precious blood, having suffered himself to be chastened for us on the cross, if we (I say) nevertheless go about to justify ourselves, and to obtain the forgiveness of our sins by our own works, as though the merits, the righteousness, and the blood of Christ were not sufficient to do it unless we put thereunto our foolish righteousness, spotted with the love of ourselves and with the respect to rewards, and with a thousand vanities; for the which we ought rather to ask of God pardon than reward: and we remember not Saint Paul's threatening of the Galatians, who being beguiled by false preachers, not believing that justification by faith was of itself sufficient, did pretend that they would be justified still by the law, to whom Saint Paul said, Christ nothing helpeth you that will justify yourselves by the law; ye are fallen from grace; we therefore look for and hope in the Spirit, to be justified through faith.

And now if the seeking of righteousness and forgiveness of sins be by the keeping of the law, that the Lord with so great glory and open miracles gave in the hill of Sinai, be a losing of Christ and his grace, what shall we say then of them that pretend and endeavor to justify themselves before God with their own law and observations? Let those persons make the comparison, and after give their judgment. Insomuch as God will not give that honor and glory to his own law, will they then that he give it to their laws and constitutions? This honor he giveth alone to his only-begotten Son: he only with the sacrifice of his passion hath made satisfaction for all our sins, past, present, and to come, as Saint Paul saith to the Hebrews, 7, 9, 10 chapters, and Saint John in his first epistle, 1, 2 chapters. Through which—as oft as we—apply by faith this satisfaction of Christ to our souls, we obtain undoubtedly forgiveness of sins, and by his righteousness we become good and righteous before God. And therefore Saint Paul saith in the third [chapter of his] epistle to the Philippians, after that he had said that as touching the righteousness which is in the law he was unrebukeable, he joineth, But the things that were vantage unto me I counted loss for Christ's sake: yea, I think all things but loss for that excellent knowledge sake of Christ Jesus my Lord, for whom I have counted all things loss, and do judge them but dung, that I might win Christ, and might be found in him, not having mine own righteousness which is of the law, but that which springeth of the faith which is in Jesus Christ; I mean the righteousness which cometh of God through faith in knowing him. O words most notable, the which every Christian man should engrave in his heart, beseeching God to make him taste the same perfectly! Behold how Saint Paul sheweth clearly that whosoever knoweth Christ truly judgeth the works of the law loss, insomuch as they draw a man from trusting in Christ (in whom we ought to settle our health), and causeth him to trust in himself; and aggravating this sentence he joineth therewith, that he judged all things," dung, that be might win Christ, and might be found incorporate in him, showing that whosoever trusteth in works, and goeth about to be justified by them, he winneth riot Christ,

neither is by any means incorporate in him, and therefore in this truth consisteth the whole mystery of faith; and to the intent that they should the better understand that he said, he joineth to it and affirmeth boldly that he refused all outward justification, all righteousness founded in the observing of the law, trusting only and assuredly unto the righteousness that God giveth by faith to them that believe that he hath chastened in Christ [all our sins, who] (as saith the same Saint Paul) was made of him our wisdom, righteousness, holiness, and redemption, or forgiveness of sins; and therefore (as it is written) he that rejoiceth let him rejoice in the Lord, and not in his own works.

Truth it is that there are found some authorities of the Holy Scripture, which being evil-understanded seem to gainsay this holy doctrine of Saint Paul, and that they should attribute the justification and forgiveness of sins to works and charity; but those authorities are declared wondrous well by some others who have evidently proved that they that understand them in that sense understand them not. Let us then (most dearly beloved brethren) follow not the foolish opinion of the bewitched Galatians, but the verity that Saint Paul teacheth, and let us give all the praise of our justification to the mercy of God, and the merits of his Son, who with his blood bath delivered us from the dominion or danger of the law, from the tyranny of sin, and from death, and bath conducted us into the kingdom of God, by giving to us eternal felicity. I say he hath delivered us from the dominion of the law, for he hath given unto us his Spirit that sheweth us all truth, and he hath made perfect satisfaction for us to the law, and hath given the same satisfaction to all his members, that is to say, to all true Christians, so that they may safely come to the judgment-seat of God, being appareled with the righteousness of Christ, and delivered by him from the curse of the law which cannot any more accuse or condemn us, nor any more stir up our affections and appetites, nor augment sin in us. And therefore saith Saint Paul, The handwriting that was against us was cancelled by Christ, and disannulled in the wooden cross, our Christ having delivered us from the dominion of the law; consequently he hath delivered us from the tyranny of sin and of death, the which cannot hold us any more oppressed, being overcome first of Christ by his resurrection, and then consequently of us that be his members, on such wise, that we may say with St Paul [and with] Hosea the prophet, Death is overcome and destroyed. O death, where is thy sting? O hell, where is thy victory? The sting of death is sin, and the strength of sin is the law; but thanks be given to God, who bath given us victory through our Lord Jesus Christ. This is that most happy seed which hath trodden down the head of the most venomous serpent, that is to say the devil; and therefore all those that believe in Christ, putting all their hope and confidence in his mercy, do overcome with Christ sin, death, the devil, and hell. This is that blessed seed of Abraham, in the which God did promise to bless all nations.

Every man ought to have trodden down severally that horrible serpent, and to have delivered himself from the malediction or curse; but that enterprise was so great that the force or power of the whole world gathered together was not sufficient to bear it. Our God then being the Father of all mercy, moved with compassion of our miseries, gave us his only-begotten Son, who hath delivered us from the venom of the serpent, and is made our blessing and justification. Let us embrace, most dearly beloved brethren, the righteousness of Jesus Christ, let us make it ours through faith, let us have a sure confidence to be righteous, not by our own works, but by the merits of Christ, and let us live with quiet conscience towards God, and with assured trust that the righteousness of Christ doth annihilate all our unrighteousness, and maketh us righteous and holy in the sight of God, who forsomuch as he seeth us made by faith one body in his Son, doth not now any more take us as the children of Adam, but as his children, and maketh us heirs with his own legitimate Son of all his riches.

Don Benedetto, The Benefit of Christ
Crucified, *1541*

3.17 SUBSTITUTION, JOHN CALVIN

Because the curse caused by our guilt was awaiting us at God's heavenly judgment seat . . . Christ's condemnation before Pontius Pilate . . . is recorded, so that we might know that the penalty to which we were subject had been inflicted on this righteous man . . . when he was arraigned before a judgment-seat, accused and put under pressure by testimony, and sentenced to death by the words of a judge, we know by these records that this role was that of a guilty wrongdoer . . . we see the role of the sinner and criminal represented in Christ, yet from his shining innocence it becomes obvious that he was burdened with the misdoing of others rather than his own. . . . This is our acquittal, that the guilt which exposed us to punishment was transferred to the head of God's Son. At every point he substituted himself in our place to pay the price of our redemption.

At every point he substituted himself in our place to pay the price of our redemption.

John Calvin, Institutes of Christian Religion

3.18 THE CROSS AND THE NEW TESTAMENT, JOHN BRADFORD

The following inscription was written by John Bradford in the New Testament of a friend of his.

This book is called, The word of the cross, because the cross always accompanies it: so that if you will be a student thereof, you must needs prepare yourself to that cross which you began to learn, before you learned your alphabet. And Christ requires it of every one that will be His disciple, therein not swerving from the common trade (manner, editor) of callings or locations, for no profession or kind of life wants its cross. So that they are far overseen (much mistaken, editor) who think that the profession of the gospel, which the devil most envies, the world does hate, and the flesh most repines at, can be without a cross. Let us therefore enable us to take up our cross by denying ourselves.

John Bradford, from prison, 18th February, 1555

3.19 JESUS IMPUTING HIS RIGHTEOUSNESS TO US, RICHARD HOOKER

Richard Hooker (March 1554–November 3, 1600) was an influential Anglican theologian. He is arguably the co-founder (with Thomas Cranmer) of Anglican theological thought.

Christ hath merited righteousness for as many as are found in him. In him God findeth us, if we be faithful; for by faith we are incorporated into him. Then, although in ourselves we be altogether sinful and unrighteous, yet even the man who in himself is impious, full of iniquity, full of sin; him being found in Christ by faith, and having his sin in hatred through repentance; him God beholdeth with a gracious eye, putteth away his sin by not imputing it, taketh quite away the punishment due thereto, by pardoning it; and accepteth him in Jesus Christ, as perfectly righteous, as if he had fulfilled all that is commanded him in the law: shall I say, more perfectly righteous than if himself had fulfilled the whole law? I must take heed what I say; but the Apostle saith, "God made him which knew no sin, to be sin for us; that we might be made the righteousness of God in him." Such we are in the sight of God the Father, as is the very Son of God himself. Let it be counted folly, or phrensy, or fury, or whatsoever. It is our wisdom, and our comfort; we care for no knowledge in the world but this, that man hath sinned, and God hath suffered; that God hath made himself the sin of men, and that men are made the righteousness of God.

Richard Hooker, "A learned discourse of Justification"
Works, *Oxford: Clarendon Press, 1865*

3.20 FOR WHOM DID CHRIST DIE?, JOHN OWEN

John Owen (1616–August 24, 1683), was an English Nonconformist church leader. He wrote numerous influential theological books, among which are: On Apostasy *(1676), a sad account of religion under the Restoration;* On the Holy Spirit *(1677-1678) and* The Doctrine of Justification *(1677).*

The Father imposed His wrath due unto, and the Son underwent punishment for, either:

All the sins of all men.

All the sins of some men, or

Some of the sins of all men.

In which case it may be said:

That if the last be true, all men have some sins to answer for, and so, none are saved.

That if the second be true, then Christ, in their stead suffered for all the sins of all the elect in the whole world, and this is the truth.

But if the first be the case, why are not all men free from the punishment due unto their sins?

You answer, "Because of unbelief."

I ask, Is this unbelief a sin, or is it not? If it be, then Christ suffered the punishment due unto it, or He did not. If He did, why must that hinder them more than their other sins for which He died? If He did not, He did not die for all their sins!"

John Owen

3.21 THE DEATH OF DEATH IN THE DEATH OF CHRIST, JOHN OWEN

In general of the end of the death of Christ, as it is in the Scripture proposed.

By the end of the death of Christ, we mean in general, both,—first, that which his Father and himself intended in it; and, secondly, that which was effectually fulfilled and accomplished by it. Concerning either we may take a brief view of the expressions used by the Holy Ghost:—

1. For the first. Will you know the end wherefore, and the intention wherewith, Christ came into the world? Let us ask himself (who knew his own mind, as also all the secrets of his Father's bosom), and he will tell us that the "Son of man came to save that which was lost," Matt. 18:11,—to recover and save poor lost sinners; that was his intent and design, as is again asserted, Luke 19:10. Ask also his apostles, who know his mind, and they will tell you the same. So Paul, 1 Tim. 1:15, "This is a faithful saying, and worthy of all acceptation, that Christ Jesus came into the world to save sinners." Now, if you will

ask who these sinners are towards whom he hath this gracious intent and purpose, himself tells you, Matt. 20:28, that he came to "give his life a ransom for many"; in other places called us, believers, distinguished from the world: for be "gave himself for our sins, that he might deliver us from this present evil world, according to the will of God and our Father," Gal. 1:4. That was the will and intention of God, that he should give himself for us, that we might be saved, being separated from the world. They are his church: Eph. 5:25-27, "He loved the church, and gave himself for it; that he might sanctify and cleanse it with the washing of water by the word, that he might present it to himself a glorious church, not having spot, or wrinkle, or any such thing; but that it should be holy and without blemish:" which last words express also the very aim and end of Christ in giving himself for any, even that they may be made fit for God, and brought nigh unto him;—the like whereof is also asserted, Titus 2:14, "He gave himself for us, that he might redeem us from all iniquity, and purify unto himself a peculiar people, zealous of good works." Thus clear, then, and apparent, is the intention and design of Christ and his Father in this great work, even what it was, and towards whom,—namely, to save us, to deliver us from the evil world, to purge and wash us, to make us holy, zealous, fruitful in good works, to render us acceptable, and to bring us unto God; for through him "we have access into the grace wherein we stand," Rom. 5:2.

2. The effect, also, and actual product of the work itself, or what is accomplished and fulfilled by the death, blood-shedding, or oblation of Jesus Christ, is no less clearly manifested, but is as fully, and very often more distinctly, expressed.

First, Reconciliation with God, by removing and slaying the enmity that was between him and us; for "when we were enemies we were reconciled to God by the death of his Son," Rom. 5:10. "God was in him reconciling the world unto himself, not imputing their trespasses unto them," 2 Cor. 5:19; yea, he hath "reconciled us to himself by Jesus Christ," verse 18. And if you would know how this reconstruction was effected, the apostle will tell you that "he abolished in his flesh the enmity, the law of commandments consisting in ordinances; for to make in himself of twain one new man, so making peace; and that he might reconcile both unto God in one body by the cross, having slain the enmity thereby," Eph. 2:l5, 16; so that "he is our peace," verse l4.

Secondly, justification, by taking away the guilt of sins, procuring remission and pardon of them, redeeming us from their power, with the curse and wrath due unto us for them; for "by his own blood he entered into the holy place, having obtained eternal redemption for us," Heb. 9:12. "He redeemed us from the curse, being made a curse for us," Gal. 3:13; "his own self bearing our sins in his own body on the tree," 1 Pet. 2:24. We have "all sinned, and come short of the glory of God"; but are "justified freely by his grace through the redemption that is in Christ Jesus, whom God hath set forth to be a propitiation through faith in his blood, to declare his righteousness for the remission of sins," Rom. 3:23-25: for "in him we have redemption through his blood, even the forgiveness of sins," Col. 1:14.

Thirdly, sanctification, by the purging away of the uncleanness and pollution of our sins, renewing in us the image of God, and supplying us with the graces of the Spirit of holiness: for "the blood of Christ, who through the eternal Spirit offered himself to God, purgeth our consciences from dead works that we may serve the living God," Heb. 9:14; yea, "the blood of Jesus Christ cleanseth us from all sin," 1 John 1:7. "By himself he purged our sins," Heb. 1:3. To "sanctify the people with his own blood, he suffered without the gate," chap. 13:12. "He gave himself for the church to sanctify and cleanse it, that it should be holy and without blemish," Eph. 5:25-27. Peculiarly amongst the graces of the Spirit, "it is given to us," in-behalf-of Christ "for Christ's sake, to believe on him," Phil 1:29; God "blessing us in him with all spiritual blessings in heavenly places," Eph. 1:3.

Fourthly, adoption, with that evangelical liberty and all those glorious privileges which appertain to the sons of God; for "God sent forth his Son, made of a woman, made under the law, to redeem them that were under the law, that we might receive the adoption of sons," Gal. 4:4, 5.

Fifthly, Neither do the effects of the death of Christ rest here; they leave us not until we are settled in heaven, in glory and immortality for ever. Our inheritance is a "purchased possession," Eph 1:14. "And for this cause he is the mediator of the new testament, that by means of death, for the redemption of the transgressions that were under the first testament, they which are called might receive the promise of eternal inheritance," Heb. 9:15.

The sum of all is,—The death and blood-shedding of Jesus Christ hath wrought, and doth effectually procure, for all those that are concerned in it, eternal redemption, consisting in grace here and glory hereafter.

John Owen,
The Death of Death in the Death of Christ

3.22 THE FOUNDATION OF JESUS' IMPUTING HIS RIGHTEOUSNESS TO US, JOHN OWEN

The foundation of the imputation is union. Hereof there are many grounds and causes . . . but that which we have immediate respect unto, as the foundation of this imputation, is that whereby the Lord Christ and believers do actually coalesce into one mystical person. This is by the Holy Spirit inhabiting in him as the head of the church in all fullness, and in all believers according to their measure, whereby they become members of his mystical body. That there is such a union between Christ and believers is the faith of the catholic church and hath been so in all ages. Those who seem in our days to deny it, or question it, either know not what they say, or their minds are influenced by their doctrine who deny the divine persons of the Son and of the Spirit (i.e., the Socinians). Upon supposition of this union, reason will grant the imputation pleaded for to be reasonable; at least, there is such a peculiar ground for it as is not to be exemplified in any things natural or political among men."

John Owen, Works, *5. 209.*

3.23 DEATH OF CHRIST, SYNOD OF DORT

THE DEATH OF CHRIST, AND THE REDEMPTION OF MEN THEREBY

Article 1

God is not only supremely merciful, but also supremely just. And His justice requires (as He has revealed Himself in His Word) that our sins committed against His infinite majesty should be punished, not only with temporal but with eternal punishments, both in body and soul; which we cannot escape, unless satisfaction be made to the justice of God.

Article 2

Since, therefore, we are unable to make that satisfaction in our own persons, or to deliver ourselves from the wrath of God, He has been pleased of His infinite mercy to give His only begotten Son for our Surety, who was made sin, and became a curse for us and in our stead, that He might make satisfaction to divine justice on our behalf.

Article 3

The death of the Son of God is the only and most perfect sacrifice and satisfaction for sin, and is of infinite worth and value, abundantly sufficient to expiate the sins of the whole world.

Article 4

This death is of such infinite value and dignity because the person who submitted to it was not only begotten Son of God, of the same eternal and infinite essence with the Father and the Holy Spirit, which qualifications were necessary to constitute Him a Savior for us; and, moreover, because it was attended with a sense of the wrath and curse of God due to us for sin.

Article 5

Moreover, the promise of the gospel is that whosoever believes in Christ crucified shall not perish, but have eternal life. This promise, together with the command to repent and believe, ought to be declared and published to all nations, and to all persons promiscuously and without distinction, to whom God out of His good pleasure sends the gospel.

Article 6

And, whereas many who are called by the gospel do not repent nor believe in Christ, but perish in unbelief, this is not owing to any defect or insufficiency in the sacrifice offered by Christ upon the cross, but is wholly to be imputed to themselves.

Article 7

But as many as truly believe, and are delivered and saved from sin and destruction through the death of Christ, are indebted for this benefit solely to the grace of God given them in Christ from everlasting, and not to any merit of their own.

Article 8

For this was the sovereign counsel and most gracious will and purpose of God the Father that the quickening and saving efficacy of the most precious death of His Son should extend to all the elect, for bestowing upon them alone the gift of justifying faith, thereby to bring them infallibly to salvation; that is, it was the will of God that Christ by the blood of the cross, whereby He confirmed the new covenant, should effectually redeem out of every people, tribe, nation, and language, all those, and those only, who were from eternity chosen to salvation and given to Him by the Father; that He should confer upon them faith, which, together with all the other saving gifts of the Holy Spirit, He purchased for them by His death; should purge them from all sin, both original and actual, whether committed before or after believing; and having faithfully preserved them even to the end, should at last bring them, free from every spot and blemish, to the enjoyment of glory in His own presence forever.

Article 9

This purpose, proceeding from everlasting love towards the elect, has from the beginning of the world to this day been powerfully accomplished, and will henceforeward still continue to be accomplished, notwithstanding all the ineffectual opposition of the gates of hell; so that the elect in due time may be gathered together into one, and that there never may be wanting a Church composed of believers, the foundation of which is laid in the blood of Christ; which may steadfastly love and faithfully serve Him as its Savior (who, as a bridegroom for his bride, laid down His life for them upon the cross); and which may celebrate His praises here and through all eternity.

Synod of Dort, November 13, 1618—May 9, 1619

3.24 CHRISTIAN'S BURDEN ROLLS AWAY, JOHN BUNYAN

Now I saw in my dream, that the highway up which Christian was to go, was fenced on either side with a wall, and that wall was called Salvation. Isaiah 26:1. Up this way, therefore, did burdened Christian run, but not without great difficulty, because of the load on his back.

He ran thus till he came at a place somewhat ascending; and upon that place stood a cross, and a little below, in the bottom, a sepulcher. So I saw in my dream, that just as Christian came up with the cross, his burden loosed from off his shoulders, and fell from off his back, and began to tumble, and so continued to do till it came to the mouth of the sepulcher, where it fell in, and I saw it no more.

Then was Christian glad and lightsome, and said with a merry heart, "He hath given me rest by his sorrow, and life by his death." Then he stood still a while, to look and wonder; for it was very surprising to him that the sight of the cross should thus ease him of his burden. He looked, therefore, and looked again, even till the springs that were in his head sent the waters down his cheeks. Zech. 12:10. Now as he stood looking and weeping, behold, three Shining Ones came to him, and saluted him with, "Peace be to thee." So the first said to him, "Thy sins be forgiven thee," Mark 2:5; the second stripped him of his rags, and clothed him with change of raiment, Zech. 3:4; the third also set a mark on his forehead, Eph. 1:13, and gave him a roll with a seal upon it, which he bid him look on as he ran, and that he should give it in at the celestial gate: so they went their way. Then Christian gave three leaps for joy, and went on singing,

"Thus far did I come laden with my sin,
Nor could aught ease the grief that I was in,
Till I came hither. What a place is this!
Must here be the beginning of my bliss?
Must here the burden fall from off my back?
Must here the strings that bound it to me crack?
Blest cross! blest sepulcher! blest rather be
The Man that there was put to shame for me!"

John Bunyan, The Pilgrim's Progress

3.25 A TREE SET ON FIRE, THOMAS TRAHERNE

No-one has ever gone into heaven except the one who came from heaven—the Son of Man. Just as Moses lifted up the snake in the desert, so the Son of Man must be lifted up, that everyone who believes in him may have eternal life (John 3:13-14).

Above everything else, our Savior's cross is the throne of delights. That center of eternity, that Tree of Life in the middle of God's paradise. There we are entertained with the wonder of the ages. There we enter into the heart of the universe.

"When I am lifted up," says the Son of Man, "I will draw all men unto me." But by what cords? The cords of a man, the cords of love. The cross is the abyss of wonders, the center of desires, the school of virtues, the house of wisdom, the throne of love, the theatre of joys, and the place of sorrows; it is the root of happiness and the gate of heaven. It is the ensign lifted up for all nations.

There we may see God's goodness, wisdom, and power displayed. There we may see man's sin and infinite value. It is a well of life beneath, in which we may see the face of heaven above: and the only mirror wherein all things appear in their proper colors; that is, sprinkled in the blood of our Lord and Savior. That cross is a tree set on fire with invisible flame, that illuminates all the world. The flame is love: the love in his heart who died on it.

Thomas Traherne, Centuries

3.26 CHRIST THE MEDIATOR, THE WESTMINSTER CONFESSION OF FAITH

1. It pleased God, in his eternal purpose, to choose and ordain the Lord Jesus, his only begotten Son, to be the Mediator between God and men, the prophet, priest, and king; the head and Savior of the Church, the heir or all things, and judge of the world; unto whom he did, from all eternity, give a people to be his seed, and to be by him in time redeemed, called, justified, sanctified, and glorified.

2. The Son of God, the second Person in the Trinity, being very and eternal God, of one substance, and equal with the Father, did, when the fullness of time was come, take upon him man's nature, with all the essential

properties and common infirmities thereof; yet without sin: being conceived by he power of the Holy Ghost, in the womb of the Virgin Mary, of her substance. So that two whole, perfect, and distinct natures, the Godhead and the manhood, were inseparably joined together in one person, without conversion, composition, or confusion. Which person is very God and very man, yet one Christ, the only Mediator between God and man.

3. The Lord Jesus in his human nature thus united to the divine, was sanctified and anointed with the Holy Spirit above measure; having in him all the treasures of wisdom and knowledge, in whom it pleased the Father that all fullness should dwell: to the end that being holy, harmless, undefiled, and full of grace and truth, he might be thoroughly furnished to execute the office of a Mediator and Surety. Which office he took not unto himself, but was thereunto called by his Father; who put all power and judgment into his hand, and gave him commandment to execute the same.

4. This office the Lord Jesus did most willingly undertake, which, that he might discharge, he was made under the law, and did perfectly fulfill it; endured most grievous torments immediately in his soul, and most painful sufferings in his body; was crucified and died; was buried, and remained under the power of death, yet saw no corruption. On the third day he arose from the dead, with the same body in which he suffered; with which also he ascended into heaven, and there sitteth at the right hand of his Father, making intercession; and shall return to judge men and angels, at the end of the world.

5. The Lord Jesus, by his perfect obedience and sacrifice of himself, which he through the eternal Spirit once offered up unto God, hath fully satisfied the justice of his Father; and purchased not only reconciliation, but an everlasting inheritance in the kingdom of heaven, for all those whom the Father hath given unto him.

6. Although the work of redemption was not actually wrought by Christ till after his incarnation, yet the virtue, efficacy, and benefits thereof were communicated into the elect, in all ages successively from the beginning of the world, in and by those promises, types, and sacrifices wherein he was revealed, and signified to be the seed of the woman, which should bruise the serpent's head, and the Lamb slain from the beginning of the world, being yesterday and today the same and for ever.

7. Christ, in the work of mediation, acteth according to both natures; by each nature doing that which is proper to itself; yet by reason of the unity of the person, that which is proper to one nature is sometimes, in Scripture, attributed to the person denominated by the other nature.

8. To all those for whom Christ hath purchased redemption, he doth certainly and effectually apply and communicate the same; making intercession for them, and revealing unto them, in and by the Word, the mysteries of salvation; effectually persuading them by his Spirit to believe and obey; and governing their hearts by his Word and Spirit; overcoming all their enemies by his almighty power and wisdom, in such manner and ways as are most consonant to his wonderful and unsearchable dispensation.

The Westminster Confession of Faith

3.27 THE WORK OF CHRIST, MEDIATOR, THE WESTMINSTER LARGER CONFESSION

Question 36: Who is the Mediator of the covenant of grace?
Answer: The only Mediator of the covenant of grace is the Lord Jesus Christ, who, being the eternal Son of God, of one substance and equal with the Father, in the fullness of time became man, and so was and continues to be God and man, in two entire distinct natures, and one person, forever.

Question 37: How did Christ, being the Son of God, become man?
Answer: Christ the Son of God became man, by taking to himself a true body, and a reasonable soul, being conceived by the power of the Holy Ghost in the womb of the virgin Mary, of her substance, and born of her, yet without sin.

Question 38: Why was it requisite that the Mediator should be God?
Answer: It was requisite that the Mediator should be God, that he might sustain and keep the human nature from sinking under the infinite wrath of God, and the power of death; give worth and efficacy to his sufferings, obedience, and intercession; and to satisfy God's justice, procure his favor, purchase a peculiar people, give his Spirit to them, conquer all their enemies, and bring them to everlasting salvation.

Question 39: Why was it requisite that the Mediator should be man?
Answer: It was requisite that the Mediator should be man, that he might advance our nature, perform obedience to the law, suffer and make intercession for us in our nature, have a fellow feeling of our infirmities; that we might receive the adoption of sons, and have comfort and access with boldness unto the throne of grace.

Question 40: Why was it requisite that the Mediator should be God and man in one person?

Answer: It was requisite that the Mediator, who was to reconcile God and man, should himself be both God and man, and this in one person, that the proper works of each nature might be accepted of God for us, and relied on by us, as the works of the whole person.

Question 41: Why was our Mediator called Jesus?
Answer: Our Mediator was called Jesus, because he saves his people from their sins.

Question 42: Why was our Mediator called Christ?
Answer: Our Mediator was called Christ, because he was anointed with the Holy Ghost above measure; and so set apart, and fully furnished with all authority and ability, to execute the offices of prophet, priest, and king of his church, in the estate both of his humiliation and exaltation.

Question 43: How does Christ execute the office of a prophet?
Answer: Christ executes the office of a prophet, in his revealing to the church, in all ages, by his Spirit and Word, in divers ways of administration, the whole will of God, in all things concerning their edification and salvation.

Question 44: How does Christ execute the office of a priest?
Answer: Christ executes the office of a priest, in his once offering himself a sacrifice without spot to God, to be a reconciliation for the sins of his people; and in making continual intercession for them.

Question 45: How does Christ execute the office of a king?
Answer: Christ executes the office of a king, in calling out of the world a people to himself, and giving them officers, laws, and censures, by

which he visibly governs them; in bestowing saving grace upon his elect, rewarding their obedience, and correcting them for their sins, preserving and supporting them under all their temptations and sufferings, restraining and overcoming all their enemies, and powerfully ordering all things for his own glory, and their good; and also in taking vengeance on the rest, who know not God, and obey not the gospel.

Question 46: What was the estate of Christ's humiliation?
Answer: The estate of Christ's humiliation was that low condition, wherein he for our sakes, emptying himself of his glory, took upon him the form of a servant, in his conception and birth, life, death, and after his death, until his resurrection.

Question 47: How did Christ humble himself in his conception and birth?
Answer: Christ humbled himself in his conception and birth, in that, being from all eternity the Son of God, in the bosom of the Father, he was pleased in the fullness of time to become the son of man, made of a woman of low estate, and to be born of her; with divers circumstances of more than ordinary abasement.

Question 48: How did Christ humble himself in his life?
Answer: Christ humbled himself in his life, by subjecting himself to the law, which he perfectly fulfilled; and by conflicting with the indignities of the world, temptations of Satan, and infirmities in his flesh, whether common to the nature of man, or particularly accompanying that his low condition.

Question 49: How did Christ humble himself in his death?
Answer: Christ humbled himself in his death, in that having been betrayed by Judas, forsaken by his disciples, scorned and rejected by the world, condemned by Pilate, and tormented by his persecutors; having also conflicted with the terrors of death, and the powers of darkness, felt and borne the weight of God's wrath, he laid down his life an offering for sin, enduring the painful,

shameful, and cursed death of the cross.

Question 50: Wherein consisted Christ's humiliation after his death?
Answer: Christ's humiliation after his death consisted in his being buried, and continuing in the state of the dead, and under the power of death till the third day; which has been otherwise expressed in these words, he descended into hell.

Question 51: What was the estate of Christ's exaltation?
Answer: The estate of Christ's exaltation comprehends his resurrection, ascension, sitting at the right hand of the Father, and his coming again to judge the world.

Question 52: How was Christ exalted in his resurrection?
Answer: Christ was exalted in his resurrection, in that, not having seen corruption in death (of which it was not possible for him to be held), and having the very same body in which he suffered, with the essential properties thereof (but without mortality, and other common infirmities belonging to this life), really united to his soul, he rose again from the dead the third day by his own power; whereby he declared himself to be the Son of God, to have satisfied divine justice, to have vanquished death, and him that had the power of it, and to be Lord of quick and dead: all which he did as a public person, the head of his church, for their justification, quickening in grace, support against enemies, and to assure them of their resurrection from the dead at the last day.

Question 53: How was Christ exalted in his ascension?
Answer: Christ was exalted in his ascension, in that having after his resurrection often appeared unto and conversed with his apostles, speaking to them of the things pertaining to the kingdom of God, and giving them commission to preach the gospel to all nations, forty days after his resurrection, he, in our nature, and as our head, triumphing over enemies, visibly went up into the highest heavens, there to receive gifts for men, to raise up our affections thither, and to prepare a

place for us, where himself is, and shall continue till his second coming at the end of the world.

Question 54: How is Christ exalted in his sitting at the right hand of God?
Answer: Christ is exalted in his sitting at the right hand of God, in that as God-man he is advanced to the highest favor with God the Father, with all fullness of joy, glory, and power over all things in heaven and earth; and does gather and defend his church, and subdue their enemies; furnishes his ministers and people with gifts and graces, and makes intercession for them.

Question 55: How does Christ make intercession?
Answer: Christ makes intercession, by his appearing in our nature continually before the Father in heaven, in the merit of his obedience and sacrifice on earth, declaring his will to have it applied to all believers; answering all accusations against them, and procuring for them quiet of conscience, notwithstanding daily failings, access with boldness to the throne of grace, and acceptance of their persons and services.

Question 56: How is Christ to be exalted in his coming again to judge the world?
Answer: Christ is to be exalted in his coming again to judge the world, in that he, who was unjustly judged and condemned by wicked men, shall come again at the last day in great power, and in the full manifestation of his own glory, and of his Father's, with all his holy angels, with a shout, with the voice of the archangel, and with the trumpet of God, to judge the world in righteousness.

Question 57: What benefits has Christ procured by his mediation?
Answer: Christ, by his mediation, has procured redemption, with all other benefits of the covenant of grace.

Question 58: How do we come to be made partakers of the benefits which Christ has procured?
Answer: We are made partakers of the benefits which Christ has procured, by the application of them unto us, which is the work especially of God the Holy Ghost.

Question 59: Who are made partakers of redemption through Christ?
Answer: Redemption is certainly applied, and effectually communicated, to all those for whom Christ has purchased it; who are in time by the Holy Ghost enabled to believe in Christ according to the gospel.

The Westminster Larger Catechism

3.28 Faith in Christ's sin-bearing death is God's gift, The Westminster Confession of Faith

Those whom God effectually calleth he also freely justifieth; not by infusing righteousness into them, but by pardoning their sins, and by accounting and accepting their persons as righteous; not for anything wrought in them, or done by them, but for Christ's sake alone; not by imputing faith itself, the act of believing, or any other evangelical obedience, to them as their righteousness; but by imputing the obedience and satisfaction of Christ unto them they receiving and resting on him and his righteousness by faith; which faith they have not of themselves; it is the gift of God.

The Westminster Confession of Faith

3.29 The Passion and death of Jesus Christ, St. Alphonsus Liguori

We read in history of a proof of love so prodigious that it will be the admiration of all ages.

There was once a king, lord of many kingdoms, who had one only son, so beautiful, so holy, so amiable, that he was the delight of his father, who loved him as much as himself. This young prince had a great affection for one of his slaves; so much so that, the slave having committed a crime for which he had been condemned to death, the prince offered himself to die for the slave; the father, being jealous of justice, was satisfied to condemn his beloved son to death, in order that the slave might remain free from the punishment that he deserved: and thus the son died a malefactor's death, and the slave was freed from punishment.

This fact, the like of which has never happened in this world, and never will happen, is related in the Gospels, where we read that the Son of God, the Lord of the universe, seeing that man was condemned to eternal death in punishment of his sins, chose to take upon Himself human flesh, and thus to pay by His death the penalty due to man: He was offered because it was His own will (Is. 53:7). And his Eternal Father caused him to die upon the cross to save us miserable sinners: He spared not his own Son, but delivered Him up for us all (Rom. 8:32). What dost thou think, O devout soul, of this love of the Son and of the Father?

Thou didst, then, O my beloved Redeemer, choose by Thy death to sacrifice Thyself in order to obtain the pardon of my sins. And what return of gratitude shall I then make to Thee? Thou hast done too much to oblige me to love Thee; I should indeed be most ungrateful to Thee if I did not love Thee with my whole heart. Thou hast given for me Thy divine life; I, miserable sinner that I am, give Thee my own life. Yes, I will at least spend that period of my life that remains to me only in loving Thee, obeying Thee, and pleasing Thee.

O men, men! let us love this our Redeemer, who, being God, has not disdained to take upon Himself our sins, in order to satisfy by His sufferings for the chastisement which we have deserved: Surely He hath borne our infirmities, and carried our sorrows (Is. 53:4)

St. Augustine says that our Lord in creating us formed us by virtue of His power, but in redeeming us He has saved us from death by means of His sufferings: "He created us in his strength; he sought us back in his weakness."

How much do I not owe Thee, O Jesus my Savior! Oh, if I were to give my blood a thousand times over,—if I were to spend a thousand lives for Thee,—it would yet be nothing. Oh, how could anyone that meditated much on the love which Thou hast shown him in Thy Passion, love anything else but Thee? Through the love with which Thou didst love us on the cross, grant me the grace to love Thee with my whole heart. I love Thee, infinite Goodness; I love Thee above every other good; and I ask nothing more of Thee but Thy holy love.

St. Alphonsus Liguori

3.30 FOR WHOM DID CHRIST DIE?, CHARLES HODGE

1. STATE OF THE QUESTION

This is a question between Augustinians and Anti-Augustinians. The former believing that God from all eternity having elected some to everlasting life, had a special reference to their salvation in the mission and work of his Son. The latter, denying that there has been any such election of a part of the human family to salvation maintain that the mission and work of Christ had an equal reference to all mankind.

The question, therefore, does not, in the first place, concern the nature of Christ's work. It is true, if it be denied that his work was a satisfaction for sin, and affirmed that it was merely didactic; that his life, sufferings, and death were designed to reveal and confirm truth; then it would follow of course that it had no reference to one class of men more than to another, or to men more than to angels. Truth is designed for the illumination of all the minds to which it is presented. But admitting the work of Christ to have been a true satisfaction for sin, its design may still be an open question. Accordingly, Lutherans and Reformed, although they agree entirely as to the nature of the atonement, differ as to its design. The former maintain that it had an equal reference to all mankind, the latter that it had special reference to the elect.

In the second place, the question does not concern the value of Christ's satisfaction. That Augustinians admit to be infinite. Its value depends on the dignity of the sacrifice; and as no limit can be placed to the dignity of the Eternal Son of God who offered Himself for our sins, so no limit can be assigned to the meritorious value of his work. It is a gross misrepresentation of the Augustinian doctrine to say that it teaches that Christ suffered so much for so many; that He would have suffered more had more been included in the purpose of salvation. This is not the doctrine of any Church on earth, and never has been. What was sufficient for one was sufficient for all. Nothing less than the light and heat of the sun is sufficient for any one plant or animal.

But what is absolutely necessary for each is abundantly sufficient for the infinite number and variety of plants and animals which fill the earth. All that Christ did and suffered would have been necessary had only one human soul been the object of redemption; and nothing different and nothing more would have been required had every child of Adam been saved through his blood.

In the third place, the question does not concern the suitableness of the atonement. What was suitable for one was suitable for all. The righteousness of Christ, the merit of his obedience and death, is needed for justification by each individual of our race, and therefore is needed by all. It is no more appropriate to one man than to another. Christ fulfilled the conditions of the covenant under which all men were placed. He rendered the obedience required of all, and suffered the penalty which all had incurred; and therefore his work is equally suited to all.

In the fourth place, the question does not concern the actual application of the redemption purchased by Christ. The parties to this controversy are agreed that some only, and not all of mankind are to be actually saved.

The whole question, therefore, concerns simply the purpose of God in the mission of his Son. What was the design of Christ's coming into the world, and doing and suffering all He actually did and suffered? Was it merely to make the salvation of all men possible; to remove the obstacles which stood in the way of the offer of pardon and acceptance to sinners? or, was it specially to render certain the salvation of his own people, i.e., of those given to Him by the Father? The latter question is affirmed by Augustinians, and denied by their opponents. It is obvious that if there be no election of some to everlasting life, the atonement can have no special reference to the elect. It must have equal reference to all mankind. But it does not follow from the assertion of its having a special reference to the elect that it had no reference to the non-elect. Augustinians readily admit that the death of Christ had a relation to man, to the whole human family, which it had not to, the fallen angels. It is the ground on which salvation is offered to every creature under heaven who hears, the gospel; but it gives no authority for a like offer to apostate angels. It moreover secures, to the whole race at large, and to all classes of men, innumerable, blessings, both providential and religious. It was, of course, designed to produce these effects; and, therefore, He died to secure them. In view of the effects which the death of Christ produces on the relation of all mankind to God, it has in all ages been customary with Augustinians to say that Christ died "*sufficienter pro omnibus, efficaciter tantum pro electis*;" sufficiently for all, efficaciously only for the elect. There is a sense, therefore, in which He died for all, and there is a sense in which He died for the elect alone. The simple question is, Had the death of Christ a reference to the elect which it had not to other men? Did He come into the world to secure the salvation of those given to Him by the Father, so that the other effects of his work are merely incidental to what was done for the attainment of that object?

2. PROOF OF THE AUGUSTINIAN DOCTRINE

That these questions must be answered in the affirmative, is evident,—

From the nature of the covenant of redemption.

a. It is admitted that there was a covenant between the Father and the Son in relation to the salvation of men. It is admitted that Christ came into the world in execution of that covenant. The nature of the covenant, therefore, determines the object of his death. According to one view, man having by his fall lost the ability of fulfilling, the conditions of the covenant of life, God, for Christ's sake, enters into a new covenant, offering men salvation upon other and easier terms; namely, as some say, faith and repentance, and others evangelical obedience. If such be the nature of the plan of salvation, then it is obvious that the work of Christ has equal reference to all mankind. According to another view, the work

of Christ was designed to secure the pardon of original sin and the gift of the Holy Spirit for all men, Jews or Gentiles, and those are saved who duly improve the grace they severally receive. The former is the doctrine of the ancient Semi-Pelagians and modern Remonstrants; the latter of the Wesleyan Arminians. The Lutherans hold that God sent his Son to make a full and real legal satisfaction for the sins of all mankind; and that on the ground of this perfect satisfaction the offer of salvation is made to all who hear the gospel; that grace is given (in the word and sacraments) which, if unresisted, is sufficient to secure their salvation. The French theologians at Saumur, in the 17th century, taught also that Christ came into the world to do whatever was necessary for the salvation of men. But God, foreseeing that, if left to themselves, men would universally reject the offers of mercy, elected some to be the subjects of his saving grace by which they are brought to faith and repentance. According to this view of the plan of salvation, election is subordinate to redemption. God first redeems all and then elects some. This is the view extensively adopted in this country. According to Augustinians, men, by their fall, having sunk into a state of sin and misery, might justly have been left, as were the fallen angels, to perish in their sins. But God, in his infinite mercy, having determined to save a multitude whom no man could number, gave them to his Son as his inheritance, provided He would assume their nature and fulfill all righteousness in their stead. In the accomplishment of this plan Christ did come into the world, and did obey and suffer in the place of those thus given to Him, and for their salvation. This was the definite object of his mission, and therefore his death had a reference to them which it could not possibly have to those whom God determined to leave to the just recompense of their sins. Now this plan only supposes that God determined from eternity to do what in time He has actually accomplished. If it were just that all men should perish on account of their sin it was just to leave a portion of the race thus to perish, while the salvation of the other portion is a matter of unmerited favor. It can hardly be denied that God did thus enter into covenant with his Son. That is, that He did promise Him the salvation of his people as the reward of his incarnation and sufferings; that Christ did come into the world and suffer and die on that condition, and, having performed the condition, is entitled to the promised reward. These are facts so clearly and so repeatedly stated in the Scriptures as not to admit of their being called into question. But if such is the plan of God respecting the salvation of men then it of necessity follows that election precedes redemption; that God had determined whom He would save before He sent his Son to save them. Therefore our Lord said that those given to Him by his Father should certainly come to Him, and that He would raise them up at the last day. These Scriptural facts cannot be admitted without its being also admitted that the death of Christ had a reference to his people, whose salvation it rendered certain, which it had not to others whom, for infinitely wise reasons, God determined to leave to themselves. It follows, therefore, from the nature of the covenant of redemption, as presented in the Bible, that Christ did not die equally for all mankind, but that He gave Himself for his people and for their redemption.

Argument from the doctrine of election
b. This follows also almost necessarily from the doctrine of election. Indeed it never was denied that Christ died specially for the elect until the doctrine of election itself was rejected. Augustine, the follower and expounder of St. Paul, taught that God out of his mere good pleasure had elected some to everlasting life, and held that Christ came into the world to suffer and die for their salvation. He purchased them with his own precious blood. The Semi-Pelagians, in denying the doctrine of election, of course denied that Christ's death had more reference to one class of men than to another. The Latin Church, so long as it held to the Augustinian doctrine of election, held also to Augustine's doctrine concerning the design and objects of Christ's death. All through the Middle Ages this was one of the distinctive doctrines of those who resisted the progress of the Semi-Pelagian party in the Western Church. At the time of

the Reformation the Lutherans, so long as they held to the one doctrine held also to the other. The Reformed, in holding fast the doctrine of election, remained faithful to their denial of the doctrine that the work of Christ had equal reference to all mankind. It was not until the Remonstrants in Holland, under the teaching of Arminius, rejected the Church doctrine of original sin, of the inability of fallen man to anything spiritually good, the sovereignty of God in election, and the perseverance of the saints, that the doctrine that the atonement had a special reference to the people of God was rejected. It is, therefore, a matter of history that the doctrine of election and the Augustinian doctrine as to the design of the work of Christ have been inseparably united. As this connection is historical so also is it logical. The one doctrine necessarily involves the other. If God from eternity determined to save one portion of the human race and not another, it seems to be a contradiction to say that the plan of salvation had equal reference to both portions; that the Father sent his Son to die for those whom He had predetermined not to save, as truly as, and in the same sense that He gave Him up for those whom He had chosen to make the heirs of salvation.

Express declarations of Scripture
c. We accordingly find numerous passages in which the design of Christ's death is declared to be, to save his people from their sins. He did not come merely to render their salvation possible, but actually to deliver them from the curse of the law, and from the power of sin. This is included in all the Scriptural representations of the nature and design of his work. No man pays a ransom without the certainty of the deliverance of those for whom it is paid. It is not a ransom unless it actually redeems. And an offering is no sacrifice unless it actually expiates and propitiates. The effect of a ransom and sacrifice may indeed be conditional, but the occurrence of the condition will be rendered certain before the costly sacrifice is offered.

There are also very numerous passages in which it is expressly declared that Christ gave Himself for his Church (Ephesians 5:25); that

He laid down his life for his sheep (John 10:15); that He laid down his life for his friends (John 15:13); that He died that He might gather together in one the children of God that are scattered abroad (John 11:52); that it was the Church which He purchased with his blood (Acts 20:28). When mankind are divided into two classes, the Church and the world, the friends and the enemies of God, the sheep and the goats, whatever is affirmed distinctively of the one class is impliedly denied of the other. When it is said that Christ loved his Church and gave Himself for it, that He laid down his life for his sheep, it is clear that something is said of the Church and of the sheep, which is not true of those who belong to neither. When it is said that a man labors and sacrifices health and strength for his children, it is thereby denied that the motive which controls him is mere philanthropy, or that the design he has in view is the good of society. He may indeed be a philanthropist, and he may recognize the fact that the well-being of his children ill promote the welfare of society, but this does not alter the case. It still remains true that love for his children is the motive, and their good his object. It is difficult, in the light of Ephesians 5:25, where the death of Christ is attributed to his love of his Church, and is said to have been designed for its sanctification and salvation, to believe that He gave Himself as much for reprobates as for those whom He intended to save. Every assertion, therefore that Christ died for a people, is a denial of the doctrine that He died equally for all men.

Argument from the special love of God
d. By the love of God is sometimes meant his goodness, of which all sensitive creatures are the objects and of whose benefits they are the recipients. Sometimes it means his special regard for the children of men, not only as rational creatures, but also as the offspring of Him who is the Father of the spirits of all men. Sometimes it means that peculiar, mysterious, sovereign, immeasurable love which passes knowledge, of which his own people, the Church of the first-born whose names are written in heaven, are the objects. Of this love it is taught,

(1.) That it is infinitely great.

(2.) That it is discriminating, fixed on some and not upon others of the children of men. It is compared to the love of a husband for his wife; which from its nature is exclusive.

(3.) That it is perfectly gratuitous and sovereign, i.e., not founded upon the special attractiveness of its objects, but like parental affection, on the mere fact that they are his children.

(4.) That it is immutable.

(5.) That it secures all saving blessings, and even all good; so that even afflictions are among its fruits intended for the greater good of the sufferer. Now to this love, not to general goodness, not to mere philanthropy, but to this peculiar and infinite love, the gift of Christ is uniformly referred. Herein is love, not that we loved God, but that He loved us, and sent his Son to be the propitiation for our sins. (1 John 4:10.) Hereby perceive we the love of God (or, hereby we know what love is), because He (Christ) laid down his life for us. (1 John 3:16.) God commendeth his love toward us, in that while we were yet sinners, Christ died for us. (Romans 5:8.) Greater love hath no man than this, that a man lay down his life for his friends. (John 15:13.) Nothing shall be able to separate us from the love of God which is in Christ Jesus. (Romans 8:35-39.) He that spared not his own Son, but delivered him up for us all, how shall he not with him also freely give us all things? (Romans 8:32.) The whole argument of the Apostle in Romans 5:1-11, and especially throughout the eighth chapter, is founded upon this infinite and immutable love of God to his people. From this he argues their absolute security for time and eternity. Because He thus loved them He gave his Son for them; and, having done this, He would certainly give them everything necessary for their salvation. No enemy should ever prevail against them; nothing could ever separate them from his love. This whole argument is utterly irreconcilable with the hypothesis that Christ died equally for all men. His death is referred to the peculiar love of God to his people, and was the pledge of all other saving gifts. This peculiar love of God is not founded upon the fact that its objects are believers, for

He loved them as enemies, as ungodly, and gave his Son to secure their being brought to faith, repentance, and complete restoration to the divine image. It cannot, therefore, be explained away into mere general benevolence or philanthropy. It is a love which secured the communication of Himself to its objects, and rendered their salvation certain; and consequently could not be bestowed upon all men, indiscriminately. This representation is so predominant in the Scriptures, namely, that the peculiar love of God to his people, to his Church, to the elect, is the source of the gift of Christ, of the mission of the Holy Spirit, and of all other saving blessings, that it cannot be ignored in any view of the plan and purpose of salvation. With this representation every other statement of the Scriptures must be consistent; and therefore the theory which denies this great and precious truth, and which assumes that the love which secured the gift of God's eternal Son, was mere benevolence which had all men for its object, many of whom are allowed to perish, must be unscriptural.

Argument from the believer's union with Christ

e. Another argument is derived from the nature of the union between Christ and his people. The Bible teaches:

(1.) That a certain portion of the human race were given to Christ.

(2.) That they were given to Him before the foundation of the world.

(3.) That all thus given to Him will certainly come to Him and be saved.

(4.) That this union, so far as it was from eternity, is not a union of nature, nor by faith, nor by the indwelling of the Holy Spirit. It was a federal union.

(5.) That Christ, therefore, was a federal head and representative. As such He came into the world, and all He did and suffered was as a representative, as a substitute, one acting in the place and for the benefit of others. But He was the representative of those given to Him, i.e., of those who were in Him. For it was this gift and the union consequent upon it, that gave Him his representative character, or constituted Him a federal head.

He was therefore the federal head, not of the human race, but of those given to Him by the Father. And, therefore, his work, so far as its main design is concerned, was for them alone. Whatever reference it had to others was subordinate and incidental. All this is illustrated and proved by the Apostle in Romans 5:12-21, in the parallel which he draws between Adam and Christ. All mankind were in Adam. He was the federal head and representative of his race. All men sinned in him and fell with him in his first transgression. The sentence of condemnation for his one offence passed upon all men. In like manner Christ was the representative of his people. He acted for them. What He did and suffered in their place, or as their representative, they in the eye of the law, did and suffered. By his obedience they are justified. As all in Adam died, so all in Christ are made alive. Such is the nature of the union in both cases, that the sin of the one rendered certain and rendered just the death of all united to Adam, and the righteousness of the other rendered certain and just the salvation of all who are in Him. The sin of Adam did not make the condemnation of all men merely possible; it was the ground of their actual condemnation. So the righteousness of Christ did not make the salvation of men merely possible, it secured the actual salvation of those for whom He wrought. As it would be unreasonable to say that Adam acted for those who were not in him; so it is unscriptural to say that Christ acted for those who were not in Him. Nevertheless, the act of Adam as the head and representative of his race, was fruitful of evil consequences, not to man only, but to the earth and all that it contains; and so the work of Christ is fruitful of good consequences to others than those for whom He acted. But this does not justify anyone in saying that Adam acted as much as the representative of the brute creation, as of his posterity; neither does it justify the assertion that Christ died for all mankind in the same sense that He died for his own people. This is all so clearly revealed in Scripture that it extorts the assent of those who are decidedly opposed to the Augustinian system. One class of those opponents, of whom Whitby may be taken as a representative, admit the truth of all that has been said of the representative character of Adam and Christ. But they maintain that as Adam represented the whole race, so also did Christ; and as in Adam all men die, so in Christ are all made alive. But they say that this has nothing to do with spiritual death in the one case, or with the salvation of the soul in the other. The death which came on all men for the sin of Adam, was merely the death of the body; and the life which comes on all through Christ, is the restoration of the life of the body at the resurrection. The Wesleyans take the same view of the representative character of Christ and of Adam. Each stood for all mankind. Adam brings upon all men the guilt of his first sin and corruption of nature. Christ secures the removal of the guilt of original sin and a seed of grace, or principle of spiritual life, for all men. So also one class of Universalists hold that as all men are condemned for the sin of Adam, so all are actually saved by the work of Christ. Rationalists also are ready to admit that Paul does teach all that Augustinians understand him to teach, but they say that this was only his Jewish mode of presenting the matter. It is not absolute truth, but a mere transient form suited to the age of the Apostles. In all these cases, however, the main fact is conceded. Christ did act as a representative; and what He did secured with certainty the benefits of his work for those for whom He acted. This being conceded, it of course follows that He acted as the representative and substitute of those only who are ultimately to be saved.

f. There is another argument on this subject generally presented, which ought not to be overlooked. The unity of the priestly office rendered the functions of the priesthood inseparable. The high-priest interceded for all those for whom he offered sacrifice. The one service did not extend beyond the other. He bore upon his breast the names of the twelve tribes. He represented them in drawing near to God. He offered sacrifices for their sins on the great day of atonement, and for them he interceded, and for no others. The sacrifice and the intercession went together. What was true of the Aaronic priests, is true of Christ. The former, we are told, were the types of the latter. Christ's functions as priest are in like manner united. He intercedes for all for whom He offered Himself as a sacrifice. He himself, however, says expressly, "I pray not for the world, but for them which thou hast given me." (John 17:9.) Him the Father heareth always, and, therefore, He cannot be assumed to intercede for those who do not actually receive the benefits of his redemption.

The church doctrine embraces all the facts of the case
g. The final test of any theory is its agreeing or disagreeing with the facts to be explained. The difficulty with all the Anti-Augustinian views as to the design of Christ's death, is that while they are consistent with more or less of the Scriptural facts connected with the subject, they are utterly irreconcilable with not less clearly revealed and equally important. They are consistent, for example, with the fact that the work of Christ lays the foundation for the offer of the gospel to all men, with the fact that men are justly condemned for the rejection of that offer; and with the fact that the Scriptures frequently assert that the work of Christ had reference to all men. All these facts can be accounted for on the assumption, that the great design of Christ's death was to make the salvation of all men possible, and that it had equal reference to every member of our race. But there are other facts which this theory leaves out of view, and with which it cannot be reconciled. On the other hand it is claimed that the Augustinian doctrine recognizes all the Scriptural assertions connected with the subject, and reconciles them all. If this be so, it must be the doctrine of the Bible. The facts which are clearly revealed concerning the death or work of Christ are,

(1.) That God from eternity gave a people to his Son.

(2.) That the peculiar and infinite love of God to his people is declared to be the motive for the gift of his Son; and their salvation the design of his mission.

(3.) That it was as their representative, head, and substitute, He came into the world, assumed our nature, fulfilled all righteousness, and bore the curse of the law.

(4.) That the salvation of all given to Him by the Father, is thus rendered absolutely certain.

That the Augustinian scheme agrees with these great Scriptural facts, is readily admitted, but it is denied that it accounts for the fact that on the ground of the work of Christ, salvation may be offered to every human being; and that all who hear and reject the gospel, are justly condemned for their unbelief. That these are Scriptural facts cannot be denied, and if the Augustinian doctrine does not provide for them, it must be false or defective. There are different grounds on which it is assumed that the Augustinian doctrine does not provide for the universal offer of the gospel. One is, the false assumption that Augustinians teach that the satisfaction of Christ was in all respects analogous to the payment of a debt, a satisfaction to commutative or commercial justice. Hence it is inferred that Christ suffered so much for so many; He paid so much for one soul, and so much for another, and of course He would have been called upon to pay more if more were to have been saved. If this be so, then it is clear that the work of Christ can justify the offer of salvation to those only whose debts He has actually cancelled. To this view of the case it may be remarked,—

(1.) That this doctrine was never held by any historical church and the ascription of it to Augustinians can only be accounted for on the ground of ignorance.

(2.) It involves the greatest confusion of ideas. It confounds the obligations which arise among men as owners of property, with the obligations of rational creatures to an infinitely holy God. A debtor is one owner, and a creditor is another. Commutative justice requires that they should settle their mutual claims equitably. But God is not one owner and the sinner another. They do not stand in relation to each other as two proprietors. The obligation which binds a debtor to pay a creditor, and the principle which impels a just God to punish sin, are entirely distinct. God is the absolute owner of all things. We own

nothing. We cannot sustain to Him, in this respect, the relation of a debtor to his creditor. The objection in question, therefore, is founded on an entire mistake or misrepresentation of the attribute of justice, to which, according to Augustinians, the satisfaction of Christ is rendered. Because the sin of Adam was the ground of the condemnation of his race, does any man infer that He sinned so much for one man and so much for another? Why then should it be said that because the righteousness of Christ is the judicial ground of our salvation, that He did and suffered so much for one man and so much for another?

(3.) As this objection is directed against a theory which no Church has ever adopted, and as it attributes to God a form of justice which cannot possibly belong to Him, so it is contrary to those scriptural representations on which the Augustinian doctrine is founded. The Scriptures teach that Christ saves us as a priest, by offering Himself as a sacrifice for our sins. But a sacrifice was not a payment of a debt, the payment of so much for so much. A single victim was sometimes a sacrifice for one individual; sometimes for the whole people. On the great day of atonement the scape-goat bore the sins of the people, whether they were more or less numerous. It had no reference at all to the number of persons for whom atonement was to be made. So Christ bore the sins of his people; whether they were to be a few hundreds, or countless millions, or the whole human family, makes no difference as to the nature of his work, or as to the value of his satisfaction. What was absolutely necessary for one, was abundantly sufficient for all.

The objection, however, is at times presented in a somewhat different form. Admitting the satisfaction of Christ to be in itself of infinite value, how can it avail for the non-elect if it was not designed for them? It does not avail for the fallen angels, because it was not intended for them; how then can it avail for the non-elect, if not designed for them? How can a ransom, whatever its intrinsic value, benefit those for whom it was not paid? In this form the objection is far more specious. It is, however, fallacious. It overlooks the peculiar nature of the case. It ignores the fact that all mankind were placed under the same constitution or covenant. What was demanded for the salvation of one was demanded for the salvation of all. Every man is required to satisfy the demands of the law. No man is required to do either more or less. If those demands are satisfied by a representative or substitute, his work is equally available for all. The secret purpose of God in providing such a substitute for man, has nothing to do with the nature of his work, or with its appropriateness. The righteousness of Christ being of infinite value or merit, and being in its nature precisely what all men need, may be offered to all men. It is thus offered to the elect and to the non-elect; and it is offered to both classes conditionally. That condition is a cordial acceptance of it as the only ground of justification. If any of the elect (being adults) fail thus to accept of it, they perish. If any of the non-elect should believe, they would be saved. What more does any Anti-Augustinian scheme provide? The advocates of such schemes say, that the design of the work of Christ was to render the salvation of all men possible. All they can mean by this is, that if any man (elect or non-elect) believes, he shall, on the ground of what Christ has done, be certainly saved. But Augustinians say the same thing. Their doctrine provides for this universal offer of salvation, as well as any other scheme. It teaches that God in effecting the salvation of his own people, did whatever was necessary for the salvation of all men, and therefore to all the offer may be, and in fact is made in the gospel. If a ship containing the wife and children of a man standing on the shore is wrecked, he may seize a boat and hasten to their rescue. His motive is love to his family; his purpose is to save them. But the boat which he has provided may be large enough to receive the whole of the ship's company. Would there be any inconsistency in his offering them the opportunity to escape? Or, would this offer prove that he had no special love to his own family and no special design to secure their safety. And if any or all of those to whom the offer was made, should refuse to accept it, some from one reason, some from

another; some because they did not duly appreciate their danger; some because they thought they could save themselves; and some from enmity to the man from whom the offer came, their guilt and folly would be just as great as though the man had no special regard to his own family, and no special purpose to effect their deliverance. Or, if a man's family were with others held in captivity, and from love to them and with the purpose of their redemption, a ransom should be offered sufficient for the delivery of the whole body of captives, it is plain that the offer of deliverance might be extended to all on the ground of that ransom, although specially intended only for a part of their number. Or, a man may make a feast for his own friends, and the provision be so abundant that he may throw open his doors to all who are willing to come. This is precisely what God, according to the Augustinian doctrine, has actually done. Out of special love to his people, and with the design of securing their salvation, He has sent his Son to do what justifies the offer of salvation to all who choose to accept of it. Christ, therefore, did not die equally for all men. He laid down his life for his sheep; He gave Himself for his Church. But in perfect consistency with all this, He did all that was necessary, so far as a satisfaction to justice is concerned, all that is required for the salvation of all men. So that all Augustinians can join with the Synod of Dort in saying, "No man perishes for want of an atonement."

If the atonement be limited in design, it must be restricted in the offer.

h. There is still another ground on which it is urged that Augustinians cannot consistently preach the gospel to every creature. Augustinians teach, it is urged, that the work of Christ is a satisfaction to divine justice. From this it follows that justice cannot condemn those for whose sins it has been satisfied. It cannot demand that satisfaction twice, first from the substitute and then from the sinner himself. This would be manifestly unjust, far worse than demanding no punishment at all. From this it is inferred that the satisfaction or righteousness of Christ, if the ground on which a sinner may be forgiven, is the ground on which he must be forgiven. It is not the ground on which he may be forgiven, unless it is the ground on which he must be forgiven. If the atonement be limited in design it must be limited in its nature, and if limited in its nature it must be limited in its offer. This objection again arises from confounding a pecuniary and a judicial satisfaction between which Augustinians are so careful to discriminate. There is no grace in accepting, a pecuniary satisfaction. It cannot be refused. It *ipso facto* liberates. The moment the debt is paid the debtor is free; and that without any condition. Nothing of this is true in the case of judicial satisfaction. If a substitute be provided and accepted it is a matter of grace. His satisfaction does not *ipso facto* liberate. It may accrue to the benefit of those for whom it is made at once or at a remote period; completely or gradually; on conditions or unconditionally; or it may never benefit them at all unless the condition on which its application is suspended be performed. These facts are universally admitted by those who hold that the work of Christ was a true and perfect satisfaction to divine justice. The application of its benefits is determined by the covenant between the Father and the Son. Those for whom it was specially rendered are not justified from eternity; they are not born in a justified state; they are by nature, or birth, the children of wrath even as others. To be the children of wrath is to be justly exposed to divine wrath. They remain in this state of exposure until they believe, and should they die (unless in infancy) before they believe they would inevitably perish notwithstanding the satisfaction made for their sins. It is the stipulations of the covenant which forbid such a result. Such being the nature of the judicial satisfaction rendered by Christ to the law, under which all men are placed, it may be sincerely offered to all men with the assurance that if they believe it shall accrue to their salvation. His work being specially designed for the salvation of his own people, renders, through the conditions of the covenant, that event certain; but this is perfectly consistent with its being made the ground of the general offer of the gospel.

Lutherans and Reformed agree entirely, as before stated, in their views of the nature of the satisfaction of Christ, and consequently, so far as that point is concerned, there is the same foundation for the general offer of the gospel according to either scheme. What the Reformed or Augustinians hold about election does not affect the nature of the atonement. That remains the same whether designed for the elect or for all mankind. It does not derive its nature from the secret purpose of God as to its application.

CERTAIN PASSAGES OF SCRIPTURE CONSIDERED

Admitting, however, that the Augustinian doctrine that Christ died specially for his own people does account for the general offer of the gospel, how is it to be reconciled with those passages which, in one form or another, teach that He died for all men? In answer to this question, it may be remarked in the first place that Augustinians do not deny that Christ died for all men. What they deny is that He died equally, and with the same design, for all men. He died for all, that He might arrest the immediate execution of the penalty of the law upon the whole of our apostate race; that He might secure for men the innumerable blessings attending their state on earth, which, in one important sense, is a state of probation; and that He might lay the foundation for the offer of pardon and reconciliation with God, on condition of faith and repentance. These are the universally admitted consequences of his satisfaction, and therefore they all come within its design. By this dispensation it is rendered manifest to every intelligent mind in heaven and upon earth, and to the finally impenitent themselves, that the perdition of those that perish is their own fault. They will not come to Christ that they may have life. They refuse to have Him to reign over them. He calls but they will not answer. He says, "Him that cometh to me, I will in no wise cast out." Every human being who does come is saved. This is what is meant when it is said, or implied in Scripture, that Christ gave Himself as a propitiation, not for our sins only, but for the sins of the whole world. He was a propitiation effectually for the sins of his people, and sufficiently for the sins of the whole world. Augustinians have no need to wrest the Scriptures. They are under no necessity of departing from their fundamental principle that it is the duty of the theologian to subordinate his theories to the Bible, and teach not what seems to him to be true or reasonable, but simply what the Bible teaches.

But, in the second place, it is to be remarked that general terms are often used indefinitely and not comprehensively. They mean all kinds, or classes, and not all and every individual. When Christ said, "I, if I be lifted up from the earth, will draw all men unto me," He meant men of all ages, classes, and conditions, and not every individual man. When God predicted that upon the advent of the Messiah He would pour out his Spirit upon all flesh, all that was foretold was a general effusion of the Holy Ghost. And when it is said that all men shall see (experience) the salvation of God, it does not mean that all men individually, but that a vast multitude of all classes shall be saved. The same remark applies to the use of the term world. It means men, mankind, as a race or order of beings. No one hesitates to call the Lord Jesus the "Salvator hominum." He is so hailed and so worshipped wherever his name is known. But no one means by this that He actually saves all mankind. What is meant is that He is our Savior, the Savior of men, not of angels, not of Jews exclusively, nor yet of the Gentiles only, not of the rich, or of the poor alone, not of the righteous only, but also of publicans and sinners. He is the Savior of all men who come unto Him. Thus when He is called the Lamb of God that bears the sin of the world, all that is meant is that He bears the sins of men; He came as a sin-offering bearing not his own, but the sins of others.

In the third place, these general terms are always to be understood in reference to the things spoken of in the context. When all things, the universe, is said to be put in subjection to Christ it is, of course, to be understood of the created universe. In 1 Corinthians 15:27, Paul expressly mentions this limitation, but in Hebrews 2:8, it is not mentioned. It is, however, just as obviously involved in the one passage as in the other. When in Romans 5:18, it is said that by the righteousness of Christ the free gift of justification of life has come upon all men, it is of necessity limited to the all in Christ of whom the Apostle is speaking. So also in 1 Corinthians 15:22, "As in Adam all die, even so in Christ shall all be made alive" (i.e., quickened with the life of Christ), it is in both members of the sentence not absolutely all, but the all in Adam and the all in Christ. This is still more obvious in Romans 8:32, where it is said that God gave up his own Son for us all. The us refers to the class of persons of which the whole chapter treats, namely, of those to whom there is no condemnation, who are led by the Spirit, for whom Christ intercedes, etc. Ephesians 1:10, and Colossians 1:20, are favorite texts with the Universalists, for they teach that all in heaven and on earth are reunited unto God by Jesus Christ. They are right in understanding these passages as teaching the salvation of all men, if by all in this connection we must understand all human beings. But why limit the word to all men? Why not include angels and even irrational creatures? The answer is, because the Bible teaches that Christ came to save men, and neither angels nor irrational animals. This is only saying that all must be limited to the objects of redemption. Who they are is to be learned not from these general terms, but from the general teaching of Scripture. The all who are to be united in one harmonious body by Jesus Christ are the all whom He came to save. The same remark applies to Hebrews 2:9, Christ tasted "death for every man." It is well known that Origen understood this of every creature; others, of every rational creature; others, of every fallen rational creature; others, of every man; others, of every one of those given to the Son by the Father. How are we to decide which of these interpretations is correct? So far as the mere signification of the words is concerned, one is as correct as another. It is only from the analogy of Scripture that the meaning of the sacred writer can be determined. Christ tasted death for every one of the objects of redemption. Whether He came to redeem all created sensuous beings, or all rational creatures, or all men, or all given to Him in the councils of eternity, the Bible must decide. The great majority of the passages quoted to prove that Christ died equally for all men come, under one or other of the classes just mentioned, and have no real bearing on the question concerning the design of his death.

There is another class of passages with which it is said that the Augustinian doctrine cannot be reconciled; such, namely, as speak of those perishing for whom Christ died. In reference to these passages it may be remarked, first, that there is a sense, as before stated, in which Christ did die for all men. His death had the effect of justifying the offer of salvation to every man; and of course was designed to have that effect. He therefore died sufficiently for all. In the second place, these passages are, in some cases at least, hypothetical. When Paul exhorts the Corinthians not to cause those to perish for whom Christ died, he merely, exhorts them not to act selfishly towards those for whom Christ had exhibited the greatest compassion. The passage neither asserts nor implies that any actually perish for whom Christ died. None perish whom He came to save; multitudes perish to whom salvation is offered on the ground of his death.

As God in the course of nature and in the dispensation of his providence, moves on in undisturbed majesty, little concerned at the apparent complication or even inconsistency of one effect or one dispensation with another; so the Spirit of God in the Bible unfolds the purposes, truths, and dealings of God, just as they are, assured that even finite minds will ultimately be able to see the consistency of all his revelations. The doctrines of foreordination, sovereignty, and effectual providential control, go hand in hand with those of the liberty and responsibility of rational creatures. Those of freedom from the law, of salvation by faith without works, and of the absolute necessity of holy living stand side by side. On the same page we find the assurance of God's love to sinners, and declarations that He would that all men should come unto Him and live, with explicit assertions that He has determined to leave multitudes to perish in their sins. In like manner, the express declarations that it was the incomprehensible and peculiar love of God for his own people, which induced Him to send his Son for their redemption; that Christ came into the world for that specific object; that He died for his sheep; that He gave Himself for his Church; and that the salvation of all for whom He thus offered Himself is rendered certain by the gift of the Spirit to bring them to faith and repentance, are intermingled with declarations of good-will to all mankind, with offers of salvation to every one who will believe in the Son of God, and denunciations of wrath against those who reject these overtures of mercy. All we have to do is not to ignore or deny either of these modes of representation, but to open our minds wide enough to receive them both, and reconcile them as best we can. Both are true, in all the cases above referred to, whether we can see their consistency or not.

In the review of this subject, it is plain that the doctrine that Christ died equally for all men with the purpose of rendering the salvation of all possible, has no advantage over the doctrine that He died specially for his own people, and with the purpose of rendering their salvation certain. It presents no higher view of the love of God, or of the value of Christ's work. It affords no better ground for the offer of salvation "to every creature," nor does it render more obvious the justice of the condemnation of those who reject the gospel. They are condemned by God, angels, and men, and by their own consciences, because they refuse to believe that Jesus is the Son of God, God manifest in the flesh, and to love, worship, trust, and obey Him accordingly. The opposite, or anti-Augustinian doctrine, is founded on a partial view of the facts of the case. It leaves out of view the clearly revealed special love of God to his peculiar people; the union between Christ and his chosen; the representative character which He assumed as their substitute; the certain efficacy of his sacrifice in virtue of the covenant of redemption; and the necessary connection between the gift of Christ and the gift of the Holy Spirit. It moreover leads to confused and inconsistent views of the plan of salvation, and to unscriptural and dangerous theories of the nature of the atonement. It therefore is the limited and meager scheme; whereas the orthodox doctrine is catholic and comprehensive; full of consolation and spiritual power, as well as of justice to all mankind.

Charles Hodge, Systematic Theology,
Volume 2, 1871

3.31 CONTEMPLATING THE CROSS IN TIMES OF DIFFICULTY, JOHN HENRY NEWMAN

His cross has put its due value upon everything which we view: all fortunes, all advantages, all ranks, all dignities, all pleasures; upon the lust of the flesh, the lust of the eyes and the pride of the life. It has a set a price on the excitements, the rivalries, the hopes, the fears, the desires, the efforts, the triumphs of mortal man . . . it has taught us how to live, how to use the world, what to expect, what to desire, what to hope.

John Henry Newman

3.32 THE CROSS: A CALL TO THE FUNDAMENTAL OF RELIGION, J. C. RYLE

John Charles Ryle, 1816-1900, noted for being thoroughly evangelical in his doctrine and uncompromising in his principles, was a prolific writer, vigorous preacher, and faithful pastor.

For 38 years he was a parish vicar, first at Helmingham and later at Stradbrooke, in Suffolk. He became a leader of the evangelical party in the Church of England and was noted for his doctrinal essays and polemical writings. In 1880, at age 64, he became the first bishop of Liverpool, at the recommendation of Prime Minister Benjamin Disraeli.

"By thy cross and passion, good Lord deliver us." The Book of Common Prayer
"God forbid that I should glory, save in the cross of our Lord Jesus Christ." Galatians 6:14

Reader,
What do you think and feel about the cross of Christ? You live in a Christian land. You probably attend the worship of a Christian Church. You have perhaps been baptized in the name of Christ. You profess and call yourself a Christian. All this is well. It is more than can be said of millions in the world. But all this is no answer to my question, "What do you think and feel about the cross of Christ?"

I want to tell you what the greatest Christian that ever lived thought of the cross of Christ. He has written down his opinion. He has given his judgment in words that cannot be mistaken. The man I mean is the Apostle Paul. The place where you will find his opinion, is in the letter which the Holy Ghost inspired him to write to the Galatians. And the words in which his judgment is set down, are these, "God forbid that I should glory, save in the cross of our Lord Jesus Christ."

Now what did Paul mean by saying this? He meant to declare strongly, that he trusted in nothing but Jesus Christ crucified for the pardon of his sins and the salvation of his soul. Let others, if they would, look elsewhere for salvation. Let others, if they were so disposed, trust in other things for pardon and peace. For his part, the apostle was determined to rest on nothing, lean on nothing, build his hope on nothing, place confidence in nothing, glory in nothing, except "the cross of Jesus Christ."

Reader, let me talk to you about this subject. Believe me, it is one of the deepest importance. This is no mere question of controversy. This is not one of those points on which men may agree to differ, and feel that differences will not shut them out of heaven. A man must be right on this subject, or he is lost forever. Heaven or hell, happiness or misery, life or death, blessing or cursing in the last day,—all hinges on the answer to this question, "What do you think about the cross of Christ?"

1. Let me show you what the Apostle Paul did not glory in.
2. Let me explain to you what he did glory in.
3. Let me show you why all Christians should think and feel about the cross like Paul.

1. WHAT DID THE APOSTLE PAUL NOT GLORY IN?

There are many things that Paul might have gloried in, if he had thought as some do in this day. If ever there was one on earth who had something to boast of in himself, that man was the great apostle of the Gentiles. Now, if he did not dare to glory, who shall?

He never gloried in his national privileges. He was a Jew by birth, and as he tells us himself,—"An Hebrew of the Hebrews." He might have said, like many of his brethren, "I have Abraham for my forefather. I am not a dark, unenlightened heathen. I am one of the favored people of God. I have been admitted into covenant with God by circumcision. I am a far better man than the ignorant Gentiles."

But he never said so. He never gloried in anything of this kind. Never for one moment!

He never gloried in his own works. None ever worked so hard for God as he did. He was more abundant in labors than any of the apostles. No living man ever preached so much, traveled so much, and endured so many hardships for Christ's cause. None ever converted so many souls, did so much good to the world, and made himself so useful to mankind. No father of the early Church, no Reformer, no Missionary, no Minister, no Layman—no one man could ever be named, who did so many good works as the Apostle Paul. But did he ever glory in them, as if they were in the least meritorious, and could save his soul? Never! never for one moment!

He never gloried in his knowledge. He was a man of great gifts naturally, and after he was converted, the Holy Spirit gave him greater gifts still. He was a mighty preacher, and a mighty speaker, and a mighty writer. He was as great with his pen as he was with his tongue. He could reason equally well with Jews and Gentiles. He could argue with infidels at Corinth, or Pharisees at Jerusalem, or self-righteous people in Galatia. He knew many deep things. He had been in the third heaven, and heard unspeakable words. He had received the spirit of prophecy, and could foretell things yet to come. But did he ever glory in his knowledge, as if it could justify him before God? Never! never! never for one moment!

He never gloried in his graces. If ever there was one who abounded in graces, that man was Paul. He was full of love. How tenderly and affectionately he used to write! He could feel for souls like a mother or a nurse feeling for her child. He was a bold man. He cared not whom he opposed when truth was at stake. He cared not what risks he ran when souls were to be won. He was a self-denying man,—in hunger and thirst often, in cold and nakedness, in watchings and fastings. He was a humble man. He thought himself less than the least of all saints, and the chief of sinners. He was a prayerful man. See how it comes out at the beginning of all his Epistles. He was a thankful man. His thanksgivings and his prayers walked side by side. But he never gloried in all this, never valued himself on it, never rested his soul's hopes in it. Oh! no! never for a moment!

He never gloried in his churchmanship. If ever there was a good churchman, that man was Paul. He was himself a chosen apostle. He was a founder of churches, and an ordainer of ministers. Timothy and Titus, and many elders, received their first commission from his hands. He was the beginner of services and sacraments in many a dark place. Many a one did he baptize. Many a one did he receive to the Lord's table. Many a meeting for prayer, and praise, and preaching, did he begin and carry on. He was the setter up of discipline in many a young church. Whatever ordinances, and rules, and ceremonies were observed in them, were first recommended by him. But did he ever glory in his office and church standing? Does he ever speak as if his churchmanship would save him, justify him, put away his sins, and make him acceptable before God? Oh! no! never! never! never for a moment!

And now, reader, mark what I say. If the apostle Paul never gloried in any of these things, who in all the world, from one end to the other, has any right to glory in them in our day? If Paul said, "God forbid that I should glory in anything whatever except the cross," who shall dare to say, "I have something to glory of—I am a better man than Paul?"

Who is there among the readers of this tract, that trusts in any goodness of his own? Who is there that is resting on his own amendments, his own morality, his own performances of any kind whatever? Who is there that is leaning the weight of his soul on anything whatever of his own in the smallest possible degree? Learn, I say, that you are very unlike the Apostle Paul. Learn that your religion is not apostolical religion.

Who is there among the readers of this tract that trusts in his churchmanship for salvation? Who is there that is valuing himself on his baptism, or his attendance at the Lord's table—his church-going on Sundays, or his daily services during the week—and saying to himself, What lack I yet? Learn, I say, this day, that you are very unlike Paul. Your

Christianity is not the Christianity of the New Testament. Paul would not glory in anything but the cross. Neither ought you.

Oh! reader, beware of self-righteousness. Open sin kills its thousands of souls. Self-righteousness kills its tens of thousands. Go and study humility with the great apostle of the Gentiles. Go and sit with Paul at the foot of the cross. Give up your secret pride. Cast away your vain ideas of your own goodness. Be thankful if you have grace, but never glory in it for a moment. Work for God and Christ with heart and soul, and mind and strength, but never dream for a second of placing confidence in any work of your own.

Think, you who take comfort in some fancied ideas of your own goodness—think, you who wrap up yourselves in the notion, "all must be right, if I keep to my church,"—think for a moment what a sandy foundation your are building upon! Think for a moment how miserably defective your hopes and pleas will look in the hour of death, and in the day of judgment! Whatever men may say of their own goodness while they are strong and healthy, they will find but little to say of it, when they are sick and dying. Whatever merit they may see in their own works here in this world, they will discover none in them when they stand before the bar of Christ. The light of that great day of assize will make a wonderful difference in the appearance of all their doings. It will strip off the tinsel, shrivel up the complexion, expose the rottenness, of many a deed that is now called good. Their wheat will prove nothing but chaff. Their gold will be found nothing but dross. Millions of so-called Christian actions, will turn out to have been utterly defective and graceless. They passed current, and were valued among men. They will prove light and worthless in the balance of God. They will be found to have been like the whitened sepulchers of old, fair and beautiful without, but full of corruption within. Alas! for the man who can look forward to the day of judgment, and lean his soul in the smallest degree on anything of his own![1]

Reader, once more I say, beware of self-righteousness in every possible shape and form. Some people get as much harm from their fancied virtues as others do from their sins. Take heed, lest you be one. Rest not, rest not till your heart beats in tune with St. Paul's. Rest not till you can say with him, "God forbid that I should glory in anything but the cross."

2. LET ME EXPLAIN, IN THE SECOND PLACE, WHAT YOU ARE TO UNDERSTAND BY THE CROSS OF CHRIST.

The cross is an expression that is used in more than one meaning in the Bible. What did St. Paul mean when he said, "I glory in the cross of Christ," in the Epistle to the Galatians? This is the point I now wish to make clear.

The cross sometimes means that wooden cross, on which the Lord Jesus was nailed and put to death on Mount Calvary. This is what St. Paul had in his mind's eye, when he told the Philippians that Christ "became obedient unto death, even the death of the cross" (Phil 2:8). This is not the cross in which St. Paul gloried. He would have shrunk with horror from the idea of glorying in a mere piece of wood. I have no doubt he would have denounced the Roman Catholic adoration of the crucifix, as profane, blasphemous, and idolatrous.

The cross sometimes means the afflictions and trials which believers in Christ have to go through if they follow Christ faithfully, for their religions' sake. This is the sense in which our Lord uses the word when He says, "He that taketh not his cross and followeth after me, cannot be my disciple" (Matt. 10:38). This also is not the sense in which Paul uses the word when he writes to the Galatians. He knew that cross well. He carried it patiently. But he is not speaking of it here.

But the cross also means in some places the doctrine that Christ died for sinners upon the cross—the atonement that He made for sinners by his suffering for them on the cross—the complete and perfect sacrifice for sin which He offered up when he gave His own body to be crucified. In short, this one word, "the cross," stands for Christ crucified, the only Savior. This is the meaning in which Paul uses the expression, when he tells the Corinthians, "the preaching of the cross is to them that perish foolishness" (1 Cor 1:18). This is the meaning in which he wrote to the Galatians, "God forbid that I should glory, save in the cross." He simply meant, "I glory in nothing but Christ crucified, as the salvation of my soul."[2]

Jesus Christ crucified was the joy and delight, the comfort and the peace, the hope and the confidence, the foundation and the resting place, the ark, and the refuge, the food and the medicine of Paul's soul. He did not think of what he had done himself, and suffered himself. He did not meditate on his own goodness, and his own righteousness. He loved to think of what Christ had done, and Christ had suffered,—of the death of Christ, the righteousness of Christ, the atonement of Christ, the blood of Christ, the finished work of Christ. In this he did glory. This was the sun of his soul.

This is the subject he loved to preach about. He was a man who went to and fro on the earth, proclaiming to sinners that the Son of God had shed His own heart's blood to save their souls. He walked up and down the world, telling people that Jesus Christ had loved them, and died for their sins upon the cross. Mark how he says to the Corinthians, "I delivered unto you first of all that which I also received, how that Christ died for our sins" (1 Cor 15:3). "I determined not to know anything among you, save Jesus Christ and him crucified" (1 Cor 2:2). He, a blaspheming, persecuting Pharisee, had been washed in Christ's blood. He could not hold his peace about it. He was never weary of telling the story of the cross.

This is the subject he loved to dwell upon when he wrote to believers. It is wonderful to observe how full his epistles generally are of the sufferings and death of Christ,—how they run over with "thoughts that breathe, and words that burn," about Christ's dying love and power. His heart seems full of the subject. He enlarges on it constantly. He returns to it continually. It is the golden thread that runs through all his doctrinal teaching and practical exhortations. He seems to think that the most advanced Christian can never hear too much about the cross.[3] This is what he lived upon all his life, from the time of his conversion. He tells the Galatians, "The life that I now live in the flesh, I live by the faith of the Son of God, who loved me, and gave himself for me" (Gal. 2:20). What made him so strong to labor? What made him so willing to work? What made him so unwearied in endeavors to save some? What made him so persevering and patient? I will tell you the secret of it all. He was always feeding by faith on Christ's body and Christ's blood. Jesus, crucified, was the meat and drink of his soul.

And, reader, you may rest assured that Paul was right. Depend upon it, the cross of Christ,—the death of Christ on the cross to make atonement for sinners,—is the center truth in the whole Bible. This is the truth we begin with when we open Genesis. The seed of the woman bruising the serpent's head, is nothing else but a prophecy of Christ crucified. This is the truth that shines out, though veiled, all through the law of Moses and the history of the Jews. The daily sacrifice, the Passover lamb, the continual shedding of blood in the tabernacle and temple,—all these were emblems of Christ crucified. This is the truth that we see honored in the vision of heaven before we close the book of Revelation. "In the midst of the throne and of the four beasts," we are told, "and in the midst of the elders, stood a lamb as it had been slain" (Rev 5:6). Even in the midst of heavenly glory we get a view of Christ crucified. Take away the cross of Christ, and the Bible is a dark book. It is like the Egyptian hieroglyphics, without the key that interprets their meaning,—curious and wonderful, but of no real use.

Reader, mark what I say. You may know a good deal about the Bible. You may know the outlines of the histories it contains, and the dates of the events described, just as a man knows the history of England. You may know the names of the men and women mentioned in it, just as a man knows Caesar, Alexander the Great, or Napoleon. You may know the several precepts of the Bible, and admire them, just as a man admires Plato, Aristotle, or Seneca. But if you have not yet found out that Christ crucified is the foundation of the whole volume, you have read your Bible hitherto to very little profit. Your religion is a heaven without a sun, an arch without a keystone, a compass without a needle, a clock without spring or weights, a lamp without oil. It will not comfort you. It will not deliver your soul from hell.

Reader, mark what I say again. You may know a good deal about Christ, by a kind of head knowledge. As the dead Oriental churches know the facts of Christianity as well as we do. You may know who Christ was, and where He was born, and what He did. You may know His miracles, His sayings, His prophecies, and his ordinances. You may know how He lived, and how he suffered, and how He died. But unless you know the power of Christ's cross by experience—unless you have reason to know that the blood shed on that cross has washed away your own particular sins,—unless you are willing to confess that your salvation depends entirely on the work that Christ did upon the cross,—unless this be the case, Christ will profit you nothing. The mere knowing Christ's name will never save you. You must know His cross, and His blood, or else you will die in your sins.[4]

Reader, as long as you live, beware of a religion in which there is not much of the cross. You live in times when the warning is sadly needful. Beware, I say again, of a religion without the cross.

There are hundreds of places of worship, in this day, in which there is every thing almost except the cross. There is carved oak and sculptured stone. There is stained glass and brilliant painting. There are solemn services and a constant round of ordinances. But the real cross of Christ is not there. Jesus crucified is not proclaimed in the pulpit. The Lamb of God is not lifted up, and salvation by faith in him is not freely proclaimed. And hence all is wrong. Beware of such places of worship. They are not apostolical. They would not have satisfied St. Paul.[5]

There are thousands of religious books published in our times, in which there is everything except the cross. They are full of directions about sacraments and praises of the church. They abound in exhortations about holy living, and rules for the attainment of perfection. They have plenty of fonts and crosses both inside and outside. But the real cross of Christ is left out. The Savior and His dying love are either not mentioned, or mentioned in an unscriptural way. And hence they are worse than useless. Beware of such books. They are not apostolical. They would never have satisfied St. Paul.

Dear reader, remember that St. Paul gloried in nothing but the cross. Strive to be like him. Set Jesus crucified fully before the eyes of your soul. Listen not to any teaching which would interpose anything between you and Him. Do not fall into the old Galatian error. Think not that any one in this day is a better guide than the apostles. Do not be ashamed of the old paths, in which men walked who were inspired by the Holy Ghost. Let not the vague talk of men who speak great swelling words about catholicity, and the church, and the ministry, disturb your peace, and make you loose your hands from the cross. Churches, ministers, and sacraments, are all useful in their way, but they are not Christ crucified. Do not give Christ's honor to another. "He that glorieth, let him glory in the Lord."

3. LET ME SHOW YOU WHY ALL CHRISTIANS OUGHT TO GLORY IN THE CROSS OF CHRIST.

I feel that I must say something on this point, because of the ignorance that prevails about it. I suspect that many see no peculiar glory and beauty in the subject of Christ's cross. On the contrary, they think it painful, humbling, and degrading. They do not see much profit in the story of His death and sufferings. They rather turn from it as an unpleasant thing.

Now I believe that such persons are quite wrong. I cannot hold with them. I believe it is an excellent thing for us all to be continually dwelling on the cross of Christ. It is a good thing to be often reminded how Jesus was betrayed into the hands of wicked men, how they condemned Him with most unjust judgment, how they spit on Him, scourged Him, beat Him, and crowned Him with thorns; how they led Him forth as a lamb to the slaughter, without His murmuring or resisting; how they drove the nails through His hands and feet, and set Him up on Calvary between two thieves; how they pierced His side with a spear, mocked Him in His sufferings, and let Him hang there naked and bleeding till He died. Of all these things, I say, it is good to be reminded. It is not for nothing that the crucifixion is described four times over in the New Testament. There are very few things that all the four writers of the Gospel describe. Generally speaking, if Matthew, Mark, and Luke tell a thing in our Lord's history, John does not tell it. But there is one thing that all the four give us most fully, and that one thing is the story of the cross. This is a telling fact, and not to be overlooked.

Men forget that all Christ's sufferings on the cross were fore-ordained. They did not come on Him by chance or accident. They were all planned, counseled, and determined from all eternity. The cross was foreseen in all the provisions of the everlasting Trinity, for the salvation of sinners. In the purposes of God the cross was set up from everlasting. Not one throb of pain did Jesus feel, not one precious drop of blood did Jesus shed, which had not been appointed long ago. Infinite wisdom planned that redemption should be by the cross. Infinite wisdom brought Jesus to the Cross in due time. He was crucified by the determinate counsel and foreknowledge of God.

Men forget that all Christ's sufferings on the cross were necessary for man's salvation. He had to bear our sins, if ever they were to be borne at all. With His stripes alone could we be healed. This was the one payment of our debt that God would accept. This was the great sacrifice on which our eternal life depended. If Christ had not gone to the cross and suffered in our stead, the just for the unjust, there would not have been a spark of hope for us. There would have been a mighty gulf between ourselves and God, which no man ever could have passed.[6]

Men forget that all Christ's sufferings were endured voluntarily and of His own free will. He was under no compulsion. Of His own choice He laid down His life. Of His own choice He went to the cross to finish the work He came to do. He might easily have summoned legions of angels with a word, and scattered Pilate and Herod and all their armies, like chaff before the wind. But he was a willing sufferer. His heart was set on the salvation of sinners. He was resolved to open a fountain for all sin and uncleanness, by shedding His own blood.

Now, when I think of all this, I see nothing painful or disagreeable in the subject of Christ's cross. On the contrary, I see in it wisdom and power, peace and hope, joy and gladness, comfort and consolation. The more I look at the cross in my mind's eye, the more fullness I seem to discern in it. The longer I dwell on the cross in my thoughts, the more I am satisfied that there is more to be learned at the foot of the cross than anywhere else in the world.

Would I know the length and breadth of God the Father's love towards a sinful world? Where shall I see it most displayed? Shall I look at His glorious sun shining down daily on the unthankful and evil? Shall I look at seed-time and harvest returning in regular yearly succession? Oh! no! I can find a stronger proof of love than anything of this sort. I look at the cross of Christ. I see in it not the cause of the Father's love, but the effect. There I see that God so loved this wicked world, that He gave His only begotten Son—gave Him to suffer and die—that whosoever believeth in Him should not perish, but have eternal life. I know that the Father loves us because He did not withhold from us His Son, His only Son. Ah! reader, I might sometimes fancy that God the Father is too high and holy to care for such miserable, corrupt creatures as we are. But I cannot, must not, dare not think it, when I look at the cross of Christ.[7]

Would I know how exceedingly sinful and abominable sin is in the sight of God? Where shall I see that most fully brought out? Shall I turn to the history of the flood, and read how sin drowned the world? Shall I go to the shore of the Dead Sea, and mark what sin brought on Sodom and Gomorrah? Shall I turn to the wandering Jews, and observe how sin has scattered them over the face of the earth? No! I can find a clearer proof still. I look at the cross of Christ. There I see that sin is so black

and damnable, that nothing but the blood of God's own Son can wash it away. There I see that sin has so separated me from my holy Maker, that all the angels in heaven could never have made peace between us. Nothing could reconcile us short of the death of Christ. Ah! if I listened to the wretched talk of proud men, I might sometimes fancy sin was not so very sinful. But I cannot think little of sin, when I look at the cross of Christ.[8]

Would I know the fullness and completeness of the salvation God has provided for sinners? Where shall I see it most distinctly? Shall I go to the general declarations in the Bible about God's mercy? Shall I rest in the general truth that God is a God of love? Oh! no! I will look at the cross of Christ. I find no evidence like that. I find no balm for a sore conscience, and a troubled heart, like the sight of Jesus dying for me on the accursed tree. There I see that a full payment has been made for all my enormous debts. The curse of that law which I have broken has come down on One who there suffered in my stead. The demands of that law are all satisfied. Payment has been made for me, even to the uttermost farthing. It will not be required twice over. Ah! I might sometimes imagine I was too bad to be forgiven. My own heart sometimes whispers that I am too wicked to be saved. But I know in my better moments this is all my foolish unbelief. I read an answer to my doubts in the blood shed on Calvary. I feel sure that there is a way to heaven for the very vilest of men, when I look at the cross.

Would I find strong reasons for being a holy man? Whither shall I turn for them? Shall I listen to the ten commandments merely? Shall I study the examples given me in the Bible of what grace can do? Shall I meditate on the rewards of heaven, and the punishments of hell? Is there no stronger motive still? Yes! I will look at the cross of Christ. There I see the love of Christ constraining me to live not unto myself, but unto Him. There I see that I am not my own now;—I am bought with a price. I am bound by the most solemn obligations to glorify Jesus with body and spirit, which are His. There I see that Jesus gave Himself for me, not only to redeem me from all iniquity, but also to purify me and make me one of a peculiar people, zealous of good works. He bore my sins in His own body on the tree, that I being dead unto sin should live unto righteousness. Ah! reader, there is nothing so sanctifying as a clear view of the cross of Christ! It crucifies the world unto us, and us unto the world. How can we love sin when we remember that because of our sins Jesus died? Surely none ought to be so holy as the disciples of a crucified Lord.

Would I learn how to be contented and cheerful under all the cares and anxieties of life? What school shall I go to? How shall I attain this state of mind most easily? Shall I look at the sovereignty of God, the wisdom of God, the providence of God, the love of God? It is well to do so. But I have a better argument still. I will look at the cross of Christ. I feel that He who spared not His only begotten Son, but delivered Him up to die for me will surely with Him give me all things that I really need. He that endured that pain for my soul, will surely not withhold from me anything that is really good. He that has done the greater things for me, will doubtless do the lesser things also. He that gave His own blood to procure me a home, will unquestionably supply me with all really profitable for me by the way. Ah! reader, there is no school for learning contentment that can be compared with the foot of the cross.

Would I gather arguments for hoping that I shall never be cast away? Where shall I go to find them? Shall I look at my own graces and gifts? Shall I take comfort in my own faith, and love, and penitence, and zeal, and prayer? Shall I turn to my own heart, and say, "This same heart will never be false and cold?" Oh! no! God forbid! I will look at the cross of Christ. This is my grand argument. This is my main stay. I cannot think that He who went through such sufferings to redeem my soul, will let that soul perish after all, when it has once cast itself on Him. Oh! no! what Jesus paid for, Jesus will surely keep. He paid dearly for it. He will not let it easily be lost. He died for me when I was yet a dark sinner. Ah! reader, when Satan tempts you to doubt whether Christ is able to keep his people from falling, bid Satan look at the cross.

And now, reader, will you marvel that I said all Christians ought to glory in the cross? Will you not rather wonder that any can hear of the cross and remain unmoved? I declare I know not greater proof of man's depravity, than the fact that thousands of so-called Christians see nothing in the cross. Well may our hearts be called stony,—well may the eyes of our mind be called blind,—well may our whole nature be called diseased,—well may we all be called dead, when the cross of Christ is heard of, and yet neglected. Surely we may take up the words of the prophet, and say, "Hear O heavens, and be astonished O earth; a wonderful and a horrible thing is done,"—Christ was crucified for sinners, and yet many Christians live as if He was never crucified at all!

Reader, the cross is the grand peculiarity of the Christian religion. Other religions have laws and moral precepts,—forms and ceremonies,—rewards and punishments. But other religions cannot tell us of a dying Savior. They cannot show us the cross. This is the crown and glory of the Gospel. This is that special comfort which belongs to it alone. Miserable indeed is that religious teaching which calls itself Christian, and yet contains nothing of the cross. A man who teaches in this way, might as well profess to explain the solar system, and yet tell his hearers nothing about the sun.

The cross is the strength of a minister. I for one would not be without it for all the world. I should feel like a soldier without arms,—like an artist without his pencil,—like a pilot without his compass,—like a laborer without his tools. Let others, if they will, preach the law and morality. Let others hold forth the terrors of hell and the joys of heaven. Let others be ever pressing upon their congregations the sacraments of the church. Give me the cross of Christ. This is the only lever which has ever turned the world upside down hitherto, and made men forsake their sins. And if this will not, nothing will. A man may begin preaching with a perfect knowledge of Latin, Greek and Hebrew. But he will do little or no good among his hearers unless he knows something of the cross. Never was there a minister who did much for the conversion of souls who did not dwell much on Christ crucified. Luther, Rutherford, Whitefield, Cecil, Simeon, Venn, were all most eminently preachers of the cross. This is the preaching that the Holy Ghost delights to bless. He loves to honor those who honor the cross.

The cross is the secret of all missionary success. Nothing but this has ever moved the hearts of the heathen. Just according as this has been lifted up missions have prospered. This is the weapon that has won victories over hearts of every kind, in every quarter of the globe. Greenlanders, Africans, South-Sea Islanders, Hindus, Chinese, all have alike felt its power. Just as that huge iron tube which crosses the Menai Straits, is more affected and bent by half an hour's sunshine than by all the dead weight that can be placed in it, so in like manner the hearts of savages have melted before the cross when every other argument seemed to move them no more than stones. "Brethren," said a North American Indian after his conversion, "I have been a heathen. I know how heathens think. Once a preacher came and began to explain to us that there was a God; but we told him to return to the place from whence he came. Another preacher came and told us not to lie, nor steal, nor drink; but we did not heed him. At last another came into my hut one day and said, 'I am come to you in the name of the Lord of heaven and earth. He sends to let you know that He will make you happy, and deliver you from misery. For this end he became a man, gave his life a ransom, and shed his blood for sinners.' I could not forget his words. I told them to the other Indians, and an awakening begun among us. I say, therefore, preach the sufferings and death of Christ, our Savior, if you wish your words to gain entrance among the heathen." Never indeed did the devil triumph so thoroughly, as when he persuaded the Jesuit missionaries in China to keep back the story of the cross!

The cross is the foundation of a church's prosperity. No church will ever be honored in which Christ crucified is not continually lifted up. Nothing whatever can make up for the want of the cross. Without it all things may be done decently and in order. Without it there may be splendid ceremonies, charming music, gorgeous churches, learned ministers, crowded communion tables, huge collections for the poor. But without the cross no good will be done. Dark hearts will not be enlightened. Proud hearts will not be humbled. Mourning hearts will not be comforted. Fainting hearts will not be cheered. Sermons about the Catholic Church and an apostolic ministry,—sermons about baptism and the Lord's supper,—sermons about unity and schism,—sermons about fast and communion,—sermons about fathers and saints,—such sermons will never make up for the absence of sermons about the cross of Christ. They may amuse some. They will feed none. A gorgeous banqueting room and splendid gold plate on the table will never make up to a hungry man for the want of food. Christ crucified is God's grand ordinance for doing good to men. Whenever a church keeps back Christ crucified, or puts anything whatever in that foremost place which Christ crucified should always have, from that moment a church ceases to be useful. Without Christ crucified in her pulpits, a church is little better than a cumberer of the ground, a dead carcass, a well without water, a barren fig tree, a sleeping watchman, a silent trumpet, a dumb witness, an ambassador without terms of peace, a messenger without tidings, a lighthouse without fire, a stumbling-block to weak believers, a comfort to infidels, a hot-bed for formalism, a joy to the devil, and an offence to God.

The cross is the grand center of union among true Christians. Our outward differences are many without doubt. And what may be the importance of those differences which now in a measure divide such as faithfully hold the head, even Christ, we cannot here enquire. But, after all, what shall we hear about most of these differences in heaven? Nothing most probably: nothing at all. Does a man really and sincerely glory in the cross of Christ? That is the grand question. If he does he is my brother; we are traveling in the same road. We are journeying towards a home where Christ is all, and everything outward in religion will be forgotten. But if he does not glory in the cross of Christ, I cannot feel comfort about him. Union on outward points only is union only for time. Union about the cross is union for eternity. Error on outward points is only a skin-deep disease. Error about the cross is disease at the heart. Union about outward points is a mere man-made union. Union about the cross of Christ can only be produced by the Holy Ghost.

Reader, I know not what you think of all this. I feel as if I had said nothing compared to what might be said. I feel as if the half of what I desire to tell you about the cross were left untold. But I do hope that I have given you something to think about. I do trust that I have shown you that I have reason for the question with which I began this tract, "What do you think and feel about the cross of Christ?" Listen to me now for a few moments, while I say something to apply the whole subject to your conscience.

Are you living in any kind of sin? Are you following the course of this world, and neglecting your soul? Hear, I beseech you, what I say to you this day: "Behold the cross of Christ." See there how Jesus loved you! See there what Jesus suffered to prepare for you a way of salvation! Yes! careless men and women, for you that blood was shed! For you those hands and feet were pierced with nails! For you that body hung in agony on the cross! You are those whom Jesus loved, and for whom He died! Surely that love ought to melt you. Surely the thought of the cross should draw you to repentance. Oh! that it might be so this very day. Oh! that you would come at once to that Savior who died for you and is willing to save. Come and cry to Him with the prayer of faith, and I know that He will listen. Come and lay hold upon the cross, and I know that He will not cast you out. Come and believe on Him who died on the cross, and this very day you will have eternal life. How will you ever escape if you neglect so great salvation? None surely will be so deep in hell as those who despise the cross!

Are you inquiring the way toward Heaven? Are you seeking salvation but doubtful whether you can find it? Are you desiring to have an interest in Christ but doubting whether Christ will receive you? To you also I say this day, "Behold the cross of Christ." Here is encouragement if you really want it. Draw near to the Lord Jesus with boldness, for nothing need keep you back. His arms are open to receive you. His heart is full of love towards you. He has made a way by which you may approach Him with confidence. Think of the cross. Draw near, and fear not.

Are you an unlearned man? Are you desirous to get to heaven and yet perplexed and brought to a stand-still by difficulties in the Bible which you cannot explain? To you also I say this day, "Behold the cross of Christ." Read there the Father's love and the Son's compassion. Surely they are written in great plain letters, which none can well mistake. What though at present you cannot reconcile your own corruption and your own responsibility? Look, I say, at the cross. Does not that cross tell you that Jesus is a mighty, loving, ready Savior? Does it not make one thing plain, and that is that if not saved it is all your own fault? Oh! get hold of that truth, and hold it fast.

Are you a distressed believer? Is your heart pressed down with sickness, tired with disappointments, overburdened with cares? To you also I say this day, "Behold the cross of Christ." Think whose hand it is that chastens you. Think whose hand is measuring to you the cup of bitterness which you are now drinking. It is the hand of Him that was crucified. It is the same hand that in love to your soul was nailed to the accursed tree. Surely that thought should comfort and hearten you. Surely you should say to yourself, "A crucified Savior will never lay upon me anything that is not for my good. There is a needs be. It must be well."

Are you a believer that longs to be more holy? Are you one that finds his heart too ready to love earthly things? To you also I say, "Behold the cross of Christ." Look at the cross. Think of the cross. Meditate on the cross, and then go and set affections on the world if you can. I believe that holiness is nowhere learned so well as on Calvary. I believe you cannot look much at the cross without feeling your will sanctified, and your tastes made more spiritual. As the sun gazed upon makes everything else look dark and dim, so does the cross darken the false splendor of this world. As honey tasted makes all other things seem to have no taste at all, so does the cross seen by faith take all the sweetness out of the pleasures of the world. Keep on every day steadily looking at the cross of Christ, and you will soon say of the world as the poet does,—

Its pleasures now no longer please,
No more content afford;
Far from my heart be joys like these,
Now I have seen the Lord.

As by the light of opening day
The stars are all conceal'd,
So earthly pleasures fade away
When Jesus is reveal'd.

Are you a dying believer? Have you gone to that bed from which something within tells you you will never come down alive? Are you drawing near to that solemn hour when soul and body must part for a season, and you must launch into a world unknown? Oh! look steadily at the cross of Christ, and you shall be kept in peace. Fix the eyes of your mind firmly on Jesus crucified, and he shall deliver you from all your fears. Though you walk through dark places, He will be with you. He will never leave you, never forsake you. Sit under the shadow of the cross to the very last, and its fruit shall be sweet to your taste. "Ah!" said a dying missionary, "there is but one thing needful on a death-bed, and that is to feel one's arms round the cross."

Reader, I lay these thoughts before your mind. What you think now about the cross of Christ I cannot tell; but I can wish you nothing better than this, that you may be able to say with the apostle Paul, before you die or meet the Lord, "God forbid that I should glory save in the cross of our Lord Jesus Christ."

Footnotes

[1] "Howsoever men when they sit at ease, do vainly tickle their own hearts with the wanton conceit of I know not what proportionable correspondence between their merits and their rewards, which in the trance of their high speculations, they dream that God hath measured and laid up as it were in bundles for them; we see notwithstanding by daily experience, in a number even of them that when the hour of death approacheth, when they secretly hear themselves summoned to appear and stand at the bar of that Judge, whose brightness causeth the eyes of angels themselves to dazzle, all those idle imaginations do then begin to hide their faces. To name merits then, is to lay their souls upon the rack. The memory of their own deeds is loathsome unto them. They forsake all things wherein they have put any trust and confidence. No staff to lean upon, no rest, no ease, no comfort then, but only in Christ Jesus." Richard Hooker.

[2] "By the cross of Christ the apostle understandeth the all-sufficient, expiatory, and satisfactory sacrifice of Christ upon the cross, with the whole work of our redemption: in the saving knowledge of, whereof he professeth he will glory and boast." Cudworth on Galatians.

"Touching these words, I do not find that any expositor, either ancient or modern, Popish or Protestant, writing on this place, doth expound the cross here mentioned of the sign of the cross, but of the profession of faith in Him that was hanged on the cross." Mayer's Commentary.

"This is rather to be understood of the cross which Christ suffered for us, than of that we suffer for Him." Leigh's Annotations.

[3] "Christ crucified is the sum of the Gospel, and contains all the riches of it. Paul was so much taken with Christ that nothing sweeter than Jesus could drop from his pen and lips. It is observed that he hath the word Jesus' five hundred times in his Epistles." Charnock.

[4] "If our faith stop in Christ's life, and do not fasten upon his blood, it will not be a justifying faith. His miracles which prepared the world for his doctrines; his holiness, which fitted himself for his sufferings, had been insufficient for us without the addition of the cross." Charnock.

[5] "Paul determined to know nothing else but Jesus Christ, and him crucified. But

many manage the ministry as if they had taken up a contrary determination, even to know anything save Jesus Christ and him crucified." Traill.

[6] "In Christ's humiliation stands our exaltation; in his weakness stands our strength; in his ignominy our glory; in his death our life." Cudworth.

"The eye of faith regards Christ sitting on the summit of the cross, as in a triumphal chariot; the devil bound to the lowest part of the same cross, and trodden under the feet of Christ." Bishop Davenant on Colossians.

[7] "The world we live in had fallen upon our heads, had it not been upheld by the pillar of the cross; had not Christ stepped in and promised a satisfaction for the sin of man. By this all things consist: not a blessing we enjoy but may put us in mind of it; they were all forfeited by sin, but merited by his blood. If we study it well we shall be sensible how God hated sin and loved a world." Charnock.

[8] "If God hateth sin so much that he would allow neither man nor angel for the redemption thereof, but only the death of his only and well-beloved Son, who will not stand in fear thereof?" Homily for Good Friday.

J. C. Ryle

3.33 THE GLORY OF THE CROSS, CHARLES KINGSLEY

Charles Kingsley, July 12, 1819–January 23, 1875, was an English novelist and Anglican clergyman, noted for his most famous book, The Water Babies.

"Father, the hour is come. Glorify thy Son, that thy Son also may glorify thee. I spoke to you lately of the beatific vision of God. I will speak of it again to-day; and say this." John 17:1

If any man wishes to see God, truly and fully, with the eyes of his soul: if any man wishes for that beatific vision of God; that perfect sight of God's perfect goodness; then must that man go, and sit down at the foot of Christ's cross, and look steadfastly upon him who hangs thereon. And there he will see, what the wisest and best among the heathen, among the Mussulmans, among all who are not Christian men, never have seen, and cannot see unto this day, however much they may feel (and some of them, thank God, do feel) that God is the Eternal Goodness, and must be loved accordingly.

And what shall we see upon the cross?

Many things, friends, and more than I, or all the preachers in the world, will be able to explain to you, though we preached till the end of the world. But one thing we shall see, if we will, which we have forgotten sadly, Christians though we be, in these very days; forgotten it, most of us, so utterly, that in order to bring you back to it, I must take a seemingly roundabout road.

Does it seem, or does it not seem, to you, that the finest thing in a man is magnanimity—what we call in plain English, greatness of soul? And if it does seem to you to be so, what do you mean by greatness of soul? When you speak of a great soul, and of a great man, what manner of man do you mean?

Do you mean a very clever man, a very far-sighted man, a very determined man, a very powerful man, and therefore a very successful man? A man who can manage everything, and every person whom he comes across, and turn and use them for his own ends, till he rises to be great and glorious—a ruler, king, or what you will?

Well—he is a great man: but I know a greater, and nobler, and more glorious stamp of man; and you do also. Let us try again, and think if we can find his likeness, and draw it for ourselves. Would he not be somewhat like this pattern?—A man who was aware that he had vast power, and yet used that power not for himself but for others; not for ambition, but for doing good? Surely the man who used his power for other people would be the greater-souled man, would he not? Let us go on, then, to find out more of his likeness. Would he be stern, or would he be tender? Would he be patient, or would he be fretful? Would he be a man who stands fiercely on his own rights, or would he be very careful of other men's rights, and very ready to waive his own rights gracefully and generously? Would he be extreme to mark what was done amiss against him, or would he be very patient when he was wronged himself, though indignant enough if he saw others wronged? Would he be one who easily lost his temper, and lost his head, and could be thrown off his balance by one foolish man? Surely not. He would be a man whom no fool, nor all fools together could throw off his balance; a man who could not lose his temper, could not lose his self-respect; a man who could bear with those who are peevish, make allowances for those who are weak and ignorant, forgive those who are insolent, and conquer those who are ungrateful, not by punishment, but by fresh kindness, overcoming their evil by his good.—A man, in short, whom no ill-usage without, and no ill-temper within, could shake out of his even path of generosity and benevolence. Is not that the truly magnanimous man; the great and royal soul? Is not that the stamp of man whom we should admire, if we met him on earth? Should we not reverence that man; esteem it an honor and a pleasure to work under that man, to take him for our teacher, our leader, in hopes that, by copying his example, our souls might become great like his?

Is it so, my friends? Then know this, that in admiring that man, you admire the likeness of God. In wishing to be like that man, you wish to be like God.

For this is God's true greatness; this is God's true glory; this is God's true royalty; the greatness, glory, and royalty of loving, forgiving, generous power, which pours itself out, untiring and undisgusted, in help and mercy to all which he has made; the glory of a Father who is perfect in this, that he causeth his rain to fall on the evil and on the good, and his sun to shine upon the just and on the unjust, and is good to the unthankful and the evil; a Father who has not dealt with us after our sins, or rewarded us after our iniquities: a Father who is not extreme to mark what is done amiss, but whom it is worth while to fear, for with him is mercy and plenteous redemption;—all this, and more—a Father who so loved a world which had forgotten him, a world whose sins must have been disgusting to him, that he spared not his only begotten Son, but freely gave him for us, and will with him freely give us all things; a Father, in one word, whose name and essence is love, even as it is the name and essence of the Son and of the Holy Ghost.

This, my friends, is the glory of God: but this glory never shone out in its full splendor till it shone upon the cross.

For—that we may go back again, to that great-souled man, of whom I spoke just now—did we not leave out one thing in his character? or at least, one thing by which his character might be proved and tried? We said that he should be generous and forgiving; we said that he should bear patiently folly, peevishness, ingratitude: but what if we asked of him, that he should sacrifice himself utterly for the peevish, ungrateful men for whose good he was toiling? What if we asked him to give up, for them, not only all which made life worth having, but to give up life itself? To die for them; and, what is bitterest of all, to die by their hands—to receive as their reward for all his goodness to them a shameful death? If he dare submit to that, then we should call his greatness of soul perfect. Magnanimity, we should say, could rise no higher; in that would be the perfection of goodness.

Surely your hearts answer, that this is true. When you hear of a father sacrificing his own life for his children; when you hear of a soldier dying for his country; when you hear of a clergyman or a physician killing himself by his work, while he is laboring to save the souls or the bodies of his fellow-creatures; then you feel—There is goodness in its highest shape. To give up our lives for others is one of the most beautiful, and noble, and glorious things on earth. But to give up our lives, willingly, joyfully for men who misunderstand us, hate us, despise us, is, if possible, a more glorious action still, and the very perfection of perfect virtue. Then, looking at Christ's cross, we see that, and even more—ay, far more than that. The cross was the perfect token of the perfect greatness of God, and of the perfect glory of God.

So on the cross, the Father justified himself to man; yea, glorified himself in the glory of his crucified Son. On the cross God proved himself to be perfectly just, perfectly good, perfectly generous, perfectly glorious, beyond all that man could ever have dared to conceive or dream. That God must be good, the wise heathens knew; but that God was so utterly good that he could stoop to suffer, to die, for men, and by men—that they never dreamed. That was the mystery of God's love, which was hid in Christ from the foundation of the world, and which was revealed at last upon the cross of Calvary by him who prayed for his murderers—'Father, forgive them, for they know not what they do.' That truly blessed sight of a God-God, who did not disdain to die the meanest and the most fearful of deaths—that, that came home at once, and has come home ever since, to all hearts which had left in them any love and respect for goodness, and melted them with the fire of divine love; as God grant it may melt yours, this day, and henceforth for ever.

I can say no more, my friends. If this good news does not come home to your hearts by its own power, it will never be brought home to you by any words of mine.

Charles Kingsley

3.34 THE LAMB, SADHU SUNDAR SINGH

Sadhu Sundar Singh, (1889-1929), a Hindu convert to Christianity, became a missionary to his people in India.

Long before the time of Jesus, families gave lambs as offerings to God. And since the first Passover, the symbolism of serving lamb is an important part in the Passover feast. Since Jesus died during Passover, his death was interpreted giving himself as an offering to God for the sins of all the world. It's for this reason the Bible calls Jesus the Lamb of God. Early Christians saw the lamb as a symbol of Jesus and continue to use it as a part of their Easter celebrations.

Sadhu Sundar Singh

3.35 THE BLESSING OF JUSTIFICATION, A. M. STIBBS

The faith of the individual must be seen as having no value in itself, but as discovering value wholly and solely through movement towards and committal to Christ. It must be seen as simply a means of finding all one's hope outside oneself in the person and work of another; and not in any sense an originating cause or objective ground of justification. For true faith is active only in the man who is wholly occupied with Christ;

its practice means that every blessing is received from another. For this reason faith is exclusive and intolerant of company; it is only truly present when any and every contribution towards his salvation on the part of the believer or on the part of the Church is absolutely and unequivocally shut out. Justification must be seen and received as a blessing dependent wholly and exclusively on Christ alone, on what he is and what he has done—a blessing enjoyed simply through being joined directly to him, through finding one's all in him, through drawing one's all from him, without the interposition of any other mediator or mediating channel whatever.

A. M. Stibbs
"Justification by Faith: the Reinstatement of
the Doctrine Today"
Evangelical Quarterly, *July, 1952*

3

POEMS, HYMNS, MEDITATIONS, AND PRAYERS ON THE DEATH OF JESUS

3.36 PRAYERS TO JESUS HANGING ON THE CROSS, ATTRIBUTED BERNARD OF CLAIRVAUX

Bernard of Clairvaux, abbot and theologian (born 1090, at Fontaines, near Dijon, France; died at Clairvaux, August 21, 1153), was the primary builder of the Cistercian order of monks.

PART I
To the feet

1. O Savior of the world, I cry to Thee; O Savior, suffering God, I worship Thee; O wounded beauteous Love, I kneel to Thee; Thou knowest, Lord, how I would follow Thee, If of Thyself Thou give Thyself to Me.

2. Thy Presence I Believe; O come to me! Behold me prostrate, Jesus; look on me! How beautiful Thou art! O turn to me! O in Thy tender mercy turn to me, And let Thy untold pity pardon me!

3. With trembling love and feet I worship Thee; I kiss the grievous nails which entered Thee, And think on those dire wounds which tortured Thee, And, grieving, lift my weeping eyes to Thee, Transfixed and dying all for love of me!

4. O wondrous grace! O gracious charity! O love of sinners in such agony! Sweet Father of the poor! O who can be Unmoved to witness this great mystery,—The Healer smitten, hanging on a tree?

5. O gentle Jesus, turn Thee unto me; What I have broken do Thou bind in me, And what is crooked make Thou straight in me; What I have lost restore Thou unto me, And what is weak and sickly heal in me.

6. O Love! with all my strength I seek for Thee; Upon and in thy Cross I look for Thee; With sorrow and with hope I turn to Thee,— That through Thy Blood new health may come to me, That washed therein Thy love may pardon me.

7. O take my heart, Thou Loved One; let it be Transfixed with those dear wounds for love of Thee, O wound it, Jesus, with pure love of Thee; And let it so be crucified with Thee, that it may be forever joined to Thee.

8. Sweet Jesus, loving God, I cry to Thee; Thou guilty, yet I come for love of Thee; O show Thyself, dear Savior, kind to me! Unworthy as I am, O turn to me, Nor at thy sacred Feet abandon me!

9. Dear Jesus, bathed in tears, I kneel to Thee; In shame and grief I lift my eyes to Thee; Prostrate before Thy Cross I bow to Thee, And thy dear Feet embrace; O look on me, Yea, from Thy Cross, O look, and pardon me.

10. O my Beloved, stretched against that Thee, Whose arms divine are now enfolding me, whose gracious Heart is now upholding me,—O my Beloved, let me wholly be Transformed, forgiven, one alone with Thee!

PART II
To the knees

1. O Jesus, King of Saints, I worship Thee; O hope of sinners, hail! I rest on Thee; True God, true man, Thou hangest on the Tree Transfixed, with quivering flesh and shaking knees, A criminal esteemed,—I worship Thee.

2. Alas, how poor, how naked, wilt Thou be! How hast Thou stript Thyself for love of me, How made Thyself a gazing-stock to be! Not forced, but, O my God! How willingly In all Thy limbs Thou sufferest on that Tree!

3. Thy Precious Blood wells forth abundantly From all Thy open wounds incessantly; All bathed therein, O God, in agony Thou standest on the Cross of infamy, Awaiting the appointed hour to die.

4. O infinite, O wondrous majesty! O terrible, unheard-of poverty! Ah, who, returning so great charity, I willing, Jesus, thus to give for Thee His blood for Thine, in faithful love for Thee?

5. O Jesus, how shall I, then, answer Thee, Who am so vile, and have not followed Thee? Or how repay the love that loveth me With such sublime, such awful charity Transfixed, from double death to set me free?

6. O Jesus, what Thy love hath been for me! O Jesus, death could never conquer Thee! Ah, with what loving care Thou keepest me Enfolded in Thine arms, lest I should be, By death of sin, a moment torn from Thee!

7. Behold, O Jesus, how for love of Thee, With all my soul I trembling cling to Thee, And Thy dear Knees embrace. O pity me! Thou knowest why—in pity bear with me, And overlook the shame that covers me!

8. O let the Blood I worship flow on me, That what I do may never anger Thee; The Blood which flows at every pore from Thee Each imperfection may it wash from me, That I may undefiled and perfect be.

9. O force me, best Beloved, to draw to Thee, Transfixed and bleeding on the shameful Tree, Despised and stretched in dying agony! All my desire, O Lord, is fixed on Thee; O call me, then, and I will follow Thee.

10. I have no other love, dear Lord, but Thee; Thou art my first and last; I cling to Thee. It is no labor, Lord; love sets me free; Then heal me, cleanse me, let me rest on Thee, For love is life, and life is love—in Thee.

PART III
To the hands

1. Hail, holy Shepherd! Lord, I worship Thee, Fatigued with combat, steeped in misery; Whose sacred Hands, outstretched in agony, All pierced and dislocated on the Tree, Are fastened to the wood of infamy.

2. Dear holy Hands, I humbly worship ye, With roses filled, fresh blossoms of that Tree; The cruel iron enters into ye, While open gashes yield unceasingly The Precious stream down-dropping from the Tree.

3. Behold, Thy Blood, O Jesus, flows on me—The price of my salvation falls on me; O ruddy as the rose, it drops on me. Sweet Precious Blood, it wells abundantly From both Thy sacred Hands to set me free.

4. My heart leaps up, O Jesus, unto Thee; Drawn by those nail-pierced Hands it flies to Thee; Drawn by those Blood-stained Hands stretched out for me, My soul breaks out with sighing unto Thee, And longs to slake its thirst, O Love, in Thee.

5. My God, what great stupendous charity— Both good and bad are welcomed here by Thee! The slothful heart Thou drawest graciously, The loving one Thou callest tenderly, And unto all a pardon grantest free.

6. Behold, I now present myself to Thee, Who dost present thy bleeding Hands to me; The sick Thou healest when they come to Thee; Thou canst not, therefore, turn away from me, Whose love Thou knowest, Lord, is all for Thee.

7. O my Beloved, fastened to the Tree, Draw, by Thy love, my senses unto Thee; My will, my intellect, my memory, And all I am, make subject unto Thee, In whose dear arms alone is liberty.

8. O draw me for Thy Cross' sake to Thee; O draw me for Thy so wide charity; Sweet Jesus, draw my heart in truth to Thee, O put an end to all my misery, And crown me with Thy Cross and victory!

9. O Jesus, place Thy sacred Hands on me, With transport let me kiss them tenderly, With groans and tears embrace them fervently; And, O for these deep wounds I worship Thee; And for the blessed drops that fall on me!

10. O dearest Jesus, I commend to Thee Myself, and all I am, most perfectly; Bathed in Thy Blood, behold, I live for Thee; O, may Thy blessed Hands encompass me, And in extremity deliver me!

PART IV
To the side

1. O Jesus, highest Good, I yearn for Thee; O Jesus, merciful, I hope in Thee, Whose sacred Body hands upon the Tree, Whose limbs, all dislocated painfully, Are stretched in torture, all for love of me!

2. Hail, sacred Side of Jesus! Verily The hidden spring of mercy lies in Thee, The source of honeyed sweetness dwells in Thee, The fountain of redemption flows from Thee, The secret well of love that cleanses me.

3. Behold, O King of Love, I draw to Thee; If I am wrong, O Jesus, pardon me; Thy love, Beloved, calls me lovingly, As I with blushing cheek gaze willingly Upon the living wound that bleeds for me.

4. O gentle opening, I worship Thee; O open door and deep, I look in Thee; O most pure stream, I gaze and gaze on Thee: More ruddy than the rose, I draw to Thee; More healing than all health, I fly to Thee.

5. More sweet than wine Thine odor is for me; The poisoned breath of sin it drives from me; Thou art the draught of life poured out for me. O ye who thirst, come, drink thereof with me; And Thou, sweet wound, O open unto me.

6. O red wound open, let me draw to Thee, And let my throbbing heart be filled from Thee! Ah, see! My heart, Beloved, faints for Thee. O my Beloved, open unto me, That I may pass and lose myself in Thee.

7. Lord, with my mouth I touch and worship Thee, With all the strength I have I cling to Thee, With all my love I plunge my heart in Thee, My very life-blood would I drawn from Thee,—O Jesus, Jesus! Draw me into Thee!

8. How Sweet Thy savor is! Who tastes of Thee, O Jesus Christ, can relish naught but Thee; Who tastes Thy living sweetness lives by Thee; All else is void—the soul must die for Thee; So faints my heart,—so would I die for thee.

9. I languish, Lord! O let me hide in Thee! In Thy sweet Side, my Love, O bury me! And may the fire divine consuming Thee Burn in my heart where it lies hid in Thee, Without a fear reposing peacefully!

10. When in the hour of death Thou callest me, O Love of loves, may my soul enter Thee; May my last breath, O Jesus fly to Thee; So no fierce beast may drive my heart from Thee, But in Thy Side may it remain with Thee!

PART V
To the breast

1. O God of my salvation, hail to Thee! O Jesus, sweetest Love, all hail to Thee! O venerable Breast, I worship Thee; O dwelling-place of love, I fly to Thee, With trembling touch adore and worship Thee.

2. Hail, throne of the Most Holy Trinity! Hail, ark immense of tender charity! Thou stay of weakness and infirmity, Sweet rest of weary souls who rest on Thee, Dear couch of loving ones who lean on Thee!

3. With reverence, O Love, I kneel to Thee, O worthy to be ever sought by me; Behold me, Jesus, looking unto Thee. O, set my heart on fire, dear Love, from Thee, And burn it in the flame that burns in Thee.

4. O make my breast a precious home for thee, A furnace of sweet love and purity, A well of holy grief and piety; Deny my will, conform it unto Thee, That grace abundant may be mine in Thee.

5. Sweet Jesus, loving Shepherd, come to me; Dear Son of God and Mary, come to me; Kind Father come, let Thy Heart pity me, And cleanse the fountain of my misery In that great fountain of Thy clemency.

6. Hail, fruitful splendor of the Deity! Hail, fruitful figure of Divinity! From the full treasure of Thy charity, O pour some gift in Thy benignity Upon the desolate who cry to Thee!

7. Dear Breast of most sweet Jesus, mine would be All Thine in its entire conformity; Absolve it from all sin, and set it free, That it may burn with ardent charity, And never, never cease to think on Thee.

8. Abyss of wisdom from eternity, The harmonies of angels worship Thee; Entrancing sweetness flows, O Breast, from thee; John tasted it as he lay rapt on Thee; O grant me thus that I may dwell in Thee!

9. Hail, fountain deep of God's benignity! The fullness of the immense Divinity Hath found at last a creature home in Thee. Ah, may the counsel that I learn from Thee All imperfection purify in me!

10. True temple of the Godhead, hail to Thee! O draw me in Thy gracious charity, Thou ark of goodness, full of grace for me. Great God of all, have mercy upon me, And on Thy right hand keep a place for me.

PART VI
To the face

1. Hail, bleeding Head of Jesus, hail to Thee! Thou thorn-crowned Head, I humbly worship Thee! O wounded Head, I lift my hands to Thee; O lovely Face besmeared, I gaze on Thee; O bruised and livid Face, look down on me!

2. Hail, beauteous Face of Jesus, bent on me, Whom angel choirs adore exultantly! Hail, sweetest Face of Jesus, bruised for me—Hail, Holy One, whose glorious Face for me Is shorn of beauty on that fatal Tree!

3. All strength, all freshness, is gone forth from Thee: What wonder! Hath not God afflicted Thee, And is not death himself approaching Thee? O Love! But death hath laid his touch on Thee, And faint and broken features turn to me.

4. O have they thus maltreated Thee, my own? O have they Thy sweet Face despised, my own? And all for my unworthy sake, my own! O in Thy beauty turn to me, my own; O turn one look of love on me, my own!

5. In this Thy Passion, Lord, remember me; In this Thy pain, O Love, acknowledge me; The honey of whose lips was shed on me, The milk of whose delights hath strengthened me Whose sweetness is beyond delight for me!

6. Despise me not, O Love; I long for Thee; Contemn me not, unworthy though I be; But now that death is fast approaching Thee, Incline Thy Head, my Love, my Love, to me, To these poor arms, and let it rest on me!

7. The holy Passion I would share with Thee, And in Thy dying love rejoice with Thee; Content if by this Cross I die with Thee; Content, Thou knowest, Lord, how willingly Where I have lived to die for love of Thee.

8. For this Thy bitter death all thanks to Thee, Dear Jesus, and Thy wondrous love for me! O gracious God, so merciful to me, Do as Thy guilty one entreateth Thee, And at the end let me be found with Thee!

9. When from this life, O Love, Thou callest me, Then, Jesus, be not wanting unto me, But in the dreadful hour of agony, O hasten, Lord, and be Thou nigh to me, Defend, protect, and O deliver me.

10. When Thou, O God, shalt bid my soul be free, Then, dearest Jesus, show Thyself to me! O condescend to show Thyself to me,—Upon Thy saving Cross, dear Lord, to me,—And let me die, my Lord, embracing Thee!

PART VII
To the sacred heart

1. Hail, sacred Heart of God's great Majesty! Hail, sweetest Heart, my heart saluteth Thee! With great desire, O Heart, I seek for Thee, And faint for joy, O Heart, embracing Thee; Then give me leave, O Love, to speak to Thee.

2. With what sweet love Thou languishedst for me! What pain and torment was that love to Thee! How didst Thou all Thyself exhaust for me! How hast Thou wholly given Thyself to me, That death no longer might have hold of me!

3. O bitter death and cruel! Can it be Thou darest so to enter greedily Into that cell divine? O can it be The Life of life, that lives there gloriously, Should feel thy bite, O death, and yield to thee?

4. For Thy death's sake which Thou didst bear for me, When Thou, O sweetest Heart, didst faint for me, O Heart most precious in its agony, See how I yearn, and longing turn to Thee! Yield to my love, and draw me unto Thee!

5. O sacred Heart, beloved most tenderly, Cleanse Thou my own; more worthy let it be, All hardened as it is with vanity; O make it tender, loving, fearing Thee, And all its icy coldness drive from me.

6. O sinner as I am, I come to Thee; My very vitals throb and call for Thee; O Love, sweet love, draw hither unto me! O Heart of Love, my heart would ravished be, And sicken with the wound of love for Thee!

7. Open, Heart of love, for me, And like a rose of wondrous fragrance be, Sweet Heart of love, united unto me; Anoint and pierce my heart, O Love, with Thee, How can he suffer, Lord, who loveth Thee?

8. O Heart of Love, who vanquished is by Thee Knows nothing, but beside himself must be; No bounds are set to that sweet liberty, No moderation,—he must fly to Thee, Or die he must of many deaths for Thee.

9. My living heart, O Love, cries out for Thee; With all its strength, O Love, my soul loves Thee; O Heart of Love, incline Thou unto me, That I with burning love may turn to Thee, And with devoted breast recline on Thee!

10. In that sweet furnace let me live for Thee, Nor let the sleep of sloth encumber me; O let me sing to Thee and weep to Thee, Adore, and magnify, and honor Thee, And always take my full delight in Thee.

11. Thou Rose of wondrous fragrance, open wide, And bring my heart into Thy wounded Side, O sweet heart, open! Draw Thy loving bride, All panting with desires intensified, And satisfy her love unsatisfied.

12. Unite my heart, O Jesus, unto Thine, And let Thy wounded love be found in mine. Ah, if my heart, dear love, be made like Thine O will it not be pierced with darts divine, the sweet reproach of love that thrills through Thine?

13. O Jesus, draw my heart within Thy Breast, That it may be by Thee alone possessed. O Love, in that sweet pain it would find rest, In that entrancing sorrow would be blest, And love itself in joy upon Thy Breast.

14. Behold, O Jesus, how it draws to Thee! O call it, that it may remain in Thee! See with what large desire it thirsts for Thee! Reprove it not, O Love; it loves but Thee: Then bid it live—by one sweet taste of Thee!

Attributed to Bernard of Clairvaux
translated by Emily Mary Shapcote

3.37 O SACRED HEAD, NOW WOUNDED,
BERNARD OF CLAIRVAUX

O sacred Head, now wounded, with grief and
shame weighed down,
Now scornfully surrounded with thorns,
Thine only crown;
How pale Thou art with anguish, with sore
abuse and scorn!
How does that visage languish, which once
was bright as morn!

What Thou, my Lord, hast suffered, was all
for sinners' gain;
Mine, mine was the transgression, but Thine
the deadly pain.
Lo, here I fall, my Savior! Tis I deserve Thy place;
Look on me with Thy favor, vouchsafe to me
Thy grace.

Men mock and taunt and jeer Thee, Thou
noble countenance,
Though mighty worlds shall fear Thee and
flee before Thy glance.
How art thou pale with anguish, with sore
abuse and scorn!
How doth Thy visage languish that once was
bright as morn!

Now from Thy cheeks has vanished their
color once so fair;
From Thy red lips is banished the splendor
that was there.
Grim death, with cruel rigor, hath robbed
Thee of Thy life;
Thus Thou hast lost Thy vigor, Thy strength
in this sad strife.

My burden in Thy Passion, Lord, Thou hast
borne for me,
For it was my transgression which brought
this woe on Thee.
I cast me down before Thee, wrath were my
rightful lot;
Have mercy, I implore Thee; Redeemer, spurn
me not!

What language shall I borrow to thank Thee,
dearest friend,

For this Thy dying sorrow, Thy pity without
end?
O make me Thine forever, and should I
fainting be,
Lord, let me never, never outlive my love to
Thee.

My Shepherd, now receive me; my Guardian,
own me Thine.
Great blessings Thou didst give me, O source
of gifts divine.
Thy lips have often fed me with words of
truth and love;
Thy Spirit oft hath led me to heavenly joys
above.

Here I will stand beside Thee, from Thee I
will not part;
O Savior, do not chide me! When breaks Thy
loving heart,
When soul and body languish in death's cold,
cruel grasp,
Then, in Thy deepest anguish, Thee in mine
arms I'll clasp.

The joy can never be spoken, above all joys
beside,
When in Thy body broken I thus with safety
hide.
O Lord of Life, desiring Thy glory now to see,
Beside Thy cross expiring, I'd breathe my soul
to Thee.

My Savior, be Thou near me when death is at
my door;
Then let Thy presence cheer me, forsake me
never more!
When soul and body languish, oh, leave me
not alone,
But take away mine anguish by virtue of
Thine own!

Be Thou my consolation, my shield when I
must die;
Remind me of Thy passion when my last
hour draws nigh.

Mine eyes shall then behold Thee, upon Thy cross shall dwell,
My heart by faith enfolds Thee. Who dieth thus dies well.

Bernard of Clairvaux
translated by Paul Gerhardt

3.38 Good Friday, John Keble

"He is despised and rejected of men." Isaiah 53:3

Is it not strange, the darkest hour
That ever dawn'd on sinful earth
Should touch the heart with softer power
For comfort, than an angel's mirth?
That to the Cross the mourner's eye should turn
Sooner than where the stars of Christmas burn?

Sooner than where the Easter sun
Shines glorious on you open grave,
And to and fro the tidings run,
"Who died to heal, is ris'n to save."
Sooner than where upon the Savior's friends
The very Comforter in light and love descends.

Yet so it is: for duly there
The bitter herbs of earth are set,
Till temper'd by the Savior's prayer,
And with the Savior's life-blood wet,
They turn to sweetness, and drop holy balm,
Soft as imprison'd martyr's deathbed calm.

All turn to sweet—but most of all
That bitterest to the lip of pride,
When hopes presumptuous fade and fall,
Or Friendship scorns us, duly tried,
Or Love, the flower that closes up for fear
When rude and selfish spirits breathe too near.

Then like a long-forgotten strain
Comes sweeping o'er the heart forlorn
What sunshine hours had taught in vain
Of JESUS suffering shame and scorn,
As in all lowly hearts he suffers still,
While we triumphant ride and have the world at will.

His pierced hands in vain would hide
His face from rude reproachful gaze,
His ears are open to abide
The wildest storm the tongue can raise,
He who with one rough word, some early day,
Their idol world and them shall sweep for aye away.

But we by Fancy may assuage
The festering sore by Fancy made,
Down in some lonely hermitage
Like wounded pilgrims safely laid.
Where gentlest breezes whisper soul   s distress'd,
That Love yet lives, and Patience shall find rest.

O shame beyond the bitterest thought
That evil spirit ever fram'd,
That sinners know what Jesus wrought,
Yet feel their haughty hearts untam'd—
That souls in refuge, holding by the Cross,
Should wince and fret at this world's little loss.

Lord of my heart, by thy last cry,
Let not thy blood on earth be spent—
Lo, at thy feet I fainting lie,
Mine eyes upon thy wounds are bent,
Upon thy streaming wounds my weary eyes
Wait like the parched earth on April skies.

Wash me, and dry these bitter tears,
O let my heart no further roam,
'Tis thine by vows, and hopes, and fears,
Long since—O call thy wanderer home;
To that dear home, safe in thy wounded side,
Where only broken hearts their sin and shame may hide.

John Keble, The Christian Year

3.39 GOOD FRIDAY, CHRISTINA ROSSETTI

Am I a stone, and not a sheep,
  That I can stand, O Christ, beneath Thy
cross,
  To number drop by drop Thy blood's
slow loss,
    And yet not weep?

Not so those women loved
  Who with exceeding grief lamented
Thee;
  Not so fallen Peter weeping bitterly;
    Not so the thief was moved;

Not so the Sun and Moon
  Which hid their faces in a starless sky,
  A horror of great darkness at broad
noon—
    I, only I.

Yet give not o'er,
  But seek Thy sheep, true Shepherd of the
flock;
  Greater than Moses, turn and look once
more
    And smite a rock.

Christina Rossetti

3.40 JESUS, THE LAMB OF GOD, HENRY NEWMAN

Behold the Lamb of God, behold Him who taketh away the sins of the world. So spoke John Baptist, when he saw our Lord coming to him. And in so speaking, he did but appeal to that title under which our Lord was known from the beginning. Just Abel showed forth his faith in Him by offering of the firstlings of his flock. Abraham, in place of his son Isaac whom God spared, offered the like for a sacrifice. The Israelites were enjoined to sacrifice once a year, at Easter time, a lamb— one lamb for each family, a lamb without blemish—to be eaten whole, all but the blood, which was sprinkled, as their protection, about their house doors. The Prophet Isaias speaks of our Lord under the same image: "He shall be led as a sheep to the slaughter, and shall be dumb as a lamb before his shearers" (53:7); and all this because "He was wounded for our iniquities, He was bruised for our sins . . . by His bruises we are healed" (53:5). And in like manner the Holy Evangelist John, in the visions of the Apocalypse, thus speaks of Him: "I saw, . . . (Apoc. 5:6), and behold a lamb standing as it were slain"; and then he saw all the blessed "fall down before the Lamb" . . . (verses 8, 9), and they sung a new canticle saying, "Thou wast slain, and hast redeemed us to God in Thy blood, out of every tribe and tongue and people and nation" (verse 9) . . . Worthy is the Lamb that was slain, to receive power, and divinity, and wisdom, and strength, and honor, and glory, and benediction" (verse 12).

This is Jesus Christ, who when darkness, sin, guilt and misery had overspread the earth, came down from Heaven, took our nature upon Him, and shed His precious blood upon the Cross for all men.

*Henry Newman, Twelve Meditations and
Intercessions for Good Friday*

3.41 Litany of the Passion, Henry Newman

Lord, have mercy.
Lord, have mercy.
Christ, have mercy.
Christ, have mercy.
Lord, have mercy.
Lord, have mercy.
Christ, hear us.
Christ, graciously hear us.

God the Father of Heaven, *Have mercy on us.*
God the Son, Redeemer of the world, *Have mercy on us.*
God the Holy Ghost, *Have mercy on us.*
Holy Trinity, one God, *Have mercy on us.*
Jesus, the Eternal Wisdom, *Have mercy on us.*
The Word made flesh, *Have mercy on us.*
Hated by the world, *Have mercy on us.*

Sold for thirty pieces of silver, *Have mercy on us.*
Sweating blood in Thy agony, *Have mercy on us.*
Betrayed by Judas, *Have mercy on us.*
Forsaken by Thy disciples, *Have mercy on us.*
Struck upon the cheek, *Have mercy on us.*
Accused by false witnesses, *Have mercy on us.*
Spit upon in the face, *Have mercy on us.*
Denied by Peter, *Have mercy on us.*
Mocked by Herod, *Have mercy on us.*
Scourged by Pilate, *Have mercy on us.*
Rejected for Barabbas, *Have mercy on us.*
Loaded with the cross, *Have mercy on us.*
Crowned with thorns, *Have mercy on us.*
Stripped of Thy garments, *Have mercy on us.*
Nailed to the tree, *Have mercy on us.*
Reviled by the Jews, *Have mercy on us.*
Scoffed at by the malefactor, *Have mercy on us.*
Wounded in the side, *Have mercy on us.*
Shedding Thy last drop of blood, *Have mercy on us.*
Forsaken by Thy Father, *Have mercy on us.*
Dying for our sins, *Have mercy on us.*
Taken down from the cross, *Have mercy on us.*
Laid in the sepulcher, *Have mercy on us.*
Rising gloriously, *Have mercy on us.*
Ascending into Heaven, *Have mercy on us.*
Sending down the Paraclete, *Have mercy on us.*
Jesus our Sacrifice, *Have mercy on us.*
Jesus our Mediator, *Have mercy on us.*

Jesus our Judge, *Have mercy on us.*

Be merciful, *spare us, O Lord.*
Be merciful, *graciously hear us, O Lord.*
From all sin, *Lord Jesus, deliver us.*
From all evil, *Lord Jesus, deliver us.*
From anger and hatred, *Lord Jesus, deliver us.*
From malice and revenge, *Lord Jesus, deliver us.*
From unbelief and hardness of heart, *Lord Jesus, deliver us.*
From blasphemy and sacrilege, *Lord Jesus, deliver us.*
From hypocrisy and covetousness, *Lord Jesus, deliver us.*
From blindness of the understanding, *Lord Jesus, deliver us.*
From contempt of Thy warnings, *Lord Jesus, deliver us.*
From relapse after Thy judgments, *Lord Jesus, deliver us.*
From danger of soul and body, *Lord Jesus, deliver us.*
From everlasting death, *Lord Jesus, deliver us.*

. . .

Lamb of God, who takest away the sins of the world,
Spare us, O Lord.
Lamb of God, who takest away the sins of the world,
Graciously hear us, O Lord.
Lamb of God, who takest away the sins of the world,
Have mercy on us.
Christ, hear us.
Christ, graciously hear us.
Lord, have mercy.
Christ, have mercy.
Lord, have mercy.
We adore Thee, O Christ, and we bless Thee,
Because through Thy Holy Cross Thou didst redeem the world.

Let us pray.
O God, who for the redemption of the world wast pleased to be born; to be circumcised; to be rejected; to be betrayed; to be bound with

thongs; to be led to the slaughter; to be shamefully gazed at; to be falsely accused; to be scourged and torn; to be spit upon, and crowned with thorns; to be mocked and reviled; to be buffeted and struck with rods; to be stripped; to be nailed to the cross; to be hoisted up thereon; to be reckoned among thieves; to have gall and vinegar to drink; to be pierced with a lance: through Thy most holy passion, which we, Thy sinful servants, call to mind, and by Thy holy cross and gracious death, deliver us from the pains of hell, and lead us whither Thou didst lead the thief who was crucified with Thee, who with the Father and the Holy Ghost livest and reignest, God, world without end.—Amen.

Henry Newman

3.42 FATHER, FORGIVE THEM, JOHN NEWTON

Luke 23:34

"Father, forgive (the Savior said)
They know not what they do:"
His heart was moved when thus he prayed
For me, my friends, and you.

He saw, that as the Jews abused
And crucified his flesh;
So he, by us, would be refused,
And crucified afresh.

Through love of sin, we long were prone
To act as Satan bid;
But now, with grief and shame we own,
We knew not what we did.
We knew not the desert of sin,
Nor whom we thus defied;

Nor where our guilty souls had been,
If JESUS had not died.

We knew not what a law we broke,
How holy, just and pure!
Nor what a God we durst provoke,
But thought ourselves secure.

But Jesus all our guilt foresaw,
And shed his precious blood
To satisfy the holy law,
And make our peace with GOD.

My sin, dear Savior, made thee bleed,
Yet didst thou pray for me!
I knew not what I did, indeed,
When ignorant of thee.

John Newton

3.43 CHRIST CRUCIFIED, RICHARD CRASHAW

Thy restless feet now cannot go
For us and our eternal good,
As they were ever wont. What though
They swim, alas! in their own flood?

Thy hands to give Thou canst not lift,
Yet will Thy hand still giving be;
It gives, but O, itself's the gift!
It gives tho' bound, tho' bound tis free!

Richard Crashaw

3.44 A HYMN TO GOD THE FATHER, BEN JONSON

Hear me, O God!
A broken heart
Is my best part.
Use still thy rod,
That I may prove
Therein thy Love.

If thou hadst not
Been stern to me,
But left me free,
I had forgot
Myself and thee.

For sin's so sweet,
As minds ill-bent
Rarely repent,
Until they meet
Their punishment.

Who more can crave
Than thou hast done,
That gav'st a Son,
To free a slave?
First made of naught;
With all since bought.

Sin, Death, and Hell
His glorious name
Quite overcame,
Yet I rebel
And slight the same.

But I'll come in
Before my loss
Me farther toss,
As sure to win
Under His cross.

Ben Jonson

3.45 HIS SAVIOR'S WORDS, GOING TO THE CROSS, ROBERT HERRICK

Have, have ye no regard, all ye
Who pass this way, to pity me
Who am a man of misery?

A man both bruis'd, and broke, and one
Who suffers not here for mine own
But for my friends' transgression?

Ah! Sion's Daughters, do not fear
The Cross, the Cords, the Nails, the Spear,

The Myrrh, the Gall, the Vinegar,
For Christ, your loving Savior, hath
Drunk up the wine of God's fierce wrath;
Only, there's left a little froth,

Less for to taste, than for to shew
What bitter cups had been your due,
Had He not drank them up for you.

Robert Herrick

3.46 THE LOOK, ELIZABETH BARRETT BROWNING

The Savior looked on Peter. Ay, no word,
No gesture of reproach! The heavens serene,
Though heavy with armed justice, did not lean
Their thunders that way! the forsaken Lord
Looked only on the traitor. None record
What that look was, none guess: for those who have seen
Wronged lovers loving through a death-pang ken,

Or pale-cheeked martyrs smiling to a sword,
Have missed Jehovah at the judgment—
"I never knew this man"—did quail and fall, call.
And Peter, from the height of blasphemy
As knowing straight that God—turned free
And went out speechless from the face of all,
And filled the silence, weeping bitterly.

Elizabeth Barrett Browning

THE MEANING OF THE LOOK, ELIZABETH BARRETT BROWNING

I think that look of Christ might seem to say,
"Thou Peter! art thou then a common stone
Which I at last must break my heart upon
For all God's charge to his high angels may
Guard my foot better? Did I yesterday
Wash *thy* feet, my beloved, that they should run
Quick to deny meneath the morning sun?
And do thy kisses, like the rest, betray?

The cock crows coldly, go, and manifest
A late contrition, but no bootless fear!
For when thy final need is dreariest,
Thou shalt not be denied, as I am here;
My voice to God and angels shall attest,
Because I KNOW this man, let him be clear."

Elizabeth Barrett Browning

THE TWO SAYINGS, ELIZABETH BARRETT BROWNING

Two sayings of the Holy Scriptures beat
Like pulses in the Church's brow and breast;
And by them we find rest in our unrest
And, heart deep in salt-tears, do yet entreat
God's fellowship as if on heavenly seat.
The first is JESUS WEPT,—whereon is prest
Full many a sobbing face that drops its best
And sweetest waters on the record sweet:
And one is where the Christ, denied and scorned

LOOKED UPON PETER. Oh, to render plain
By help of having loved a little and mourned,
That look of sovran love and sovran pain
Which HE, who could not sin yet suffered, turned
On him who could reject but not sustain!

Elizabeth Barrett Browning

3.47 IT IS A THING MOST WONDERFUL, WILLIAM W. HOW

It is a thing most wonderful,
Almost too wonderful to be,
That God's own Son should come from Heav'n,
And die to save a child like me.

And yet I know that it is true;
He chose a poor and humble lot,
And wept, and toiled, and mourned, and died,
For love of those who loved Him not.

I cannot tell how He could love
A child so weak and full of sin;

His love must be most wonderful,
If He could die my love to win.

It is most wonderful to know
His love for me so free and sure;
But tis more wonderful to see
My love for Him so faint and poor.

And yet I want to love Thee, Lord;
Oh, light the flame within my heart,
And I will love Thee more and more,
Until I see Thee as Thou art.

William W. How

3.48 RIDE ON, RIDE ON, IN MAJESTY!, HENRY H. MILMAN

Ride on, ride on, in majesty!
Hark! all the tribes Hosanna cry;
O Savior meek, pursue Thy road
With palms and scattered garments strowed.

Ride on, ride on, in majesty!
In lowly pomp ride on to die!
O Christ! Thy triumph now begin
Over captive death and conquered sin.

Ride on, ride on, in majesty!
The wingèd squadrons of the sky
Look down with sad and wondering eyes
To see the approaching sacrifice.

Ride on, ride on, in majesty!
Thy last and fiercest strife is nigh;
The Father, on His sapphire throne,
Expects His own anointed Son.

Ride on, ride on, in majesty!
In lowly pomp ride on to die;
Bow Thy meek head to mortal pain,
Then take, O God, Thy power, and reign.

Henry H. Milman

3.49 ALAS! AND DID MY SAVIOR BLEED, ISAAC WATTS

Alas! and did my Savior bleed
And did my Sovereign die?
Would He devote that sacred head
For sinners such as I?
[originally, For such a worm as I?]

Refrain
At the cross, at the cross where I first saw the light,
And the burden of my heart rolled away,
It was there by faith I received my sight,

And now I am happy all the day!
Thy body slain, sweet Jesus, Thine—
And bathed in its own blood—
While the firm mark of wrath divine,
His Soul in anguish stood.

Was it for crimes that I had done
He groaned upon the tree?
Amazing pity! grace unknown!
And love beyond degree!

Well might the sun in darkness hide
And shut his glories in,
When Christ, the mighty Maker died,

For man the creature's sin.
Thus might I hide my blushing face
While His dear cross appears,
Dissolve my heart in thankfulness,
And melt my eyes to tears.

But drops of grief can ne'er repay
The debt of love I owe:
Here, Lord, I give my self away
'Tis all that I can do.

Isaac Watts

3.50 WHEN I SURVEY THE WONDROUS CROSS, ISAAC WATTS

When I survey the wondrous cross
On which the Prince of glory died,
My richest gain I count but loss,
And pour contempt on all my pride.

Forbid it, Lord, that I should boast,
Save in the death of Christ my God!
All the vain things that charm me most,
I sacrifice them to His blood.

See from His head, His hands, His feet,
Sorrow and love flow mingled down!

Did e'er such love and sorrow meet,
Or thorns compose so rich a crown?

His dying crimson, like a robe,
Spreads o'er His body on the tree;
Then I am dead to all the globe,
And all the globe is dead to me.

Were the whole realm of nature mine,
That were a present far too small;
Love so amazing, so divine,
Demands my soul, my life, my all.

Isaac Watts

3.51 AM I A SOLDIER OF THE CROSS? ISAAC WATTS

Am I a soldier of the cross,
A follower of the Lamb,
And shall I fear to own His cause,
Or blush to speak His Name?

Must I be carried to the skies
On flowery beds of ease,

While others fought to win the prize,
And sailed through bloody seas?

Are there no foes for me to face?
Must I not stem the flood?
Is this vile world a friend to grace,
To help me on to God?

Sure I must fight if I would reign;
Increase my courage, Lord.
I'll bear the toil, endure the pain,
Supported by Thy Word.

Thy saints in all this glorious war
Shall conquer, though they die;

They see the triumph from afar,
By faith's discerning eye.

When that illustrious day shall rise,
And all Thy armies shine
In robes of victory through skies,
The glory shall be Thine.

Isaac Watts

3.52 Rock of Ages, cleft for me, Augustus M. Toplady

Rock of Ages, cleft for me,
Let me hide myself in Thee;
Let the water and the blood,
From Thy wounded side which flowed,
Be of sin the double cure;
Save from wrath and make me pure.

Not the labor of my hands
Can fulfill Thy law's demands;
Could my zeal no respite know,
Could my tears forever flow,
All for sin could not atone;
Thou must save, and Thou alone.

Nothing in my hand I bring,
Simply to the cross I cling;

Naked, come to Thee for dress;
Helpless look to Thee for grace;
Foul, I to the fountain fly;
Wash me, Savior, or I die.

While I draw this fleeting breath,
When mine eyes shall close in death,
[originally When my eye-strings break in death]
When I soar to worlds unknown,
See Thee on Thy judgment throne,
Rock of Ages, cleft for me,
Let me hide myself in Thee.

Augustus M. Toplady

3.53 Good Friday 1613. Riding Westward, John Donne

Let man's Soul be a Sphere, and then, in this,
The intelligence that moves, devotion is,
And as the other Spheres, by being grown
Subject to foreign motions, lose their own,
And being by others hurried every day,
Scarce in a year their natural form obey:
Pleasure of business, so, our Souls admit
For their first mover, and are whirled by it.
Hence is't, that I am carried towards the West
This day, when my Soul's form bends towards
the East.
There I should see a Sun, by rising set,
And by that setting endless day beget;

But that Christ on this Cross, did rise and fall,
Sin had eternally benighted all.
Yet dare I almost be glad, I do not see
That spectacle of too much weight for me.
Who sees God's face, that is self life, must die;
What a death were it then to see God die?

It made his own Lieutenant Nature shrink,
It made his footstool crack, and the Sun wink.
Could I behold those hands which span the
Poles,
And tune all spheres at once, pierc'd with
those holes?

Could I behold that endless height which is
Zenith to us, and our Antipodes,
Humbled below us? or that blood which is
The seat of all our Souls, if not of his,
Made dirt of dust, or that flesh which was
worn
By God, for his apparel, ragg'd, and torn?
If on these things I durst not look, durst I
Upon his miserable mother cast mine eye,
Who was God's partner here, and furnish'd
thus
Half of that Sacrifice, which ransom'd us?
Though these things, as I ride, be from mine eye,

They are present yet unto my memory,
For that looks towards them; and thou look'st
towards me,
O Savior, as Thou hang'st upon the tree;
I turn my back to Thee, but to receive
Corrections, till Thy mercies bid Thee leave.
O think me worth Thine anger, punish me,
Burn off my rusts, and my deformity,
Restore Thine Image, so much, by Thy grace,
That Thou may'st know me, and I'll turn my
face.

John Donne

3.54 Spit in my face, John Donne

Spit in my face you Jews, and pierce my side,
Buffet, and scoff, scourge, and crucify me, For
I have sinned, and sinned, and only he Who
could do no iniquity hath died:
    But by my death can not be satisfied My
sins, which pass the Jews' impiety: They killed
once an inglorious man, but I Crucify him
daily, being now glorified.

Oh let me, then, his strange love still admire:
Kings pardon, but he bore our punishment.
And Jacob came clothed in vile harsh attire
But to supplant, and with gainful intent: God
clothed himself in vile man's flesh, that so He
might be weak enough to suffer woe.

John Donne

3.55 The work of Christ, John Donne

Donne pictures how Jesus' incarnation and death are foils to the evil work of Satan. Jesus buys back what Satan had previously stolen.

HOLY SONNETS XV

Wilt thou love God as he thee? then digest,
My soul, this wholesome meditation,
How God the Spirit, by angels waited on
In heaven, doth make His temple in thy breast.
The Father having begot a Son most blest,
And still begetting—for he ne'er begun—
Hath deign'd to choose thee by adoption,
Co-heir to His glory, and Sabbath' endless rest.
And as a robb'd man, which by search doth find

His stolen stuff sold, must lose or buy it
again,
The Sun of glory came down, and was slain,
Us whom He had made, and Satan stole, to
unbind.
'Twas much, that man was made like God
before,
But, that God should be made like man,
much more.

John Donne

3.56 THE CROSS, JOHN DONNE

Donne wrote these words to go with a signet ring that he gave to Isaac Walton. On the ring was an engraving of Christ crucified with the cross in the shape of an anchor.

The Cross, my seal in baptism, spread below
Doth by that form into an anchor grow,
Crosses grow anchors, bear as thou should'st do
Thy cross, and that cross grows an anchor too.

But he that makes our crosses anchors thus
Is Christ, Who there is crucified for us.

John Donne

3.57 ON A HIGH HILL, JOHN DONNE

On a high hill,
Craggy and steep, Truth stands and he that will
Reach her, about must, and about must go.

John Donne

3.58 BENEATH THE CROSS OF JESUS, ELIZABETH C. CLEPHANE

Beneath the cross of Jesus I fain would take my stand,
The shadow of a mighty rock within a weary land;
A home within the wilderness, a rest upon the way,
From the burning of the noontide heat, and the burden of the day.

O safe and happy shelter, O refuge tried and sweet,
O trysting place where Heaven's love and Heaven's justice meet!
As to the holy patriarch that wondrous dream was given,
So seems my Savior's cross to me, a ladder up to heaven.

There lies beneath its shadow but on the further side
The darkness of an awful grave that gapes both deep and wide

And there between us stands the cross two arms outstretched to save
A watchman set to guard the way from that eternal grave.

Upon that cross of Jesus mine eye at times can see
The very dying form of One Who suffered there for me;
And from my stricken heart with tears two wonders I confess;
The wonders of redeeming love and my unworthiness.

I take, O cross, thy shadow for my abiding place;
I ask no other sunshine than the sunshine of His face;
Content to let the world go by to know no gain or loss,
My sinful self my only shame, my glory all the cross.

Elizabeth C. Clephane

3.59 There is a fountain filled with blood, William Cowper

There is a fountain filled with blood drawn from Emmanuel's veins;
And sinners plunged beneath that flood lose all their guilty stains.
Lose all their guilty stains, lose all their guilty stains;
And sinners plunged beneath that flood lose all their guilty stains.

The dying thief rejoiced to see that fountain in his day;
And there have I, though vile as he, washed all my sins away.
Washed all my sins away, washed all my sins away;
And there have I, though vile as he, washed all my sins away.

Dear dying Lamb, Thy precious blood shall never lose its power
Till all the ransomed church of God be saved, to sin no more.
Be saved, to sin no more, be saved, to sin no more;
Till all the ransomed church of God be saved, to sin no more.

E'er since, by faith, I saw the stream Thy flowing wounds supply,
Redeeming love has been my theme, and shall be till I die.
And shall be till I die, and shall be till I die;
Redeeming love has been my theme, and shall be till I die.

Then in a nobler, sweeter song, I'll sing Thy power to save,
When this poor lisping, stammering tongue lies silent in the grave.
Lies silent in the grave, lies silent in the grave;
When this poor lisping, stammering tongue lies silent in the grave.

Lord, I believe Thou hast prepared, unworthy though I be,
For me a blood bought free reward, a golden harp for me!
'Tis strung and tuned for endless years, and formed by power divine,
To sound in God the Father's ears no other name but Thine.

William Cowper

3.60 The Dream of the Rood, Author unknown

This eighth-century poem and meditation on the death of Christ is most unusually presented from the point of view of the rood (or cross) on which Christ was crucified.

Hear while I tell about the best of dreams
Which came to me the middle of one night
While humankind were sleeping in their beds.
It was as though I saw a wondrous tree
Towering in the sky suffused with light . . .
. . . the best
Of woods began to speak these words to me:

It was long past—I still remember it—
That I was cut down at the copse's end,

Moved from my roots. Strong enemies there took me,
Told me to hold aloft their criminals,
Made me a spectacle. Men carried me
Upon their shoulders, set me on a hill,
A host of enemies there fastened me.
And then I saw the Lord of all mankind
Hasten with eager zeal that He might mount
Upon me. I durst not against God's word
Bend down or break, when I saw tremble all

The surface of the earth. Although I might
Have struck down all the foes, yet stood I fast.
Then the young hero (who was God almighty)
Got ready, resolute and strong in heart.
He climbed onto the lofty gallows-tree,
Bold in the sight of many watching men,
When he intended to redeem mankind.
I trembled as the warrior embraced me.
But still I dared not bend down to the earth,
Fall to the ground. Upright I had to stand.
A rood I was raised up; and I held high
The noble King, the Lord of heaven above.
I dared not stoop. They pierced me with dark nails;
The scars can still be clearly seen on me,
The open wounds of malice. Yet might I
Not harm them. They reviled us both together.

I was made wet all over with the blood
Which poured out from His side, after He had
Sent forth His spirit. And I underwent
Full many a dire experience on that hill.
I saw the God of hosts stretched grimly out.
Darkness covered the Ruler's corpse with clouds,
His shining beauty; the shadows passed across,
Black in the darkness. All creation wept,

Bewailed the King's death; Christ was on the cross.
And yet I saw men coming from afar,
Hastening to the Prince. I watched it all.

Author unknown

3.61 *REX TRAGICUS,* OR CHRIST GOING TO HIS CROSS, ROBERT HERRICK

Put off thy robe of purple, then go on
To the sad place of execution:
Thine hour is come; and the tormentor stands
Ready, to pierce thy tender feet, and hands.
Long before this, the base, the dull, the rude,
Th' inconstant and unpurged multitude
Yawn for thy coming; some ere this time cry,
How he defers, how loath he is to die!
Amongst this scum, the soldier with his spear,
And that sour fellow, with his vinegar,
His sponge, and stick, do ask why thou dost stay?
So do the scurf and bran too: Go thy way,
Thy way, thou guiltless Man, and satisfy
By thine approach, each their beholding eye.
Not as a thief, shalt thou ascend the mount,
But like a person of some high account:
The cross shall be thy stage; and thou shalt there

The spacious field have for thy theatre.
Thou art that Roscius, and that marked-out man,
That must this day act the tragedian,

To wonder and affrightment: Thou art He,
Whom all the flux of nations comes to see;
Not those poor thieves that act their parts with Thee:
Those act without regard, when once a King,
And God, as thou art, comes to suffering.
No, no, this scene from thee takes life and sense,
And soul and spirit, plot and excellence.
Then begin, great King! ascend thy throne,
And thence proceed to act thy passion
To such a height, to such a period raised,
As hell, and earth, and heaven may stand amazed.
God, and good angels guide thee; and so bless
Thee in thy several parts of bitterness;
That those, who see thee nailed unto the tree,
May (though they scorn Thee) praise and pity Thee.
And we (Thy lovers) while we see Thee keep
The laws of action, will both sigh and weep;
And bring our spices, and embalm Thee dead;
That done, we'll see Thee sweetly buried.

Robert Herrick

5

QUOTATION COLLECTION ON THE CROSS OF JESUS

There is a green hill far away,
    Without a city wall,
Where the dear Lord was crucified,
    Who died to save us all.

C. F. Alexander

His sinless life and substitutionary atonement alone are sufficient for our justification and reconciliation to the Father.

Alliance of Confessing Evangelicals, The Cambridge Declaration

What will move you?
    Will pity? Here is distress never the like.
    Will duty? Here is a person never the like.
    Will fear? Here is wrath never the like.
    Will remorse? Here are sins never the like.
    Will kindness? Here is love never the like.
    Will bounty? Here are benefits never the like. Will all these?
    Here they be all, all in the highest degree.

Lancelot Andrewes

O hidden strength! A man hanging on a cross lifts the weight of eternal death; a man fixed on wood frees the world from everlasting death. O hidden power!

Anselm

Why did the Son of God have to suffer for us? There was a great need, and it can be considered in a twofold way: in the first place, as a remedy for sin, and secondly, as an example of how to act.

Thomas Aquinas

All my theology is reduced to this narrow compass—Christ Jesus came into the world to save sinners.

Archibald Arnold

Anyone who has not been troubled by the scandal of Christ's suffering and his complete humiliation is ignorant of the meaning of belief in him.

Johann Heinrich Arnold

He who alone was free among the dead—because he was free to lay down his life and free to take it up again—was for us both victor and victim. . . . and it is because he was the victim that he was also the victor.

Augustine

Jesus Christ is risen today,
Our triumphant holy day;
Who did once upon the cross
Suffer to redeem our loss.

Author unknown, Latin hymn

The cross is the way of the lost.
The cross is the staff of the lame.
The cross is the guide of the blind.
The cross is the strength of the weak.
The cross is the hope of the hopeless.
The cross is the freedom of the slaves.
The cross is the water of the seeds.
The cross is the consolation of the enslaved laborers.
The cross is the source of those who seek water.
The cross is the cloth of the naked.

Author unknown, tenth-century African hymn

The love on the cross is not what God suddenly became but what God always was and ever shall be.

William Barclay

Onward, Christian soldiers,
    Marching as to war,

With the Cross of Jesus
Going on before.

Sabine Baring-Gould

The Cross is the Gate of Heaven.

Karl Barth

To conquer evil, the good must crucify itself.

Nicolas Berdyaev

Justification is a judicial act of God, in which He declares, on the basis of the righteousness of Jesus Christ, that all the claims of the law are satisfied with respect to the sinner.

L. Berkhof

Man of Sorrows! what a name
For the Son of God, who came
Ruined sinners to reclaim!
Hallelujah, what a Savior!

Philip Paul Bliss

He drained the cup of God's wrath bone dry, leaving not a drop for us to drink.

Richard Allen Bodey

Limited Atonement: If from eternity God has planned to save one portion of the human race and not another, it seems to be a contradiction to say that His work has equal reference to both portions, or that He sent His Son to die for those whom He had predetermined not to save, as truly as, and in the same sense that He was sent to die for those whom He had chosen for salvation. These two doctrines must stand or fall together. We cannot logically accept one and reject the other. If God has elected some and not others to eternal life, then plainly the primary purpose of Christ's work was to redeem the elect.

Loraine Boettner

The cross means this: Jesus taking our place to satisfy the demands of God's justice and turning aside God's wrath.

James M. Boice

Any gospel that talks about the love of God without pointing out that his love led him to pay the ultimate price for sin in the person of his Son on the cross is a false gospel.

James M. Boice

If the death of Christ on the cross is the true meaning of the Incarnation, then there is no gospel without the cross.

James M. Boice

Had it not been for this [Christ's] dying, grace and guilt could not have looked each other in the face.

Horatius Bonar

If Christ is not the Substitute, He is nothing to the sinner. If He did not die as the Sin-bearer, He has died in vain.

Horatius Bonar

The cross is God's truth about us, and therefore it is the only power which can make us truthful. When we know the cross we are no longer afraid of the truth.

Dietrich Bonhoeffer

The cross of Christ destroyed the equation "religion equals happiness."

Dietrich Bonhoeffer

The cross is laid on every Christian.

Dietrich Bonhoeffer

Anybody who has once been horrified by the dreadfulness of his own sin that nailed Jesus to the Cross will no longer be horrified by even the rankest sins of a brother.

Dietrich Bonhoeffer

By Thine agony and bloody sweat; by Thy cross and passion; by Thy precious death and burial; by Thy glorious resurrection and ascension: and by the coming of the Holy Ghost, good Lord, deliver us.

Book of Common Prayer

In the cross of Christ excess in men is met by excess in God, excess of evil is mastered by excess of love.

Louis Bourdaloue

In the cross of Christ I glory,
Towering o'er the wrecks of time;
All the light of sacred story
Gathers round its head sublime.

John Bowring

Christ's blood is heaven's key.

Thomas Brooks

When Christ brings his cross, he brings his presence; and where he is, none is desolate, and there is no room for despair.

Elizabeth Barrett Browning

By his dying, Jesus released into the world an entirely new kind of life, life that has flowed down through the tragic centuries like water through a dry land, making alive and whole all who will only kneel to drink.

Frederick Buechner

"Thus far did I come laden with my sin,
Nor could aught ease the grief that I was in,
Till I came hither. What a place is this!
Must here be the beginning of my bliss?
Must here the burden fall from off my back?
Must here the strings that bound it to me crack?
Blest cross! blest sepulcher blest rather be
The Man that there was put to shame for me!"

John Bunyan, The Pilgrim's Progress

He was condemned, that thou mightest be justified, and was killed, that thou mightest live.

John Bunyan

If he hides the sin, or lesseneth it, He is faulty; if He leaves it still upon us, we die. He must then take our iniquity to Himself, make it His own, and so deliver us; for thus having taken the sin upon Himself, as lawfully He may, and lovingly He doth, it followeth that we live if He lives; and who can desire more?

John Bunyan

The Crucifixion accuses human nature, accuses all of us in the very things that we think are our righteousness.

Herbert Butterfield

Our attitude to the Crucifixion must be that of self-identification with the rest of human nature—we must say, "We did it."

Herbert Butterfield

If Christ had died only a bodily death, it would have been ineffectual. Unless his soul shared in the punishment, he would have been the Redeemer of bodies alone. He paid a greater and more excellent price in suffering in his soul the terrible torments of a condemned and forsaken man.

John Calvin

His death was sufficient for all: it was efficient in the case of many.

John Calvin

The Atonement *per se* saves no one. It merely makes salvation possible.

James M. Campbell

The death of God's Son is the only and entirely complete sacrifice and satisfaction for sins; it is of infinite value and worth, more than sufficient to atone for the sins of the whole world.

Canons of Dort

Do you wish to see God's love? Look at the cross. Do you wish to see God's wrath? Look at the cross.

D. A. Carson

Nails were not enough to hold God-and-man nailed and fastened on the Cross, had not love held Him there.

Catherine of Siena

When Jesus Christ shed his blood on the cross, it was not the blood of a martyr; or the blood of one man for another; it was the life of God poured out to redeem the world.

Oswald Chambers

Jesus Christ hates the wrong in man, and Calvary is the estimate of His hatred.

Oswald Chambers

The symbol of God's nature is the cross, whose arms stretch out to limitless reaches.

Oswald Chambers

The doctrine of the death of Christ is the substance of the gospel.

Stephen Charnock

God gave his only begotten Son to be crucified on the cross so that this world could be saved and redeemed. That is God's uppermost goal—the redemption of souls.

Dr David Yonggi Cho
pastor of the largest church in the world, in
Seoul, South Korea

Listen to the Lord's appeal. My body was stretched on the cross as a symbol, not of how much I suffered, but of my all-embracing love.

Peter Chrysologus

The Cross uprooted us from the depths of evil and elevated us to the summit of virtue.

John Chrysostom

By the cross we know the gravity of sin and the greatness of God's love towards us.

John Chrysostom

Lovely was the death
Of him whose life was love.

Samuel Taylor Coleridge

When God wanted to defeat sin, his ultimate weapon was the sacrifice of his own Son.

Charles Colson

The Cross!
There, and there only (though the deist rave,
And atheist, if Earth bears so base a slave);
There and there only, is the power to save.

William Cowper

Dear dying Lamb, Thy precious blood shall never lose its power
Till all the ransomed church of God be saved, to sin no more.

William Cowper

O my Savior, make me see
How dearly thou hast paid for me.

Richard Crawshaw

Christ stretched out His hands on the Cross, that He might embrace the ends of the world; for this Golgotha is the very center of the earth.

Cyril of Jerusalem

To put the matter at its simplest, Jesus Christ came to make bad men good.

James Denney

An atonement that does not regenerate is not an atonement in which men can be asked to believe.

James Denney

The cross is the ladder to heaven.

Thomas Draxe

The necessity of Christ's satisfaction to divine justice is, as it were, the center and hinge of all doctrines of pure revelation.

Jonathan Edwards

Death by crucifixion was, in every sense of the word, excruciating (Latin, *excruciates*, or "out of the cross").

William D. Edwards

While the Lamb of God hanged on the cross delivered the world from Death and Hell.

Ephrem the Syrian

If we consider how utterly undeserved [the crucifixion] was, we call it grace;
if we consider the cost, we call it atonement;
if we consider the effect, we call it new life, redemption, sanctification.

Austin Farrer

In respect of God, Christ's death was justice and mercy. In respect of men, it was murder and cruelty. In respect of himself, it was obedience and humility.

John Flavel

A crucified style best suits the preachers of a crucified Christ.

John Flavel

You do not understand Christ till you understand the cross.

P. T. Forsyth

Love, not anger, brought Jesus to the Cross.
Richard J. Foster

The more we lack in this world, the more we discover the best thing the world has to offer us: the Cross.
Charles de Foucauld

A man who was completely innocent, offered himself as a sacrifice for the good of others, including his enemies, and became the ransom of the world. It was a perfect act.
Mahatma Gandhi

O sacred head, sore wounded,
  Defiled and put to scorn;
O kingly head, surrounded
  With mocking crown of thorn:
What sorrow mars thy grandeur?
  Can death thy bloom deflower?
O countenance whose splendor
  The hosts of heaven adore!
In thy most bitter passion
  My heart to share doth cry,
With thee for my salvation
  Upon the cross to die.
Ah, keep my heart thus movèd
  To stand thy cross beneath,
To mourn thee, well-belovèd,
  Yet thank thee for thy death.
Paul Gerhardt

Christ died for all mankind, he suffered for all mankind. He forgave as he was tortured and killed.
Mel Gibson

God came to earth to do the one thing he could not do in heaven. Die.
Ken Gire

There were no cords could have held him to the whipping-post but those of love; no nails have fastened him to the cross but those of love.
Thomas Goodwin

From the darkness round the cross there rings out this voice so sure that God is love.
A. J. Gossip

The blood of Christ may seem to be a grim, repulsive subject to those who do not realize its true significance, but to those who have accepted his redemption and have been set free from sin's chains, the blood of Christ is precious.
Billy Graham

It was love that kept Jesus from calling 12,000 angels who had already drawn their swords to come to his rescue.
Billy Graham

Only the way of the cross leads home.
Billy Graham

In the cross of Christ I see three things:
First, a description of the depth of man's sin.
Second, the overwhelming love of God.
Third, the only way of salvation.
Billy Graham

The knowledge of the Cross is concealed in the sufferings of the Cross.
Gregory I (the Great)

A few drops of Blood renew the whole world.
Gregory I (the Great)

Yesterday I hung on the cross with Christ;
today I am glorified with him;
yesterday I was dying with him; today I am brought to life with him;
yesterday I was buried with him; today I rise with him.
Gregory of Nyssa

At the supreme moment of his dying Jesus so identified himself with men and the depths of their predicament and agony that no man can now sink so low that God has not gone lower.
Os Guinness

Christ never lost a battle even when He lost His life.
William Gurnall

Pilate missed Christ on the bench, while the poor thief finds Him, and heaven with Him, on the cross.
William Gurnall

If your love for the Lord is pure, you will love him as much on Calvary as on Mount Tabor.

Jeanne Guyon

God gives us the cross, and then the cross gives us God.

Jeanne Guyon

Come, and see the victories of the cross. Christ's wounds are thy healings, His agonies thy repose, His conflicts thy conquests, His groans thy songs, His pains thine ease, His shame thy glory, His death thy life, His sufferings, thy salvation.

Matthew Henry

Though God loved Christ as his Son he frowned upon him as a Surety.

Matthew Henry

Christ did not die that God might love us, but He died because God loved us.

Charles Hodge

If o'er the dial glides a shade, redeem
The time for lo! It passes like a dream:
But if tis all a blank, then mark the loss
Of hours unblest by shadows from the cross.

Inscription, on a sun dial in a churchyard at Shenstone, England

The cross is the door to mysteries.

Isaac of Syria

Through a tree we were made debtors to God; so through a tree we have our debt canceled.

Irenaeus

After the Savior's sufferings, the Cross became the sign of the Son of Man, that is, the Cross signifies the Lord Himself, incarnate and suffering for our salvation.

John of Kronstadt

He who seeks not the cross of Christ seeks not the glory of Christ.

John of the Cross

At the cross God wrapped his heart in flesh and blood and let it be nailed to the cross for our redemption.

E. Stanley Jones

"He bore in his own body our sins upon a tree." Don't ask me to explain it. I can't explain it, I bow in humility and repentance at, the cross at the wonder of it, that God should give himself for me. I bow and am redeemed!

E. Stanley Jones

The more we meditate on the Cross, the deeper our companionship and knowledge gets of Christ the Lord.

Pishoy Kamel

Suffering love, the cross, stands at the heart of the church.

T.Z. Koo

Comfort yourself with him who nails you to the cross.

Brother Lawrence

May the Cross of Christ be the glory of Christians.

William Law

The whole world in comparison with the cross of Christ is one grand impertinence.

Robert Leighton

Thy Cross is a well of blessing for all, and a cause for thanksgiving for all.

Leo I

It costs God nothing, so far as we know, to create nice things: but to convert rebellious wills cost him crucifixion.

C. S. Lewis

We are told that Christ was killed for us, that His death has washed out our sins, and that by dying He disabled death itself. That is the formula. That is Christianity. That is what has to be believed.

C. S. Lewis

It was not for societies or states, that Christ died, but for men.

C. S. Lewis

There is only one answer to the question as to why Christ had to die—the holiness of God!

D. Martyn Lloyd-Jones

Our Lord's death on the Cross is the supreme manifestation of the love of God.

> D. Martyn Lloyd-Jones

It was not we who brought God's Son to the cross. It was God.

> D. Martyn Lloyd-Jones

We are also told in Isaiah 53 that Christ's death is to be vicarious.

> D. Martyn Lloyd-Jones

In Christ my guilt is removed.

> D. Martyn Lloyd-Jones

The blood of Christ does not cover your sins, conceal your sins, postpone your sins, or diminish your sins. It takes away your sins.

> Max Lucado

The cross is where God forgave his children without lowering his standards.

> Max Lucado

Lord Jesus, you are my righteousness, I am your sin. You have taken upon yourself what is mine and given me what is yours. You have become what you were not so that I might become what I was not.

> Martin Luther

In Christ crucified is the true theology and the knowledge of God.

> Martin Luther

Christ, our Sin-bearer is not like Moses who only shows sin, but rather like Aaron who bears sin.

> Martin Luther

Jesus became the greatest liar, perjurer, thief, adulterer and murderer than mankind has ever known—not because he committed these sins but because he was actually made sin for us.

> Martin Luther

One drop of Christ's blood is worth more than heaven and earth.

> Martin Luther

Take this to heart and doubt not that you are the one who killed Christ. Your sins certainly did, and when you see the nails driven through his hands, be sure that you are pondering, and when the thorns pierce his brow, know that they are your evil thoughts.

> Martin Luther

Christians are righteous because they believe in Christ, whose righteousness covers them and is imputed to them.

> Martin Luther

Either sin is with you, lying on your shoulders, or it is lying on Christ, the Lamb of God. Now if it is lying on your back, you are lost; but if it is resting on Christ, you are free, and you will be saved.

> Martin Luther

This is the mystery of the riches of divine grace for sinners; for by a wonderful exchange our sins are now not ours but Christ's, and Christ's righteousness is not Christ's but ours.

> Martin Luther

The purpose of the cross is to repair the irreparable.

> Erwin Lutzer

Christ's death on the cross included a sacrifice for all our sins, past, present, and future.

> Erwin Lutzer

Hold thou thy cross
    before my closing eyes;
Shine through the gloom,
    and point me to the skies;
Heaven's morning breaks,
    and earth's vain shadows flee;
In life, in death, O Lord,
    abide with me.

> Henry Francis Lyte

The cross is proof of both the immense love of God and the profound wickedness of sin.

> John F. MacArthur

On the cross, God treated Jesus as if he lived your life so he could treat you as if you had lived his. That's imputation; that's substitution.

> John F. McArthur

The story of God's self-sacrifice … is the story with a cross at its center but not at its end: its plot moves toward the upsetting of all things, the Great Reversal in which the dead Jesus was raised from the tomb, and along with him our hope that death be swallowed up by life eternal.

David McCullough

The wounds of Christ were the greatest outlets of his glory that ever were. The divine glory shone more out of his wounds than out of all his life before.

Robert Murray M'Cheyne

Jesus was crucified not in a cathedral between two candles, but on a cross between two thieves.

George F. MacLeod

In most trials, people are tried for what they have done, but this was not true of Christ's. Jesus was tried for who he was.

Josh McDowell

Each of Christ's wounds is a token of the loving care of a compassionate God.

Alister McGrath

Each nail hammered into the body of the Savior of the world shouts out these words— "He loves us!"

Alister McGrath

Christ on the cross is not a mere theological precondition for salvation. He is God's enduring Word to the world saying, "See how much I love you. See how you must love one another."

Brennan Manning

In one and the same movement, our Savior's passion raises men and women from the depths, lifts them up from the earth, and sets them in the heights.

Maximus of Turin

The cross is seen as the saving act of Christ, but even more than this, it is seen as the final place of reconciliation between God and humanity.

Calvin Miller

One cannot even begin to understand the life of Christ without understanding His death.

Calvin Miller

The symbol of the cross in the church points to the God who was crucified not between two candles on an altar, but between two thieves in the place of the skull, where the outcasts belong, outside the gates of the city.

Jurgen Moltmann

In all truth, Wisdom is the Cross and the Cross is Wisdom.

Louis de Montfort

I must die or get somebody to die for me. If the Bible doesn't teach that, it doesn't teach anything. And that is where the atonement of Jesus Christ comes in.

D. L. Moody

And in the garden secretly,
    And on the cross on high,
Should teach his brethren, and inspire
    To suffer and to die.

J. H. Newman

Every time real preaching occurs the crucifixion is realized again: for no preacher can bring anyone to the light without having entered the darkness of the cross himself.

Henri Nouwen

If there be no sin, the Son of God would not have had to become a lamb, nor would he have had to become incarnate and be put to death.

Origen

Christ died for all men; I am a man: therefore, Christ died for me.

John Owen

Christ did not die for any upon condition, if they do believe; but He died for all God's elect, that they should believe.

John Owen

He suffered not as God, but he who suffered was God.

John Owen

There is no death of sin without the death of Christ.

John Owen

The Cross saves.

J. I. Packer

Christ's death made satisfaction precisely by being the punishment of our sins in his person. Satisfaction, in other words, was by substitution; vicarious sin-bearing by the Son of God is the ground of our justification and hope.

J. I. Packer

The death of Christ was an act of obedient substitution on Christ's part, an acceptance in his own person of the penalty due to us, in virtue of which the holy Judge declares guilty sinners immune from punishment and righteous in his sight.

J. I. Packer

The doctrine of justification by faith is like Atlas. It bears a whole world on its shoulders, the entire evangelical knowledge of God the Savior.

J. I. Packer

Calvary not merely made possible the salvation of those for whom Christ died; it ensured that they would be brought to faith and their salvation made actual.

J. I. Packer

Jesus Christ is a God whom we approach without pride and before whom we humble ourselves without despair.

Blaise Pascal

The knowledge of God without that of man's misery causes pride. The knowledge of man's misery without that of God causes despair. The knowledge of Jesus Christ constitutes the middle course, because in Him we find both God and our misery.

Blaise Pascal

When you feel the assaults of passion and anger, then is the time to be silent as Jesus was silent in the midst of His ignominies and sufferings.

Paul of the Cross

The atonement was not the cause but the effect of God's love.

A. W. Pink

They are nice to wear for jewelry, but nobody wants to die on one.

John Piper

God did not spare his own Son, because it was the only way he could spare us.

John Piper

The wisdom of God has ordained a way for the love of God to deliver us from the wrath of God without compromising the justice of God.

John Piper

Man asserts himself against God and puts himself where only God deserves to be; God sacrifices himself for man and puts himself where only man deserves to be.

Rebecca Manley Pippert

The death of Christ was the most dreadful blow ever given to the empire of darkness.

William S. Plumer

I do not believe we can repeat too often the dust-raising truth that if common sense had been enough, Jesus Christ would not have needed to die!

Eugenia Price

Repentance as such does not expiate sin and pay for sin.

Cornelius Pronk

The cross is our tree of life.

Vic Reasoner

Two thousand years ago there was One here on this earth who lived the grandest life that ever has been lived yet: a life that every thinking man, with deeper or shallower meaning, has agreed to call divine.

F. W. Robertson

Death stung himself to death when he stung Christ.

William Romaine

Apart from the cross there is no other ladder by which we may get to heaven.

Rose of Lima

Socrates dies with honor, surrounded by his disciples listening to the most tender words—the easiest death that one could wish to die. Jesus dies in pain, dishonor, mockery, the object of universal cursing—the most horrible death that one could fear. At the receipt of the cup of poison, Socrates blesses him who could not give it to him without tears; Jesus, while suffering the sharpest pains, prays for His most bitter enemies. If Socrates lived and died like a philosopher, Jesus lived and died like a god.

Jean-Jacques Rousseau

The cross of Christ, on which he was extended, points, in the length of it, to heaven and earth, reconciling them together; and in the breadth of it, to former and following ages, as being equally salvation to both.

Samuel Rutherford

Christ would have lived, and taught, and preached, and prophesied, and wrought miracles in vain, if he had not crowned all by dying for our sins as our substitute!

J. C. Ryle

You must know His Cross, and His blood, or else you will die in your sins.

J. C. Ryle

Take away the cross from the Bible, and it's a dark book.

J. C. Ryle

The cross of Christ is the summary of all; the central point, from which radiate Justification, Sanctification, and the Future Glory.

Adolph Saphir

What is the cross? It is a minus turned into a plus.

Robert H. Schuller

From my many years experience I can unhesitatingly say that the cross bears those who bear the cross.

Sadhu Sundar Singh

We know more about the details of the hours immediately before and the actual death of Jesus, in and near Jerusalem, than we know about the death of any other one man in all the ancient world.

Wilbur Smith

See the greatness of your sins which required so vast a sacrifice.

C. H. Spurgeon

The heaviest end of the cross lies ever on His shoulders. If He bids us carry a burden, He carries it also.

C. H. Spurgeon

If we would live aright it must be by the contemplation of Christ's death.

C. H. Spurgeon

I would rather believe a limited atonement that is efficacious for all men for whom it was intended, than a universal atonement that is not efficacious for anybody, except the will of men be added to it.

C. H. Spurgeon

Christ crucified is of no practical value to us without the work of the Holy Spirit.

C. H. Spurgeon

No scene in sacred history ever gladdens the soul like Calvary's tragedy.

C. H. Spurgeon

Christ died our death in order that we might be forgiven.

John Stott

The accumulated sins of all human history were laid upon Christ.

John Stott

The cross bids us accept injury, love our enemies, and leave the outcome to God.

John Stott

If you are talking of atonement, the means by which we sinners can be reconciled to the God of holy love, why then, yes, I don't think we can escape the truth of the divine substitution.

John Stott

Christ took our nature, sin guilt and judgment upon him in his death.

John Stott

Grant, O Lord, that in your wounds I may find my safety, in your stripes my cure, in your pain my peace, in your cross my victory, in your resurrection my triumph, and a crown of righteousness in the glories of your eternal kingdom.

Jeremy Taylor

We deny that any view of the Atonement that rejects the substitutionary satisfaction of divine justice, accomplished vicariously for believers, is compatible with the teaching of the Gospel.

The gospel of Jesus Christ: An evangelical celebration

In the cross there is safety.

Thomas à Kempis

Jesus now has many lovers of His heavenly kingdom, but few bearers of his cross.

Thomas à Kempis

To glory in tribulation is no hard thing for him that loveth, for so to glory is to glory in the cross of the Lord.

Thomas à Kempis

We must do something about the cross, and one of two things only we can do—flee it or die upon it.

A. W. Tozer

The cross of Christ is the most revolutionary thing ever to appear among men.

A. W. Tozer

The cross is a symbol of death. It stands for the abrupt, violent death of a human being. The man in Roman times who took up his cross and started down the road had already said good-by to his friends. He was not coming back. He was going out to have it

ended. The cross made no compromise, modified nothing, spared nothing; it slew all of the man, completely and for good. It did not try to keep on good terms with its victim. It struck cruel and hard, and when it had finished its work, the man was no more.

A. W. Tozer

The cross is a tree set on fire with invisible flame, that illumines all the world. The flame is love.

Thomas Traherne

The cross is the abyss of wonders, the center of desire, the school of virtues, the house of wisdom, the throne of love, the theater of joys, and the place of sorrows; it is the root of happiness, and the gate of heaven.

Thomas Traherne

In the blood of Christ, which fulfilled the law for us, may every person that repents, believes, loves the law and mourns for strength to fulfill it, rejoice, be he ever so weak a sinner.

William Tyndale

Heaven comes by Christ's blood.

William Tyndale

The Cross will either cause offence to man's pride and intelligence or it will be the pinnacle of God's wisdom, power, glory and grace to man.

Arthur Wallis

The cross is a picture of violence, yet the key to peace, a picture of suffering, yet the key to healing, a picture of death, yet the key to life.

David Watson

Christ's blood has value enough to redeem the whole world, but the virtue of it is applied only to such as believe.

Thomas Watson

When I survey the wondrous cross,
On which the Prince of Glory died,
My richest gain I count by loss,
And pour contempt on all my pride.

Isaac Watts

At the heart of the story stands the cross of Christ where evil did its worst and met its match.

John W. Wenham

The divine King rules forever by dying.

B. F. Westcott

The wood and the nails and the spear all taken together were not our Lord's real cross. His real cross was sin; our sin laid on His hands, and on His imagination, and on His conscience, till it was all but His very own sin.

Alexander Whyte

The cross reveals the vast difference between a god who proves himself through power and One who proves himself through love.

Philip Yancey

Part Four

THE RESURRECTION, ASCENSION AND RETURN OF JESUS

INTRODUCTION

Belief in the literal, bodily resurrection of Jesus has always been an important non-negotiable doctrine of the Christian faith for most Christians.

The idea of any kind of human resurrection, let alone Jesus' resurrection, has never been a popular concept. The ancient Greeks poured scorn on the notion that the body could ever be raised. It is little wonder that when Paul in Athens spoke about "the resurrection of the dead," the Greeks mocked his message (Acts 17:32).

In Jesus' day the idea of the resurrection of the body was rejected by the Sadducees (Matthew 22:23; Acts 23:6-8). It seems that belief in Jesus' resurrection has been attacked and rejected by leading religious authorities in every age.

Then there are attacks by atheists on any kind of resurrection. An article in the *Soviet Encyclopedia* asserts that the concept of the resurrection is in "decisive contradiction with scientific natural knowledge."

Some Christians who do not enjoy the support of a close Christian fellowship often feel overwhelmed by the constant barrage of attacks on the possibility of Jesus ever rising from the dead. Other Christians are so cocooned that they are unaware of any arguments that could ever make anyone doubt Jesus' resurrection.

In Part Four of *The Encyclopedia of Jesus' Life and Time* Christian theologians emphasize both the historic fact of the event of Jesus' resurrection and the necessity of having personal faith in the risen Lord Jesus Christ. They believe that there is no need at all for Christians to be doubtful, or apologetic, about the resurrection of Jesus.

The New Testament teaching on the ascension of Jesus and his return are also included here in Part Four.

1

COMPARING MODERN VIEWPOINTS ON THE RESURRECTION OF JESUS

4.1 BILLY GRAHAM

THE FACT OF THE RESURRECTION

Upon that great fact [of Jesus' resurrection] hangs the entire plan of the redemptive program of God. Without the resurrection there could be no salvation. Christ predicted His resurrection many times. He said on one occasion, "For as Jonah was three days and three nights in the whale's belly; so shall the Son of man be three days and three nights in the heart of the earth" (Matthew 12:40). As He predicted, He rose!

There are certain laws of evidence which hold in the establishment of any historic event. There must be documentation of the event in question made by reliable contemporary witnesses. There is more evidence that Jesus rose from the dead than there is that Julius Caesar ever lived or that Alexander the Great died at the age of thirty-three. It is strange that historians will accept thousands of facts for which they can produce only shreds of evidence. But in the face of the overwhelming evidence of the resurrection of Jesus Christ they cast a skeptical eye and hold intellectual doubts. The trouble with these people is that they do not want to believe. Their spiritual vision is so blinded and they are so completely prejudiced that they cannot accept the glorious fact of the resurrection of Christ on Bible testimony alone.

The resurrection meant:

First, that Christ was undeniably God. He was what He claimed to be. Christ was Deity in the flesh.

Second, it meant that God had accepted His atoning work on the cross, which was necessary to our salvation. (See Romans 4:25.)

Third, it assures mankind of a righteous judgment. . . . (See Romans 5:19.)

Fourth, it guarantees that our bodies also will be raised in the end. (See 1 Corinthians 15:20.)

And, fifth, it means that death will ultimately be abolished. (See Psalm 23:4.)

Billy Graham, Peace with God, *Word Publishing, 1955*

4.2 C. S. LEWIS

HALLUCINATION?

Any theory of hallucination breaks down on the fact (and if it is invention [rather than fact], it is the oddest invention that ever entered the mind of man) that on three separate occasions this hallucination was not immediately recognized as Jesus (Luke 24:13-31; John 20:15; 21:4). Even granting that God sent a holy hallucination to teach truths already widely believed without it, and far more easily taught by other methods, and certain to be completely obscured by this, might we not at least hope that he would get the face of the hallucination right? Is he who made all faces such a bungler that he cannot even work up a recognizable likeness of the Man who was himself?

C. S. Lewis, Miracles, *New York: Macmillan, 1960*

4.3 M. Lloyd-Jones

SANCTIFICATION IN THE LIGHT OF THE RESURRECTION

"Who was delivered for our offences, and was raised again for our justification." Romans 4:25

It is only in the light of the resurrection that I finally have an assurance of my sins forgiven. It is only in the light of the resurrection that I ultimately know that I stand in the presence of God absolved from guilt and shame and every condemnation. I can now say with Paul, "There is therefore now no condemnation to them which are in Christ Jesus, (Romans 8:1) because I look at the fact of the resurrection. It is there that I know it.

You notice how Paul argues in 1 Corinthians 15:17 when he says, "If Christ be not raised, your faith is vain; ye are yet in your sins." If it is not a fact that Christ literally rose from the grave, then you are still guilty before God. Your punishment has not been borne, your sins have not been dealt with, you are yet in your sins. It matters that much: without the resurrection you have not standing at all. You are still uncertain as to whether you are forgiven and whether you are a child of God. And when one day you come to your death-bed you will not know, you will be uncertain as to where you are going and what is going to happen to you. "Who was delivered for our offences, and was raised again for our justification" (Romans 4:25). It is there in the resurrection that I stand before God free and absolved and without a fear and know that I am indeed a child of God. So you see the importance of holding on to this doctrine and why we must insist upon the details of doctrine, and not be content with some vague general belief in the Lord Jesus Christ?

M. Lloyd-Jones
Sanctified through the truth, *Crossway Books, Wheaton, 1989*

4.4 J. I. Packer

WHAT IF JESUS HAD STAYED DEAD?

Suppose that Jesus, having died on the cross, had stayed dead. Suppose that, like Socrates or Confucius, he was now no more than a beautiful memory. Would it matter? Had Jesus not risen, but stayed dead, the bottom would drop out of Christianity, for four things would then be true.

First, to quote Paul, 1 Cor. 15:17: "If Christ has not been raised, your faith is futile and you are still in your sins."

Second, there is then no hope of your rising either; we must expect to say dead too.

Third, if Jesus Christ is not risen, then he is not reigning and will not return . . . .

Fourth, Christianity cannot be what the first Christians thought it was—fellowship with a living Lord who is identical with the Jesus of the Gospels. The Jesus of the Gospels can still be your hero, but he cannot be your Savior.

[He rose on] . . . "the third day," counting inclusively (the ancient's way) from the day when Jesus was "crucified under Pontius Pilate" in about A. D. 30. On that precise day, in Jerusalem, capital of Palestine, Jesus came alive and vacated a rock tomb, and death was conquered for all time.

Can we be sure it happened? The evidence is solid. The tomb was empty, and nobody could produce the body. For more than a month after, the disciples kept meeting Jesus alive, always unexpectedly, usually in groups (from two to 500). Hallucinations don't happen this way!

The disciples, for their part, were sure that the risen Christ was no fancy, and tirelessly proclaimed his rising in face of ridicule, persecution, and even death—a most effective way of scotching the malicious rumor that they stole Jesus' body (cf. Matthew 28:11-15).

J. I. Packer, Growing in Christ, *Crossway Books, Wheaton, 1994*

4.5 JOHN STOTT

EVIDENCES FOR THE RESURRECTION

It was the resurrection which transformed Peter's fear into courage and James' doubt into faith. It was the resurrection which changed the Sabbath into Sunday and the Jewish remnant into the Christian church. It was the resurrection which changed Saul, the Pharisee, into Paul, the Apostle, the fanatical persecutor into a preacher of the very faith he previously tried to destroy. These are the evidences for the resurrection. The body had disappeared. The grave cloths remained undisturbed. The Lord was seen. And the disciples were transformed. There was no adequate explanation of these phenomena other than the great Christian affirmation: The Lord is risen indeed!'

John Stott, Basic Christianity, *Grand Rapids: Eerdmans, 1972*

THE LINK BETWEEN JESUS' DEATH AND RESURRECTION

There can be no question that, although Christ's saving career is one, it is principally by his death that men may be saved. We read in 1 Corinthians 15:3ff. . . . that "Christ died for our sins," not that "Christ rose for our sins." Certainly the apostle goes on in this primitive statement of the gospel to say "he was raised" and that "he appeared" to various chosen witnesses, but his resurrection did not in itself accomplish our salvation, but rather gave public evidence of its accomplishment by Christ's death, with which the Father was well pleased. That is why Paul can write later in the same chapter: "if Christ has not been raised, then our preaching is in vain and your faith is in vain. . . If Christ has not been raised, your faith is futile and you are still in your sins" (verses 14, 17). If Jesus never rose from the dead, men are still unsaved sinners, not because the resurrection would have saved them, but because without the resurrection, the death of Jesus is shown to have been without saving efficacy.

John Stott, The Preacher's Portrait, *Grand Rapids: Eerdmans, 1961*

THEOLOGIANS AND CHRISTIAN WRITERS ON THE RESURRECTION OF JESUS

4.6 DAMASUS WILL RISE AGAIN, ST. DAMASUS

He who walking on the sea could calm the bitter waves, who gives life to the dying seeds of the earth; he who was able to loose the mortal chains of death, and after three days' darkness could bring again to the upper world the brother for his sister Martha: he, I believe, will make Damasus rise again from the dust.

St. Damasus, from an epitaph written for himself

4.7 THE RESURRECTION OF CHRIST, MARTIN LUTHER

The history of the resurrection of Christ, teaching that which human wit and wisdom of itself cannot believe, that "Christ is risen from the dead," was declared to the weaker and sillier creatures, women, and such as were perplexed and troubled.

Silly, indeed, before God, and before the world: first, before God, in that they "sought the living among the dead"; second, before the world, for they forgot the "great stone which lay at the mouth of the sepulcher," and prepared spices to anoint Christ, which was all in vain. But spiritually is hereby signified this: if the "great stone," namely, the law and human traditions, whereby the consciences are bound and snared, be not rolled away from the heart, then we cannot find Christ, or believe that he is risen from the dead. For through him we are delivered from the power of sin and death, Rom. 8, so that the hand-writing of the conscience can hurt us no more.

Martin Luther, Table Talk, *195*

4.8 THE ARISING OF JESUS, ALFRED EDERSHEIM

St. Matt. 28:1-10; Mark 16:1-11; Luke 24:1-12; John 20:1-18; St. Matt. 28:11-15; Mark 16:12, 13; Luke 24:13-35; 1 Cor. 15:5; Mark 16:14; Luke 24:36-43; John 20:19-25; John 20:26-29; St. Matt. 28:16; John 21:1-24; St. Matt. 28:17-20; Mark 16:15-28; 1 Cor. 15:6; Luke 24:44-53; Mark 16:19, 20; Acts 1:3-12.

Grey dawn was streaking the sky, when they who had so lovingly watched Him to His Burying were making their lonely way to the rock-hewn Tomb in the Garden. Considerable as are the difficulties of exactly harmonizing the details in the various narratives, if, indeed, importance attaches to such attempts, we are thankful to know that any hesitation only attaches to the arrangement of minutes particulars, and not to the great facts of the case. And even these minute details would, as we shall have occasion to show, be harmonious, if only we knew all the circumstances.

The difference, if such it may be called, in the names of the women, who at early morn went to the Tomb, scarce requires elaborate discussion. It may have been, that there were two parties, starting from different places to meet at the Tomb, and that this also accounts for the slight difference in the details of what they saw and heard at the Grave. At any rate, the mention of the two Marys and Joanna is supplemented in Luke by that of the "other women with them," while, if John speaks only of Mary Magdalene, her report to Peter and John: "We know not where they have laid Him," implies, that she had not gone alone to the Tomb. It was the first day of the week, an expression which exactly answers to the Rabbinic, according to Jewish reckoning the third day from His Death; Friday, Saturday, Sunday.

The narrative leaves the impression that the Sabbath's rest had delayed their visit to the Tomb; but it is at least a curious coincidence that the relatives and friends of the deceased were in the habit of going to the grave up to the third day (when presumably corruption was supposed to begin), so as to make sure that those laid there were really dead. Commenting on this, that Abraham described Mount Moriah on the third day, the Rabbis insist on the importance of "the third day" in various events connected with Israel, and specially speak of it in connection with the resurrection of the dead, referring in proof to Hos. 6:2. In another place, appealing to the same prophetic saying, they infer from Gen. 42:7, that God never leaves the just more than three days in anguish.

In mourning also the third day formed a sort of period, because it was thought that the soul hovered round the body till the third day, when it finally parted from its tabernacle.

Although these things are here mentioned, we need scarcely say that no such thoughts were present with the holy mourners who, in the grey of that Sunday-morning, went to the Tomb. Whether or not there were two groups of women who started from different places to meet at the Tomb, the most prominent figure among them was Mary Magdalene as prominent among the pious women as Peter was among the Apostles.

She seems to have reached the Grave, and, seeing the great stone that had covered its entrance rolled away, hastily judged that the Body of the lord had been removed. Without waiting for further inquiry, she ran back to inform Peter and John of the fact. The Evangelist here explains, that there had been a great earthquake, and that the Angel of the Lord, to human sight as lightning and in brilliant white garment, had rolled back the stone, and sat upon it, when the guard, affrighted by what they heard and saw, and especially by the look and attitude of heavenly power in the Angel, had been seized with mortal faintness. Remembering the events connected with the Crucifixion, which had no doubt been talked about among the soldiery, and bearing in mind the impression of such a sight on such minds, we could readily understand the effect on the two sentries who that long night had kept guard over the solitary Tomb.

The event itself (we mean: as regards the rolling away of the stone), we suppose to have taken place after the Resurrection of Christ, in the early dawn, while the holy women were on their way to the Tomb. The earth-quake cannot have been one in the ordinary sense, but a shaking of the place, when the Lord of Life burst the gates of Hades to re-tenant His Glorified Body, and the lightning-like Angel descended from heaven to roll away the stone. To have left it there, when the Tomb was empty, would have implied what was no longer true. But there is a sublime irony in the contrast between man's elaborate precautions and the ease with which the Divine Hand can sweep them aside, and which, as throughout the history of Christ and of His Church, recalls the prophetic declaration: He that sitteth in the heavens shall laugh at them.'

While the Magdalene hastened, probably by another road, to the abode of Peter and John, the other women also had reached the Tomb, either in one party, or, it may be, in two companies. They had wondered and feared how they could accomplish their pious purpose, for, who would roll away the stone for them? But, as often, the difficulty apprehended no longer existed. Perhaps they thought that the now absent Mary Magdalene had obtained help for this. At any rate, they now entered the vestibule of the Sepulcher. Here the appearance of the Angel filled them with fear. But the heavenly Messenger bade them dismiss apprehension; he told them that Christ was not there, nor yet any longer dead, but risen, as indeed, He had foretold in Galilee to His disciples; finally, he bade them hasten with the announcements to the disciples, and with this message, that, as Christ had directed them before, they were to meet Him in Galilee.

It was not only that this connected, so to speak, the wondrous present with the familiar past, and helped them to realize that it was their very Master; nor yet that in the retirement, quiet, and security of Galilee, there would be best opportunity for fullest manifestation, as to the five hundred, and for final conversation and instruction. But the main reason, and that which explains the otherwise strange, almost exclusive, promi-

nence given at such a moment to the direction to meet Him in Galilee, has already been indicated in a previous chapter. . . . With the scattering of the Eleven in Gethsemane on the night of Christ's betrayal, the Apostolic College was temporarily broken up. They continued, indeed, still to meet together as individual disciples, but the bond of the Apostolate was for the moment, dissolved.

And the Apostolic circle was to be reformed, and the Apostolic Commission renewed and enlarged, in Galilee; not, indeed, by its Lake, where only seven of the Eleven seem to have been present, John 21:2, but on the mountain where He had directed them to meet Him, Matt. 28:16. Thus was the end to be like the beginning. Where He had first called, and directed them for their work, there would He again call them, give fullest directions, and bestow new and amplest powers. His appearances in Jerusalem were intended to prepare them for all this, to assure them completely and joyously of the fact of His Resurrection, the full teaching of which would be given in Galilee. And when the women, perplexed and scarcely conscious, obeyed the command to go in and examine for themselves the now empty niche in the Tomb, they saw two Angels

They waited no longer, but hastened, without speaking to anyone, to carry to the disciples the tidings of which they could not even yet grasp the full import. In the Fourth Gospel, Mary Magdalene hastens from the Tomb, and ran to the lodging of Peter and to that of John. Her startling tidings induced them to go at once, and they went towards the sepulcher. "But they began to run, the two together," probably so soon as they were outside the town and near the Garden. John, as the younger, outran Peter. It may be regarded as a specimen of what one might designate as the imputation of sinister motives to the Evangelists, when the most advanced negative criticism describes this legend as implying the contest between Jewish and Gentile Christianity (Peter and John) in which the younger gains the race!

Similarly, we are informed that the penitent on the Cross is intended to indicate the Gentiles, the impenitent the Jews! But no language can be to strong to repudiate the imputation, that so many parts of the Gospels were intended as covert attacks by certain tendencies in the early Church against others, the Petrine and Jacobine against the Johannine and Pauline directions.

Reaching the Sepulcher, and stooping down, he seeth the linen clothes, but, from his position, not the napkin which lay apart by itself. If reverence and awe prevented John from entering the Sepulcher, his impulsive companion, who arrived immediately after him, thought of nothing else than the immediate and full clearing up of the mystery.

As he entered the sepulcher, he steadfastly (intently) beholds in one place the linen swathes that had bound about His Head. There was no sign of haste, but all was orderly, leaving the impression of One Who had leisurely divested Himself of what no longer befitted Him. Soon the other disciples followed Peter. The effect of what he saw was, that he now believed in his heart that the Master was risen, for till then they had not yet derived from Holy Scripture the knowledge that He must rise again. And this also is most instructive. It was not the belief previously derived from Scripture, that the Christ was to rise from the Dead, which led to expectancy of it, but the evidence that He had risen which led them to the knowledge of what Scripture taught on the subject.

Yet whatever light had risen in the inmost sanctuary of John's heart, he spake not his thoughts to the Magdalene, whether she had reached the Sepulcher ere the two left it, or met them by the way. The two Apostles returned to their home, either feeling that nothing more could be learned at the Tomb, or wait for further teaching and guidance. Or it might even have been partly due to a desire not to draw needless attention to the empty Tomb. But the love of the Magdalene could not rest satisfied, while doubt hung over the fate of His Sacred Body. It must be remembered that she knew only of the empty Tomb. For a time she gave away the agony of her sorrow; then, as she wiped away her tears, she stopped to take one more look into the Tomb, which she thought empty, when, as she

"intently gazed," the Tomb seemed no longer empty.

At the head and feet, where the Sacred Body had lain, were seated two Angels in white. Their question, so deeply true from their knowledge that Christ had risen: "Woman, why weepest thou?" seems to have come upon the Magdalene with such overpowering suddenness, that, without being able to realize, perhaps in the semi-gloom who it was that had asked it, she spake, bent only on obtaining the information she sought: "Because they have taken away my Lord, and I know not where they have laid Him."

So is it often with us, that, weeping, we ask the question of doubt or fear, which, if we only knew, would never risen to out lips; nay, that heaven's own "Why?" fails to impress us, even when the Voice of its Messengers would gently recall us from the error of our impatience.

But already another was to given to the Magdalene. As she spake, she became conscious of another Presence close to her. Quickly turning round, she gazed on One Whom she recognized not, but regarded as the gardener, from His presence there and from His question: "Woman, why weepest thou? Whom seekest thou?" The hope, that she might now learn what she sought, gave wings to her words, intensity and pathos. If the supposed gardener had borne to another place the Sacred Body, she would take It away, if she only knew where It was laid. This depth and agony of love, which made the Magdalene forget even the restraints of a Jewish woman's intercourse with a stranger, was the key that opened the Lips of Jesus. A moment's pause, and He spake her name in those well-remembered accents, that had first unbound her from sevenfold demoniac power and called her into a new life.

It was as another unbinding, another call into a new life. She had not known His appearance, just as the others did not know at first, so unlike, and yet so like, was the glorified Body to that which they had known. But she could not mistake the Voice, especially when It spake to her, and spake her name. So do we also often fail to recognize the Lord when He comes to us "in another form," Mark 16:12, than we had known. But we cannot fail to recognize Him when He speaks to us and speaks our name.

Perhaps we may here be allowed to pause, and, from the non recognition of the Risen Lord till He spoke, ask this question: With what body shall we rise? Like or unlike the past? Assuredly, most like. Our bodies will then be true; for the soul will body itself forth according to its past history, not only impress itself, as now on the features, but express itself, so that a man may be known by what he is, and as what he is. Thus, in this respect also, has the Resurrection a moral aspects, and is the completion of the history of mankind and of each man. And the Christ also must have borne in His glorified Body all that He was, all that even His most intimate disciples had not known nor understood while He was with them, which they now failed to recognize, but knew at once when He spake to them.

It was precisely this which now prompted the action of the Magdalene, prompted also, and explains, the answer of the Lord. As in her name she recognized His Name, the rush of old feeling came over her, and with the familiar "Rabboni!" my Master, she would fain have grasped Him. Was it the unconscious impulse to take hold on the precious treasure which she had thought for ever lost; the unconscious attempt to make sure that it was not merely an apparition of Jesus from heaven, but the real Christ in His corporeity on earth; or a gesture of generation, the beginning of such acts of worship as her heart prompted? Probably all these; and yet probably she was not at the moment distinctly conscious of either or of any of these feelings.

But to them all there was one answer, and in it a higher direction, given by the words of the Lord: "Touch Me not, for I am not yet ascended to the Father." Not the Jesus appearing from heaven, for He had not yet ascended to the Father; not the former intercourse, not the former homage and worship. There was yet a future of completion before Him in the Ascension, of which Mary knew not. Between that future of completion and the past of work, the present was a gap, belonging partly to the past and partly to the future. The past could not be recalled, the future could not be anticipated.

The present was of reassurance, of consolation, of preparation, of teaching. Let the Magdalene go and tell His "brethren" of the Ascension. So would she best and most truly tell them that she had seen Him; so also would they best learn how the Resurrection linked the past of His Work of love for them to the future: "I ascend unto My Father, and your Father, and to my God, and your God." Thus, the fullest teaching of the past, the clearest manifestation of the present, and the brightest teaching of the future, all as gathered up in the Resurrection, came to the Apostles through the mouth of love of her out of whom He had cast seven devils.

Yet another scene on that Easter morning does Matthew relate, in explanation of how the well-known Jewish Calumny had arisen that the disciples had stolen away the Body of Jesus. He tells, how the guard had reported to the chief priests what had happened, and how they had turn had bribed the guard to spread this rumor, at the same time promising that if the fictitious account of their having slept while the disciples robbed the Sepulcher should reach Pilate, they would intercede on their behalf. Whatever else may be said, we know that from the time of Justin Martyr this has been the Jewish explanation.

It was the early afternoon of that spring-day perhaps soon after the early meal, when two men from that circle of disciples left the City. Their narrative affords deeply interesting glimpses into the circle of the Church in those first days. The impression conveyed to us is of utter bewilderment, in which only some things stood out unshaken and firm: love to the Person of Jesus; love among the brethren; mutual confidence and fellowship; together with a dim hope of something yet to come, if not Christ in His Kingdom, yet some manifestation of, or approach to it. The Apostolic College seems broken up into units; even the two chief Apostles, Peter and John, are only "certain of them that were with us." And no wonder; for they are no longer "Apostles," sent out. Who is to send them forth? Not a dead Christ!

And what would be their commission, and to whom and whither? And above all rested a cloud of utter uncertainty and perplexity. Jesus was a Prophet mighty in word and deed before God and all the people. But their rulers had crucified Him. What was to be their new relation to Jesus; what to their rulers? And what of the great hope of the Kingdom, which they had connected with Him?

Thus they were unclear on that very Easter Day even as to His Mission and Work: unclear as to the past, the present, and the future. What need for the Resurrection, and for the teaching which the Risen One alone could bring! These two men had on that very day been in communication with Peter and John. And it leaves on us the impression, that, amidst the general confusion, all had brought such tidings as they, or had come to hear them, and had tried but failed, to put it all into order or to see light around it. "The women" had come to tell of the empty Tomb and of their vision of Angels, who said that He was alive. But as yet the Apostles had no explanation to offer. Peter and John had gone to see for themselves.

They had brought back confirmation of the report that the Tomb was empty, but they had seen neither Angels nor Him Whom they were said to have declared alive. And, although the two had evidently left the circle of the disciples, if not Jerusalem, before the Magdalene came, yet we know that even her account did not carry conviction to the minds of those that heard it, Mark 16:11.

Of the two, who on that early spring afternoon left the City in company, we know that one bore the name of Cleopas. The other, unnamed, has for that very reason, and because the narrative of that work bears in its vividness the character of personal recollection, been identified with Luke himself. If so, then, as has been finely remarked, by Godet, each of the Gospels would, like a picture, bear in some dim corner the indication of its author: the first, that of the "publican"; that by Mark, that of the young man, who, in the night of the Betrayal, had fled from his captors; that of Luke in the Companion of Cleopas; and that of John, in the disciple whom Jesus loved. Uncertainty, almost equal to that about the second traveler to Emmaus, rests on the identification of that place.

. . . It may have been where the two roads from Lifta and Kolonieh meet, that the mysterious Stranger, Whom they knew not, their eyes being "holden," joined the two friends. Yet all these six or seven miles (60 furlongs about = 7 1/2 miles) their converse had been of Him, and even now their flushed faces bore the marks of sadness on account of those events of which they had been speaking, disappointed hopes, all the more bitter for the perplexing tidings about the empty Tomb and the absent Body of the Christ.

So is Christ often near to us when our eyes are holden, and we know Him not; and so do ignorance and unbelief often fill our hearts with sadness, even when truest joy would most become us. To the question of the Stranger about the topics of a conversation which had so visibly affected them, they replied in language which shows that they were so absorbed by it themselves, as scarcely to understand how even a festive pilgrim and stranger in Jerusalem could have failed to know it, or perceive its supreme importance. Yet, strangely unsympathetic as from His question He might seem, there was that in His Appearance which unlocked their inmost hearts.

They told Him their thoughts about this Jesus; how He had showed Himself a prophet mighty in deed and word before God and all the people; then, how their rules had crucified Him; and, lastly, how fresh perplexity had come to them from the tidings which the women had brought, and which Peter and John had so far confirmed, but were unable to explain. Their words were almost childlike in their simplicity, deeply truthful, and with a pathos and earnest craving for guidance and comfort that goes straight to the heart.

To such souls it was, that the Risen Savior would give His first teaching. The very rebuke with which He opened it must have brought its comfort. We also, in our weakness, are sometimes sore distrest when we hear what, at the moment, seem to us insuperable difficulties raised to any of the great of our holy faith; and, in perhaps equal weakness, feel comforted and strengthened, when some "great one" turns them aside, or avows himself in face of them a believing disciple of Christ. As if man's puny height could reach up to heaven's mysteries, or any big infant's strength were needed to steady the building which God has reared on that great Cornerstone! But Christ's rebuke was not of such kind.

Their sorrow arose from their folly in looking only at the things seen, and this, from their slowness to believe what the prophets had spoken. Had they attended to this, instead of allowing it all. Did not the Scriptures with one voice teach this twofold truth about the Messiah, that He was to suffer and to enter into His glory? Then why wonder, why not rather expect, that He had suffered, and that Angels had proclaimed Him alive again?

He spake it, and fresh hope sprang up in their hearts, new thoughts rose in their minds. Their eager gaze was fastened on Him as He now opened up, one by one, the Scriptures, from Moses and all the prophets, and in each well-remembered passage interpreted to them the things concerning Himself. Oh, that we had been there to hear, though in silence of our hearts also, if only we crave for it, and if we walk with Him, He sometimes so opens from the Scriptures, nay, from all the Scriptures, that which comes not to us by critical study: "the things concerning Himself." All too quickly fled the moments. The brief space was traversed, and the Stranger seemed about to pass on from Emmaus, not the feigning it, but really: for, the Christ will only abide with us if our longing and loving constrain Him. But they could not part with Him.

"They constrained Him." Love made them ingenious. It was toward evening; the day was far spent; He must even abide with them. What rush of thought and feeling comes to us, as we think of it all, and try to realize time, scenes, circumstances in our experience, that are blessedly akin to it.

The Master allowed Himself to be constrained. He went in to be their guest, as they thought, for the night. The simple evening-meal was spread. He sat down with them to the frugal board. And now He was no longer the Stranger; He was the Master. No one asked, or questioned, as He took the bread and spake the words of blessing, then, breaking, gave it to them.

But that moment it was, as if an unfelt Hand had been taken from their eyelids, as if suddenly the film had been cleared from their sight. And as they knew Him, He vanished from their view, for, that which He had come to do had been done. They were unspeakably rich and happy now. But, amidst it all, one thing forced itself ever anew upon them, that, even while their eyes had yet been holden, their hearts had burned within them, while He spake to them and opened to them the Scriptures. So, then, they had learned to full the Resurrection-lesson, not only that He was risen indeed, but that it needed not His seen Bodily Presence, if only He opened up to the heart and mind all the Scriptures concerning Himself.

And this, concerning those other words about "holding" and "touching" Him, about having converse and fellowship with Him as the Risen One, had been also the lesson taught the Magdalene, when He would not suffer her loving, worshipful touch, pointing her to the Ascension before Him. This is the great lesson concerning the Risen One, which the Church fully learned in the Day of Pentecost.

That same afternoon, in circumstances and manner to us unknown, the Lord had appeared to Peter, 1 Cor. 15:5. We may perhaps suggest, that it was after His manifestation at Emmaus. This would complete the cycle of mercy: first, to the loving sorrow of the woman; next, to the loving perplexity of the disciples; then, to the anxious heart of the stricken Peter, last, in the circle of the Apostles, which was again drawing together around the assured fact of His Resurrection.

These two in Emmaus could not have kept the good tidings to themselves. Even if they had not remembered the sorrow and perplexity in which they had left their fellow-disciples in Jerusalem that forenoon, they could not have kept it to themselves, could not have remained in Emmaus, but must have gone to their brethren in the City. So they left the uneaten meal, and hastened back the road they had traveled with the now well-known Stranger, but, ah, with what lighter hearts and steps!

They knew well the trysting-place where to find "the Twelve," nay, not the Twelve now, but "the Eleven," and even thus their circle was not complete, for, as already stated, it was broken up, and at least Thomas was not with the others on that Easter-Evening of the first "Lord's Day." But, as Luke is careful to inform us, Luke 24:33, with the others who then associated with them. This is of extreme importance, as marking that the words which the Risen Christ spake on that occasion were addressed not to the Apostles as such, a thought forbidden also by the absence of Thomas, but to the Church, although it may be as personified and represented by such of the "Twelve,"or rather "Eleven," as were present on the occasion.

When the two from Emmaus arrived, they found the little band as sheep sheltering within the fold from the storm. Whether they apprehended persecution simply as disciples, or because the tidings of the empty Tomb, which had reached the authorities, would stir the fears of the Sanhedrists, special precautions had been taken. The outer and inner doors were shut, alike to conceal their gathering and to prevent surprise. But those assembled were now sure of at least one thing. Christ was risen. And when they from Emmaus told their wondrous story, the others could antiphonally reply by relating how He had appeared, not only to the Magdalene, but also to Peter. And still they seem not yet to have understood His Resurrection; to have regarded it as rather an Ascension to Heaven, from which He had made manifestation, that as the reappearance of His real, though glorified Corporeity.

They were sitting at meat, Mark 16:14, if we may infer from the notice of Mark, and from what happened immediately afterwards, discussing, not without considerable doubt and misgiving, the real import of these appearances of Christ. That to the Magdalene seems to have been put aside, at least, it is not mentioned, and, even in regard to the others, they seem to have been considered, at any rate by some, rather as what we might call spectral appearances. But all at once He stood in the midst of them. The common salutation, on His Lips not common, but a reality, fell on their hearts at first with terror rather than joy.

They had spoken of spectral appearances, and now they believed they were "gazing! On "a spirit." This the Savior first, and once for all, corrected, by the exhibition of the glorified marks of His Sacred Wounds, and by bidding them handle Him to convince themselves, that His was a real Body, and what they saw not a disembodied spirit.

The unbelief of doubt now gave place to the not daring to believe all that it meant, for very gladness, and for wondering whether there could now be any longer fellowship or bond between this Risen Christ and them in their bodies. It was to remove this also, which, though from another aspect, was equally unbelief, that the Savior now partook before them of their supper of broiled fish, thus holding with them true human fellowship as of old. Such seems to me the meaning of His eating; any attempt at explaining, we willingly forego in our ignorance of the conditions of a glorified body, just as we refuse to discuss the manner in which He suddenly appeared in the room while the doors were shut. But I at least cannot believe, that His body was then in a "transition state," not perfected not quite glorified till His Ascension.

It was this lesson of His continuity, in the strictest sense, with the past, which was required in order that the Church might be, so to speak, reconstituted now in the Name, Power, and Spirit of the Risen One Who had lived and died. Once more He spake the "Peace be unto you!" and now it was to them not occasion of doubt or fear, but the well-known salvation of their old Lord and Master. It was followed by the re-gathering and constituting of the Church as that of Jesus Christ, the Risen One. The Church of the Risen One was to be the Ambassador of Christ, as He had been the Delegate of the Father. The Apostles were commissioned to carry on Christ's work, and not to begin a new one.

"As the Father has sent Me [in the past, for His Mission was completed], even so send I you [in the constant, present, till His coming again]." This marks the threefold relation of the Church to the Son, to the Father, and to the world, and her position in it.

In the same manner, for the same purpose, nay, so far as possible, with the same qualification and the same authority as the Father had sent Christ, does He commission His Church. And so it was that He made it a very real commission when He breathed on them, not individually but as an assembly, and said: "Take ye the Holy Ghost"; and this, manifestly not in the absolute sense, since the Holy Ghost was not yet given, but as the connecting link with, and the qualification for, the authority bestowed on the Church.

Or, to set forth another aspect of it by somewhat inverting the order of the words: Alike the Mission of the Church and her authority to forgive or retain sins are connected with a personal qualification: "Take ye the Holy Ghost"; in which the word "take" should also be marked. This is the authority which the Church possesses, not *ex opere operato,* but as not connected with the taking and the indwelling of the Holy Ghost in the Church.

It still remains to explain, so far as we can, these two points: in what this power of forgiving and retaining sins consists, and in what manner it resides in the Church. In regard to the former we must first inquire what idea it would convey to those to whom Christ spake the words. The power of "loosing" and "binding" referred to the legislative authority claimed by, and conceded to, the Rabbinic College. Similarly, that here referred to applied to their juridical or judicial power, according to which they pronounced a person either, *"Zakkai,"* innocent or "free;" absolved, *"Patur"*; or else "liable," "guilty," *"Chayyabh"* (whether liable to punishment or sacrifice.)

In the true sense, therefore, this is rather administrative, disciplinary power, "the power of the keys," such as St. Paul would have had the Corinthian Church put in force, the power of admission and exclusion, of the authoritative declaration of the forgiveness of sins, in the exercise of which power (as it seems to the present writer) the authority for the administration of the Holy Sacraments is also involved. And yet it is not, as is sometimes represented, "absolution from sin," which belongs only to God and to Christ as Head of the Church, but absolution of the sinner, which He has delegated to His Church: "Whosoever sins ye forgive, they are forgiven." These words also teach us, that the Rabbis claimed in virtue of their office, that the Lord bestowed on His Church in virtue of her receiving, and of the indwelling of, the Holy Ghost.

In answering the second question proposed, we must bear in mind one important point. The power of "binding" and "loosing" had been primarily committed to the Apostles, Matt. 16:19; 18:18, and exercised by them in connection with the Church, Acts 15:22, 23. On the other hand, that of forgiving and retaining sins, in the sense explained, was primarily bestowed on the Church, and exercised by her through her representatives, the Apostles, and those to whom they committed rule, 1 Cor. 5:4, 5, 12, 13; 2 Cor. 2:6, 10. Although, therefore, the Lord on that night committed this power to His Church, it was in the person of her representatives and rulers. The Apostles alone could exercise legislative function, but the Church, has to the end of time "the power of the keys."

There had been absent from the circle of disciples on that Easter-Evening one of the Apostles, Thomas. Even when told of the marvelous events at that gathering, he refused to believe, unless he had personal and sensuous evidence of the truth of the report. It can scarcely have been, that Thomas did not believe in the fact that Christ's Body had quitted the Tomb, or that He had really appeared. But he held fast by what we may term the Vision-hypothesis, or, in this case, rather the spectral theory. But until this Apostle also had come to conviction of the Resurrection in the only real sense, of the identical though glorified Corporeity of the Lord, and hence of the continuity of the past with the present and future, it was impossible to re-form the Apostolic Circle, or to renew the Apostolic commission, since its primal message was testimony concerning the Risen One.

This, if we may so suggest, seems the reason why the Apostles still remain in Jerusalem, instead of hastening, as directed, to meet the Master in Galilee.

A quiet week had passed, during which, and this also may be for our twofold learning, the Apostles excluded not Thomas, nor yet Thomas withdrew from the Apostles. Once more the day of days had come, the Octave of the Feast. From that Easter-Day onwards the Church must, even without special institution, have celebrated the weekly-recurring memorial of His Resurrection, as that when He breathed on the Church the breath of anew life, and consecrated it to be His Representative. Thus, it was not only the memorial of His Resurrection, but the birthday of the Church, even as Pentecost was her baptism day.

On that Octave, then, the disciples were again gathered, under circumstances precisely similar to those of Easter, but now Thomas was also with them. Once more, and it is again specially marked: "the doors being shut," the Risen Savior appeared in the midst of the disciples with the well-known salutation. He now offered to Thomas the demanded evidence; but it was no longer either needed or sought. With a full rush of feeling he yielded himself to the blessed conviction, which once formed, must immediately have passed into act of adoration: "My Lord and my God!" The fullest confession this hitherto made, and which truly embraced the whole outcome of the new conviction concerning the reality of Christ Resurrection. We remember how, under similar circumstances, Nathaniel had been the first to utter fullest confession, John 1:45-51.

We also remember the analogous reply of the Savior. As then, so now, He pointed to the higher: to a faith which was not the outcome of sight, and therefore limited and bounded by sight, whether of the sense or of perception by the intellect. As Westcott has finely remarked: "This last and greatest of the Beatitudes is the peculiar heritage of the later Church," and thus most aptly comes as the consecration gift of that Church.

The next scene presented to us is once again by the Lake of Galilee. The manifestation to Thomas, and, with it, the restoration of unity in the Apostolic Circle, had originally concluded the Gospel of John, John 20:30, 31. But the report which had spread in the early Church, that Disciple whom Jesus loved was not to die, led him to add to his Gospel, by way of Appendix, and account of the events with which this expectancy and connected itself. It is most instructive to the critic, when challenged at every step to explain why one or another fact is not mentioned or mentioned only in one Gospel, to find that, but for the correction of a possible misapprehension in regard to the aged Apostle, the Fourth Gospel would have contained no reference to the manifestation of Christ in Galilee, nay, to the presence of the disciples there before the Ascension.

Yet, for all that John had it in his mind. And should we not learn from this, that what appear to us strange omissions, which, when held by the side of the other Gospel-narratives, seem to involve discrepancies, may be capable of the most satisfactory explanation, if we only knew all the circumstance?

The history itself sparkles like a gem in its own peculiar setting. It is of green Galilee, and of the blue Lake, and recalls the early days and scenes of this history. As Matthew has it, Matt. 28:16, "the eleven disciples went away into Galilee," probably immediately after that Octava of the Easter. The account of Luke, in Luke 24:44-48, is a condensed narrative, without distinction of time or place, of what occurred during all the forty days.

It can scarcely be doubted, that they made known not only the fact of the Resurrection, but the trysting which the Risen One had given them, perhaps at that Mountain where He had spoken His first "Sermon." And so it was, that "some doubted," Matt. 28:17, and that He afterwards appeared to the five hundred at once, 1 Cor. 15:6. But on that morning there were by the Lake of Tiberias only seven of the disciples. Five of them only are named. They are those who most closely kept in company with Him, perhaps also they who lived nearest the Lake.

The scene is introduced by Peter's proposal to go a-fishing. It seems as if the old habits had come back to them with the old associations. Peter's companions naturally proposed to join him. All that still, clear night they were on the Lake, but caught nothing. Did not this recall to them for former event, when James and John, and Peter and Andrew were called to be Apostles, and did it not specially recall to Peter the searching and sounding of his heart on the morning that followed? But so utterly self-unconscious were they, and, let us add, so far is this history from any trace of legendary design, that not the slightest indication of this appears.

Early morning was breaking, and under the rosy glow above the cool shadows were still lying on the pebbly "beach." There stood the Figure of One Whom they recognized not, nay, not even when He spake. Yet His Words were intended to bring them this knowledge. The direction to cast the net to the right side of the ship brought them, as He had said, the haul for which they had toiled all night in vain. And more than this: such a multitude of fishes, enough for "the disciple whom Jesus loved," and whose heart may previously have misgiven him. He whispered it to Peter: "It is the Lord," and Simon, only reverently gathering about him his fisher's upper garment, cast himself into the sea.

Yet even so, except to be sooner by the side of Christ, Peter seems to have gained nothing by his haste. The others, leaving the ship, and transferring themselves to a small boat, which must have been attached to it followed, rowing the short distance of about one hundred yards, and dragging after them the net, weighted with the fishes.

They stepped on the beach, hallowed by His Presence, in silence, as if they had entered Church or Temple. They dared not even dispose of the netful of fishes which they had dragged on shore, until He directed them what to do. This only they notice, that some unseen hand had prepared the morning meal, which, when asked by the Master, they had admitted they had not of their own. And now Jesus directed them to bring the fish they had caught. When Peter dragged up the weight net, it was found full of great fishes, not less than a hundred and fifty-three in number. There is no need to attach any symbolic import to that number, as the Fathers and later writers have done. We can quite understand, nay, it seems almost natural, that, in the peculiar circumstances, they should have counted the large fishes in that miraculous draught that still left the net unbroken.

It may have been, that they were told to count the fishes, partly, also, to show the reality of what had taken place. But on the fire the coals there seems to have been only one fish, and beside it only one bread. To this meal He now bade them, for they seem still to have hung back in reverent awe, nor durst they ask him, Who He was, well knowing it was the Lord. This, as John notes, was the third appearance of Christ to the disciples as a body.

And still this morning of blessing was not ended. The frugal meal was past, with all its significant teaching of just sufficient provision for His servants, and abundant supply in the unbroken net beside them. But some special teaching was needed, more even than that to Thomas, for him whose work was to be so prominent among the Apostles, whose love was so ardent, and yet in its very ardor so full of danger to himself. For, our dangers spring not only from deficiency, but it may be from excess of feeling, when that feeling is not commensurate with inward strength.

Had Peter not confessed, quite honestly, yet, as the event proved, mistakenly, that his love to Christ would endure even an ordeal that would disperse all the others? Matt. 26:33; John 13:37. And had he not, almost immediately afterwards, and though prophetically warned of it, thrice denied his Lord? Jesus had, indeed, since then appeared specially to Peter as the Risen One. But this threefold denial still, stood, as it were, uncancelled before the other disciples, nay, before Peter himself. It was to this that the threefold question to the Risen Lord now referred. Turning to Peter, with pointed though most gentle allusion to be danger of self-confidence, a confidence springing from only a sense of personal affection, even though genuine, He asked: "Simon, son of Jona," as it were with fullest reference to what he was naturally, "lovest thou Me more than these?" Peter understood it all.

No longer with confidence in self, avoiding the former reference to the others, and even with marked choice of a different word to express his affection from that which the Savior had used, he replied, appealing rather to his Lord's, than to his own consciousness: "Yea, Lord, Thou knowest that

I love Thee." And even here the answer of Christ is characteristic. It was to set him first the humblest work, that which needed most tender care and patience: "Feed [provide with food] My Lambs."

Yet a second time came the same question, although now without the reference to the others, and, with the same answer by Peter, the now varied and enlarged commission: "Feed [shepherd] My Sheep." Yet a third time did Jesus repeat the same question, now adopting in it the very word which Peter had used to express his affection. Peter was grieved at this threefold repetition. It recalled only to bitterly his threefold denial. And yet the Lord was not doubtful of Peter's love, for each time He followed up His question with a fresh Apostle commission; but now that He put it for the third time, Peter would have the Lord send down the sounding-line quite into the lowest deep of this heart: "Lord, Thou knowest all things, Thou perceivest that I love Thee!" And now the Savior spake it: "Feed [provide food for] My sheep." His Lamb, His Sheep, to be provided for, to be tended as such! And only love can do such service.

Yes, and Peter did love the Lord Jesus. He had loved Him when he said it, only to confident in the strength of his feelings, that he would follow the Master even unto death. And Jesus saw it all, yea, and how this love of the ardent temperament which had once made him rove at wild liberty, would give place to patient work of love, and be crowed with that martyrdom which, when the beloved disciple wrote, was already matter of the past. And the very manner of death by which he was to glorify God was indicated in the words of Jesus.

As He spake them, He joined the symbolic action to His "Follow Me." This command, and the encouragement of being in death literally made like Him, following Him, were Peter's best strength. He obeyed; but as he turned to do so, he saw another following. As John himself puts it, it seems almost to convey that he had longed to share Peter's call, with all that it implied. For, John speak of himself as the disciple whom Jesus loves, and he reminds us that in that night of betrayal he

had been specially a sharer with Peter, nay, had spoken what the other had silently asked of him. Was it impatience, was it a touch of the old Peter, or was it a simple inquiry of brotherly interest which prompted the question, as he pointed to John: "Lord, and this man, what?"

Whatever had been the motive, to him, as to us all, when perplexed about those who seem to follow Christ, we ask it, sometimes is bigoted narrowness, sometimes in ignorance, folly, or jealousy, is this answer: "What is that to thee? follow thou Me." For John also had his life-work for Christ. It was to "tarry" while He was coming. So Canon Westcott renders the meaning. The "coming" might refer to the second Coming, to the destruction of Jerusalem, or even to the firm establishment of the Church. John was to tarry those many years in patient labor, while Christ was coming.

But what did it mean? The saying went aboard among the brethren that John was not to die, but to tarry till Jesus came again to reign, when death would be swallowed up in victory. But Jesus had not so said, only: "If I will that he tarry while I am coming." What that "Coming" was, Jesus had not said, and John knew not. So, then, there are things, and connected with His Coming, on which Jesus has left the evil, only to be lifted by His own Hand, which He means us not to know at present, and which we should be content to leave as He has left them.

Beyond this narrative we have only briefest notices: by St. Paul, of Christ manifesting Himself to James, which probably finally decided him for Christ, and the Eleven meeting Him at the mountain, where He had appointed them; by Luke, of the teaching in the Scriptures during the forty days of communication between the Risen Christ and the disciples.

But this twofold testimony comes to us from Matthew and Mark, that then the worshipping disciples were once more formed into the Apostolic Circle, Apostles, now, of the Risen Christ. And this was the warrant of their new commission: "All power (authority) has been given to Me in heaven and on earth." And this was their new commission: "Go ye, therefore, and make disciples of all the nations, baptizing them into the Name of the Father, and of the Son, and of the Holy Ghost." And this was their work: "Teaching them to observe all things whatsoever I commanded you." And this is His final and sure promise: "And lo, I am with you always, even unto the end of the world."

We are once more in Jerusalem, whither He had bidden them go to tarry for the fulfillment of the great promise. The Pentecost was drawing nigh. And on that last, day the day of His Ascension, He led them forth to the well-remembered Bethany. From where He had made His last triumphal Entry into Jerusalem before His Crucifixion, would He make His triumphant Entry visibly into Heaven. Once more would they have asked Him about that which seemed to them the final consummation, the restoration of the Kingdom to Israel. But such questions became them not. Theirs was to be work, not rest; suffering, not triumph. The great promise before them was of spiritual, not outward, power: of the Holy Ghost, and their call not yet to reign with Him, but to bear witness for Him.

And, as He so spake, He lifted His Hands in blessing upon them, and, as He was visibly taken up, a cloud received Him. And still they gazed, with upturned faces, on that luminous cloud which had received Him, and two Angels spake to them this last message from him, that He should so come in like manner, as they had beheld Him going into heaven.

And so their last question to Him, ere He had parted from them, was also answered, and with blessed assurance. Reverently they worshipped Him; then, with great joy, returned to Jerusalem. So it was all true, all real, and Christ "sat down at the Right Hand of God"! Henceforth, neither doubting, ashamed, nor yet afraid, they "were continually in the Temple, blessing God." "And they went forth and preached everywhere, the Lord working with them, and confirming the word by the signs that follows. Amen."

Amen! It is so. Ring out the bells of heaven; sing forth the Angelic welcome of worship; carry it to the utmost bound of earth! Shine forth from Bethany, Thou Sun of Righteousness, and chase away earth's mist and darkness, for Heaven's golden day has broken!

Our task is ended, and we also worship and look up. And we go back from this sight into a hostile world, to love, and to live, and to work for Risen Christ. But as earth's day if growing dim, and, with earth's gathering darkness, breaks over it heaven's storm, we ring out, as of old they were wont, from church-tower, to the mariners that hugged a rock-bound coast, our Easter-bells to guide them who are belated, over the storm-tossed sea, beyond the breakers, into the desired haven. Ring out, earth, all thy Easter-chimes; bring you offerings, all ye people; worship in faith, for, "This Jesus, Who was received up from you into heaven, shall so come, in like manner as ye beheld Him going into heaven." "Even so, Lord Jesus, come quickly!"

Alfred Edersheim, Life and Times of Jesus the Messiah
Book 5, Chapter XVII, 1886

4.9 Resurrection of Christ, *Easton's Bible Dictionary*

One of the cardinal facts and doctrines of the gospel. If Christ be not risen, our faith is vain (1 Corinthians 15:14). The whole of the New Testament revelation rests on this as an historical fact. On the day of Pentecost Peter argued the necessity of Christ's resurrection from the prediction in Psalms 16 (Acts 2:24-28). In his own discourses, also, our Lord clearly intimates his resurrection (Matthew 20:19; Mark 9:9; 14:28; Luke 18:33; John 2:19-22).

Appearances of the risen Jesus:

To Mary Magdalene at the sepulcher alone. This is recorded at length only by (John 20:11-18), and alluded to by (Mark 16:9-11).

To certain women, "the other Mary," Salome, Joanna, and others, as they returned from the sepulcher. (Matthew 28:1-10) alone gives an account of this. (Compare Mark 16:1-8, and Luke 24:1-11.)

To Simon Peter alone on the day of the resurrection. (See Luke 24:34; 1 Corinthians 15:5.)

To the two disciples on the way to Emmaus on the day of the resurrection, recorded fully only by (Luke 24:13-35. Compare Mark 16:12, 13).

To the ten disciples (Thomas being absent) and others "with them," at Jerusalem on the evening of the resurrection day. One of the evangelists gives an account of this appearance (John 20:19-24).

To the disciples again (Thomas being present) at Jerusalem (Mark 16:14-18; Luke 24:33-40; John 20:26-28. See also 1 Corinthians 15:5).

To the disciples when fishing at the Sea of Galilee. Of this appearance also (John 21:1-23) alone gives an account.

To the eleven, and above 500 brethren at once, at an appointed place in Galilee (1 Corinthians 15:6; Compare Matthew 28:16-20).

To James, but under what circumstances we are not informed (1 Corinthians 15:7).

To the apostles immediately before the ascension. They accompanied him from Jerusalem to Mount Olivet, and there they saw him ascend "till a cloud received him out of their sight" (Mark 16:19; Luke 24:50-52; Acts 1:4-10). It is worthy of note that it is distinctly related that on most of these occasions our Lord afforded his disciples the amplest opportunity of testing the fact of his resurrection. He conversed with them face to face. They touched him (Matthew 28:9; Luke 24:39; John 20:27), and he ate bread with them (Luke 24:42, 43; John 21:12, 13).

In addition to the above, mention might be made of Christ's manifestation of himself to Paul at Damascus, who speaks of it as an appearance of the risen Savior (Acts 9:3-9, 17; 1 Corinthians 15:8; 9:1). It is implied in the words of Luke (Acts 1:3) that there may have been other appearances of which we have no record.

The resurrection is spoken of as the act:

(1) of God the Father (Psalms 16:10; Acts 2:24; 3:15; Romans 8:11; Ephesians 1:20; Colossians 2:12; Hebrews 13:20);

(2) of Christ himself (John 2:19; 10:18); and

(3) of the Holy Spirit (1 Peter 3:18).

The resurrection is a public testimony of Christ's release from his undertaking as surety, and an evidence of the Father's acceptance of his work of redemption. It is a victory over death and the grave for all his followers.

The importance of Christ's resurrection will be seen when we consider that if he rose the gospel is true, and if he rose not it is false. His resurrection from the dead makes it manifest that his sacrifice was accepted. Our justification was secured by his obedience to the death, and therefore he was raised from the dead (Romans 4:25). His resurrection is a proof that he made a full atonement for our sins, that his sacrifice was accepted as a satisfaction to divine justice, and his blood a ransom for sinners. It is also a pledge and an earnest of the resurrection of all believers (Romans 8:11; 1 Corinthians 6:14; 15:47-49; Phil 3:21; 1 John 3:2). As he lives, they shall live also.

It proved him to be the Son of God, inasmuch as it authenticated all his claims (John 2:19; 10:17). "If Christ did not rise, the whole scheme of redemption is a failure, and all the predictions and anticipations of its glorious results for time and for eternity, for men and for angels of every rank and order, are proved to be chimeras. But now is Christ risen from the dead, and become the first-fruits of them that slept. Therefore the Bible is true from Genesis to Revelation. The kingdom of darkness has been overthrown, Satan has fallen as lightning from heaven, and the triumph of truth over error, of good over evil, of happiness over misery is for ever secured." Hodge.

With reference to the report which the Roman soldiers were bribed (Matthew 28:12-14) to circulate concerning Christ's resurrection, "his disciples came by night and stole him away while we slept," Matthew Henry in his *Commentary*, under John 20:1-10, fittingly remarks, "The grave-clothes in which Christ had been buried were found in very good order, which serves for an evidence that his body was not 'stolen away while men slept.' Robbers of tombs have been known to take away 'the clothes' and leave the body; but none ever took away 'the body' and left the clothes, especially when they were 'fine linen' and new (Mark 15:46). Any one would rather choose to carry a dead body in its clothes than naked. Or if they that were supposed to have stolen it would have left the grave-clothes behind, yet it cannot be supposed they would find leisure to fold up the linen."

M. G. Easton, Easton's Bible Dictionary, *1890*

4.10 THE RESURRECTION OF CHRIST, C. H. SPURGEON

The resurrection of Christ was effected by the power of the Holy Spirit! and here we have a vivid illustration of His omnipotence. If you could you have stepped, as the angels did, into the grave of Jesus, and seen His sleeping body, you would have found it cold as any other corpse. Lift up the hand; it falls by the side. Look at the eye; it is glazed. And there is the gaping wound in His side which must have annihilated His life. See His hands: the blood no longer drips from them. They are cold and motionless. Can that body live? Can it rise up? Yes; and it is an illustration of the power of the Holy Spirit. For when the power of the Holy Spirit came on Him, as it was when it fell upon the dry bones of the valley, "He arose in the majesty of His divinity, and, bright and shining, astonished the Roman soldiers guarding the tomb so that they ran away; yes, He arose never to die again, but to live forever, King of kings and Prince of the kings of the earth."

C. H. Spurgeon

4.11 The resurrection of Christ: an historical fact, B. B. Warfield

It is a somewhat difficult matter to distinguish between Christian doctrines and facts. The doctrines of Christianity are doctrines only because they are facts; and the facts of Christianity become its most indispensable doctrines. The Incarnation of the eternal God is necessarily a dogma: no human eye could witness his stooping to man's estate, no human tongue could bear witness to it as a fact. And yet, if it be not a fact, our faith is vain, we are yet in our sins. On the other hand, the Resurrection of Christ is a fact, an external occurrence within the cognizance of men to be established by their testimony. And yet, it is the cardinal doctrine of our system: on it all other doctrines hang.

There have been some, indeed, who have refused to admit the essential importance of this fact to our system; and even so considerable a critic as Keim has announced himself as occupying this standpoint. Strauss saw, however, with more unclouded eye, truly declaring the fact of Christ's resurrection to be "the center of the center, the real heart of Christianity," on which its truth stands or falls. To this, indeed, an older and deeper thinker than Strauss had long ago abundantly witnessed. The modern skeptic does but echo the words of the apostle Paul. Come what may, therefore, modern skepticism must be rid of the resurrection of Christ. It has recognized the necessity and has bent all its energies to the endeavor.

But the early followers of the Savior also themselves recognized the paramount importance of this fact; and the records of Christianity contain a mass of proof for it, of such cogent variety and convincing power, that Hume's famous dilemma recoils on his own head. It is more impossible that the laws of testimony should be so far set aside, that such witness should be mistaken, than that the laws of nature should be so far set aside that a man should rise from the dead. The opponents of revelation themselves being witnesses, the testimony of the historical books of the New Testament if the testimony of eyewitnesses is amply sufficient to establish this, to them, absolutely crushing fact. It is admitted well-nigh universally that the Gospels contain testimony for the resurrection of Christ, which, if it stand, proves that fact; and that if Christ rose from the dead all motive for, and all possibility of, denial of any supernatural fact of Christianity is forever removed.

Of course, it has become necessary, then, for the deniers of a supernatural origin to Christianity to impeach the credibility of these witnesses. It is admitted that if the Gospel account be truly the testimony of eye-witnesses, then Christ did rise from the dead; but it is immediately added that the Gospels are late compositions which first saw the light in the second century-that they represent, not the testimony of eye-witnesses, but the wild dreams of a mythological fancy or the wilder inventions of unscrupulous forgery; and that, therefore, they are unworthy of credit and valueless as witnesses to fact. Thus, it is proclaimed, this alleged occurrence of the rising of Jesus from the dead, is stripped of all the pretended testimony of eye-witnesses; and all discussion of the question whether it be fact or not is forever set aside-the only question remaining being that which concerns itself with the origin and propagation of this fanatical belief.

It is in this position that we find skepticism entrenched—a strong position assuredly and chosen with consummate skill. It is not, however, impregnable. There are at least two courses open to us in attacking it. We may either directly storm the works, or, turning their flank, bring our weapons to bear on them from the rear. The authenticity of our Gospels is denied. We may either prove their authenticity and hence the autoptic character of the testimony they contain; or, we may waive all question of the books attacked, and, using only those which are by the skeptics themselves acknowledged to be genuine, prove from them that the resurrection of Christ actually occurred.

The first course, as being the most direct, is the one usually adopted. Here the battle is intense; but the issue is not doubtful. Internally, those books evince themselves as genuine. Not only do they proclaim a teaching absolutely original and patently divine, but they have presented a biography to the world such as no man or body of men could have concocted. No mythologists could have invented a divine-human personality and assigned the exact proportions in which his divinity and humanity should be exhibited in his life, and then dramatized this character through so long a course of teaching and action without a single contradiction or inconsistency. That simple peasants have succeeded in a task wherein a body of philosophers would have assuredly hopelessly failed, can be accounted for only on the hypothesis that they were simply detailing actual facts.

Again, there are numerous evidently undesigned coincidences in minute points to be observed between the book of Acts and those Epistles of Paul acknowledged to be genuine, which prove beyond a peradventure that book to be authentic history. The authenticity of Acts carries that of the Gospel of Luke with it; and the witness of these two establishes the Resurrection.

But, aside from all internal evidence, the external evidence for the authenticity of the New Testament historical books is irrefragable. The immediate successors of the apostles possessed them all and esteemed them as the authoritative documents of their religion. One of the writers of this age (placed by Hilgenfeld in the first century) quotes Matthew as Scripture: another explicitly places Acts among the "Holy Books," a collection containing on common terms the Old Testament and at least a large part of the New: all quote these historical books with respect and reverence. There is on external, historical grounds no room left for denying the genuineness of the Gospels and Acts; and hence, no room left for denying the fact of the

Resurrection. The result of a half-century's conflict on this line of attack has resulted in the triumphant vindication of the credibility of the Christian records.

We do not propose, however, to fight this battle over again at this time. The second of the courses above pointed out has been less commonly adopted, but leads to equally satisfactory results. To exhibit this is our present object. The most extreme schools of skepticism admit that the book of Revelation is by John; and that Romans, 1 and 2 Corinthians, and Galatians are genuine letters of St. Paul. Most leaders of anti-Christian thought admit other epistles also; but we wish to confine ourselves to the narrowest ground. Our present task, then, is, waiving all reference to disputed books, to show that the testimony of these confessedly genuine writings of the apostles is enough to establish the fact of the Resurrection. We are even willing to assume narrower ground. The Revelation is admitted to be written by an eye-witness of the death of Christ and the subsequent transactions; and the Book of Revelation testifies to Christ's resurrection. In it he is described as One who was dead and yet came to life (2:8), and as the first-begotten of the dead (1:5). Here, then, is one admitted to have been an eye-witness testifying of the Resurrection. For the sake of simplifying our argument, however, we will omit the testimony of Revelation and ask only what witness the four acknowledged Epistles of Paul-Romans, 1 and 2 Corinthians, and Galatians bear to the fact that Christ rose from the dead.

It is plain on the very first glance into these Epistles that they have a great deal to say about this Resurrection. Our task is to draw out the evidential value of their references.

We would note, then, in the first place, that Paul claims to be himself an eye-witness of a risen Christ. After stating as a fact that Christ rose from the dead and enumerating his various appearances to his followers, he adds: "And last of all, as unto one born out of due time, he appeared to me also" (1 Cor. 15:8). And again, he bases his apostleship on this sight, saying (1 Cor. 9:1), "Am I not an apostle? Have I not seen Jesus our Lord?" His "sight" of the Lord Jesus was, therefore of such a kind that it constituted a call to the apostleship. It was not, then, a simple sight of Jesus before his crucifixion: as is also proved from the fact that it was after all the appearances which he vouchsafed after his resurrection to his other followers, that Paul saw him (1 Cor. 15:8). It remains true, then, that Paul claims to be an eye-witness of the fact that Christ had risen. It will not do to say that Paul claims only to have had a "theophany" as it were a "sight" of Christ's spirit living, which would not imply the resurrection of his body. As Beyschlag has long ago pointed out, the whole argument in 1 Cor. 15 being meant to prove the bodily resurrection of believers from the resurrection of Christ, necessitates the sense that Paul, like the other witnesses there adduced saw Christ in the body. Nor is it difficult to determine when Paul claims to have seen Christ: it is admitted by all that it was this "sight" that produced his conversion and called him to the apostleship. According to Gal. 1:19 both calls were simultaneous.

Tracing his conversion thus to, and basing his apostleship on, the resurrection of Christ, it is not strange that Paul has not been able to keep his Epistles from bristling with marks of his intense conviction of the fact of the Resurrection. Compare, e.g., Romans 1:4; 4:24, 25; 5:10; 6:4, 5, 8, 9 10, 11, 13; 7:4; 8:11, 34; 10:7, 9; 14:9. We cannot, therefore, without stultification deny that Paul was thoroughly convinced that he had seen the risen Jesus; and the skeptics themselves feel forced to admit this fact.

What, then, shall we do with this claim of Paul to be an eye-witness? Shall we declare his "sight" to have been no true sight, but a deceiving vision? Paul certainly thought it bodily and a sight. But we are told that Paul was given to seeing visions-that he was in fact of that enthusiastic spiritual temperament-like Francis of Assisi for instance-which fails to distinguish between vivid subjective ideas and external facts. But, while it must be admitted that Paul did see visions, all sober criticism must wholly deny that he was a visionary. Waiving the fact that even Paul's visions were externally communicated to him and not the projections of a diseased imagination, as well as all general discussion of the elements of Paul's character, this visionary hypothesis is shattered on the simple fact that Paul knew the difference between this "sight" of Jesus and his visions, and draws the distinction sharply between them. This "sight" was, as he himself tells us, the last of all; and the only vision which on our opponents' principles can be attributed to him, that recorded in 2 Cor. 12 is described by Paul in such a manner as to draw the contrast very strongly between his confidence in this "sight" and his uncertainty as to what had happened to him then. Of course, no appeal can be properly made to the "false" history of the Acts; but, if attempted, it is sufficient to say that according to Acts Paul saw Jesus after this sight of 1 Cor. 15; but that this was in a trance (Acts 22:18 ff.), and in spite of it the sight of 1 Cor. 15 was the "last" time Jesus was seen. In other words, Paul once more draws a strict distinction between his "visions" and this "sight."

It is instructive to note the methods by which it is attempted to make this visionary hypothesis more credible. A graphic picture is drawn by Baur, Strauss, and Renan, of the physical and psychological condition of St. Paul. He had been touched by the steadfastness of the Christians; he was deeply moved by the grandeur of Stephen's death; had begun to doubt within himself whether the resurrection of Christ had not really occurred; and, sick in body and distracted in mind, smitten by the sun or the lightning of some sudden storm, was prostrated on his way to Damascus and saw in his delirium his awful self-imagined vision. It would be easy to show that the important points of this picture are contradicted by Paul himself: he knows nothing of distraction of mind or of opening doubts before the coming of the catastrophe (cf. Gal. 1:13 ff.). It would be easy, again, to show that, brilliant as it is, this picture fails to account for the facts, notably for the immense moral change (recognized by Paul himself) by which he was transformed from the most bloodthirsty of fanatics to the tenderest of saints. But, it will be sufficient for our present purpose to not only that all that renders it plausible is its connection with certain facts recorded only in that "unbelievable" history, the Acts. We find ourselves, then, in this dilemma: if Acts be no true history, then these facts cannot be so used; if Acts be true history, then Paul's conversion occurred quite otherwise; and again, if Acts be true, then so is Luke's Gospel; and Acts and Luke are enough to authenticate the resurrection of Christ. In either case, our cause is won.

In regard to this whole visionary scheme we have one further remark to make: it is to be noted that even were it much more plausible than it is, it still would not be worth further consideration. For, Paul believed in the fact of the resurrection of Christ not only because he had seen the Lord, but also on the testimony of others. For, we would note in the second place that Paul introduces us to other eye-witnesses of the resurrection of Christ. He founded his gospel on this fact; and in Gal. 2:6 ff. he tells us his gospel was the same as was preached by Peter, James, and John. Peter, James, and John, then, believed with the same intensity that Christ rose from the dead. We have already seen that this testimony as to John at least, is supported by what he himself has written in the Apocalypse. In consistency with the inference, again, Paul explicitly declares in 1 Cor. 15:3 ff., that the risen Christ was seen not only by himself but by Cephas, James, and indeed all the apostles; and that, more than once. Even more: he states that he was seen by over five hundred brethren at once, the most of whom were still living when Paul wrote this letter, and whose witness-bearing he invokes. Here, Paul brings before us a cloud of witnesses.

In respect to them the following facts are worth pointing out. These witnesses were numerous; there were at least five hundred of them. They were not a mere unknown mob: we know somewhat of several of them and know them as practical men. The most of them were still living when Paul wrote, and he could appeal to them to bear testimony to the Corinthians.

The result of all of which is that this notice in 1 Cor. is equivalent to their individual testimony. Paul is admitted to be a sober and trustworthy writer; this Epistle is admitted to be genuinely his; and he here in a

contemporary document challenges an appeal to living eye-witnesses. He could not have made this confident appeal had not these men really professed, soberly and earnestly, to have seen the risen Christ. We have, then, not only Paul claiming to be an eye-witness of the Resurrection; but a large number of men, over two hundred and fifty of whom were known to be still living when he wrote. We have to account not for the claim of one man that he had seen Jesus alive after he had died, but for the same claim put in by a multitude. Will any arguing that Paul sometimes saw visions serve our purpose here? And there is still another point which is worth remarking. The witnesses here appealed to are the original disciples and apostles of our Lord. From this, two facts follow: the one, the original disciples believed they had seen the risen Lord; and the other, they claimed to have seen him on the third day after his burial (1 Cor. 15:4). This, according to Paul, is certain fact.

Then note once more, in the third place, that this testimony (as already pointed out) was not only absolutely convincing to the Apostle Paul, but it was so also to the whole body of Christians. Not only did Paul base the truth of all Christianity on the truth of this testimony, and found his conversion on it; but so did all Christians. He could count on all his readers being just as firmly persuaded of this fact as he was. To the Corinthians, Galatians, Romans-this is the dogma of Christianity. When Paul wishes to prove his apostleship to the Corinthians or Galatians he is not afraid to base it on the therefore admitted fact of the resurrection of Christ (1 Cor. 9:1; Gal. 1:1): when he wishes to make our justification seem sure to the Romans, he appeals to Christ's resurrection in its proof (Rom. 4:24, 25). These are but specimens of his practice. Both purposed and incidental allusions are made to the Resurrection through all four of these Epistles of such character as to prove that it was felt by Paul that he could count on it above all other facts as the starting-point of Christianity in the minds of his readers. Whether he is writing to Corinthians, Galatians, or Romans, this is alike true. Now, consider the force of this. In some of these churches, it is to be remembered, there were dissensions, divisions, parties arrayed in bitter hostility against one another, parties with contumely denying the apostleship, or discarding the leadership of Paul. Yet all these parties believe in the resurrection of Christ: Paul can appeal to all alike to accept a doctrine based on that. It is to his bitterest opponents that he will prove his apostleship by claiming to have seen the risen Lord. It is plain, then, that the resurrection of Christ was in Paul's day deemed a primordial, universal, and essential doctrine of Christianity.

Again, some of Paul's readers were far removed from credulous simplicity. There was a party in the Corinthian Church, for instance, who, with all the instincts of modern philosophical criticism, claimed the right to try at the bar of reason the doctrines submitted to their acceptance. They could not accept such an absurdity as the resurrection of the bodies of those who slept in the Lord: "If the dead be raised, With what body do they come?" was but one of their argumentative queries. The same class of difficulties in regard to the resurrection of men, as would in modern times start up in the minds of scientific inquirers, was evidently before their minds. Yet they believed firmly in the resurrection of Christ. When Paul wishes to argue with them in regard to our resurrection, he bases his argument on the therefore common ground of the resurrection of Christ. It is plain, then, that unthinking credulity will not account for the universal acceptance of this doctrine: men able and more than willing to apply critical tests to evidence were firm believers in it.

And still again, one of these letters is addressed to a church with which Paul had no personal connection. It was not founded by him; it had never been visited by him; it had not before been addressed by him. There were those in it who were opposed to his dearest teachings: there were those in it who had been humble followers of Christ while he was still raging against his Church. Yet, they all believed as firmly as he did in the resurrection of Christ. He could prove his doctrines to them best by basing on this common faith. It is plain, then, that this doctrine was not of late growth in the Church; nor had its origin from

Paul. It had always been the universal belief in the Church: men did not believe it because Paul preached it only, but they and Paul alike believed it from the convincing character of the evidence. When had a belief, thus universally accepted as a part of aboriginal Christianity in A.D. 58, had an opportunity to mythically grow into being? And, if it grew, what of the testimony of those over two hundred and fifty still living eye-witnesses to the fact?

Here we may fitly pause to gather up results. It seems indisputably evident from these four Epistles of Paul:

First, That the resurrection of Christ was universally believed in the Christian Church when these Epistles were written: whatever party lines there were, however near they came, yet did they not cut through this dogma.

Second, That the original followers of Christ, including his apostles, claimed to be eye-witnesses of the fact of his resurrection; and, therefore, from the beginning (third day) the whole Church had been convinced of its truth. Over two hundred and fifty of these eye-witnesses were living when Paul wrote.

Third, That the Church believed universally that it owed its life, as it certainly owed its continued existence and growth, to its firm belief in this dogma. What has to be accounted for, then, is:

1. Not the belief of one man that he had seen the Lord, but of something over five hundred.

2. Not the conviction of a party, and that after some time, that the Lord had risen, but the universal and immediate belief of the whole Church.

3. The effect of this faith in absolutely changing the characters and filling with enthusiasm its first possessors.

And 4. Their power in propagating their faith, in building up on this strange dogma a large and fast-growing communion, all devoted to it as the first and ground element of their faith.

There are only three theories which can be possibly stated to account for these facts. Either, the original disciples of Christ were deceivers and deliberately concocted the story of the Resurrection; or, they were woefully deluded; or the Resurrection was a fact.

I. THE FIRST OF THESE THEORIES, OLD AS IT IS (MATT. 28:11 FF.), IS NOW ADMITTED ON ALL SIDES TO BE RIDICULOUS.

Strauss and Volkmar, for example, both scorn it as an impossible explanation. We may, therefore, pass it over in few words. The dead body of Christ lying in his grave ready to be produced by the Jews at any moment, of itself destroys this theory. For we must remember that the belief in the Resurrection dates from the third day. Or, if the body no longer lay in the grave, where was it? It must have been either removed by their enemies, in which case it would have been produced in disproof of the Resurrection; or stolen by the disciples themselves. We are shut up to these two hypotheses, for the only possible third one (that the body had never been buried but thrown upon the dunghill) is out of the question, eye-witnesses expressly witnessing, according to Paul, that it was buried (1 Cor. 15:4 f.). No one will so stultify himself in this age as to seriously contend that the disciples stole the body. Not only is it certain that they could not possibly have summoned courage to make the attempt; but the very idea of Christianity owing its life to such an act is worse than absurd. Imagine, if one can, this band of disheartened disciples assembled and coolly plotting to conquer the world to themselves by proclaiming what must have been seen to be the absurd promise of everlasting life through One who had himself died—had died and had not risen again. Imagine them not expecting a resurrection nor dreaming of its possibility, determining to steal the body of their dead Lord, pretend that he had risen, and, then, to found on their falsehood a system of the most marvelous truth—on this act of rapine a system of the most perfect morals. Imagine the body stolen and brought into their midst—who can think they could be stirred up to noble endeavor by the sight? "Can a more appalling spectacle be imagined," exclaims Dr. Nott, "than that of a dead Christ stolen from his sepulcher and surrounded by his hopeless, heaven-deserted

followers? And was it here, think you, in this cadaverous chamber . . . in this haunt of sin, of falsehood, of misery, and of putrefaction, that the transcendent and immortal system of Christian faith and morals was adopted? Was this stolen, mangled, lifeless corpse the only rallying point of Christians? Was it the sight of this that . . . fortified, and filled with the most daring courage, the most deathless hopes, the whole body of the disciples?" Well have our opponents declared this supposition absurd. Christ rose from the dead, or else his disciples were a body of woefully deluded men.

II. THEN, WILL THIS SECOND THEORY MEET THE CASE?

Is the admitted fact that Christ's earliest followers were all convinced that he rose from the dead, adequately explained by the supposition that they were the victims of a delusion? We must remember that the testimony of eye-witnesses declares that Christ rose on the third day; and that we have thus to account for immediate faith. But, then, there is the dead body of Jesus lying in the grave! How could the whole body of those men be so deceived in so momentous a matter with the means of testing its truth ready at their hand? Hence, it is commonly admitted that the grave was now empty. Strauss alone resorts to the sorry hypothesis that the appearances of the risen Christ were all in Galilee, and that before the forty days which intervened before the disciples returned to Jerusalem had passed, the site of the grave (or dunghill) had been wholly forgotten by friend and foe alike. But, there is that unimpeachable testimony of eye-witnesses that the appearances began on the third day; and the equally assured fact (Rom. 6:4; 1 Cor. 15:4), that the body was not thrown on a dunghill but that there was a veritable grave. So that the empty grave stares us still in the face. If Christ did not rise, how came the grave empty? Here is the crowning difficulty which all the ingenuity of the whole modern critical school has not been able to lay aside. Was it emptied by Christ's own followers? That would have been imposture, and the skeptics scorn such a resort: moreover, the hypothesis that the apostles were impostors has been laid aside already (in the preceding paragraph). Was it, then, emptied by his enemies? How soon would the body have been produced, then, to confront and confound the so rapidly growing heresy! Or, if this were not possible, how soon would overwhelming proof of the removal of the body have been brought forward! Then, how was that grave emptied? Shall we say that Jesus was not really dead, and reviving from the swoon, himself crept from the tomb? This was the hypothesis of Schleiermacher. But not only is it in direct contradiction with the eye-witness testimony (1 Cor. 15:3; 2 Cor. 5:15; Rom. 14:9, *et saepe*), which is explicit that Christ died; but it has been felt by all the leaders of skeptical thought to be inadequate as an explanation. Strauss has himself executed justice on it. It not only casts a stigma on the moral character of our Lord; but it is itself laden with absurdity. "It would have been impossible thus to mistake a wounded man, dying from exhaustion, for the Messiah of Jewish expectations, or then to magnify this into a resurrection from the dead." A dying man in hiding, the center of Christianity's life! This fill with enthusiasm and death-defying courage the founders of the Church! Besides all which, the hypothesis makes the apostles either knaves or fools, neither of which, as the skeptics admit, is possible truth. Hence, they themselves unite with us in rejecting as wholly absurd this dream of Schleiermacher. Once more, then, how can we account for the empty grave? We hazard nothing in asserting that this one fact is destructive to all the theories of Christ's resurrection which have been started in the nervous effort to be rid of its reality. That empty grave is alone enough to found all Christianity upon.

But, suppose for a moment, we assume the impossible, and allow to Strauss that the site of the grave was already lost. What then? The disciples were still convinced that Christ had risen. How shall we account for this invincible conviction? The only possible resort is to the worn-out vision-hypothesis. Renan draws a beautiful picture of Mary Magdalene in her love and grief fancying she saw her longed-for Lord; and a not so beautiful one of the abject and idiotic credulity of the disciples who believed her, and then, because they believed her, fancied they had seen him themselves. But will all this fine picturing of what might have been, stand the test of facts? That grave stares us in the face again: if the body was still in it, there was no place left for visions of it as living and out of it; if not in it, how came it out?

But laying aside this final argument as premised, even then the theory cannot stand.

1. There was no expectation of a resurrection, and hence no ground for visions. So far we can go here. Could we appeal to the Gospels we could go farther and show that the disciples had lost all heart and "so far was their imagination from creating the sensible presence of Jesus, that at the first they did not recognize him." Renan gains all the facts on which he founds his theory from the Gospels: let him be refuted from the same records. How could Mary Magdalene's own mind have created the vision of Jesus when she did not recognize him as Jesus when he appeared?

2. There was no time for belief in the Resurrection to mythically grow. That well-established third day meets us here. And within forty days the whole Christian community, over five hundred in number, not only firmly believed in the Resurrection, but believed, each man of them, that he had himself seen the Lord. We must account for this.

3. These five hundred are too many visionaries to create. Was all Palestine inhabited by Francises of Assisi? What might be plausibly urged of Paul or Mary loses all plausibility when urged of all their contemporaries. And thus we cannot but conclude that all attempts to explain the belief of the early followers of Christ in his resurrection as a delusion, utterly fail. If it was not founded on fraud or delusion, then, was it not on fact? There seems no other alternative: eye-witnesses in abundance witness to the fact; if they were neither deceivers nor deceived, then Christ did rise from the dead.

We must not imagine, however, that this is all the proof we have of that great fact. We have been only very inadequately working one single vein. There is another very convincing course of argumentation which might be based on the results of the resurrection of Christ-in transforming those who believed in it-in founding a Church. And, then, there is that other form of argument already pointed out which consists in the not very difficult task of vindicating the authority of our Gospels and Acts, or of the account included in them. Taking all lines of proof together, it is by no means extravagant to assert that no fact in the history of the world is so well authenticated as the fact of Christ's resurrection. And that established, all Christianity is established too. Its supernatural element is vindicated its supernatural origin evinced. Then, our faith is not in vain, and we are not still in our sins. Then, the world has been redeemed unto our God, and all flesh can see his salvation. Then, the All-Wise is the All-Loving, too, and has vindicated his love forever. Then, the supreme song of heaven may be fitly repeated on earth: "Worthy is the Lamb that hath been slain to receive the power, and riches, and wisdom, and might, and honor, and glory, and blessing." Then, we can know that nothing can separate us from his love-that even death has failed in the attempt; and that it is thus given to mortals to utter in triumph the immortal cry, "Death is swallowed up in victory!"

B. B. Warfield, The Journal of Christian Philosophy
vol. 3., 1884, pp. 305-318.

4.12 THE RESURRECTION OF CHRIST, J. GRESHAM MACHEN

John Gresham Machen (1881-1937) was an influential American Presbyterian theologian in the early 20th century. He was the Professor of New Testament at Princeton Seminary between 1915 and 1929, and led a conservative revolt against modernist theology at Princeton and formed Westminster Seminary as a more orthodox alternative. This split was irreconcilable, and Machen led others to form the Orthodox Presbyterian Church.

Machen is considered to be the last of the great Princeton Theologians who had, since the formation of the college in the early 19th century, developed Princeton Theology—a conservative and Calvinist form of Evangelical Christianity. Although Machen can be compared to the great Princeton Theologians (Archibald Alexander, Charles Hodge, A. A. Hodge and B. B. Warfield) he was neither a lecturer in theology (he was a New Testament scholar) nor did he ever become the seminary's principal.

Machen's influence can still be felt today through the existence of both institutions that he founded—Westminster Seminary and the Orthodox Presbyterian Church.

Some nineteen hundred years ago, in an obscure corner of the Roman Empire, there lived one who, to a casual observer might have seemed to be a remarkable man. Up to the age of about thirty years. He lived an obscure life in the midst of an humble family. Then He began a remarkable course of ethical and religious teaching, accompanied by a ministry of healing. At first He was very popular. Great crowds followed Him gladly, and the intellectual men of His people were interested in what He had to say. But His teaching presented revolutionary features, and He did not satisfy the political expectations of the populace. And so, before long, after some three years, He fell a victim to the jealousy of the leaders of His people and the cowardice of the Roman governor. He died the death of the criminals of those days, on the cross. At His death, the disciples whom He had gathered about Him were utterly discouraged. In Him had centered all their loftiest hopes. And now that He was taken from them by a shameful death, their hopes were shattered. They fled from Him in cowardly fear in the hour of His need, and an observer would have said that never was a movement more hopelessly dead. These followers of Jesus had evidently been far inferior to Him in spiritual discernment and in courage. They had not been able, even when He was with them, to understand the lofty teachings of their leader. How, then, could they understand Him when He was gone? The movement depended, one might have said, too much on one extraordinary man, and when He was taken away, then surely the movement was dead.

But then the astonishing thing happened. The plain fact, which no one doubts, is that those same weak, discouraged men who had just fled in the hour of their Master's need, and who were altogether hopeless on account of His death, suddenly began in Jerusalem, a very few days or weeks after their Master's death, what is certainly the most remarkable spiritual movement that the world has ever seen. At first, the movement thus begun remained within the limits of the Jewish people. But soon it broke the bands of Judaism, and began to be planted in all the great cities of the Roman world. Within three hundred years, the Empire itself had been conquered by the Christian faith.

But this movement was begun in those few decisive days after the death of Jesus. What was it which caused the striking change in those weak, discouraged disciples, which made them the spiritual conquerors of the world?

Historians of today are perfectly agreed that something must have happened, something decisive, after the death of Jesus, in order to begin this new movement. It was not just an ordinary continuation of the influence of Jesus' teaching. The modern historians are at least agreed that some striking change took place after the death of Jesus, and before the beginning of the Christian missionary movement. They are agreed, moreover, to some extent even about the question what the change was; they are agreed in holding that

this new Christian movement was begun by the belief of the disciples in the resurrection of Jesus; they are agreed in holding that in the minds and hearts of the disciples there was formed the conviction that Jesus had risen from the dead. Of course, that was not formerly admitted by everyone. It used to be maintained, in the early days of modern skepticism, that the disciples of Jesus only pretended that He had risen from the dead. Such hypotheses have long ago been placed in the limbo of discarded theories. The disciples of Jesus, the intimate friends of Jesus, it is now admitted, in a short time after His death came to be believe honestly that He had risen from the dead. The only difference of opinion comes when we ask what in turn produced this belief.

The New Testament answer to this question is perfectly plain. According to the New Testament, the disciples believed in the resurrection of Jesus because Jesus really, after His death, came out of the tomb, appeared to them, and held extended intercourse with them, so that their belief in the resurrection was simply based on fact.

Of course, this explanation is rejected by those modern men who are unwilling to recognize in the origin of Christianity an entrance of the creative power of God, in distinction from the laws which operate in nature. And so another explanation has been proposed. It is that the belief of the disciples in the resurrection was produced by certain hallucinations in which they thought they saw Jesus, their teacher, and heard perhaps words of His ringing in their ears. A hallucination is a phenomenon well known to students of pathology. In an hallucination, the optic nerve is affected, and the patient therefore does actually in one sense "see" someone or something. But this effect is produced, not by an external object, but by the pathological condition of the subject himself. That is the view of the "appearances" of the risen Christ which is held today by those who reject the miraculous in connection with the origin of Christianity.

It is also held, it is true, that what was decisive in the resurrection faith of the early disciples was the impression which they had received of Jesus' person. Without that impression, it is supposed, they could never have had those pathological experiences which they called appearances of the risen Christ, so that those pathological experiences were merely the necessary form in which the continued impression of Jesus' person made itself felt in the life of the first disciples. But after all, on this hypothesis, the resurrection faith of the disciples, upon which the Christian church is founded, was really based upon a pathological experience in which these men thought they saw Jesus, and heard perhaps a word or two of His ringing in their ears, when there was nothing in the external world to make them think that they were in His presence.

Formerly, it is true, there were other explanations. It used to be held sometimes that the disciples came to believe in the resurrection because Jesus was not really dead. When He was placed in the cool air of the tomb, He revived and came out, and the disciples thought that He had arisen. A noteworthy scholar of today is said to have revived this theory, because he is dissatisfied with the prevailing idea. But the great majority of scholars today believe that this faith of the disciples was caused by hallucinations, which are called "appearances" of the risen Lord. But let us examine the New Testament account of the resurrection of Jesus, and of the related events. This account is contained particularly in six of the New Testament books. Of course, all the New Testament books presuppose the resurrection, and witness is borne to it in all of them. But there are six of these books, above all others, which provide the details of the Resurrection. These are the four Gospels, the Book of Acts, and the First Epistle of Paul to the Corinthians.

According to these six books, if their witness be put together, Jesus died on a Friday. His body was not allowed to remain and decompose on the cross, but was buried that same evening. He was placed in a grave chosen by a leader of the people, a member of the Sanhedrin. His burial was witnessed by certain women. He remained in the grave during the Sabbath. But on the morning of the first day of the week, He arose. Certain women who came to the grave found it empty, and saw angels who told them He had risen from the dead. He appeared to these women. The grave was visited that same morning by Peter and the beloved disciple. In the course of the day Jesus appeared to Peter. In the evening He appeared to two unnamed disciples who were walking to Emmaus, and apparently later on the same evening He appeared to all the apostles save Thomas. Then a week later He appeared again to the apostles, Thomas being present. Then He appeared in Galilee, as we learn from Matthew 28. Paul is probably mentioning this same appearance when he says that "He appeared to above five hundred brethren at once," 1 Corinthians 15:6. It was probably then, also, that He appeared to the seven disciples on the sea of Galilee, John 21. Then He appeared in Jerusalem, and ascended from the Mount of Olives. Some time in the course of the appearances there was one to James, His own brother, 1 Corinthians 15:7. Later on He appeared to Paul. Such is the New Testament account of the resurrection appearances of our Lord.

There are two features of this account to which great prominence has been given in recent discussions. These are,

1. the place, and

2. the character, of the appearances of Jesus.

1. THE PLACE

According to the New Testament, the place was first Jerusalem, then Galilee, and then Jerusalem again. The appearances took place, not only in Galilee and in Jerusalem, but both in Jerusalem and in Galilee; and the first appearances took place in Jerusalem.

2. THE CHARACTER

So much for the place of the appearances. As for the character of the appearances, they were, according to the New Testament, of a plain, physical kind. In the New Testament Jesus is represented even as holding table companionship with His disciples after His resurrection, and as engaging in rather extended intercourse with them. There is, it is true, something mysterious about this intercourse; it is not just a continuation of the old Galilean relationship. Jesus' body is independent of conditions of time and space in a way that appeared only rarely in His previous ministry. There was a change. But there is also continuity. The body of Jesus came out of the tomb and appeared to the disciples in such a way that a man could put his finger in the mark of the nails in His hands.

In two particulars, this account is contradicted by modern scholars. In the first place, the character of the appearances, is supposed to have been different. The disciples of Jesus, it is supposed, saw Him just for a moment in glory, and perhaps heard a word or two ringing in their ears. Of course this was not, according to the modern naturalistic historians, a real seeing and hearing, but an hallucination. But the point is, that those who regard these appearances as hallucinations are not able to take the New Testament account and prove from it that these appearances were hallucinations and were not founded upon the real presence of the body of Jesus; but are obliged first to reduce the New Testament account to manageable proportions. The reason is that there are limits to an hallucination. No sane men could think that they had had extended companionship with one who was not really present, or could believe that they had walked with Him and talked with Him after His death. You cannot enter upon the modern explanation of these happenings as genuine experiences but at the same time mere visions, until you modify the account that is given of the appearance themselves. And if this modified account be true, there must be a great deal in the New Testament account that is legendary. You must admit this, and you are going to explain these appearances as hallucinations. So there is a difference concerning the nature of the appearances, according to modern reconstruction, as over against the New Testament.

And there is a difference also concerning the place of the appearances. According to the customary modern view of naturalistic historians, the first appearances took place in Galilee, and not in Jerusalem. But what is the importance of that difference of opinion? It looks at first sight as though it were a mere matter of detail. But in reality it is profoundly important for the whole modern reconstruction. If you are going to explain these experiences as hallucinations, the necessary psychological conditions must have prevailed in order for the disciples to have had the experiences. Therefore modern historians are careful to allow time for the profound discouragement of the disciples to be gotten rid of—for the disciples to return to Galilee, and to live again in the scenes where they had lived with Jesus; to muse upon Him, and be ready to have these visions of Him. Time must be permitted, and the place must be favorable. And then there is another important element.

We come here to one of the most important things of all—the empty tomb. If the first appearances were in Jerusalem, why did not the disciples or the enemies investigate the tomb, and refute this belief of finding the body of Jesus still there? This argument is thought to be refuted by the Galilean hypothesis regarding the first appearances. If the first appearances took place not till weeks afterward and in Galilee, this mystery is thought to be explained. There would be no opportunity to investigate the tomb until it was too late; and so the matter could have been allowed to pass, and the resurrection faith could have arisen. Of course, this explanation is not quite satisfactory, because one cannot see how the disciples would not have been stimulated to investigate the tomb, whenever and wherever the appearances took place. We have not quite explained the empty tomb even by this Galilean hypothesis. But you can understand the insistence of the modern writers that the first appearances took place in Galilee.

So there is a difference between the modern historian and the New Testament account in the matters of the manner and of the place of these experiences. Were they of a kind such that they could be explained as hallucinations or were they such that they could only be regarded as real appearances? Was the first appearance three days after Jesus' death, and near the tomb, or later on in Galilee?

Let us come now to the New Testament account. The first source that we should consider is the first Epistle of Paul to the Corinthians. It is probably the earliest of the sources. But what is still more important—the authorship and date of this particular source of information have been agreed upon even by the opponents of Christianity. So this is not only a source of first-rate historical importance but it is a source of admitted importance. We have here a fixed starting-point in all controversy.

We must examine, then, this document with some care. It was probably written, roughly speaking, about A.D. 55, about twenty-five years after the death of Jesus, about as long after the death of Jesus as 1924 is after the Spanish-American War (1898). That is not such a very long period of time. And of course, there is one vital element in the testimony here, which does not prevail in the case of the Spanish War. Most people have forgotten many details of the Spanish-American War, because they have not had them continuously in mind.

But it would not be so in the case now under consideration. The resurrection of Jesus was the thing which formed the basis of all the thought of the early Christians, and so the memory of it when it was twenty-five years past was very much fresher than the memory of an event like the Spanish-American War of twenty-five years ago, which has passed out of our consciousness.

Let us turn, then, to 1 Corinthians 15, and read the first verses, "Moreover, brethren, I declare unto you the gospel which I preached unto you, which also ye have received, and wherein ye stand; by which also ye are saved, if ye keep in memory what I preached unto you, unless ye have believed in vain. For I delivered unto you first of all that which I also received." "First of all," or "among the first things," may mean first in point of time, or first in point of importance. At any rate, this was a part of Paul's fundamental preaching in Corinth, in about the year 51 or 52. So we get back a little farther than the time when the Epistle was written. But these things were evidently also first and fundamental in Paul's preaching in

other places, so that you are taken back an indefinite period in the ministry of Paul for this evidence. But then you are taken back by the next words farther still—"that which I also received." There is a common agreement as to the source from which Paul "received" this information; it is pretty generally agreed that he received it from the Jerusalem church. According to the Epistle to the Galatians, he had been in conference with Peter and James only three years after his conversion. That was the time for Paul to receive this tradition. Historians are usually willing to admit that this information is nothing less than the account which the primitive Church, including Peter and James, gave of the events which lay at the foundation of the Church. So you have here, even in the admission of modern men, a piece of historical information of priceless value.

"For I delivered unto you first of all that which I also received, how that Christ died for our sins according to the Scriptures; and that he was buried, and that he rose again the third day according to the Scriptures." Why does Paul mention the burial of Jesus? The impression which the mention of the burial produces upon every reader who comes to It as for the first time is that Paul means to say that the body of Jesus was laid in the tomb. The burial, in other words, implies the empty tomb. And yet a great many modern historians say that Paul "knows nothing" about the empty tomb! Surely such an assertion is quite false. Paul does not indeed mention the empty tomb in so many words; he does not give a detailed description of it here. But that does not mean that he knew nothing about it. Those to whom he was writing believed in it already, and he is simply reviewing a previous argument in order to draw inferences from it with regard to the resurrection of Christians. To say that Paul knows nothing about the empty tomb ignores the fact that the mention of the burial is quite meaningless unless Paul had in mind the empty tomb. I do not see how any one can get any other impression. Moreover is not that what resurrection means, after all? Modern historians say that Paul was interested simply in the continued life of Jesus in a new body which had nothing to do with the body which lay in the tomb. That is rather strange in this connection. Paul is arguing, in this passage, not against men who denied the immortality of the soul, but against men who held the Greek view of the immortality of the soul without the body. The view that they were holding, would logically make of the resurrection of Jesus just the simple continuance of His personal life. There is no point at all, then, in what Paul says against them unless he is referring to the resurrection from the tomb. Unless he is referring to this, he is playing into the hands of his opponents. But many men nowadays have such a strangely unhistorical notion of what "resurrection" meant to the early disciples. They talk as though the resurrection faith meant that those disciples simply believed that Jesus continued to exist after His crucifixion. This is absurd. Those men believed in the continued existence after death of every man. There is not the slightest doubt about that. They were thoroughly imbued with this belief. They were not Sadducees. Even in those first three days after Jesus' crucifixion, they still believed that He was alive. If that is all that resurrection meant, there was nothing in it to cause joy. Conviction of the continued life of Jesus would not make Him any different from other men. But what changed sadness into joy and brought about the founding of the Church was the substitution, for a belief in the continued existence of Jesus, of a belief in the emergence of His body from the tomb. And Paul's words imply that as clear as day.

"And that he rose again the third day." Of all the important things that Paul says, this is perhaps the most important, from the point of view of modern discussion. There are few words in the New Testament that are more disconcerting to modern naturalistic historians than the words, "on the third day." We have just observed what the modern reconstruction is. The disciples went back to Galilee, it is supposed, and there, some time after the crucifixion, they came to believe that Jesus was alive. But if the first appearance took place on the third day, this explanation is not possible. The modern reconstruction disap-

pears altogether if you believe that the first appearances were on the third day. If Paul's words are to be taken at their face value, the whole elaborate psychological reconstruction of the conditions in the disciples' minds, leading up to the hallucinations in Galilee, disappears.

Many men, it is true, have an answer ready. "Let us not," they say in effect, "go beyond what Paul actually says! Paul does not say that the first appearance occurred on the third day, but only that Christ rose on that day. He might have risen some time before He first appeared to them; the resurrection might have occurred on the third day and yet the first appearance might have occurred some weeks after, in Galilee."

But why, if nothing in particular happened on the third day, and if the first appearance occurred some weeks after, did the disciples hit upon just the third day as the day of the supposed resurrection? Surely it was very strange for them to suppose that Jesus had really risen a considerable time before He appeared to them and had left them all that time in their despair. So strange a supposition on the part of the disciples surely requires an explanation. Why was it, if nothing happened on the third day, that the disciples ever came to suppose that the resurrection occurred on that day and not on some other day?

One proposed explanation is that the third day was hit upon as the day of the supposed resurrection because Scripture was thought to require it. Paul says, it will be remembered, that Jesus rose the third day according to the Scriptures. But where will you find in the Old Testament Scriptures any clear reference to the third day, as the day of the resurrection of Christ. No doubt there is the "sign of Jonah." And there is also Hosea 6-2. We are certainly not denying that these passages (at least the former) are true prophecies of the resurrection on the third day. But could they ever have been understood before the fulfillment had come? That is more than doubtful. Indeed it is not even quite clear whether Paul means the words "according to the Scriptures" to refer to the third day at all, and not merely to the central fact of the resurrection itself. At any rate the Scripture passages never could have suggested the third day to the disciples unless something had actually happened on that day to indicate that Christ had then risen.

But had not Jesus Himself predicted that He would rise on the third day, and might not this prediction have caused the disciples to suppose that He had risen on that day even if the first appearance did not occur till long afterwards? This is an obvious way out of the difficulty, but it is effectually closed to the modern naturalistic historian. For it would require us to suppose that Jesus' predictions of His resurrection, recorded in the Gospels, are historical. But the naturalistic historians are usually concerned with few things more than with the denial of the authenticity of these predictions. According to the ordinary "liberal" view, Jesus certainly could not have predicted that He would rise from the dead in the manner recorded in the Gospels. So for the "liberal" historians this explanation of "the third day" becomes impossible. The explanation would perhaps explain "the third day" in the belief of the disciples, but it would also destroy the whole account of the "liberal Jesus."

Accordingly it becomes necessary to seek explanations farther afield. Some have appealed to a supposed belief in antiquity to the effect that the soul of a dead person hovered around the body for three days and then departed. This belief, it is said, might have seemed to the disciples to make it necessary to put the supposed resurrection not later than the third day. But how far did this belief prevail in Palestine in the first century? The question is perhaps not capable of satisfactory answer. Moreover, it is highly dangerous from the point of view of the modern naturalistic historians to appeal to this belief, since it would show that some interest was taken in the body of Jesus; and yet that is what these modern historians are most concerned to deny. For if interest was taken in the body, the old question arises again why the tomb was not investigated. And the whole vision hypothesis breaks down. Since these explanations have proved unsatisfactory, some modern scholars have had recourse to a fourth explanation. There was in ancient times, they say, a pagan belief about a god who died and

rose again. On the first day the worshiper of the god were to mourn, but on the third day they were to rejoice, because of the resurrection of the god. So it is thought that the disciples may have been influenced by this pagan belief. But surely this is a desperate expedient. It is only a very few students of the history of religions who would be quite so bold as to believe that in Palestine, in the time of Christ, there was any prevalence of this pagan belief with its dying and rising god. Indeed the importance and clearness of this belief have been enormously exaggerated in recent works—particularly as regards the rising of the god on the third day.

The truth is that the third day in the primitive account of the resurrection of Christ remains, and that there is no satisfactory means of explaining it away. Indeed some naturalistic historians are actually coming back to the view that perhaps we cannot explain this third day away, and that perhaps something did happen on the third day to produce the faith of the disciples. But if this conclusion be reached, then the whole psychological reconstruction disappears, and particularly the modern hypothesis about the place of the appearances. Something must have happened to produce the disciples' belief in the resurrection not far off in Galilee but near to the tomb in Jerusalem. But if so, there would be no time for the elaborate psychological process which is supposed to have produced the visions, and there would be ample opportunity for the investigation of the tomb.

It is therefore a fact of enormous importance that it is just Paul in the passage where he is admittedly reproducing the tradition of the primitive Jerusalem Church, who mentions the third day.

Then, after mentioning the third day, Paul gives a detailed account which is not quite complete, of the resurrection appearances. He leaves out the account of the appearances to the women, because he is merely giving the official list of the appearances to the leaders in the Jerusalem church.

So much for the testimony of Paul. This testimony is sufficient of itself to refute the modern naturalistic reconstruction. But it is time to glance briefly at the testimony in the Gospels.

If you take the shortest Gospel, the Gospel according to Mark, you will find, first, that Mark gives an account of the burial, which is of great importance. Modern historians cannot deny that Jesus was buried, because that is attested by the universally accepted source of information, I Corinthians 15. Mark is here confirmed by the Jerusalem tradition as preserved by Paul. But the account of the burial in Mark is followed by the account of the empty tomb, and the two things are indissolubly connected. If one is historical, it is difficult to reject the other. Modern naturalistic historians are in a divided condition about this matter of the empty tomb. Some admit that the tomb was empty. Others deny that it ever was. Some say what we have just outlined—that the tomb was never investigated at all until it was too late, and that then the account of the empty tomb grew up as a legend in the Church. But other historians are clear-sighted enough to see that you cannot get rid of the empty tomb in any such fashion.

But if the tomb was empty, why was it empty? The New Testament says that it was empty because the body of Jesus had been raised out of it. But if this be not the case, then why was the tomb empty? Some say that the enemies of Jesus took the body away. If so, they have done the greatest possible service to the resurrection faith which they so much hated. Others have said that the disciples stole the body away to make the people believe that Jesus was risen. But no one holds that view now. Others have said that Joseph of Arimathea changed the place of burial. That is difficult to understand, because if such were the case, why should Joseph of Arimathea have kept silence when the resurrection faith arose? Other explanations, no doubt, have been proposed. But it cannot be said that these hypotheses have altogether satisfied even those historians who have proposed them. The empty tomb has never been successfully explained away.

We might go on to consider the other accounts. But I think we have pointed out some of the most important parts of the evidence. The resurrection was of a bodily kind, and appears in connection with the empty tomb. It is quite a misrepresentation of the state of affairs when people talk about "interpreting" the New Testament in accordance with the modern view of natural law as operating in connection with the origin of Christianity. What is really being engaged in is not an interpretation of the New Testament but a complete contradiction of the New Testament at its central point. In order to explain the resurrection faith of the disciples as caused by hallucinations, you must first pick and choose in the sources of information, and reconstruct a statement of the case for which you have no historical information. You must first reconstruct this account, different from that which is given in the only sources of information, before you can even begin to explain the appearances as hallucinations. And even then you are really no better off. It is after all quite preposterous to explain the origin of the Christian Church as being due to pathological experiences of weak-minded men. So mighty a building was not founded upon so small a pin-point.

So the witness of the whole New Testament has not been put out of the way. It alone explains the origin of the Church, and the change of the disciples from weak men into the spiritual conquerors of the world.

Why is it, then, if the evidence be so strong, that so many modern men refuse to accept the New Testament testimony to the resurrection of Christ? The answer is perfectly plain. The resurrection, if it be a fact, is a stupendous miracle and against the miraculous or the supernatural there is a tremendous opposition in the modern mind.

But is the opposition well grounded? It would perhaps be well-grounded if the direct evidence for the resurrection stood absolutely alone—If it were simply a question whether a man of the first century, otherwise unknown, really rose from the dead. There would in that case be a strong burden of proof against the belief in the resurrection. But as a matter of fact the question is not whether any ordinary man rose from the dead, but whether Jesus rose from the dead. We know something of

Jesus from the Gospels, and as thus made known He is certainly different from all other men. A man who comes into contact with His tremendous personality will say to himself, "It is impossible that Jesus could ever have been hoiden [held] of death." Thus when the extraordinary testimony to the resurrection faith which has been outlined above comes to us, we add to this our tremendous impression of Jesus' Person, gained from the reading of the Gospels, and we accept this strange belief which comes to us and fills us with joy, that the Redeemer really triumphed over death and the grave and sin.

And if He be living, we come to Him today. And thus finally we add to the direct historical evidence our own Christian experience. If He be a living Savior, we come to Him for salvation today, and we add to the evidence from the New Testament documents an immediacy of conviction which delivers us from fear. The Christian man should indeed never say, as men often say, "Because of my experience of Christ in my soul I am independent of the basic facts of Christianity; I am independent of the question whether Jesus rose from the grave or not." But Christian experience, though it cannot make us Christians whether Jesus rose or not, still can add to the direct historical evidence a confirming witness that, as a matter of fact, Christ did really rise from the dead on the third day, according to the Scriptures. The "witness of the Spirit" is not, as it is often quite falsely represented today, independent of the Bible; on the contrary it is a witness by the Holy Spirit, who is the author of the Bible, to the fact that the Bible is true.

J. Gresham Machen, Historic Christianity, *1935*

4.13 THE POST-RESURRECTION APPEARANCES OF JESUS, WILLIAM HENDRIKSEN

(1) To Mary Magdalene (Mark 16:9; John 20:11-18).

(2) To the women (Matt. 28:9, 10).

(3) To Cleopas and his companion (Luke 24:13-35).

(4) To Simon (Luke 24:34; 1 Cor. 15:15).

(5) To the disciples except Thomas (John 20:19-23).

(6) To the disciples, Thomas being present (John 20:24-29). All of these occurred in Jerusalem. After the disciples have gone to Galilee, in obedience to the instructions which they had received from the Lord, Jesus appears again:

(7) To the seven at the Sea of Tiberias (21:1-14).

(8) To the disciples on a "mountain" in Galilee, where Jesus made a great claim, gave the great commission, and proclaimed the great presence (28:16-20). By many commentators this appearance is identifed with Number 9.

(9) To the five hundred (1 Cor. 15:6).

(10) To James, the Lord's brother (1 Cor. 15:7). Whether this took place in Galilee or in Judea is not stated. The disciples having returned to Jerusalem:

(11) To the eleven on Olivet, near Jerusalem (Acts 1:4-11; cf. Luke 24:50, 51). The next appearance that is specifically recorded is by the Lord from heaven:

(12) To Paul, when he was on his way to Damascus (Acts 9:3-7; 22:6-10; 26:12-18; 1 Cor. 9:1; 15:8).

There may have been several others. How many there were we do not know (cf. Acts 1:3).

William Hendriksen, The Gospel According to John
Grand Rapids: Baker Book House, 1953

3

POEMS, HYMNS, MEDITATIONS, AND PRAYERS ON THE RESURRECTION OF JESUS

4.14 Most glorious Lord of life, Edmund Spenser

Most glorious Lord of life, that on this day,
Didst make thy triumph over death and sin:
And having harrow'd hell, didst bring away
Captivity thence captive, us to win:
This joyous day, dear Lord, with joy begin,
And grant that we for whom thou diddest die,
Being with thy dear blood clean wash'd
from sin,

May live for ever in felicity.
And that thy love we weighing worthily,
May likewise love thee for the same again:
And for thy sake, that all like dear didst buy,
With love may one another entertain.
So let us love, dear love, like as we ought,
Love is the lesson which the Lord us taught.

Edmund Spenser, Amoretti 68

4.15 Christ, the Lord, is risen today, Alleluia!, Charles Wesley

Christ, the Lord, is risen today, Alleluia!
Sons of men and angels say, Alleluia!
Raise your joys and triumphs high, Alleluia!
Sing, ye heavens, and earth, reply, Alleluia!

Love's redeeming work is done, Alleluia!
Fought the fight, the battle won, Alleluia!
Lo! the Sun's eclipse is over, Alleluia!
Lo! He sets in blood no more, Alleluia!

Vain the stone, the watch, the seal, Alleluia!
Christ hath burst the gates of hell, Alleluia!
Death in vain forbids His rise, Alleluia!
Christ hath opened Paradise, Alleluia!

Lives again our glorious King, Alleluia!
Where, O death, is now thy sting? Alleluia!

Once He died our souls to save, Alleluia!
Where thy victory, O grave? Alleluia!

Soar we now where Christ hath led, Alleluia!
Following our exalted Head, Alleluia!
Made like Him, like Him we rise, Alleluia!
Ours the cross, the grave, the skies, Alleluia!

Hail, the Lord of earth and heaven, Alleluia!
Praise to Thee by both be given, Alleluia!
Thee we greet triumphant now, Alleluia!
Hail, the resurrection day, Alleluia!

King of glory, Soul of bliss, Alleluia!
Everlasting life is this, Alleluia!
Thee to know, Thy power to prove, Alleluia!
Thus to sing and thus to love, Alleluia!

Hymns of praise then let us sing, Alleluia!
Unto Christ, our heavenly King, Alleluia!
Who endured the cross and grave, Alleluia!
Sinners to redeem and save. Alleluia!

But the pains that He endured, Alleluia!
Our salvation have procured, Alleluia!
Now above the sky He's King, Alleluia!
Where the angels ever sing. Alleluia!

Jesus Christ is risen today, Alleluia!
Our triumphant holy day, Alleluia!
Who did once upon the cross, Alleluia!
Suffer to redeem our loss. Alleluia!

Charles Wesley

4.16 CHRIST IS ARISEN, JOHANN WOLFGANG VON GOETHE

Christ is arisen,
Joy to thee, mortal!
Out of His prison,
Forth from its portal!
Christ is not sleeping,
Seek Him no longer;
Strong was His keeping,
Jesus was stronger.

Christ is arisen,
Seek Him not here;
Lonely His prison,
Empty His bier;
Vain His entombing,

Spices and lawn,
Vain the perfunimg,
Jesus is gone.

Christ is arisen,
Joy to thee, mortal!
Empty His prison,
Broken its portal
Rising, He giveth
His shroud to the sod:
Risen, He liveth,
and liveth to God.

Johann Wolfgang von Goethe

4.17 UP FROM THE GRAVE HE AROSE, ROBERT LOWRY

Low in the grave He lay, Jesus my Savior,
Waiting the coming day, Jesus my Lord!

Refrain
Up from the grave He arose,
With a mighty triumph o'er His foes,
He arose a Victor from the dark domain,
And He lives forever, with His saints to reign.
He arose! He arose!
Hallelujah! Christ arose!

Vainly they watch His bed, Jesus my Savior;
Vainly they seal the dead, Jesus my Lord!

Refrain

Death cannot keep its Prey, Jesus my Savior;
He tore the bars away, Jesus my Lord!

Refrain

Robert Lowry

4.18 JESUS CHRIST IS RISEN TODAY, ALLELUIA!, AUTHOR UNKNOWN

Jesus Christ is risen to-day, Alleluia!
Our triumphant holy day, Alleluia!
Who did once, upon the Cross, Alleluia!
Suffer to redeem our loss. Alleluia!

Hymns of praise then let us sing, Alleluia!
Unto Christ, our heavenly King, Alleluia!
Who endured the Cross and grave, Alleluia!
Sinners to redeem and save. Alleluia!
But the pains that he endured, Alleluia!
Our salvation have procured; Alleluia!

Now above the sky he's King, Alleluia!
Where the angels ever sing. Alleluia!

Sing we to our God above, Alleluia!
Praise eternal as His love, Alleluia!
Praise Him, all you heavenly host, Alleluia!
Father, Son, and Holy Ghost, Alleluia!

Author unknown, translated from a fourteent-
century Bohemian Latin carol
Surrexit Christus hodie.

4.19 HIPPOLYTUS OF ROME, CHRIST IS RISEN! THE WORLD BELOW LIES DESOLATE.

Christ is risen! The world below lies desolate.
Christ is risen! The spirits of evil are fallen.
Christ is risen! The angels of God rejoice.
Christ is risen! The tombs of the dead are empty.

Christ is risen indeed from the dead—
the first of the sleepers. And glory and power
are his forever and ever, Amen.

Hippolytus of Rome

4.20 A BETTER RESURRECTION, CHRISTINA ROSSETTI

I have no wit, no words, no tears;
My heart within me like a stone
Is numb'd too much for hopes or fears;
Look right, look left, I dwell alone;
I lift mine eyes, but dimm'd with grief
No everlasting hills I see;
My life is in the falling leaf:
O Jesus, quicken me.

My life is like a faded leaf,
My harvest dwindled to a husk:
Truly my life is void and brief
And tedious in the barren dusk;

My life is like a frozen thing,
No bud nor greenness can I see:
Yet rise it shall—the sap of Spring;
O Jesus, rise in me.

My life is like a broken bowl,
A broken bowl that cannot hold
One drop of water for my soul
Or cordial in the searching cold;
Cast in the fire the perish'd thing;
Melt and remould it, till it be
A royal cup for Him, my King:
O Jesus, drink of me.

Christina Rossetti

4

QUOTATION COLLECTION ON THE RESURRECTION OF JESUS

Men and women disbelieve the Easter story not because of the evidence but in spite of it. It is not that they weigh the evidence with open minds, assess its relevance and cogency and finally decide that it is suspect or inadequate. Instead, they start with the a priori conviction that the resurrection of Christ would constitute such an incredible event that it could not be accepted or believed without scientific demonstration of an irrefutable nature. But it is idle to demand proof of this sort for any event in history. Historical evidence, from its very nature, can never amount to more than a very high degree of probability.

J. N. D. Anderson

I know of no one fact in the history of mankind which is proved by better evidence of every sort, to the understanding of a fair enquirer, than the great sign which God has given us that Christ died and rose from the dead.

Thomas Arnold

If He did not rise, but is still dead, how is it that He routs and persecutes and overthrows the false gods, whom unbelievers think to be alive, and the evil spirits whom they worship?

Athanasius

The immortal Son of God, fulfilled all justice in restoring mankind to immortality by the promise of the resurrection.

Athanasius

Our faith is strengthened by the resurrection of Christ.

Augustine

The historical Jesus Christ was an amazing power in the lives of men years after his death. It is not so much the fact that a miracle happened. . . . The chief reason that the disciples spoke so often about it was that Jesus was alive and with them again.

Oliver Barclay

Earth to earth, ashes to ashes, dust to dust; in sure and certain hope of the Resurrection into eternal life . . . .

Book of Common Prayer

The resurrection is not merely a victory over death (though it is that) but a proof that the atonement was a satisfactory atonement in the sight of the Father.

James Montgomery Boice

This is the end, but for me it is the beginning of life.

Dietrich Bonhoeffer, as he was taken away to be executed

If that vital spark that we find in a grain of wheat can pass unchanged through countless deaths and resurrections, will the spirit of man be unable to pass from this body to another?

William Jennings Bryan

An historical fact which involves a resurrection from the dead is utterly inconceivable.

Rudolph Bultmann

The claims of Jesus Christ, namely his resurrection, has led me as often as I have tried to examine the evidence to believe it as a fact beyond dispute.

Lord Caldecote

Although we have complete salvation through his death, because we are reconciled to God by it, it is by his resurrection, not his death, that we are said to be born to a living hope (1 Peter 1:3).

John Calvin

Let us always remember that the end of the resurrection is eternal happiness.

John Calvin

Accordingly in the death and burial of Christ a twofold blessing is set before us, namely, deliverance from death, to which we were enslaved, and the mortification of our flesh.

John Calvin

Let us always remember that the end of the resurrection is eternal happiness, of whose excellence scarcely the minutist part can be described by all that human tongues can say. For though we are truly told that the kingdom of God will be full of light, and gladness, and felcity, and glory, yet the things meant by these words remain most remote from sense, and as it were involved in enigma, until the day arrive on which he will manifest his glory to us face to face.

John Calvin

The most celebrated event in the New Testament is the resurrection of Christ.

Edward John Carnell

Certainly no event since the world began has been so fully proved by the concurrent testimonies of so many people.

Edward John Carnell

Christ has turned all our sunsets into dawns.

Clement of Alexander

Let us look at the resurrection which happens regularly. Day and night show us a resurrection; night goes to sleep, day rises: day departs, night arrives.

Clement of Rome

Nothing less than a resurrected Christ could have caused those men to maintain to their dying whispers that Jesus is alive and is Lord.

Chuck Colson

I know pretty well what evidence is; and I tell you, such evidence as that for the resurrection has never broken down yet.

John Singleton Copley, former Attorney General

No intelligent jury in the world could fail to bring in a verdict that the resurrection story is true.

Lord Darling, former Lord Chief Justice of England

The entire New Testament is witness that the real presence of Christ was not withdrawn when the resurrection "appearances" ceased.

C. H. Dodd

When that great Christian and scientist Sir Michael Faraday was dying, journalists questioned him about his speculations for a life after death. "Speculations!" said Faraday, "I know nothing of speculations. I'm resting on certainties. I know that my Redeemer liveth, and because He lives, I shall live also."

Michael Faraday

The body of Benjamin Franklin, Printer (like the cover of an old book, its contents torn out and stripped of its lettering and gilding), lies here, food for worms; but the work shall not be lost, for it will (as he believed) appear once more in a new and more elegant edition, revised and corrected by the Author.

Benjamin Franklin, Epitaph, composed by Franklin

To consign the resurrection to the category of myth is a typical species of modern laziness or a typically lazy modernism.

Hans Frei

The resurrection is the heart of the gospel.

Norman Geisler

There is more evidence that Jesus rose from the dead than there is that Julius Caesar ever lived or that Alexander the Great died at the age of thirty-three.

Billy Graham

Jesus came to do three days work.

Billy Graham

The evidence in favor of this astonishing fact [of Jesus' resurrection] is overwhelming.

Michael Green

Christianity does not hold the resurrection to be one among many tenets of belief. Without faith in the resurrection there would be no Christianity at all. . . . Once disprove it, and you have disposed of Christianity.

Michael Green

The Resurrection was the belief that turned brokenhearted followers of a crucified rabbi into the courageous witness and martyrs of the early church. . . . You could imprison them, flog them, but you could not make them deny their conviction that "on the third day, he rose again."

Michael Green

Without faith in the resurrection there would be no Christianity at all.

Michael Green

There is more evidence for the historical fact of the resurrection of Jesus Christ than for just about any other event in history.

Simon Greenleaf, Dane Professor of Law at Harvard University

The simple faith of the Christian who believes in the Resurrection is nothing compared to the credulity of the skeptic who will accept the wildest and most improbable romances rather than admit the plain witness of historical certainties.

George Hanson

If the resurrection is not historic fact, then the power of death remains unbroken, and with it the effect of sin.

James Hastings

Thou hast conquered, O Galilaean.

George Herbert

The resurrection of Jesus is the ultimate sign that our salvation comes only when we cease trying to interpret Jesus' story in the light of our history, and instead we interpret ourselves in the light of his.

Stanley Hauerwas

The head that once was crowned with thorns is crowned with glory now.

Thomas Kelley

The most certain assurance of life after death for the Christian is the historical, literal resurrection of Christ.

Peter Kreeft

Receive every day as a resurrection from death, as a new enjoyment of life.

William Law

Jesus has forced open a door that has been locked since the death of the first man. He has met, fought and beaten the King of Death. Everything is different because he has done so.

C. S. Lewis

The first fact in the history of Christendom is a number of people who say that they have seen the Resurrection.

C. S. Lewis

The Resurrection is the central theme in every Christian sermon reported in the Acts.

C. S. Lewis

If the thing happened, it was the central event in the history of the earth.

C. S. Lewis

We must both, I'm afraid, recognize that, as we grow older, we become like old cars— more and more repairs and replacements are necessary. We must just look forward to the fine new machines (latest Resurrection model) which are waiting for us, we hope, in the Divine garage.

C. S. Lewis

Jesus' supreme credential to authentic his claim to deity was his resurrection from the dead. Five times in the course of his life he predicted he would die. He also predicted how he would die and that three days later he would rise from the dead and appear to his disciples.

Paul E. Little

The mightiest foes, the devil, death, and hell have already been vanquished, and the resurrection of Christ is the proof of it.

D. Martyn Lloyd-Jones

Without Christ's resurrection you have not standing at all.

D. Martyn Lloyd-Jones

Our Lord has written the promise of the resurrection, not in books alone but in every leaf in springtime.

Martin Luther

I know pretty well what evidence is; and, I tell you, such evidence as that for the resurrection has never broken down yet.

Lord Lyndhurst

If [Jesus' resurrection] is unique, then, by definition, there will be no analogous events. That makes it a lot harder to believe. It also makes it worth believing.

Alister E. McGrath

His resurrection was all for others. That miracle was wrought in him, not for him.

George MacDonald

The seed dies into a new life, and so does man.

George MacDonald

The one proof of a life beyond the grave is the resurrection of Jesus Christ.

Alexander Maclaren

If all the evidence is weighed carefully and fairly, it is indeed justifiable, according to the cannons of historical research, to conclude that the sepulcher of Joseph of Arimathea, in which Jesus was buried, was actually empty (Jesus was resurrected) on the morning of the first Easter. And no thread of evidence has yet been discovered in literary sources, epigraphy, or archaeology that would disprove this statement.

Paul L. Maier, Professor of ancient history at Western Michigan University

Because of Christ's resurrection the thief ascends to paradise.

Maximus of Turin

Christ is risen. His rising brings life to the dead, forgiveness to sinners, and glory to the saints.

Maximus of Turin

The resurrection of Jesus Christ is the epicenter of Christianity.

Calvin Miller

The resurrection is the faith requirement through which seekers become followers.

Calvin Miller

Christian faith lives from the raising of the crucified Christ.

Jürgen Moltmann

One day soon you will hear that I am dead. Do not believe it. I will then be alive as never before.

Dwight Moody

The bodily resurrection of Jesus Christ from the dead is the crowning proof of Christianity. If the resurrection did not take place, then Christianity is a false religion. If it did take place, then Christ is God and the Christian faith is absolute truth.

Henry Morris

The same power that brought Christ back from the dead is operative within those who are Christ's.

Leon Morris

The Resurrection is an ongoing thing.

Leon Morris

The origin of Christianity must remain an unsolved enigma for any historian who refuses to take seriously the only explanation offered by the Church itself.

C. F. D. Moule

Our old history ends with the Cross; our new history begins with the resurrection.

Watchman Nee

The purpose of revelation is restoration, the renewal in us of that likeness to God which man lost by sin.

Stephen Neill

There is probably no event in human history that has had such importance, while remaining, at the same time, so unspectacular. The world didn't notice it; only those few to whom Jesus had chosen to show himself, and whom he wanted to send out to announce God's love to the world just as he had done.

Henri J. M. Nouwen

The resurrection of Jesus Christ is the glorious manifestation of the victory of love over death.

Henri J. M. Nouwen

No single example can be produced of belief in the resurrection of an historical personage such as Jesus was: none at least on which anything was ever founded. The Christian resurrection is thus a fact without historical analogy.

James Orr

It really is harder to disbelieve the resurrection than to accept it, much harder.

J. I. Packer

The cooperate experience of the Christian church over nineteen centuries chimes in with the belief that Jesus rose.

J. I. Packer

To echo the words of ex-doubter Thomas, "My Lord and my God," is certainly more than an exercise of reason, but in the face of the evidence it is the only reasonable thing a person can do.

J. I. Packer

What reason have atheists for saying that we cannot rise again? Which is the more difficult, to be born, or to rise again? That which has never been, should be, or that which has been, should be again? Is it more difficult to come into being than to return to it?

Blaise Pascal

The historical evidence for the resurrection is stronger than for any other miracle anywhere narrated.

William Lyon Phelps

The resurrection stands within the realm of historical factuality, and constitutes excellent motivation for a person to trust Christ as Savior.

Clark Pinnock

The empty tomb of Christ has been the cradle of the Church.

Edmond de Pressensé

In both ecclesiastical history and creedal history the resurrection is affirmed from the earliest times. It is mentioned in Clement of Rome, Epistle to the Corinthians (A.D. 95), the earliest document of church history and so continuously throughout all of the patristic period. It appears in all forms of the Apostles' Creed and is never debated.

Bernard Ramm

No Resurrection, no Christianity.

Michael Ramsey

So utterly new and foreign to the expectations of men was this doctrine [of Jesus' resurrection], that it seems hard to doubt that only historical events could have created it.

Michael Ramsey

The recent mythological view (of the resurrection of Jesus) fails to do justice to the scriptural evidence. Many in fact will continue to find it easier to believe that the empty tomb produced the disciples' faith than that the disciples' faith produced the empty tomb.

J. A. T. Robinson

If Christ were not risen, he would not be present alongside us today.

Brother Roger of Taizé

If Christ were not risen, he would just be a remarkable personality in the history of humanity.

Brother Roger of Taizé

If Christ were not risen, it would not be possible to discover a communion in him, to share with him through prayer.

Brother Roger of Taizé

[The disciples] had seen the strong hands of God twist the crown of thorns into a crown of glory, and in hands as strong as that they knew themselves safe.

Dorothy L. Sayers

Without His Resurrection the death of Christ would be of no avail, and His grave would be the grave of all our hopes.

Philip Schaff

The bodies of men after death return to dust, but their spirits return immediately to God—the righteous to rest with Him; the wicked to be reserved under darkness to the judgment. At the last day, the bodies of all the dead, both just and unjust, will be raised.

Southern Baptist Theological Seminary

The meaning of the resurrection is a theological matter, but the fact of the resurrection is a historical matter; the nature of the resurrection body of Jesus may be a mystery, but the fact that the body disappeared from the tomb is a matter to be decided upon by historical evidence.

Wilbur Smith

Next to Christology, the Resurrection is undoubtedly the doctrine which held the chief place in early Christian literature.

W. J. Sparrow-Simpson

A glance at these graveclothes proved the reality, and indicated the nature, of the resurrection.

John Stott

Christianity is in its very essence a resurrection religion. The concept of resurrection lies at its heart. If you remove it, Christianity is destroyed.

John Stott

Condemned for blasphemy, he was now designated Son of God by the resurrection.

John Stott

It was not Christ's personality that survived death, or his influence but his literal body that was raised from the dead.

John Stott

Perhaps the transformation of the disciples of Jesus is the greatest evidence for the resurrection. It was the resurrection which transformed Peter's fear into courage, and James' doubt into faith. It was the resurrection which changed the Sabbath into Sunday and the Jewish remnant into the Christian Church. It was the resurrection which changed Saul the Pharisee into Paul the Apostle and turned his persecuting into preaching.

John Stott

Christ is unique in his resurrection.

John Stott

We live and die. Christ died and lived!

John Stott

Christianity is in its every essence a resurrection religion. The concept of resurrection lies at its heart. If you remove it, Christianity is destroyed.

John Stott

It was not Christ's personality that survived death, or his influence but his literal body that was raised from the dead.

John Stott

If Christ be not risen, the dreadful consequence is not that death ends life, but that we are still in our sins.

G. A. Studdert-Kennedy

Our life's a flying shadow, God's the pole,
The index pointing at Him is our soul;
Death the horizon, when our sun is set,
Which will through Christ a resurrection get.

Sun dial inscription, formerly on the wall of Glasgow Cathedral

How fair and lovely is the hope which the Lord gave to the dead when he lay down like them beside them. Rise up and come forth and sing praise to him who has raised you from destruction.

Syrian Orthodox Liturgy

No man would be willing to die unless he knew he had the truth.

Tertullian

We affirm that the bodily resurrection of Christ from the dead is essential to the biblical Gospel.

The gospel of Jesus Christ: An evangelical celebration

Something tremendous must have happened to account for such a radical and astounding moral transformation as this. Nothing short of the fact of the resurrection, of their having seen the risen Lord, will explain it.

R. A. Torrey

The death and resurrection of Jesus Christ puts the issue beyond doubt. Ultimately goodness, laughter, peace, compassion, gentleness, forgiveness, and reconciliation will have the last word and prevail over their ghastly counterparts. The victory over apartheid is proof positive of this truth.

Desmond Tutu

Christ himself deliberately staked his whole claim to the credit of men upon his resurrection. When asked for a sign he pointed to this sign as his single and sufficient credential.

B. B. Warfield

Unless we believe as literally in the Resurrection as we do in the Passion and the Death, we are not Christians at all.

B. F. Westcott

Taking all the evidence together, it is not too much to say that there is no historic incident better or more variously supported than the resurrection of Christ. Nothing but the antecedent assumption that it must be false could have suggested the idea of deficiency in the proof of it.

B. F. Westcott

The Gospels do not explain the resurrection; the resurrection explains the Gospels. Belief in the resurrection is not an appendage to the Christian faith; it is the Christian faith.

John S. Whale

There is no mystery in heaven or earth so great as this—a suffering Deity, an almighty Savior nailed to a Cross.

Samuel Zwemer

JESUS' ASCENSION

4.21 JESUS' CONSTANT PRESENCE, WILLIAM TEMPLE

The ascension of Christ is his liberation from all restrictions of time and space. It does not represent his removal from the earth, but his constant presence everywhere on earth.

William Temple

4.22 ASCENSION, W. H. GRIFFITH THOMAS

W. H. Griffith Thomas (1861—1924) was a leading evangelical writer and Anglican vicar of the central London parish of St. Paul's at the turn of the twentieth century. His commentary on 2 Peter is still in print.

Most modern lives of Christ commence at Bethlehem and end with the Ascension, but Christ's life began earlier and continued later. The Ascension is not only a great fact of the New Testament, but a great factor in the life of Christ and Christians, and no complete view of Jesus Christ is possible unless the Ascension its consequences are included. It is the consummation of His redemptive work. The Christ of the Gospels is the Christ of history, the Christ of the past, but the full New Testament picture of Christ is that of a living Christ, the Christ of heaven, the Christ of experience, the Christ of the present and the future. The New Testament passages referring to the Ascension need close study and their teaching careful observation.

I. IN THE GOSPELS
1. Anticipations
The Ascension is alluded to in several passages in the Gospels in the course of our Lord's earthly ministry (Luke 9:31, Luke 9:51; John 6:62; John 7:33; John 12:32; John 14:12, John 14:28; John 16:5, John 16:10, John 16:17, John 16:28; John 20:17). These passages show that the event was constantly in view, and anticipated by our Lord. The Ascension is also clearly implied in the allusions to His coming to earth on clouds of heaven (Matthew 24:30; Matthew 26:64).

2. Records
If with most modern scholars we regard Mark's Gospel as ending with Mark 16:8, it will be seen to stop short at the resurrection, though the present ending speaks of Christ being received up into heaven, of His sitting at the right hand of God, and of His working with the disciples as they went preaching the word (Mark 16:19-20). In any case this is a bare summary only. The close of the Third Gospel includes an evident reference to the fact of the Ascension (Luke 24:28-53), even if the last six words of Luke 24:51, "and was carried up into heaven" are not authentic. No difficulty need be felt at the omission of the Fourth Gospel to refer to the fact of the Ascension, though it was universally accepted at the time the apostle wrote (John 20:17). As Dr. Hort has pointed

out, "The Ascension did not lie within the proper scope of the Gospels. . . . its true place was at the head of the Acts of the Apostles" (quoted Swete, The Ascended Christ, 2).

II. IN THE ACTS.
1. Record
The story in Acts 1:6-12 is clear. Jesus Christ was on the Mount of Olives. There had been conversation between Him and His disciples, and in the course of it He was taken up; and a cloud received Him out of their sight (Acts 1:9). His body was uplifted till it disappeared, and while they continued to gaze up they saw two men who assured them that He would come back exactly as He had gone up. The three Greek words rendered "taken up" (*eperthe*) (Acts 1:9); "went" (*poreuomenou*) (Acts 1:10); "received up" (*analemphtheis*) (Acts 1:11); deserve careful notice. This account must either be attributed to invention, or to the testimony of an eye-witness. But Luke's historicity now seems abundantly proved.

2. References
The Ascension is mentioned or implied in several passages in Acts 2:33 ff.; Acts 3:21; Acts 7:55 ff.; Acts 9:3-5; Acts 22:6-8; Acts 26:13-15. All these passages assert the present life and activity of Jesus Christ in heaven.

III. IN THE PAULINE EPISTLES
1. Romans
In Romans 8:34 the apostle states four facts connected with Christ Jesus: His death; His resurrection; His session at God's right hand; His intercession. The last two are clearly the culminating points of a series of redemptive acts.

2. Ephesians
While for its purpose Romans necessarily lays stress on the Resurrection, Ephesians has as part of its special aim an emphasis on the Ascension. In Ephesians 1:20 God's work wrought in Christ is shown to have gone much farther than the Resurrection, and to have "made him to sit at his right hand in the heavenly places," thereby constituting Him the supreme authority over all things, and

especially Head of the church (Ephesians 1:20-23). This idea concerning Christ is followed in Ephesians 2:6 by the association of believers with Christ "in the heavenly places," and the teaching finds its completest expression in Ephesians 4:8-11, where the Ascension is connected with the gift of the heavenly Christ as the crowning feature of His work. Nothing is more striking than the complementary teaching of Romans and Ephesians respectively in their emphasis on the Resurrection and Ascension.

3. Philippians
In Philippians 2:6-11 the exaltation of Christ is shown to follow His deep humiliation. He who humbled Himself is exalted to the place of supreme authority. In Philippians 3:20 Christians are taught that their common-wealth is in heaven, "whence also we wait for a Savior."

4. Thessalonians
The emphasis placed on the second advent of Christ in 1 Thess. is an assumption of the fact of the Ascension. Christians are waiting for God's Son from heaven (1 Thessalonians 1:10) who is to "descend from heaven, with a shout, with the voice of the archangel, and with the trump of God" (1 Thessalonians 4:16).

5. Timothy
The only allusion to the Ascension in the Pastoral Epistles is found in the closing statement of what seems to be an early Christian song in 1 Timothy 3:16. He who was "manifested in the flesh . . . . received up in glory."

IV. IN HEBREWS
In Hebrews there is more recorded about the Ascension and its consequences than in any other part of the New Testament. The facts of the Ascension and Session are first of all stated (Hebrews 1:3) with all that this implies of definite position and authority (Hebrews 1:4-13). Christians are regarded as contemplating Jesus as the Divine Man in heaven (Hebrews 2:9), though the meaning of the phrase, "crowned with glory and honor" is variously

interpreted, some thinking that it refers to the result and outcome of His death, others thinking that He was "crowned for death" in the event of the Transfiguration (Matheson in Bruce, Hebrews, 83). Jesus Christ is described as "a great High Priest, who hath passed through the heavens" (Hebrews 4:14), as a Forerunner who is entered within the veil for us, and as a High Priest for ever after the order of Melchizedek (Hebrews 6:20). As such He "abideth for ever," and "ever liveth to make intercession" (Hebrews 7:24-25). The chief point of the epistle itself is said to be "such a high priest, who sat down on the right hand of the throne of the Majesty in the heavens" (Hebrews 8:1), and His position there implies that He has obtained eternal redemption for His people and is appearing before God on their behalf (Hebrews 9:12, Hebrews 9:24). This session at God's right hand is also said to be with a view to His return to earth when His enemies will have become His footstool (Hebrews 10:12-13), and one of the last exhortations bids believers to look unto Jesus as the Author and Perfecter of faith who has "sat down at the right hand of the throne of God" (Hebrews 12:2).

V. IN THE PETRINE EPISTLES
The only reference to the Ascension is in 1 Peter 3:22, where Christ's exaltation after His sufferings is set forth as the pattern and guarantee of Christian glorification after endurance of persecution.

VI. IN THE JOHANNINE WRITINGS
1. Epistles
Nothing is recorded of the actual Ascension, but 1 John 2:1 says that "we have an Advocate with the Father." The word "Advocate" is the same as "Comforter" in John 14:16, where it is used of the Holy Spirit. Christ is the Comforter "in relation to the Father," and the Holy Spirit is the Comforter dwelling in the soul.

2. Apocalypse
All the references in the Apocalypse either teach or imply the living Christ who is in heaven, as active in His church and as coming again (Revelation 1:7; 1:13; 5:5-13; 6:9-17; 14:1-5).

VII. SUMMARY OF NEW TESTAMENT TEACHING
1. The fact
The New Testament calls attention to the fact of Ascension and the fact of the Session at God's right hand. Three words are used in the Greek in connection with the Ascension: *anabainein* (*ascendere*), "to go up"; *analambanesthai* (*adsumi*), "to be taken up"; *poreuesthai* "to go." The Session is connected with Ps. 110, and this Old Testament passage finds frequent reference or allusion in all parts of the New Testament. But it is used especially in Hebrews in connection with Christ's priesthood, and with His position of authority and honor at God's right hand (Swete, The Ascended Christ, 10-15). But the New Testament emphasizes the fact of Christ's exaltation rather than the mode, the latter being quite secondary. Yet the acceptance of the fact must be carefully noticed, for it is impossible to question that this is the belief of all the New Testament writers. They base their teaching on the fact and do not rest content with the moral or theological aspects of the Ascension apart from the historic reality. The Ascension is regarded as the point of contact between the Christ of the gospels and of the epistles. The gift of the Spirit is said to have come from the ascended Christ. The Ascension is the culminating point of Christ's glorification after His Resurrection, and is regarded as necessary for His heavenly exaltation. The Ascension was proved and demanded by the Resurrection, though there was no need to preach it as part of the evangelistic message. Like the Virgin birth, the Ascension involves doctrine for Christians rather than non-Christians. It is the culmination of the Incarnation, the reward of Christ's redemptive work, and the entrance upon a wider sphere of work in His glorified condition, as the Lord and Priest of His church (John 7:39; John 16:7).

2. The Message
We may summarize what the New Testament tells us of our Lord's present life in heaven by observing carefully what is recorded in the various passages of the New Testament. He

ascended into heaven (Mark 16:19; Luke 24:51; Acts 1:9); He is seated on the right hand of God (Colossians 3:1; Hebrews 1:3; Hebrews 8:1; Hebrews 10:12); He bestowed the gift of the Holy Spirit on the Day of Pentecost (Acts 4:9, Acts 4:33); He added disciples to the church (Acts 2:47); He worked with the disciples as they went forth preaching the gospel (Mark 16:20); He healed the impotent man (Acts 3:16); He stood to receive the first martyr (Acts 7:56); He appeared to Saul of Tarsus (Acts 9:5); He makes intercession for His people (Romans 8:26; Hebrews 7:25); He is able to succor the tempted (Hebrews 2:18); He is able to sympathize (Hebrews 4:15); He is able to save to the uttermost (Hebrews 7:25); He lives forever (Hebrews 7:24; Revelation 1:18); He is our Great High Priest (Hebrews 7:26; Hebrews 8:1; Hebrews 10:21); He possesses an intransmissible or inviolable priesthood (Hebrews 7:24); He appears in the presence of God for us (Hebrews 9:24); He is our Advocate with the father (1 John 2:1); He is waiting until all opposition to Him is overcome (Hebrews 10:13). This includes all the teaching of the New Testament concerning our Lord's present life in heaven.

VIII. PROBLEMS

There are two questions usually associated with the Ascension which need our attention.

1. Relation to the laws of nature

There is no greater difficulty in connection with the Ascension than with the Resurrection, or the Incarnation. Of our Lord's resurrection body we know nothing. All we can say is that it was different from the body laid in the tomb and yet essentially the same; the same and yet essentially different. The Ascension was the natural close of Our Lord's earthly life, and as such, is inseparable from the Resurrection. Whatever, therefore, may be said of the Resurrection in regard to the laws of nature applies equally to the Ascension.

2. Localization of the spiritual world

The record in Acts is sometimes objected to because it seems to imply the localization of heaven above the earth. But is not this taking the narrative in too absolutely bald and literal

a sense? Heaven is at once a place and a state, and as personality necessarily implies locality, some place for our Lord's Divine, yet human person is essential. To speak of heaven as "above" may be only symbolical, but the ideas of fact and locality must be carefully adhered to. And yet it is not merely local, and "we have to think less of a transition from one locality than of a transition from one condition to another. . . . the real meaning of the ascension is that . . . our Lord withdrew from a world of limitations" to that higher existence where God is (Milligan, Ascension and Heavenly Priesthood, 26). It matters not that our conception today of the physical universe is different from that of New Testament times. We still speak of the sun setting and rising, though strictly these are not true. The details of the Ascension are really unimportant. Christ disappeared from view, and no question need be raised either of distance or direction. We accept the fact without any scientific explanation. It was a change of conditions and mode of existence; the essential fact is that He departed and disappeared. Even Keim admits that "the ascension of Jesus follows from all the facts of His career" (quoted, Milligan, 13), and Weiss is equally clear that the Ascension is as certain as the Resurrection, and stands and fails therewith (Milligan, 14).

IX. ITS RELATION TO CHRIST HIMSELF

The Ascension was the exaltation and glory of Jesus Christ after His work was accomplished (Philippians 2:9). He had a threefold glory: (1) as the Son of God before the Incarnation (John 17:5); (2) as God manifest in the flesh (John 1:14); (3) as the exalted Son of God after the Resurrection and Ascension (Luke 24:26; 1 Peter 1:21). The Ascension meant very much to Christ Himself, and no study of subject must overlook this aspect of New Testament teaching. His exaltation to the right hand of meant:

    (1) the proof of victory (Ephesians 4:8);
    (2) the position of honor (Psalms 110:1);
    (3) the place of power (Acts 2:33);
    (4) the place of happiness (Psalms 26:11);
    (5) the place of rest ("seated");
    (6) the place of permanence ("for ever").

X. ITS TEACHING FOR CHRISTIANS

The importance of the Ascension for Christians lies mainly in the fact that it was the introduction to our Lord's present life in heaven which means so much in the believer's life. The spiritual value of the Ascension lies, not in Christ's physical remoteness, but in His spiritual nearness. He is free from earthly limitations, and His life above is the promise and guarantee of ours. "Because I live ye shall live also."

1. Redemption accomplished

The Ascension and Session are regarded as the culminating point of Christ's redemptive work (Hebrews 8:1), and at the same time the demonstration of the sufficiency of His righteousness on man's behalf. For sinful humanity to reach heaven two essential features were necessary: (a) the removal of sin (negative); and (b) the presence of righteousness (positive). The Resurrection demonstrated the sufficiency of the atonement for the former, and the Ascension demonstrated the sufficiency of righteousness for the latter. The Spirit of God was to convict the world of "righteousness" "because I go to the Father" (John 16:10). In accord with this we find that in the Epistle to the Hebrews every reference to our Lord's atonement is in the past, implying completeness and perfection, "once for all."

2. High priesthood

This is the peculiar and special message of He. Priesthood finds its essential features in the representation of man to God, involving access into the Divine presence (Hebrews 5:1). It means drawing near and dwelling near to God. In Hebrews, Aaron is used as typical of the work, and Melchizedek as typical of the person of the priest; and the two acts mainly emphasized are the offering in death and the entrance into heaven. Christ is both priest and priestly victim. He offered propitiation and then entered into heaven, not "with," but "through" His own blood (Hebrews 9:12), and as High Priest, at once human and Divine, He is able to sympathize (Hebrews 4:15); able to succor (Hebrews 2:18); and able to save (Hebrews 7:25).

3. Lordship

The Ascension constituted Christ as Head of the church (Ephesians 1:22; Ephesians 4:10, Ephesians 4:15; Colossians 2:19). This Headship teaches that He is the Lord and Life of the church. He is never spoken of as King in relation to His Body, the Church, only as Head and Lord. The fact that He is at the right hand of God suggests in the symbolical statement that He is not yet properly King on His own throne, as He will be hereafter as "King of the Jews," and "King of Kings."

4. Intercession

In several New Testament passages this is regarded as the crowning point of our Lord's work in heaven (Romans 8:33-34). He is the perfect Mediator between God and man (1 Timothy 2:5; Hebrews 8:6); our Advocate with the Father (1 John 2:1). His very presence at God's right hand pleads on behalf of His people. There is no presentation, or representation, or pleading, of Himself, for His intercession is never associated with any such relation to the sacrifice of Calvary. Nor is there any hint in the New Testament of a relation between the Eucharist and His life and work in heaven. This view, popularized by the late Dr. William Milligan (The Ascension, etc., 266), and endorsed from other standpoints in certain aspects of Anglican teaching (Swete, The Ascended Christ, 46), does not find any support in the New Testament. As Westcott says, "The modern conception of Christ, pleading in heaven His passion, offering His blood, on behalf of man, has no foundation in this epistle" (Hebrews, 230). And Hort similarly remarks, "The words, Still. . . . His prevailing death He pleads' have no apostolic warrant, and cannot even be reconciled with apostolic doctrine" (Life and Letters, II, 213). our Lord's intercession is He says as in what He is. He pleads by His presence on His Father's throne, and he is able to save to the uttermost through His intercession, because of His perpetual life and His inviolable, undelegated, intransmissible priesthood (Hebrews 7:24-25).

5. The gift of the Spirit

There is an intimate and essential connection between the Ascension of Christ and the descent of the Holy Spirit. The Holy Spirit was given to Christ as the acknowledgment and reward of His work done, and having received this "Promise of the Father" He bestowed Him upon His people (Acts 2:33). By means of the Spirit the twofold work is done, of convincing sinners (John 16:9), and of edifying believers (John 14:12; see also John 14:25-26; John 16:14-15).

6. Presence

It is in connection with the Ascension and our Lord's life in heaven that we understand the force of such a passage as "Lo, I am with you always" (Matthew 28:20). "He ever liveth" is the supreme inspiration of the individual Christian and of the whole church. All through the New Testament from the time of the Ascension onward, the one assurance is that Christ is living; and in His life we live, hold fellowship with God, receive grace for daily living and rejoice in victory over sin, sorrow and death.

7. Expectation

Our Lord's life in heaven looks forward to a consummation. He is "expecting till his enemies be made his footstool" (Hebrews 10:13, the King James Version). He is described as our Forerunner (Hebrews 6:18 ff.), and His presence above is the assurance that His people will share His life hereafter. But His Ascension is also associated with His coming again (Philippians 3:20-21; 1 Thessalonians 4:16; Hebrews 9:28). At this coming there will be the resurrection of dead saints, and the transformation of living ones (1 Thessalonians 4:16-17), to be followed by the Divine tribunal with Christ as Judge (Romans 2:16; 2 Timothy 4:1, 2 Timothy 4:8). To His own people this coming will bring joy, satisfaction and glory (Acts 3:21; Romans 8:19); to His enemies defeat and condemnation (1 Corinthians 15:25; Hebrews 2:8; Hebrews 10:13).

CONCLUSION

Reviewing all the teaching of our Lord's present life in heaven, appearing on our behalf, interceding by His presence, bestowing the Holy Spirit, governing and guiding the church, sympathizing, helping and saving His people, we are called upon to up "lift our hearts," for it is in occupation with the living that we find the secret of peace, the assurance of access, and the guaranty of our permanent relation to God. Indeed, we are clearly taught in He that it is in fellowship with the present life of Christ in heaven that Christians realize the difference between spiritual immaturity and maturity (Hebrews 6:1; Hebrews 10:1), and it is the purpose of this epistle to emphasize this truth above all others. Christianity is "the religion of free access to God," and in proportion as we realize, in union with Christ in heaven, this privilege of drawing near and keeping near, we shall find in the attitude of "lift up your hearts" the essential features of a strong, vigorous, growing, joyous Christian life.

W. H. Griffith Thomas in International
Standard Bible Encyclopedia
General Editor, James Orr, 1915

4.23 Christ's ascension into heaven, Martin Luther

This sermon was preached in 1523.

Now we must consider the ascension of the Lord Jesus Christ. In the first place, it is easily said and understood that the Lord ascended into heaven and sits at the right hand of God. But they are dead words to the understanding if they are not grasped with the heart.

24. We must, therefore, conceive of his ascension and Lordship as something active, energetic and continuous, and must not imagine that he sits above while we hold the reins of government down here. Nay, he ascended up thither for the reason that there he can best do his work and exercise dominion. Had he remained upon earth in visible form, before the people, he could not have wrought so effectually, for all the people could not have been with him and heard him. Therefore, he inaugurated an expedient which made it possible for him to be in touch with all and reign in all, to preach to all and be heard by all, and to be with all. Therefore, beware lest you imagine within yourself that he has gone, and now is, far away from us. The very opposite is true: While he was on earth, he was far away from us; now he is very near.

25. Reason cannot comprehend how this can be. Therefore it is an article of faith. Here one must close his eyes and not follow his reason, but lay hold of all by faith. For how can reason grasp the thought that there should be a being like ourselves, who is all-seeing and knows all hearts and gives all men faith and the Spirit; or that he sits above in heaven, and yet is present with us and in us and rules over us? Therefore, strive not to comprehend, but say: This is Scripture and this is God's Word, which is immeasurably higher than all understanding and reason. Cease your reasoning and lay hold of the Scriptures, which testify of this being—how he ascended to heaven and sits at the right hand of God and exercises dominion. Let us examine some Scripture bearing upon this matter.

26. In the first place, Ps. 8:4-6 says of Christ: "What is man, that thou visitest him?

For thou hast made him but little lower than God, and crownest him with glory and honor. Thou makest him to have dominion over the works of thy hands; thou hast put all things under his feet." Here the prophet speaks to God concerning a man and marvels that God humbled, for a time, that man, when he suffered him to die, humbled him to the extent that it seemed as if God were not with him. But after a little while God exalted him, so that all things must obey him, both in heaven and on earth. To these words we must hold, to these words we must cling, in these words we must believe; for reason will not submit nor adapt itself to them, but says they are lies. Now, if all things are to be subject to this being and to fall at his feet, he must sit where he can look into the whole world, into heaven and hell and every heart; where he can see all sin and all righteousness, and can not only see all things, but can rule accordingly.

27. Hence, these are majestic and powerful words. They afford the heart great comfort, so that they who believe this are filled with joy and courage and defiantly say: My Lord Jesus Christ is Lord over death, Satan, sin, righteousness, body, life, foes and friends. What shall I fear? For while my enemies stand before my very door and plan to slay me, my faith reasons thus: Christ is ascended into heaven and become Lord over all creatures, hence my enemies, too, must be subject to him and thus it is not in their power to do me harm. I challenge them to raise a finger against me or to injure a hair of my head against the will of my Lord Jesus Christ. When faith grasps and stands upon this article, it stands firm and waxes bold and defiant, so as even to say: If my Lord so wills that they, mine enemies, slay me, blessed am I; I gladly depart. Thus you will see that he is ascended into heaven, not to remain in indifference, but to exercise dominion; and all for our good, to afford us comfort and joy. This is one passage.

28. Furthermore, in the second Psalm, verses 7 and 8, we read that God says to

Christ: "Thou art my son; this day have I begotten thee. Ask of me and I will give thee the nations for thine inheritance, and the uttermost parts of the earth for thy possessions." Here you see again that Christ is appointed of God a Lord over all the earth. Now, if he is my friend and I am persuaded that he died for me and gave me all things and for my sake sits in heaven and watches over me, who then can do aught to me? Or if any man should do aught, what harm can come of it?

29. Furthermore, David says again in the 110th Psalm, verse 1: "Jehovah saith unto my lord, sit thou at my right hand, until I make thine enemies thy footstool." And further on, in verses 5, 6, 7: "The Lord at thy right hand will strike through kings in the day of his wrath. He will judge among the nations, he will fill the places with dead bodies; he will strike through the head in many countries. He will drink of the brook in the way; therefore will he lift up the head."

30. Again in still another Psalm, David says (Ps. 68:18): "Thou hast ascended on high, thou hast led away captives; thou hast received gifts among men, yea among the rebellious also, that Jehovah God might dwell with them." And all the prophets took great pains to describe Christ's ascension and his kingdom. For, as his sufferings and death are deeply founded in the Scriptures, so are also his kingdom, his resurrection and ascension. In this manner we must view the ascension of Christ. Otherwise it will afford us neither pleasure nor profit. For what good will it do you if you merely preach that he ascended up to heaven and sits there with folded hands? This is what the prophet would say in the Psalm: Christ is ascended on high and has led captivity captive. That is to say, not only does he sit up there but he is also down here. And for this purpose did he ascend up thither, that he might be down here, that he might fill all things and be everywhere present; which thing he could not do had he remained on earth, for here in the body he could not have been present with all. He ascended to heaven, where all hearts can see him, where he can deal with all men, that he might fill all creation. He is present everywhere and all things are filled with his fullness. Nothing is

so great, be it in heaven or on earth, but he has power over it, and it must be in perfect obedience to him. He not only governs and fills all creation (that would not help my faith any nor take away my sins), but also has led captivity captive.

31. This captivity some have interpreted to mean that he delivered the sainted patriarchs out of the stronghold of hell; but that interpretation does not benefit our faith any either, for it is not particularly edifying to faith. Therefore, we must simply understand the matter thus: that he means that captivity which captures us and holds us captive. I am Adam's child, full of sin and foully besmirched; therefore, the law has taken me captive, so that I am fettered in conscience and sentenced to death.

32. From this captivity no one can free himself, save only that one man Christ. What did he do? He made sin, death, and Satan his debtors. Sin fell upon him as though it would vanquish him, but it lost the day; he devoured sin. And Satan, death, and hell fared the same way. But we are unable to do this unless he be present to aid us. Alone, we must needs perish. But he, since he had done no sin and was full of righteousness, trod under foot Satan, death and hell, and devoured them, and took everything captive that fain would capture us, so that sin and death no longer can do harm.

33. This, then, is the power he causes to be preached, that all who believe in him are released from captivity. I believe in him by whom sin, death, and all things that afflict us, were led captive. It is a pleasing discourse, and full of comfort, when we are told that death is taken away and slain, so that it is no longer felt. However, it affords pleasure and comfort only to those who believe it. You will not find release from captivity in your works, fastings, prayers, castigations, tonsures, and gowns, and whatever more things you may do; but only in the place where Christ sits, whither he ascended and whither he led captivity with him. Hence, he who would be freed from sin and delivered from Satan and death, must come thither where Christ is. Now, where is he? He is here with us, and for this purpose did he sit down in heaven, that he might be

near unto us. Thus, we are with him up there and he is with us down here. Through the word he comes down and through faith we ascend up.

34. So, we see everywhere in the Scriptures that faith is such an unspeakably great thing that we can never preach about it sufficiently nor reach it with words. It cannot be heard and seen, therefore it must be believed. Such is the nature of faith that it feels nothing at all, but merely follows the words which it hears, and clings to them. If you believe, you have; if you believe not, you have not. In this wise must we understand this article of faith, that Christ is ascended into heaven and sitteth at the right hand of God.

Martin Luther

4.24 OF THE ASCENSION OF CHRIST TO HEAVEN, JOHN GILL

The ascension of Christ to heaven was, at his death, burial, and resurrection, according to the scriptures; he himself gave hints of it to his disciples, even before his death, as well as after his resurrection; "What and if ye shall see the Son of man ascend up where he was before?" John 6:62; 16:28; 20:17. It was pre-signified both by scripture prophecies, and by scripture types.

1. First by scripture prophecies; of which there are many; some more obscurely, others more clearly point unto it. As,

1a. First, A passage in Ps. 47:5, "God is gone up with a shout, the Lord with the sound of a trumpet." The whole Psalm is applied, by some Jewish writers, to the times of the Messiah, and this verse particularly, who is the great King over all the earth, Ps. 47:2, 7 and more manifestly appeared so at his ascension, when he was made and declared Lord and Christ; and who subdued the Gentile world, Ps. 47:3, through the ministration of his gospel; by which, after his ascension, he went into it, conquering and to conquer; and caused his ministers to triumph in it. And though it was in his human nature that he went up from earth to heaven; yet it was in that, as in union with his divine Person; so that it may be truly said, that God went up to heaven; in like sense as God is said to purchase the church with his blood; even God in our nature; God manifest in the flesh; Immanuel, God with us: and though the circumstance of his ascension, being attended with a shout, and with the sound of a trumpet, is not mentioned in the New Testament, in the account of it; yet there is no doubt to be made of it, since the angels present at it, told the disciples on the spot, that this same Jesus should so come, in like manner as they saw him go into heaven: now it is certain, that Christ will descend from heaven with the voice of an archangel, and with the trump of God: and also, since he was attended in his ascension with the angels of God, and with some men who rose after his resurrection; there is scarce any question to be made of it, that he ascended amidst their shouts and acclamations; and the rather, since he went up as a triumphant conqueror, over all his and our enemies, leading captivity captive.

1b. Secondly, The words of the Psalmist, in Ps. 110:1. "The Lord said unto my Lord, Sit thou at my right hand"; though they do not express, yet they plainly imply, the ascension of Christ to heaven; for unless he ascended to heaven, how could he sit down at the right hand of God there? and hence the apostle Peter thus argues and reasons upon them; "For David is not ascended into the heavens"; not in his body, and therefore the words are not spoken of him, but of one that is ascended; "But he himself saith," not of himself, but another, even of his Lord the Messiah; "The Lord said unto my Lord," &c. Acts 2:34, 35.

1c. Thirdly, The vision Daniel had of the Son of man in Dan. 7:13, 14 is thought by some to have respect to the ascension of Christ to heaven; he is undoubtedly meant by "one like unto the Son of man"; that is, really and truly man; as he is said to be "in the likeness of men," and to be "found in fashion as a man"; the same "came in the clouds of heaven"; so a cloud received Christ, and conveyed him to heaven, at his ascension; and he was "brought near to the Ancient of days," to God, who is from everlasting to everlasting; and was received with a welcome by him; and there were given him "dominion, glory, and a kingdom"; as Christ, at his ascension, was made, or made manifest, openly declared Lord and Christ, Head and King of his church. Though this vision will have a farther accomplishment at the second coming of Christ, when his glorious kingdom will commence in the personal reign; who will deliver up the kingdom until that reign is ended. Once more,

1d. Fourthly, The prophecy in Mic 2:13 may be understood as referring to this matter; "The breaker up is come up before them"; which, in the latter part of the verse, is thus explained; "And their King shall pass before them, and the Lord on the head of them"; so that a divine Person is meant, who is head and king of the church, and plainly points to Christ, who may be called Phorez, "the breaker"; as Pharez had his name from the same word, because he broke forth before his brother; as Christ, at his birth, broke forth into the world in an uncommon way, being born of a virgin; and at his death, broke through the troops of hell, and spoiled principalities and powers; broke down the middle wall of partition, that stood between Jews and Gentiles; and at his resurrection, broke the cords of death, as Samson did his withs, with which he could be no more nor longer held by them, than he with them; and at his ascension he broke up, and broke his way through the region of the air, and through legions of devils; at the head of those that were raised with him when he rose, angels and men shouting as he passed along. But,

1e. Fifthly, What most clearly foretold the ascension of Christ to heaven, is in Ps. 68:18

which is, by the apostle Paul, quoted and applied to the ascension of Christ, Eph 4:8-10 and all the parts of it agree with him: he is spoken of in the context, in the words both before and after. He is the Lord that was among the angels in Sinai, who spoke to Moses there; and from whom he received the oracles of God, to give to Israel: and he is the God of salvation, the author of it to his people. And of him it may be truly said, that he "ascended on high," far above all heavens, the visible heavens, the airy and starry heavens, and into the third heaven, the more glorious seat of the divine Majesty: he has led "captivity captive"; either such as had been prisoners in the grave, but freed by him, and who went with him to heaven; or the enemies of his people, who have led them captive, as Satan and his principalities; the allusion is to leading captives in triumph for victories obtained. Christ "received," upon his ascension, "gifts for men"; and, as the apostle expresses it, "gave" them to men; he received them in order to give them; and he gave them, in consequence of receiving them: and even he received them for, and gave them to, "rebellious" men, as all by nature are "foolish and disobedient"; and even those be to whom he gives gifts fitting for public usefulness; and such an one was the apostle Paul, as the account of him and his own confessions show, who received a large measure of those gifts of grace; the end of bestowing which gifts was, "That the Lord God might dwell among men," gathered out of the world, through the ministry of the word, into gospel churches, which are built up for an habitation for God, through the Spirit.

2. Secondly, The ascension of Christ was presignified by scripture types; personal ones, as those of Enoch and Elijah. The one in the times of the patriarchs, before the flood, and before the law; the other in the times of the prophets, after the flood, and after the law was given. Enoch, a man that walked with God, and had communion with him, "was not"; he was not on earth, after he had been some time on it; "God took him" from thence up to heaven, soul and body, Gen. 5:24. Elijah went up to heaven in a whirlwind, in a chariot, and

horses of fire; was carried up by angels, who appeared in such a form; when he and Elisha had been conversing together, 2 Kgs. 2:11. So Christ was carried up to heaven, received by a cloud, attended by angels, while he was blessing his disciples: more especially, the high priest was a type of Christ in this respect, when he entered into the holiest of all once a year, with blood and incense; which were figures of Christ's entering into heaven with his blood, and to make intercession for men, Heb. 9:23, 24. The ark in which the two tables were, was a type of Christ, who is the fulfilling end of the law for righteousness; and the bringing up of the ark from the place where it was to mount Zion, which some think was the occasion of penning the twenty fourth Psalm, in which are these words, "Be ye lift up, ye everlasting doors, and the King of Glory shall come in"; and of the forty seventh Psalm, where are the above words, "God is gone up with a shout", &c. the bringing up of which ark to Zion, may be considered as an emblem of Christ's ascension to heaven, sometimes signified by mount Zion.

Now as it was foretold by prophecies and types, that Christ should ascend to heaven, so it is matter of fact, that he has ascended thither; concerning which may be observed,

2a. First, The evidence of it; as the angels of God, who were witnesses of it; for as Christ went up to heaven in the sight of his apostles, "two men stood by them in white apparel," who were angels, that appeared in an human form, and thus arrayed, to denote their innocence and purity; and other angels attended him in his ascent, when it was that he was seen "of angels," who were eyewitnesses of his ascension; see Acts 1:10 1; Tim. 3:16. The eleven apostles were together, and others with them, when this great event was; and while he was pronouncing a blessing on them, he was parted from them, and carried up to heaven; they beheld him, and looked steadfastly towards heaven, as he went up, until a cloud received him out of their sight, Luke 24:33, 50, 51; Acts 1:9, 10. Yea, after this, when he had ascended to heaven, and had entered into it, and was set down on the right hand of God, he was seen by Stephen the proto-martyr, and by the apostle Paul: while Stephen was

suffering, looking steadfastly to heaven, he saw the glory of God, and Jesus standing at the right hand of God; and at the same time declared it to the Jews, that he saw the heavens opened, and the Son of man standing on the right hand of God, Acts 7:55, 56. Christ "appeared" to the apostle Paul at his conversion, when he was caught up into the third heaven, and heard and saw things not to be uttered; and afterwards, when in a trance in the temple, he says, "I saw him," Acts 26:16; 22:18 see also 1 Cor. 15:8. Moreover, the extraordinary effusion of the Spirit, on the day of Pentecost, is a proof of Christ's ascension to heaven, Acts 2:33 for before this time, the Spirit was not given in an extraordinary manner; "Because Jesus was not yet glorified"; but when he was glorified, and having ascended to heaven, and being at the right hand of God, then the Spirit was given; and the gift of him was a proof of his ascension and glorification, John 7:39.

2b. Secondly, The time of Christ's ascension, which was forty days from his resurrection; which time he continued on earth that his disciples might have full proof, and be at a certainty of the truth of his resurrection; "to whom he showed himself alive after his passion, by many infallible proofs, being seen of them forty days"; not that he was with them all that forty days, but at several times in that interval: on the first day he appeared to many, and on that day week again to his disciples; at another time at the sea of Tiberias; and again on a mountain in Galilee. Now by these various interviews the apostles had opportunities of making strict and close observation, of looking wisely at him, of handling him, of conversing with him, of eating and drinking with him, of reasoning upon things in their own minds, and of having their doubts resolved, if they entertained any; and had upon the whole infallible proofs of the truth of his resurrection: in this space of time also he renewed their commission and enlarged it, and sent them into the whole world to preach and baptize, and further to instruct those that were taught and baptized by them; now it was he opened the understandings of his apostles, that they might more clearly understand the scriptures concerning himself, which he explained unto them, that so they might be the more fitted for their ministerial work; he also spoke to them "of the things pertaining to the kingdom of God," the gospel church state; of the nature of a gospel church, of the officers of it, of ordinances in it, and discipline to be observed therein; wherefore all that they afterwards delivered out and practised, were according to the directions and prescriptions given by him: and as all this required time, such a length of time was taken as that of forty days; yet longer it was not proper he should continue with them in this state, lest his apostles should think he was about to set up a temporal kingdom on earth, which their minds were running upon, and inquiring after and expecting, Acts 1:5, 6, and besides, it was proper that they should be endued with the Holy Ghost in an extraordinary manner, to qualify them for the important work Christ gave them a commission to do; and which they could not receive until Christ was ascended and glorified.

2c. Thirdly, The place from whence, and the place whither Christ ascended, may next be considered.

2c(i). The earth on which he was when he became incarnate, the world into which he came to save men, out of which he went when he had done his work, John 16:28, the particular spot of ground from whence he ascended was mount Olivet, as appears from Acts 1:12, a place he frequented much in the latter part of his life; and it was in a garden at the bottom of the mount where his sufferings began, where his soul was exceeding sorrowful, even unto death; and where he put up that prayer, "Father, if it be possible, let this cup pass from me;" and where he was in such an agony, that his sweat was as drops of blood falling to the ground; and from this very spot he ascended to his God and Father, to enjoy his presence, and all the pleasures of it, and partake of the glory promised him, Luke 21:37; 22:39, 44. One of the evangelists tells us, that he led his disciples as far as Bethany, and there blessed them, and was parted from them; which must not be understood of the town of Bethany, but of a part of mount Olivet near to Bethany, and

which bore that name, and which signifies the house of affliction, from whence Christ went to heaven; and as it was necessary he should suffer the things he did, and enter into his glory, so his people must through many tribulations enter the kingdom, Luke 24:50, 51; 21:26; Acts 14:22.

2c(ii). The place whither he ascended, heaven, even the third heaven; hence Christ is often said to be carried up into heaven, taken up into heaven, towards which the disciples were gazing as he went up; passed into heaven, and was received into heaven, where he remains; and which is to be understood, not merely of a glorious state, into which he passed, exchanging a mean, uncomfortable, and suffering one, for a glorious, happy, and comfortable one; which is meant by the two witnesses ascending to heaven, even a more glorious state of the church, Rev. 11:12, but a place in which he is circumscribed in his human nature, where he is, and not elsewhere, nor everywhere; which has received him, and where he is, and will be retained until the times of the restitution of all things; from whence he is expected, and from whence he will descend at the last day; he is gone to his Father there, and has taken his place at his right hand; who, though everywhere, being omnipresent, yet heaven is more especially the place where he displays his glory; and who is called "Our Father," and Christ's Father, who is "in heaven"; and of going to him at his ascension he often spoke, John 16:10, 16, 17, 28; 20:17.

2d. Fourthly, The manner of Christ's ascension, or in what sense he might be said to ascend; not "figuratively," as God is sometimes said to go down and to go up, Gen. 11:6; 17:22, which must be understood consistent with the omnipresence of God; not of any motion from place to place, but of some exertion of his power, or display of himself; nor in appearance only, as it might seem to beholders, but in reality and truth; nor was it a "disappearance" of him merely, as in Luke 24:31, for he was seen going up, and was gazed at till a cloud received him out of sight; nor was it in a "visionary" way, as the apostle Paul was caught up into the third heaven, not knowing whether in the body or out of the body; nor in a "spiritual" manner, in mind and affections, in which sense saints ascend to heaven, when in spiritual frames of soul; but "really, visibly", and "locally": this ascension of Christ was a real motion of his human nature, which was visible to the apostles, and was by change of place, even from earth to heaven; and was sudden, swift, and glorious, in a triumphant manner: and he went up as he will come again, in a cloud, in a bright cloud, a symbol of his divine majesty, either literally taken; or if understood of the appearance of angels in the form of a bright cloud, as by Dr. Hammond, it is expressive of the same; nor does it at all affect the reality, locality, and visibility of Christ's ascension, so to understand it: nor can Luke, as an historian, be chargeable with an impropriety in his relation of it in such sense, any more than in the same account by representing angels as appearing in an human form, and in white apparel; nor than that the author of the book of Kings is, in relating the ascent of Elijah to heaven in a chariot and horses of fire, generally understood of angels in such a form, 2 Kgs. 2:11, as the horses and chariots of fire also are in 2 Kgs. 6:17 which yet were really and visibly seen; and the rather it may be thought that the angels are intended in the account of Christ's ascension, since as the Lord makes the clouds his chariots, Ps. 104:3; so certain it is, the angels are the twenty thousand chariots of God among whom Christ was, and inclosed, as in a bright cloud when he ascended on high, Ps. 68:17, 18, all which serve to set forth the grandeur and majesty in which Christ ascended.

2e. Fifthly, The cause or causes of Christ's ascension; it was a work of almighty power to cause a body to move upwards with such swiftness, and to such a distance; it is ascribed to the right hand of God, that is, of God the Father; to the power of God, by which he is said to be lifted up and exalted, Acts 2:33; 5:31, and therefore it is sometimes passively expressed, that he was "carried up, taken up," and "received up" into heaven; and sometimes actively, as done by himself, by his own power; so it is said, "he went up," he lifted up his own body through the union of it to his divine person, and carried it up to heaven; so "God

went up with a shout"; see Acts 1:10; and often he speaks of it as his own act, "What if the son of man ascend," &c. "I ascend to my God," &c. the "efficient" cause of it is God; and being a work "ad extra," Father, Son, and Spirit were concerned in it. The "procuring" or "meritorious" cause of it was the "blood" of Christ; by which he made full satisfaction to divine justice, and obtained eternal redemption for his people: and therefore having done the work he engaged to do, it was but fit and just that he should be, not only raised from the dead, but ascend to heaven, and be received there; hence it is said, "by his own blood," through the virtue of it, and in consequence of what he had done by it, "he entered in once into the holy place, having obtained eternal redemption for us," Heb. 9:12. The "instrumental" or ministering causes, were the "cloud" and the attending angels.

2f. Sixthly, The effects of Christ's Ascension, or the ends to be answered, and which have been answered, are,

2f(i). To fulfill the prophecies and types concerning it, and particularly that of the high priest's entering into the holiest of all once a year, to officiate for the people; and so Christ has entered into heaven itself, figured by the most holy place, there to make, and where he ever lives to make, intercession for the saints.

2f(ii). To take upon him more openly the exercise of his kingly office; to this purpose is the parable of the nobleman, Luke 19:12, by the "nobleman" is meant Christ himself; see Jer. 33:21; by the "far country" he went into, heaven, even the third heaven, which is far above the visible ones; his end in going there, was "to receive a kingdom for himself," to take possession of it, and exercise kingly power; to be made and declared Lord and Christ, as he was upon his ascension, Acts 2:36, which kingdom will be delivered up at the close of his personal reign, and not before.

2f(iii). To receive gifts for men, both extraordinary and ordinary; and this end has been answered, he has received them, and he has given them; extraordinary gifts he received for, and bestowed upon the apostles on the day of Pentecost; and ordinary ones, which he has given since, and still continues to give, to fit men for the work of the ministry, and for the good of his churches and interest in all succeeding ages, Eph 4:8-13.

2f(v). To open the way into heaven for his people, and to prepare a place for them there; he has by his blood entered into heaven himself, and made the way into the holiest of all manifest; and given boldness and liberty to his people through it to enter thither also, even by a new and living way, consecrated through the vail of his flesh, Heb. 9:8, 12; 10:19, 20, he is the forerunner for them entered, and is gone beforehand to prepare by his presence and intercession mansions of glory for them in his Father's house, Heb. 6:20; John 14:2, 3.

2f(vi). To assure the saints of their ascension also; for it is to his God and their God, to his Father and their Father, that he is ascended; and therefore they shall ascend also, and be where he is, and be glorified together with him; and all this is to draw up their minds to heaven, to seek things above, where Jesus is; and to set their affections, not on things on earth, but on things in heaven; and to have their conversation there; and to expect and believe that they shall be with Christ for evermore.

John Gill, A Body of Doctrinal and Practical Divinity

Poems, hymns, meditations, and prayers on the ascension of Jesus

4.25 Hail the day that sees Him rise, Alleluia!, Charles Wesley

Hail the day that sees Him rise, Alleluia!
To His throne above the skies, Alleluia!
Christ, awhile to mortals given, Alleluia!
Reascends His native heaven, Alleluia!

There the glorious triumph waits, Alleluia!
Lift your heads, eternal gates, Alleluia!
Christ hath conquered death and sin, Alleluia!
Take the King of glory in, Alleluia!

Circled round with angel powers, Alleluia!
Their triumphant Lord, and ours, Alleluia!
Conqueror over death and sin, Alleluia!
"Take the King of glory in! Alleluia!"

Him though highest Heav'n receives, Alleluia!
Still He loves the earth He leaves, Alleluia!
Though returning to His throne, Alleluia!
Still He calls mankind His own, Alleluia!

See! He lifts His hands above, Alleluia!
See! He shows the prints of love, Alleluia!
Hark! His gracious lips bestow, Alleluia!
Blessings on His church below, Alleluia!

Still for us His death He pleads, Alleluia!
Prevalent He intercedes, Alleluia!
Near Himself prepares our place, Alleluia!
Harbinger of human race, Alleluia!

Master, (will we ever say), Alleluia!
Taken from our head to day, Alleluia!
See Thy faithful servants, see, Alleluia!
Ever gazing up to Thee, Alleluia!

Grant, though parted from our sight, Alleluia!
Far above yon azure height, Alleluia!
Grant our hearts may thither rise, Alleluia!
Seeking Thee beyond the skies, Alleluia!

Ever upward let us move, Alleluia!
Wafted on the wings of love, Alleluia!
Looking when our Lord shall come, Alleluia!
Longing, gasping after home, Alleluia!

There we shall with Thee remain, Alleluia!
Partners of Thy endless reign, Alleluia!
There Thy face unclouded see, Alleluia!
Find our heaven of heavens in Thee, Alleluia!
Charles Wesley

QUOTATION COLLECTION ON THE ASCENSION OF JESUS

Jesus departed from our sight that he might return to our heart. He departed, and behold, he is here.

Augustine

As sign and wonder this exaltation is a pointer to the revelation that occurred in His resurrection, of Jesus Christ as the heart of all powers in heaven and earth.

Karl Barth

For God to adorn His Son with all this glory in His ascension, thus to make Him ride conqueror up into the clouds, thus to go up with sound of trumpet, with shout of angels and with songs of praises, and let me add, to be accompanied also with those that rose from the dead after His resurrection, who were the very price of His blood—this does greatly demonstrate that Jesus Christ, by what he has done, has paid a full price to God for the souls of sinners, and obtained eternal redemption for them: he had not else rode thus triumph to heaven.

John Bunyan

When Christ returned to heaven, he withdrew his physical presence from our sight. He didn't stop being with the disciples but by the ascension fulfilled his promise to be with us to the end of the world. As his body was raised to heaven, so his power and reign have spread to the uttermost parts.

John Calvin

The Ascension placed Jesus Christ back in the glory which he had with the Father before the world was. The Ascension, not the Resurrection, is the completion of the Transfiguration.

Oswald Chambers

At his ascension our Lord entered heaven, and he keeps the door open for humanity to enter.

Oswald Chambers

In the Christian story God descends to re-ascend.

C. S. Lewis

If upward you can soar and let God have his way,
Then this has in your spirit become Ascension Day.

Angelus Silesius

Christ is gone from our eyes, but abides in our hearts.

C. H. Spurgeon

Jesus' Return

4.26 The second coming, John Bunyan

The talk they had with the Shining Ones was about the glory of the place; who told them that the beauty and glory of it was inexpressible. There, said they, is the "Mount Zion, the heavenly Jerusalem, the innumerable company of angels, and the spirits of just men made perfect" (Heb. 12:22-24). You are going now, said they, to the paradise of God, wherein you shall see the tree of life, and eat of the never-fading fruits thereof; and when you come there, you shall have white robes given you, and your walk and talk shall be every day with the King, even all the days of eternity (Rev. 2:7; 3:4; 22:5). There you shall not see again such things as you saw when you were in the lower region upon the earth, to wit, sorrow, sickness, affliction, and death, "for the former things are passed away." You are now going to Abraham, to Isaac, and Jacob, and to the prophets-men that God hath taken away from the evil to come, and that are now resting upon their beds, each one walking in his righteousness (Is. 57:1, 2; 65:17). The men then asked, What must we do in the holy place? To whom it was answered, You must there receive the comforts of all your toil, and have joy for all your sorrow; you must reap what you have sown, even the fruit of all your prayers, and tears, and sufferings for the King by the way (Gal. 6:7). In that place you must wear crowns of gold, and enjoy the perpetual sight and vision of the Holy One, for "there you shall see Him as He is" (1 John 3:2). There also you shall serve Him continually with praise, with shouting and thanksgiving, whom you desired to serve in the world, though with much difficulty, because of the infirmity of your flesh. There your eyes shall be delighted with seeing, and your ears with hearing the pleasant voice of the Mighty One. There you shall enjoy your friends again, that are gone thither before you; and there you shall with joy receive, even every one that follows into the holy place after you. There also shall you be clothed with glory and majesty, and put into an equipage fit to ride out with the King of glory. When He shall come with sound of trumpet in the clouds, as upon the wings of the wind, you shall come with Him; and when He shall sit upon the throne of judgment, you shall sit by Him; yea, and when He shall pass sentence upon all the workers of iniquity, let them be angels or men, you also shall have a voice in that judgment, because they were His and your enemies (1 Thess. 4:13-17; Jude 14; Dan. 7:9, 10; 1 Cor. 6:2, 3). Also when He shall again return to the city, you shall go too, with sound of trumpet, and be ever with Him.

John Bunyan, The Pilgrim's Progress

4.27 Of the second coming of Christ, and his personal appearance, John Gill

The personal appearance of Christ will be before the resurrection of the just, which is the first resurrection; that will be at the coming of Christ, which might properly have been treated of before that resurrection; but that I chose to lay before the reader in one connected view, the separate state of the soul after the death of the body, until the resurrection, and the resurrection of it: and for the same reason I have treated of the doctrine of the resurrection in both its branches together, of the just, and of the unjust; though the one will be a thousand years before the other; and many events will intervene between them; as the conflagration of the world, the making of the new heavens and the new earth, and the dwelling and reigning of Christ with his saints therein, and the binding of Satan during that time; all which will follow the personal appearance of Christ, and will be treated of after that, in their order.

There have been various appearances of Christ already; many in an human form before his incarnation, as a presage and pledge of it; but his principal appearance, and what may be called his "first" appearance and coming, was at his incarnation; there were several appearances of him to his disciples after his resurrection, and to Stephen, and to the apostle Paul, after his ascension; and there was a coming of him in his kingdom and power sometime after to take vengeance on the Jewish nation for their rejection of him, and the persecution of his followers. There is now an appearance of Christ in heaven as the advocate of his people; and there is a spiritual appearance of him at conversion, and in after visits of his love, and communion with him; and in the latter day there will be a great appearance of Christ in a spiritual manner, or a coming of him by the effusion of his Spirit upon his people, when his spiritual reign will take place, elsewhere treated of; after which will be the personal appearance of Christ to reign in a still more glorious manner. Hence

his appearance and kingdom are joined together, when he will judge both quick and dead, 2 Tim. 4:1, and this will be attended with great glory, and is called his "glorious appearing," Titus 2:13, and in distinction from his first coming and appearance at his incarnation, it is called his "second," Heb. 9:28, which will now be treated of:

1. By giving the proof of the certainty of it, that Christ will most surely appear personally to judge the world, and reign with his people; which may be most firmly believed, depended upon, and looked for; and this will appear,

1a. First, from what the patriarchs before and after the flood have said of it; for so early has it been spoken of, as may be observed from the prophecy of Enoch, the seventh from Adam, recorded by the apostle Jude 1:14, 15. "Saying, Behold, the Lord cometh with ten thousand of his saints to execute judgment upon all"; which prophecy, whether it was written or not, is not certain, nor how the apostle came by it, whether by tradition, as the apostle Paul had the names of the magicians of Egypt, or by divine revelation; however, it is made authentic by the Spirit of God, and is to be depended on as fact; and is to be understood, not of the first, but of the second coming of Christ, as appears by his attendants, "ten thousands his saints"; such and such a number of them were not with him when he came in the flesh, but his second coming will be "with all his saints," 1 Thess. 3:13, and by the work he is to do, to execute judgment on all, and to convince of and punish wicked men for their words and works; see Eccl. 12:14; John 3:17. Job also declared his faith, that Christ his living Redeemer should "stand at the latter day on the earth," that is, the latter or last day of the present world; since it is connected with the resurrection of the dead he believed in, and the future judgment, Job 19:25-27, 29. Also

David the patriarch, as he is called, Acts 2:29 ,speaks of the coming of Christ to judge the earth and world, and the people of it with righteousness; and which is repeated, to denote the certainty of it, Ps. 96:13; 98:9.

1b. Secondly, the certainty of Christ's second coming and personal appearance may be confirmed from what the prophets have said concerning it; for it has been "spoken of by the mouth of them all," Acts 3:21, and though the prophecies greatly respect his spiritual reign, yet are intermixed with many things concerning his personal coming and appearance; and it requires skill and care, being attended with some difficulty, to distinguish and separate the one from the other; and besides these, there are some which chiefly and plainly respect his personal appearance and kingdom; as,

1b(i). The prophecy in Dan. 7:13, 14 where, after the destruction of Antichrist and the AntiChristian states in the spiritual reign, signified by the slaying and burning of the "fourth beast," follows in a natural order the coming of the "Son of man" to take possession of his kingdom; Christ said to be like one, either in conformity to the language of the former visions, his kingdom being humane, gentle, just, and wise, as well as powerful, and not beastly, as the others; or because he was not yet become man; or rather the "as" or "like" is not an "as" of similitude but of certainty, as in Matt. 14:5; John 1:14; Phil. 2:7, and being described as coming "with the clouds of heaven," fixes it to his second and personal coming, which is always so described, Matt. 24:30; 26:64; Rev. 1:7. The "Ancient of days" he is said to come to, is God the Father, the eternal God; they that brought him near him are either the saints, who hasten his coming by their prayers; or the angels: or it may be impersonally read, and "he was brought"; which denotes the august and magnificent manner in which he will be personally and visibly put into the possession of his kingdom and dominion; which will have a "glory" beyond all expression, and will be "everlasting"; it will never be succeeded by another; and though Christ's personal reign on earth will be but a thousand years, yet his whole reign, personal and spiritual, will be of

a long duration, and which in scripture is called "everlasting," Gen. 17:8; Lev. 16:34. Besides, this kingdom, when delivered up, will not cease, but will be connected with, and issue in the ultimate glory, in which Christ will reign with his saints for ever.

1b(ii). Another prophecy in Dan. 12:1-3 respects the second and personal coming of Christ; for he is meant by Michael, who is "as God," as his name signifies, equal to him; the "great prince," the prince of the kings of the earth, and the head of all principalities and powers. "Who standeth for the children of Daniel's people"; meaning the election of grace among the Jews, on whose behalf Christ will stand at the time of their conversion in the latter day; previous to which it will be a time of great trouble; both to the saints, when will be the slaying of the witnesses; and to the antichristian states, when the vials will be poured out upon them, which will bring on the spiritual reign; after which will be the personal coming of Christ, here implied, since the resurrection of the dead will follow, and when such will be rewarded in the kingdom of Christ, who have been eminently serviceable in his interest; and the rest of the chapter is taken up about the time when these things shall be.

1b(iii). The prophecy in Zech. 14:4, 5 respects the second and personal coming of Christ; since "all the saints" will come with him, and descend with him on earth; when his feet shall stand on the mount of Olives, and when Christ will be king over all the earth, Zech. 14:10, and the saints will be in a sinless state, Zech. 14:20, 21, though there are some things which respect the spiritual reign of Christ, and a time of distress previous to it, Zech. 14:1-3, 6-8.

1b(iv). The prophecy in Mal. 4:1-3 respects not the first but the second coming of Christ, when the day of the Lord shall "burn like an oven"; the elements shall melt with fervent heat, and the earth and all that therein is shall be burnt up; and "all the wicked" shall perish in the conflagration; be burnt up "like stubble," and be properly "ashes under the soles of the feet" of them that fear the Lord; to whom it will be a glorious day, on whom the sun of righteousness shall arise, Mal. 4:4.

1c. Thirdly, the certainty of Christ's second and personal coming to reign on earth, may be evinced from several sayings and parables delivered by him. Not to omit the petition directed to in the prayer commonly called the "Lord's Prayer; Thy kingdom come," connected with another, "thy will be done on earth as it is done in heaven;" the sense of which is, that the kingdom of God might come, and so come, that the will of God might be done by men on earth as it is done by the angels in heaven; which petition, though it has been put up thousands of times, has never yet been fulfilled, nor never can be but in a perfect state; and there will be no such on earth till the resurrection state takes place, and Christ personally appears in his kingdom and glory.

1c(i). First, the answer of Christ to the question of his disciples, "What shall be the sign of thy coming, and of the end of the world?" Matt. 24:3 given in the following part of the chapter, seems to respect the second and personal coming of Christ; for though it is so expressed as that it may be applied to his coming in his kingdom and power to destroy the Jewish nation, and so to be the end of their world, church and state; yet what is said of that, and of the signs of it, may be considered as types, symbols, and emblems of, and to have a further accomplishment in the second coming of Christ, and the end of the present world; whose coming will be like lightning, swift, sudden, at an unawares, and local and visible; for "then shall appear the sign of the son of man in heaven," Matt. 24:27, 30, that is, the son of man himself, as the sign of Jonah is Jonah himself; who will personally appear in the lower heaven, so as to be seen by all the tribes of the earth, who shall mourn on that account: and "they shall see the son of man coming in the clouds of heaven"; which, as has been before observed, is a distinguishing and peculiar characteristic of the second coming of Christ; which will be "with power," seen in raising the dead, burning the world, binding Satan, making new heavens and a new earth, and setting up his glorious kingdom in it; and so "with great glory," his own, his Father's, and that of the holy angels; and then he will "send his angels

with a great sound of a trumpet," Matt. 24:31, and with such an one, and with his angels shall he descend in person from heaven, 1 Thess. 4:16; 2 Thess. 1:7, and those he will employ to "gather together his elect from the four winds, from one end of heaven to the other"; that is, the raised saints, who will rise at this time in the several parts of the world where they died and were buried; and whom the angels shall collect together, and bring with the living saints changed, to Christ in the air, where he will be seen. But of "the day and hour" of Christ's coming "knoweth no man, no not the angels in heaven," Matt. 24:36. Moreover the coming of the son of man will be "like the days of Noah" for carnality, sensuality, and security, Matt. 24:37, etc. which agrees with the accounts other scriptures give; as that it will be like that of a thief in the night, sudden and at unawares; and that when persons are crying peace, peace, great pleasure and happiness, sudden destruction comes upon them; and therefore, since the son of man comes in an hour unthought of, persons ought to be "ready" for it, Matt. 24:44, for nothing is more certain than death, the coming of Christ, and the judgment day.

1c(ii). Secondly, The parables in Matt. 25:1-46 all respect the second coming of Christ. The parable of the wise and foolish virgins, describes the state of the church under the gospel dispensation, as consisting of true believers, and formal professors, and their different behavior, until the coming of Christ; when the door will be shut, the door of the word and ordinances; for after the spiritual reign, and in the millennium state, they will be no more administered, and Christ, and his gospel, will be no more preached; and so no more a door of faith and hope for sinners. Before the personal coming of Christ, all the virgins, both wise and foolish, will be asleep, unconcerned about his coming, off of their watch and guard, and in no expectation of it; and, having little faith about it, "When the Son of man cometh, shall he find faith on the earth?" To this state answers the Laodicean church state, lukewarm, indifferent, and regardless of divine things; which will bring on, and issue in the last judgment of the people, as its name signifies. Christ, in this parable, is all along represented as a bridegroom, and as such he shall come, Matt. 25:1, 5, 6, 10 when the church, his bride, will be made ready, and come down from God out of heaven, as a bride adorned for her husband; when she, the bride, the Lamb's wife, having the glory of God upon her, shall dwell with him in the new Jerusalem state; which is the marriage chamber they that are ready shall enter into with him.

The parable of the talents, in the same chapter, respects the same time, and describes our Lord's giving gifts to men, upon his ascension to heaven, and since; to some more, and others less, of which they make a different improvement: and also his "coming" again, after a long time, and reckoning with them; which will be done when he personally appears; and who will, in the resurrection state, distribute honors and rewards to his servants, according as they have made use of the talents committed to them.

The chapter is closed with an account of the Son of man coming in his glory, and all the holy angels with him, and sitting on the throne of his glory, summoning all nations before him, and separating the good from the bad, and passing the definitive sentence on each, and executing it.

1c(iii). Thirdly, the parable of the nobleman, in Luke 19:12, etc. is similar to that of the talents, in Matt. 25:1-46. By the nobleman is meant Christ, who is of noble extract indeed; as the Son of God, he is the only begotten of the Father; as man, he sprung from the Jewish ancestors, Abraham, Isaac, and Jacob, and from a race of kings of the line of David. By the "far country" he went into, heaven is designed; which is the better country, a land afar off, from whence Christ came at his incarnation, and whither he went after his ascension, and where he will remain till his second coming. His end in going thither, was "to receive for himself a kingdom"; to take open possession of a kingdom that was appointed for him; and which he did, in some sort, at his ascension, when he was made, or declared, Lord and Christ; and more fully will, in the spiritual reign, when the kingdoms of this world shall

become his; but most openly, clearly, and plainly, at his personal appearing and kingdom; which will be the time of his "return," when he will appear manifestly instated in it, and possessed of it; and then will he call his servants to an, account for the money he committed to them, to make use of in his absence; and according to the use it shall appear they have made of them, they will be rewarded in the millennium state, signified by giving them authority over more or fewer cities.

1c(iv). Fourthly, the words of Christ in John 14:2, 3 cannot well be neglected; "In my Father's house are many mansions; I go to prepare a place for you, and I will come again, and receive you unto myself." By Christ's "Father's house" is meant heaven, the house not made with hands, eternal in the heavens; in which there are many mansions, dwelling, resting places for the "many sons" he, the great Captain of their salvation, must, and will bring to glory; and hither Christ is gone, as the forerunner, both to take possession of heaven for them, and to prepare it for their reception of it; for though it is a kingdom prepared from the foundation of the world, in the purpose, council, and covenant of God; yet Christ is further preparing and fitting it for them, by his personal presence, and powerful mediation, while they are preparing and working up for the self-same thing, by his Spirit within them; and when they are all gathered in, and made ready, he will come again in person, and raise their bodies, and reunite their souls to them, and take them, soul and body, to himself, to be with him where he is, first in the millennium state, and then in the ultimate glory.

1d. Fourthly, that Christ will come personally on earth a second time, may be most certainly concluded from the words of the angels, in Acts 1:11 at the ascension of Christ to heaven; "This same Jesus which is taken up from you into heaven, shall so come in like manner as ye have seen him go into heaven." The angels reproved the apostles, that they stood gazing at Jesus, as he went up to heaven, being desirous of seeing the last of him, as if they were never to see him any more; whereas he would come again from heaven, in like manner as they saw him go thither: as he ascended in person, in his human nature, united to his divine person, as the Son of God; so he should descend in person, in the same human nature thus united; "The Lord himself shall descend from heaven" and as his ascension to heaven was visible, he was seen of angels, and by the apostles; so his descent from thence will be visible; "Every eye shall see him"; not a few only, as then, but all: and as a cloud received him out of their sight, when he went to hearer; so when he comes again, he will come in the clouds of heaven: and as he was attended by angels, who escorted him through the regions of the air; so he will be revealed from heaven, with his mighty angels: and though no mention is made in this narrative, of his ascension with a shout, and the sound of a trumpet attending it; yet, as it was foretold in prophecy and type, no doubt is to be made of it; "God is gone up with a shout, the Lord with the sound of a trumpet!" Ps. 47:5, and certain it is, he will descend in such manner; "The Lord himself shall descend from heaven with a shout, with the voice of the archangel, and with the trump of God!" 1 Thess. 4:16 and as his ascent was from the mount of Olives, Acts 1:12, it is very probable his descent will be on that very spot; since it is said, that when the Lord shall come with all his saints, "his feet shall stand in that day on the mount of Olives," Zech. 14:4, 5.

1e. Fifthly, the second coming and appearance of Christ, may be confirmed from various passages in the sermons, discourses, and epistles of the apostles. And,

1e(i). From the words of Peter, Acts 3:19-21. From whence it appears, that there was then to come, and still is to come, "a time of the restitution of all things"; which cannot be understood of the gospel dispensation, called the time of "reformation;" for that had taken place already; nor of the restitution of the brute creatures to their estate of paradise, of which some interpret Isa 11:6, 9; Ro 8:19-23, for which I can see no need nor use of, in a perfect state, as these times will be; nor of the restitution of gospel doctrines, ordinances, discipline, and worship, to their former purity and perfection, which will be accomplished in the spiritual reign; but of the restitution of all the bodies of the saints, a resurrection of them from the dead, and a restoration of them to their souls; and of the renovation of the world, which will be at the second coming of Christ: and when the time fixed for it is come, then will God "send Jesus Christ" from heaven, where he now is, and where he will be retained till that time, and then he will descend from thence, when the saints in their resurrection state shall be judged; and though their sins are already "blotted out" by the blood of Christ, and for his sake; and a comfortable application of it is made to the consciences of all penitent and converted persons; yet there will be then a public blotting of them out, or a declaration that they are blotted out, never to be seen nor read more; which will be done before angels and men; and then it will be "a time of refreshing" indeed, "from the presence of the Lord"; for the tabernacle of God will now be with men, and he will dwell with them; and there shall be no more sorrow and weeping, crying and pain, Rev. 21:3, 4.

1e(ii). There are various passages, in which express mention is made of the coming of Christ; of his appearing a second time, unto the salvation of his people; of their waiting for his coming, looking for, and hastening unto it, and loving it, Heb. 9:28; 1 Cor. 1:7; Titus 2:13; 2 Pet. 3:12; 2 Tim. 4:8, and of what the saints shall be, and shall have then; that they shall appear in glory with Christ, and shall be like him, and shall have grace given them, and a crown of glory likewise; and shall be the joy and crown of rejoicing of Christ's ministers, Col. 3:4; 1 John 3:2; 1 Pet. 1:13; 5:4; 2 Tim. 4:8; 1 Thess. 2:19, and also of what shall then be done by Christ; all the saints shall be brought with him; the dead in him shall be raised, and both quick and dead be judged; and the counsels of all hearts shall be made manifest, 1 Thess. 3:13; 4:14, 16; 2 Tim. 4:1; 1 Cor. 4:5.

1e(iii). In all those places in which mention is made of "that day," that famous, that well known day, so much spoken of and expected, 2 Tim. 1:12, 18; 4:8 and of the day of the Lord, 1 Thess. 5:2; 2 Pet. 3:10; and of the day of the Lord Jesus, 1 Cor. 1:8; 5:5; 2 Cor. 1:14; Phil. 1:6, and of the day of redemption, Eph 4:30, the time of Christ's second coming, and personnel appearance, is meant; which will be sudden, and at an unawares, like a thief in the night; till which time the saints commit themselves into his hands; and when the work of grace, in its utmost extent and influence on soul and body, will be completed, and they will be unblameable before him, and their bodies redeemed from mortality, corruption, and death.

1f. Sixthly, in the book of the Revelation, frequent mention is made of the visible, quick, and speedy coming of Christ, and of what shall be then done by him; as in Rev. 1:7; 3:11; 22:7, 12, 20, and in particular of his descent from heaven, for the binding of Satan the space of a thousand years, Rev. 20:1-3, where he is described by his office, an Angel, not a created, but the uncreated one; nor is it unusual for Christ to be called an Angel; he is that Angel who appeared to Moses in the bush; and who went before the children of Israel in the wilderness; and who is called "the Angel of God's presence", and the Angel, or "Messenger, of the covenant:" and he is described by his descent "from heaven," whither he went at his ascension, and where he is now retained, and from whence he will come at the last day; and by what he had in his hand, a "key" and a "great chain"; a key to open the bottomless pit, to pat Satan into it, and shut him up therein; and who so proper to have this key, as he who has "the keys of hell and death"? Rev. 1:18, and a great chain to bind him therewith; and which will be greater, though shorter, than what he is now held with; and with which he will be bound faster and closer, and laid under greater restraints than he now is; so that he shall not be able to do the harm and mischief, and practice the deceit among the nations he now does, by instilling evil principles into them, and stirring them up to evil practices; and so will he remain bound, shut up, and sealed, for the space of a thousand years.

2. The locality of Christ's second coming, and personal appearance; or the place from whence he will come, and where he will appear.

2a. The place from whence he will come; heaven, the third heaven, where he now is in human nature, into which he was received at his ascension; and where he will continue till his second coming, and from thence he will then be revealed; he will descend from heaven to earth; he came down from heaven to earth at his incarnation; but that his coming was not local, not by change of place, which cannot agree with him as the omnipresent God; but by assumption of nature: but as his ascent to heaven in human nature, having assumed it, and done his work in it, which he came about, was local, by change of place from earth to heaven; so when he comes again from heaven to earth, it will be local, by change of place, which his human nature is capable of.

2b. The place whither he shall come, is the earth; for, as Job says, he shall stand on the earth in the latter day; though he shall not descend upon it at once; when he appears from the third heaven, he shall descend into the air, and there stay some time, until the dead saints are raised, and the living ones changed; and both brought unto him there; and till the new earth is made and prepared for him and them; when he and they will come down from heaven to earth, and they shall reign with him on it a thousand years; and he shall reign before his ancients gloriously.

3. The visibility of Christ's personal appearance; he will appear in human nature, visible to all; the sign of the Son of man, that is, the Son of man himself, shall appear in heaven, in the air; and "every eye shall see him," all the inhabitants of the earth: such will be the agility of his glorious body, that he will swiftly move from one end of the heaven to the other, like lightning, to which his coming is compared, Matt. 24:27, so that he will be seen by all the tribes, kindreds, and nations of the earth: he will be seen by all good men, by the living saints, that will be changed; by the dead, who will be raised, and both caught up together to meet him in the air; when he appears, they shall appear with him, and see him as he is: and he will be seen by them in the millennium state, and

throughout the whole of it; for he will reign before his ancients, in the sight of them, in a glorious manner; and then, as Job says, when they shall both stand together upon the earth, in their flesh, and with their fleshly eyes shall they see God in human nature, and that for themselves, and not another: and he will be seen by bad men; by all the wicked living on earth, at his first appearance, who will wail and mourn because of him, fearing his wrath and vengeance they justly deserve; and when they, even the greatest personages among them, shall flee, and call to the rocks and mountains to fall on them, and hide them from his face, terrible to them. And at the end of a thousand years, when they will be all raised, they will see him as their Judge on a throne of glory, and stand before him, small and great, and tremble at the sight of him, as the devils also will.

4. The glory of Christ's second coming. His first coming was in a very low, mean, and abject manner, without observation, pomp, and splendor; but his second coming will be in "great glory," Matt. 24:30; Luke 9:26, and therefore is, with great propriety, called, "The glorious appearing of the great God!" Titus 2:13.

4a. First, Christ will come in the "glory of his Father;" this is sometimes said alone, and when no mention is made of his own glory with it, Matt. 16:27; Mark 8:38, the glory of the Father, and the glory of Christ, as the only begotten of the Father, are the same; the same is the glory of him that begot, and the glory of him that is begotten; Christ is the brightness of his Father's glory, and the express image of his person; having the same nature and perfections, and so the same glory, with which he shall now appear: or by his Father's glory may be meant, the glory he promised him in covenant, on doing the work of redemption and salvation of men, proposed to him, and to which he agreed; wherefore when he came the first time, when he had finished his work, he pleaded the promised reward, John 17:4, 5, and which promised glory took place, first upon the resurrection of Christ from the dead; for "God raised him from the dead, and gave him glory"; and at his ascension he

"highly exalted him, and gave him a name above every name"; and now by faith we see him "crowned with glory and honor"! and thus glorified, exalted, and crowned, will he come a second time. Besides, he will come as a Judge, to which office he is appointed by his Father; under whom, as such he will act; and will therefore come with a commission from him, and clothed with authority by him; for he hath "given him authority to execute judgment also, because he is the Son of man"; that Son of man whom the Father has appointed to judge the world in righteousness; and so will come with the power, pomp, and majesty of a judge; and shall sit on a "throne of glory," with thousands and ten thousands ministering unto him, called "a great white throne"; "great," suitable to the greatness of his person and office; and "white," to denote the purity, uprightness, and righteousness of his proceedings.

4b. Secondly, he will come "in his own glory:" this is sometimes also spoken of singly; and no mention made of his Father's glory, Matt. 25:31. And this his own glory, in which he will come, is twofold.

4b(i). He will come in the glory of his divine nature, and the perfections of it, as a divine Person, as God over all. At first he came as a man; and because he appeared so mean, was taken by the Jews to be a mere man, as he still is by many; but when he comes a second time, his appearing will be the appearing of "the great God," the most high God; and so his coming is called, "the coming of the day of God," Titus 2:13; 2 Pet. 3:12; see Zech. 14:5; his divine perfections will be very illustriously displayed, particularly his omnipotence; upon his coming, voices will he heard in heaven, the church, loud proclamations made; "The Lord God omnipotent reigneth!" Rev. 19:6, he will come "with power," with almighty power; which will appear by raising his dead saints, and changing his living ones; by burning the world, the heavens and the earth, and making all things new; by summoning all nations before him, setting them in their proper posture and distance, passing the decisive sentence, and carrying it into execution; especially on the wicked, who will be "punished with everlasting destruction from the presence of the Lord, and from the glory of his power," 2 Thess. 1:9. Also his omniscience will be clearly discerned; he will let all the churches, and all the world know, that he is he who searcheth the reins and hearts, and who needs no testimony from men; for he knows what is in men, and is done by them; for he will bring to light the hidden things of darkness, and every secret thing into judgment; and neither men nor things shall escape his all seeing eye. Likewise the glory of his holiness and justice will be very conspicuous; he will appear as the Judge of the whole earth, who will do right, and will truly claim the character of a "righteous Judge"; and his judgment be "righteous judgment;" and, as in all his other offices, so in the execution of this, "righteousness will be the girdle of his loins, and faithfulness the girdle of his reins." There will be also large displays of grace and mercy, made at the appearance of Christ; hence saints are exhorted, "to hope to the end for the grace that is to be brought unto them, at the revelation of Jesus Christ"; and to "look for the mercy of our Lord Jesus Christ, unto eternal life!" 1 Pet. 1:13; Jude 1:21; 2 Tim. 1:16, 18.

4b(ii). Christ will come in the glory of his human nature. The apostle takes notice of this remarkable circumstance, which will attend the second coming and appearance of Christ, that it will be "without sin," the disgrace of human nature, Heb. 9:28. The human nature of Christ, when first assumed by him, was without sin, without original sin, the taint and contagion of corrupt nature, which is in all the ordinary descendants of Adam; hence it is called, the "holy thing"; and throughout his whole life it was free from all actual transgressions; no act of sin was ever committed by him: but then he was not without the appearance of sin; though his flesh was not sinful flesh, yet he was "sent in the likeness of sinful flesh"; being born of a sinful woman, brought up among sinful men, and conversed with some of the chief of them in life, and was numbered among transgressors at his death: and moreover, he had all the sins of his people imputed to him; he was made sin by imputation, who knew none: he bore all the sins of his people, and the punishment due to them, in his body on the

tree; but having thereby made satisfaction for them, upon his resurrection from the dead, he was discharged, acquitted, and justified: so that when he comes a second time, he will appear as without sin inherent in him he never had, and without sin done by him he never did; so without sin imputed to him, this being satisfied for by him, and he discharged from it. Likewise, whereas he bore our sorrows, and carried our griefs, and was attended with the sinless infirmities of our nature, and was at last crucified through weakness; now he will appear without any such; as hunger, thirst, weariness, and pain: and whereas, what with one thing and another, his visage was more marred than any man's, and his form than the sons of men; now his body is become a glorious one; of the glory of which his transfiguration on the Mount was an emblem, when his face did shine as the sun: and if the righteous, whose bodies will be fashioned like to Christ's glorious body, shall shine as the sun in the kingdom of their Father, with what luster and splendor will Christ appear in his glorified body?

4c. Thirdly, Christ will come in the glory of his holy angels; this circumstance is always observed in the account of his glorious coming. This will add to the glory and solemnity of the day. So kings, when they go abroad, are attended by their guards, not only for their safety, but for the glory of their majesty; and thus, when God descended on mount Sinai, to give the law to Israel, he came with ten thousand of his saints, his Holy Ones, the holy angels: and when Christ ascended on high, his chariots were twenty thousand, even thousands of angels; and when he shall descend from heaven, he will be revealed from thence with his mighty angels: nor will they be only used for the glory of his Majesty; but they will be employed by him in certain services; as to gather out of his kingdom all things that offend, to bind the tares in bundles and east them into the furnace of fire; and, to collect together from the four winds, the saints raised from the dead, in the several parts of the world, and bring them to Christ, to meet him in the air, and come along with him.

5. The time of Christ's second coming and personal appearance, may next be enquired into; but to put a stop to enquiries of this kind, at least a boundary to them, it should be observed what our Lord says; "Of that day and hour knoweth no man, no not the angels; but my Father only," Matt. 24:36. Another evangelist has it; "Neither the Son," that is, as man; the human nature of Christ not being possessed of divine perfections, and so not of omniscience: to "know the times and seasons" of Christ's personal appearance and kingdom, is not for us; these the "Father has put in his own power," and keeps them secret there, Acts 1:6, 7. Some good men, in the last age, fixed the time of Christ's second coming, of his personal reign, and the millennium; in which being mistaken, it has brought the doctrine into disgrace, and great neglect: their mistake arose greatly from their confounding the spiritual and personal reign of Christ; as if they commenced together; namely, upon the destruction of antichrist, pope, and Turk; the calling of the Jews, and the large conversions of the Gentiles; whereas there is a distant space between the one and the other, and which is entirely unknown; the spiritual reign, indeed, will take place upon the above events, and there are dates given of them; namely, of the reign of antichrist, the witnesses prophesying in sackcloth, the holy city being given to the Gentiles to be trodden under foot, and the church in the wilderness; and the dates of these arc the same, forty two months, or one thousand two hundred and sixty days, which are alike; for forty two months, reckoning thirty days in a month, as was the usual reckoning, are just one thousand two hundred and sixty days, and which design so many years; so that these things took place, go on, and will end together; see Rev. 11:2, 3; 12:6; 13:5. Now these dates are given to exercise the minds, the study, and diligence of men: and though men good and learned, have hitherto been mistaken in fixing the end of these dates, arising from the difficulty of knowing the time of their commencement, this should not discourage a modest and humble enquiry into them; for, for what end else are these dates given? could we find out the time when antichrist began his reign, the

end of it could easily be fixed to a year. There is a hint given of his first appearance in 2 Thess. 2:6-8. "Now ye know, what withholdeth that he" (antichrist before described) "might be revealed in his time; for the mystery of iniquity doth already work"; it was not only in embryo, but was got to some size, and was busy and operative, though secret and hidden; "only he who now letteth will let, until he be taken out of the way, and then shall that wicked one be revealed," the man of sin, or antichrist: now that which let, seems to be rightly interpreted by many, of the Roman emperor, who stood in the way of the bishop of Rome, appearing in that pomp and power he was thirsting after; and which seemed to bid fair to be fulfilling, when Augustulus, the last of the emperors, delivered up the empire to Odoacer, a king of the Goths; and the seat of the empire was removed from Rome to Ravenna, whereby way was made for the bishop of Rome to take his seat, and appear in the grandeur he was aiming at. Now this seemed to be a probable area to begin the reign of antichrist; and as this was in the year four hundred and seventy six, if one thousand two hundred and sixty years are added thereunto, the fall of antichrist must have happened in the year one thousand seven hundred and thirty six; this some learned men were very confident of, particularly Lloyd, bishop of Worcester, a great calculator of times, affirmed, that all the devils in hell could not support the pope of Rome, longer than one thousand seven hundred and thirty six. But we have lived to see him mistaken; more than thirty years have since passed, yet the popish antichrist is still in his seat; though his civil power has been weakening, and still is weakening; so that it might be hoped, he will, ere long, come to his end. Nor should we be altogether discouraged from searching into the date of his reign: there is another zero which bids fair to be the beginning of it; and that is, when the emperor Phocas gave the grant of universal bishop to the pope of Rome; and this was done in the year six hundred and six: and the rather this date should be attended to, since within a little time after, Mahomet, the Eastern antichrist, arose; so that as they appeared about the same time, and go on together, they will end together. Now if to the above date are added one thousand two hundred and sixty years, the end of antichrist's reign will fall in the year one thousand eight hundred and sixty six: according to this computation, antichrist has almost an hundred years more to reign: and if the date of his reign is to be taken from his arriving to a greater degree of pride and power, or from the year six hundred and sixty six, which is the number of the beast, Rev. 13:18, it will be protracted still longer. It may be observed, that the dates in Dan. 12:11, 12 and in the Revelation, somewhat differ; they are larger in the former; instead of one thousand two hundred and sixty days, as in the latter, it is one thousand two hundred and ninety days; thirty days, that is, thirty years, more; which, after the fall of antichrist, may be taken up in the conversion of the Jews, and the settlement of them in their own land: and the date is still further increased in the next verse; "Blessed is he that waiteth, and cometh to the thousand three hundred and thirty five days"; which make forty five days, or years, more; and which may be employed in the destruction of the Ottoman empire; and in the spread of the gospel through the whole world; and therefore happy will he be that comes to this date; these will be happy, halcyon days indeed! But now supposing these dates could be settled with any precision, as they cannot, until more light is thrown upon them, which perhaps may be, when nearer their accomplishment; yet the time of the second coming, and personal appearance of Christ, and of the millennium, or thousand years reign upon it, cannot be known hereby; because the spiritual reign of Christ, will only take place upon the above events; and how long that will last, none can say: nor have we any chronological dates, nor hints, concerning the duration of it; only the Philadelphian church state, in which it will be; but as that is not yet begun, so neither do we know when it will; nor when it will end: and after that, there will be another state of lukewarmness, drowsiness, and carnal security; which the Laodicean church state will bring on, and will continue till Christ's personal appearance; for such will be the state of things when the Son

of man comes; which will be like the times of Noah and Lot; and how long this state will last cannot be said; unless the "seven months," allowed for the burial of Gog and his multitude, Eze 39:12, can be thought to be the duration of this state; which, if understood of prophetic time, takes in a compass of two hundred and ten years; but this is uncertain. So that it seems impracticable and impossible, to know the time of the second coming of Christ; and therefore it must be vain and needless, if not criminal, to enquire into it. However, it is known to God, who has appointed a day in which he will judge the world by Christ; and as there was a set time for his first coming into the world, so there is for his second coming; and God in his own appointed time will send him, show him, and set him forth. And it is often said by our Lord in the book of the Revelation, that he would "come quickly," Rev. 3:11; 22:7, 12, 20 to quicken saints to an expectation of it; and yet it is seemingly deferred, to try the faith and patience of saints, and to render the wicked inexcusable: but the chief reason is what the apostle gives, 2 Pet. 3:9; that "the Lord is long suffering to us-ward," the beloved of the Lord, 2 Pet. 3:8; the elect of God he wrote unto; "not willing that any" of those his beloved and chosen ones "should but that all should come to repentance"; and when they are all brought to repentance towards God, and to faith in Christ, he will stay no longer, "but the day of the Lord will come" immediately.

6. The signs of Christ's appearance and kingdom. The more remote ones are such as Christ gives in answer to the question of the apostles to him; "What shall be the sign of thy coming, and of the end of the world?" whether they meant his second coming, or his coming to destroy Jerusalem, and the end of the Jewish world, church and state, Christ gave them signs which answer to both; the destruction of Jerusalem being a presage and emblem of the destruction of the world at the second coming of Christ; such as wars and rumors of wars, famines, pestilences, and earthquakes; persecutions of good men, false teachers, the preaching of the gospel

throughout the world: all which had an accomplishment before the coming of Christ to destroy Jerusalem: and they have been fulfilling again and again in all ages since; and perhaps will be more frequent before the destruction of the world at the second coming of Christ. The more near signs, or what will more nearly precede Christ's second and personal coming, are the spiritual reigns, and what will introduce that? the destruction of antichrist, the call of the Jews, and numerous conversions of Gentiles, through the general spread of the gospel; and after that, great coolness and indifference in religion, and great defection in faith and practice. But after all, it seems as if there would be an uncertainty of it until the sign of the Son of man, which is himself, as before observed, appears in the heavens; for the Son of man will come in an hour unthought of by good men; and as a thief in the night to wicked men; suddenly and at an unawares; and to both wise and foolish professors, while they are slumbering and sleeping.

7. The ends to be answered by the second and personal coming of Christ.

7a. The putting of the saints into the full possession of salvation, Heb. 9:28. Christ's first coming into the world was to work out the salvation of his people; this he has obtained, he is become the author of it, and which is published in the gospel; and an application of it is made to particular persons, by the Spirit of God, at conversion: but the full enjoyment of it is yet to come, Ro 13:11, to which saints are kept by the power of God; and of which they are now heirs, and when Christ shall appear he will put them into the possession of their inheritance, Matt. 25:34.

7b. The destruction of all his and our enemies; all wicked men, the beast and false prophet, and Satan, who will be cast by Christ into the lake which burns with fire and brimstone; even all those who would not have him to reign over them: and by all this, the ultimate end of all, the glory of God; will be answered; the glory of his divine perfections, in the salvation of his people, and in the destruction of the wicked; and the glorification of Christ in all them that believe, 2 Thess. 1:10.

John Gill, A Body of Doctrinal and Practical Divinity

4.28 *PAROUSIA*, BURTON SCOTT EASTON

I. THE APOSTOLIC DOCTRINE
1. Terms
The second coming of Christ (a phrase not found in the Bible) is expressed by the apostles in the following special terms:

(1) "Parousia," a word fairly common in Greek, with the meaning "presence" (2 Corinthians 10:10; Philippians 2:12). More especially it may mean "presence after absence," "arrival" (but not "return," unless this is given by the context), as in 1 Corinthians 16:17; 2 Corinthians 7:6, 7; Philippians 1:26. And still more particularly it is applied to the Coming of Christ in 1 Corinthians 15:23; 1 Thessalonians 2:19; 3:13; 4:15; 5:23; 2 Thessalonians 2:1, 8; James 5:7, 8; 2 Peter 1:16; 3:4, 12; 1 John 2:28—in all 13 times, besides 2 Thessalonians 2:9, where it denotes the coming of Anti-christ.

(2) "Epiphany," "manifestation," used of the Incarnation in 2 Timothy 1:10, but of the Second Coming in 2 Thessalonians 2:8; 1 Timothy 6:14; 2 Timothy 4:1, 8; Titus 2:13. The word was used like Parousia in Hellenistic Greek to denote the ceremonial arrival of rulers.

(3) "Apocalypse," "revelation," denotes the Second Coming in 1 Corinthians 1:7;

2 Thessalonians 1:7; 1 Peter 1:7, 13; 4:13.

(4) "Day of the Lord," more or less modified, but referring to Christ in 1 Corinthians 1:8; 5:5; 2 Corinthians 1:14; Philippians 1:6, 10; 2:16; 1 Thessalonians 5:2; 2 Thessalonians 2:2. The phrase is used of the Father in the strict Old Testament sense in Acts 2:20; 2 Peter 3:12; Revelation 1:6-14, and probably in 2 Peter 3:10. Besides, as in the Old Testament and the intermediate literature, "day of wrath," "last day," or simply "day" are used very frequently.

Of the first three of the above terms, only Parousia is found in the Gospels, 4 times, all in Matthew 24:3, 17, 37, 39, and in the last three of these all in the set phrase "so shall be the Parousia of the Son of Man." As Christ spoke in Aramaic, the use of "Parousia" here is of course due to Matthew's adoption of the current Greek word.

2. Data and sources

The last of the 4 terms above brings the apostolic doctrine of the Parousia into connection with the eschatology (Messianic or otherwise) of the Old Testament and of the intermediate writings. But the connection is far closer than that supplied by this single term only, for newly every feature in the apostolic doctrine can be paralleled directly from the Jewish sources. The following summary does not begin to give complete references to even such Jewish material as is extant, but enough is presented to show how closely allied are the eschatologies of Judaism and of early Christianity.

The end is not to be expected instantly. There are still signs to come to pass (2 Thessalonians 2:3), and in especial the determined number of martyrs must be filled up (Revelation 6:11). There is need of patience (James 5:7). But it is at hand (1 Peter 4:7; Revelation 1:3; 22:10). "Yet a little while" (Hebrews 10:37), "The night is far spent" (Romans 13:12), "The Lord is at hand" (Philippians 4:5). "We that are alive" expect to see it (1 Thessalonians 4:15; 1 Corinthians 15:51); the time is shortened henceforth (1 Corinthians 7:29). Indeed, there is hardly

time for repentance even (Revelation 22:11, ironical), certainly there is no time left for self-indulgence (1 Thessalonians 5:3; 1 Peter 4:2; 2 Peter 3:11; Revelation 3:3), and watchfulness is urgently demanded (1 Thessalonians 5:6; Revelation 3:3).

An outpouring of the Spirit is a sign of the end (Acts 2:17, 18). But the world is growing steadily worse, for the godly and intense trials are coming, although those especially favored may be spared suffering (Revelation 3:10). This is the beginning of Judgment (1 Peter 4:17). Iniquity increases and false teachers are multiplied (Jude 1:18; 2 Peter 3:3; 2 Timothy 3:13). Above all there is to be an outburst of diabolic malevolence in the antichrist (1 John 2:18, 22; 4:3; 2 John 1:7; 2 Thessalonians 2:8-10; Revelation 19:19), who will gather all nations to his ensign (Revelation 19:19; 2 Thessalonians 2:10). Plagues fall upon men and natural portents occur (Acts 2:19, 20;). But the conversion of the Jews (Romans 11:26) is brought about by these plagues (Revelation 11:13). Then Christ is manifested and Antichrist is slain or captured (2 Thessalonians 2:8). In Revelation 20:3 the Millennium follows. The general resurrection then follows.

The Father holds the judgment in Hebrews 10:30; 12:23; 13:4; James 4:11, 12; 1 Peter 1:17; Revelation 14:7; 20:11, and probably in Jude 1:14, 15. Christ is judge in Acts 10:42; 2 Corinthians 5:10; 2 Timothy 4:1. The two concepts are interwoven in Romans 14:9, 10. God mediates judgment through Christ in Acts 17:31; Romans 2:16, and probably in Romans 2:2-6; 3:6. In 2 Thessalonians Christ appears as the executor of punishment. Then all nature is renewed (Romans 8:21) or completely destroyed (1 Corinthians 7:31; Hebrews 12:27; Revelation 21:1); by fire in 2 Peter 3:10, so as to leave only the eternal verities (Hebrews 12:27), or to be replaced with a new heaven and a new earth (Revelation 21:1). And the righteous receive the New Jerusalem (Galatians 4:26; Hebrews 12:22; Revelation 3:12; 21:2, 10).

Burton Scott Easton, International Standard Bible Encyclopedia
General Editor, James Orr, 1915

Check-list

4.29 The second coming of Jesus, R. A. Torrey

Reuben Archer Torrey (1856-1928) was an American evangelist, pastor, educator, and writer. He held evangelistic meetings all over the world with song leader Charles Alexander. D. L. Moody persuaded him to head up the Bible Institute of the Chicago Evangelization Society (now Moody Bible Institute). He wrote more than forty books.

TIME OF, UNKNOWN
Matthew 24:36; Mark 13:32

CALLED THE
Times of refreshing from the presence of the Lord
Acts 3:19
Times of restitution of all things
Acts 3:21; Romans 8:21
Last time
1 Peter 1:5
Appearing of Jesus Christ
1 Peter 1:7
Revelation of Jesus Christ
1 Peter 1:13
Glorious appearing of the great God and our Savior
Titus 2:13
Coming of the day of God
2 Peter 3:12
Day of our Lord Jesus Christ
1 Corinthians 1:8

FORETOLD BY
Prophets
Daniel 7:13; Jude 1:14
Himself
Matthew 25:31; John 14:3
Apostles
Acts 3:20; 1 Timothy 6:14
Angels
Acts 1:10, 11

SIGNS PRECEDING
Matthew 24:3-51

THE MANNER OF
In clouds
Matthew 24:30; 26:64; Revelation 1:7

In the glory of his Father
Matthew 16:27
In his own glory
Matthew 25:31
In flaming fire
2 Thessalonians 1:8
With power and great glory
Matthew 24:30
As he ascended
Acts 1:9, 11
With a shout and the voice of the Archangel
1 Thessalonians 4:16
Accompanied by Angels
Matthew 16:27; 25:31; Mark 8:38; 2 Thessalonians 1:7
With his saints
1 Thessalonians 3:13; Jude 1:14
Suddenly
Mark 13:36
Unexpectedly
Matthew 24:44; Luke 12:40
As a thief in the night
1 Thessalonians 5:2; 2 Peter 3:10; Revelation 16:15
As the lightning
Matthew 24:27

THE HEAVENS AND EARTH SHALL BE DISSOLVED AT
2 Peter 3:10, 12

THOSE WHO SHALL HAVE DIED IN CHRIST SHALL RISE FIRST AT
1 Thessalonians 4:16

THE SAINTS ALIVE AT, SHALL BE CAUGHT UP TO MEET HIM
1 Thessalonians 4:17

IS NOT TO MAKE ATONEMENT
Hebrews 9:28; Romans 6:9, 10; Hebrews 10:14

THE PURPOSE OF, ARE TO
Complete the salvation of saints
Hebrews 9:28; 1 Peter 1:5
Be glorified in his saints
2 Thessalonians 1:10
Be admired in them that believe
2 Thessalonians 1:10
Bring to light the hidden things of darkness
1 Corinthians 4:5
Judge
Psalms 50:3, 4; John 5:22; 2 Timothy 4:1; Jude 1:15; Revelation 20:11-13
Reign
Isaiah 24:23; Daniel 7:14; Revelation 11:15
Destroy death
1 Corinthians 15:25, 26

EVERY EYE SHALL SEE HIM AT
Revelation 1:7

SHOULD BE ALWAYS CONSIDERED AS AT HAND
Romans 13:12; Philippians 4:5; 1 Peter 4:7

BLESSEDNESS OF BEING PREPARED FOR
Matthew 24:46; Luke 12:37, 38

SAINTS (CHRISTIANS)
Assured of
Job 19:25, 26
Love
2 Timothy 4:8
Look for
Philippians 3:20; Titus 2:13
Wait for
1 Corinthians 1:7; 1 Thessalonians 1:10
Haste to
2 Peter 3:12
Pray for
Revelation 22:20
Should be ready for
Matthew 24:44; Luke 12:40
Should watch for
Matthew 24:42; Mark 13:35-37; Luke 21:36
Should be patient to
2 Thessalonians 3:5; James 5:7, 8

SHALL BE PRESERVED TO
Philippians 1:6; 2 Timothy 4:18; 1 Peter 1:5; Jude 1:24

SHALL NOT BE ASHAMED AT
1 John 2:28; 4:17

SHALL BE BLAMELESS AT
1 Corinthians 1:8; 1 Thessalonians 3:13; 5:23; Jude 1:24

SHALL BE LIKE HIM AT
Philippians 3:21; 1 John 3:2

SHALL SEE HIM AS HE IS, AT
1 John 3:2

SHALL APPEAR WITH HIM IN GLORY AT
Colossians 3:4

SHALL RECEIVE A CROWN OF GLORY AT
2 Timothy 4:8; 1 Peter 5:4

SHALL REIGN WITH HIM AT
Daniel 7:27; 2 Timothy 2:12; Revelation 5:10; 20:6; 22:5

FAITH OF, SHALL BE FOUND TO PRAISE AT
1 Peter 1:7

THE WICKED
Scoff at
2 Peter 3:3, 4
Presume upon the delay of
Matthew 24:48
Shall be surprised by
Matthew 24:37-39; 1 Thessalonians 5:3; 2 Peter 3:10
Shall be punished at
2 Thessalonians 1:8, 9

THE MAN OF SIN TO BE DESTROYED AT
2 Thessalonians 2:8

ILLUSTRATED
Matthew 25:6; Luke 12:36, 39; 19:12, 15

R. A. Torrey, The New Topical Text Book, *1897*

4.30 THE PERSONAL ADVENT OF CHRIST, CHARLES HODGE

It is admitted that the words "coming of the Lord" are often used in Scripture for any signal manifestation of his presence either for judgment or for mercy. When Jesus promised to manifest Himself to his disciples, "Judas saith unto Him, not Iscariot, Lord, how is it that thou wilt manifest thyself unto us, and not unto the world? Jesus answered and said unto him, If a man love me he will keep my words: and my Father will love him, and we will come unto him, and make our abode with him." (John 14:22, 23.) There is a coming of Christ, true and real, which is not outward and visible. Thus also in the epistle to the Church in Pergamos it is said: "Repent; or else I will come unto thee quickly." (Rev. 2:16.) This form of expression is used frequently in the Bible. There are, therefore, many commentators who explain everything said in the New Testament of the second coming of Christ, of the spiritual manifestation of his power. Thus Mr. Alger, to cite a single example of this school, says: "The Hebrews called any signal manifestation of power—especially any dreadful calamity— a coming of the Lord. It was a coming of Jehovah when his vengeance strewed the ground with the corpses of Sennacherib's host; when its storm swept Jerusalem as with fire, and bore Israel into bondage; when its sword came down upon Idumea and was bathed in blood upon Edom. 'The day of the Lord' is another term of precisely similar import. It occurs in the Old Testament about fifteen times. In every instance it means some mighty manifestation of God's power in calamity. These occasions are pictured forth with the most astounding figures of speech." On the following page he says he fully believes that the evangelists and early Christians understood the language of Christ in reference to his second coming, as predictions of a personal and visible advent, connected with a resurrection and a general judgment, but he more than doubts whether such was the meaning of Christ Himself. (1.) Because he says nothing of a resurrection of the dead. (2.) The figures which He uses are precisely those which the Jewish prophets employed in predicting "great and signal events on the earth." (3.) Because He "fixed the date of the events He referred to within that generation." Christ, he thinks, meant to teach that his "truths shall prevail and shall be owned as the criteria of Divine judgment. According to them," he understands Christ to say, "all the righteous shall be distinguished as my subjects, and all the iniquitous shall be separated from my kingdom. Some of those standing here shall not taste death till all these things be fulfilled. Then it will be seen that I am the Messiah, and that through the eternal principles of truth which I have proclaimed I shall sit upon a throne of glory, not literally, in person, as you thought, blessing the Jews and cursing the Gentiles, but spiritually, in the truth, dispensing joy to good men and woe to bad men, according to their deserts." It is something to have it admitted that the Apostles and early Christians believed in the personal advent of Christ. What the Apostles believed we are bound to believe; for John said "He that knoweth God, heareth us." That the New Testament does teach a

> second,
> visible, and
> glorious appearing

of the Son of God, is plain:—

1. From the analogy between the first and second advents.

The rationalistic Jews would have had precisely the same reasons for believing in a more spiritual coming of the Messiah as modern rationalists have for saying that his second coming is to be spiritual. The advent in both cases is predicted in very nearly the same terms. If, therefore, his first coming was in person and visible, so his second coming must be. The two advents are often spoken of in connection, the one illustrating the other. He came the first time as the Lamb of God bearing the sins of the world; He is to come "the second time, without sin, unto salvation."

(Heb. 9:28.) God, said the apostle Peter, "shall send Jesus Christ, which before was preached unto you: whom the heaven must receive until the times of restitution of all things, which God hath spoken by the mouth of all his holy prophets since the world began." (Acts 3:20, 21.) Christ is now invisible to us, having been received up into heaven. He is to remain thus invisible, until God shall send him at the restitution of all things.

2. In many places it is directly asserted that his appearing is to be personal and visible.
At the time of his ascension, the angels said to his disciples: "Ye men of Galilee, why stand ye gazing up into heaven? This same Jesus, which is taken up from you into heaven, shall so come in like manner as ye have seen him go into heaven." (Acts 1:11.) His second coming is to be as visible as his ascension. They saw Him go; and they shall see him come. In Matt. 26:64, it is said, "Hereafter shall ye see the Son of Man sitting on the right hand of power, and coming in the clouds of heaven"; Matt. 24:30, "Then shall all the tribes of the earth mourn, and they shall see the Son of Man coming in the clouds of heaven with power and great glory." Luke 21:27, "Then shall they see the Son of Man coming in a cloud."

3. The circumstances attending the second advent prove that it is to be personal and visible.
It is to be in the clouds; with power and great glory; with the holy angels and all the saints; and it is to be with a shout and the voice of the archangel.

4. The effects ascribed to his advent prove the same thing.
All the tribes of the earth shall mourn; the dead, both small and great are to arise; the wicked shall call on the rocks and hills to cover them; the saints are to be caught up to meet the Lord in the air; and the earth and the heavens are to flee away at his presence.

5. That the Apostles understood Christ to predict his second coming in person does not admit of doubt.

Indeed almost all the rationalistic commentators teach that the Apostles fully believed and even taught that the second advent with all its glorious consequences would occur in their day. Certain it is that they be. lieved that He would come visibly and with great glory, and that they held his coming as the great object of expectation and desire. Indeed Christians are described as those who "are waiting for the coming of our Lord Jesus Christ" (1 Cor. 1:7); as those who are "looking for that blessed hope, and the glorious appearing of the great God and our Savior Jesus Christ" (Titus 2:13) (it is to them who look for Him, He is to "appear the second time, without sin unto salvation," Heb. 9:28); as those who are expecting and earnestly desiring the coming of the day of God. (2 Pet. 3:12.) It is a marked charac-teristic of the apostolic writings that they give such prominence to the doctrine of the second advent. "Judge nothing before the time, until the Lord come." (1 Cor. 4:5.) "Christ the first-fruits; afterwards they that are Christ's at his coming." (1 Cor. 15:23.) Ye are our rejoicing "in the day of the Lord Jesus." (2 Cor. 1:14.) "He. . . . will perform it until the day of Jesus Christ." (Phil. 1:6.) "That I may rejoice in the day of Christ." (2:16.) "Our conversation is in heaven, from whence also we look for the Savior, the Lord Jesus Christ." (3:20.) "When Christ, who is our life, shall appear, then shall ye also appear with Him in glory." (Col. 3:4.) "To wait for his Son from heaven, whom he raised from the dead, even Jesus, which delivered us from the wrath to come." (1 Thess. 1:10.) "What is our hope, . . . are not even ye in the presence of our Lord Jesus Christ at his coming?" (2:19.) "Unblamable in holiness . . . at the coming of our Lord Jesus Christ with all his saints." (3:13.) "We which are alive and remain unto the coming of the Lord . . . shall be caught up . . . in the clouds, to meet the Lord in the air: and so shall we ever be with the Lord." (4:15-17.) In his second epistle he assures the Thessalonians that they shall have rest, "when the Lord Jesus shall be revealed from heaven." (2 Thess. 1:7.) The coming of Christ, however, he tells them was not at hand; there must come a great falling away first. Paul said to Timothy, "Keep this commandment without spot, unrebukable, until the appearing of our Lord Jesus Christ." (1 Tim. 6:14.) "There is laid up for me a crown of righteousness, which the Lord, the righteous judge, shall give me at that day: and not to me only, but unto all them also that love his appearing." (2 Tim. 4:8.) The epistles of Peter afford the same evidence of the deep hold which the promise of Christ's second coming had taken on the minds of the Apostles and of all the early Christians. He tells his readers that they "are kept by the power of God through faith unto salvation, ready to be revealed in the last time . . . that the trial of your faith, . . might be found unto praise, and honor, and glory, at the appearing of Jesus Christ." (1 Pet. 1:5-7.) Men are to "give account to Him that is ready to judge the quick and the dead." (4:5.) "Rejoice that, when his glory shall be revealed, ye may be glad also with exceeding joy." (verse 13.) "When the chief Shepherd shall appear, ye shall receive a crown of glory." (5:4.) " We have not followed cunningly devised fables, when we made known unto you the power and coming of our Lord Jesus Christ, but were eye-witnesses of his majesty." (2 Pet. 1:16). The transfiguration on the mount was a type and pledge of the glory of the second advent. The Apostle warns the disciples that scoffers would come "saying, Where is the promise of his coming? for since the fathers fell asleep, all things continue as they were from the beginning of the creation." In answer to this objection, he reminds them that the threatened deluge was long delayed, but came at last; that time is not with God as it is with us; that with Him a thousand years are as one day, and one day as a thousand years. He repeats the assurance that "the day of the Lord will come as a thief in the night; in the which the heavens shall pass away with a great noise, and the elements shall melt with fervent heat; the earth also and the works that are therein, shall be burned up." (2 Peter 3:3-10.)

From all these passages, and from the whole drift of the New Testament, it is plain,

(1.) That the Apostles fully believed that there is to be a second coming of Christ.

(2.) That his coming is to be in person, visible and glorious.

(3.) That they kept this great event constantly before their own minds, and urged it on the attention of the people, as a motive to patience, constancy, joy, and holy living.

(4.) That the Apostles believed that the second advent of Christ would be attended by the general resurrection, the final judgment, and the end of the world.

As already intimated, it is objected to this view of the prophecies of the New Testament referring to the Second Advent:

1. That the first advent of Christ is predicted in the Old Testament in nearly as glowing terms as his second coming is set forth in the New Testament.

He was to come in the clouds of heaven; with great pomp and power; all nations were to be subject to Him; all people were to be gathered before Him; the stars were to fall from heaven; the sun was to be darkened, and the moon to be turned into blood. These descriptions were not realized by the event; and are understood to refer to the great changes in the state of the world to be effected by his coming. It is unreasonable, therefore, as it is agreed, to expect anything like a literal fulfilment of these New Testament prophecies.

To this it may be answered,

(1.) That in the Old Testament the Messianic period is described as a whole. The fact that the Messiah was to come and establish an everlasting kingdom which was to triumph over all opposition, and experience a glorious consummation, is clearly foretold. All these events were, so to speak, included in the same picture; but the perspective was not preserved. The prophecies were not intended to give the chronological order of the events foretold. Hence the consummation of the Messiah's kingdom is depicted as in immediate proximity with his appearance in the flesh. This led almost all the Jews, and even the disciples of Christ themselves, before the day of Pentecost, to look for the immediate establishment of the Messiah's kingdom in its glory. Such being the character of the Old Testament prophecies, it cannot be fairly inferred that they have as yet received their full accomplishment; or that they are now being fulfilled in the silent progress of the Gospel.

They include the past and the present, but much remains to be accomplished in the future more in accordance with their literal meaning.

(2.) The character of the predictions in the New Testament does not admit of their being made to refer to any spiritual coming of Christ or to the constant progress of his Church. They evidently refer to a single event; to an event in the future, not now in progress; an event which shall attract the attention of all nations, and be attended by the resurrection of the dead, the complete salvation of the righteous, and the condemnation of the wicked.

(3.) A third answer to the objection under consideration is, that the Apostles, as is conceded, understood the predictions of Christ concerning his second coming, in the way in which they have been understood by the Church, as a whole, from that day to this.

2. A second objection to the common Church view of the echatology of the New Testament is, that our Lord expressly says that the events which He foretold were to come to pass during that generation. His words are, "Verily, I say unto you, This generation shall not pass, till all these things be fulfilled." This objection is founded upon the pregnant discourse of Christ recorded in the twenty-fourth and twenty-fifth chapters of Matthew. It is to be remarked that those chapters contain the answer which Christ gave to three questions addressed to Him by his disciples; first, when the destruction of the temple and of Jerusalem was to occur second, what was to be the sign of His coming; and third, when the end of the world was to take place. The difficulty in interpreting this discourse is, to determine its relation to these several questions. There are three methods of interpretation which have been applied to this passage. The first assumes that the whole of our Lord's discourse refers but to one question, namely, When was Jerusalem to be destroyed and Christ's kingdom to be inaugurated; the second adopts the theory of what used to be called the double sense of prophecy; that is, that the same words or prediction refer to one event in one sense, and

to a different event in a higher sense; the third assumes that one part of our Lord's predictions refers exclusively to one of the questions asked, and that other portions refer exclusively to the other questions.

The rationalistic interpreters adopt the first method and refer everything to the overthrow of the Jewish polity, the destruction of Jerusalem, and the inaugnration of the Church which is to do its work of judgment in the earth. Some evangelical interpreters also assume that our Lord answers the three questions put to Him as one, as they constituted in fact but one in the minds of his disciples, since they believed that the three events, the destruction of Jerusalem, the second coming of Christ, and the end of the world, were all to occur together. Thus Luthardt says: "There are three questions according to the words; but only one in the minds of the disciples, as they did not consider the three events, the destruction of Jerusalem, the second coming of Christ, and the end of the world, as separated chronologically; but as three great acts in the final drama of the world s history." In this sense our Lord, he adds, answered their inquiries. He does not separate the different subjects, so as to speak first of one and then of another; but he keeps all ever in view. "It is the method," he says, "of Biblical prophecy, which our Lord observes, always to predict the one great end and all else and what is preparatory, only so far as it stands in connection with that end and appears as one of its elements." Although, therefore, the prophecy of Christ extends to events in the distant future, He could say that that generation should not pass away until all was fulfilled; for the destruction of Jerusalem was the commencement of that work of judgment which Christ foretold.

According to this view, the first method of interpretation differs very little from the second of those above mentioned. Both suppose that the same words or descriptions are intended to refer to two or more events very different in their nature and in the time of their occurrence. Isaiah's prediction of the great deliverance which God was to effect for his people, was so framed as to answer both to the redemption of the Jews from their captivity in Babylon, and to the greater redemption by the Messiah. It was in fact and equally a prediction of both events. The former was the type, and the first step toward the accomplishment of the other. So also in the fourteenth chapter of Zechariah, the prophecy of the destruction of Jerusalem, the spiritual redemption, and the final judgment, are blended together. As, therefore, in the Old Testament the Messianic prophecies took in the whole scope of God's dealings with his people, including their deliverance from Babylon and their redemption by Christ, so as to make it doubtful what refers to the former and what to the latter event; so this discourse of Christ may be considered as taking in the whole history of his kingdom, including his great work of judgment in casting out the Jews and calling the Gentiles, as well as the final consummation of his work. Thus everything predicted of the final judgment had its counterpart in what was fulfilled in that generation.

The third method of interpretation is greatly to be preferred, if it can be successfully carried out. Christ does in fact answer the three questions presented by his disciples. He told when the temple and the city were to be destroyed; it was when they should see Jerusalem compassed about with armies. He told them that the sign of the coming of the Son of Man was to be great defection in the Church, dreadful persecutions, and all but irresistible temptations, and that with his coming were to be connected the final judgment and the end of the world; but that the time when those events were to occur, was not given unto them to know, nor even to the angels of heaven. (Matt. 24:36.)

If this be the method of interpreting these important predictions, then the declaration contained in Matt. 24:34, "This generation shall not pass, till all these things be fulfilled," must be restricted to the "all things spoken of," referring to the destruction of Jerusalem and the inauguration of the Church as Christ's kingdom on earth. There is, however, high authority for making "all things spoken of" here and in the parallel passages, Mark 13:30 and Luke 21:32, refer to Israel as a people or race; in this case the meaning would be that the Jews would not cease to be a distinct people until his predictions were fulfilled. There is nothing, therefore, in this discourse of Christ's inconsistent with the common Church doctrine as to the nature and concomitants of his Second Advent.

Charles Hodge, Systematic Theology,
Part IV, Chapter III

POEMS, HYMNS, MEDITATIONS, AND PRAYERS ON THE RETURN OF JESUS

4.31 LO! HE COMES WITH CLOUDS DESCENDING, JOHN CENNICK

Lo! He comes with clouds descending,
Once for favored sinners slain;
Thousand thousand saints attending,
Swell the triumph of His train:
Hallelujah! Hallelujah!
God appears on earth to reign.

Every eye shall now behold Him
Robed in dreadful majesty;
Those who set at naught and sold Him,
Pierced and nailed Him to the tree,
Deeply wailing, deeply wailing,
Shall the true Messiah see.

Every island, sea, and mountain,
Heav'n and earth, shall flee away;
All who hate Him must, confounded,
Hear the trump proclaim the day:
Come to judgment! Come to judgment!
Come to judgment! Come away!

Now redemption, long expected,
See in solemn pomp appear;
All His saints, by man rejected,
Now shall meet Him in the air:

Hallelujah! Hallelujah!
See the day of God appear!

Answer Thine own bride and Spirit,
Hasten, Lord, the general doom!
The new Heav'n and earth t'inherit,
Take Thy pining exiles home:
All creation, all creation,
Travails! groans! and bids Thee come!

The dear tokens of His passion
Still His dazzling body bears;
Cause of endless exultation
To His ransomed worshippers;
With what rapture, with what rapture
Gaze we on those glorious scars!

Yea, Amen! let all adore Thee,
High on Thine eternal throne;
Savior, take the power and glory,
Claim the kingdom for Thine own;
O come quickly! O come quickly!
Everlasting God, come down!

John Cennick

4.32 THE BATTLE HYMN OF THE REPUBLIC, JULIA WARD HOWE

Mine eyes have seen the glory of the coming
of the Lord;
He is trampling out the vintage where the
grapes of wrath are stored;
He hath loosed the fateful lightning of His
terrible swift sword;
His truth is marching on.
Glory! Glory! Hallelujah!
Glory! Glory! Hallelujah!
Glory! Glory! Hallelujah!
His truth is marching on.

I have seen Him in the watch fires of a
hundred circling camps
They have builded Him an altar in the
evening dews and damps;
I can read His righteous sentence by the dim
and flaring lamps;
His day is marching on.
Glory! Glory! Hallelujah!
Glory! Glory! Hallelujah!
Glory! Glory! Hallelujah!
His day is marching on.

I have read a fiery Gospel writ in burnished
rows of steel;
"As ye deal with My contemners, so with
you My grace shall deal;"
Let the Hero, born of woman, crush the
serpent with His heel,
Since God is marching on.
Glory! Glory! Hallelujah!
Glory! Glory! Hallelujah!
Glory! Glory! Hallelujah! Since
God is marching on.

He has sounded forth the trumpet that shall
never call retreat;
He is sifting out the hearts of men before
His judgment seat;
Oh, be swift, my soul, to answer Him! be
jubilant, my feet;
Our God is marching on.
Glory! Glory! Hallelujah!
Glory! Glory! Hallelujah!
Glory! Glory! Hallelujah!
Our God is marching on.

In the beauty of the lilies Christ was born
across the sea,
With a glory in His bosom that transfigures
you and me:
As He died to make men holy, *let us live to
make men free;
While God is marching on.
Glory! Glory! Hallelujah!
Glory! Glory! Hallelujah!
Glory! Glory! Hallelujah!
While God is marching on.

He is coming like the glory of the morning
on the wave,
He is wisdom to the mighty, He is honor to
the brave;
So the world shall be His footstool, and the
soul of wrong His slave,
Our God is marching on.
Glory! Glory! Hallelujah!
Glory! Glory! Hallelujah!
Glory! Glory! Hallelujah!
Our God is marching on.

Julia Ward Howe

*[originally ...let us die to make men free]

10

QUOTATION COLLECTION ON THE RETURN OF JESUS

Christ will return at the consummation to judge.

Augsburg Confession

He who loves the coming of the Lord is not he who affirms it is far off, nor is it he who says it is near. It is he who, whether it be far or near, awaits it with sincere faith, steadfast hope, and fervent love.

Augustine

I hope that when Christ comes He will find me either praying or preaching.

Augustine

I waken, and I hear the birds twittering, twittering, twittering, and I expect to hear the Trumpet break in upon their song.

Andrew Bonar

There is nothing left for the faithful but with wakeful mind to be always intent on His second coming.

John Calvin

For Christ will descend from heaven in visible form, in like manner as he was seen to ascend, and appear to all, with the ineffable majesty of his kingdom, the splendor of immortality, the boundless power of divinity, and an attending company of angels.

John Calvin

We should live our lives as though Christ were coming this afternoon.

Jimmy Carter, Speech in March 1976

Our anticipation of Jesus' coming ought to make us modest, self-disciplined, and faithful.

François Fénelon

The Second Coming of Christ is necessary to complete the work begun in his Incarnation. There are, in other words, two great events in God's conquest of the powers of evil, two invasions of God into history: the Incarnation and the Second Coming.

George Eldon Ladd

The doctrine of the Second Coming teaches us that we do not and cannot know when the world drama will end.

C. S. Lewis

We must never speak to simple, excitable people about "the Day" without emphasizing again and again the utter impossibility of prediction.

C. S. Lewis

I only have two dates on my calendar—today and that day.

Martin Luther

I hope that the day is near at hand when the advent of the great God will appear, for all things everywhere are boiling, burning, moving, falling, sinking, groaning.

Martin Luther

If Christ were coming again tomorrow, I would plant a tree today.

Martin Luther

Many Christians long for the Rapture, not because of their intense love for the Lord, but because it symbolizes an escape from the distress of our age.

Erwin W. Lutzer

You will be incomplete Christians if you do not look for the coming again of the Lord Jesus.

Robert Murray M'Cheyne

F. B. Meyer once asked D. L. Moody, "What is the secret of your success?" Moody replied, "For many years I have never given an address without the consciousness that the Lord may come before I have finished."

D. L. Moody

I never lay my head upon the pillow without thinking that maybe before the morning breaks, the final morning may have dawned.

Campbell Morgan

I never begin my work in the morning without thinking that perhaps He may interrupt my work and begin His Own.

Campbell Morgan

If our hopes really lie in this world instead of in the eternal order, we shall find it difficult to accept the New Testament teaching of the Second Coming.

J. B. Phillips

Ardently I desire the day of Christ. I half call His absence cruel—O when shall we meet!

Samuel Rutherford

I do not think that in the last forty years I have lived one conscious hour that was not influenced by the thought of our Lord's return.

Lord Shaftsbury

We talk of the second coming, half the world has never heard of the first.

Oswald J. Smith

Let me be buried somewhere in a quiet spot, where the leaves fall, and the robins play, and the dewdrops gleam in the sunshine; and if there must be a line about me, let it be: "Here lies the body of John Ploughman, waiting for the appearing of his Lord and Savior, Jesus Christ."

C. H. Spurgeon

Only Christ at his second coming will eradicate evil and enthrone righteousness for ever. For that day we wait with eagerness.

John Stott

We are not a post-war generation; but a pre-peace generation. Jesus is coming.

Corrie ten Boom

I wish that he would come during my lifetime so that I could take my crown and lay it at his feet.

Queen Victoria, after hearing a clergyman preach on the Second Coming

I believe that as Jesus Christ has once come in grace, so also is he to come a second time in glory.

B. B. Warfield

I am daily waiting for the coming of the Son of God.

George Whitefield

Jesus is going to come back with his arms full of toys.

Richard Wurmbrand

Part Five

DEVOTIONAL RESPONSES TO JESUS

INTRODUCTION

Christians have always, and always will, need to be encouraged in their belief in Jesus and in their walk with him.

The writer of the letter to the Hebrews opens his penultimate chapter with the well-known and encouraging words: "Therefore, since we are surrounded by such a great cloud of witnesses, let us throw off everything that hinders and the sin that so easily entangles, and let us run with perseverance the race marked out for us. Let us fix our eyes on Jesus, the author and perfecter of our faith, who for the joy set before him endured the cross, scorning its shame, and sat down at the right hand of the throne of God. Consider him who endured such opposition from sinful men, so that you will not grow weary and lose heart. In your struggle against sin, you have not yet resisted to the point of shedding your blood." Hebrews 12:1-4 NIV.

Part Five focuses on a number of individuals and their writings who make up this "cloud of witnesses." Today many Christians have the great privilege of having the treasures of the Christian heritage readily available to them. This can only help Christians in their lifelong task of following Jesus' challenging words: "'Love the Lord your God with all your heart and with all your soul and with all your strength and with all your mind;' and, 'Love your neighbor as yourself.'" Luke 10:27 NIV

1
JESUS AND CHRISTIANS

5.1 CHRIST AND SALVATION, JOHN CALVIN

If we seek salvation, we are taught by the very name of Jesus that it is "of him."
If we seek redemption, it lies in his passion;
if acquittal, in his condemnation;
if remission of the curse, in his cross;
if satisfaction, in his sacrifice;
if purification, in his blood;
if reconciliation, in his descent into hell;
if mortification of the flesh, in his tomb;
if newness of life, in his resurrection;
if immortality, in the same;
if inheritance of the Heavenly Kingdom, in his entrance into heaven;
if protection, if security, if abundant supply of all blessings, in his Kingdom;
if untroubled expectation of judgment, in the power given to him to judge.

John Calvin

5.2 THE GOD OF CHRISTIANS, BLAISE PASCAL

The God of Christians is not a God who is simply the author of mathematical truths, or of the order of the elements; that is the view of heathens and Epicureans. He is not merely a God who exercises His providence over the life and fortunes of men, to bestow on those who worship Him a long and happy life. That was the portion of the Jews. But the God of Abraham, the God of Isaac, the God of Jacob, the God of Christians, is a God of love and of comfort, a God who fills the soul and heart of those whom He possesses, a God who makes them conscious of their inward wretchedness, and His infinite mercy, who unites Himself to their inmost soul, who fills it with humility and joy, with confidence and love, who renders them incapable of any other end than Himself.

All who seek God without Jesus Christ, and who rest in nature, either find no light to satisfy them, or come to form for themselves a means of knowing God and serving Him without a mediator. Thereby they fall either into atheism, or into deism, two things which the Christian religion abhors almost equally.

Blaise Pascal

5.3 Think of Christ, C. H. Spurgeon

You may think of a doctrine forever, and get no good from it, if you are not already saved; but think of the person of Christ, and that will give you faith. Take him everywhere, wherever you go, and try to meditate on him in your leisure moments, and then he will reveal himself to you, and give you peace.

C. H. Spurgeon

5.4 How we share in Christ's redemption, The Westminster Shorter Catechism

QUESTION 29: How are we made partakers of the redemption purchased by Christ?
ANSWER: We are made partakers of the redemption purchased by Christ, by the effectual application of it to us by his Holy Spirit.

John 1:12-13. But as many as received him, to them gave he power to become the sons of God, even to them that believe on his name: which were born, not of blood, nor of the will of the flesh, nor of the will of man, but of God.

John 3:5-6. Jesus answered, Verily, verily, I say unto thee, Except a man be born of water and of the Spirit, he cannot enter into the kingdom of God. . . That which is born of the flesh is flesh; and that which is born of the Spirit is spirit.

Titus 3:5-6. Not by works of righteousness which we have done, but according to his mercy he saved us, by the washing of regeneration, and renewing of the Holy Ghost; which he shed on us abundantly through Jesus Christ our Savior.

The Westminster Shorter Catechism

5.5 How we share in Christ's redemption, Matthew Henry

1. IS REDEMPTION PURCHASED BY CHRIST?

Yes: he obtained eternal redemption for us, Heb. 9:12. Is he then the Author of it? Yes: he became the Author of salvation, Heb. 5:9. Is it redemption by price? Yes: Ye are bought with a price, 1 Cor. 6:20. Is it a redemption by power? Yes: for he hath led captivity captive, Ps. 68:18. Is this redemption offered to all? Yes: he hath proclaimed liberty to the captives, Is. 61:1. May all that will take the benefit of it? Yes: Ho, every one that thirsteth, come ye to the waters, Is. 55:1. Have all the world therefore some benefit by it? Yes: Go into all the world, and preach the gospel to every creature, Mark 16:15. But have all the world a like benefit by it? No: Thou wilt manifest thyself to us, and not unto the world, John 14:22.

2. IS IT ENOUGH THAT THERE IS A REDEMPTION PURCHASED?

No: for there are those who deny the Lord who bought them, 2 Pet. 2:1. Is it enough to hear of it? No: for to some it is a savor of death unto death, 2 Cor. 2:16. Is it enough to have a name among the redeemed? No: Thou hast a name that thou livest, and art dead, Rev. 3:1. Is it necessary therefore that we be partakers of the redemption? Yes: that we may say, Who loved me, and gave himself for me, Gal. 2:20. Do all partake of it? No: Thou hast neither part nor lot in this matter, Acts 8:21. Do all believers partake of it? Yes: We are made partakers of Christ, Heb. 2:14. Do they receive the Redeemer? Yes: We have received Christ Jesus the Lord, Col. 2:6. Do any receive this of themselves? No: A man can receive nothing except it be given him from above, John 3:27.

3. MUST THE REDEMPTION BE APPLIED TO US?

Yes: It is Christ in you the hope of glory, Col. 1:27. Is it the Spirit's work to apply it? Yes: for it is the Spirit that quickens, John 6:68. Is he sent for that purpose? Yes: He shall take of mine, and shall show it unto you, John 16:15. Is he sent in Christ's name? Yes: He is the Comforter, which is the Holy Ghost, whom the Father will send in my name, John 14:26. Have we as much need of the Spirit to apply the redemption to us, as of the Son to purchase it for us? Yes: for when Christ had purchased it, it was expedient for us he should go away, that he might send the Comforter, John 16:7.

4. IS THE SPIRIT GIVEN TO THE CHURCH IN GENERAL?

Yes: Another Comforter shall abide with you for ever, John 14:16. Is he promised to particular persons? Yes: Turn ye at my reproof; behold, I will pour out my Spirit unto you, Prov. 1:28. Are we to pray for the Spirit then? Yes: our heavenly Father will give the Holy Spirit to them that ask him, Luke 11:13. Do all believers receive of the Spirit? Yes: God hath sent forth the Spirit of his Son into your hearts, Gal. 4:6. Is he their teacher? Yes: he shall teach them all things. Is he their remembrancer? Yes: he shall bring all things to their remembrance, John 14:26. Is he the earnest? Yes: he hath given the earnest of the Spirit in our hearts, 2 Cor. 1:22. Does he begin the good work of grace in the heart? Yes: for when he is come, he shall convince, John 16:8. And does he perfect it? Yes: for he hath wrought us for the selfsame thing, 2 Cor. 5:5.

Matthew Henry, A Scripture Catechism in the method of the Assembly's

---

5.6 THE BENEFITS BELIEVERS RECEIVE FROM CHRIST AT DEATH, *THE WESTMINSTER SHORTER CATECHISM*

QUESTION 37: What benefits do believers receive from Christ at death?
ANSWER: The souls of believers are at their death made perfect in holiness, and do immediately pass into glory; and their bodies, being still united to Christ, do rest in their graves till the resurrection.

Luke 23:43. And Jesus said unto him, Verily I say unto thee, To day shalt thou be with me in paradise.
Luke 16:23. And in hell he lift up his eyes, being in torments, and seeth Abraham afar off, and Lazarus in his bosom.

Philippians 1:23. For I am in a strait betwixt two, having a desire to depart, and to be with Christ; which is far better.

2 Corinthians 5:6-8. Therefore we are always confident, knowing that, whilst we are at home in the body, we are absent from the Lord: (for we walk by faith, not by sight:) we are confident, I say, and willing rather to be absent from the body, and to be present with the Lord.

1 Thessalonians 4:14. For if we believe that Jesus died and rose again, even so them also which sleep in Jesus will God bring with him.

Romans 8:23. And not only they, but ourselves also, which have the firstfruits of the Spirit, even we ourselves groan within

ourselves, waiting for the adoption, to wit, the redemption of our body.

1 Thessalonians 4:14. For if we believe that Jesus died and rose again, even so them also which sleep in Jesus will God bring with him.

The Westminster Shorter Catechism

5.7 THE BENEFITS BELIEVERS RECEIVE FROM CHRIST AT DEATH, MATTHEW HENRY

1. IS THE HAPPINESS OF BELIEVERS CONFINED TO THIS PRESENT LIFE?

No: if in this life only we have hope in Christ, we are of all men most miserable, 1 Cor. 15:19. Is the best of their happiness in this life? No: for in the world ye shall have tribulation, John 16:33. Must they die as well as others? Yes: it is appointed unto men once to die, Heb. 9:27. Must the best and most useful die? Yes: the righteous perisheth, and merciful men are taken away, Is. 57:1. Ought they then to wait for it? Yes: All the days of my appointed time will I wait, till my change come, Job 14:14. And to prepare for it? Yes: Therefore be ye also ready, Matt. 24:44.

2. IS DEATH LOSS TO A GOOD CHRISTIAN?

No: for to me to live is Christ, and to die is gain, Phil. 1:21. Should it therefore be a terror? No: for the righteous hath hope in his death, Prov 14:32. Does God take special care of the death of his people? Yes: for precious in the sight of the Lord is the death of his saints, Ps. 116:15. Is death in the covenant? Yes: All is yours, whether life or death, 1 Cor. 3:22. Can it separate them from the love of God? No: neither death nor life can do that, Rom. 8:38.

3. ARE BELIEVERS PERFECT IN HOLINESS IN THIS LIFE?

No: I have not yet attained, neither am I already perfect, Phil. 3:12. Are their souls made perfect at death? Yes: the spirits of just men are made perfect, Heb. 12:23. Are they

delivered from sin? Yes: he that is dead is freed from sin, Rom. 6:7. Are they made perfect in knowledge? Yes: Then shall I know, even as also I am known, 1 Cor. 13:12. And perfect in holiness? Yes: for they are come to the perfect man, to the measure of the stature of the fullness of Christ, Eph. 4:13. Might they pass into glory without being made perfect in holiness? No: for corruption cannot inherit incorruption, 1 Cor. 15:50. Being made perfect in holiness, are they confirmed in it? Yes: He that is holy, let him be holy still, Rev. 22:11.

4. DO THE SOULS OF BELIEVERS AT DEATH SLEEP WITH THEIR BODIES?

No: for when we are absent from the body, we are present with the Lord, 2 Cor. 5:8. Do they go to Christ? Yes: Having a desire to depart and to be with Christ, Phil. 1:23. And will he receive them? Yes: Lord Jesus, receive my spirit, Acts 7:59. Shall they be where he is? Yes: That where I am there ye may be also, John 14:3. Will they be with him in heaven? Yes: We have a house not made with hands, eternal in the heavens, 2 Cor. 5:1. Do they pass into this glory at death? Yes: That when ye fail ye may be received into everlasting habitations, Luke 16:9. Do they immediately pass into it? Yes: This day shalt thou be with me in paradise, Luke 23:43. Are they guarded by angels thither? Yes: he was carried by angels into Abraham's bosom, Luke 16:22. Are they happy then in their death? Yes: Blessed are the dead which die in the Lord, Rev. 14:13. Happier than in life? Yes: The day of their death is better than the day of their birth, Eccl. 7:1. And is their end peace? Yes: Mark the perfect man, and behold the upright, for the end of that man is peace, Ps. 37:37.

5. IS DEATH GAIN TO THE WICKED MAN?

No: for when a wicked man dies, his expectation shall perish, Prov. 11:7. Is it therefore a terror to the wicked? Yes: this night thy soul shall be required of thee, Luke 12:20. Do the souls of the wicked, at death go into torment? Yes: the rich man died, and was buried, and in hell he lifted up his eyes, being in torment, Luke 16:22, 23. Do they go away under the guilt of their sins? Yes: If ye believe not that I am he, ye shall die in your sins, John 8:24. Is it a fearful thing to fall into the hands of the living God? Yes: for our God is a consuming fire, Heb. 12:29. Are the souls of believers distinguished from them? Yes: But God will redeem my soul from the power of the grave, Ps. 49:15.

6. ARE THE BODIES OF BELIEVERS WELL PROVIDED FOR AT DEATH?

Yes: for the Lord is for the body, 1 Cor. 6:13. May they be cheerfully committed to the grave? Yes; My flesh also shall rest in hope, Ps. 16:9. Do they still remain united to Christ? Yes: for they sleep in Jesus, 1 Thess. 4:14. Do they rest in their graves? Yes: for there the weary be at rest, Job 3:17. Is the grave a good Christian's bed? Yes: He shall enter into peace, they shall rest in their beds, Is. 57:2. May the saints triumph over the grave then? Yes: O

grave where is thy victory? 1 Cor. 15:55. And need they to fear no evil in it? No: for the sucking child shall play upon the hole of the asp, Is. 11:8. Are all who are regenerate delivered from the second death? Yes: Blessed and holy is he that hath part in the first resurrection, on such the second death shall have no power, Rev. 20:6.

7. SHALL THE DEAD BE RAISED AGAIN?

Yes: there shall be a resurrection of the dead, both of the just and of the unjust, Acts 24:15. Shall the same body be raised again? Yes: Though after my skin worms destroy this body, yet in my flesh shall I see God, Job 19:26. Shall it be done by the power of Christ? Yes: for as in Adam all die, so in Christ shall all be made alive, 1 Cor. 15:22 Shall there be a vast difference between the godly and the wicked at the resurrection? Yes: for some shall awake to everlasting life, and some to shame and everlasting contempt, Dan 12:2. Has Christ himself assured us of this? Yes: the hour is coming when all that are in the graves shall hear his voice, and shall come forth; they that have done good unto the resurrection of life, and they that have done evil to the resurrection of condemnation, John 5:28, 29. Is it certain when this shall be? Yes: for he hath appointed a day, Acts 17:31. But is it known to us? No: for of that day and hour knoweth no man, Mark 13:32.

Matthew Henry, A Scripture Catechism in the method of the Assembly's

---

5.8 THE BENEFITS BELIEVERS RECEIVE FROM CHRIST AT THE RESURRECTION, *THE WESTMINSTER SHORTER CATECHISM*

QUESTION 38: What benefits do believers receive from Christ at the resurrection?
ANSWER: At the resurrection, believers being raised up in glory, shall be openly Zacknowledged and acquitted in the day of

judgment, and made perfectly blessed in the full enjoyment of God to all eternity.

1 Corinthians 15:42-43. So also is the resurrection of the dead. It is sown in corruption; it is raised in incorruption: It is

sown in dishonor; it is raised in glory: it is sown in weakness; it is raised in power.

Matthew 25:33-34. And he shall set the sheep on his right hand, but the goats on the left. Then shall the King say unto them on his right hand, Come, ye blessed of my Father, inherit the kingdom prepared for you from the foundation of the world.

Matthew 10:32. Whosoever therefore shall confess me before men, him will I confess also before my Father which is in heaven.

Psalm 16:11. Thou wilt shew me the path of life: in thy presence is fullness of joy; at thy right hand there are pleasures for evermore.

1 Corinthians 2:9. But as it is written, Eye hath not seen, nor ear heard, neither have entered into the heart of man, the things which God hath prepared for them that love him.

1 Thessalonians 4:17. Then we which are alive and remain shall be caught up together with them in the clouds, to meet the Lord in the air: and so shall we ever be with the Lord.

The Westminster Shorter Catechism

5.9 The benefits believers receive from Christ at the resurrection, Matthew Henry

1. SHALL THE DEAD BODIES OF BELIEVERS BE RAISED?

Yes: For the dead shall be raised, 1 Cor. 15:52, Is it possible that the same body should return to life again? Yes: Why should it seem a thing incredible with you that God should raise the dead? Acts 26:8. Is it certain that they shall be raised? Yes: for if there be no resurrection of the dead, then is Christ not risen, 1 Cor. 15:13. Has Christ undertaken for the resurrection of believers? Yes: I am the resurrection and the life, John 11:15. Are they in error who deny it? Yes: Ye do err, not knowing the Scriptures, nor the power of God, Matt. 22:29.

2. SHALL THE BELIEVER'S BODY BE RAISED UP IN GLORY?

Yes: it is sown in dishonor, it is raised in glory, 1 Cor. 15:43. Shall it be the glory of Christ's glorified body? Yes: he shall change our vile bodies, that they may be fashioned like unto his glorious body, Phil. 3:21. Shall they be raised by virtue of their union with Christ? Yes: Together with my dead body shall they arise, Is. 26:19. Shall they be raised to such a life as we now live? No: for in the resurrection they neither marry, nor are given in marriage, Matt. 22:30. Shall they be raised to an immortal life? Yes: for this mortal must put

off immortality, 1 Cor. 15:53. Shall they that are found alive be changed? Yes: Behold, I show you a mystery, we shall not all sleep, but we shall all be changed, 1 Cor. 15:51.

3. SHALL ALL THE SAINTS AT THAT DAY BE BROUGHT TO JESUS CHRIST?

Yes: at the coming of our Lord Jesus Christ there shall be a gathering together unto him, 2 Thess. 2:1. Shall they be separated from the wicked? Yes: as the Shepherd divideth the sheep from the goats, Matt. 25:32. Shall all the saints be then together? Yes: for he shall gather his elect from the four winds, Matt. 24:31. And none but saints? Yes: for he shall gather out of his kingdom all things that offend, Matt. 13:41. And saints made perfect? Yes: for then that which is perfect is come, 1 Cor. 13:10. Shall they attend upon Christ at his coming? Yes: Behold the Lord cometh with ten thousand of his saints, Jude 14. Shall they be assessors with him in his judgment. Yes: for the saints shall judge the world, 1 Cor. 6:2.

4. SHALL THEY BE OPENLY ACKNOWLEDGED IN THE DAY OF JUDGMENT?

Yes: Him will I confess before my Father which is in heaven, Matt. 10:32. Will God own them as his own? Yes: They shall be mine, saith the Lord, in that day when I make up my jewels, Mal. 3:17. And will that be their honor? Yes: If any man serve me, him will my Father honor, John 12:26. Shall they be openly acquitted? Yes: for their sins shall be blotted out when the times of refreshing come, Acts 3:19.

5. SHALL THE WICKED BE CONDEMNED THEN?
Yes: he shall say to them on his left hand, Depart from me. Shall they be sent away with a blessing? No: Depart ye cursed. Shall they go into a place of ease? No: into fire. Into ordinary fire? No: into fire prepared. Shall it be for a short time? No: but into everlasting fire. Shall they have good company? No: but the devil and his angels, Matt. 25:41. Will the salvation of the saints aggravate their condemnation? Yes: for they shall see Abraham, and Isaac, and Jacob in the kingdom of heaven, Luke 13:28.

6. SHALL THE SAINTS AT THE DAY OF JUDGMENT BE PUT IN POSSESSION OF ETERNAL LIFE?
Yes: the righteous into life eternal, Matt. 25:4, 6. Shall they be blessed? Yes: Come, ye blessed of my Father, Matt. 25:34. Shall they be perfectly blessed? Yes: for in thy presence is fullness of joy, Ps. 16:11. Shall there be any sin in heaven? No: for they are as the angels of God in heaven, Matt. 22:30. Shall there be any sorrow there? No: for God shall wipe away all tears from their eyes, Rev. 21:4. Shall there be any dying there? No: there shall be no more death, Rev. 21:4.

7. IS HEAVEN A PLACE OF REST?
Yes: there remaineth a rest for the people of God, Heb. 4:9. Is it light? Yes: it is the inheritance of the saints in light, Col. 1:12. Is it honor? Yes: it is a crown of glory that fades not away, 1 Pet. 5:4. Is it wealth? Yes: it is an inheritance incorruptible, 1 Pet. 1:4. Is it joy? Yes: Enter thou into the joy of thy Lord, Matt. 25:21.

8. SHALL WE IN HEAVEN SEE GOD?
Yes: when he shall appear we shall be like him, for we shall see him as he is, 1 John 3:2. Shall we see him clearly? Yes: now we see through a glass darkly, but then face to face, 1 Cor. 13:12. Shall we enjoy him? Yes: God himself shall be with them, and be their God, Rev. 21.

9. SHALL WE BE SATISFIED IN THE VISION AND FRUITION OF GOD?
Yes: I shall be satisfied when I awake with thy likeness, Ps. 17:15. Shall this be everlasting? Yes: So shall we ever be with the Lord, 1 Thess. 4:17.

10. IS THIS HAPPINESS PURCHASED?
Yes: it is the purchased possession, Eph. 1:14. Is it promised? Yes: it is eternal life which God, that cannot lie, promised, Titus 1:2. Is it sure to all good Christians? Yes: even the poor in the world, if rich in faith, are heirs of the kingdom, Jam. 2:5. Should we not be solicitous that it may be sure with us? Yes: What shall I do that I may inherit eternal life? Luke 18:18. Should we not then have it much in our eye? Yes: for we look not at the things that are seen, but the things that are not seen, 2 Cor. 4:18. And should we not be comforted and encouraged with the prospect of it? Yes: for the sufferings of this present time are not worthy to be compared with the glory which shall be revealed, Rom. 8:18.

Matthew Henry, A Scripture Catechism in the method of the Assembly's

5.10 WHAT FAITH IN JESUS CHRIST IS, *THE WESTMINSTER SHORTER CATECHISM*

QUESTION 86: What is faith in Jesus Christ?

ANSWER: Faith in Jesus Christ is a saving grace, whereby we receive and rest upon him alone for salvation, as he is offered to us in the gospel.

Hebrews 10:39. But we are not of them who draw back unto perdition; but of them that believe to the saving of the soul.

John 1:12. But as many as received him, to them gave he power to become the sons of God, even to them that believe on his name.

Isaiah 26:3-4. Thou wilt keep him in perfect peace, whose mind is stayed on thee; because he trusteth in thee. Trust ye in the Lord for ever: for in the Lord Jehovah is everlasting strength.

Philippians 3:9. And be found in him, not having mine own righteousness, which is of the law, but that which is through the faith of Christ, the righteousness which is of God by faith.

John 6:40. And this is the will of him that sent me, that every one which seeth the Son, and believeth on him, may have everlasting life: and I will raise him up at the last day.

Galatians 2:16. Knowing that a man is not justified by the works of the law, but by the faith of Jesus Christ, even we have believed in Jesus Christ, that we might be justified by the works of the law: for by the works of the law shall no flesh be justified.

The Westminster Shorter Catechism

5.11 WHAT FAITH IN JESUS CHRIST IS, MATTHEW HENRY

1. ARE WE TO BELIEVE IN JESUS CHRIST?

Yes: Ye believe in God, believe also in me, John 14:1. Is Christ in the word the object of our faith? Yes: For the word is nigh thee, Rom. 10:8. Is faith in Christ a grace? Yes: it is not of ourselves, it is the gift of God, Eph. 2:8. Is it free grace? Yes: To you it is given on the behalf of Christ to believe in him, Phil. 1:29. Is it a saving grace? Yes: for we believe to the saving of the soul, Heb. 10:39. Is it that by which we live? Yes: The just shall five by his faith, Rom. 1:17. Is unbelief the great damning sin? Yes: They could not enter in because of unbelief, Heb. 3:19.

2. DO WE BY FAITH ASSENT TO GOSPEL TRUTHS?

Yes: He that has received his testimony hath set to his seal that God is true, John 3:33. Do we by faith consent to gospel terms? Yes: Take my yoke upon you, and learn of me, Matt. 11:29. Must both these go together? Yes: He said, Lord, I believe, and he worshipped him, John 9:38. Is there good reason for both? Yes: for it is both a faithful saying, and worthy of all acceptation, 1 Tim. 1:15.

3. IS THIS RECEIVING CHRIST?

Yes: Ye have received Christ Jesus the Lord, Col. 2:6. Is it applying the righteousness of Christ to ourselves? Yes: Who loved me, and gave himself for me, Gal. 2:20. And consenting to it? Yes: We have now received the atonement, Rom. 5:11. Must we receive Christ to rule us as well as to save us? Yes: For him hath God exalted to be both a Prince and a Savior, Acts 5:31. And is it enough only to receive him? No: as we have received him, so we must walk in him, Col. 2:6.

4. DO WE BY FAITH REST ON CHRIST ALONE FOR SALVATION?

Yes: in his name shall the Gentiles trust, Matt. 12:21. And rely on his righteousness? Yes: That I may win Christ, and be found in him, not having my own righteousness, which is of the law, but that which is through the faith of Christ, Phil. 3:9. And do we rejoice in him? Yes: for we are the circumcision that rejoice in Christ Jesus, Phil. 3:3.

5. WILL FAITH IN CHRIST PRODUCE GOOD AFFECTIONS?

Yes: for it works by love, Gal. 5:6. Will it purify the heart? Yes: Purifying their hearts by faith, Acts 15:9. Will it overcome the world? Yes: This is the victory, overcoming the world, even your faith, 1 John 5:4. Will it resist the temptations of Satan? Yes: Yes: the shield of faith quenches the fiery darts of the wicked, Eph. 6:16. Does it exert itself in obedience? Yes: for the gospel is made known to all nations for the obedience of faith, Rom. 16:26. And does it subject the soul to the grace and government of the Lord Jesus? Yes: My Lord, and my God, John 20:28.

Matthew Henry, A Scripture Catechism in the method of the Assembly's

---

5.12 THE OUTWARD MEANS BY WHICH CHRIST GIVES US THE BENEFITS OF REDEMPTION, *THE WESTMINSTER SHORTER CATECHISM*

QUESTION 88: What are the outward means whereby Christ communicates to us the benefits of redemption?

ANSWER: The outward and ordinary means whereby Christ communicates to us the benefits of redemption, are his ordinances, especially the word, sacraments, and prayer; all which are made effectual to the elect for salvation.

Matthew 28:19-20. Go ye therefore, and teach all nations, baptizing them in the name of the Father, and of the Son, and of the Holy Ghost: teaching them to observe all things whatsoever I have commanded you: and, lo, I am with you alway, even unto the end of the world. Amen.

Acts 2:41-42, 46-47. Then they that gladly received his word were baptized: and the same day there were added unto them about three thousand souls. And they continued steadfastly in the apostles' doctrine and fellowship, and in breaking of bread, and in prayers. . . And they, continuing daily with one accord in the temple, and breaking bread from house to house, did eat their meat with gladness and singleness of heart, praising God, and having favor with all the people. And the Lord added to the church daily such as should be saved.

The Westminster Shorter Catechism

5.13 THE OUTWARD MEANS BY WHICH CHRIST GIVES US THE BENEFITS OF REDEMPTION, MATTHEW HENRY

1. DOES CHRIST COMMUNICATE THE BENEFITS OF REDEMPTION?

Yes: for of his fullness have all we received, John 1:16. Does he ordinarily communicate them by means? Yes: I will for this be inquired of, Ezek. 36:37. Is he tied to those means? No: for the Spirit, as the wind, bloweth where he listeth, John 3:8. But are we tied to the use of them? Yes: Where I record my name, I will come to thee, and will bless thee, Ex. 20:24. Are the ordinances the outward and ordinary means of grace? Yes: I the Lord do sanctify Israel, when my sanctuary shall be in the midst of them, Ezek. 37:28.

2. ARE THE WORD, SACRAMENTS, AND PRAYER, THE GREAT GOSPEL ORDINANCES?

Yes: Then they that gladly received his Word were baptized, and they continued steadfastly in the apostles' doctrine and fellowship, and in breaking bread, and in prayers, Acts 2:41, 42. Is singing of psalms also a gospel ordinance? Yes: Speaking to yourselves in psalms, and hymns, and spiritual songs, Eph. 5:19. Is it appointed for our own consolation? Yes: Is any

merry, let him sing psalms, Jam. 5:13. And for mutual instruction? Yes: Teaching and admonishing one another in psalms, Col. 3:16. And for God's glory? Yes: Singing with grace in your heart to the Lord, Col. 3:16.

3. HAS CHRIST APPOINTED MINISTERS OF THE GOSPEL?

Yes: he hath given pastors and teachers for the edifying of the body of Christ, Eph. 4:11, 12. Is the administration of ordinances committed to them? Yes: for they are the stewards of the mysteries of God, 1 Cor. 4:1. And must they attend that service? Yes: We will give ourselves to prayer, and to the ministry of the word, Acts 6:4.

4. ARE GOSPEL ORDINANCES MADE EFFECTUAL TO ALL FOR SALVATION?

No: for with many of them God was not well pleased, 1 Cor. 10:5. But are they made effectual to the elect? Yes: As many as were ordained to eternal life believed, Acts 13:48.

Matthew Henry, A Scripture Catechism in the method of the Assembly's

---

CHECK-LIST

5.14 BIBLE STUDY ON BEING "IN CHRIST"

The Bible version used in this section is the NIV.

1. What we are "in Christ Jesus"
2. What we are "in Jesus"
3. What we are "in Christ"
4. What we are "with Christ"

1. WHAT WE ARE "IN CHRIST JESUS"

Several days later Felix came with his wife

Drusilla, who was a Jewess. He sent for Paul and listened to him as he spoke about faith in Christ Jesus.

Acts 24:24

In the same way, count yourselves dead to sin but alive to God in Christ Jesus.

Romans 6:11

Therefore, there is now no condemnation for those who are in Christ Jesus.

Romans 8:1

. . . neither height nor depth, nor anything else in all creation, will be able to separate us from the love of God that is in Christ Jesus our Lord.

Romans 8:39

Therefore I glory in Christ Jesus in my service to God.

Romans 15:17

Greet Priscilla and Aquila, my fellow workers in Christ Jesus.

Romans 16:3

To the church of God in Corinth, to those sanctified in Christ Jesus and called to be holy, together with all those everywhere who call on the name of our Lord Jesus Christ—their Lord and ours.

1 Corinthians 1:2

I always thank God for you because of his grace given you in Christ Jesus.

1 Corinthians 1:4

It is because of him that you are in Christ Jesus, who has become for us wisdom from God—that is, our righteousness, holiness and redemption.

1 Corinthians 1:30

Even though you have ten thousand guardians in Christ, you do not have many fathers, for in Christ Jesus I became your father through the gospel.

1 Corinthians 4:15

For this reason I am sending to you Timothy, my son whom I love, who is faithful in the Lord. He will remind you of my way of life in Christ Jesus, which agrees with what I teach everywhere in every church.

1 Corinthians 4:17

I die every day—I mean that, brothers—just as surely as I glory over you in Christ Jesus our Lord.

1 Corinthians 15:31

My love to all of you in Christ Jesus. Amen.

1 Corinthians 16:24

. . . because some false brothers had infiltrated our ranks to spy on the freedom we have in Christ Jesus and to make us slaves.

Galatians 2:4

. . . know that a man is not justified by observing the law, but by faith in Jesus Christ. So we, too, have put our faith in Christ Jesus that we may be justified by faith in Christ and not by observing the law, because by observing the law no one will be justified.

Galatians 2:16

You are all sons of God through faith in Christ Jesus.

Galatians 3:26

There is neither Jew nor Greek, slave nor free, male nor female, for you are all one in Christ Jesus.

Galatians 3:28

For in Christ Jesus neither circumcision nor uncircumcision has any value. The only thing that counts is faith expressing itself through love.

Galatians 5:6

Paul, an apostle of Christ Jesus by the will of God, To the saints in Ephesus, the faithful in Christ Jesus.

Ephesians 1:1

And God raised us up with Christ and seated us with him in the heavenly realms in Christ Jesus.

Ephesians 2:6

. . . in order that in the coming ages he might show the incomparable riches of his grace, expressed in his kindness to us in Christ Jesus.

Ephesians 2:7

For we are God's workmanship, created in Christ Jesus to do good works, which God prepared in advance for us to do.

Ephesians 2:10

But now in Christ Jesus you who once were far away have been brought near through the blood of Christ.

Ephesians 2:13

This mystery is that through the gospel the Gentiles are heirs together with Israel, members together of one body, and sharers together in the promise in Christ Jesus.

Ephesians 3:6

. . . according to his eternal purpose which he accomplished in Christ Jesus our Lord.

Ephesians 3:11

. . . to him be glory in the church and in Christ Jesus throughout all generations, for ever and ever! Amen.

Ephesians 3:21

Paul and Timothy, servants of Christ Jesus, To all the saints in Christ Jesus at Philippi, together with the overseers and deacons.

Philippians 1:1

So that through my being with you again your joy in Christ Jesus will overflow on account of me.

Philippians 1:26

For it is we who are the circumcision, we who worship by the Spirit of God, who glory in Christ Jesus, and who put no confidence in the flesh.

Philippians 3:3

I press on toward the goal to win the prize for which God has called me heavenward in Christ Jesus.

Philippians 3:14

And the peace of God, which transcends all understanding, will guard your hearts and your minds in Christ Jesus.

Philippians 4:7

And my God will meet all your needs according to his glorious riches in Christ Jesus.

Philippians 4:19

Greet all the saints in Christ Jesus. The brothers who are with me send greetings.

Philippians 4:21

. . . because we have heard of your faith in Christ Jesus and of the love you have for all the saints.

Colossians 1:4

For you, brothers, became imitators of God's churches in Judea, which are in Christ Jesus: You suffered from your own countrymen the same things those churches suffered from the Jews.

1 Thessalonians 2:14

. . . give thanks in all circumstances, for this is God's will for you in Christ Jesus.
1 Thessalonians 5:18

The grace of our Lord was poured out on me abundantly, along with the faith and love that are in Christ Jesus.

1 Timothy 1:14

Those who have served well gain an excellent standing and great assurance in their faith in Christ Jesus.

1 Timothy 3:13

Paul, an apostle of Christ Jesus by the will of God, according to the promise of life that is in Christ Jesus.

2 Timothy 1:1

. . . who has saved us and called us to a holy life—not because of anything we have done but because of his own purpose and grace. This grace was given us in Christ Jesus before the beginning of time.

2 Timothy 1:9

What you heard from me, keep as the pattern of sound teaching, with faith and love in Christ Jesus.

2 Timothy 1:13

You then, my son, be strong in the grace that is in Christ Jesus.

2 Timothy 2:1

Therefore I endure everything for the sake of the elect, that they too may obtain the salvation that is in Christ Jesus, with eternal glory.

2 Timothy 2:10

In fact, everyone who wants to live a godly life in Christ Jesus will be persecuted.

2 Timothy 3:12

. . . and how from infancy you have known the holy Scriptures, which are able to make you wise for salvation through faith in Christ Jesus.

2 Timothy 3:15

Epaphras, my fellow prisoner in Christ Jesus, sends you greetings.

Philemon 1:23

2. WHAT WE ARE "IN JESUS"

Paul said, "John's baptism was a baptism of repentance. He told the people to believe in the one coming after him, that is, in Jesus."

Acts 19:4

This righteousness from God comes through faith in Jesus Christ to all who believe. There is no difference.

Romans 3:22

. . . he did it to demonstrate his justice at the present time, so as to be just and the one who justifies those who have faith in Jesus.

Romans 3:26

. . . know that a man is not justified by observing the law, but by faith in Jesus Christ. So we, too, have put our faith in Christ Jesus that we may be justified by faith in Christ and not by observing the law, because by observing the law no one will be justified.

Galatians 2:16

But the Scripture declares that the whole world is a prisoner of sin, so that what was promised, being given through faith in Jesus Christ, might be given to those who believe.

Galatians 3:22

Surely you heard of him and were taught in him in accordance with the truth that is in Jesus.

Ephesians 4:21

I, John, your brother and companion in the suffering and kingdom and patient endurance that are ours in Jesus, was on the island of Patmos because of the word of God and the testimony of Jesus.

Revelation 1:9

3. WHAT WE ARE "IN CHRIST"

I speak the truth in Christ—I am not lying, my conscience confirms it in the Holy Spirit.

Romans 9:1

. . . so in Christ we who are many form one body, and each member belongs to all the others.

Romans 12:5

Greet Andronicus and Junias, my relatives who have been in prison with me. They are outstanding among the apostles, and they were in Christ before I was.

Romans 16:7

Greet Urbanus, our fellow worker in Christ, and my dear friend Stachys.

Romans 16:9

Greet Apelles, tested and approved in Christ. Greet those who belong to the household of Aristobulus.

Romans 16:10

Brothers, I could not address you as spiritual but as worldly—mere infants in Christ.

1 Corinthians 3:1

We are fools for Christ, but you are so wise in Christ! We are weak, but you are strong! You are honored, we are dishonored!

1 Corinthians 4:10

Even though you have ten thousand guardians in Christ, you do not have many fathers, for in Christ Jesus I became your father through the gospel.

1 Corinthians 4:15

Then those also who have fallen asleep in Christ are lost.

1 Corinthians 15:18

If only for this life we have hope in Christ, we are to be pitied more than all men.

1 Corinthians 15:19

For as in Adam all die, so in Christ all will be made alive.

1 Corinthians 15:22

For no matter how many promises God has made, they are "Yes" in Christ. And so through him the "Amen" is spoken by us to the glory of God.

2 Corinthians 1:20

Now it is God who makes both us and you stand firm in Christ. He anointed us . . .

2 Corinthians 1:21

But thanks be to God, who always leads us in triumphal procession in Christ and through us spreads everywhere the fragrance of the knowledge of him.

2 Corinthians 2:14

Unlike so many, we do not peddle the word of God for profit. On the contrary, in Christ we speak before God with sincerity, like men sent from God.

2 Corinthians 2:17

But their minds were made dull, for to this day the same veil remains when the old covenant is read. It has not been removed, because only in Christ is it taken away.

2 Corinthians 3:14

Therefore, if anyone is in Christ, he is a new creation; the old has gone, the new has come!

2 Corinthians 5:17

. . . that God was reconciling the world to himself in Christ, not counting men's sins against them. And he has committed to us the message of reconciliation.

2 Corinthians 5:19

I know a man in Christ who fourteen years ago was caught up to the third heaven. Whether it was in the body or out of the body I do not know—God knows.

2 Corinthians 12:2

Have you been thinking all along that we have been defending ourselves to you? We have been speaking in the sight of God as those in Christ; and everything we do, dear friends, is for your strengthening.

2 Corinthians 12:19

I was personally unknown to the churches of Judea that are in Christ.

Galatians 1:22

. . . know that a man is not justified by observing the law, but by faith in Jesus Christ. So we, too, have put our faith in Christ Jesus that we may be justified by faith in Christ and not by observing the law, because by observing the law no one will be justified.

Galatians 2:16

If, while we seek to be justified in Christ, it becomes evident that we ourselves are sinners, does that mean that Christ promotes sin? Absolutely not!

Galatians 2:17

Praise be to the God and Father of our Lord Jesus Christ, who has blessed us in the heavenly realms with every spiritual blessing in Christ.

Ephesians 1:3

And he made known to us the mystery of his will according to his good pleasure, which he purposed in Christ.

Ephesians 1:9

. . . in order that we, who were the first to hope in Christ, might be for the praise of his glory.

Ephesians 1:12

And you also were included in Christ when you heard the word of truth, the gospel of your salvation. Having believed, you were marked in him with a seal, the promised Holy Spirit.

Ephesians 1:13

. . . which he exerted in Christ when he raised him from the dead and seated him at his right hand in the heavenly realms.

Ephesians 1:20

And God raised us up with Christ and seated us with him in the heavenly realms in Christ Jesus.

Ephesians 2:6

But now in Christ Jesus you who once were far away have been brought near through the blood of Christ.

Ephesians 2:13

Be kind and compassionate to one another, forgiving each other, just as in Christ God forgave you.

Ephesians 4:32

. . . and be found in him, not having a righteousness of my own that comes from the law, but that which is through faith in Christ—the righteousness that comes from God and is by faith.

Philippians 3:9

I press on toward the goal to win the prize for which God has called me heavenward in Christ Jesus.

Philippians 3:14

To the holy and faithful brothers in Christ at Colosse: Grace and peace to you from God our Father.

Colossians 1:2

We proclaim him, admonishing and teaching everyone with all wisdom, so that we may present everyone perfect in Christ.

Colossians 1:28

For though I am absent from you in body, I am present with you in spirit and delight to see how orderly you are and how firm your faith in Christ is.

Colossians 2:5

For in Christ all the fullness of the Deity lives in bodily form.

Colossians 2:9

. . . and you have been given fullness in Christ, who is the head over every power and authority.

Colossians 2:10

These are a shadow of the things that were to come; the reality, however, is found in Christ.

Colossians 2:17

For the Lord himself will come down from heaven, with a loud command, with the voice of the archangel and with the trumpet call of God, and the dead in Christ will rise first.

1 Thessalonians 4:16

I pray that you may be active in sharing your faith, so that you will have a full understanding of every good thing we have in Christ.

Philemon 1:6

Therefore, although in Christ I could be bold and order you to do what you ought to do.

Philemon 1:8

I do wish, brother, that I may have some benefit from you in the Lord; refresh my heart in Christ.

Philemon 1:20

We have come to share in Christ if we hold firmly till the end the confidence we had at first.

Hebrews 3:14

. . . keeping a clear conscience, so that those who speak maliciously against your good behavior in Christ may be ashamed of their slander.

1 Peter 3:16

And the God of all grace, who called you to his eternal glory in Christ, after you have suffered a little while, will himself restore you and make you strong, firm and steadfast.

1 Peter 5:10

Greet one another with a kiss of love. Peace to all of you who are in Christ.

1 Peter 5:14

4. WHAT WE ARE "WITH CHRIST"

Now if we died with Christ, we believe that we will also live with him.

Romans 6:8

Now if we are children, then we are heirs—heirs of God and coheirs with Christ, if indeed we share in his sufferings in order that we may also share in his glory.

Romans 8:17

The body is a unit, though it is made up of many parts; and though all its parts are many, they form one body. So it is with Christ.

1 Corinthians 12:12

I have been crucified with Christ and I no longer live, but Christ lives in me. The life I live in the body, I live by faith in the Son of God, who loved me and gave himself for me.

Galatians 2:20

. . . for all of you who were baptized into Christ have clothed yourselves with Christ.

Galatians 3:27

. . . made us alive with Christ even when we were dead in transgressions—it is by grace you have been saved.

Ephesians 2:5

And God raised us up with Christ and seated us with him in the heavenly realms in Christ Jesus.

Ephesians 2:6

. . . built on the foundation of the apostles and prophets, with Christ Jesus himself as the chief cornerstone.

Ephesians 2:20

I am torn between the two: I desire to depart and be with Christ, which is better by far.

Philippians 1:23

If you have any encouragement from being united with Christ, if any comfort from his love, if any fellowship with the Spirit, if any tenderness and compassion . . .

Philippians 2:1

When you were dead in your sins and in the uncircumcision of your sinful nature, God made you [2:13 Some manuscripts us] alive with Christ. He forgave us all our sins . . .

Colossians 2:13

Since you died with Christ to the basic principles of this world, why, as though you still belonged to it, do you submit to its rules . . .

Colossians 2:20

Since, then, you have been raised with Christ, set your hearts on things above, where Christ is seated at the right hand of God.

Colossians 3:1

For you died, and your life is now hidden with Christ in God.

Colossians 3:3

I saw thrones on which were seated those who had been given authority to judge. And I saw the souls of those who had been beheaded because of their testimony for Jesus and because of the word of God. They had not worshiped the beast or his image and had not received his mark on their foreheads or their hands. They came to life and reigned with Christ a thousand years.

Revelation 20:4

2

JESUS' CONTINUING PRESENCE

5.15 THREEFOLD COMING OF THE LORD, BERNARD OF CLAIRVAUX

"And the Word became flesh and dwelt among us, full of grace and truth." John 1:14

We have come to know a threefold coming of the Lord. The third coming takes place between the other two. They are clearly manifest but the third is not.

In the first coming the Lord was seen on earth and lived among men in the days when, as he himself bears witness, they saw him and hated him.

In his last coming "all flesh shall see the salvation of our God." And "they shall look on him whom they have pierced."

The other coming is hidden. In it, only the chosen see him within themselves and their souls are saved.

In brief, his first coming was in the flesh and in weakness, the intermediary coming is in the spirit and in power, the last coming will be in glory and majesty. This intermediary coming is like a road leading from the first to the last coming. In the first coming Christ was our redemption, in the last he will appear as our life, in this intermediary coming he is our rest and consolation. Do not imagine that what we are saying about the intermediary coming is simply our own fabrication. Listen to Christ himself, "If a man loves me he will keep my words, and my Father will love him, and we will come to him."

Bernard of Clairvaux, On Advent 5

5.16 THE PRACTICE OF THE PRESENCE OF GOD, BROTHER LAWRENCE

Brother Lawrence (c. 1605—1691) was born Nicolas Hermanin Hériménal, near Lunéville in the Lorraine district of France. His parents were pious and his uncle was a Discalced Carmelite brother, and there was a monastery of Carmelite nuns in Lunéville. At the age of 18 he had a sudden, overwhelming experience of the grandeur and presence of God. In his First Conversation he records that, "One day in winter while he was looking at a tree stripped of its leaves, and he realized that in a little while its leaves would reappear, followed by its flowers and fruit, he received a profound insight into God's providence that has never been erased from his soul. This insight completely freed him from the world, and gave him such a love for God that he could not say it had increased during the more than forty years that had passed." This was the beginning of his life-long practice of the presence of God.

THIRD CONVERSATION:
FAITH WORKING BY LOVE
OUTWARD BUSINESS NO DETRIMENT
PERFECT RESIGNATION THE SURE WAY

He told me, that the foundation of the spiritual life in him had been a high notion and esteem of God in faith; which when he had once well conceived, he had no other care at first, but faithfully to reject every other thought, that he might perform all his actions for the love of God. That when sometimes he had not thought of God for a good while, he did not disquiet himself for it; but after having acknowledged his wretchedness to God, he returned to Him with so much the greater trust in Him, by how much he found himself more wretched to have forgot Him.

That the trust we put in God honors Him much, and draws down great graces.

That it was impossible, not only that God should deceive, but also that He should long let a soul suffer which is perfectly resigned to Him, and resolved to endure everything for His sake.

That he had so often experienced the ready succors of Divine Grace upon all occasions, that from the same experience, when he had business to do, he did not think of it beforehand; but when it was time to do it, he found in God, as in a clear mirror, all that was fit for him to do. That of late he had acted thus, without anticipating care; but before the experience above mentioned, he had used it in his affairs.

When outward business diverted him a little from the thought of God, a fresh remembrance coming from God invested his soul, and so inflamed and transported him that it was difficult for him to contain himself.

That he was more united to God in his outward employments, than when he left them for devotion in retirement.

That he expected hereafter some great pain of body or mind; that the worst that could happen to him was, to lose that sense of God, which he had enjoyed so long; but that the goodness of God assured him He would not forsake him utterly, and that He would give him strength to bear whatever evil He permitted to happen to him; and therefore that he feared nothing, and had no occasion to consult with anybody about his state. That when he had attempted to do it, he had always come away more perplexed; and that as he was conscious of his readiness to lay down his life for the love of God, he had no apprehension of danger. That perfect resignation to God was a sure way to heaven, a way in which we had always sufficient light for our conduct.

That in the beginning of the spiritual life, we ought to be faithful in doing our duty and denying ourselves; but after that unspeakable pleasures followed: that in difficulties we need only have recourse to Jesus Christ, and beg His grace, with which everything became easy.

That many do not advance in the Christian progress, because they stick in penances, and particular exercises, while they neglect the love of God, which is the end. That this appeared plainly by their works, and was the reason why we see so little solid virtue.

That there needed neither art nor science for going to God, but only a heart resolutely determined to apply itself to nothing but Him, or for His sake, and to love Him only.

Brother Lawrence
The Practice of the Presence of God: The Best Rule of Holy Life

5.17 CHRIST OUR FOOD, C. H. SPURGEON

Without bread, I become thin like a skeleton; and, in time, I will die. Without thought, my mind becomes dwarfed, yes, and it deteriorates until I become an idiot, with a soul that just has life, but little more. And without Christ, my spirit must become a vague, shadowy emptiness. It cannot live unless it feeds on that heavenly manna which came down from heaven. Now the Christian can say, "The life that I live is Christ"; because Christ is the food on which he feeds, and the sustenance of his newborn spirit.

C. H. Spurgeon

5.18 *QUO VADIS?*, HENRYK SIENKIEWICZ

Henryk Adam Aleksander Pius Sienkiewicz (May 5, 1846–November 15, 1916) was a Polish novelist, one of the outstanding writers of the second half of the 19th century. Serializing his novels in newspapers, he became immensely popular in his time and, over a century later, is still highly valued by readers of prose. In Poland he is best known for his colorful historical novels depicting the daring deeds of Polish heroes; abroad—for his novel, Quo Vadis, *set in the reign of the Roman emperor Nero.*

CHAPTER 68

News of the miraculous rescue of Lygia was circulated quickly among those scattered Christians who had escaped destruction. Confessors came to look at her to whom Christ's favor had been shown clearly. First came Nazarius and Miriam, with whom Peter the Apostle was hiding thus far; after them came others. All, as well as Vinicius, Lygia, and the Christian slaves of Petronius, listened with attention to the narrative of Ursus about the voice which he had heard in his soul, and which commanded him to struggle with the wild bull. All went away consoled, hoping that Christ would not let His followers be exterminated on earth before His coming at the day of judgment. And hope sustained their hearts, for persecution had not ceased yet. Whoever was declared a Christian by public report was thrown into prison at once by the city watches. It is true that the victims were fewer, for the majority of confessors had been seized and tortured to death. The Christians who remained had either left Rome to wait out the storm in distant provinces, or had hidden most carefully, not daring to assemble in common prayer, unless in sand-pits outside the city. They were persecuted yet, however, and though the games were at an end, the newly arrested were reserved for future games or punished specially. Though it was believed in Rome no longer that Christians had caused the conflagration, they were declared enemies of humanity and the State, and the edict against them remained in former force.

The Apostle Peter did not venture for a long time to appear in the house of Petronius, but at last on a certain evening Nazarius announced his arrival. Lygia, who was able to walk alone now, and Vinicius ran out to meet him, and fell to embracing his feet. He greeted them with emotion all the greater that not many sheep in that flock over which Christ had given him authority, and over the fate of which his great heart was weeping, remained to him. So when Vinicius said, "Lord, because of thee the Redeemer returned her to me," he answered: "He returned her because of thy faith, and so that not all the lips which profess His name should grow silent." And evidently he was thinking then of those thousands of his children torn by wild beasts, of those crosses with which the arena had been filled, and those fiery pillars in the gardens of the "Beast"; for he spoke with great sadness. Vinicius and Lygia noticed also that his hair had grown entirely white, that his whole form was bent, and that in his face there was as much sadness and suffering as if he had passed through all those pains and torments which the victims of Nero's rage and madness had endured. But both understood that since Christ had given Himself to torture and to death, no one was permitted to avoid it. Still their hearts were cut at sight of the Apostle, bent by years, toil, and pain. So Vinicius, who intended to take Lygia soon to Naples, where they would meet Pomponia and go to Sicily, implored him to leave Rome in their company.

But the Apostle placed his hand on the tribune's head and answered, "In my soul I hear these words of the Lord, which He spoke to me on the Lake of Tiberias: 'When thou wert young, thou didst gird thyself, and walk whither thou wouldst; but when thou shalt be old, thou shalt stretch forth thy hands, and another shall gird thee, and carry thee whither thou wouldst not.' Therefore it is proper that I follow my flock."

And when they were silent, not knowing the sense of his speech, he added, "My toil is nearing its end; I shall find entertainment and rest only in the house of the Lord."

Then he turned to them saying: "Remember me, for I have loved you as a father loves his children; and whatever ye do in life, do it for the glory of God."

Thus speaking, he raised his aged, trembling hands and blessed them; they nestled up to him, feeling that to be the last blessing, perhaps, which they should receive from him.

It was destined them, however, to see him once more. A few days later Petronius brought terrible news from the Palatine. It had been discovered there that one of Caesar's freedmen was a Christian; and on this man were found letters of the Apostles Peter and Paul, with letters of James, John, and Judas. Peter's

presence in Rome was known formerly to Tigellinus, but he thought that the Apostle had perished with thousands of other confessors. Now it transpired that the two leaders of the new faith were alive and in the capital. It was determined, therefore, to seize them at all costs, for it was hoped that with their death the last root of the hated sect would be plucked out. Petronius heard from Vestinius that Caesar himself had issued an order to put Peter and Paul in the Mamertine prison within three days, and that whole detachments of pretorians had been sent to search every house in the Trans-Tiber.

When he heard this, Vinicius resolved to warn the Apostle. In the evening he and Ursus put on Gallic mantles and went to the house of Miriam, where Peter was living. The house was at the very edge of the Trans-Tiber division of the city, at the foot of the Janiculum. On the road they saw houses surrounded by soldiers, who were guided by certain unknown persons. This division of the city was alarmed, and in places crowds of curious people had assembled. Here and there centurions interrogated prisoners touching Simon Peter and Paul of Tarsus.

Ursus and Vinicius were in advance of the soldiers, and went safely to Miriam's house, in which they found Peter surrounded by a handful of the faithful. Timothy, Paul's assistant, and Linus were at the side of the Apostle.

At news of the approaching danger, Nazarius led all by a hidden passage to the garden gate, and then to deserted stone quarries, a few hundred yards distant from the Janiculum Gate. Ursus had to carry Linus, whose bones, broken by torture, had not grown together yet. But once in the quarry, they felt safe; and by the light of a torch ignited by Nazarius they began to consult, in a low voice, how to save the life of the Apostle who was so dear to them.

"Lord," said Vinicius, "let Nazarius guide thee at daybreak to the Alban Hills. There I will find thee, and we will take thee to Antium, where a ship is ready to take us to Naples and Sicily. Blessed will the day and the hour be in which thou shalt enter my house, and thou wilt bless my hearth."

The others heard this with delight, and pressed the Apostle, saying, "Hide thyself, sacred leader; remain not in Rome. Preserve the living truth, so that it perish not with us and thee. Hear us, who entreat thee as a father."

"Do this in Christ's name!" cried others, grasping at his robes.

"My children," answered Peter, "who knows the time when the Lord will mark the end of his life?"

But he did not say that he would not leave Rome, and he hesitated what to do; for uncertainty, and even fear, had been creeping into his soul for some time. His flock was scattered; the work was wrecked; that church, which before the burning of the city had been flourishing like a splendid tree, was turned into dust by the power of the "Beast." Nothing remained save tears, nothing save memories of torture and death. The sowing had yielded rich fruit, but Satan had trampled it into the earth. Legions of angels had not come to aid the perishing,—and Nero was extending in glory over the earth, terrible, mightier than ever, the lord of all seas and all lands. More than once had that fisherman of the Lord stretched his hands heavenward in loneliness and asked: "Lord, what must I do? How must I act? And how am I, a feeble old man, to fight with this invincible power of Evil, which Thou hart permitted to rule, and have victory?"

And he called out thus in the depth of his immense pain, repeating in spirit: "Those sheep which Thou didst command me to feed are no more, Thy church is no more; loneliness and mourning are in Thy capital; what dost Thou command me to do now? Am I to stay here, or lead forth the remnant of the flock to glorify Thy name in secret somewhere beyond the sea?"

And he hesitated. He believed that the living truth would not perish, that it must conquer; but at moments he thought that the hour had not come yet, that it would come only when the Lord should descend to the earth in the day of judgment in glory and power a hundred times greater than the might of Nero.

Frequently it seemed to him that if he left Rome, the faithful would follow; that he would lead them then far away to the shady groves of Galilee, to the quiet surface of the Lake of Tiberias, to shepherds as peaceful as doves, or as sheep, who feed there among thyme and pepperwort. And an increasing desire for peace and rest, an increasing yearning for the lake and Galilee, seized the heart of the fisherman; tears came more frequently to the old man's eyes.

But at the moment when he made the choice, sudden alarm and fear came on him. How was he to leave that city, in which so much martyrs' blood had sunk into the earth, and where so many lips had given the true testimony of the dying? Was he alone to yield? And what would he answer the Lord on hearing the words, "These have died for the faith, but thou didst flee?"

Nights and days passed for him in anxiety and suffering. Others, who had been torn by lions, who had been fastened to crosses, who had been burnt in the gardens of Caesar, had fallen asleep in the Lord after moments of torture; but he could not sleep, and he felt greater tortures than any of those invented by executioners for victims. Often was the dawn whitening the roofs of houses while he was still crying from the depth of his mourning heart: "Lord, why didst Thou command me to come hither and found Thy capital in the den of the 'Beast?'"

For thirty-three years after the death of his Master he knew no rest. Staff in hand, he had gone through the world and declared the "good tidings." His strength had been exhausted in journeys and toil, till at last, when in that city, which was the head of the world, he had established the work of his Master, one bloody breath of wrath had burned it, and he saw that there was need to take up the struggle anew. And what a struggle! On one side Caesar, the Senate, the people, the legions holding the world with a circle of iron, countless cities, countless lands,—power such as the eye of man had not seen; on the other side he, so bent with age and toil that his trembling hand was hardly able to carry his staff.

At times, therefore, he said to himself that it was not for him to measure with the Caesar of Rome,—that Christ alone could do that.

All these thoughts were passing through his care-filled head, when he heard the prayers of the last handful of the faithful. They, surrounding him in an ever narrowing circle, repeated with voices of entreaty, "Hide thyself, Rabbi, and lead us away from the power of the 'Beast.'"

Finally Linus also bowed his tortured head before him.

"O lord," said he, "the Redeemer commanded thee to feed His sheep, but they are here no longer or to-morrow they will not be here; go, therefore, where thou mayst find them yet. The word of God is living still in Jerusalem, in Antioch, in Ephesus, and in other cities. What wilt thou do by remaining in Rome? If thou fall, thou wilt merely swell the triumph of the 'Beast.' The Lord has not designated the limit of John's life; Paul is a Roman citizen, they cannot condemn him without trial; but if the power of hell rise up against thee, O teacher, those whose hearts are dejected will ask, 'Who is above Nero?' Thou art the rock on which the church of God is founded. Let us die, but permit not the victory of Antichrist over the vicegerent of God, and return not hither till the Lord has crushed him who shed innocent blood."

"Look at our tears!" repeated all who were present.

Tears flowed over Peter's face too. After a while he rose, and, stretching his hands over the kneeling figures, said, "May the name of the Lord be magnified, and may His will be done!"

CHAPTER 69

About dawn of the following day two dark figures were moving along the Appian Way toward the Campania.

One of them was Nazarius; the other the Apostle Peter, who was leaving Rome and his martyred co-religionists.

The sky in the east was assuming a light tinge of green, bordered gradually and more distinctly on the lower edge with saffron color. Silver-leafed trees, the white marble of villas, and the arches of aqueducts, stretching through the plain toward the city, were emerging from shade. The greenness of the sky was clearing gradually, and becoming permeated with gold. Then the east began to grow rosy and illuminate the Alban Hills, which seemed marvelously beautiful, lily-colored, as if formed of rays of light alone.

The light was reflected in trembling leaves of trees, in the dew-drops. The haze grew thinner, opening wider and wider views on the plain, on the houses dotting it, on the cemeteries, on the towns, and on groups of trees, among which stood white columns of temples.

The road was empty. The villagers who took vegetables to the city had not succeeded yet, evidently, in harnessing beasts to their vehicles. From the stone blocks with which the road was paved as far as the mountains, there came a low sound from the bark shoes on the feet of the two travelers.

Then the sun appeared over the line of hills; but at once a wonderful vision struck the Apostle's eyes. It seemed to him that the golden circle, instead of rising in the sky, moved down from the heights and was advancing on the road. Peter stopped, and asked, "Seest thou that brightness approaching us?"

"I see nothing," replied Nazarius.

But Peter shaded his eyes with his hand, and said after a while,

"Some figure is coming in the gleam of the sun." But not the slightest sound of steps reached their ears. It was perfectly still all around. Nazarius saw only that the trees were quivering in the distance, as if some one were shaking them, and the light was spreading more broadly over the plain. He looked with wonder at the Apostle.

"Rabbi! what ails thee?" cried he, with alarm.

The pilgrim's staff fell from Peter's hands to the earth; his eyes were looking forward, motionless; his mouth was open; on his face were depicted astonishment, delight, rapture.

Then he threw himself on his knees, his arms stretched forward; and this cry left his lips, "O Christ! O Christ!"

He fell with his face to the earth, as if kissing some one's feet.

The silence continued long; then were heard the words of the aged man, broken by sobs, "Quo vadis, Domine?"

Nazarius did not hear the answer; but to Peter's ears came a sad and sweet voice, which said, "If thou desert my people, I am going to Rome to be crucified a second time."

The Apostle lay on the ground, his face in the dust, without motion or speech. It seemed to Nazarius that he had fainted or was dead; but he rose at last, seized the staff with trembling hands, and turned without a word toward the seven hills of the city.

The boy, seeing this, repeated as an echo, "Quo vadis, Domine?"

"To Rome," said the Apostle, in a low voice.

And he returned.

Paul, John, Linus, and all the faithful received him with amazement; and the alarm was the greater, since at daybreak, just after his departure, pretorians had surrounded Miriam's house and searched it for the Apostle. But to every question he answered only with delight and peace, "I have seen the Lord!"

And that same evening he went to the Ostian cemetery to teach and baptize those who wished to bathe in the water of life.

And thenceforward he went there daily, and after him went increasing numbers. It seemed that out of every tear of a martyr new confessors were born, and that every groan on the arena found an echo in thousands of breasts. Caesar was swimming in blood, Rome and the whole pagan world was mad. But those who had had enough of transgression and madness, those who were trampled upon, those whose lives were misery and oppression, all the weighed down, all the sad, all the unfortunate, came to hear the wonderful tidings of God, who out of love for men had given Himself to be crucified and redeem their sins.

When they found a God whom they could love, they had found that which the society of the time could not give any one,— happiness and love.

And Peter understood that neither Caesar nor all his legions could overcome the living truth,—that they could not overwhelm it with tears or blood, and that now its victory was beginning. He understood with equal force why the Lord had turned him back on the road. That city of pride, crime, wickedness, and power was beginning to be His city, and the double capital, from which would flow out upon the world government of souls and bodies.

Henryk Sienkiewicz, Quo Vadis? *1896*

5.19 "THROWN INTO A DEEP WELL," SADHU SUNDAR SINGH

I often remember that day when, for preaching the Gospel in Tibet, I was thrown into a deep well. For three days I was in that well without food and water. The door was locked and it was quite dark. There was nothing, but dead bodies and bones in that well. It was like hell. There I was tempted: "Is your Christ going to save you, now you have been put into this prison?"

But I remember a wonderful peace and joy came to me in those hours of persecution, when my arm was broken, and there was such a bad smell. That hell seemed like heaven. I felt the presence of Living Christ. He is always with us as he has promised. I never thought that I could have any Cross with this kind of peace, but there I had that experience. After that was a wonderful thing, I was thinking that my time had come and I would be called to Heaven, when somebody opened the door. I could see no one. Then I knew what a wonderful power had delivered me. Perhaps someone will think that this was a dream, or that somebody set me free from that well, but the Man who made me free, who touched my arm—it was all right in a few minutes—was no human being. A human being could not do that, only the power of God. Now I preach, not because I know Christ through what is written about him, but because I know him from my own experience. He is the Living Savior. If Jesus Christ were not the Living Christ, I would not be preaching the gospel.

Sadhu Sundar Singh

3
TESTIMONIES TO JESUS

5.20 JESUS IN EVERY BIBLE BOOK

Jesus is the theme of the Bible. He is:
Promised: Genesis,
Revealed: the law,
Prefigured: its history,
Praised: its poetry,
Proclaimed: its prophecy
Provided: its Gospels,
Proved, its Acts,
Preeminent: its letters and
Prevails: in the book of Revelation.

OLD TESTAMENT

In Genesis
Jesus is the Seed of the woman
Jesus is the Creator God
Jesus is the ram at Abraham's altar

In Exodus
Jesus is the Passover Lamb
Jesus is our Deliverer

In Leviticus
Jesus is our High Priest
Jesus is our sacrifice for sin

In Numbers
Jesus is the Star of Jacob
Jesus is our " Lifted-up One" as the bronze serpent (Num. 21:9; John 3:14)
Jesus is the cloud and the fire

In Deuteronomy
Jesus is the true Prophet like Moses
Jesus is the great Rock
Jesus is the city of our refuge

In Joshua
Jesus is the Captain of the Lord of Hosts
The Captain of our salvation

In Judges
Jesus is the Messenger of Jehovah
The Judge and Lawgiver

In Ruth
Jesus is our Kinsman Redeemer
Jesus is our Faithful Bridegroom

In 1 Samuel
Jesus is the Judge
Jesus is the Prophet of the Lord
Jesus is our King

In 2 Samuel
Jesus is the anointed King
Jesus is the Prophet of the Lord
Jesus is the descendant of David

In 1 Kings
Jesus is the reigning King
Jesus is our temple

In 2 Kings
Jesus is the Holiest of all
Jesus is our King

In 1 Chronicles
Jesus is our King
Jesus is our Shepherd
Jesus is our Ark
Jesus is the God of our salvation

In 2 Chronicles
Jesus is our King
Jesus is our Temple

In Ezra
Jesus is the Lord of heaven and earth
Jesus is the faithful Scribe
Jesus is the Restorer of our inner temple

In Nehemiah
Jesus is the Builder
Jesus is the Rebuilder of the broken walls

In Esther
Jesus is our Mordecai
Jesus is the judging King
Jesus, the Savior of Israel, is our Advocate

In Job
Jesus is our Redeemer
Jesus is our friend who stays closer than a brother

In Psalms
Jesus is the Son of God
The Good Shepherd

In Proverbs
Jesus is our wisdom

In Ecclesiastes
Jesus is the wisdom of God

In Song of Songs
Jesus is the Lover of our souls
Jesus is the Bridegroom

In Isaiah
Jesus is the suffering Servant
Jesus is the glorified Servant
Jesus is the Prince of Peace
Jesus is the Messiah
Jesus is the mighty God

In Jeremiah
Jesus is the Lord our righteousness
Jesus is the righteous Branch
Jesus is our new covenant
Jesus is the weeping Prophet

In Lamentations
Jesus is the man of sorrows

In Ezekiel
Jesus is the glorious God
Jesus is the Son of Man
Jesus is our Shepherd

In Daniel
Jesus is the Messiah
Jesus is the fourth man in the fiery furnace
Jesus is our Rescuer

In Hosea
Jesus is the risen Son of God
Jesus is the Healer of the backslider
Jesus is the forgiving Lover

In Joel
Jesus is the giver of the Spirit
Jesus is the restorer

In Amos
Jesus is the champion of social justice

In Obadiah
Jesus is the forgiving Christ
Jesus is the mighty Savior

In Jonah
Jesus is the risen prophet
The forgiving God

In Micah
Jesus is the Messiah born in Bethlehem
The Messenger with the beautiful feet bringing the gospel

In Nahum
Jesus is our strong tower in the day of trouble
Jesus is the bringer of good news

In Habakkuk
Jesus is the Lord in his Temple
Jesus is the great Evangelist
Jesus is the God of our salvation

In Zephaniah
Jesus is the Merciful Christ
The restorer of God's lost heritage

In Haggai
Jesus is the desired of all nations

In Zechariah
Jesus is the righteous Branch
Jesus is the pierced One
Jesus is our Righteousness
Jesus is the Messiah
Jesus is the triumphant king humbly riding on a donkey
Jesus is the One sold for thirty pieces of silver

In Malachi
Jesus is the sun of righteousness with healing wings

NEW TESTAMENT

In Matthew
Jesus is the King of the Jews
Jesus is the long-awaited Messiah

In Mark
Jesus is the Servant

In Luke
Jesus is the Son of Man

In John
Jesus is the Son of God

In Acts
Jesus is the ascended Lord
Jesus is the giver of the Holy Spirit

In Romans
Jesus is our righteousness
Jesus is the justifier

In 1 Corinthians
Jesus is our resurrection

In 2 Corinthians
Jesus is the God of all comfort

In Galatians
Jesus is the Redeemer from the Law

In Ephesians
Jesus is the head of the Church
Jesus is the chief cornerstone

In Philippians
Jesus is our joy
Jesus is the supplier of our every need

In Colossians
Jesus is the fullness of the Godhead

In 1 Thessalonians
Jesus is the returning Lord

In 2 Thessalonians
Jesus is the returning Lord

In 1 Timothy
Jesus is the Mediator
Jesus is the King of kings, and Lord of lords
Jesus is our Teacher

In 2 Timothy
Jesus is our example
Jesus is the giver of a crown of righteousness

In Titus
Jesus is our great God and Savior

In Philemon
Jesus is the Friend, closer than a brother

In Hebrews
Jesus is our Intercessor
Jesus is our High Priest

In James
Jesus is the Lord drawing near
Jesus is our example in faith and deeds

In 1 Peter
Jesus is our vicarious Sufferer

In 2 Peter
Jesus is the Lord of Glory

In 1 John
Jesus is the Way
Jesus is the assurance of our salvation.

In 2 John
Jesus is the Truth

In 3 John
Jesus is the Life

In Jude
Jesus keeps us from falling

In Revelation
Jesus is the Lion of the Tribe of Judah
Jesus is the Lamb of God
Jesus is the Bright and Morning Star
Jesus is the King of kings and Lord of lords.
Jesus is the Alpha and Omega, the beginning
and the end

TESTIMONIES

TESTIMONIES IN THE BIBLE

5.21 BIBLE STUDY: INSTANCES OF FAITH IN CHRIST ORVILLE, J. NAVE

The Gospels
The wise men from the east
Matthew 2:1, 2, 11
Peter
Matthew 4:18-22; Mark 1:16-20; Luke 5:4,
5; John 6:68, 69
Andrew
Matthew 4:18-22; Mark 1:16-20; John 1:41
James and John
Matthew 4:21, 22; Mark 1:19, 20
The woman with the issue of blood
Matthew 9:21, 22
Jairus, for the healing of his daughter
Matthew 9:18, 23-25
Two blind men
Matthew 9:29, 30
Blind Bartimaeus and a fellow blind man
Matthew 20:30-34; Mark 10:46-52; Luke
18:35-42
The Samaritan leper
Luke 17:11-19
The sick people of Gennesaret
Matthew 14:36; Mark 3:10; 6:54-56
Those who brought the paralyzed man to
Jesus
Luke 5:18-20

The Syrophoenician woman
Matthew 15:22-28; Mark 7:25-30
The woman who anointed Jesus' feet
Luke 7:36-50
Those who brought those who were sick with
palsy
Matthew 9:2
Philip
John 1:45, 46
Nathanael
John 1:49
The Samaritans, who believed
Through the preaching of Jesus
John 4:39-42
Through the preaching of Philip
Acts 8:9-12
The nobleman whose child was sick
John 4:46-53
Abraham
John 8:56
The blind man whom Jesus healed on the
Sabbath
John 9:13-38
Mary, the sister of Martha
Luke 10:38-42; John 11:32
John the disciple
John 20:8

The disciples, through the miracle at Cana of Galilee
John 2:11
Jews at Jerusalem
John 2:23; 8:30; 11:45; 12:11
About three-thousand people on the day of Pentecost

Acts
Acts 2:41
About five-thousand people
Acts 4:4
Multitudes
Acts 5:14
The crippled man at Lystra
Acts 14:9
Stephen
Acts 6:8
The Ethiopian eunuch
Acts 8:37
The people of Lydda
Acts 9:35
The people of Joppa
Acts 9:42
The people of Antioch
Acts 11:21-24
Barnabas
Acts 11:24

Eunice, Lois, and Timothy
2 Timothy 1:5; Acts 16:1
Lydia
Acts 16:14
The Philippian jailor
Acts 16:31-34
Crispus
Acts 18:8
The Corinthians
Acts 18:8; 1 Corinthians 15:11
Jews at Rome
Acts 28:24

The letters
Ephesians
Ephesians 1:13, 15
Colossians
Colossians 1:2, 4
Thessalonians
1 Thessalonians 1:6; 3:6-8; 2 Thessalonians 1:3, 4
Philemon
Philemon 1:5

The book of Revelation
The congregation at Thyatira
Revelation 2:19

Orville J. Nave, Topical Bible, *1896*

TESTIMONIES FROM THE PAST 2,000 YEARS

5.22 THE NAME OF JESUS, MARTIN LUTHER

I know nothing of Jesus Christ but only his name; I have not heard or seen him corporally, yet I have, God be praised, learned so much out of the Scriptures, that I am well and thoroughly satisfied; therefore I desire neither to see nor to hear him in the body. When left and forsaken of all men, in my highest weakness, in trembling, and in fear of death, when persecuted of the wicked world, then I felt most deeply the divine power which this name, Christ Jesus, communicated unto me.

Martin Luther, Table Talk, *232*

5.23 Christ strengthens our faith, Martin Luther

It was a wonderful thing when our Savior Christ ascended up into heaven, in full view of his disciples. Some, no doubt, thought in themselves: We did eat and drink with him, and now he is taken from us, and carried up into heaven; are all these things right? Such reasonings, doubtless, some of them had, for they were not all alike strong in faith, as St Matthew writes: "When the eleven saw the Lord, they worshipped, but some doubted." And during those forty days, from the resurrection until the ascension, the Lord taught them by manifold arguments, and instructed them in all necessary things; he strengthened their faith, and put them in mind of what he had told them before, to the end they should in nowise doubt of his person.

Yet his words made little impression, for when the Lord appeared in the midst of them, on Easter-day, at evening, and said: "Peace be with you," they were perplexed and affrighted, supposing they saw a spirit; nor would Thomas believe that the other disciples had seen the Lord, until he saw the print of the nails in his hands. And though for the space of forty days he had communed with them concerning the kingdom of God, and was even ready to ascend, yet, notwithstanding, they asked him, "Lord! wilt thou at this time restore again the kingdom to Israel?"

But after this, on Whitsunday, when they had received the Holy Ghost, then they were of another mind; they then stood no more in fear of the Jews, but rose up boldly, and with great joyfulness preached Christ to the people. And Peter said to the lame man: "Silver and gold have I none, but what I have, that give I thee; in the name of Jesus Christ of Nazareth, rise up and walk." Yet notwithstanding all this, the Lord was fain to show unto him, through a vision, that the Gentiles should be partakers of the promise of life, although, before his ascension, he had heard this command from the Lord himself: "Go ye into all the world, and preach the gospel to every creature." And "Teach all nations."

The apostles themselves did not know every thing, even after they had received the Holy Ghost; yea, and sometimes they were weak in faith. When all Asia turned from St Paul, and some of his own disciples had departed from him, and many false spirits that were in high esteem set themselves against him, then with sorrow of heart he said: "I was with you in weakness, fear, and in much trembling." And, "We were troubled on every side; without were fightings, and within were fears." Hereby it is evident that he was fain to comfort him, saying: "My grace is sufficient for thee, for my power is strong in weakness."

This is to me, and to all true Christians, a comfortable doctrine; for I persuade myself also that I have faith, though it is but small, and might well be better; yet I teach the faith to others, and know, that my teaching is right. Sometimes I commune thus with myself: Thou preachest indeed God's Word; this office is committed to thee, and thou art called thereunto without thy seeking, which is not fruitless, for many thereby are reformed; but when I consider and behold my own weakness, that I eat, drink, sometimes am merry, yea, also, now and then am overtaken, being off my guard, then I begin to doubt and say: Ah! that we could but only believe.

Therefore, confident professors are troublesome and dangerous people; who, when they have but only looked on the outside of the Bible, or heard a few sermons, presently think they have the Holy Ghost, and understand and know all. But good and godly hearts are of another mind, and pray daily: "Lord, strengthen our faith."

Martin Luther, Table Talk, *229*

5.24 63 TESTIMONIES TO JESUS, JOHN CALVIN'S WRITINGS

1. Christ was vividly represented in the person of the high priest . . . [who] bore the people itself upon his shoulders and before his breast, in such a manner that in the person of one, all might be presented familiarly before God.

Comment on Exodus 39:1.

2. Christ . . . the Lamb of God, whose offering blotted out the sins of the world.

Comment on Leviticus 16:7.

3. The salvation brought by Christ is common to the whole human race, inasmuch as Christ, the author of salvation, is descended from Adam, the common father of us all.

Institutes, 2. 13:3.

4. He alone bore the punishment of many, because the guilt of the whole world was laid upon Him. It is evident from other passages . . . that "many" sometimes denotes "all" . . . That, then, is how our Lord Jesus bore the sins and iniquities of many. But in fact, this word "many" is often as good as equivalent to "all." And indeed, our Lord Jesus was offered to all the world. For it is not speaking of three or four when it says: "God so loved the world, that He spared not His only Son." But yet we must notice what the Evangelist adds in this passage: "That whosoever believes in Him shall not perish but obtain eternal life." Our Lord Jesus suffered for all and there is neither great nor small who is not inexcusable today, for we can obtain salvation in Him. Unbelievers who turn away from Him and who deprive themselves of Him by their malice are today doubly culpable. For how will they excuse their ingratitude in not receiving the blessing in which they could share by faith? And let us realize that if we come flocking to our Lord Jesus Christ, we shall not hinder one another and prevent Him being sufficient for each of us . . . Let us not fear to come to Him in great numbers, and each one of us bring his neighbors, seeing that He is sufficient to save us all.

Sermons on Isaiah 53.

5. The Son of God went to face death of His own will, to reconcile the world to the Father . . . the spontaneous sacrifice by which all the world's transgressions were blotted out.

Comment on Matthew 26:1-2.

6. [Christ's] grave would be of sweet savor to breathe life and salvation upon all the world.

Comment on Matthew 26:12.

7. Christ offered Himself as a Victim for the salvation of the human race.

Comment on Matthew 26:14-20.

8. The sacrifice [of Christ] was ordained by the eternal decree of God, to expiate the sins of the world.

Comment on Matthew 26:24.

9. [Christ was] burdened with the sins of the whole world.

Comment on Matthew 26:39.

10. Christ . . . won acquittal for the whole human race.

Comment on Matthew 27:12.

11. God had ordained [Christ] to be the . . . (sacrificial outcast) for the expiation of the world's sins.

Comment on Matthew 27:15.

12. First, whence could that confidence in pardon have sprung, if [the thief] did not sense in Christ's death . . . a sacrifice of sweet odor, able to expiate the sins of the world?

Comment on Luke 23:42.

13. [Christ] must be Redeemer of the world . . . He was there, as it were, in the place of all cursed ones and of all transgressors, and of those who had deserved eternal death.

Sermons on Christ's Passion.

14. [God] willed that [Christ] be the sacrifice to wipe out the sins of the world.

Sermons on Christ's Passion.

15. Our Lord made effective for [the pardoned thief on the cross] His death and passion which He suffered and endured for all mankind.

Sermons on Christ's Passion.

16. The Lord Jesus [was] found before the seat-seat of God in the name of all poor sinners (for He was there, as it were, having to sustain all our burdens) . . . The death and passion of our Lord Jesus . . . served . . . to wipe away the iniquities of the world.

Sermons on Christ's Passion.

17. And when he says the sin of the world he extends this kindness indiscriminately to the whole human race, that the Jews might not think the Redeemer has been sent to them alone . . . John, therefore, by speaking of the sin of the world in general, wanted to make us feel our own misery and exhort us to seek the remedy. Now it is for us to embrace the blessing offered to all, that each may make up his mind that there is nothing to hinder him from finding reconciliation in Christ if only, led by faith, he comes to Him.

Comment on John 1:29.

18. Christ . . .was offered as our Savior . . . Christ brought life because the heavenly Father does not wish the human race that He loves to perish . . . But we should remember . . . that the secret love in which our heavenly Father embraced us to Himself is, since it flows from His eternal good pleasure, precedent to all other causes; but the grace which He wants to be testified to us and by which we are stirred to the hope of salvation, begins with the reconciliation provided through Christ . . . Thus before we can have any feeling of His Fatherly kindness, the blood of Christ must intercede to reconcile God to us . . . And He has used a general term [whosoever], both to invite indiscriminately all to share in life and to cut off every excuse from unbelievers. Such is also the significance of the term "world" which He had used before. For although there is nothing in the world deserving of God's favor, He nevertheless shows He is favorable to the whole world when He calls all without exception to the faith of Christ, which is indeed an entry into life.

Moreover, let us remember that although life is promised generally to all who believe in Christ, faith is not common to all. Christ is open to all and displayed to all, but God opens the eyes only of the elect that they may seek Him by faith . . . And whenever our sins press hard on us, whenever Satan would drive us to despair, we must hold up this shield, that God does not want us to be overwhelmed in everlasting destruction, for He has ordained His Son to be the Savior of the world.

Comment on John 3:16.

19. As also it is said in John 3:16 that God so loved the world that He spared not His own Son, but delivered Him to death for our sakes. *Sermons on Christ's Passion.*

20. Again, when they proclaim that Jesus is the Savior of the world and the Christ, they have undoubtedly learned this from hearing Him . . . And He declared that the salvation He had brought was common to the whole world, so that they should understand more easily that it belonged to them also.

Comment on John 4:42.

21. It is no small consolation to godly teachers that, although the larger part of the world does not listen to Christ, He has His sheep whom He knows and by whom He is also known. They must do their utmost to bring the whole world into Christ's fold, but when they do not succeed as they would wish, they must be satisfied with the single thought that those who are sheep will be collected together by their work.

Comment on John 10:27.

22. Christ . . . offers salvation to all indiscriminately and stretches out His arms to embrace all, that all may be the more encouraged to repent. And yet He heightens by an important detail the crime of rejecting an invitation so kind and gracious; for it is as if He had said: See, I have come to call all; and forgetting the role of judge, my one aim is to attract and rescue from destruction those who

already seem doubly ruined.' Hence no man is condemned for despising the Gospel save he who spurns the lovely news of salvation and deliberately decides to bring destruction on himself.

Comment on John 12:47.

23. For [by Christ's death] we know that by the expiation of sins the world has been reconciled to God.

Comment on John 17:1.

24. He openly declares that He does not pray for the world, for He is solicitous only for His own flock [the disciples] which He received from the Father's hand. But this might seem absurd; for no better rule of prayer can be found than to follow Christ as our Guide and Teacher. But we are commanded to pray for all, and Christ Himself afterwards prayed for all indiscriminately, "Father, forgive them; for they know not what they do." I reply, the prayers which we utter for all are still limited to God's elect. We ought to pray that this and that and every man may be saved and so embrace the whole human race, because we cannot yet distinguish the elect from the reprobate . . . we pray for the salvation of all whom we know to have been created in God's image and who have the same nature as ourselves; and we leave to God's judgment those whom He knows to be reprobate.

Comment on John 17:9.

25. Moreover, we offer up our prayers unto Thee, O most Gracious God and most merciful Father, for all men in general, that as Thou art pleased to be acknowledged the Savior of the whole human race by the redemption accomplished by Jesus Christ Thy Son, so those who are still strangers to the knowledge of him, and immersed in darkness, and held captive by ignorance and error, may, by Thy Holy Spirit shining upon them, and by Thy gospel sounding in their ears, be brought back to the right way of salvation, which consists in knowing Thee the true God and Jesus Christ whom Thou hast sent.

Forms of Prayer for the Church Tracts, Vol. 2.

26. The draught appointed to Christ was to suffer the death of the cross for the reconciliation of the world.

Comment on John 18:11.

27. And surely there is nothing that ought to be more effective in spurring on pastors to devote themselves more eagerly to their duty than if they reflect that it is to themselves that the price of the blood of Christ has been entrusted. For it follows from this, that unless they are faithful in putting out their labor on the Church, not only are they made accountable for lost souls, but they are guilty of sacrilege, because they have profaned the sacred blood of the Son of God, and have made useless the redemption acquired by Him, as far as they are concerned. But it is a hideous and monstrous crime if, by our idleness, not only the death of Christ becomes worthless, but also the fruit of it is destroyed and perishes.

Comment on Acts 20:28.

28. For we ought to have a zeal to have the Church of God enlarged, and increase rather than diminish. We ought to have a care also of our brethren, and to be sorry to see them perish: for it is no small matter to have the souls perish which were bought by the blood of Christ.

Sermons on Timothy and Titus.

29. Because God does not work effectually in all men, but only when the Spirit shines in our hearts as the inward teacher, he adds to every one that believeth. The Gospel is indeed offered to all for their salvation, but its power is not universally manifest . . . When, therefore, the Gospel invites all to partake of salvation without any difference, it is rightly termed the doctrine of salvation. For Christ is there offered, whose proper office is to save that which had been lost, and those who refuse to be saved by Him shall find Him their Judge.

Comment on Romans 1:16.

30. Faith is the beginning of godliness, from which all those for whom Christ died were estranged . . . [God] loved us of His own good pleasure, as John tells us (John 3:16) . . . We

have been reconciled to God by the death of Christ, Paul holds, because His was an expiatory sacrifice by which the world was reconciled to God.

Comment on Romans 5:6-10.

31. Paul makes grace common to all men, not because it in fact extends to all, but because it is offered to all. Although Christ suffered for the sins of the world, and is offered by the goodness of God without distinction to all men, yet not all receive him.

Comment on Romans 5:18.

32. The price of the blood of Christ is wasted when a weak conscience is wounded, for the most contemptible brother has been redeemed by the blood of Christ. It is intolerable, therefore, that he should be destroyed for the gratification of the belly.

Comment on Romans 14:15.

33. For one can imagine nothing more despicable than this, that while Christ did not hesitate to die so that the weak might not perish, we, on the other hand, do not care a straw for the salvation of the men and women who have been redeemed at such a price. This is a memorable saying, from which we learn how precious the salvation of our brothers ought to be to us, and not only that of all, but of each individual, in view of the fact that the blood of Christ was poured out for each one . . . If the soul of every weak person costs the price of the blood of Christ, anyone, who, for the sake of a little bit of meat, is responsible for the rapid return to death of a brother redeemed by Christ, shows just how little the blood of Christ means to him. Contempt like that is therefore an open insult to Christ.

Comment on 1 Corinthians 8:11.

34. God was in Christ and then that by this intervention He was reconciling the world to Himself . . . Although Christ's coming had its source in the overflowing love of God for us, yet, until men know that God has been propitiated by a mediator, there cannot but be on their side a separation which prevents them from having access to God . . . [Paul] says again that a commission to offer this

reconciliation to us has been given to ministers of the Gospel . . . He says that as He once suffered, so now every day He offers the fruit of His sufferings to us through the Gospel which He has given to the world as a sure and certain record of His completed work of reconciliation. Thus the duty of ministers is to apply to us the fruit of Christ's death.

Comment on 2 Corinthians 5:19.

35. When Christ appeared, salvation was sent to the whole world.

Comment on 2 Corinthians 6:2.

36. Pighius speaks . . . that Christ, the Redeemer of the whole world, commands the Gospel to be preached promiscuously to all does not seem congruent with special election. But the Gospel is an embassy of peace by which the world is reconciled to God, as Paul teaches (2 Cor. 5:18); and on the same authority it is announced that those who hear are saved. I answer briefly that Christ was so ordained for the salvation of the whole world that He might save those who are given to Him by the Father, that He might be their life whose head He is, and that He might receive those into participation of His benefits whom God by His gratuitous good pleasure adopted as heirs for Himself. Which of these things can be denied? . . . Even those opposed to me will concede that the universality of the grace of Christ is not better judged than from the preaching of the Gospel. But the solution of the difficulty lies in seeing how the doctrine of the Gospel offers salvation to all. That it is salvific for all I do not deny. But the question is whether the Lord in His counsel here destines salvation equally for all. All are equally called to penitence and faith; the same mediator is set forth for all to reconcile them to the Father—so much is evident. But it is equally evident that nothing can be perceived except by faith, that Paul's word should be fulfilled: the Gospel is the power of God for salvation to all that believe (Rom. 1:16). But what can it be for others but a savor of death to death? as he elsewhere says (2 Cor. 2:16).

Further, since it is clear that out of the many whom God calls by His external voice very few believe, if I prove that the greater part remain unbelieving because God honors with illumination none but those whom He will, then I draw another conclusion. The mercy of God is offered equally to both kinds of men, so that those who are not inwardly taught are rendered only inexcusable.

Concerning the Eternal Predestination of God.

37. It is not enough to regard Christ as having died for the salvation of the world; each man must claim the effect and possession of this grace for himself personally.

Comment on Galatians 2:20.

38. God commends to us the salvation of all men without exception, even as Christ suffered for the sins of the whole world.

Comment on Galatians 5:12.

39. And he contenteth not himself to say, that Christ gave himself for the world in common, for that had been but a slender saying: but (sheweth that) every of us must apply to himself particularly, the virtue of the death and passion of our Lord Jesus Christ. Whereas it is said that the Son of God was crucified, we must not only think that the same was done for the redemption of the world: but also every of us must on his own behalf join himself to our Lord Jesus Christ, and conclude, It is for me that he hath suffered . . . But when we once know that the thing was done for the redemption of the whole world, pertaineth to every of us severally: it behoveth every of us to say also on his own behalf, The Son of God hath loved me so dearly, that he hath given himself to death for me . . . we be very wretches if we accept not such a benefit when it is offered to us . . . Lo here a warrant for our salvation, so as we ought to think ourselves thoroughly assured of it.

Sermons on Galatians.

40. Christ is in a general view the Redeemer of the world, yet his death and passion are of no advantage to any but such as receive that which St Paul shows here. And so we see that when we once know the benefits brought to us by Christ, and which he daily offers us by his gospel, we must also be joined to him by faith.

Sermons on Ephesians.

41. Also we ought to have good care of thos e tha t have been redeemed with the blood of our Lord Jesus Christ. If we see souls which have been so precious to God go to perdition, and we make nothing of it, that is to despise the blood of our Lord Jesus Christ.

Sermons on Ephesians.

42. For the wretched unbelievers and the ignorant have great need to be pleaded for with God; behold them on the way to perdition. If we saw a beast at the point of perishing, we would have pity on it. And what shall we do when we see souls in peril, which are so precious before God, as he has shown in that he has ransomed them with the blood of his own Son. If we see then a poor soul going thus to perdition, ought we not to be moved with compassion and kindness, and should we not desire God to apply the remedy? So then, St. Paul's meaning in this passage is not that we should let the wretched unbelievers alone without having any care for them. We should pray generally for all men.

Sermons on Ephesians.

43. He says that this redemption was procured by the blood of Christ, for by the sacrifice of His death all the sins of the world have been expiated.

Comment on Colossians 1:14.

44. For although it is true that we must not try to decide what is God's will by prying into His secret counsel, when He has made it plain to us by external signs, yet that does not mean that God has not determined secretly within Himself what He wishes to do with every single man.

But I pass from that point which is not relevant to the present context, for the apostle's meaning here is simply that no nation of the earth and no rank of society is excluded from salvation, since God wills to offer the Gospel to all without exception. . . For as there is one God, the Creator and Father of all, so, he declares, there is one Mediator, through whom access to God is not given only to one nation, or to few men of a particular class, but to all, for the benefit of the sacrifice, by which He has expiated for our sins, applies to all . . . The universal term "all" must always be referred to classes of men but never to individuals. It is as if he had said, "Not only Jews, but also Greeks, not only people of humble rank but also princes have been redeemed by the death of Christ." Since therefore He intends the benefit of His death to be common to all, those who hold a view that would exclude any from the hope of salvation do Him an injury.

Comment on 1 Timothy 2:3-5.

45. No one unless deprived of sense and judgment can believe that salvation is ordained in the secret counsel of God equally for all . . . Who does not see that the reference [1 Tim. 2:4] is to orders of men rather than individual men? Nor indeed does the distinction lack substantial ground: what is meant is not individuals of nations but nations of individuals. At any rate, the context makes it clear that no other will of God is intended than that which appears in the external preaching of the Gospel. Thus Paul means that God wills the salvation of all whom He mercifully invites by the preaching of Christ.

Concerning the Eternal Predestination of God.

46. So then, seeing it is God his will that all men should be partakers of that salvation which he hath sent in the person of his only begotten Son . . . yet we must mark that Saint Paul speaketh not here of every particular man, but of all sorts, and of all people: Therefore, when he saith, that God will have all men to be saved, we must not think that he speaketh here of Peter, or John, but his meaning is this, that whereas in times past he chose out one certain people for himself, he meaneth now to show mercy to all the world . . . but when Jesus Christ came to be a common Savior for all in general, he offered the grace of God his father, to the end that all might receive it . . . Let us see now, whether God will draw all the world to [the Gospel] or not. No, no: for then had our Lord Jesus Christ said in vain No man can come to me, unless God my Father teach him (John 6:44). . . .

It followeth then, that before the world was made, (as Saint Paul saith in the first to the Ephesians) God chose such as it pleased him: and it pertaineth not to us to know, why this man, more than that man, we know not the reason . . . Saint Paul speaketh not here of every particular man, but he speaketh of all people . . . now God showeth himself a Savior of all the world . . . Saint Paul speaketh not in this place, of the strait counsel of God, neither that he meaneth to lead us to this everlasting election and choice which was before the beginning of the world, but only sheweth us what God his will and pleasure is, so far forth as we may know it. Truth it is, that God changeth not, neither hath he two wills, neither does he use any counterfeit dealing, as though he meant one thing, but would not have it so. And yet doth the Scripture speak unto us after two sorts touching the will of God . . . God doeth exhort all men generally, thereby we may judge, that it is the will of God, that all men should be saved, as he saith also by the Prophet Ezekiel I will not the death of a sinner, but that he turn himself and live (Ezek. 18:23) . . . For Jesus Christ is not a Savior of three or four, but he offereth himself to all . . . And is he not the Savior of the whole world as well? Is Jesus Christ come to be the Mediator between two or three men only? No, no: but he is the Mediator between God and men.

Sermons on Timothy and Titus.

47. Repentance and faith must needs go together . . . God receiveth us to mercy, and daily pardoneth our faults through his free goodness: and that we be justified because Jesus Christ hath reconciled him unto us, inasmuch as he accepteth us for righteous though we be wretched sinners: in preaching this, it behoveth us to add, how it is upon condition that we return unto God: as was spoken of heretofore by the prophets.

Sermons on Timothy and Titus.

48. Indeed the death of Christ was life for the whole world.

Comment on Hebrews 8:2.

49. He suffered death in the common way of men, but He made divine atonement for the sins of the world as a Priest.

Comment on Hebrews 8:4.

50. To bear the sins means to free those who have sinned from their guilt by his satisfaction. He says many meaning all, as in Rom. 5:15. It is of course certain that not all enjoy the fruits of Christ's death, but this happens because their unbelief hinders them.

Comment on Hebrews 9:27.

51. He brought His own blood into the heavenly sanctuary in order to atone for the sins of the world.

Comment on Hebrews 13:12.

52. So we must beware, or souls redeemed by Christ may perish by our carelessness, for their salvation to some degree was put into our hands by God.

Comment on James 5:20.

53. It was not a common or a small favor that God put off the manifestation of Christ to their time, when He had ordained Him by His eternal counsel for the salvation of the world . . . a remedy for mankind . . . He ordained that Christ should be the Redeemer, who would deliver the lost race of man from ruin . . . [but] the manifestation of Christ does not refer to all indiscriminately, but belongs only to those whom He illumines by the Gospel.

Comment on 1 Peter 1:20.

54. We have the Gospel in its entirety, when we know that He who had long been promised as Redeemer came down from heaven, put on our flesh, lived in the world, experienced death and then rose again; and secondly when we see the purpose and fruits of all these things in the fact that He was God with us, that He gave us in Himself a sure pledge of our adoption, that by the grace of His Spirit He has cleansed us from the stains of our carnal iniquities and consecrated us to be temples to God, that He has raised us from the depths to heaven, that by His sacrificial death He has made atonement for the sins of the world, that He has reconciled us to the Father, and that He has been the source of righteousness and life for us. Whoever holds to these things has rightly grasped the Gospel.

Comment on 2 Peter 1:16.

55. Christ redeemed us to have us as a people separated from all the iniquities of the world, devoted to holiness and purity. Those who throw over the traces and plunge themselves into every kind of license are not unjustly said to deny Christ, by whom they were redeemed.

Comment on 2 Peter 2:1.

56. This is His wondrous love towards the human race, that He desires all men to be saved, and is prepared to bring even the perishing to safety . . . It could be asked here, if God does not want any to perish, why do so many in fact perish? My reply is that no mention is made here of the secret decree of God by which the wicked are doomed to their own ruin, but only of His loving-kindness as it is made known to us in the Gospel. There God stretches out His hand to all alike, but He only grasps those (in such a way as to lead to Himself) whom He has chosen before the foundation of the world.

Comment on 2 Peter 3:9.

57. He put this in for amplification, that believers might be convinced that the expiation made by Christ extends to all who by faith embrace the Gospel. But here the question may be asked as to how the sins of the whole world have been expiated. I pass over the dreams of the fanatics, who make this a reason to extend salvation to all the reprobate and even to Satan himself. Such a monstrous idea is not worth refuting. Those who want to avoid this absurdity have said that Christ suffered sufficiently for the whole world but effectively only for the elect. This solution has commonly prevailed in the schools. Although I allow the truth of this, I deny that it fits the passage. For John's purpose was only to make this blessing common to the whole church. Therefore, under the word "all" he does not include the reprobate, but refers to all who would believe and those who were scattered through various regions of the earth. For, as is meet, the grace of Christ is really made clear when it is declared to be the only salvation of the world.

Comment on 1 John 2:2.

58. Georgius thinks he argues very acutely when he says: Christ is the propitiation for the sins of the whole world; and hence those who wish to exclude the reprobate from participation in Christ must place them outside the world. For this, the common solution does not avail, that Christ suffered sufficiently for all, but efficaciously only for the elect. By this great absurdity, this monk has sought applause in his own fraternity, but it has no weight with me. Wherever the faithful are dispersed throughout the world, John [1 John 2:2] extends to them the expiation wrought by Christ's death. But this does not alter the fact that the reprobate are mixed up with the elect in the world. It is incontestable that Christ came for the expiation of the sins of the whole world. But the solution lies close at hand, that whosoever believes in Him should not perish but should have eternal life (John 3:15). For the present question is not how great the power of Christ is or what efficacy it has in itself, but to whom He gives Himself to be enjoyed. If possession lies in faith and faith emanates from the Spirit of adoption, it follows that only he is reckoned in the number of God's children who will be a partaker of Christ. The evangelist John sets forth the office of Christ as nothing else than by His death to gather the children of God into one (John 11:52). Hence, we conclude that, though reconciliation is offered to all through Him, yet the benefit is peculiar to the elect, that they may be gathered into the society of life. However, while I say it is offered to all, I do not mean that this embassy, by which on Paul's testimony (2 Cor. 5:18) God reconciles the world to Himself, reaches to all, but that it is not sealed indiscriminately on the hearts of all to whom it comes so as to be effectual.

Concerning the Eternal Predestination of God.

60. He again shows the cause of Christ's coming and His office when he says that He was sent to be the propitiation for sins . . . For propitiation strictly refers to the sacrifice of His death. Hence we see that to Christ alone belongs this honor of expiating for the sins of the world and taking away the enmity between God and us.

Comment on 1 John 4:10.

61. Certainly, in 2 Pet. 2:1, there is reference only to Christ, and He is called Master there. Denying . . . Christ, he says, of those who have been redeemed by His blood, and now enslave themselves again to the devil, frustrating (as best they may) that incomparable boon.

Comment on Jude 4.

62. Christ, who is the salvation of the world.

Catechism of the Church of Geneva,
Tracts, Vol. 2.

63. I John Calvin, servant of the Word of God in the church of Geneva, weakened by many illnesses . . . thank God that he has not only shown mercy to me, his poor creature . . . and suffered me in all sins and weaknesses, but what is more than that, he has made me a partaker of his grace to serve him through my work . . . I confess to live and die in this faith which he has given me, inasmuch as I have no other hope or refuge than his predestination upon which my entire salvation is grounded. I embrace the grace which he has offered me in our Lord Jesus Christ, and accept the merits of his suffering and dying that through him all my sins are buried; and I humbly beg him to wash me and cleanse me with the blood of our great Redeemer, as it was shed for all poor sinners so that I, when I appear before his face, may bear his likeness.

John Calvin's Last Will, April 25, 1564.

5.25 PROOFS OF JESUS CHRIST, BLAISE PASCAL

Blaise Pascal (June 19, 1623–August 19, 1662) was a French mathematician, physicist, and religious philosopher. Important contributions by Pascal to the natural sciences include the construction of mechanical calculators, considerations on probability theory, the study of fluids, and clarification of concepts such as pressure and vacuum. Following his conversion to Christ in 1654, he devoted himself to reflection and writing about philosophy and theology. In honor to his scientific contributions the name pascal has been given to a unit of pressure and to a programming language, as well as to many mathematical concepts, such as Pascal's Triangle.

Pascal's most influential theological work, the Pensées *is an examination of and defense of the Christian faith.*

737. Therefore I reject all other religions. In that way I find an answer to all objections. It is right that a God so pure should only reveal Himself to those whose hearts are purified. Hence this religion is lovable to me, and I find it now sufficiently justified by so divine a morality. But I find more in it.

I find it convincing that, since the memory of man has lasted, it was constantly announced to men that they were universally corrupt, but that a Redeemer should come; that it is not one man who said it, but innumerable men, and a whole nation expressly made for the purpose and prophesying for four thousand years. This is a nation which is more ancient than every other nation. Their books, scattered abroad, are four thousand years old.

The more I examine them, the more truths I find in them: an entire nation foretell Him before His advent, and an entire nation worship Him after His advent; what has preceded and what has followed; in short, people without idols and kings, this synagogue which was foretold, and these wretches who frequent it and who, being our enemies, are admirable witnesses of the truth of these prophecies, wherein their wretchedness and even their blindness are foretold.

I find this succession, this religion, wholly divine in its authority, in its duration, in its perpetuity, in its morality, in its conduct, in its doctrine, in its effects.

So I hold out my arms to my Redeemer, who, having been foretold for four thousand years, has come to suffer and to die for me on earth, at the time and under all the circumstances foretold. By His grace, I await death in peace, in the hope of being eternally united to Him. Yet I live with joy, whether in the prosperity which it pleases Him to bestow upon me, or in the adversity which He sends for my good, and which He has taught me to bear by His example.

738. The prophecies having given different signs which should all happen at the advent of the Messiah, it was necessary that all these signs should occur at the same time. So it was necessary that the fourth monarchy should have come, when the seventy weeks of Daniel were ended; and that the scepter should have then departed from Judah. And all this happened without any difficulty. Then it was necessary that the Messiah should come; and Jesus Christ then came, who was called the Messiah. And all this again was without difficulty. This indeed shows the truth of the prophecies.

739. The prophets foretold, and were not foretold. The saints again were foretold, but did not foretell. Jesus Christ both foretold and was foretold.

740. Jesus Christ, whom the two Testaments regard, the Old as its hope, the New as its model, and both as their center.

741. The two oldest books in the world are those of Moses and Job, the one a Jew and the other a Gentile. Both of them look upon Jesus Christ as their common center and object: Moses in relating the promises of God to Abraham, Jacob, etc., and his prophecies; and Job, "for I know that my redeemer liveth." See Job 19:23-25.

742. The Gospel only speaks of the virginity of the Virgin up to the time of the birth of Jesus Christ. All with reference to Jesus Christ.

748. In the time of the Messiah the people divided themselves. The spiritual embraced the Messiah, and the coarser-minded remained to serve as witnesses of Him.

751. What do the prophets say of Jesus Christ? That He will be clearly God? No; but that He is a God truly hidden; that He will be slighted; that none will think that it is He; that He will be a stone of stumbling, upon which many will stumble, etc. Let people then reproach us no longer for want of clearness, since we make profession of it.

756. What can we have but reverence for a man who foretells plainly things which come to pass, and who declares his intention both to blind and to enlighten, and who intersperses obscurities among the clear things which come to pass?

761. The Jews, in slaying Him in order not to receive Him as the Messiah, have given Him the final proof of being the Messiah.

765. Source of contradictions.—A God humiliated, even to the death on the cross; a Messiah triumphing over death by his own death. Two natures in Jesus Christ, two advents, two states of man's nature.

768. Jesus Christ typified by Joseph, the beloved of his father, sent by his father to see his brethren, etc., innocent, sold by his brethren for twenty pieces of silver, and thereby becoming their lord, their savior, the savior of strangers and the savior of the world; which had not been but for their plot

to destroy him, their sale and their rejection of him.

In prison, Joseph innocent between two criminals; Jesus Christ on the cross between two thieves. Joseph foretells freedom to the one, and death to the other, from the same omens. Jesus Christ saves the elect, and condemns the outcast for the same sins. Joseph foretells only; Jesus Christ acts. Joseph asks him who will be saved to remember him, when he comes into his glory; and he whom Jesus Christ saves asks that He will remember him, when He comes into His kingdom.

771. Jesus Christ came to blind those who saw clearly, and to give sight to the blind; to heal the sick, and leave the healthy to die; to call to repentance, and to justify sinners, and to leave the righteous in their sins; to fill the needy, and leave the rich empty.

785. I consider Jesus Christ in all persons and in ourselves: Jesus Christ as a Father in His Father, Jesus Christ as a Brother in His Brethren, Jesus Christ as poor in the poor, Jesus Christ as rich in the rich, Jesus Christ as Doctor and Priest in priests, Jesus Christ as Sovereign in princes, etc. For by His glory He is all that is great, being God; and by His mortal life He is all that is poor and abject. Therefore He has taken this unhappy condition, so that He could be in all persons and the model of all conditions.

793. Jesus Christ, without riches and without any external exhibition of knowledge, is in His own order of holiness. He did not invent; He did not reign. But He was humble, patient, holy, holy to God, terrible to devils, without any sin. Oh! in what great pomp and in what wonderful splendor He is come to the eyes of the heart, which perceive wisdom!

It is most absurd to take offence at the lowliness of Jesus Christ, as if His lowliness were in the same order as the greatness which He came to manifest. If we consider this greatness in His life, in His passion, in His obscurity, in His death, in the choice of His disciples, in their desertion, in His secret resurrection, and the rest, we shall see it to be so immense that we shall have no reason for being offended at a lowliness which is not of that order.

797. Jesus Christ said great things so simply that it seems as though He had not thought them great; and yet so clearly that we easily see what He thought of them. This clearness, joined to this simplicity, is wonderful.

801. The supposition that the apostles were impostors is very absurd. Let us think it out. Let us imagine those twelve men, assembled after the death of Jesus Christ, plotting to say that He was risen. By this they attack all the powers. The heart of man is strangely inclined to fickleness, to change, to promises, to gain. However little any of them might have been led astray by all these attractions, nay more, by the fear of prisons, tortures, and death, they were lost. Let us follow up this thought.

802. The apostles were either deceived or deceivers. Either supposition has difficulties; for it is not possible to mistake a man raised from the dead.

While Jesus Christ was with them, He could sustain them. But, after that, if He did not appear to them, who inspired them to act?

Blaise Pascal, Pensées, *Section 12*

5.26 "A STATE IN CHRIST JESUS," GEORGE FOX

George Fox (July 1624–January 13, 1691) was an English Dissenter and the founder of the Society of Friends, commonly known as the Quakers. Living in a time of great social upheaval, he rebelled against the religious and political consensus by proposing an unusual and uncompromising approach to the Christian faith. His Journal *is a text popular even among non-Quakers for its vivid account of his personal spiritual journey.*

Now I was come up in spirit through the flaming sword, into the paradise of God. All things were new; and all the creation gave unto me another smell than before, beyond what words can utter. I knew nothing but pureness, and innocence, and righteousness; being renewed into the image of God by Christ Jesus, to the state of Adam, which he was in before he fell. The creation was opened to me; and it was showed me how all things had their names given them according to their nature and virtue.

I was at a stand in my mind whether I should practice physic for the good of mankind, seeing the nature and virtues of things were so opened to me by the Lord. But I was immediately taken up in spirit to see into another or more steadfast state than Adam's innocence, even into a state in Christ Jesus that should never fall. And the Lord showed me that such as were faithful to Him, in the power and light of Christ, should come up into that state in which Adam was before he fell; in which the admirable works of the creation, and the virtues thereof, may be known, through the openings of that divine Word of wisdom and power by which they were made.

Great things did the Lord lead me into, and wonderful depths were opened unto me, beyond what can by words be declared; but as people come into subjection to the Spirit of God, and grow up in the image and power of the Almighty, they may receive the Word of wisdom that opens all things, and come to know the hidden unity in the Eternal Being.

George Fox, Journal

5.27 THY RIGHTEOUSNESS IS IN HEAVEN, JOHN BUNYAN

The scene is set for Bunyan's "waking dream" in John Brown's biography of John Bunyan.

A VOICE DID SUDDENLY DART FROM HEAVEN INTO MY SOUL

There are some natures to whom the great spiritual world of the unseen is always present as the background of life. It was so with Shakespeare. It was so also with Bunyan, though in a different way. Even when he was a child, the wrong things of the day were followed by the remorse, and fears, and dread dreams of the night. But the real struggle began later, when after his marriage and the reading of his wife's books, he was seen "going to church twice a day, and with the foremost." He had not done this long before there arose a fight with his conscience about Sunday sports, in the course of which there came the weird voices that seemed to be shouted into his ear on Elstow Green.

Somewhere on the sward round the broken pillar of the old Market Cross he was one Sunday in the middle of a game of cat [a forerunner of cricket]. He had struck it one blow from the hole and was about to strike it the second time, when, as he says, "A voice did suddenly dart from heaven into my soul, which said, Wilt thou leave thy sins and go to heaven, or have thy sins and go to hell? At this I was put to an exceeding maze. Wherefore, leaving my cat upon the ground, I looked up to heaven, and was as if I had with the eyes of my understanding, seen the Lord Jesus looking down upon me, as being very hotly displeased with me."

Thus conscience-stricken he afterwards made a desperate fling to be rid of conscience altogether, only to find, as other men have, that its grip was tighter than he thought. . . .

HIS WONDERFUL POWER OF DREAMING WAKING DREAMS

Then blossomed into shape his wonderful power of dreaming waking dreams. There were these good people at Bedford sitting on the sunny side of a mountain, while he was separated from them by a wall all about, and shivering in the cold. Round and round that wall he goes to see if there be no opening, be it ever so narrow, and at last he finds one. But it is narrow, indeed so narrow that none can get through but those who are in downright earnest, and who leave the wicked world behind them. There is just room for body and soul, but not for body and soul and sin. It must be a strait gate through which a man gets rid of self; but by dint of sidling and striving he first gets in his head, then his shoulders, and then his whole body, at which he is exceeding glad, for now too he is in the sunshine and is comforted. But as yet this is only in a dream, and dreams tarry not. . . .

"Methought I saw with the eye of my soul, Jesus Christ at God's right hand . . . One day as he was passing into the field, still with some fears in his heart, suddenly this sentence fell into his soul, 'Thy righteousness is in heaven:' and methought withal I saw with the eye of my soul, Jesus Christ at God's right hand. I saw, moreover, that it was not my good frame of heart that made my righteousness better, not yet my bad frame that made my righteousness worse; for my righteousness was Jesus Christ Himself, the same yesterday, today, and for ever. Now did my chains fall from my legs indeed; I was loosed from my afflictions and irons. Oh, methought, Christ! Christ! there was nothing but Christ that was before my eyes! I could look from myself to Him and should reckon that all those graces of God that now were green on me, were yet like those crack-groats and fourpence halfpennies that rich men carry in their purses, when their gold is in their trunks at home! Oh, I saw my gold was in my trunk at home! Oh, I saw my gold was in my trunk at home! In Christ my Lord and Savior! Now Christ was all; all my wisdom, all my righteousness, all my sanctification, and all my redemption! . . .

"Further, the Lord did also lead me into the mystery of union with the Son of God, that I was joined to him, that I was flesh of his flesh, and bone of his bone, and now was that a sweet word to me in Ephesians 5:30. By this also was my faith in him, as my righteousness, the more confirmed to me; for if he and I were one, then his righteousness was mine, his merits mine, his victory also mine. Now could I see myself in heaven and earth at once; in heaven by my Christ, by my head, by my righteousness and life, though on earth by my body or person.

"Now I saw Christ Jesus was looked on of God, and should also be looked upon by us, as that common or public person, in whom all the whole body of his elect are always to be considered and reckoned; that we fulfilled the law by him, died by him, rose from the dead by him, got the victory over sin, death, the devil, and hell, by him; when he died, we died; and so of his resurrection. 'Thy dead men shall live, together with my dead body shall they arise,' saith he (Isa 26:19). And again, 'After two days will he revive us: in the third day he will raise us up, and we shall live in his sight' (Hosea 6:2); which is now fulfilled by the sitting down of the Son of man on the right hand of the Majesty in the heavens, according to that to the Ephesians, he 'hath raised us up together, and made us sit together in heavenly places in Christ Jesus'" (Eph 2:6).

John Brown, John Bunyan
And John Bunyan, Grace Abounding to the Chief of Sinners

5.28 "I FELT MY HEART STRANGELY WARMED," JOHN WESLEY

John Wesley was an 18th century preacher and the founder of the Methodist denomination of Protestant Christianity.

He was born at Epworth, England (23 miles north-west of Lincoln) June 28, 1703, and died in London March 2, 1791.

Wesley traveled constantly, generally on horseback, preaching several times a day. He formed societies, opened chapels, examined and commissioned preachers, administered discipline, raised funds for schools, chapels, and charities, prescribed for the sick, helped to pioneer the use of electric shock for the treatment of illness, superintended schools and orphanages, wrote commentaries and other religious literature, replied to attacks on Methodism, conducted controversies, and carried on a prodigious correspondence. He is believed to have traveled more than 250,000 miles in the course of his ministry, and to have preached more than 40,000 times.

Monday, Tuesday, and Wednesday, I had continual sorrow and heaviness in my heart.

WEDNESDAY, MAY 24, 1738

I think it was about five this morning that I opened my Testament on those words, "There are given unto us exceeding great and precious promises, even that ye should be partakers of the divine nature" [2 Peter 1:4]. Just as I went out, I opened it again on those words, "Thou art not far from the kingdom of God" [Mark 12:34]. In the afternoon I was asked to go to St. Paul's. The anthem was, "Out of the deep have I called unto Thee, O Lord: Lord, hear my voice. Oh, let Thine ears consider well the voice of my complaint. If Thou, Lord, wilt be extreme to mark what is done amiss, O Lord, who may abide it? For there is mercy with Thee; therefore shalt Thou be feared. O Israel, trust in the Lord: for with the Lord there is mercy, and with Him is plenteous redemption. And He shall redeem Israel from all his sins."

"I FELT MY HEART STRANGELY WARMED"

In the evening I went very unwillingly to a society in Aldersgate Street, where one was reading Luther's preface to the Epistle to the Romans. About a quarter before nine, while he was describing the change which God works in the heart through faith in Christ, I felt my heart strangely warmed. I felt I did trust in Christ, Christ alone, for salvation; and an assurance was given me that He had taken away my sins, even mine, and saved me from the law of sin and death.

I began to pray with all my might for those who had in a more especial manner despitefully used me and persecuted me. I then testified openly to all there what I now first felt in my heart. But it was not long before the enemy suggested, "This cannot be faith; for where is thy joy?" Then was I taught that peace and victory over sin are essential to faith in the Captain of our salvation; but that, as to the transports of joy that usually attend the beginning of it, especially in those who have mourned deeply, God sometimes giveth, sometimes withholdeth, them according to the counsels of His own will.

After my return home, I was much buffeted with temptations, but I cried out, and they fled away. They returned again and again. I as often lifted up my eyes, and He "sent me help from his holy place." And herein I found the difference between this and my former state chiefly consisted. I was striving, yea, fighting with all my might under the law, as well as under grace. But then I was sometimes, if not often, conquered; now, I was always conqueror.

THURSDAY, 25

The moment I awakened, "Jesus, Master," was in my heart and in my mouth; and I found all my strength lay in keeping my eye fixed upon Him and my soul waiting on Him continually. Being again at St. Paul's in the afternoon, I could taste the good word of God in the anthem which began, "My song shall be always of the loving-kindness of the Lord: with my mouth will I ever be showing forth thy truth from one generation to another." Yet the enemy injected a fear, "If thou dost believe, why is there not a more sensible change?" I answered (yet not I), "That I know not. But, this I know, I have now peace with God. And I sin not today, and Jesus my Master has forbidden me to take thought for the morrow."

John Wesley, Journal

5.29 FOLLOWING CHRIST, JONATHAN EDWARDS

The first instance, that I remember, of that sort of inward, sweet delight in God and divine things, that I have lived much in since, was on reading those words, I Timothy 1:17. Now unto the King eternal, immortal, invisible, the only wise God, be honor and glory for ever and ever, Amen. As I read the words, there came into my soul, and was as it were diffused through it, a sense of the glory of the Divine Being; a new sense, quite different

from any thing I ever experienced before. Never any words of Scripture seemed to me as these words did. I thought with myself, how excellent a Being that was, and how happy I should be, if I might enjoy that God, and be rapt up to him in heaven, and be as it were swallowed up in him for ever! I kept saying, and as it were singing, over these words of scripture to myself; and went to pray to God that I might enjoy Him, and prayed in a manner quite different from what I used to do; with a new sort of affection. But it never came into my thought, that there was any thing spiritual, or of a saving nature in this.

From about that time, I began to have a new kind of apprehensions and ideas of Christ, and the work of redemption, and the glorious way of salvation by Him. An inward, sweet sense of these things, at times, came into my heart; and my soul was led away in pleasant views and contemplations of them. And my mind was greatly engaged to spend my time in readings and mediating on Christ, on the beauty and excellency of His person, and the lovely way of salvation by free grace in Him. . . .

On January 12, 1723, I made a solemn dedication of myself to God, and I wrote it down; giving up myself, and all that I had to God; to be for the future, in no respect, my own; to act as one that had no right to himself, in any respect. And solemnly vowed, to take God for my whole portion and felicity; looking on nothing else, as any part of my happiness, nor acting as if it were; and His law for the constant rule of my obedience: engaging to fight, with all my might. against the world, the flesh, and the devil, to the end of my life. But I have reason to be infinitely humbled, when I consider, how much I have failed, of answering my obligation. . . .

I have loved the doctrines of the Gospel; they have been to my soul like green pastures. The Gospel has seemed to me the richest treasure; the treasure that I have most desired, and longed that is might dwell richly in me. The way of salvation by Christ, has appeared, in general way, glorious and excellent, most pleasant and most beautiful. It has often seemed to me, that it would, in a great measure, spoil heaven, to receive it in any other way. That text has often been affecting and delightful to me, Isaiah 32:2, And a man shall be as an hiding place from the wind, and a covert from the tempest, . . .

It has often appeared to me delightful, to be united to Christ; to have Him for my head, and to be a member of His body; also to have Christ for my teacher and prophet. I very often think with sweetness, and longings, and pantings of soul, of being a little child, taking

hold of Christ, to be led by Him through the wilderness of this world. That text, Matthew 18:3, has often been sweet to me, Except ye be converted, and become as little children . . . I love to think of coming to Christ, to receive salvation of Him, poor in spirit, and quite empty of self, humbly exalting Him alone; cut off entirely from my own root, in order to grow into, and out of Christ: to have God in Christ to be all in all; and to live by faith on the Son of God, a life of humble, unfeigned confidence in Him. . . .

Once, as I rode out into the woods for my health, in 1737, having alighted from my horse in a retired place, as my manner commonly has been, to walk for divine contemplation and prayer, I had a view, that for me was extraordinary, of the glory of the Son of God, as mediator between God and man, and His wonderful, great, full, pure and sweet grace and love, and meek and gentle condescension. This grace that appeared so calm and sweet, appeared also great above the heavens. The person of Christ appeared ineffably excellent, with an excellency great enough to swallow up all thought and conception which continued, as near as I can judge, about an hour; which kept me the greater part of the time, in a flood of tears, and weeping aloud. I felt an ardency of soul to be, what I know not otherwise how to express, emptied and annihilated; to lie in the dust, and to be full of Christ alone; to love him with a holy and pure love; to trust in Him; to live upon Him; to serve and follow Him; and to be perfectly sanctified and made pure, with a divine and heavenly purity. I have, several other times, had views very much of the same nature, and which have had the same effects.

I have, many times, had a sense of the glory of the Third Person in the Trinity, in His office of Sanctifier; in His Holy operations, communicating divine light and life to the soul. God in the communications of His Holy Spirit, has appeared as an infinite fountain of divine glory and sweetness; being full and sufficient to fill and satisfy the soul; pouring forth itself in sweet communications, like the sun in its glory, sweetly and pleasantly diffusing light and life. And I have sometimes had an affecting sense of the excellency of the

Word of God as a Word of life; as the Light of life; a sweet, excellent, life-giving Word; accompanied with a thirsting after that Word, that it might dwell richly in my heart . . . .

Though it seems to me, that in some respects, I was a far better Christian, for two or three years after my first conversion, than I am now; and lived in a more constant delight and pleasure; yet of late years, I have had a more full and constant sense of the absolute sovereignty of God, and a delight in that sovereignty; and have had more of a sense of the glory of Christ, as a Mediator revealed in the Gospel. On one Saturday night, in particular, I had such a discovery of the excellency of the Gospel above all other doctrines, that I could not but to say to myself, "This is my chosen light, my chosen doctrine," and of Christ, "This is my chosen Prophet." It appeared sweet, beyond all expression, to follow Christ, and to be taught, and enlightened, and instructed by Him; to learn of Him, and live to Him.

Jonathan Edwards

5.30 "LOOK UNTO ME," C. H. SPURGEON

In my conversion, the very point lay in making the discovery that I had nothing to do but to look at Christ, and I should be saved. I believe that I had been a very good, attentive hearer; my own impression about myself was that nobody ever listened much better than I did. For years, as a child, I tried to learn the way of salvation; and either did not hear it set forth, which I think cannot quite have been the case, or else I was spiritually blind and deaf, and could not see it and could not hear it; but the good news that I was, as a sinner, to look away from myself to Christ, as much startled me, and came as fresh to me, as any news I ever heard in my life. Had I never read my Bible? Yes, and read it earnestly. Had I never been taught by Christian people? Yes, I had, by mother, and father, and others. Had I not heard the Gospel? Yes, I think I had; and yet, somehow, it was like a new revelation to me that I was to believe and live. I confess to have been tutored in piety, put into my cradle by prayerful; hands, and lulled to sleep by songs concerning Jesus; but after having heard the gospel continually, with line upon line, precept upon precept, here much and there much, yet, when the Word of the Lord came to me with power, it was as new as if I had lived among the unvisited tribes of Central Africa, and had never heard the tidings of the cleansing fountain filled with blood, drawn from the Savior's veins.

When, for the first time, I received the gospel to my soul's salvation, I thought that I had never really heard it before, and I began to think that the preachers to whom I had listened had not truly preached it. But, on looking back, I am inclined to believe that I had heard the gospel fully preached many hundreds of times before, and that this was the difference, that I then heard it as though I heard it not; and when I did hear it, the message may not have been any more clear in itself than it had been at former times, but the power of the Holy Spirit was present to open my ear, and to guide the message to my heart.

I sometimes think I might have been in darkness and despair until now had it not been for the goodness of God in sending a snowstorm, one Sunday morning, while I was going to a certain place of worship. When I could go no further, I turned down a side street, and came to a little Primitive Methodist Chapel. In that chapel there may have been a dozen or fifteen people. I had heard of the Primitive Methodists, how they sang so loudly that they made people's heads ache; but that did not matter to me. I wanted to know how I might be saved, and if they could tell me that, I did not care how much they made my head ache. The minister did not come that morning; he was snowed up, I suppose. At last, a very thin-looking man, a shoemaker, or tailor, or something of that sort, went up into the pulpit to preach. Now, it is well that preachers should be instructed; but this man was really stupid. He was obliged to stick to his text, for the simple reason that he had little else to say. The text was, look unto me, and be ye saved, all the ends of the earth.' He did not even pronounce the word rightly, but that did not matter. There was, I thought, a glimpse of hope for me in that text. The preacher began thus: "My dear friends, this is a very simple text indeed. It says, 'Look.' Now lookin' don't take a deal of pains. It ain't liftin' your foot or your finger; it is just, 'Look.' Well, a man needn't go to College to learn to look. You may be the biggest fool, and yet you can look. A man needn't be worth a thousand a year to be able to look. Anyone can look; even a child can look. But then the text says, 'Look unto Me.' Ay!" said he, in broad Essex, "many on ye are lookin' to yourselves, but it's no use lookin' there. You'll never find any comfort in yourselves. Some look to God the Father. No, look to Him by-and-by. Jesus Christ says, 'Look unto Me.' Some says, 'We must wait for the Spirit's workin'.' You have no business with that just now. Look to Christ. The text says, 'Look unto Me.'"

Then the good man followed up his text in this way: "Look unto Me; I am sweatin' great drops of blood. Look unto Me; I am hangin' on the cross. Look unto Me; I am dead and buried. Look unto Me; I rise again. Look unto Me; I ascend to Heaven. Look unto Me; I am sittin' at the Father's right hand. O poor sinner, look unto Me! Look unto Me!"

When he had gone to about that length, and managed to spin out ten minutes or so, he was at the end of his tether. Then he looked at me under the gallery, and I dare say, with so few present, he knew me to be a stranger. Just fixing his eyes on me, as if he knew all my heart, he said, "Young man, you look very miserable." Well, I did, but I had not been accustomed to have remarks made from the pulpit on my personal appearance before. However, it was a good blow, struck right at home. He continued, "and you always will be miserable, miserable in life, and miserable in death, if you don't obey my text; but if you obey now, this moment, you will be saved." Then, lifting up his hands, he shouted, as only a Primitive Methodist could do, "Young man, look to Jesus Christ. Look! Look! Look! You have nothing to do but to look and live."

I saw at once the way of salvation. I know not what else he said,—I did not take notice of it,—I was so possessed with that one thought. Like when the brazen serpent was lifted up, the people only looked and were healed, so it was with me. I had been waiting to do fifty things, but when I heard that word, Look!' what a charming word it seemed to me! Oh! I looked until I could almost have looked my eyes away. There and then the cloud was gone, the darkness had rolled away, and that moment I saw the sun; and I could have risen that instant, and sung with the most enthusiastic of them, of the precious blood or Christ, and the simple faith which looks alone to Him. Oh, that somebody had told me this before, "Trust Christ, and you shall be saved."

It is not everyone who can remember the very day and hour of his deliverance; but, as Richard Knill said, "At such a time of day, clang went every harp in Heaven, for Richard Knill was born again," it was e'en so with me. The clock of mercy struck in Heaven the hour and moment of my emancipation, for the time had come. Between half-past ten o'clock, when I entered that chapel, and half-past twelve o'clock, when I was back home again, what a change had taken place in me! I had passed from darkness into marvelous light, from death to life. Simply by looking to Jesus, I had been delivered from despair, and I was brought into such a joyous state of mind that, when they saw me at home, they said to me, "Something wonderful has happened to you"; and I was eager to tell them all about it. . . .

I have always considered, with Luther and Calvin, that the sum and substance of the gospel lies in that word substitution,—Christ standing in the stead of man. If I understand the gospel, it is this: I deserve to be lost for ever; the only reason why I should not be damned is, that Christ was punished in my stead, and there is no need to execute a sentence twice for sin. On the other hand, I know I cannot enter Heaven unless I have a perfect righteousness; I am absolutely certain I shall never have one of my own, for I find I sin every day; but then Christ had a perfect righteousness, and He said, "There, poor sinner, take My garment, and put it on; you shall stand before God as if you were Christ, and I will stand before God as if I had been the sinner; I will suffer in the sinner's stead, and you shall be rewarded for works which you did not do, but which I did for you." I find it very convenient every day to come to Christ as a sinner, as I came at the first. "You are no saint," says the devil. Well, if I am not, I am a sinner, and Jesus Christ came into the world to save sinners. Sink or swim, I go to Him; other hope I have none. By looking to Him, I received all the faith which inspired me with confidence in His grace; and the word that first drew my soul "Look unto Me," still rings its clarion note in my ears. There I once found conversion, and there I shall ever find refreshing renewal.

C. H. Spurgeon

5.31 DECEMBER 16, 1904, SADHU SUNDAR SINGH

Sundar Singh was brought up in the state of Punjab, in north-west India. After his mother died he became so depressed that he contemplated suicide, but was prevented from doing this by the following vision of Jesus.

I found nothing in Hindu philosophy. Only in Jesus Christ whom I used to hate, I found peace. I was spiritually blind, but in Him I found what I had been seeking for a long time. I shall never forget that day, December 16, 1904 when I burnt the Bible in the fire and my father said, "Why are you doing such a foolish thing?"

I said, "The western religion is false; we must destroy it." So I destroyed the Bible and thought I had done my duty. On the third day, I saw the power of the Living Christ. That third day I was going to commit suicide, because I had no peace in my heart. I woke up in the early morning; it was winter and I took a cold bath. Then began to pray, but not to the Christ of Christianity, but I prayed like an atheist for I had lost my faith in God. I said, "If there be a God you must show me the way of salvation or I will commit suicide." From 3:00 to 4:30 early in the morning I was praying. About 5:00 I was going to commit suicide by placing my head on the railway line, so I had only half an hour more.

Then something happened which I never expected; the room was filled with a wonderful light I saw a glorious figure standing in the room. I thought it was Buddha, Krishna or some other saint whom I used to worship and was quite prepared to worship him, but I was surprised to hear these words; "How long are you going to persecute me? I died for thee. For thee I gave my life." I could not understand, could not speak a single word. And then I saw the scars of the Living Christ, whom I thought of as a great man who used to live in Palestine and was now dead; but I found he was living, the Living Christ, not dead and gone. I was now prepared to worship Him. I saw his loving face. Though I had burnt the Bible the day before yesterday, he was not angry. I was changed! There I knew the Living Christ, the savior of the world, and my heart was full of joy and peace, which I cannot express. When I got up he disappeared. I went to tell my father. He could not believe it. "Only the day before yesterday you burnt the Bible, how can it be that you are now a Christian?" "Because now I have seen His power; He is the Living Christ. It was not an imagination that I saw Him, because before the vision I hated Him and did not worship him. If I had seen Buddha you might say it was an imagination, because I used to worship him. It was not a dream. After taking a cold bath nobody can dream. There was reality, the Living Christ."

Sadhu Sundar Singh

4

THEOLOGIANS AND CHRISTIAN RESPONSES TO JESUS

5.32 ENFOLDED IN JESUS' LOVE, JULIAN OF NORWICH

It was at that time that the Lord gave me a spiritual understanding of the warm friendliness of his love. I saw that he is everything which is good and comfortable. He is our clothing: out of love for us he wraps us around, fastens the clasp, and enfolds us in his love, so that he will never leave us. I saw that he is everything that is good for us.

Julian of Norwich, Revelations of Divine Love

5.33 I AM NOTHING, WILLIAM HILTON

I am nothing, I have nothing. I desire nothing but the love of Jesus in Jerusalem.

Walter Hilton, The Scale of Perfection

5.34 IMITATING CHRIST AND DESPISING ALL EARTHLY VANITIES, THOMAS À KEMPIS

"He who follows Me, walks not in darkness," says the Lord, John 8:12. By these words of Christ we are advised to imitate His life and habits, if we wish to be truly enlightened and free from all blindness of heart. Let our chief effort, therefore, be to study the life of Jesus Christ.

The teaching of Christ is more excellent than all the advice of the saints, and he who has His spirit will find in it a hidden manna. Now, there are many who hear the Gospel often but care little for it because they have not the spirit of Christ. Yet whoever wishes to understand fully the words of Christ must try to pattern his whole life on that of Christ.

What good does it do to speak learnedly about the Trinity if, lacking humility, you displease the Trinity? Indeed it is not learning that makes a man holy and just, but a virtuous life makes him pleasing to God. I would rather feel contrition than know how to define it. For what would it profit us to know the whole Bible by heart and the principles of all the philosophers if we live without grace and the love of God? Vanity of vanities and all is vanity, except to love God and serve Him alone.

This is the greatest wisdom—to seek the kingdom of heaven through contempt of the world. It is vanity, therefore, to seek and trust in riches that perish. It is vanity also to court honor and to be puffed up with pride. It is vanity to follow the lusts of the body and to desire things for which severe punishment later must come. It is vanity to wish for long life and to care little about a well-spent life. It is vanity to be concerned with the present only and not to make provision for things to come. It is vanity to love what passes quickly and not to look ahead where eternal joy abides.

Thomas à Kempis, Imitation of Christ, *1.1*

5.35 BEARING THE CROSS, THOMAS À KEMPIS

WE OUGHT TO DENY OURSELVES AND IMITATE CHRIST THROUGH BEARING THE CROSS

The voice of Christ

My child, the more you depart from yourself, the more you will be able to enter into Me. As the giving up of exterior things brings interior peace, so the forsaking of self unites you to God. I will have you learn perfect surrender to My will, without contradiction or complaint.

Follow Me. I am the Way, the Truth, and the Life. Without the Way, there is no going. Without the Truth, there is no knowing. Without the Life, there is no living. I am the Way which you must follow, the Truth which you must believe, the Life for which you must hope. I am the inviolable Way, the infallible Truth, the unending Life. I am the Way that is straight, the supreme Truth, the Life that is true, the blessed, the uncreated Life. If you abide in My Way you shall know the Truth, and the Truth shall make you free, and you shall attain life everlasting.

If you wish to enter into life, keep My commandments. If you will know the truth, believe in Me. If you will be perfect, sell all. If you will be My disciple, deny yourself. If you will possess the blessed life, despise this present life. If you will be exalted in heaven, humble yourself on earth. If you wish to reign with Me, carry the Cross with Me. For only the servants of the Cross find the life of blessedness and of true light.

The disciple

Lord Jesus, because Your way is narrow and despised by the world, grant that I may despise the world and imitate You. For the servant is not greater than his Lord, nor the disciple above the Master. Let Your servant be trained in Your life, for there is my salvation and true holiness. Whatever else I read or hear does not fully refresh or delight me.

The voice of Christ

My child, now that you know these things and have read them all, happy will you be if you do them. He who has My commandments and keeps them, he it is that loves Me. And I will love him and will show Myself to him, and will bring it about that he will sit down with Me in My Father's Kingdom.

The disciple

Lord Jesus, as You have said, so be it, and what You have promised, let it be my lot to win. I have received the cross, from Your hand I have received it. I will carry it, carry it even unto death as You have laid it upon me. Truly, the life of a good religious man is a cross, but it leads to paradise. We have begun—we may not go back, nor may we leave off.

Take courage, brethren, let us go forward together and Jesus will be with us. For Jesus' sake we have taken this cross. For Jesus' sake let us persevere with it. He will be our help as He is also our leader and guide. Behold, our

King goes before us and will fight for us. Let us follow like men. Let no man fear any terrors. Let us be prepared to meet death valiantly in battle. Let us not suffer our glory to be blemished by fleeing from the Cross.

Thomas à Kempis, The Imitation of Christ

5.36 Loving Jesus above all things, Thomas à Kempis

Blessed is he who appreciates what it is to love Jesus and who despises himself for the sake of Jesus. Give up all other love for His, since He wishes to be loved alone above all things.

Affection for creatures is deceitful and inconstant, but the love of Jesus is true and enduring. He who clings to a creature will fall with its frailty, but he who gives himself to Jesus will ever be strengthened.

Love Him, then; keep Him as a friend. He will not leave you as others do, or let you suffer lasting death. Sometime, whether you will or not, you will have to part with everything. Cling, therefore, to Jesus in life and death; trust yourself to the glory of Him who alone can help you when all others fail.

Your Beloved is such that He will not accept what belongs to another—He wants your heart for Himself alone, to be enthroned therein as King in His own right. If you but knew how to free yourself entirely from all creatures, Jesus would gladly dwell within you.

You will find, apart from Him, that nearly all the trust you place in men is a total loss. Therefore, neither confide in nor depend upon a wind-shaken reed, for "all flesh is grass" (Is. 15:6), and all its glory, like the flower of grass, will fade away.

You will quickly be deceived if you look only to the outward appearance of men, and you will often be disappointed if you seek comfort and gain in them. If, however, you seek Jesus in all things, you will surely find Him. Likewise, if you seek yourself, you will find yourself—to your own ruin. For the man who does not seek Jesus does himself much greater harm than the whole world and all his enemies could ever do.

Thomas à Kempis, The Imitation of Christ

5.37 Few love the Cross of Jesus, Thomas à Kempis

Jesus has always many who love His heavenly kingdom, but few who bear His cross. He has many who desire consolation, but few who care for trial. He finds many to share His table, but few to take part in His fasting. All desire to be happy with Him; few wish to suffer anything for Him. Many follow Him to the breaking of bread, but few to the drinking of the chalice of His passion. Many revere His miracles; few approach the shame of the Cross. Many love Him as long as they encounter no hardship; many praise and bless Him as long as they receive some comfort from Him. But if Jesus hides Himself and leaves them for a while, they fall either into complaints or into deep dejection. Those, on the contrary, who love Him for His own sake and not for any comfort of their own, bless Him in all trial and anguish of heart as well as in the bliss of consolation. Even if He should never give them consolation, yet they would continue to praise Him and wish always to give Him thanks. What power there is in pure love for Jesus—love that is free from all self-interest and self-love!

Do not those who always seek consolation deserve to be called mercenaries? Do not those who always think of their own profit and gain prove that they love themselves rather than Christ? Where can a man be found who desires to serve God for nothing? Rarely indeed is a man so spiritual as to strip himself of all things. And who shall find a man so truly poor in spirit as to be free from every creature? His value is like that of things brought from the most distant lands.

If a man give all his wealth, it is nothing; if he do great penance, it is little; if he gain all knowledge, he is still far afield; if he have great virtue and much ardent devotion, he still lacks a great deal, and especially, the one thing that is most necessary to him. What is this one thing? That leaving all, he forsake himself, completely renounce himself, and give up all private affections. Then, when he has done all that he knows ought to be done, let him consider it as nothing, let him make little of what may be considered great; let him in all honesty call himself an unprofitable servant. For truth itself has said: "When you shall have done all these things that are commanded you, say: we are unprofitable servants'" (Luke 17:10).

Then he will be truly poor and stripped in spirit, and with the prophet may say: "I am alone and poor," Ps. 24:16. No one, however, is more wealthy than such a man; no one is more powerful, no one freer than he who knows how to leave all things and think of himself as the least of all.

Thomas à Kempis, The Imitation of Christ

5.38 TRANSFORMED BY THE BEHOLDING OF CHRIST, RICHARD SIBBES

The very beholding of Christ is a transforming sight. The Spirit that makes us new creatures, and stirs us up to behold this Savior, causes it to be a transforming beholding. If we look upon him with the eye of faith, it will make us like Christ; for the gospel is a mirror, and such a mirror, that when we a look into it, and see ourselves interested in it, we are changed from glory to glory, 2 Cor. 3:18. A man cannot look upon the love of God and of Christ in the gospel, but it will change him to be like God and Christ For how can we see Christ, and God in Christ, but we shall see how God hates sin, and this will transform us to hate it as God cloth, who hated it so that it could not be expiated but with the blood of Christ, God man. So, seeing the holiness of God in it, it will transform us to be holy. When we see the love of God in the gospel, and the love of Christ giving himself for us, this will transform us to love God. When we see the humility and obedience of Christ, when we look on Christ as God's chosen servant in all this, and as our surety and head, it transforms us to the like humility and obedience. Those that find not their dispositions in some comfortable measure wrought to this blessed transformation, they have not yet those eyes that the Holy Ghost requireth here. Behold my servant whom I have chosen, my beloved in whom my soul delighteth.'

Richard Sibbes, A Description of Christ

5.39 CLOTHED WITH CHRIST, DON BENEDETTO

Don Benedetto, a student of the Spanish Reformer Juan de Valdes, was an Italian Reformation writer. The following extract comes from one of the most popular books of the Italian Reformation. About 60,000 copies of The Benefit of Christ Crucified *were printed between 1541-1548.*

HOW THE CHRISTIAN MAN APPARELED OR CLOTHETH HIMSELF WITH CHRIST.

To talk of Christ and of his gifts to a good Christian can never seem tedious nor painful, although a thing were repeated a thousand times. I say, that the Christian knoweth Christ to be his by faith, with all his righteousness, holiness, and innocence. And as a man appareled himself with a very fair and precious garment when he will present himself to the presence of a great lord, so the Christian, appareled and covered with the innocence of Christ and with all his perfections, presenteth himself before God the Lord of all, putting his trust in the merits of Christ none otherwise than if he had merited and obtained [them all]; faith (without doubt) causeth that we possess Christ and all that is his, as every one of us possesseth his own garment. And therefore to apparel ourselves with Christ is none other thing than to believe assuredly that Christ is ours (as true it is if we believe it), and to believe that by this heavenly garment we be dearly beloved and acceptable in the presence of God; because it is most certain that he is a most kind Father, hath given unto us his Son, and willeth that all his righteousness and all that he is, that he may and that he hath wrought, be in our jurisdiction and rule, in such manner that it is lawful for us to glory as though we by our own power had gotten and wrought them. Whosoever then believeth this shall without fail find that which he believeth to be very true, as we have above shewed. Then the Christian man ought to have a firm faith and trust that all the goods, all the grace, and all the riches of Christ be his; for God having given us Christ, how may it be that he giveth not us all things with him?

If this be true (as indeed it is) the Christian man may say truly, I am the son of God, Christ is my brother, I am lord of heaven and earth, of hell, of death, and of the law; and therefore the law cannot accuse nor say evil of me, being made mine the righteousness of my Christ. This faith is that only which maketh a man to be called a Christian, and it appareled him with Christ, as we have said. And this may properly be called a great mystery, under which are contained the things of Almighty God both marvelous and unheard, the which cannot enter into the heart of man, if God do not mollify it with his grace, as he promiseth by the mouth of Ezekiel, saying, A new heart will I give you, and a new spirit will I put into you: as for that stony heart I will take it out of your body, and give you a fleshly heart. He then which doth not believe in this manner, that is to say, that Christ is his with all his goods that he possesseth, he (I say) cannot call himself a true Christian, nor never can have a merry and a quiet conscience, nor a good and a fervent mind to work well, and shall fall very soon from good works, or rather he can never do any that may be truly called good works. This only faith and trust that we have in the merits of Christ maketh men true Christians, strong, rejoicing, merry, in love with God, ready to do good works, possessors of the kingdom of God, and his dearly beloved children, in whom truly and certainly the Holy Ghost dwelleth.

What mind is so abject, or lewd, vile, and cold, that considering the inestimable greatness of the gift which God hath given unto us, giving us his most dearly-beloved Son with all his perfections, is not inflamed with most ardent desire to be like unto him in good works, forsomuch as he is also given to us of the Father for an example, whom we ought always to behold, forming on such manner our life and conversation that it should be a representation of following the life of Christ; for, as Saint Peter saith, Christ suffered for us, leaving us an example that we should follow his steps. By considering of this springeth the other manner of appareling us with Christ, the which we may call example; for the Christian ought to rule all his life by the example of Christ, conforming himself like unto him in all his thoughts, words, and works, leaving his ill life past, and appareling himself [with] a new life, that is to say, with the life of Christ. Whereupon Saint Paul saith, Let us cast away the works of darkness, and [let] us apparel ourselves with the armor of light: let us walk honestly as it were in daylight, not in banqueting [and] drunkenness, neither in chambering and wantonness, neither in strife and envying; but let us put upon us our Lord Jesus Christ, and let us not make provision for the flesh to fulfill the lusts of it. Wherefore the true Christian man being enamored on Christ, saith thus within himself, Since Christ having no need of me, hath recovered me with his own blood, and became poor to make me rich, I will in like manner again give my goods and my life for the love and health of my neighbor; and even as I am appareled with Christ through the love that he hath borne to me, so will I that my neighbor in Christ for the love that I bare unto him for Christ's sake be appareled with me and my goods. And if a man do not in this manner, then is be not yet a true Christian man, and therefore let not any man brag or say, I love Christ, if he love not the members and the brethren of Christ; for if we love not our neighbor for whose sake Christ hath shed his own precious blood, we cannot say truly that we do love Christ, who being equal with God, was obedient to the Father, even to the death of the cross, and hath loved and redeemed us, giving unto us himself with all his works and with all that he possesseth. In this same self manner, forsomuch as we be abundantly rich with the goods of Christ, we ought to be obedient to God again, and to offer and give our works, and all that is ours and ourselves, likewise to our neighbors and brethren in Christ, serving them in all their needs, and being to them, as a man might say,

another Christ. And even as Christ was humble, meek, and most far off from contention and strife, so ought we to give ourselves altogether to humbleness and meekness, fleeing all strife and contention, no less those that consist in words and disputations, than those that consist in deeds. Even as Christ suffered all the persecutions and shames of the world for the glory of God, so ought we joyfully to sustain the shames and persecutions that the false Christians do to all those who will live godly in Christ. Christ did give his life for his enemies and prayed for them on the cross, and so we ought ever to pray for our enemies, and give our life gladly for their health. And this is to follow Christ's footsteps, as Saint Peter saith. For when we know Christ with all his riches to be our own, which is to clothe us with Christ, and to become clean and pure of all spots, there resteth then none other thing for us to do but to glorify God through the following of Christ, and to do the selfsame thing to our brethren that Christ hath done to us; and that, through his own word, we bear in mind without ceasing, that whatsoever good or benefit we do to his brethren and ours he accepteth as benefit done to him. And without doubt, forsomuch as the true Christians are the members of Christ, we can do neither good nor evil unto the true Christian man, but we do evil or good to Christ, forasmuch as he rejoiceth and suffereth in his members. Then as Christ is our apparel, by faith, so ought we through love to be the apparel of our brethren, and the selfsame care and regard that we have of our own body we ought to have of theirs who are true members of our body, of the which Christ is the head. This is that godly love and charity which springeth up out of the unfeigned faith wherewith God inspireth his elects, of the which Saint Paul saith that it worketh through love.

But forasmuch as the life of Christ, with the imitation or following of which we ought to apparel ourselves, was a perpetual cross, full of tribulation, shame, and persecutions; if we will conform ourselves and become like unto his life, it is needful that we do bear continually the cross, as he himself saith, If any man will follow me let him deny himself, and take up his cross daily, and follow me. The chief cause of this cross is that our Lord God with this exercise will mortify in us the affections of the mind and the appetites and lusts of the flesh, to the intent that we may comprehend in ourselves that perfection in the which we are comprehended of Christ, through the incorporation and being made one body in him, and will that our faith, fined as gold in the furnace of adversity, shine to his praise. And moreover, he will that by our infirmities we shall illustrate and set forth his mighty power, the which the world (in despite of itself) seeth in us when our frailness through tribulations and persecutions become strong, and the more it is beaten down and oppressed, so much the more it becometh strong and stable or steadfast. Whereupon St. Paul saith, We have this treasure in earthen vessels, that the excellency of the power might be of God, and not ours. We are troubled on every side, yet are we not utterly without shift; we are in poverty, but not utterly without somewhat; we suffer persecution, but are not forsaken therein; we are cast down, nevertheless we perish not; and always we bear about in our body the dying of our Lord Jesus, that the life of Jesus might appear in our bodies.

Then seeing Christ and his dear disciples have glorified God with their tribulations, let us also embrace them joyfully, saying with Saint Paul, God forbid that I should glory but in the cross of our Lord Jesus Christ. And let us work and behave ourselves in such sort that the world (to his own hurt) may know and see with his eyes the marvelous effects that God worketh in them that sincerely embrace the grace of the Gospel; let the man of the world (I say) see with how much tranquility and quietness of mind the true Christians

sustain the loss of goods, the death of their children, slanders, infirmities of the body, and the persecutions of the false Christians; let them see how these only do honor God in the spirit and truth, thankfully taking at the hand of him all that happeneth to them, counting for good, just, and holy, all that he doeth; and in all prosperity and adversity praising and thanking him as a most good and merciful Father, and knowledging it for a great gift of God to suffer, and specially for the gospel and following of Christ before all things, knowing that tribulation bringeth patience, patience bringeth experience, experience bringeth hope, and hope makes not ashamed. I say that patience worketh experience; for God having promised to help in tribulations them that trust in him, we know it by experience whilst we stand strong and constant and be holden up by the hand of God, which thing we cannot do by our own strength. Then through patience we have experience, that the Lord bringeth the help that he hath promised in our need, through which our hope is established; therefore it should be to him much ingratitude and unthankfulness not to abide and look for that help and favor at his hand which we had before by experience found so certain and constant. But what needeth so many words? it ought to be sufficient and enough to know that the true Christian men through tribulations apparel themselves with the image and likeness of Christ crucified, which if we shall beer willingly we shall apparel ourselves afterward with the image of Christ glorified; for even as the afflictions of Christ now abound in us, even so through Christ shall also abound our consolation and comfort; and if we suffer with him we shall reign together with him.

Don Benedetto, Benefit of Christ Crucified, *1541*

5.40 CONVERTED TO CHRIST, JOHN OWEN

The corrupt principle of sin works early in our natures, and for the most part prevents grace from working in us (Ps. 58:3). As we grow mentally and physically, our natures increasingly become the willing instruments of unrighteousness (Rom. 6:13). This perverse ruling principle in us reveals itself more and more as we grow older (Eccl. 11:10). So the child, as it grows, begins to commit actual sins, e.g., lying.

SIN INCREASES

As men grow in their unregenerate state, sin gains ground subjectively and objectively. The natural subjective desires of the body grow stronger, and objectively the physical organs for the fulfillment of these desires are developing. But those subjective desires ruled by sin become sinful desires, and the organs for the fulfilling of those desires become instruments of sin. Thus when Paul was confronted by God's commandments which forbade him to fulfill those sinful desires, he was tempted more strongly to satisfy his lusts (Rom. 7:8). Timothy is warned to flee youthful lusts' (2 Tim. 2:22). David prayed that the sins of his youth would not be remembered and held against him (Ps. 25:7). It is these sins of youth that are often the torment of old age (Job 20:11).

God often allows men to fall into great actual sins in order to awaken their consciences or as a judgment on them (Acts 2:36, 37). He allows them to fulfill the desires of their heart. Then a dominant habit of sinning takes hold of men. Men become hardened in sin and lose all sense of shame.

Yet there is still hope, even for the worst of sinners (1 Cor. 6:9, 11; Matt. 12:31, 32; Luke 12:10). Firstly, because, in spite of the depravity of nature, various feelings, fears, forebodings, or what they have been taught or heard in sermons may stir up the nearly extinguished "celestial fire" within men. These are inbred notions of good and evil, right and wrong, rewards and punishments, coupled with the sense that God can see us, and that he may be willing to help us, if only we did not dread facing him. And

secondly, God works on men by his Spirit through many outward means to make them consider him. "God is not in all their thoughts" (Ps. 10:4). Whatever they do in religion it is not to glorify God (Amos 5:25).

VARIETY IN GOD'S WAYS

God may begin his work in several ways. He may begin it by sudden, startling judgments (Rom. 1:18; Ps. 107:25-28; Jonah 1:4, 7; Ex. 9:28). He may begin it by personal affliction and disaster (Job 33:19, 20; Ps. 78:34, 35; Hos. 5:15; 1 Kings 17:18; Gen. 42:21, 22; Eccl. 7:14). He may begin it by remarkable deliverances from death along with other great mercies (2 Kings 5:15). He may begin it by the witness of others (1 Pet. 3:1, 2). He may begin it by the Word of God (1 Cor 14:24, 25; Rom. 7:7).

Yet in spite of all these, men often take no notice because their minds are still dark. They think they are as good as they can be. They love to be popular and fear losing their friends. They have good intentions which come to nothing. Satan blinds their minds and they are full of love for their lusts and pleasures.

THE SPIRIT CONVINCES OF SIN

In calling men to God the Holy Spirit first convinces them of sin. The sinner is made to consider his sin, and feel its guilt on his conscience.

The Holy Spirit convinces of sin by the preaching of the law (Ps. 50:21; Rome 7:7; John 16:8).

Some lose all sense of conviction because the power of their own lusts dulls this conviction. They are healed superficially but there has been no real repentance. Thus they are led into a false sense of peace with God. The world draws them back into its evil clutches (Prov. 1:11, 14). They are not immediately punished for their sins (Eccl. 8:11; 2 Pet. 3:4).

In others the Holy Spirit is pleased to carry on this work of conviction until it results in conversion. A conflict between corruptions and convictions is aroused (Rom. 7:7, 9). Promises to be and do better are made (Hos. 6:4). Great distress may arise in the soul as it is torn between the power of corruption and the terror of conviction.

The Holy Spirit awakens in them a dread about their eternal destiny. They feel sorrow and shame (Gen. 3:7; Acts 2:37). They begin to fear eternal wrath and damnation (Heb. 2:15; Gen. 3:8, 10). They want to know the way of salvation (Mic. 6:6, 7; Acts 2:37; 16:30). They begin to pray for salvation, abstain from sin and make every effort to live a better life. They are brought under the spirit of bondage to fear (Rom. 8:15; Gal. 4:22, 24).

These fears are not required as a duty man must fulfill before he can be saved. He may indeed feel these fears, but God could quite easily convert him without them. God deals with each person differently. But two things are necessary.

The sinner must be brought to acknowledge his guilt before God without excuses or blaming others (Rom. 3:19; Gal. 3:22). He must acknowledge his need of a physician.

As his only hope of salvation lies in receiving and believing the gospel, this he must do or he will not be saved. His duty then is clear. He must receive the revelation of Jesus Christ and the righteousness of God in him (John 1:12). He must accept the sentence of the law (Rom. 3:4, 19, 20; 7:12, 13). He must be careful not to believe everything that is put to him as to how he can be saved (Mic 6:6, 7). In particular he must beware of false religious cults, and of believing that he can somehow save himself by his own self-righteousness.

There are two dangers of which to beware. The first is thinking, I have not sorrowed enough or truly repented of my sin'. No degrees of sorrow are prescribed in the gospel. God alone can work true repentance in you. Repentance is his gift to you.

The second great danger is thinking that you are so bad a sinner that Christ cannot possibly save you. Remember, the more difficult the disease is to cure, the more glory does the physician get when he cures it. Christ calls to himself the worst of sinners, so that he might get the greater glory for their salvation.

FAITH IN CHRIST

God completes his work of conversion by regenerating the sinner and so enabling him to turn from his sins and believe on the Lord Jesus Christ. This is the special work of the gospel (John 1:17; Rom. 1:16; 1 Pet. 1:23; James 1:18; Eph. 3:8, 10). The gospel must be preached (Rom. 10:13, 15). The preaching of the gospel is accompanied with a revelation of God's will (John 6:29). 'Believe on the Lord Jesus Christ, and you will be saved' (Acts 16:31). To reject this call makes God a liar because it shows contempt for his love and grace (1 John 5:10; John 3:33).

Christ must be preached as crucified (John 3:14, 15; Gal. 3:1; Is. 55:1, 3; 65:1), and seen as the only Savior of sinners (Matt. 1:21; 1 Thess. 1:10). There is a way of escape from the curse of the law (Ps. 130:4; Job 33:24; Acts 4:12; Rom. 3:25; 2 Cor. 5:21; Gal. 3:13)! God is well pleased with Christ's atonement and wants us to accept it (2 Cor. 5:18, 20; Is. 53:11, 12; Rom. 5:10, 11). If we believe, we shall be pardoned (Rom. 8:1, 3, 4; 10:3, 4; 1 Cor. 1:30, 31; 2 Cor. 5:21; Eph. 2:8, 10).

The gospel is filled with such reasons, invitations, encouragements, exhortations and promises to persuade us to receive Christ. They are all designed to explain and declare the love, grace, faithfulness and good will of God in Christ.

In preaching, God often causes some special word to fix itself on the mind of the sinner, and by the effectual working of the Holy Spirit that word is made the means of bringing the sinner to conversion.

THE HOLY SPIRIT GIVES A DESIRE TO OBEY CHRIST

When the Holy Spirit brings a sinner to put his faith in Christ, his heart is also filled by the same Holy Spirit with a holy desire wholeheartedly to obey Christ and turn from all sin.

Those thus converted to Christ, are, on their confession or profession of faith, admitted into the society of the church and into all the mysteries of the faith.

John Owen, The Work of Conversion

5.41 JOY IN JESUS, BLAISE PASCAL

The year of grace 1654, Monday, 23 November, feast of St. Clement, pope and martyr, and others in the martyrology. Vigil of St. Chrysogonus, martyr, and others.
From about half past ten at night until about half past midnight,
FIRE.
God of Abraham, God of Isaac, God of Jacob not of the philosophers and of the learned.
Certitude. Certitude. Feeling. Joy. Peace.
God of Jesus Christ.
My God and your God.
Your God will be my God.
Forgetfulness of the world and of everything, except God.
He is only found by the ways taught in the Gospel.
Grandeur of the human soul.
Righteous Father, the world has not known you, but I have known you.
Joy, joy, joy, tears of joy.

I have departed from him:
They have forsaken me, the fount of living water.
My God, will you leave me?
Let me not be separated from him forever.
This is eternal life, that they know you, the one true God, and the one that you sent, Jesus Christ.
Jesus Christ.
Jesus Christ.
I left him; I fled him, renounced, crucified.
Let me never be separated from him.
He is only kept securely by the ways taught in the Gospel:
Renunciation, total and sweet.
Complete submission to Jesus Christ and to my director.
Eternally in joy for a day's exercise on the earth.
May I not forget your words. Amen.

Blaise Pascal

5.42 JESUS IS THE WAY AND THE TRUTH AND THE LIFE, FRANÇOIS FÉNELON

François de Salignac de la Mothe, more commonly known as François Fénelon (1651–1715), was a French Roman Catholic theologian, poet and writer. Fénelon was appointed Archbishop of Cambrai in 1695, however the publication of his Explanation of the Sayings of the Saints on the Interior Life *was condemned and Fénelon retired.*

Christ is "the way, and the truth, and the life." The grace which sanctifies as well as that which justifies, is by Him and through Him. He is the true and living way; and no man can gain the victory over sin, and be brought into union with God, without Christ. And when, in some mitigated sense, we may be said to have arrived at the end of the way by being brought home to the Divine fold and reinstated in the Divine image, it would be sad indeed if we should forget the way itself, as Christ is sometimes called. At every period

of our progress, however advanced it may be, our life is derived from God through Him and for Him. The most advanced souls are those which are most possessed with the thoughts and the presence of Christ.

Any other view would be extremely pernicious. It would be to snatch from the faithful eternal life, which consists in knowing the only true God and Jesus Christ His Son, whom he has sent.

François Fénelon, Maxims of the Saints

5.43 Conformity to the life of Jesus Christ, François Fénelon

We must imitate Jesus; live as He lived, think as He thought, and be conformed to his image, which is the seal of our sanctification.

What a contrast! Nothingness strives to be something, and the Omnipotent becomes nothing! I will be nothing with Thee, my Lord! I offer Thee the pride and vanity which have possessed me hitherto. Help Thou my will; remove from me occasions of my stumbling; turn away mine eyes from beholding vanity (Psalm 118:37); let me behold nothing but Thee and myself in thy presence, that I may understand what I am and what Thou art.

Jesus Christ was born in a stable; he was obliged to fly into Egypt; thirty years of his life were spent in a workshop; he suffered hunger, thirst, and weariness; he was poor, despised and miserable; he taught the doctrines of Heaven, and no one would listen. The great and the wise persecuted and took him, subjected him to frightful torments, treated him as a slave and put him to death between two malefactors, having preferred to give liberty to a robber, rather than to suffer him to escape. Such was the life which our Lord chose; while we are horrified at any kind of humiliation, and cannot bear the slightest appearance of contempt.

Let us compare our lives with that of Jesus Christ, reflecting that he was the Master and that we are the servants; that He was all-powerful, and that we are but weakness; that he was abased and that we are exalted. Let us so constantly bear our wretchedness in mind, that we may have nothing but contempt for ourselves. With what face can we despise others, and dwell upon their faults, when we ourselves are filled with nothing else? Let us begin to walk in the path which our Savior has marked out, for it is the only one that can lead us to Him.

And how can we expect to find Jesus if we do not seek Him in the states of his earthly life, in loneliness and silence, in poverty and suffering, in persecution and contempt, in annihilation and the cross? The saints find him in heaven, in the splendors of glory and in unspeakable pleasures; but it is only after having dwelt with Him on earth in reproaches, in pain and in humiliation. To be a Christian is to be an imitator of Jesus Christ. In what can we imitate Him if not in his humiliation? Nothing else can bring us near to Him. We may adore him as Omnipotent, fear him as just, love him with all our heart as good and merciful,—but we can only imitate him as humble, submissive, poor and despised.

Let us not imagine that we can do this by our own efforts; everything that is written is opposed to it; but we may rejoice in the presence of God. Jesus has chosen to be made partaker of all our weaknesses; He is a compassionate high-priest who has voluntarily submitted to be tempted in all points like as we are; let us, then, have all our strength in Him who became weak that he might strengthen us; let us enrich ourselves out of his poverty, confidently exclaiming, I can do all things through Christ which strengtheneth me. (Phil. 4:13.)

Let me follow in thy footsteps, O Jesus! I would imitate Thee, but cannot without the aid of thy grace! O humble and lowly Savior, grant me the knowledge of the true Christian, and that I may willingly despise myself; let me learn the lesson, so incomprehensible to the mind of man, that I must die to myself by an abandonment that shall produce true humility.

Let us earnestly engage in this work, and change this hard heart, so rebellious to the heart of Jesus Christ. Let us make some approaches toward the holy soul of Jesus; let Him animate our souls and destroy all our repugnances. O lovely Jesus! who hast suffered so many injuries and reproaches for my sake, let me esteem and love them for thine, and let me desire to share thy life of humiliation!

François Fénelon, Spiritual Progress

5.44 Abandonment to Divine Providence, Jean-Pierre de Caussade

Jean-Pierre de Caussade, 1675–1751, was an outstanding Jesuit who contributed greatly to the life of the Christian Church. De Caussade is best known for his book, Abandonment to Divine Providence.

A SHORT WAY TO PERFECTION. THIS ABANDONMENT IS THE SHORTEST WAY TO ARRIVE AT PERFECT LOVE AND PERFECTION.

Your letter, my dear Sister, put me in mind of the Gospel, where we see a young man approaching our Lord to ask Him the way to eternal life. Our good Master replied that he should keep the commandments, and when the young man answered that he had kept them faithfully from his youth, our Lord said, "If you would be perfect, go, sell all that you have and give to the poor, and come, follow Me." Your request is exactly the same as that of the young man. You want me to show you the shortest and surest way to attain perfection which is the fullness of life eternal.

If I did not know you as I do I should answer that the first thing to do is to keep your rule, because the rule is to every Religious the only sure road to perfection. But I am aware that you have kept it with scrupulous fidelity for a long time: therefore, what you wish to learn at present is by what particular practice a Religious who faithfully fulfils all her duties can arrive at a high degree of sanctity. To this question, my dear Sister, my reply will be exactly similar to that of our good Master. If you would be perfect, divest yourself of your own views, of all high notions of yourself, of studied elegance, of all reflexion of your own conduct; in fine, of all that you can call your own, and give yourself up without reserve and for ever to the guidance and good pleasure of God. Abandonment, yes, entire, blind, absolute abandonment; this, for souls circumstanced as you are is the height and the whole of perfection, because perfection consists in perfect love, and because for you

the practice of abandonment is another word for the practice of pure love.

It is true that love, even the purest, does not exclude in the soul the desire of its own salvation and perfection; but it is equally incontestable that the nearer the soul approaches the perfect purity of divine love the more its thoughts and reflexions are turned away from itself and fixed on the infinite goodness of God. This divine goodness does not compel us to repudiate the happiness it destines for us, but it has every right, doubtless, to be loved for itself alone without any reflexion on our own interests: This love which includes the love of ourselves but is independent of it, is what theologians call pure love, and all agree in recognizing that the soul is so much the more perfect according to the measure in which it habitually acts under the influence of this love, and the extent to which it divests itself of all self-seeking, at any rate unless its own interests are subordinated to the interests of God. Therefore total renunciation without reserve or limit has no thought of self-interest—it thinks but of God, of His good pleasure, of His wishes, of His glory; it neither knows, nor desires to know aught else. Far from making its own interests a reason for its love, the soul, truly detached, generously accepts and embraces all that tends to annihilate them; darkness, uncertainty, weakness; humiliations! all these things give it pleasure directly it perceives that it so pleases the Beloved, because the pleasure and satisfaction of its Beloved form all its own pleasure and satisfaction. It neither has a will, nor a desire, nor a life of its own but is completely lost, engulfed, and, as it were, annihilated in the depth of the dark abyss of the will of Him whom it loves.

I could tell you of souls known to me, which, having crossed this terrible pass of total abandonment, and thrown themselves into the deep abyss of the incomprehensible will of God, could not refrain from crying out in a transport of joy and holy confidence, "Oh! will of my God! how infinitely holy, just, and adorable it is, and still more lovable and beneficent. If it be entirely accomplished in me, I shall infallibly find true satisfaction in this life and eternal happiness in the next. Infinite mercy could not permit anything which did not tend to the greater good of His poor creatures. These only can be lost by the perversion of their own will, and by preventing the accomplishment of those designs which are always holy and most merciful. Give me then, oh my God, the grace to destroy by complete detachment this foolish resistance, and henceforth be assured that Your holy will shall be done in me; while I shall be equally assured of salvation and perfection."

Jean-Pierre de Caussade, Letter 2

5.45 Christ our Advocate, Charles G. Finney

Charles, G. Finney, 1792-1875, influenced revivals in America like no other person. In America, Finney was considered the father of modern revivalism with over 500,000 conversions resulting from his ministry. Historians claim that in many ways, Finney laid a well-paved road for mass evangelists who would come after him, such as Dwight L. Moody, Billy Sunday, and Billy Graham.

"And if any man sin we have an Advocate with the Father, Jesus Christ, the righteous. And he is the propitiation for our sins; and not for ours only, but also for the sins of the whole world."
1 John 2:1, 2

The Bible abounds with governmental analogies. These are designed for our instruction; but if we receive instruction from them, it is because there is a real analogy in many points between the government of God and human governments.

I propose to inquire,

I. WHAT IS AN ADVOCATE?

What is the idea of an advocate when the term is used to express a governmental office or relation?

An advocate is one who pleads the cause of another; who represents another, and acts in his name; one who uses his influence in behalf of another by his request.

II. PURPOSES FOR WHICH AN ADVOCATE MAY HE EMPLOYED.

1. To secure justice, in case any question involving justice is to be tried.

2. To defend the accused. If one has been accused of committing a crime, an advocate may be employed to conduct his trial on his behalf; to defend him against the charge, and prevent his conviction if possible.

3. An advocate may be employed to secure a pardon, when a criminal has been justly condemned, and is under sentence. That is, an advocate may be employed either to secure justice for his client, or to obtain mercy for him, in case he is condemned; may be employed either to prevent his conviction, or when convicted, may be employed in

setting aside the execution of the law upon the criminal.

III. THE SENSE IN WHICH CHRIST IS THE ADVOCATE OF SINNERS.

He is employed to plead the cause of sinners, not at the bar of justice; not to defend them against the charge of sin, because the question of their guilt is already settled. The Bible represents them as condemned already; and such is the fact, as every sinner knows. Every sinner in the world knows that he has sinned, and that consequently he must be condemned by the law of God. This office, then, is exercised by Christ in respect to sinners; not at the bar of justice, but at the throne of grace, at the footstool of sovereign mercy. He is employed, not to prevent the conviction of the sinner, but to prevent his execution; not to prevent his being condemned, but being already condemned, to prevent his being damned.

IV. WHAT IS IMPLIED IN HIS BEING THE ADVOCATE OF SINNERS.

1. His being employed at a throne of grace and not at the bar of justice, to plead for sinners, as such, and not for those who are merely charged with sin, but the charge not established. This implies that the guilt of the sinner is already ascertained, the verdict of guilty given, the sentence of the law pronounced, and that the sinner awaits his execution.

2. His being appointed by God as the Advocate of sinners implies a merciful disposition in God. If God had not been mercifully disposed towards sinners, no Advocate had been appointed, no question of forgiveness had been raised.

3. It implies also that the exercise of mercy on certain conditions is possible. Not only is God mercifully disposed, but to manifest this disposition in the actual pardon of sin is possible. Had not this been the case, no Advocate had been appointed.

4. It implies that there is hope, then, for the condemned. Sinners are prisoners; but in this world they are not yet prisoners of despair, but are prisoners of hope.

5. It implies that there is a governmental necessity for the interposition of an advocate;

that the sinner's relations are such, and his character such, that he can not be admitted to plead his own cause in his own name. He is condemned, he is no longer on trial. In this respect he is under sentence for a capital crime; consequently he is an outlaw, and the government can not recognize him as being capable of performing any legal act. His relations to the government forbid that in his own name, or in his own person, he should appear before God. So far as his own personal influence with the government is concerned, he is as a dead man—he is civilly dead. Therefore, he must appear by his next friend, or by his advocate, if he is heard at all. He may not appear in his own name and in his own person, but must appear by an advocate who is acceptable to the government.

V. THE ESSENTIAL QUALIFICATIONS OF AN ADVOCATE UNDER SUCH CIRCUMSTANCES.

1. He must be the uncompromising friend of the government. Observe, he appears to pray for mercy to be extended to the guilty party whom he represents. Of course he must not himself be the enemy of the government of whom he asks so great a favor; but he should be known to be the devoted friend of the government whose mercy he prays may be extended to the guilty.

2. He must be the uncompromising friend of the dishonored law. The sinner has greatly dishonored, and by his conduct denounced, both the law and the Law-giver. By his uniform disobedience the sinner has proclaimed, in the most emphatic manner, that the law is not worthy of obedience, and that the Law-giver is a tyrant. Now the Advocate must be a friend to this law; he must not sell himself to the dishonor of the law nor consent to its dishonor. He must not reflect upon the law; for in this case he places the Law-giver in a position in which, if he should set aside the penalty and exercise mercy, he would consent to the dishonor of the law, and by a public act himself condemn the law. The Advocate seeks to dispense with the execution of the law; but he must not offer, as a reason, that the law is unreasonable and unjust. For in this case he renders it impossible for the Law-

giver to set aside the execution without consenting to the assertion that the law is not good. In that case the Law-giver would condemn himself instead of the sinner. It is plain, then, that he must be the uncompromising friend of the law, or he can never secure the exercise of mercy without involving the Law-giver himself in the crime of dishonoring the law.

3. The Advocate must be righteous; that is, he must be clear of any complicity in the crime of the sinner. He must have no fellowship with his crime; there must be no charge or suspicion of guilt resting upon the Advocate. Unless he himself be clear of the crime of which the criminal is accused, he is not the proper person to represent him before a throne of mercy.

4. He must be the compassionate friend of the sinner—not of his sins, but of the sinner himself. This distinction is very plain. Every one knows that a parent can be greatly opposed to the wickedness of his children, while he has great compassion for their person. He is not a true friend to the sinner who really sympathizes with his sins. I have several times heard sinners render as an excuse for not being Christians, that their friends were opposed to it. They have a great many dear friends who are opposed to their becoming Christians and obeying God. They desire them to live on in their sins. They do not want them to change and be come holy, but desire them to remain in their worldly-mindedness and sinfulness. I tell such persons that those are their friends in the same sense that the devil is their friend.

And would they call the devil their good friend, their kind friend, because he sympathizes with their sins, and wishes them not to become Christians? Would you call a man your friend, who wished you to commit murder, or robbery, to tell a lie, or commit any crime? Suppose he should come and appeal to you, and because you are his friend should desire you to commit some great crime, would you regard that man as your friend?

No! No man is a true friend of a sinner, unless he is desirous that he should abandon his sins. If any person would have you continue in your sins, he is the adversary of your soul. Instead of being in any proper sense your friend, he is playing the devil's part to ruin you.

Now observe: Christ is the compassionate friend of sinners, a friend in the best and truest sense. He does not sympathize with your sins, but His heart is set upon saving you from your sins. I said He must be the compassionate friend of sinners; and His compassion must be stronger than death, or He will never meet the necessities of the case.

5. Another qualification must be, that He is able sufficiently to honor the law, which sinners by their transgression have dishonored. He seeks to avoid the execution of the dishonored law of God. The law having been dishonored by sin in the highest degree, must either be honored by its execution on the criminal, or the Law-giver must in some other way bear testimony in favor of the law, before He can justly dispense with the execution of its penalty. The law is not to be repealed; the law must not be dishonored. It is the law of God's nature, the unalterable law of His government, the eternal law of heaven, the law for the government of moral agents in all worlds, and in all time, and to all eternity. Sinners have borne their most emphatic testimony against it, by pouring contempt upon it in utterly refusing to obey it. Now sin must not be treated lightly—this law must be honored.

God might pour a flash of glory over it by executing its penalty upon the whole race that have despised it. This would be the solemn testimony of God to sustain its authority and vindicate its claims. If our Advocate appears before God to ask for the remission of sin, that the penalty of this law may be set aside and not executed, the question immediately arises, But how shall the dishonor of this law be avoided? What shall compensate for the reckless and blasphemous contempt with which this law has been treated? How shall sin be forgiven without apparently making light of it?

It is plain that sin has placed the whole question in such a light that God's testimony must in some way be borne in a most emphatic manner against sin, and to sustain the authority of this dishonored law. It behooves the Advocate of sinners to provide Himself with a plea that shall meet this difficulty. He must meet this necessity, if He would secure the setting aside of the penalty. He must be able to provide an adequate substitute for its execution. He must be able to do that which will as effectually bear testimony in favor of the law and against sin, as the execution of the law upon the criminal would do. In other words, He must be able to meet the demands of public justice.

6. He must be willing to volunteer a gratuitous service. He can not be called upon in justice to volunteer a service, or suffer for the sake of sinners. He may volunteer His service and it may be accepted; but if He does volunteer His service, He must be able and willing to endure whatever pain or sacrifice is necessary to meet the case.

If the law must be honored by obedience; if, "without the shedding of blood, there can be no remission"; if an emphatic governmental testimony must be borne against sin, and in honor of the law; if He must become the representative of sinners, offering Himself before the whole universe as a propitiation for sin, He must be willing to meet the case and make the sacrifice.

7. He must have a good plea. In other words, when He appears before the mercy-seat, He must be able to present such considerations as shall really meet the necessities of the case, and render it safe, proper, honorable, glorious in God to forgive.

VI. WHAT HIS PLEA IN BEHALF OF SINNERS IS.

1. It should be remembered that the appeal is not to justice. Since the fall of man, God has plainly suspended the execution of strict justice upon our race. To us, as a matter of fact, He has set upon a throne of mercy. Mercy, and not justice, has been the rule of His administration, since men were involved in sin.

This is simple fact. Men do sin, and they are not cut off immediately and sent to hell. The execution of justice is suspended; and God is represented as seated upon a throne of grace, or upon a mercy-seat. It is here at a

mercy-seat that Christ executes the office of Advocate for sinners.

2. Christ's plea for sinners can not be that they are not guilty. They are guilty, and condemned. No question can be raised as it respects their guilt and their ill-desert; such questions are settled. It has often appeared strange to me that men overlook the fact that they are condemned already, and that no question respecting their guilt or desert of punishment can ever be raised.

3. Christ as our Advocate can not, and need not, plead a justification. A plea of justification admits the fact charged; but asserts that under the circumstances the accused had a right to do as he did. This plea Christ can never make. This is entirely out of place, the case having been already tried, and sentence passed.

4. He may not plead what will reflect, in any wise, upon the law. He can not plead that the law was too strict in its precept, or too severe in its penalty; for in that case he would not really plead for mercy, but for justice. He would plead in that case that no injustice might be done the criminal. For if he intimates that the law is not just, then the sinner does not deserve the punishment; hence it would be unjust to punish him, and his plea would amount to this, that the sinner be not punished, because he does not deserve it. But if this plea should be allowed to prevail, it would be a public acknowledgment on the part of God that His law was unjust. But this may never be.

5. He may not plead anything that shall reflect upon the administration of the Law-giver. Should he plead that men had been hardly treated by the Law-giver, either in their creation, or by His providential arrangements, or by suffering them to be so tempted—or if, in any wise, he brings forward a plea that reflects upon the Law-giver, in creation, or in the administration of His government, the Law-giver can not listen to his plea, and forgive the sinner, without condemning Himself. In that case, instead of insisting that the sinner should repent, virtually the Law-giver would be called upon Himself to repent.

6. He may not plead any excuse whatever for the sinner in mitigation of his guilt, or in

extenuation of his conduct. For if he does, and the Law-giver should forgive in answer to such a plea, He would confess that He had been wrong, and that the sinner did not deserve the sentence that had been pronounced against him.

He must not plead that the sinner does not deserve the damnation of hell; for, should he urge this plea, it would virtually accuse the justice of God, and would be equivalent to begging that the sinner might not be sent unjustly to hell. This would not be a proper plea for mercy, but rather an issue with justice. It would be asking that the sinner might not be sent to hell, not because of the mercy of God, but because the justice of God forbids it. This will never be.

7. He can not plead as our Advocate that He has paid our debt, in such a sense that He can demand our discharge on the ground of justice. He has not paid our debt in such a sense that we do not still owe it. He has not atoned for our sins in such a sense that we might not still be justly punished for them. Indeed, such a thing is impossible and absurd. One being can not suffer for another in such a sense as to remove the guilt of that other. He may suffer for another's guilt in such a sense that it will be safe to forgive the sinner, for whom the suffering has been endured; but the suffering of the substitute can never, in the least degree, diminish the intrinsic guilt of the criminal. Our Advocate may urge that He has borne such suffering for us to honor the law that we had dishonored, that now it is safe to extend mercy to us; but He never can demand our discharge on the ground that we do not deserve to be punished. The fact of our intrinsic guilt remains, and must forever remain; and our forgiveness is just as much an act of sovereign mercy, as if Christ had never died for us.

8. But Christ may plead His sin-offering to sanction the law, as fulfilling a condition, upon which we may be forgiven.

This offering is not to be regarded as the ground upon which justice demands our forgiveness. The appeal of our Advocate is not to this offering as payment in such a sense that now in justice He can demand that we shall be set free. No. As I said before, it is simply the fulfilling of a condition, upon which it is safe for the mercy of God to arrest and set aside the execution of the law, in the case of the penitent sinner.

Some theologians appear to me to have been unable to see this distinction. They insist upon it that the atonement of Christ is the ground of our forgiveness. They seem to assume that He literally bore the penalty for us in such a sense that Christ now no longer appeals to mercy, but demands justice for us. To be consistent they must maintain that Christ does not plead at a mercy-seat for us, but having paid our debt, appears before a throne of justice, and demands our discharge.

I cannot accept this view. I insist that His offering could not touch the question of our intrinsic desert of damnation. His appeal is to the infinite mercy of God, to His loving disposition to pardon; and He points to His atonement, not as demanding our release, but as fulfilling a condition upon which our release is honorable to God. His obedience to the law and the shedding of His blood He may plead as a substitute for the execution of the law upon us—in short, He may plead the whole of His work as God-man and Mediator. Thus He may give us the full benefit of what He has done to sustain the authority of law and to vindicate the character of the Law-giver, as fulfilling conditions that have rendered it possible for God to be just and still justify the penitent sinner.

9. But the plea is directed to the merciful disposition of God. He may point to the promise made to him in Isaiah, chap. 52d, from v. 13 to the end, and chap. 53, vs. 1, 2: "Behold, my servant shall deal prudently, he shall be exalted and extolled, and be very high. As many were astonished at thee; (his visage was so marred more than any man, and his form more than the sons of men:)

"So shall he sprinkle many nations; the kings shall shut their mouths at him: for that which had not been told them shall they see; and that which they had not heard shall they consider." "Who hath believed our report? and to whom is the arm of the Lord revealed?

"For he shall grow up before him as a tender plant, and as a root out of a dry ground: he hath no form nor comeliness; and when we shall see him, there is no beauty that we should desire him."

10. He may plead also that He becomes our surety, that He undertakes for us, that He is our wisdom, and righteousness, and sanctification, and redemption; and point to His official relations. His infinite fullness, willingness, and ability to restore us to obedience, and to fit us for the service, the employments, and enjoyments of heaven. It is said that He is made the surety of a better covenant than the legal one; and a covenant founded upon better promises.

11. He may urge as a reason for our pardon the great pleasure it will afford to God, to set aside the execution of the law. "Mercy rejoiceth against judgment." Judgment is His strange work; but He delighteth in mercy.

It is said of Victoria that when her prime minister presented a pardon, and asked her if she would sign a pardon in the case of some individual who was sentenced to death, she seized the pen, and said, "Yes! with all my heart!" Could such an appeal be made to a woman's heart, think you, without its leaping for joy to be placed in a position in which it could save the life of a fellow-being?

It is said that "there is joy in the presence of the angels of God over one sinner that repenteth"; and think you not that it affords God the sincerest joy to be able to forgive the wretched sinner, and save him from the doom of hell? He has no pleasure in our death. It is a grief to Him to be obliged to execute His law on sinners; and no doubt it affords Him infinitely higher pleasure to forgive us, than it does us to be forgiven. He knows full well what are the unutterable horrors of hell and damnation. He knows the sinner can not bear it. He says, "Can thine heart endure, and can thine hands be strong in the day that I shall

deal with thee? And what wilt thou do when I shall punish thee?" Our Advocate knows that to punish the sinner is that in which God has no delight—that He will forgive and sign the pardon with all His heart.

And think you such an appeal to the heart of God, to His merciful disposition, will have no avail? It is said of Christ, our Advocate, that "for the joy set before Him, He endured the cross, and despised the shame." So great was the love of our Advocate for us that He regarded it a pleasure and a joy so great to save us from hell, that He counted the shame and agony of the cross as a mere trifle. He despised them. This, then, is a disclosure of the heart of our Advocate. And how surely may He assume that it will afford God the sincerest joy, eternal joy, to be able honorably to seal to us a pardon.

12. He may urge the glory that will redound to the Son of God, for the part that He has taken in this work.

Will it not be eternally honorable in the Son to have advocated the cause of sinners? to have undertaken at so great expense to Himself a cause so desperate? and to have carried it through at the expense of such agony and blood?

Will not the universe of creatures forever wonder and adore, as they see this Advocate surrounded with the innumerable throng of souls, for whom His advocacy has prevailed?

13. Our Advocate may plead the gratitude of the redeemed, and the profound thanks and praise of all good beings.

Think you not that the whole family of virtuous beings will forever feel obliged for the intervention of Christ as out Advocate, and for the mercy, forbearance, and love that has saved our race?

Charles G. Finney, Christ our Advocate,
1861

5.46 Meditate on Christ, C. H. Spurgeon

I urge you to meditate on Christ, as a piece of scented substance that was perfumed in heaven. It does not matter what you have in your house; this will make it like the fragrance of Paradise—will make it smell like those breezes that once blew through the garden of Eden, carrying the odor of flowers. Oh! there is nothing that can so comfort your spirits, and relieve all your distresses and troubles, as the feeling that now you can meditate on the person of Jesus Christ.

C. H. Spurgeon

5.47 The anchor of Calvary, C. H. Spurgeon

There was an evil hour once when I released the anchor of my faith; I cut the cable of my belief; I no longer moored myself tight to the coasts of the Revelation of God; I allowed my vessel to drift with the wind; I said to reason, "You be my captain"; I said to my own brain, "You be my rudder"; and I started on my mad voyage. Thank God, it is all over now; but I will tell you its brief history. It was one hurried sailing over the tempestuous ocean of free thought. I went on, and as I went, the skies began to darken; but to make up for that deficiency, the waters were brilliant with the glitter of brilliancy. I saw sparks flying upward that pleased me, and I thought, "If this is free thought, it is a good thing." My thoughts seemed like gems, and I scattered stars with both my hands; but before long, instead of these flashes of glory, I saw grim fiends, fierce and horrible, come up from the waters, and as I rushed on, they gnashed their teeth, and grinned at me; they seized the bow of my ship and dragged me on, while I, in part, was impressed at the swiftness of my motion, but yet shuddered at the terrific rate with which I passed the old landmarks of my faith. As I hurried forward with an awful speed, I began to doubt my very existence; I doubted if there were a world, I doubted if there were such a thing, as myself. I went to the very verge of the dreamy realms of unbelief. I went to the very bottom of the sea of Unbelief. I doubted everything. But here the devil foiled himself: for the very extravagance of the doubt, proved its absurdity. Just when I saw the bottom of that sea, there came a voice which said, "And can this doubt be true?" At this very thought I awoke. I started from that death-dream, which, God knows, might have damned my Soul, and ruined my body, if I had not awoke. When I arose, faith took the helm; from that moment I no longer doubted. Faith steered me back; faith cried, "Away, away!" I cast my anchor on Calvary; I lifted my eye to God; and here I am, "alive, and out of hell."

C. H. Spurgeon

5.48 LOOK TO CHRIST!, C. H. SPURGEON

From the cross of Calvary, where the bleeding hands of Jesus drop mercy; from the garden of Gethsemane, where the bleeding pores of the Savior sweat pardons, the cry comes, "Look to me, and be saved, all you ends of the earth." From Calvary's summit, where Jesus cries, "It is finished," I hear a shout, "Look, and be saved." But there comes a vile cry from our soul, "No, look to yourself! Look to yourself!" Ah, look to yourself, and you will be damned. That certainly will come of it. As long as you look to yourself there is no hope for you. It is not a consideration of what you are, but a consideration of what God is, and what Christ is, that can save you. It is looking from yourself to Jesus. Oh! there are men that quite misunderstand the gospel; they think that righteousness qualifies them to come to Christ; whereas sin is the only qualification for man to come to Jesus. Good old Crisp says, "Righteousness keeps me from Christ: those who are healthy have no need of a physician, but only they that are sick. Sin makes me come to Jesus, when sin is felt; and in coming to Christ, the more sin I have the more cause I have to hope for mercy."

C. H. Spurgeon

5.49 THE NATIONAL PRAYER BREAKFAST IN WASHINGTON, DC, MOTHER TERESA OF CALCUTTA

Mother Teresa of Calcutta, missionary to "the poorest of the poor" and founder of the Missionaries of Charity religious order, died on September 5, 1997 in Calcutta, India, at the age of 87.

Mother Teresa of Calcutta addressed an audience of powerful politicians, including President Clinton, in February 1994 when she spoke at the National Prayer Breakfast in Washington, DC

Love always hurts
"I want this child!"
The greatness of the poor
A sign of care

On the last day, Jesus will say to those at his right hand, "Come, enter the Kingdom. For I was hungry and you gave me food, I was thirsty and you gave me drink, I was sick and you visited me."

Then Jesus will turn to those on his left hand and say, "Depart from me because I was hungry and you did not feed me, I was thirsty and you did not give me drink, I was sick and you did not visit me."

These will ask him, "When did we see you hungry, or thirsty, or sick, and did not come to your help?"

And Jesus will answer them, "Whatever you neglected to do unto one of the least of these, you neglected to do unto me!"

As we have gathered here to pray together, I think it will be beautiful if we begin with a prayer that expresses very well what Jesus wants us to do for the least. St. Francis of Assisi understood very well these words of Jesus and his life is very well expressed by a prayer. And this prayer, which we say every day after Holy Communion, always surprises me very much, because it is very fitting for each one of us. And I always wonder whether eight hundred years ago when St. Francis lived, they had the same difficulties that we have today. I think that some of you already have this prayer of peace, so we will pray it together.

Let us thank God for the opportunity he has given us today to have come here to pray together. We have come here especially to pray for peace, joy, and love. We are reminded that Jesus came to bring the good news to the poor. He had told us what that good news is when he said, "My peace I leave with you, my peace I give unto you."

He came not to give the peace of the world, which is only that we don't bother each other. He came to give peace of heart which comes from loving—from doing good to others.

And God loved the world so much that he gave his son. God gave his son to the Virgin Mary, and what did she do with him? As soon as Jesus came into Mary's life, immediately she went in haste to give that good news. And as she came into the house of her cousin, Elizabeth, Scripture tells us that the unborn child—the child in the womb of Elizabeth—leapt with joy. While still in the womb of Mary, Jesus brought peace to John the Baptist, who leapt for joy in the womb of Elizabeth.

And as if that were not enough—as if it were not enough that God the Son should become one of us and bring peace and joy while still in the womb, Jesus also died on the Cross to show that greater love. He died for you and for me, and for that leper and for that man dying of hunger and that naked person lying in the street—not only of Calcutta, but of Africa, of everywhere. Our Sisters serve these poor people in 105 countries throughout the world. Jesus insisted that we love one another as he loves each one of us. Jesus gave his life to love us, and he tells us

that he loves each one of us. Jesus gave his life to love us, and he tells us that we also have to give whatever it takes to do good to one another. And in the Gospel Jesus says very clearly, " Love as I have loved you."

Jesus died on the Cross because that is what it took for him to do good for us—to save us from our selfishness and sin. He gave up everything to do the Father's will, to show us that we too must be willing to give everything to do God's will, to love one another as he loves each of us. If we are not willing to give whatever it takes to do good for one another, sin is still in us. That is why we too must give to each other until it hurts.

LOVE ALWAYS HURTS

It is not enough for us to say, "I love God." But I also have to love my neighbor. John says that you are a liar if you say you love God and you don't love your neighbor. How can you love God whom you do not see, if you do not love your neighbor whom you see, whom you touch, with whom you live? And so it is very important for us to realize that love, to be true, has to hurt. I must be willing to give whatever it takes not to harm other people and, in fact, to do good to them. This requires that I be willing to give until it hurts. Otherwise, there is no true love in me and I bring injustice, not peace, to those around me.

It hurt Jesus to love us. We have been created in his image for greater things, to love and to be loved. We must "put on Christ," as Scripture tells us. And so we have been created to love as he loves us. Jesus makes himself the hungry one, the naked one, the homeless one, the unwanted one, and he says, "You did it to me." On the last day he will say to those on his right, "Whatever you did to the least of these, you did to me," and he will also say to those on his left, "whatever you neglected to do for the least of these, you neglected to do it for me."

When he was dying on the Cross, Jesus said, "I thirst." Jesus is thirsting for our love, and this is the thirst for everyone, poor and rich alike. We all thirst for the love of others, that they go out of their way to avoid harming us and to do good to us. This is the meaning of true love, to give until it hurts.

I can never forget the experience I had in visiting a home where they kept all these old parents of sons and daughters who had just put them into an institution and, maybe, forgotten them. I saw that in that home these old people had everything: good food, comfortable place, television—everything. But everyone was looking toward the door. And I did not see a single one with a smile on his face.

I turned to Sister and I asked, "Why do these people, who have every comfort here— why are they all looking toward the door? Why are they not smiling?" (I am so used to seeing the smiles on our people. Even the dying ones smile.) And Sister said, "This is the way it is, nearly everyday. They are expecting—they are hoping—that a son or daughter will come to visit them. They are hurt because they are forgotten."

See, this neglect to love brings spiritual poverty. Maybe in our family we have somebody who is feeling lonely, who is feeling sick, who is feeling worried. Are we there? Are we willing to give until it hurts, in order to be with our families? Or do we put our own interests first? These are the questions we must ask ourselves, especially as we begin this Year of the Family. We must remember that love begins at home, and we must also remember that "the future of humanity passes through the family."

I was surprised in the West to see so many young boys and girls given to drugs. And I tried to find out why. Why is it like that, when those in the West have so many more things than those in the East? And the answer was, "Because there is no one in the family to receive them." Our children depend on us for everything: their health, their nutrition, their security, their coming to know and love God. For all of this, they look to us with trust, hope, and expectation. But often father and mother are so busy that they have no time for their children, or perhaps they are not even married, or have given up on their marriage. So the children go to the streets, and get involved in drugs, or other things. We are talking of love of the child, which is where love and peace must begin. These are the things that break peace.

But I feel that the greatest destroyer of peace today is abortion, because it is a war against the child—a direct killing of the innocent child—murder by the mother herself. And if we accept that a mother can kill even her own child, how can we tell other people not to kill one another? How do we persuade a woman not to have an abortion? As always, we must persuade her with love, and we remind ourselves that love means to be willing to give until it hurts. Jesus gave even his life to love us. So the mother who is thinking of abortion, should be helped to love—that is, to give until it hurts her plans, or her free time, to respect the life of her child. The father of that child, whoever he is, must also give until it hurts. By abortion, the mother does not learn to love, but kills even her own child to solve her problems. And by abortion, the father is told that he does not have to take any responsibility at all for the child he has brought into the world. That father is likely to put other women into the same trouble. So abortion just leads to more abortion. Any country that accepts abortion is not teaching the people to love, but to use any violence to get what they want. That is why the greatest destroyer of love and peace is abortion.

Many people are very, very concerned with the children of India, with the children of Africa, where quite a few die of hunger, and so on. Many people are also concerned about all the violence in this great country of the United States. These concerns are very good. But often these same people are not concerned with the millions who are being killed by the deliberate decision of their own mothers. And this is what is the greatest destroyer of peace today: abortion, which brings people to such blindness.

"I WANT THIS CHILD!"

And for this I appeal in India and I appeal everywhere: "Let us bring the child back." The child is God's gift to the family. Each child is created in the special image and likeness of God for greater things—to love and to be loved. In this Year of the Family we must bring the child back to the center of our care and concern. This is the only way that our world can survive, because our children are the only hope for the future. As other people are called to God, only their children can take their places.

But what does God say to us? He says, "Even if a mother could forget her child, I will not forget you. I have carved you in the palm of my hand." We are carved in the palm of his hand; that unborn child has been carved in the hand of God from conception, and is called by God to love and to be loved, not only now in this life, but forever. God can never forget us.

I will tell you something beautiful. We are fighting abortion by adoption—by care of the mother and adoption for her baby. We have saved thousands of lives. We have sent word to the clinics, to the hospitals, and police stations: "Please don't destroy the child; we will take the child." So we always have someone tell the mothers in trouble: "Come, we will take care of you, we will get a home for your child."

And we have a tremendous demand from couples who cannot have a child. But I never give a child to a couple who has done something not to have a child. Jesus said, "Anyone who receives a child in my name, receives me." By adopting a child, these couples receive Jesus, but by aborting a child, a couple refuses to receive Jesus.

Please don't kill the child. I want the child. Please give me the child. I am willing to accept any child who would be aborted, and to give that child to a married couple who will love the child, and be loved by the child. From our children's home in Calcutta alone, we have saved over 3,000 children from abortions. These children have brought such love and joy to their adopting parents, and have grown up so full of love and joy! I know that couples have to plan their family, and for that there is natural family planning. The way to plan the family is natural family planning, not contraception. In destroying the power of giving life, through contraception, a husband or wife is doing something to self. This turns the attention to self, and so it destroys the gift of love in him or her. In loving, the husband and wife must turn the attention to each other, as happens in natural family planning, and not

to self, as happens in contraception. Once that living love is destroyed by contraception, abortion follows very easily.

THE GREATNESS OF THE POOR

I also know that there are great problems in the world—that many spouses do not love each other enough to practice natural family planning. We cannot solve all the problems in the world, but let us never bring in the worst problem of all, and that is to destroy love. This is what happens when we tell people to practice contraception and abortion.

The poor are very great people. They can teach us so many beautiful things. Once one of them came to thank us for teaching them natural family planning, and said: "You people—who have practiced chastity—you are the best people to teach us natural family planning, because it is nothing more than self-control out of love for each other." And what this poor person said is very true. These poor people maybe have nothing to eat, maybe they have not a home to live in, but they can still be great people when they are spiritually rich. Those who are materially poor can be wonderful people. One evening we went out and we picked up four people from the street. And one of them was in a most terrible condition. I told the Sisters: "You take care of the other three; I will take care of the one who looks worse." So I did for her all that my love can do. I put her in bed, and there was a beautiful smile on her face. She took hold of my hand, and she said one thing only: "Thank you." Then she died.

I could not help but examine my conscience before her. I asked, "What would I say if I were in her place?" And my answer was very simple. I would have tried to draw a little attention to myself. I would have said, "I am hungry, I am dying, I am cold, I am in pain," or something like that. But she gave me much more—she gave me her grateful love. And she died with a smile on her face.

Then there was the man we picked up from the drain, half-eaten by worms. And after we had brought him to the home, he only said, "I have lived like an animal in the street, but am going to die as an angel, loved and cared for." Then, after we had removed all the worms from this body, all he said—with a big smile—was: "Sister, I am going home to God." And he died. It was so wonderful to see the greatness of that man, who could speak like that without blaming anybody, without comparing anything. Like an angel—this is the greatness of people who are spiritually rich, even when they are materially poor.

A SIGN OF CARE

We are not social workers. We may be doing social work in the eyes of some people, but we must be contemplatives in the heart of the world. For we must bring that presence of God into your family, for the family that prays together, stays together. There is so much hatred, so much misery, and we with our prayer, with our sacrifice, are beginning at home. Love begins at home, and it is not how much we do, but how much love we put into what we do.

If we are contemplatives in the heart of the world with all its problems, these problems can never discourage us. We must always remember what God tells us in the Scripture: Even if the mother could forget the child in her womb—something that is impossible, but even if she could forget—I will never forget you. And so here I am talking with you. I want you to find the poor here, right in your own home first. And begin love there. Bear the good news to your own people first. And find out about your next-door neighbors. Do you know who they are?

I had the most extraordinary experience of love of a neighbor from a Hindu family. A gentleman came to our house and said, "Mother Teresa, there is a family who have not eaten for so long. Do something." So I took some rice and went there immediately. And I saw the children, their eyes shining with hunger. (I don't know if you have ever seen hunger, but I have seen it very often.) And the mother of the family took the rice I gave her, and went out. When she came back, I asked her, "Where did you go? What did

you do?" And she gave me a very simple answer: "They are hungry also." What struck me was that she knew. And who were "they?" A Muslim family. And she knew. I didn't bring any more rice that evening, because I wanted them—Hindus and Muslims—to enjoy the joy of sharing.

But there were those children, radiating joy, sharing the joy and peace with their mother because she had the love to give until it hurts. And you see this is where love begins: at home in the family. God will never forget us, and there is something you and I can always do. We can keep the joy of loving Jesus in our hearts, and share that joy with all we come in contact with. Let us make that one point: that no child will be unwanted, unloved, uncared for, or killed and thrown away. And give until it hurts—with a smile.

Because I talk so much of giving with a smile, once a professor from the United States asked me, "Are you married?" And I said, "Yes, and I find it sometimes very difficult to smile at my spouse—Jesus—because he can be very demanding—sometimes this is really something true. And there is where love comes in—when it is demanding, and yet we can give it with joy."

One of the most demanding things for me is traveling everywhere, and with publicity. I have said to Jesus that if I don't go to heaven for anything else, I will be going to heaven for all the traveling with all the publicity, because it has purified me and sacrificed me and made me really ready to go to heaven. If we remember that God loves us, and that we can love others as he loves us, then America can become a sign of peace for the world. From here, a sign of care for the weakest of the weak—the unborn child—must go out to the world. If you become a burning light of justice and peace in the world, then really you will be true to what the founders of this country stood for. God bless you!

Mother Teresa of Calcutta

5

POEMS, HYMNS, MEDITATIONS, AND PRAYERS

5.50 LATE HAVE I LOVED YOU, AUGUSTINE

Late have I loved you, O Beauty, so ancient and so new, late have I loved you! And behold, you were within me and I was outside, and there I sought for you, and in my deformity I rushed headlong into the well-formed things that you have made. You were with me, and I was not with you. Those outer beauties held me far from you, yet if they had not been in you, they would not have existed at all. You called, and cried out to me and broke open my deafness; you shone forth upon me and you scattered my blindness. You breathed fragrance, and I drew in my breath and I now pant for you. I tasted, and I hunger and thirst; you touched me, and I burned for your peace.

Augustine, Confessions

5.51 BREASTPLATE PRAYER, ST. PATRICK

I arise today
Through a mighty strength, the invocation of
the Trinity,
Through the belief in the threeness,
Through confession of the oneness
Of the Creator of Creation.

I arise today
Through the strength of Christ's birth with
his baptism,
Through the strength of his crucifixion with
his burial,
Through the strength of his resurrection with
his ascension,
Through the strength of his descent for the
judgment of Doom.

I arise today
Through the strength of the love Cherubim,
In obedience of angels,
In the service of archangels,
In hope of resurrection to meet with reward,

In prayers of patriarchs,
In predictions of prophets,
In preaching of apostles,
In faith of confessors,
In innocence of holy virgins,
In deeds of righteous men.

I arise today
Through the strength of heaven:
Light of sun,
Radiance of moon,
Splendor of fire,
Speed of lightning,
Swiftness of wind,
Depth of sea,
Stability of earth,
Firmness of rock.

I arise today
Through God's strength to pilot me:
God's might to uphold me,
God's wisdom to guide me,

God's eye to look before me,
God's ear to hear me,
God's word to speak for me,
God's hand to guard me,
God's way to lie before me,
God's shield to protect me,
God's host to save me
From snares of devils,
From temptations of vices,
From everyone who shall wish me ill,
Afar and anear,
Alone and in multitude.

I summon today all these powers between me
and those evils,
Against every cruel merciless power that may
oppose my body and soul,
Against incantations of false prophets,
Against black laws of pagandom
Against false laws of heretics,
Against craft of idolatry,
Against spells of witches and smiths and
wizards,
Against every knowledge that corrupts man's
body and soul.

Christ to shield me today
Against poison, against burning,
Against drowning, against wounding,
So that there may come to me abundance of
reward.
Christ with me, Christ before me, Christ
behind me,
Christ in me, Christ beneath me, Christ
above me,
Christ on my right, Christ on my left,
Christ when I lie down, Christ when I sit
down, Christ when I arise,
Christ in the heart of every man who thinks of me,
Christ in the mouth of everyone who speaks
of me,

Christ in every eye that sees me,
Christ in every ear that hears me.

I arise today
Through a mighty strength, the invocation of
the Trinity,
Through belief in the threeness,
Through confession of the oneness,
Of the Creator of Creation.

St. Patrick

THE BREASTPLATE

I bind unto myself today
The power of God to hold and lead,
His eye to watch, his might to stay,
His ear to hearken to my need.
The wisdom of my God to teach,
His hand to guide, his shield to ward;
The word of God to give me speech,
His heavenly host to be my guard.

Christ be with me, Christ within me,
Christ behind me, Christ before me,
Christ beside me, Christ to win me,
Christ to comfort and restore me,
Christ beneath me, Christ above me,
Christ in quiet, Christ in danger,
Christ in mouth of friend and stranger.

I bind unto myself the name,
The strong name of the Trinity;
By invocation of the same,
The Three in One, the One in Three,
Of whom all nature hath creation;
Eternal Father, Spirit, Word,
Praise to the Lord of my salvation,
Salvation is of Christ the Lord.

St. Patrick

5.52 Jesus, Thou Joy of loving hearts, Bernard of Clairvaux

Jesus, Thou Joy of loving hearts,
Thou Fount of life, Thou Light of men,
From the best bliss that earth imparts,
We turn unfilled to Thee again.

Thy truth unchanged hath ever stood;
Thou savest those that on Thee call;
To them that seek Thee Thou art good,
To them that find Thee all in all.

We taste Thee, O Thou living Bread,
And long to feast upon Thee still;
We drink of Thee, the Fountainhead,
And thirst our souls from Thee to fill.

Our restless spirits yearn for Thee,
Wherever our changeful lot is cast;
Glad when Thy gracious smile we see,
Blessed when our faith can hold Thee fast.

O Jesus, ever with us stay,
Make all our moments calm and bright;
Chase the dark night of sin away,
Shed over the world Thy holy light.
Bernard of Clairvaux, translated by Ray Palmer

5.53 Drop, drop, slow tears, Phineas Fletcher

Drop, drop, slow tears,
    And bathe those beauteous feet
Which brought from Heaven
    The news and Prince of Peace:
Cease not, wet eyes,
    His mercy to entreat;
To cry for vengeance

    Sin doth never cease.
In your deep floods
    Drown all my faults and fears;
Nor let His eye
    See sin, but through my tears.
Phineas Fletcher, A Litany

5.54 My song is love unknown, Samuel Crossman

My song is love unknown,
My Savior's love to me,
Love to the loveless shown,
That they might lovely be.
O, who am I,
That for my sake
My Lord should take
Frail flesh, and die?

He came from his blest throne,
Salvation to bestow:
But men made strange, and none
The longed-for Christ would know.
But O, my Friend,
My Friend indeed,
Who at my need
His life did spend!

Here might I stay and sing,
No story so divine;
Never was love, dear King,
Never was grief like thine!

This is my Friend,
In whose sweet praise
I all my days
Could gladly spend.

Samuel Crossman

5.55 By the love of thy cross, Thomas Ken

By the love of thy cross, O Jesu, I live; in that I will only glory, that above all things will I study, that before all things will I value; by the love of thy cross I will take up my cross daily, and follow thee.

Thomas Ken

5.56 Jesus shall reign where'er the sun, Isaac Watts

Jesus shall reign where'er the sun
Does his successive journeys run;
His kingdom stretch from shore to shore,
Till moons shall wax and wane no more.

People and realms of every tongue
Dwell on His love with sweetest song;
And infant voices shall proclaim
Their early blessings on His Name.

Blessings abound wherever He reigns;
The prisoner leaps to lose his chains;
The weary find eternal rest,
And all the sons of want are blessed.

Let every creature rise and bring
Peculiar honors to our King;
Angels descend with songs again,
And earth repeat the loud amen!

Isaac Watts

5.57 O for a thousand tongues to sing, Charles Wesley

O for a thousand tongues to sing
My great Redeemer's praise,
The glories of my God and King,
The triumphs of His grace!

My gracious Master and my God,
Assist me to proclaim,
To spread through all the earth abroad
The honors of Thy name.

Jesus! the name that charms our fears,
That bids our sorrows cease;

'Tis music in the sinner's ears,
'Tis life, and health, and peace.

He breaks the power of canceled sin,
He sets the prisoner free;
His blood can make the foulest clean,
His blood availed for me.

He speaks, and, listening to His voice,
New life the dead receive,
The mournful, broken hearts rejoice,
The humble poor believe.

Hear Him, ye deaf; His praise, ye dumb,
Your loosened tongues employ;

Ye blind, behold your Savior come,
And leap, ye lame, for joy.

Charles Wesley

5.58 JESUS, LOVER OF MY SOUL, LET ME TO THY BOSOM FLY, CHARLES WESLEY

Jesus, lover of my soul, let me to Thy bosom fly,
While the nearer waters roll, while the tempest still is high.
Hide me, O my Savior, hide, till the storm of life is past;
Safe into the haven guide; O receive my soul at last.

Other refuge have I none, hangs my helpless soul on Thee;
Leave, ah! leave me not alone, still support and comfort me.
All my trust on Thee is stayed, all my help from Thee I bring;
Cover my defenseless head with the shadow of Thy wing.

Wilt Thou not regard my call? Wilt Thou not accept my prayer?
Lo! I sink, I faint, I fall—Lo! on Thee I cast my care;
Reach me out Thy gracious hand! While I of Thy strength receive,
Hoping against hope I stand, dying, and behold, I live.

Thou, O Christ, art all I want, more than all in Thee I find;
Raise the fallen, cheer the faint, heal the sick, and lead the blind.
Just and holy is Thy Name, I am all unrighteousness;
False and full of sin I am; Thou art full of truth and grace.

Plenteous grace with Thee is found, grace to cover all my sin;
Let the healing streams abound; make and keep me pure within.
Thou of life the fountain art, freely let me take of Thee;
Spring Thou up within my heart; rise to all eternity.

Charles Wesley

5.59 AMAZING GRACE! HOW SWEET THE SOUND, JOHN NEWTON

Amazing grace! How sweet the sound
That saved a wretch like me!
I once was lost, but now am found;
Was blind, but now I see.

'Twas grace that taught my heart to fear,
And grace my fears relieved;

How precious did that grace appear
The hour I first believed.

Through many dangers, toils and snares,
I have already come;
'Tis grace hath brought me safe thus far,
And grace will lead me home.

And then, never more shall the fears,
The trials, temptations, and woes,
Which darken this valley of tears,
Intrude on my blissful repose.

Or, if yet remembered above,
Remembrance no sadness shall raise;

They will be but new signs of thy love,
New themes for my wonder and praise.

Thus the strokes which from sin and from pain
Shall set me eternally free,
Will but strengthen and rivet the chain
Which binds me, my Savior, to thee.

William Cowper

5.62 LOVEST THOU ME?—JOHN 21:16, WILLIAM COWPER

Hark, my soul! it is the Lord:
'Tis thy Savior, hear his word;
Jesus speaks, and speaks to thee:
"Say, poor sinner, lovest thou me?

"I deliver'd thee when bound,
And when bleeding, heal'd thy wound;
Sought thee wandering, set thee right,
Turn'd thy darkness into light.

"Can a woman's tender care
Cease towards the child she bare?
Yes, she may forgetful be,
Yet will I remember thee.

"Mine is an unchanging love,
Higher than the heights above;
Deeper than the depths beneath,
Free and faithful, strong as death.

"Thou shalt see my glory soon,
When the work of grace is done;
Partner of my throne shalt be:—
Say, poor sinner, lovest thou me?"

Lord, it is my chief complaint,
That my love is weak and faint;
Yet I love thee and adore:
Oh for grace to love thee more!

William Cowper

5.63 JUST AS I AM, WITHOUT ONE PLEA, CHARLOTTE ELLIOTT

Just as I am, without one plea
But that thy blood was shed for me,
And that thou bidd'st me come to thee,
O Lamb of God, I come.

Just as I am, though tossed about
With many a conflict, many a doubt,
Fightings within, and fears without,
O Lamb of God, I come.

Just as I am, poor, wretched, blind;
Sight, riches, healing of the mind,
Yea all I need, in thee to find,
O Lamb of God, I come.

Just as I am, thou wilt receive,
Wilt welcome, pardon, cleanse, relieve:
Because thy promise I believe,
O Lamb of God, I come.

Just as I am (thy love unknown
Has broken every barrier down),
Now to be thine, yea thine alone,
O Lamb of God, I come.

Just as I am, of that free love
The breadth, length, depth and height to prove,
Here for a season then above,
O Lamb of God, I come.

Charlotte Elliott

5.64 LORD JESUS, WHO WOULD THINK THAT I AM THINE?, CHRISTINA ROSSETTI

Lord Jesus, who would think that I am Thine?
    Ah, who would think
Who sees me ready to turn back or sink,
    That Thou art mine?
I cannot hold Thee fast tho' Thou art mine:

    Hold Thou me fast,
So earth shall know at last and heaven at last
    That I am Thine.

Christina Rossetti

5.65 IMMANUEL, C. H. SPURGEON

When once I mourned a load of sin;
When conscience felt a wound within;
When all my works were thrown away;
When on my knees I knelt to pray,
Then, blissful hour, remembered well,
I learned Thy love, Immanuel.

When storms of sorrow toss my soul;
When waves of care around me roll;
When comforts sink, when joys shall flee;
When hopeless griefs shall gape for me,
One word the tempest's rage shall quell—
That word, Thy name, Immanuel.

When for the truth I suffer shame;
When foes pour scandal on my name;
When cruel taunts and jeers abound;
When "Bulls of Bashan" gird me round,
Secure within Thy tower I'll dwell—
That tower, Thy grace, Immanuel.

When hell enraged lifts up her roar;
When Satan stops my path before;
When fiends rejoice and wait my end;
When legioned hosts their arrows send,
Fear not, my soul, but hurl at hell
Thy battle-cry, Immanuel.

When down the hill of life I go;
When o'er my feet death's waters flow;
When in the deep'ning flood I sink;
When friends stand weeping on the brink,
I'll mingle with my last farewell
Thy lovely name, Immanuel.

When tears are banished from mine eye;
When fairer worlds than these are nigh;
When heaven shall fill my ravished sight;
When I shall bathe in sweet delight,
One joy all joys shall far excel,
To see Thy face, Immanuel.

C. H. Spurgeon

5.66 HIDDEN IN THE HOLLOW, FRANCES R. HAVERGAL

Hidden in the hollow
Of His blessed hand,
Never foe can follow,
Never traitor stand;
Not a surge of worry,

Not a shade of care,
Not a blast of hurry
Touch the Spirit there.

Frances R. Havergal

The Lord has promised good to me,
His Word my hope secures;
He will my Shield and Portion be,
As long as life endures.

When we've been there ten thousand years,
Bright shining as the sun,
We've no less days to sing God's praise
Than when we'd first begun.

John Newton

5.60 How sweet the name of Jesus sounds, John Newton

How sweet the name of Jesus sounds
In a believer's ear!
It soothes his sorrows, heals his wounds,
And drives away his fear.

It makes the wounded spirit whole,
And calms the troubled breast;
'Tis manna to the hungry soul,
And to the weary, rest.

Dear name! the rock on which I build,
My shield and hiding-place;
My never-failing treasury, filled
With boundless stores of grace.

By thee my prayers acceptance gain,
Although with sin defiled;

Satan accuses me in vain,
And I am owned a child.

Jesus, my Shepherd, Husband, Friend,
My Prophet, Priest, and King,
My Lord, my Life, my Way, my End,
Accept the praise I bring.

Weak is the effort of my heart,
And cold my warmest thought;
But when I see thee as thou art,
I'll praise thee as I ought.

Till then, I would thy love proclaim
With every fleeting breath;
And may the music of thy name
Refresh my soul in death!

John Newton

5.61 Longing to be with Christ, William Cowper

To Jesus, the Crown of my hope,
My soul is in haste to be gone:
O bear me, ye cherubim, up,
And waft me away to his throne!

My Savior, whom absent I love,
Whom, not having seen, I adore;
Whose name is exalted above
All glory, dominion, and power;

Dissolve thou these bonds, that detain
My soul from her portion in thee;

Ah! strike off this adamant chain,
And make me eternally free.

When that happy era begins,
When arrayed in thy glories I shine,
Nor grieve any more, by my sins,
The bosom on which I recline:

Oh, then shall the veil be removed,
And round me thy brightness be poured;
I shall meet him whom absent I loved,
I shall see whom unseen I adored.

5.67 JESUS, I AM RESTING, RESTING, JEAN S. PIGOTT

Jesus, I am resting, resting,
In the joy of what Thou art;
I am finding out the greatness
Of Thy loving heart.
Thou hast bid me gaze upon Thee,
And Thy beauty fills my soul,
For by Thy transforming power,
Thou hast made me whole.

Refrain
Jesus, I am resting, resting,
In the joy of what Thou art;
I am finding out the greatness
Of Thy loving heart.

O, how great Thy loving kindness,
Vaster, broader than the sea!
O, how marvelous Thy goodness,
Lavished all on me!
Yes, I rest in Thee, Belovèd,
Know what wealth of grace is Thine,
Know Thy certainty of promise,
And have made it mine.

Refrain

Simply trusting Thee, Lord Jesus,
I behold Thee as Thou art,
And Thy love, so pure, so changeless,
Satisfies my heart;
Satisfies its deepest longings,
Meets, supplies its every need,
Compasseth me round with blessings:
Thine is love indeed!

Refrain

Ever lift Thy face upon me
As I work and wait for Thee;
Resting 'neath Thy smile, Lord Jesus,
Earth's dark shadows flee.
Brightness of my Father's glory,
Sunshine of my Father's face,
Keep me ever trusting, resting,
Fill me with Thy grace.

Refrain

Jean S. Pigott

5.68 FACE TO FACE, AUTHOR UNKNOWN

Many Christians can empathize with the desire
to spread the message of Jesus expressed in this
anonymous poem.

I had walked life's way with an easy tread,
Had followed where comfort and pleasures led,
Until one day in a quiet place
I met the Master face to face.

With station and rank and wealth for my
goal,
Much thought for my body, but none for my
soul,
I had entered to win in life's mad race,
When I met the Master face to face.

I met Him, and knew Him and blushed to see
That His eyes full of sorrow, were fixed on me;
And I faltered and fell at His feet that day,
While my castles melted and vanished away.

Melted and vanished and in their place
Naught else did I see but the Master's face.
And I cried aloud, "Oh, make me meet
To follow the steps of Thy wounded feet."

My thought is now for the souls of men,
I have lost my life to find it again,
E'er since one day in a quite place
I met the Master face to face.

Author unknown

5.69 HOW THE GREAT GUEST CAME, EDWIN MARKHAM

Before the Cathedral in grandeur rose
At Ingelburg where the Danube goes;
Before its forest of silver spires
Went airily up to the clouds and fires;
Before the oak had ready a beam,
While yet the arch was stone and dream—
There where the altar was later laid,
Conrad the cobbler plied his trade.

It happened one day at the year's white end—
Two neighbors called on their old-time friend;
And they found his shop, so meager and mean,
Made gay with a hundred boughs of green.
Conrad was stitching with face ashine,
But suddenly stopped as he twitched a twine:
"Good news, old friends! At dawn today,
As the cocks were scaring the night away,
The Lord appeared in a dream to me,
And said, 'I am coming, your Guest to be!'
So I've been busy with feet astir,
Strewing the floor with branches of fir.
The wall is washed and the shelf is shined,
And over the rafter the holly twined.
He comes today, and the table is spread
With milk and honey and wheaten bread."

His friends went home. Conrad's face grew still
As he watched for the shadow across the sill.
He lived all the moments o'er and o'er,
When the Lord should enter his lowly door—
The knock, the call, the latch pulled up,
The lighted face, the offered cup.
He would wash the feet where the spikes had been,
He would kiss the hands where the nails went in,

And then at the last would sit with Him
And break the bread as the day grew dim.

While the cobbler mused there passed his pane
A beggar drenched by the driving rain.
He called him in from the stony street
And gave him shoes for his hurting feet.
The beggar went and there came a crone,
Her face with wrinkles of sorrow sown,
A bundle of faggots bowed her back,
And she was spent with the wrench and rack.
He gave her his loaf and steadied her load,
As she went her way on the weary road.
Then to his door came a little child,
Lost and afraid in the world so wild,
In the big dark world. Catching him up,
He gave him the milk in the waiting cup,
And led him home to his mother's arms,
Out of the reach of the world's alarms.

The day went down in the crimson west
And with it the hope of the blessed Guest,
And Conrad sighed as the world turned gray:
"Why is it Lord that your feet delay?
Did You forget that this was the day?"
Then soft in the silence a voice he heard:
"Lift up your heart, for I kept my word.
Three times I came to your friendly door!
Three times my shadow was on your floor!
I was the beggar with the hurting feet;
I was the woman you gave to eat;
I was the child on the homeless street!"

Edwin Markham

5.70 The Hound of Heaven, Francis Thompson

Francis Thompson (December 18, 1859–November 13, 1907) was an English poet. His most famous poem, The Hound of Heaven *describes the pursuit of the human soul by God.*

I fled Him, down the nights and down the days;
I fled Him, down the arches of the years;
I fled Him, down the labyrinthine ways
Of my own mind; and in the mist of tears
I hid from Him, and under running laughter.
Up vistaed hopes I sped;
And shot, precipitated,
Adown Titanic glooms of chasmèd fears,
From those strong Feet that followed, followed after.
But with unhurrying chase,
And unperturbèd pace,
Deliberate speed, majestic instancy,
They beat—and a Voice beat
More instant than the Feet—
"All things betray thee, who betrayest Me."

I pleaded, outlaw-wise,
By many a hearted casement, curtained red,
Trellised with intertwining charities;
(For, though I knew His love Who followèd,
Yet was I sore adread
Lest, having Him, I must have naught beside.)
But, if one little casement parted wide,
The gust of His approach would clash it to:
Fear wist not to evade, as Love wist to pursue.
Across the margent of the world I fled,
And troubled the gold gateways of the stars,
Smiting for shelter on their clangèd bars:
Fretted to dulcet jars
And silvern chatter the pale ports o' the moon.
I said to Dawn: Be sudden—to Eve: Be soon;
With thy young skiey blossoms heap me over
From this tremendous Lover—
Float thy vague veil about me, lest He see!
I tempted all His servitors, but to find
My own betrayal in their constancy,
In faith to Him their fickleness to me,
Their traitorous trueness, and their loyal deceit.
To all swift things for swiftness did I sue;
Clung to the whistling mane of every wind.

But whether they swept, smoothly fleet,
The long savannahs of the blue;
Or whether, Thunder-driven,
They clanged his chariot thwart a heaven,
Plashy with flying lightnings round the spurn o' their feet:—
Fear wist not to evade as Love wist to pursue.
Still with unhurrying chase,
And unperturbèd pace,
Deliberate speed, majestic instancy,
Came on the following Feet,
And a Voice above their beat—
"Naught shelters thee, who wilt not shelter Me."

I sought no more that after which I strayed
In face of man or maid;
But still within the little children's eyes
Seems something, something that replies,
They at least are for me, surely for me!
I turned me to them very wistfully;
But just as their young eyes grew sudden fair
With dawning answers there,
Their angel plucked them from me by the hair.
"Come then, ye other children, Nature's—share
With me" (said I) "your delicate fellowship;
Let me greet you lip to lip,
Let me twine you with caresses,
Wantoning
With our Lady-Mother's vagrant tresses,
Banqueting
With her in her wind-walled palace,
Underneath her azured dais,
Quaffing, as your taintless way is,
From a chalice
Lucent-weeping out of the dayspring."

So it was done:
I in their delicate fellowship was one—
Drew the bolt of Nature's secrecies.
I knew all the swift importings

On the wilful face of skies;
I knew how the clouds arise
Spuméd of the wild sea-snortings;
All that's born or dies
Rose and drooped with; made them shapers
Of mine own moods, or wailful or divine;
With them joyed and was bereaven.
I was heavy with the even,
When she lit her glimmering tapers
Round the day's dead sanctities.
I laughed in the morning's eyes.
I triumphed and I saddened with all weather,
Heaven and I wept together,
And its sweet tears were salt with mortal mine;
Against the red throb of its sunset-heart
I laid my own to beat,
And share commingling heat;
But not by that, by that, was eased my human
smart.
In vain my tears were wet on Heaven's grey
cheek.
For ah! we know not what each other says,
These things and I; in sound I speak—
Their sound is but their stir, they speak by
silences.
Nature, poor stepdame, cannot slake my
drouth;
Let her, if she would owe me,
Drop yon blue bosom-veil of sky, and show me
The breasts o' her tenderness:
Never did any milk of hers once bless
My thirsting mouth.
Nigh and nigh draws the chase,
With unperturbèd pace,
Deliberate speed, majestic instancy;
And past those noised Feet
A voice comes yet more fleet—
"Lo! naught contents thee, who content'st not
Me."

Naked I wait Thy love's uplifted stroke!
My harness piece by piece Thou hast hewn
from me,
And smitten me to my knee;
I am defenceless utterly.
I slept, methinks, and woke,
And, slowly gazing, find me stripped in sleep.
In the rash lustihead of my young powers,
I shook the pillaring hours
And pulled my life upon me; grimed with
smears,

I stand amid the dust o' the mounded years—
My mangled youth lies dead beneath the
heap.
My days have crackled and gone up in smoke,
Have puffed and burst as sun-starts on a
stream.
Yea, faileth now even dream
The dreamer, and the lute the lutanist.
Even the linked fantasies, in whose blossomy
twist
I swung the earth a trinket at my wrist,
Are yielding; cords of all too weak account
For earth with heavy griefs so overplussed.
Ah! is Thy love indeed
A weed, albeit an amaranthine weed,
Suffering no flowers except its own to mount?
Ah! must—
Designer infinite!—
Ah! must Thou char the wood ere Thou can'st
limn with it?
My freshness spent its wavering shower i' the
dust;
And now my heart is as a broken fount,
Wherein tear-drippings stagnate, spilt down
ever
From the dank thoughts that shiver
Upon the sighful branches of my mind.
Such is; what is to be?
The pulp so bitter, how shall taste the rind?
I dimly guess what Time in mists confounds;
Yet ever and anon a trumpet sounds
From the hid battlements of Eternity;
Those shaken mists a space unsettle, then
Round the half-glimpséd turrets slowly wash
again.
But not ere him who summoneth
I first have seen, enwound
With glooming robes purpureal, cypress-
crowned;
His name I know, and what his trumpet saith.
Whether man's heart or life it be which yields
Thee harvest, must Thy harvest-fields
Be dunged with rotten death?

Now of that long pursuit
Comes on at hand the bruit;
That Voice is round me like a bursting sea:
"And is thy earth so marred,
Shattered in shard on shard?
Lo, all things fly thee, for thou fliest Me!
Strange, piteous, futile thing!

Werefore should any set thee love apart?
Seeing none but I makes much of naught"
(He said),
"And human love needs human meriting:
 How hast thou merited—
Of all man's clotted clay the dingiest clot?
Alack, thou knowest not
How little worthy of any love thou art!
Whom wilt thou find to love ignoble thee,
Save Me, save only Me?
All which I took from thee I did but take,
Not for thy harms,

But just that thou might'st seek it in My arms.
All which thy child's mistake
Fancies as lost, I have stored for thee at home:
Rise, clasp My hand, and come!"
Halts by me that footfall:
Is my gloom, after all,
Shade of His hand, outstretched caressingly?
"Ah, fondest, blindest, weakest,
I am He Whom thou seekest!
Thou dravest love from thee, who dravest
Me."

Francis Thompson

6

QUOTATION COLLECTION OF
DEVOTIONAL RESPONSES TO JESUS

I confess Jesus Christ, the son of God, with my whole being. Those whom you call gods are idols; they are made by hands.

Alban, first British martyr, when asked to offer sacrifices to the gods Jupiter and Apollo

If you seek the example of love: Greater love than this no man has, than to lay down his life for his friends. Such a man was Christ on the cross. And if he gave his life for us, then it should not be difficult to bear whatever hardships arise for his sake.

Thomas Aquinas

I am nothing without Christ.

Augustine

When Jesus comes, the shadows depart.

Author unknown, Inscription on the wall of a castle in Scotland

We do not really love Christ unless we are prepared to face His task and to take up His Cross.

William Barclay

Jesus loves me! This I know, for the Bible tells me so.

Karl Barth's response to the question, "What is the greatest thought that has ever passed through your mind?"

Christians indeed must be self-denying Cross-bearers.

Richard Baxter

If Christ is the wisdom of God and the power of God in the experience of those who trust and love Him, there needs no further argument of His divinity.

Henry Ward Beecher

Jesus is honey in the mouth, music in the ear, a song of gladness in the heart.

Bernard of Clairvaux

The word of Christ is the great stabilizer of our lives. Listening to Him leads us into truth and freedom.

Klaus Bockmuehl

Only the person who follows the command of Jesus without reserve and submits unresistingly to his yoke, finds his burden easy.

Dietrich Bonhoeffer

I say, the acknowledgement of God in Christ
Accepted by thy reason, solves for thee
All questions in the earth and out of it.

Robert Browning

Methought I saw, with the eyes of my soul, Jesus Christ at God's right hand; there I say, was my righteousness; so that wherever I was, or whatever I was doing, God could not say of me, he wants my righteousness, for that was just before him.

John Bunyan

Christ was given to us by God's generosity, to be grasped and possessed by us in faith. By partaking of him, we principally receive a double grace.

John Calvin

[The glory of Jesus' transfiguration was seen and not just expounded on so that] the disciples could taste in part what could not be fully comprehended.

John Calvin

Our speech, our thoughts, our actions, our reactions, our relationships, our goals, our values—all are transformed if only we live in the self-conscious enjoyment of the love of Christ.

D. A. Carson

Love him totally who gave himself totally for your love.

Clare of Assisi

Our Savior Christ is both the first beginner of our spiritual life (who first begetteth us into God his Father), and also afterwards he is or lively food and spiritual life.

Thomas Cranmer

I believe there is nothing lovelier, deeper, more sympathetic and more perfect than the Savior; I say to myself with jealous love that not only is there no one else like him, but that there could be no one.

Fyodor Dostoevsky

I am never alone. Christ is always present.

Elizabeth of the Trinity

We have proved beyond any doubt that He means what He says-His grace is sufficient, nothing can separate us from the love of Christ.

Elisabeth Elliot

The Christian's love to Christ takes fire at Christ's love to him.

William Gurnall

Christ is in very truth in the Father by his eternal generation; we are in very truth in Christ, and he likewise is in us.

St. Hilary

The principal acts of saving faith are, accepting, receiving, and resting upon Christ alone for justification, sanctification, and eternal life, by virtue of the covenant of grace.

A. A. Hodge

Christ, who was called the Son of God before the ages, was manifested in the fullness of time, in order that He might cleanse us through His blood, who were under the power of sin, presenting us as pure sons to His Father, if we yield ourselves obediently to the chastisement of the Spirit.

Irenaeus

We get no deeper into Christ than we allow him to get into us.

J. H. Jowett

When Christians say the Christ-life is in them, they do not mean simply something mental or moral. When they speak of being "in Christ" or of Christ being "in them," this is not simply a way of saying that they are thinking about Christ or copying Him. They mean that Christ is actually operating through them.

C. S. Lewis

What will you do with Jesus,
Neutral you can not be,
One day your heart will be asking,
What will He do with me.

C. S. Lewis

If we are in Christ, we are dead to sin, dead to Satan, dead to the world, dead to our old selves.

D. Martyn Lloyd-Jones

I will place no value on anything I have or may possess except in relation to the Kingdom of Christ.

David Livingstone

You will never find Jesus so precious as when the world is one vast howling wilderness. Then he is like a rose blooming in the midst of the desolation, a rock rising above the storm.

Robert Murray M'Cheyne

The love I bear Christ is but a faint and feeble spark, but it is an emanation from himself: He kindled it and he keeps it alive; and because it is his work, I trust many waters shall not quench it.

John Newton

What can be more satisfactory, more full of glory unto the souls of believers, than clearly to comprehend the mystery of the wisdom, grace, and love of God in Christ?

John Owen

In a sense, Jesus' living in us is like the hand in the glove. Jesus Christ clothes himself and uses me for his purpose. I want to allow the indwelling Christ to mold me and use me and bend me any way he pleases as long as he accomplishes his will.

Luis Palau

Christianity, no dichotomy or hierarchy between the body and the soul.

Francis A. Schaeffer

True religion is a union of God with the soul, a real participation of the divine nature, the very image of God drawn upon the soul. It is Christ formed in us.

Henry Scougal

All God's love and the fruits of it come to us as we are in Christ.

Richard Sibbes

Christ is my Savior. He is my life. He is everything to me in heaven and earth.

Sadhu Sundar Singh

The primary response of our faith in Christ is a holy love for Christ and for our fellow Christians.

R. C. Sproul

Jesus chose us, loved us, bought us, cleansed us, robed us, kept us, glorified us: we are here entirely through the Lord Jesus.

C. H. Spurgeon

I have a great need for Christ; I have a great Christ for my need.

C. H. Spurgeon

When Christ came into my life, I came about like a well-handled ship.

Robert Louis Stevenson

Life in Christ is one long string of action verbs: grow . . . praise . . . love . . . learn . . . stretch . . . reach . . . put on . . . put off . . . press on . . . follow . . . hold . . . cleave . . . run . . . weep . . . produce . . . stand . . . fight.

Joni Eareckson Tada

Our relation to Christ is based on His death and resurrection and this means His Lordship.

W. H. Griffith Thomas

If in everything you seek Jesus, you will doubtless find him. But if you seek yourself, you will indeed find yourself, to your own ruin.

Thomas à Kempis

All his glory and beauty come from within, and there he delights to dwell, his visits there are frequent, his conversation sweet, his comforts refreshing; and his peace passing all understanding.

Thomas à Kempis

My greatest help in Christ is that moment by moment I can pass my distress over to him.

George Verwer

Jesus loves me, this I know
For the Bible tells me so.

Anna Bartlett Warner

Worship is nothing more or less than love on its knees before the beloved; just as mission is love on its feet to serve the beloved—and just as the Eucharist, as the climax of worship, is love embracing the beloved and so being strengthened for service.

N. T. Wright

In Jesus—and Jesus alone—we get God.

Ravi Zacharias

INDEXES

INDEX OF AUTHORS AND COUNCILS AND CATECHISMS

An index of authors of poems, hymns, meditations, and prayers follows this index. The first index of authors relates to all entries except those included in quotation collections and in the index of authors of poems, hymns, meditations, and prayers.

Barclay, William, 1907-78
Scottish theologian, author of *The Daily Study Bible*. See 3.7.

Benedetto, Don,? -1554
Italian Reformation writer. See 3.16; 5.39.

Bernard of Clairvaux, 1090-53
Author of a monastic Rule and several mystical works. See 5.15.

Beza, Theodore, 1519-1605
French nobleman; leading exponent of Reformed theology. See 1.31

Bradford, John, 1510-55
English Protestant martyr. See 3.18.

Brown, Colin, twentieth century
Theological professor. See 2.34.

Brown, David, 1803-97
Bible commentator. See 2.26; 2.35.

Bruce, A. B., nineteenth century
Author of *The Training of the Twelve: Timeless Principles for Leadership Development*. See 2.31; 2.44

Bunyan, John, 1628-88
English nonconformist minister and writer; author of *The Pilgrim's Progress*. See 1.2; 3.30; 3.24; 4.26; 5.27.

Calvin, John, 1509-64

Leading Reformation theologian; born in France, settled in Geneva. See 1.5; 1.37; 2.2; 2.46; 3.17; 5.1; 5.24.

Chalcedon, Council of, 451
Produced orthodox definition of faith about the person of Jesus. See 1.27.

Check-lists. See 1.7; 1.8; 1.9; 1.10; 1.47; 1.48; 5.14; 5.20; 5.21.

Damasus, St., fourth century
Pope from 366 to 384, a Spaniard; a zealous opponent of the Arians and a friend of Jerome. See 4.6.

de Caussade, Jean-Pierre,?-1751
Jesuit ascetic writer. See 5.44.

Denney, James, 1856-1917
Scottish theologian. See 1.52

Dickens, Charles, 1812-70
English novelist. See 1.1.

Dominguez, Jerome, twentieth century
Medical doctor and writer on the Bible. See 1.7; 1.8; 1.9; 1.10

Dort, Synod of, 1619
The Synod of Dort ratified the beliefs of the Dutch Reformed Church. See 3.23.

Dosker, Henry E., 1855-1926
Dutch theologian. See 3.9.

Easton, Burton Scott, twentieth century
Christian writer. See 4.28.

Easton, M. G., nineteenth century
Author of *Easton's Bible Dictionary, 1890*. See 2.4; 4.9.

Edersheim, Alfred, 1825-89
English biblical scholar, author of *Life and Times of Jesus the Messiah*. See 2.21; 2.32; 2.42; 2.51; 4.8

Edwards, Jonathan, 1703-58
Leading American theologian in Reformed tradition. See 1.43; 2.50; 5.29.

Farrar, F. W., 1831-1903
English theologian, author of *The Life of Christ*. See 2.12; 2.49.

Fénelon, François 1651-1715
Archbishop of Cambrai; author of many letters of spiritual guidance. See 5.42; 5.43.

Finney, Charles G., 1792-1875
U.S. evangelist. See 5.45.

Flavel, John, 1630-91
English Presbyterian minister. See 1.38.

Fox, George, 1624-91
English preacher; founder of the Quakers. See 5.26.

Gill, John, 1697-1771
English nonconformist theologian and predecessor to C. H. Spurgeon at the Metropolitan Tabernacle, London. See 1.6; 1.32; 4.24; 4.27.

Graham, Billy, b. 1918-
U.S. evangelist. See 1.16; 3.1; 4:1.

Hendriksen, William, twentieth century
Bible commentator. See 4.13.

Henry, Matthew, 1662-1714
English nonconformist minister and Bible commentator. See 1.40; 1.42; 5.5; 5.7; 5.9; 5.11; 5.13.

Hilton, William,?-1396
English Augustinian canon and mystic; author of *The Scale of Perfection*. See 5.33.

Hodge, A. A., 1823-86
Son of Charles Hodge, and leading defender of Old Princeton Theology. See 1.28.

Hodge, Charles, 1797-1878
Principal of Princeton Seminary between 1851 and 1878. See 1.49; 2.47; 3.30.

Hooker, Richard, 1554-1600
English Anglican theologian. See 3.19.

Ignatius of Antioch, c. 35-c. 107
Author of letters to several of the early churches; martyred in Rome. See 1.22.

Irenaeus, c. 130-c. 200
Bishop of Lyons; biblical theologian. See 1.4; 1.23.

Julian of Norwich, c. 1342-c. 1415
English mystic and author of *Revelations of Divine Love*. See 1.34; 3.11; 3.12; 5.32.

Kingsley, Charles, 1819-75
English clergyman and social reformer; author of *The Water Babies*. See 3.33.

Lawrence, Brother, 1605-91
French Carmelite lay brother and mystic; author of *The Practice of the Presence of God*. See 5.16.

Leo the Great, d. 461
Also known as Leo I; became pope in 440; author of *Tome of Leo*. See 1.26.

Lewis, C. S., 1898-1963
English literature professor and writer of popular Christian apologetics. See 1.17; 2.13; 2.29; 3.2; 4:2.

Liddon, H. P., 1829-1890
English clergyman. See 2.28.

Liguori, Alphonsus, 1696-1787
Italian moral theologian. See 2.8; 3.29.

Lloyd-Jones, M., 1899-1981
Welsh Nonconformist doctor and minister noted for his expository preaching at London's Westminster Chapel. See 1.18; 2.33; 3.3; 4.3.

Luther, Martin, 1483-1546
German theologian who led the Protestant Reformation and translated the Bible into

Stott, John, b. 1921
Leading English Bible teacher. See 1.21; 3.5; 4.5.

Tasker R. V. G., twentieth century
Bible commentator. See 3.8.

Temple, William, 1887-1944
Archbishop of Canterbury. See 4.21.

Teresa of Calcutta, Mother, 1910-97
Missionary nun noted for her care for the poor and dying. See 5.49.

Tertullian, c. 150-c. 212
North African theologian. See 1.24.

Thielicke, Helmut, 1908-86
German Lutheran theologian. See 2.14.

Thomas à Kempis, 1380-1471
German devotional theologian, author of *the Imitation of Christ*. See 1.35; 5.34; 5.35; 5.36; 5.37.

Thomas, W. H. Griffith, 1861-1924
English evangelical author. See 4.22.

Torrey, R. A., 1856-1928
American Congregationalist evangelist. See 4.29.

Traherne, Thomas, 1636-74
English clergyman and poet. See 3.25.

Trench, R. C., 1807-86
Anglican Archbishop of Dublin, author of books on miracles and parables. See 2.27; 2.36.

Wallace, Lew, 1827-1905
American soldier, statesman, scholar, and author of *Ben-Hur*. See 2.10; 2.11; 3.10.

Warfield, B. B, 1851-1921
American theologian, and professor at Princeton. See 1.13; 1.50; 1.51; 2.23; 2.40; 4.11.

Watson, Thomas, d. 1686
English Puritan. See 2.9.

Wesley, John, 1703-91
English clergyman and founder of Methodism. See 5.28.

Westminster Confession of Faith, 1646
See 3.26. 3.28.

Westminster Larger Confession, 1646
See 3.27.

Westminster Shorter Catechism, The, 1647
Statement of faith of the English church in Parliamentary times, and more permanently, of the Church of Scotland and other Presbyterians. See 1.39; 1.41; 5.4; 5.6; 5.8; 5.10; 5.12.

Whitefield, George, 1714-1770
English clergyman and evangelist who attracted large crowds in England and America. See 2.43.

Whyte, Alexander, 1836-1921
Scottish Presbyterian preacher and author. See 1.29.

INDEX OF AUTHORS OF POEMS, HYMNS, MEDITATIONS, AND PRAYERS

Longfellow, Henry Wadsworth
Blind Bartimeus. See 2.62.
Lowry, Robert
Up from the grave He arose. See 4.17.

Markham, Edwin
How the great guest came. See 5.69.
Milman, Henry H.
Ride on, ride on, in majesty! See 3.48.
Montgomery, James
Angels from the realms of glory. See 2.18.
Murray, James, R.
Away in a manger. See 2.20.

Newman, Henry
Jesus, the Lamb of God. See 3.40.
Litany of the Passion. See 3.41.
Newton, John
Amazing grace! How sweet the sound. See
5.59
Father, forgive them. See 3.42.
How sweet the name of Jesus sounds. See
5.60.
The blasted fig-tree. See 2.59.

Patrick, St.
Breastplate Prayer, I bind unto myself
today. See 5.51.
Pigott, Jean S.
Jesus, I am resting, resting. See 5.67.

Rossetti, Christina
A better resurrection. See 4.20.

Good Friday. See 3.39.
In the bleak mid-winter. See 2.19.
Lord Jesus, who would think that I am
Thine? See 5.64.

Spenser, Edmund
Most glorious Lord of life. See 4.14.
Spurgeon, Charles
Immanuel. See 5.65.

Tennyson, Alfred, Lord
Lazarus. See 2.61.
Thompson, Francis
The Hound of Heaven. See 5.70.
Toplady, Augustus M.
Rock of ages. See 3.52.

Watts, Isaac
Alas! and did my Savior bleed. See 3.49.
Am I a soldier of the cross? See 3.51.
Jesus shall reign where'er the sun. See 5.56.
When I survey the wondrous cross. See
3.50.
Wesley, Charles
Christ, the Lord, is risen today, Alleluia!
See 4.15.
Hark! The herald angels sing. See 2.17.
Hail the day that sees Him rise, Alleluia!
See 4.25.
Jesus, lover of my soul, let me to Thy
bosom fly. See 5.58.
O for a thousand tongues to sing. See
5.57.